"This book is a very useful tool for anyone who wants to 'look under the hood' so to speak, and really start putting the power of Linux to work. What I find particularly frustrating about man pages is that they never include examples. Sobell, on the other hand, outlines very clearly what the command does and then gives several common, easy-to-understand examples that make it a breeze to start shell programming on one's own. As with Sobell's other works, this is simple, straight-forward, and easy to read. It's a great book and will stay on the shelf at easy arm's reach for a long time."

—*Ray Bartlett*
Travel Writer

"Overall I found this book to be quite excellent, and it has earned a spot on the very front of my bookshelf. It covers the real 'guts' of Linux— the command line and its utilities—and does so very well. Its strongest points are the outstanding use of examples, and the Command Reference section. Highly recommended for Linux users of all skill levels. Well done to Mark Sobell and Prentice Hall for this outstanding book!"

—*Dan Clough*
Electronics Engineer and
Slackware Linux user

"Totally unlike most Linux books, this book avoids discussing everything via GUI and jumps right into making the power of the command line your friend."

—*Bjorn Tipling*
Software Engineer
ask.com

"This book is the best distro-agnostic, foundational Linux reference I've ever seen, out of dozens of Linux-related books I've read. Finding this book was a real stroke of luck. If you want to really understand how to get things done at the command line, where the power and flexibility of free UNIX-like OSes really live, this book is among the best tools you'll find toward that end."

—Chad Perrin
Writer, TechRepublic

Praise for Other Books by Mark G. Sobell

"I keep searching for books that collect everything you want to know about a subject in one place, and keep getting disappointed. Usually the books leave out some important topic, while others go too deep in some areas and must skim lightly over the others. *A Practical Guide to Red Hat® Linux®* is one of those rare books that actually pulls it off. Mark G. Sobell has created a single reference for Red Hat Linux that can't be beat! This marvelous text (with a 4-CD set of Linux Fedora Core 2 included) is well worth the price. This is as close to an 'everything you ever needed to know' book that I've seen. It's just that good and rates 5 out of 5."

—Ray Lodato
Slashdot contributor

"Mark Sobell has written a book as approachable as it is authoritative."

—Jeffrey Bianchine
Advocate, Author, Journalist

"Excellent reference book, well suited for the sysadmin of a Linux cluster, or the owner of a PC contemplating installing a recent stable Linux. Don't be put off by the daunting heft of the book. Sobell has strived to be as inclusive as possible, in trying to anticipate your system administration needs."

—Wes Boudville
Inventor

"*A Practical Guide to Red Hat® Linux®* is a brilliant book. Thank you Mark Sobell."

—C. Pozrikidis
University of California
at San Diego

"This book presents the best overview of the Linux operating system that I have found. . . . [It] should be very helpful and understandable no matter what the reader's background: traditional UNIX user, new Linux devotee, or even Windows user. Each topic is presented in a clear, complete fashion, and very few assumptions are made about what the reader knows. . . . The book is extremely useful as a reference, as it contains a 70-page glossary of terms and is very well indexed. It is organized in such a way that the reader can focus on simple tasks without having to wade through more advanced topics until they are ready."

—Cam Marshall
Marshall Information Service LLC
Member of Front Range UNIX
Users Group [FRUUG]
Boulder, Colorado

"Conclusively, this is THE book to get if you are a new Linux user and you just got into the RH/Fedora world. There's no other book that discusses so many different topics and in such depth."

—Eugenia Loli-Queru
Editor in Chief
OSNews.com

A Practical Guide to Linux® Commands, Editors, and Shell Programming

SECOND EDITION

A Practical Guide to Linux® Commands, Editors, and Shell Programming

SECOND EDITION

Mark G. Sobell

PRENTICE
HALL

Upper Saddle River, NJ • Boston • Indianapolis • San Francisco
New York • Toronto • Montreal • London • Munich • Paris • Madrid
Capetown • Sydney • Tokyo • Singapore • Mexico City

Many of the designations used by manufacturers and sellers to distinguish their products are claimed as trademarks. Where those designations appear in this book, and the publisher was aware of a trademark claim, the designations have been printed with initial capital letters or in all capitals.

The author and publisher have taken care in the preparation of this book, but make no expressed or implied warranty of any kind and assume no responsibility for errors or omissions. No liability is assumed for incidental or consequential damages in connection with or arising out of the use of the information or programs contained herein.

The publisher offers excellent discounts on this book when ordered in quantity for bulk purchases or special sales, which may include electronic versions and/or custom covers and content particular to your business, training goals, marketing focus, and branding interests. For more information, please contact:

U.S. Corporate and Government Sales
(800) 382-3419
corpsales@pearsontechgroup.com

For sales outside the United States, please contact:

International Sales
international@pearson.com

Visit us on the Web: informit.com/ph

Library of Congress Cataloging-in-Publication Data
Sobell, Mark G.
 A practical guide to Linux commands, editors, and shell programming /
Mark G. Sobell.—2nd ed.
    p. cm.
 Includes bibliographical references and index.
 ISBN 978-0-13-136736-4 (pbk.)
 1. Linux. 2. Operating systems (Computers) I. Title.
 QA76.76.O63S59483 2009
 005.4'32—dc22
                                2009038191

ISBN-13: 978-0-13-136736-4
ISBN-10:   0-13-136736-6
Text printed in the United States on recycled paper at Edwards Brothers in Ann Arbor,
Michigan
Fourth printing, October 2011

With love for my guys,
Zach, Max, and Sam

BRIEF CONTENTS

Contents

CHAPTER 4: THE FILESYSTEM   77

CHAPTER 5: THE SHELL   117

PART II THE EDITORS 147

CHAPTER 6: THE vim EDITOR 149

CHAPTER 7: THE emacs EDITOR   205

PART III THE SHELLS 267

CHAPTER 8: THE BOURNE AGAIN SHELL 269

Chapter 9: The TC Shell   349

PART IV   PROGRAMMING TOOLS   395

CHAPTER 11: THE PERL SCRIPTING LANGUAGE   485

CHAPTER 12: THE AWK PATTERN PROCESSING LANGUAGE   531

CHAPTER 13: THE sed EDITOR   565

CHAPTER 14: THE rsync SECURE COPY UTILITY   583

PART V   COMMAND REFERENCE   597

PART VI   APPENDIXES   885

APPENDIX A: REGULAR EXPRESSIONS   887

PREFACE

Linux   *A Practical Guide to Linux® Commands, Editors, and Shell Programming, Second Edition*, explains how to work with the Linux operating system from the command line. The first few chapters of this book quickly bring readers with little computer experience up to speed. The rest of the book is appropriate for more experienced computer users. This book does not describe a particular release or distribution of Linux but rather pertains to all recent versions of Linux.

Mac OS X   This book also explains how to work with the UNIX/Linux foundation of Mac OS X. It looks "under the hood," past the traditional graphical user interface (GUI) that most people think of as a Macintosh, and explains how to use the powerful command-line interface (CLI) that connects you directly to OS X. As with the Linux releases, this book does not describe a particular release of OS X but rather pertains to all recent releases. Where this book refers to Linux, it implicitly refers to Mac OS X as well and makes note of differences between the two operating systems.

Command-line interface (CLI)   In the beginning there was the command-line (textual) interface (CLI), which enabled you to give Linux commands from the command line. There was no mouse to point with or icons to drag and drop. Some programs, such as emacs, implemented rudimentary windows using the very minimal graphics available in the ASCII character set. Reverse video helped separate areas of the screen.

Linux was born and raised in this environment, so naturally all the original Linux tools were invoked from the command line. The real power of Linux still lies in this environment, which explains why many Linux professionals work *exclusively* from the command line. Using clear descriptions and lots of examples, this book shows you how to get the most out of your Linux system using the command-line interface.

Linux distributions   A Linux distribution comprises the Linux kernel, utilities, and application programs. Many distributions are available, including Ubuntu, Fedora, Red Hat, Mint, OpenSUSE, Mandriva, CentOS, and Debian. Although the distributions differ from one another in various ways, all of them rely on the Linux kernel, utilities, and applications. This book is based on the code that is common to most distributions. As a consequence you can use it regardless of which distribution you are running.

New in this edition   This edition includes a wealth of new and updated material:

- Coverage of the Mac OS X command-line interface (throughout the book). Part V covers utilities and highlights the differences between utility options used under Linux and those used under Mac OS X.

- An all-new chapter on the Perl scripting language (Chapter 11; page 485).

- New coverage of the rsync secure copy utility (Chapter 14; page 583).

- Coverage of more than 15 new utilities in Part V, including some utilities available under Mac OS X only.

- Three indexes to make it easier to find what you are looking for quickly. These indexes indicate where you can locate tables (page numbers followed by the letter t) and definitions (italic page numbers). They also differentiate between light and comprehensive coverage (page numbers in light and standard fonts, respectively).

  - The File Tree index (page 989) lists, in hierarchical fashion, most files mentioned in this book. These files are also listed in the Main index.

  - The Utility index (page 991) locates all utilities mentioned in this book. A page number in a light font indicates a brief mention of the utility; use of the regular font indicates more substantial coverage.

  - The completely revised Main index (page 995) is designed for ease of use.

Overlap   If you read *A Practical Guide to Red Hat® Linux®: Fedora™ and Red Hat Enterprise Linux, Fourth Edition,* or *A Practical Guide to Ubuntu Linux®, Second Edition,* or a subsequent edition of either book, you will notice some overlap between those books and the one you are reading now. The introduction, the appendix on regular expressions, and the chapters on the utilities (Chapter 3 of this book—*not* Part V), the filesystem, the Bourne Again Shell (bash), and Perl are very similar in the books. Chapters that appear in this book but not in the other two books include those covering the vim and emacs editors, the TC Shell (tcsh), the AWK and sed languages, the rsync utility, and Part V, which describes 97 of the most useful Linux and Mac OS X utility programs in detail.

Audience   This book is designed for a wide range of readers. It does not require programming experience, although some experience using a computer is helpful. It is appropriate for the following readers:

- **Students** taking a class in which they use Linux or Mac OS X

- **Power users** who want to explore the power of Linux or Mac OS X from the command line

- **Professionals** who use Linux or Mac OS X at work

- **Beginning Macintosh users** who want to know what UNIX/Linux is, why everyone keeps saying it is important, and how to take advantage of it

- **Experienced Macintosh users** who want to know how to take advantage of the power of UNIX/Linux that underlies Mac OS X

- **UNIX users** who want to adapt their UNIX skills to the Linux or Mac OS X environment

- **System administrators** who need a deeper understanding of Linux or Mac OS X and the tools that are available to them, including the bash and Perl scripting languages

- **Computer science students** who are studying the Linux or Mac OS X operating system

- **Programmers** who need to understand the Linux or Mac OS X programming environment

- **Technical executives** who want to get a grounding in Linux or Mac OS X

Benefits *A Practical Guide to Linux® Commands, Editors, and Shell Programming, Second Edition,* gives you an in-depth understanding of how to use Linux and Mac OS X from the command line. Regardless of your background, it offers the knowledge you need to get on with your work: You will come away from this book with an understanding of how to use Linux/OS X, and this text will remain a valuable reference for years to come.

A large amount of free software has always been available for Macintosh systems. In addition, the Macintosh shareware community is very active. By introducing the UNIX/Linux aspects of Mac OS X, this book throws open to Macintosh users the vast store of free and low-cost software available for Linux and other UNIX-like systems.

In this book, *Linux* refers to *Linux* and *Mac OS X*

tip The UNIX operating system is the common ancestor of Linux and Mac OS X. Although the graphical user interfaces (GUIs) of these two operating systems differ significantly, the command-line interfaces (CLIs) are very similar and in many cases identical. This book describes the CLIs of both Linux and Mac OS X. To make it more readable, this book uses the term *Linux* to refer to both *Linux* and *Mac OS X*. It makes explicit note of where the two operating systems differ.

FEATURES OF THIS BOOK

This book is organized for ease of use in different situations. For example, you can read it from cover to cover to learn command-line Linux from the ground up. Alternatively, once you are comfortable using Linux, you can use this book as a reference: Look up a topic of interest in the table of contents or index and read about it. Or, refer to one of the utilities covered in Part V, "Command Reference."

You can also think of this book as a catalog of Linux topics: Flip through the pages until a topic catches your eye. The book also includes many pointers to Web sites where you can obtain additional information: Consider the Internet to be an extension of this book.

A Practical Guide to Linux® Commands, Editors, and Shell Programming, Second Edition, offers the following features:

- **Optional sections** allow you to read the book at different levels, returning to more difficult material when you are ready to tackle it.

- **Caution boxes** highlight procedures that can easily go wrong, giving you guidance *before* you run into trouble.

- **Tip boxes** highlight places in the text where you can save time by doing something differently or when it may be useful or just interesting to have additional information.

- **Security boxes** point out ways you can make a system more secure.

- The **Supporting Web site** at www.sobell.com includes corrections to the book, downloadable examples from the book, pointers to useful Web sites, and answers to even-numbered exercises.

- Concepts are illustrated by **practical examples** found throughout the book.

- The many useful **URLs** (Internet addresses) identify sites where you can obtain software and information.

- **Chapter summaries** review the important points covered in each chapter.

- **Review exercises** are included at the end of each chapter for readers who want to hone their skills. Answers to even-numbered exercises are available at www.sobell.com.

- Important **GNU tools**, including gcc, GNU Configure and Build System, make, gzip, and many others, are described in detail.

- Pointers throughout the book provide help in obtaining **online documentation** from many sources, including the local system and the Internet.

- Important command-line utilities that were developed by Apple specifically for Mac OS X are covered in detail, including diskutil, ditto, dscl, GetFileInfo, launchctl, otool, plutil, and SetFile.

- Descriptions of Mac OS X **extended attributes** include **file forks, file attributes, attribute flags,** and **Access Control Lists (ACLs).**

- Appendix D, "Mac OS X Notes," lists some differences between Mac OS X and Linux.

CONTENTS

This section describes the information that each chapter covers and explains how that information can help you take advantage of the power of Linux. You may want to review the table of contents for more detail.

- **Chapter 1—Welcome to Linux and Mac OS X**
  Presents background information on Linux and OS X. This chapter covers the **history of Linux,** profiles the OS X **Mach kernel,** explains how the GNU Project helped Linux get started, and discusses some of **Linux's important features** that distinguish it from other operating systems.

PART I: THE LINUX AND MAC OS X OPERATING SYSTEMS

Experienced users may want to skim Part I

tip If you have used a UNIX/Linux system before, you may want to skim or skip some or all of the chapters in Part I. All readers should take a look at "Conventions Used in This Book" (page 24), which explains the typographic conventions that this book uses, and "Where to Find Documentation" (page 33), which points you toward both local and remote sources of Linux documentation.

Part I introduces Linux and gets you started using it.

- **Chapter 2—Getting Started**
  Explains the **typographic conventions** this book uses to make explanations clearer and easier to read. This chapter provides basic information and explains how to log in, **change your password,** give Linux commands using the shell, and **find system documentation.**

- **Chapter 3—The Utilities**
  Explains the **command-line interface** (CLI) and briefly introduces **more than 30 command-line utilities.** Working through this chapter gives you a feel for Linux and introduces some of the tools you will use day in and day out. The utilities covered in this chapter include

  - grep, which **searches through files** for strings of characters;
  - unix2dos, which **converts Linux text files** to Windows format;
  - tar, which **creates archive files** that can hold many other files;
  - bzip2 and gzip, which **compress files** so that they take up less space on disk and allow you to transfer them over a network more quickly; and
  - diff, which **displays the differences** between two text files.

- Chapter 4—The Filesystem
Discusses the Linux hierarchical filesystem, covering files, filenames, **pathnames**, working with directories, **access permissions**, and hard and **symbolic links**. Understanding the filesystem allows you to **organize your data** so that you can find information quickly. It also enables you to **share some of your files** with other users while **keeping other files private**.

- Chapter 5—The Shell
Explains how to use shell features to make your work faster and easier. All of the features covered in this chapter work with both bash and tcsh. This chapter discusses

  - Using **command-line options** to modify the way a command works;

  - Making minor changes in a command line to **redirect input** to a command so that it comes from a file instead of the keyboard;

  - **Redirecting output** from a command to go to a file instead of the screen;

  - Using **pipes** to send the output of one utility directly to another utility so you can solve problems right on the command line;

  - Running programs in the **background** so you can work on one task while Linux is working on a different one; and

  - Using the shell to **generate filenames** to save time spent on typing and help you when you do not remember the exact name of a file.

PART II: THE EDITORS

Part II covers two classic, powerful Linux command-line text editors. Most Linux distributions include the vim text editor, an "improved" version of the widely used vi editor, as well as the popular GNU emacs editor. Text editors enable you to create and modify text files that can hold programs, shell scripts, memos, and input to text formatting programs. Because Linux system administration involves editing text-based configuration files, skilled Linux administrators are adept at using text editors.

- Chapter 6—The vim Editor
Starts with a **tutorial** on vim and then explains how to use many of the **advanced features** of vim, including special characters in search strings, the General-Purpose and Named buffers, parameters, markers, and execution of commands from within vim. The chapter concludes with a **summary of vim commands**.

- Chapter 7—The emacs Editor
Opens with a **tutorial** and then explains many of the features of the emacs editor as well as how to use the META, ALT, and ESCAPE keys. In addition, this

chapter covers key bindings, buffers, and **incremental and complete searching** for both character strings and regular expressions. It details the relationship between Point, the cursor, Mark, and Region. It also explains how to take advantage of the extensive **online help** facilities available from emacs. Other topics covered include cutting and pasting, using multiple windows and frames, and working with emacs modes—specifically **C mode**, which aids programmers in writing and debugging C code. Chapter 7 concludes with a **summary of emacs commands**.

PART III: THE SHELLS

Part III goes into more detail about bash and introduces the TC Shell (tcsh).

- **Chapter 8—The Bourne Again Shell**
  Picks up where Chapter 5 left off, covering more advanced aspects of working with a shell. For examples it uses the Bourne Again Shell—bash, the shell used almost exclusively for system shell scripts. Chapter 8 describes how to

  - Use shell **startup files**, shell options, and shell features to **customize the shell**;

  - Use **job control** to stop jobs and move jobs from the foreground to the background, and vice versa;

  - Modify and reexecute commands using the **shell history** list;

  - Create **aliases** to customize commands;

  - Work with **user-created and keyword variables** in shell scripts;

  - Set up **functions**, which are similar to shell scripts but are executed more quickly;

  - Write and execute simple **shell scripts**; and

  - **Redirect error messages** so they go to a file instead of the screen.

- **Chapter 9—The TC Shell**
  Describes tcsh and covers features common to and different between bash and tcsh. This chapter explains how to

  - Run tcsh and **change your default shell** to tcsh;

  - **Redirect error messages** so they go to files instead of the screen;

  - Use **control structures** to alter the flow of control within shell scripts;

  - Work with tcsh **array and numeric variables**; and

  - Use shell **builtin commands**.

PART IV: PROGRAMMING TOOLS

Part IV covers important programming tools that are used extensively in Linux and Mac OS X system administration and general-purpose programming.

Chapter 10—Programming the Bourne Again Shell
Continues where Chapter 8 left off, going into greater depth about advanced shell programming using bash, with the discussion enhanced by extensive examples. This chapter discusses

- **Control structures** such as **if...then...else** and **case;**
- **Variables,** including locality of variables;
- **Arithmetic and logical (Boolean) expressions;** and
- Some of the most useful **shell builtin commands,** including exec, trap, and getopts.

Once you have mastered the basics of Linux, you can use your knowledge to build more complex and specialized programs, using the shell as a programming language.

Chapter 10 poses two complete **shell programming problems** and then shows you how to solve them step by step. The first problem uses **recursion** to create a hierarchy of directories. The second problem develops a quiz program, shows you how to set up a shell script that **interacts with a user,** and explains how the script processes data. (The examples in Part V also demonstrate many features of the utilities you can use in shell scripts.)

- **Chapter 11—The Perl Scripting Language**
Introduces the popular, feature-rich Perl programming language. This chapter covers

    - Perl **help tools** including perldoc;
    - Perl **variables** and **control structures;**
    - **File handling;**
    - **Regular expressions;** and
    - Installation and use of **CPAN modules.**

Many Linux administration scripts are written in Perl. After reading Chapter 11 you will be able to better understand these scripts and start writing your own. This chapter includes many examples of Perl scripts.

- **Chapter 12—The AWK Pattern Processing Language**
Explains how to write programs using the powerful AWK language that filter data, **write reports,** and **retrieve data from the Internet.** The advanced programming section describes how to set up **two-way communication** with another program using a **coprocess** and how to obtain input over a network instead of from a local file.

- **Chapter 13—The sed Editor**
  Describes sed, the **noninteractive stream editor** that finds many applications as a filter within shell scripts. This chapter discusses how to use sed's buffers to write **simple yet powerful programs** and includes many examples.

- **Chapter 14—The rsync Secure Copy Utility**
  Covers rsync, a secure utility that copies an ordinary file or directory hierarchy locally or between the local system and another system on a network. As you write programs, you can use this utility to back them up to another system.

PART V: COMMAND REFERENCE

Linux includes hundreds of utilities. Chapters 12, 13, and 14 as well as Part V provide extensive examples of the use of 100 of the **most important utilities** with which you can solve problems without resorting to programming in C. If you are already familiar with UNIX/Linux, this part of the book will be a valuable, **easy-to-use reference**. If you are not an experienced user, it will serve as a useful supplement while you are mastering the earlier sections of the book.

Although the descriptions of the utilities in Chapters 12, 13, and 14 and Part V are presented in a format similar to that used by the Linux manual (man) pages, they are much easier to read and understand. These utilities are included because you will work with them **day in and day out** (for example, ls and cp), because they are **powerful tools** that are especially useful in shell scripts (sort, paste, and test), because they help you **work with a Linux system** (ps, kill, and fsck), or because they enable you to **communicate with other systems** (ssh, scp, and ftp). Each utility description includes complete explanations of its most useful options, differentiating between options supported under Mac OS X and those supported under Linux. The "Discussion" and "Notes" sections present **tips and tricks** for taking full advantage of the utility's power. The **"Examples" sections** demonstrate how to use these utilities in real life, alone and together with other utilities to generate reports, summarize data, and extract information. Take a look at the "Examples" sections for AWK (more than 20 pages, starting on page 541), ftp (page 707), and sort (page 819) to see how extensive these sections are.

PART VI: APPENDIXES

Part VI includes the appendixes, the glossary, and three indexes.

- **Appendix A—Regular Expressions**
  Explains how to use **regular expressions** to take advantage of the **hidden power of Linux**. Many utilities, including grep, sed, vim, AWK, and Perl, accept regular expressions in place of simple strings of characters. A single regular expression can match many simple strings.

- **Appendix B—Help**
  Details the steps typically used to **solve the problems** you may encounter with a Linux system. This appendix also includes many **links to Web sites** that offer **documentation**, useful Linux and Mac OS X information, mailing lists, and **software**.

- **Appendix C—Keeping the System Up-to-Date**
  Describes how to use tools to download software and **keep a system current**. This appendix includes information on

  - yum—Downloads software from the Internet, keeping a system up-to-date and **resolving dependencies** as it goes.

  - apt-get—An alternative to yum for keeping a system current.

  - **BitTorrent**—Good for distributing large amounts of data such as Linux installation CDs.

- **Appendix D—Mac OS X Notes**
  This appendix is a brief guide to Mac OS X features and quirks that may be unfamiliar to users who have been using Linux or other UNIX-like systems.

- **Glossary**
  Defines more than 500 terms that pertain to the use of Linux and Mac OS X.

- **Indexes**

  - **File Tree Index**—Lists, in hierarchical fashion, most files mentioned in this book. These files are also listed in the Main index.

  - **Utility Index**—Locates all utilities mentioned in this book.

  - **Main Index**—Helps you find the information you want quickly.

SUPPLEMENTS

The author's home page (www.sobell.com) contains downloadable listings of the longer programs from this book as well as pointers to many interesting and useful Linux- and OS X-related sites on the World Wide Web, a list of corrections to the book, answers to even-numbered exercises, and a solicitation for corrections, comments, and suggestions.

THANKS

First and foremost I want to thank my editor at Prentice Hall, Mark L. Taub, who encouraged me and kept me on track. Mark is unique in my experience: He is an editor who works with the tools I am writing about. Because Mark runs Linux on his home computer, we share experiences as I write. His comments and direction were invaluable. Thank you, Mark T.

Molly Sharp of ContentWorks worked with me during the day-by-day production of this book, providing help, listening to my rants, and keeping everything on track. Thanks to Jill Hobbs, Copyeditor, who made the book readable, understandable, and consistent; and Andrea Fox, Proofreader, who made each page sparkle and found the mistakes that the author left behind.

Thanks also to the folks at Prentice Hall who helped bring this book to life, especially Julie Nahil, Full-Service Production Manager, who oversaw production of the book; John Fuller, Managing Editor, who kept the large view in check; Brandon Prebynski, Marketing Manager; Curt Johnson, Executive Marketing Manager; Kim Boedigheimer, Editorial Assistant, who attended to the many details involved in publishing this book; Heather Fox, Publicist; Cheryl Lenser, Senior Indexer; Sandra Schroeder, Design Manager; Chuti Prasertsith, Cover Designer; and everyone else who worked behind the scenes to make this book come into being.

A big "Thank You" to the folks who read through the drafts of the book and made comments that caused me to refocus parts of the book where things were not clear or were left out altogether: David L. Adam; Joe Barker, Ubuntu Forums LoCo Admin; Mike Basinger, Ubuntu Forum Administrator; Michael Davis, Systems Analyst, CSC; Andy Lester, author of *Land the Tech Job You Love: Why Skill and Luck Are Not Enough,* who helped extensively with the Perl chapter; John Peters, J&J Associates; Rich Rosen, Interactive Data; Max Sobell, New York University; Leon Towns-von Stauber; and Jarod Wilson, Senior Software Engineer, Red Hat, Inc.

I am also indebted to Denis Howe, the editor of *The Free On-Line Dictionary of Computing* (FOLDOC). Denis has graciously permitted me to use entries from his compilation. Be sure to visit the dictionary (www.foldoc.org).

Dr. Brian Kernighan and Rob Pike graciously allowed me to reprint the **bundle** script from their book, *The UNIX Programming Environment* (Prentice Hall, 1984).

Thanks also to the people who helped with the first edition of this book: Lars Kellogg-Stedman, Harvard University; Jim A. Lola, Principal Systems Consultant, Privateer Systems, LLC; Eric S. Raymond, cofounder, Open Source Initiative; Scott Mann; Randall Lechlitner, Independent Computer Consultant; Jason Wertz, Computer Science Instructor, Montgomery County Community College; Justin Howell, Solano Community College; Ed Sawicki, The Accelerated Learning Center; David Mercer, Contechst; Jeffrey Bianchine, Advocate, Author, Journalist; John Kennedy; Chris Karr; and Jim Dennis, Starshine Technical Services.

Parts of *A Practical Guide to Linux® Commands, Editors, and Shell Programming, Second Edition,* have grown from my previous Linux books and I want to thank the people who helped with those books. Thank you to John Dong, Ubuntu Developer, Forums Council Member; Matthew Miller, Senior Systems Analyst/Administrator, BU Linux Project, Boston University Office of Information Technology; George Vish II, Senior Education Consultant, Hewlett-Packard; James Stockford, Systemateka, Inc.;

Stephanie Troeth, Book Oven; Doug Sheppard; Bryan Helvey, IT Director, OpenGeo-Solutions; Vann Scott, Baker College of Flint; David Chisnall, computer scientist extraordinaire; Thomas Achtemichuk, Mansueto Ventures; Scott James Remnant, Ubuntu Development Manager and Desktop Team Leader; Daniel R. Arfsten, Pro/Engineer Drafter/Designer; Chris Cooper, Senior Education Consultant, Hewlett-Packard Education Services; Sameer Verma, Associate Professor of Information Systems, San Francisco State University; Valerie Chau, Palomar College and Programmers Guild; James Kratzer; Sean McAllister; Nathan Eckenrode, New York Ubuntu Local Community Team; Christer Edwards; Nicolas Merline; Michael Price; Sean Fagan, Apple Computer; Paul M. Lambert, Apple Computer; Nicolas Roard; Stephen Worotynec, Engineering Services, Alias Systems; Gretchen Phillips, Independent Consultant, GP Enterprises; Peggy Fenner; Carsten Pfeiffer, Software Engineer and KDE Developer; Aaron Weber, Ximian; Cristof Falk, Software Developer at CritterDesign; Steve Elgersma, Computer Science Department, Princeton University; Scott Dier, University of Minnesota; and Robert Haskins, Computer Net Works.

Thanks also to Dustin Puryear, Puryear Information Technology; Gabor Liptak, Independent Consultant; Bart Schaefer, Chief Technical Officer, iPost; Michael J. Jordan, Web Developer, Linux Online Inc.; Steven Gibson, owner of SuperAnt.com; John Viega, founder and Chief Scientist, Secure Software, Inc.; K. Rachael Treu, Internet Security Analyst, Global Crossing; Kara Pritchard, K & S Pritchard Enterprises, Inc.; Glen Wiley, Capital One Finances; Karel Baloun, Senior Software Engineer, Looksmart, Ltd.; Matthew Whitworth; Dameon D. Welch-Abernathy, Nokia Systems; Josh Simon, Consultant; Stan Isaacs; Dr. Eric H. Herrin II, Vice President, Herrin Software Development, Inc. And thanks to Doug Hughes, long-time system designer and administrator, who gave me a big hand with the sections on system administration, networks, the Internet, and programming.

More thanks go to consultants Lorraine Callahan and Steve Wampler; Ronald Hiller, Graburn Technology, Inc.; Charles A. Plater, Wayne State University; Bob Palowoda; Tom Bialaski, Sun Microsystems; Roger Hartmuller, TIS Labs at Network Associates; Kaowen Liu; Andy Spitzer; Rik Schneider; Jesse St. Laurent; Steve Bellenot; Ray W. Hiltbrand; Jennifer Witham; Gert-Jan Hagenaars; and Casper Dik.

A Practical Guide to Linux® Commands, Editors, and Shell Programming, Second Edition, is based in part on two of my previous UNIX books: *UNIX System V: A Practical Guide* and *A Practical Guide to the UNIX System.* Many people helped me with those books, and thanks here go to Pat Parseghian, Dr. Kathleen Hemenway, Brian LaRose; Byron A. Jeff, Clark Atlanta University; Charles Stross; Jeff Gitlin, Lucent Technologies; Kurt Hockenbury; Maury Bach, Intel Israel Ltd.; Peter H. Salus; Rahul Dave, University of Pennsylvania; Sean Walton, Intelligent Algorithmic Solutions; Tim Segall, Computer Sciences Corporation; Behrouz Forouzan, DeAnza College; Mike Keenan, Virginia Polytechnic Institute and State University; Mike Johnson, Oregon State University; Jandelyn Plane, University of Maryland; Arnold Robbins and Sathis Menon, Georgia Institute of Technology; Cliff Shaffer, Virginia Polytechnic Institute and State University; and Steven Stepanek, California State University, Northridge.

I continue to be grateful to the many people who helped with the early editions of my UNIX books. Special thanks are due to Roger Sippl, Laura King, and Roy Harrington for introducing me to the UNIX system. My mother, Dr. Helen Sobell, provided invaluable comments on the original manuscript at several junctures. Also, thanks go to Isaac Rabinovitch, Professor Raphael Finkel, Professor Randolph Bentson, Bob Greenberg, Professor Udo Pooch, Judy Ross, Dr. Robert Veroff, Dr. Mike Denny, Joe DiMartino, Dr. John Mashey, Diane Schulz, Robert Jung, Charles Whitaker, Don Cragun, Brian Dougherty, Dr. Robert Fish, Guy Harris, Ping Liao, Gary Lindgren, Dr. Jarrett Rosenberg, Dr. Peter Smith, Bill Weber, Mike Bianchi, Scooter Morris, Clarke Echols, Oliver Grillmeyer, Dr. David Korn, Dr. Scott Weikart, and Dr. Richard Curtis.

I take responsibility for any errors and omissions in this book. If you find one or just have a comment, let me know (mgs@sobell.com) and I will fix it in the next printing. My home page (www.sobell.com) contains a list of errors and credits those who found them. It also offers copies of the longer scripts from the book and pointers to many interesting Linux pages.

Mark G. Sobell
San Francisco, California

1

WELCOME TO LINUX AND MAC OS X

An operating system is the low-level software that schedules tasks, allocates storage, and handles the interfaces to peripheral hardware, such as printers, disk drives, the screen, keyboard, and mouse. An operating system has two main parts: the *kernel* and the *system programs*. The kernel allocates machine resources—including memory, disk space, and *CPU* (page 949) cycles—to all other programs that run on the computer. The system programs include device drivers, libraries, utility programs, shells (command interpreters), configuration scripts and files, application programs, servers, and documentation. They perform higher-level housekeeping tasks, often acting as servers in a client/server relationship. Many of the libraries, servers, and utility programs were written by the GNU Project, which is discussed shortly.

Linux kernel   The Linux *kernel* was developed by Finnish undergraduate student Linus Torvalds, who used the Internet to make the source code immediately available to others for free. Torvalds released Linux version 0.01 in September 1991.

The new operating system came together through a lot of hard work. Programmers around the world were quick to extend the kernel and develop other tools, adding functionality to match that already found in both BSD UNIX and System V UNIX (SVR4) as well as new functionality. The name *Linux* is a combination of *Linus* and *UNIX*.

The Linux operating system, which was developed through the cooperation of many, many people around the world, is a *product of the Internet* and is a *free* (*open source*; page 969) operating system. In other words, all the source code is free. You are free to study it, redistribute it, and modify it. As a result, the code is available free of cost—no charge for the software, source, documentation, or support (via newsgroups, mailing lists, and other Internet resources). As the GNU Free Software Definition (www.gnu.org/philosophy/free-sw.html) puts it:

Free beer   "Free software" is a matter of liberty, not price. To understand the concept, you should think of "free" as in "free speech," not as in "free beer."

Mach kernel   OS X runs the Mach kernel, which was developed at Carnegie Mellon University (CMU) and is free software. CMU concluded its work on the project in 1994, although other groups have continued this line of research. Much of the Mac OS X software is *open source:* the Mac OS X kernel is based on Mach and FreeBSD code, utilities come from BSD and the GNU project, and system programs come mostly from BSD code, although Apple has developed a number of new programs.

Linux, OS X, and UNIX

tip   Linux and OS X are closely related to the UNIX operating system. This book describes Linux and OS X. To make reading easier, this book talks about Linux when it means OS X and Linux, and points out where OS X behaves differently from Linux. For the same reason, this chapter frequently uses the term Linux to describe both Linux and OS X features.

THE HISTORY OF UNIX AND GNU–LINUX

This section presents some background on the relationships between UNIX and Linux and between GNU and Linux. Go to www.levenez.com/unix for an impressive diagram of the history of UNIX.

THE HERITAGE OF LINUX: UNIX

The UNIX system was developed by researchers who needed a set of modern computing tools to help them with their projects. The system allowed a group of people working together on a project to share selected data and programs while keeping other information private.

Universities and colleges played a major role in furthering the popularity of the UNIX operating system through the "four-year effect." When the UNIX operating system became widely available in 1975, Bell Labs offered it to educational institutions at nominal cost. The schools, in turn, used it in their computer science programs, ensuring that computer science students became familiar with it. Because UNIX was such an advanced development system, the students became acclimated to a sophisticated programming environment. As these students graduated and went into industry, they expected to work in a similarly advanced environment. As more of them worked their way up the ladder in the commercial world, the UNIX operating system found its way into industry.

BSD (Berkeley) UNIX

In addition to introducing students to the UNIX operating system, the Computer Systems Research Group (CSRG) at the University of California at Berkeley made significant additions and changes to it. In fact, it made so many popular changes that one version of the system is called the Berkeley Software Distribution (BSD) of the UNIX system (or just Berkeley UNIX). The other major version is UNIX System V (SVR4), which descended from versions developed and maintained by AT&T and UNIX System Laboratories. Mac OS X inherits much more strongly from the BSD branch of the tree.

FADE TO 1983

Richard Stallman (www.stallman.org) announced[1] the GNU Project for creating an operating system, both kernel and system programs, and presented the GNU Manifesto,[2] which begins as follows:

> GNU, which stands for Gnu's Not UNIX, is the name for the complete UNIX-compatible software system which I am writing so that I can give it away free to everyone who can use it.

Some years later, Stallman added a footnote to the preceding sentence when he realized that it was creating confusion:

> The wording here was careless. The intention was that nobody would have to pay for *permission* to use the GNU system. But the words don't make this clear, and people often interpret them as saying that copies of GNU should always be distributed at little or no charge. That was never the intent; later on, the manifesto mentions the possibility of companies providing the service of distribution for a profit. Subsequently I have learned to distinguish carefully between "free" in the sense of freedom and "free" in the sense of price. Free software is software that users have the freedom to distribute and change. Some users may obtain copies at no charge, while others pay to obtain copies—and if the funds help support improving the software, so much the better. The important thing is that everyone who has a copy has the freedom to cooperate with others in using it.

---

1. www.gnu.org/gnu/initial-announcement.html
2. www.gnu.org/gnu/manifesto.html

In the manifesto, after explaining a little about the project and what has been accomplished so far, Stallman continues:

Why I Must Write GNU

I consider that the golden rule requires that if I like a program I must share it with other people who like it. Software sellers want to divide the users and conquer them, making each user agree not to share with others. I refuse to break solidarity with other users in this way. I cannot in good conscience sign a nondisclosure agreement or a software license agreement. For years I worked within the Artificial Intelligence Lab to resist such tendencies and other inhospitalities, but eventually they had gone too far: I could not remain in an institution where such things are done for me against my will.

So that I can continue to use computers without dishonor, I have decided to put together a sufficient body of free software so that I will be able to get along without any software that is not free. I have resigned from the AI Lab to deny MIT any legal excuse to prevent me from giving GNU away.

NEXT SCENE, 1991

The GNU Project has moved well along toward its goal. Much of the GNU operating system, except for the kernel, is complete. Richard Stallman later writes:

By the early '90s we had put together the whole system aside from the kernel (and we were also working on a kernel, the GNU Hurd,[3] which runs on top of Mach[4]). Developing this kernel has been a lot harder than we expected, and we are still working on finishing it.[5]

...[M]any believe that once Linus Torvalds finished writing the kernel, his friends looked around for other free software, and for no particular reason most everything necessary to make a UNIX-like system was already available.

What they found was no accident—it was the GNU system. The available free software[6] added up to a complete system because the GNU Project had been working since 1984 to make one. The GNU Manifesto had set forth the goal of developing a free UNIX-like system, called GNU. The Initial Announcement of the GNU Project also outlines some of the original plans for the GNU system. By the time Linux was written, the [GNU] system was almost finished.[7]

---

3. www.gnu.org/software/hurd/hurd.html
4. www.gnu.org/software/hurd/gnumach.html
5. www.gnu.org/software/hurd/hurd-and-linux.html
6. www.gnu.org/philosophy/free-sw.html
7. www.gnu.org/gnu/linux-and-gnu.html

Today the GNU "operating system" runs on top of the FreeBSD (www.freebsd.org) and NetBSD (www.netbsd.org) kernels with complete Linux binary compatibility and on top of Hurd pre-releases and Darwin (developer.apple.com/opensource) without this compatibility.

THE CODE IS FREE

The tradition of free software dates back to the days when UNIX was released to universities at nominal cost, which contributed to its portability and success. This tradition eventually died as UNIX was commercialized and manufacturers came to regard the source code as proprietary, making it effectively unavailable. Another problem with the commercial versions of UNIX related to their complexity. As each manufacturer tuned UNIX for a specific architecture, the operating system became less portable and too unwieldy for teaching and experimentation.

MINIX Two professors created their own stripped-down UNIX look-alikes for educational purposes: Doug Comer created XINU and Andrew Tanenbaum created MINIX. Linus Torvalds created Linux to counteract the shortcomings in MINIX. Every time there was a choice between code simplicity and efficiency/features, Tanenbaum chose simplicity (to make it easy to teach with MINIX), which meant this system lacked many features people wanted. Linux went in the opposite direction.

You can obtain Linux at no cost over the Internet. You can also obtain the GNU code via the U.S. mail at a modest cost for materials and shipping. You can support the Free Software Foundation (www.fsf.org) by buying the same (GNU) code in higher-priced packages, and you can buy commercial packaged releases of Linux (called *distributions;* e.g., Ubuntu, Red Hat, openSUSE), that include installation instructions, software, and support.

GPL Linux and GNU software are distributed under the terms of the GNU General Public License (GPL, www.gnu.org/licenses/licenses.html). The GPL says you have the right to copy, modify, and redistribute the code covered by the agreement. When you redistribute the code, however, you must also distribute the same license with the code, thereby making the code and the license inseparable. If you get source code off the Internet for an accounting program that is under the GPL and then modify that code and redistribute an executable version of the program, you must also distribute the modified source code and the GPL agreement with it. Because this arrangement is the reverse of the way a normal copyright works (it *gives* rights instead of *limiting* them), it has been termed a *copyleft.* (This paragraph is not a legal interpretation of the GPL; it is intended merely to give you an idea of how it works. Refer to the GPL itself when you want to make use of it.)

HAVE FUN!

Two key words for Linux are "Have Fun!" These words pop up in prompts and documentation. The UNIX—now Linux—culture is steeped in humor that can be seen throughout the system. For example, less is more—GNU has replaced the UNIX paging utility named more with an improved utility named less. The utility to view PostScript documents is named ghostscript, and one of several replacements for the vi editor is named elvis. While machines with Intel processors have "Intel Inside" logos on their outside, some Linux machines sport "Linux Inside" logos. And Torvalds himself has been seen wearing a T-shirt bearing a "Linus Inside" logo.

What Is So Good About Linux?

In recent years Linux has emerged as a powerful and innovative UNIX work-alike. Its popularity has surpassed that of its UNIX predecessors. Although it mimics UNIX in many ways, the Linux operating system departs from UNIX in several significant ways: The Linux kernel is implemented independently of both BSD and System V, the continuing development of Linux is taking place through the combined efforts of many capable individuals throughout the world, and Linux puts the power of UNIX within easy reach of both business and personal computer users. Using the Internet, today's skilled programmers submit additions and improvements to the operating system to Linus Torvalds, GNU, or one of the other authors of Linux.

Standards   In 1985, individuals from companies throughout the computer industry joined together to develop the POSIX (Portable Operating System Interface for Computer Environments) standard, which is based largely on the UNIX System V Interface Definition (SVID) and other earlier standardization efforts. These efforts were spurred by the U.S. government, which needed a standard computing environment to minimize its training and procurement costs. Released in 1988, POSIX is a group of IEEE standards that define the API (application program interface; page 941), shell, and utility interfaces for an operating system. Although aimed at UNIX-like systems, the standards can apply to any compatible operating system. Now that these standards have gained acceptance, software developers are able to develop applications that run on all conforming versions of UNIX, Linux, and other operating systems.

Applications   A rich selection of applications is available for Linux—both free and commercial— as well as a wide variety of tools: graphical, word processing, networking, security, administration, Web server, and many others. Large software companies have recently seen the benefit in supporting Linux and now have on-staff programmers whose job it is to design and code the Linux kernel, GNU, KDE, or other software that runs on Linux. For example, IBM (www.ibm.com/linux) is a major Linux supporter. Linux conforms increasingly more closely to POSIX standards, and some distributions and parts of others meet this standard. These developments indicate that Linux is becoming mainstream and is respected as an attractive alternative to other popular operating systems.

Peripherals   Another aspect of Linux that appeals to users is the amazing range of peripherals that is supported and the speed with which support for new peripherals emerges. Linux often supports a peripheral or interface card before any company does. Unfortunately some types of peripherals—particularly proprietary graphics cards—lag in their support because the manufacturers do not release specifications or source code for drivers in a timely manner, if at all.

Software   Also important to users is the amount of software that is available—not just source code (which needs to be compiled) but also prebuilt binaries that are easy to install and ready to run. These programs include more than free software. Netscape, for example, has been available for Linux from the start and included Java support before it was available from many commercial vendors. Its sibling Mozilla/Thunderbird/Firefox is also a viable browser, mail client, and newsreader, performing many other functions as well.

Platforms   Linux is not just for Intel-based platforms (which now include Apple computers): It has been ported to and runs on the Power PC—including older Apple computers (ppclinux), Compaq's (née Digital Equipment Corporation) Alpha-based machines, MIPS-based machines, Motorola's 68K-based machines, various 64-bit systems, and IBM's S/390. Nor is Linux just for single-processor machines: As of version 2.0, it runs on multiple-processor machines (*SMPs;* page 978). It also includes an O(1) scheduler, which dramatically increases scalability on SMP systems.

Emulators   Linux supports programs, called *emulators,* that run code intended for other operating systems. By using emulators you can run some DOS, Windows, and Macintosh programs under Linux. For example, Wine (www.winehq.com) is an open-source implementation of the Windows API that runs on top of the X Window System and UNIX/Linux.

Virtual machines   A virtual machine (VM or guest) appears to the user and to the software running on it as a complete physical machine. It is, however, one of potentially many such VMs running on a single physical machine (the host). The software that provides the virtualization is called a virtual machine monitor (VMM) or hypervisor. Each VM can run a different operating system from the other VMs. For example, on a single host you could have VMs running Windows, Ubuntu 7.10, Ubuntu 9.04, and Fedora 10.

A multitasking operating system allows you to run many programs on a single physical system. Similarly, a hypervisor allows you to run many operating systems (VMs) on a single physical system.

VMs provide many advantages over single, dedicated machines:

- **Isolation**—Each VM is isolated from the other VMs running on the same host: Thus, if one VM crashes or is compromised, the others are not affected.

- **Security**—When a single server system running several servers is compromised, all servers are compromised. If each server is running on its own VM, only the compromised server is affected; other servers remain secure.

- **Power consumption**—Using VMs, a single powerful machine can replace many less powerful machines, thereby cutting power consumption.

- **Development and support**—Multiple VMs, each running a different version of an operating system and/or different operating systems, can facilitate development and support of software designed to run in many environments. With this organization you can easily test a product in different environments before releasing it. Similarly, when a user submits a bug, you can reproduce the bug in the same environment it occurred in.

- **Servers**—In some cases, different servers require different versions of system libraries. In this instance, you can run each server on its own VM, all on a single piece of hardware.

- **Testing**—Using VMs, you can experiment with cutting-edge releases of operating systems and applications without concern for the base (stable) system, all on a single machine.

- **Networks**—You can set up and test networks of systems on a single machine.

- **Sandboxes**—A VM presents a sandbox—an area (system) that you can work in without regard for the results of your work or for the need to clean up.

- **Snapshots**—You can take snapshots of a VM and return the VM to the state it was in when you took the snapshot simply by reloading the VM from the snapshot.

Xen   Xen, which was created at the University of Cambridge and is now being developed in the open-source community, is an open-source VMM. Xen introduces minimal performance overhead when compared with running each of the operating systems natively.

This book does not cover the installation or use of Xen. For more information on Xen, refer to the Xen home page at www.cl.cam.ac.uk/research/srg/netos/xen and to wiki.xensource.com/xenwiki

VMware   VMware, Inc. (www.vmware.com) offers VMware Server, a free, downloadable, proprietary product you can install and run as an application under Linux. VMware Server enables you to install several VMs, each running a different operating system, including Windows and Linux. VMware also offers a free VMware player that enables you to run VMs you create with the VMware Server.

KVM   The Kernel-based Virtual Machine (KVM; kvm.qumranet.com and libvirt.org) is an open-source VM and runs as part of the Linux kernel. It works only on systems based on the Intel VT (VMX) CPU or the AMD SVM CPU.

Qemu   Qemu (bellard.org/qemu), written by Fabrice Bellard, is an open-source VMM that runs as a user application with no CPU requirements. It can run code written for a different CPU than that of the host machine.

VirtualBox   VirtualBox (www.virtualbox.org) is an open-source VM developed by Sun Microsystems.

WHY LINUX IS POPULAR WITH HARDWARE COMPANIES AND DEVELOPERS

Two trends in the computer industry set the stage for the growing popularity of UNIX and Linux. First, advances in hardware technology created the need for an operating system that could take advantage of available hardware power. In the mid-1970s, minicomputers began challenging the large mainframe computers because, in many applications, minicomputers could perform the same functions less expensively. More recently, powerful 64-bit processor chips, plentiful and inexpensive memory, and lower-priced hard disk storage have allowed hardware companies to install multiuser operating systems on desktop computers.

Proprietary operating systems

Second, with the cost of hardware continually dropping, hardware manufacturers could no longer afford to develop and support proprietary operating systems. A *proprietary* operating system is one that is written and owned by the manufacturer of the hardware (for example, DEC/Compaq owns VMS). Today's manufacturers need a generic operating system that they can easily adapt to their machines.

Generic operating systems

A *generic* operating system is written outside of the company manufacturing the hardware and is sold (UNIX, OS X, Windows) or given (Linux) to the manufacturer. Linux is a generic operating system because it runs on different types of hardware produced by different manufacturers. Of course, if manufacturers can pay only for development and avoid per-unit costs (which they have to pay to Microsoft for each copy of Windows they sell), they are much better off. In turn, software developers need to keep the prices of their products down; they cannot afford to create new versions of their products to run under many different proprietary operating systems. Like hardware manufacturers, software developers need a generic operating system.

Although the UNIX system once met the needs of hardware companies and researchers for a generic operating system, over time it has become more proprietary as manufacturers added support for their own specialized features and introduced new software libraries and utilities. Linux emerged to serve both needs: It is a generic operating system that takes advantage of available hardware.

LINUX IS PORTABLE

A *portable* operating system is one that can run on many different machines. More than 95 percent of the Linux operating system is written in the C programming language, and C is portable because it is written in a higher-level, machine-independent language. (The C compiler is written in C.)

Because Linux is portable, it can be adapted (ported) to different machines and can meet special requirements. For example, Linux is used in embedded computers, such as the ones found in cellphones, PDAs, and the cable boxes on top of many

TVs. The file structure takes full advantage of large, fast hard disks. Equally important, Linux was originally designed as a multiuser operating system—it was not modified to serve several users as an afterthought. Sharing the computer's power among many users and giving them the ability to share data and programs are central features of the system.

Because it is adaptable and takes advantage of available hardware, Linux runs on many different microprocessor-based systems as well as mainframes. The popularity of the microprocessor-based hardware drives Linux; these microcomputers are getting faster all the time, at about the same price point. Linux on a fast microcomputer has become good enough to displace workstations on many desktops. This widespread acceptance benefits both users, who do not like having to learn a new operating system for each vendor's hardware, and system administrators, who like having a consistent software environment.

The advent of a standard operating system has given a boost to the development of the software industry. Now software manufacturers can afford to make one version of a product available on machines from different manufacturers.

THE C PROGRAMMING LANGUAGE

Ken Thompson wrote the UNIX operating system in 1969 in PDP-7 assembly language. Assembly language is machine dependent: Programs written in assembly language work on only one machine or, at best, on one family of machines. For this reason, the original UNIX operating system could not easily be transported to run on other machines (it was not portable).

To make UNIX portable, Thompson developed the B programming language, a machine-independent language, from the BCPL language. Dennis Ritchie developed the C programming language by modifying B and, with Thompson, rewrote UNIX in C in 1973. Originally, C was touted as a "portable assembler." The revised operating system could be transported more easily to run on other machines.

That development marked the start of C. Its roots reveal some of the reasons why it is such a powerful tool. C can be used to write machine-independent programs. A programmer who designs a program to be portable can easily move it to any computer that has a C compiler. C is also designed to compile into very efficient code. With the advent of C, a programmer no longer had to resort to assembly language to get code that would run well (that is, quickly—although an assembler will always generate more efficient code than a high-level language).

C is a good systems language. You can write a compiler or an operating system in C. It is a highly structured but is not necessarily a high-level language. C allows a programmer to manipulate bits and bytes, as is necessary when writing an operating system. At the same time, it has high-level constructs that allow for efficient, modular programming.

In the late 1980s the American National Standards Institute (ANSI) defined a standard version of the C language, commonly referred to as *ANSI C* or *C89* (for the

Figure 1-1   A layered view of the Linux operating system

year the standard was published). Ten years later the C99 standard was published; it is mostly supported by the GNU Project's C compiler (named gcc). The original version of the language is often referred to as *Kernighan & Ritchie* (or *K&R*) C, named for the authors of the book that first described the C language.

Another researcher at Bell Labs, Bjarne Stroustrup, created an object-oriented programming language named C++, which is built on the foundation of C. Because object-oriented programming is desired by many employers today, C++ is preferred over C in many environments. Another language of choice is Objective-C, which was used to write the first Web browser. The GNU Project's C compiler supports C, C++, and Objective-C.

OVERVIEW OF LINUX

The Linux operating system has many unique and powerful features. Like other operating systems, it is a control program for computers. But like UNIX, it is also a well-thought-out family of utility programs (Figure 1-1) and a set of tools that allow users to connect and use these utilities to build systems and applications.

LINUX HAS A KERNEL PROGRAMMING INTERFACE

The Linux kernel—the heart of the Linux operating system—is responsible for allocating the computer's resources and scheduling user jobs so each one gets its fair share of system resources, including access to the CPU; peripheral devices, such as hard disk, DVD, and CD-ROM storage; printers; and tape drives. Programs interact with the kernel through *system calls,* special functions with well-known names. A programmer can use a single system call to interact with many kinds of devices. For example, there is one **write**() system call, rather than many device-specific ones. When a program issues a **write**() request, the kernel interprets the context and passes the request to the appropriate device. This flexibility allows old utilities to work with devices that did not exist when the utilities were written. It also makes it possible to move programs to new versions of the operating system without rewriting them (provided the new version recognizes the same system calls).

LINUX CAN SUPPORT MANY USERS

Depending on the hardware and the types of tasks the computer performs, a Linux system can support from 1 to more than 1,000 users, each concurrently running a different set of programs. The per-user cost of a computer that can be used by many people at the same time is less than that of a computer that can be used by only a single person at a time. It is less because one person cannot generally take advantage of all the resources a computer has to offer. That is, no one can keep all the printers going constantly, keep all the system memory in use, keep all the disks busy reading and writing, keep the Internet connection in use, and keep all the terminals busy at the same time. By contrast, a multiuser operating system allows many people to use all of the system resources almost simultaneously. The use of costly resources can be maximized and the cost per user can be minimized—the primary objectives of a multiuser operating system.

LINUX CAN RUN MANY TASKS

Linux is a fully protected multitasking operating system, allowing each user to run more than one job at a time. Processes can communicate with one another but remain fully protected from one another, just as the kernel remains protected from all processes. You can run several jobs in the background while giving all your attention to the job being displayed on the screen, and you can switch back and forth between jobs. If you are running the X Window System (page 16), you can run different programs in different windows on the same screen and watch all of them. This capability helps users be more productive.

LINUX PROVIDES A SECURE HIERARCHICAL FILESYSTEM

A *file* is a collection of information, such as text for a memo or report, an accumulation of sales figures, an image, a song, or an executable program. Each file is stored under a unique identifier on a storage device, such as a hard disk. The Linux filesystem provides a structure whereby files are arranged under *directories,* which are like folders or boxes. Each directory has a name and can hold other files and directories. Directories, in turn, are arranged under other directories, and so forth, in a treelike organization. This structure helps users keep track of large numbers of files by grouping related files in directories. Each user has one primary directory and as many subdirectories as required (Figure 1-2).

Standards   With the idea of making life easier for system administrators and software developers, a group got together over the Internet and developed the Linux Filesystem Standard (FSSTND), which has since evolved into the Linux Filesystem Hierarchy Standard (FHS). Before this standard was adopted, key programs were located in different places in different Linux distributions. Today you can sit down at a Linux system and expect to find any given standard program at a consistent location (page 91).

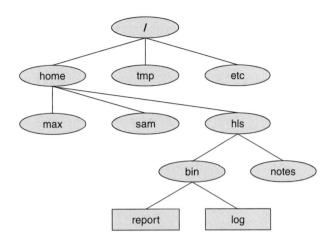

Figure 1-2   The Linux filesystem structure

Links   A *link* allows a given file to be accessed by means of two or more names. The alternative names can be located in the same directory as the original file or in another directory. Links can make the same file appear in several users' directories, enabling those users to share the file easily. Windows uses the term *shortcut* in place of *link* to describe this capability. Macintosh users will be more familiar with the term *alias*. Under Linux, an *alias* is different from a *link;* it is a command macro feature provided by the shell (page 324).

Security   Like most multiuser operating systems, Linux allows users to protect their data from access by other users. It also allows users to share selected data and programs with certain other users by means of a simple but effective protection scheme. This level of security is provided by file access permissions, which limit the users who can read from, write to, or execute a file. More recently, Linux has implemented Access Control Lists (ACLs), which give users and administrators finer-grained control over file access permissions.

THE SHELL: COMMAND INTERPRETER AND PROGRAMMING LANGUAGE

In a textual environment, the shell—the command interpreter—acts as an interface between you and the operating system. When you enter a command on the screen, the shell interprets the command and calls the program you want. A number of shells are available for Linux. The four most popular shells are

- The Bourne Again Shell (bash), an enhanced version of the original Bourne Shell (the original UNIX shell).

- The Debian Almquist Shell (dash), a smaller version of bash, with fewer features. Most startup shell scripts call dash in place of bash to speed the boot process.

- The TC Shell (tcsh), an enhanced version of the C Shell, developed as part of BSD UNIX.

- The Z Shell (zsh), which incorporates features from a number of shells, including the Korn Shell.

Because different users may prefer different shells, multiuser systems can have several different shells in use at any given time. The choice of shells demonstrates one of the advantages of the Linux operating system: the ability to provide a customized interface for each user.

Shell scripts   Besides performing its function of interpreting commands from a keyboard and sending those commands to the operating system, the shell is a high-level programming language. Shell commands can be arranged in a file for later execution (Linux calls these files *shell scripts;* Windows calls them *batch files*). This flexibility allows users to perform complex operations with relative ease, often by issuing short commands, or to build with surprisingly little effort elaborate programs that perform highly complex operations.

FILENAME GENERATION

Wildcards and ambiguous file references   When you type commands to be processed by the shell, you can construct patterns using characters that have special meanings to the shell. These characters are called *wildcard* characters. The patterns, which are called *ambiguous file references,* are a kind of shorthand: Rather than typing in complete filenames, you can type patterns; the shell expands these patterns into matching filenames. An ambiguous file reference can save you the effort of typing in a long filename or a long series of similar filenames. For example, the shell might expand the pattern **mak✳** to **make-3.80.tar.gz**. Patterns can also be useful when you know only part of a filename or cannot remember the exact spelling of a filename.

COMPLETION

In conjunction with the Readline library, the shell performs command, filename, pathname, and variable completion: You type a prefix and press ESCAPE, and the shell lists the items that begin with that prefix or completes the item if the prefix specifies a unique item.

DEVICE-INDEPENDENT INPUT AND OUTPUT

Redirection   Devices (such as a printer or a terminal) and disk files appear as files to Linux programs. When you give a command to the Linux operating system, you can instruct it to send the output to any one of several devices or files. This diversion is called output *redirection.*

Device independence   In a similar manner, a program's input, which normally comes from a keyboard, can be redirected so that it comes from a disk file instead. Input and output are *device independent;* that is, they can be redirected to or from any appropriate device.

As an example, the cat utility normally displays the contents of a file on the screen. When you run a cat command, you can easily cause its output to go to a disk file instead of the screen.

SHELL FUNCTIONS

One of the most important features of the shell is that users can use it as a programming language. Because the shell is an interpreter, it does not compile programs written for it but rather interprets programs each time they are loaded from the disk. Loading and interpreting programs can be time-consuming.

Many shells, including the Bourne Again Shell, support shell functions that the shell holds in memory so it does not have to read them from the disk each time you execute them. The shell also keeps functions in an internal format so it does not have to spend as much time interpreting them.

JOB CONTROL

Job control is a shell feature that allows users to work on several jobs at once, switching back and forth between them as desired. When you start a job, it is frequently run in the foreground so it is connected to the terminal. Using job control, you can move the job you are working with to the background and continue running it there while working on or observing another job in the foreground. If a background job then needs your attention, you can move it to the foreground so it is once again attached to the terminal. (The concept of job control originated with BSD UNIX, where it appeared in the C Shell.)

A LARGE COLLECTION OF USEFUL UTILITIES

Linux includes a family of several hundred utility programs, often referred to as *commands*. These utilities perform functions that are universally required by users. The sort utility, for example, puts lists (or groups of lists) in alphabetical or numerical order and can be used to sort lists by part number, last name, city, ZIP code, telephone number, age, size, cost, and so forth. The sort utility is an important programming tool that is part of the standard Linux system. Other utilities allow users to create, display, print, copy, search, and delete files as well as to edit, format, and typeset text. The man (for manual) and info utilities provide online documentation for Linux.

INTERPROCESS COMMUNICATION

Pipes and filters   Linux enables users to establish both pipes and filters on the command line. A *pipe* sends the output of one program to another program as input. A *filter* is a special kind of pipe that processes a stream of input data to yield a stream of output data. A filter processes another program's output, altering it as a result. The filter's output then becomes input to another program.

Pipes and filters frequently join utilities to perform a specific task. For example, you can use a pipe to send the output of the sort utility to head (a filter that lists the first ten lines of its input); you can then use another pipe to send the output of head to a third utility, lpr, that sends the data to a printer. Thus, in one command line, you can use three utilities together to sort and print part of a file.

SYSTEM ADMINISTRATION

On a Linux system the system administrator is frequently the owner and only user of the system. This person has many responsibilities. The first responsibility may be to set up the system, install the software, and possibly edit configuration files. Once the system is up and running, the system administrator is responsible for downloading and installing software (including upgrading the operating system), backing up and restoring files, and managing such system facilities as printers, terminals, servers, and a local network. The system administrator is also responsible for setting up accounts for new users on a multiuser system, bringing the system up and down as needed, monitoring the system, and taking care of any problems that arise.

ADDITIONAL FEATURES OF LINUX

The developers of Linux included features from BSD, System V, and Sun Microsystems' Solaris, as well as new features, in their operating system. Although most of the tools found on UNIX exist for Linux, in some cases these tools have been replaced by more modern counterparts. This section describes some of the popular tools and features available under Linux.

GUIs: GRAPHICAL USER INTERFACES

X11 The X Window System (also called X or X11) was developed in part by researchers at the Massachusetts Institute of Technology (MIT) and provides the foundation for the GUIs available with Linux. Given a terminal or workstation screen that supports X, a user can interact with the computer through multiple windows on the screen, display graphical information, or use special-purpose applications to draw pictures, monitor processes, or preview formatted output. X is an across-the-network protocol that allows a user to open a window on a workstation or computer system that is remote from the CPU generating the window.

Aqua Mac OS X comes with two graphical interfaces that can be used simultaneously. Most Macintosh users are familiar with Aqua, the standard Mac OS X graphical interface. Aqua is based on a rendering technology named Quartz and has a standard look and feel for applications. Mac OS X also supports X11, which also uses Quartz.

Desktop manager Usually two layers run on top of X: a desktop manager and a window manager. A *desktop manager* is a picture-oriented user interface that enables you to interact with system programs by manipulating icons instead of typing the corresponding commands to a shell. Most Linux distributions run the GNOME desktop manager (www.gnome.org) by default, but they can also run KDE (www.kde.org) and a number of other desktop managers. Mac OS X handles the desktop in Aqua, not in X11, so there is no desktop manager under X11.

Window manager   A *window manager* is a program that runs under the desktop manager and allows you to open and close windows, run programs, and set up a mouse so it has different effects depending on how and where you click. The window manager also gives the screen its personality. Whereas Microsoft Windows allows you to change the color of key elements in a window, a window manager under X allows you to customize the overall look and feel of the screen: You can change the way a window looks and works (by giving it different borders, buttons, and scrollbars), set up virtual desktops, create menus, and more.

Several popular window managers run under X and Linux. Most Linux distributions provide both Metacity (the default under GNOME) and kwin (the default under KDE). Other window managers, such as Sawfish and WindowMaker, are also available.

Under Mac OS X, most windows are managed by a Quartz layer, which applies the Apple Aqua look and feel. For X11 applications only, this task is performed by quartz-wm, which mimics the Apple Aqua look and feel so X11 applications on the Mac desktop have the same appearance as native Mac OS X applications.

(INTER)NETWORKING UTILITIES

Linux network support includes many utilities that enable you to access remote systems over a variety of networks. In addition to sending email to users on other systems, you can access files on disks mounted on other computers as if they were located on the local system, make your files available to other systems in a similar manner, copy files back and forth, run programs on remote systems while displaying the results on the local system, and perform many other operations across local area networks (LANs) and wide area networks (WANs), including the Internet.

Layered on top of this network access is a wide range of application programs that extend the computer's resources around the globe. You can carry on conversations with people throughout the world, gather information on a wide variety of subjects, and download new software over the Internet quickly and reliably.

SOFTWARE DEVELOPMENT

One of Linux's most impressive strengths is its rich software development environment. Linux supports compilers and interpreters for many computer languages. Besides C and C++, languages available for Linux include Ada, Fortran, Java, Lisp, Pascal, Perl, and Python. The bison utility generates parsing code that makes it easier to write programs to build compilers (tools that parse files containing structured information). The flex utility generates scanners (code that recognizes lexical patterns in text). The make utility and the GNU Configure and Build System make it easier to manage complex development projects. Source code management systems, such as CVS, simplify version control. Several debuggers, including ups and gdb, can help you track down and repair software defects. The GNU C compiler (gcc) works with the gprof profiling utility to help programmers identify potential bottlenecks in a program's performance. The C compiler includes options to perform extensive checking of C code, thereby making the code more portable and reducing debugging time. Table B-4 on page 904 lists some sites you can download software from. Under OS X, Apple's Xcode development environment provides a unified graphical front end to most of these tools as well as other options and features.

CHAPTER SUMMARY

The Linux operating system grew out of the UNIX heritage to become a popular alternative to traditional systems (that is, Windows) available for microcomputer (PC) hardware. UNIX users will find a familiar environment in Linux. Distributions of Linux contain the expected complement of UNIX utilities, contributed by programmers around the world, including the set of tools developed as part of the GNU Project. The Linux community is committed to the continued development of this system. Support for new microcomputer devices and features is added soon after the hardware becomes available, and the tools available on Linux continue to be refined. Given the many commercial software packages available to run on Linux platforms and the many hardware manufacturers offering Linux on their systems, it is clear that the system has evolved well beyond its origin as an undergraduate project to become an operating system of choice for academic, commercial, professional, and personal use.

EXERCISES

1. What is free software? List three characteristics of free software.

2. Why is Linux popular? Why is it popular in academia?

3. What are multiuser systems? Why are they successful?

4. What is the Free Software Foundation/GNU? What is Linux? Which parts of the Linux operating system did each provide? Who else has helped build and refine this operating system?

5. In which language is Linux written? What does the language have to do with the success of Linux?

6. What is a utility program?

7. What is a shell? How does it work with the kernel? With the user?

8. How can you use utility programs and a shell to create your own applications?

9. Why is the Linux filesystem referred to as *hierarchical*?

10. What is the difference between a multiprocessor and a multiprocessing system?

11. Give an example of when you would want to use a multiprocessing system.

12. Approximately how many people wrote Linux? Why is this project unique?

13. What are the key terms of the GNU General Public License?

PART I
THE LINUX AND MAC OS X OPERATING SYSTEMS

2

GETTING STARTED

One way or another you are sitting in front of a screen that is connected to a computer that is running Linux. You may be working with a graphical user interface (GUI) or a textual interface. This book is about the textual interface, also called the command-line interface (CLI). If you are working with a GUI, you will need to use a terminal emulator such as xterm, Konsole, GNOME Terminal, Terminal (under Mac OS X), or a virtual console (page 40) to follow the examples in this book.

This chapter starts with a discussion of the typographical conventions this book uses, followed by a section about logging in on the system. The next section introduces the shell and explains how to fix mistakes on the command line. Next come a brief reminder about the powers of working with **root** privileges and suggestions about how to avoid making mistakes that will make your system inoperable or hard to work with. The chapter continues with a discussion about where to find more information about Linux. It concludes with additional information on logging in, including how to change your password.

23

Be sure to read the warning about the dangers of misusing the powers of working with **root** privileges on page 31. While heeding that warning, feel free to experiment with the system: Give commands, create files, follow the examples in this book, and have fun.

Conventions Used in This Book

This book uses conventions to make its explanations shorter and clearer. The following paragraphs describe these conventions.

Mac OS X The term **Mac OS X** refers to both **Mac OS X** and **Mac OS X Server**. This book points out important differences between the two.

Mac OS X versions References to **Mac OS X** refer to version **10.5** (Leopard). Because the book focuses on the underlying operating system, which changes little from one release of OS X to the next, the text will remain relevant through several future releases. The author's Web site (www.sobell.com) provides corrections and updates as appropriate.

Text and examples The text is set in this type, whereas examples are shown in a `monospaced font` (also called a fixed-width font):

```
$ cat practice
This is a small file I created
with a text editor.
```

Items you enter Everything you enter at the keyboard is shown in a bold typeface. Within the text, **this bold typeface** is used; within examples and screens, **this one** is used. In the previous example, the dollar sign (**$**) on the first line is a prompt that Linux displays, so it is not bold; the remainder of the first line is entered by a user, so it is bold.

Utility names Names of utilities are printed in this sans serif typeface. This book references the emacs text editor and the ls utility or ls command (or just ls) but instructs you to enter **ls –a** on the command line. In this way the text distinguishes between utilities, which are programs, and the instructions you give on the command line to invoke the utilities.

Filenames Filenames appear in a bold typeface. Examples are **memo5**, **letter.1283**, and **reports**. Filenames may include uppercase and lowercase letters; however, the popular Linux **ext2**, **ext3**, and **ext4** filesystems are *case sensitive* (page 945), so **memo5**, **MEMO5**, and **Memo5** refer to three different files.

The default Mac OS X filesystem, HFS+, is not case sensitive; under OS X, **memo5**, **MEMO5**, and **Memo5** refer to the same file. For more information refer to "Case Sensitivity" on page 927.

Character strings Within the text, characters and character strings are marked by putting them in a bold typeface. This convention avoids the need for quotation marks or other delimiters before and after a string. An example is the following string, which is displayed by the passwd utility: **Sorry, passwords do not match.**

Keys and characters   This book uses SMALL CAPS for three kinds of items:

- Keyboard keys, such as the SPACE bar and the RETURN,[1] ESCAPE, and TAB keys.

- The characters that keys generate, such as the SPACES generated by the SPACE bar.

- Keyboard keys that you press with the CONTROL key, such as CONTROL-D. (Even though D is shown as an uppercase letter, you do not have to press the SHIFT key; enter CONTROL-D by holding the CONTROL key down and pressing d.)

Prompts and RETURNS   Most examples include the *shell prompt*—the signal that Linux is waiting for a command—as a dollar sign ($), a hash symbol or pound sign (#), or sometimes a percent sign (%). The prompt does not appear in a bold typeface in this book because you do not enter it. Do not type the prompt on the keyboard when you are experimenting with examples from this book. If you do, the examples will not work.

Examples *omit* the RETURN keystroke that you must use to execute them. An example of a command line is

```
$ vim memo.1204
```

To use this example as a model for running the vim text editor, give the command **vim memo.1204** and press the RETURN key. (Press ESCAPE ZZ to exit from vim; see page 151 for a vim tutorial.) This method of entering commands makes the examples in the book correspond to what appears on the screen.

Definitions   All glossary entries marked with FOLDOC are courtesy of Denis Howe, editor of the Free On-Line Dictionary of Computing (foldoc.org), and are used with permission. This site is an ongoing work containing definitions, anecdotes, and trivia.

optional   **OPTIONAL INFORMATION**

Passages marked as optional appear in a gray box. This material is not central to the ideas presented in the chapter but often involves more challenging concepts. A good strategy when reading a chapter is to skip the optional sections and then return to them when you are comfortable with the main ideas presented in the chapter. This is an optional paragraph.

URLs (Web addresses)   Web addresses, or URLs, have an implicit **http://** prefix, unless **ftp://** or **https://** is shown. You do not normally need to specify a prefix in a browser when the prefix is **http://**, but you must use a prefix when you specify an FTP or secure HTTP site. Thus you can specify a URL in a browser exactly as shown in this book.

---

1. Different keyboards use different keys to move the *cursor* (page 949) to the beginning of the next line. This book always refers to the key that ends a line as the RETURN key. Your keyboard may have a RET, NEWLINE, ENTER, RETURN, or other key. Use the corresponding key on your keyboard each time this book asks you to press RETURN.

Tip, caution, and
security boxes

The following boxes highlight information that may be helpful while you are using or administrating a Linux system.

This is a tip box

tip

A tip box may help you avoid repeating a common mistake or may point toward additional information.

This box warns you about something

caution

A caution box warns you about a potential pitfall.

This box marks a security note

security

A security box highlights a potential security issue. These notes are usually for system administrators, but some apply to all users.

LOGGING IN FROM A TERMINAL OR TERMINAL EMULATOR

Above the login prompt on a terminal, terminal emulator, or other textual device, many systems display a message called *issue* (stored in the **/etc/issue** file). This message usually identifies the version of Linux running on the system, the name of the system, and the device you are logging in on. A sample issue message follows:

```
Ubuntu 9.10 tiny tty1
```

The issue message is followed by a prompt to log in. Enter your username and password in response to the system prompts. The following example shows Max logging in on the system named **tiny**:

```
tiny login: max
Password:
Last login: Wed Mar 10 19:50:38 from dog
[max@tiny max]$
```

If you are using a *terminal* (page 983) and the screen does not display the **login:** prompt, check whether the terminal is plugged in and turned on, and then press the RETURN key a few times. If **login:** still does not appear, try pressing CONTROL-Q (Xon).

Did you log in last?

security

As you are logging in to a textual environment, after you enter your username and password, the system displays information about the last login on this account, showing when it took place and where it originated. You can use this information to determine whether anyone has accessed the account since you last used it. If someone has, perhaps an unauthorized user has learned your password and logged in as you. In the interest of maintaining security, advise the system administrator of any circumstances that make you suspicious and change your password.

If you are using an Apple, PC, another Linux system, or a *workstation* (page 988), open the program that runs ssh (secure; page 828), telnet (not secure; page 852), or whichever communications/emulation software you use to log in on the system, and give it the name or IP address (page 960) of the system you want to log in on. Log in, making sure you enter your username and password as they were specified when your account was set up; the routine that verifies the username and password is case sensitive. Like most systems, Linux does not display your password when you enter it. By default Mac OS X does not allow remote logins (page 936).

telnet **is not secure**

security   One of the reasons **telnet** is not secure is that it sends your username and password over the network in *cleartext* (page 947) when you log in, allowing someone to capture your login information and log in on your account. The **ssh** utility encrypts all information it sends over the network and, if available, is a better choice than **telnet**. The **ssh** program has been implemented on many operating systems, not just Linux. Many user interfaces to **ssh** include a terminal emulator.

Following is an example of logging in using **ssh** from a Linux system:

```
$ ssh max@tiny
max@tiny's password:
Permission denied, please try again.
max@tiny's password:
Last login: Wed Mar 10 21:21:49 2005 from dog
[max@tiny max]$
```

In the example Max mistyped his password, received an error message and another prompt, and retyped the password correctly. If your username is the same on the system you are logging in from and the system you are logging in on, you can omit your username and the following at sign (@). In the example, Max would have given the command **ssh tiny**.

After you log in, the *shell prompt* (or just *prompt*) appears, indicating you have successfully logged in; it shows the system is ready for you to give a command. The first shell prompt may be preceded by a short message called the *message of the day,* or **motd**, which is stored in the **/etc/motd** file.

The usual prompt is a dollar sign ($). Do not be concerned if you have a different prompt; the examples in this book will work regardless of what the prompt looks like. In the previous example, the $ prompt (last line) is preceded by the username (**max**), an at sign (@), the system name (**tiny**), and the name of the directory Max is working in (**max**). For information on how to change the prompt, refer to page 299 (bash) or page 373 (tcsh).

Make sure **TERM** is set correctly

tip   The **TERM** shell variable establishes the pseudographical characteristics of a character-based terminal or terminal emulator. Typically **TERM** is set for you—you do not have to set it manually. If things on the screen do not look right, refer to "Specifying a Terminal" on page 906.

WORKING WITH THE SHELL

Before the introduction of the graphical user interface (GUI), UNIX and then Linux provided only a textual interface (also called a command-line interface or CLI). Today, a textual interface is available when you log in from a terminal, a terminal emulator, or a textual virtual console, or when you use ssh or telnet to log in on a system.

When you log in and are working in a textual (nongraphical) environment, and when you are using a terminal emulator window in a graphical environment, you are using the shell as a command interpreter. The shell displays a prompt that indicates it is ready for you to enter a command. In response to the prompt, you type a command. The shell executes this command and then displays another prompt.

Advantages of the textual interface
Although the concept may seem antiquated, a textual interface has a place in modern computing. In some cases an administrator may use a command-line tool either because a graphical equivalent does not exist or because the graphical tool is not as powerful or flexible as the textual one. When logging in using a dial-up line or network connection, using a GUI may not be practical because of the slow connection speed. Frequently, on a server system, a graphical interface may not even be installed. The first reason for this omission is that a GUI consumes a lot of system resources; on a server, those resources are better dedicated to the main task of the server. Additionally, security mandates that a server system run as few tasks as possible because each additional task can make the system more vulnerable to attack. Also, some users prefer a textual interface because it is cleaner and more efficient than a GUI. Some simple tasks, such as changing file access permissions, can be done more easily from the command line (see chmod on page 626).

Pseudographical interface
Before the introduction of GUIs, resourceful programmers created textual interfaces that included graphical elements such as boxes, borders outlining rudimentary windows, highlights, and, more recently, color. These textual interfaces, called *pseudographical interfaces,* bridge the gap between textual and graphical interfaces. An example of a modern utility that uses a pseudographical interface is the dpkg-reconfigure utility, which reconfigures an installed software package.

This section explains how to identify the shell you are using and describes the keystrokes you can use to correct mistakes on the command line. It covers how to abort a running command and briefly discusses how to edit a command line. Several chapters of this book are dedicated to shells: Chapter 5 introduces shells, Chapter 8 goes into more detail about the Bourne Again Shell with some coverage of the TC Shell, Chapter 9 covers the TC Shell exclusively, and Chapter 10 discusses writing programs (shell scripts) using the Bourne Again Shell.

WHICH SHELL ARE YOU RUNNING?

This book discusses both the Bourne Again Shell (bash) and the TC Shell (tcsh). You are probably running bash, but you may be running tcsh or another shell such as the

Z Shell (zsh). You can identify the shell you are running by using the ps utility (page 796). Type **ps** in response to the shell prompt and press RETURN.

```
$ ps
  PID TTY          TIME CMD
 2402 pts/5     00:00:00 bash
 7174 pts/5     00:00:00 ps
```

This command shows that you are running two utilities or commands: bash and ps. If you are running tcsh, ps will display **tcsh** instead of **bash**. If you are running a different shell, ps will display its name.

CORRECTING MISTAKES

This section explains how to correct typographical and other errors you may make while you are logged in on a textual display. Because the shell and most other utilities do not interpret the command line or other text until after you press RETURN, you can readily correct typing mistakes before you press RETURN.

You can correct typing mistakes in several ways: erase one character at a time, back up a word at a time, or back up to the beginning of the command line in one step. After you press RETURN, it is too late to correct a mistake: You must either wait for the command to run to completion or abort execution of the program (page 30).

ERASING A CHARACTER

While entering characters from the keyboard, you can back up and erase a mistake by pressing the *erase key* once for each character you want to delete. The erase key backs over as many characters as you wish. It does not, in general, back up past the beginning of the line.

The default erase key is BACKSPACE. If this key does not work, try pressing DELETE or CONTROL-H. If these keys do not work, give the following stty[2] command to set the erase and line kill (see "Deleting a Line" on the next page) keys to their default values:

```
$ stty ek
```

See page 838 for more information on stty.

DELETING A WORD

You can delete a word you entered by pressing CONTROL-W. A *word* is any sequence of characters that does not contain a SPACE or TAB. When you press CONTROL-W, the cursor moves left to the beginning of the current word (as you are entering a word) or the previous word (when you have just entered a SPACE or TAB), removing the word.

---

2. The command stty is an abbreviation for *set teletypewriter,* the first terminal that UNIX was run on. Today stty is commonly thought of as meaning *set terminal.*

CONTROL-Z **suspends a program**

tip   Although it is not a way of correcting a mistake, you may press the suspend key (typically CONTROL-Z) by mistake and wonder what happened. If the system displays a message containing the word **Stopped**, you have just stopped your job using job control. Give the command **fg** to continue your job in the foreground, and you should return to where you were before you pressed the suspend key. For more information refer to "Moving a Job from the Foreground to the Background" on page 135.

DELETING A LINE

Any time before you press RETURN, you can delete the line you are entering by pressing the *(line) kill key*. When you press this key, the cursor moves to the left, erasing characters as it goes, back to the beginning of the line. The default line kill key is CONTROL-U. If this key does not work, try CONTROL-X. If these keys do not work, give the stty command described under "Erasing a Character."

ABORTING EXECUTION

Sometimes you may want to terminate a running program. For example, you may want to stop a program that is performing a lengthy task such as displaying the contents of a file that is several hundred pages long or copying a file that is not the one you meant to copy.

To terminate a program from a textual display, press the *interrupt key* (CONTROL-C or sometimes DELETE or DEL). If you would like to use another key as your interrupt key, see "Special Keys and Characteristics" on page 838.

If this method does not terminate the program, try stopping the program with the suspend key (typically CONTROL-Z), giving a **jobs** command to verify the number of the job running the program, and using kill to abort the job. The job number is the number within the brackets at the left end of the line that jobs displays ([**1**] in the next example). In the following example, the user uses the **–TERM** option to kill to send a termination signal to the job specified by the job number, which is preceded by a percent sign (**%1**). You can omit **–TERM** from the command as kill sends a termination signal by default.

```
$ bigjob
CONTROL-Z
[1]+  Stopped                 bigjob
$ jobs
[1]+  Stopped                 bigjob
$ kill -TERM %1
$ RETURN
[1]+  Killed                  bigjob
```

The **kill** command returns a prompt; press RETURN again to see the confirmation message. If the terminal interrupt signal does not appear to work, wait ten seconds and press RETURN. If there is no message indicating the job was killed, use the kill (**–KILL**) signal. A running program cannot usually ignore a kill signal; it is almost sure to abort the program. For more information refer to "Running a Command in the Background" on page 134 and kill on page 729.

optional When you press the interrupt key, the Linux operating system sends a terminal interrupt signal to the program you are running and to the shell. Exactly what effect this signal has depends on the program.

A program may stop execution and exit immediately (most common), it may ignore the signal, or it may receive the signal and take another action based on a custom signal handler procedure.

The Bourne Again Shell has a custom signal handler procedure for the terminal interrupt signal. The behavior of this signal handler depends on whether the shell is waiting for the user to finish typing a command or waiting for a program to finish executing. If the shell is waiting for the user, the signal handler discards the partial line and displays a prompt. If the shell is waiting for a program, the signal handler does nothing; the shell keeps waiting. When the program finishes executing, the shell displays a prompt.

REPEATING/EDITING COMMAND LINES

To repeat a previous command under bash or tcsh, press the UP ARROW key. Each time you press this key, the shell displays an earlier command line. To reexecute the displayed command line, press RETURN. Press the DOWN ARROW key to browse through the command lines in the other direction.

The RIGHT and LEFT ARROW keys move the cursor back and forth along the displayed command line. At any point along the command line, you can add characters by typing them. Use the erase key to remove characters from the command line. For information about more complex command-line editing, see page 310 (bash) and page 363 (tcsh).

su/sudo: CURBING YOUR POWER (root PRIVILEGES)

UNIX and Linux systems have always had a privileged user named **root**. When you are working as the **root** user ("working with *root privileges*"), you have extraordinary systemwide powers. A user working with **root** privileges is sometimes referred to as *Superuser* or *administrator*. When working with **root** privileges, you can read from or write to any file on the system, execute programs that ordinary users cannot, and more. On a multiuser system you may not be permitted to gain **root** privileges and so may not be able to run certain programs. Nevertheless, someone—the *system administrator*—can, and that person maintains the system.

Do not experiment while you are working with root privileges

caution Feel free to experiment when you are *not* working with **root** privileges. When you *are* working with **root** privileges, do only what you have to do and make sure you know exactly what you are doing. After you have completed the task at hand, revert to working as yourself. When working with **root** privileges, you can damage the system to such an extent that you will need to reinstall Linux to get it working again.

Under a conventional setup, you can gain **root** privileges in one of two ways. First you can log in as the user named **root**; when you do so you are working with **root** privileges until you log off. Alternatively, while you are working as yourself, you can use the su (substitute user) utility to execute a single command with **root** privileges or to gain **root** privileges temporarily so you can execute several commands. Logging in as **root** and running su to gain **root** privileges require you to enter the **root** password. The following example shows how to use su to execute a single command.

```
$ ls -l /lost+found
ls: cannot open directory /lost+found: Permission denied
$ su -c 'ls -l /lost+found'
Password:                    Enter the root password
total 0
$
```

The first command in the preceding example shows that a user who does not have **root** privileges is not permitted to list the files in the **/lost+found** directory: ls displays an error message. The second command uses su with the –c (command) option to execute the same command with **root** privileges. Single quotation marks enclose the command to ensure the shell interprets the command properly. When the command finishes executing (ls shows there are no files in the directory), the user no longer has **root** privileges. Without any arguments, su spawns a new shell running with **root** privileges. Typically the shell displays a hash or pound sign (#) prompt when you are working with **root** privileges. Give an **exit** command to return to the normal prompt and nonroot privileges.

```
$ su
Password:                    Enter the root password
# ls -l /lost+found
total 0
# exit
exit
$
```

Some distributions (e.g., Ubuntu) ship with the **root** account locked—there is no **root** password—and rely on the sudo (www.sudo.ws) utility to allow users to gain **root** privileges. The sudo utility requires you to enter *your* password (not the **root** password) to gain **root** privileges. The following example allows the user to gain **root** privileges to view the contents of the **/lost+found** directory.

```
$ sudo ls -l /lost+found
[sudo] password for sam:     Enter your password
total 0
$
```

With an argument of –i, sudo spawns a new shell running with **root** privileges. Typically the shell displays a hash or pound sign (#) prompt when you are working with **root** privileges. Give an **exit** command to return to the normal prompt and nonroot privileges.

```
$ sudo -i
[sudo] password for sam:        Enter your password
# ls -l /lost+found
total 0
# exit
logout
$
```

WHERE TO FIND DOCUMENTATION

Distributions of Linux do not typically come with hardcopy reference manuals. However, its online documentation has always been one of Linux's strengths. The man (or manual) and info pages have been available via the man and info utilities since early releases of the operating system. Not surprisingly, with the ongoing growth of Linux and the Internet, the sources of documentation have expanded as well. This section discusses some of the places you can look for information on Linux. See Appendix B as well.

THE --help OPTION

Most GNU utilities provide a **--help** option that displays information about the utility. Non-GNU utilities may use a **–h** or **–help** option to display help information.

```
$ cat --help
Usage: cat [OPTION] [FILE]...
Concatenate FILE(s), or standard input, to standard output.

  -A, --show-all             equivalent to -vET
  -b, --number-nonblank      number nonblank output lines
  -e                         equivalent to -vE
  -E, --show-ends            display $ at end of each line
...
```

If the information that **--help** displays runs off the screen, send the output through the less pager (page 34) using a pipe (page 56):

```
$ ls --help | less
```

man: DISPLAYS THE SYSTEM MANUAL

The man utility (page 759) displays (man) pages from the system documentation in a textual environment. This documentation is helpful when you know which utility you want to use but have forgotten exactly how to use it. You can also refer to the man pages to get more information about specific topics or to determine which features are available with Linux. You can search for topics covered by man pages using the apropos utility (page 35). Because the descriptions in the system documentation are often terse, they are most helpful if you already understand the basic functions of a utility.

```
MAN(1)                    Manual pager utils                    MAN(1)

NAME
        man - an interface to the on-line reference manuals

SYNOPSIS
        man  [-c|-w|-tZ] [-H[browser]] [-T[device]] [-X[dpi]] [-adhu7V] [-i|-I]
        [-m system[,...]] [-L locale] [-p string]  [-C file]  [-M path]  [-P
        pager]  [-r  prompt]  [-S  list] [-e extension] [--warnings [warnings]]
        [[section] page ...] ...
        man -l [-7] [-tZ] [-H[browser]] [-T[device]] [-X[dpi]] [-p string]  [-P
        pager] [-r prompt] [--warnings[warnings]] file ...
        man -k [apropos options] regexp ...
        man -f [whatis options] page ...

DESCRIPTION
        man  is  the  system's  manual pager. Each page argument given to man is
        normally the name of a program, utility or function.  The  manual  page
        associated  with each of these arguments is then found and displayed. A
        section, if provided, will direct man to look only in that  section  of
        the  manual.   The  default action is to search in all of the available
        sections, following a pre-defined order and to show only the first page
        found, even if page exists in several sections.

        The table below shows the section numbers of the manual followed by the
        types of pages they contain.

Manual page man(1) line 1
```

Figure 2-1   The man utility displaying information about itself

Online man pages

tip   The tldp.org/manpages/man.html site holds links to copies of most man pages. In addition to presenting man pages in an easy-to-read HTML format, this site does not require you to install a utility to read the man page.

To find out more about a utility, give the command **man,** followed by the name of the utility. Figure 2-1 shows man displaying information about itself; the user entered a **man man** command.

less (pager)   The man utility automatically sends its output through a *pager*—usually less, which displays one screen at a time. When you access a manual page in this manner, less displays a prompt [e.g., **Manual page man(1) line 1**] at the bottom of the screen after it displays each screen of text and waits for you to request another screen of text by pressing the SPACE bar. Pressing **h** (help) displays a list of less commands. Pressing **q** (quit) stops less and causes the shell to display a prompt. For more information refer to page 48.

Manual sections   Based on the FHS (Filesystem Hierarchy Standard; page 91), the Linux system manual and the man pages are divided into ten sections, where each section describes related tools:

1. User Commands
2. System Calls
3. Subroutines
4. Devices
5. File Formats
6. Games
7. Miscellaneous
8. System Administration
9. Kernel
10. New

This layout closely mimics the way the set of UNIX manuals has always been divided. Unless you specify a manual section, man displays the earliest occurrence in the manual of the word you specify on the command line. Most users find the information they need in sections 1, 6, and 7; programmers and system administrators frequently need to consult the other sections.

In some cases the manual contains entries for different tools with the same name. For example, the following command displays the man page for the passwd utility from section 1 of the system manual:

```
$ man passwd
```

To see the man page for the **passwd** file from section 5, enter this command:

```
$ man 5 passwd
```

The preceding command instructs man to look only in section 5 for the man page. In documentation you may see this man page referred to as **passwd(5)**. Use the **–a** option (see the adjacent tip) to view all man pages for a given subject (press **q**RETURN to display the next man page). For example, give the command **man –a passwd** to view all man pages for **passwd**.

Options

> **tip** An option modifies the way a utility or command works. Options are usually specified as one or more letters preceded by one or two hyphens. An option typically appears following the name of the utility you are calling and a SPACE. Other *arguments* (page 941) to the command follow the option and a SPACE. For more information refer to "Options" on page 119.

apropos: SEARCHES FOR A KEYWORD

When you do not know the name of the command you need to carry out a particular task, you can use apropos with a keyword to search for it. This utility searches for the keyword in the short description line (the top line) of all man pages and displays those that contain a match. The man utility, when called with the **–k** (keyword) option, provides the same output as apropos.

The database apropos uses, named **whatis**, is not available on many Linux systems when they are first installed, but is built automatically by cron (see crontab on page 649 for a discussion of cron).

The following example shows the output of apropos when you call it with the **who** keyword. The output includes the name of each command, the section of the manual that contains it, and the brief description from the top of the man page. This list includes the utility that you need (who) and identifies other, related tools that you might find useful:

```
$ apropos who
at.allow (5)         - determine who can submit jobs via at or batch
at.deny (5)          - determine who can submit jobs via at or batch
from (1)             - print names of those who have sent mail
w (1)                - Show who is logged on and what they are doing.
w.procps (1)         - Show who is logged on and what they are doing.
who (1)              - show who is logged on
whoami (1)           - print effective userid
```

```
File: coreutils.info,  Node: Top,  Next: Introduction,  Up: (dir)

GNU Coreutils
*************

This manual documents version 6.10 of the GNU core utilities, including
the standard programs for text and file manipulation.

   Copyright (C) 1994-1996, 2000-2008 Free Software Foundation, Inc.

     Permission is granted to copy, distribute and/or modify this
     document under the terms of the GNU Free Documentation License,
     Version 1.2 or any later version published by the Free Software
     Foundation; with no Invariant Sections, with no Front-Cover Texts,
     and with no Back-Cover Texts.  A copy of the license is included
     in the section entitled "GNU Free Documentation License".

* Menu:

* Introduction::                        Caveats, overview, and authors.
* Common options::                      Common options.
* Output of entire files::              cat tac nl od
* Formatting file contents::            fmt pr fold
* Output of parts of files::            head tail split csplit
* Summarizing files::                   wc sum cksum md5sum sha1sum sha2
* Operating on sorted files::           sort shuf uniq comm ptx tsort
--zz-Info: (coreutils.info.gz)Top, 318 lines --Top-----------------------------
Welcome to Info version 4.11. Type ? for help, m for menu item.
```

Figure 2-2   The initial screen **info coreutils** displays

whatis The whatis utility is similar to apropos but finds only complete word matches for the name of the utility:

```
$ whatis who
who                        (1)  - show who is logged on
```

info: DISPLAYS INFORMATION ABOUT UTILITIES

The textual info utility is a menu-based hypertext system developed by the GNU project (page 3) and distributed with Linux. The info utility can display documentation on many Linux shells, utilities, and programs developed by the GNU project. See www.gnu.org/software/texinfo/manual/info for the info manual. Figure 2-2 shows the screen that info displays when you give the command **info coreutils** (the **coreutils** software package holds the Linux core utilities).

man and info display different information

tip The info utility displays more complete and up-to-date information on GNU utilities than does man. When a man page displays abbreviated information on a utility that is covered by info, the man page refers to info. The man utility frequently displays the only information available on non-GNU utilities. When info displays information on non-GNU utilities, it is frequently a copy of the man page.

Because the information on this screen is drawn from an editable file, your display may differ from the screens shown in this section. When you see the initial info screen, you can press any of the following keys or key combinations:

- **?** lists info commands
- SPACE scrolls through the menu of items for which information is available
- **m** followed by the name of a menu displays that menu
- **m** followed by a SPACE displays a list of menus
- **q** or CONTROL-C quits info

```
* chroot invocation::           Run a command with a different root directory
* env invocation::              Run a command in a modified environment
* nice invocation::             Run a command with modified niceness
* nohup invocation::            Run a command immune to hangups
* su invocation::               Run a command with substitute user and group ID

Process control

* kill invocation::             Sending a signal to processes.

Delaying

* sleep invocation::            Delay for a specified time

Numeric operations

* factor invocation::           Print prime factors
* seq invocation::              Print numeric sequences

File permissions

* Mode Structure::              Structure of file mode bits.
* Symbolic Modes::              Mnemonic representation of file mode bits.
* Numeric Modes::               File mode bits as octal numbers.
* Directory Setuid and Setgid:: Set-user-ID and set-group-ID on directories.

--zz-Info: (coreutils.info.gz)Top, 318 lines --83%--------------------------------
```

Figure 2-3 The screen **info coreutils** displays after you type **/sleep**RETURN twice

The notation info uses to describe keyboard keys may not be familiar to you. The notation **C-h** is the same as CONTROL-H. Similarly **M-x** means hold down the META or ALT key and press **x**. On some systems you need to press ESCAPE and then **x** to duplicate the function of META-X. For more information refer to "Keys: Notation and Use" on page 216. For Mac keyboards see "Activating the META key" on page 935.

You may find pinfo **easier to use than** info

tip   The pinfo utility is similar to info but is more intuitive if you are not familiar with the emacs editor. This utility runs in a textual environment, as does info. When it is available, pinfo uses color to make its interface easier to use. You may have to install pinfo before you can use it; see Appendix C.

After giving the command **info coreutils**, type **/sleep**RETURN to search for the string **sleep**. When you type **/**, the cursor moves to the bottom line of the screen and displays **Search for string [***string***]:** where *string* is the last string you searched for. Press RETURN to search for *string* or enter the string you want to search for. Typing **sleep** displays **sleep** on that line, and pressing RETURN displays the next occurrence of **sleep**.

Next, type **/**RETURN (or **/sleep**RETURN) to search for the second occurrence of **sleep** as shown in Figure 2-3. The asterisk at the left end of the line indicates that this entry is a menu item. Following the asterisk is the name of the menu item, two colons, and a description of the item.

Each menu item is a link to the info page that describes that item. To jump to that page, use the ARROW keys to move the cursor to the line containing the menu item and press RETURN. Alternatively, you can type the name of the menu item in a menu command to view the information. To display information on **sleep**, for example, you can give the command **m sleep**, followed by RETURN. When you type **m** (for *menu*), the cursor moves to the bottom line of the window (as it did when you typed **/**) and displays **Menu item:**. Typing **sleep** displays **sleep** on that line, and pressing RETURN displays information about the menu item you have chosen.

```
File: coreutils.info,  Node: sleep invocation,  Up: Delaying

24.1 `sleep': Delay for a specified time
========================================

`sleep' pauses for an amount of time specified by the sum of the values
of the command line arguments.  Synopsis:

     sleep NUMBER[smhd]...

     Each argument is a number followed by an optional unit; the default
is seconds.  The units are:

`s'
     seconds

`m'
     minutes

`h'
     hours

`d'
     days

     Historical implementations of `sleep' have required that NUMBER be
--zz-Info: (coreutils.info.gz)sleep invocation, 36 lines --Top-----------------
```

Figure 2-4   The info page on the sleep utility

Figure 2-4 shows the *top node* of information on sleep. A node groups a set of information you can scroll through with the SPACE bar. To display the next node, press **n**. Press **p** to display the previous node. (The **sleep** item has only one node.)

As you read through this book and learn about new utilities, you can use man or info to find out more about those utilities. If you can print PostScript documents, you can print a manual page by using the man utility with the **–t** option. For example, **man –t cat | lpr** prints information about the cat utility. You can also use a Web browser to display the documentation at www.tldp.org and print the desired information from the browser.

HOWTOs: Finding Out How Things Work

A HOWTO document explains in detail how to do something related to Linux—from setting up a specialized piece of hardware to performing a system administration task to setting up specific networking software. Mini-HOWTOs offer shorter explanations. As with Linux software, one person or a few people generally are responsible for writing and maintaining a HOWTO document, but many people may contribute to it.

The Linux Documentation Project (LDP; page 40) site houses most HOWTO and mini-HOWTO documents. Use a Web browser to visit www.tldp.org, click **HOW-TOs**, and pick the index you want to use to find a HOWTO or mini-HOWTO. You can also use the LDP search feature on its home page to find HOWTOs and other documents.

Getting Help with the System

This section describes several places you can look for help in using a Linux system.

Figure 2-5   Google reporting on an error message

FINDING HELP LOCALLY

/usr/share/doc   The **/usr/share/doc** and **/usr/src/linux/Documentation** (present only if you installed the kernel source code) directories often contain more detailed and different information about a utility than man or info provides. Frequently this information is meant for people who will be compiling and modifying the utility, not just using it. These directories hold thousands of files, each containing information on a separate topic.

For example, the following commands display information on grep and info. The second command uses zcat (page 618) to allow you to view a compressed file by decompressing it and sending it through the less pager (page 34).

```
$ less /usr/share/doc/grep/README
```

```
$ zcat /usr/share/doc/info/README.gz | less
```

USING THE INTERNET TO GET HELP

The Internet provides many helpful sites related to Linux. Aside from sites that offer various forms of documentation, you can enter an error message from a program you are having a problem with in a search engine such as Google (www.google.com, or its Linux-specific version at www.google.com/linux). Enclose the error message within double quotation marks to improve the quality of the results. The search will likely yield a post concerning your problem and suggestions about how to solve it. See Figure 2-5.

GNU   GNU manuals are available at www.gnu.org/manual. In addition, you can visit the GNU home page (www.gnu.org) for more documentation and other GNU resources. Many of the GNU pages and resources are available in a variety of languages.

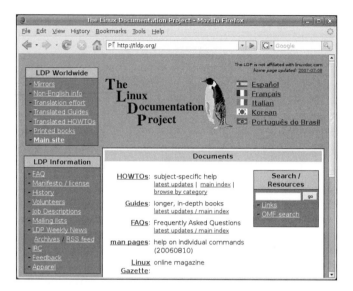

Figure 2-6   The Linux Documentation Project home page

The Linux Documentation Project   The Linux Documentation Project (www.tldp.org; Figure 2-6), which has been around for almost as long as Linux, houses a complete collection of guides, HOW-TOs, FAQs, man pages, and Linux magazines. The home page is available in English, Portuguese, Spanish, Italian, Korean, and French. It is easy to use and supports local text searches. It also provides a complete set of links you can use to find almost anything you want related to Linux (click **Links** in the Search box or go to www.tldp.org/links). The **links** page includes sections on general information, events, getting started, user groups, mailing lists, and newsgroups, with each section containing many subsections.

MORE ABOUT LOGGING IN

This section discusses how to use virtual consoles, what to do if you have a problem logging in, and how to change your password.

USING VIRTUAL CONSOLES

When running Linux on a personal computer, you will frequently work with the display and keyboard attached to the computer. Using this physical console, you can access as many as 63 *virtual consoles* (also called *virtual terminals*). Some are set up to allow logins; others act as graphical displays. To switch between virtual consoles, hold the CONTROL and ALT keys down and press the function key that corresponds to the console you want to view. For example, CONTROL-ALT-F5 displays the fifth virtual console. This book refers to the console you see when you press CONTROL-ALT-F1 as the *system console,* or just *console*.

Typically, six virtual consoles are active and have textual login sessions running. When you want to use both textual and graphical interfaces, you can set up a textual session on one virtual console and a graphical session on another. No matter which virtual console you start a graphical session from, the graphical session runs on the first unused virtual console (typically number seven).

WHAT TO DO IF YOU CANNOT LOG IN

If you enter either your username or password incorrectly, the system displays an error message after you enter *both* your username *and* your password. This message indicates you have entered either the username or the password incorrectly or they are not valid. It does not differentiate between an unacceptable username and an unacceptable password—a strategy meant to discourage unauthorized people from guessing names and passwords to gain access to the system.

Following are some common reasons why logins fail:

- **The username and password are case sensitive.** Make sure the CAPS LOCK key is off and enter your username and password exactly as specified or as you set them up.

- **You are not logging in on the right machine.** The login/password combination may not be valid if you are trying to log in on the wrong machine. On a larger, networked system, you may have to specify the machine you want to connect to before you can log in.

- **Your username is not valid.** The login/password combination may not be valid if you have not been set up as a user. Check with the system administrator.

LOGGING OUT

To log out from a character-based interface, press CONTROL-D in response to the shell prompt. This action sends the shell an EOF (end of file) signal. Alternatively, you can give the command **exit**. Exiting from a shell does not end a graphical session; it just exits from the shell you are working with. For example, exiting from the shell that GNOME terminal provides closes the GNOME terminal window.

CHANGING YOUR PASSWORD

If someone else assigned you a password, it is a good idea to give yourself a new one. For security reasons none of the passwords you enter is displayed by any utility.

Protect your password

security   Do not allow someone to find out your password: *Do not* put your password in a file that is not encrypted, allow someone to watch you type your password, or give your password to someone you do not know (a system administrator never needs to know your password). You can always write your password down and keep it in a safe, private place.

Choose a password that is difficult to guess

security   Do not use phone numbers, names of pets or kids, birthdays, words from a dictionary (not even a foreign language), and so forth. Do not use permutations of these items or a l33t-speak variation of a word: Modern dictionary crackers may also try these permutations.

Differentiate between important and less important passwords

security   It is a good idea to differentiate between important and less important passwords. For example, Web site passwords for blogs or download access are not very important; it is acceptable to use the same password for these types of sites. However, your login, mail server, and bank account Web site passwords are critical: Use different passwords for each and never use these passwords for an unimportant Web site.

To change your password, give the command **passwd**. The first item passwd asks for is your current (old) password. This password is verified to ensure that an unauthorized user is not trying to alter your password. Then the system requests a new password.

pwgen **can help you pick a password**

security   The pwgen utility (which you may need to install; see Appendix C) generates a list of almost random passwords. With a little imagination, you can pronounce, and therefore remember, some of these passwords.

After you enter your new password, the system asks you to retype it to make sure you did not make a mistake when you entered it the first time. If the new password is the same both times you enter it, your password is changed. If the passwords differ, it means that you made an error in one of them, and the system displays this error message:

```
Sorry, passwords do not match
```

If your password is not long enough, the system displays the following message:

```
You must choose a longer password
```

When it is too simple, the system displays this message:

```
Bad: new password is too simple
```

If the system displays an error message, you need to start over. Press RETURN a few times until the shell displays a prompt and run passwd again.

When you successfully change your password, you change the way you log in. If you forget your password, someone working with **root** privileges can run passwd to change it and tell you your new password.

Under OS X, the passwd utility changes your login password, but does not change your Keychain password. The Keychain password is used by various graphical applications. You can change the Keychain password using the Keychain Access application.

Secure passwords   To be relatively secure, a password should contain a combination of numbers, upper-case and lowercase letters, and punctuation characters and meet the following criteria:

- Must be at least four to six or more characters long (depending on how the administrator sets up the system). Seven or eight characters is a good compromise between length and security.
- Should not be a word in a dictionary of any language, no matter how seemingly obscure.
- Should not be the name of a person, place, pet, or other thing that might be discovered easily.
- Should contain at least two letters and one digit or punctuation character.
- Should not be your username, the reverse of your username, or your username shifted by one or more characters.

Only the first item is mandatory. Avoid using control characters (such as CONTROL-H) because they may have a special meaning to the system, making it impossible for you to log in. If you are changing your password, the new password should differ from the old one by at least three characters. Changing the case of a character does not make it count as a different character.

CHAPTER SUMMARY

As with many operating systems, your access to a Linux system is authorized when you log in. You enter your username in response to the **login:** prompt, followed by a password. You can use passwd to change your password any time while you are logged in. Choose a password that is difficult to guess and that conforms to the criteria imposed by the system administrator.

The system administrator is responsible for maintaining the system. On a single-user system, you are the system administrator. On a small, multiuser system, you or another user will act as the system administrator, or this job may be shared. On a large, multiuser system or network of systems, there is frequently a full-time system administrator. When extra privileges are required to perform certain system tasks, the system administrator gains root privileges by logging in as **root,** or running su or sudo. On a multiuser system, several trusted users may be allowed to gain **root** privileges.

Do not work with **root** privileges as a matter of course. When you have to do something that requires **root** privileges, work with **root** privileges for only as long as you need to; revert to working as yourself as soon as possible.

The man utility provides online documentation on system utilities. This utility is helpful both to new Linux users and to experienced users who must often delve into the system documentation for information on the fine points of a utility's behavior. The info utility helps the beginner and the expert alike. It includes documentation on many Linux utilities.

EXERCISES

1. The following message is displayed when you attempt to log in with an incorrect username *or* an incorrect password:

   ```
   Login incorrect
   ```

   This message does not indicate whether your username, your password, or both are invalid. Why does it not tell you this information?

2. Give three examples of poor password choices. What is wrong with each? Include one that is too short. Give the error message the system displays.

3. Is **fido** an acceptable password? Give several reasons why or why not.

4. What would you do if you could not log in?

5. Try to change your password to **dog**. What happens? Now change it to a more secure password. What makes that password relatively secure?

ADVANCED EXERCISES

6. Change your login shell to tcsh without using **root** privileges.

7. How many man pages are in the **Devices** subsection of the system manual? (*Hint:* **Devices** is a subsection of **Special Files**.)

8. The example on page 35 shows that man pages for **passwd** appear in sections 1 and 5 of the system manual. Explain how you can use man to determine which sections of the system manual contain a manual page with a given name.

9. How would you find out which Linux utilities create and work with archive files?

3

THE UTILITIES

When Linus Torvalds introduced Linux and for a long time thereafter, Linux did not have a graphical user interface (GUI): It ran using a textual interface, also referred to as a command-line interface (CLI). All the tools ran from a command line. Today the Linux GUI is important but many people—especially system administrators—run many command-line utilities. Command-line utilities are often faster, more powerful, or more complete than their GUI counterparts. Sometimes there is no GUI counterpart to a textual utility; some people just prefer the hands-on feeling of the command line.

When you work with a command-line interface, you are working with a shell (Chapters 5, 8, and 10). Before you start working with a shell, it is important that you understand something about the characters that are special to the shell, so this chapter starts with a discussion of special characters. The chapter then describes five basic utilities: ls, cat, rm, less, and hostname. It continues by describing several other file manipulation utilities as well as utilities that display who is logged in; that communicate with other users; that print, compress, and decompress files; and that pack and unpack archive files.

SPECIAL CHARACTERS

Special characters, which have a special meaning to the shell, are discussed in "File-name Generation/Pathname Expansion" on page 136. These characters are men-tioned here so you can avoid accidentally using them as regular characters until you understand how the shell interprets them. For example, it is best to avoid using any of the following characters in a filename (even though emacs and some other programs do) because they make the file harder to reference on the command line:

    & ; | * ? ' " ` [ ] ( ) $ < > { } # / \ ! ~

Whitespace   Although not considered special characters, RETURN, SPACE, and TAB have special mean-ings to the shell. RETURN usually ends a command line and initiates execution of a command. The SPACE and TAB characters separate elements on the command line and are collectively known as *whitespace* or *blanks*.

Quoting special characters   If you need to use a character that has a special meaning to the shell as a regular character, you can *quote* (or *escape*) it. When you quote a special character, you keep the shell from giving it special meaning. The shell treats a quoted special character as a regular character. However, a slash (/) is always a separator in a pathname, even when you quote it.

Backslash   To quote a character, precede it with a backslash (\). When two or more special characters appear together, you must precede each with a backslash (for example, you would enter ** as **). You can quote a backslash just as you would quote any other special character—by preceding it with a backslash (\\).

Single quotation marks   Another way of quoting special characters is to enclose them between single quota-tion marks: '**'. You can quote many special and regular characters between a pair of single quotation marks: '**This is a special character: >**'. The regular charac-ters are interpreted as usual, and the shell also interprets the special characters as regular characters.

The only way to quote the erase character (CONTROL-H), the line kill character (CONTROL-U), and other control characters (try CONTROL-M) is by preceding each with a CONTROL-V. Single quotation marks and backslashes do not work. Try the following:

```
$ echo 'xxxxxxCONTROL-U'
$ echo xxxxxxCONTROL-V CONTROL-U
```

optional   Although you cannot see the CONTROL-U displayed by the second of the preceding pair of commands, it is there. The following command sends the output of echo (page 57) through a pipe (page 56) to od (octal display; page 776) to display CONTROL-U as octal 25 (025):

```
$ echo xxxxxxCONTROL-V CONTROL-U | od -c
0000000   x   x   x   x   x   x 025  \n
0000010
```

The **\n** is the NEWLINE character that echo sends at the end of its output.

BASIC UTILITIES

One of the important advantages of Linux is that it comes with thousands of utilities that perform myriad functions. You will use utilities whenever you work with Linux, whether you use them directly by name from the command line or indirectly from a menu or icon. The following sections discuss some of the most basic and important utilities; these utilities are available from a textual interface. Some of the more important utilities are also available from a GUI; others are available only from a GUI.

Run these utilities from a command line

tip This chapter describes command-line, or textual, utilities. You can experiment with these utilities from a terminal, a terminal emulator within a GUI, or a virtual console (page 40).

Folder/directory The term *directory* is used extensively in the next sections. A directory is a resource that can hold files. On other operating systems, including Windows and Mac OS X, and frequently when speaking about a Linux GUI, a directory is referred to as a *folder*. That is a good analogy: A traditional manila folder holds files just as a directory does.

In this chapter you work in your home directory

tip When you log in on the system, you are working in your *home directory*. In this chapter that is the only directory you use: All the files you create in this chapter are in your home directory. Chapter 4 goes into detail about directories.

ls: LISTS THE NAMES OF FILES

Using the editor of your choice, create a small file named **practice**. (A tutorial on the vim editor appears on page 151 and a tutorial on emacs appears on page 208.) After exiting from the editor, you can use the ls (list) utility to display a list of the names of the files in your home directory. In the first command in Figure 3-1, ls lists the name of the **practice** file. (You may also see files that the system or a program created automatically.) Subsequent commands in Figure 3-1 display the contents of the file and remove the file. These commands are described next. Refer to page 745 or give the command **info coreutils 'ls invocation'** for more information.

```
$ ls
practice
$ cat practice
This is a small file that I created
with a text editor.
$ rm practice
$ ls
$ cat practice
cat: practice: No such file or directory
$
```

Figure 3-1 Using ls, cat, and rm on the file named **practice**

cat: DISPLAYS A TEXT FILE

The cat utility displays the contents of a text file. The name of the command is derived from *catenate*, which means to join together, one after the other. (Figure 5-8 on page 127 shows how to use cat to string together the contents of three files.)

A convenient way to display the contents of a file to the screen is by giving the command **cat**, followed by a SPACE and the name of the file. Figure 3-1 shows cat displaying the contents of **practice**. This figure shows the difference between the ls and cat utilities: The ls utility displays the *name* of a file, whereas cat displays the *contents* of a file. Refer to page 618 or give the command **info coreutils 'cat invocation'** for more information.

rm: DELETES A FILE

The rm (remove) utility deletes a file. Figure 3-1 shows rm deleting the file named **practice**. After rm deletes the file, ls and cat show that **practice** is no longer in the directory. The ls utility does not list its filename, and cat says that no such file exists. Use rm carefully. Refer to page 804 or give the command **info coreutils 'rm invocation'** for more information. If you are running Mac OS X, see "Many Utilities Do Not Respect Apple Human Interface Guidelines" on page 936.

A safer way of removing files

tip   You can use the interactive form of rm to make sure that you delete only the file(s) you intend to delete. When you follow rm with the **–i** option (see page 35 for a tip on options) and the name of the file you want to delete, rm displays the name of the file and then waits for you to respond with **y** (yes) before it deletes the file. It does not delete the file if you respond with a string that begins with a character other than **y**.

```
$ rm -i toollist
rm: remove regular file 'toollist'? y
```

Optional: You can create an alias (page 324) for **rm –i** and put it in your startup file (page 82) so rm always runs in interactive mode.

less Is more: DISPLAY A TEXT FILE ONE SCREEN AT A TIME

Pagers   When you want to view a file that is longer than one screen, you can use either the less utility or the more utility. Each of these utilities pauses after displaying a screen of text; press the SPACE bar to display the next screen of text. Because these utilities show one page at a time, they are called *pagers*. Although less and more are very similar, they have subtle differences. At the end of the file, for example, less displays an **END** message and waits for you to press **q** before returning you to the shell. In contrast, more returns you directly to the shell. While using both utilities you can press **h** to display a Help screen that lists commands you can use while paging through a file. Give the commands **less practice** and **more practice** in place of the **cat** command in Figure 3-1 to see how these commands work. Use the command **less /usr/share/dict/words** instead if you want to experiment with a longer file. Refer to page 735 or to the less and more man pages for more information on less and more.

hostname: Displays the System Name

The hostname utility displays the name of the system you are working on. Use this utility if you are not sure you are logged in on the right machine. Refer to the hostname man page for more information.

```
$ hostname
dog
```

Working with Files

This section describes utilities that copy, move, print, search through, display, sort, and compare files. If you are running Mac OS X, see "Resource forks" on page 929.

Filename completion

tip After you enter one or more letters of a filename (following a command) on a command line, press TAB and the Bourne Again Shell will complete as much of the filename as it can. When only one filename starts with the characters you entered, the shell completes the filename and places a SPACE after it. You can keep typing or you can press RETURN to execute the command at this point. When the characters you entered do not uniquely identify a filename, the shell completes what it can and waits for more input. When pressing TAB does not change the display, press TAB again (Bourne Again Shell, page 320) or CONTROL-D (TC Shell, page 360) to display a list of possible completions.

cp: Copies a File

The cp (copy) utility (Figure 3-2) makes a copy of a file. This utility can copy any file, including text and executable program (binary) files. You can use cp to make a backup copy of a file or a copy to experiment with.

The cp command line uses the following syntax to specify source and destination files:

cp source-file destination-file

The **source-file** is the name of the file that cp will copy. The **destination-file** is the name that cp assigns to the resulting (new) copy of the file.

```
$ ls
memo
$ cp memo memo.copy
$ ls
memo memo.copy
```

Figure 3-2   cp copies a file

The cp command line in Figure 3-2 copies the file named **memo** to **memo.copy**. The period is part of the filename—just another character. The initial ls command shows that **memo** is the only file in the directory. After the cp command, a second ls shows two files in the directory, **memo** and **memo.copy**.

Sometimes it is useful to incorporate the date in the name of a copy of a file. The following example includes the date January 30 (**0130**) in the copied file:

```
$ cp memo memo.0130
```

Although it has no significance to Linux, the date can help you find a version of a file you created on a certain date. Including the date can also help you avoid overwriting existing files by providing a unique filename each day. For more information refer to "Filenames" on page 79.

Refer to page 640 or give the command **info coreutils 'cp invocation'** for more information. Use scp (page 810), ftp (page 704), or rsync (page 583) when you need to copy a file from one system to another on a common network.

cp can destroy a file

caution   If the *destination-file* exists *before* you give a cp command, cp overwrites it. Because cp over-writes (and destroys the contents of) an existing *destination-file* without warning, you must take care not to cause cp to overwrite a file that you need. The cp **–i** (interactive) option prompts you before it overwrites a file. See page 35 for a tip on options.

The following example assumes that the file named **orange.2** exists before you give the cp command. The user answers **y** to overwrite the file:

```
$ cp -i orange orange.2
cp: overwrite 'orange.2'? y
```

mv: Changes the Name of a File

The mv (move) utility can rename a file without making a copy of it. The mv command line specifies an existing file and a new filename using the same syntax as cp:

mv existing-filename new-filename

The command line in Figure 3-3 changes the name of the file **memo** to **memo.0130**. The initial ls command shows that **memo** is the only file in the directory. After you give the mv command, **memo.0130** is the only file in the directory. Compare this result to that of the cp example in Figure 3-2.

The mv utility can be used for more than changing the name of a file. Refer to "mv, cp: Move or Copy Files" on page 90. Also refer to page 771 or give the command **info coreutils 'mv invocation'** for more information.

mv can destroy a file

caution   Just as cp can destroy a file, so can mv. Also like cp, mv has a **–i** (interactive) option. See the caution box labeled "cp can destroy a file."

```
$ ls
memo
$ mv memo memo.0130
$ ls
memo.0130
```

Figure 3-3   mv renames a file

lpr: PRINTS A FILE

The lpr (line printer) utility places one or more files in a print queue for printing. Linux provides print queues so that only one job is printed on a given printer at a time. A queue allows several people or jobs to send output simultaneously to a single printer with the expected results. On systems that have access to more than one printer, you can use **lpstat –p** to display a list of available printers. Use the **–P** option to instruct lpr to place the file in the queue for a specific printer—even one that is connected to another system on the network. The following command prints the file named **report**:

```
$ lpr report
```

Because this command does not specify a printer, the output goes to the default printer, which is *the* printer when you have only one printer.

The next command line prints the same file on the printer named **mailroom**:

```
$ lpr -P mailroom report
```

You can see which jobs are in the print queue by giving an **lpstat –o** command or by using the lpq utility:

```
$ lpq
lp is ready and printing
Rank  Owner    Job Files               Total Size
active max       86 (standard input)     954061 bytes
```

In this example, Max has one job that is being printed; no other jobs are in the queue. You can use the job number (86 in this case) with the lprm utility to remove the job from the print queue and stop it from printing:

```
$ lprm 86
```

You can send more than one file to the printer with a single command. The following command line prints three files on the printer named **laser1**:

```
$ lpr -P laser1 05.txt 108.txt 12.txt
```

Refer to pages 132 and 742 or to the lpr man page for more information.

```
$ cat memo

Helen:

In our meeting on June 6 we
discussed the issue of credit.
Have you had any further thoughts
about it?

              Max

$ grep 'credit' memo
discussed the issue of credit.
```

Figure 3-4   grep searches for a string

grep: SEARCHES FOR A STRING

The grep[1] utility searches through one or more files to see whether any contain a specified string of characters. This utility does not change the file it searches but simply displays each line that contains the string.

The grep command in Figure 3-4 searches through the file **memo** for lines that contain the string **credit** and displays the single line that meets this criterion. If **memo** contained such words as **discredit, creditor,** or **accreditation,** grep would have displayed those lines as well because they contain the string it was searching for. The **–w** (words) option causes grep to match only whole words. Although you do not need to enclose the string you are searching for in single quotation marks, doing so allows you to put SPACEs and special characters in the search string.

The grep utility can do much more than search for a simple string in a single file. Refer to page 719 or to the grep man page for more information. See also Appendix A, "Regular Expressions."

head: DISPLAYS THE BEGINNING OF A FILE

By default the head utility displays the first ten lines of a file. You can use head to help you remember what a particular file contains. For example, if you have a file named **months** that lists the 12 months of the year in calendar order, one to a line, then head displays **Jan** through **Oct** (Figure 3-5).

This utility can display any number of lines, so you can use it to look at only the first line of a file, at a full screen, or even more. To specify the number of lines

---

1. Originally the name grep was a play on an ed—an original UNIX editor, available on Linux—command: g/re/p. In this command **g** stands for global, **re** is a regular expression delimited by slashes, and **p** means print.

```
$ head months
Jan
Feb
Mar
Apr
May
Jun
Jul
Aug
Sep
Oct

$ tail -5 months
Aug
Sep
Oct
Nov
Dec
```

Figure 3-5   head displays the first lines of a file; tail displays the last lines of a file

displayed, include a hyphen followed by the number of lines you want head to display. For example, the following command displays only the first line of **months**:

```
$ head -1 months
Jan
```

The head utility can also display parts of a file based on a count of blocks or characters rather than lines. Refer to page 727 or give the command **info coreutils 'head invocation'** for more information.

tail: DISPLAYS THE END OF A FILE

The tail utility is similar to head but by default displays the *last* ten lines of a file. Depending on how you invoke it, this utility can display fewer or more than ten lines, use a count of blocks or characters rather than lines to display parts of a file, and display lines being added to a file that is changing. The tail command in Figure 3-5 displays the last five lines (**Aug** through **Dec**) of the **months** file.

You can monitor lines as they are added to the end of the growing file named **logfile** with the following command:

```
$ tail -f logfile
```

Press the interrupt key (usually CONTROL-C) to stop tail and display the shell prompt. Refer to page 843 or give the command **info coreutils 'tail invocation'** for more information.

```
$ cat days
Monday
Tuesday
Wednesday
Thursday
Friday
Saturday
Sunday

$ sort days
Friday
Monday
Saturday
Sunday
Thursday
Tuesday
Wednesday
```

Figure 3-6   sort displays the lines of a file in order

sort: DISPLAYS A FILE IN ORDER

The sort utility displays the contents of a file in order by lines; it does not change the original file. Figure 3-6 shows cat displaying the file named **days**, which contains the name of each day of the week on a separate line in calendar order. The sort utility then displays the file in alphabetical order.

The sort utility is useful for putting lists in order. The **–u** option generates a sorted list in which each line is unique (no duplicates). The **–n** option puts a list of numbers in numerical order. Refer to page 817 or give the command **info coreutils 'sort invocation'** for more information.

uniq: REMOVES DUPLICATE LINES FROM A FILE

The uniq (unique) utility displays a file, skipping adjacent duplicate lines, but does not change the original file. If a file contains a list of names and has two successive entries for the same person, uniq skips the duplicate line (Figure 3-7).

If a file is sorted before it is processed by uniq, this utility ensures that no two lines in the file are the same. (Of course, sort can do that all by itself with the **–u** option.) Refer to page 872 or give the command **info coreutils 'uniq invocation'** for more information.

diff: COMPARES TWO FILES

The diff (difference) utility compares two files and displays a list of the differences between them. This utility does not change either file; it is useful when you want to compare two versions of a letter or a report or two versions of the source code for a program.

The diff utility with the **–u** (unified output format) option first displays two lines indicating which of the files you are comparing will be denoted by a plus sign (**+**)

```
$ cat dups
Cathy
Fred
Joe
John
Mary
Mary
Paula

$ uniq dups
Cathy
Fred
Joe
John
Mary
Paula
```

Figure 3-7   uniq removes duplicate lines

and which by a minus sign (–). In Figure 3-8, a minus sign indicates the **colors.1** file; a plus sign indicates the **colors.2** file.

The **diff –u** command breaks long, multiline text into *hunks*. Each hunk is preceded by a line starting and ending with two at signs (**@@**). This hunk identifier indicates the starting line number and the *number of lines* from each file for this hunk. In Figure 3-8, the hunk covers the section of the **colors.1** file (indicated by a minus sign) from the first line through the sixth line. The **+1,5** then indicates that the hunk covers **colors.2** from the first line through the fifth line.

Following these header lines, **diff –u** displays each line of text with a leading minus sign, a leading plus sign, or a SPACE. A leading minus sign indicates that the line occurs only in the file denoted by the minus sign. A leading plus sign indicates that the line occurs only in the file denoted by the plus sign. A line that begins with a SPACE (neither a plus sign nor a minus sign) occurs in both files in the same location. Refer to page 663 or to the diff info page for more information.

```
$ diff -u colors.1 colors.2
--- colors.1   2009-07-29 16:41:11.000000000 -0700
+++ colors.2   2009-07-29 16:41:17.000000000 -0700
@@ -1,6 +1,5 @@
 red
+blue
 green
 yellow
-pink
-purple
 orange
```

Figure 3-8   diff displaying the unified output format

file: Identifies the Contents of a File

You can use the file utility to learn about the contents of a file without having to open and examine the file yourself. In the following example, file reports that **letter_e.bz2** contains data that was compressed by the bzip2 utility (page 60):

```
$ file letter_e.bz2
letter_e.bz2: bzip2 compressed data, block size = 900k
```

Next file reports on two more files:

```
$ file memo zach.jpg
memo:      ASCII text
zach.jpg: JPEG image data, ... resolution (DPI), 72 x 72
```

Refer to page 686 or to the file man page for more information.

| (Pipe): Communicates Between Processes

Because pipes are integral to the functioning of a Linux system, this chapter introduces them for use in examples. Pipes are covered in detail beginning on page 131. If you are running Mac OS X, see the tip "Pipes do not work with resource forks" on page 929.

A *process* is the execution of a command by Linux (page 306). Communication between processes is one of the hallmarks of both UNIX and Linux. A *pipe* (written as a vertical bar [|] on the command line and appearing as a solid or broken vertical line on a keyboard) provides the simplest form of this kind of communication. Simply put, a pipe takes the output of one utility and sends that output as input to another utility. Using UNIX/Linux terminology, a pipe takes standard output of one process and redirects it to become standard input of another process. (For more information refer to "Standard Input and Standard Output" on page 123.) Most of what a process displays on the screen is sent to standard output. If you do not redirect it, this output appears on the screen. Using a pipe, you can redirect standard output so it becomes standard input of another utility. For example, a utility such as head can take its input from a file whose name you specify on the command line following the word **head**, or it can take its input from standard input. The following command line sorts the lines of the **months** file (Figure 3-5, page 53) and uses head to display the first four months of the sorted list:

```
$ sort months | head -4
Apr
Aug
Dec
Feb
```

The next command line displays the number of files in a directory (assuming no filenames include SPACEs). The wc (word count) utility with the **–w** (words) option displays the number of words in its standard input or in a file you specify on the command line:

```
$ ls | wc -w
14
```

```
$ ls
memo  memo.0714  practice
$ echo Hi
Hi
$ echo This is a sentence.
This is a sentence.
$ echo star: *
star: memo memo.0714 practice
$
```

Figure 3-9   echo copies the command line (but not the word **echo**) to the screen

You can use a pipe to send output of a program to the printer:

```
$ tail months | lpr
```

FOUR MORE UTILITIES

The echo and date utilities are two of the most frequently used members of the large collection of Linux utilities. The script utility records part of a session in a file, and todos or unix2dos makes a copy of a text file that can be read on a machine running Windows or Mac OS X.

echo: DISPLAYS TEXT

The echo utility copies the characters you type on the command line after **echo** to the screen. Figure 3-9 shows some examples. The last example shows how the shell treats an unquoted asterisk (*) on the command line: It expands the asterisk into a list of filenames in the directory.

The echo utility is a good tool for learning about the shell and other Linux utilities. Some examples on page 138 use echo to illustrate how special characters, such as the asterisk, work. Throughout Chapters 5, 8, and 10, echo helps explain how shell variables work and how you can send messages from shell scripts to the screen. Refer to page 680 or give the command **info coreutils 'echo invocation'** for more information. See the bash and tcsh man pages for information about the versions of echo that are built into those shells.

optional   You can use echo to create a file by redirecting its output to a file:

```
$ echo 'My new file.' > myfile
$ cat myfile
My new file.
```

The greater than (>) sign tells the shell to send the output of echo to the file named **myfile** instead of to the screen. For more information refer to "Redirecting Standard Output" on page 126.

date: DISPLAYS THE TIME AND DATE

The date utility displays the current date and time:

```
$ date
Wed Mar 18 17:12:20 PDT 2009
```

The following example shows how you can choose the format and select the contents of the output of date:

```
$ date +"%A %B %d"
Wednesday March 18
```

Refer to page 655 or give the command **info coreutils 'date invocation'** for more information.

script: RECORDS A SHELL SESSION

The script utility records all or part of a login session, including your input and the system's responses. This utility is useful only from character-based devices, such as a terminal or a terminal emulator. It does capture a session with vim; however, because vim uses control characters to position the cursor and display different typefaces, such as bold, the output will be difficult to read and may not be useful. When you cat a file that has captured a vim session, the session quickly passes before your eyes.

By default script captures the session in a file named **typescript**. To specify a different filename, follow the script command with a SPACE and the filename. To append to a file, use the **–a** option after **script** but before the filename; otherwise script overwrites an existing file. Following is a session being recorded by script:

```
$ script
Script started, file is typescript
$ whoami
sam
$ ls -l /bin | head -5
total 5024
-rwxr-xr-x 1 root root   2928 Sep 21 21:42 archdetect
-rwxr-xr-x 1 root root   1054 Apr 26 15:37 autopartition
-rwxr-xr-x 1 root root   7168 Sep 21 19:18 autopartition-loop
-rwxr-xr-x 1 root root 701008 Aug 27 02:41 bash
$ exit
exit
Script done, file is typescript
```

Use the exit command to terminate a script session. You can then view the file you created using cat, less, more, or an editor. Following is the file that was created by the preceding script command:

```
$ cat typescript
Script started on Thu Sep 24 20:54:59 2009
$ whoami
sam
```

```
$ ls -l /bin | head -5
total 5024
-rwxr-xr-x 1 root root    2928 Sep 21 21:42 archdetect
-rwxr-xr-x 1 root root    1054 Apr 26 15:37 autopartition
-rwxr-xr-x 1 root root    7168 Sep 21 19:18 autopartition-loop
-rwxr-xr-x 1 root root  701008 Aug 27 02:41 bash
$ exit
exit

Script done on Thu Sep 24 20:55:29 2009
```

If you will be editing the file with vim, emacs, or another editor, you can use fromdos or dos2unix (both below) to eliminate from the **typescript** file the **^M** characters that appear at the ends of the lines. Refer to the script man page for more information.

todos/unix2dos: CONVERTS LINUX AND MAC OS X FILES TO WINDOWS FORMAT

If you want to share a text file you created on a Linux system with someone on a system running Windows or Mac OS X, you need to convert the file before the person on the other system can read it easily. The todos (to DOS; part of the **tofrodos** package) or unix2dos (UNIX to DOS; part of the **unix2dos** package) utility converts a Linux text file so it can be read on a Windows or OS X system. Give the following command to convert a file named **memo.txt** (created with a text editor) to a DOS-format file:

```
$ todos memo.txt
```

or

```
$ unix2dos memo.txt
```

You can now email the file as an attachment to someone on a Windows or OS X system. Without any options, todos overwrites the original file. Use the **–b** (backup) option to cause todos to make a copy of the file with a **.bak** filename extension before modifying it. Use the **–n** (new) option to cause unix2dos to write the modified file to a new file as specified by a second argument (**unix2dos** *old new*).

fromdos/dos2unix   You can use the fromdos (from DOS; part of the **tofrodos** package) or dos2unix (DOS to UNIX; part of the **dos2unix** package) utility to convert Windows or OS X files so they can be read on a Linux system:

```
$ fromdos memo.txt
```

or

```
$ dos2unix memo.txt
```

See the todos and fromdos or unix2dos and dos2unix man pages for more information.

optional

tr   You can also use tr (translate; page 864) to change a Windows or OS X text file into a Linux text file. In the following example, the **–d** (delete) option causes tr to remove RETURNS (represented by **\r**) as it makes a copy of the file:

```
$ cat memo | tr -d '\r' > memo.txt
```

The greater than (**>**) symbol redirects the standard output of tr to the file named **memo.txt**. For more information refer to "Redirecting Standard Output" on page 126. Converting a file the other way without using todos or unix2dos is not as easy.

COMPRESSING AND ARCHIVING FILES

Large files use a lot of disk space and take longer than smaller files to transfer from one system to another over a network. If you do not need to look at the contents of a large file often, you may want to save it on a CD, DVD, or another medium and remove it from the hard disk. If you have a continuing need for the file, retrieving a copy from another medium may be inconvenient. To reduce the amount of disk space a file occupies without removing the file, you can compress the file without losing any of the information it holds. Similarly a single archive of several files packed into a larger file is easier to manipulate, upload, download, and email than multiple files. You may download compressed, archived files from the Internet. The utilities described in this section compress and decompress files and pack and unpack archives.

bzip2: COMPRESSES A FILE

The bzip2 utility compresses a file by analyzing it and recoding it more efficiently. The new version of the file looks completely different. In fact, because the new file contains many nonprinting characters, you cannot view it directly. The bzip2 utility works particularly well on files that contain a lot of repeated information, such as text and image data, although most image data is already in a compressed format.

The following example shows a boring file. Each of the 8,000 lines of the **letter_e** file contains 72 e's and a NEWLINE character that marks the end of the line. The file occupies more than half a megabyte of disk storage.

```
$ ls -l
-rw-rw-r--  1 sam sam 584000 Mar  1 22:31 letter_e
```

The **–l** (long) option causes ls to display more information about a file. Here it shows that **letter_e** is 584,000 bytes long. The **–v** (verbose) option causes bzip2 to report how much it was able to reduce the size of the file. In this case, it shrank the file by 99.99 percent:

```
$ bzip2 -v letter_e
letter_e: 11680.00:1, 0.001 bits/byte, 99.99% saved, 584000 in, 50 out.
```

```
$ ls -l
-rw-rw-r--  1 sam sam 50 Mar  1 22:31 letter_e.bz2
```

.bz2 filename extension   Now the file is only 50 bytes long. The bzip2 utility also renamed the file, appending **.bz2** to its name. This naming convention reminds you that the file is compressed; you would not want to display or print it, for example, without first decompressing it. The bzip2 utility does not change the modification date associated with the file, even though it completely changes the file's contents.

Keep the original file by using the –k option

tip The bzip2 utility (and its counterpart, bunzip2) remove the original file when they compress or decompress a file. Use the **–k** (keep) option to keep the original file.

In the following, more realistic example, the file **zach.jpg** contains a computer graphics image:

```
$ ls -l
-rw-r--r--  1 sam sam 33287 Mar  1 22:40 zach.jpg
```

The bzip2 utility can reduce the size of the file by only 28 percent because the image is already in a compressed format:

```
$ bzip2 -v zach.jpg
zach.jpg:  1.391:1,  5.749 bits/byte, 28.13% saved, 33287 in, 23922 out.
```

```
$ ls -l
-rw-r--r--  1 sam sam 23922 Mar  1 22:40 zach.jpg.bz2
```

Refer to page 615 or to the bzip2 man page for more information. See also www.bzip.org, and the *Bzip2 mini-HOWTO* (see page 38 for instructions on obtaining this document).

bunzip2 AND bzcat: DECOMPRESS A FILE

You can use the bunzip2 utility to restore a file that has been compressed with bzip2:

```
$ bunzip2 letter_e.bz2
$ ls -l
-rw-rw-r--  1 sam sam 584000 Mar  1 22:31 letter_e
$ bunzip2 zach.jpg.bz2
$ ls -l
-rw-r--r--  1 sam sam  33287 Mar  1 22:40 zach.jpg
```

The bzcat utility displays a file that has been compressed with bzip2. The equivalent of cat for **.bz2** files, bzcat decompresses the compressed data and displays the decompressed data. Like cat, bzcat does not change the source file. The pipe in the following example redirects the output of bzcat so instead of being displayed on the screen it becomes the input to head, which displays the first two lines of the file:

```
$ bzcat letter_e.bz2 | head -2
eeeeeeeeeeeeeeeeeeeeeeeeeeeeeeeeeeeeeeeeeeeeeeeeeeeeeeeeeeeeeeeeeeeeeeeee
eeeeeeeeeeeeeeeeeeeeeeeeeeeeeeeeeeeeeeeeeeeeeeeeeeeeeeeeeeeeeeeeeeeeeeeee
```

After running bzcat, the contents of **letter_e.bz2** is unchanged; the file is still stored on the disk in compressed form.

bzip2recover   The bzip2recover utility supports limited data recovery from media errors. Give the command **bzip2recover** followed by the name of the compressed, corrupted file from which you want to recover data.

gzip: COMPRESSES A FILE

gunzip and zcat   The gzip (GNU zip) utility is older and less efficient than bzip2. Its flags and operation are very similar to those of bzip2. A file compressed by gzip is marked by a **.gz** filename extension. Linux stores manual pages in gzip format to save disk space; likewise, files you download from the Internet are frequently in gzip format. Use gzip, gunzip, and zcat just as you would use bzip2, bunzip2, and bzcat, respectively. Refer to page 724 or to the gzip man page for more information.

compress   The compress utility can also compress files, albeit not as well as gzip. This utility marks a file it has compressed by adding .Z to its name.

gzip **versus** zip

tip   Do not confuse gzip and gunzip with the zip and unzip utilities. These last two are used to pack and unpack zip archives containing several files compressed into a single file that has been imported from or is being exported to a system running Windows. The zip utility constructs a zip archive, whereas unzip unpacks zip archives. The zip and unzip utilities are compatible with PKZIP, a Windows program that compresses and archives files.

tar: PACKS AND UNPACKS ARCHIVES

The tar utility performs many functions. Its name is short for *tape archive,* as its original function was to create and read archive and backup tapes. Today it is used to create a single file (called a *tar file, archive,* or *tarball*) from multiple files or directory hierarchies and to extract files from a tar file. The cpio utility (page 644) performs a similar function.

In the following example, the first ls shows the sizes of the files **g, b,** and **d.** Next tar uses the −c (create), −v (verbose), and −f (write to or read from a file) options to create an archive named **all.tar** from these files. Each line of output displays the name of the file tar is appending to the archive it is creating.

The tar utility adds overhead when it creates an archive. The next command shows that the archive file **all.tar** occupies about 9,700 bytes, whereas the sum of the sizes of the three files is about 6,000 bytes. This overhead is more appreciable on smaller files, such as the ones in this example.

```
$ ls -l g b d
-rw-r--r--  1 zach  other  1178 Aug 20 14:16 b
-rw-r--r--  1 zach  zach   3783 Aug 20 14:17 d
-rw-r--r--  1 zach  zach   1302 Aug 20 14:16 g

$ tar -cvf all.tar g b d
g
b
d
```

```
$ ls -l all.tar
-rw-r--r--   1 zach        zach         9728 Aug 20 14:17 all.tar

$ tar -tvf all.tar
-rw-r--r-- zach /zach        1302 2009-08-20 14:16 g
-rw-r--r-- zach /other       1178 2009-08-20 14:16 b
-rw-r--r-- zach /zach        3783 2009-08-20 14:17 d
```

The final command in the preceding example uses the –t option to display a table of contents for the archive. Use –x instead of –t to extract files from a tar archive. Omit the –v option if you want tar to do its work silently.[2]

Compressed tar files   You can use bzip2, compress, or gzip to compress tar files, making them easier to store and handle. Many files you download from the Internet will already be in one of these formats. Files that have been processed by tar and compressed by bzip2 frequently have a filename extension of **.tar.bz2** or **.tbz**. Those processed by tar and gzip have an extension of **.tar.gz**, **.tgz**, or **.gz**, whereas files processed by tar and compress use **.tar.Z** as the extension.

You can unpack a tarred and gzipped file in two steps. (Follow the same procedure if the file was compressed by bzip2, but use bunzip2 instead of gunzip.) The next example shows how to unpack the GNU make utility after it has been downloaded (ftp.gnu.org/pub/gnu/make/make-3.81.tar.gz):

```
$ ls -l mak*
-rw-r--r-- 1 sam sam 1564560 Mar 26 18:25 make-3.81.tar.gz

$ gunzip mak*
$ ls -l mak*
-rw-r--r-- 1 sam sam 6072320 Mar 26 18:25 make-3.81.tar

$ tar -xvf mak*
make-3.81/
make-3.81/config/
make-3.81/config/dospaths.m4
make-3.81/config/gettext.m4
make-3.81/config/iconv.m4
...
make-3.81/tests/run_make_tests
make-3.81/tests/run_make_tests.pl
make-3.81/tests/test_driver.pl
```

The first command lists the downloaded tarred and gzipped file: **make-3.81.tar.gz** (about 1.2 megabytes). The asterisk (*) in the filename matches any characters in any filenames (page 138), so ls displays a list of files whose names begin with **mak**; in this case there is only one. Using an asterisk saves typing and can improve accuracy with long filenames. The gunzip command decompresses the file and yields

---

2. Although the original UNIX tar did not use a leading hyphen to indicate an option on the command line, the GNU/Linux version accepts hyphens, but works as well without them. This book precedes tar options with a hyphen for consistency with most other utilities.

make-3.81.tar (no .gz extension), which is about 4.8 megabytes. The tar command creates the **make-3.81** directory in the working directory and unpacks the files into it.

```
$ ls -ld mak*
drwxr-xr-x 8 sam sam    4096 Mar 31  2006 make-3.81
-rw-r--r-- 1 sam sam 6072320 Mar 26 18:25 make-3.81.tar

$ ls -l make-3.81
total 2100
-rw-r--r-- 1 sam sam  53838 Mar 31  2006 ABOUT-NLS
-rw-r--r-- 1 sam sam   2810 Mar 19  2006 AUTHORS
-rw-r--r-- 1 sam sam  18043 Dec 10  1996 COPYING
-rw-r--r-- 1 sam sam 106390 Mar 31  2006 ChangeLog
...
-rw-r--r-- 1 sam sam  16907 Feb 11  2006 vmsjobs.c
-rw-r--r-- 1 sam sam  17397 Feb 11  2006 vpath.c
drwxr-xr-x 6 sam sam   4096 Mar 31  2006 w32
```

After tar extracts the files from the archive, the working directory contains two files whose names start with **mak: make-3.81.tar** and **make-3.81**. The **–d** (directory) option causes ls to display only file and directory names, not the contents of directories as it normally does. The final ls command shows the files and directories in the **make-3.81** directory. Refer to page 846 or to the tar man page for more information.

tar: the –x option may extract a lot of files

caution Some tar archives contain many files. To list the files in the archive without unpacking them, run tar with the **–t** option and the name of the tar file. In some cases you may want to create a new directory (mkdir [page 86]), move the tar file into that directory, and expand it there. That way the unpacked files will not mingle with existing files, and no confusion will occur. This strategy also makes it easier to delete the extracted files. Depending on how they were created, some tar files automatically create a new directory and put the files into it; the **–t** option indicates where tar will place the files you extract.

tar: the –x option can overwrite files

caution The **–x** option to tar overwrites a file that has the same filename as a file you are extracting. Follow the suggestion in the preceding caution box to avoid overwriting files.

optional You can combine the gunzip and tar commands on one command line with a pipe (|), which redirects the output of gunzip so that it becomes the input to tar:

```
$ gunzip -c make-3.81.tar.gz | tar -xvf -
```

The **–c** option causes gunzip to send its output through the pipe instead of creating a file. The final hyphen (–) causes tar to read from standard input. Refer to "Pipes" (page 131), gzip (pages 62 and 724), and tar (page 846) for more information about how this command line works.

A simpler solution is to use the **–z** option to tar. This option causes tar to call gunzip (or gzip when you are creating an archive) directly and simplifies the preceding command line to

```
$ tar -xvzf make-3.81.tar.gz
```
In a similar manner, the –j option calls bzip2 or bunzip2.

LOCATING COMMANDS

The whereis and slocate utilities can help you find a command whose name you have forgotten or whose location you do not know. When multiple copies of a utility or program are present, which tells you which copy you will run. The slocate utility searches for files on the local system.

which AND whereis: LOCATE A UTILITY

Search path   When you give Linux a command, the shell searches a list of directories for a program with that name and runs the first one it finds. This list of directories is called a *search path*. For information on how to change the search path see page 298. If you do not change the search path, the shell searches only a standard set of directories and then stops searching. However, other directories on the system may also contain useful utilities.

which   The which utility locates utilities by displaying the full pathname of the file for the utility. (Chapter 4 contains more information on pathnames and the structure of the Linux filesystem.) The local system may include several utilities that have the same name. When you type the name of a utility, the shell searches for the utility in your search path and runs the first one it finds. You can find out which copy of the utility the shell will run by using which. In the following example, which reports the location of the tar utility:

```
$ which tar
/bin/tar
```

The which utility can be helpful when a utility seems to be working in unexpected ways. By running which, you may discover that you are running a nonstandard version of a tool or a different one from the one you expected. ("Important Standard Directories and Files" on page 91 provides a list of standard locations for executable files.) For example, if tar is not working properly and you find that you are running **/usr/local/bin/tar** instead of **/bin/tar**, you might suspect that the local version is broken.

whereis   The whereis utility searches for files related to a utility by looking in standard locations instead of using your search path. For example, you can find the locations for files related to tar:

```
$ whereis tar
tar: /bin/tar /usr/include/tar.h /usr/share/man/man1/tar.1.gz
```

In this example whereis finds three references to tar: the tar utility file, a tar header file, and the tar man page.

which **versus** whereis

tip   Given the name of a utility, which looks through the directories in your *search path* (page 297), in order, and locates the utility. If your search path includes more than one utility with the specified name, which displays the name of only the first one (the one you would run).

The whereis utility looks through a list of *standard directories* and works independently of your search path. Use whereis to locate a binary (executable) file, any manual pages, and source code for a program you specify; whereis displays all the files it finds.

which, whereis, **and builtin commands**

caution   Both the which and whereis utilities report only the names for utilities as they are found on the disk; they do not report shell builtins (utilities that are built into a shell; see page 141). When you use whereis to try to find where the echo command (which exists as both a utility program and a shell builtin) is kept, you get the following result:

```
$ whereis echo
echo: /bin/echo /usr/share/man/man1/echo.1.gz
```

The whereis utility does not display the echo builtin. Even the which utility reports the wrong information:

```
$ which echo
/bin/echo
```

Under bash you can use the type builtin (page 447) to determine whether a command is a builtin:

```
$ type echo
echo is a shell builtin
```

slocate/locate: SEARCHES FOR A FILE

The slocate (secure locate) or locate utility searches for files on the local system:

```
$ slocate motd
/usr/share/app-install/icons/xmotd.xpm
/usr/share/app-install/desktop/motd-editor.desktop
/usr/share/app-install/desktop/xmotd.desktop
/usr/share/base-files/motd.md5sums
/usr/share/base-files/motd
...
```

You may need to install slocate or locate; see Appendix C. Before you can use slocate or locate the updatedb utility must build or update the slocate database. Typically the database is updated once a day by a cron script (see page 649 for information on crontab and cron).

If you are not on a network, skip the rest of this chapter

tip   If you are the only user on a system that is not connected to a network, you may want to skip the rest of this chapter. If you are not on a network but are set up to send and receive email, read "Email" on page 72.

OBTAINING USER AND SYSTEM INFORMATION

This section covers utilities that provide information about who is using the system, what those users are doing, and how the system is running.

To find out who is using the local system, you can employ one of several utilities that vary in the details they provide and the options they support. The oldest utility, who, produces a list of users who are logged in on the local system, the device each person is using, and the time each person logged in.

The w and finger utilities show more detail, such as each user's full name and the command line each user is running. You can use the finger utility to retrieve information about users on remote systems if the local system is attached to a network. Table 3-1 on page 70 summarizes the output of these utilities.

who: LISTS USERS ON THE SYSTEM

The who utility displays a list of users who are logged in on the local system. In Figure 3-10 the first column who displays shows that Sam, Max, and Zach are logged in. (Max is logged in from two locations.) The second column shows the device that each user's terminal, workstation, or terminal emulator is connected to. The third column shows the date and time the user logged in. An optional fourth column shows (in parentheses) the name of the system that a remote user logged in from.

The information that who displays is useful when you want to communicate with a user on the local system. When the user is logged in, you can use write (page 70) to establish communication immediately. If who does not list the user or if you do not need to communicate immediately, you can send email to that person (page 72).

If the output of who scrolls off the screen, you can redirect the output through a pipe (|, page 56) so that it becomes the input to less, which displays the output one screen at a time. You can also use a pipe to redirect the output through grep to look for a specific name.

If you need to find out which terminal you are using or what time you logged in, you can use the command **who am i**:

```
$ who am i
max        tty2          2009-07-25 16:42
```

```
$ who
sam        tty4          2009-07-25 17:18
max        tty2          2009-07-25 16:42
zach       tty1          2009-07-25 16:39
max        pts/4         2009-07-25 17:27 (coffee)
```

Figure 3-10   who lists who is logged in

```
$ finger
Login      Name            Tty        Idle  Login Time   Office ...
max        Max Wild        *tty2            Jul 25 16:42
max        Max Wild         pts/4        3  Jul 25 17:27 (coffee)
sam        Sam the Great   *tty4       29  Jul 25 17:18
zach       Zach Brill      *tty1     1:07  Jul 25 16:39
```

Figure 3-11   finger I: lists who is logged in

finger: LISTS USERS ON THE SYSTEM

You can use finger to display a list of users who are logged in on the local system. In addition to usernames, finger supplies each user's full name along with information about which device the user's terminal is connected to, how recently the user typed something on the keyboard, when the user logged in, and available contact information. If the user has logged in over the network, the name of the remote system is shown as the user's location. For example, in Figure 3-11 Max is logged in from the remote system named **coffee**. The asterisks (*) in front of the device names in the **Tty** column indicate that the user has blocked messages sent directly to his terminal (refer to "mesg: Denies or Accepts Messages" on page 71).

finger **can be a security risk**

security   On systems where security is a concern, the system administrator may disable finger. This utility can reveal information that can help a malicious user break into a system.

Mac OS X disables remote finger support by default.

You can also use finger to learn more about an individual by specifying a username on the command line. In Figure 3-12, finger displays detailed information about Max. Max is logged in and actively using one of his terminals (**tty2**); he has not used his other terminal (**pts/4**) for 3 minutes and 7 seconds. You also learn from finger that if you want to set up a meeting with Max, you should contact Zach at extension 1693.

.plan and .project   Most of the information in Figure 3-12 was collected by finger from system files. The information shown after the heading **Plan:**, however, was supplied by Max. The finger utility searched for a file named **.plan** in Max's home directory and displayed its contents.

```
$ finger max
Login: max                               Name: Max Wild
Directory: /home/max                     Shell: /bin/tcsh
On since Fri Jul 25 16:42 (PDT) on tty2 (messages off)
On since Fri Jul 25 17:27 (PDT) on pts/4 from coffee
    3 minutes 7 seconds idle
New mail received Sat Jul 25 17:16 2009 (PDT)
     Unread since Sat Jul 25 16:44 2009 (PDT)
Plan:
I will be at a conference in Hawaii all next week.
If you need to see me, contact Zach Brill, x1693.
```

Figure 3-12   finger II: lists details about one user

(Filenames that begin with a period, such as **.plan**, are not normally listed by ls and are called hidden filenames [page 82].) You may find it helpful to create a **.plan** file for yourself; it can contain any information you choose, such as your schedule, interests, phone number, or address. In a similar manner, finger displays the contents of the **.project** and **.pgpkey** files in your home directory. If Max had not been logged in, finger would have reported only his user information, the last time he logged in, the last time he read his email, and his plan.

You can also use finger to display a user's username. For example, on a system with a user named Helen Simpson, you might know that Helen's last name is Simpson but might not guess her username is **hls**. The finger utility, which is not case sensitive, can search for information on Helen using her first or last name. The following commands find the information you seek as well as information on other users whose names are Helen or Simpson:

```
$ finger HELEN
Login: hls                              Name: Helen Simpson.
...
$ finger simpson
Login: hls                              Name: Helen Simpson.
...
```

See page 695 for more information about finger.

w: LISTS USERS ON THE SYSTEM

The w utility displays a list of the users who are logged in on the local system. As discussed in the section on who, the information that w displays is useful when you want to communicate with someone at your installation.

The first column in Figure 3-13 shows that Max, Zach, and Sam are logged in. The second column shows the name of the device file each user's terminal is connected to. The third column shows the system that a remote user is logged in from. The fourth column shows the time each user logged in. The fifth column indicates how long each user has been idle (how much time has elapsed since the user pressed a key on the keyboard). The next two columns identify how much computer processor time each user has used during this login session and on the task that user is running. The last column shows the command each user is running.

The first line the w utility displays includes the time of day, the period of time the computer has been running (in days, hours, and minutes), the number of users

```
$ w
 17:47:35 up 1 day,  8:10,  4 users,  load average: 0.34, 0.23, 0.26
USER     TTY      FROM            LOGIN@   IDLE   JCPU   PCPU WHAT
sam      tty4     -               17:18    29:14m 0.20s  0.00s vi memo
max      tty2     -               16:42    0.00s  0.20s  0.07s w
zach     tty1     -               16:39    1:07   0.05s  0.00s run_bdgt
max      pts/4    coffee          17:27    3:10m  0.24s  0.24s -bash
```

Figure 3-13   The w utility

logged in, and the load average (how busy the system is). The three load average numbers represent the number of jobs waiting to run, averaged over the past 1, 5, and 15 minutes. Use the uptime utility to display just this line. Table 3-1 compares the w, who, and finger utilities.

Table 3-1   Comparison of w, who, and finger

Information displayed	w	who	finger
Username	X	X	X
Terminal-line identification (tty)	X	X	X
Login time (and day for old logins)	X		
Login date and time		X	X
Idle time	X		X
Program the user is executing	X		
Location the user logged in from			X
CPU time used	X		
Full name (or other information from **/etc/passwd**)			X
User-supplied vanity information			X
System uptime and load average	X		

COMMUNICATING WITH OTHER USERS

You can use the utilities discussed in this section to exchange messages and files with other users either interactively or through email.

write: SENDS A MESSAGE

The write utility sends a message to another user who is logged in. When you and another user use write to send messages to each other, you establish two-way communication. Initially a write command displays a banner on the other user's terminal, saying that you are about to send a message (Figure 3-14).

The syntax of a write command line is

> write **username** [**terminal**]

```
$ write max
Hi Max, are you there? o
```

Figure 3-14   The write utility I

```
$ write max
Hi Max, are you there? o

Message from max@bravo.example.com on pts/0 at 16:23 ...
Yes Zach, I'm here. o
```

Figure 3-15   The write utility II

The *username* is the username of the user you want to communicate with. The *terminal* is an optional device name that is useful if the user is logged in more than once. You can display the usernames and device names of all users who are logged in on the local system by using who, w, or finger.

To establish two-way communication with another user, you and the other user must each execute write, specifying the other's username as the *username*. The write utility then copies text, line by line, from one keyboard/display to the other (Figure 3-15). Sometimes it helps to establish a convention, such as typing o (for "over") when you are ready for the other person to type and typing oo (for "over and out") when you are ready to end the conversation. When you want to stop communicating with the other user, press CONTROL-D at the beginning of a line. Pressing CONTROL-D tells write to quit, displays **EOF** (end of file) on the other user's terminal, and returns you to the shell. The other user must do the same.

If the **Message from** banner appears on your screen and obscures something you are working on, press CONTROL-L or CONTROL-R to refresh the screen and remove the banner. Then you can clean up, exit from your work, and respond to the person who is writing to you. You have to remember who is writing to you, however, because the banner will no longer appear on the screen.

mesg: DENIES OR ACCEPTS MESSAGES

By default, messages to your screen are blocked. Give the following mesg command to allow other users to send you messages:

```
$ mesg y
```

If Max had not given this command before Zach tried to send him a message, Zach might have seen the following message:

```
$ write max
write: max has messages disabled
```

You can block messages by entering **mesg n**. Give the command **mesg** by itself to display **is y** (for "yes, messages are allowed") or **is n** (for "no, messages are not allowed").

If you have messages blocked and you write to another user, write displays the following message because, even if you are allowed to write to another user, the user will not be able to respond to you:

```
$ write max
write: write: you have write permission turned off.
```

EMAIL

Email enables you to communicate with users on the local system and, if the installation is part of a network, with other users on the network. If you are connected to the Internet, you can communicate electronically with users around the world.

Email utilities differ from write in that email utilities can send a message when the recipient is not logged in. In this case the email is stored until the recipient reads it. These utilities can also send the same message to more than one user at a time.

Many email programs are available for Linux, including the original character-based mailx program, Mozilla/Thunderbird, pine, mail through emacs, KMail, and evolution. Another popular graphical email program is sylpheed (sylpheed.sraoss.jp/en).

Two programs are available that can make any email program easier to use and more secure. The procmail program (www.procmail.org) creates and maintains email servers and mailing lists; preprocesses email by sorting it into appropriate files and directories; starts various programs depending on the characteristics of incoming email; forwards email; and so on. The GNU Privacy Guard (GPG or GNUpg; www.gnupg.org) encrypts and decrypts email and makes it almost impossible for an unauthorized person to read.

Network addresses   If the local system is part of a LAN, you can generally send email to and receive email from users on other systems on the LAN by using their usernames. Someone sending Max email on the Internet would need to specify his *domain name* (page 952) along with his username. Use this address to send email to the author of this book: **mgs@sobell.com**.

CHAPTER SUMMARY

The utilities introduced in this chapter are a small but powerful subset of the many utilities available on a typical Linux system. Because you will use them frequently and because they are integral to the following chapters, it is important that you become comfortable using them.

The utilities listed in Table 3-2 manipulate, display, compare, and print files.

Table 3-2   File utilities

Utility	Function
cp	Copies one or more files (page 49)
diff	Displays the differences between two files (page 54)
file	Displays information about the contents of a file (page 56)
grep	Searches file(s) for a string (page 52)

Table 3-2   File utilities (continued)

Utility	Function
head	Displays the lines at the beginning of a file (page 52)
lpq	Displays a list of jobs in the print queue (page 51)
lpr	Places file(s) in the print queue (page 51)
lprm	Removes a job from the print queue (page 51)
mv	Renames a file or moves file(s) to another directory (page 50)
sort	Puts a file in order by lines (page 54)
tail	Displays the lines at the end of a file (page 53)
uniq	Displays the contents of a file, skipping adjacent duplicate lines (page 54)

To reduce the amount of disk space a file occupies, you can compress it with the bzip2 utility. Compression works especially well on files that contain patterns, as do most text files, but reduces the size of almost all files. The inverse of bzip2—bunzip2—restores a file to its original, decompressed form. Table 3-3 lists utilities that compress and decompress files. The bzip2 utility is the most efficient of these.

Table 3-3   (De)compression utilities

Utility	Function
bunzip2	Returns a file compressed with bzip2 to its original size and format (page 61)
bzcat	Displays a file compressed with bzip2 (page 61)
bzip2	Compresses a file (page 60)
compress	Compresses a file (not as well as bzip2 or gzip; page 62)
gunzip	Returns a file compressed with gzip or compress to its original size and format (page 62)
gzip	Compresses a file (not as well as bzip2; page 62)
zcat	Displays a file compressed with gzip (page 62)

An archive is a file, frequently compressed, that contains a group of files. The tar utility (Table 3-4) packs and unpacks archives. The filename extensions **.tar.bz2**, **.tar.gz**, and **.tgz** identify compressed tar archive files and are often seen on software packages obtained over the Internet.

Table 3-4   Archive utility

Utility	Function
tar	Creates or extracts files from an archive file (page 62)

The utilities listed in Table 3-5 determine the location of a utility on the local system. For example, they can display the pathname of a utility or a list of C++ compilers available on the local system.

Table 3-5   Location utilities

Utility	Function
locate	Searches for files on the local system (page 66)
whereis	Displays the full pathnames of a utility, source code, or man page (page 65)
which	Displays the full pathname of a command you can run (page 65)

Table 3-6 lists utilities that display information about other users. You can easily learn a user's full name, the user's login status, the login shell of the user, and other items of information maintained by the system.

Table 3-6   User and system information utilities

Utility	Function
finger	Displays detailed information about users, including their full names (page 68)
hostname	Displays the name of the local system (page 49)
w	Displays detailed information about users who are logged in on the local system (page 69)
who	Displays information about users who are logged in on the local system (page 67)

The utilities shown in Table 3-7 can help you stay in touch with other users on the local network.

Table 3-7   User communication utilities

Utility	Function
mesg	Permits or denies messages sent by write (page 71)
write	Sends a message to another user who is logged in (page 70)

Table 3-8 lists miscellaneous utilities.

Table 3-8   Miscellaneous utilities

Utility	Function
date	Displays the current date and time (page 58)
echo	Copies its *arguments* (page 941) to the screen (page 57)

EXERCISES

1. Which commands can you use to determine who is logged in on a specific terminal?

2. How can you keep other users from using write to communicate with you? Why would you want to?

3. What happens when you give the following commands if the file named **done** already exists?

   ```
   $ cp to_do done
   $ mv to_do done
   ```

4. How can you display the following line on the screen you are working on?

   ```
   Hi $2, I'm number * (guess)!
   ```

5. How can you find the phone number for **Ace Electronics** in a file named **phone** that contains a list of names and phone numbers? Which command can you use to display the entire file in alphabetical order? How can you display the file without any adjacent duplicate lines? How can you display the file without any duplicate lines?

6. What happens when you use diff to compare two binary files that are not identical? (You can use gzip to create the binary files.) Explain why the diff output for binary files is different from the diff output for ASCII files.

7. Create a **.plan** file in your home directory. Does finger display the contents of your **.plan** file?

8. What is the result of giving the which utility the name of a command that resides in a directory that is *not* in your search path?

9. Are any of the utilities discussed in this chapter located in more than one directory on the local system? If so, which ones?

10. Experiment by calling the file utility with the names of files in **/usr/bin**. How many different types of files are there?

11. Which command can you use to look at the first few lines of a file named **status.report**? Which command can you use to look at the end of the file?

ADVANCED EXERCISES

12. Re-create the **colors.1** and **colors.2** files used in Figure 3-8 on page 55. Test your files by running **diff –u** on them. Do you get the same results as in the figure?

13. Try giving these two commands:

    ```
    $ echo cat
    $ cat echo
    ```

    Explain the differences between the output of each command.

14. Repeat exercise 5 using the file **phone.gz**, a compressed version of the list of names and phone numbers. Consider more than one approach to answer each question, and explain how you made your choices.

15. Find existing files or create files that

    a. gzip compresses by more than 80 percent.

    b. gzip compresses by less than 10 percent.

    c. Get larger when compressed with gzip.

    d. Use **ls –l** to determine the sizes of the files in question. Can you characterize the files in a, b, and c?

16. Older email programs were not able to handle binary files. Suppose that you are emailing a file that has been compressed with gzip, which produces a binary file, and the recipient is using an old email program. Refer to the man page on uuencode, which converts a binary file to ASCII. Learn about the utility and how to use it.

    a. Convert a compressed file to ASCII using uuencode. Is the encoded file larger or smaller than the compressed file? Explain. (If uuencode is not on the local system, you can install it using yum or aptitude [both in Appendix C]; it is part of the **sharutils** package.)

    b. Would it ever make sense to use uuencode on a file before compressing it? Explain.

4

THE FILESYSTEM

A *filesystem* is a set of *data structures* (page 950) that usually resides on part of a disk and that holds directories of files. Filesystems store user and system data that are the basis of users' work on the system and the system's existence. This chapter discusses the organization and terminology of the Linux filesystem, defines ordinary and directory files, and explains the rules for naming them. It also shows how to create and delete directories, move through the filesystem, and use absolute and relative pathnames to access files in various directories. It includes a discussion of important files and directories as well as file access permissions and Access Control Lists (ACLs), which allow you to share selected files with other users. It concludes with a discussion of hard and symbolic links, which can make a single file appear in more than one directory.

In addition to reading this chapter, you may want to refer to the df, fsck, mkfs, and tune2fs utilities in Part V for more information on filesystems. If you are running Mac OS X, see "Filesystems" on page 927.

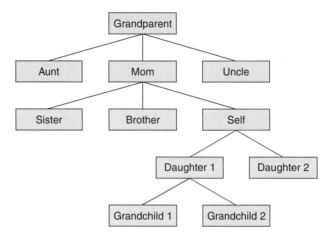

Figure 4-1   A family tree

THE HIERARCHICAL FILESYSTEM

Family tree   A *hierarchical* structure (page 957) frequently takes the shape of a pyramid. One example of this type of structure is found by tracing a family's lineage: A couple has a child, who may in turn have several children, each of whom may have more children. This hierarchical structure is called a *family tree* (Figure 4-1).

Directory tree   Like the family tree it resembles, the Linux filesystem is called a *tree*. It consists of a set of connected files. This structure allows you to organize files so you can easily find any particular one. On a standard Linux system, each user starts with one directory, to which the user can add subdirectories to any desired level. By creating multiple levels of subdirectories, a user can expand the structure as needed.

Subdirectories   Typically each subdirectory is dedicated to a single subject, such as a person, project, or event. The subject dictates whether a subdirectory should be subdivided further. For example, Figure 4-2 shows a secretary's subdirectory named **correspond**. This directory contains three subdirectories: **business**, **memos**, and **personal**. The **business** directory contains files that store each letter the secretary types. If you expect many letters to go to one client, as is the case with **milk_co**, you can dedicate a subdirectory to that client.

One major strength of the Linux filesystem is its ability to adapt to users' needs. You can take advantage of this strength by strategically organizing your files so they are most convenient and useful for you.

DIRECTORY FILES AND ORDINARY FILES

Like a family tree, the tree representing the filesystem is usually pictured upside down, with its *root* at the top. Figures 4-2 and 4-3 show that the tree "grows"

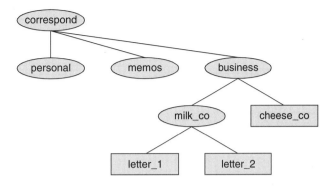

Figure 4-2   A secretary's directories

downward from the root, with paths connecting the root to each of the other files. At the end of each path is either an ordinary file or a directory file. Special files, which can also appear at the ends of paths, provide access to operating system features. *Ordinary files*, or simply *files*, appear at the ends of paths that cannot support other paths. *Directory files*, also referred to as *directories* or *folders*, are the points that other paths can branch off from. (Figures 4-2 and 4-3 show some empty directories.) When you refer to the tree, *up* is toward the root and *down* is away from the root. Directories directly connected by a path are called *parents* (closer to the root) and *children* (farther from the root). A *pathname* is a series of names that trace a path along branches from one file to another. See page 83 for more information about pathnames.

FILENAMES

Every file has a *filename*. The maximum length of a filename varies with the type of filesystem; Linux supports several types of filesystems. Although most of today's filesystems allow files with names up to 255 characters long, some filesystems

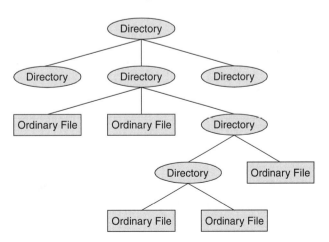

Figure 4-3   Directories and ordinary files

restrict filenames to fewer characters. While you can use almost any character in a filename, you will avoid confusion if you choose characters from the following list:

- Uppercase letters (A–Z)
- Lowercase letters (a–z)
- Numbers (0–9)
- Underscore (_)
- Period (.)
- Comma (,)

Like the children of one parent, no two files in the same directory can have the same name. (Parents give their children different names because it makes good sense, but Linux requires it.) Files in different directories, like the children of different parents, can have the same name.

The filenames you choose should mean something. Too often a directory is filled with important files with such unhelpful names as **hold1**, **wombat**, and **junk**, not to mention **foo** and **foobar**. Such names are poor choices because they do not help you recall what you stored in a file. The following filenames conform to the suggested syntax *and* convey information about the contents of the file:

- correspond
- january
- davis
- reports
- 2001
- acct_payable

Filename length When you share your files with users on other systems, you may need to make long filenames differ within the first few characters. Systems running DOS or older versions of Windows have an 8-character filename body length limit and a 3-character filename extension length limit. Some UNIX systems have a 14-character limit and older Macintosh systems have a 31-character limit. If you keep the filenames short, they are easy to type; later you can add extensions to them without exceeding the shorter limits imposed by some filesystems. The disadvantage of short filenames is that they are typically less descriptive than long filenames.

The stat utility (page 835) can display the maximum length of a filename. In the following example, the number following **Namelen:** is the maximum number of characters permitted in a filename on the specified filesystem (**/home**).

```
$ stat -f /home | grep -i name
    ID: ff1f5275f648468b Namelen: 255      Type: ext2/ext3
```

The **–f** option tells stat to display filesystem status instead of file status. The **–i** (case insensitive) option tells grep to not consider case in its search.

Long filenames enable you to assign descriptive names to files. To help you select among files without typing entire filenames, shells support filename completion. For more information about this feature, see the "Filename completion" tip on page 49.

Case sensitivity You can use uppercase and/or lowercase letters within filenames, but be careful: Many filesystems are case sensitive. For example, the popular **ext** family of filesystems and the UFS filesystem are case sensitive, so files named **JANUARY, January,** and **january** refer to three distinct files. The FAT family of filesystems (used mostly for removable media) is not case sensitive, so those three filenames represent the same file. The HFS+ filesystem, which is the default OS X filesystem, is case preserving but not case sensitive; refer to "Case Sensitivity" on page 927 for more information.

Do not use SPACEs within filenames

caution Although you can use SPACEs within filenames, it is a poor idea. Because a SPACE is a special character, you must quote it on a command line. Quoting a character on a command line can be difficult for a novice user and cumbersome for an experienced user. Use periods or underscores instead of SPACEs: **joe.05.04.26, new_stuff.**

If you are working with a filename that includes a SPACE, such as a file from another operating system, you must quote the SPACE on the command line by preceding it with a backslash or by placing quotation marks on either side of the filename. The two following commands send the file named **my file** to the printer.

```
$ lpr my\ file
$ lpr "my file"
```

FILENAME EXTENSIONS

A *filename extension* is the part of the filename following an embedded period. In the filenames listed in Table 4-1, filename extensions help describe the contents of the file. Some programs, such as the C programming language compiler, default to specific filename extensions; in most cases, however, filename extensions are optional. Use extensions freely to make filenames easy to understand. If you like, you can use several periods within the same filename—for example, **notes.4.10.01** or **files.tar.gz.** Under Mac OS X, some applications use filename extensions to identify files, but many use type codes and creator codes (page 931).

Table 4-1 Filename extensions

Filename with extension	Meaning of extension
compute.c	A C programming language source file
compute.o	The object code file for **compute.c**
compute	The executable file for **compute.c**
memo.0410.txt	A text file
memo.pdf	A PDF file; view with **xpdf** or **kpdf** under a GUI
memo.ps	A PostScript file; view with **gs** or **kpdf** under a GUI
memo.Z	A file compressed with **compress** (page 62); use **uncompress** or **gunzip** (page 62) to decompress
memo.tgz or **memo.tar.gz**	A tar (page 62) archive of files compressed with **gzip** (page 62)
memo.gz	A file compressed with **gzip** (page 62); view with **zcat** or decompress with **gunzip** (both on page 62)

Table 4-1   Filename extensions (continued)

Filename with extension	Meaning of extension
memo.bz2	A file compressed with **bzip2** (page 60); view with **bzcat** or decompress with **bunzip2** (both on page 61)
memo.html	A file meant to be viewed using a Web browser, such as Firefox
photo.gif, **photo.jpg**, **photo.jpeg**, **photo.bmp**, **photo.tif**, or **photo.tiff**	A file containing graphical information, such as a picture

HIDDEN FILENAMES

A filename that begins with a period is called a *hidden filename* (or a *hidden file* or sometimes an *invisible file*) because ls does not normally display it. The command **ls –a** displays *all* filenames, even hidden ones. Names of startup files (page 82) usually begin with a period so that they are hidden and do not clutter a directory listing. The **.plan** file (page 68) is also hidden. Two special hidden entries—a single and double period (**.** and **..**)—appear in every directory (page 88).

THE WORKING DIRECTORY

pwd   While you are logged in on a character-based interface to a Linux system, you are always associated with a directory. The directory you are associated with is called the *working directory* or *current directory*. Sometimes this association is referred to in a physical sense: "You are *in* (or *working in*) the **zach** directory." The pwd (print working directory) shell builtin (page 141) displays the pathname of the working directory.

YOUR HOME DIRECTORY

When you first log in, the working directory is your *home directory*. To display the pathname of your home directory, use pwd just after you log in (Figure 4-4). Linux home directories are typically located in **/home** while Mac OS X home directories are located in **/Users**.

When used without any arguments, the ls utility displays a list of the files in the working directory. Because your home directory has been the only working directory you have used so far, ls has always displayed a list of files in your home directory. (All the files you have created up to this point were created in your home directory.)

STARTUP FILES

Startup files, which appear in your home directory, give the shell and other programs information about you and your preferences. Under Mac OS X these files are

```
login: max
Password:
Last login: Wed Oct 20 11:14:21 from bravo
$ pwd
/home/max
```

Figure 4-4   Logging in and displaying the pathname of your home directory called *configuration files* or *preference files* (page 936). Frequently one of these files tells the shell what kind of terminal you are using (page 906) and executes the stty (set terminal) utility to establish the erase (page 29) and line kill (page 30) keys.

Either you or the system administrator can put a shell startup file containing shell commands in your home directory. The shell executes the commands in this file each time you log in. Because the startup files have hidden filenames, you must use the ls –a command to see whether one is in your home directory. See page 271 (bash) and page 352 (tcsh) for more information about startup files.

PATHNAMES

Every file has a *pathname,* which is a trail from a directory through part of the directory hierarchy to an ordinary file or a directory. Within a pathname, a slash (/) to the right of a filename indicates that the file is a directory file. The file following the slash can be an ordinary file or a directory file. The simplest pathname is a simple filename, which points to a file in the working directory. This section discusses absolute and relative pathnames and explains how to use each. If you are running Mac OS X, refer also to page 928 for information on Carbon pathnames.

ABSOLUTE PATHNAMES

/ (root)   The root directory of the filesystem hierarchy does not have a name; it is referred to as the *root directory* and is represented by a / (slash) standing alone or at the left end of a pathname.

An *absolute pathname* starts with a slash (/), which represents the root directory. The slash is followed by the name of a file located in the root directory. An absolute pathname continues, tracing a path through all intermediate directories, to the file identified by the pathname. String all the filenames in the path together, following each directory with a slash (/). This string of filenames is called an absolute pathname because it locates a file absolutely by tracing a path from the root directory to the file. Typically the absolute pathname of a directory does not include the trailing slash, although that format may be used to emphasize that the pathname specifies a directory (e.g., **/home/zach/**). The part of a pathname following the final slash is called a *simple filename, filename,* or *basename.* Figure 4-5 (next page) shows the absolute pathnames of directories and ordinary files in part of a filesystem hierarchy.

Using an absolute pathname, you can list or otherwise work with any file on the local system, assuming you have permission to do so, regardless of the working directory at the time you give the command. For example, Sam can give the following command while working in his home directory to list the files in the **/usr/bin** directory:

```
$ pwd
/home/sam
$ ls /usr/bin
7z                          kwin
7za                         kwin_killer_helper
822-date                    kwin_rules_dialog
...
```

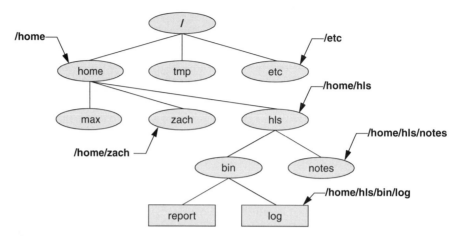

Figure 4-5   Absolute pathnames

~ (TILDE) IN PATHNAMES

In another form of absolute pathname, the shell expands the characters ~/ (a tilde followed by a slash) at the start of a pathname into the pathname of your home directory. Using this shortcut, you can display your **.bashrc** startup file (page 272) with the following command, no matter which directory is the working directory:

```
$ less ~/.bashrc
```

A tilde quickly references paths that start with your or someone else's home directory. The shell expands a tilde followed by a username at the beginning of a pathname into the pathname of that user's home directory. For example, assuming he has permission to do so, Max can examine Sam's **.bashrc** file with the following command:

```
$ less ~sam/.bashrc
```

Refer to "Tilde Expansion" on page 337 for more information.

RELATIVE PATHNAMES

A *relative pathname* traces a path from the working directory to a file. The pathname is *relative* to the working directory. Any pathname that does not begin with the root directory (represented by /) or a tilde (~) is a relative pathname. Like absolute pathnames, relative pathnames can trace a path through many directories. The simplest relative pathname is a simple filename, which identifies a file in the working directory. The examples in the next sections use absolute and relative pathnames.

SIGNIFICANCE OF THE WORKING DIRECTORY

To access any file in the working directory, you need only a simple filename. To access a file in another directory, you *must* use a pathname. Typing a long pathname is tedious and increases the chance of making a mistake. This possibility is less likely under a GUI, where you click filenames or icons. You can choose a working directory for any particular task to reduce the need for long pathnames. Your choice of a

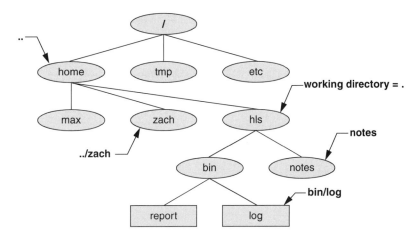

Figure 4-6 Relative pathnames

working directory does not allow you to do anything you could not do otherwise—it just makes some operations easier.

When using a relative pathname, know which directory is the working directory

caution The location of the file that you are accessing with a relative pathname is dependent on (is relative to) the working directory. Always make sure you know which directory is the working directory before you use a relative pathname. Use pwd to verify the directory. If you are creating a file using vim and you are not where you think you are in the file hierarchy, the new file will end up in an unexpected location.

It does not matter which directory is the working directory when you use an absolute pathname. Thus, the following command always edits a file named **goals** in your home directory:

```
$ vim ~/goals
```

Refer to Figure 4-6 as you read this paragraph. Files that are children of the working directory can be referenced by simple filenames. Grandchildren of the working directory can be referenced by short relative pathnames: two filenames separated by a slash. When you manipulate files in a large directory structure, using short relative pathnames can save you time and aggravation. If you choose a working directory that contains the files used most often for a particular task, you need use fewer long, cumbersome pathnames. (The . and .. entries are explained on page 88.)

WORKING WITH DIRECTORIES

This section discusses how to create directories (mkdir), switch between directories (cd), remove directories (rmdir), use pathnames to make your work easier, and move and copy files and directories between directories. It concludes with a section that lists and describes briefly important standard directories and files in the Linux filesystem.

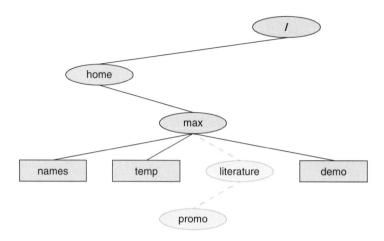

Figure 4-7   The file structure developed in the examples

mkdir: CREATES A DIRECTORY

The mkdir utility creates a directory. The *argument* (page 941) to mkdir becomes the pathname of the new directory. The following examples develop the directory structure shown in Figure 4-7. In the figure, the directories that are added appear in a lighter shade than the others and are connected by dashes.

In Figure 4-8, pwd shows that Max is working in his home directory (**/home/max**) and ls shows the names of the files in his home directory: **demo, names,** and **temp.** Using mkdir, Max creates a directory named **literature** as a child of his home directory. He uses a relative pathname (a simple filename) because he wants the **literature** directory to be a child of the working directory. Max could have used an absolute pathname to create the same directory: **mkdir /home/max/literature** or **mkdir ~max/literature.**

The second ls in Figure 4-8 verifies the presence of the new directory. The **–F** option to ls displays a slash after the name of each directory and an asterisk after each executable

```
$ pwd
/home/max
$ ls
demo  names  temp
$ mkdir literature
$ ls
demo  literature  names  temp
$ ls -F
demo  literature/  names  temp
$ ls literature
$
```

Figure 4-8   The mkdir utility

file (shell script, utility, or application). When you call it with an argument that is the name of a directory, ls lists the contents of that directory. The final ls does not display anything because there are no files in the **literature** directory.

The following commands show two ways to create the **promo** directory as a child of the newly created **literature** directory. The first way checks that **/home/max** is the working directory and uses a relative pathname:

```
$ pwd
/home/max
$ mkdir literature/promo
```

The second way uses an absolute pathname:

```
$ mkdir /home/max/literature/promo
```

Use the **–p** (parents) option to mkdir to create both the **literature** and **promo** directories with one command:

```
$ pwd
/home/max
$ ls
demo   names   temp
$ mkdir -p literature/promo
```

or

```
$ mkdir -p /home/max/literature/promo
```

cd: CHANGES TO ANOTHER WORKING DIRECTORY

The cd (change directory) utility makes another directory the working directory but does *not* change the contents of the working directory. Figure 4-9 shows two ways to make the **/home/max/literature** directory the working directory, as verified by pwd. First Max uses cd with an absolute pathname to make **literature** his working directory—it does not matter which is the working directory when you give a command with an absolute pathname.

A pwd command confirms the change made by Max. When used without an argument, cd makes your home directory the working directory, as it was when you logged in. The second cd command in Figure 4-9 does not have an argument so it

```
$ cd /home/max/literature
$ pwd
/home/max/literature
$ cd
$ pwd
/home/max
$ cd literature
$ pwd
/home/max/literature
```

Figure 4-9   cd changes the working directory

makes Max's home directory the working directory. Finally, knowing that he is working in his home directory, Max uses a simple filename to make the **literature** directory his working directory (**cd literature**) and confirms the change using pwd.

The working directory versus your home directory

The working directory is not the same as your home directory. Your home directory remains the same for the duration of your session and usually from session to session. Immediately after you log in, you are always working in the same directory: your home directory.

Unlike your home directory, the working directory can change as often as you like. You have no set working directory, which explains why some people refer to it as the *current directory*. When you log in and until you change directories using cd, your home directory is the working directory. If you were to change directories to Sam's home directory, then Sam's home directory would be the working directory.

THE . AND .. DIRECTORY ENTRIES

The mkdir utility automatically puts two entries in each directory it creates: a single period (.) and a double period (..). See Figure 4-6 on page 85. The . is synonymous with the pathname of the working directory and can be used in its place; the .. is synonymous with the pathname of the parent of the working directory. These entries are hidden because their filenames begin with a period.

With the **literature** directory as the working directory, the following example uses .. three times: first to list the contents of the parent directory (**/home/max**), second to copy the **memoA** file to the parent directory, and third to list the contents of the parent directory again.

```
$ pwd
/home/max/literature
$ ls ..
demo  literature  names  temp
$ cp memoA ..
$ ls ..
demo  literature  memoA  names  temp
```

After using cd to make **promo** (a subdirectory of **literature**) his working directory, Max can use a relative pathname to call vim to edit a file in his home directory.

```
$ cd promo
$ vim ../../names
```

You can use an absolute or relative pathname or a simple filename virtually anywhere a utility or program requires a filename or pathname. This usage holds true for ls, vim, mkdir, rm, and most other Linux utilities.

rmdir: DELETES A DIRECTORY

The rmdir (remove directory) utility deletes a directory. You cannot delete the working directory or a directory that contains files other than the . and .. entries. If you need to delete a directory that has files in it, first use rm to delete the files and then delete the directory. You do not have to (nor can you) delete the . and .. entries; rmdir removes them automatically. The following command deletes the **promo** directory:

```
$ rmdir /home/max/literature/promo
```

The rm utility has a **–r** option (**rm –r** *filename*) that recursively deletes files, including directories, within a directory and also deletes the directory itself.

Use rm –r carefully, if at all

caution Although **rm –r** is a handy command, you must use it carefully. Do not use it with an ambiguous file reference such as ∗. It is frighteningly easy to wipe out your entire home directory with a single short command.

Using Pathnames

touch Use a text editor to create a file named **letter** if you want to experiment with the examples that follow. Alternatively you can use touch (page 862) to create an empty file:

```
$ cd
$ pwd
/home/max
$ touch letter
```

With **/home/max** as the working directory, the following example uses cp with a relative pathname to copy the file **letter** to the **/home/max/literature/promo** directory. (You will need to create **promo** again if you deleted it earlier.) The copy of the file has the simple filename **letter.0610**:

```
$ cp letter literature/promo/letter.0610
```

If Max does not change to another directory, he can use vim as shown to edit the copy of the file he just made:

```
$ vim literature/promo/letter.0610
```

If Max does not want to use a long pathname to specify the file, he can use cd to make **promo** the working directory before using vim:

```
$ cd literature/promo
$ pwd
/home/max/literature/promo
$ vim letter.0610
```

To make the parent of the working directory (named **/home/max/literature**) the new working directory, Max can give the following command, which takes advantage of the .. directory entry:

```
$ cd ..
$ pwd
/home/max/literature
```

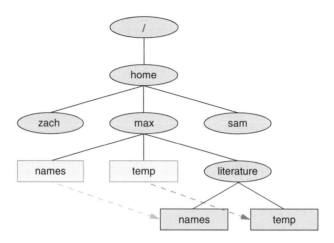

Figure 4-10 Using mv to move **names** and **temp**

mv, cp: MOVE OR COPY FILES

Chapter 3 discussed the use of mv to rename files. However, mv works even more generally: You can use this utility to move files from one directory to another (change the pathname of a file) as well as to change a simple filename. When used to move one or more files to a new directory, the mv command has this syntax:

> *mv existing-file-list directory*

If the working directory is **/home/max**, Max can use the following command to move the files **names** and **temp** from the working directory to the **literature** directory:

```
$ mv names temp literature
```

This command changes the absolute pathnames of the **names** and **temp** files from **/home/max/names** and **/home/max/temp** to **/home/max/literature/names** and **/home/max/literature/temp**, respectively (Figure 4-10). Like most Linux commands, mv accepts either absolute or relative pathnames.

As you work with Linux and create more files, you will need to create new directories using mkdir to keep the files organized. The mv utility is a useful tool for moving files from one directory to another as you extend your directory hierarchy.

The cp utility works in the same way as mv does, except that it makes copies of the *existing-file-list* in the specified *directory*.

mv: MOVES A DIRECTORY

Just as it moves ordinary files from one directory to another, so mv can move directories. The syntax is similar except that you specify one or more directories, not ordinary files, to move:

> *mv existing-directory-list new-directory*

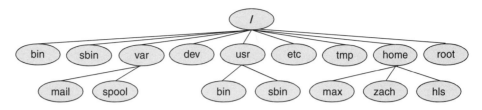

Figure 4-11   A typical FHS-based Linux filesystem structure

If *new-directory* does not exist, the *existing-directory-list* must contain just one directory name, which mv changes to *new-directory* (mv renames the directory). Although you can rename directories using mv, you cannot copy their contents with cp unless you use the −r (recursive) option. Refer to the explanations of tar (page 846) and cpio (page 644) for other ways to copy and move directories.

IMPORTANT STANDARD DIRECTORIES AND FILES

Originally files on a Linux system were not located in standard places within the directory hierarchy. The scattered files made it difficult to document and maintain a Linux system and just about impossible for someone to release a software package that would compile and run on all Linux systems. The first standard for the Linux filesystem, the FSSTND (Linux Filesystem Standard), was released early in 1994. In early 1995 work was started on a broader standard covering many UNIX-like systems: FHS (Linux Filesystem Hierarchy Standard; proton.pathname.com/fhs). More recently FHS has been incorporated in LSB (Linux Standard Base; www.linuxfoundation.org/en/LSB), a workgroup of FSG (Free Standards Group). Finally, FSG combined with Open Source Development Labs (OSDL) to form the Linux Foundation (www.linuxfoundation.org). Figure 4-11 shows the locations of some important directories and files as specified by FHS. The significance of many of these directories will become clear as you continue reading.

The following list describes the directories shown in Figure 4-11, some of the directories specified by FHS, and some other directories. Most Linux distributions do not use all the directories specified by FHS. Be aware that you cannot always determine the function of a directory by its name. For example, although **/opt** stores add-on software, **/etc/opt** stores configuration files for the software in **/opt**.

/   **Root** The root directory, present in all Linux filesystem structures, is the ancestor of all files in the filesystem.

/bin   **Essential command binaries** Holds the files needed to bring the system up and run it when it first comes up in single-user or recovery mode.

/boot   **Static files of the boot loader** Contains all files needed to boot the system.

/dev   **Device files** Contains all files that represent peripheral devices, such as disk drives, terminals, and printers. Previously this directory was filled with all possible devices. The udev utility provides a dynamic device directory that enables **/dev** to contain only devices that are present on the system.

/etc   **Machine–local system configuration files** Holds administrative, configuration, and other system files. One of the most important is **/etc/passwd**, which contains a list of all users who have permission to use the system. Mac OS X uses Open Directory (page 926) in place of **/etc/passwd**.

/etc/opt   **Configuration files for add-on software packages kept in /opt**

/etc/X11   **Machine–local configuration files for the X Window System**

/home   **User home directories** Each user's home directory is typically one of many subdirectories of the **/home** directory. As an example, assuming that users' directories are under **/home**, the absolute pathname of Zach's home directory is **/home/zach**. On some systems the users' directories may not be found under **/home** but instead might be spread among other directories such as **/inhouse** and **/clients**. Under Mac OS X user home directories are typically located in **/Users**.

/lib   **Shared libraries**

/lib/modules   **Loadable kernel modules**

/mnt   **Mount point for temporarily mounting filesystems**

/opt   **Add-on (optional) software packages**

/proc   **Kernel and process information virtual filesystem**

/root   **Home directory for the root account**

/sbin   **Essential system binaries** Utilities used for system administration are stored in **/sbin** and **/usr/sbin**. The **/sbin** directory includes utilities needed during the booting process, and **/usr/sbin** holds utilities used after the system is up and running. In older versions of Linux, many system administration utilities were scattered through several directories that often included other system files (**/etc, /usr/bin, /usr/adm, /usr/include**).

/sys   **Device pseudofilesystem**

/tmp   **Temporary files**

/Users   **User home directories** Under Mac OS X, each user's home directory is typically one of many subdirectories of the **/Users** directory. Linux typically stores home directories in **/home**.

/usr   **Second major hierarchy** Traditionally includes subdirectories that contain information used by the system. Files in **/usr** subdirectories do not change often and may be shared by several systems.

/usr/bin   **Most user commands** Contains standard Linux/OS X utility programs—that is, binaries that are not needed in single-user or recovery mode.

/usr/games   **Games and educational programs**

/usr/include   **Header files used by C programs**

/usr/lib   **Libraries**

/usr/local   **Local hierarchy** Holds locally important files and directories that are added to the system. Subdirectories can include **bin, games, include, lib, sbin, share,** and **src**.

/usr/sbin Nonvital system administration binaries See **/sbin.**

/usr/share **Architecture-independent data** Subdirectories can include **dict, doc, games, info,** **locale, man, misc, terminfo,** and **zoneinfo.**

/usr/share/doc Documentation

/usr/share/info GNU info system's primary directory

/usr/share/man Online manuals

/usr/src Source code

/var **Variable data** Files with contents that vary as the system runs are kept in subdirectories under **/var.** The most common examples are temporary files, system log files, spooled files, and user mailbox files. Subdirectories can include **cache, lib, lock, log, mail, opt, run, spool, tmp,** and **yp.** Older versions of Linux scattered such files through several subdirectories of **/usr** (**/usr/adm, /usr/mail, /usr/spool, /usr/tmp**).

/var/log **Log files** Contains **lastlog** (a record of the last login by each user), **messages** (system messages from **syslogd**), and **wtmp** (a record of all logins/logouts), among other log files.

/var/spool **Spooled application data** Contains **anacron, at, cron, lpd, mail, mqueue, samba,** and other directories. The file **/var/spool/mail** is typically a link to **/var/mail.**

ACCESS PERMISSIONS

Linux supports two methods of controlling who can access a file and how they can access it: traditional Linux access permissions and Access Control Lists (ACLs). This section describes traditional Linux access permissions. See page 99 for a discussion of ACLs, which provide finer-grained control of access permissions than do traditional access permissions.

Three types of users can access a file: the owner of the file (*owner*), a member of a group that the file is associated with (*group*), and everyone else (*other*). A user can attempt to access an ordinary file in three ways: by trying to *read from, write to,* or *execute* it.

ls –l: DISPLAYS PERMISSIONS

When you call ls with the –l option and the name of one or more ordinary files, ls displays a line of information about the file. The following example displays information for two files. The file **letter.0610** contains the text of a letter, and **check_spell** contains a shell script, a program written in a high-level shell programming language:

```
$ ls -l letter.0610 check_spell
-rwxr-xr-x 1 max pubs  852 Jul 31 13:47 check_spell
-rw-r--r-- 1 max pubs 3355 Jun 22 12:44 letter.0610
```

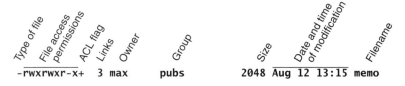

Figure 4-12   The columns displayed by the **ls −l** command

From left to right, the lines that an **ls −l** command displays contain the following information (refer to Figure 4-12):

- The type of file (first character)
- The file's access permissions (the next nine characters)
- The ACL flag (present if the file has an ACL, page 99)
- The number of links to the file (page 104)
- The name of the owner of the file (usually the person who created the file)
- The name of the group the file is associated with
- The size of the file in characters (bytes)
- The date and time the file was created or last modified
- The name of the file

Type of file   The type of file (first column) for **letter.0610** is a hyphen (−) because it is an ordinary file. Directory files have a **d** in this column; see Figure V-19 on page 748 for a list of other characters that can appear in this position.

Permissions   The next three characters specify the access permissions for the *owner* of the file: **r** (in the first position) indicates read permission, **w** (in the second position) indicates write permission, and **x** (in the third position) indicates execute permission. A − in one of the positions indicates that the owner does *not* have the permission associated with that position.

In a similar manner the next three characters represent permissions for the *group*, and the final three characters represent permissions for *other* (everyone else). In the preceding example, the owner of **letter.0610** can read from and write to the file, whereas the group and others can only read from the file and no one is allowed to execute it. Although execute permission can be allowed for any file, it does not make sense to assign execute permission to a file that contains a document, such as a letter. The **check_spell** file is an executable shell script, so execute permission is appropriate for it. (The owner, group, and others have execute permission.) For more information refer to "Discussion" on page 748.

chmod: CHANGES ACCESS PERMISSIONS

The Linux file access permission scheme lets you give other users access to the files you want to share yet keep your private files confidential. You can allow other users to read from *and* write to a file (handy if you are one of several people working on a joint project). You can allow others only to read from a file (perhaps a project specification you are proposing). Or you can allow others only to write to a file (similar to an inbox or mailbox, where you want others to be able to send you mail but do not want them to read your mail). Similarly you can protect entire directories from being scanned (covered shortly).

A user with **root** privileges can access any file on the system

security There is an exception to the access permissions described in this section. Anyone who can gain **root** privileges has full access to *all* files, regardless of the file's owner or access permissions.

The owner of a file controls which users have permission to access the file and how those users can access it. When you own a file, you can use the chmod (change mode) utility to change access permissions for that file. You can specify symbolic (relative) or numeric (absolute) arguments to chmod.

SYMBOLIC ARGUMENTS TO chmod

The following example, which uses symbolic arguments to chmod, adds (**+**) read and write permissions (**rw**) for all (**a**) users:

```
$ ls -l letter.0610
-rw------- 1 max pubs 3355 Jun 22 12:44 letter.0610
$ chmod a+rw letter.0610
$ ls -l letter.0610
-rw-rw-rw- 1 max pubs 3355 Jun 22 12:44 letter.0610
```

You must have read permission to execute a shell script

tip Because a shell needs to read a shell script (a text file containing shell commands) before it can execute the commands within that script, you must have read permission for the file containing the script to execute it. You also need execute permission to execute a shell script directly from the command line. In contrast, binary (program) files do not need to be read; they are executed directly. You need only execute permission to run a binary program.

Using symbolic arguments with chmod modifies existing permissions; the change a given argument makes depends on (is relative to) the existing permissions. In the next example, chmod removes (**–**) read (**r**) and execute (**x**) permissions for other (**o**) users. The owner and group permissions are not affected.

```
$ ls -l check_spell
-rwxr-xr-x 1 max pubs 852 Jul 31 13:47 check_spell
$ chmod o-rx check_spell
$ ls -l check_spell
-rwxr-x--- 1 max pubs 852 Jul 31 13:47 check_spell
```

In addition to **a** (all) and **o** (other), you can use **g** (group) and **u** (user, although *user* refers to the *owner* of the file who may or may not be the user of the file at any given time) in the argument to chmod. For example, **chmod a+x** adds execute permission for all users (other, group, and owner) and **chmod go–rwx** removes all permissions for all but the owner of the file.

chmod: **o** for other, **u** for owner

tip When using chmod, many people assume that the **o** stands for *owner;* it does not. The **o** stands for *other,* whereas **u** stands for *owner* (*user*). The acronym UGO (user-group-other) may help you remember how permissions are named.

NUMERIC ARGUMENTS TO chmod

You can also use numeric arguments to specify permissions with chmod. In place of the letters and symbols specifying permissions used in the previous examples, numeric arguments comprise three octal digits. (A fourth, leading digit controls set-uid and setgid permissions and is discussed next.) The first digit specifies permissions for the owner, the second for the group, and the third for other users. A **1** gives the specified user(s) execute permission, a **2** gives write permission, and a **4** gives read permission. Construct the digit representing the permissions for the owner, group, or others by ORing (adding) the appropriate values as shown in the following examples. Using numeric arguments sets file permissions absolutely; it does not modify existing permissions as symbolic arguments do.

In the following example, chmod changes permissions so only the owner of the file can read from and write to the file, regardless of how permissions were previously set. The **6** in the first position gives the owner read (**4**) and write (**2**) permissions. The 0s remove all permissions for the group and other users.

```
$ chmod 600 letter.0610
$ ls -l letter.0610
-rw------- 1 max pubs 3355 Jun 22 12:44 letter.0610
```

Next, **7** (**4** + **2** + **1**) gives the owner read, write, and execute permissions. The **5** (**4** + **1**) gives the group and other users read and execute permissions:

```
$ chmod 755 check_spell
$ ls -l check_spell
-rwxr-xr-x 1 max pubs 852 Jul 31 13:47 check_spell
```

Refer to Table V-8 on page 628 for more examples of numeric permissions.

Refer to page 278 for more information on using chmod to make a file executable and to page 626 for information on absolute arguments and chmod in general.

SETUID AND SETGID PERMISSIONS

When you execute a file that has setuid (set user ID) permission, the process executing the file takes on the privileges of the file's owner. For example, if you run a set-uid program that removes all files in a directory, you can remove files in any of the file owner's directories, even if you do not normally have permission to do so. In a similar manner, setgid (set group ID) permission gives the process executing the file the privileges of the group the file is associated with.

Minimize use of setuid and setgid programs owned by root

security Executable files that are setuid and owned by **root** have **root** privileges when they run, even if they are not run by **root**. This type of program is very powerful because it can do anything that **root** can do (and that the program is designed to do). Similarly executable files that are setgid and belong to the group **root** have extensive privileges.

Because of the power they hold and their potential for destruction, it is wise to avoid indiscriminately creating and using setuid programs owned by **root** and setgid programs belonging to the group **root**. Because of their inherent dangers, many sites minimize the use of these programs. One necessary setuid program is passwd.

The following example shows a user working with **root** privileges and using symbolic arguments to chmod to give one program setuid privileges and another program setgid privileges. The ls –l output (page 93) shows setuid permission by displaying an **s** in the owner's executable position and setgid permission by displaying an **s** in the group's executable position:

```
$ ls -l myprog*
-rwxr-xr-x 1 root pubs 19704 Jul 31 14:30 myprog1
-rwxr-xr-x 1 root pubs 19704 Jul 31 14:30 myprog2

# chmod u+s myprog1
# chmod g+s myprog2

$ ls -l myprog*
-rwsr-xr-x 1 root pubs 19704 Jul 31 14:30 myprog1
-rwxr-sr-x 1 root pubs 19704 Jul 31 14:30 myprog2
```

The next example uses numeric arguments to chmod to make the same changes. When you use four digits to specify permissions, setting the first digit to **1** sets the *sticky bit* (page 980), setting it to **2** specifies setgid permissions, and setting it to **4** specifies setuid permissions:

```
$ ls -l myprog*
-rwxr-xr-x 1 root pubs 19704 Jul 31 14:30 myprog1
-rwxr-xr-x 1 root pubs 19704 Jul 31 14:30 myprog2

# chmod 4755 myprog1
# chmod 2755 myprog2

$ ls -l myprog*
-rwsr-xr-x 1 root pubs 19704 Jul 31 14:30 myprog1
-rwxr-sr-x 1 root pubs 19704 Jul 31 14:30 myprog2
```

Do not write setuid shell scripts

security Never give shell scripts setuid permission. Several techniques for subverting them are well known.

DIRECTORY ACCESS PERMISSIONS

Access permissions have slightly different meanings when they are used with directories. Although the three types of users can read from or write to a directory, the directory cannot be executed. Execute permission is redefined for a directory: It means that you can cd into the directory and/or examine files that you have permission to read from in the directory. It has nothing to do with executing a file.

When you have only execute permission for a directory, you can use ls to list a file in the directory if you know its name. You cannot use ls without an argument to list the entire contents of the directory. In the following exchange, Zach first verifies that he is logged in as himself. He then checks the permissions on Max's info directory. You can view the access permissions associated with a directory by running ls with the –d (directory) and –l (long) options:

```
$ who am i
zach        pts/7   Aug 21 10:02
$ ls -ld /home/max/info
drwx-----x   2 max pubs 512 Aug 21 09:31 /home/max/info
$ ls -l /home/max/info
ls: /home/max/info: Permission denied
```

The **d** at the left end of the line that ls displays indicates that **/home/max/info** is a directory. Max has read, write, and execute permissions; members of the pubs group have no access permissions; and other users have execute permission only, indicated by the **x** at the right end of the permissions. Because Zach does not have read permission for the directory, the ls –l command returns an error.

When Zach specifies the names of the files he wants information about, he is not reading new directory information but rather searching for specific information, which he is allowed to do with execute access to the directory. He has read permission for **notes** so he has no problem using cat to display the file. He cannot display **financial** because he does not have read permission for it:

```
$ ls -l /home/max/info/financial /home/max/info/notes
-rw-------   1 max pubs 34 Aug 21 09:31 /home/max/info/financial
-rw-r--r--   1 max pubs 30 Aug 21 09:32 /home/max/info/notes
$ cat /home/max/info/notes
This is the file named notes.
$ cat /home/max/info/financial
cat: /home/max/info/financial: Permission denied
```

Next Max gives others read access to his **info** directory:

```
$ chmod o+r /home/max/info
```

When Zach checks his access permissions on **info**, he finds that he has both read and execute access to the directory. Now ls –l can list the contents of the **info** directory, but Zach still cannot read **financial**. (This restriction is an issue of file permissions, not directory permissions.) Finally, Zach tries to create a file named **newfile** using touch (page 862). If Max were to give him write permission to the **info** directory, Zach would be able to create new files in it:

```
$ ls -ld /home/max/info
drwx---r-x   2 max pubs 512 Aug 21 09:31 /home/max/info
$ ls -l /home/max/info
total 8
-rw-------   1 max pubs 34 Aug 21 09:31 financial
-rw-r--r--   1 max pubs 30 Aug 21 09:32 notes
$ cat /home/max/info/financial
cat: financial: Permission denied
$ touch /home/max/info/newfile
touch: cannot touch '/home/max/info/newfile': Permission denied
```

ACLs: Access Control Lists

Access Control Lists (ACLs) provide finer-grained control over which users can access specific directories and files than do traditional Linux permissions (page 93). Using ACLs you can specify the ways in which each of several users can access a directory or file. Because ACLs can reduce performance, do not enable them on filesystems that hold system files, where the traditional Linux permissions are sufficient. Also be careful when moving, copying, or archiving files: Not all utilities preserve ACLs. In addition, you cannot copy ACLs to filesystems that do not support ACLs.

An ACL comprises a set of rules. A rule specifies how a specific user or group can access the file that the ACL is associated with. There are two kinds of rules: *access rules* and *default rules*. (The documentation refers to *access ACLs* and *default ACLs,* even though there is only one type of ACL: There is one type of list [ACL] and there are two types of rules that an ACL can contain.)

An access rule specifies access information for a single file or directory. A default ACL pertains to a directory only; it specifies default access information (an ACL) for any file in the directory that is not given an explicit ACL.

Most utilities do not preserve ACLs

caution   When used with the **–p** (preserve) or **–a** (archive) option, cp preserves ACLs when it copies files. The mv utility also preserves ACLs. When you use cp with the **–p** or **–a** option and it is not able to copy ACLs, and in the case where mv is unable to preserve ACLs, the utility performs the operation and issues an error message:

```
$ mv report /tmp
mv: preserving permissions for '/tmp/report': Operation not supported
```

Other utilities, such as tar, cpio, and dump, do not support ACLs. You can use cp with the **–a** option to copy directory hierarchies, including ACLs.

You can never copy ACLs to a filesystem that does not support ACLs or to a filesystem that does not have ACL support turned on.

ENABLING ACLS

The following explanation of how to enable ACLs pertains to Linux. See page 933 if you are running Mac OS X.

Before you can use ACLs you must install the **acl** software package as explained in Appendix C.

Linux officially supports ACLs on **ext2**, **ext3**, and **ext4** filesystems only, although informal support for ACLs is available on other filesystems. To use ACLs on an **ext** filesystem, you must mount the device with the **acl** option (**no_acl** is the default). For example, if you want to mount the device represented by **/home** so you can use ACLs on files in **/home**, you can add **acl** to its options list in **/etc/fstab**:

```
$ grep home /etc/fstab
LABEL=/home              /home           ext3    defaults,acl        1 2
```

After changing **fstab**, you need to remount **/home** before you can use ACLs. If no one else is using the system, you can unmount it and mount it again (working with **root** privileges) as long as the working directory is not in the **/home** hierarchy. Alternatively you can use the **remount** option to mount to remount **/home** while the device is in use:

```
# mount -v -o remount /home
/dev/hda3 on /home type ext3 (rw,acl)
```

WORKING WITH ACCESS RULES

The setfacl utility modifies a file's ACL and getfacl displays a file's ACL. These utilities are available under Linux only. If you are running OS X you must use chmod as explained on page 933. When you use getfacl to obtain information about a file that does not have an ACL, it displays the same information as an **ls -l** command, albeit in a different format:

```
$ ls -l report
-rw-r--r--  1 max max 9537 Jan 12 23:17 report

$ getfacl report
# file: report
# owner: max
# group: max
user::rw-
group::r--
other::r--
```

The first three lines of the getfacl output comprise the header; they specify the name of the file, the owner of the file, and the group the file is associated with. For more information refer to "ls -l: Displays Permissions" on page 93. The **--omit-header** (or just **--omit**) option causes getfacl not to display the header:

```
$ getfacl --omit-header report
user::rw-
group::r--
other::r--
```

In the line that starts with **user**, the two colons (**::**) with no name between them indicate that the line specifies the permissions for the owner of the file. Similarly, the two colons in the **group** line indicate that the line specifies permissions for the group the file is associated with. The two colons following **other** are there for consistency: No name can be associated with **other**.

The setfacl **--modify** (or **-m**) option adds or modifies one or more rules in a file's ACL using the following format:

> setfacl --modify *ugo:name:permissions file-list*

where *ugo* can be either **u, g,** or **o** to indicate that the command sets file permissions for a user, a group, or all other users, respectively; *name* is the name of the user or group that permissions are being set for; *permissions* is the permissions in either symbolic or absolute format; and *file-list* is the list of files the permissions are to be applied to. You must omit *name* when you specify permissions for other users (**o**). Symbolic permissions use letters to represent file permissions (**rwx, r-x,** and so on), whereas absolute permissions use an octal number. While chmod uses three sets of permissions or three octal numbers (one each for the owner, group, and other users), setfacl uses a single set of permissions or a single octal number to represent the permissions being granted to the user or group represented by *ugo* and *name*. See the discussion of chmod on page 94 for more information about symbolic and absolute representations of file permissions.

For example, both of the following commands add a rule to the ACL for the **report** file that gives Sam read and write permission to that file:

```
$ setfacl --modify u:sam:rw- report
```

or

```
$ setfacl --modify u:sam:6 report
$ getfacl report
# file: report
# owner: max
# group: max
user::rw-
user:sam:rw-
group::r--
mask::rw-
other::r--
```

The line containing **user:sam:rw-** shows that Sam has read and write access (**rw-**) to the file. See page 93 for an explanation of how to read access permissions. See the following optional section for a description of the line that starts with **mask**.

When a file has an ACL, ls **-l** displays a plus sign (**+**) following the permissions, even if the ACL is empty:

```
$ ls -l report
-rw-rw-r--+ 1 max max 9537 Jan 12 23:17 report
```

optional EFFECTIVE RIGHTS MASK

The line that starts with **mask** specifies the *effective rights mask*. This mask limits the effective permissions granted to ACL groups and users. It does not affect the owner of the file or the group the file is associated with. In other words, it does not affect traditional Linux permissions. However, because setfacl always sets the effective rights mask to the least restrictive ACL permissions for the file, the mask has no effect unless you set it explicitly after you set up an ACL for the file. You can set the mask by specifying **mask** in place of *ugo* and by not specifying a *name* in a setfacl command.

The following example sets the effective rights mask to **read** for the **report** file:

```
$ setfacl -m mask::r-- report
```

The **mask** line in the following getfacl output shows the effective rights mask set to read (**r--**). The line that displays Sam's file access permissions shows them still set to read and write. However, the comment at the right end of the line shows that his effective permission is read.

```
$ getfacl report
# file: report
# owner: max
# group: max
user::rw-
user:sam:rw-                          #effective:r--
group::r--
mask::r--
other::r--
```

As the next example shows, setfacl can modify ACL rules and can set more than one ACL rule at a time:

```
$ setfacl -m u:sam:r--,u:zach:rw- report

$ getfacl --omit-header report
user::rw-
user:sam:r--
user:zach:rw-
group::r--
mask::rw-
other::r--
```

The **–x** option removes ACL rules for a user or a group. It has no effect on permissions for the owner of the file or the group that the file is associated with. The next example shows setfacl removing the rule that gives Sam permission to access the file:

```
$ setfacl -x u:sam report

$ getfacl --omit-header report
user::rw-
user:zach:rw-
group::r--
mask::rw-
other::r--
```

You must not specify *permissions* when you use the **–x** option. Instead, specify only the *ugo* and *name*. The **–b** option, followed by a filename only, removes all ACL rules and the ACL itself from the file or directory you specify.

Both setfacl and getfacl have many options. Use the **––help** option to display brief lists of options or refer to the man pages for details.

Setting Default Rules for a Directory

The following example shows that the **dir** directory initially has no ACL. The setfacl command uses the **–d** (default) option to add two default rules to the ACL for **dir**. These rules apply to all files in the **dir** directory that do not have explicit ACLs. The rules give members of the **pubs** group read and execute permissions and give members of the **admin** group read, write, and execute permissions.

```
$ ls -ld dir
drwx------ 2 max max 4096 Feb 12 23:15 dir
$ getfacl dir
# file: dir
# owner: max
# group: max
user::rwx
group::---
other::---

$ setfacl -d -m g:pubs:r-x,g:admin:rwx dir
```

The following ls command shows that the **dir** directory now has an ACL, as indicated by the **+** to the right of the permissions. Each of the default rules that getfacl displays starts with **default:**. The first two default rules and the last default rule specify the permissions for the owner of the file, the group that the file is associated with, and all other users. These three rules specify the traditional Linux permissions and take precedence over other ACL rules. The third and fourth rules specify the permissions for the **pubs** and **admin** groups. Next is the default effective rights mask.

```
$ ls -ld dir
drwx------+ 2 max max 4096 Feb 12 23:15 dir
$ getfacl dir
# file: dir
# owner: max
# group: max
user::rwx
group::---
other::---
default:user::rwx
default:group::---
default:group:pubs:r-x
default:group:admin:rwx
default:mask::rwx
default:other::---
```

Remember that the default rules pertain to files held in the directory that are not assigned ACLs explicitly. You can also specify access rules for the directory itself.

When you create a file within a directory that has default rules in its ACL, the effective rights mask for that file is created based on the file's permissions. In some cases the mask may override default ACL rules.

In the next example, touch creates a file named **new** in the **dir** directory. The ls command shows that this file has an ACL. Based on the value of umask (see the bash man page), both the owner and the group that the file is associated with have read and write permissions for the file. The effective rights mask is set to read and write so that the effective permission for **pubs** is read and the effective permissions for **admin** are read and write. Neither group has execute permission.

```
$ cd dir
$ touch new
$ ls -l new
-rw-rw----+ 1 max max 0 Feb 13 00:39 new
$ getfacl --omit new
user::rw-
group::---
group:pubs:r-x          #effective:r--
group:admin:rwx         #effective:rw-
mask::rw-
other::---
```

If you change the file's traditional permissions to read, write, and execute for the owner and the group, the effective rights mask changes to read, write, and execute and the groups specified by the default rules gain execute access to the file.

```
$ chmod 770 new
$ ls -l new
-rwxrwx---+ 1 max max 0 Feb 13 00:39 new
$ getfacl --omit new
user::rwx
group::---
group:pubs:r-x
group:admin:rwx
mask::rwx
other::---
```

LINKS

A *link* is a pointer to a file. Each time you create a file using vim, touch, cp, or by another other means, you are putting a pointer in a directory. This pointer associates a filename with a place on the disk. When you specify a filename in a command, you are indirectly pointing to the place on the disk that holds the information you want.

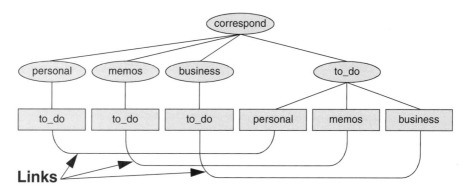

Figure 4-13   Using links to cross-classify files

Sharing files can be useful when two or more people are working on the same project and need to share some information. You can make it easy for other users to access one of your files by creating additional links to the file.

To share a file with another user, first give the user permission to read from and write to the file (page 94). You may also have to change the access permissions of the parent directory of the file to give the user read, write, or execute permission (page 98). Once the permissions are appropriately set, the user can create a link to the file so that each of you can access the file from your separate directory hierarchies.

A link can also be useful to a single user with a large directory hierarchy. You can create links to cross-classify files in your directory hierarchy, using different classifications for different tasks. For example, if you have the file layout depicted in Figure 4-2 on page 79, a file named **to_do** might appear in each subdirectory of the **correspond** directory—that is, in **personal, memos,** and **business.** If you find it difficult to keep track of everything you need to do, you can create a separate directory named **to_do** in the **correspond** directory. You can then link each subdirectory's to-do list into that directory. For example, you could link the file named **to_do** in the **memos** directory to a file named **memos** in the **to_do** directory. This set of links is shown in Figure 4-13.

Although it may sound complicated, this technique keeps all your to-do lists conveniently in one place. The appropriate list is easily accessible in the task-related directory when you are busy composing letters, writing memos, or handling personal business.

About the discussion of hard links

tip   Two kinds of links exist: hard links and symbolic (soft) links. Hard links are older and becoming outdated. The section on hard links is marked as optional; you can skip it, although it discusses inodes and gives you insight into the structure of the filesystem.

optional

HARD LINKS

A hard link to a file appears as another file. If the file appears in the same directory as the linked-to file, the links must have different filenames because two files in the same directory cannot have the same name. You can create a hard link to a file only from within the filesystem that holds the file.

ln: CREATES A HARD LINK

The ln (link) utility (without the –s or ––symbolic option) creates a hard link to an existing file using the following syntax:

ln existing-file new-link

The next command shows Zach making the link shown in Figure 4-14 by creating a new link named **/home/max/letter** to an existing file named **draft** in Zach's home directory:

```
$ pwd
/home/zach
$ ln draft /home/max/letter
```

The new link appears in the **/home/max** directory with the filename **letter**. In practice, Max may need to change directory access permissions so Zach will be able to create the link. Even though **/home/max/letter** appears in Max's directory, Zach is the owner of the file because he created it.

The ln utility creates an additional pointer to an existing file but it does *not* make another copy of the file. Because there is only one file, the file status information—such as access permissions, owner, and the time the file was last modified—is the same for all links; only the filenames differ. When Zach modifies **/home/zach/draft**, for example, Max sees the changes in **/home/max/letter**.

Figure 4-14   Two links to the same file: **/home/max/letter** and **/home/zach/draft**

cp VERSUS ln

The following commands verify that ln does not make an additional copy of a file. Create a file, use ln to make an additional link to the file, change the contents of the file through one link, and verify the change through the other link:

```
$ cat file_a
This is file A.
$ ln file_a file_b
$ cat file_b
This is file A.
$ vim file_b
...
$ cat file_b
This is file B after the change.
$ cat file_a
This is file B after the change.
```

If you try the same experiment using cp instead of ln and change a *copy* of the file, the difference between the two utilities will become clearer. Once you change a *copy* of a file, the two files are different:

```
$ cat file_c
This is file C.
$ cp file_c file_d
$ cat file_d
This is file C.
$ vim file_d
...
$ cat file_d
This is file D after the change.
$ cat file_c
This is file C.
```

ls and link counts You can use ls with the –l option, followed by the names of the files you want to compare, to confirm that the status information is the same for two links to the same file and is different for files that are not linked. In the following example, the 2 in the links field (just to the left of **max**) shows there are two links to **file_a** and **file_b** (from the previous example):

```
$ ls -l file_a file_b file_c file_d
-rw-r--r-- 2 max pubs 33  May 24 10:52 file_a
-rw-r--r-- 2 max pubs 33  May 24 10:52 file_b
-rw-r--r-- 1 max pubs 16  May 24 10:55 file_c
-rw-r--r-- 1 max pubs 33  May 24 10:57 file_d
```

Although it is easy to guess which files are linked to one another in this example, ls does not explicitly tell you.

ls and inodes Use ls with the –i option to determine without a doubt which files are linked. The –i option lists the *inode* (page 959) number for each file. An inode is the control structure for a file. (HFS+, the default filesystem under Mac OS X, does not have inodes but, through an elaborate scheme, appears to have inodes.) If the two filenames have the same inode number, they share the same control structure and are links to the same file. Conversely, when two filenames have different inode numbers, they are different files. The following example shows that **file_a** and **file_b** have the same inode number and that **file_c** and **file_d** have different inode numbers:

```
$ ls -i file_a file_b file_c file_d
3534 file_a    3534 file_b    5800 file_c    7328 file_d
```

All links to a file are of equal value: The operating system cannot distinguish the order in which multiple links were created. When a file has two links, you can remove either one and still access the file through the remaining link. You can remove the link used to create the file, for example, and, as long as one link remains, still access the file through that link.

SYMBOLIC LINKS

In addition to hard links, Linux supports *symbolic links,* also called *soft links* or *symlinks.* A hard link is a pointer to a file (the directory entry points to the inode), whereas a symbolic link is an *indirect* pointer to a file (the directory entry contains the pathname of the pointed-to file—a pointer to the hard link to the file).

Advantages of symbolic links
Symbolic links were developed because of the limitations inherent in hard links. You cannot create a hard link to a directory, but you can create a symbolic link to a directory.

In most cases the Linux file hierarchy encompasses several filesystems. Because each filesystem keeps separate control information (that is, separate inode tables or filesystem structures) for the files it holds, it is not possible to create hard links between files in different filesystems. A symbolic link can point to any file, regardless of where it is located in the file structure, but a hard link to a file must be in the same filesystem as the other hard link(s) to the file. When you create links only among files in your home directory, you will not notice this limitation.

A major advantage of a symbolic link is that it can point to a nonexistent file. This ability is useful if you need a link to a file that is periodically removed and re-created. A hard link keeps pointing to a "removed" file, which the link keeps alive even after a new file is created. In contrast, a symbolic link always points to the newly created file and does not interfere when you delete the old file. For example, a symbolic link could point to a file that gets checked in and out under a source code control system, a .o file that is re-created by the C compiler each time you run make, or a log file that is repeatedly archived.

Although they are more general than hard links, symbolic links have some disadvantages. Whereas all hard links to a file have equal status, symbolic links do not have the same status as hard links. When a file has multiple hard links, it is analogous to a person having multiple full legal names, as many married women do. In contrast, symbolic links are analogous to nicknames. Anyone can have one or more nicknames, but these nicknames have a lesser status than legal names. The following sections describe some of the peculiarities of symbolic links. See page 932 for information on Mac OS X Finder aliases.

ln: CREATES SYMBOLIC LINKS

The ln utility with the **--symbolic** (or **-s**) option creates a symbolic link. The following example creates a symbolic link **/tmp/s3** to the file **sum** in Max's home directory. When you use an ls –l command to look at the symbolic link, ls displays the name of the link and the name of the file it points to. The first character of the listing is l (for link).

```
$ ln --symbolic /home/max/sum /tmp/s3
$ ls -l /home/max/sum /tmp/s3
-rw-rw-r--   1 max max 38 Jun 12 09:51 /home/max/sum
lrwxrwxrwx   1 max max 14 Jun 12 09:52 /tmp/s3 -> /home/max/sum
$ cat /tmp/s3
This is sum.
```

The sizes and times of the last modifications of the two files are different. Unlike a hard link, a symbolic link to a file does not have the same status information as the file itself.

You can also use ln to create a symbolic link to a directory. When you use the **--symbolic** option, ln works as expected whether the file you are creating a link to is an ordinary file or a directory.

Use absolute pathnames with symbolic links

tip Symbolic links are literal and are not aware of directories. A link that points to a relative pathname, including a simple filename, assumes the relative pathname is relative to the directory that the link was created *in* (not the directory the link was created *from*). In the following example, the link points to the file named **sum** in the **/tmp** directory. Because no such file exists, cat gives an error message:

```
$ pwd
/home/max
$ ln --symbolic sum /tmp/s4
$ ls -l sum /tmp/s4
lrwxrwxrwx   1 max     max            3 Jun 12 10:13 /tmp/s4 -> sum
-rw-rw-r--   1 max     max           38 Jun 12 09:51 sum
$ cat /tmp/s4
cat: /tmp/s4: No such file or directory
```

optional cd AND SYMBOLIC LINKS

When you use a symbolic link as an argument to cd to change directories, the results can be confusing, particularly if you did not realize that you were using a symbolic link.

If you use cd to change to a directory that is represented by a symbolic link, the pwd shell builtin (page 141) lists the name of the symbolic link. The pwd utility

(**/bin/pwd**) lists the name of the linked-to directory, not the link, regardless of how you got there.

```
$ ln -s /home/max/grades /tmp/grades.old
$ pwd
/home/max
$ cd /tmp/grades.old
$ pwd
/tmp/grades.old
$ /bin/pwd
/home/max/grades
```

When you change directories back to the parent, you end up in the directory holding the symbolic link:

```
$ cd ..
$ pwd
/tmp
$ /bin/pwd
/tmp
```

Under Mac OS X, **/tmp** is a symbolic link to **/private/tmp**. When you are running OS X, after you give the **cd ..** command in the previous example, the working directory is **/private/tmp**.

rm: REMOVES A LINK

When you create a file, there is one hard link to it. You can then delete the file or, using Linux terminology, remove the link with the rm utility. When you remove the last hard link to a file, the operating system releases the space the file occupied on the disk and you can no longer access the information that was stored in the file. This space is released even if symbolic links to the file remain. When there is more than one hard link to a file, you can remove a hard link and still access the file from any remaining link. Unlike DOS and Windows, Linux does not provide an easy way to undelete a file once you have removed it. A skilled hacker, however, can sometimes piece the file together with time and effort.

When you remove all hard links to a file, you will not be able to access the file through a symbolic link. In the following example, cat reports that the file **total** does not exist because it is a symbolic link to a file that has been removed:

```
$ ls -l sum
-rw-r--r-- 1 max pubs 981  May 24 11:05 sum
$ ln -s sum total
$ rm sum
$ cat total
cat: total: No such file or directory
$ ls -l total
lrwxrwxrwx 1 max pubs 6  May 24 11:09 total -> sum
```

When you remove a file, be sure to remove all symbolic links to it. Remove a symbolic link in the same way you remove other files:

```
$ rm total
```

CHAPTER SUMMARY

Linux has a hierarchical, or treelike, file structure that makes it possible to organize files so you can find them quickly and easily. The file structure contains directory files and ordinary files. Directories contain other files, including other directories; ordinary files generally contain text, programs, or images. The ancestor of all files is the root directory and is represented by / standing alone or at the left end of a pathname.

Most Linux filesystems support 255-character filenames. Nonetheless, it is a good idea to keep filenames simple and intuitive. Filename extensions can help make filenames more meaningful.

When you are logged in, you are always associated with a working directory. Your home directory is the working directory from the time you log in until you use cd to change directories.

An absolute pathname starts with the root directory and contains all the filenames that trace a path to a given file. The pathname starts with a slash, representing the root directory, and contains additional slashes following all the directories in the path, except for the last directory in the case of a path that points to a directory file.

A relative pathname is similar to an absolute pathname but traces the path starting from the working directory. A simple filename is the last element of a pathname and is a form of a relative pathname; it represents a file in the working directory.

A Linux filesystem contains many important directories, including **/usr/bin**, which stores most of the Linux utility commands, and **/dev**, which stores device files, many of which represent physical pieces of hardware. An important standard file is **/etc/passwd**; it contains information about users, such as each user's ID and full name.

Among the attributes associated with each file are access permissions. They determine who can access the file and how the file may be accessed. Three groups of users can potentially access the file: the owner, the members of a group, and all other users. An ordinary file can be accessed in three ways: read, write, and execute. The ls utility with the –l option displays these permissions. For directories, execute access is redefined to mean that the directory can be searched.

The owner of a file or a user working with **root** privileges can use the chmod utility to change the access permissions of a file. This utility specifies read, write, and execute permissions for the file's owner, the group, and all other users on the system.

Access Control Lists (ACLs) provide finer-grained control over which users can access specific directories and files than do traditional Linux permissions. Using ACLs you can specify the ways in which each of several users can access a directory or file. Few utilities preserve ACLs when working with files.

An ordinary file stores user data, such as textual information, programs, or images. A directory is a standard-format disk file that stores information, including names, about ordinary files and other directory files. An inode is a data structure, stored on disk, that defines a file's existence and is identified by an inode number. A directory relates each of the filenames it stores to an inode.

A link is a pointer to a file. You can have several links to a file so you can share the file with other users or have the file appear in more than one directory. Because only one copy of a file with multiple links exists, changing the file through any one link causes the changes to appear in all the links. Hard links cannot link directories or span filesystems, whereas symbolic links can.

Table 4-2 summarizes the utilities introduced in this chapter.

Table 4-2   Utilities introduced in Chapter 4

Utility	Function
cd	Associates you with another working directory (page 87)
chmod	Changes access permissions on a file (page 94)
getfacl	Displays a file's ACL (page 100)
ln	Makes a link to an existing file (page 106)
mkdir	Creates a directory (page 86)
pwd	Displays the pathname of the working directory (page 82)
rmdir	Deletes a directory (page 88)
setfacl	Modifies a file's ACL (page 100)

EXERCISES

1. Is each of the following an absolute pathname, a relative pathname, or a simple filename?

   a. **milk_co**

   b. **correspond/business/milk_co**

c. **/home/max**

d. **/home/max/literature/promo**

e. **..**

f. **letter.0610**

2. List the commands you can use to perform these operations:

a. Make your home directory the working directory

b. Identify the working directory

3. If the working directory is **/home/max** with a subdirectory named **literature,** give three sets of commands that you can use to create a subdirectory named **classics** under **literature.** Also give several sets of commands you can use to remove the **classics** directory and its contents.

4. The df utility displays all mounted filesystems along with information about each. Use the df utility with the **–h** (human-readable) option to answer the following questions.

a. How many filesystems are mounted on your Linux system?

b. Which filesystem stores your home directory?

c. Assuming that your answer to exercise 4a is two or more, attempt to create a hard link to a file on another filesystem. What error message do you get? What happens when you attempt to create a symbolic link to the file instead?

5. Suppose you have a file that is linked to a file owned by another user. How can you ensure that changes to the file are no longer shared?

6. You should have read permission for the **/etc/passwd** file. To answer the following questions, use cat or less to display **/etc/passwd.** Look at the fields of information in **/etc/passwd** for the users on your system.

a. Which character is used to separate fields in **/etc/passwd**?

b. How many fields are used to describe each user?

c. How many users are on the local system?

d. How many different login shells are in use on your system? (*Hint:* Look at the last field.)

e. The second field of **/etc/passwd** stores user passwords in encoded form. If the password field contains an **x,** your system uses shadow passwords and stores the encoded passwords elsewhere. Does your system use shadow passwords?

7. If **/home/zach/draft** and **/home/max/letter** are links to the same file and the following sequence of events occurs, what will be the date in the opening of the letter?

a. Max gives the command **vim letter**.

b. Zach gives the command **vim draft**.

c. Zach changes the date in the opening of the letter to January 31, 2009, writes the file, and exits from vim.

d. Max changes the date to February 1, 2009, writes the file, and exits from vim.

8. Suppose a user belongs to a group that has all permissions on a file named **jobs_list**, but the user, as the owner of the file, has no permissions. Describe which operations, if any, the user/owner can perform on **jobs_list**. Which command can the user/owner give that will grant the user/owner all permissions on the file?

9. Does the root directory have any subdirectories you cannot search as an ordinary user? Does the root directory have any subdirectories you cannot read as a regular user? Explain.

10. Assume you are given the directory structure shown in Figure 4-2 on page 79 and the following directory permissions:

```
d--x--x---   3 zach pubs 512 Mar 10 15:16 business
drwxr-xr-x   2 zach pubs 512 Mar 10 15:16 business/milk_co
```

For each category of permissions—owner, group, and other—what happens when you run each of the following commands? Assume the working directory is the parent of **correspond** and that the file **cheese_co** is readable by everyone.

a. **cd correspond/business/milk_co**

b. **ls –l correspond/business**

c. **cat correspond/business/cheese_co**

ADVANCED EXERCISES

11. What is an inode? What happens to the inode when you move a file within a filesystem?

12. What does the **..** entry in a directory point to? What does this entry point to in the root (**/**) directory?

13. How can you create a file named **–i**? Which techniques do not work, and why do they not work? How can you remove the file named **–i**?

14. Suppose the working directory contains a single file named **andor**. What error message do you get when you run the following command line?

    ```
    $ mv andor and\/or
    ```

    Under what circumstances is it possible to run the command without producing an error?

15. The **ls –i** command displays a filename preceded by the inode number of the file (page 107). Write a command to output inode/filename pairs for the files in the working directory, sorted by inode number. (*Hint:* Use a pipe.)

16. Do you think the system administrator has access to a program that can decode user passwords? Why or why not? (See exercise 6.)

17. Is it possible to distinguish a file from a hard link to a file? That is, given a filename, can you tell whether it was created using an **ln** command? Explain.

18. Explain the error messages displayed in the following sequence of commands:

    ```
    $ ls -l
    total 1
    drwxrwxr-x   2 max pubs 1024 Mar  2 17:57 dirtmp
    $ ls dirtmp
    $ rmdir dirtmp
    rmdir: dirtmp: Directory not empty
    $ rm dirtmp/*
    rm: No match.
    ```

5

THE SHELL

This chapter takes a close look at the shell and explains how to use some of its features. It discusses command-line syntax and describes how the shell processes a command line and initiates execution of a program. In addition the chapter explains how to redirect input to and output from a command, construct pipes and filters on the command line, and run a command in the background. The final section covers filename expansion and explains how you can use this feature in your everyday work.

Except as noted, everything in this chapter applies to the Bourne Again (bash) and TC (tcsh) Shells. The exact wording of the shell output differs from shell to shell: What the shell you are using displays may differ slightly from what appears in this book. For shell-specific information, refer to Chapters 8 (bash) and 9 (tcsh). Chapter 10 covers writing and executing bash shell scripts.

The Command Line

The shell executes a program when you give it a command in response to its prompt. For example, when you give an ls command, the shell executes the utility program named ls. You can cause the shell to execute other types of programs— such as shell scripts, application programs, and programs you have written—in the same way. The line that contains the command, including any arguments, is called the *command line*. This book uses the term *command* to refer to both the characters you type on the command line and the program that action invokes.

Syntax

Command-line syntax dictates the ordering and separation of the elements on a command line. When you press the RETURN key after entering a command, the shell scans the command line for proper syntax. The syntax for a basic command line is

command [arg1] [arg2] ... *[argn]* RETURN

One or more SPACEs must separate elements on the command line. The **command** is the name of the command, **arg1** through **argn** are arguments, and RETURN is the keystroke that terminates all command lines. The brackets in the command-line syntax indicate that the arguments they enclose are optional. Not all commands require arguments: Some commands do not allow arguments; other commands allow a variable number of arguments; and still others require a specific number of arguments. Options, a special kind of argument, are usually preceded by one or two hyphens (also called a dash or minus sign: –).

Command Name

Usage message Some useful Linux command lines consist of only the name of the command without any arguments. For example, ls by itself lists the contents of the working directory. Commands that require arguments typically give a short error message, called a *usage message,* when you use them without arguments, with incorrect arguments, or with the wrong number of arguments.

Arguments

On the command line each sequence of nonblank characters is called a *token* or *word*. An *argument* is a token, such as a filename, string of text, number, or other object that a command acts on. For example, the argument to a vim or emacs command is the name of the file you want to edit.

The following command line shows cp copying the file named **temp** to **tempcopy**:

```
$ cp temp tempcopy
```

Arguments are numbered starting with the command itself, which is argument zero. In this example, **cp** is argument zero, **temp** is argument one, and **tempcopy** is argument two. The cp utility requires at least two arguments on the command line; see page 640. Argument one is the name of an existing file. Argument two is the name of the file that cp is creating or overwriting. Here the arguments are not optional; both arguments must be present for the command to work. When you do

```
$ ls
hold    mark    names    oldstuff  temp  zach
house   max     office   personal  test
$ ls -r
zach  temp       oldstuff  names  mark   hold
test  personal   office    max    house
$ ls -x
hold       house    mark   max    names  office
oldstuff   personal temp   test   zach
$ ls -rx
zach    test   temp   personal  oldstuff  office
names   max    mark   house     hold
```

Figure 5-1   Using options

not supply the right number or kind of arguments, cp displays a usage message. Try typing **cp** and then pressing RETURN.

OPTIONS

An *option* is an argument that modifies the effects of a command. You can frequently specify more than one option, modifying the command in several different ways. Options are specific to and interpreted by the program the command line calls, not by the shell.

By convention options are separate arguments that follow the name of the command and usually precede other arguments, such as filenames. Most utilities require you to prefix options with a single hyphen. However, this requirement is specific to the utility and not the shell. GNU program options are frequently preceded by two hyphens in a row. For example, **--help** generates a (sometimes extensive) usage message.

Figure 5-1 first shows the output of an ls command without any options. By default ls lists the contents of the working directory in alphabetical order, vertically sorted in columns. Next the **–r** (reverse order; because this is a GNU utility, you can also use **--reverse**) option causes the ls utility to display the list of files in reverse alphabetical order, still sorted in columns. The **–x** option causes ls to display the list of files in horizontally sorted rows.

Combining options   When you need to use several options, you can usually group multiple single-letter options into one argument that starts with a single hyphen; do not put SPACEs between the options. You cannot combine options that are preceded by two hyphens in this way. Specific rules for combining options depend on the program you are running. Figure 5-1 shows both the **–r** and **–x** options with the ls utility. Together these options generate a list of filenames in horizontally sorted columns, in reverse alphabetical order. Most utilities allow you to list options in any order; thus **ls –xr** produces the same results as **ls –rx**. The command **ls –x –r** also generates the same list.

Option arguments   Some utilities have options that themselves require arguments. For example, the gcc utility has a **–o** option that must be followed by the name you want to give the executable file that gcc generates. Typically an argument to an option is separated from its option letter by a SPACE:

```
$ gcc -o prog prog.c
```

Displaying readable file sizes: the –h option

tip   Most utilities that report on file sizes specify the size of a file in bytes. Bytes work well when you are dealing with smaller files, but the numbers can be difficult to read when you are working with file sizes that are measured in megabytes or gigabytes. Use the **–h** (or **––human-readable**) option to display file sizes in kilo-, mega-, and gigabytes. Experiment with the **df –h** (disk free) and **ls –lh** commands.

Arguments that start with a hyphen   Another convention allows utilities to work with arguments, such as filenames, that start with a hyphen. If a file's name is –l, the following command is ambiguous:

```
$ ls -l
```

This command could mean you want ls to display a long listing of all files in the working directory or a listing of the file named –l. It is interpreted as the former. Avoid creating files whose names begin with hyphens. If you do create them, many utilities follow the convention that a –– argument (two consecutive hyphens) indicates the end of the options (and the beginning of the arguments). To disambiguate the preceding command, you can type

```
$ ls -- -l
```

You can use an alternative format in which the period refers to the working directory and the slash indicates that the name refers to a file in the working directory:

```
$ ls ./-l
```

Assuming you are working in the **/home/max** directory, the preceding command is functionally equivalent to

```
$ ls /home/max/-l
```

The following command displays a long listing of this file:

```
$ ls -l -- -l
```

These are conventions, not hard-and-fast rules, and a number of utilities do not follow them (e.g., find). Following such conventions is a good idea and makes it easier for users to work with your program. When you write shell scripts that require options, follow the Linux option conventions. You can use xargs (page 881) in a shell script to help follow these conventions.

PROCESSING THE COMMAND LINE

As you enter a command line, the Linux tty device driver (part of the Linux kernel) examines each character to see whether it must take immediate action. When you press CONTROL-H (to erase a character) or CONTROL-U (to kill a line), the device driver immediately adjusts the command line as required; the shell never sees the character(s) you erased or the line you killed. Often a similar adjustment occurs when you press CONTROL-W (to erase a word). When the character you entered does not require immediate action, the device driver stores the character in a buffer and waits for additional characters. When you press RETURN, the device driver passes the command line to the shell for processing.

Parsing the command line   When the shell processes a command line, it looks at the line as a whole and *parses* (breaks) it into its component parts (Figure 5-2). Next the shell looks for the name of the command. Usually the name of the command is the first item on the command line

The --help option

tip Many utilities display a (sometimes extensive) help message when you call them with an argument of **--help**. All utilities developed by the GNU Project (page 3) accept this option. An example follows.

```
$ bzip2 --help
bzip2, a block-sorting file compressor.  Version 1.0.5, 10-Dec-2007.

   usage: bunzip2 [flags and input files in any order]

   -h --help           print this message
   -d --decompress     force decompression
   -z --compress       force compression
   -k --keep           keep (don't delete) input files
   -f --force          overwrite existing output files
...
   If invoked as 'bzip2', default action is to compress.
             as 'bunzip2',  default action is to decompress.
             as 'bzcat', default action is to decompress to stdout.
...
```

after the prompt (argument zero). The shell typically takes the first characters on the command line up to the first blank (TAB or SPACE) and then looks for a command with that name. The command name (the first token) can be specified on the command line

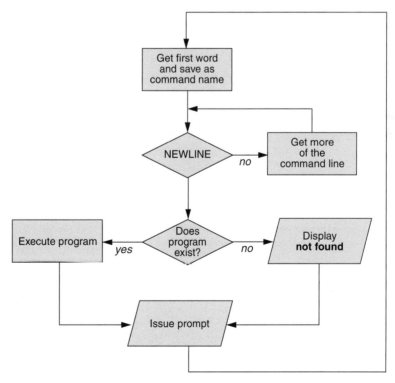

Figure 5-2   Processing the command line

either as a simple filename or as a pathname. For example, you can call the ls command in either of the following ways:

```
$ ls
$ /bin/ls
```

optional   The shell does not require that the name of the program appear first on the command line. Thus you can structure a command line as follows:

```
$ >bb <aa cat
```

This command runs cat with standard input coming from the file named **aa** and standard output going to the file named **bb**. When the shell recognizes the redirect symbols (page 126), it recognizes and processes them and their arguments before finding the name of the program that the command line is calling. This is a properly structured—albeit rarely encountered and possibly confusing—command line.

Absolute versus relative pathnames   When you give an absolute pathname of a program on the command line or a relative pathname that is not a simple filename (i.e., any pathname that includes at least one slash), the shell looks in the specified directory (**/bin** in the case of the **/bin/ls** command) for a file that has the name you specified and that you have permission to execute. When you give a simple filename of a program, the shell searches through a list of directories for a filename that matches the specified name and for which you have execute permission. The shell does not look through all directories but only the ones specified by the variable named **PATH**. Refer to page 297 (bash) or page 373 (tcsh) for more information on **PATH**. Also refer to the discussion of the which and whereis utilities on page 65.

When it cannot find the executable file, the Bourne Again Shell (bash) displays a message such as the following:

```
$ abc
bash: abc: command not found
```

One reason the shell may not be able to find the executable file is that it is not in a directory in your **PATH**. Under bash the following command temporarily adds the working directory (.) to **PATH**:

```
$ PATH=$PATH:.
```

For security reasons, you may not want to add the working directory to **PATH** permanently; see the tip on the next page and the one on page 298.

When the shell finds the program but cannot execute it (i.e., because you do not have execute permission for the file that contains the program), it displays a message similar to

```
$ def
bash: ./def: Permission denied
```

See "ls –l: Displays Permissions" on page 93 for information on displaying access permissions for a file and "chmod: Changes Access Permissions" on page 94 for instructions on how to change file access permissions.

Figure 5-3 The command does not know where standard input comes from or where standard output and standard error go

Try giving a command as *./command*

tip You can always execute an executable file in the working directory by prepending **./** to the name of the file. For example, if **myprog** is an executable file in the working directory, you can execute it with the following command, regardless of how **PATH** is set:

```
$ ./myprog
```

EXECUTING THE COMMAND LINE

Process If it finds an executable file with the same name as the command, the shell starts a new process. A *process* is the execution of a command by Linux (page 306). The shell makes each command-line argument, including options and the name of the command, available to the called program. While the command is executing, the shell waits for the process to finish. At this point the shell is in an inactive state called *sleep*. When the program finishes execution, it passes its exit status (page 440) to the shell. The shell then returns to an active state (wakes up), issues a prompt, and waits for another command.

The shell does not process arguments Because the shell does not process command-line arguments but merely passes them to the called program, the shell has no way of knowing whether a particular option or other argument is valid for a given program. Any error or usage messages about options or arguments come from the program itself. Some utilities ignore bad options.

EDITING THE COMMAND LINE

You can repeat and edit previous commands and edit the current command line. See page 31, page 310 (bash), and page 363 (tcsh) for more information.

STANDARD INPUT AND STANDARD OUTPUT

Standard output is a place a program can send information, such as text. The program never "knows" where the information it sends to standard output is going (Figure 5-3). The information can go to a printer, an ordinary file, or the screen. The following sections show that by default the shell directs standard output from a command to the screen[1] and describe how you can cause the shell to redirect this output to an ordinary file.

---

1. This book uses the term *screen* to refer to a screen, terminal emulator window, or workstation—in other words, to the device that the shell displays its prompt and messages on.

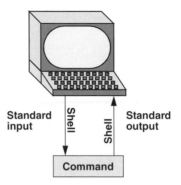

Figure 5-4   By default, standard input comes from the keyboard and
standard output goes to the screen

Standard input is a place that a program gets information from. As with standard
output the program never "knows" where the information comes from. The following sections explain how to redirect standard input to a command so that it comes
from an ordinary file instead of from the keyboard (the default).

In addition to standard input and standard output, a running program normally has
a place to send error messages: *standard error*. Refer to page 275 (bash) and
page 359 (tcsh) for more information on working with standard error.

optional   By convention, a process expects that the program that called it (frequently the
shell) has set up standard input, standard output, and standard error so the process
can use them immediately. The called process does not *have* to know which files or
devices are connected to standard input, standard output, or standard error.

However, a process *can* query the kernel to get information about the device that
standard input, standard output, or standard error is connected to. For example,
the ls utility displays output in multiple columns when the output goes to the screen,
but generates a single column of output when the output is redirected to a file or
another program. The ls utility uses the **isatty**() system call to determine if output is
going to the screen (a tty). In addition, ls can use another system call to determine
the width of the screen it is sending output to. It then modifies its output to fit the
width of the screen. Compare the output of ls by itself and when you send it
through a pipe to less.

THE SCREEN AS A FILE

Chapter 4 introduced ordinary files, directory files, and hard and soft links. Linux
and OS X have an additional type of file: a *device file*. A device file resides in the
Linux file structure, usually in the **/dev** directory, and represents a peripheral device,
such as a screen and keyboard, printer, or disk drive.

The device name that the who utility displays after your username is the filename of
the screen and keyboard. For example, when who displays the device name **pts/4**,
the pathname of the screen and keyboard is **/dev/pts/4**. In a graphical environment,

```
$ cat
This is a line of text.
This is a line of text.
Cat keeps copying lines of text
Cat keeps copying lines of text
until you press CONTROL-D at the beginning
until you press CONTROL-D at the beginning
of a line.
of a line.
CONTROL-D
$
```

Figure 5-5   The cat utility copies standard input to standard output

when you work with multiple windows, each window has its own device name. You can also use the tty utility to display the name of the device that you give the command from. Although you would not normally have occasion to do so, you can read from and write to this file as though it were a text file. Writing to it displays what you write on the screen; reading from it reads what you enter on the keyboard.

THE KEYBOARD AND SCREEN AS STANDARD INPUT AND STANDARD OUTPUT

When you first log in, the shell directs standard output of your commands to the device file that represents the screen (Figure 5-4). Directing output in this manner causes it to appear on the screen. The shell directs standard input to come from the same file, so your commands receive as input anything you type on the keyboard.

cat   The cat utility provides a good example of the way the keyboard and screen function as standard input and standard output, respectively. When you use cat, it copies a file to standard output. Because the shell directs standard output to the screen, cat displays the file on the screen.

Up to this point cat has taken its input from the filename (argument) you specify on the command line. When you do not give cat an argument (that is, when you give the command **cat** followed immediately by RETURN), cat takes its input from standard input. Thus, when called without an argument, cat copies standard input to standard output, one line at a time.

To see how cat works, type **cat** and press RETURN in response to the shell prompt. Nothing happens. Enter a line of text and press RETURN. The same line appears just under the one you entered. The cat utility is working. Because the shell associates cat's standard input with the keyboard and cat's standard output with the screen, when you type a line of text cat copies the text from standard input (the keyboard) to standard output (the screen). Figure 5-5 shows this exchange.

CONTROL-D   The cat utility keeps copying text until you enter CONTROL-D on a line by itself. Pressing
signals EOF   CONTROL-D sends an EOF (end of file) signal to cat to indicate that it has reached the end of standard input and there is no more text for it to copy. The cat utility then finishes execution and returns control to the shell, which displays a prompt.

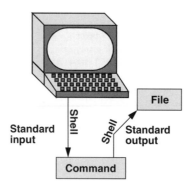

Figure 5-6   Redirecting standard output

REDIRECTION

The term *redirection* encompasses the various ways you can cause the shell to alter where standard input of a command comes from and where standard output goes to. By default the shell associates standard input and standard output of a command with the keyboard and the screen. You can cause the shell to redirect standard input or standard output of any command by associating the input or output with a command or file other than the device file representing the keyboard and the screen. This section demonstrates how to redirect input from and output to ordinary files.

REDIRECTING STANDARD OUTPUT

The *redirect output symbol* (>) instructs the shell to redirect the output of a command to the specified file instead of to the screen (Figure 5-6). The format of a command line that redirects output is

> *command [arguments] > filename*

where **command** is any executable program (such as an application program or a utility), **arguments** are optional arguments, and **filename** is the name of the ordinary file the shell redirects the output to.

Figure 5-7 uses cat to demonstrate output redirection. This figure contrasts with Figure 5-5, where standard input *and* standard output are associated with the keyboard and screen. The input in Figure 5-7 comes from the keyboard. The redirect output symbol on the command line causes the shell to associate cat's standard output with the **sample.txt** file specified on the command line.

After giving the command and typing the text shown in Figure 5-7, the **sample.txt** file contains the text you entered. You can use cat with an argument of **sample.txt** to display this file. The next section shows another way to use cat to display the file.

Figure 5-7 shows that redirecting standard output from cat is a handy way to create a file without using an editor. The drawback is that once you enter a line

```
$ cat > sample.txt
This text is being entered at the keyboard and
cat is copying it to a file.
Press CONTROL-D to signal the end of file.
CONTROL-D
$
```

Figure 5-7   cat with its output redirected

Redirecting output can destroy a file I

Use caution when you redirect output to a file. If the file exists, the shell will overwrite it and destroy its contents. For more information see the tip "Redirecting output can destroy a file II" on page 129.

and press RETURN, you cannot edit the text. While you are entering a line, the erase and kill keys work to delete text. This procedure is useful for creating short, simple files.

Figure 5-8 shows how to use cat and the redirect output symbol to *catenate* (join one after the other—the derivation of the name of the cat utility) several files into one larger file. The first three commands display the contents of three files: **stationery**, **tape**, and **pens**. The next command shows cat with three filenames as arguments. When you call it with more than one filename, cat copies the files, one at a time, to standard output. This command redirects standard output to the file **supply_orders**. The final cat command shows that **supply_orders** holds the contents of all three original files.

```
$ cat stationery
2,000 sheets letterhead ordered:    10/7/08

$ cat tape
1 box masking tape ordered:         10/14/08
5 boxes filament tape ordered:      10/28/08

$ cat pens
12 doz. black pens ordered:         10/4/08

$ cat stationery tape pens > supply_orders

$ cat supply_orders
2,000 sheets letterhead ordered:    10/7/08
1 box masking tape ordered:         10/14/08
5 boxes filament tape ordered:      10/28/08
12 doz. black pens ordered:         10/4/08
$
```

Figure 5-8   Using cat to catenate files

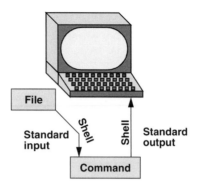

Figure 5-9   Redirecting standard input

REDIRECTING STANDARD INPUT

Just as you can redirect standard output, so you can redirect standard input. The *redirect input symbol* (<) instructs the shell to redirect a command's input to come from the specified file instead of from the keyboard (Figure 5-9). The format of a command line that redirects input is

> *command [arguments] < filename*

where *command* is any executable program (such as an application program or a utility), *arguments* are optional arguments, and *filename* is the name of the ordinary file the shell redirects the input from.

Figure 5-10 shows cat with its input redirected from the **supply_orders** file created in Figure 5-8 and standard output going to the screen. This setup causes cat to display the sample file on the screen. The system automatically supplies an EOF signal at the end of an ordinary file.

Utilities that take input from a file or standard input Giving a cat command with input redirected from a file yields the same result as giving a cat command with the filename as an argument. The cat utility is a member of a class of Linux utilities that function in this manner. Other members of this class of utilities include lpr, sort, grep, and Perl. These utilities first examine the command line you call them with. If you include a filename on the command line, the utility takes its input from the file you specify. If you do not specify a filename, the utility takes its input from standard input. It is the utility or program—not the shell or operating system—that functions in this manner.

```
$ cat < supply_orders
2,000 sheets letterhead ordered:     10/7/08
1 box masking tape ordered:          10/14/08
5 boxes filament tape ordered:       10/28/08
12 doz. black pens ordered:          10/4/08
```

Figure 5-10   cat with its input redirected

noclobber: AVOIDS OVERWRITING FILES

The shell provides the **noclobber** feature that prevents overwriting a file using redirection. Under bash you can enable this feature by setting **noclobber** using the command **set −o noclobber**. The same command with **+o** unsets **noclobber**. Under tcsh use **set noclobber** and **unset noclobber**. With **noclobber** set, if you redirect output to an existing file, the shell displays an error message and does not execute the command. The following example, run under bash and tcsh, creates a file using touch, sets **noclobber**, attempts to redirect the output from echo to the newly created file, unsets **noclobber**, and performs the redirection again:

bash
```
$ touch tmp
$ set -o noclobber
$ echo "hi there" > tmp
bash: tmp: cannot overwrite existing file
$ set +o noclobber
$ echo "hi there" > tmp
$
```

tcsh
```
tcsh $ touch tmp
tcsh $ set noclobber
tcsh $ echo "hi there" > tmp
tmp: File exists.
tcsh $ unset noclobber
tcsh $ echo "hi there" > tmp
$
```

Redirecting output can destroy a file II

caution   Depending on which shell you are using and how the environment is set up, a command such as the following may yield undesired results:

```
$ cat orange pear > orange
cat: orange: input file is output file
```

Although cat displays an error message, the shell destroys the contents of the existing **orange** file. The new **orange** file will have the same contents as **pear** because the first action the shell takes when it sees the redirection symbol (**>**) is to remove the contents of the original **orange** file. If you want to catenate two files into one, use cat to put the two files into a temporary file and then use mv to rename the temporary file:

```
$ cat orange pear > temp
$ mv temp orange
```

What happens in the next example can be even worse. The user giving the command wants to search through files **a**, **b**, and **c** for the word **apple** and redirect the output from grep (page 52) to the file **a.output**. Unfortunately the user enters the filename as **a output**, omitting the period and inserting a SPACE in its place:

```
$ grep apple a b c > a output
grep: output: No such file or directory
```

The shell obediently removes the contents of **a** and then calls grep. The error message may take a moment to appear, giving you a sense the command is running correctly. Even after you see the error message, it may take a while to realize you have destroyed the contents of **a**.

You can override **noclobber** by putting a pipe symbol (tcsh uses an exclamation point) after the redirect symbol (>l). In the following example, the user creates a file by redirecting the output of date. Next the user sets the **noclobber** variable and redirects output to the same file again. The shell displays an error message. Then the user places a pipe symbol after the redirect symbol and the shell allows the user to overwrite the file.

```
$ date > tmp2
$ set -o noclobber
$ date > tmp2
bash: a: cannot overwrite existing file
$ date >| tmp2
$
```

For more information on using **noclobber** under tcsh, refer to page 377.

APPENDING STANDARD OUTPUT TO A FILE

The *append output symbol* (>>) causes the shell to add new information to the end of a file, leaving existing information intact. This symbol provides a convenient way of catenating two files into one. The following commands demonstrate the action of the append output symbol. The second command accomplishes the catenation described in the preceding caution box:

```
$ cat orange
this is orange
$ cat pear >> orange
$ cat orange
this is orange
this is pear
```

The first command displays the contents of the **orange** file. The second command appends the contents of the **pear** file to the **orange** file. The final cat displays the result.

Do not trust **noclobber**

caution   Appending output is simpler than the two-step procedure described in the preceding caution box but you must be careful to include both greater than signs. If you accidentally use only one and the **noclobber** feature is not set, the shell will overwrite the **orange** file. Even if you have the **noclobber** feature turned on, it is a good idea to keep backup copies of the files you are manipulating in case you make a mistake.

Although it protects you from overwriting a file using redirection, **noclobber** does not stop you from overwriting a file using cp or mv. These utilities include the **–i** (interactive) option that helps protect you from this type of mistake by verifying your intentions when you try to overwrite a file. For more information see the tip "cp can destroy a file" on page 50.

The next example shows how to create a file that contains the date and time (the output from date), followed by a list of who is logged in (the output from who). The first line in Figure 5-11 redirects the output from date to the file named **whoson**. Then cat displays the file. Next the example appends the output from who to the **whoson** file. Finally cat displays the file containing the output of both utilities.

```
$ date > whoson
$ cat whoson
Fri Mar 27 14:31:18 PST 2009
$ who >> whoson
$ cat whoson
Fri Mar 27 14:31:18 PST 2009
sam         console       Mar 27 05:00(:0)
max         pts/4         Mar 27 12:23(:0.0)
max         pts/5         Mar 27 12:33(:0.0)
zach        pts/7         Mar 26 08:45 (bravo.example.com)
```

Figure 5-11   Redirecting and appending output

/dev/null: MAKING DATA DISAPPEAR

The **/dev/null** device is a *data sink*, commonly referred to as a *bit bucket*. You can redirect output that you do not want to keep or see to **/dev/null** and the output will disappear without a trace:

```
$ echo "hi there" > /dev/null
$
```

When you read from **/dev/null**, you get a null string. Give the following cat command to truncate a file named **messages** to zero length while preserving the ownership and permissions of the file:

```
$ ls -l messages
-rw-r--r--   1 max pubs 25315 Oct 24 10:55 messages
$ cat /dev/null > messages
$ ls -l messages
-rw-r--r--   1 max pubs 0 Oct 24 11:02 messages
```

PIPES

The shell uses a *pipe* to connect standard output of one command to standard input of another command. A pipe (sometimes referred to as a *pipeline*) has the same effect as redirecting standard output of one command to a file and then using that file as standard input to another command. A pipe does away with separate commands and the intermediate file. The symbol for a pipe is a vertical bar (|). The syntax of a command line using a pipe is

command_a [arguments] | command_b [arguments]

The preceding command line uses a pipe on a single command line to generate the same result as the following three command lines:

command_a [arguments] > temp
command_b [arguments] < temp
rm temp

In the preceding sequence of commands, the first line redirects standard output from *command_a* to an intermediate file named *temp*. The second line redirects

```
$ ls > temp
$ lpr temp
$ rm temp

or

$ ls | lpr
```

Figure 5-12   A pipe

standard input for *command_b* to come from *temp*. The final line deletes *temp*. The command using a pipe is not only easier to type, but is more efficient because it does not create a temporary file.

tr   You can use a pipe with any of the Linux utilities that accept input either from a file specified on the command line or from standard input. You can also use pipes with utilities that accept input only from standard input. For example, the tr (translate; page 864) utility takes its input from standard input only. In its simplest usage tr has the following format:

> tr *string1* *string2*

The tr utility accepts input from standard input and looks for characters that match one of the characters in *string1*. Upon finding a match, it translates the matched character in *string1* to the corresponding character in *string2*. (The first character in *string1* translates into the first character in *string2*, and so forth.) The tr utility sends its output to standard output. In both of the following examples, tr displays the contents of the **abstract** file with the letters **a**, **b**, and **c** translated into **A**, **B**, and **C**, respectively:

```
$ cat abstract | tr abc ABC
$ tr abc ABC < abstract
```

The tr utility does not change the contents of the original file; it cannot change the original file because it does not "know" the source of its input.

lpr   The lpr (line printer; page 742) utility accepts input from either a file or standard input. When you type the name of a file following lpr on the command line, it places that file in the print queue. When you do not specify a filename on the command line, lpr takes input from standard input. This feature enables you to use a pipe to redirect input to lpr. The first set of commands in Figure 5-12 shows how you can use ls and lpr with an intermediate file (**temp**) to send a list of the files in the working directory to the printer. If the **temp** file exists, the first command overwrites its contents. The second set of commands uses a pipe to send the same list (with the exception of **temp**) to the printer.

The commands in Figure 5-13 redirect the output from the who utility to **temp** and then display this file in sorted order. The sort utility (page 54) takes its input from the file specified on the command line or, when a file is not specified, from standard input; it sends its output to standard output. The sort command line in Figure 5-13

```
$ who > temp
$ sort < temp
max        pts/4           Mar 24 12:23
max        pts/5           Mar 24 12:33
sam        console         Mar 24 05:00
zach       pts/7           Mar 23 08:45
$ rm temp
```

Figure 5-13   Using a temporary file to store intermediate results

takes its input from standard input, which is redirected (**<**) to come from **temp**. The output that sort sends to the screen lists the users in sorted (alphabetical) order.

Because sort can take its input from standard input or from a filename on the command line, omitting the **<** symbol from Figure 5-13 yields the same result.

Figure 5-14 achieves the same result without creating the **temp** file. Using a pipe, the shell redirects the output from who to the input of sort. The sort utility takes input from standard input because no filename follows it on the command line.

When many people are using the system and you want information about only one of them, you can send the output from who to grep (page 52) using a pipe. The grep utility displays the line(s) containing the string you specify—**sam** in the following example:

```
$ who | grep 'sam'
sam        console         Mar 24 05:00
```

Another way of handling output that is too long to fit on the screen, such as a list of files in a crowded directory, is to use a pipe to send the output through less or more (both on page 48).

```
$ ls | less
```

The less utility displays text one screen at a time. To view another screen, press the SPACE bar. To view one more line, press RETURN. Press **h** for help and **q** to quit.

FILTERS

A *filter* is a command that processes an input stream of data to produce an output stream of data. A command line that includes a filter uses a pipe to connect standard output of one command to the filter's standard input. Another pipe connects

```
$ who | sort
max        pts/4           Mar 24 12:23
max        pts/5           Mar 24 12:33
sam        console         Mar 24 05:00
zach       pts/7           Mar 23 08:45
```

Figure 5-14   A pipe doing the work of a temporary file the filter's standard output to standard input of another command. Not all utilities can be used as filters.

In the following example, sort is a filter, taking standard input from standard output of who and using a pipe to redirect standard output to standard input of lpr. This command line sends the sorted output of who to the printer:

```
$ who | sort | lpr
```

The preceding example demonstrates the power of the shell combined with the versatility of Linux utilities. The three utilities who, sort, and lpr were not specifically designed to work with each other, but they all use standard input and standard output in the conventional way. By using the shell to handle input and output, you can piece standard utilities together on the command line to achieve the results you want.

tee: SENDS OUTPUT IN TWO DIRECTIONS

The tee (page 851) utility copies its standard input both to a file and to standard output. This utility is aptly named: It takes a single stream of input and sends the output in two directions. In Figure 5-15 the output of who is sent via a pipe to standard input of tee. The tee utility saves a copy of standard input in a file named **who.out** and also sends a copy to standard output. Standard output of tee goes via a pipe to standard input of grep, which displays only those lines containing the string **sam**. Use the −a (append) option to cause tee to append to a file instead of overwriting it.

```
$ who | tee who.out | grep sam
sam         console    Mar 24 05:00
$ cat who.out
sam         console    Mar 24 05:00
max         pts/4      Mar 24 12:23
max         pts/5      Mar 24 12:33
zach        pts/7      Mar 23 08:45
```

Figure 5-15   tee copies standard input to a file and to standard output

RUNNING A COMMAND IN THE BACKGROUND

Foreground   All commands up to this point have been run in the foreground. When you run a command in the *foreground,* the shell waits for it to finish before displaying another prompt and allowing you to continue. When you run a command in the *background,* you do not have to wait for the command to finish before running another command.

Jobs   A *job* is a series of one or more commands that can be connected by pipes. You can have only one foreground job in a window or on a screen, but you can have many background jobs. By running more than one job at a time, you are using one of

Linux's important features: multitasking. Running a command in the background can be useful when the command will run for a long time and does not need supervision. It leaves the screen free so you can use it for other work. Of course, when you are using a GUI, you can open another window to run another job.

Job number,
PID number

To run a job in the background, type an ampersand (&) just before the RETURN that ends the command line. The shell assigns a small number to the job and displays this *job number* between brackets. Following the job number, the shell displays the *process identification (PID) number*—a larger number assigned by the operating system. Each of these numbers identifies the job running in the background. The shell then displays another prompt and you can enter another command. When the background job finishes, the shell displays a message giving both the job number and the command line used to run the command.

The next example runs in the background; it sends the output of ls through a pipe to lpr, which sends it to the printer.

```
$ ls -l | lpr &
[1] 22092
$
```

The [1] following the command line indicates that the shell has assigned job number 1 to this job. The **22092** is the PID number of the first command in the job. (The TC Shell shows PID numbers for all commands in the job.) When this background job completes execution, the shell displays the message

```
[1]+ Done          ls -l | lpr
```

(In place of **ls –l**, the shell may display something similar to **ls ––color=always –l**. This difference is due to the fact that **ls** is aliased [page 324] to **ls ––color=always**.)

MOVING A JOB FROM THE FOREGROUND TO THE BACKGROUND

CONTROL-Z

You can suspend a foreground job (stop it from running without aborting the job) by pressing the suspend key, usually CONTROL-Z. The shell then stops the process and disconnects standard input from the keyboard. You can put a suspended job in the background and restart it by using the **bg** command followed by the job number. You do not need to specify the job number when there is only one stopped job.

Only the foreground job can take input from the keyboard. To connect the keyboard to a program running in the background, you must bring it to the foreground. To do so, type **fg** without any arguments when only one job is in the background. When more than one job is in the background, type **fg**, or a percent sign (%), followed by the number of the job you want to bring into the foreground. The shell displays the command you used to start the job (**promptme** in the following example), and you can enter any input the program requires to continue:

```
bash $ fg 1
promptme
```

Redirect the output of a job you run in the background to keep it from interfering with whatever you are working on in the foreground (on the screen). See page 285 for more information on job control. Refer to "| and & Separate Commands and Do Something Else" on page 283 for more detail about background tasks.

kill: ABORTING A BACKGROUND JOB

The interrupt key (usually CONTROL-C) cannot abort a background process; you must use kill (page 729) for this purpose. Follow **kill** on the command line with either the PID number of the process you want to abort or a percent sign (**%**) followed by the job number.

Determining the PID of a process using ps   If you forget a PID number, you can use the ps (process status; page 796) utility to display it. The following example runs a **tail –f outfile** command (the **–f** [follow] option causes tail to watch **outfile** and display new lines as they are written to the file) as a background job, uses ps to display the PID number of the process, and aborts the job with kill:

```
$ tail -f outfile &
[1] 18228
$ ps | grep tail
18228 pts/4     00:00:00 tail
$ kill 18228
[1]+  Terminated              tail -f outfile
$
```

Determining the number of a job using jobs   If you forget a job number, you can use the jobs command to display a list of job numbers. The next example is similar to the previous one except it uses the job number instead of the PID number to identify the job to be killed. Sometimes the message saying the job is terminated does not appear until you press RETURN after the RETURN that executes the kill command.

```
$ tail -f outfile &
[1] 18236
$ bigjob &
[2] 18237
$ jobs
[1]-  Running                 tail -f outfile &
[2]+  Running                 bigjob &
$ kill %1
$ RETURN
[1]-  Terminated              tail -f outfile
$
```

FILENAME GENERATION/PATHNAME EXPANSION

Wildcards, globbing   When you give the shell abbreviated filenames that contain *special characters*, also called *metacharacters*, the shell can generate filenames that match the names of existing files. These special characters are also referred to as *wildcards* because they act much as the jokers do in a deck of cards. When one of these characters appears in an argument on the command line, the shell expands that argument in sorted order into a list of filenames and passes the list to the program called by the command line. Filenames that contain these special characters are called *ambiguous file references* because they do not refer to any one specific file. The process that the shell performs on these filenames is called *pathname expansion* or *globbing*.

Ambiguous file references refer to a group of files with similar names quickly, saving the effort of typing the names individually. They can also help find a file whose name you do not remember in its entirety. If no filename matches the ambiguous file reference, the shell generally passes the unexpanded reference—special characters and all—to the program.

The ? Special Character

The question mark (?) is a special character that causes the shell to generate filenames. It matches any single character in the name of an existing file. The following command uses this special character in an argument to the lpr utility:

```
$ lpr memo?
```

The shell expands the **memo?** argument and generates a list of files in the working directory that have names composed of **memo** followed by any single character. The shell then passes this list to lpr. The lpr utility never "knows" the shell generated the filenames it was called with. If no filename matches the ambiguous file reference, the shell passes the string itself (**memo?**) to lpr or, if it is set up to do so, passes a null string (see **nullglob** on page 333).

The following example uses ls first to display the names of all files in the working directory and then to display the filenames that **memo?** matches:

```
$ ls
mem     memo12  memo9  memomax    newmemo5
memo    memo5   memoa  memos
$ ls memo?
memo5   memo9   memoa  memos
```

The **memo?** ambiguous file reference does not match **mem**, **memo**, **memo12**, **memomax**, or **newmemo5**. You can also use a question mark in the middle of an ambiguous file reference:

```
$ ls
7may4report  may4report     mayqreport  may_report
may14report  may4report.79  mayreport   may.report
$ ls may?report
may.report  may4report  may_report  mayqreport
```

You can use echo and ls to practice generating filenames. The echo utility displays the arguments that the shell passes to it:

```
$ echo may?report
may.report may4report may_report mayqreport
```

The shell first expands the ambiguous file reference into a list of all files in the working directory that match the string **may?report**. It then passes this list to echo, just as though you had entered the list of filenames as arguments to echo. The echo utility displays the list of filenames.

A question mark does not match a leading period (one that indicates a hidden filename; page 82). When you want to match filenames that begin with a period, you must explicitly include the period in the ambiguous file reference.

THE * SPECIAL CHARACTER

The asterisk (*) performs a function similar to that of the question mark but matches any number of characters, *including zero characters,* in a filename. The following example first shows all files in the working directory and then shows three commands that display all the filenames that begin with the string **memo**, end with the string **mo**, and contain the string **sam**:

```
$ ls
amemo    memo.0612    memosally    memsam       user.memo
mem      memoa        memosam.0620 sallymemo
memo     memorandum   memosam.keep typescript
$ echo memo*
memo memo.0612 memoa memorandum memosally memosam.0620 memosam.keep
$ echo *mo
amemo memo sallymemo user.memo
$ echo *sam*
memosam.0620 memosam.keep memsam
```

The ambiguous file reference **memo*** does not match **amemo, mem, sallymemo,** or **user.memo**. Like the question mark, an asterisk does *not* match a leading period in a filename.

Hidden filenames   The **–a** option causes ls to display hidden filenames. The command **echo *** does not display . (the working directory), .. (the parent of the working directory), **.aaa**, or **.profile**. In contrast, the command **echo .*** displays only those four names:

```
$ ls
aaa         memo.sally  sally.0612  thurs
memo.0612   report      saturday
$ ls -a
.     .aaa     aaa         memo.sally  sally.0612  thurs
..    .profile memo.0612   report      saturday
$ echo *
aaa memo.0612 memo.sally report sally.0612 saturday thurs
$ echo .*
. .. .aaa .profile
```

In the following example, **.p*** does not match **memo.0612, private, reminder,** or **report**. The **ls .*** command causes ls to list **.private** and **.profile** in addition to the contents of the . directory (the working directory) and the .. directory (the parent of the working directory). When called with the same argument, echo displays the names of files (including directories) in the working directory that begin with a dot (.), but not the contents of directories.

```
$ ls -a
.           .private    memo.0612   reminder
..          .profile    private     report
$ echo .p*
.private .profile
$ ls .*
.private .profile

.:
memo.0612   private     reminder    report

..:
.
.

$ echo .*
. .. .private .profile
```

You can plan to take advantage of ambiguous file references when you establish conventions for naming files. For example, when you end all text filenames with **.txt**, you can reference that group of files with ***.txt**. The next command uses this convention to send all text files in the working directory to the printer. The ampersand (**&**) causes lpr to run in the background.

```
$ lpr *.txt &
```

THE [ ] SPECIAL CHARACTERS

A pair of brackets surrounding a list of characters causes the shell to match filenames containing the individual characters. Whereas **memo?** matches **memo** followed by any character, **memo[17a]** is more restrictive: It matches only **memo1**, **memo7**, and **memoa**. The brackets define a *character class* that includes all the characters within the brackets. (GNU calls this a *character list*; a GNU *character class* is something different.) The shell expands an argument that includes a character-class definition, by substituting each member of the character class, *one at a time*, in place of the brackets and their contents. The shell then passes the list of matching filenames to the program it is calling.

Each character-class definition can replace only a single character within a filename. The brackets and their contents are like a question mark that substitutes only the members of the character class.

The first of the following commands lists the names of all files in the working directory that begin with **a**, **e**, **i**, **o**, or **u**. The second command displays the contents of the files named **page2.txt**, **page4.txt**, **page6.txt**, and **page8.txt**.

```
$ echo [aeiou]*
...
$ less page[2468].txt
...
```

A hyphen within brackets defines a range of characters within a character-class definition. For example, **[6–9]** represents **[6789]**, **[a–z]** represents all lowercase letters in English, and **[a–zA–Z]** represents all letters, both uppercase and lowercase, in English.

The following command lines show three ways to print the files named **part0**, **part1**, **part2**, **part3**, and **part5**. Each of these command lines causes the shell to call lpr with five filenames:

```
$ lpr part0 part1 part2 part3 part5
$ lpr part[01235]
$ lpr part[0-35]
```

The first command line explicitly specifies the five filenames. The second and third command lines use ambiguous file references, incorporating character-class definitions. The shell expands the argument on the second command line to include all files that have names beginning with **part** and ending with any of the characters in the character class. The character class is explicitly defined as **0**, **1**, **2**, **3**, and **5**. The third command line also uses a character-class definition but defines the character class to be all characters in the range **0–3** plus **5**.

The following command line prints 39 files, **part0** through **part38**:

```
$ lpr part[0-9] part[12][0-9] part3[0-8]
```

The first of the following commands lists the files in the working directory whose names start with **a** through **m**. The second lists files whose names end with **x**, **y**, or **z**.

```
$ echo [a-m]*
. . .
$ echo *[x-z]
. . .
```

optional When an exclamation point (!) or a caret (^) immediately follows the opening bracket ([) that defines a character class, the string enclosed by the brackets matches any character *not* between the brackets. Thus **[^tsq]*** matches any filename that does *not* begin with **t**, **s**, or **q**.

The following examples show that ***[^ab]** matches filenames that do not end with the letters **a** or **b** and that **[^b-d]*** matches filenames that do not begin with **b**, **c**, or **d**.

```
$ ls
aa  ab  ac  ad  ba  bb  bc  bd  cc  dd
$ ls *[^ab]
ac  ad  bc  bd  cc  dd
$ ls [^b-d]*
aa  ab  ac  ad
```

You can cause a character class to match a hyphen (–) or a closing bracket (]) by placing it immediately before the final closing bracket.

The next example demonstrates that the ls utility cannot interpret ambiguous file references. First ls is called with an argument of **?old**. The shell expands **?old** into a matching filename, **hold**, and passes that name to ls. The second command is the same as the first, except the **?** is quoted (refer to "Special Characters" on page 46). The shell does not recognize this question mark as a special character and passes it to ls. The ls utility generates an error message saying that it cannot find a file named **?old** (because there is no file named **?old**).

```
$ ls ?old
hold
$ ls \?old
ls: ?old: No such file or directory
```

Like most utilities and programs, ls cannot interpret ambiguous file references; that work is left to the shell.

The shell expands ambiguous file references

tip *The shell does the expansion* when it processes an ambiguous file reference, not the program that the shell runs. In the examples in this section, *the utilities* (ls, cat, echo, lpr) *never see the ambiguous file references.* The shell expands the ambiguous file references and passes a list of ordinary filenames to the utility.

BUILTINS

A *builtin* is a utility (also called a *command*) that is built into a shell. Each of the shells has its own set of builtins. When it runs a builtin, the shell does not fork a new process. Consequently builtins run more quickly and can affect the environment of the current shell. Because builtins are used in the same way as utilities, you will not typically be aware of whether a utility is built into the shell or is a stand-alone utility.

The echo utility, for example, is a shell builtin. The shell always executes a shell builtin before trying to find a command or utility with the same name. See page 446 for an in-depth discussion of builtin commands, page 459 for a list of bash builtins, and page 387 for a list of tcsh builtins.

Listing bash builtins   To display a list of bash builtins, give the command **info bash** and select the **Shell Builtin Commands** menu. Then select the **Bourne Shell Builtins** and/or **Bash Builtins** menus. See page 36 for information on using info. The bash info page is part of the **bash-doc** package—you can view only the man page (even using info) if this package is not installed. See Appendix C for information on installing software packages.

Because bash was written by GNU, the info page has better information than does the man page. If you want to read about builtins in a man page, refer to the **builtins** man page.

Listing tcsh builtins   For tcsh, give the command **man tcsh** to display the tcsh man page and then search with the following command: **/Builtin commands$** (search for the string at the end of a line).

CHAPTER SUMMARY

The shell is the Linux command interpreter. It scans the command line for proper syntax, picking out the command name and any arguments. The first argument is argument one, the second is argument two, and so on. The name of the command itself is argument zero. Many programs use options to modify the effects of a command. Most Linux utilities identify an option by its leading one or two hyphens.

When you give it a command, the shell tries to find an executable program with the same name as the command. When it does, the shell executes the program. When it does not, the shell tells you that it cannot find or execute the program. If the command is a simple filename, the shell searches the directories given in the variable **PATH** in an attempt to locate the command.

When it executes a command, the shell assigns one file to the command's standard input and another file to its standard output. By default the shell causes a command's standard input to come from the keyboard and its standard output to go to the screen. You can instruct the shell to redirect a command's standard input from or standard output to any file or device. You can also connect standard output of one command to standard input of another command using a pipe. A filter is a command that reads its standard input from standard output of one command and writes its standard output to standard input of another command.

When a command runs in the foreground, the shell waits for it to finish before it displays a prompt and allows you to continue. When you put an ampersand (&) at the end of a command line, the shell executes the command in the background and displays another prompt immediately. Run slow commands in the background when you want to enter other commands at the shell prompt. The jobs builtin displays a list of suspended jobs and jobs running in the background; it includes the job number of each.

The shell interprets special characters on a command line to generate filenames. A question mark represents any single character, and an asterisk represents zero or more characters. A single character may also be represented by a character class: a list of characters within brackets. A reference that uses special characters (wildcards) to abbreviate a list of one or more filenames is called an ambiguous file reference.

A builtin is a utility that is built into a shell. Each shell has its own set of builtins. When it runs a builtin, the shell does not fork a new process. Consequently builtins run more quickly and can affect the environment of the current shell.

UTILITIES AND BUILTINS INTRODUCED IN THIS CHAPTER

Table 5-1 lists the utilities introduced in this chapter.

Table 5-1 New utilities

Utility	Function
tr	Maps one string of characters to another (page 132)
tee	Sends standard input to both a file and standard output (page 134)
bg	Moves a process to the background (page 135)
fg	Moves a process to the foreground (page 135)
jobs	Displays a list of suspended jobs and jobs running in the background (page 136)

EXERCISES

1. What does the shell ordinarily do while a command is executing? What should you do if you do not want to wait for a command to finish before running another command?

2. Using sort as a filter, rewrite the following sequence of commands:

```
$ sort list > temp
$ lpr temp
$ rm temp
```

3. What is a PID number? Why are these numbers useful when you run processes in the background? Which utility displays the PID numbers of the commands you are running?

4. Assume that the following files are in the working directory:

```
$ ls
intro     notesb    ref2      section1    section3    section4b
notesa    ref1      ref3      section2    section4a   sentrev
```

Give commands for each of the following, using wildcards to express file-names with as few characters as possible.

a. List all files that begin with **section**.

b. List the **section1**, **section2**, and **section3** files only.

c. List the **intro** file only.

d. List the **section1**, **section3**, **ref1**, and **ref3** files.

5. Refer to Part V or the man pages to determine which command will

   a. Output the number of lines in the standard input that contain the *word* a or **A**.

   b. Output only the names of the files in the working directory that contain the pattern $(.

   c. List the files in the working directory in reverse alphabetical order.

   d. Send a list of files in the working directory to the printer, sorted by size.

6. Give a command to

   a. Redirect standard output from a sort command to a file named **phone_list**. Assume the input file is named **numbers**.

   b. Translate all occurrences of the characters [and { to the character (, and all occurrences of the characters] and } to the character) in the file **permdemos.c**. (*Hint:* Refer to tr on page 864.)

   c. Create a file named **book** that contains the contents of two other files: **part1** and **part2**.

7. The lpr and sort utilities accept input either from a file named on the command line or from standard input.

   a. Name two other utilities that function in a similar manner.

   b. Name a utility that accepts its input only from standard input.

8. Give an example of a command that uses grep

   a. With both input and output redirected.

   b. With only input redirected.

   c. With only output redirected.

   d. Within a pipe.

   In which of the preceding cases is grep used as a filter?

9. Explain the following error message. Which filenames would a subsequent ls display?

```
$ ls
abc   abd   abe   abf   abg   abh
$ rm abc ab*
rm: cannot remove 'abc': No such file or directory
```

ADVANCED EXERCISES

10. When you use the redirect output symbol (>) with a command, the shell creates the output file immediately, before the command is executed. Demonstrate that this is true.

11. In experimenting with shell variables, Max accidentally deletes his **PATH** variable. He decides he does not need the **PATH** variable. Discuss some of the problems he may soon encounter and explain the reasons for these problems. How could he *easily* return **PATH** to its original value?

12. Assume your permissions allow you to write to a file but not to delete it.

    a. Give a command to empty the file without invoking an editor.

    b. Explain how you might have permission to modify a file that you cannot delete.

13. If you accidentally create a filename that contains a nonprinting character, such as a CONTROL character, how can you remove the file?

14. Why does the **noclobber** variable *not* protect you from overwriting an existing file with cp or mv?

15. Why do command names and filenames usually not have embedded SPACEs? How would you create a filename containing a SPACE? How would you remove it? (This is a thought exercise, not recommended practice. If you want to experiment, create and work in a directory that contains only your experimental file.)

16. Create a file named **answer** and give the following command:

    ```
    $ > answers.0102 < answer cat
    ```

    Explain what the command does and why. What is a more conventional way of expressing this command?

PART II
THE EDITORS

6

THE vim EDITOR

This chapter begins with a history and description of vi, the original, powerful, sometimes cryptic, interactive, visually oriented text editor. The chapter continues with a tutorial that explains how to use vim (vi improved—a vi clone supplied with or available for most Linux distributions) to create and edit a file. Much of the tutorial and the balance of the chapter apply to vi and other vi clones. Following the tutorial, the chapter delves into the details of many vim commands and explains how to use parameters to customize vim to meet your needs. It concludes with a quick reference/summary of vim commands.

History

Before vi was developed, the standard UNIX system editor was ed (available on most Linux systems), a line-oriented editor that made it difficult to see the context of your editing. Next came ex,[1] a superset of ed. The most notable advantage that ex has over ed is a display-editing facility that allows you to work with a full screen of text instead of just a line. While using ex, you can bring up the display-editing facility by giving a vi (Visual mode) command. People used this display-editing facility so extensively that the developers of ex made it possible to start the editor with the display-editing facility already running, rather than having to start ex and then give a **vi** command. Appropriately they named the program vi. You can call the Visual mode from ex, and you can go back to ex while you are using vi. Start by running ex; give a **vi** command to switch to Visual mode, and give a **Q** command while in Visual mode to use ex. The **quit** command exits from ex.

vi clones   Linux offers a number of versions, or *clones*, of vi. The most popular of these clones are elvis (elvis.the-little-red-haired-girl.org), nvi (an implementation of the original vi editor, www.bostic.com/vi), vile (invisible-island.net/vile/vile.html), and vim (www.vim.org). Each clone offers additional features beyond those provided by the original vi.

The examples in this book are based on vim. Several Linux distributions support multiple versions of vim. For example, Red Hat provides **/bin/vi**, a minimal build of vim that is compact and faster to load but offers fewer features, and **/usr/bin/vim**, a full-featured version of vim.

If you use one of the clones other than vim, or vi itself, you may notice slight differences from the examples presented in this chapter. The vim editor is compatible with almost all vi commands and runs on many platforms, including Windows, Macintosh, OS/2, UNIX, and Linux. Refer to the vim home page (www.vim.org) for more information and a very useful Tips section.

What vim is not   The vim editor is not a text formatting program. It does not justify margins or provide the output formatting features of a sophisticated word processing system such as OpenOffice.org Writer. Rather, vim is a sophisticated text editor meant to be used to write code (C, HTML, Java, and so on), short notes, and input to a text formatting system, such as groff or troff. You can use fmt (page 697) to minimally format a text file you create with vim.

Reading this chapter   Because vim is so large and powerful, this chapter describes only some of its features. Nonetheless, if vim is completely new to you, you may find even this limited set of commands overwhelming. The vim editor provides a variety of ways to accomplish most editing tasks. A useful strategy for learning vim is to begin by learning a subset of commands to accomplish basic editing tasks. Then, as you become more comfortable with the editor, you can learn other commands that enable you to edit a file more quickly and efficiently. The following tutorial section

---

1. The ex program is usually a link to vi, which is a version of vim on some systems.

introduces a basic, useful set of vim commands and features that will enable you to create and edit a file.

TUTORIAL: USING vim TO CREATE AND EDIT A FILE

This section explains how to start vim, enter text, move the cursor, correct text, save the file to the disk, and exit from vim. The tutorial discusses three of the modes of operation of vim and explains how to switch from one mode to another.

---

vimtutor and vim help files are not installed by default

tip   To run vimtutor and to get help as described on page 155, you must install the **vim-runtime** or **vim-enhanced** package; see Appendix C.

---

vimtutor   In addition to working with this tutorial, you may want to try vim's instructional program, named vimtutor. Give its name as a command to run it.

Specifying a terminal   Because vim takes advantage of features that are specific to various kinds of terminals, you must tell it which type of terminal or terminal emulator you are using. On many systems, and usually when you work on a terminal emulator, your terminal type is set automatically. If you need to specify your terminal type explicitly, refer to "Specifying a Terminal" on page 906.

STARTING vim

Start vim with the following command to create and edit a file named **practice**:

```
$ vim practice
```

When you press RETURN, vim replaces the command line with a screen that looks similar to the one shown in Figure 6-1.

```
"practice" [New File]
```

Figure 6-1   Starting vim

The tildes (~) at the left of the screen indicate that the file is empty. They disappear as you add lines of text to the file. If your screen looks like a distorted version of the one shown in Figure 6-1, your terminal type is probably not set correctly; see page 906.

If you start vim with a terminal type that is not in the **terminfo** database, vim displays an error message and the terminal type defaults to **ansi**, which works on many terminals. In the following example, the user mistyped **vt100** and set the terminal type to **vg100**:

```
E558: Terminal entry not found in terminfo
'vg100' not known. Available builtin terminals are:
    builtin_ansi
    builtin_xterm
    builtin_iris-ansi
    builtin_dumb
defaulting to 'ansi'
```

The vi **command may run** vim

tip   On some Linux systems the command **vi** runs vim in vi-compatible mode (page 158).

Emergency exit   To reset the terminal type, press ESCAPE and then give the following command to exit from vim and display the shell prompt:

  :q!

When you enter the colon (:), vim moves the cursor to the bottom line of the screen. The characters **q!** tell vim to quit without saving your work. (You will not ordinarily exit from vim this way because you typically want to save your work.) You must

Figure 6-2   Starting vim without a filename

press RETURN after you give this command. Once the shell displays a prompt, refer to "Specifying a Terminal" on page 906, and then start vim again.

If you call vim without specifying a filename on the command line, vim assumes that you are a novice and tells you how to get started (Figure 6-2).

The **practice** file is new so it does not contain any text. Thus vim displays a message similar to the one shown in Figure 6-1 on the status (bottom) line of the terminal to indicate that you are creating a new file. When you edit an existing file, vim displays the first few lines of the file and gives status information about the file on the status line.

COMMAND AND INPUT MODES

Two of vim's modes of operation are *Command mode* (also called *Normal mode*) and *Input mode* (Figure 6-3). While vim is in Command mode, you can give vim commands. For example, you can delete text or exit from vim. You can also command vim to enter Input mode. In Input mode, vim accepts anything you enter as text and displays it on the screen. Press ESCAPE to return vim to Command mode. By default the vim editor informs you about which mode it is in: It displays **INSERT** at the lower-left corner of the screen while it is in Insert mode. See the tip on page 160 if vim does not display **INSERT** when it is in Insert mode.

The following command causes vim to display line numbers next to the text you are editing:

```
:set number RETURN
```

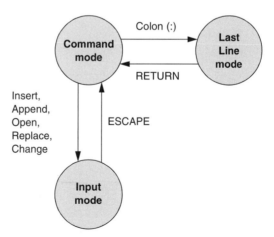

Figure 6-3 Modes in vim

Figure 6-4   Entering text with vim

Last Line mode   The colon (**:**) in the preceding command puts vim into another mode, *Last Line mode*. While in this mode, vim keeps the cursor on the bottom line of the screen. When you press RETURN to finish entering the command, vim restores the cursor to its place in the text. Give the command **:set nonumber** RETURN to turn off line numbers.

ENTERING TEXT

i/a (Input mode)   When you start vim, you must put it in Input mode before you can enter text. To put vim in Input mode, press the **i** (insert before cursor) key or the **a** (append after cursor) key.

vim **is case sensitive**

tip   When you give vim a command, remember that the editor is case sensitive. In other words, vim interprets the same letter as two different commands, depending on whether you enter an upper-case or lowercase character. Beware of the CAPS LOCK (SHIFTLOCK) key. If you activate this key to enter uppercase text while you are in Input mode and then exit to Command mode, vim interprets your commands as uppercase letters. It can be confusing when this happens because vim does not appear to be executing the commands you are entering.

If you are not sure whether vim is in Input mode, press the ESCAPE key; vim returns to Command mode if it is in Input mode or beeps, flashes, or does nothing if it is already in Command mode. You can put vim back in Input mode by pressing the **i** or **a** key again.

While vim is in Input mode, you can enter text by typing on the keyboard. If the text does not appear on the screen as you type, vim is not in Input mode.

```
*help.txt*      For Vim version 7.1.  Last change: 2006 Nov 07

                        VIM - main help file
                                                               k
          Move around:  Use the cursor keys, or "h" to go left,    h    l
                        "j" to go down, "k" to go up, "l" to go right.    j
    Close this window:  Use ":q<Enter>".
       Get out of Vim:  Use ":qa!<Enter>" (careful, all changes are lost!).

    Jump to a subject:  Position the cursor on a tag (e.g. |bars|) and hit CTRL-].
        With the mouse:  ":set mouse=a" to enable the mouse (in xterm or GUI).
                        Double-click the left mouse button on a tag, e.g. |bars|.
           Jump back:  Type CTRL-T or CTRL-O (repeat to go further back).

    Get specific help:  It is possible to go directly to whatever you want help
                        on, by giving an argument to the |:help| command.
                        It is possible to further specify the context:
                                                        *help-context*
                            WHAT            PREPEND    EXAMPLE
                        Normal mode command    (nothing)   :help x
    help.txt [Help][RO]
    If you are not sure whether vim is in Input mode, press the ESCAPE key;
    vim returns to Command mode if it is in Input mode or beeps, flashes,
    or does nothing if it is already in Command mode. You can put vim back in
    Input mode by pressing the i or a key again.

    practice
    "help.txt" [readonly] 216L, 8010C
```

Figure 6-5   The main vim Help screen

To continue with this tutorial, enter the sample paragraph shown in Figure 6-4, pressing the RETURN key at the end of each line. If you do not press RETURN before the cursor reaches the right side of the screen or window, vim wraps the text so that it appears to start a new line. Physical lines will not correspond to programmatic (logical) lines in this situation, so editing will be more difficult. While you are using vim, you can always correct any typing mistakes you make. If you notice a mistake on the line you are entering, you can correct it before you continue (page 156); you can correct other mistakes later. When you finish entering the paragraph, press ESCAPE to return vim to Command mode.

GETTING HELP

To use vim's help system, you must install the **vim-runtime** package; see Appendix C.

To get help while you are using vim, give the command **:help** [*feature*] followed by RETURN (you must be in Command mode when you give this command). The colon moves the cursor to the last line of the screen. If you type **:help**, vim displays an introduction to vim Help (Figure 6-5). Each area of the screen that displays a file, such as the two areas shown in Figure 6-5, is a vim "window." The dark band at the bottom of each vim window names the file that is displayed above it. In Figure 6-5, the **help.txt** file occupies most of the screen (the upper vim window). The file that is being edited (**practice**) occupies a few lines in the lower portion of the screen (the lower vim window).

Read through the introduction to Help by scrolling the text as you read. Press **j** or the DOWN ARROW key to move the cursor down one line at a time; press CONTROL-D or CONTROL-U to scroll the cursor down or up half a window at a time. Give the command **:q** to close the Help window.

```
<insert>        or                                  *i* *insert* *<Insert>*
i                       Insert text before the cursor [count] times.
                        When using CTRL-O in Insert mode |i_CTRL-O| the count
                        is not supported.

                                                    *I*
I                       Insert text before the first non-blank in the line
                        [count] times.
                        When the 'H' flag is present in 'cpoptions' and the
                        line only contains blanks, insert start just before
                        the last blank.

                                                    *gI*
gI                      Insert text in column 1 [count] times.  {not in Vi}

                                                    *gi*
gi                      Insert text in the same position as where Insert mode
                        was stopped last time in the current buffer.
                        This uses the |'^| mark.  It's different from "`^i"
                        when the mark is past the end of the line.
insert.txt [Help][RO]
If you are not sure whether vim is in Input mode, press the ESCAPE key;
vim returns to Command mode if it is in Input mode or beeps, flashes,
or does nothing if it is already in Command mode. You can put vim back in
Input mode by pressing the i or a key again.

practice
"insert.txt" [readonly] 1880L, 77090C
```

Figure 6-6   Help with insert commands

You can display information about the insert commands by giving the command **:help insert** while vim is in Command mode (Figure 6-6).

CORRECTING TEXT AS YOU INSERT IT

The keys that back up and correct a shell command line serve the same functions when vim is in Input mode. These keys include the erase, line kill, and word kill keys (usually CONTROL-H, CONTROL-U, and CONTROL-W, respectively). Although vim may not remove deleted text from the screen as you back up over it using one of these keys, the editor does remove it when you type over the text or press RETURN.

MOVING THE CURSOR

To delete, insert, and correct text, you need to move the cursor on the screen. While vim is in Command mode, you can use the RETURN key, the SPACE bar, and the ARROW keys to move the cursor. If you prefer to keep your hand closer to the center of the keyboard, if your terminal does not have ARROW keys, or if the emulator you are using does not support them, you can use the **h, j, k,** and **l** (lowercase "l") keys to move the cursor left, down, up, and right, respectively.

DELETING TEXT

x (Delete character)
dw (Delete word)
dd (Delete line)

You can delete a single character by moving the cursor until it is over the character you want to delete and then giving the command **x.** You can delete a word by positioning the cursor on the first letter of the word and then giving the command **dw** (Delete word). You can delete a line of text by moving the cursor until it is anywhere on the line and then giving the command **dd.**

UNDOING MISTAKES

u (Undo)   If you delete a character, line, or word by mistake or give any command you want to reverse, give the command **u** (Undo) immediately after the command you want to undo. The vim editor will restore the text to the way it was before you gave the last command. If you give the **u** command again, vim will undo the command you gave before the one it just undid. You can use this technique to back up over many of your actions. With the **compatible** parameter (page 158) set, however, vim can undo only the most recent change.

:redo (Redo)   If you undo a command you did not mean to undo, give a Redo command: CONTROL-R or **:redo** (followed by a RETURN). The vim editor will redo the undone command. As with the Undo command, you can give the Redo command many times in a row. With the **compatible** parameter (page 158) set, however, vim can redo only the most recent undo.

ENTERING ADDITIONAL TEXT

i (Insert)
a (Append)   When you want to insert new text within existing text, move the cursor so it is on the character that follows the new text you plan to enter. Then give the **i** (Insert) command to put vim in Input mode, enter the new text, and press ESCAPE to return vim to Command mode. Alternatively, you can position the cursor on the character that precedes the new text and use the **a** (Append) command.

o/O (Open)   To enter one or more lines, position the cursor on the line above where you want the new text to go. Give the command **o** (Open). The vim editor opens a blank line below the line the cursor was on, puts the cursor on the new, empty line, and enters Input mode. Enter the new text, ending each line with a RETURN. When you are finished entering text, press ESCAPE to return vim to Command mode. The **O** command works in the same way as the **o** command, except it opens a blank line *above* the current line.

CORRECTING TEXT

To correct text, use **dd**, **dw**, or **x** to remove the incorrect text. Then use **i**, **a**, **o**, or **O** to insert the correct text.

For example, to change the word **pressing** to **hitting** in Figure 6-4 on page 154, you might use the ARROW keys to move the cursor until it is on top of the **p** in **pressing**. Then give the command **dw** to delete the word **pressing**. Put vim in Input mode by giving an **i** command, enter the word **hitting** followed by a SPACE, and press ESCAPE. The word is changed and vim is in Command mode, waiting for another command. A shorthand for the two commands **dw** followed by the **i** command is **cw** (Change word). The **cw** command puts vim into Input mode.

Page breaks for the printer

tip   CONTROL-L tells the printer to skip to the top of the next page. You can enter this character anywhere in a document by pressing CONTROL-L while you are in Input mode. If **^L** does not appear, press CONTROL-V before CONTROL-L.

ENDING THE EDITING SESSION

While you are editing, vim keeps the edited text in an area named the *Work buffer*. When you finish editing, you must write the contents of the Work buffer to a disk file so the edited text is saved and available when you next want it.

Make sure vim is in Command mode, and use the ZZ command (you must use uppercase Zs) to write the newly entered text to the disk and end the editing session. After you give the ZZ command, vim returns control to the shell. You can exit with :q! if you do not want to save your work.

Do not confuse ZZ with CONTROL-Z

caution   When you exit from vim with **ZZ**, make sure that you type **ZZ** and not CONTROL-Z (which is typically the suspend key). When you press CONTROL-Z, vim disappears from your screen, almost as though you had exited from it. In fact, vim will continue running in the background with your work unsaved. Refer to "Job Control" on page 285. If you try to start editing the same file with a new **vim** command, vim displays a message about a swap file (Figure 6-7, page 162).

THE compatible PARAMETER

The **compatible** parameter makes vim more compatible with vi. By default this parameter is not set. To get started with vim you can ignore this parameter.

Setting the **compatible** parameter changes many aspects of how vim works. For example, when the **compatible** parameter is set, the Undo command (page 157) can undo only the most recent change; in contrast, with the **compatible** parameter unset, you can call Undo repeatedly to undo many changes. This chapter notes when the **compatible** parameter affects a command. To obtain more details on the **compatible** parameter, give the command :help compatible RETURN. To display a complete list of vim's differences from the original vi, use :help vi-diff RETURN. See page 155 for a discussion of the **help** command.

On the command line, use the –C option to set the **compatible** parameter and the –N option to unset it. Refer to "Setting Parameters from Within vim" on page 175 for information on changing the **compatible** parameter while you are running vim.

INTRODUCTION TO vim FEATURES

This section covers online help, modes of operation, the Work buffer, emergency procedures, and other vim features. To see which features are incorporated in a particular build, give a **vim** command followed by the ––version option.

ONLINE HELP

As covered briefly earlier, vim provides help while you are using it. Give the command :help *feature* to display information about *feature*. As you scroll through the various help texts, you will see words with a bar on either side, such as |tutor|. These words are *active links:* Move the cursor on top of an active link and press CONTROL-] to jump to the linked text. Use CONTROL-o (lowercase "o") to jump back to where you were in the help text. You can also use the active link words in place of *feature*. For example, you might see the reference |credits|; you could enter **:help credits** RETURN to read more about credits. Enter **:q!** to close a help window.

Some common *features* that you may want to investigate by using the help system are **insert, delete,** and **opening-window.** Although *opening-window* is not intuitive, you will get to know the names of *features* as you spend more time with vim. You can also give the command **:help doc-file-list** to view a complete list of the help files. Although vim is a free program, the author requests that you donate the money you would have spent on similar software to help the children in Uganda (give the command **:help iccf** for more information).

TERMINOLOGY

This chapter uses the following terms:

Current character   The character the cursor is on.

Current line   The line the cursor is on.

Status line   The last or bottom line of the screen. This line is reserved for Last Line mode and status information. Text you are editing does not appear on this line.

MODES OF OPERATION

The vim editor is part of the ex editor, which has five modes of operation:

- ex Command mode
- ex Input mode
- vim Command mode
- vim Input mode
- vim Last Line mode

While in Command mode, vim accepts keystrokes as commands, responding to each command as you enter it. It does not display the characters you type in this mode. While in Input mode, vim accepts and displays keystrokes as text that it eventually puts into the file you are editing. All commands that start with a colon (:) put vim in Last Line mode. The colon moves the cursor to the status line of the screen, where you enter the rest of the command.

In addition to the position of the cursor, there is another important difference between Last Line mode and Command mode. When you give a command in Command mode, you do not terminate the command with a RETURN. In contrast, you must terminate all Last Line mode commands with a RETURN.

You do not normally use the ex modes. When this chapter refers to Input and Command modes, it means the vim modes, not the ex modes.

When an editing session begins, vim is in Command mode. Several commands, including Insert and Append, put vim in Input mode. When you press the ESCAPE key, vim always reverts to Command mode.

The Change and Replace commands combine the Command and Input modes. The Change command deletes the text you want to change and puts vim in Input mode so you can insert new text. The Replace command deletes the character(s) you over-write and inserts the new one(s) you enter. Figure 6-3 on page 153 shows the modes and the methods for changing between them.

Watch the mode and the CAPS LOCK **key**

tip   Almost anything you type in Command mode means something to vim. If you think vim is in Input mode when it is in Command mode, typing in text can produce confusing results. When you are learning to use vim, make sure the **showmode** parameter (page 188) is set (it is by default) to remind you which mode you are using. You may also find it useful to turn on the status line by giving a **:set laststatus=2** command (page 187).

Also keep your eye on the CAPS LOCK key. In Command mode, typing uppercase letters produces different results than typing lowercase ones. It can be disorienting to give commands and have vim give the "wrong" responses.

THE DISPLAY

The vim editor uses the status line and several symbols to give information about what is happening during an editing session.

STATUS LINE

The vim editor displays status information on the bottom line of the display area. This information includes error messages, information about the deletion or addition of blocks of text, and file status information. In addition, vim displays Last Line mode commands on the status line.

REDRAWING THE SCREEN

Sometimes the screen may become garbled or overwritten. When vim puts characters on the screen, it sometimes leaves @ on a line instead of deleting the line. When output from a program becomes intermixed with the display of the Work buffer, things can get even more confusing. The output *does not* become part of the Work buffer but affects only the display. If the screen gets overwritten, press ESCAPE to make sure vim is in Command mode, and press CONTROL-L to redraw (refresh) the screen.

TILDE (~) SYMBOL

If the end of the file is displayed on the screen, vim marks lines that would appear past the end of the file with a tilde (~) at the left of the screen. When you start editing a new file, the vim editor marks each line on the screen (except the first line) with this symbol.

CORRECTING TEXT AS YOU INSERT IT

While vim is in Input mode, you can use the erase and line kill keys to back up over text so you can correct it. You can also use CONTROL-W to back up over words.

WORK BUFFER

The vim editor does all its work in the Work buffer. At the beginning of an editing session, vim reads the file you are editing from the disk into the Work buffer. During the editing session, it makes all changes to this copy of the file but does not change the file on the disk until you write the contents of the Work buffer back to the disk. Normally when you end an editing session, you tell vim to write the contents of the Work buffer, which makes the changes to the text final. When you edit a new file, vim creates the file when it writes the contents of the Work buffer to the disk, usually at the end of the editing session.

Storing the text you are editing in the Work buffer has both advantages and disadvantages. If you accidentally end an editing session without writing out the contents of the Work buffer, your work is lost. However, if you unintentionally make some major changes (such as deleting the entire contents of the Work buffer), you can end the editing session without implementing the changes.

To look at a file but not to change it while you are working with vim, you can use the view utility:

```
$ view filename
```

Calling the view utility is the same as calling the vim editor with the **–R** (readonly) option. Once you have invoked the editor in this way, you cannot write the contents of the Work buffer back to the file whose name appeared on the command line. You can always write the Work buffer out to a file with a different name. If you have installed mc (Midnight Commander), the **view** command calls mcview and not vim.

LINE LENGTH AND FILE SIZE

The vim editor operates on files of any format, provided the length of a single line (that is, the characters between two NEWLINE characters) can fit into available memory. The total length of the file is limited only by available disk space and memory.

WINDOWS

The vim editor allows you to open, close, and hide multiple windows, each of which allows you to edit a different file. Most of the window commands consist of CONTROL-W followed by another letter. For example, CONTROL-W **s** opens another window (splits the screen) that is editing the same file. CONTROL-W **n** opens a second window that is editing an empty file. CONTROL-W **w** moves the cursor between windows, and CONTROL-W **q** (or **:q**) quits (closes) a window. Give the command **:help windows** to display a complete list of windows commands.

FILE LOCKS

When you edit an existing file, vim displays the first few lines of the file, gives status information about the file on the status line, and locks the file. When you try to open a locked file with vim, you will see a message similar to the one shown in

```
E325: ATTENTION
Found a swap file by the name ".practice.swp"
          owned by: mark    dated: Mon Mar 23 16:37:55 2009
         file name: ~mark/practice
          modified: no
         user name: mark    host name: coffee
        process ID: 25914 (still running)
While opening file "practice"
             dated: Mon Mar 23 16:37:50 2009

(1) Another program may be editing the same file.
    If this is the case, be careful not to end up with two
    different instances of the same file when making changes.
    Quit, or continue with caution.

(2) An edit session for this file crashed.
    If this is the case, use ":recover" or "vim -r practice"
    to recover the changes (see ":help recovery").
    If you did this already, delete the swap file ".practice.swp"
    to avoid this message.
"practice" 1L, 262C
Press ENTER or type command to continue█
```

Figure 6-7   Attempting to open a locked file

Figure 6-7. You will see this type of message in two scenarios: when you try to edit a file that someone is already editing (perhaps you are editing it in another window, in the background, or on another terminal) and when you try to edit a file that you were editing when vim or the system crashed.

Although it is advisable to follow the instructions that vim displays, a second user can edit a file and write it out with a different filename. Refer to the next sections for more information.

ABNORMAL TERMINATION OF AN EDITING SESSION

You can end an editing session in one of two ways: When you exit from vim, you can save the changes you made during the editing session or you can abandon those changes. You can use the **ZZ** or **:wq** command from Command mode to save the changes and exit from vim (see "Ending the Editing Session" on page 158).

To end an editing session without writing out the contents of the Work buffer, give the following command:

:q!

Use the **:q!** command cautiously. When you use this command to end an editing session, vim does not preserve the contents of the Work buffer, so you will lose any work you did since the last time you wrote the Work buffer to disk. The next time you edit or use the file, it will appear as it did the last time you wrote the Work buffer to disk.

Sometimes you may find that you created or edited a file but vim will not let you exit. For example, if you forgot to specify a filename when you first called vim, you will get a message saying **No file name** when you give a **ZZ** command. If vim does not let you exit normally, you can use the Write command (**:w**) to name the file and write it to disk before you quit vim. Give the following command, substituting the name of the file for *filename* (remember to follow the command with a RETURN):

:w filename

After you give the Write command, you can use **:q** to quit using vim. You do not need to include the exclamation point (as in **q!**); it is necessary only when you have made changes since the last time you wrote the Work buffer to disk. Refer to page 183 for more information about the Write command.

When you cannot write to a file

tip It may be necessary to write a file using **:w** *filename* if you do not have write permission for the file you are editing. If you give a **ZZ** command and see the message **"***filename***" is read only**, you do not have write permission for the file. Use the Write command with a temporary filename to write the file to disk under a different filename. If you do not have write permission for the working directory, however, **vim** may not be able to write the file to the disk. Give the command again, using an absolute pathname of a dummy (nonexistent) file in your home directory in place of the filename. (For example, Max might give the command **:w /home/max/temp** or **:w ~/temp**.)

If vim reports **File exists**, you will need to use **:w!** *filename* to overwrite the existing file (make sure you want to overwrite the file). Refer to page 184.

RECOVERING TEXT AFTER A CRASH

The vim editor temporarily stores the file you are working on in a *swap file*. If the system crashes while you are editing a file with vim, you can often recover its text from the swap file. When you attempt to edit a file that has a swap file, you will see a message similar to the one shown in Figure 6-7 on page 162. If someone else is editing the file, quit or open the file as a readonly file.

In the following example, Max uses the **–r** option to check whether the swap file exists for a file named **memo**, which he was editing when the system crashed:

```
$ vim -r
Swap files found:
   In current directory:
1.    .party.swp
          owned by: max    dated: Sat Jan 26 11:36:44 2008
          file name: ~max/party
          modified: YES
          user name: max    host name: coffee
         process ID: 18439
2.    .memo.swp
          owned by: max    dated: Mon Mar 23 17:14:05 2009
          file name: ~max/memo
          modified: no
          user name: max    host name: coffee
         process ID: 27733 (still running)
   In directory ~/tmp:
      -- none --
   In directory /var/tmp:
      -- none --
   In directory /tmp:
-- none --
```

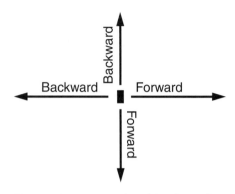

Figure 6-8   Forward and backward

With the **–r** option, vim displays a list of swap files it has saved (some may be old). If your work was saved, give the same command followed by a SPACE and the name of the file. You will then be editing a recent copy of your Work buffer. Give the command **:w** *filename* immediately to save the salvaged copy of the Work buffer to disk under a name different from the original file; then check the recovered file to make sure it is OK. Following is Max's exchange with vim as he recovers **memo**. Subsequently he deletes the swap file:

```
$ vim -r memo
Using swap file ".memo.swp"
Original file "~/memo"
Recovery completed. You should check if everything is OK.
(You might want to write out this file under another name
and run diff with the original file to check for changes)
Delete the .swp file afterwards.

Hit ENTER or type command to continue
:w memo2
:q
$ rm .memo.swp
```

You must recover files on the system you were using

tip   The recovery feature of **vim** is specific to the system you were using when the crash occurred. If you are running on a cluster, you must log in on the system you were using before the crash to use the **–r** option successfully.

COMMAND MODE: MOVING THE CURSOR

While vim is in Command mode, you can position the cursor over any character on the screen. You can also display a different portion of the Work buffer on the screen. By manipulating the screen and cursor position, you can place the cursor on any character in the Work buffer.

Figure 6-9   Moving the cursor by characters

You can move the cursor forward or backward through the text. As illustrated in Figure 6-8, *forward* means toward the right and bottom of the screen and the end of the file. *Backward* means toward the left and top of the screen and the beginning of the file. When you use a command that moves the cursor forward past the end (right) of a line, the cursor generally moves to the beginning (left) of the next line. When you move it backward past the beginning of a line, the cursor generally moves to the end of the previous line.

Long lines   Sometimes a line in the Work buffer may be too long to appear as a single line on the screen. In such a case vim wraps the current line onto the next line (unless you set the **nowrap** option [page 187]).

You can move the cursor through the text by any *Unit of Measure* (that is, character, word, line, sentence, paragraph, or screen). If you precede a cursor-movement command with a number, called a *Repeat Factor,* the cursor moves that number of units through the text. Refer to pages 193 through page 196 for precise definitions of these terms.

MOVING THE CURSOR BY CHARACTERS

l/h   The SPACE bar moves the cursor forward, one character at a time, toward the right side of the screen. The l (lowercase "l") key and the RIGHT ARROW key (Figure 6-9) do the same thing. For example, the command 7 SPACE or 7l moves the cursor seven characters to the right. These keys cannot move the cursor past the end of the current line to the beginning of the next line. The **h** and LEFT ARROW keys are similar to the l and RIGHT ARROW keys but work in the opposite direction.

MOVING THE CURSOR TO A SPECIFIC CHARACTER

f/F   You can move the cursor to the next occurrence of a specified character on the current line by using the Find command. For example, the following command moves the cursor from its current position to the next occurrence of the character **a**, if one appears on the same line:

    fa

You can also find the previous occurrence by using a capital **F**. The following command moves the cursor to the position of the closest previous **a** in the current line:

    Fa

A semicolon (;) repeats the last Find command.

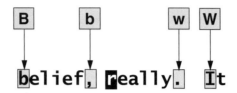

Figure 6-10   Moving the cursor by words

MOVING THE CURSOR BY WORDS

w/W   The **w** (word) key moves the cursor forward to the first letter of the next word (Figure 6-10). Groups of punctuation count as words. This command goes to the next line if the next word is located there. The command **15w** moves the cursor to the first character of the fifteenth subsequent word.

The **W** key is similar to the **w** key but moves the cursor by blank-delimited words, including punctuation, as it skips forward. (Refer to "Blank-Delimited Word" on page 194.)

b/B   The **b** (back) key moves the cursor backward to the first letter of the previous word.

e/E   The **B** key moves the cursor backward by blank-delimited words. Similarly the **e** key moves the cursor to the end of the next word; **E** moves it to the end of the next blank-delimited word.

MOVING THE CURSOR BY LINES

j/k   The RETURN key moves the cursor to the beginning of the next line; the **j** and DOWN ARROW keys move the cursor down one line to the character just below the current character (Figure 6-11). If no character appears immediately below the current character, the cursor moves to the end of the next line. The cursor will not move past the last line of text in the work buffer.

The **k** and UP ARROW keys are similar to the **j** and DOWN ARROW keys but work in the opposite direction. The minus (–) key is similar to the RETURN key but works in the opposite direction.

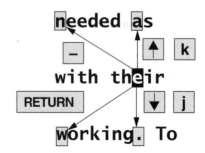

Figure 6-11   Moving the cursor by lines

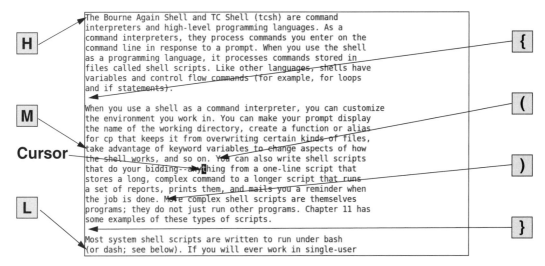

Figure 6-12   Moving the cursor by sentences, paragraphs, H, M, and L

MOVING THE CURSOR BY SENTENCES AND PARAGRAPHS

)/(The) and } keys move the cursor forward to the beginning of the next sentence or
}/{   the next paragraph, respectively (Figure 6-12). The (and { keys move the cursor
backward to the beginning of the current sentence or paragraph, respectively. You
can find more information on sentences and paragraphs starting on page 194.

MOVING THE CURSOR WITHIN THE SCREEN

H/M/L   The **H** (home) key positions the cursor at the left end of the top line of the screen,
the **M** (middle) key moves the cursor to the middle line, and the **L** (lower) key
moves it to the bottom line (Figure 6-12).

VIEWING DIFFERENT PARTS OF THE WORK BUFFER

The screen displays a portion of the text that is in the Work buffer. You can display
the text preceding or following the text on the screen by *scrolling* the display. You
can also display a portion of the Work buffer based on a line number.

CONTROL-D   Press CONTROL-D to scroll the screen down (forward) through the file so that vim dis-
CONTROL-U   plays half a screen of new text. Use CONTROL-U to scroll the screen up (backward) by
the same amount. If you precede either of these commands with a number, vim
scrolls that number of lines each time you press CONTROL-D or CONTROL-U for the rest of
the session (unless you again change the number of lines to scroll). See page 188 for
a discussion of the **scroll** parameter.

CONTROL-F   The CONTROL-F (forward) and CONTROL-B (backward) keys display almost a *whole* screen
CONTROL-B   of new text, leaving a couple of lines from the previous screen for continuity. On
many keyboards you can use the PAGE DOWN and PAGE UP keys in place of CONTROL-F and
CONTROL-B, respectively.

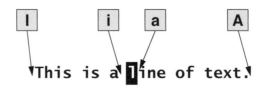

Figure 6-13 The I, i, a, and A commands

Line numbers (**G**) When you enter a line number followed by **G** (goto), vim positions the cursor on that line in the Work buffer. If you press **G** without a number, vim positions the cursor on the last line in the Work buffer. Line numbers are implicit; the file does not need to have actual line numbers for this command to work. Refer to "Line numbers" on page 187 if you want vim to display line numbers.

INPUT MODE

The Insert, Append, Open, Change, and Replace commands put vim in Input mode. While vim is in this mode, you can put new text into the Work buffer. To return vim to Command mode when you finish entering text, press the ESCAPE key. Refer to "Show mode" on page 188 if you want vim to remind you when it is in Input mode (it does by default).

INSERTING TEXT

Insert (**i/I**) The **i** (Insert) command puts vim in Input mode and places the text you enter before the current character. The **I** command places text at the beginning of the current line (Figure 6-13). Although the **i** and **I** commands sometimes overwrite text on the screen, the characters in the Work buffer are not changed; only the display is affected. The overwritten text is redisplayed when you press ESCAPE and vim returns to Command mode. Use **i** or **I** to insert a few characters or words into existing text or to insert text in a new file.

APPENDING TEXT

Append (**a/A**) The **a** (Append) command is similar to the **i** command, except that it places the text you enter after the current character (Figure 6-13). The **A** command places the text after the last character on the current line.

OPENING A LINE FOR TEXT

Open (**o/O**) The **o** (Open) and **O** commands open a blank line within existing text, place the cursor at the beginning of the new (blank) line, and put vim in Input mode. The **O** command opens a line above the current line; the **o** command opens one below the current line. Use these commands when you are entering several new lines within existing text.

REPLACING TEXT

Replace (**r/R**)   The **r** and **R** (Replace) commands cause the new text you enter to overwrite (replace) existing text. The single character you enter following an **r** command overwrites the current character. After you enter that character, vim returns to Command mode—you do not need to press the ESCAPE key.

The **R** command causes *all* subsequent characters to overwrite existing text until you press ESCAPE to return vim to Command mode.

Replacing TABs

tip   The Replace commands may appear to behave strangely when you replace TAB characters. TAB characters can appear as several SPACES—until you try to replace them. A TAB is one character and is replaced by a single character. Refer to "Invisible characters" on page 187 for information on displaying TABs as visible characters.

QUOTING SPECIAL CHARACTERS IN INPUT MODE

CONTROL-V   While you are in Input mode, you can use the Quote command, CONTROL-V, to enter any character into the text, including characters that normally have special meaning to vim. Among these characters are CONTROL-L (or CONTROL-R), which redraws the screen; CONTROL-W, which backs the cursor up a word to the left; CONTROL-M, which enters a NEWLINE; and ESCAPE, which ends Input mode.

To insert one of these characters into the text, type CONTROL-V followed by the character. CONTROL-V quotes the single character that follows it. For example, to insert the sequence ESCAPE[2J into a file you are creating in vim, you would type the character sequence CONTROL-V ESCAPE[2J. This character sequence clears the screen of a DEC VT-100 and other similar terminals. Although you would not ordinarily want to type this sequence into a document, you might want to use it or another ESCAPE sequence in a shell script you are creating in vim. Refer to Chapter 10 for information about writing shell scripts.

COMMAND MODE: DELETING AND CHANGING TEXT

This section describes the commands to delete and replace, or change, text in the document you are editing. The Undo command is covered here because it allows you to restore deleted or changed text.

UNDOING CHANGES

Undo (**u/U**)   The **u** command (Undo) restores text that you just deleted or changed by mistake. A single Undo command restores only the most recently deleted text. If you delete a line and then change a word, the first Undo restores only the changed word; you have to give a second Undo command to restore the deleted line. With the **compatible** parameter (page 158) set, vim can undo only the most recent change. The U command restores the last line you changed to the way it was before you started changing it, even after several changes.

DELETING CHARACTERS

Delete character **(x/X)** The **x** command deletes the current character. You can precede the **x** command by a Repeat Factor (page 196) to delete several characters on the current line, starting with the current character. The X command deletes the character to the left of the cursor.

DELETING TEXT

Delete **(d/D)** The **d** (Delete) command removes text from the Work buffer. The amount of text that **d** removes depends on the Repeat Factor and the Unit of Measure (page 193). After the text is deleted, vim is still in Command mode.

Use **dd** to delete a single line

tip The command **d** RETURN deletes two lines: the current line and the following one. Use **dd** to delete just the current line, or precede **dd** by a Repeat Factor (page 196) to delete several lines.

You can delete from the current cursor position up to a specific character on the same line. To delete up to the next semicolon (;), give the command **dt;** (see page 173 for more information on the **t** command). To delete the remainder of the current line, use **D** or **d$**. Table 6-1 lists some Delete commands. Each command, except the last group that starts with **dd**, deletes *from/to* the current character.

Exchange characters and lines

tip If two characters are out of order, position the cursor on the first character and give the commands **xp**.

If two lines are out of order, position the cursor on the first line and give the commands **ddp**.

See page 181 for more information on the Put commands.

Table 6-1   Delete command examples

Command	Result
dl	Deletes current character (same as the **x** command)
d0	Deletes from beginning of line
d^	Deletes from first character of line (not including leading SPACEs or TABs)
dw	Deletes to end of word
d3w	Deletes to end of third word
db	Deletes from beginning of word
dW	Deletes to end of blank-delimited word

Table 6-1 Delete command examples (continued)

Command	Result
dB	Deletes from beginning of blank-delimited word
d7B	Deletes from seventh previous beginning of blank-delimited word
d)	Deletes to end of sentence
d4)	Deletes to end of fourth sentence
d(	Deletes from beginning of sentence
d}	Deletes to end of paragraph
d{	Deletes from beginning of paragraph
d7{	Deletes from seventh paragraph preceding beginning of paragraph
d/*text*	Deletes up to next occurrence of word ***text***
df*c*	Deletes on current line up to and including next occurrence of character ***c***
dt*c*	Deletes on current line up to next occurrence of ***c***
D	Deletes to end of line
d$	Deletes to end of line
dd	Deletes current line
5dd	Deletes five lines starting with current line
dL	Deletes through last line on screen
dH	Deletes from first line on screen
dG	Deletes through end of Work buffer
d1G	Deletes from beginning of Work buffer

CHANGING TEXT

Change (**c/C**) The c (Change) command replaces existing text with new text. The new text does not have to occupy the same space as the existing text. You can change a word to several words, a line to several lines, or a paragraph to a single character. The C command replaces the text from the cursor position to the end of the line.

The c command deletes the amount of text specified by the Repeat Factor and the Unit of Measure (page 193) and puts vim in Input mode. When you finish entering the new text and press ESCAPE, the old word, line, sentence, or paragraph is changed to the new one. Pressing ESCAPE without entering new text deletes the specified text (that is, it replaces the specified text with nothing).

Table 6-2 lists some Change commands. Except for the last two, each command changes text *from/to* the current character.

Table 6-2   Change command examples

Command	Result
cl	Changes current character
cw	Changes to end of word
c3w	Changes to end of third word
cb	Changes from beginning of word
cW	Changes to end of blank-delimited word
cB	Changes from beginning of blank-delimited word
c7B	Changes from beginning of seventh previous blank-delimited word
c$	Changes to end of line
c0	Changes from beginning of line
c)	Changes to end of sentence
c4)	Changes to end of fourth sentence
c(	Changes from beginning of sentence
c}	Changes to end of paragraph
c{	Changes from beginning of paragraph
c7{	Changes from beginning of seventh preceding paragraph
ct*c*	Changes on current line up to next occurrence of *c*
C	Changes to end of line
cc	Changes current line
5cc	Changes five lines starting with current line

dw works differently from cw

tip   The **dw** command deletes all characters through (including) the SPACE at the end of a word. The **cw** command changes only the characters in the word, leaving the trailing SPACE intact.

REPLACING TEXT

Substitute (**s/S**)   The **s** and **S** (Substitute) commands also replace existing text with new text (Table 6-3). The **s** command deletes the current character and puts vim into Input mode. It has the effect of replacing the current character with whatever you type until you press ESCAPE. The **S** command does the same thing as the **cc** command: It changes the current line. The **s** command replaces characters only on the current line. If you specify a Repeat Factor before an **s** command and this action would replace more characters than are present on the current line, **s** changes characters only to the end of the line (same as **C**).

Table 6-3   Substitute command examples

Command	Result
s	Substitutes one or more characters for current character
S	Substitutes one or more characters for current line
5s	Substitutes one or more characters for five characters, starting with current character

CHANGING CASE

The tilde (~) character changes the case of the current character from uppercase to lowercase, or vice versa. You can precede the tilde with a number to specify the number of characters you want the command to affect. For example, the command 5~ transposes the next five characters starting with the character under the cursor, but will not transpose characters past the end of the current line.

SEARCHING AND SUBSTITUTING

Searching for and replacing a character, a string of text, or a string that is matched by a regular expression is a key feature of any editor. The vim editor provides simple commands for searching for a character on the current line. It also provides more complex commands for searching for—and optionally substituting for—single and multiple occurrences of strings or regular expressions anywhere in the Work buffer.

SEARCHING FOR A CHARACTER

Find (**f/F**) You can search for and move the cursor to the next occurrence of a specified character on the current line using the **f** (Find) command. Refer to "Moving the Cursor to a Specific Character" on page 165.

Find (**t/T**) The next two commands are used in the same manner as the Find commands. The **t** command places the cursor on the character before the next occurrence of the specified character. The **T** command places the cursor on the character after the previous occurrence of the specified character.

A semicolon (;) repeats the last **f**, **F**, **t**, or **T** command.

You can combine these search commands with other commands. For example, the command **d2fq** deletes the text from the current character to the second occurrence of the letter **q** on the current line.

SEARCHING FOR A STRING

Search (/ /?) The vim editor can search backward or forward through the Work buffer to find a string of text or a string that matches a regular expression (Appendix A). To find the next occurrence of a string (forward), press the forward slash (/) key, enter the text you want to find (called the *search string*), and press RETURN. When you press the slash key, vim displays a slash on the status line. As you enter the string of text, it is also displayed on the status line. When you press RETURN, vim searches for the string. If this search is successful, vim positions the cursor on the first character of the string. If you use a question mark (?) in place of the forward slash, vim searches for the previous occurrence of the string. If you need to include a forward slash in a forward search or a question mark in a backward search, you must quote it by preceding it with a backslash (\).

Two distinct ways of quoting characters

tip You use CONTROL-V to quote special characters in text that you are entering into a file (page 169). This section discusses the use of a backslash (\) to quote special characters in a search string. The two techniques of quoting characters are not interchangeable.

Next (n/N) The N and n keys repeat the last search but do not require you to reenter the search string. The n key repeats the original search exactly, and the N key repeats the search in the opposite direction of the original search.

If you are searching forward and vim does not find the search string before it gets to the end of the Work buffer, the editor typically *wraps around* and continues the search at the beginning of the Work buffer. During a backward search, vim wraps around from the beginning of the Work buffer to the end. Also, vim normally performs case-sensitive searches. Refer to "Wrap scan" (page 189) and "Ignore case in searches" (page 187) for information about how to change these search parameters.

NORMAL VERSUS INCREMENTAL SEARCHES

When vim performs a normal search (its default behavior), you enter a slash or question mark followed by the search string and press RETURN. The vim editor then moves the cursor to the next or previous occurrence of the string you are searching for.

When vim performs an incremental search, you enter a slash or question mark. As you enter each character of the search string, vim moves the highlight to the next or previous occurrence of the string you have entered so far. When the highlight is on the string you are searching for, you must press RETURN to move the cursor to the highlighted string. If the string you enter does not match any text, vim does not highlight anything.

The type of search that vim performs depends on the **incsearch** parameter (page 187). Give the command **:set incsearch** to turn on incremental searching; use **noincsearch** to turn it off. When you set the **compatible** parameter (page 158), vim turns off incremental searching.

SPECIAL CHARACTERS IN SEARCH STRINGS

Because the search string is a regular expression, some characters take on a special meaning within the search string. The following paragraphs list some of these characters. See also "Extended Regular Expressions" on page 893.

The first two items in the following list (^ and $) always have their special meanings within a search string unless you quote them by preceding them with a backslash (\). You can turn off the special meanings within a search string for the rest of the items in the list by setting the **nomagic** parameter. For more information refer to "Allow special characters in searches" on page 186.

^   BEGINNING-OF-LINE INDICATOR

When the first character in a search string is a caret (also called a circumflex), it matches the beginning of a line. For example, the command **/^the** finds the next line that begins with the string **the**.

$ END-OF-LINE INDICATOR

A dollar sign matches the end of a line. For example, the command **/!$** finds the next line that ends with an exclamation point and **/ $** matches the next line that ends with a SPACE.

.   ANY-CHARACTER INDICATOR

A period matches *any* character, anywhere in the search string. For example, the command **/l..e** finds **line, followed, like, included, all memory**, or any other word or character string that contains an **l** followed by any two characters and an **e**. To search for a period, use a backslash to quote the period (\.).

\>   END-OF-WORD INDICATOR

This pair of characters matches the end of a word. For example, the command **/s\>** finds the next word that ends with an **s**. Whereas a backslash (\) is typically used to *turn off* the special meaning of a character, the character sequence \> has a special meaning, while > alone does not.

\<   BEGINNING-OF-WORD INDICATOR

This pair of characters matches the beginning of a word. For example, the command **/\<The** finds the next word that begins with the string **The**. The beginning-of-word indicator uses the backslash in the same, atypical way as the end-of-word indicator.

*   ZERO OR MORE OCCURRENCES

This character is a modifier that will match zero or more occurrences of the character immediately preceding it. For example, the command **/dis*m** will match the string **di** followed by zero or more **s** characters followed by an **m**. Examples of successful matches would include **dim**, or **dism**, and **dissm**.

[] CHARACTER-CLASS DEFINITION

Brackets surrounding two or more characters match any *single* character located between the brackets. For example, the command **/dis[ck]** finds the next occurrence of *either* disk or disc.

There are two special characters you can use within a character-class definition. A caret (^) as the first character following the left bracket defines the character class to be *any except the following characters*. A hyphen between two characters indicates a range of characters. Refer to the examples in Table 6-4.

Table 6-4 Search examples

Search string	What it finds
/and	Finds the next occurrence of the string **and**
	Examples: sand and standard slander andiron
/\<and\>	Finds the next occurrence of the word **and**
	Example: and
/^The	Finds the next line that starts with **The**
	Examples:
	The . . .
	There . . .
/^[0-9][0-9])	Finds the next line that starts with a two-digit number followed by a right parenthesis
	Examples:
	77)...
	01)...
	15)...
/\<[adr]	Finds the next word that starts with **a**, **d**, or **r**
	Examples: apple drive road argument right
/^[A-Za-z]	Finds the next line that starts with an uppercase or lowercase letter
	Examples:
	will not find a line starting with the number 7 . . .
	Dear Mr. Jones . . .
	in the middle of a sentence like this . . .

SUBSTITUTING ONE STRING FOR ANOTHER

A Substitute command combines the effects of a Search command and a Change command. That is, it searches for a string (regular expression) just as the **/** command does, allowing the same special characters discussed in the previous section. When it finds the string or matches the regular expression, the Substitute command changes the string or regular expression it matches. The syntax of the Substitute command is

:*[g][address]*s/*search-string*/*replacement-string[/option]*

As with all commands that begin with a colon, vim executes a Substitute command from the status line.

THE SUBSTITUTE ADDRESS

If you do not specify an *address,* Substitute searches only the current line. If you use a single line number as the *address,* Substitute searches that line. If the *address* is two line numbers separated by a comma, Substitute searches those lines and the lines between them. Refer to "Line numbers" on page 187 if you want vim to display line numbers. Wherever a line number is allowed in the *address,* you may also use an *address* string enclosed between slashes. The vim editor operates on the next line that the *address* string matches. When you precede the first slash of the *address* string with the letter **g** (for global), vim operates on all lines in the file that the *address* string matches. (This **g** is not the same as the one that goes at the end of the Substitute command to cause multiple replacements on a single line; see "Searching for and Replacing Strings" on the next page).

Within the *address,* a period represents the current line, a dollar sign represents the last line in the Work buffer, and a percent sign represents the entire Work buffer. You can perform *address* arithmetic using plus and minus signs. Table 6-5 shows some examples of *address*es.

Table 6-5   Addresses

Address	Portion of Work buffer addressed
5	Line 5
77,100	Lines 77 through 100 inclusive
1,.	Beginning of Work buffer through current line
.,$	Current line through end of Work buffer
1,$	Entire Work buffer
%	Entire Work buffer
/pine/	The next line containing the word **pine**
g/pine/	All lines containing the word **pine**
.,.+10	Current line through tenth following line (11 lines in all)

SEARCHING FOR AND REPLACING STRINGS

An **s** comes after the *address* in the command syntax, indicating that this is a Substitute command. A delimiter follows the **s**, marking the beginning of the *search-string*. Although the examples in this book use a forward slash, you can use as a delimiter any character that is not a letter, number, blank, or backslash. You must use the same delimiter at the end of the *search-string*.

Next comes the *search-string*. It has the same format as the search string in the **/** command and can include the same special characters (page 175). (The *search-string* is a regular expression; refer to Appendix A for more information.) Another delimiter marks the end of the *search-string* and the beginning of the *replacement-string*.

The *replacement-string* replaces the text matched by the *search-string* and is typically followed by the delimiter character. You can omit the final delimiter when no option follows the *replacement-string;* a final delimiter is required if an option is present.

Several characters have special meanings in the *search-string*, and other characters have special meanings in the *replacement-string*. For example, an ampersand (&) in the *replacement-string* represents the text that was matched by the *search-string*. A backslash in the *replacement-string* quotes the character that follows it. Refer to Table 6-6 and Appendix A.

Table 6-6   Search and replace examples

Command	Result
:s/bigger/biggest/	Replaces the first occurrence of the string **bigger** on the current line with **biggest**
	Example:
	bigger $\longrightarrow$ **biggest**
:1,.s/Ch 1/Ch 2/g	Replaces every occurrence of the string **Ch 1**, before or on the current line, with the string **Ch 2**
	Examples:
	Ch 1 $\longrightarrow$ **Ch 2**
	Ch 12 $\longrightarrow$ **Ch 22**
:1,$s/ten/10/g	Replaces every occurrence of the string **ten** with the string **10**
	Examples:
	ten $\longrightarrow$ **10**
	often $\longrightarrow$ **of10**
	tenant $\longrightarrow$ **10ant**
:g/chapter/s/ten/10/	Replaces the first occurrence of the string **ten** with the string **10** on all lines containing the word **chapter**
	Examples:
	chapter ten $\longrightarrow$ **chapter 10**
	chapters will often $\longrightarrow$ **chapters will of10**

Table 6-6   Search and replace examples (continued)

Command	Result
:%s/\<ten\>/10/g	Replaces every occurrence of the word **ten** with the string **10**
	Example:
	ten $\longrightarrow$ **10**
:.,.+10s/every/each/g	Replaces every occurrence of the string **every** with the string **each** on the current line through the tenth following line
	Examples:
	every $\longrightarrow$ **each**
	everything $\longrightarrow$ **eachthing**
:s/\<short\>/"&"/	Replaces the word **short** on the current line with **"short"** (enclosed within quotation marks)
	Example:
	the shortest of the short $\longrightarrow$ **the shortest of the "short"**

Normally, the Substitute command replaces only the first occurrence of any text that matches the *search-string* on a line. If you want a global substitution—that is, if you want to replace all matching occurrences of text on a line—append the **g** (global) option after the delimiter that ends the *replacement-string*. Another useful option, **c** (check), causes vim to ask whether you would like to make the change each time it finds text that matches the *search-string*. Pressing y replaces the *search-string*, **q** terminates the command, l (last) makes the replacement and quits, **a** (all) makes all remaining replacements, and **n** continues the search without making that replacement.

The *address* string need not be the same as the *search-string*. For example,

```
:/candle/s/wick/flame/
```

substitutes **flame** for the first occurrence of **wick** on the next line that contains the string **candle**. Similarly,

```
:g/candle/s/wick/flame/
```

performs the same substitution for the first occurrence of **wick** on each line of the file containing the string **candle** and

```
:g/candle/s/wick/flame/g
```

performs the same substitution for all occurrences of **wick** on each line that contains the string **candle**.

If the *search-string* is the same as the *address*, you can leave the *search-string* blank. For example, the command **:/candle/s//lamp/** is equivalent to the command **:/candle/s/candle/lamp/**.

MISCELLANEOUS COMMANDS

This section describes three commands that do not fit naturally into any other groups.

JOIN

Join (**J**) The **J** (Join) command joins the line below the current line to the end of the current line, inserting a SPACE between what was previously two lines and leaving the cursor on this SPACE. If the current line ends with a period, vim inserts two SPACEs.

You can always "unjoin" (break) a line into two lines by replacing the SPACE or SPACEs where you want to break the line with a RETURN.

STATUS

Status (CONTROL-G) The Status command, CONTROL-G, displays the name of the file you are editing, information about whether the file has been modified or is a readonly file, the number of the current line, the total number of lines in the Work buffer, and the percentage of the Work buffer preceding the current line. You can also use **:f** to display status information. Following is a sample status line:

```
"/usr/share/dict/words" [readonly] line 28501 of 98569 --28%-- col 1
```

. (PERIOD)

. The **.** (period) command repeats the most recent command that made a change. If you had just given a **d2w** command (delete the next two words), for example, the **.** command would delete the next two words. If you had just inserted text, the **.** command would repeat the insertion of the same text. This command is useful if you want to change some occurrences of a word or phrase in the Work buffer. Search for the first occurrence of the word (use **/**) and then make the change you want (use **cw**). You can then use **n** to search for the next occurrence of the word and **.** to make the same change to it. If you do not want to make the change, give the **n** command again to find the next occurrence.

COPYING, MOVING, AND DELETING TEXT

The vim editor has a General-Purpose buffer and 26 Named buffers that can hold text during an editing session. These buffers are useful if you want to move or copy a portion of text to another location in the Work buffer. A combination of the Delete and Put commands removes text from one location in the Work buffer and places it in another location in the Work buffer. The Yank and Put commands copy text to another location in the Work buffer, without changing the original text.

THE GENERAL-PURPOSE BUFFER

The vim editor stores the text that you most recently changed, deleted, or yanked (covered below) in the General-Purpose buffer. The Undo command retrieves text from the General-Purpose buffer when it restores text.

COPYING TEXT TO THE BUFFER

Yank (y/Y)   The Yank command (**y**) is identical to the Delete (**d**) command except that it does not delete text from the Work buffer. The vim editor places a *copy* of the yanked text in the General-Purpose buffer. You can then use a Put command to place another copy of it elsewhere in the Work buffer. Use the Yank command just as you use the Delete command. The uppercase **Y** command yanks an entire line into the General-Purpose buffer.

Use yy to yank one line

tip   Just as **d** RETURN deletes two lines, so **y** RETURN yanks two lines. Use the **yy** command to yank and **dd** to delete the current line.

D works differently from Y

tip   The **D** command (page 170) does not work in the same manner as the **Y** command. Whereas **D** deletes to the end of the line, **Y** yanks the entire line regardless of the cursor position.

COPYING TEXT FROM THE BUFFER

Put (p/P)   The Put commands, **p** and **P**, copy text from the General-Purpose buffer to the Work buffer. If you delete or yank characters or words into the General-Purpose buffer, **p** inserts them after the current *character,* and **P** inserts them before this character. If you delete or yank lines, sentences, or paragraphs, **P** inserts the contents of the General-Purpose buffer before the current *line,* and **p** inserts them after the current line.

Put commands do not destroy the contents of the General-Purpose buffer. Thus you can place the same text at several points within the file by giving one Delete or Yank command and several Put commands.

DELETING TEXT COPIES IT INTO THE BUFFER

Any of the Delete commands described earlier in this chapter (page 169) place the deleted text in the General-Purpose buffer. Just as you can use the Undo command to put the deleted text back where it came from, so you can use a Put command to put the deleted text at another location in the Work buffer.

Suppose you delete a word from the middle of a sentence by giving the **dw** command and then move the cursor to a SPACE between two words and give a **p** command; vim places the word you just deleted at the new location. If you delete a line using the **dd** command and then move the cursor to the line *below* the line where you want the deleted line to appear and give a **P** command, vim places the line at the new location.

optional

NAMED BUFFERS

You can use a Named buffer with any of the Delete, Yank, or Put commands. Each of the 26 Named buffers is named by a letter of the alphabet. Each Named buffer can store a different block of text and you can recall each block as needed. Unlike the General-Purpose buffer, vim does not change the contents of a Named buffer unless you issue a command that specifically overwrites that buffer. The vim editor maintains the contents of the Named buffers throughout an editing session.

The vim editor stores text in a Named buffer if you precede a Delete or Yank command with a double quotation mark (") and a buffer name (for example, "kyy yanks a copy of the current line into buffer k). You can put information from the Work buffer into a Named buffer in two ways. First, if you give the name of the buffer as a lowercase letter, vim overwrites the contents of the buffer when it deletes or yanks text into the buffer. Second, if you use an uppercase letter for the buffer name, vim appends the newly deleted or yanked text to the end of the buffer. This feature enables you to collect blocks of text from various sections of a file and deposit them at one place in the file with a single command. Named buffers are also useful when you are moving a section of a file and do not want to give a Put command immediately after the corresponding Delete command, and when you want to insert a paragraph, sentence, or phrase repeatedly in a document.

If you have one sentence you use throughout a document, you can yank that sentence into a Named buffer and put it wherever you need it by using the following procedure: After entering the first occurrence of the sentence and pressing ESCAPE to return to Command mode, leave the cursor on the line containing the sentence. (The sentence must appear on a line or lines by itself for this procedure to work.) Then yank the sentence into Named buffer **a** by giving the "**ayy** command (or "**a2yy** if the sentence takes up two lines). Now anytime you need the sentence, you can return to Command mode and give the command "**ap** to put a copy of the sentence below the current line.

This technique provides a quick and easy way to insert text that you use frequently in a document. For example, if you were editing a legal document, you might store the phrase **The Plaintiff alleges that the Defendant** in a Named buffer to save yourself the trouble of typing it every time you want to use it. Similarly, if you were creating a letter that frequently used a long company name, such as **National Standards Institute,** you might put it into a Named buffer.

NUMBERED BUFFERS

In addition to the 26 Named buffers and 1 General-Purpose buffer, 9 Numbered buffers are available. They are, in one sense, readonly buffers. The vim editor fills them with the nine most recently deleted chunks of text that are at least one line long. The most recently deleted text is held in "**1**, the next most recent in "**2**, and so on. If you delete a block of text and then give other vim commands so that you cannot reclaim the deleted text with an Undo command, you can use **"1p** to paste the most recently deleted chunk of text below the location of the cursor. If you have deleted several blocks of text and want to reclaim a specific one, proceed as follows: Paste the contents of the first buffer with **"1p**. If the first buffer does not hold the text you are looking for, undo the paste operation with **u** and then give the period (.) command to repeat the previous command. The Numbered buffers work in a unique way with the period command: Instead of pasting the contents of buffer **"1**, the period command pastes the contents of the next buffer (**"2**). Another **u** and period would replace the contents of buffer **"2** with that of buffer **"3**, and so on through the nine buffers.

READING AND WRITING FILES

Exit (**ZZ**) The vim editor reads a disk file into the Work buffer when you specify a filename on the command line you use to call vim. A **ZZ** command that terminates an editing session writes the contents of the Work buffer back to the disk file. This section discusses other ways of reading text into the Work buffer and writing it to a file.

READING FILES

Read (**:r**) The Read command reads a file into the Work buffer. The new file does not overwrite any text in the Work buffer but rather is positioned following the single address you specify (or the current line if you do not specify an address). You can use an address of 0 to read the file into the beginning of the Work buffer. The Read command has the following syntax:

> :[address]r [filename]

As with other commands that begin with a colon, when you enter the colon it appears on the status line. The *filename* is the pathname of the file that you want to read and must be terminated by RETURN. If you omit the *filename*, vim reads from the disk the file you are editing.

WRITING FILES

Write (**:w**) The Write command writes part or all of the Work buffer to a file. You can specify an address to write part of the Work buffer and a filename to specify a file to receive the text. If you do not specify an address or filename, vim writes the entire contents of the Work buffer to the file you are editing, updating the file on the disk.

During a long editing session, it is a good idea to use the Write command occasionally. If a problem develops later, a recent copy of the Work buffer is then safe on the disk. If you use a **:q!** command to exit from vim, the disk file reflects the version of the Work buffer at the time you last used a Write command.

The Write command has two formats:

:[address]w[!] [filename]
:[address]w>> filename

The second format appends text to an existing file. The *address* specifies the portion of the Work buffer vim will write to the file. The *address* follows the form of the *address* that the Substitute command uses (page 177). If you do not specify an *address*, vim writes the entire contents of the Work buffer. The optional *filename* is the pathname of the file you are writing to. If you do not specify a *filename*, vim writes to the file you are editing.

w! Because the Write command can quickly destroy a large amount of work, vim demands that you enter an exclamation point (!) following the **w** as a safeguard against accidentally overwriting a file. The only times you do not need an exclamation point are when you are writing out the entire contents of the Work buffer to the file being edited (using no *address* and no *filename*) and when you are writing part or all of the Work buffer to a new file. When you are writing part of the file to the file being edited or when you are overwriting another file, you must use an exclamation point.

IDENTIFYING THE CURRENT FILE

The File command (:f) provides the same information as the Status command (CONTROL-G; page 180). The filename the File command displays is the one the Write command uses if you give a :w command without a filename.

SETTING PARAMETERS

You can tailor the vim editor to your needs and habits by setting vim parameters. Parameters perform such functions as displaying line numbers, automatically inserting RETURNs, and establishing incremental and nonstandard searches.

You can set parameters in several ways. For example, you can set them to establish the environment for the current editing session while you are using vim. Alternatively, you can set the parameters in your **~/.bash_profile** (bash) or **~/.tcshrc** (tcsh) shell startup file or in the vim startup file, **~/.vimrc**. When you set the parameters in any of these files, the same customized environment will be available each time vim starts and you can begin editing immediately.

SETTING PARAMETERS FROM WITHIN vim

To set a parameter while you are using vim, enter a colon (:), the word **set**, a SPACE, and the parameter (refer to "Parameters" on page 185). The command appears on the status line as you type it and takes effect when you press RETURN. The following command establishes incremental searches for the current editing session:

```
:set incsearch
```

SETTING PARAMETERS IN A STARTUP FILE

VIMINIT   If you are using bash, you can put a line with the following format in your ~/**.bash_profile** startup file (page 272):

> *export VIMINIT='set param1 param2 ...'*

Replace *param1* and *param2* with parameters selected from Table 6-7. **VIMINIT** is a shell variable that vim reads. The following statement causes vim to ignore the case of characters in searches, display line numbers, use the TC Shell to execute Linux commands, and wrap text 15 characters from the right edge of the screen:

```
export VIMINIT='set ignorecase number shell=/bin/tcsh wrapmargin=15'
```

If you use the parameter abbreviations, it looks like this:

```
export VIMINIT='set ic nu sh=/bin/tcsh wm=15'
```

If you are using tcsh, put the following line in your ~/**.tcshrc** startup file (page 352):

> *setenv VIMINIT 'set param1 param2 ...'*

Again, replace *param1* and *param2* with parameters from Table 6-7. The values between the single quotation marks are the same as those shown in the preceding examples.

THE .vimrc STARTUP FILE

Instead of setting vim parameters in your shell startup file, you can create a ~/**.vimrc** file in your home directory and set the parameters there. Creating a **.vimrc** file causes vim to start with the **compatible** parameter unset (page 158). Lines in a **.vimrc** file follow this format:

> *set param1 param2 ...*

Following are examples of **.vimrc** files that perform the same function as **VIMINIT** described previously:

```
$ cat ~/.vimrc
set ignorecase
set number
set shell=/bin/tcsh
set wrapmargin=15

$ cat ~/.vimrc
set ic nu sh=/bin/tcsh wm=15
```

Parameters set by the **VIMINIT** variable take precedence over those set in the **.vimrc** file.

PARAMETERS

Table 6-7 lists some of the most useful vim parameters. The vim editor displays a complete list of parameters and indicates how they are currently set when you give the command **:set all** followed by a RETURN. The command **:set** RETURN displays a list of options that are set to values other than their default values. Two classes of parameters exist: those that contain an equal sign (and can take on a value) and those that are optionally prefixed with **no** (switches that are on or off). You can change the sense of a switch parameter by giving the command **:set [no]***param*. For example, give the command **:set number** (or **:set nonumber**) to turn on (or off) line numbering. To change the value of a parameter that takes on a value (and uses an equal sign), give a command such as **:set shiftwidth=15**.

Most parameters have abbreviations—for example, **nu** for **number, nonu** for **nonumber,** and **sw** for **shiftwidth**. The abbreviations are listed in the left column of Table 6-7, following the name of the parameter.

Table 6-7   Parameters

Parameter	Effect
Allow special characters in searches **magic**	Refer to "Special Characters in Search Strings" on page 175. By default the following characters have special meanings when used in a search string: . [ ] * When you set the **nomagic** parameter, these characters no longer have special meanings. The **magic** parameter restores their special meanings. The **^** and **$** characters always have special meanings within search strings, regardless of how you set this parameter.
Automatic indention **autoindent, ai**	The automatic indention feature works with the **shiftwidth** parameter to provide a regular set of indentions for programs or tabular material. This feature is off by default. You can turn it on by setting **autoindent** and turn it off by setting **noautoindent**. When automatic indention is on and vim is in Input mode, pressing CONTROL-T moves the cursor from the left margin (or an indention) to the next indention position, pressing RETURN moves the cursor to the left side of the next line under the first character of the previous line, and pressing CONTROL-D backs up over indention positions. The CONTROL-T and CONTROL-D keys work only before text is placed on a line.
Automatic write **autowrite, aw**	By default vim asks you before writing out the Work buffer when you have not explicitly told it to do so (as when you give a **:n** command to edit the next file). The **autowrite** option causes vim to write the Work buffer automatically when you use commands, such as **:n**, to edit to another file. You can disable this parameter by setting the **noautowrite** or **noaw** option.
Flash **flash, fl**	The vim editor normally causes the terminal to beep when you give an invalid command or press ESCAPE when it is in Command mode. Setting the parameter **flash** causes the terminal to flash instead of beep. Set **noflash** to cause it to beep. Not all terminals and emulators support this parameter.

Table 6-7   Parameters (continued)

Parameter	Effect
Ignore case in searches **ignorecase, ic**	The vim editor normally performs case-sensitive searches, differentiating between uppercase and lowercase letters. It performs case-insensitive searches when you set the **ignorecase** parameter. Set **noignorecase** to restore case-sensitive searches.
Incremental search **incsearch, is**	Refer to "Normal Versus Incremental Searches" on page 174. By default vim does not perform incremental searches. To cause vim to perform incremental searches, set the parameter **incsearch**. To cause vim not to perform incremental searches, set the parameter **noincsearch**.
Invisible characters **list**	To cause vim to display each TAB as ^I and to mark the end of each line with a **$**, set the **list** parameter. To display TABs as whitespace and not mark ends of lines, set **nolist**.
Status line **laststatus=*n*, ls=*n***	This parameter displays a status line that shows the name of the file you are editing, a **[+]** if the file has been changed since it was last written out, and the position of the cursor. When setting the parameter **laststatus=*n*, *n*** equal to **0** (zero) turns off the status line, **1** displays the status line when at least two vim windows are displayed, and **2** always displays the status line.
Line numbers **number, nu**	The vim editor does not normally display the line number associated with each line. To display line numbers, set the parameter **number**. To cause line numbers not to be displayed, set the parameter **nonumber**. Line numbers are not part of the file, are not stored with the file, and are not displayed when the file is printed. They appear on the screen only while you are using vim.
Line wrap **wrap**	The line wrap controls how vim displays lines that are too long to fit on the screen. To cause vim to wrap long lines and continue them on the next line, set **wrap** (set by default). If you set **nowrap**, vim truncates long lines at the right edge of the screen.
Line wrap margin **wrapmargin=*nn*, wm=*nn***	The line wrap margin causes vim to break the text that you are inserting at approximately the specified number of characters from the right margin. The vim editor breaks the text by inserting a NEWLINE character at the closest blank-delimited word boundary. Setting the line wrap margin is handy if you want all the text lines to be approximately the same length. This feature relieves you of the need to remember to press RETURN to end each line of input. When setting the parameter **wrapmargin=*nn*, *nn*** is the number of characters *from the right side of the screen* where you want vim to break the text. This number is not the column width of the text but rather the distance from the end of the text to the right edge of the screen. Setting the wrap margin to **0** (zero) turns this feature off. By default the line wrap margin is off (set to **0**).

Table 6-7   Parameters (continued)

Parameter	Effect
Report **report=**_nn_	This parameter causes vim to display a report on the status line whenever you make a change that affects at least _nn_ lines. For example, if **report** is set to **7** and you delete seven lines, vim displays the message **7 lines deleted**. When you delete six or fewer lines, vim does not display a message. The default for **report** is **5**.
Scroll **scroll=**_nn_, **scr=**_nn_	This parameter controls the number of lines that CONTROL-D and CONTROL-U (page 167) scroll text on the screen. By default **scroll** is set to half the window height. There are two ways to change the value of **scroll**. First you can enter a number before pressing CONTROL-D or CONTROL-U; vim sets **scroll** to that number. Alternatively, you can set **scroll** explicitly with **scroll=**_nn_, where _nn_ is the number of lines you want to scroll with each CONTROL-D or CONTROL-U command.
Shell **shell=**_path_, **sh=**_path_	While you are using vim, you can cause it to spawn a new shell. You can either create an interactive shell (if you want to run several commands) or run a single command. The **shell** parameter determines which shell vim invokes. By default vim sets the **shell** parameter to your login shell. To change it, set the parameter **shell=**_path_, where _path_ is the absolute pathname of the shell you want to use.
Shift width **shiftwidth=**_nn_, **sw=**_nn_	This parameter controls the functioning of CONTROL-T and CONTROL-D in Input mode when automatic indention is on (see "Automatic indention" in this table). When setting the parameter **shiftwidth=**_nn_, _nn_ is the spacing of the indention positions (**8** by default). Setting the shift width is similar to setting the TAB stops on a typewriter; with **shiftwidth**, however, the distance between TAB stops remains constant.
Show match **showmatch**, **sm**	This parameter is useful for programmers who are working in languages that use braces (**{ }**) or parentheses as expression delimiters (Lisp, C, Tcl, and so on). When **showmatch** is set and you are entering code (in Input mode) and type a closing brace or parenthesis, the cursor jumps briefly to the matching opening brace or parenthesis (that is, the preceding corresponding element at the same nesting level). After it highlights the matching element, the cursor resumes its previous position. When you type a right brace or parenthesis that does not have a match, vim beeps. Use **noshowmatch** to turn off automatic matching.
Show mode **showmode**, **smd**	Set the parameter **showmode** to display the mode in the lower-right corner of the screen when vim is in Input mode (default). Set **noshowmode** to cause vim not to display the mode.

Table 6-7   Parameters (continued)

Parameter	Effect
vi compatibility **compatible**, **cp**	Refer to "The compatible Parameter" on page 158. By default, vim does not attempt to be compatible with vi. To cause vim to be compatible with vi, set the parameter **compatible**. To cause vim not to be compatible with vi, set the parameter **nocompatible**.
Wrap scan **wrapscan**, **ws**	By default, when a search for the next occurrence of a search string reaches the end of the Work buffer, vim continues the search at the beginning of the Work buffer. The reverse is true with a search for the previous occurrence of a search string. The **nowrapscan** parameter stops the search at either end of the Work buffer. Set the **wrapscan** parameter if you want searches to wrap around the ends of the Work buffer.

ADVANCED EDITING TECHNIQUES

This section presents several commands you may find useful once you have become comfortable using vim.

optional

USING MARKERS

While you are using vim, you can set and use markers to make addressing more convenient. Set a marker by giving the command **m***c*, where *c* is any character. (Letters are preferred because some characters, such as a single quotation mark, have special meanings when used as markers.) The vim editor does not preserve markers when you exit from vim.

Once you have set a marker, you can use it in a manner similar to a line number. You can move the cursor to the beginning of a line that contains a marker by preceding the marker name with a single quotation mark. For example, to set marker **t**, position the cursor on the line you want to mark and give the command **mt**. During the remainder of this editing session, unless you reset marker **t** or delete the line it marks, you can return to the beginning of the line you marked by giving the command **'t**.

You can delete all text from the current line through the line containing marker **r** with the following command:

   d'r

You can use a back tick (` , also called a grave accent or reverse single quotation mark) to go to the exact position of the marker on the line. After setting marker **t**, you can move the cursor to the location of this marker (not the beginning of the line that holds the marker) with the command `t. The following command deletes all the text from the current line up to the character where the marker **r** was placed; the rest of the line containing the marker remains intact:

    d`r

You can use markers in addresses of commands instead of line numbers. The following command replaces all occurrences of **The** with **THE** on all lines from marker **m** to the current line (marker **m** must precede the current line):

    :'m,.s/The/THE/g

EDITING OTHER FILES

The following command causes vim to edit the file you specify with *filename*:

    :e[!] [filename]

If you want to save the contents of the Work buffer, you must write it out (using **:w**) before you give this command. If you do not want to save the contents of the Work buffer, vim insists you use an exclamation point to acknowledge that you will lose the work you did since the last time you wrote out the Work buffer. If you do not supply a *filename*, vim edits the file you are working on.

:e! The command **:e!** starts an editing session over again. This command returns the Work buffer to the state it was in the last time you wrote it out or, if you have not written it out, the state it was in when you started editing the file. It is useful when you make mistakes while editing a file and decide that it would be easier to start over than to fix the mistakes.

Because the **:e** command does not destroy the contents of the General-Purpose or Named buffers, you can store text from one file in a buffer, use a **:e** command to edit a second file, and put text from the buffer in the second file.

:e# The command **:e#** closes the current file and opens the last file you were editing, placing the cursor on the line that it was on when you last closed the file. If you do not save the file you are working on before you give this command, vim prompts you to do so. Setting the **autowrite** parameter (page 186) will not stop vim from prompting you.

:n
:rew The **:e#** command can help you copy blocks of text from one file to another. When you call vim with the names of several files as arguments, you can use **:n** to edit the next file, **:e#** to edit the file you just edited, and **:rew** to rewind the sequence of files so that you are editing the first file again. As you move between files, you can copy text from one file into a buffer and paste that text into another file. You can use **:n!** to force vim to close a file without writing out changes before it opens the next file.

MACROS AND SHORTCUTS

:map The vim editor allows you to create both macros and shortcuts. The **:map** command defines a key or sequence of keys that perform some action in Command mode. The following command maps CONTROL-X to the commands that will find the next left bracket on the current line (**f[**), delete all characters from that bracket to the next right bracket (**df]**) on the same line, delete the next character (**x**), move the cursor down two lines (**2j**), and finally move the cursor to the beginning of the line (**0**):

```
:map ^X f[df]x2j0
```

Although you can use ESCAPE and CONTROL sequences, it is a good idea to avoid remapping characters or sequences that are vim commands. Type **:map** by itself to see a list of the current mappings. You may need to use CONTROL-V (page 169) to quote some of the characters you want to enter into the **:map** string.

:abbrev The **:abbrev** command is similar to **:map** but creates abbreviations you can use while in Input mode. When you are in Input mode and type a string you have defined with **:abbrev**, followed by a SPACE, vim replaces the string and the SPACE with the characters you specified when you defined the string. For ease of use, avoid common sequences of characters when creating abbreviations. The following command defines **ZZ** as an abbreviation for **Sam the Great**:

```
:abbrev ZZ Sam the Great
```

Even though **ZZ** is a vim command, it is used only in Command mode. It has no special meaning in Input mode, where you use abbreviations.

EXECUTING SHELL COMMANDS FROM WITHIN vim

:sh You can execute shell commands in several ways while you are using vim. For instance, you can spawn a new interactive shell by giving the following command and pressing RETURN:

```
:sh
```

The vim **shell** parameter (page 188) determines which shell is spawned (usually bash or tcsh). By default **shell** is the same as your login shell.

After you have finished your work in the shell, you can return to vim by exiting from the shell (press CONTROL-D or give an **exit** command).

If :sh does not work correctly

tip The **:sh** command may behave strangely depending on how the shell has been configured. You may get warnings with the **:sh** command or it may even hang. Experiment with the **:sh** command to be sure it works correctly with your configuration. If it does not, you might want to set the vim **shell** parameter to another shell before using **:sh**. For example, the following command causes vim to use tcsh with the **:sh** command:

```
:set shell=/bin/tcsh
```

You may need to change the **SHELL** environment variable after starting **:sh** to show the correct shell.

Edit only one copy of a file

caution   When you create a new shell by giving the command **:sh**, remember you are still using vim. A common mistake is to try to edit the same file from the new shell, forgetting that vim is already editing the file from a different shell. Because you can lose information by editing the same file from two instances of an editor, vim warns you when you make this mistake. Refer to "File Locks" on page 161 to see an example of the message that vim displays.

:!command   You can execute a shell command line from vim by giving the following command, replacing *command* with the command line you want to execute and terminating the command with a RETURN:

> *:!command*

The vim editor spawns a new shell that executes the *command*. When the *command* runs to completion, the newly spawned shell returns control to the editor.

:!!command   You can execute a command from vim and have it replace the current line with the output from the command. If you do not want to replace any text, put the cursor on a blank line before giving the following command:

> *!!command*

Nothing happens when you enter the first exclamation point. When you enter the second one, vim moves the cursor to the status line and allows you to enter the command you want to execute. Because this command puts vim in Last Line mode, you must end the command with a RETURN (as you would end most shell commands).

You can also execute a command from vim with standard input to the command coming from all or part of the file you are editing and standard output from the command replacing the input in the file you are editing. This type of command is handy for sorting a list in place within a file.

To specify the block of text that will become standard input for the command, move the cursor to one end of the block of text. Then enter an exclamation point followed by a command that would normally move the cursor to the other end of the block of text. For example, if the cursor is at the beginning of the file and you want to specify the whole file, give the command **!G**. If you want to specify the part of the file between the cursor and marker **b**, give the command **! ' b**. After you give the cursor-movement command, vim displays an exclamation point on the status line and waits for you to enter a shell command.

To sort a list of names in a file, move the cursor to the beginning of the list and set marker **q** with an **mq** command. Then move the cursor to the end of the list and give the following command:

> **! ' qsort**

Press RETURN and wait. After a few seconds, the sorted list should replace the original list on the screen. If the command did not behave as expected, you can usually undo the change with a **u** command. Refer to page 817 for more information on sort.

! can destroy a file

caution   If you enter the wrong command or mistype a command, you can destroy a file (for example, if the command hangs or stops vim from working). For this reason it is a good idea to save your file before using this command. The Undo command (page 169) can be a lifesaver. A **:e!** command (page 190) will get rid of the changes, returning the buffer to the state it was in last time you saved it.

As with the **:sh** command, the default shell may not work properly with the **!** command. You may want to test the shell with a sample file before executing this command with your real work. If the default shell does not work properly, change the **shell** parameter.

UNITS OF MEASURE

Many vim commands operate on a block of text—ranging from one character to many paragraphs. You specify the size of a block of text with a *Unit of Measure*. You can specify multiple Units of Measure by preceding a Unit of Measure with a Repeat Factor (page 196). This section defines the various Units of Measure.

CHARACTER

A character is one character—visible or not, printable or not—including SPACEs and TABs. Some examples of characters are

    a   q   A   .   5   R   -   >   TAB SPACE

WORD

A word, similar to a word in the English language, is a string of one or more characters bounded on both sides by any combination of one or more of the following elements: a punctuation mark, SPACE, TAB, numeral, or NEWLINE. In addition, vim considers each group of punctuation marks to be a word (Table 6-8).

Table 6-8   Words

Word count	Text
1	pear
2	pear!
2	pear!)
3	pear!) The
4	pear!) "The
11	This is a short, concise line (no frills).

BLANK-DELIMITED WORD

A blank-delimited word is the same as a word but includes adjacent punctuation. Blank-delimited words are separated by one or more of the following elements: a SPACE, TAB, or NEWLINE (Table 6-9).

Table 6-9   Blank-delimited words

Word count	Text
1	pear
1	pear!
1	pear!)
2	pear!) The
2	pear!) "The
8	This is a short, concise line (no frills).

LINE

A line is a string of characters bounded by NEWLINEs that is not necessarily displayed as a single physical line on the screen. You can enter a very long single (logical) line that wraps around (continues on the next physical line) several times or disappears off the right edge of the display. It is a good idea to avoid creating long logical lines; ideally you would terminate lines with a RETURN before they reach the right side of the screen. Terminating lines in this manner ensures that each physical line contains one logical line and avoids confusion when you edit and format text. Some commands do not *appear* to work properly on physical lines that are longer than the width of the screen. For example, with the cursor on a long logical line that wraps around several physical lines, pressing RETURN once appears to move the cursor down more than one line. You can use fmt (page 697) to break long logical lines into shorter ones.

SENTENCE

A sentence is an English sentence or the equivalent. A sentence starts at the end of the previous sentence and ends with a period, exclamation point, or question mark, followed by two SPACEs or a NEWLINE (Table 6-10).

Table 6-10   Sentences

Sentence count	Text
One: only one SPACE after the first period and a NEWLINE after the second period	That's it. This is one sentence.

Table 6-10   Sentences (continued)

Sentence count	Text
Two: two SPACES after the first period and a NEWLINE after the second period	`That's it.  This is two sentences.`
Three: two SPACES after the first two question marks and a NEWLINE after the exclamation point	`What?  Three sentences?  One line!`

One: NEWLINE after the period	`This sentence takes`
	`up a total of`
	`three lines.`

PARAGRAPH

A paragraph is preceded and followed by one or more blank lines. A blank line is composed of two NEWLINE characters in a row (Table 6-11).

Table 6-11   Paragraphs

Paragraph count	Text
One: blank line before and after text	`One paragraph`

One: blank line before and after text	`          This may appear to be`
	`more than one paragraph.`
	`          Just because there are`
	`two indentions does not mean`
	`it qualifies as two paragraphs.`

Three: three blocks of text separated by blank lines	`Even though in`
	
	`English this is only`
	`one sentence,`
	
	`vim considers it to be`
	`three paragraphs.`

SCREEN (WINDOW)

Under vim, a screen or terminal emulator window can display one or more logical windows of information. A window displays all or part of a Work buffer. Figure 6-5 on page 155 shows a screen with two windows.

REPEAT FACTOR

A number that precedes a Unit of Measure (page 193) is a Repeat Factor. Just as the 5 in *5 inches* causes you to consider *5 inches* as a single Unit of Measure, so a Repeat Factor causes vim to group more than one Unit of Measure and consider it as a single Unit of Measure. For example, the command **w** moves the cursor forward 1 word, the command **5w** moves it forward 5 words, and the command **250w** moves it forward 250 words. If you do not specify a Repeat Factor, vim assumes a Repeat Factor of 1. If the Repeat Factor would move the cursor past the end of the file, the cursor is left at the end of the file.

CHAPTER SUMMARY

This summary of vim includes all the commands covered in this chapter, plus a few more. Table 6-12 lists some of the ways you can call vim from the command line.

Table 6-12 Calling vim

Command	Result
vim *filename*	Edits *filename* starting at line 1
vim +*n* ***filename***	Edits *filename* starting at line *n*
vim + *filename*	Edits *filename* starting at the last line
vim +/*pattern* ***filename***	Edits *filename* starting at the first line containing *pattern*
vim –r *filename*	Recovers *filename* after a system crash
vim –R *filename*	Edits *filename* readonly (same as opening the file with view)

You must be in Command mode to use commands that move the cursor by Units of Measure (Table 6-13). You can use these Units of Measure with Change, Delete, and Yank commands. Each of these commands can be preceded by a Repeat Factor.

Table 6-13 Moving the cursor by Units of Measure

Command	Moves the cursor
SPACE, **l** (ell), *or* RIGHT ARROW	Space to the right
h *or* LEFT ARROW	Space to the left
w	Word to the right

Table 6-13   Moving the cursor by Units of Measure (continued)

Command	Moves the cursor
W	Blank-delimited word to the right
b	Word to the left
B	Blank-delimited word to the left
$	End of line
e	End of word to the right
E	End of blank-delimited word to the right
0 (zero)	Beginning of line (cannot be used with a Repeat Factor)
RETURN	Beginning of next line
j *or* DOWN ARROW	Down one line
–	Beginning of previous line
k *or* UP ARROW	Up one line
)	End of sentence
(	Beginning of sentence
}	End of paragraph
{	Beginning of paragraph
%	Move to matching brace of same type at same nesting level

Table 6-14 shows the commands that enable you to view different parts of the Work buffer.

Table 6-14   Viewing the Work buffer

Command	Moves the cursor
CONTROL-D	Forward one-half window
CONTROL-U	Backward one-half window
CONTROL-F *or* PAGE DOWN	Forward one window
CONTROL-B *or* PAGE UP	Backward one window
*n***G**	To line *n* (without *n*, to the last line)
H	To top of window
M	To middle of window
L	To bottom of window

The commands in Table 6-15 enable you to add text to the buffer. All these commands, except **r**, leave vim in Input mode. You must press ESCAPE to return to Command mode.

Table 6-15 Adding text

Command	Adds text
i	Before cursor
I	Before first nonblank character on line
a	After cursor
A	At end of line
o	Opens a line below current line
O	Opens a line above current line
r	Replaces current character (no ESCAPE needed)
R	Replaces characters, starting with current character (overwrite until ESCAPE)

Table 6-16 lists commands that delete and change text. In this table *M* is a Unit of Measure that you can precede with a Repeat Factor, *n* is an optional Repeat Factor, and *c* is any character.

Table 6-16 Deleting and changing text

Command	Result
*n*x	Deletes the number of characters specified by *n*, starting with the current character
*n*X	Deletes *n* characters before the current character, starting with the character preceding the current character
d*M*	Deletes text specified by *M*
*n*dd	Deletes *n* lines
dt*c*	Deletes to the next character *c* on the current line
D	Deletes to end of the line
n~	Changes case of the next *n* characters

The following commands leave vim in Input mode. You must press ESCAPE to return to Command mode.

*n*s	Substitutes *n* characters

Table 6-16 Deleting and changing text (continued)

Command	Result
S	Substitutes for the entire line
c*M*	Changes text specified by *M*
*n*cc	Changes *n* lines
ct*c*	Changes to the next character *c* on the current line
C	Changes to end of line

Table 6-17 lists search commands. Here *rexp* is a regular expression that can be a simple string of characters.

Table 6-17 Searching

Command	Result
/*rexp*RETURN	Searches forward for *rexp*
?*rexp* RETURN	Searches backward for *rexp*
n	Repeats original search exactly
N	Repeats original search, in the opposite direction
/RETURN	Repeats original search forward
?RETURN	Repeats original search backward
f*c*	Positions the cursor on the next character *c* on the current line
F*c*	Positions the cursor on the previous character *c* on the current line
t*c*	Positions the cursor on the character before (to the left of) the next character *c* on the current line
T*c*	Positions the cursor on the character after (to the right of) the previous character *c* on the current line
;	Repeats the last **f**, **F**, **t**, or **T** command

The format of a Substitute command is

> :[*address*]s/*search-string*/*replacement-string*[/g]

where *address* is one line number or two line numbers separated by a comma. A . (period) represents the current line, **$** represents the last line, and % represents the entire file. You can use a marker or a search string in place of a line number. The *search-string* is a regular expression that can be a simple string of characters. The *replacement-string* is the replacement string. A **g** indicates a global replacement (more than one replacement per line).

Table 6-18 lists miscellaneous vim commands.

Table 6-18   Miscellaneous commands

Command	Result
J	Joins the current line and the following line
.	Repeats the most recent command that made a change
:w *filename*	Writes the contents of the Work buffer to *filename* (or to the current file if there is no *filename*)
:q	Quits vim
ZZ	Writes the contents of the Work buffer to the current file and quits vim
:f *or* CONTROL-G	Displays the filename, status, current line number, number of lines in the Work buffer, and percentage of the Work buffer preceding the current line
CONTROL-V	Inserts the next character literally even if it is a vim command (use in Input mode)

Table 6-19 lists commands that yank and put text. In this table *M* is a Unit of Measure that you can precede with a Repeat Factor and *n* is a Repeat Factor. You can precede any of these commands with the name of a buffer using the form **"*x*,** where *x* is the name of the buffer (**a–z**).

Table 6-19   Yanking and putting text

Command	Result
y*M*	Yanks text specified by *M*
***n*yy**	Yanks *n* lines
Y	Yanks to end of line
P	Puts text before or above
p	Puts text after or below

Table 6-20 lists advanced vim commands.

Table 6-20   Advanced commands

Command	Result
m*x*	Sets marker *x*, where *x* is a letter from **a** to **z**.
' ' (two single quotation marks)	Moves cursor back to its previous location.

Table 6-20   Advanced commands (continued)

Command	Result
' *x*	Moves cursor to line with marker *x*.
` *x*	Moves cursor to character with marker *x*.
:e *filename*	Edits *filename*, requiring you to write changes to the current file (with **:w** or **autowrite**) before editing the new file. Use **:e!** *filename* to discard changes to the current file. Use **:e!** without a filename to discard changes to the current file and start editing the saved version of the current file.
:n	Edits the next file when **vim** is started with multiple filename arguments. Requires you to write changes to the current file (with **:w** or **autowrite**) before editing the next file. Use **:n!** to discard changes to the current file and edit the next file.
:rew	Rewinds the filename list when **vim** is started with multiple filename arguments and starts editing with the first file. Requires you to write changes to the current file (with **:w** or **autowrite**) before editing the first file. Use **:rew!** to discard changes to the current file and edit the first file.
:sh	Starts a shell. Exit from the shell to return to vim.
:!*command*	Starts a shell and executes *command*.
!!*command*	Starts a shell, executes *command*, and places output in the Work buffer, replacing the current line.

EXERCISES

1. How can you cause vim to enter Input mode? How can you make vim revert to Command mode?

2. What is the Work buffer? Name two ways of writing the contents of the Work buffer to the disk.

3. Suppose that you are editing a file that contains the following paragraph and the cursor is on the second tilde (~):

```
The vim editor has a command, tilde (~),
that changes lowercase letters to
uppercase, and vice versa.
The ~ command works with a Unit of Measure or
a Repeat Factor, so you can change
the case of more than one character at a time.
```

How can you

a. Move the cursor to the end of the paragraph?

b. Move the cursor to the beginning of the word **Unit**?

c. Change the word **character** to **letter**?

4. While working in vim, with the cursor positioned on the first letter of a word, you give the command **x** followed by **p**. Explain what happens.

5. What are the differences between the following commands?

a. **i** and **I**

b. **a** and **A**

c. **o** and **O**

d. **r** and **R**

e. **u** and **U**

6. Which command would you use to search backward through the Work buffer for lines that start with the word **it**?

7. Which command substitutes all occurrences of the phrase **this week** with the phrase **next week**?

8. Consider the following scenario: You start vim to edit an existing file. You make many changes to the file and then realize that you deleted a critical section of the file early in your editing session. You want to get that section back but do not want to lose all the other changes you made. What would you do?

9. How can you move the current line to the beginning of the file?

10. Use vim to create the **letter_e** file of e's used on page 60. Use as few vim commands as possible. Which vim commands did you use?

ADVANCED EXERCISES

11. Which commands can you use to take a paragraph from one file and insert it in a second file?

12. Create a file that contains the following list, and then execute commands from within vim to sort the list and display it in two columns. (*Hint:* Refer to page 794 for more information on pr.)

```
Command mode
Input mode
Last Line mode
Work buffer
General-Purpose buffer
```

```
Named buffer
Regular Expression
Search String
Replacement String
Startup File
Repeat Factor
```

13. How do the Named buffers differ from the General-Purpose buffer?

14. Assume that your version of vim does not support multiple Undo commands. If you delete a line of text, then delete a second line, and then a third line, which commands would you use to recover the first two lines that you deleted?

15. Which command would you use to swap the words **hither** and **yon** on any line with any number of words between them? (You need not worry about special punctuation, just uppercase and lowercase letters and spaces.)

7

THE emacs EDITOR

In 1956 the Lisp (List processing) language was developed at MIT by John McCarthy. In its original conception, Lisp had only a few scalar (*atomic*) data types and only one *data structure* (page 950): a list. Lists could contain atomic data or other lists. Lisp supported recursion and nonnumeric data (exciting concepts in those Fortran and COBOL days) and, in the Cambridge culture at least, was once the favored implementation language. Richard Stallman and Guy Steele were part of this MIT Lisp culture. In 1975 they collaborated on emacs, which Stallman maintained by himself for a long time. This chapter discusses the emacs editor as implemented by the Free Software Foundation (GNU), version 22. The emacs home page is www.gnu.org/software/emacs.

HISTORY

The emacs editor was prototyped as a series of extension commands or macros for the late 1960s text editor TECO (Text Editor and COrrector). Its acronymic name, Editor MACroS, reflects this origin, although there have been many humorous reinterpretations, including ESCAPE META ALT CONTROL SHIFT, Emacs Makes All Computing Simple, and the unkind translation Eight Megabytes And Constantly Swapping.

EVOLUTION

Over time emacs has grown and evolved through more than 20 major revisions to the mainstream GNU version. The emacs editor, which is coded in C, contains a complete Lisp interpreter and fully supports the X Window System and mouse interaction. The original TECO macros are long gone, but emacs is still very much a work in progress. Version 22 has significant internationalization upgrades: an extended UTF-8 internal character set four times bigger than Unicode, along with fonts and keyboard input methods for more than 30 languages. Also, the user interface is moving in the direction of a WYSIWYG (what you see is what you get) word processor, which makes it easier for beginners to use the editor.

The emacs editor has always been considerably more than a text editor. Not having been developed originally in a UNIX environment, it does not adhere to the UNIX/Linux philosophy. Whereas a UNIX/Linux utility is typically designed to do one thing and to be used in conjunction with other utilities, emacs is designed to "do it all." Taking advantage of the underlying programming language (Lisp), emacs users tend to customize and extend the editor rather than to use existing utilities or create new general-purpose tools. Instead they share their ~/.emacs (customization) files.

Well before the emergence of the X Window System, Stallman put a great deal of thought and effort into designing a window-oriented work environment, and he used emacs as his research vehicle. Over time he built facilities within emacs for reading and composing email messages, reading and posting netnews, giving shell commands, compiling programs and analyzing error messages, running and debugging these programs, and playing games. Eventually it became possible to enter the emacs environment and not come out all day, switching from window to window and from file to file. If you had only an ordinary serial, character-based terminal, emacs gave you tremendous leverage.

In an X Window System environment, emacs does not need to control the whole display. Instead, it usually operates only one or two windows. The original, character-based work environment is still available and is covered in this chapter.

As a *language-sensitive* editor, emacs has special features that you can turn on to help edit text, nroff, TeX, Lisp, C, Fortran, and so on. These feature sets are called *modes*, but they are not related to the Command and Input modes found in vi, vim, and other editors. Because you never need to switch emacs between Input and Command modes, emacs is a *modeless* editor.

emacs VERSUS vim

See en.wikipedia.org/wiki/Editor_war for an interesting discussion of the ongoing editor wars; or search the Web for **emacs vs vi**.

Like vim, emacs is a display editor: It displays on the screen the text you are editing and changes the display as you type each command or insert new text. Unlike vim, emacs does not require you to keep track of whether you are in Command mode or Insert mode: Commands always use CONTROL or other special keys. The emacs editor inserts ordinary characters into the text you are editing (as opposed to using ordinary characters as commands), another trait of modeless editing. For many people this approach is convenient and natural.

As with vim, you use emacs to edit a file in a work area, or *buffer,* and have the option of writing this buffer back to the file on the disk when you are finished. With emacs, however, you can have many work buffers and switch among them without having to write the buffer out and read it back in. Furthermore, you can display multiple buffers at one time, each in its own window within emacs. This way of displaying files is often helpful when you are cutting and pasting text or when you want to keep C declarations visible while editing related code in another part of a file.

Like vim, emacs has a rich, extensive command set for moving about in the buffer and altering text. This command set is not "cast in concrete"—you can change or customize commands at any time. Any key can be coupled (*bound*) to any command to match a particular keyboard better or to fulfill a personal whim. Usually key bindings are set in the ~/.emacs startup file, but they can also be changed interactively during a session. All the key bindings described in this chapter are standard on the current versions of GNU emacs.

Too many key bindings

caution If you change too many key bindings, you may produce a command set that you will not remember or that will make it impossible for you to return to the standard bindings in the same session.

Finally, and very unlike vim, emacs allows you to use Lisp to write new commands or override old ones. Stallman calls this feature *online extensibility,* but it would take a gutsy Lisp guru to write and debug a new command while editing text. It is much more common to add debugged commands to the **.emacs** file, where they are loaded when you start emacs. Experienced emacs users often write modes, or environments, that are conditionally loaded by emacs for specific tasks. For more information on the **.emacs** file, see page 250.

The screen and emacs windows

tip In this chapter, the term *screen* denotes a character-based terminal screen or a terminal emulator window in a graphical environment. The term *window* refers to an emacs window within a screen.

emacs **and the X Window System**

tip   Since version 19, GNU emacs has fully embraced the X Window System environment. If you start emacs from a terminal emulator window running in a graphical environment, you will bring up the X interface (GUI) to emacs. This book does not cover the graphical interface; use the **–nw** option when you start emacs to bring up the textual interface in any environment. See "Starting emacs" below.

COMMAND-LINE emacs VERSUS GRAPHICAL emacs

This book is about the command-line interface to Linux. This chapter is mostly about the command-line interface to emacs. See page 215 for a look at some of the graphical features emacs offers.

TUTORIAL: GETTING STARTED WITH emacs

The emacs editor has many, many features, and there are many ways to use it. Its complete manual includes more than 35 chapters. Nevertheless, you can do a considerable amount of meaningful work with a relatively small subset of the commands. This section describes a simple editing session, explaining how to start and exit from emacs and how to move the cursor and delete text. Coverage of some issues is postponed or simplified in the interest of clarity.

emacs **online tutorial**

tip   The emacs editor provides an online tutorial. After starting emacs, press CONTROL-H **t** to start the tutorial. Press CONTROL-X CONTROL-C to exit from emacs. If you have more than one emacs window open, see the tip "Closing the help window" on page 223.

STARTING emacs

To edit a file named **sample** using emacs as a text-based editor, enter the following command:

```
$ emacs -nw -q sample
```

The **–nw** option, which must be the first option on the emacs command line, tells emacs not to use its X interface (GUI). The **–q** option tells emacs *not* to read the **~/.emacs** startup file. Not reading this file guarantees that emacs will behave in a standard manner and can be useful for beginners or for other users who want to bypass a .emacs file.

The preceding command starts emacs, reads the file named **sample** into a buffer, and displays its contents on the screen or window. If no file has this name, emacs displays a blank screen with (**New File**) at the bottom (Figure 7-1). If the file exists, emacs displays the file and a different message (Figure 7-3, page 211). If you start emacs without naming a file on the command line, it displays a welcome screen that includes usage information and a list of basic commands (Figure 7-2).

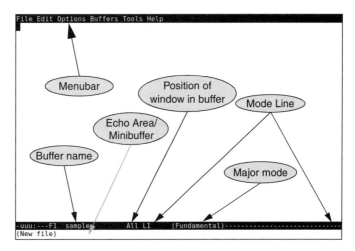

Figure 7-1   The emacs new file screen

Initially, emacs displays a single window. At the top of the window is a reverse-video menubar that you can access using a mouse or keyboard. From the keyboard, F10, META-` (back tick), or META-x **tmm-menubar** RETURN displays the Menubar Completion List window. For more information refer to "Using the Menubar from the Keyboard" on page 221.

At the bottom of the emacs window is a reverse-video titlebar called the *Mode Line*. At a minimum, the Mode Line shows which buffer the window is viewing, whether the buffer has been changed, which major and minor modes are in effect, and how far down the buffer the window is positioned. When multiple windows appear on the screen, one Mode Line appears in each window. At the bottom of the screen,

Figure 7-2   The emacs welcome screen

emacs leaves a single line open. This *Echo Area* and *Minibuffer* line (they coexist on one line) is used for messages and special one-line commands.

The emacs manual

tip   The emacs manual is available from within emacs. While you are running emacs, give the command CONTROL-H **r**. Then use the ARROW keys to scroll to the section you want to view and press RETURN. Alternatively, type **m** (which moves the cursor to the Minibuffer) followed by the name of the section (menu) you want to view. Type TAB to cause emacs to complete the menu name; menu completion works similarly to pathname completion (page 233). See the tip on page 223 for instructions on how to close the Help window and page 223 for more information on online help.

For example, to view the Minibuffer section of the online manual, give the command CONTROL-H **r m minibuffer** RETURN. You can also give the command CONTROL-H **r m min** TAB RETURN.

If you make an error while you are typing in the Minibuffer, emacs displays the error message in the Echo Area. The error message overwrites the command you were typing, but emacs restores the command in a few seconds. The brief display of the error messages gives you time to read it before you continue typing the command from where you left off. More detailed information is available from the Minibuffer menu of the emacs online manual (see the preceding tip).

A cursor is either in the window or in the Minibuffer. All input and nearly all editing take place at the cursor. As you type ordinary characters, emacs inserts them at the cursor position. If characters are under the cursor or to its right, they are pushed to the right as you type, so no characters are lost.

EXITING

The command to exit from emacs is CONTROL-X CONTROL-C. You can give this command at almost any time (in some modes you may have to press CONTROL-G first). It stops emacs gracefully, asking if you want to keep the changes you made during the editing session.

If you want to cancel a half-typed command or stop a running command before it is done, press CONTROL-G. The emacs editor displays **Quit** in the Echo Area and waits for another command.

INSERTING TEXT

Typing an ordinary (printing) character pushes the cursor and any characters to the right of the cursor one position to the right and inserts the new character in the space opened by moving the characters.

DELETING CHARACTERS

Depending on the keyboard and the emacs startup file, different keys may delete characters in different ways. CONTROL-D typically deletes the character under the cursor, as do DELETE and DEL. BACKSPACE typically deletes the character to the left of the cursor. Try each of these keys and see what it does.

More about deleting characters

tip If the instructions described in this section do not work, read the emacs info section on **deletion**.
Give this command from a shell prompt:

$ `info emacs`

From info give the command **m deletion** to display a document that describes in detail how to
delete small amounts of text. Use the SPACE bar to scroll through the document. Type **q** to exit from
info. You can read the same information in the emacs online manual (CONTROL-H **r**; page 223)

Start emacs and type a few lines of text. If you make a mistake, correct the error
using the deletion characters discussed previously. The RETURN key inserts an invisible
end-of-line character in the buffer and returns the cursor to the left margin, one line
down. It is possible to back up past the start of a line and up to the end of the previous line. Figure 7-3 shows a sample buffer.

Use the ARROW keys

tip Sometimes the easiest way to move the cursor is by using the LEFT, RIGHT, UP, and DOWN ARROW keys.

MOVING THE CURSOR

You can position the cursor over any character in the emacs window and move the
window so it displays any portion of the buffer. You can move the cursor forward
or backward through the text (Figure 6-8, page 164) by various textual units—for
example, characters, words, sentences, lines, and paragraphs. Any of the cursor-
movement commands can be preceded by a repetition count (CONTROL-U followed by a
numeric argument), which causes the cursor to move that number of textual units
through the text. Refer to page 218 for a discussion of numeric arguments.

Figure 7-3   Sample buffer

CONTROL-B   CONTROL-F

Figure 7-4   Moving the cursor by characters

MOVING THE CURSOR BY CHARACTERS

CONTROL-F   Pressing the RIGHT ARROW key or CONTROL-F moves the cursor forward (to the right) one character. If the cursor is at the end of a line, these commands wrap it to the beginning of the next line. For example, the command CONTROL-U 7 CONTROL-F moves the cursor seven characters forward.

CONTROL-B   Pressing the LEFT ARROW key or CONTROL-B moves the cursor backward (to the left) one character. For example, the command CONTROL-U 7 CONTROL-B moves the cursor seven characters backward. The command CONTROL-B works in a manner similar to CONTROL-F (Figure 7-4).

MOVING THE CURSOR BY WORDS

META-f   Pressing META-f moves the cursor forward one word. To invoke this command, hold down the META or ALT key while you press **f**. If the keyboard you are using does not have either of these keys, press ESCAPE, release it, and then press **f**. This command leaves the cursor on the first character that is not part of the word the cursor started on. The command CONTROL-U 4 META-f moves the cursor forward one space past the end of the fourth word. For more information refer to "Keys: Notation and Use" on page 216.

META-b   Pressing META-b moves the cursor backward one word, leaving the cursor on the first letter of the word it started on. If the cursor was on the first letter of a word, META-b moves the cursor to the first letter of the preceding word. The command META-b works in a manner similar to META-f (Figure 7-5).

MOVING THE CURSOR BY LINES

CONTROL-A
CONTROL-E
CONTROL-P
CONTROL-N

Pressing CONTROL-A moves the cursor to the beginning of the line it is on; CONTROL-E moves it to the end. Pressing the UP ARROW key or CONTROL-P moves the cursor up one line to the position directly above where the cursor started; pressing the DOWN ARROW key or CONTROL-N moves it down. As with the other cursor-movement keys, you can precede CONTROL-P and CONTROL-N with CONTROL-U and a numeric argument to move the cursor up or down multiple lines. You can also use pairs of these commands to move the cursor up to the beginning of the previous line, down to the end of the following line, and so on (Figure 7-6).

Figure 7-5   Moving the cursor by words

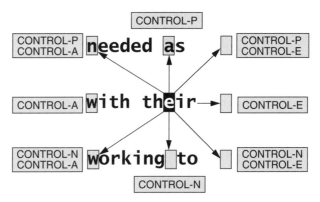

Figure 7-6   Moving the cursor by lines

MOVING THE CURSOR BY SENTENCES, PARAGRAPHS, AND WINDOW POSITION

META-a, META-e   Pressing META-a moves the cursor to the beginning of the sentence the cursor is on;
META-{, META-}   META-e moves the cursor to the end. META-{ moves the cursor to the beginning of the
paragraph the cursor is on; META-} moves it to the end. (Sentences and paragraphs are
defined starting on page 241.) You can precede any of these commands with a repetition count (CONTROL-U followed by a numeric argument) to move the cursor by that
many sentences or paragraphs.

META-r   Pressing META-r moves the cursor to the beginning of the middle line of the window.
You can precede this command with CONTROL-U and a line number (here CONTROL-U does
not indicate a repetition count but rather a screen line number). The command CON-
TROL-U 0 META-r moves the cursor to the beginning of the top line (line zero) in the window. The command CONTROL-U – (minus sign) moves the cursor to the beginning of the
last line of the window (Figure 7-7).

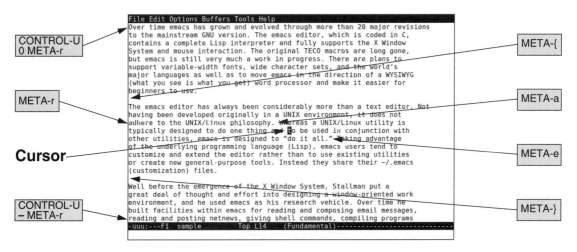

Figure 7-7   Moving the cursor by sentences, paragraphs, and window position

EDITING AT THE CURSOR POSITION

Entering text requires no commands once you position the cursor in the window at the location you want to enter text. When you type text, emacs displays that text at the position of the cursor. Any text under or to the right of the cursor is pushed to the right. If you type enough characters so the text would extend past the right edge of the window, emacs displays a backslash (\) near the right edge of the window and wraps the text to the next line. The backslash appears on the screen but is not saved as part of the file and is never printed. Although you can create an arbitrarily long line, some Linux tools have problems with text files containing such lines. To split a line into two lines, position the cursor at the location you want to split the line and press RETURN.

Deleting text   Pressing BACKSPACE removes characters to the left of the cursor. The cursor and the remainder of the text on this line both move to the left each time you press BACKSPACE. To join a line with the line above it, position the cursor on the first character of the second line and press BACKSPACE.

Press CONTROL-D to delete the character under the cursor. The cursor remains stationary, but the remainder of the text on the line moves left to replace the deleted character. See the tip "More about deleting characters" on page 211 if either of these keys does not work as described here.

SAVING AND RETRIEVING THE BUFFER

No matter what changes you make to a buffer during an emacs session, the associated file does not change until you save the buffer. If you leave emacs without saving the buffer (emacs allows you to do so if you are persistent), the file is not changed and emacs discards the work you did during the session.

Backups   As it writes a buffer's edited contents back to the file, emacs may optionally first make a backup of the original file. You can choose to make no backups, one level of backup (default), or an arbitrary number of levels of backups. The level one backup filenames are formed by appending a tilde (~) to the original filename. The multilevel backups have .~n~ appended to the filename, where *n* is the sequential backup number, starting with 1. The **version-control** variable dictates how emacs saves backups. See page 250 for instructions on assigning a value to an emacs variable.

Saving the buffer   The command CONTROL-X CONTROL-S saves the current buffer in its associated file. The emacs editor confirms a successful save by displaying an appropriate message in the Echo Area.

Visiting another file   When you are editing a file with emacs and want to edit another file (emacs documentation refers to editing a file as *visiting* a file), you can copy the new file into a new emacs buffer by giving the command CONTROL-X CONTROL-F. The emacs editor prompts for a filename, reads that file into a new buffer, and displays that buffer in the current window. Having two files open in one editing session is more convenient than exiting from emacs, returning to the shell, and then starting a new copy of emacs to edit a second file.

Visiting a file with CONTROL-X CONTROL-F

tip   When you give the command CONTROL-X CONTROL-F to visit a file, emacs displays the pathname of
the directory in which it assumes the file is located. Normally it displays the pathname of the working directory, but in some situations emacs displays a different pathname, such as the pathname
of your home directory. Edit this pathname if it is not pointing to the correct directory. This command provides pathname completion (page 233).

THE emacs GUI

The emacs editor originally ran on serial ASCII (textual) terminals. Over time, with
the introduction of graphical displays, emacs has become more graphically oriented. Full mouse support was introduced in version 19. The emacs editor is still
evolving toward full internationalization, accessibility, and a simplified user experience that appeals to the widest possible audience. New features include a colorful
menubar and toolbar, mixed text and graphics, tooltips, drag and drop editing, and
new GUIs for browsing directories and selecting fonts. Many of these features are
available from the emacs GUI only.

This chapter discusses how to use emacs from the keyboard

tip   Because of the command-line orientation of this book, this chapter discusses how to use emacs
from the keyboard. This section provides a brief introduction to the emacs GUI for readers who
want to pursue that path.

To see what graphical mode looks like, start emacs without the **–nw** option from a
terminal emulator window in a graphical environment; emacs displays a welcome
screen (Figure 7-8) that includes clickable hyperlinks to local help files and to the

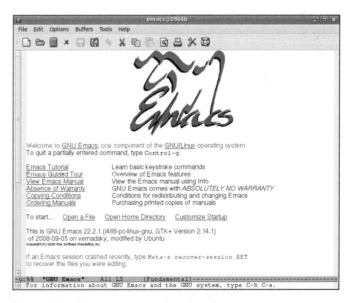

Figure 7-8   The emacs graphical welcome screen

GNU home page. The emacs GUI presents a menubar and toolbar you can make selections from using a mouse. All keyboard commands in this chapter work while emacs displays its GUI.

BASIC EDITING COMMANDS

This section takes a more detailed look at the fundamental emacs editing commands. It covers editing a single file in a single emacs window.

KEYS: NOTATION AND USE

Although emacs has been internationalized, its keyboard input is still an evolved and extended ASCII code, usually with one keystroke producing one byte. ASCII keyboards have a typewriter-style SHIFT key and a CONTROL key. Some keyboards also have a META (diamond or ALT) key that controls the eighth bit. It takes seven bits to describe an ASCII character; the eighth bit of an eight-bit byte can be used to communicate additional information. Because so much of the emacs command set is in the nonprinting CONTROL or META case, Stallman was one of the first to develop a nonnumeric notation for describing keystrokes.

His solution, which is still used in the emacs community, is clear and unambiguous (Table 7-1). It uses the capital letters **C** and **M** to denote holding down the CONTROL and META (or ALT) keys, respectively, and a few simple acronyms for the most common special characters, such as RET (this book uses RETURN), LFD (LINEFEED), DEL (DELETE), ESC (ESCAPE), SPC (SPACE), and TAB. Most emacs documentation, including the online help, uses this notation.

Table 7-1   emacs key notation

Character	Classic emacs notation
(lowercase) a	a
(uppercase) SHIFT-a	A
CONTROL-a	C-a
CONTROL-A	C-a (do *not* use SHIFT), equivalent to CONTROL-a
META-a	M-a
META-A	M-A (*do* use SHIFT), different from M-a
CONTROL-META-a	C-M-a
META-CONTROL-a	M-C-a (not used frequently)

The emacs use of keys had some problems. Many keyboards had no META key, and some operating systems discarded the META bit. In addition, the emacs command set clashes with the increasingly outdated XON-XOFF flow control, which also uses CONTROL-S and CONTROL-Q.

Under OS X, most keyboards do not have a META or ALT key. See page 935 for an explanation of how to set up the OPTION key to perform the same functions as the META key on a Macintosh.

The missing META key issue was resolved by making an optional two-key sequence starting with ESCAPE equate to a META character. If the keyboard you are using does not have a META or ALT key, you can use the two-key ESCAPE sequence by pressing the ESCAPE key, releasing it, and then pressing the key following the META key in this book. For example, you can type ESCAPE a instead of META-a or type ESCAPE CONTROL-A instead of CONTROL-META-a.

Stallman considers XON-XOFF flow control to be a historical issue, and has no plans to change the emacs command set. However, the online help emacs FAQ offers several workarounds for this issue.

The notation used in this book

tip   This book uses an uppercase letter following the CONTROL key and a lowercase letter following the META key. In either case *you do not have to hold down the* SHIFT *key while entering a* CONTROL *or* META *character.* Although the META uppercase character (that is, META-A) is a different character, it is usually set up to cause no action or to have the same effect as its lowercase counterpart.

KEY SEQUENCES AND COMMANDS

In emacs the relationship between key sequences (one or more keys that you press together or in sequence to issue an emacs command) and commands is very flexible, and there is considerable opportunity for exercising your personal preference. You can translate and remap key sequences to other commands and replace or reprogram commands.

Although most emacs documentation glosses over the details and talks about keystrokes as though they were the commands, it is important to recognize that the underlying machinery remains separate from the key sequences and to understand that you can change the behavior of the key sequences and the commands. For more information refer to "Customizing emacs" on page 249.

META-x: RUNNING A COMMAND WITHOUT A KEY BINDING

The emacs keymaps (the tables, or vectors, that emacs uses to translate key sequences into commands [page 251]) are very crowded, and often it is not possible to bind every command to a key sequence. You can execute any command by name by preceding it with META-x. When you press META-x, the emacs editor prompts you for a command in the Echo Area. After you enter the command name and press RETURN, it executes the command.

Smart completion   When a command has no common key sequence, it is sometimes described as META-x *command-name*. The emacs editor provides *smart completion* for most answers it prompts for. After you type part of a response to a prompt, press SPACE or TAB to cause emacs to complete, if possible, to the end of the current word or the whole command, respectively. Forcing a completion past the last unambiguous point or typing a question mark (?) opens a Completion List window that displays a list of alternatives. Smart completion works in a manner similar to pathname completion (page 233).

NUMERIC ARGUMENTS

Some of the emacs editing commands accept a numeric argument as a repetition count. Place this argument immediately before the key sequence for the command. The absence of an argument almost always means a count of 1. Even an ordinary alphabetic character can have a numeric argument, which means "insert this many times." Use either of the following techniques to give a numeric argument to a command:

- Press META with each digit (0–9) or the minus sign (–). For example, to insert 10 z characters, type META-1 META-0 z.

- Use CONTROL-U to begin a string of digits, including the minus sign. For example, to move the cursor forward 20 words, type CONTROL-U 20 META-f.

CONTROL-U   For convenience, CONTROL-U defaults to *multiply by 4* when you do not follow it with a string of one or more digits. For example, entering CONTROL-U r means insert **rrrr** (4 * 1), whereas CONTROL-U CONTROL-U r means insert **rrrrrrrrrrrrrrrr** (4 * 4 * 1). For quick partial scrolling of a tall window, you may find it convenient to use repeated sequences of CONTROL-U CONTROL-V to scroll down 4 lines, CONTROL-U META-v to scroll up 4 lines, CONTROL-U CONTROL-U CONTROL-V to scroll down 16 lines, or CONTROL-U CONTROL-U META-v to scroll up 16 lines.

POINT AND THE CURSOR

Point is the place in a buffer where editing takes place and is where the cursor is positioned. Strictly speaking, Point is at the left edge of the cursor—think of it as lying *between* two characters.

Each window has its own Point, but there is only one cursor. When the cursor is in a window, moving the cursor also moves Point. Switching the cursor out of a window does not change that window's Point; it is in the same place when you switch the cursor back to that window.

All of the cursor-movement commands described previously also move Point.

SCROLLING THROUGH A BUFFER

CONTROL-V   A buffer is likely to be much larger than the window through which it is viewed, so
META-v   you need a way of moving the display of the buffer contents up or down so as to
CONTROL-L   position the interesting part in the window. *Scrolling forward* refers to moving the

text upward, with new lines entering at the bottom of the window. Press CONTROL-V or the PAGE DOWN key to scroll forward one window (minus two lines for context). *Scrolling backward* refers to moving the text downward, with new lines entering at the top of the window. Press META-v or the PAGE UP key to scroll backward one window (again leaving two lines for context). Pressing CONTROL-L clears the screen and repaints it, moving the line the cursor is on to the middle line of the window. This command is useful if the screen becomes garbled.

A numeric argument to CONTROL-V or META-v means "scroll that many lines"; for example, CONTROL-U 10 CONTROL-V means scroll forward ten lines. A numeric argument to CONTROL-L means "scroll the text so the cursor is on that line of the window," where 0 means the top line and –1 means the bottom line, just above the Mode Line. Scrolling occurs automatically if you exceed the window limits when pressing CONTROL-P or CONTROL-N.

META-<
META->

You can move the cursor to the beginning of the buffer with META-< or to the end of the buffer with META->.

Erasing Text

Delete versus kill

When you erase text you can discard it or move it into a holding area and optionally bring it back later. The term *delete* means *permanently discard,* and the term *kill* means *move to a holding area.* The holding area, called the *Kill Ring,* can hold several pieces of killed text. You can use the text in the Kill Ring in many ways (refer to "Cut and Paste: Yanking Killed Text" on page 228).

META-d
CONTROL-K

The META-d command kills from the cursor forward to the end of the current word. CONTROL-K kills from the cursor forward to the end of the current line. It does *not* delete the line-ending LINEFEED character unless Point and the cursor are just to the left of the LINEFEED. This setup allows you to reach the left end of a line with CONTROL-A, kill the whole line with CONTROL-K, and then immediately type a replacement line without having to reopen a hole for the new line. Another consequence is that, from the beginning of the line, it takes the command CONTROL-K CONTROL-K (or CONTROL-U 2 CONTROL-K) to kill the text and close the hole.

Searching for Text

The emacs editor allows you to search for text in the following ways:

- Incrementally for a character string

- Incrementally for a regular expression (possible but uncommon)

- For a complete character string

- For a complete regular expression (Appendix A)

You can run each of the four types of searches either forward or backward in the buffer.

The *complete* searches behave in the same manner as searches carried out in other editors. Searching begins only when the search string is complete. In contrast, an *incremental* search begins when you type the first character of the search string and keeps going as you enter additional characters. Initially this approach may sound confusing, but it is surprisingly useful.

INCREMENTAL SEARCHES

CONTROL-S
CONTROL-R

A single command selects the direction of and starts an incremental search. CONTROL-S starts a forward incremental search and CONTROL-R starts a reverse incremental search.

When you start an incremental search, emacs prompts you with **I-search:** in the Echo Area. When you enter a character, it immediately searches for that character in the buffer. If it finds that character, emacs moves Point and cursor to that position so you can see the search progress. If the search fails, emacs tells you so.

After you enter each character of the search string, you can take one of several actions depending on the result of the search to that point. The following paragraphs list results and corresponding actions.

- The search finds the string you are looking for, leaving the cursor positioned just to its right. You can stop the search and leave the cursor in its new position by pressing RETURN. (Any emacs command not related to searching will also stop the search but remembering exactly which ones apply can be difficult. For a new user, RETURN is safer.)

- The search finds a string but it is not the one you are looking for. You can refine the search string by adding another letter, press CONTROL-R or CONTROL-S to look for the next occurrence of this search string, or press RETURN to stop the search and leave the cursor where it is.

- The search hits the beginning or end of the buffer and reports **Failing I-Search.** You can proceed in one of the following ways:

  - If you mistyped the search string, press BACKSPACE as needed to remove characters from the search string. The text and cursor in the window jump backward in step as you remove characters.

  - If you want to wrap past the beginning or end of the buffer and continue searching, you can force a wrap by pressing CONTROL-R or CONTROL-S.

  - If the search has not found the string you are looking for but you want to leave the cursor at its current position, press RETURN to stop the search.

  - If the search has gone wrong and you just want to get back to where you started, press CONTROL-G (the quit character). From an unsuccessful search, a single CONTROL-G backs out all the characters in the search string that could not be found. If this action returns you to a place you wish to continue searching from, you can add characters to the search string again. If you do not want to continue the search from that position, pressing CONTROL-G a second time stops the search and leaves the cursor where it was initially.

NONINCREMENTAL SEARCHES

CONTROL-S RETURN
CONTROL-R RETURN

If you prefer that your searches succeed or fail without showing all the intermediate results, you can give the nonincremental command CONTROL-S RETURN to search forward or CONTROL-R RETURN to search backward. Searching does not begin until you enter a search string in response to the emacs prompt and press RETURN again. Neither of these commands wraps past the end of the buffer.

REGULAR EXPRESSION SEARCHES

You can perform both incremental and nonincremental regular expression searching in emacs. Use the commands listed in Table 7-2 to begin a regular expression search.

Table 7-2   Searching for regular expressions

Command	Result
META-CONTROL-s	Incrementally searches forward for a regular expression; prompts for a regular expression one character at a time
META-CONTROL-r	Incrementally searches backward for a regular expression; prompts for a regular expression one character at a time
META-CONTROL-s RETURN	Prompts for and then searches forward for a complete regular expression
META-CONTROL-r RETURN	Prompts for and then searches backward for a complete regular expression

USING THE MENUBAR FROM THE KEYBOARD

This section describes how to use the keyboard to make selections from the emacs menubar (Figure 7-1, page 209). In a graphical environment you can also use a mouse for this purpose. The menubar selections are appropriate to the Major mode emacs is in (see "Major Modes: Language-Sensitive Editing" on page 239). For example, when you are editing a C program, the menubar includes a C menu that holds commands specific to editing and indenting C programs.

To make a selection from the menubar, first press the F10 function key, META-` (back tick), or META-x **tmm-menubar** RETURN. The emacs editor displays the Menubar Completion List window populated with the top-level menubar selections (File, Edit,

```
File Edit Options Buffers Tools Minibuf Help
Over time emacs has grown and evolved through more than 20 major revisions
to the mainstream GNU version. The emacs editor, which is coded in C,
contains a complete Lisp interpreter and fully supports the X Window
System and mouse interaction. The original TECO macros are long gone,
but emacs is still very much a work in progress. There are plans to
support variable-width fonts, wide character sets, and the world's
major languages as well as to move emacs in the direction of a WYSIWYG
(what you see is what you get) word processor and make it easier for
beginners to use.

The emacs editor has always been considerably more than a text editor. Not
having been developed originally in a UNIX environment, it does not
adhere to the UNIX/Linux philosophy. Whereas a UNIX/Linux utility is
typically designed to do one thing and to be used in conjunction with
-uuu:---F1  sample        Top L1     (Fundamental)--------------------------
Press PageUp key to reach this buffer from the minibuffer.
Alternatively, you can use Up/Down keys (or your History keys) to change
the item in the minibuffer, and press RET when you are done, or press the
marked letters to pick up your choice.  Type C-g or ESC ESC ESC to cancel.
In this buffer, type RET to select the completion near point.

Possible completions are:
f==>File                           e==>Edit
o==>Options                        b==>Buffers
t==>Tools                          h==>Help
-uuu:%*-F1  *Completions*   All L1    (Completion List)--------------------
Menu bar (up/down to change, PgUp to menu): f==>File
```

Figure 7-9   The top-level Menubar Completion List window

Options, and so on), with the current selection displayed in the Minibuffer. Figure 7-9 shows the Menubar Completion List window with **File** as the current selection in the Minibuffer.

With the Menubar Completion List window open, you can perform any of the following actions:

- Cancel the menu selection by pressing CONTROL-G or ESCAPE ESCAPE ESCAPE. The display returns to the state it was in before you opened the Menubar Completion List window.

- Use the UP ARROW and DOWN ARROW keys to display successive menu selections in the Minibuffer. Press RETURN to choose the displayed selection.

- Type the one-character abbreviation of a selection as shown in the Menubar Completion List window to choose the selection. You do not need to press RETURN.

- Press PAGE UP or META-v to move the cursor to the Menubar Completion List window. Use the ARROW keys to move the cursor between selections. Press RETURN to choose the selection the cursor is on. You can type ESCAPE ESCAPE ESCAPE to back out of this window and return the cursor to the Minibuffer.

When you make a choice from the top-level menu, emacs displays the corresponding second-level menu in the Menubar Completion List window. Repeat one of the preceding actions to make a selection from this menu. When you make a final selection, emacs closes the Menubar Completion List window and takes the action you selected. More information is available from the Menu Bar menu of the emacs online manual (see the tip on page 210).

ONLINE HELP

CONTROL-H The emacs help system is always available. With the default key bindings, you can start it with CONTROL-H. The help system then prompts you for a one-letter help command. If you do not know which help command you want, type **?** or CONTROL-H to switch the current window to a list of help commands, each with a one-line description; emacs again requests a one-letter help command. If you decide you do not want help after all, type CONTROL-G to cancel the help request and return to the former buffer.

If the help output is only a single line, it appears in the Echo Area. If it is more than one line, the output appears in its own window. Use CONTROL-V and META-v to scroll forward and backward through the buffer (page 218). You can move the cursor between windows with CONTROL-X o (lowercase "o"). See page 236 for a discussion of working with multiple windows.

Closing the help window

tip To delete the help window while the cursor is in the window that holds the text you are editing, type CONTROL-X **1** (one). Alternatively, you can move the cursor to the help window (CONTROL-X **o** [lowercase "o"]) and type CONTROL-X **0** (zero) to delete the current window.

If help displays a window that occupies the entire screen, as is the case with CONTROL-H **n** (emacs news) and CONTROL-H **t** (emacs tutorial), you can kill the help buffer by pressing CONTROL-X **k** or switch buffers by pressing CONTROL-X **b** (both discussed on page 235).

On many terminals the BACKSPACE or LEFT ARROW key generates CONTROL-H. If you forget that you are using emacs and try to back over a few characters, you may unintentionally enter the help system. This action does not pose a danger to the buffer you are editing, but it can be unsettling to lose the window contents and not have a clear picture of how to restore it. While you are being prompted for the type of help you want, you can type CONTROL-G to remove the prompt and return to editing the buffer. Some users elect to put help on a different key (page 251). Table 7-3 lists some of the help commands.

Table 7-3 Help commands

Command	Type of help offered
CONTROL-H a	Prompts for a string and displays a list of commands whose names contain that string.

Table 7-3   Help commands (continued)

Command	Type of help offered
CONTROL-H b	Displays a long table of the key bindings in effect.
CONTROL-H c *key-sequence*	Displays the name of the command bound to *key-sequence*. Multiple key sequences are allowed. For a long key sequence where only the first part is recognized, the command describes the first part and quietly inserts the unrecognized part into the buffer. This can happen with three-character function keys (F1, F2, and so on, on the keyboard) that generate character sequences such as ESCAPE [SHIFT.
CONTROL-H f	Prompts for the name of a Lisp function and displays the documentation for it. Because commands are Lisp functions, you can use a command name with this command.
CONTROL-H i	Displays the top info (page 36) menu where you can browse for emacs or other documentation.
CONTROL-H k *key-sequence*	Displays the name and documentation of the command bound to *key-sequence*. (See the notes on CONTROL-H **c**.)
CONTROL-H l (lowercase "l")	Displays the last 100 characters typed. The record is kept *after* the first-stage keyboard translation. If you have customized the keyboard translation table, you must make a mental reverse translation.
CONTROL-H m	Displays the documentation and special key bindings for the current Major mode (Text, C, Fundamental, and so on, [page 240]).
CONTROL-H n	Displays the emacs news file, which lists recent changes to emacs, ordered with the most recent changes first.
CONTROL-H r	Displays the emacs manual.
CONTROL-H t	Runs an emacs tutorial session.
CONTROL-H v	Prompts for a Lisp variable name and displays the documentation for that variable.
CONTROL-H w	Prompts for a command name and identifies any key sequence bound to that command. Multiple key sequences are allowed. (See the notes on CONTROL-H **c**.)

optional   As this abridged presentation makes clear, you can use the help system to browse through the emacs internal Lisp system. For the curious, following is Stallman's list of strings that match many names in the Lisp system. To get a view of the internal functionality of emacs, you can use any of these strings with CONTROL-H **a** (help system list of commands) or META-x **apropos** (prompts for a string and lists variables whose names contain that string).

backward	dir	insert	previous	view
beginning	down	kill	region	what
buffer	end	line	register	window
case	file	list	screen	word
change	fill	mark	search	yank
char	find	mode	sentence	
defun	forward	next	set	
delete	goto	page	sexp	
describe	indent	paragraph	up	

ADVANCED EDITING

The basic emacs commands suffice for many editing tasks but the serious user will quickly discover the need for more power. This section presents some of the more advanced emacs capabilities.

UNDOING CHANGES

An editing session begins when you read a file into an emacs buffer. At that point the buffer content matches the file exactly. As you insert text and give editing commands, the buffer content becomes increasingly more different from the file. If you are satisfied with the changes, you can write the altered buffer back out to the file and end the session.

Near the left end of the Mode Line (Figure 7-1, page 209) is an indicator that shows the modification state of the buffer displayed in the window. The three possible states are –– (not modified), ** (modified), and %% (readonly).

The emacs editor keeps a record of all keys you have pressed (text and commands) since the beginning of the editing session, up to a limit currently set at 20,000 characters. If you are within this limit, it is possible to undo the entire session for this buffer, one change at a time. If you have multiple buffers (page 235), each buffer has its own undo record.

Undoing is considered so important that it has a backup key sequence, in case a keyboard cannot easily handle the primary sequence. The two sequences are CONTROL-_ (underscore, which on old ASR-33 TTY keyboards was LEFT ARROW) and CONTROL-X **u**. When you type CONTROL-_, emacs undoes the last command and moves the cursor to the position of the change in the buffer so you can see what happened. If you type CONTROL-_ a second time, the next-to-last command is undone, and so on. If you keep typing CONTROL-_, eventually the buffer will be returned to its original unmodified state and the ✷✷ Mode Line indicator will change to −−.

When you break the string of Undo commands by typing text or giving any command except Undo, all reverse changes you made during the string of undos become a part of the change record and can themselves be undone. This strategy offers a way to redo some or all of the undo operations. If you decide you backed up too far, type a command (something innocuous that does not change the buffer, such as CONTROL-F), and begin undoing your changes in reverse. Table 7-4 lists some examples of Undo commands.

Table 7-4   Undo commands

Commands	Result
CONTROL-_	Undoes the last change
CONTROL-_ CONTROL-F CONTROL-_	Undoes the last change and changes it back again
CONTROL-_ CONTROL-_	Undoes the last two changes
CONTROL-_ CONTROL-_ CONTROL-F CONTROL-_ CONTROL-_	Undoes two changes and changes them both back again
CONTROL-_ CONTROL-_ CONTROL-F CONTROL-_	Undoes two changes and changes the most recent one back again

If you do not remember the last change you made, you can type CONTROL-_ and undo it. If you wanted to make this change, type CONTROL-F CONTROL-_ to make the change again. If you modified a buffer by accident, you can keep typing CONTROL-_ until the Mode Line indicator shows −− once more.

If the buffer is completely ruined and you want to start over, issue the command META-x **revert-buffer** to discard the current buffer contents and reread the associated file. The emacs editor asks you to confirm your intentions.

POINT, MARK, AND REGION

Point is the current editing position in a buffer. You can move Point anywhere within the buffer by moving the cursor. It is also possible to set a marker called *Mark* in the buffer. The contiguous characters between Point and Mark (either one may come first) are called *Region*. Many commands operate on a buffer's Region, not just on the characters near Point.

MOVING MARK AND ESTABLISHING REGION

Mark is not as easy to move as Point. Once set, Mark can be moved only by setting it somewhere else. Each buffer has only one Mark. The CONTROL-@ (or CONTROL-SPACE) command explicitly sets Mark at the current cursor (and Point) position. Some keyboards generate CONTROL-@ when you type CONTROL-Q. Although this is not really a backup key binding, it is occasionally a convenient alternative. You can use CONTROL-X CONTROL-X to exchange Point and Mark (and move the cursor to the new Point).

To establish Region, you usually position the cursor (and Point) at one end of the desired Region, set Mark with CONTROL-@, and then move the cursor (and Point) to the other end of Region. If you forget where you left Mark, you can move the cursor back to it again by giving the command CONTROL-X CONTROL-X. You can move the cursor back and forth with repeated CONTROL-X CONTROL-X commands to show Region more clearly.

If a Region boundary is not to your liking, you can swap Point and Mark using CONTROL-X CONTROL-X to move the cursor from one end of Region to the other and then move Point. Continue until you are satisfied with Region.

OPERATING ON REGION

Table 7-5 lists selected commands that operate on Region. Give the command CONTROL-H **a region** to see a complete list of these commands.

Table 7-5   Operating on Region

Command	Result
META-w	Copies Region nondestructively (without killing it) to the Kill Ring
CONTROL-W	Kills Region
META-x print-region	Sends Region to the printer
META-x append-to-buffer	Prompts for a buffer and appends Region to that buffer
META-x append-to-file	Prompts for a filename and appends Region to that file
META-x capitalize-region	Converts Region to uppercase
CONTROL-X CONTROL-L	Converts Region to lowercase

THE MARK RING

Each time you set Mark in a buffer, you are also pushing Mark's former location onto the buffer's *Mark Ring*. The Mark Ring is organized as a FIFO (first in, first out) list and holds the 16 most recent locations where Mark was set. Each buffer has its own Mark Ring. This record of recent Mark history is useful because it often holds locations that you want to jump back to quickly. Jumping to a location pointed to by the Mark Ring can be faster and easier than scrolling or searching your way through the buffer to find the site of a previous change.

CONTROL-U
CONTROL-@
To work your way backward along the trail of former Mark locations, use the command CONTROL-U CONTROL-@ one or more times. Each time you give the command, emacs

- Moves Point (and the cursor) to the current Mark location
- Saves the current Mark location at the *oldest* end of the Mark Ring
- Pops off the *youngest* (most recent) Mark Ring entry and sets Mark

Each additional CONTROL-U CONTROL-@ command causes emacs to move Point and the cursor to the previous entry on the Mark Ring.

Although this process may seem complex, it really just makes a safe jump to a previous Mark location. It is safe because each jump's starting point is recirculated through the Mark Ring, where it is easy to find again. You can jump to all previous locations on the Mark Ring (it may be fewer than 16) by giving the command CONTROL-U CONTROL-@ repeatedly. You can go around the ring as many times as you like and stop whenever you want.

SETTING MARK AUTOMATICALLY

Some commands set Mark automatically: The idea is to leave a bookmark before moving Point a long distance. For example, META-> sets Mark before jumping to the end of the buffer. You can then return to your starting position with CONTROL-U CONTROL-@. Searches behave similarly. To help you avoid surprises the message **Mark Set** appears in the Echo Area whenever Mark is set, either explicitly or implicitly.

CUT AND PASTE: YANKING KILLED TEXT

Recall that killed text is not discarded but rather is kept in the Kill Ring. The Kill Ring holds the last 30 pieces of killed text and is visible from all buffers.

Retrieving text from the Kill Ring is called *yanking*. The meaning of this term in emacs is the opposite of that used in vim: In vim *yanking* pulls text from the buffer, and *putting* puts text into the buffer. Killing and yanking—which are roughly analogous to cutting and pasting—are emacs's primary mechanisms for moving and copying text. Table 7-6 lists the most common kill and yank commands.

Table 7-6   Common kill and yank commands

Command	Result
META-d	Kills to end of current word
META-D	Kills from beginning of previous word
CONTROL-K	Kills to end of line, not including LINEFEED
CONTROL-U 1 CONTROL-K	Kills to end of line, including LINEFEED
CONTROL-U 0 CONTROL-K	Kills from beginning of line
META-w	Copies Region to the Kill Ring but does *not* erase Region from the buffer

Table 7-6   Common kill and yank commands (continued)

Command	Result
CONTROL-W	Kills Region
META-z *char*	Kills up to next occurrence of *char*
CONTROL-Y	Yanks the most recently killed text into the current buffer at Point, sets Mark at the beginning of this text, and positions Point and the cursor at the end; follow with CONTROL-Y to swap Point and Mark
META-y	Erases the just-yanked text, rotates the Kill Ring, and yanks the next item (only after CONTROL-Y or META-y)

To move two lines of text, move Point to the beginning of the first line and then enter CONTROL-U 2 CONTROL-K to kill two lines. Move Point to the destination position and then enter CONTROL-Y.

To copy two lines of text, move Point to the beginning of the first line and give the commands CONTROL-U 2 CONTROL-K CONTROL-Y to kill the lines and then yank them back immediately. Move Point to the destination position and type CONTROL-Y.

To copy a larger piece of the buffer, set Region to cover this piece and type CONTROL-W CONTROL-Y to kill Region and yank it back. Next move Point to the destination and type CONTROL-Y. You can also set Region and use META-w to copy Region to the Kill Ring.

The Kill Ring is organized as a fixed-length FIFO list, with each new entry causing the eldest to be discarded (once you build up to 30 entries). Simple cut-and-paste operations generally use only the newest entry. The older entries are retained to give you time to change your mind about a deletion. If you do change your mind, you can "mine" the Kill Ring like an archaeological dig, working backward through time and down through the strata of killed material to copy a specific item back into the buffer.

To view every entry in the Kill Ring, begin a yanking session by pressing CONTROL-Y. This action copies the youngest entry in the Kill Ring to the buffer at the current cursor position. If this entry is not the item you want, continue the yanking session by pressing META-y. This action erases the previous yank and copies the next youngest entry to the buffer at the current cursor position. If this still is not the item you wanted, press META-y again to erase it and retrieve a copy of the next entry, and so on. You can continue giving META-y commands all the way back to the oldest entry. If you continue to press META-y, you will eventually wrap back to the youngest entry again. In this manner you can examine each entry as many times as you wish.

The sequence used in a yanking session consists of CONTROL-Y followed by any mixture of CONTROL-Y and META-y. If you type any other command after META-y, the sequence is broken and you must give the CONTROL-Y command again to start another yanking session.

As you work backward in the Kill Ring, it is useful to think of this process as advancing a Last Yank pointer back through history to increasingly older entries.

This pointer is *not* reset to the youngest entry until you give a new kill command. Using this technique, you can work backward partway through the Kill Ring with CONTROL-Y and a few META-y commands, give some commands that do not kill, and then pick up where you left off with another CONTROL-Y and a succession of META-y commands.

It is also possible to position the Last Yank pointer with positive or negative numeric arguments to META-y. Refer to the online documentation for more information.

INSERTING SPECIAL CHARACTERS

As stated earlier, emacs inserts everything that is not a command into the buffer at the position of the cursor. To insert characters that would ordinarily be emacs commands, you can use the emacs escape character: CONTROL-Q. There are two ways of using this escape character:

- CONTROL-Q followed by any other character inserts that character in the buffer, no matter which command interpretation it was supposed to have.

- CONTROL-Q followed by three octal digits inserts a byte with that value in the buffer.

CONTROL-Q

tip   Depending on the way your terminal is set up, CONTROL-Q may clash with software flow control. If CONTROL-Q seems to have no effect, it is most likely being used for flow control. In that case you must bind another key to the command **quoted-insert** (page 251).

GLOBAL BUFFER COMMANDS

The vim editor and its predecessors have global commands for bufferwide search and replace operations. They operate on the entire buffer. The emacs editor has a similar family of commands. They operate on the portion of the buffer between Point and the end of the buffer. If you wish to operate on the entire buffer, use META-< to move Point to the beginning of the buffer before issuing the command.

LINE-ORIENTED OPERATIONS

The commands listed in Table 7-7 take a regular expression and apply it to the lines between Point and the end of the buffer.

Table 7-7   Line-oriented operations

Command	Result
META-x occur	Prompts for a regular expression and copies each line with a match for the expression to a buffer named *Occur*
META-x delete-matching-lines	Prompts for a regular expression and deletes each line with a match for the expression

Table 7-7   Line-oriented operations (continued)

Command	Result
META-x delete-non-matching-lines	Prompts for a regular expression and deletes each line that does *not* have a match for that expression

The META-x **occur** command puts its output in a special buffer named ✳Occur✳, which you can peruse and discard or use as a jump menu to reach each line quickly. To use the ✳Occur✳ buffer as a jump menu, switch to it (CONTROL-X **o** [lowercase "o"]), move the cursor to the copy of the desired destination line, and give the command CONTROL-C CONTROL-C. This command moves the cursor to the buffer that was searched and positions it on the line that the regular expression matched.

As with any buffer change, you can undo the effect of the delete commands.

UNCONDITIONAL AND INTERACTIVE REPLACEMENT

The commands listed in Table 7-8 operate on the characters between Point and the end of the buffer, changing every string match or regular expression match. An unconditional replacement makes all replacements automatically. An interactive replacement gives you the opportunity to see and approve each replacement before it is made.

Table 7-8   Replacement commands

Command	Result
META-x replace-string	Prompts for *string* and *newstring* and replaces every instance of *string* with *newstring*. Point is left at the site of the last replacement, but Mark is set when you give the command, so you can return to it with CONTROL-U CONTROL-@.
META-x replace-regexp	Prompts for *regexp* and *newstring* and replaces every match for *regexp* with *newstring*. Point is left at the site of the last replacement, but Mark is set when you give the command, so you can return to it with CONTROL-U CONTROL-@.
META-% *string or* META-x query-replace	The first form uses *string;* the second form prompts for *string*. Both forms prompt for *newstring*, query each instance of *string*, and, depending on your response, replace it with *newstring*. Point is left at the site of the last replacement, but Mark is set when you give the command, so you can return to it with CONTROL-U CONTROL-@.
META-x query-replace-regexp	Prompts for *regexp* and *newstring*, queries each match for *regexp*, and, depending on your response, replaces it with *newstring*. Point is left at the site of the last replacement, but Mark is set when you give the command, so you can return to it with CONTROL-U CONTROL-@.

If you perform an interactive replacement, emacs displays each instance of *string* or match for *regexp* and prompts you for an action to take. Table 7-9 lists some of the possible responses.

Table 7-9   Responses to interactive replacement prompts

Response	Meaning
RETURN	Do not do any more replacements; quit now.
SPACE	Make this replacement and go on.
DELETE	Do *not* make this replacement. Skip it and go on.
, (comma)	Make this replacement, display the result, and ask for another command. Any command is legal except DELETE is treated like SPACE and does not undo the change.
. (period)	Make this replacement and quit searching.
! (exclamation point)	Replace this and all remaining instances without asking any more questions.

VISITING AND SAVING FILES

When you *visit* (emacs terminology for "call up") a file, emacs reads it into a buffer (page 235), allows you to edit the buffer, and eventually usually saves the buffer back to the file. The commands discussed here relate to visiting and saving files.

META-x **pwd**
META-x **cd**

Each emacs buffer keeps a record of its default directory (the directory the file was read from or the working directory, if it is a new file) that is prepended to any relative pathname you specify. This convenience is meant to save some typing. Enter META-x **pwd** to print the default directory for the current buffer or META-x **cd** to prompt for a new default directory and assign it to this buffer. The next section discusses pathname completion, which you can use when emacs prompts for a pathname.

VISITING FILES

The emacs editor works well when you visit a file that has already been called up and whose image is now in a buffer. After a check of the modification time to ensure that the file has not been changed since it was last called up, emacs simply switches to that buffer. Table 7-10 lists commands used to visit files.

Table 7-10   Visiting files

Command	Result
CONTROL-X CONTROL-F	Prompts for a filename and reads its contents into a new buffer. Assigns the file's simple filename as the buffer name. Other buffers are unaffected. It is common practice and often useful to have several files open simultaneously for editing.
CONTROL-X CONTROL-V	Prompts for a filename and replaces the current buffer with a buffer containing the contents of the requested file. The current buffer is destroyed.

Table 7-10   Visiting files (continued)

Command	Result
CONTROL-X 4 CONTROL-F	Prompts for a filename and reads its contents into a new buffer. Assigns the file's simple filename as the buffer name. Creates a new window for this buffer and selects that window. The window selected before the command still displays the buffer it was showing before this operation, although the new window may cover up part of the old window.

To create a new file, simply call it up. An empty buffer is created and properly named so you can eventually save it. The message (**New File**) appears in the Echo Area, reflecting emacs's understanding of the situation. If this new file grew out of a typographical error, you can give the command CONTROL-X CONTROL-V and enter the correct name.

PATHNAME COMPLETION

When you are prompted for the pathname of a file in the Minibuffer, you can type the pathname followed by a RETURN. Alternatively, you can use pathname completion, which is similar to bash filename completion (page 320), to help you enter a pathname.

While you are entering a pathname in the Minibuffer, press TAB and emacs will complete the pathname as far as possible. If the completed pathname is satisfactory, press RETURN. In some cases, emacs cannot complete a pathname. For example, a directory in the pathname you entered may not exist or you may not have permission to read it. If emacs cannot complete a pathname, it displays a message in the Echo Area. If the characters following the rightmost slash (/) in the pathname you are typing match more than one filename, when you press TAB emacs displays [**Complete, but not unique**]. If you press TAB a second time, emacs opens a Pathname Completion List window that displays a list of possible completions (Figure 7-10). You can open this window manually while you are entering a pathname by typing a question mark (?).

Figure 7-10   A Pathname Completion List window

With the Pathname Completion List window open, you can

- Cancel the selection by pressing CONTROL-G or ESCAPE ESCAPE ESCAPE. The display returns to the state it was in before you opened the Pathname Completion List window.

- Type more characters in the Minibuffer to finish the pathname. Press RETURN to select the pathname; emacs closes the completion window.

- Type more characters in the Minibuffer to make the completion unambiguous and press TAB again.

- Press META-v or PAGE UP to move the cursor into the Pathname Completion List window. Use the ARROW keys to move the cursor between selections. Press RETURN to choose the selection the cursor is on. You can press CONTROL-G or ESCAPE ESCAPE ESCAPE to back out of this window and return the cursor to the Minibuffer.

When you press RETURN, emacs closes the Pathname Completion List window, adds the filename you selected to the end of the pathname you were typing, and moves the cursor to the end of the pathname you were typing in the Minibuffer. You can continue typing in the Minibuffer and perform more completions before you press RETURN to accept the pathname. More information is available from the Completion and Completion Commands menus of the Minibuffer menu of the emacs online manual (see the tip on page 210).

Saving Files

You save a buffer by copying its contents back to the original file you called up. Table 7-11 lists the relevant commands.

You can exit without first getting a warning

caution Clearing the modified flag (META-~) allows you to exit without saving a modified buffer with no warning. Make sure you know what you are doing when you use META-~.

Did you modify a buffer by mistake?

caution When you give a CONTROL-X **s** command, you may discover files whose buffers were modified by mistake as emacs tries to save the wrong changes back to the file. When emacs prompts you to confirm the save, *do not* answer **y** if you are not sure. First exit from the CONTROL-X **s** dialog by typing **n** to any saves you are not sure about. You then have several options:

- Save the suspicious buffer to a temporary file with CONTROL-X CONTROL-W and analyze it later.
- Undo the changes with a string of CONTROL-_ commands until the ** indicator disappears from the buffer's Mode Line.
- If you are sure that all the changes are wrong, use META-x **revert-buffer** to get a fresh copy of the file.
- Kill the buffer outright. Because it is modified, emacs asks whether you are sure before carrying out this command.
- Give the META-~ (tilde) command to clear the modified condition and ** indicator. A subsequent CONTROL-X **s** then believes that the buffer does not need to be written.

Table 7-11 Saving files

Command	Result
CONTROL-X CONTROL-S	This workhorse file-saving command saves the current buffer into its original file. If the current buffer is not modified, emacs displays the message **(No changes need to be saved)**.
CONTROL-X s	For each modified buffer, you are asked whether you wish to save it. Answer **y** or **n**. This command is given automatically as you exit from emacs and allows you to save any buffers that have been modified but not yet written out. Give this command to save intermediate copies of your work.
META-x set-visited-file-name	Prompts for a filename and sets this name as the "original" name for the current buffer.
CONTROL-X CONTROL-W	Prompts for a filename, sets this name as the "original" name for the current buffer, and saves the current buffer into that file. Equivalent to META-x **set-visited-file-name** followed by CONTROL-X CONTROL-S.
META-~ (tilde)	Clears the modified flag from the current buffer. If you mistakenly type META-~ against a buffer with changes you want to keep, you need to make sure the modified condition and its ** indicator are turned back on before leaving emacs, or all the changes you made will be lost. One easy way to mark a buffer as modified is to insert a SPACE and then remove it using DELETE.

BUFFERS

An emacs buffer is a storage object that you can edit. It often holds the contents of a file but can also exist without being associated with a file. You can select only one buffer at a time, designated as the *current buffer*. Most commands operate only on the current buffer, even when windows show multiple buffers on the screen. For the most part each buffer is its own world: It has its own name, its own modes, its own file associations, its own modified state, and perhaps its own special key bindings. You can use the commands shown in Table 7-12 to create, select, list, and manipulate buffers.

Table 7-12 Working with buffers

Command	Result
CONTROL-X b	Prompts for a buffer name and selects it. If the buffer you name does not exist, this command creates it.
CONTROL-X 4 b	Prompts for a buffer name and selects it in another window. The existing window is not disturbed, although the new window may overlap it.

Table 7-12   Working with buffers (continued)

Command	Result
CONTROL-X CONTROL-B	Creates a buffer named *✱**Buffer List**✱ and displays it in another window. The existing window is not disturbed, although the new window may overlap it. The new buffer is not selected. In the ✱**Buffer List**✱ buffer, each buffer's data is shown along with the name, size, mode(s), and original filename. A % appears for a readonly buffer, a ✱ indicates a modified buffer, and . appears for the selected buffer.
META-x rename-buffer	Prompts for a new buffer name and gives this new name to the current buffer.
CONTROL-X CONTROL-Q	Toggles the current buffer's readonly status and the associated %% Mode Line indicator. This command can prevent you from accidentally modifying a buffer or allow you to modify a buffer when visiting a readonly file.
META-x append-to-buffer	Prompts for a buffer name and appends Region to the end of that buffer.
META-x prepend-to-buffer	Prompts for a buffer name and prepends Region to the beginning of that buffer.
META-x copy-to-buffer	Prompts for a buffer name and deletes the contents of the buffer before copying Region to that buffer.
META-x insert-buffer	Prompts for a buffer name and inserts the contents of that buffer in the current buffer at Point.
CONTROL-X k	Prompts for a buffer name and deletes that buffer. If the buffer has been modified but not saved, emacs asks you to confirm the operation.
META-x kill-some-buffers	Goes through the list of buffers and offers the chance to delete each buffer. As with CONTROL-X **k**, emacs asks you to confirm the kill command if a modified buffer has not been saved.

WINDOWS

An emacs *window* is a viewport that looks into a buffer. The emacs screen begins by displaying a single window, but this screen space can later be divided among two or more windows. On the screen the *current window* holds the cursor and views the *current buffer*. For a tip on terminology, see "The screen and emacs windows" on page 207.

CONTROL-X **b**
buffer-name

A window displays one buffer at a time. The command CONTROL-X **b** *buffer-name* switches the buffer that the current window displays. Multiple windows can display

Figure 7-11 Splitting a window horizontally

the same buffer with each window displaying a different part of the buffer. Any change to a buffer is reflected in all windows displaying that buffer. Also, a buffer can exist without a window open on it.

SPLITTING A WINDOW

One way to divide the screen is to split the starting window explicitly into two or more pieces. The command CONTROL-X 2 splits the current window in two, with one new window appearing above the other. A numeric argument is taken as the size of the upper window in lines. The command CONTROL-X 3 splits the current window in two, with the new windows being arranged side by side (Figure 7-11). A numeric argument is taken as the number of columns to give the left window. For example, CONTROL-U CONTROL-X 2 splits the current window in two; because of the special "times 4" interpretation of CONTROL-U standing alone, the upper window is given four lines (barely enough to be useful).

Although these commands split the current window, both windows continue to view the same buffer. You can select a new buffer in either or both new windows, or you can scroll each window to show different portions of the same buffer.

MANIPULATING WINDOWS

CONTROL-X o
META-CONTROL-V

You can use CONTROL-X o (lowercase "o") to select the other window. If more than two windows appear on the screen, a sequence of CONTROL-X o commands cycles through them in top-to-bottom, left-to-right order. The META-CONTROL-V command scrolls the other window. If more than two windows are visible, the command scrolls the window that CONTROL-X o would select next. You can use either a positive or negative scrolling argument, just as with CONTROL-V scrolling in the current window.

OTHER-WINDOW DISPLAY

CONTROL-X **4b**
CONTROL-X **4f**

In normal emacs operation, explicit window splitting is not nearly as common as the implicit splitting done by the family of CONTROL-X **4** commands. The CONTROL-X **4b** command, for example, prompts for a *buffer name* and selects it in the other window. If no other window exists, this command begins with a half-and-half split that arranges the windows one above the other. The CONTROL-X **4f** command prompts for a *filename*, calls the file up in the other window, and selects the other window. If no other window exists, this command begins with a half-and-half split that arranges the windows one above the other.

ADJUSTING AND DELETING WINDOWS

CONTROL-X **0**
CONTROL-X **1**

Windows may be destroyed when they get in the way. No data is lost in the window's associated buffer with this operation, and you can make another window whenever you like. The CONTROL-X **0** (zero) command deletes the current window and gives its space to its neighbors; CONTROL-X **1** deletes all windows except the current window.

META-x **shrink-window**
CONTROL-X **^**
CONTROL-X **}**
CONTROL-X **{**

You can also adjust the dimensions of the current window at the expense of its neighbors. To make a window shorter, give the command META-x **shrink-window**. Press CONTROL-X **^** to increase the height of a window, CONTROL-X **}** to make the window wider, and CONTROL-X **{** to make the window narrower. Each of these commands adds or subtracts one line or column to or from the window, unless you precede the command with a numeric argument.

The emacs editor has its own guidelines for a window's minimum useful size and may destroy a window before you force one of its dimensions to zero. Although the window may disappear, the buffer remains intact.

FOREGROUND SHELL COMMANDS

The emacs editor can run a subshell (a shell that is a child of emacs—refer to "Executing a Command" on page 308) to execute a single command line, optionally with standard input coming from Region of the current buffer and optionally with standard output replacing Region (Table 7-13). This process is analogous to executing a shell command from the vim editor and having the input come from the file you are editing and the output go back to the same file (page 192). As with vim, how well this process works depends in part on the capabilities of the shell.

Table 7-13   Foreground shell commands

Command	Result
META-! (exclamation point)	Prompts for a shell command, executes it, and displays the output
CONTROL-U META-! (exclamation point)	Prompts for a shell command, executes it, and inserts the output at Point
META-| (vertical bar)	Prompts for a shell command, gives Region as input, filters it through the command, and displays the output

Table 7-13   Foreground shell commands (continued)

Command	Result
CONTROL-U META-| (vertical bar)	Prompts for a shell command, gives Region as input, filters it through the command, deletes the old Region, and inserts the output in that position

The emacs editor can also start an interactive subshell that runs continuously in its own buffer. See "Shell Mode" on page 248 for more information.

BACKGROUND SHELL COMMANDS

The emacs editor can run processes in the background, with their output being fed into a growing emacs buffer that does not have to remain in view. You can continue editing while the background process runs and look at its output later. Any shell command can be run in this way.

The growing output buffer is always named ***compilation***. You can read it, copy from it, or edit it in any way, without waiting for the background process to finish. Most commonly this buffer is used to review the output of program compilation and to correct any syntax errors found by the compiler.

META-x **compile**   To run a process in the background, give the command META-x **compile** to prompt for a shell command and begin executing it as a background process. The screen splits in half to show the ***compilation*** buffer.

You can switch to the ***compilation*** buffer and watch the execution, if you wish. To make the display scroll as you watch, position the cursor at the very end of the text with a META-> command. If you are not interested in this display, just remove the window with CONTROL-X 0 (zero) if you are in it or CONTROL-X 1 otherwise and keep working. You can switch back to the ***compilation*** buffer later with CONTROL-X **b**.

To kill the background process give the command META-x **kill-compilation**. The emacs editor asks for confirmation and then kills the background process.

If standard format error messages appear in ***compilation***, you can automatically visit the line in the file where each error occurred. Give the command CONTROL-X ` (back tick) to split the screen into two windows and visit the file and line of the next error message. Scroll the **\*compilation\*** buffer until this error message appears at the top of its window. Use CONTROL-U CONTROL-X ` to start over with the first error message and visit that file and line.

MAJOR MODES: LANGUAGE-SENSITIVE EDITING

The emacs editor has a large collection of feature sets, each specific to a certain variety of text. The feature sets are called *Major modes*. A buffer can have only one Major mode at a time.

A buffer's Major mode is private to the buffer and does not affect editing in any other buffer. If you switch to a new buffer having a different mode, rules for the new mode take effect immediately. To avoid confusion, the name of a buffer's Major mode appears in the Mode Line of any window viewing that buffer (Figure 7-1 on page 209).

The three classes of Major modes are used for the following tasks:

- Editing human languages (for example, text, nroff, TeX)
- Editing programming languages (for example, C, Fortran, Lisp)
- Special purposes (for example, shell, mail, dired, ftp)

In addition, one Major mode—Fundamental—does nothing special. A Major mode usually sets up the following:

- Special commands unique to the mode, possibly with their own key bindings. Whereas languages may have just a few special commands, special-purpose modes may have dozens.
- Mode-specific character syntax and regular expressions defining word-constituent characters, delimiters, comments, whitespace, and so on. This setup conditions the behavior of commands oriented to syntactic units, such as words, sentences, comments, or parenthesized expressions.

SELECTING A MAJOR MODE

META-x *modename*   The emacs editor chooses and sets a mode when a file is called up by matching the filename against a set of regular expression patterns describing the filename and filename extension. The explicit command to enter a Major mode is META-x *modename*. This command is used mostly to correct the Major mode when emacs guesses wrong.

To have a file define its own mode, include the text –*– **modename** –*– somewhere in the first nonblank line of the file, possibly inside a comment suitable for the programming language the file is written in.

HUMAN-LANGUAGE MODES

A *human* language is meant eventually to be used by humans, possibly after being formatted by a text-formatting program. Human languages share many conventions about the structure of words, sentences, and paragraphs. With regard to these textual units, the major human language modes all behave in the same way.

Beyond this area of commonality, each mode offers additional functionality oriented to a specific text formatter, such as TeX, LaTeX, or nroff/troff. Text-formatter extensions are beyond the scope of this chapter; the focus here is on the commands relating to human textual units.

WORDS

As mnemonic aids, the bindings for words are defined parallel to the character-oriented bindings CONTROL-F, CONTROL-B, CONTROL-D, DELETE, and CONTROL-T.

META-f
META-b
Just as CONTROL-F and CONTROL-B move forward and backward over characters, so META-f and META-b move forward and backward over words. They may start from a position inside or outside the word to be traversed, but in all cases Point finishes just beyond the word, adjacent to the last character skipped over. Both commands accept a numeric argument specifying the number of words to be traversed.

META-d
META-DELETE
Just as CONTROL-D and DELETE delete characters forward and backward, so the keys META-d and META-DELETE kill words forward and backward. They leave Point in exactly the same finishing position as META-f and META-b do, but they kill the words they pass over. They also accept a numeric argument.

META-t
META-t transposes the word before Point with the word after Point.

SENTENCES

META-a
META-e
CONTROL-X DELETE
META-k
As mnemonic aids, three of the bindings for sentences are defined parallel to the line-oriented bindings: CONTROL-A, CONTROL-E, and CONTROL-K. The META-a command moves backward to the beginning of a sentence; META-e moves forward to the end of a sentence. In addition, CONTROL-X DELETE kills backward to the beginning of a sentence; META-k kills forward to the end of a sentence.

The emacs editor recognizes the ends of sentences by referring to a regular expression that is kept in a variable named **sentence-end**. Briefly, emacs looks for the characters ., ?, or ! followed by two SPACEs or an end-of-line marker, possibly with close quotation marks or close braces. Give the command CONTROL-H v **sentence-end** RETURN to display the value of this variable.

The META-a and META-e commands leave Point adjacent to the first or last nonblank character in the sentence. They accept a numeric argument specifying the number of sentences to traverse; a negative argument runs them in reverse.

The META-k and CONTROL-X DELETE commands kill sentences forward and backward, in a manner analogous to CONTROL-K line kill. They leave Point in the same position as META-a and META-e do, but they kill the sentences they pass over. They also accept a numeric argument. CONTROL-X DELETE is useful for quickly backing out of a half-finished sentence.

PARAGRAPHS

META-{
META-}
META-h
The META-{ command moves backward to the most recent paragraph beginning; META-} moves forward to the next paragraph ending. The META-h command marks the paragraph the cursor is on as Region (that is, it puts Point at the beginning and Mark at the end), or marks the next paragraph if the cursor is between paragraphs.

The META-} and META-{ commands leave Point at the beginning of a line, adjacent to the first character or last character, respectively, of the paragraph. They accept a numeric argument specifying the number of paragraphs to traverse and run in reverse if given a negative argument.

In human-language modes, paragraphs are separated by blank lines and text-formatter command lines, and an indented line starts a paragraph. Recognition is based on the regular expressions stored in the variables **paragraph-separate** and **paragraph-start**. A paragraph is composed of complete lines, including the final line terminator. If a paragraph starts following one or more blank lines, the last blank line before the paragraph belongs to the paragraph.

FILL

The emacs editor can *fill* a paragraph to fit a specified width, breaking lines and rearranging them as necessary. It breaks lines between words and does not hyphenate words. The emacs editor can fill automatically as you type or in response to an explicit command.

META-x **auto-fill-mode**

The META-x **auto-fill-mode** command toggles Auto Fill mode on and off. When this mode is on, emacs automatically breaks lines when you press SPACE or RETURN and are currently beyond the specified line width. This feature is useful when you are entering new text.

META-q
META-x **fill-region**

Auto Fill mode does not automatically refill the entire paragraph you are currently working on. If you add new text in the middle of a paragraph, Auto Fill mode breaks the new text as you type but does not refill the complete paragraph. To refill a complete paragraph or Region of paragraphs, use either META-q to refill the current paragraph or META-x **fill-region** to refill each paragraph in Region (between Point and Mark).

You can change the filling width from its default value of 70 by setting the **fill-column** variable. Give the command CONTROL-X f to set **fill-column** to the current cursor position and the command CONTROL-U *nnn* CONTROL-X f to set **fill-column** to *nnn*, where 0 is the left margin.

CASE CONVERSION

The emacs editor can force words or Regions to all uppercase, all lowercase, or initial caps (the first letter of each word uppercase, the rest lowercase) characters. Refer to Table 7-14.

Table 7-14　Case conversion

Command	Result
META-l (lowercase "l")	Converts word to the right of Point to lowercase
META-u	Converts word to the right of Point to uppercase
META-c	Converts word to the right of Point to initial caps
CONTROL-X CONTROL-L	Converts Region to lowercase
CONTROL-X CONTROL-U	Converts Region to uppercase

The word-oriented conversions move Point over the word just converted (just as META-f does), allowing you to walk through text and convert each word with META-l, META-u, or META-c, or skip over words to be left alone with META-f. A positive numeric argument converts that number of words to the right of Point, moving Point as it goes. A negative numeric argument converts that number of words to the left of Point but leaves Point stationary. This feature is useful for quickly changing the case of words you have just typed. Table 7-15 shows some examples.

Table 7-15   Examples of case conversion

Characters and commands	Result
HELLOMETA--META-l (lowercase "l")	**hello**
helloMETA--META-u	**HELLO**
helloMETA--META-c	**Hello**

When the cursor (Point) is in the middle of a word, the case conversion commands convert the characters to the left of the cursor.

TEXT MODE

META-x **text-mode**   With very few exceptions, the commands for human-language textual units are always turned on and available, even when the programming-language modes are activated. Text mode adds very little to these basic commands but is still worth turning on just to activate the TAB key function (next). Use the command META-x **text-mode** to activate Text mode.

META-x **edit-tab-stops**   In Text mode, pressing TAB runs the function **tab-to-tab-stop**. By default TAB stops are set every eight columns. You can adjust them with META-x **edit-tab-stops**, which switches to a special *Tab Stops* buffer. The current TAB stops are laid out in this buffer on a scale for you to edit. The new stops are installed when or if you type CONTROL-C CONTROL-C. You can kill this buffer (CONTROL-X k) or switch away from it (CONTROL-X b) without changing the TAB stops.

The TAB stops you set with the META-x **edit-tab-stops** command affect only the interpretation of TAB characters arriving from the keyboard. The emacs editor automatically inserts enough spaces to reach the TAB stop. This command does not affect the interpretation of TAB characters already in the buffer or the underlying file. If you edit the TAB stops and then use them, when you print the file the hard copy will look the same as the text on the screen.

C MODE

Programming languages are read by humans but are interpreted by machines. Besides continuing to handle some of the human-language text units (for example, words and sentences), the major programming-language modes address several additional issues:

- Handling *balanced expressions* enclosed by parentheses, brackets, or braces as textual units

- Handling comments as textual units
- Indention

The emacs editor includes Major modes to support C, Fortran, and several variants of Lisp. In addition, many users have contributed modes for their favorite languages. In these modes the commands for human textual units are still available, with occasional redefinitions. For example, a paragraph is bounded only by blank lines and indention does not signal a paragraph start. In addition, each mode has custom code to handle the language-specific conventions for balanced expressions, comments, and indention. This chapter discusses only C mode.

EXPRESSIONS

The emacs Major modes are limited to lexical analysis. They can recognize most tokens (for example, symbols, strings, and numbers) and all matched sets of parentheses, brackets, and braces. This is enough for Lisp but not for C. The C mode lacks a full-function syntax analyzer and is not prepared to recognize all of C's possible expressions.[1]

Table 7-16 lists the emacs commands applicable to parenthesized expressions and some tokens. By design the bindings run parallel to the CONTROL commands for characters and the META commands for words. All of these commands accept a numeric argument and run in reverse if that argument is negative.

Table 7-16   Commands for expressions and tokens

Command	Result
CONTROL-META-f	Moves forward over an expression. The exact behavior depends on which character lies to the right of Point (or left of Point, depending on which direction you are moving Point).
	• If the first nonwhitespace is an opening delimiter (parenthesis, bracket, or brace), Point is moved just past the matching closing delimiter.
	• If the first nonwhitespace is a token, Point is moved just past the end of this token.
CONTROL-META-b	Moves backward over an expression.
CONTROL-META-k	Kills an expression forward. This command leaves Point at the same finishing position as CONTROL-META-f but kills the expression it traverses.
CONTROL-META-@	Sets Mark at the position CONTROL-META-f would move to but does not change Point. To see the marked Region clearly, give a pair of CONTROL-X CONTROL-X commands to exchange Point and Mark.

---

1. In the emacs documentation the recurring term *sexp* refers to the Lisp term *S-expression*. Unfortunately, it is sometimes used interchangeably with *expression*, even though the language might not be Lisp.

FUNCTION DEFINITIONS

In emacs a balanced expression at the outermost level is considered to be a function definition and is often called a *defun*, even though that term is specific to Lisp. More generally it is understood to be a function definition in the language at hand.

In C mode a function definition includes the return data type, the function name, and the argument declarations appearing before the { character. Table 7-17 shows the commands for operating on function definitions.

Function indention style

caution   The emacs editor assumes an opening brace at the left margin is part of a function definition. This heuristic speeds up the reverse scan for a definition's leading edge. If your code has an indention style that puts the opening brace elsewhere, you may get unexpected results.

Table 7-17   Function definition commands

Command	Result
CONTROL-META-a	Moves to the beginning of the most recent function definition. Use this command to scan backward through a buffer one function at a time.
CONTROL-META-e	Moves to the end of the next function definition. Use this command to scan forward through a buffer one function at a time.
CONTROL-META-h	Marks as Region the current function definition (or next function definition, if the cursor is between two functions). This command sets up an entire function definition for a Region-oriented operation such as kill.

INDENTION

The emacs C mode has extensive logic to control the indention of C programs. You can adjust this logic for many different styles of C indention (Table 7-18).

Table 7-18   Indention commands

Command	Result
TAB	Adjusts the indention of the current line. TAB inserts or deletes whitespace at the beginning of the line until the indention conforms to the current context and rules in effect. Point is not moved unless it lies in the whitespace area; in that case it is moved to the end of the whitespace. TAB inserts leading SPACES; you can press TAB with the cursor at any position on the line. If you want to insert a TAB in the text, use META-i or CONTROL-Q TAB.
LINEFEED	Shorthand for RETURN followed by TAB. The LINEFEED key is a convenience for entering new code, giving you an autoindent as you begin each line.

Table 7-18   Indention commands (continued)

Command	Result
The next two commands indent multiple lines with a single command.	
CONTROL-META-q	Reindents all lines inside the next pair of matched braces. CONTROL-META-q assumes the left brace is correctly indented and drives the indention from there. If you need to adjust the left brace, type TAB just to the left of the brace before giving this command. All lines up to the matching brace are indented as if you had typed TAB on each one.
CONTROL-META-\	Reindents all lines in Region. Put Point just to the left of a left brace and then give the command. All lines up to the matching brace are indented as if you had typed TAB on each one.

CUSTOMIZING INDENTION

Many styles of C programming have evolved, and emacs does its best to support automatic indention for all of them. The indention coding was completely rewritten for emacs version 19; it supports C, C++, Objective-C, and Java. The new emacs syntactic analysis is much more precise and can classify each syntactic element of each line of a program into a single syntactic category (out of about 50), such as *statement, string,* or *else-clause.* Based on that analysis, emacs refers to the offset table named **c-offsets-alist** to look up how much each line should be indented from the preceding line.

To customize indention, you must change the offset table. Although you can define a completely new offset table for each customized style, it is typically more convenient to feed in a short list of exceptions to the standard rules. Each mainstream style (GNU, K&R [Kernighan and Ritchie], BSD, and so on) has such an exception list; all are collected in **c-style-alist**. Here is one entry from **c-style-alist**:

```
("gnu"
(c-basic-offset . 2)
(c-comment-only-line-offset . (0 . 0))
(c-offsets-alist . ((statement-block-intro . +)
    (knr-argdecl-intro . 5)
    (substatement-open . +)
    (label . 0)
    (statement-case-open . +)
    (statement-cont . +)
    (arglist-intro . c-lineup-arglist-intro-after-paren)
    (arglist-close . c-lineup-arglist)
    ))
)
```

Constructing a custom style is beyond the scope of this book. If you are curious, the long story is available in emacs info beginning at "Customizing C Indentation." The sample **.emacs** file given in this chapter (page 253) adds a very simple custom style and arranges to use it on every **.c** file that is edited.

COMMENTS

Each buffer has its own **comment-column** variable, which you can view with the CONTROL-H **v** **comment-column** RETURN help command. Table 7-19 lists commands that facilitate working with comments.

Table 7-19   Comment commands

Command	Result
META-;	Inserts a comment on the current line or aligns an existing comment. This command's behavior differs according to the situation. • If no comment is on this line, META-; creates an empty comment at the value of **comment-column**. • If text already on this line overlaps the position of **comment-column**, META-; creates an empty comment one SPACE after the end of the text. • If a comment is already on this line but not at the current value of **comment-column**, META-; realigns the comment at that column. If text is in the way, it places the comment one SPACE after the end of the text. Once an aligned (possibly empty) comment exists on the line, Point moves to the start of the comment text.
CONTROL-X ;	Sets **comment-column** to the column after Point. The left margin is column 0.
CONTROL-U − CONTROL-X ;	Kills the comment on the current line. This command sets **comment-column** from the first comment found above this line and then performs a META-; command to insert or align a comment at that position.
CONTROL-U CONTROL-X ;	Sets **comment-column** to the position of the first comment found above this line and then executes a META-; command to insert or align a comment on this line.

SPECIAL-PURPOSE MODES

The emacs editor includes a third family of Major modes that are not oriented toward a particular language or toward ordinary editing. Instead, these modes perform some special function. The following modes may define their own key bindings and commands to accomplish that function:

• Rmail: reads, archives, and composes email

• Dired: moves around an **ls −l** display and operates on files

• VIP: simulates a complete vi environment

• VC: allows you to drive version-control systems (including RCS, CVS, and Subversion) from within emacs

- GUD (Grand Unified Debugger): allows you to run and debug C (and other) programs from within emacs

- Tramp: allows you to edit files on any remote system you can reach with ftp or scp

- Shell: runs an interactive subshell from inside an emacs buffer

This book discusses only Shell mode.

SHELL MODE

One-time shell commands and Region filtering were discussed earlier under "Foreground Shell Commands" on page 238. Each emacs buffer in Shell mode has an underlying interactive shell permanently associated with it. This shell takes its input from the last line of the buffer and sends its output back to the buffer, advancing Point as it goes. If you do not edit the buffer, it holds a record of the complete shell session.

The shell runs asynchronously, whether or not you have its buffer in view. The emacs editor uses idle time to read the shell's output and add it to the buffer.

META-x **shell**   Type META-x **shell** to create a buffer named ✳shell✳ and start a subshell. If a buffer named ✳shell✳ already exists, emacs just switches to that buffer. The shell that this command runs is taken from one of the following sources:

- The Lisp variable **explicit-shell-file-name**

- The environment variable **ESHELL**

- The environment variable **SHELL**

To start a second shell, first give the command META-x **rename-buffer** to change the name of the existing shell's buffer, and then give the command META-x **shell** to start another shell. You can create as many subshells and buffers as you like, all running in parallel.

A special set of commands is defined in Shell mode (Table 7-20). These commands are bound mostly to two-key sequences starting with CONTROL-C. Each sequence is similar to the ordinary control characters found in Linux but uses a leading CONTROL-C.

Table 7-20   Shell mode commands

Command	Result
RETURN	If Point is at the end of the buffer, emacs inserts the RETURN and sends this (the last) line to the shell. If Point is elsewhere, it copies this line to the end of the buffer, peeling off the old shell prompt (see the regular expression **shell-prompt-pattern**), if one existed. Then this copied line—now the last in the buffer—is sent to the shell.
CONTROL-C CONTROL-D	Sends CONTROL-D to the shell or its subshell.
CONTROL-C CONTROL-C	Sends CONTROL-C to the shell or its subshell.
CONTROL-C CONTROL-\	Sends a quit signal to the shell or its subshell.

Table 7-20   Shell mode commands (continued)

Command	Result
CONTROL-C CONTROL-U	Kills the text on the current line not yet completed.
CONTROL-C CONTROL-R	Scrolls back to the beginning of the last shell output, putting the first line of output at the top of the window.
CONTROL-C CONTROL-O	Deletes the last batch of shell output.

optional

Customizing emacs

At the heart of emacs is a Lisp interpreter written in C. This version of Lisp is significantly extended and includes many special editing commands. The interpreter's main task is to execute the Lisp-coded system that implements the look-and-feel of emacs.

Reduced to its essentials, this system implements a continuous loop that watches keystrokes arrive, parses them into commands, executes those commands, and updates the screen. This behavior can be customized in a number of ways.

- As single keystrokes arrive, they are mapped immediately through a keyboard translation table. By changing the entries in this table, it is possible to swap keys. If you are used to vi or vim, for example, you might want to swap DELETE and CONTROL-H. Then CONTROL-H backspaces as it does in vim, and DELETE (which is not used by vim) is the help key. If you use DELETE as an interrupt key, you may want to choose another key to swap with CONTROL-H.

- The mapped keystrokes are gathered into small groups called *key sequences*. A key sequence may be only a single key, such as CONTROL-N, or may include two or more keys, such as CONTROL-X CONTROL-F. Once gathered, the key sequences are used to select a particular procedure to be executed. The rules for gathering each key sequence and the specific procedure name to be executed when that sequence comes in are codified in a series of tables called *keymaps*. By altering the keymaps, you can change the gathering rules or change which procedure is associated with which sequence. For example, if you are used to vi's or vim's use of CONTROL-W to back up over the word you are entering, you may want to change emacs's CONTROL-W binding from the standard **kill-region** to **delete-word-backward**.

- The command behavior is often conditioned by one or more global variables or options. It may be possible to get the behavior you want by setting some of these variables.

- The command itself is usually a Lisp program that can be reprogrammed to make it behave as desired. Although this task is not appropriate for beginners, the Lisp source to nearly all commands is available and the internal Lisp system is fully documented. As mentioned earlier, it is common practice to load customized Lisp code at startup time, even if you did not write the code yourself.

Most emacs documentation glosses over the translation, gathering, and procedure selection steps and talks about keystrokes as though they were commands. However, it is important to know that the underlying machinery exists and to understand that you can change its behavior.

THE .emacs STARTUP FILE

Each time you start emacs, it loads the file of Lisp code named ~/.emacs. Using this file is the most common way to customize emacs. Two command-line options control the use of the .emacs file. The –q option ignores the .emacs file so emacs starts without it; this is one way to get past a bad .emacs file. The –u *user* option uses the ~*user*/.emacs file (the .emacs file from the home directory of *user*).

The .emacs startup file is generally concerned only with key bindings and option settings; it is possible to write the Lisp statements for this file in a straightforward style. Each parenthesized Lisp statement is a Lisp function call. Inside the parentheses the first symbol is the function name; the rest of the SPACE-separated tokens are arguments to that function.

Assigning a value to a variable   The most common function in the .emacs file, **setq**, is a simple assignment to a global variable. The first argument is the name of the variable to set and the second argument is its value. The following example sets the variable named **c-indent-level** to 8:

```
(setq c-indent-level 8)
```

Displaying the value of a variable   While you are running emacs, the command CONTROL-H **v** prompts for the name of a variable. When you enter the name of a variable and press RETURN, emacs displays the value of the variable.

Setting the default value of a variable   You can set the default value for a variable that is buffer-private by using the function named **setq-default**. To set a specific element of a vector, use the function name **aset**. The first argument is the name of the vector, the second is the offset, and the third is the value of the target entry. In the startup file the new values are usually constants. Table 7-21 shows the formats of these constants.

Table 7-21   Formats of constants in **.emacs**

Command	Result
Numbers	Decimal integers, with an optional minus sign
Strings	Similar to C strings but with extensions for CONTROL and META characters: **\C-s** yields CONTROL-S, **\M-s** yields META-s, and **\M-\C-s** yields CONTROL-META-s
Characters	*Not* like C characters; start with **?** and continue with a printing character or with a backslash escape sequence (for example, **?a**, **?\C-i**, **?\033**)

Table 7-21   Formats of constants in **.emacs (continued)**

Command	Result
Booleans	*Not* **1** and **0**; use **t** for *true* and **nil** for *false*
Other Lisp objects	Begin with a single quotation mark and continue with the object's name

REMAPPING KEYS

The emacs command loop begins each cycle by translating incoming keystrokes into the name of the command to be executed. The basic translation operation uses the ASCII value of the incoming character to index a 128-element vector called a *keymap*.

Sometimes a character's eighth bit is interpreted as the META *case*, but this cannot always be relied on. At the point of translation all META characters appear with the ESCAPE prefix, whether or not they were typed that way.

Each position in this vector is one of the following:

- Not defined: No translation possible in this map.

- The name of another keymap: Switches to that keymap and waits for the next character to arrive.

- The name of a Lisp function to be called: Translation process is done; call this command.

Because keymaps can reference other keymaps, an arbitrarily complex recognition tree can be set up. The mainstream emacs bindings use at most three keys, with a very small group of well-known *prefix keys*, each with its well-known keymap name.

Each buffer can have a *local keymap* that is used first for any keystrokes arriving while a window into that buffer is selected. The local keymap allows the regular mapping to be extended or overridden on a per-buffer basis and is most often used to add bindings for a Major mode.

The basic translation flow runs as follows:

- Map the first character through the buffer's local keymap. If it is defined as a Lisp function name, translation is done and emacs executes that function. If it is not defined, use this same character to index the global top-level keymap.

- Map the first character through the top-level global keymap **global-map**. At this and each following stage, the following conditions hold:

    - If the entry for this character is not defined, it is an error. Send a bell to the terminal and discard all the characters entered in this key sequence.

    - If the entry for this character is defined as a Lisp function name, translation is done and the function is executed.

• If the entry for this character is defined as the name of another keymap, switch to that keymap and wait for another character to select one of its elements.

Everything input during the remapping process must be either a command or an error. Ordinary characters that are to be inserted in the buffer are usually bound to the command **self-insert-command**. Each of the well-known prefix characters is each associated with a keymap (Table 7-22).

Table 7-22   Keymap prefixes

Keymap prefix	Applies to
ctl-x-map	For characters following CONTROL-X
ctl-x-4-map	For characters following CONTROL-X **4**
esc-map	For characters following ESCAPE (including META characters)
help-map	For characters following CONTROL-H
mode-specific-map	For characters following CONTROL-C

To see the current state of the keymaps, type CONTROL-H **b**. They appear in the following order: local, global, and shorter maps for each prefix key. Each line specifies the name of the Lisp function to be called; the documentation for that function can be retrieved with the command CONTROL-H **f** *function-name* or CONTROL-H **k** *key-sequence*.

The most common type of keymap customization is making small changes to the global command assignments without creating any new keymaps or commands. This type of customization is most easily done in the **.emacs** file using the Lisp function **define-key**. The **define-key** function takes three arguments:

• The keymap name
• A single character defining a position in that map
• The command to be executed when this character appears

For instance, to bind the command **backward-kill-word** to CONTROL-W, use the statement

```
(define-key global-map "\C-w" 'backward-kill-word)
```

The \ character causes **C-w** to be interpreted as CONTROL-W instead of three letters (equivalent to \^w). The unmatched single quotation mark in front of the command name is correct. This Lisp escape character keeps the name from being evaluated too soon. To bind the command **kill-region** to CONTROL-X CONTROL-K, use the statement

```
(define-key ctl-x-map "\C-k" 'kill-region)
```

A SAMPLE .emacs FILE

The following ~/.emacs file produces a plain editing environment that minimizes surprises for vi and vim users. If any section or any line is not appropriate for your situation, you can edit it or make it a comment by placing one or more semicolons (;) beginning in column 1.

```
;;; Preference Variables

(setq make-backup-files nil)      ;Do not make backup files
(setq backup-by-copying t)        ;If you do, at least do not destroy links
(setq delete-auto-save-files t)   ;Delete autosave files when writing orig
(setq blink-matching-paren nil)   ;Do not blink opening delim
(setq require-final-newline 'ask) ;Ask about missing final newline

;; Reverse mappings for C-h and DEL.
;; Sometimes useful to get DEL character from the Backspace key,
;; and online help from the Delete key.
;; NB: F1 is always bound to online help.
(keyboard-translate ?\C-h ?\177)
(keyboard-translate ?\177 ?\C-h)

;; Some vi sugar: emulate the CR command
;; that positions us to first non-blank on next line.
(defun forward-line-1-skipws ()
  "Position to first nonwhitespace character on next line."
  (interactive)
  (if (= (forward-line) 0)         ;if moved OK to start of next line
      (skip-chars-forward " \t"))) ;skip over horizontal whitespace

;; Bind this to M-n. ("enhanced next-line")
;; C-M-n is arguably more "correct" but (1) it takes three fingers
;; and (2) C-M-n is already bound to forward-list.
(define-key esc-map "n" 'forward-line-1-skipws)


;; C mode customization: set vanilla (8-space bsd) indention style

(require 'cc-mode)                 ;kiss: be sure it's here

(setq c-default-style
  '(
    (java-mode . "java")
    (awk-mode . "awk")
    (c-mode . "bsd")
    (other . "gnu")
  ))

;; See also CC Mode in online help for more style setup examples.

;; end of c mode style setup
```

MORE INFORMATION

A lot of emacs documentation is available in both paper and electronic form. The emacs info page and emacs help functions (page 223) provide an abundance of information. See also the GNU emacs Web page at www.gnu.org/software/emacs.

The comp.emacs and gnu.emacs.help newsgroups offer support for and a general discussion about emacs.

ACCESS TO emacs

The emacs editor is included in the repositories of most Linux distributions. You can download and install emacs with apt-get (page 916) or yum (page 910). You can download the latest version of the source code from www.gnu.org.

The Free Software Foundation can be reached at these addresses:

Mail: Free Software Foundation, Inc.
51 Franklin Street, Fifth Floor
Boston, MA 02110-1301, USA

Email: gnu@gnu.org

Phone: +1 617-542-5942

Fax +1 617 542 2652

World Wide Web www.gnu.org

CHAPTER SUMMARY

You can precede many of the commands in the following tables with a numeric argument to make the command repeat the number of times specified by the argument. Precede a numeric argument with CONTROL-U to keep emacs from entering the argument as text.

Table 7-23 lists commands that move the cursor.

Table 7-23   Moving the cursor

Command	Result
CONTROL-F	Forward by characters
CONTROL-B	Backward by characters
META-f	Forward by words
META-b	Backward by words
META-e	To end of sentence

Table 7-23   Moving the cursor (continued)

Command	Result
META-a	To beginning of sentence
META-}	To end of paragraph
META-{	To beginning of paragraph
META->	Forward to end of buffer
META-<	Backward to beginning of buffer
CONTROL-ESCAPE	To end of line
CONTROL-A	To beginning of line
CONTROL-N	Forward (down) one line
CONTROL-P	Backward (up) one line
CONTROL-V	Scroll forward (down) one window
META-v	Scroll backward (up) one window
CONTROL-L	Clear and repaint screen, and scroll current line to center of window
META-r	To beginning of middle line
CONTROL-U *num* META-r	To beginning of line number *num* (0 = top, – = bottom)

Table 7-1 lists commands that kill and delete text.

Table 7-1   Killing and deleting text

Command	Result
CONTROL-DELETE	Deletes character under cursor
DELETE	Deletes character to left of cursor
META-d	Kills forward to end of current word
META-DELETE	Kills backward to beginning of previous word
META-k	Kills forward to end of sentence
CONTROL-X DELETE	Kills backward to beginning of sentence
CONTROL-K	Kills forward to, but not including, line-ending LINEFEED; if there is no text between the cursor and the LINEFEED, kills the LINEFEED
CONTROL-U 1 CONTROL-K	Kills from cursor forward to and including LINEFEED
CONTROL-U 0 CONTROL-K	Kills from cursor backward to beginning of line
META-z *char*	Kills forward to, but not including, next occurrence of *char*

Table 7-1 Killing and deleting text (continued)

Command	Result
META-w	Copies Region to Kill Ring (does not delete Region from buffer)
CONTROL-W	Kills Region (deletes Region from buffer)
CONTROL-Y	Yanks most recently killed text into current buffer at Point; sets Mark at beginning of this text, with Point and cursor at the end
META-y	Erases just-yanked text, rotates Kill Ring, and yanks next item (only after CONTROL-Y or META-y)

Table 7-2 lists commands that search for strings and regular expressions.

Table 7-2 Search commands

Command	Result
CONTROL-S	Prompts incrementally for a string and searches forward
CONTROL-S RETURN	Prompts for a complete string and searches forward
CONTROL-R	Prompts incrementally for a string and searches backward
CONTROL-R RETURN	Prompts for a complete string and searches backward
META-CONTROL-S	Prompts incrementally for a regular expression and searches forward
META- CONTROL-S RETURN	Prompts for a complete regular expression and searches forward
META-CONTROL-R	Prompts incrementally for a regular expression and searches backward
META- CONTROL-R RETURN	Prompts for a complete regular expression and searches backward

Table 7-3 lists commands that provide online help.

Table 7-3 Online help

Command	Result
CONTROL-H a	Prompts for *string* and displays a list of commands whose names contain *string*
CONTROL-H b	Displays a (long) table of all key bindings now in effect
CONTROL-H c *key-sequence*	Displays the name of the command bound to *key-sequence*
CONTROL-H k *key-sequence*	Displays the name of and documentation for the command bound to *key-sequence*
CONTROL-H f	Prompts for the name of a Lisp function and displays the documentation for that function

Table 7-3 Online help *(continued)*

Command	Result
CONTROL-H i (lowercase "i")	Displays the top menu of info (page 36)
CONTROL-H l (lowercase "l")	Displays the last 100 characters typed
CONTROL-H m	Displays the documentation and special key bindings for the current Major mode
CONTROL-H n	Displays the emacs news file
CONTROL-H t	Starts an emacs tutorial session
CONTROL-H v	Prompts for a Lisp variable name and displays the documentation for that variable
CONTROL-H w	Prompts for a command name and displays the key sequence, if any, bound to that command

Table 7-4 lists commands that work with a Region.

Table 7-4 Working with a Region

Command	Result
META-W	Copies Region nondestructively to the Kill Ring
CONTROL-W	Kills (deletes) Region
META-x print-region	Copies Region to the print spooler
META-x append-to-buffer	Prompts for buffer name and appends Region to that buffer
META-x append-to-file	Prompts for filename and appends Region to that file
CONTROL-X CONTROL-U	Converts Region to uppercase
CONTROL-X CONTROL-L	Converts Region to lowercase

Table 7-5 lists commands that work with lines.

Table 7-5 Working with lines

Command	Result
META-x occur	Prompts for a regular expression and lists each line containing a match for the expression in a buffer named ☀**Occur**☀
META-x delete-matching-lines	Prompts for a regular expression and deletes lines from Point forward that have a match for the regular expression
META-x delete-non-matching-lines	Prompts for a regular expression and deletes lines from Point forward that do *not* have a match for the regular expression

Table 7-6 lists commands that replace strings and regular expressions unconditionally and interactively.

Table 7-6   Commands that replace text

Command	Result
META-x replace-string	Prompts for two strings and replaces each instance of the first string with the second string from Mark forward; sets Mark at the start of the command
META-% *or* META-x query-replace	As above but queries for each replacement (see Table 7-7 for a list of responses)
META-x replace-regexp	Prompts for a regular expression and a string, and replaces each match for the regular expression with the string; sets Mark at the start of the command
META-x query-replace-regexp	As above but queries for each replacement (see Table 7-7 for a list of responses)

Table 7-7 lists responses to replacement queries.

Table 7-7   Responses to replacement queries

Command	Result
RETURN	Quits searching (does not make or query for any more replacements)
SPACE	Makes this replacement and continues querying
DELETE	Does *not* make this replacement and continues querying
, (comma)	Makes this replacement, displays the result, and asks for another command
. (period)	Makes this replacement and does not make or query for any more replacements
! (exclamation point)	Replaces this and all remaining instances without querying

Table 7-8 lists commands that work with windows.

Table 7-8   Working with windows

Command	Result
CONTROL-X b	Prompts for and displays a different buffer in current window
CONTROL-X 2	Splits current window vertically into two
CONTROL-X 3	Splits current window horizontally into two

Table 7-8   Working with windows (continued)

Command	Result
CONTROL-X o (lowercase "o")	Selects other window
META-CONTROL-V	Scrolls other window
CONTROL-X 4b	Prompts for buffer name and selects it in other window
CONTROL-X 4f	Prompts for filename and selects it in other window
CONTROL-X 0 (zero)	Deletes current window
CONTROL-X 1 (one)	Deletes all windows except current window
META-x shrink-window	Makes current window one line shorter
CONTROL-X ^	Makes current window one line taller
CONTROL-X }	Makes current window one character wider
CONTROL-X {	Makes current window one character narrower

Table 7-9 lists commands that work with files.

Table 7-9   Working with files

Command	Result
CONTROL-X CONTROL-F	Prompts for a filename and reads its contents into a new buffer; assigns the file's simple filename as the buffer name.
CONTROL-X CONTROL-V	Prompts for a filename and reads its contents into the current buffer (overwriting the contents of the current buffer).
CONTROL-X 4 CONTROL-F	Prompts for a filename and reads its contents into a new buffer; assigns the file's simple filename as the buffer name. Creates a new window for the new buffer and selects that window. This command splits the screen in half if you begin with only one window.
CONTROL-X CONTROL-S	Saves the current buffer to the original file.
CONTROL-X s	Prompts for whether to save each modified buffer (**y**/**n**).
META-x set-visited-file-name	Prompts for a filename and sets the current buffer's "original" name to that filename.
CONTROL-X CONTROL-W	Prompts for a filename, sets the current buffer's "original" name to that filename, and saves the current buffer in that file.
META-~ (tilde)	Clears modified flag from the current buffer. Use with caution.

Table 7-10 lists commands that work with buffers.

Table 7-10   Working with buffers

Command	Result
CONTROL-X CONTROL-S	Saves current buffer in its associated file.
CONTROL-X CONTROL-F	Prompts for filename and visits (opens) that file.
CONTROL-X b	Prompts for buffer name and selects it. If that buffer does not exist, creates it.
CONTROL-X 4b	Prompts for buffer name and displays that buffer in another window. The existing window is not disturbed, although the new window may overlap it.
CONTROL-X CONTROL-B	Creates a buffer named ✻**Buffer List**✻ and displays it in another window. The existing window is not disturbed, although the new window may overlap it. The new buffer is not selected. In the ✻**Buffer List**✻ buffer, each buffer's data is displayed with its name, size, mode(s), and original filename.
META-x rename-buffer	Prompts for a new buffer name and assigns this new name to the current buffer.
CONTROL-X CONTROL-Q	Toggles the current buffer's readonly status and the associated %% Mode Line indicator.
META-x append-to-buffer	Prompts for buffer name and appends Region to the end of that buffer.
META-x prepend-to-buffer	Prompts for buffer name and prepends Region to the beginning of that buffer.
META-x copy-to-buffer	Prompts for buffer name, deletes contents of that buffer, and copies Region to that buffer.
META-x insert-buffer	Prompts for buffer name and inserts entire contents of that buffer in current buffer at Point.
CONTROL-X k	Prompts for buffer name and deletes that buffer.
META-x kill-some-buffers	Goes through the entire buffer list and offers the chance to delete each buffer.

Table 7-11 lists commands that run shell commands in the foreground. These commands may not work with all shells.

Table 7-11   Foreground shell commands

Command	Result
META-! (exclamation point)	Prompts for shell command, executes it, and displays the output
CONTROL-U META-! (exclamation point)	Prompts for shell command, executes it, and inserts the output at Point
META-| (vertical bar)	Prompts for shell command, supplies Region as input to that command, and displays output of command
CONTROL-U META-| (vertical bar)	Prompts for shell command, supplies Region as input to that command, deletes old Region, and inserts output of command in place of Region

Table 7-12 lists commands that run shell commands in the background.

Table 7-12   Background shell commands

Command	Result
META-x compile	Prompts for shell command and runs that command in the background, with output going to the buffer named *compilation*
META-x kill-compilation	Kills background process

Table 7-13 lists commands that convert text from uppercase to lowercase, and vice versa.

Table 7-13   Case conversion commands

Command	Result
META-l (lowercase "l")	Converts word to right of Point to lowercase
META-u	Converts word to right of Point to uppercase
META-c	Converts word to right of Point to initial caps
CONTROL-X CONTROL-L	Converts Region to lowercase
CONTROL-X CONTROL-U	Converts Region to uppercase

Table 7-14 lists commands that work in C mode.

Table 7-14 C mode commands

Command	Result
CONTROL-META-f	Moves forward over expression
CONTROL-META-b	Moves backward over expression
CONTROL-META-k	Moves forward over expression and kills it
CONTROL-META-@	Sets Mark at the position CONTROL-META-f would move to, without changing Point
CONTROL-META-a	Moves to beginning of the most recent function definition
CONTROL-META-e	Moves to end of the next function definition
CONTROL-META-h	Moves Point to beginning and Mark to end of current (or next, if between) function definition

Type META-x **shell** to create a buffer named ✳**shell**✳ and start a subshell. Table 7-15 lists commands that work on this buffer.

Table 7-15 Shell mode commands

Command	Result
RETURN	Sends current line to the shell
CONTROL-C CONTROL-D	Sends CONTROL-D to shell or its subshell
CONTROL-C CONTROL-C	Sends CONTROL-C to shell or its subshell
CONTROL-C CONTROL-\	Sends quit signal to shell or its subshell
CONTROL-C CONTROL-U	Kills text on the current line not yet completed
CONTROL-C CONTROL-R	Scrolls back to beginning of last shell output, putting first line of output at the top of the window
CONTROL-C CONTROL-O (uppercase "O")	Deletes last batch of shell output

EXERCISES

1. Given a buffer full of English text, answer the following questions:

   a. How would you change every instance of **his** to **hers**?

   b. How would you make this change only in the final paragraph?

    c. Is there a way to look at every usage in context before changing it?

    d. How would you deal with the possibility that **His** might begin a sentence?

2. Which command moves the cursor to the end of the current paragraph? Can you use this command to skip through the buffer in one-paragraph steps?

3. Suppose that you get lost in the middle of typing a long sentence.

    a. Is there an easy way to kill the botched sentence and start over?

    b. What if only one word is incorrect? Is there an alternative to backspacing one letter at a time?

4. After you have been working on a paragraph for a while, most likely some lines will have become too short and others too long. Is there a command to "neaten up" the paragraph without rebreaking all the lines by hand?

5. Is there a way to change the entire contents of the buffer to capital letters? Can you think of a way to change just one paragraph?

6. How would you reverse the order of two paragraphs?

7. How would you reverse two words?

8. Imagine that you saw a Usenet posting with something particularly funny in it and saved the posting to a file. How would you incorporate this file into your own buffer? What if you wanted to use only a couple of paragraphs from the posting? How would you add > to the beginning of each included line?

9. On the keyboard alone emacs has always offered a full set of editing possibilities. Generally several techniques will accomplish the same goal for any editing task. In the X environment the choice is enlarged still further with a new group of mouse-oriented visual alternatives. From these options you must select the way that you like to solve a given editing puzzle best.

Consider this Shakespearean fragment:

```
1. Full fathom five thy father lies;
2.   Of his bones are coral made;
3. Those are pearls that were his eyes:
4.   Nothing of him that doth fade,
5. But doth suffer a sea-change
6. Into something rich and strange.
7. Sea-nymphs hourly ring his knell:
8.           Ding-dong.
9. Hark! now I hear them--
10.     Ding-dong, bell!
```

The following fragment has been typed with some errors:

```
1. Full fathiom five tyy father lies;
2. These are pearls that were his eyes:
3.   Of his bones are coral made;
4.   Nothin of him that doth fade,
5. But doth susffer a sea-change
6. Into something rich and strange.
7. Sea-nymphs hourly ring his knell:
8.           Ding=dong.
9. Hard! now I hear them--
10.      Ding-dong, bell!
```

Use only the keyboard to answer the following:

a. How many ways can you think of to move the cursor to the spelling errors?

b. Once the cursor is on or near the errors, how many ways can you think of to fix them?

c. Are there ways to fix errors without explicitly navigating to or searching for them? How many can you think of?

d. Lines 2 and 3 in the retyped material are transposed. How many ways can you think of to correct this situation?

ADVANCED EXERCISES

10. Assume that your buffer contains the C code shown here, with the Major mode set for C and the cursor positioned at the end of the **while** line as shown by the black square:

```c
/*
 * Copy string s2 to s1.  s1 must be large enough
 * return s1
 */
char *strcpy(char *s1, char *s2)
{
        char *os1;

        os1 = s1;
        while (*s1++ = *s2++)
                ;
        return os1;
}

/*
 * Copy source into dest, stopping after '\0' is copied, and
 * return a pointer to the '\0' at the end of dest. Then our caller
 * can catenate to the dest  * string without another strlen call.
 */
```

```
char *stpcpy (char *dest, char *source)
{
        while ((*dest++ = *source++) != '\0') ■
               ; /* void loop body */
        return (dest - 1);
}
```

a. Which command moves the cursor to the opening brace of **strcpy**? Which command moves the cursor past the closing brace? Can you use these commands to skip through the buffer in one-procedure steps?

b. Assume the cursor is just past the closing parenthesis of the **while** condition. How do you move to the matching opening parenthesis? How do you move back to the matching close parenthesis again? Does the same command set work for matched [] (square brackets) and {} (braces)? How does this differ from the vim % command?

c. One procedure is indented in the Berkeley indention style; the other is indented in the GNU style. Which command reindents a line in accordance with the current indention style you have set up? How would you reindent an entire procedure?

d. Suppose that you want to write five string procedures and intend to use **strcpy** as a starting point for further editing. How would you make five copies of the **strcpy** procedure?

e. How would you compile the code without leaving emacs?

PART III
The Shells

8

THE BOURNE AGAIN SHELL

This chapter picks up where Chapter 5 left off by focusing on the Bourne Again Shell (bash). It notes where tcsh implementation of a feature differs from that of bash and, if appropriate, directs you to the page that discusses the alternative implementation. Chapter 10 expands on this chapter, exploring control flow commands and more advanced aspects of programming the Bourne Again Shell (bash). The bash home page is www.gnu.org/software/bash. The bash info page is a complete Bourne Again Shell reference.

The Bourne Again Shell and TC Shell (tcsh) are command interpreters and high-level programming languages. As command interpreters, they process commands you enter on the command line in response to a prompt. When you use the shell as a programming language, it processes commands stored in files called *shell scripts*. Like other languages, shells have variables and control flow commands (for example, **for** loops and **if** statements).

When you use a shell as a command interpreter, you can customize the environment you work in. You can make your prompt display the name of the working directory, create a function or an alias for cp that keeps it from overwriting certain kinds of files, take advantage of keyword variables to change

269

aspects of how the shell works, and so on. You can also write shell scripts that do your bidding—anything from a one-line script that stores a long, complex command to a longer script that runs a set of reports, prints them, and mails you a reminder when the job is done. More complex shell scripts are themselves programs; they do not just run other programs. Chapter 10 has some examples of these types of scripts.

Most system shell scripts are written to run under bash (or dash; see below). If you will ever work in single-user or recovery mode—when you boot the system or perform system maintenance, administration, or repair work, for example—it is a good idea to become familiar with this shell.

This chapter expands on the interactive features of the shell described in Chapter 5, explains how to create and run simple shell scripts, discusses job control, introduces the basic aspects of shell programming, talks about history and aliases, and describes command-line expansion. Chapter 9 covers interactive use of the TC Shell and TC Shell programming, and Chapter 10 presents some more challenging shell programming problems.

BACKGROUND

The Bourne Again Shell is based on the Bourne Shell (the early UNIX shell; this book refers to it as the *original Bourne Shell* to avoid confusion), which was written by Steve Bourne of AT&T's Bell Laboratories. Over the years the original Bourne Shell has been expanded but it remains the basic shell provided with many commercial versions of UNIX.

sh Shell   Because of its long and successful history, the original Bourne Shell has been used to write many of the shell scripts that help manage UNIX systems. Some of these scripts appear in Linux as Bourne Again Shell scripts. Although the Bourne Again Shell includes many extensions and features not found in the original Bourne Shell, bash maintains compatibility with the original Bourne Shell so you can run Bourne Shell scripts under bash. On UNIX systems the original Bourne Shell is named sh.

On some Linux systems sh is a symbolic link to bash ensuring that scripts that require the presence of the Bourne Shell still run. When called as sh, bash does its best to emulate the original Bourne Shell.

dash Shell   The bash executable file is about 800 kilobytes, has many features, and is well suited as a user login shell. The dash (Debian Almquist) shell is about 100 kilobytes, offers Bourne Shell compatibility for shell scripts (noninteractive use), and, because of its size, can load and execute shell scripts much more quickly than bash. Most system scripts are set up to run sh, which under some systems, such as Ubuntu, is a symbolic link to dash. This setup allows the system to boot and run system shell scripts quickly.

Korn Shell   System V UNIX introduced the Korn Shell (ksh), written by David Korn. This shell extended many features of the original Bourne Shell and added many new features.

Some features of the Bourne Again Shell, such as command aliases and command-line editing, are based on similar features from the Korn Shell.

POSIX The POSIX (Portable Operating System Interface) family of related standards is being developed by PASC (IEEE's Portable Application Standards Committee, www.pasc.org). A comprehensive FAQ on POSIX, including many links, appears at www.opengroup.org/austin/papers/posix_faq.html.

POSIX standard 1003.2 describes shell functionality. The Bourne Again Shell provides the features that match the requirements of this standard. Efforts are under way to make the Bourne Again Shell fully comply with the POSIX standard. In the meantime, if you invoke bash with the --posix option, the behavior of the Bourne Again Shell will closely match the POSIX requirements.

The **bash-doc** package holds Bourne Again Shell info **documentation**

tip Without the **bash-doc** package installed, the bash man page is available. Installing this package provides the more complete bash info pages. See page 36 for information on info and Appendix C for information on installing software packages.

SHELL BASICS

This section covers writing and using startup files, redirecting standard error, writing and executing simple shell scripts, separating and grouping commands, implementing job control, and manipulating the directory stack.

chsh: **changes your login shell**

tip The person who sets up your account determines which shell you use when you first log in on the system or when you open a terminal emulator window in a GUI environment. Under most Linux distributions, bash is the default shell. You can run any shell you like once you are logged in. Enter the name of the shell you want to use (bash, tcsh, or another shell) and press RETURN; the next prompt will be that of the new shell. Give an **exit** command to return to the previous shell. Because shells you call in this manner are nested (one runs on top of the other), you will be able to log out only from your original shell. When you have nested several shells, keep giving **exit** commands until you reach your original shell. You will then be able to log out.

Use the chsh utility to change your login shell permanently. First give the command **chsh**. In response to the prompts, enter your password and the absolute pathname of the shell you want to use (**/bin/bash**, **/bin/tcsh**, or the pathname of another shell). When you change your login shell in this manner using a terminal emulator (page 26) under a GUI, subsequent terminal emulator windows will not reflect the change until you log out of the system and log back in.

STARTUP FILES

When a shell starts, it runs startup files to initialize itself. Which files the shell runs depends on whether it is a login shell, an interactive shell that is not a login shell (such as you get by giving the command **bash**), or a noninteractive shell (one used to execute a shell script). You must have read access to a startup file to execute the commands in it. Typically Linux distributions put appropriate commands in some of these files. This section covers bash startup files. See page 352 for information on tcsh startup files and page 936 for information on startup files under Mac OS X.

LOGIN SHELLS

The files covered in this section are executed by login shells and shells that you start with the bash ––login option. Login shells are, by their nature, interactive.

/etc/profile   The shell first executes the commands in **/etc/profile**. A user working with **root** privileges can set up this file to establish systemwide default characteristics for users running bash.

.bash_profile
.bash_login
.profile

Next the shell looks for **~/.bash_profile**, **~/.bash_login**, and **~/.profile** (**~/** is shorthand for your home directory), in that order, executing the commands in the first of these files it finds. You can put commands in one of these files to override the defaults set in **/etc/profile**. A shell running on a virtual terminal does not execute commands in these files.

.bash_logout   When you log out, bash executes commands in the **~/.bash_logout** file. This file often holds commands that clean up after a session, such as those that remove temporary files.

INTERACTIVE NONLOGIN SHELLS

The commands in the preceding startup files are not executed by interactive, nonlogin shells. However, these shells inherit values from the login shell variables that are set by these startup files.

/etc/bashrc   Although not called by bash directly, many **~/.bashrc** files call **/etc/bashrc**. This setup allows a user working with **root** privileges to establish systemwide default characteristics for nonlogin bash shells.

.bashrc   An interactive nonlogin shell executes commands in the **~/.bashrc** file. Typically a startup file for a login shell, such as **.bash_profile**, runs this file, so both login and nonlogin shells run the commands in **.bashrc**.

NONINTERACTIVE SHELLS

The commands in the previously described startup files are not executed by noninteractive shells, such as those that runs shell scripts. However, these shells inherit login shell variables that are set by these startup files.

BASH_ENV   Noninteractive shells look for the environment variable **BASH_ENV** (or **ENV** if the shell is called as sh) and execute commands in the file named by this variable.

SETTING UP STARTUP FILES

Although many startup files and types of shells exist, usually all you need are the **.bash_profile** and **.bashrc** files in your home directory. Commands similar to the following in **.bash_profile** run commands from **.bashrc** for login shells (when **.bashrc** exists). With this setup, the commands in **.bashrc** are executed by login and nonlogin shells.

```
if [ -f ~/.bashrc ]; then . ~/.bashrc; fi
```

The [**–f ~/.bashrc**] tests whether the file named **.bashrc** in your home directory exists. See pages 399, 401, and 854 for more information on test and its synonym [ ]. See page 274 for information on the . (dot) builtin.

Use .bash_profile to set PATH

tip   Because commands in **.bashrc** may be executed many times, and because subshells inherit exported variables, it is a good idea to put commands that add to existing variables in the **.bash_profile** file. For example, the following command adds the **bin** subdirectory of the **home** directory to **PATH** (page 297) and should go in **.bash_profile**:

```
PATH=$PATH:$HOME/bin
```

When you put this command in **.bash_profile** and not in **.bashrc**, the string is added to the **PATH** variable only once, when you log in.

Modifying a variable in **.bash_profile** causes changes you make in an interactive session to propagate to subshells. In contrast, modifying a variable in **.bashrc** overrides changes inherited from a parent shell.

Sample **.bash_profile** and **.bashrc** files follow. Some commands used in these files are not covered until later in this chapter. In any startup file, you must export variables and functions that you want to be available to child processes. For more information refer to "Locality of Variables" on page 436.

```
$ cat ~/.bash_profile
if [ -f ~/.bashrc ]; then
    . ~/.bashrc                    # Read local startup file if it exists
fi
PATH=$PATH:.                       # Add the working directory to PATH
export PS1='[\h \W \!]\$ '         # Set prompt
```

The first command in the preceding **.bash_profile** file executes the commands in the user's **.bashrc** file if it exists. The next command adds to the **PATH** variable (page 297). Typically **PATH** is set and exported in **/etc/profile** so it does not need to be exported in a user's startup file. The final command sets and exports **PS1** (page 299), which controls the user's prompt.

A sample **.bashrc** file is shown on the next page. The first command executes the commands in the **/etc/bashrc** file if it exists. Next the file sets and exports the **LANG** (page 304) and **VIMINIT** (for vim initialization) variables and defines several aliases. The final command defines a function (page 327) that swaps the names of two files.

```
$ cat ~/.bashrc
if [ -f /etc/bashrc ]; then
    source /etc/bashrc            # read global startup file if it exists
fi

set -o noclobber                 # prevent overwriting files
unset MAILCHECK                  # turn off "you have new mail" notice
export LANG=C                    # set LANG variable
export VIMINIT='set ai aw'       # set vim options
alias df='df -h'                 # set up aliases
alias rm='rm -i'                 # always do interactive rm's
alias lt='ls -ltrh | tail'
alias h='history | tail'
alias ch='chmod 755 '

function switch()                # a function to exchange the names
{                                # of two files
    local tmp=$$switch
    mv "$1" $tmp
    mv "$2" "$1"
    mv $tmp "$2"
}
```

. (DOT) OR source: RUNS A STARTUP FILE IN THE CURRENT SHELL

After you edit a startup file such as **.bashrc**, you do not have to log out and log in again to put the changes into effect. Instead, you can run the startup file using the **.** (dot) or source builtin (they are the same command under bash; only source is available under tcsh [page 390]). As with all other commands, the **.** must be followed by a SPACE on the command line. Using **.** or source is similar to running a shell script, except these commands run the script as part of the current process. Consequently, when you use **.** or source to run a script, changes you make to variables from within the script affect the shell you run the script from. If you ran a startup file as a regular shell script and did not use the **.** or source builtin, the variables created in the startup file would remain in effect only in the subshell running the script—not in the shell you ran the script from. You can use the **.** or source command to run any shell script—not just a startup file—but undesirable side effects (such as changes in the values of shell variables you rely on) may occur. For more information refer to "Locality of Variables" on page 436.

In the following example, **.bashrc** sets several variables and sets **PS1**, the prompt, to the name of the host. The **.** builtin puts the new values into effect.

```
$ cat ~/.bashrc
export TERM=vt100                # set the terminal type
export PS1="$(hostname -f): "    # set the prompt string
export CDPATH=:$HOME             # add HOME to CDPATH string
stty kill '^u'                   # set kill line to control-u

$ . ~/.bashrc
bravo.example.com:
```

COMMANDS THAT ARE SYMBOLS

The Bourne Again Shell uses the symbols (,), [,], and $ in a variety of ways. To minimize confusion, Table 8-1 lists the most common use of each of these symbols, even though some of them are not introduced until later in this book.

Table 8-1   Builtin commands that are symbols

Symbol	Command
( )	Subshell (page 284)
$( )	Command substitution (page 340)
(( ))	Arithmetic evaluation; a synonym for let (use when the enclosed value contains an equal sign; page 460)
$(( ))	Arithmetic expansion (not for use with an enclosed equal sign; page 338)
[ ]	The test command (pages 399, 401, and 854)
[[ ]]	Conditional expression; similar to [ ] but adds string comparisons (page 461)

REDIRECTING STANDARD ERROR

Chapter 5 covered the concept of standard output and explained how to redirect standard output of a command. In addition to standard output, commands can send output to *standard error*. A command can send error messages to standard error to keep them from getting mixed up with the information it sends to standard output.

Just as it does with standard output, by default the shell directs standard error to the screen. Unless you redirect one or the other, you may not know the difference between the output a command sends to standard output and the output it sends to standard error. This section describes the syntax used by the Bourne Again Shell to redirect standard error and to distinguish between standard output and standard error. See page 359 if you are using the TC Shell.

File descriptors   A *file descriptor* is the place a program sends its output to and gets its input from. When you execute a program, Linux opens three file descriptors for the program: 0 (standard input), 1 (standard output), and 2 (standard error). The redirect output symbol (> [page 126]) is shorthand for 1>, which tells the shell to redirect standard output. Similarly < (page 128) is short for 0<, which redirects standard input. The symbols 2> redirect standard error. For more information refer to "File Descriptors" on page 431.

The following examples demonstrate how to redirect standard output and standard error to different files and to the same file. When you run the cat utility with the name of a file that does not exist and the name of a file that does exist, cat sends an error message to standard error and copies the file that does exist to standard output. Unless you redirect them, both messages appear on the screen.

```
$ cat y
This is y.
$ cat x
cat: x: No such file or directory

$ cat x y
cat: x: No such file or directory
This is y.
```

When you redirect standard output of a command, output sent to standard error is not affected and still appears on the screen.

```
$ cat x y > hold
cat: x: No such file or directory
$ cat hold
This is y.
```

Similarly, when you send standard output through a pipe, standard error is not affected. The following example sends standard output of cat through a pipe to tr, which in this example converts lowercase characters to uppercase. (See page 864 for more information on tr.) The text that cat sends to standard error is not translated because it goes directly to the screen rather than through the pipe.

```
$ cat x y | tr "[a-z]" "[A-Z]"
cat: x: No such file or directory
THIS IS Y.
```

The following example redirects standard output and standard error to different files. The token following **2>** tells the shell where to redirect standard error (file descriptor 2). The token following **1>** tells the shell where to redirect standard output (file descriptor 1). You can use > in place of **1>**.

```
$ cat x y 1> hold1 2> hold2
$ cat hold1
This is y.
$ cat hold2
cat: x: No such file or directory
```

Combining standard output and standard error
In the next example, the **&>** token redirects standard output and standard error to a single file. The **>&** token performs the same function under tcsh (page 359).

```
$ cat x y &> hold
$ cat hold
cat: x: No such file or directory
This is y.
```

Duplicating a file descriptor
In the next example, first **1>** redirects standard output to **hold** and then **2>&1** declares file descriptor 2 to be a duplicate of file descriptor 1. As a result, both standard output and standard error are redirected to **hold**.

```
$ cat x y 1> hold 2>&1
$ cat hold
cat: x: No such file or directory
This is y.
```

In this case, **1> hold** precedes **2>&1**. If they had been listed in the opposite order, standard error would have been made a duplicate of standard output before standard output was redirected to **hold**. Only standard output would have been redirected to **hold** in that scenario.

The next example declares file descriptor 2 to be a duplicate of file descriptor 1 and sends the output for file descriptor 1 through a pipe to the tr command.

```
$ cat x y 2>&1 | tr "[a-z]" "[A-Z]"
CAT: X: NO SUCH FILE OR DIRECTORY
THIS IS Y.
```

Sending errors to standard error

You can use **1>&2** to redirect standard output of a command to standard error. Shell scripts use this technique to send the output of echo to standard error. In the following script, standard output of the first echo is redirected to standard error:

```
$ cat message_demo
echo This is an error message. 1>&2
echo This is not an error message.
```

If you redirect standard output of **message_demo**, error messages such as the one produced by the first echo appear on the screen because you have not redirected standard error. Because standard output of a shell script is frequently redirected to another file, you can use this technique to display on the screen any error messages generated by the script. The **lnks** script (page 406) uses this technique. You can also use the exec builtin to create additional file descriptors and to redirect standard input, standard output, and standard error of a shell script from within the script (page 451).

The Bourne Again Shell supports the redirection operators shown in Table 8-2.

Table 8-2 Redirection operators

Operator	Meaning
< *filename*	Redirects standard input from *filename*.
> *filename*	Redirects standard output to *filename* unless *filename* exists and **noclobber** (page 129) is set. If **noclobber** is not set, this redirection creates *filename* if it does not exist and overwrites it if it does exist.
>| *filename*	Redirects standard output to *filename*, even if the file exists and **noclobber** (page 129) is set.
>> *filename*	Redirects and appends standard output to *filename* unless *filename* exists and **noclobber** (page 129) is set. If **noclobber** is not set, this redirection creates *filename* if it does not exist.
&> *filename*	Redirects standard output and standard error to *filename*.
<&*m*	Duplicates standard input from file descriptor *m* (page 432).
[n]>&*m*	Duplicates standard output or file descriptor *n* if specified from file descriptor *m* (page 432).
[n]<&−	Closes standard input or file descriptor *n* if specified (page 432).
[n]>&−	Closes standard output or file descriptor *n* if specified.

Writing a Simple Shell Script

A *shell script* is a file that holds commands that the shell can execute. The commands in a shell script can be any commands you can enter in response to a shell prompt. For example, a command in a shell script might run a Linux utility, a compiled program, or another shell script. Like the commands you give on the command line, a command in a shell script can use ambiguous file references and can have its input or output redirected from or to a file or sent through a pipe. You can also use pipes and redirection with the input and output of the script itself.

In addition to the commands you would ordinarily use on the command line, *control flow* commands (also called *control structures*) find most of their use in shell scripts. This group of commands enables you to alter the order of execution of commands in a script in the same way you would alter the order of execution of statements using a structured programming language. Refer to "Control Structures" on page 398 (bash) and page 378 (tcsh) for specifics.

The shell interprets and executes the commands in a shell script, one after another. Thus a shell script enables you to simply and quickly initiate a complex series of tasks or a repetitive procedure.

chmod: Makes a File Executable

To execute a shell script by giving its name as a command, you must have permission to read and execute the file that contains the script (refer to "Access Permissions" on page 93). Read permission enables you to read the file that holds the script. Execute permission tells the shell and the system that the owner, group, and/or public has permission to execute the file; it implies that the content of the file is executable.

When you create a shell script using an editor, the file does not typically have its execute permission set. The following example shows a file named **whoson** that contains a shell script:

```
$ cat whoson
date
echo "Users Currently Logged In"
who

$ ./whoson
bash: ./whoson: Permission denied
```

You cannot execute **whoson** by giving its name as a command because you do not have execute permission for the file. The shell does not recognize **whoson** as an executable file and issues the error message **Permission denied** when you try to execute it. (See the tip on the next page if you get a **command not found** error message.) When you give the filename as an argument to bash (**bash whoson**), bash takes the argument to be a shell script and executes it. In this case **bash** is executable and **whoson** is an argument that bash executes so you do not need to have execute permission to **whoson**. You must have read permission. You can do the same with tcsh script files.

```
$ ls -l whoson
-rw-rw-r--   1 max group 40 May 24 11:30 whoson

$ chmod u+x whoson
$ ls -l whoson
-rwxrw-r--   1 max group 40 May 24 11:30 whoson

$ ./whoson
Fri May 22 11:40:49 PDT 2009
Users Currently Logged In
zach     pts/7    May 21 18:17
hls      pts/1    May 22 09:59
sam      pts/12   May 22 06:29 (bravo.example.com)
max      pts/4    May 22 09:08
```

Figure 8-1   Using chmod to make a shell script executable

The chmod utility changes the access privileges associated with a file. Figure 8-1 shows ls with the –l option displaying the access privileges of **whoson** before and after chmod gives execute permission to the file's owner.

The first ls displays a hyphen (–) as the fourth character, indicating that the owner does not have permission to execute the file. Next chmod gives the owner execute permission: **u+x** causes chmod to add (**+**) execute permission (**x**) for the owner (**u**). (The **u** stands for *user*, although it means the owner of the file.) The second argument is the name of the file. The second ls shows an **x** in the fourth position, indicating that the owner has execute permission.

Command not found?

tip   If you give the name of a shell script as a command without including the leading ./, the shell typically displays the following error message:

```
$ whoson
bash: whoson: command not found
```

This message indicates the shell is not set up to search for executable files in the working directory. Give this command instead:

```
$ ./whoson
```

The ./ tells the shell explicitly to look for an executable file in the working directory. To change the environment so the shell searches the working directory automatically, see the section about **PATH** on page 297.

If other users will execute the file, you must also change group and/or public access permissions for the file. Any user must have execute access to use the file's name as a command. If the file is a shell script, the user trying to execute the file must have read access to the file as well. You do not need read access to execute a binary executable (compiled program).

The final command in Figure 8-1 shows the shell executing the file when its name is given as a command. For more information refer to "Access Permissions" on page 93 as well as the discussions of ls and chmod in Part V.

#! SPECIFIES A SHELL

You can put a special sequence of characters on the first line of a shell script to tell the operating system which shell (or other program) should execute the file. Because the operating system checks the initial characters of a program before attempting to execute it using **exec**, these characters save the system from making an unsuccessful attempt. If **#!** are the first two characters of a script, the system interprets the characters that follow as the absolute pathname of the utility that should execute the script. This can be the pathname of any program, not just a shell. The following example specifies that bash should run the script:

```
$ cat bash_script
#!/bin/bash
echo "This is a Bourne Again Shell script."
```

The **#!** characters are useful if you have a script that you want to run with a shell other than the shell you are running the script from. The next example shows a script that should be executed by tcsh:

```
$ cat tcsh_script
#!/bin/tcsh
echo "This is a tcsh script."
set person = zach
echo "person is $person"
```

Because of the **#!** line, the operating system ensures that tcsh executes the script no matter which shell you run it from.

You can use **ps –f** within a shell script to display the name of the shell that is executing the script. The three lines that ps displays in the following example show the process running the parent bash shell, the process running the tcsh script, and the process running the ps command:

```
$ cat tcsh_script2
#!/bin/tcsh
ps -f

$ ./tcsh_script2
UID        PID  PPID  C STIME TTY          TIME CMD
max       3031  3030  0 Nov16 pts/4    00:00:00 -bash
max       9358  3031  0 21:13 pts/4    00:00:00 /bin/tcsh ./tcsh_script2
max       9375  9358  0 21:13 pts/4    00:00:00 ps -f
```

If you do not follow **#!** with the name of an executable program, the shell reports that it cannot find the command that you asked it to run. You can optionally follow **#!** with SPACEs. If you omit the **#!** line and try to run, for example, a tcsh script from bash, the script will run under bash and may generate error messages or not run properly. See page 578 for an example of a stand-alone sed script that uses **#!**.

BEGINS A COMMENT

Comments make shell scripts and all code easier to read and maintain by you and others. The comment syntax is common to both the Bourne Again and the TC Shells.

If a pound sign (#) in the first character position of the first line of a script is not immediately followed by an exclamation point (!) or if a pound sign occurs in any other location in a script, the shell interprets it as the beginning of a comment. The shell then ignores everything between the pound sign and the end of the line (the next NEWLINE character).

EXECUTING A SHELL SCRIPT

fork and **exec** system calls A command on the command line causes the shell to **fork** a new process, creating a duplicate of the shell process (a subshell). The new process attempts to **exec** (execute) the command. Like **fork**, the **exec** routine is executed by the operating system (a system call). If the command is a binary executable program, such as a compiled C program, **exec** succeeds and the system overlays the newly created subshell with the executable program. If the command is a shell script, **exec** fails. When **exec** fails, the command is assumed to be a shell script, and the subshell runs the commands in the script. Unlike a login shell, which expects input from the command line, the subshell takes its input from a file—namely, the shell script.

As discussed earlier, you can run commands in a shell script file that you do not have execute permission for by using a bash command to **exec** a shell that runs the script directly. In the following example, bash creates a new shell that takes its input from the file named **whoson**:

```
$ bash whoson
```

Because the bash command expects to read a file containing commands, you do not need execute permission for **whoson**. (You do need read permission.) Even though bash reads and executes the commands in **whoson**, standard input, standard output, and standard error remain directed from/to the terminal.

Although you can use bash to execute a shell script, this technique causes the script to run more slowly than giving yourself execute permission and directly invoking the script. Users typically prefer to make the file executable and run the script by typing its name on the command line. It is also easier to type the name, and this practice is consistent with the way other kinds of programs are invoked (so you do not need to know whether you are running a shell script or an executable file). However, if bash is not your interactive shell or if you want to see how the script runs with different shells, you may want to run a script as an argument to **bash** or **tcsh**.

SEPARATING AND GROUPING COMMANDS

Whether you give the shell commands interactively or write a shell script, you must separate commands from one another. This section, which applies to the Bourne Again and the TC Shells, reviews the ways to separate commands that were covered in Chapter 5 and introduces a few new ones.

; AND NEWLINE SEPARATE COMMANDS

The NEWLINE character is a unique command separator because it initiates execution of the command preceding it. You have seen this behavior throughout this book each time you press the RETURN key at the end of a command line.

The semicolon (;) is a command separator that *does not* initiate execution of a command and *does not* change any aspect of how the command functions. You can execute a series of commands sequentially by entering them on a single command line and separating each from the next with a semicolon (;). You initiate execution of the sequence of commands by pressing RETURN:

```
$ x ; y ; z
```

If **x**, **y**, and **z** are commands, the preceding command line yields the same results as the next three commands. The difference is that in the next example the shell issues a prompt after each of the commands (**x**, **y**, and **z**) finishes executing, whereas the preceding command line causes the shell to issue a prompt only after **z** is complete:

```
$ x
$ y
$ z
```

Whitespace   Although the whitespace around the semicolons in the earlier example makes the command line easier to read, it is not necessary. None of the command separators needs to be surrounded by SPACEs or TABs.

\ CONTINUES A COMMAND

When you enter a long command line and the cursor reaches the right side of the screen, you can use a backslash (\) character to continue the command on the next line. The backslash quotes, or escapes, the NEWLINE character that follows it so the shell does not treat the NEWLINE as a command terminator. Enclosing a backslash within single quotation marks or preceding it with another backslash turns off the power of a backslash to quote special characters such as NEWLINE (not tcsh; see **prompt2** on page 374). Enclosing a backslash within double quotation marks has no effect on the power of the backslash (not tcsh).

Although you can break a line in the middle of a word (token), it is typically simpler to break a line immediately before or after whitespace.

optional   Under bash, you can enter a RETURN in the middle of a quoted string on a command line without using a backslash. (See **prompt2** on page 374 for tcsh behavior). The NEWLINE (RETURN) you enter will then be part of the string:

```
$ echo "Please enter the three values
> required to complete the transaction."
Please enter the three values
required to complete the transaction.
```

In the three examples in this section, bash does not interpret RETURN as a command terminator because it occurs within a quoted string. The greater than (>) sign is a secondary prompt (**PS2**; page 300) indicating the shell is waiting for you to continue the unfinished command. In the next example, the first RETURN is quoted (escaped) so the shell treats it as a separator and does not interpret it literally.

```
$ echo "Please enter the three values \
> required to complete the transaction."
Please enter the three values required to complete the transaction.
```

Single quotation marks cause the shell to interpret a backslash literally:

```
$ echo 'Please enter the three values \
> required to complete the transaction.'
Please enter the three values \
required to complete the transaction.
```

| AND & SEPARATE COMMANDS AND DO SOMETHING ELSE

The pipe symbol (|) and the background task symbol (&) are also command separators. They *do not* start execution of a command but *do* change some aspect of how the command functions. The pipe symbol alters the source of standard input or the destination of standard output. The background task symbol causes the shell to execute the task in the background and display a prompt immediately; you can continue working on other tasks.

Each of the following command lines initiates a single job comprising three tasks:

```
$ x | y | z
$ ls -l | grep tmp | less
```

In the first job, the shell redirects standard output of task **x** to standard input of task **y** and redirects **y**'s standard output to **z**'s standard input. Because it runs the entire job in the foreground, the shell does not display a prompt until task **z** runs to completion: Task **z** does not finish until task **y** finishes, and task **y** does not finish until task **x** finishes. In the second job, task **x** is an **ls –l** command, task **y** is **grep tmp**, and task **z** is the pager **less**. The shell displays a long (wide) listing of the files in the working directory that contain the string **tmp**, piped through **less**.

The next command line executes tasks **d** and **e** in the background and task **f** in the foreground:

```
$ d & e & f
[1] 14271
[2] 14272
```

The shell displays the job number between brackets and the PID number for each process running in the background. It displays a prompt as soon as **f** finishes, which may be before **d** or **e** finishes.

Before displaying a prompt for a new command, the shell checks whether any background jobs have completed. For each completed job, the shell displays its job number, the word **Done**, and the command line that invoked the job; the shell then displays a prompt. When the job numbers are listed, the number of the last job started is followed by a + character and the job number of the previous job is followed by a – character.

Other jobs are followed by a SPACE character. After running the last command, the shell displays the following lines before issuing a prompt:

```
[1]-  Done                    d
[2]+  Done                    e
```

The next command line executes all three tasks as background jobs. The shell displays a prompt immediately:

```
$ d & e & f &
[1] 14290
[2] 14291
[3] 14292
```

You can use pipes to send the output from one task to the next task and an ampersand (&) to run the entire job as a background task. Again the shell displays the prompt immediately. The shell regards the commands joined by a pipe as a single job. That is, it treats all pipes as single jobs, no matter how many tasks are connected with the pipe (|) symbol or how complex they are. The Bourne Again Shell reports only one process in the background (although there are three):

```
$ d | e | f &
[1] 14295
```

The TC Shell shows three processes (all belonging to job 1) placed in the background:

```
tcsh $ d | e | f &
[1] 14302 14304 14306
```

optional   ( ) GROUPS COMMANDS

You can use parentheses to group commands. The shell creates a copy of itself, called a *subshell*, for each group. It treats each group of commands as a job and creates a new process to execute each command (refer to "Process Structure" on page 306 for more information on creating subshells). Each subshell (job) has its own environment, meaning that it has its own set of variables whose values can differ from those found in other subshells.

The following command line executes commands **a** and **b** sequentially in the background while executing **c** in the background. The shell displays a prompt immediately.

```
$ (a ; b) & c &
[1] 15520
[2] 15521
```

The preceding example differs from the earlier example **d & e & f &** in that tasks **a** and **b** are initiated sequentially, not concurrently.

Similarly the following command line executes **a** and **b** sequentially in the background and, at the same time, executes **c** and **d** sequentially in the background. The subshell running **a** and **b** and the subshell running **c** and **d** run concurrently. The shell displays a prompt immediately.

```
$ (a ; b) & (c ; d) &
[1] 15528
[2] 15529
```

The next script copies one directory to another. The second pair of parentheses creates a subshell to run the commands following the pipe. Because of these parentheses, the output of the first tar command is available for the second tar command despite the intervening cd command. Without the parentheses, the output of the first tar command would be sent to cd and lost because cd does not process input from standard input. The shell variables **$1** and **$2** represent the first and second command-line arguments (page 441), respectively. The first pair of parentheses, which creates a subshell to run the first two commands, allows users to call **cpdir** with relative pathnames. Without them, the first cd command would change the working directory of the script (and consequently the working directory of the second cd command). With them, only the working directory of the subshell is changed.

```
$ cat cpdir
(cd $1 ; tar -cf - . ) | (cd $2 ; tar -xvf - )
$ ./cpdir /home/max/sources /home/max/memo/biblio
```

The **cpdir** command line copies the files and directories in the **/home/max/sources** directory to the directory named **/home/max/memo/biblio**. This shell script is almost the same as using cp with the **–r** option. Refer to Part V for more information on cp and tar.

JOB CONTROL

A *job* is a command pipeline. You run a simple job whenever you give the shell a command. For example, if you type **date** on the command line and press RETURN, you have run a job. You can also create several jobs with multiple commands on a single command line:

```
$ find . -print | sort | lpr & grep -l max /tmp/* > maxfiles &
[1] 18839
[2] 18876
```

The portion of the command line up to the first & is one job consisting of three processes connected by pipes: find (page 688), sort (pages 54 and 817), and lpr (pages 51 and 742). The second job is a single process running grep. The trailing & characters put each job in the background, so bash does not wait for them to complete before displaying a prompt.

Using job control you can move commands from the foreground to the background (and vice versa), stop commands temporarily, and list all commands that are running in the background or stopped.

jobs: LISTS JOBS

The jobs builtin lists all background jobs. Following, the sleep command runs in the background and creates a background job that jobs reports on:

```
$ sleep 60 &
[1] 7809
$ jobs
[1] + Running                     sleep 60 &
```

fg: BRINGS A JOB TO THE FOREGROUND

The shell assigns a job number to each command you run in the background. For each job run in the background, the shell lists the job number and PID number immediately, just before it issues a prompt:

```
$ xclock &
[1] 1246
$ date &
[2] 1247
$ Tue Dec 2 11:44:40 PST 2008
[2]+ Done            date
$ find /usr -name ace -print > findout &
[2] 1269
$ jobs
[1]- Running        xclock &
[2]+ Running        find /usr -name ace -print > findout &
```

Job numbers, which are discarded when a job is finished, can be reused. When you start or put a job in the background, the shell assigns a job number that is one more than the highest job number in use.

In the preceding example, the jobs command lists the first job, xclock, as job 1. The date command does not appear in the jobs list because it finished before jobs was run. Because the date command was completed before find was run, the find command became job 2.

To move a background job to the foreground, use the fg builtin followed by the job number. Alternatively, you can give a percent sign (%) followed by the job number as a command. Either of the following commands moves job 2 to the foreground. When you move a job to the foreground, the shell displays the command it is now executing in the foreground.

```
$ fg 2
find /usr -name ace -print > findout
```

or

```
$ %2
find /usr -name ace -print > findout
```

You can also refer to a job by following the percent sign with a string that uniquely identifies the beginning of the command line used to start the job. Instead of the preceding command, you could have used either **fg %find** or **fg %f** because both uniquely identify job 2. If you follow the percent sign with a question mark and a string, the string can match any part of the command line. In the preceding example, **fg %?ace** also brings job 2 to the foreground.

Often the job you wish to bring to the foreground is the only job running in the background or is the job that jobs lists with a plus (+). In these cases fg without an argument brings the job to the foreground.

SUSPENDING A JOB

Pressing the suspend key (usually CONTROL-Z) immediately suspends (temporarily stops) the job in the foreground and displays a message that includes the word **Stopped**.

```
CONTROL-Z
[2]+  Stopped                        find /usr -name ace -print > findout
```

For more information refer to "Moving a Job from the Foreground to the Background" on page 135.

bg: SENDS A JOB TO THE BACKGROUND

To move the foreground job to the background, you must first suspend the job (above). You can then use the **bg** builtin to resume execution of the job in the background.

```
$ bg
[2]+ find /usr -name ace -print > findout &
```

If a background job attempts to read from the terminal, the shell stops the program and displays a message saying the job has been stopped. You must then move the job to the foreground so it can read from the terminal.

```
$ (sleep 5; cat > mytext) &
[1] 1343
$ date
Tue Dec  2 11:58:20 PST 2008
[1]+ Stopped                    ( sleep 5; cat >mytext )
$ fg
( sleep 5; cat >mytext )
Remember to let the cat out!
CONTROL-D
$
```

In the preceding example, the shell displays the job number and PID number of the background job as soon as it starts, followed by a prompt. Demonstrating that you can give a command at this point, the user gives the command **date** and its output appears on the screen. The shell waits until just before it issues a prompt (after **date** has finished) to notify you that job 1 is stopped. When you give an **fg** command, the shell puts the job in the foreground and you can enter the data the command is waiting for. In this case the input needs to be terminated with CONTROL-D, which sends an EOF (end of file) signal to the shell. The shell then displays another prompt.

The shell keeps you informed about changes in the status of a job, notifying you when a background job starts, completes, or stops, perhaps because it is waiting for input from the terminal. The shell also lets you know when a foreground job is suspended. Because notices about a job being run in the background can disrupt your work, the shell delays displaying these notices until just before it displays a prompt. You can set **notify** (page 333) to cause the shell to display these notices without delay.

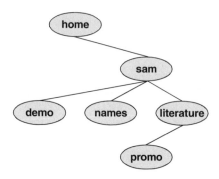

Figure 8-2   The directory structure in the examples

If you try to exit from a shell while jobs are stopped, the shell issues a warning and does not allow you to exit. If you then use jobs to review the list of jobs or you immediately try to exit from the shell again, the shell allows you to exit. If **huponexit** (page 333) is not set (the default), stopped and background jobs keep running in the background. If it is set, the shell terminates the jobs.

MANIPULATING THE DIRECTORY STACK

Both the Bourne Again and the TC Shells allow you to store a list of directories you are working with, enabling you to move easily among them. This list is referred to as a *stack*. It is analogous to a stack of dinner plates: You typically add plates to and remove plates from the top of the stack, so this type of stack is named a last in, first out (LIFO) stack.

dirs: DISPLAYS THE STACK

The dirs builtin displays the contents of the directory stack. If you call dirs when the directory stack is empty, it displays the name of the working directory:

```
$ dirs
~/literature
```

Figure 8-3   Creating a directory stack

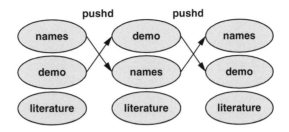

Figure 8-4 Using pushd to change working directories

The dirs builtin uses a tilde (~) to represent the name of a user's home directory. The examples in the next several sections assume that you are referring to the directory structure shown in Figure 8-2.

pushd: PUSHES A DIRECTORY ON THE STACK

When you supply the pushd (push directory) builtin with one argument, it pushes the directory specified by the argument on the stack, changes directories to the specified directory, and displays the stack. The following example is illustrated in Figure 8-3:

```
$ pushd ../demo
~/demo ~/literature
$ pwd
/home/sam/demo
$ pushd ../names
~/names ~/demo ~/literature
$ pwd
/home/sam/names
```

When you use pushd without an argument, it swaps the top two directories on the stack, makes the new top directory (which was the second directory) the new working directory, and displays the stack (Figure 8-4):

```
$ pushd
~/demo ~/names ~/literature
$ pwd
/home/sam/demo
```

Using pushd in this way, you can easily move back and forth between two directories. You can also use **cd –** to change to the previous directory, whether or not you have explicitly created a directory stack. To access another directory in the stack, call pushd with a numeric argument preceded by a plus sign. The directories in the stack are numbered starting with the top directory, which is number 0. The following pushd command continues with the previous example, changing the working directory to **literature** and moving **literature** to the top of the stack:

```
$ pushd +2
~/literature ~/demo ~/names
$ pwd
/home/sam/literature
```

Figure 8-5   Using popd to remove a directory from the stack

popd: POPS A DIRECTORY OFF THE STACK

To remove a directory from the stack, use the popd (pop directory) builtin. As the following example and Figure 8-5 show, without an argument, popd removes the top directory from the stack and changes the working directory to the new top directory:

```
$ dirs
~/literature ~/demo ~/names
$ popd
~/demo ~/names
$ pwd
/home/sam/demo
```

To remove a directory other than the top one from the stack, use popd with a numeric argument preceded by a plus sign. The following example removes directory number 1, **demo**. Removing a directory other than directory number 0 does not change the working directory.

```
$ dirs
~/literature ~/demo ~/names
$ popd +1
~/literature ~/names
```

PARAMETERS AND VARIABLES

Variables   Within a shell, a *shell parameter* is associated with a value that is accessible to the user. There are several kinds of shell parameters. Parameters whose names consist of letters, digits, and underscores are often referred to as *shell variables,* or simply *variables.* A variable name must start with a letter or underscore, not with a number. Thus **A76**, **MY_CAT**, and **___X___** are valid variable names, whereas **69TH_STREET** (starts with a digit) and **MY-NAME** (contains a hyphen) are not.

User-created variables   Shell variables that you name and assign values to are *user-created variables.* You can change the values of user-created variables at any time, or you can make them *readonly* so that their values cannot be changed. You can also make user-created variables *global.* A global variable (also called an *environment variable*) is available to all shells and other programs you fork from the original shell. One naming convention is to use only uppercase letters for global variables and to use mixed-case or lowercase letters for other variables. Refer to "Locality of Variables" on page 436 for more information on global variables.

To assign a value to a variable in the Bourne Again Shell, use the following syntax:

VARIABLE=value

There can be no whitespace on either side of the equal sign (=). An example assignment follows:

```
$ myvar=abc
```

Under the TC Shell the assignment must be preceded by the word **set** and the SPACEs on either side of the equal sign are optional:

```
$ set myvar = abc
```

The Bourne Again Shell permits you to put variable assignments on a command line. This type of assignment creates a variable that is local to the command shell—that is, the variable is accessible only from the program the command runs. The **my_script** shell script displays the value of **TEMPDIR**. The following command runs **my_script** with **TEMPDIR** set to **/home/sam/temp**. The echo builtin shows that the interactive shell has no value for **TEMPDIR** after running **my_script**. If **TEMPDIR** had been set in the interactive shell, running **my_script** in this manner would have had no effect on its value.

```
$ cat my_script
echo $TEMPDIR
$ TEMPDIR=/home/sam/temp ./my_script
/home/sam/temp
$ echo $TEMPDIR

$
```

Keyword variables   *Keyword shell variables* (or simply *keyword variables*) have special meaning to the shell and usually have short, mnemonic names. When you start a shell (by logging in, for example), the shell inherits several keyword variables from the environment. Among these variables are **HOME**, which identifies your home directory, and **PATH**, which determines which directories the shell searches and in what order to locate commands that you give the shell. The shell creates and initializes (with default values) other keyword variables when you start it. Still other variables do not exist until you set them.

You can change the values of most keyword shell variables. It is usually not necessary to change the values of keyword variables initialized in the **/etc/profile** or **/etc/csh.cshrc** systemwide startup files. If you need to change the value of a bash keyword variable, do so in one of your startup files (for bash see page 271; for tcsh see page 352). Just as you can make user-created variables global, so you can make keyword variables global—a task usually done automatically in startup files. You can also make a keyword variable readonly.

Positional and special parameters   The names of positional and special parameters do not resemble variable names. Most of these parameters have one-character names (for example, **1**, **?**, and **#**) and are referenced (as are all variables) by preceding the name with a dollar sign (**$1**, **$?**, and **$#**). The values of these parameters reflect different aspects of your ongoing interaction with the shell.

Whenever you give a command, each argument on the command line becomes the value of a *positional parameter* (page 440). Positional parameters enable you to access command-line arguments, a capability that you will often require when you write shell scripts. The set builtin (page 442) enables you to assign values to positional parameters.

Other frequently needed shell script values, such as the name of the last command executed, the number of command-line arguments, and the status of the most recently executed command, are available as *special parameters* (page 438). You cannot assign values to special parameters.

USER-CREATED VARIABLES

The first line in the following example declares the variable named **person** and initializes it with the value **max** (use **set person = max** in tcsh):

```
$ person=max
$ echo person
person
$ echo $person
max
```

Parameter
substitution
Because the echo builtin copies its arguments to standard output, you can use it to display the values of variables. The second line of the preceding example shows that **person** does not represent **max**. Instead, the string **person** is echoed as **person**. The shell substitutes the value of a variable only when you precede the name of the variable with a dollar sign ($). Thus the command **echo $person** displays the value of the variable **person**; it does not display **$person** because the shell does not pass **$person** to echo as an argument. Because of the leading **$**, the shell recognizes that **$person** is the name of a variable, *substitutes* the value of the variable, and passes that value to echo. The echo builtin displays the value of the variable—not its name—never "knowing" that you called it with a variable.

Quoting the $
You can prevent the shell from substituting the value of a variable by quoting the leading **$**. Double quotation marks do not prevent the substitution; single quotation marks or a backslash (\) do.

```
$ echo $person
max
$ echo "$person"
max
$ echo '$person'
$person
$ echo \$person
$person
```

SPACES Because they do not prevent variable substitution but do turn off the special meanings of most other characters, double quotation marks are useful when you assign values to variables and when you use those values. To assign a value that contains SPACES or TABS to a variable, use double quotation marks around the value. Although double quotation marks are not required in all cases, using them is a good habit.

```
$ person="max and zach"
$ echo $person
max and zach
$ person=max and zach
bash: and: command not found
```

When you reference a variable whose value contains TABs or multiple adjacent SPACES, you need to use quotation marks to preserve the spacing. If you do not quote the variable, the shell collapses each string of blank characters into a single SPACE before passing the variable to the utility:

```
$ person="max    and    zach"
$ echo $person
max and zach
$ echo "$person"
max    and    zach
```

Pathname expansion in assignments When you execute a command with a variable as an argument, the shell replaces the name of the variable with the value of the variable and passes that value to the program being executed. If the value of the variable contains a special character, such as * or ?, the shell *may* expand that variable.

The first line in the following sequence of commands assigns the string **max*** to the variable **memo**. The Bourne Again Shell does *not expand the string* because bash does not perform pathname expansion (page 136) when it assigns a value to a variable. All shells process a command line in a specific order. Within this order bash (but not tcsh) expands variables before it interprets commands. In the following echo command line, the double quotation marks quote the asterisk (*) in the expanded value of **$memo** and prevent bash from performing pathname expansion on the expanded **memo** variable before passing its value to the echo command:

```
$ memo=max*
$ echo "$memo"
max*
```

All shells interpret special characters as special when you reference a variable that contains an unquoted special character. In the following example, the shell expands the value of the **memo** variable because it is not quoted:

```
$ ls
max.report
max.summary
$ echo $memo
max.report max.summary
```

Here the shell expands the **$memo** variable to **max***, expands **max*** to **max.report** and **max.summary**, and passes these two values to echo.

optional

Braces   The *$VARIABLE* syntax is a special case of the more general syntax *${VARIABLE}*, in which the variable name is enclosed by ${}. The braces insulate the variable name from adjacent characters. Braces are necessary when catenating a variable value with a string:

```
$ PREF=counter
$ WAY=$PREFclockwise
$ FAKE=$PREFfeit
$ echo $WAY $FAKE

$
```

The preceding example does not work as planned. Only a blank line is output because, although the symbols **PREFclockwise** and **PREFfeit** are valid variable names, they are not set. By default the shell evaluates an unset variable as an empty (null) string and displays this value (bash) or generates an error message (tcsh). To achieve the intent of these statements, refer to the **PREF** variable using braces:

```
$ PREF=counter
$ WAY=${PREF}clockwise
$ FAKE=${PREF}feit
$ echo $WAY $FAKE
counterclockwise counterfeit
```

The Bourne Again Shell refers to the arguments on its command line by position, using the special variables **$1**, **$2**, **$3**, and so forth up to **$9**. If you wish to refer to arguments past the ninth argument, you must use braces: **${10}**. The name of the command is held in **$0** (page 441).

unset: REMOVES A VARIABLE

Unless you remove a variable, it exists as long as the shell in which it was created exists. To remove the *value* of a variable but not the variable itself, assign a null value to the variable (use **set person =** in tcsh):

```
$ person=
$ echo $person

$
```

You can remove a variable using the unset builtin. The following command removes the variable **person**:

```
$ unset person
```

VARIABLE ATTRIBUTES

This section discusses attributes and explains how to assign them to variables.

readonly: MAKES THE VALUE OF A VARIABLE PERMANENT

You can use the readonly builtin (not in tcsh) to ensure that the value of a variable cannot be changed. The next example declares the variable **person** to be readonly. You must assign a value to a variable *before* you declare it to be readonly; you cannot change its value after the declaration. When you attempt to unset or change the value of a readonly variable, the shell displays an error message:

```
$ person=zach
$ echo $person
zach
$ readonly person
$ person=helen
bash: person: readonly variable
```

If you use the readonly builtin without an argument, it displays a list of all readonly shell variables. This list includes keyword variables that are automatically set as readonly as well as keyword or user-created variables that you have declared as readonly. See page 296 for an example (**readonly** and **declare –r** produce the same output).

declare AND typeset: ASSIGN ATTRIBUTES TO VARIABLES

The declare and typeset builtins (two names for the same command, neither of which is available in tcsh) set attributes and values for shell variables. Table 8-3 lists five of these attributes.

Table 8-3   Variable attributes (typeset or declare)

Attribute	Meaning
–a	Declares a variable as an array (page 434)
–f	Declares a variable to be a function name (page 327)
–i	Declares a variable to be of type integer (page 296)
–r	Makes a variable readonly; also readonly (page 295)
–x	Exports a variable (makes it global); also export (page 436)

The following commands declare several variables and set some attributes. The first line declares **person1** and assigns it a value of **max**. This command has the same effect with or without the word **declare**.

```
$ declare person1=max
$ declare -r person2=zach
$ declare -rx person3=helen
$ declare -x person4
```

The readonly and export builtins are synonyms for the commands **declare –r** and **declare –x**, respectively. You can declare a variable without assigning a value to it, as the preceding declaration of the variable **person4** illustrates. This declaration makes **person4** available to all subshells (i.e., makes it global). Until an assignment is made to the variable, it has a null value.

You can list the options to declare separately in any order. The following is equivalent to the preceding declaration of **person3**:

```
$ declare -x -r person3=helen
```

Use the **+** character in place of **–** when you want to remove an attribute from a variable. You cannot remove the readonly attribute. After the following command is given, the variable **person3** is no longer exported but it is still readonly.

```
$ declare +x person3
```

You can use typeset instead of declare.

Listing variable attributes
Without any arguments or options, declare lists all shell variables. The same list is output when you run set (page 442) without any arguments.

If you use a declare builtin with options but no variable names as arguments, the command lists all shell variables that have the indicated attributes set. For example, the command **declare –r** displays a list of all readonly shell variables. This list is the same as that produced by the **readonly** command without any arguments. After the declarations in the preceding example have been given, the results are as follows:

```
$ declare -r
declare -ar BASH_VERSINFO='([0]="3" [1]="2" [2]="39" [3]="1" ... )'
declare -ir EUID="500"
declare -ir PPID="936"
declare -r SHELLOPTS="braceexpand:emacs:hashall:histexpand:history:..."
declare -ir UID="500"
declare -r person2="zach"
declare -rx person3="helen"
```

The first five entries are keyword variables that are automatically declared as read-only. Some of these variables are stored as integers (**–i**). The **–a** option indicates that **BASH_VERSINFO** is an array variable; the value of each element of the array is listed to the right of an equal sign.

Integer
By default the values of variables are stored as strings. When you perform arithmetic on a string variable, the shell converts the variable into a number, manipulates it, and then converts it back to a string. A variable with the integer attribute is stored as an integer. Assign the integer attribute as follows:

```
$ declare -i COUNT
```

KEYWORD VARIABLES

Keyword variables either are inherited or are declared and initialized by the shell when it starts. You can assign values to these variables from the command line or from a startup file. Typically you want these variables to apply to all subshells you start as well as to your login shell. For those variables not automatically exported by the shell, you must use export (bash; page 436) or setenv (tcsh; page 366) to make them available to child shells.

HOME: YOUR HOME DIRECTORY

By default your home directory is the working directory when you log in. Your home directory is established when your account is set up; under Linux its name is stored in the **/etc/passwd** file. Mac OS X uses Open Directory (page 926) to store this information.

```
$ grep sam /etc/passwd
sam:x:501:501:Sam S. x301:/home/sam:/bin/bash
```

When you log in, the shell inherits the pathname of your home directory and assigns it to the variable **HOME**. When you give a **cd** command without an argument, cd makes the directory whose name is stored in **HOME** the working directory:

```
$ pwd
/home/max/laptop
$ echo $HOME
/home/max
$ cd
$ pwd
/home/max
```

This example shows the value of the **HOME** variable and the effect of the cd builtin. After you execute cd without an argument, the pathname of the working directory is the same as the value of **HOME**: your home directory.

Tilde (~) The shell uses the value of **HOME** to expand pathnames that use the shorthand tilde (~) notation (page 84) to denote a user's home directory. The following example uses echo to display the value of this shortcut and then uses ls to list the files in Max's **laptop** directory, which is a subdirectory of his home directory:

```
$ echo ~
/home/max
$ ls ~/laptop
tester        count        lineup
```

PATH: WHERE THE SHELL LOOKS FOR PROGRAMS

When you give the shell an absolute or relative pathname rather than a simple filename as a command, it looks in the specified directory for an executable file with the specified filename. If the file with the pathname you specified does not exist, the shell reports **command not found**. If the file exists as specified but you do not have execute permission for it, or in the case of a shell script you do not have read and execute permission for it, the shell reports **Permission denied**.

If you give a simple filename as a command, the shell searches through certain directories (your search path) for the program you want to execute. It looks in several directories for a file that has the same name as the command and that you have execute permission for (a compiled program) or read and execute permission for (a shell script). The **PATH** shell variable controls this search.

The default value of **PATH** is determined when bash or tcsh is compiled. It is not set in a startup file, although it may be modified there. Normally the default specifies that the shell search several system directories used to hold common commands. These system directories include **/bin** and **/usr/bin** and other directories appropriate to the local system. When you give a command, if the shell does not find the executable—and, in the case of a shell script, readable—file named by the command in any of the directories listed in **PATH**, the shell generates one of the aforementioned error messages.

Working directory The **PATH** variable specifies the directories in the order the shell should search them. Each directory must be separated from the next by a colon. The following command sets **PATH** so that a search for an executable file starts with the **/usr/local/bin** directory. If it does not find the file in this directory, the shell looks next in **/bin**, and then in **/usr/bin**. If the search fails in those directories, the shell looks in the **~/bin** directory, a subdirectory of the user's home directory. Finally the shell looks in the working directory. Exporting **PATH** makes its value accessible to subshells:

```
$ export PATH=/usr/local/bin:/bin:/usr/bin:~/bin:
```

A null value in the string indicates the working directory. In the preceding example, a null value (nothing between the colon and the end of the line) appears as the last element of the string. The working directory is represented by a leading colon (not recommended; see the following security tip), a trailing colon (as in the example), or two colons next to each other anywhere in the string. You can also represent the working directory explicitly with a period (.). See "**PATH**" on page 373 for a tcsh example.

Because Linux stores many executable files in directories named **bin** (*binary*), users typically put their own executable files in their own **~/bin** directories. If you put your own **bin** directory at the end of your **PATH**, as in the preceding example, the shell looks there for any commands that it cannot find in directories listed earlier in **PATH**.

PATH and security

security Do not put the working directory first in **PATH** when security is a concern. If you are working as **root**, you should *never* put the working directory first in **PATH**. It is common for **root**'s **PATH** to omit the working directory entirely. You can always execute a file in the working directory by prepending **./** to the name: **./myprog**.

Putting the working directory first in **PATH** can create a security hole. Most people type **ls** as the first command when entering a directory. If the owner of a directory places an executable file named **ls** in the directory, and the working directory appears first in a user's **PATH**, the user giving an **ls** command from the directory executes the ls program in the working directory instead of the system ls utility, possibly with undesirable results.

If you want to add directories to **PATH**, you can reference the old value of the **PATH** variable in setting **PATH** to a new value (but see the preceding security tip). The following command adds **/usr/local/bin** to the beginning of the current **PATH** and the **bin** directory in the user's home directory (**~/bin**) to the end:

```
$ PATH=/usr/local/bin:$PATH:~/bin
```

MAIL: WHERE YOUR MAIL IS KEPT

The **MAIL** variable (**mail** under tcsh) contains the pathname of the file that holds your mail (your *mailbox*, usually **/var/mail/*name***, where ***name*** is your username). If **MAIL** is set and **MAILPATH** (next) is not set, the shell informs you when mail arrives in the file specified by **MAIL**. In a graphical environment you can unset **MAIL** so the shell does not display mail reminders in a terminal emulator window (assuming you are using a graphical mail program).

Most Mac OS X systems do not use local files for incoming mail; mail is typically kept on a remote mail server instead. The **MAIL** variable and other mail-related shell variables do not do anything unless you have a local mail server.

The **MAILPATH** variable (not available under tcsh) contains a list of filenames separated by colons. If this variable is set, the shell informs you when any one of the files is modified (for example, when mail arrives). You can follow any of the filenames in the list with a question mark (**?**), followed by a message. The message replaces the **you have mail** message when you receive mail while you are logged in.

The **MAILCHECK** variable (not available under tcsh) specifies how often, in seconds, the shell checks for new mail. The default is 60 seconds. If you set this variable to zero, the shell checks before each prompt.

PS1: USER PROMPT (PRIMARY)

The default Bourne Again Shell prompt is a dollar sign (**$**). When you run bash with **root** privileges, bash typically displays a pound sign (#) prompt. The **PS1** variable (**prompt** under tcsh, page 373) holds the prompt string that the shell uses to let you know that it is waiting for a command. When you change the value of **PS1** or **prompt**, you change the appearance of your prompt.

You can customize the prompt displayed by **PS1**. For example, the assignment

```
$ PS1="[\u@\h \W \!]$ "
```

displays the following prompt:

[user@host directory event]$

where ***user*** is the username, ***host*** is the hostname up to the first period, ***directory*** is the basename of the working directory, and ***event*** is the event number (page 309) of the current command.

If you are working on more than one system, it can be helpful to incorporate the system name into your prompt. For example, you might change the prompt to the name of the system you are using, followed by a colon and a SPACE (a SPACE at the end of the prompt makes the commands you enter after the prompt easier to read). This command uses command substitution (page 340) in the string assigned to **PS1**:

```
$ PS1="$(hostname): "
bravo.example.com: echo test
test
bravo.example.com:
```

Use the following command under tcsh:

```
tcsh $ set prompt = "`hostname`: "
```

The first example that follows changes the prompt to the name of the local host, a SPACE, and a dollar sign (or, if the user is running with **root** privileges, a pound sign). The second example changes the prompt to the time followed by the name of the user. The third example changes the prompt to the one used in this book (a pound sign for **root** and a dollar sign otherwise):

```
$ PS1='\h \$ '
bravo $

$ PS1='\@ \u $ '
09:44 PM max $

$ PS1='\$ '
$
```

Table 8-4 describes some of the symbols you can use in **PS1**. See Table 9-4 on page 373 for the corresponding tcsh symbols. For a complete list of special characters you can use in the prompt strings, open the bash man page and search for the second occurrence of **PROMPTING** (give the command **/PROMPTING** and then press **n**).

Table 8-4   **PS1** symbols

Symbol	Display in prompt
\$	# if the user is running with **root** privileges; otherwise, **$**
\w	Pathname of the working directory
\W	Basename of the working directory
\!	Current event (history) number (page 313)
\d	Date in Weekday Month Date format
\h	Machine hostname, without the domain
\H	Full machine hostname, including the domain
\u	Username of the current user
\@	Current time of day in 12-hour, AM/PM format
\T	Current time of day in 12-hour HH:MM:SS format
\A	Current time of day in 24-hour HH:MM format
\t	Current time of day in 24-hour HH:MM:SS format

PS2: USER PROMPT (SECONDARY)

The **PS2** variable holds the secondary prompt (tcsh uses **prompt2**; page 374). On the first line of the next example, an unclosed quoted string follows echo. The shell assumes the command is not finished and, on the second line, gives the default secondary prompt (>). This prompt indicates the shell is waiting for the user to continue the command line. The shell waits until it receives the quotation mark that closes the string. Only then does it execute the command:

```
$ echo "demonstration of prompt string
> 2"
demonstration of prompt string
2
$ PS2="secondary prompt: "
$ echo "this demonstrates
secondary prompt: prompt string 2"
this demonstrates
prompt string 2
```

The second command changes the secondary prompt to **secondary prompt:** followed by a SPACE. A multiline echo demonstrates the new prompt.

PS3: MENU PROMPT

The **PS3** variable holds the menu prompt (tcsh uses **prompt3**; page 374) for the **select** control structure (page 428).

PS4: DEBUGGING PROMPT

The **PS4** variable holds the bash debugging symbol (page 410; not under tcsh).

IFS: SEPARATES INPUT FIELDS (WORD SPLITTING)

The **IFS** (Internal Field Separator) shell variable (not under tcsh) specifies the characters you can use to separate arguments on a command line. It has the default value of SPACE TAB NEWLINE. Regardless of the value of **IFS**, you can always use one or more SPACE or TAB characters to separate arguments on the command line, provided these characters are not quoted or escaped. When you assign **IFS** character values, these characters can also separate fields—but only if they undergo expansion. This type of interpretation of the command line is called *word splitting*.

Be careful when changing IFS

caution   Changing **IFS** has a variety of side effects, so work cautiously. You may find it useful to save the value of **IFS** before changing it. Then you can easily restore the original value if you get unexpected results. Alternatively, you can fork a new shell with a **bash** command before experimenting with **IFS**; if you get into trouble, you can **exit** back to the old shell, where **IFS** is working properly.

The following example demonstrates how setting **IFS** can affect the interpretation of a command line:

```
$ a=w:x:y:z

$ cat $a
cat: w:x:y:z: No such file or directory
$ IFS=":"

$ cat $a
cat: w: No such file or directory
cat: x: No such file or directory
cat: y: No such file or directory
cat: z: No such file or directory
```

The first time cat is called, the shell expands the variable **a**, interpreting the string **w:x:y:z** as a single word to be used as the argument to cat. The cat utility cannot find a file named **w:x:y:z** and reports an error for that filename. After **IFS** is set to a colon (**:**), the shell expands the variable **a** into four words, each of which is an argument to cat. Now cat reports errors for four files: **w**, **x**, **y**, and **z**. Word splitting based on the colon (**:**) takes place only *after* the variable **a** is expanded.

The shell splits all *expanded* words on a command line according to the separating characters found in **IFS**. When there is no expansion, there is no splitting. Consider the following commands:

```
$ IFS="p"
$ export VAR
```

Although **IFS** is set to **p**, the **p** on the **export** command line is not expanded, so the word **export** is not split.

The following example uses variable expansion in an attempt to produce an **export** command:

```
$ IFS="p"
$ aa=export
$ echo $aa
ex ort
```

This time expansion occurs, so the character **p** in the token **export** is interpreted as a separator (as the echo command shows). Now when you try to use the value of the **aa** variable to export the **VAR** variable, the shell parses the **$aa VAR** command line as **ex ort VAR**. The effect is that the command line starts the **ex** editor with two filenames: **ort** and **VAR**.

```
$ $aa VAR
2 files to edit
"ort" [New File]
Entering Ex mode.  Type "visual" to go to Normal mode.
:q
E173: 1 more file to edit
:q
$
```

If you unset **IFS**, only SPACEs and TABs work as field separators.

Multiple separator characters

tip   Although the shell treats sequences of multiple SPACE or TAB characters as a single separator, it treats *each occurrence* of another field-separator character as a separator.

CDPATH: BROADENS THE SCOPE OF cd

The **CDPATH** variable (**cdpath** under tcsh) allows you to use a simple filename as an argument to the cd builtin to change the working directory to a directory other than a child of the working directory. If you have several directories you typically work out of, this variable can speed things up and save you the tedium of using cd with longer pathnames to switch among them.

When **CDPATH** or **cdpath** is not set and you specify a simple filename as an argument to cd, cd searches the working directory for a subdirectory with the same name as the argument. If the subdirectory does not exist, cd displays an error message. When **CDPATH** or **cdpath** is set, cd searches for an appropriately named subdirectory in the directories in the **CDPATH** list. If it finds one, that directory becomes the working directory. With **CDPATH** or **cdpath** set, you can use cd and a simple filename to change the working directory to a child of any of the directories listed in **CDPATH** or **cdpath**.

The **CDPATH** or **cdpath** variable takes on the value of a colon-separated list of directory pathnames (similar to the **PATH** variable). It is usually set in the **~/.bash_profile** (bash) or **~/.tcshrc** (tcsh) startup file with a command line such as the following:

```
export CDPATH=$HOME:$HOME/literature
```

Use the following format for tcsh:

```
setenv cdpath $HOME\:$HOME/literature
```

These commands cause cd to search your home directory, the **literature** directory, and then the working directory when you give a cd command. If you do not include the working directory in **CDPATH** or **cdpath**, cd searches the working directory if the search of all the other directories in **CDPATH** or **cdpath** fails. If you want cd to search the working directory first, include a null string, represented by two colons (::), as the first entry in **CDPATH**:

```
export CDPATH=::$HOME:$HOME/literature
```

If the argument to the cd builtin is an absolute pathname—one starting with a slash (/)—the shell does not consult **CDPATH** or **cdpath**.

KEYWORD VARIABLES: A SUMMARY

Table 8-5 presents a list of bash keyword variables. See page 371 for information on tcsh variables.

Table 8-5   bash keyword variables

Variable	Value
BASH_ENV	The pathname of the startup file for noninteractive shells (page 272)
CDPATH	The cd search path (page 302)
COLUMNS	The width of the display used by **select** (page 427)
FCEDIT	The name of the editor that fc uses by default (page 312)
HISTFILE	The pathname of the file that holds the history list (default: **~/.bash_history**; page 308)
HISTFILESIZE	The maximum number of entries saved in **HISTFILE** (default: 500; page 308)
HISTSIZE	The maximum number of entries saved in the history list (default: 500; page 308)

Table 8-5   bash keyword variables *(continued)*

Variable	Value
HOME	The pathname of the user's home directory (page 297); used as the default argument for cd and in tilde expansion (page 84)
IFS	Internal Field Separator (page 301); used for word splitting (page 341)
INPUTRC	The pathname of the Readline startup file (default: ~/.inputrc; page 321)
LANG	The locale category when that category is not specifically set with an LC_* variable
LC_*	A group of variables that specify locale categories including LC_COLLATE, LC_CTYPE, LC_MESSAGES, and LC_NUMERIC; use the locale builtin to display a complete list with values
LINES	The height of the display used by **select** (page 427)
MAIL	The pathname of the file that holds a user's mail (page 299)
MAILCHECK	How often, in seconds, bash checks for mail (page 299)
MAILPATH	A colon-separated list of file pathnames that bash checks for mail in (page 299)
PATH	A colon-separated list of directory pathnames that bash looks for commands in (page 297)
PROMPT_COMMAND	A command that bash executes just before it displays the primary prompt
PS1	Prompt String 1; the primary prompt (page 299)
PS2	Prompt String 2; the secondary prompt (default: '> '; page 300)
PS3	The prompt issued by **select** (page 427)
PS4	The bash debugging symbol (page 410)
REPLY	Holds the line that read accepts (page 448); also used by **select** (page 427)

SPECIAL CHARACTERS

Table 8-6 lists most of the characters that are special to the bash and tcsh shells.

Table 8-6   Shell special characters

Character	Use
NEWLINE	Initiates execution of a command (page 282)
;	Separates commands (page 282)

Table 8-6   Shell special characters (continued)

Character	Use
( )	Groups commands (page 284) for execution by a subshell or identifies a function (page 327)
(( ))	Expands an arithmetic expression (page 338)
&	Executes a command in the background (pages 134 and 283)
|	Sends standard output of the preceding command to standard input of the following command (pipe; page 283)
>	Redirects standard output (page 126)
>>	Appends standard output (page 130)
<	Redirects standard input (page 128)
<<	Here document (page 429)
*	Any string of zero or more characters in an ambiguous file reference (page 138)
?	Any single character in an ambiguous file reference (page 137)
\	Quotes the following character (page 46)
'	Quotes a string, preventing all substitution (page 46)
"	Quotes a string, allowing only variable and command substitution (pages 46 and 292)
` ... `	Performs command substitution (page 340)
[ ]	Character class in an ambiguous file reference (page 139)
$	References a variable (page 290)
. (dot builtin)	Executes a command (page 274)
#	Begins a comment (page 281)
{ }	Surrounds the contents of a function (page 327)
: (null builtin)	Returns *true* (page 455)
&& (Boolean AND)	Executes command on right only if command on left succeeds (returns a zero exit status; page 466)
|| (Boolean OR)	Executes command on right only if command on left fails (returns a nonzero exit status; page 466)
! (Boolean NOT)	Reverses exit status of a command
$() (not in tcsh)	Performs command substitution (preferred form; page 340)
[ ]	Evaluates an arithmetic expression (page 338)

PROCESSES

A *process* is the execution of a command by the Linux kernel. The shell that starts when you log in is a command, or a process, like any other. When you give the name of a Linux utility on the command line, you initiate a process. When you run a shell script, another shell process is started and additional processes are created for each command in the script. Depending on how you invoke the shell script, the script is run either by the current shell or, more typically, by a subshell (child) of the current shell. A process is not started when you run a shell builtin, such as cd.

PROCESS STRUCTURE

fork system call   Like the file structure, the process structure is hierarchical, with parents, children, and even a *root*. A parent process *forks* a child process, which in turn can fork other processes. (The term *fork* indicates that, as with a fork in the road, one process turns into two. Initially the two forks are identical except that one is identified as the parent and one as the child. You can also use the term *spawn;* the words are interchangeable.) The operating system routine, or *system call,* that creates a new process is named **fork**().

When Linux begins execution when a system is started, it starts init, a single process called a *spontaneous process,* with PID number 1. This process holds the same position in the process structure as the root directory does in the file structure: It is the ancestor of all processes the system and users work with. When a command-line system is in multiuser mode, init runs getty or mingetty processes, which display **login:** prompts on terminals. When a user responds to the prompt and presses RETURN, getty hands control over to a utility named login, which checks the username and password combination. After the user logs in, the login process becomes the user's shell process.

PROCESS IDENTIFICATION

PID numbers   Linux assigns a unique PID (process identification) number at the inception of each process. As long as a process exists, it keeps the same PID number. During one session the same process is always executing the login shell. When you fork a new process—for example, when you use an editor—the PID number of the new (child) process is different from that of its parent process. When you return to the login shell, it is still being executed by the same process and has the same PID number as when you logged in.

The following example shows that the process running the shell forked (is the parent of) the process running ps. When you call it with the –f option, ps displays a full listing of information about each process. The line of the ps display with **bash** in the CMD column refers to the process running the shell. The column headed by **PID** identifies the PID number. The column headed **PPID** identifies the PID number of the *parent* of the process. From the PID and PPID columns you can see that the process running the shell (PID 21341) is the parent of the process running sleep (PID 22789). The parent PID number of sleep is the same as the PID number of the shell (21341).

```
$ sleep 10 &
[1] 22789
$ ps -f
UID          PID  PPID  C STIME TTY          TIME CMD
max        21341 21340  0 10:42 pts/16   00:00:00 bash
max        22789 21341  0 17:30 pts/16   00:00:00 sleep 10
max        22790 21341  0 17:30 pts/16   00:00:00 ps -f
```

Refer to page 796 for more information on ps and the columns it displays with the –f option. A second pair of **sleep** and **ps –f** commands shows that the shell is still being run by the same process but that it forked another process to run sleep:

```
$ sleep 10 &
[1] 22791
$ ps -f
UID          PID  PPID  C STIME TTY          TIME CMD
max        21341 21340  0 10:42 pts/16   00:00:00 bash
max        22791 21341  0 17:31 pts/16   00:00:00 sleep 10
max        22792 21341  0 17:31 pts/16   00:00:00 ps -f
```

You can also use pstree (or **ps ––forest**, with or without the –e option) to see the parent–child relationship of processes. The next example shows the –p option to pstree, which causes it to display PID numbers:

```
$ pstree -p
init(1)-+-acpid(1395)
        |-atd(1758)
        |-crond(1702)
        ...
        |-kdeinit(2223)-+-firefox(8914)---run-mozilla.sh(8920)---firefox-bin(8925)
        |               |-gaim(2306)
        |               |-gqview(14062)
        |               |-kdeinit(2228)
        |               |-kdeinit(2294)
        |               |-kdeinit(2314)-+-bash(2329)---ssh(2561)
        |               |               |-bash(2339)
        |               |               '-bash(15821)---bash(16778)
        |               |-kdeinit(16448)
        |               |-kdeinit(20888)
        |               |-oclock(2317)
        |               '-pam-panel-icon(2305)---pam_timestamp_c(2307)
        ...
        |-login(1823)---bash(20986)-+-pstree(21028)
        |                           '-sleep(21026)
        ...
```

The preceding output is abbreviated. The line that starts with **–kdeinit** shows a graphical user running many processes, including **firefox**, **gaim**, and **oclock**. The line that starts with **–login** shows a textual user running sleep in the background and running pstree in the foreground. Refer to "$$: PID Number" on page 439 for a description of how to instruct the shell to report on PID numbers.

EXECUTING A COMMAND

fork and **sleep**   When you give the shell a command, it usually forks [spawns using the **fork**() system call] a child process to execute the command. While the child process is executing the command, the parent process *sleeps* [implemented as the **sleep**() system call]. While a process is sleeping, it does not use any computer time; it remains inactive, waiting to wake up. When the child process finishes executing the command, it tells its parent of its success or failure via its exit status and then dies. The parent process (which is running the shell) wakes up and prompts for another command.

Background process   When you run a process in the background by ending a command with an ampersand (**&**), the shell forks a child process without going to sleep and without waiting for the child process to run to completion. The parent process, which is executing the shell, reports the job number and PID number of the child process and prompts for another command. The child process runs in the background, independent of its parent.

Builtins   Although the shell forks a process to run most of the commands you give it, some commands are built into the shell. The shell does not need to fork a process to run builtins. For more information refer to "Builtins" on page 141.

Variables   Within a given process, such as your login shell or a subshell, you can declare, initialize, read, and change variables. By default, however, a variable is local to a process. When a process forks a child process, the parent does not pass the value of a variable to the child. You can make the value of a variable available to child processes (global) by using the export builtin under bash (page 436) or the setenv builtin under tcsh (page 366).

HISTORY

The history mechanism, a feature adapted from the C Shell, maintains a list of recently issued command lines, also called *events,* that provides a quick way to reexecute any of the events in the list. This mechanism also enables you to execute variations of previous commands and to reuse arguments from them. You can use the history list to replicate complicated commands and arguments that you used earlier in this login session or in a previous one and enter a series of commands that differ from one another in minor ways. The history list also serves as a record of what you have done. It can prove helpful when you have made a mistake and are not sure what you did or when you want to keep a record of a procedure that involved a series of commands.

The history builtin (in both bash and tcsh) displays the history list. If it does not, read the next section, which describes the variables you need to set.

VARIABLES THAT CONTROL HISTORY

The TC Shell's history mechanism is similar to bash's but uses different variables and has other differences. See page 354 for more information.

The value of the **HISTSIZE** variable determines the number of events preserved in the history list during a session. A value in the range of 100 to 1,000 is normal.

When you exit from the shell, the most recently executed commands are saved in the file whose name is stored in the **HISTFILE** variable (the default is **~/.bash_history**). The next time you start the shell, this file initializes the history list. The value of the **HISTFILESIZE** variable determines the number of lines of history saved in **HISTFILE**. See Table 8-7.

history **can help track down mistakes**

tip When you have made a mistake on a command line (not an error within a script or program) and are not sure what you did wrong, look at the history list to review your recent commands. Sometimes this list can help you figure out what went wrong and how to fix things.

Table 8-7 History variables

Variable	Default	Function
HISTSIZE	500 events	Maximum number of events saved during a session
HISTFILE	**~/.bash_history**	Location of the history file
HISTFILESIZE	500 events	Maximum number of events saved between sessions

Event number The Bourne Again Shell assigns a sequential *event number* to each command line. You can display this event number as part of the bash prompt by including \! in **PS1** (page 299). Examples in this section show numbered prompts when they help to illustrate the behavior of a command.

Give the following command manually, or place it in **~/.bash_profile** to affect future sessions, to establish a history list of the 100 most recent events:

```
$ HISTSIZE=100
```

The following command causes bash to save the 100 most recent events across login sessions:

```
$ HISTFILESIZE=100
```

After you set **HISTFILESIZE**, you can log out and log in again, and the 100 most recent events from the previous login session will appear in your history list.

Give the command **history** to display the events in the history list. This list is ordered so that the oldest events appear at the top. A tcsh history list includes the time the command was executed. The following history list includes a command to modify the bash prompt so it displays the history event number. The last event in the history list is the **history** command that displayed the list.

```
32 $ history | tail
   23  PS1="\! bash$ "
   24  ls -l
   25  cat temp
   26  rm temp
   27  vim memo
   28  lpr memo
   29  vim memo
   30  lpr memo
   31  rm memo
   32  history | tail
```

As you run commands and your history list becomes longer, it may run off the top of the screen when you use the history builtin. Pipe the output of history through less to browse through it, or give the command **history 10** or **history | tail** to look at the ten most recent commands.

A handy history alias

tip   Creating the following aliases makes working with history easier. The first allows you to give the command **h** to display the ten most recent events. The second alias causes the command **hg** *string* to display all events in the history list that contain *string*. Put these aliases in your ~/.**bashrc** file to make them available each time you log in. See page 324 for more information.

```
$ alias 'h=history | tail'
$ alias 'hg=history | grep'
```

Reexecuting and Editing Commands

You can reexecute any event in the history list. This feature can save you time, effort, and aggravation. Not having to reenter long command lines allows you to reexecute events more easily, quickly, and accurately than you could if you had to retype the command line in its entirety. You can recall, modify, and reexecute previously executed events in three ways: You can use the fc builtin (covered next), the exclamation point commands (page 313), or the Readline Library, which uses a one-line vi- or emacs-like editor to edit and execute events (page 318).

Which method to use?

tip   If you are more familiar with vi or emacs and less familiar with the C or TC Shell, use fc or the Readline Library. If you are more familiar with the C or TC Shell, use the exclamation point commands. If it is a toss-up, try the Readline Library; it will benefit you in other areas of Linux more than learning the exclamation point commands will.

fc: Displays, Edits, and Reexecutes Commands

The fc (fix command) builtin (not in tcsh) enables you to display the history list and to edit and reexecute previous commands. It provides many of the same capabilities as the command-line editors.

Viewing the History List

When you call fc with the –l option, it displays commands from the history list. Without any arguments, **fc –l** lists the 16 most recent commands in a numbered list, with the oldest appearing first:

```
$ fc -l
1024     cd
1025     view calendar
1026     vim letter.adams01
1027     aspell -c letter.adams01
1028     vim letter.adams01
1029     lpr letter.adams01
1030     cd ../memos
```

```
1031     ls
1032     rm *0405
1033     fc -l
1034     cd
1035     whereis aspell
1036     man aspell
1037     cd /usr/share/doc/*aspell*
1038     pwd
1039     ls
1040     ls man-html
```

The fc builtin can take zero, one, or two arguments with the –l option. The arguments specify the part of the history list to be displayed:

*fc –l [**first** [**last**]]*

The fc builtin lists commands beginning with the most recent event that matches *first*. The argument can be an event number, the first few characters of the command line, or a negative number, which is taken to be the *n*th previous command. Without *last*, fc displays events through the most recent. If you include *last*, fc displays commands from the most recent event that matches *first* through the most recent event that matches *last*.

The next command displays the history list from event 1030 through event 1035:

```
$ fc -l 1030 1035
1030     cd ../memos
1031     ls
1032     rm *0405
1033     fc -l
1034     cd
1035     whereis aspell
```

The following command lists the most recent event that begins with **view** through the most recent command line that begins with **whereis**:

```
$ fc -l view whereis
1025     view calendar
1026     vim letter.adams01
1027     aspell -c letter.adams01
1028     vim letter.adams01
1029     lpr letter.adams01
1030     cd ../memos
1031     ls
1032     rm *0405
1033     fc -l
1034     cd
1035     whereis aspell
```

To list a single command from the history list, use the same identifier for the first and second arguments. The following command lists event 1027:

```
$ fc -l 1027 1027
1027     aspell -c letter.adams01
```

EDITING AND REEXECUTING PREVIOUS COMMANDS

You can use fc to edit and reexecute previous commands.

fc [–e editor] [first [last]]

When you call fc with the –e option followed by the name of an editor, fc calls the editor with event(s) in the Work buffer, assuming the editor you specify is installed. By default, fc invokes the nano editor. Without *first* and *last*, it defaults to the most recent command. The next example invokes the vim editor to edit the most recent command:

```
$ fc -e vi
```

The fc builtin uses the stand-alone vim editor. If you set the **FCEDIT** variable, you do not need to use the –e option to specify an editor on the command line. Because the value of **FCEDIT** has been changed to **/usr/bin/emacs** and fc has no arguments, the following command edits the most recent command using the emacs editor (part of the **emacs** package; not installed by default):

```
$ export FCEDIT=/usr/bin/emacs
$ fc
```

If you call it with a single argument, fc invokes the editor on the specified command. The following example starts the editor with event 1029 in the Work buffer. When you exit from the editor, the shell executes the command:

```
$ fc 1029
```

As described earlier, you can identify commands with numbers or by specifying the first few characters of the command name. The following example calls the editor to work on events from the most recent event that begins with the letters **vim** through event 1030:

```
$ fc vim 1030
```

Clean up the fc buffer

caution   When you execute an fc command, the shell executes whatever you leave in the editor buffer, possibly with unwanted results. If you decide you do not want to execute a command, delete everything from the buffer before you exit from the editor.

REEXECUTING COMMANDS WITHOUT CALLING THE EDITOR

You can reexecute previous commands without using an editor. If you call fc with the –s option, it skips the editing phase and reexecutes the command. The following example reexecutes event 1029:

```
$ fc -s 1029
lpr letter.adams01
```

The next example reexecutes the previous command:

```
$ fc -s
```

When you reexecute a command, you can tell fc to substitute one string for another. The next example substitutes the string **john** for the string **adams** in event 1029 and executes the modified event:

```
$ fc -s adams=john 1029
lpr letter.john01
```

USING AN EXCLAMATION POINT (!) TO REFERENCE EVENTS

The C Shell history mechanism uses an exclamation point to reference events. This technique, which is available under bash and tcsh, is frequently more cumbersome to use than fc but nevertheless has some useful features. For example, the **!!** command reexecutes the previous event, and the shell replaces the **!$** token with the last word on the previous command line.

You can reference an event by using its absolute event number, its relative event number, or the text it contains. All references to events, called event designators, begin with an exclamation point (!). One or more characters follow the exclamation point to specify an event.

You can put history events anywhere on a command line. To escape an exclamation point so that the shell interprets it literally instead of as the start of a history event, precede the exclamation point with a backslash (\) or enclose it within single quotation marks.

EVENT DESIGNATORS

An event designator specifies a command in the history list. See Table 8-8 on the next page for a list of event designators.

!! reexecutes the previous event
You can reexecute the previous event by giving a **!!** command. In the following example, event 45 reexecutes event 44:

```
44 $ ls -l text
-rw-rw-r--   1 max group 45 Apr 30 14:53 text
45 $ !!
ls -l text
-rw-rw-r--   1 max group 45 Apr 30 14:53 text
```

The **!!** command works whether or not your prompt displays an event number. As this example shows, when you use the history mechanism to reexecute an event, the shell displays the command it is reexecuting.

!*n* event number
A number following an exclamation point refers to an event. If that event is in the history list, the shell executes it. Otherwise, the shell displays an error message. A negative number following an exclamation point references an event relative to the current event. For example, the command **!–3** refers to the third preceding event. After you issue a command, the relative event number of a given event changes (event **–3** becomes event **–4**). Both of the following commands reexecute event 44:

```
51 $ !44
ls -l text
-rw-rw-r--   1 max group 45 Apr 30 14:53 text
52 $ !-8
ls -l text
-rw-rw-r--   1 max group 45 Apr 30 14:53 text
```

!string event text   When a string of text follows an exclamation point, the shell searches for and executes the most recent event that *began* with that string. If you enclose the string within question marks, the shell executes the most recent event that *contained* that string. The final question mark is optional if a RETURN would immediately follow it.

```
68 $ history 10
   59   ls -l text*
   60   tail text5
   61   cat text1 text5 > letter
   62   vim letter
   63   cat letter
   64   cat memo
   65   lpr memo
   66   pine zach
   67   ls -l
   68   history
69 $ !l
ls -l
...
70 $ !lpr
lpr memo
71 $ !?letter?
cat letter
...
```

Table 8-8   Event designators

Designator	Meaning
!	Starts a history event unless followed immediately by SPACE, NEWLINE, =, or (.
!!	The previous command.
!*n*	Command number *n* in the history list.
!–*n*	The *n*th preceding command.
!*string*	The most recent command line that started with *string*.
!?*string*[?]	The most recent command that contained *string*. The last ? is optional.
!#	The current command (as you have it typed so far).
!{*event*}	The *event* is an event designator. The braces isolate *event* from the surrounding text. For example, !{–3}3 is the third most recently executed command followed by a 3.

optional   WORD DESIGNATORS

A *word designator* specifies a word (token) or series of words from an event. (Table 8-9 on page 316 lists word designators.) The words are numbered starting with 0 (the first word on the line—usually the command), continuing with 1 (the first word following the command), and ending with *n* (the last word on the line).

To specify a particular word from a previous event, follow the event designator (such as !14) with a colon and the number of the word in the previous event. For example, !14:3 specifies the third word following the command from event 14. You can specify the first word following the command (word number 1) using a caret (^) and the last word using a dollar sign ($). You can specify a range of words by separating two word designators with a hyphen.

```
72 $ echo apple grape orange pear
apple grape orange pear
73 $ echo !72:2
echo grape
grape
74 $ echo !72:^
echo apple
apple
75 $ !72:0 !72:$
echo pear
pear
76 $ echo !72:2-4
echo grape orange pear
grape orange pear
77 $ !72:0-$
echo apple grape orange pear
apple grape orange pear
```

As the next example shows, !$ refers to the last word of the previous event. You can use this shorthand to edit, for example, a file you just displayed with cat:

```
$ cat report.718
...
$ vim !$
vim report.718
...
```

If an event contains a single command, the word numbers correspond to the argument numbers. If an event contains more than one command, this correspondence does not hold true for commands after the first. In the following example, event 78 contains two commands separated by a semicolon so the shell executes them sequentially; the semicolon is word number 5.

```
78 $ !72 ; echo helen zach barbara
echo apple grape orange pear ; echo helen zach barbara
apple grape orange pear
helen zach barbara
79 $ echo !78:7
echo helen
helen
80 $ echo !78:4-7
echo pear ; echo helen
pear
helen
```

Table 8-9   Word designators

Designator	Meaning
n	The *nth* word. Word 0 is normally the command name.
^	The first word (after the command name).
$	The last word.
m–n	All words from word number *m* through word number *n; m* defaults to 0 if you omit it (0–*n*).
n∗	All words from word number *n* through the last word.
∗	All words except the command name. The same as **1**∗.
%	The word matched by the most recent *?string?* search.

MODIFIERS

On occasion you may want to change an aspect of an event you are reexecuting. Perhaps you entered a complex command line with a typo or incorrect pathname or you want to specify a different argument. You can modify an event or a word of an event by putting one or more modifiers after the word designator, or after the event designator if there is no word designator. Each modifier must be preceded by a colon (:).

Substitute modifier   The following example shows the *substitute modifier* correcting a typo in the previous event:

```
$ car /home/zach/memo.0507 /home/max/letter.0507
bash: car: command not found
$ !!:s/car/cat
cat /home/zach/memo.0507 /home/max/letter.0507
...
```

The substitute modifier has the following syntax:

[g]s/*old*/*new*/

where *old* is the original string (not a regular expression) and *new* is the string that replaces *old*. The substitute modifier substitutes the first occurrence of *old* with *new*. Placing a **g** before the **s** (as in *gs/old/new/*) causes a global substitution, replacing all occurrences of *old*. Although / is the delimiter in the examples, you can use any character that is not in either *old* or *new*. The final delimiter is optional if a RETURN would immediately follow it. As with the vim Substitute command, the history mechanism replaces an ampersand (&) in *new* with *old*. The shell replaces a null old string (*s//new/*) with the previous old string or string within a command that you searched for with *?string?*.

Quick substitution   An abbreviated form of the substitute modifier is *quick substitution*. Use it to reexecute the most recent event while changing some of the event text. The quick substitution character is the caret (^). For example, the command

```
$ ^old^new^
```

produces the same results as

```
$ !!:s/old/new/
```

Thus substituting **cat** for **car** in the previous event could have been entered as

```
$ ^car^cat
cat /home/zach/memo.0507 /home/max/letter.0507
...
```

You can omit the final caret if it would be followed immediately by a RETURN. As with other command-line substitutions, the shell displays the command line as it appears after the substitution.

Other modifiers   Modifiers (other than the substitute modifier) perform simple edits on the part of the event that has been selected by the event designator and the optional word designators. You can use multiple modifiers, each preceded by a colon (:).

The following series of commands uses ls to list the name of a file, repeats the command without executing it (**p** modifier), and repeats the last command, removing the last part of the pathname (**h** modifier) again without executing it:

```
$ ls /var/log/messages
/var/log/messages
$ !!:p
ls /var/log/messages
$ !!:h:p
ls /var/log
```

Table 8-10 lists event modifiers other than the substitute modifier.

Table 8-10   Event modifiers

Modifier		Function
e	(extension)	Removes all but the filename extension
h	(head)	Removes the last part of a pathname
p	(print-not)	Displays the command, but does not execute it
q	(quote)	Quotes the substitution to prevent further substitutions on it
r	(root)	Removes the filename extension
t	(tail)	Removes all elements of a pathname except the last
x		Like **q** but quotes each word in the substitution individually

THE READLINE LIBRARY

Command-line editing under the Bourne Again Shell is implemented through the *Readline Library,* which is available to any application written in C. Any application that uses the Readline Library supports line editing that is consistent with that provided by bash. Programs that use the Readline Library, including bash, read ~/.inputrc (page 321) for key binding information and configuration settings. The ––noediting command-line option turns off command-line editing in bash.

vi mode   You can choose one of two editing modes when using the Readline Library in bash: emacs or vi(m). Both modes provide many of the commands available in the stand-alone versions of the emacs and vim editors. You can also use the ARROW keys to move around. Up and down movements move you backward and forward through the history list. In addition, Readline provides several types of interactive word completion (page 320). The default mode is emacs; you can switch to vi mode with the following command:

```
$ set -o vi
```

emacs mode   The next command switches back to emacs mode:

```
$ set -o emacs
```

vi EDITING MODE

Before you start, make sure the shell is in vi mode.

When you enter bash commands while in vi editing mode, you are in Input mode (page 153). As you enter a command, if you discover an error before you press RETURN, you can press ESCAPE to switch to vim Command mode. This setup is different from the stand-alone vim editor's initial mode. While in Command mode you can use many vim commands to edit the command line. It is as though you were using vim to edit a copy of the history file with a screen that has room for only one command. When you use the **k** command or the UP ARROW to move up a line, you access the previous command. If you then use the **j** command or the DOWN ARROW to move down a line, you return to the original command. To use the **k** and **j** keys to move between commands, you must be in Command mode; you can use the ARROW keys in both Command and Input modes.

The stand-alone editor starts in Command mode

tip   The stand-alone vim editor starts in Command mode, whereas the command-line vim editor starts in Input mode. If commands display characters and do not work properly, you are in Input mode. Press ESCAPE and enter the command again.

In addition to cursor-positioning commands, you can use the search-backward (?) command followed by a search string to look *back* through your history list for the most recent command containing that string. If you have moved back in your history list, use a forward slash (/) to search *forward* toward your most recent command. Unlike the search strings in the stand-alone vim editor, these search strings cannot contain regular expressions. You can, however, start the search string with a caret (^)

to force the shell to locate commands that start with the search string. As in vim, pressing **n** after a successful search looks for the next occurrence of the same string.

You can also use event numbers to access events in the history list. While you are in Command mode (press ESCAPE), enter the event number followed by a **G** to go to the command with that event number.

When you use **/**, **?**, or **G** to move to a command line, you are in Command mode, not Input mode: You can edit the command or press RETURN to execute it.

Once the command you want to edit is displayed, you can modify the command line using vim Command mode editing commands such as **x** (delete character), **r** (replace character), **~** (change case), and **.** (repeat last change). To change to Input mode, use an Insert (**i**, **I**), Append (**a**, **A**), Replace (**R**), or Change (**c**, **C**) command. You do not have to return to Command mode to execute a command; simply press RETURN, even if the cursor is in the middle of the command line.

Refer to page 196 for a summary of vim commands.

emacs Editing Mode

Unlike the vim editor, emacs is modeless. You need not switch between Command mode and Input mode because most emacs commands are control characters (page 216), allowing emacs to distinguish between input and commands. Like vim, the emacs command-line editor provides commands for moving the cursor on the command line and through the command history list and for modifying part or all of a command. However, in a few cases, the emacs command-line editor commands differ from those in the stand-alone emacs editor.

In emacs you perform cursor movement by using both CONTROL and ESCAPE commands. To move the cursor one character backward on the command line, press CONTROL-B. Press CONTROL-F to move one character forward. As in vim, you may precede these movements with counts. To use a count you must first press ESCAPE; otherwise, the numbers you type will appear on the command line.

Like vim, emacs provides word and line movement commands. To move backward or forward one word on the command line, press ESCAPE **b** or ESCAPE **f**. To move several words using a count, press ESCAPE followed by the number and the appropriate escape sequence. To move to the beginning of the line, press CONTROL-A; to the end of the line, press CONTROL-E; and to the next instance of the character *c*, press CONTROL-X CONTROL-F followed by *c*.

You can add text to the command line by moving the cursor to the position you want to enter text and typing the desired text. To delete text, move the cursor just to the right of the characters that you want to delete and press the erase key (page 29) once for each character you want to delete.

CONTROL-D **can terminate your screen session**

tip If you want to delete the character directly under the cursor, press CONTROL-D. If you enter CONTROL-D at the beginning of the line, it may terminate your shell session.

If you want to delete the entire command line, type the line kill character (page 30). You can type this character while the cursor is anywhere in the command line. If you want to delete from the cursor to the end of the line, press CONTROL-K.

Refer to page 254 for a summary of emacs commands.

READLINE COMPLETION COMMANDS

You can use the TAB key to complete words you are entering on the command line. This facility, called *completion,* works in both vi and emacs editing modes and is similar to the completion facility available in tcsh. Several types of completion are possible, and which one you use depends on which part of a command line you are typing when you press TAB.

COMMAND COMPLETION

If you are typing the name of a command (usually the first word on the command line), pressing TAB initiates *command completion,* in which bash looks for a command whose name starts with the part of the word you have typed. If no command starts with the characters you entered, bash beeps. If there is one such command, bash completes the command name. If there is more than one choice, bash does nothing in vi mode and beeps in emacs mode. Pressing TAB a second time causes bash to display a list of commands whose names start with the prefix you typed and allows you to continue typing the command name.

In the following example, the user types **bz** and presses TAB. The shell beeps (the user is in emacs mode) to indicate that several commands start with the letters **bz**. The user enters another TAB to cause the shell to display a list of commands that start with **bz** followed by the command line as the user had entered it so far:

```
$ bz ⟶TAB (beep) ⟶TAB
bzcat          bzdiff        bzip2          bzless
bzcmp          bzgrep        bzip2recover  bzmore
$ bz█
```

Next the user types **c** and presses TAB twice. The shell displays the two commands that start with **bzc**. The user types **a** followed by TAB. At this point the shell completes the command because only one command starts with **bzca**.

```
$ bzc ⟶TAB (beep) ⟶TAB
bzcat  bzcmp
$ bzca ⟶TAB ⟶ t █
```

PATHNAME COMPLETION

Pathname completion, which also uses TABs, allows you to type a portion of a pathname and have bash supply the rest. If the portion of the pathname you have typed is sufficient to determine a unique pathname, bash displays that pathname. If more than one pathname would match it, bash completes the pathname up to the point where there are choices so that you can type more.

When you are entering a pathname, including a simple filename, and press TAB, the shell beeps (if the shell is in emacs mode—in vi mode there is no beep). It then extends the command line as far as it can.

```
$ cat films/dar  →TAB (beep) cat films/dark_█
```

In the **films** directory every file that starts with **dar** has **k_** as the next characters, so bash cannot extend the line further without making a choice among files. The shell leaves the cursor just past the _ character. At this point you can continue typing the pathname or press TAB twice. In the latter case bash beeps, displays your choices, redisplays the command line, and again leaves the cursor just after the _ character.

```
$ cat films/dark_  →TAB (beep)  →TAB
dark_passage   dark_victory
$ cat films/dark_█
```

When you add enough information to distinguish between the two possible files and press TAB, bash displays the unique pathname. If you enter **p** followed by TAB after the _ character, the shell completes the command line:

```
$ cat films/dark_p  →TAB  →assage
```

Because there is no further ambiguity, the shell appends a SPACE so you can finish typing the command line or just press RETURN to execute the command. If the complete pathname is that of a directory, bash appends a slash (**/**) in place of a SPACE.

VARIABLE COMPLETION

When you are typing a variable name, pressing TAB results in *variable completion*, wherein bash attempts to complete the name of the variable. In case of an ambiguity, pressing TAB twice displays a list of choices:

```
$ echo $HO  →TAB  →TAB
$HOME        $HOSTNAME  $HOSTTYPE
$ echo $HOM  →TAB  →E
```

Pressing RETURN executes the command

caution Pressing RETURN causes the shell to execute the command regardless of where the cursor is on the command line.

.inputrc: CONFIGURING THE READLINE LIBRARY

The Bourne Again Shell and other programs that use the Readline Library read the file specified by the **INPUTRC** environment variable to obtain initialization information. If **INPUTRC** is not set, these programs read the **~/.inputrc** file. They ignore lines of **.inputrc** that are blank or that start with a pound sign (#).

VARIABLES

You can set variables in **.inputrc** to control the behavior of the Readline Library using the following syntax:

set *variable value*

Table 8-11 lists some variables and values you can use. See **Readline Variables** in the bash man or info page for a complete list.

Table 8-11   Readline variables

Variable	Effect
editing-mode	Set to **vi** to start Readline in vi mode. Set to **emacs** to start Readline in emacs mode (the default). Similar to the **set −o vi** and **set −o emacs** shell commands (page 318).
horizontal-scroll-mode	Set to **on** to cause long lines to extend off the right edge of the display area. Moving the cursor to the right when it is at the right edge of the display area shifts the line to the left so you can see more of the line. You can shift the line back by moving the cursor back past the left edge. The default value is **off**, which causes long lines to wrap onto multiple lines of the display.
mark-directories	Set to **off** to cause Readline not to place a slash (/) at the end of directory names it completes. The default value is **on**.
mark-modified-lines	Set to **on** to cause Readline to precede modified history lines with an asterisk. The default value is **off**.

KEY BINDINGS

You can specify bindings that map keystroke sequences to Readline commands, allowing you to change or extend the default bindings. Like the emacs editor, the Readline Library includes many commands that are not bound to a keystroke sequence. To use an unbound command, you must map it using one of the following forms:

> *keyname: command_name*
> "*keystroke_sequence*": *command_name*

In the first form, you spell out the name for a single key. For example, CONTROL-U would be written as **control-u**. This form is useful for binding commands to single keys.

In the second form, you specify a string that describes a sequence of keys that will be bound to the command. You can use the emacs-style backslash escape sequences to represent the special keys CONTROL (\C), META (\M), and ESCAPE (\e). Specify a backslash by escaping it with another backslash: \\. Similarly, a double or single quotation mark can be escaped with a backslash: \" or \'.

The **kill-whole-line** command, available in emacs mode only, deletes the current line. Put the following command in **.inputrc** to bind the **kill-whole-line** command (which is unbound by default) to the keystroke sequence CONTROL-R:

```
control-r: kill-whole-line
```

bind Give the command **bind −P** to display a list of all Readline commands. If a command is bound to a key sequence, that sequence is shown. Commands you can use in vi mode start with **vi**. For example, **vi-next-word** and **vi-prev-word** move the cursor to the beginning of the next and previous words, respectively. Commands that do not begin with **vi** are generally available in emacs mode.

Use **bind −q** to determine which key sequence is bound to a command:

```
$ bind -q kill-whole-line
kill-whole-line can be invoked via "\C-r".
```

You can also bind text by enclosing it within double quotation marks (emacs mode only):

```
"QQ": "The Linux Operating System"
```

This command causes bash to insert the string **The Linux Operating System** when you type **QQ**.

CONDITIONAL CONSTRUCTS

You can conditionally select parts of the **.inputrc** file using the **$if** directive. The syntax of the conditional construct is

> *$if test[=value]*
> > *commands*
> *[$else*
> > *commands]*
> *$endif*

where *test* is **mode, term,** or **bash**. If *test* equals *value* (or if *test* is *true* when *value* is not specified), this structure executes the first set of *commands*. If *test* does not equal *value* (or if *test* is *false* when *value* is not specified), this construct executes the second set of *commands* if they are present or exits from the structure if they are not present.

The power of the **$if** directive lies in the three types of tests it can perform.

1. You can test to see which mode is currently set.

   ```
   $if mode=vi
   ```

   The preceding test is *true* if the current Readline mode is **vi** and *false* otherwise. You can test for **vi** or **emacs**.

2. You can test the type of terminal.

   ```
   $if term=xterm
   ```

   The preceding test is *true* if the **TERM** variable is set to **xterm**. You can test for any value of **TERM**.

3. You can test the application name.

   ```
   $if bash
   ```

   The preceding test is *true* when you are running **bash** and not another program that uses the Readline Library. You can test for any application name.

These tests can customize the Readline Library based on the current mode, the type of terminal, and the application you are using. They give you a great deal of power and flexibility when you are using the Readline Library with bash and other programs.

The following commands in **.inputrc** cause CONTROL-Y to move the cursor to the beginning of the next word regardless of whether bash is in vi or emacs mode:

```
$ cat ~/.inputrc
set editing-mode vi
$if mode=vi
        "\C-y": vi-next-word
    $else
        "\C-y": forward-word
$endif
```

Because bash reads the preceding conditional construct when it is started, you must set the editing mode in **.inputrc**. Changing modes interactively using set will not change the binding of CONTROL-Y.

For more information on the Readline Library, open the bash man page and give the command **/^READLINE**, which searches for the word **READLINE** at the beginning of a line.

If Readline commands do not work, log out and log in again

tip   The Bourne Again Shell reads **~/.inputrc** when you log in. After you make changes to this file, you must log out and log in again before the changes will take effect.

ALIASES

An *alias* is a (usually short) name that the shell translates into another (usually longer) name or (complex) command. Aliases allow you to define new commands by substituting a string for the first token of a simple command. They are typically placed in the **~/.bashrc** (bash) or **~/.tcshrc** (tcsh) startup files so that they are available to interactive subshells.

Under bash the syntax of the alias builtin is

> *alias [name[=value]]*

Under tcsh the syntax is

> *alias [name[value]]*

In the bash syntax no SPACEs are permitted around the equal sign. If *value* contains SPACEs or TABs, you must enclose *value* within quotation marks. Unlike aliases under tcsh, a bash alias does not accept an argument from the command line in *value*. Use a bash function (page 327) when you need to use an argument.

An alias does not replace itself, which avoids the possibility of infinite recursion in handling an alias such as the following:

```
$ alias ls='ls -F'
```

You can nest aliases. Aliases are disabled for noninteractive shells (that is, shell scripts). To see a list of the current aliases, give the command **alias**. To view the alias for a particular name, give the command **alias** followed by the name of the alias. You can use the unalias builtin to remove an alias.

When you give an alias builtin command without any arguments, the shell displays a list of all defined aliases:

```
$ alias
alias ll='ls -l'
alias l='ls -ltr'
alias ls='ls -F'
alias zap='rm -i'
```

Most Linux distributions define at least some aliases. Give an **alias** command to see which aliases are in effect. You can delete the aliases you do not want from the appropriate startup file.

SINGLE VERSUS DOUBLE QUOTATION MARKS IN ALIASES

The choice of single or double quotation marks is significant in the alias syntax when the alias includes variables. If you enclose *value* within double quotation marks, any variables that appear in *value* are expanded when the alias is created. If you enclose *value* within single quotation marks, variables are not expanded until the alias is used. The following example illustrates the difference.

The **PWD** keyword variable holds the pathname of the working directory. Max creates two aliases while he is working in his home directory. Because he uses double quotation marks when he creates the **dirA** alias, the shell substitutes the value of the working directory when he creates this alias. The **alias dirA** command displays the **dirA** alias and shows that the substitution has already taken place:

```
$ echo $PWD
/home/max
$ alias dirA="echo Working directory is $PWD"
$ alias dirA
alias dirA='echo Working directory is /home/max'
```

When Max creates the **dirB** alias, he uses single quotation marks, which prevent the shell from expanding the **$PWD** variable. The **alias dirB** command shows that the **dirB** alias still holds the unexpanded **$PWD** variable:

```
$ alias dirB='echo Working directory is $PWD'
$ alias dirB
alias dirB='echo Working directory is $PWD'
```

After creating the **dirA** and **dirB** aliases, Max uses cd to make **cars** his working directory and gives each of the aliases as commands. The alias he created using double quotation marks displays the name of the directory he created the alias in as the working directory (which is wrong). In contrast, the **dirB** alias displays the proper name of the working directory:

```
$ cd cars
$ dirA
Working directory is /home/max
$ dirB
Working directory is /home/max/cars
```

How to prevent the shell from invoking an alias

tip The shell checks only simple, unquoted commands to see if they are aliases. Commands given as relative or absolute pathnames and quoted commands are not checked. When you want to give a command that has an alias but do not want to use the alias, precede the command with a back-slash, specify the command's absolute pathname, or give the command as *./command*.

EXAMPLES OF ALIASES

The following alias allows you to type **r** to repeat the previous command or **r abc** to repeat the last command line that began with **abc**:

```
$ alias r='fc -s'
```

If you use the command **ls –ltr** frequently, you can create an alias that substitutes **ls –ltr** when you give the command **l**:

```
$ alias l='ls -ltr'
$ l
total 41
-rw-r--r--  1 max    group    30015 Mar  1 2008 flute.ps
-rw-r-----  1 max    group     3089 Feb 11 2009 XTerm.ad
-rw-r--r--  1 max    group      641 Apr  1 2009 fixtax.icn
-rw-r--r--  1 max    group      484 Apr  9 2009 maptax.icn
drwxrwxr-x  2 max    group     1024 Aug  9 17:41 Tiger
drwxrwxr-x  2 max    group     1024 Sep 10 11:32 testdir
-rwxr-xr-x  1 max    group      485 Oct 21 08:03 floor
drwxrwxr-x  2 max    group     1024 Oct 27 20:19 Test_Emacs
```

Another common use of aliases is to protect yourself from mistakes. The following example substitutes the interactive version of the rm utility when you give the command **zap**:

```
$ alias zap='rm -i'
$ zap f*
rm: remove 'fixtax.icn'? n
rm: remove 'flute.ps'? n
rm: remove 'floor'? n
```

The **–i** option causes rm to ask you to verify each file that would be deleted, thereby helping you avoid deleting the wrong file. You can also alias rm with the **rm –i** command: **alias rm='rm –i'**.

The aliases in the next example cause the shell to substitute **ls –l** each time you give an **ll** command and **ls –F** each time you use **ls**:

```
$ alias ls='ls -F'
$ alias ll='ls -l'
$ ll
total 41
drwxrwxr-x  2 max    group     1024 Oct 27 20:19 Test_Emacs/
drwxrwxr-x  2 max    group     1024 Aug 9 17:41 Tiger/
-rw-r-----  1 max    group     3089 Feb 11 2009 XTerm.ad
-rw-r--r--  1 max    group      641 Apr 1 2009 fixtax.icn
-rw-r--r--  1 max    group    30015 Mar 1 2008 flute.ps
-rwxr-xr-x  1 max    group      485 Oct 21 08:03 floor*
-rw-r--r--  1 max    group      484 Apr 9 2009 maptax.icn
drwxrwxr-x  2 max    group     1024 Sep 10 11:32 testdir/
```

The **–F** option causes ls to print a slash (**/**) at the end of directory names and an asterisk (*****) at the end of the names of executable files. In this example, the string that replaces the alias ll (ls –l) itself contains an alias (ls). When it replaces an alias with its value, the shell looks at the first word of the replacement string to see whether it is an alias. In the preceding example, the replacement string contains the alias ls, so a second substitution occurs to produce the final command ls –F –l. (To avoid a *recursive plunge,* the ls in the replacement text, although an alias, is not expanded a second time.)

When given a list of aliases without the *=value* or *value* field, the alias builtin responds by displaying the value of each defined alias. The alias builtin reports an error if an alias has not been defined:

```
$ alias ll l ls zap wx
alias ll='ls -l'
alias l='ls -ltr'
alias ls='ls -F'
alias zap='rm -i'
bash: alias: wx: not found
```

You can avoid alias substitution by preceding the aliased command with a backslash (****):

```
$ \ls
Test_Emacs XTerm.ad  flute.ps  maptax.icn
Tiger      fixtax.icn floor     testdir
```

Because the replacement of an alias name with the alias value does not change the rest of the command line, any arguments are still received by the command that gets executed:

```
$ ll f*
-rw-r--r--  1 max   group    641 Apr  1 2009 fixtax.icn
-rw-r--r--  1 max   group  30015 Mar  1 2008 flute.ps
-rwxr-xr-x  1 max   group    485 Oct 21 08:03 floor*
```

You can remove an alias with the unalias builtin. When the **zap** alias is removed, it is no longer displayed with the alias builtin and its subsequent use results in an error message:

```
$ unalias zap
$ alias
alias ll='ls -l'
alias l='ls -ltr'
alias ls='ls -F'
$ zap maptax.icn
bash: zap: command not found
```

FUNCTIONS

A bash shell function (tcsh does not have functions) is similar to a shell script in that it stores a series of commands for execution at a later time. However, because the shell stores a function in the computer's main memory (RAM) instead of in a file on the disk, the shell can access it more quickly than the shell can access a script. The shell also preprocesses (parses) a function so that it starts up more quickly than a script. Finally the shell executes a shell function in the same shell that called it. If you define too many functions, the overhead of starting a subshell (as when you run a script) can become unacceptable.

You can declare a shell function in the **~/.bash_profile** startup file, in the script that uses it, or directly from the command line. You can remove functions with the **unset** builtin. The shell does not retain functions after you log out.

Removing variables and functions

tip   If you have a shell variable and a function with the same name, using **unset** removes the shell variable. If you then use **unset** again with the same name, it removes the function.

The syntax that declares a shell function is

[function] function-name ()
{
        commands
}

where the word *function* is optional, **function-name** is the name you use to call the function, and *commands* comprise the list of commands the function executes when you call it. The *commands* can be anything you would include in a shell script, including calls to other functions.

The opening brace ({) can appear on the same line as the function name. Aliases and variables are expanded when a function is read, not when it is executed. You can use the **break** statement (page 420) within a function to terminate its execution.

Shell functions are useful as a shorthand as well as to define special commands. The following function starts a process named **process** in the background, with the output normally displayed by **process** being saved in **.process.out**:

```
start_process() {
process > .process.out 2>&1 &
}
```

The next example creates a simple function that displays the date, a header, and a list of the people who are logged in on the system. This function runs the same commands as the **whoson** script described on page 278. In this example the function is being entered from the keyboard. The greater than (**>**) signs are secondary shell prompts (**PS2**); do not enter them.

```
$ function whoson ()
> {
>   date
>   echo "Users Currently Logged On"
>   who
> }

$ whoson
Sun Aug 9 15:44:58 PDT 2009
Users Currently Logged On
hls       console    Aug  8 08:59  (:0)
max       pts/4      Aug  8 09:33  (0.0)
zach      pts/7      Aug  8 09:23  (bravo.example.com)
```

Functions in
startup files

If you want to have the **whoson** function always be available without having to enter it each time you log in, put its definition in **~/.bash_profile**. Then run **.bash_profile**, using the . (dot) command to put the changes into effect immediately:

```
$ cat ~/.bash_profile
export TERM=vt100
stty kill '^u'
whoson ()
{
    date
    echo "Users Currently Logged On"
    who
}
$ . ~/.bash_profile
```

You can specify arguments when you call a function. Within the function these arguments are available as positional parameters (page 440). The following example shows the **arg1** function entered from the keyboard:

```
$ arg1 ( ) {
> echo "$1"
> }

$ arg1 first_arg
first_arg
```

See the function **switch** () on page 274 for another example of a function. "Functions" on page 437 discusses the use of local and global variables within a function.

optional   The following function allows you to export variables using tcsh syntax. The env builtin lists all environment variables and their values and verifies that **setenv** worked correctly:

```
$ cat .bash_profile
...
# setenv - keep tcsh users happy
function setenv()
{
    if [ $# -eq 2 ]
        then
            eval $1=$2
            export $1
        else
            echo "Usage: setenv NAME VALUE" 1>&2
    fi
}
$ . ~/.bash_profile
$ setenv TCL_LIBRARY /usr/local/lib/tcl
$ env | grep TCL_LIBRARY
TCL_LIBRARY=/usr/local/lib/tcl
```

eval   The **$#** special parameter (page 441) takes on the value of the number of command-line arguments. This function uses the **eval** builtin to force bash to scan the command **$1=$2** *twice*. Because **$1=$2** begins with a dollar sign ($), the shell treats the entire string as a single token—a command. With variable substitution performed, the command name becomes **TCL_LIBRARY=/usr/local/lib/tcl**, which results in an error. Using eval, a second scanning splits the string into the three desired tokens, and the correct assignment occurs.

CONTROLLING bash: FEATURES AND OPTIONS

This section explains how to control bash features and options using command-line options and the set and shopt builtins.

COMMAND-LINE OPTIONS

Two kinds of command-line options are available: short and long. Short options consist of a hyphen followed by a letter; long options have two hyphens followed by multiple characters. Long options must appear before short options on a command line that calls bash. Table 8-12 lists some commonly used command-line options.

Table 8-12   Command-line options

Option	Explanation	Syntax
Help	Displays a usage message.	**--help**
No edit	Prevents users from using the Readline Library (page 318) to edit command lines in an interactive shell.	**--noediting**
No profile	Prevents reading these startup files (page 271): **/etc/profile**, **~/.bash_profile**, **~/.bash_login**, and **~/.profile**.	**--noprofile**
No rc	Prevents reading the **~/.bashrc** startup file (page 272). This option is on by default if the shell is called as **sh**.	**--norc**
POSIX	Runs bash in POSIX mode.	**--posix**
Version	Displays bash version information and exits.	**--version**
Login	Causes bash to run as though it were a login shell.	**-l** (lowercase "l")
shopt	Runs a shell with the *opt* shopt option (next page). A **-O** (uppercase "O") sets the option; **+O** unsets it.	[±]**O** [*opt*]
End of options	On the command line, signals the end of options. Subsequent tokens are treated as arguments even if they begin with a hyphen (–).	**--**

SHELL FEATURES

You can control the behavior of the Bourne Again Shell by turning features on and off. Different features use different methods to turn features on and off. The set builtin controls one group of features, while the shopt builtin controls another group. You can also control many features from the command line you use to call bash.

Features, options, variables?

tip To avoid confusing terminology, this book refers to the various shell behaviors that you can control as *features*. The bash info page refers to them as "options" and "values of variables controlling optional shell behavior."

set ±o: TURNS SHELL FEATURES ON AND OFF

The bash set builtin (there is a set builtin in tcsh, but it works differently), when used with the **–o** or **+o** option, enables, disables, and lists certain bash features. For example, the following command turns on the **noclobber** feature (page 129):

```
$ set -o noclobber
```

You can turn this feature off (the default) by giving the command

```
$ set +o noclobber
```

The command **set –o** without an option lists each of the features controlled by set, followed by its state (on or off). The command **set +o** without an option lists the same features in a form you can use as input to the shell. Table 8-13 (next page) lists bash features.

shopt: TURNS SHELL FEATURES ON AND OFF

The shopt (shell option) builtin (not available in tcsh) enables, disables, and lists certain bash features that control the behavior of the shell. For example, the following command causes bash to include filenames that begin with a period (.) when it expands ambiguous file references (the **–s** stands for *set*):

```
$ shopt -s dotglob
```

You can turn this feature off (the default) by giving the following command (the **–u** stands for *unset*):

```
$ shopt -u dotglob
```

The shell displays how a feature is set if you give the name of the feature as the only argument to shopt:

```
$ shopt dotglob
dotglob         off
```

The command **shopt** without any options or arguments lists the features controlled by shopt and their state. The command **shopt –s** without an argument lists the features controlled by shopt that are set or on. The command **shopt –u** lists the features that are unset or off. Table 8-13 lists bash features.

Setting set ±o features using shopt

tip You can use shopt to set/unset features that are otherwise controlled by **set ±o**. Use the regular shopt syntax with **–s** or **–u** and include the **–o** option. For example, the following command turns on the **noclobber** feature:

```
$ shopt -o -s noclobber
```

Table 8-13   bash features

Feature	Description	Syntax	Alternate syntax
allexport	Automatically exports all variables and functions you create or modify after giving this command.	**set −o allexport**	**set −a**
braceexpand	Causes bash to perform brace expansion (the default; page 336).	**set −o braceexpand**	**set −B**
cdspell	Corrects minor spelling errors in directory names used as arguments to cd.	**shopt −s cdspell**	
cmdhist	Saves all lines of a multiline command in the same history entry, adding semicolons as needed.	**shopt −s cmdhist**	
dotglob	Causes shell special characters (wildcards; page 136) in an ambiguous file reference to match a leading period in a filename. By default special characters do not match a leading period. You must always specify the filenames . and .. explicitly because no pattern ever matches them.	**shopt −s dotglob**	
emacs	Specifies emacs editing mode for command-line editing (the default; page 319).	**set −o emacs**	
errexit	Causes bash to exit when a simple command (not a control structure) fails.	**set −o errexit**	**set −e**
execfail	Causes a shell script to continue running when it cannot find the file that is given as an argument to exec. By default a script terminates when exec cannot find the file that is given as its argument.	**shopt −s execfail**	
expand_aliases	Causes aliases (page 324) to be expanded (by default it is on for interactive shells and off for noninteractive shells).	**shopt −s expand_alias**	
hashall	Causes bash to remember where commands it has found using **PATH** (page 297) are located (default).	**set −o hashall**	**set −h**
histappend	Causes bash to append the history list to the file named by **HISTFILE** (page 308) when the shell exits. By default bash overwrites this file.	**shopt −s histappend**	
histexpand	Turns on the history mechanism (which uses exclamation points by default; page 313). Turn this feature off to turn off history expansion.	**set −o histexpand**	**set −H**

Table 8-13 bash features (continued)

Feature	Description	Syntax	Alternate syntax
history	Enables command history (on by default; page 308).	**set −o history**	
huponexit	Specifies that bash send a SIGHUP signal to all jobs when an interactive login shell exits.	**shopt −s huponexit**	
ignoreeof	Specifies that bash must receive ten EOF characters before it exits. Useful on noisy dial-up lines.	**set −o ignoreeof**	
monitor	Enables job control (on by default, page 285).	**set −o monitor**	**set −m**
nocaseglob	Causes ambiguous file references (page 136) to match filenames without regard to case (off by default).	**shopt −s nocaseglob**	
noclobber	Helps prevent overwriting files (off by default; page 129).	**set −o noclobber**	**set −C**
noglob	Disables pathname expansion (off by default; page 136).	**set −o noglob**	**set −f**
notify	With job control (page 285) enabled, reports the termination status of background jobs immediately. The default behavior is to display the status just before the next prompt.	**set −o notify**	**set −b**
nounset	Displays an error and exits from a shell script when you use an unset variable in an interactive shell. The default is to display a null value for an unset variable.	**set −o nounset**	**set −u**
nullglob	Causes bash to expand ambiguous file references (page 136) that do not match a filename to a null string. By default bash passes these file references without expanding them.	**shopt −s nullglob**	
posix	Runs bash in POSIX mode.	**set −o posix**	
verbose	Displays command lines as bash reads them.	**set −o verbose**	**set −v**
vi	Specifies vi editing mode for command-line editing (page 318).	**set −o vi**	
xpg_echo	Causes the echo builtin to expand backslash escape sequences without the need for the −e option (page 424).	**shopt −s xpg_echo**	
xtrace	Turns on shell debugging (page 410).	**set −o xtrace**	**set −x**

PROCESSING THE COMMAND LINE

Whether you are working interactively or running a shell script, bash needs to read a command line before it can start processing it—bash always reads at least one line before processing a command. Some bash builtins, such as **if** and **case**, as well as functions and quoted strings, span multiple lines. When bash recognizes a command that covers more than one line, it reads the entire command before processing it. In interactive sessions, bash prompts you with the secondary prompt (**PS2**, **>** by default; page 300) as you type each line of a multiline command until it recognizes the end of the command:

```
$ echo 'hi
> end'
hi
end
$ function hello () {
> echo hello there
> }
$
```

After reading a command line, bash applies history expansion and alias substitution to the line.

HISTORY EXPANSION

"Reexecuting and Editing Commands" on page 310 discusses the commands you can give to modify and reexecute command lines from the history list. History expansion is the process that bash uses to turn a history command into an executable command line. For example, when you give the command **!!**, history expansion changes that command line so it is the same as the previous one. History expansion is turned on by default for interactive shells; **set +o histexpand** turns it off. History expansion does not apply to noninteractive shells (shell scripts).

ALIAS SUBSTITUTION

Aliases (page 324) substitute a string for the first word of a simple command. By default aliases are turned on for interactive shells and off for noninteractive shells. Give the command **shopt –u expand_aliases** to turn aliases off.

PARSING AND SCANNING THE COMMAND LINE

After processing history commands and aliases, bash does not execute the command immediately. One of the first things the shell does is to *parse* (isolate strings of characters in) the command line into tokens or words. The shell then scans each token for special characters and patterns that instruct the shell to take certain actions. These actions can involve substituting one word or words for another. When the shell parses the following command line, it breaks it into three tokens (**cp**, **~/letter**, and **.**):

```
$ cp ~/letter .
```

After separating tokens and before executing the command, the shell scans the tokens and performs *command-line expansion*.

COMMAND-LINE EXPANSION

Both interactive and noninteractive shells transform the command line using *command-line expansion* before passing the command line to the program being called. You can use a shell without knowing much about command-line expansion, but you can use what a shell has to offer to a better advantage with an understanding of this topic. This section covers Bourne Again Shell command-line expansion; TC Shell command-line expansion is covered starting on page 354.

The Bourne Again Shell scans each token for the various types of expansion and substitution in the following order. Most of these processes expand a word into a single word. Only brace expansion, word splitting, and pathname expansion can change the number of words in a command (except for the expansion of the variable "$@"—see page 444).

1. Brace expansion (page 336)

2. Tilde expansion (page 337)

3. Parameter and variable expansion (page 338)

4. Arithmetic expansion (page 338)

5. Command substitution (page 340)

6. Word splitting (page 341)

7. Pathname expansion (page 341)

8. Process substitution (page 343)

Quote removal After bash finishes with the preceding list, it removes from the command line single quotation marks, double quotation marks, and backslashes that are not a result of an expansion. This process is called *quote removal*.

ORDER OF EXPANSION

The order in which bash carries out these steps affects the interpretation of commands. For example, if you set a variable to a value that looks like the instruction for output redirection and then enter a command that uses the variable's value to perform redirection, you might expect bash to redirect the output.

```
$ SENDIT="> /tmp/saveit"
$ echo xxx $SENDIT
xxx > /tmp/saveit
$ cat /tmp/saveit
cat: /tmp/saveit: No such file or directory
```

In fact, the shell does *not* redirect the output—it recognizes input and output redirection before it evaluates variables. When it executes the command line, the shell checks for redirection and, finding none, evaluates the **SENDIT** variable. After replacing the variable with **> /tmp/saveit**, bash passes the arguments to echo, which dutifully copies its arguments to standard output. No **/tmp/saveit** file is created.

The following sections provide more detailed descriptions of the steps involved in command processing. Keep in mind that double and single quotation marks cause the shell to behave differently when performing expansions. Double quotation marks permit parameter and variable expansion but suppress other types of expansion. Single quotation marks suppress all types of expansion.

BRACE EXPANSION

Brace expansion, which originated in the C Shell, provides a convenient way to specify filenames when pathname expansion does not apply. Although brace expansion is almost always used to specify filenames, the mechanism can be used to generate arbitrary strings; the shell does not attempt to match the brace notation with the names of existing files.

Brace expansion is turned on in interactive and noninteractive shells by default; you can turn it off with **set +o braceexpand**. The shell also uses braces to isolate variable names (page 294).

The following example illustrates how brace expansion works. The ls command does not display any output because there are no files in the working directory. The echo builtin displays the strings that the shell generates with brace expansion. In this case the strings do not match filenames (because there are no files in the working directory).

```
$ ls
$ echo chap_{one,two,three}.txt
chap_one.txt chap_two.txt chap_three.txt
```

The shell expands the comma-separated strings inside the braces in the echo command into a SPACE-separated list of strings. Each string from the list is prepended with the string **chap_**, called the *preamble*, and appended with the string **.txt**, called the *postscript*. Both the preamble and the postscript are optional. The left-to-right order of the strings within the braces is preserved in the expansion. For the shell to treat the left and right braces specially and for brace expansion to occur, at least one comma and no unquoted whitespace characters must be inside the braces. You can nest brace expansions.

Brace expansion is useful when there is a long preamble or postscript. The following example copies four files—**main.c, f1.c, f2.c,** and **tmp.c**—located in the **/usr/local/src/C** directory to the working directory:

```
$ cp /usr/local/src/C/{main,f1,f2,tmp}.c .
```

You can also use brace expansion to create directories with related names:

```
$ ls -F
file1  file2  file3
$ mkdir vrs{A,B,C,D,E}
$ ls -F
file1  file2  file3  vrsA/  vrsB/  vrsC/  vrsD/  vrsE/
```

The **−F** option causes ls to display a slash (**/**) after a directory and an asterisk (**∗**) after an executable file.

If you tried to use an ambiguous file reference instead of braces to specify the directories, the result would be different (and not what you wanted):

```
$ rmdir vrs*
$ mkdir vrs[A-E]
$ ls -F
file1  file2  file3  vrs[A-E]/
```

An ambiguous file reference matches the names of existing files. In the preceding example, because it found no filenames matching **vrs[A–E]**, bash passed the ambiguous file reference to mkdir, which created a directory with that name. Brackets in ambiguous file references are discussed on page 139.

TILDE EXPANSION

Chapter 4 introduced a shorthand notation to specify your home directory or the home directory of another user. This section provides a more detailed explanation of *tilde expansion.*

The tilde (**~**) is a special character when it appears at the start of a token on a command line. When it sees a tilde in this position, bash looks at the following string of characters—up to the first slash (**/**) or to the end of the word if there is no slash—as a possible username. If this possible username is null (that is, if the tilde appears as a word by itself or if it is immediately followed by a slash), the shell substitutes the value of the **HOME** variable for the tilde. The following example demonstrates this expansion, where the last command copies the file named **letter** from Max's home directory to the working directory:

```
$ echo $HOME
/home/max
$ echo ~
/home/max
$ echo ~/letter
/home/max/letter
$ cp ~/letter .
```

If the string of characters following the tilde forms a valid username, the shell substitutes the path of the home directory associated with that username for the tilde and name. If the string is not null and not a valid username, the shell does not make any substitution:

```
$ echo ~zach
/home/zach
$ echo ~root
/root
$ echo ~xx
~xx
```

Tildes are also used in directory stack manipulation (page 288). In addition, **~+** is a synonym for **PWD** (the name of the working directory), and **~–** is a synonym for **OLDPWD** (the name of the previous working directory).

PARAMETER AND VARIABLE EXPANSION

On a command line, a dollar sign (**$**) that is not followed by an open parenthesis introduces parameter or variable expansion. *Parameters* include both command-line, or positional, parameters (page 440) and special parameters (page 438). *Variables* include both user-created variables (page 292) and keyword variables (page 296). The bash man and info pages do not make this distinction.

Parameters and variables are not expanded if they are enclosed within single quotation marks or if the leading dollar sign is escaped (i.e., preceded with a backslash). If they are enclosed within double quotation marks, the shell expands parameters and variables.

ARITHMETIC EXPANSION

The shell performs *arithmetic expansion* by evaluating an arithmetic expression and replacing it with the result. See page 368 for information on arithmetic expansion under tcsh. Under bash the syntax for arithmetic expansion is

   $((expression))

The shell evaluates *expression* and replaces *$((expression))* with the result of the evaluation. This syntax is similar to the syntax used for command substitution [*$(...)*] and performs a parallel function. You can use *$((expression))* as an argument to a command or in place of any numeric value on a command line.

The rules for forming *expression* are the same as those found in the C programming language; all standard C arithmetic operators are available (see Table 10-8 on page 463). Arithmetic in bash is done using integers. Unless you use variables of type integer (page 296) or actual integers, however, the shell must convert string-valued variables to integers for the purpose of the arithmetic evaluation.

You do not need to precede variable names within *expression* with a dollar sign (**$**). In the following example, after read (page 447) assigns the user's response to **age**, an arithmetic expression determines how many years are left until age 60:

```
$ cat age_check
#!/bin/bash
echo -n "How old are you? "
read age
echo "Wow, in $((60-age)) years, you'll be 60!"

$ ./age_check
How old are you? 55
Wow, in 5 years, you'll be 60!
```

You do not need to enclose the *expression* within quotation marks because bash does not perform filename expansion on it. This feature makes it easier for you to use an asterisk (*****) for multiplication, as the following example shows:

```
$ echo There are $((60*60*24*365)) seconds in a non-leap year.
There are 31536000 seconds in a non-leap year.
```

The next example uses wc, cut, arithmetic expansion, and command substitution (page 340) to estimate the number of pages required to print the contents of the file **letter.txt**. The output of the wc (word count) utility (page 876) used with the –l option is the number of lines in the file, in columns (character positions) 1 through 4, followed by a SPACE and the name of the file (the first command following). The cut utility (page 652) with the –c1–4 option extracts the first four columns.

```
$ wc -l letter.txt
351 letter.txt
$ wc -l letter.txt | cut -c1-4
351
```

The dollar sign and single parenthesis instruct the shell to perform command substitution; the dollar sign and double parentheses indicate arithmetic expansion:

```
$ echo $(( $(wc -l letter.txt | cut -c1-4)/66 + 1))
6
```

The preceding example sends standard output from wc to standard input of cut via a pipe. Because of command substitution, the output of both commands replaces the commands between the $(and the matching) on the command line. Arithmetic expansion then divides this number by 66, the number of lines on a page. A 1 is added because the integer division results in any remainder being discarded.

Fewer dollar signs ($)

tip   When you use variables within **$((** and **))**, the dollar signs that precede individual variable references are optional:

```
$ x=23 y=37
$ echo $((2*$x + 3*$y))
157
$ echo $((2*x + 3*y))
157
```

Another way to get the same result without using cut is to redirect the input to wc instead of having wc get its input from a file you name on the command line. When you redirect its input, wc does not display the name of the file:

```
$ wc -l < letter.txt
   351
```

It is common practice to assign the result of arithmetic expansion to a variable:

```
$ numpages=$(( $(wc -l < letter.txt)/66 + 1))
```

let builtin   The let builtin (not available in tcsh) evaluates arithmetic expressions just as the **$(( ))** syntax does. The following command is equivalent to the preceding one:

```
$ let "numpages=$(wc -l < letter.txt)/66 + 1"
```

The double quotation marks keep the SPACEs (both those you can see and those that result from the command substitution) from separating the expression into separate arguments to let. The value of the last expression determines the exit status of let. If the value of the last expression is 0, the exit status of let is 1; otherwise, its exit status is 0.

You can supply let with multiple arguments on a single command line:

```
$ let a=5+3 b=7+2
$ echo $a $b
8 9
```

When you refer to variables when doing arithmetic expansion with let or $(( )), the shell does not require a variable name to begin with a dollar sign ($). Nevertheless, it is a good practice to do so for consistency, as in most places you must precede a variable name with a dollar sign.

COMMAND SUBSTITUTION

Command substitution replaces a command with the output of that command. The preferred syntax for command substitution under bash follows:

$(command)

Under bash you can also use the following, older syntax, which is the only syntax allowed under tcsh:

`command`

The shell executes *command* within a subshell and replaces *command,* along with the surrounding punctuation, with standard output of *command.*

In the following example, the shell executes pwd and substitutes the output of the command for the command and surrounding punctuation. Then the shell passes the output of the command, which is now an argument, to echo, which displays it.

```
$ echo $(pwd)
/home/max
```

The next script assigns the output of the pwd builtin to the variable **where** and displays a message containing the value of this variable:

```
$ cat where
where=$(pwd)
echo "You are using the $where directory."
$ ./where
You are using the /home/zach directory.
```

Although it illustrates how to assign the output of a command to a variable, this example is not realistic. You can more directly display the output of pwd without using a variable:

```
$ cat where2
echo "You are using the $(pwd) directory."
$ ./where2
You are using the /home/zach directory.
```

The following command uses find to locate files with the name **README** in the directory tree rooted at the working directory. This list of files is standard output of find and becomes the list of arguments to ls.

```
$ ls -l $(find . -name README -print)
```

The next command line shows the older `command` syntax:

```
$ ls -l `find . -name README -print`
```

One advantage of the newer syntax is that it avoids the rather arcane rules for token handling, quotation mark handling, and escaped back ticks within the old syntax. Another advantage of the new syntax is that it can be nested, unlike the old syntax. For example, you can produce a long listing of all **README** files whose size exceeds the size of *./README* with the following command:

```
$ ls -l $(find . -name README -size +$(echo $(cat ./README | wc -c)c ) -print )
```

Try giving this command after giving a **set –x** command (page 410) to see how bash expands it. If there is no **README** file, you just get the output of ls –l.

For additional scripts that use command substitution, see pages 406, 425, and 455.

$((Versus $(

tip The symbols **$((** constitute a single token. They introduce an arithmetic expression, not a command substitution. Thus, if you want to use a parenthesized subshell (page 284) within **$()**, you must insert a SPACE between the **$(** and the following **(**.

WORD SPLITTING

The results of parameter and variable expansion, command substitution, and arithmetic expansion are candidates for word splitting. Using each character of **IFS** (page 301) as a possible delimiter, bash splits these candidates into words or tokens. If **IFS** is unset, bash uses its default value (SPACE-TAB-NEWLINE). If **IFS** is null, bash does not split words.

PATHNAME EXPANSION

Pathname expansion (page 136), also called *filename generation* or *globbing,* is the process of interpreting ambiguous file references and substituting the appropriate list of filenames. Unless **noglob** (page 333) is set, the shell performs this function when it encounters an ambiguous file reference—a token containing any of the unquoted characters ∗, ?, [, or]. If bash cannot locate any files that match the specified pattern, the token with the ambiguous file reference is left alone. The shell does not delete the token or replace it with a null string but rather passes it to the program as is (except see **nullglob** on page 333). The TC Shell generates an error message.

In the first echo command in the following example, the shell expands the ambiguous file reference **tmp∗** and passes three tokens (**tmp1**, **tmp2**, and **tmp3**) to echo. The echo builtin displays the three filenames it was passed by the shell. After rm removes the three **tmp*** files, the shell finds no filenames that match **tmp*** when it tries to expand it. It then passes the unexpanded string to the echo builtin, which displays the string it was passed.

```
$ ls
tmp1 tmp2 tmp3
$ echo tmp*
tmp1 tmp2 tmp3
$ rm tmp*
$ echo tmp*
tmp*
```

By default the same command causes the TC Shell to display an error message:

```
tcsh $ echo tmp*
echo: No match
```

A period that either starts a pathname or follows a slash (/) in a pathname must be matched explicitly unless you have set **dotglob** (page 332). The option **nocaseglob** (page 333) causes ambiguous file references to match filenames without regard to case.

Quotation marks Putting double quotation marks around an argument causes the shell to suppress pathname and all other kinds of expansion except parameter and variable expansion. Putting single quotation marks around an argument suppresses all types of expansion. The second echo command in the following example shows the variable **$max** between double quotation marks, which allow variable expansion. As a result the shell expands the variable to its value: **sonar**. This expansion does not occur in the third echo command, which uses single quotation marks. Because neither single nor double quotation marks allow pathname expansion, the last two commands display the unexpanded argument **tmp***.

```
$ echo tmp* $max
tmp1 tmp2 tmp3 sonar
$ echo "tmp* $max"
tmp* sonar
$ echo 'tmp* $max'
tmp* $max
```

The shell distinguishes between the value of a variable and a reference to the variable and does not expand ambiguous file references if they occur in the value of a variable. As a consequence you can assign to a variable a value that includes special characters, such as an asterisk (*****).

Levels of expansion In the next example, the working directory has three files whose names begin with **letter**. When you assign the value **letter*** to the variable **var**, the shell does not expand the ambiguous file reference because it occurs in the value of a variable (in the assignment statement for the variable). No quotation marks surround the string **letter***; context alone prevents the expansion. After the assignment the set builtin (with the help of grep) shows the value of **var** to be **letter***.

```
$ ls letter*
letter1 letter2  letter3
$ var=letter*
```

```
$ set | grep var
var='letter*'
$ echo '$var'
$var
$ echo "$var"
letter*
$ echo $var
letter1 letter2 letter3
```

The three **echo** commands demonstrate three levels of expansion. When **$var** is quoted with single quotation marks, the shell performs no expansion and passes the character string $var to echo, which displays it. With double quotation marks, the shell performs variable expansion only and substitutes the value of the **var** variable for its name, preceded by a dollar sign. No pathname expansion is performed on this command because double quotation marks suppress it. In the final command, the shell, without the limitations of quotation marks, performs variable substitution and then pathname expansion before passing the arguments to echo.

PROCESS SUBSTITUTION

A special feature of the Bourne Again Shell is the ability to replace filename arguments with processes. An argument with the syntax <*(command)* causes *command* to be executed and the output written to a named pipe (FIFO). The shell replaces that argument with the name of the pipe. If that argument is then used as the name of an input file during processing, the output of *command* is read. Similarly an argument with the syntax >*(command)* is replaced by the name of a pipe that *command* reads as standard input.

The following example uses sort (pages 54 and 817) with the **–m** (merge, which works correctly only if the input files are already sorted) option to combine two word lists into a single list. Each word list is generated by a pipe that extracts words matching a pattern from a file and sorts the words in that list.

```
$ sort -m -f <(grep "[^A-Z]..$" memo1 | sort) <(grep ".*aba.*" memo2 |sort)
```

CHAPTER SUMMARY

The shell is both a command interpreter and a programming language. As a command interpreter, it executes commands you enter in response to its prompt. As a programming language, the shell executes commands from files called shell scripts. When you start a shell, it typically runs one or more startup files.

Running a shell script Assuming the file holding a shell script is in the working directory, there are three basic ways to execute the shell script from the command line.

1. Type the simple filename of the file that holds the script.

2. Type a relative pathname, including the simple filename preceded by ./.

3. Type **bash** or **tcsh** followed by the name of the file.

Technique 1 requires that the working directory be in the **PATH** variable. Techniques 1 and 2 require that you have execute and read permission for the file holding the script. Technique 3 requires that you have read permission for the file holding the script.

Job control   A job is one or more commands connected by pipes. You can bring a job running in the background into the foreground using the fg builtin. You can put a foreground job into the background using the bg builtin, provided that you first suspend the job by pressing the suspend key (typically CONTROL-Z). Use the jobs builtin to see which jobs are running or suspended.

Variables   The shell allows you to define variables. You can declare and initialize a variable by assigning a value to it; you can remove a variable declaration using unset. Variables are local to a process unless they are exported using the export (bash) or setenv (tcsh) builtin to make them available to child processes. Variables you declare are called *user-created* variables. The shell defines *keyword* variables. Within a shell script you can work with the command-line (*positional*) parameters the script was called with.

Process   Each process has a unique identification (PID) number and is the execution of a single Linux command. When you give it a command, the shell forks a new (child) process to execute the command, unless the command is built into the shell. While the child process is running, the shell is in a state called sleep. By ending a command line with an ampersand (&), you can run a child process in the background and bypass the sleep state so that the shell prompt returns immediately after you press RETURN. Each command in a shell script forks a separate process, each of which may in turn fork other processes. When a process terminates, it returns its exit status to its parent process. An exit status of zero signifies success; nonzero signifies failure.

History   The history mechanism, a feature adapted from the C Shell, maintains a list of recently issued command lines, also called *events,* that provides a way to reexecute previous commands quickly. There are several ways to work with the history list; one of the easiest is to use a command-line editor.

Command-line editors   When using an interactive Bourne Again Shell, you can edit a command line and commands from the history file, using either of the Bourne Again Shell's command-line editors (vim or emacs). When you use the vim command-line editor, you start in Input mode, unlike vim. You can switch between Command and Input modes. The emacs editor is modeless and distinguishes commands from editor input by recognizing control characters as commands.

Aliases   An alias is a name that the shell translates into another name or (complex) command. Aliases allow you to define new commands by substituting a string for the first token of a simple command. The Bourne Again and TC Shells use different syntaxes to define an alias, but aliases in both shells work similarly.

Functions   A shell function is a series of commands that, unlike a shell script, is parsed prior to being stored in memory. As a consequence shell functions run faster than shell scripts. Shell scripts are parsed at runtime and are stored on disk. A function can be defined on the command line or within a shell script. If you want the function definition to remain in effect across login sessions, you can define it in a startup file.

Like functions in many programming languages, a shell function is called by giving its name followed by any arguments.

Shell features   There are several ways to customize the shell's behavior. You can use options on the command line when you call bash. You can use the bash set and shopt builtins to turn features on and off.

Command-line expansion   When it processes a command line, the Bourne Again Shell may replace some words with expanded text. Most types of command-line expansion are invoked by the appearance of a special character within a word (for example, a leading dollar sign denotes a variable). Table 8-6 on page 304 lists these special characters. The expansions take place in a specific order. Following the history and alias expansions, the common expansions are parameter and variable expansion, command substitution, and pathname expansion. Surrounding a word with double quotation marks suppresses all types of expansion except parameter and variable expansion. Single quotation marks suppress all types of expansion, as does quoting (escaping) a special character by preceding it with a backslash.

EXERCISES

1. Explain the following unexpected result:

```
$ whereis date
date: /bin/date ...
$ echo $PATH
.:/usr/local/bin:/usr/bin:/bin
$ cat > date
echo "This is my own version of date."
$ ./date
Fri May 22 11:45:49 PDT 2009
```

2. What are two ways you can execute a shell script when you do not have execute permission for the file containing the script? Can you execute a shell script if you do not have read permission for the file containing the script?

3. What is the purpose of the **PATH** variable?

a. Set the **PATH** variable so that it causes the shell to search the following directories in order:

- /usr/local/bin
- /usr/bin
- /bin
- /usr/kerberos/bin
- The **bin** directory in your home directory
- The working directory

b. If there is a file named **doit** in **/usr/bin** and another file with the same name in your **~/bin** directory, which one will be executed? (Assume that you have execute permission for both files.)

c. If your **PATH** variable is not set to search the working directory, how can you execute a program located there?

d. Which command can you use to add the directory **/usr/games** to the end of the list of directories in **PATH**?

4. Assume you have made the following assignment:

   $ **person=zach**

   Give the output of each of the following commands:

   a. echo $person

   b. echo '$person'

   c. echo "$person"

5. The following shell script adds entries to a file named **journal-file** in your home directory. This script helps you keep track of phone conversations and meetings.

```
$ cat journal
# journal: add journal entries to the file
# $HOME/journal-file

file=$HOME/journal-file
date >> $file
echo -n "Enter name of person or group: "
read name
echo "$name" >> $file
echo >> $file
cat >> $file
echo "-----------------------------------------------" >> $file
echo >> $file
```

a. What do you have to do to the script to be able to execute it?

b. Why does the script use the read builtin the first time it accepts input from the terminal and the cat utility the second time?

6. Assume the **/home/zach/grants/biblios** and **/home/zach/biblios** directories exist. Give Zach's working directory after he executes each sequence of commands given. Explain what happens in each case.

a.
```
$ pwd
/home/zach/grants
$ CDPATH=$(pwd)
$ cd
$ cd biblios
```

b.
```
$ pwd
/home/zach/grants
$ CDPATH=$(pwd)
$ cd $HOME/biblios
```

7. Name two ways you can identify the PID number of the login shell.

8. Give the following command:

```
$ sleep 30 | cat /etc/inittab
```

Is there any output from sleep? Where does cat get its input from? What has to happen before the shell displays another prompt?

ADVANCED EXERCISES

9. Write a sequence of commands or a script that demonstrates variable expansion occurs before pathname expansion.

10. Write a shell script that outputs the name of the shell executing it.

11. Explain the behavior of the following shell script:

```
$ cat quote_demo
twoliner="This is line 1.
This is line 2."
echo "$twoliner"
echo $twoliner
```

a. How many arguments does each echo command see in this script? Explain.

b. Redefine the **IFS** shell variable so that the output of the second echo is the same as the first.

12. Add the exit status of the previous command to your prompt so that it behaves similarly to the following:

```
$ [0] ls xxx
ls: xxx: No such file or directory
$ [1]
```

13. The dirname utility treats its argument as a pathname and writes to standard output the path prefix—that is, everything up to but not including the last component:

```
$ dirname a/b/c/d
a/b/c
```

If you give **dirname** a simple filename (no **/** characters) as an argument, **dirname** writes a **.** to standard output:

```
$ dirname simple
.
```

Implement dirname as a bash function. Make sure that it behaves sensibly when given such arguments as /.

14. Implement the basename utility, which writes the last component of its pathname argument to standard output, as a bash function. For example, given the pathname **a/b/c/d**, basename writes **d** to standard output:

```
$ basename a/b/c/d
d
```

15. The Linux basename utility has an optional second argument. If you give the command **basename** *path suffix*, basename removes the *suffix* and the prefix from *path*:

```
$ basename src/shellfiles/prog.bash .bash
prog
$ basename src/shellfiles/prog.bash .c
prog.bash
```

Add this feature to the function you wrote for exercise 14.

9

THE TC SHELL

The TC Shell (tcsh) performs the same function as the Bourne Again Shell and other shells: It provides an interface between you and the Linux operating system. The TC Shell is an interactive command interpreter as well as a high-level programming language. Although you use only one shell at any given time, you should be able to switch back and forth comfortably between shells as the need arises. In fact, you may want to run different shells in different windows. Chapters 8 and 10 apply to tcsh as well as to bash so they provide a good background for this chapter. This chapter explains tcsh features that are not found in bash and those that are implemented differently from their bash counterparts. The tcsh home page is www.tcsh.org.

The TC Shell is an expanded version of the C Shell (csh), which originated on Berkeley UNIX. The "T" in TC Shell comes from the TENEX and TOPS-20 operating systems, which inspired command completion and other features in the TC Shell. A number of features not found in csh are present in tcsh, including file and username completion, command-line editing, and spelling correction. As with csh, you can customize tcsh to make it more tolerant of mistakes and easier to use. By setting the proper shell variables, you can have tcsh warn you when you appear to be accidentally logging out or overwriting a file. Many popular features of the original C Shell are now shared by bash and tcsh.

Assignment statement Although some of the functionality of tcsh is present in bash, differences arise in the syntax of some commands. For example, the tcsh assignment statement has the following syntax:

set *variable* = *value*

Having SPACEs on either side of the equal sign, although illegal in bash, is allowed in tcsh. By convention shell variables in tcsh are generally named with lowercase letters, not uppercase (you can use either). If you reference an undeclared variable (one that has had no value assigned to it), tcsh generates an error message, whereas bash does not. Finally the default tcsh prompt is a greater than sign (>), but it is frequently set to a single $ character followed by a SPACE. The examples in this chapter use a prompt of **tcsh $** to avoid confusion with the bash prompt.

Do not use tcsh as a programming language

tip If you have used UNIX and are comfortable with the C or TC Shell, you may want to use tcsh as your login shell. However, you may find that the TC Shell is not as good a programming language as bash. If you are going to learn only one shell programming language, learn bash. The Bourne Again Shell and dash (page 270), which is a subset of bash, are used throughout Linux to program many system administration scripts.

SHELL SCRIPTS

The TC Shell can execute files containing tcsh commands, just as the Bourne Again Shell can execute files containing bash commands. Although the concepts of writing and executing scripts in the two shells are similar, the methods of declaring and assigning values to variables and the syntax of control structures are different.

You can run bash and tcsh scripts while using any one of the shells as a command interpreter. Various methods exist for selecting the shell that runs a script. Refer to "#! Specifies a Shell" on page 280 for more information.

If the first character of a shell script is a pound sign (#) and the following character is *not* an exclamation point (!), the TC Shell executes the script under tcsh. If the first character is anything other than #, tcsh calls the sh link to dash or bash to execute the script.

echo: getting rid of the RETURN

tip The tcsh echo builtin accepts either a **–n** option or a trailing **\c** to get rid of the RETURN that echo normally displays at the end of a line. The bash echo builtin accepts only the **–n** option (refer to "read: Accepts User Input" on page 447).

Shell game

tip When you are working with an interactive TC Shell, if you run a script in which # is *not* the first character of the script and you call the script *directly* (without preceding its name with tcsh), tcsh calls the sh link to dash or bash to run the script. The following script was written to be run under tcsh but, when called from a tcsh command line, is executed by bash. The set builtin (page 442) works differently under bash and tcsh. As a result the following example (from page 371) issues a prompt but does not wait for you to respond:

```
tcsh $ cat user_in
echo -n "Enter input: "
set input_line = "$<"
echo $input_line

tcsh $ user_in
Enter input:
```

Although in each case the examples are run from a tcsh command line, the following one calls tcsh explicitly so that tcsh executes the script and it runs correctly:

```
tcsh $ tcsh user_in
Enter input: here is some input
here is some input
```

ENTERING AND LEAVING THE TC SHELL

chsh You can execute tcsh by giving the command **tcsh**. If you are not sure which shell you are using, use the ps utility to find out. It shows whether you are running tcsh, bash, sh (linked to bash), or possibly another shell. The finger command followed by your username displays the name of your login shell, which is stored in the **/etc/passwd** file. (Mac OS X uses Open Directory [page 926] in place of this file.) If you want to use tcsh as a matter of course, you can use the chsh (change shell) utility to change your login shell:

```
bash $ chsh
Changing shell for sam.
Password:
New shell [/bin/bash]: /bin/tcsh
Shell changed.
bash $
```

The shell you specify will remain in effect for your next login and all subsequent logins until you specify a different login shell. The **/etc/passwd** file stores the name of your login shell.

You can leave tcsh in several ways. The approach you choose depends on two factors: whether the shell variable **ignoreeof** is set and whether you are using the shell that you logged in on (your login shell) or another shell that you created after you logged in. If you are not sure how to exit from tcsh, press CONTROL-D on a line by itself with no leading SPACEs, just as you would to terminate standard input to a program. You will either exit or receive instructions on how to exit. If you have not set ignoreeof (page 377) and it has not been set for you in a startup file, you can exit from any shell by using CONTROL-D (the same procedure you use to exit from the Bourne Again Shell).

When **ignoreeof** is set, CONTROL-D does not work. The **ignoreeof** variable causes the shell to display a message telling you how to exit. You can always exit from tcsh by giving an **exit** command. A **logout** command allows you to exit from your login shell only.

STARTUP FILES

When you log in on the TC Shell, it automatically executes various startup files. These files are normally executed in the order described in this section, but you can compile tcsh so that it uses a different order. You must have read access to a startup file to execute the commands in it. See page 271 for information on bash startup files and page 936 for information on startup files under Mac OS X.

/etc/csh.cshrc and /etc/csh.login   The shell first executes the commands in **/etc/csh.cshrc** and **/etc/csh.login**. A user working with **root** privileges can set up these files to establish systemwide default characteristics for tcsh users. They contain systemwide configuration information, such as the default **path**, the location to check for mail, and so on.

.tcshrc and .cshrc   Next the shell looks for **~/.tcshrc** or, if it does not exist, **~/.cshrc** (**~/** is shorthand for your home directory; page 84). You can use these files to establish variables and parameters that are local to your shell. Each time you create a new shell, tcsh reinitializes these variables for the new shell. The following **.tcshrc** file sets several shell variables, establishes two aliases (page 357), and adds two directories to **path**—one at the beginning of the list and one at the end:

```
tcsh $ cat ~/.tcshrc
set noclobber
set dunique
set ignoreeof
set history=256
set path = (~/bin $path /usr/games)
alias h history
alias ll ls -l
```

.history   Login shells rebuild the history list from the contents of **~/.history**. If the **histfile** variable exists, tcsh uses the file that **histfile** points to in place of **.history**.

.login   Login shells read and execute the commands in **~/.login**. This file contains commands that you want to execute once, at the beginning of each session. You can use setenv (page 366) to declare environment (global) variables here. You can also declare the type of terminal you are using and set some terminal characteristics in your **.login** file.

```
tcsh $ cat ~/.login
setenv history 200
```

```
setenv mail /var/spool/mail/$user
if ( -z $DISPLAY ) then
        setenv TERM vt100
    else
        setenv TERM xterm
endif
stty erase '^h' kill '^u' -lcase tab3
date '+Login on %A %B %d at %I:%M %p'
```

The preceding **.login** file establishes the type of terminal you are using by setting the **TERM** variable (the **if** statement [page 378] determines whether you are using a graphical interface and therefore which value should be assigned to **TERM**). It then runs stty (page 838) to set terminal characteristics and date (page 655) to display the time you logged in.

/etc/csh.logout The TC Shell runs the **/etc/csh.logout** and **~/.logout** files, in that order, when you
and .logout exit from a login shell. The following sample **.logout** file uses date to display the time you logged out. The sleep command ensures that echo has time to display the message before the system logs you out. The delay may be useful for dial-up lines that take some time to display the message.

```
tcsh $ cat ~/.logout
date '+Logout on %A %B %d at %I:%M %p'
sleep 5
```

FEATURES COMMON TO THE BOURNE AGAIN AND
TC SHELLS

Most of the features common to both bash and tcsh are derived from the original C Shell:

- Command-line expansion (also called substitution; page 354)
- History (page 354)
- Aliases (page 357)
- Job control (page 358)
- Filename substitution (page 358)
- Directory stack manipulation (page 359)
- Command substitution (page 359)

The chapters on bash discuss these features in detail. This section focuses on the differences between the bash and tcsh implementations.

COMMAND-LINE EXPANSION (SUBSTITUTION)

Refer to "Processing the Command Line" on page 334 for an introduction to command-line expansion in the Bourne Again Shell. The tcsh man page uses the term *substitution* instead of *expansion;* the latter is used by bash. The TC Shell scans each token for possible expansion in the following order:

1. History substitution (below)

2. Alias substitution (page 357)

3. Variable substitution (page 366)

4. Command substitution (page 359)

5. Filename substitution (page 358)

6. Directory stack substitution (page 359)

HISTORY

The TC Shell assigns a sequential *event number* to each command line. You can display this event number as part of the tcsh prompt (refer to "prompt" on page 373). Examples in this section show numbered prompts when they help illustrate the behavior of a command.

THE history BUILTIN

As in bash, the tcsh history builtin displays the events in your history list. The list of events is ordered with the oldest events at the top. The last event in the history list is the **history** command that displayed the list. In the following history list, which is limited to ten lines by the argument of **10** to the **history** command, command 23 modifies the tcsh prompt to display the history event number. The time each command was executed appears to the right of the event number.

```
32 $ history 10
   23   23:59   set prompt = "! $ "
   24   23:59   ls -l
   25   23:59   cat temp
   26   0:00    rm temp
   27   0:00    vim memo
   28   0:00    lpr memo
   29   0:00    vim memo
   30   0:00    lpr memo
   31   0:00    rm memo
   32   0:00    history
```

HISTORY EXPANSION

The same event and word designators work in both shells. For example, **!!** refers to the previous event in tcsh, just as it does in bash. The command **!328** executes event number **328**; **!?txt?** executes the most recent event containing the string **txt**. For more information refer to "Using an Exclamation Point (!) to Reference Events" on page 313. Table 9-1 lists the few tcsh word modifiers not found in bash.

Table 9-1   Word modifiers

Modifier	Function
u	Converts the first lowercase letter into uppercase
l	Converts the first uppercase letter into lowercase
a	Applies the next modifier globally within a single word

You can use more than one word modifier in a command. For instance, the **a** modifier, when used in combination with the **u** or **l** modifier, enables you to change the case of an entire word.

```
tcsh $ echo $VERSION
VERSION: Undefined variable.
tcsh $ echo !!:1:al
echo $version
tcsh 6.14.00 (Astron) 2005-03-25 (i486-intel-linux) options wide,nls,dl,...
```

In addition to using event designators to access the history list, you can use the command-line editor to access, modify, and execute previous commands (page 363).

VARIABLES

The variables you set to control the history list in tcsh are different from those used in bash. Whereas bash uses **HISTSIZE** and **HISTFILESIZE** to determine the number of events that are preserved during and between sessions, respectively, tcsh uses **history** and **savehist** (Table 9-2) for these purposes.

Table 9-2   History variables

Variable	Default	Function
history	100 events	Maximum number of events saved during a session
histfile	~/.history	Location of the history file
savehist	not set	Maximum number of events saved between sessions

history and savehist   When you exit from a tcsh shell, the most recently executed commands are saved in your **~/.history** file. The next time you start the shell, this file initializes the history list. The value of the **savehist** variable determines the number of lines saved in the **.history** file (not necessarily the same as the **history** variable). If **savehist** is not set, tcsh does not save history information between sessions. The **history** and **savehist** variables must be local (i.e., declared with **set**, not **setenv**). The **history** variable holds the number of events remembered during a session and the **savehist** variable holds the number remembered between sessions. See Table 9-2.

If you set the value of **history** too high, it can use too much memory. If it is unset or set to zero, the shell does not save any commands. To establish a history list of the 500 most recent events, give the following command manually or place it in your ~/.tcshrc startup file:

```
tcsh $ set history = 500
```

The following command causes tcsh to save the 200 most recent events across login sessions:

```
tcsh $ set savehist = 200
```

You can combine these two assignments into a single command:

```
tcsh $ set history=500 savehist=200
```

After you set **savehist**, you can log out and log in again; the 200 most recent events from the previous login sessions will appear in your history list after you log back in. Set **savehist** in your ~/.tcshrc file if you want to maintain your event list from login to login.

histlit   If you set the variable **histlit** (history literal), history displays the commands in the history list exactly as they were typed in, without any shell interpretation. The following example shows the effect of this variable (compare the lines numbered 32):

```
tcsh $ cat /etc/csh.cshrc
...
tcsh $ cp !!:1 ~
cp /etc/csh.cshrc ~
tcsh $ set histlit
tcsh $ history
...
    31  9:35     cat /etc/csh.cshrc
    32  9:35     cp !!:1 ~
    33  9:35     set histlit
    34  9:35     history
tcsh $ unset histlit
tcsh $ history
...
    31  9:35     cat /etc/csh.cshrc
    32  9:35     cp /etc/csh.cshrc ~
    33  9:35     set histlit
    34  9:35     history
    35  9:35     unset histlit
    36  9:36     history
```

optional   The bash and tcsh Shells expand history event designators differently. If you give the command !250w, bash replaces it with command number 250 with a character **w** appended to it. In contrast, tcsh looks back through your history list for an event that begins with the string **250w** to execute. The reason for the difference: bash interprets the first three characters of **250w** as the number of a command, whereas tcsh interprets those characters as part of the search string **250w**. (If the 250 stands alone, tcsh treats it as a command number.)

If you want to append **w** to command number 250, you can insulate the event number from the **w** by surrounding it with braces:

```
!{250}w
```

ALIASES

The alias/unalias feature in tcsh closely resembles its counterpart in bash (page 324). However, the alias builtin has a slightly different syntax:

*alias **name value***

The following command creates an alias for **ls**:

```
tcsh $ alias ls "ls -1F"
```

The tcsh alias allows you to substitute command-line arguments, whereas bash does not:

```
$ alias nam "echo Hello, \!^ is my name"
$ nam Sam
Hello, Sam is my name
```

The string **\!*** within an alias expands to all command-line arguments:

```
$ alias sortprint "sort \!* | lpr"
```

The next alias displays its second argument:

```
$ alias n2 "echo \!:2"
```

SPECIAL ALIASES

Some alias names, called *special aliases*, have special meaning to tcsh. If you define an alias with one of these names, tcsh executes it automatically as explained in Table 9-3. Initially all special aliases are undefined.

To see a list of current aliases, give the command **alias**. To view the alias for a particular name, give the command **alias** followed by the name.

Table 9-3   Special aliases

Alias	When executed
beepcmd	Whenever the shell would normally ring the terminal bell. Gives you a way to have other visual or audio effects take place at those times.
cwdcmd	Whenever you change to another working directory.
periodic	Periodically, as determined by the number of minutes in the **tperiod** variable. If **tperiod** is unset or has the value 0, **periodic** has no meaning.
precmd	Just before the shell displays a prompt.
shell	Gives the absolute pathname of the shell that you want to use to run scripts that do not start with **#!** (page 280).

HISTORY SUBSTITUTION IN ALIASES

You can substitute command-line arguments by using the history mechanism, where a single exclamation point represents the command line containing the alias. Modifiers are the same as those used by history (page 313). In the following example, the exclamation points are quoted so the shell does not interpret them when building the aliases:

```
21 $ alias last echo \!:$
22 $ last this is just a test
test
23 $ alias fn2 echo \!:2:t
24 $ fn2 /home/sam/test /home/zach/temp /home/barbara/new
temp
```

Event 21 defines for **last** an alias that displays the last argument. Event 23 defines for **fn2** an alias that displays the simple filename, or tail, of the second argument on the command line.

JOB CONTROL

Job control is similar in both bash (page 285) and tcsh. You can move commands between the foreground and the background, suspend jobs temporarily, and get a list of the current jobs. The % character references a job when it is followed by a job number or a string prefix that uniquely identifies the job. You will see a minor difference when you run a multiple-process command line in the background from each shell. Whereas bash displays only the PID number of the last background process in each job, tcsh displays the numbers for all processes belonging to a job. The example from page 285 looks like this under tcsh:

```
tcsh $ find . -print | sort | lpr & grep -l zach /tmp/* > zachfiles &
[1] 18839   18840   18841
[2] 18876
```

FILENAME SUBSTITUTION

The TC Shell expands the characters *, ?, and [] in a pathname just as bash does (page 136). The * matches any string of zero or more characters, ? matches any single character, and [] defines a character class, which is used to match single characters appearing within a pair of brackets.

The TC Shell expands command-line arguments that start with a tilde (~) into filenames in much the same way that bash does (page 361), with the ~ standing for the user's home directory or the home directory of the user whose name follows the tilde. The bash special expansions ~+ and ~- are not available in tcsh.

Brace expansion (page 336) is available in tcsh. Like tilde expansion, it is regarded as an aspect of filename substitution even though brace expansion can generate strings that are not the names of actual files.

In tcsh and its predecessor csh, the process of using patterns to match filenames is referred to as *globbing* and the pattern itself is called a *globbing pattern*. If tcsh is unable to identify one or more files that match a globbing pattern, it reports an error (unless the pattern contains a brace). Setting the shell variable **noglob** suppresses filename substitution, including both tilde and brace interpretation.

MANIPULATING THE DIRECTORY STACK

Directory stack manipulation in tcsh does not differ much from that in bash (page 288). The dirs builtin displays the contents of the stack, and the pushd and popd builtins push directories onto and pop directories off of the stack.

COMMAND SUBSTITUTION

The $(...) format for command substitution is *not* available in tcsh. In its place you must use the original `...` format. Otherwise, the implementation in bash and tcsh is identical. Refer to page 340 for more information on command substitution.

REDIRECTING STANDARD ERROR

Both bash and tcsh use a greater than symbol (>) to redirect standard output, but tcsh does *not* use the bash notation 2> to redirect standard error. Under tcsh you use a greater than symbol followed by an ampersand (>&) to combine and redirect standard output and standard error. Although you can use this notation under bash, few people do. The following examples, like the bash examples on page 276, reference file **x**, which does not exist, and file **y**, which contains a single line:

```
tcsh $ cat x
cat: x: No such file or directory
tcsh $ cat y
This is y.
tcsh $ cat x y >& hold
tcsh $ cat hold
cat: x: No such file or directory
This is y.
```

With an argument of **y** in the preceding example, cat sends a string to standard output. An argument of **x** causes cat to send an error message to standard error.

Unlike bash, tcsh does not provide a simple way to redirect standard error separately from standard output. A work-around frequently provides a reasonable solution. The following example runs cat with arguments of **x** and **y** in a subshell (the parentheses ensure that the command within them runs in a subshell; see page 284). Also within the subshell, a > redirects standard output to the file **outfile**. Output sent to standard error is not touched by the subshell but rather is sent to the parent shell, where both it and standard output are sent to **errfile**. Because standard output has already been redirected, **errfile** contains only output sent to standard error.

```
tcsh $ (cat x y > outfile) >& errfile
tcsh $ cat outfile
This is y.
tcsh $ cat errfile
cat: x: No such file or directory
```

It can be useful to combine and redirect output when you want to execute a command that runs slowly in the background and do not want its output cluttering up the terminal screen. For example, because the find utility (page 688) often takes some time to complete, it may be a good idea to run it in the background. The next command finds in the filesystem hierarchy all files that contain the string **biblio** in their name. This command runs in the background and sends its output to the **findout** file. Because the find utility sends to standard error a report of directories that you do not have permission to search, the **findout** file contains a record of any files that are found as well as a record of the directories that could not be searched.

```
tcsh $ find / -name "*biblio*" -print >& findout &
```

In this example, if you did not combine standard error with standard output and redirected only standard output, the error messages would appear on the screen and **findout** would list only files that were found.

While a command that has its output redirected to a file is running in the background, you can look at the output by using tail (page 843) with the **–f** option. The **–f** option causes tail to display new lines as they are written to the file:

```
tcsh $ tail -f findout
```

To terminate the tail command, press the interrupt key (usually CONTROL-C).

WORKING WITH THE COMMAND LINE

This section covers word completion, editing the command line, and correcting spelling.

WORD COMPLETION

The TC Shell completes filenames, commands, and variable names on the command line when you prompt it to do so. The generic term used to refer to all these features under tcsh is *word completion*.

FILENAME COMPLETION

The TC Shell can complete a filename after you specify a unique prefix. Filename completion is similar to filename generation, but the goal of filename completion is to select a single file. Together these capabilities make it practical to use long, descriptive filenames.

To use filename completion when you are entering a filename on the command line, type enough of the name to identify the file in the directory uniquely and press TAB; tcsh fills in the name and adds a SPACE, leaving the cursor so you can enter additional arguments or press RETURN. In the following example, the user types the command **cat trig1A** and presses TAB; the system fills in the rest of the filename that begins with **trig1A**:

```
tcsh $ cat trig1A  —→TAB  —→cat trig1A.302488 ■
```

If two or more filenames match the prefix that you have typed, tcsh cannot complete the filename without obtaining more information from you. The shell attempts to maximize the length of the prefix by adding characters, if possible, and then beeps to signify that additional input is needed to resolve the ambiguity:

```
tcsh $ ls h*
help.hist  help.trig01  help.txt
tcsh $ cat h  —→TAB  —→cat help. (beep)
```

You can fill in enough characters to resolve the ambiguity and then press the TAB key again. Alternatively, you can press CONTROL-D to cause tcsh to display a list of matching filenames:

```
tcsh $ cat help.  —→CONTROL-D
help.hist     help.trig01  help.txt
tcsh $ cat help.■
```

After displaying the filenames, tcsh redraws the command line so you can disambiguate the filename (and press TAB again) or finish typing the filename manually.

TILDE COMPLETION

The TC Shell parses a tilde (~) appearing as the first character of a word and attempts to expand it to a username when you enter a TAB:

```
tcsh $ cd ~za  —→TAB  —→cd ~zach/■  —→RETURN
tcsh $ pwd
/home/zach
```

By appending a slash (/), tcsh indicates that the completed word is a directory. The slash also makes it easy to continue specifying the pathname.

COMMAND AND VARIABLE COMPLETION

You can use the same mechanism that you use to list and complete filenames with command and variable names. Unless you give a full pathname, the shell uses the variable **path** in an attempt to complete a command name. The choices tcsh lists may be located in different directories.

```
tcsh $ up —→TAB (beep) —→CONTROL-D
up2date              updatedb              uptime
up2date-config       update-mime-database
up2date-nox          updmap
tcsh $ up —→t —→TAB —→uptime ■ —→RETURN
9:59am up 31 days, 15:11, 7 users, load average: 0.03, 0.02, 0.00
```

If you set the **autolist** variable as in the following example, the shell lists choices automatically when you invoke completion by pressing TAB. You do not have to press CONTROL-D.

```
tcsh $ set autolist
tcsh $ up —→TAB (beep)
up2date              updatedb              uptime
up2date-config       update-mime-database
up2date-nox          updmap
tcsh $ up —→t —→TAB —→uptime ■ —→RETURN
10:01am up 31 days, 15:14, 7 users, load average: 0.20, 0.06, 0.02
```

If you set **autolist** to **ambiguous**, the shell lists the choices when you press TAB *only* if the word you enter is the longest prefix of a set of commands. Otherwise, pressing TAB causes the shell to add one or more characters to the word until it is the longest prefix; pressing TAB again then lists the choices:

```
tcsh $ set autolist=ambiguous
tcsh $ echo $h —→TAB (beep)
histfile history home
tcsh $ echo $h■ —→i —→TAB —→echo $hist■ —→TAB
histfile history
tcsh $ echo $hist■ —→o —→TAB —→echo $history ■ —→RETURN
1000
```

The shell must rely on the context of the word within the input line to determine whether it is a filename, a username, a command, or a variable name. The first word on an input line is assumed to be a command name; if a word begins with the special character $, it is viewed as a variable name; and so on. In the following example, the second which command does not work properly: The context of the word **up** makes it look like the beginning of a filename rather than the beginning of a command. The TC Shell supplies which with an argument of **updates** (a nonexecutable file) and which displays an error message:

```
tcsh $ ls up*
updates
tcsh $ which updatedb ups uptime
/usr/bin/updatedb
/usr/local/bin/ups
/usr/bin/uptime
tcsh $ which up —→TAB —→which updates
updates: Command not found.
```

Editing the Command Line

bindkey The tcsh command-line editing feature is similar to that available under bash. You can use either emacs mode commands (default) or vi(m) mode commands. Change to vi(m) mode commands by using **bindkey –v** and to emacs mode commands by using **bindkey –e**. The ARROW keys are bound to the obvious motion commands in both modes, so you can move back and forth (up and down) through the history list as well as left and right on the current command line.

Without an argument, the bindkey builtin displays the current mappings between editor commands and the key sequences you can enter at the keyboard:

```
tcsh $ bindkey
Standard key bindings
"^@"            -> set-mark-command
"^A"            -> beginning-of-line
"^B"            -> backward-char
"^C"            -> tty-sigintr
"^D"            -> delete-char-or-list-or-eof
...
Multi-character bindings
"^[[A"          -> up-history
"^[[B"          -> down-history
"^[[C"          -> forward-char
"^[[D"          -> backward-char
...
Arrow key bindings
down            -> down-history
up              -> up-history
left            -> backward-char
right           -> forward-char
home            -> beginning-of-line
end             -> end-of-line
```

The ^ indicates a CONTROL character (^B = CONTROL-B). The ^[indicates a META or ALT character; in this case you press and hold the META or ALT key while you press the key for the next character. If this substitution does not work or if the keyboard you are using does not have a META or ALT key, press and release the ESCAPE key and then press the key for the next character. For ^[[F you would press META-[or ALT-[followed by the F key or else ESCAPE [F. The **down/up/left/right** indicate ARROW keys, and **home/end** indicate the HOME and END keys on the numeric keypad. See page 216 for more information on the META key.

Under OS X, most keyboards do not have a META or ALT key. See page 935 for an explanation of how to set up the OPTION key to perform the same functions as the META key on a Macintosh.

The preceding example shows the output from bindkey with the user in emacs mode. Change to vi(m) mode (**bindkey –v**) and give another bindkey command to display the vi(m) key bindings. You can pipe the output of bindkey through less to make it easier to read.

CORRECTING SPELLING

You can have tcsh attempt to correct the spelling of command names, filenames, and variables (but only using emacs-style key bindings). Spelling correction can take place only at two times: before and after you press RETURN.

BEFORE YOU PRESS RETURN

For tcsh to correct a word or line before you press RETURN, you must indicate that you want it to do so. The two functions for this purpose are **spell-line** and **spell-word**:

```
$ bindkey | grep spell
"^[$"           -> spell-line
"^[S"           -> spell-word
"^[s"           -> spell-word
```

The output from bindkey shows that **spell-line** is bound to META-$ (ALT-$ or ESCAPE $) and **spell-word** is bound to META-s and META-s (ALT-s or ESCAPE s and ALT-S or ESCAPE S). To correct the spelling of the word to the left of the cursor, press META-s. Pressing META-$ invokes the **spell-line** function, which attempts to correct all words on a command line:

```
tcsh $ ls
bigfile.gz
tcsh $ gunzipp  →META-s →gunzip bigfele.gz  →META-s →gunzip bigfile.gz
tcsh $ gunzip bigfele.gz  →META-$ →gunzip bigfile.gz
tcsh $ ecno $usfr  →META-$ →echo $user
```

AFTER YOU PRESS RETURN

The variable named **correct** controls what tcsh attempts to correct or complete *after* you press RETURN and before it passes the command line to the command being called. If you do not set **correct**, tcsh will not correct anything:

```
tcsh $ unset correct
tcsh $ ls morning
morning
tcsh $ ecno $usfr morbing
usfr: Undefined variable.
```

The shell reports the error in the variable name and not the command name because it expands variables before it executes the command (page 354). When you give a bad command name without any arguments, the shell reports on the bad command name.

Set **correct** to **cmd** to correct only commands; to **all** to correct commands, variables, and filenames; or to **complete** to complete commands:

```
tcsh $ set correct = cmd
tcsh $ ecno $usfr morbing

CORRECT>echo $usfr morbing (y|n|e|a)? y
usfr: Undefined variable.
```

```
tcsh $ set correct = all
tcsh $ echo $usfr morbing

CORRECT>echo $user morning (y|n|e|a)? y
zach morning
```

With **correct** set to **cmd**, tcsh corrects the command name from **ecno** to **echo**. With **correct** set to **all**, tcsh corrects both the command name and the variable. It would also correct a filename if one was present on the command line.

The TC Shell displays a special prompt that lets you enter **y** to accept the modified command line, **n** to reject it, **e** to edit it, or **a** to abort the command. Refer to "prompt3" on page 374 for a discussion of the special prompt used in spelling correction.

In the next example, after setting the **correct** variable the user mistypes the name of the ls command; tcsh then prompts for a correct command name. Because the command that tcsh has offered as a replacement is not ls, the user chooses to edit the command line. The shell leaves the cursor following the command so the user can correct the mistake:

```
tcsh $ set correct=cmd
tcsh $ 1x -1 ⟶RETURN (beep)
CORRECT>1ex -1 (y|n|e|a)? e
tcsh $ 1x -1█
```

If you assign the value **complete** to the variable **correct**, tcsh attempts command name completion in the same manner as filename completion (page 360). In the following example, after setting **correct** to **complete** the user enters the command **up**. The shell responds with **Ambiguous command** because several commands start with these two letters but differ in the third letter. The shell then redisplays the command line. The user could press TAB at this point to get a list of commands that start with **up** but decides to enter **t** and press RETURN. The shell completes the command because these three letters uniquely identify the uptime utility:

```
tcsh $ set correct = complete
tcsh $ upRETURN
Ambiguous command
tcsh $ up ⟶tRETURN ⟶uptime
4:45pm  up 5 days,  9:54,  5 users,  load average: 1.62, 0.83, 0.33
```

VARIABLES

Although tcsh stores variable values as strings, you can work with these variables as numbers. Expressions in tcsh can use arithmetic, logical, and conditional operators. The **@** builtin can evaluate integer arithmetic expressions.

This section uses the term *numeric variable* to describe a string variable that contains a number that tcsh uses in arithmetic or logical arithmetic computations. However, no true numeric variables exist in tcsh.

Variable name   A tcsh variable name consists of 1 to 20 characters, which can be letters, digits, and underscores (_). The first character cannot be a digit but can be an underscore.

VARIABLE SUBSTITUTION

Three builtins declare, display, and assign values to variables: set, @, and setenv. The set and setenv builtins both assume nonnumeric string variables. The @ builtin works only with numeric variables. Both set and @ declare local variables. The setenv builtin declares a variable *and* places it in the calling environment of all child processes (makes it global). Using setenv is similar to assigning a value to a variable and then using export in the Bourne Again Shell. See "Locality of Variables" on page 436 for a discussion of local and environment variables.

Once the value—or merely the existence—of a variable has been established, tcsh substitutes the value of that variable when the name of the variable, preceded by a dollar sign ($), appears on a command line. If you quote the dollar sign by preceding it with a backslash or enclosing it within single quotation marks, the shell does not perform the substitution. When a variable is within double quotation marks, the substitution occurs even if you quote the dollar sign by preceding it with a backslash.

STRING VARIABLES

The TC Shell treats string variables similarly to the way the Bourne Again Shell does. The major difference lies in their declaration and assignment: tcsh uses an explicit command, set (or setenv), to declare and/or assign a value to a string variable.

```
tcsh $ set name = fred
tcsh $ echo $name
fred
tcsh $ set
argv    ()
cwd     /home/zach
home    /home/zach
name    fred
path    (/usr/local/bin /bin /usr/bin /usr/X11R6/bin)
prompt  $
shell   /bin/tcsh
status  0
term    vt100
user    zach
```

The first line in the example declares the variable **name** and assigns the string **fred** to it. Unlike bash, tcsh allows—but does not require—SPACEs around the equal sign. The next line displays the value of **name**. When you give a set command without any arguments, it displays a list of all local shell variables and their values (your list will be longer than the one in the example). When you give a set command with the name of a variable and no value, the command sets the value of the variable to a null string.

You can use the unset builtin to remove a variable:

```
tcsh $ set name
tcsh $ echo $name

tcsh $ unset name
tcsh $ echo $name
name: Undefined variable.
```

setenv   With setenv you must separate the variable name from the string being assigned to it by inserting one or more SPACEs and omitting the equal sign. In the following example, the **tcsh** command creates a subshell, echo shows that the variable and its value are known to the subshell, and **exit** returns to the original shell. Try this example, using set in place of setenv:

```
tcsh $ setenv SRCDIR /usr/local/src
tcsh $ tcsh
tcsh $ echo $SRCDIR
/usr/local/src
tcsh $ exit
```

If you use setenv with no arguments, it displays a list of the environment (global) variables—variables that are passed to the shell's child processes. By convention, environment variables are named using uppercase letters.

As with set, giving setenv a variable name without a value sets the value of the variable to a null string. Although you can use unset to remove environment and local variables, unsetenv can remove *only* environment variables.

ARRAYS OF STRING VARIABLES

An *array* is a collection of strings, each of which is identified by its index (1, 2, 3, and so on). Arrays in tcsh use one-based indexing (i.e., the first element of the array has the subscript 1). Before you can access individual elements of an array, you must declare the entire array by assigning a value to each element of the array. The list of values must be enclosed in parentheses and separated by SPACEs:

```
8 $ set colors = (red green blue orange yellow)
9 $ echo $colors
red green blue orange yellow
10 $ echo $colors[3]
blue
11 $ echo $colors[2-4]
green blue orange
12 $ set shapes = ('' '' '' '' '')
13 $ echo $shapes

14 $ set shapes[4] = square
15 $ echo $shapes[4]
square
```

Event 8 declares the array of string variables named **colors** to have five elements and assigns values to each of them. If you do not know the values of the elements at the time you declare an array, you can declare an array containing the necessary number of null elements (event 12).

You can reference an entire array by preceding its name with a dollar sign (event 9). A number in brackets following a reference to the array refers to an element of the array (events 10, 14, and 15). Two numbers in brackets, separated by a hyphen, refer to two or more adjacent elements of the array (event 11). Refer to "Special Variable Forms" on page 371 for more information on arrays.

NUMERIC VARIABLES

The @ builtin assigns the result of a numeric calculation to a numeric variable (as described under "Variables" on page 365, tcsh has no true numeric variables). You can declare single numeric variables with @, just as you can use **set** to declare nonnumeric variables. However, if you give it a nonnumeric argument, @ displays an error message. Just as **set** does, the @ command used without any arguments lists all shell variables.

Many of the expressions that the @ builtin can evaluate and the operators it recognizes are derived from the C programming language. The following format shows a declaration or assignment using @ (the SPACE after the @ is required):

> @ *variable-name operator expression*

The *variable-name* is the name of the variable you are assigning a value to. The *operator* is one of the C assignment operators: =, +=, −=, *=, /=, or %=. (See Table 12-4 on page 537 for a description of these operators.) The *expression* is an arithmetic expression that can include most C operators (see the next section). You can use parentheses within the expression for clarity or to change the order of evaluation. Parentheses must surround parts of the expression that contain any of the following characters: <, >, &, or l.

Do not use $ when assigning a value to a variable

tip   As with bash, variables having a value assigned to them (those on the left of the operator) must not be preceded by a dollar sign (**$**) in tcsh. Thus

```
tcsh $ @ $answer = 5 + 5
```

will yield

```
answer: Undefined variable.
```

or, if **answer** is defined,

```
@: Variable name must begin with a letter.
```

whereas

```
tcsh $ @ answer = 5 + 5
```

assigns the value 10 to the variable **answer**.

EXPRESSIONS

An expression can be composed of constants, variables, and most of the bash operators (page 463). Expressions that involve files rather than numeric variables or strings are described in Table 9-8 on page 379.

Expressions follow these rules:

1. The shell evaluates a missing or null argument as 0.

2. All results are decimal numbers.

3. Except for != and ==, the operators act on numeric arguments.

4. You must separate each element of an expression from adjacent elements by a SPACE, unless the adjacent element is &, |, <, >, (, or).

Following are some examples that use @:

```
216 $ @ count = 0
217 $ echo $count
0
218 $ @ count = ( 10 + 4 ) / 2
219 $ echo $count
7
220 $ @ result = ( $count < 5 )
221 $ echo $result
0
222 $ @ count += 5
223 $ echo $count
12
224 $ @ count++
225 $ echo $count
13
```

Event 216 declares the variable **count** and assigns it a value of 0. Event 218 shows the result of an arithmetic operation being assigned to a variable. Event 220 uses @ to assign the result of a logical operation involving a constant and a variable to **result**. The value of the operation is *false* (= 0) because the variable **count** is not less than 5. Event 222 is a compressed form of the following assignment statement:

```
tcsh $ @ count = $count + 5
```

Event 224 uses a postfix operator to increment **count** by 1.

Postincrement and postdecrement operators
You can use the postincrement (++) and postdecrement (−−) operators only in expressions containing a single variable name, as shown in the following example:

```
tcsh $ @ count = 0
tcsh $ @ count++
tcsh $ echo $count
1
tcsh $ @ next = $count++
@: Badly formed number.
```

Unlike in the C programming language and bash, expressions in tcsh cannot use preincrement and predecrement operators.

ARRAYS OF NUMERIC VARIABLES

You must use the set builtin to declare an array of numeric variables before you can use @ to assign values to the elements of that array. The set builtin can assign any values to the elements of a numeric array, including zeros, other numbers, and null strings.

Assigning a value to an element of a numeric array is similar to assigning a value to a simple numeric variable. The only difference is that you must specify the element, or index, of the array. The syntax is

> @ *variable-name[index] operator expression*

The *index* specifies the element of the array that is being addressed. The first element has an index of 1. The *index* cannot be an expression but rather must be either a numeric constant or a variable. In the preceding syntax the brackets around *index* are part of the syntax and do not indicate that *index* is optional. If you specify an *index* that is too large for the array you declared with set, tcsh displays **@: Subscript out of range.**

```
226 $ set ages = (0 0 0 0 0)
227 $ @ ages[2] = 15
228 $ @ ages[3] = ($ages[2] + 4)
229 $ echo $ages[3]
19
230 $ echo $ages
0 15 19 0 0
231 $ set index = 3
232 $ echo $ages[$index]
19
233 $ echo $ages[6]
ages: Subscript out of range.
```

Elements of a numeric array behave as though they were simple numeric variables. Event 226 declares an array with five elements, each having a value of 0. Events 227 and 228 assign values to elements of the array, and event 229 displays the value of one of the elements. Event 230 displays all the elements of the array, event 232 specifies an element by using a variable, and event 233 demonstrates the out-of-range error message.

BRACES

Like bash, tcsh allows you to use braces to distinguish a variable from the surrounding text without the use of a separator:

```
$ set bb=abc
$ echo $bbdef
bbdef: Undefined variable.
$ echo ${bb}def
abcdef
```

Special Variable Forms

The special variable with the following syntax has the value of the number of elements in the *variable-name* array:

$#variable-name

You can determine whether *variable-name* has been set by looking at the value of the variable with the following syntax:

$?variable-name

This variable has a value of 1 if *variable-name* is set and 0 otherwise:

```
tcsh $ set days = (mon tues wed thurs fri)
tcsh $ echo $#days
5
tcsh $ echo $?days
1
tcsh $ unset days
tcsh $ echo $?days
0
```

Reading User Input

Within a tcsh shell script, you can use the set builtin to read a line from the terminal and assign it to a variable. The following portion of a shell script prompts the user and reads a line of input into the variable **input_line**:

```
echo -n "Enter input: "
set input_line = "$<"
```

The value of the shell variable $< is a line from standard input. The quotation marks around $< keep the shell from assigning only the first word of the line of input to the variable **input_line**.

Shell Variables

TC Shell variables may be set by the shell, inherited by the shell from the environment, or set by the user and used by the shell. Some variables take on significant values (for example, the PID number of a background process). Other variables act as switches: *on* if they are declared and *off* if they are not. Many of the shell variables are often set from one of tcsh's two startup files: **~/.login** and **~/.tcshrc** (page 352).

Shell Variables That Take on Values

argv   Contains the command-line arguments (positional parameters) from the command line that invoked the shell. Like all tcsh arrays, this array uses one-based indexing; **argv[1]** contains the first command-line argument. You can abbreviate references to

$argv[*n*]* as *$n*. The token **argv[*]** references all the arguments together; you can abbreviate it as $*. Use $0 to reference the name of the calling program. Refer to "Positional Parameters" on page 440. The Bourne Again Shell does not use the **argv** form, only the abbreviated form. You cannot assign values to the elements of **argv**.

$#argv *or* $# Holds the number of elements in the **argv** array. Refer to "Special Variable Forms" on page 371.

autolist Controls command and variable completion (page 361).

autologout Enables tcsh's automatic logout facility, which logs you out if you leave the shell idle for too long. The value of the variable is the number of minutes of inactivity that tcsh waits before logging you out. The default is 60 minutes except when you are running in a graphical environment, in which case this variable is initially unset.

cdpath Affects the operation of cd in the same way as the **CDPATH** variable does in bash (page 302). The **cdpath** variable is assigned an array of absolute pathnames (see **path**, later in this section) and is usually set in the ~/.login file with a line such as the following:

```
set cdpath = (/home/zach /home/zach/letters)
```

When you call cd with a simple filename, it searches the working directory for a subdirectory with that name. If one is not found, cd searches the directories listed in **cdpath** for the subdirectory.

correct Set to **cmd** for automatic spelling correction of command names, to **all** to correct the entire command line, and to **complete** for automatic completion of command names. This variable works on corrections that are made after you press RETURN. Refer to "After You Press RETURN" on page 364.

cwd The shell sets this variable to the name of the working directory. When you access a directory through a symbolic link (page 108), tcsh sets **cwd** to the name of the symbolic link.

dirstack The shell keeps the stack of directories used with the pushd, popd, and dirs builtins in this variable. For more information refer to "Manipulating the Directory Stack" on page 288.

fignore Holds an array of suffixes that tcsh ignores during filename completion.

gid The shell sets this variable to your group ID.

histfile Holds the full pathname of the file that saves the history list between login sessions (page 355). The defaults is ~/.history.

history Specifies the size of the history list. Refer to "History" on page 354.

home *or* HOME Holds the pathname of the user's home directory. The cd builtin refers to this variable, as does the filename substitution of ~ (page 337).

mail Specifies files and directories, separated by whitespace, to check for mail. The TC Shell checks for new mail every 10 minutes unless the first word of **mail** is a number, in which case that number specifies how often the shell should check in seconds.

owd   The shell keeps the name of your previous (old) working directory in this variable, which is equivalent to ~~ in bash.

path *or* PATH   Holds a list of directories that tcsh searches for executable commands (page 297). If this array is empty or unset, you can execute commands only by giving their full pathnames. You can set **path** with a command such as the following:

```
tcsh $ set path = ( /usr/bin /bin /usr/local/bin /usr/bin/X11 ~/bin . )
```

prompt   Holds the primary prompt, similar to the bash **PS1** variable (page 299). If it is not set, the prompt is >, or # when you are working with **root** privileges. The shell expands an exclamation point in the prompt string to the current event number. The following is a typical line from a .tcshrc file that sets the value of **prompt**:

```
set prompt = '! $ '
```

Table 9-4 lists some of the formatting sequences you can use in **prompt** to achieve special effects.

Table 9-4   **prompt** formatting sequences

Sequence	Displays in prompt
%/	Value of **cwd** (the working directory)
%~	Same as %/, but replaces the path of the user's home directory with a tilde
%! *or* %h *or* !	Current event number
%d	Day of the week
%D	Day of the month
%m	Hostname without the domain
%M	Full hostname, including the domain
%n	User's username
%t	Time of day through the current minute
%p	Time of day through the current second
%W	Month as **mm**
%y	Year as **yy**
%Y	Year as **yyyy**
%#	A pound sign (#) if the user is running with **root** privileges; otherwise, a greater than sign (>)
%?	Exit status of the preceding command

prompt2 Holds the secondary prompt, which tcsh uses to indicate it is waiting for additional input. The default value is **%R?**. The TC Shell replaces **%R** with nothing when it is waiting for you to continue an unfinished command, the word **foreach** while iterating through a **foreach** structure (page 383), and the word **while** while iterating through a **while** structure (page 385).

When you press RETURN in the middle of a quoted string on a command line without ending the line with a backslash, tcsh displays an error message regardless of whether you use single or double quotation marks:

```
% echo "Please enter the three values
Unmatched ".
```

In the next example, the first RETURN is quoted (escaped); the shell interprets it literally. Under tcsh, single and double quotation marks produce the same result. The secondary prompt is a question mark (**?**).

```
% echo "Please enter the three values \
? required to complete the transaction."
Please enter the three values
> required to complete the transaction.
```

prompt3 Holds the prompt used during automatic spelling correction. The default value is **CORRECT>%R (y|n|e|a)?**, where **R** is replaced by the corrected string.

savehist Specifies the number of commands saved from the history list when you log out. These events are saved in a file named **~/.history**. The shell uses these events as the initial history list when you log in again, causing your history list to persist across login sessions (page 355).

shell Holds the pathname of the shell you are using.

shlvl Holds the level of the shell. The TC Shell increments this variable each time you start a subshell and decrements it each time you exit a subshell. The value is set to 1 for a login shell.

status Contains the exit status returned by the last command. Similar to **$?** in bash (page 440).

tcsh Holds the version number of tcsh you are running.

time Provides two functions: automatic timing of commands using the time builtin and the format used by time. You can set this variable to either a single numeric value or an array holding a numeric value and a string. The numeric value is used to control automatic timing; any command that takes more than that number of CPU seconds to run has time display the command statistics when it finishes execution. A value of 0 results in statistics being displayed after every command. The string controls the formatting of the statistics using formatting sequences, including those listed in Table 9-5.

Table 9-5   time formatting sequences

Sequence	Displays
%U	Time the command spent running user code, in CPU seconds (user mode)
%S	Time the command spent running system code, in CPU seconds (kernel mode)
%E	Wall clock time (total elapsed) taken by the command
%P	Percentage of time the CPU spent on this task during this period, computed as (%U+%S)/%E
%W	Number of times the command's processes were swapped out to disk
%X	Average amount of shared code memory used by the command, in kilobytes
%D	Average amount of data memory used by the command, in kilobytes
%K	Total memory used by the command (as %X+%D), in kilobytes
%M	Maximum amount of memory used by the command, in kilobytes
%F	Number of major page faults (pages of memory that had to be read from disk)
%I	Number of input operations
%O	Number of output operations

By default the time builtin uses the string

```
"%Uu %Ss %E %P%   %X+%Dk %I+%Oio %Fpf+%Ww"
```

which generates output in the following format:

```
tcsh $ time
0.200u 0.340s 17:32:33.27 0.0%     0+0k 0+0io 1165pf+0w
```

You may want to time commands when concerns arise about system performance. If your commands consistently show many page faults and swaps, the system probably does not have enough memory; you should consider adding more. You can use the information that time reports to compare the performance of various system configurations and program algorithms.

tperiod   Controls how often, in minutes, the shell executes the special **periodic** alias (page 357).

user   The shell sets this variable to your username.

version   The shell sets this variable to contain detailed information about the version of tcsh that the system is running.

watch   Set to an array of user and terminal pairs to watch for logins and logouts. The word **any** means any user or any terminal, so (**any any**) monitors all logins and logouts on all terminals, whereas (**zach ttyS1 any console $user any**) watches for **zach** on **ttyS1**, any user who accesses the system console, and any logins and logouts that use your account (presumably to catch intruders). By default logins and logouts are checked once every 10 minutes, but you can change this value by beginning the array with a numeric value giving the number of minutes between checks. If you set **watch** to (**1 any console**), logins and logouts by any user on the console will be checked once per minute. Reports are displayed just before a new shell prompt is issued. Also, the log builtin forces an immediate check whenever it is executed. See **who** (next) for information about how you can control the format of the **watch** messages.

who Controls the format of the information displayed in **watch** messages (Table 9-6).

Table 9-6 **who** formatting sequence

Sequence	Displays
%n	Username
%a	Action taken by the user
%l	Terminal on which the action took place
%M	Full hostname of remote host (or **local** if none) from which the action took place
$m	Hostname without domain name

The default string used for watch messages when **who** is unset is **"%n has %a %l from %m"**, which generates the following line:

```
sam has logged on tty2 from local
```

$ As in bash, this variable contains the PID number of the current shell; use it as **$$**.

SHELL VARIABLES THAT ACT AS SWITCHES

The following shell variables act as switches; their values are not significant. If the variable has been declared, the shell takes the specified action. If not, the action is not taken or is negated. You can set these variables in your **~/.tcshrc** startup file, in a shell script, or from the command line.

autocorrect Causes the shell to attempt spelling correction automatically, just before each attempt at completion (page 364).

dunique Normally pushd blindly pushes the new working directory onto the directory stack, meaning that you can end up with many duplicate entries on this stack. Set **dunique** to cause the shell to look for and delete any entries that duplicate the one it is about to push.

echo Causes the shell to display each command before it executes that command. Set **echo** by calling tcsh with the **–x** option or by using set.

filec Enables filename completion (page 360) when running tcsh as csh (and csh is linked to tcsh).

histlit Displays the commands in the history list exactly as entered, without interpretation by the shell (page 356).

ignoreeof Prevents you from using CONTROL-D to exit from a shell so you cannot accidentally log out. When this variable is declared, you must use **exit** or **logout** to leave a shell.

listjobs Causes the shell to list all jobs whenever a job is suspended.

listlinks Causes the ls–F builtin to show the type of file each symbolic link points to instead of marking the symbolic link with an @ symbol.

loginsh Set by the shell if the current shell is running as a login shell.

nobeep Disables all beeping by the shell.

noclobber Prevents you from accidentally overwriting a file when you redirect output and prevents you from creating a file when you attempt to append output to a nonexistent file (Table 9-7). To override **noclobber**, add an exclamation point to the symbol you use for redirecting or appending output (for example, >! and >>!). For more information see page 129.

Table 9-7 How **noclobber** works

Command line	noclobber not declared	noclobber declared
x > *fileout*	Redirects standard output from process **x** to *fileout*. Overwrites *fileout* if it exists.	Redirects standard output from process **x** to *fileout*. The shell displays an error message if *fileout* exists, and does not overwrite the file.
x >> *fileout*	Redirects standard output from process **x** to *fileout*. Appends new output to the end of *fileout* if it exists. Creates *fileout* if it does not exist.	Redirects standard output from process **x** to *fileout*. Appends new output to the end of *fileout* if it exists. The shell displays an error message if *fileout* does not exist, and does not create the file.

noglob Prevents the shell from expanding ambiguous filenames. Allows you to use *, ?, ~, and [] literally on the command line or in a shell script without quoting them.

nonomatch Causes the shell to pass an ambiguous file reference that does not match a filename to the command being called. The shell does not expand the file reference. When you do not set **nonomatch**, tcsh generates a **No match** error message and does not execute the command.

```
tcsh $ cat questions?
cat: No match
tcsh $ set nonomatch
tcsh $ cat questions?
cat: questions?: No such file or directory
```

notify When set, tcsh sends a message to the screen immediately whenever a background job completes. Ordinarily tcsh notifies you about job completion just before displaying the next prompt. Refer to "Job Control" on page 285.

pushdtohome Causes a call to pushd without any arguments to change directories to your home directory (equivalent to **pushd –**).

pushdsilent Causes pushd and popd not to display the directory stack.

rmstar   Causes the shell to request confirmation when you give an **rm** * command.

verbose   Causes the shell to display each command after a history expansion (page 354). Set **verbose** by calling tcsh with the **–v** option or by using set.

visiblebell   Causes audible beeps to be replaced by flashing the screen.

CONTROL STRUCTURES

The TC Shell uses many of the same control structures as the Bourne Again Shell. In each case the syntax is different, but the effects are the same. This section summarizes the differences between the control structures in the two shells. For more information refer to "Control Structures" on page 398.

if

The syntax of the **if** control structure is

if (expression) simple-command

The **if** control structure works only with simple commands, not with pipes or lists of commands. You can use the **if...then** control structure (page 382) to execute more complex commands.

```
tcsh $ cat if_1
#!/bin/tcsh
# Routine to show the use of a simple if control structure.
#
if ( $#argv == 0 ) echo "if_1: There are no arguments."
```

The **if_1** script checks whether it was called with zero arguments. If the expression enclosed in parentheses evaluates to *true*—that is, if zero arguments were on the command line—the **if** structure displays a message.

In addition to logical expressions such as the one the **if_1** script uses, you can use expressions that return a value based on the status of a file. The syntax for this type of expression is

–n filename

where *n* is one of the values listed in Table 9-8.

If the result of the test is *true,* the expression has a value of 1; if it is *false,* the expression has a value of 0. If the specified file does not exist or is not accessible, tcsh evaluates the expression as 0. The following example checks whether the file specified on the command line is an ordinary or directory file (and not a device or other special file):

```
tcsh $ cat if_2
#!/bin/tcsh
if -f $1 echo "$1 is an ordinary or directory file."
```

Table 9-8   Value of *n*

n	Meaning
b	File is a block special file
c	File is a character special file
d	File is a directory file
e	File exists
f	File is an ordinary or directory file
g	File has the set-group-ID bit set
k	File has the sticky bit (page 980) set
l	File is a symbolic link
o	File is owned by user
p	File is a named pipe (FIFO)
r	The user has read access to the file
S	File is a socket special file
s	File is not empty (has nonzero size)
t	File descriptor (a single digit replacing *filename*) is open and connected to the screen
u	File has the set-user-ID bit set
w	User has write access to the file
X	File is either a builtin or an executable found by searching the directories in **$path**
x	User has execute access to the file
z	File is 0 bytes long

You can combine operators where it makes sense. For example, **–ox filename** is *true* if you own and have execute permission for the file. This expression is equivalent to **–o filename && –x filename**.

Some operators return useful information about a file other than reporting *true* or *false*. They use the same *–n filename* format, where *n* is one of the values shown in Table 9-9 on the next page.

Table 9-9 Value of *n*

n	Meaning
A	The last time the file was accessed.*
A:	The last time the file was accessed displayed in a human-readable format.
M	The last time the file was modified.*
M:	The last time the file was modified displayed in a human-readable format.
C	The last time the file's inode was modified.*
C:	The last time the file's inode was modified displayed in a human-readable format.
D	Device number for the file. This number uniquely identifies the device (a disk partition, for example) on which the file resides.
I	Inode number for the file. The inode number uniquely identifies a file on a particular device.
F	A string of the form **device:inode**. This string uniquely identifies a file anywhere on the system.
N	Number of hard links to the file.
P	The file's permissions, shown in octal, without a leading 0.
U	Numeric user ID of the file's owner.
U:	Username of the file's owner.
G	Numeric group ID of the file's group.
G:	Name of the file's group.
Z	Number of bytes in the file.

*Time measured in seconds from the *epoch* (usually the start of January 1, 1970).

You can use only one of these operators in a given test, and it must appear as the last operator in a multiple-operator sequence. Because 0 (zero) can be a valid response from some of these operators (for instance, the number of bytes in a file might be 0), most return −1 on failure instead of the 0 that the logical operators return on failure. The one exception is F, which returns a colon if it cannot determine the device and inode for the file.

When you want to use one of these operators outside of a control structure expression, you can use the filetest builtin to evaluate a file test and report the result:

```
tcsh $ filetest -z if_1
0
tcsh $ filetest -F if_1
2051:12694
tcsh $ filetest -Z if_1
131
```

goto

The **goto** statement has the following syntax:

goto label

A **goto** builtin transfers control to the statement beginning with *label:*. The following script fragment demonstrates the use of **goto**:

```
tcsh $ cat goto_1
#!/bin/tcsh
#
# test for 2 arguments
#
if ($#argv == 2) goto goodargs
echo "Usage: $0 arg1 arg2"
exit 1
goodargs:
...
```

The **goto_1** script displays a usage message (page 402) when it is called with more or fewer than two arguments.

INTERRUPT HANDLING

The **onintr** (on interrupt) statement transfers control when you interrupt a shell script. The format of an **onintr** statement is

onintr label

When you press the interrupt key during execution of a shell script, the shell transfers control to the statement beginning with *label:*. This statement allows you to terminate a script gracefully when it is interrupted. You can use it to ensure that when you interrupt a shell script, the script removes temporary files before returning control to the parent shell.

The following script demonstrates the use of **onintr**. It loops continuously until you press the interrupt key, at which time it displays a message and returns control to the shell:

```
tcsh $ cat onintr_1
#!/bin/tcsh
# demonstration of onintr
onintr close
while ( 1 )
    echo "Program is running."
    sleep 2
end
close:
echo "End of program."
```

If a script creates temporary files, you can use **onintr** to remove them.

```
close:
rm -f /tmp/$$*
```

The ambiguous file reference **/tmp/$$*** matches all files in **/tmp** that begin with the PID number of the current shell. Refer to page 439 for a description of this technique for naming temporary files.

if...then...else

The **if...then...else** control structure has three forms. The first form, an extension of the simple **if** structure, executes more complex *commands* or a series of *commands* if *expression* is *true*. This form is still a one-way branch.

> *if (**expression**) then*
>   *commands*
> *endif*

The second form is a two-way branch. If *expression* is *true,* the first set of *commands* is executed. If it is *false,* the set of *commands* following **else** is executed.

> *if (**expression**) then*
>   *commands*
> *else*
>   *commands*
> *endif*

The third form is similar to the **if...then...elif** structure (page 405). It performs tests until it finds an *expression* that is *true* and then executes the corresponding *commands.*

> *if (**expression**) then*
>   *commands*
> *else if (**expression**) then*
>   *commands*
>   . . .
> *else*
>   *commands*
> *endif*

The following program assigns a value of 0, 1, 2, or 3 to the variable **class** based on the value of the first command-line argument. The program declares the variable **class** at the beginning for clarity; you do not need to declare it before its first use. Also for clarity, the script assigns the value of the first command-line argument to **number.**

```
tcsh $ cat if_else_1
#!/bin/tcsh
# routine to categorize the first
# command-line argument
set class
set number = $argv[1]
#
```

```
if ($number < 0) then
    @ class = 0
else if (0 <= $number && $number < 100) then
    @ class = 1
else if (100 <= $number && $number < 200) then
    @ class = 2
else
    @ class = 3
endif
#
echo "The number $number is in class ${class}."
```

The first **if** statement tests whether **number** is less than 0. If it is, the script assigns 0 to **class** and transfers control to the statement following **endif**. If it is not, the second **if** tests whether the number is between 0 and 100. The **&&** Boolean AND operator yields a value of *true* if the expression on each side is *true*. If the number is between 0 and 100, 1 is assigned to **class** and control is transferred to the statement following **endif**. A similar test determines whether the number is between 100 and 200. If it is not, the final **else** assigns 3 to **class**. The **endif** closes the **if** control structure. The final statement uses braces ({}) to isolate the variable **class** from the following period. The braces isolate the period for clarity; the shell does not consider a punctuation mark to be part of a variable name. The braces would be required if you wanted other characters to follow immediately after the variable.

foreach

The **foreach** structure parallels the bash **for...in** structure (page 411). The syntax is

> *foreach **loop-index** (argument-list)*
>   *commands*
> *end*

This structure loops through *commands*. The first time through the loop, the structure assigns the value of the first argument in *argument-list* to *loop-index*. When control reaches the **end** statement, the shell assigns the value of the next argument from *argument-list* to *loop-index* and executes the commands again. The shell repeats this procedure until it exhausts *argument-list*.

The following tcsh script uses a **foreach** structure to loop through the files in the working directory containing a specified string of characters in their filename and to change the string. For example, you can use it to change the string **memo** in filenames to **letter**. Thus the filenames **memo.1**, **dailymemo**, and **memories** would be changed to **letter.1**, **dailyletter**, and **letterries**, respectively.

This script requires two arguments: the string to be changed (the old string) and the new string. The *argument-list* of the **foreach** structure uses an ambiguous file reference to loop through all files in the working directory with filenames that contain the first argument. For each filename that matches the ambiguous file reference, the mv utility changes the filename. The echo and sed commands appear within back ticks (`) that indicate command substitution: Executing the commands within the back ticks replaces the back ticks and everything between them. Refer to "Command Substitution" on page 340 for more information. The sed utility (page 565) substitutes the first argument for the second argument in the filename. The **$1** and **$2** are abbreviated forms of **$argv[1]** and **$argv[2]**, respectively.

```
tcsh $ cat ren
#!/bin/tcsh
# Usage:        ren arg1 arg2
#               changes the string arg1 in the names of files
#               in the working directory into the string arg2
if ($#argv != 2) goto usage
foreach i ( *$1* )
    mv $i `echo $i | sed -n s/$1/$2/p`
end
exit 0

usage:
echo "Usage: ren arg1 arg2"
exit 1
```

optional   The next script uses a **foreach** loop to assign the command-line arguments to the elements of an array named **buffer**:

```
tcsh $ cat foreach_1
#!/bin/tcsh
# routine to zero-fill argv to 20 arguments
#
set buffer = (0 0 0 0 0 0 0 0 0 0 0 0 0 0 0 0 0 0 0 0)
set count = 1
#
if ($#argv > 20) goto toomany
#
foreach argument ($argv[*])
    set buffer[$count] = $argument
    @ count++
end
# REPLACE command ON THE NEXT LINE WITH
# THE PROGRAM YOU WANT TO CALL.
exec command $buffer[*]
#
toomany:
echo "Too many arguments given."
echo "Usage: foreach_1 [up to 20 arguments]"
exit 1
```

The **foreach_1** script calls another program named **command** with a command line guaranteed to contain 20 arguments. If **foreach_1** is called with fewer than 20 arguments, it fills the command line with zeros to complete the 20 arguments for **command**. Providing more than 20 arguments causes it to display a usage message and exit with an error status of 1.

The **foreach** structure loops through the commands one time for each command-line argument. Each time through the loop, **foreach** assigns the value of the next argument from the command line to the variable **argument**. Then the script assigns each of these values to an element of the array **buffer**. The variable **count** maintains the index for the **buffer** array. A postfix operator increments the **count** variable using @ (@ **count++**). The **exec** builtin (bash and tcsh; page 450) calls **command** so that a new process is not initiated. (Once **command** is called, the process running this routine is no longer needed so a new process is not required.)

while

The syntax of the **while** structure is

while (expression)
    commands
end

This structure continues to loop through *commands* while *expression* is *true*. If *expression* is *false* the first time it is evaluated, the structure never executes *commands*.

```
tcsh $ cat while_1
#!/bin/tcsh
# Demonstration of a while control structure.
# This routine sums the numbers between 1 and n;
# n is the first argument on the command line.
#
set limit = $argv[1]
set index = 1
set sum = 0
#
while ($index <= $limit)
    @ sum += $index
    @ index++
end
#
echo "The sum is $sum"
```

This program computes the sum of all integers up to and including *n*, where *n* is the first argument on the command line. The **+=** operator assigns the value of **sum + index** to **sum**.

break AND continue

You can interrupt a **foreach** or **while** structure with a **break** or **continue** statement. These statements execute the remaining commands on the line before they transfer control. The **break** statement transfers control to the statement after the **end** statement, terminating execution of the loop. The **continue** statement transfers control to the **end** statement, which continues execution of the loop.

switch

The **switch** structure is analogous to the bash **case** structure (page 421):

*switch (**test-string**)*

> *case **pattern:***
> > *commands*
>
> *breaksw*
>
> *case **pattern:***
> > *commands*
>
> *breaksw*
>
> *...*
>
> *default:*
> > *commands*
>
> *breaksw*

endsw

The **breaksw** statement transfers control to the statement following the **endsw** statement. If you omit **breaksw**, control falls through to the next command. You can use any of the special characters listed in Table 10-2 on page 423 within *pattern* except the pipe symbol (|).

```
tcsh $ cat switch_1
#!/bin/tcsh
# Demonstration of a switch control structure.
# This routine tests the first command-line argument
# for yes or no in any combination of uppercase and
# lowercase letters.
#
# test that argv[1] exists
if ($#argv != 1) then
    echo "Usage: $0 [yes|no]"
    exit 1
else
    # argv[1] exists, set up switch based on its value
    switch ($argv[1])
    # case of YES
        case [yY][eE][sS]:
        echo "Argument one is yes."
        breaksw
    #
    # case of NO
        case [nN][oO]:
        echo "Argument one is no."
    breaksw
    #
```

```
        # default case
            default:
            echo "Argument one is not yes or no."
            breaksw
        endsw
    endif
```

BUILTINS

Builtins are commands that are part of (built into) the shell. When you give a simple filename as a command, the shell first checks whether it is the name of a builtin. If it is, the shell executes it as part of the calling process; the shell does not fork a new process to execute the builtin. The shell does not need to search the directory structure for builtin programs because they are immediately available to the shell.

If the simple filename you give as a command is not a builtin, the shell searches the directory structure for the program you want, using the **PATH** variable as a guide. When it finds the program, the shell forks a new process to execute the program.

Although they are not listed in Table 9-10, the control structure keywords (**if**, **foreach**, **endsw**, and so on) are builtins. Table 9-10 describes many of the tcsh builtins, some of which are also built into other shells.

Table 9-10   tcsh builtins

Builtin	Function
% *job*	A synonym for the fg builtin. The *job* is the job number of the job you want to bring to the foreground (page 286).
% *job* &	A synonym for the bg builtin. The *job* is the number of the job you want to put in the background (page 287).
@	Similar to the set builtin but evaluates numeric expressions. Refer to "Numeric Variables" on page 368.
alias	Creates and displays aliases; bash uses a different syntax than tcsh. Refer to "Aliases" on page 357.
alloc	Displays a report of the amount of free and used memory.
bg	Moves a suspended job into the background (page 287).
bindkey	Controls the mapping of keys to the tcsh command-line editor commands.
	bindkey Without any arguments, bindkey lists all key bindings (page 363).
	bindkey –l Lists all available editor commands and gives a short description of each.
	bindkey –e Puts the command-line editor in emacs mode (page 363).

Table 9-10   tcsh builtins (continued)

Builtin	Function
bindkey –v	Puts the command-line editor in vi(m) mode (page 363).
bindkey *key* *command*	Attaches the editor command *command* to the key *key*.
bindkey –b *key* *command*	Similar to the previous form but allows you to specify control keys by using the form C–x (where x is the character you type while you press the CONTROL key), specify meta key sequences as M-x (on most keyboards used with Linux, the ALT key is the META key; Mac OS X uses the OPTION key [but you have to set an option in the Terminal utility to use it; see page 935]), and specify function keys as F-x.
bindkey –c *key* *command*	Binds the key *key* to the command *command*. Here the *command* is not an editor command but rather a shell builtin or an executable program.
bindkey –s *key* *string*	Causes tcsh to substitute *string* when you press *key*.
builtins	Displays a list of all builtins.
cd or chdir	Changes the working directory (page 87).
dirs	Displays the directory stack (page 288).
echo	Displays its arguments. You can prevent echo from displaying a RETURN at the end of a line by using the **–n** option (see "Reading User Input" on page 371) or by using a trailing \c (see "read: Accepts User Input" on page 447). The echo builtin is similar to the echo utility (page 680).
eval	Scans and evaluates the command line. When you put eval in front of a command, the command is scanned twice by the shell before it is executed. This feature is useful with a command that is generated through command or variable substitution. Because of the order in which the shell processes a command line, it is sometimes necessary to repeat the scan to achieve the desired result (page 329).
exec	Overlays the program currently being executed with another program in the same shell. The original program is lost. Refer to "exec: Executes a Command or Redirects File Descriptors" on page 450 for more information; also refer to source on page 390.
exit	Exits from a TC Shell. When you follow exit with a numeric argument, tcsh returns that number as the exit status (page 440).
fg	Moves a job into the foreground (page 285).
filetest	Takes one of the file inquiry operators followed by one or more filenames and applies the operator to each filename (page 380). Returns the results as a SPACE-separated list.

Table 9-10 tcsh builtins (continued)

Builtin	Function
glob	Like echo, but does not display SPACES between its arguments and does not follow its display with a NEWLINE.
hashstat	Reports on the efficiency of tcsh's hash mechanism. The hash mechanism speeds the process of searching through the directories in your search path. See also rehash (page 390) and unhash (page 391).
history	Displays a list of recent commands (page 354).
jobs	Displays a list of jobs (suspended commands and those running in the background).
kill	Terminates a job or process (page 456).
limit	Limits the computer resources that the current process and any processes it creates can use. You can put limits on the number of seconds of CPU time the process can use, the size of files that the process can create, and so forth.
log	Immediately produces the report that the watch shell variable (page 375) would normally cause tcsh to produce every 10 minutes.
login	Logs in a user. Can be followed by a username.
logout	Ends a session if you are using your original (login) shell.
ls–F	Similar to ls –F (page 746) but faster. (This builtin is the characters ls–F without any SPACES.)
nice	Lowers the processing priority of a command or a shell. This builtin is useful if you want to run a command that makes large demands on the system and you do not need the output right away. If you are working with **root** privileges, you can use nice to raise the priority of a command. Refer to page 773 for more information on the nice builtin and the nice utility.
nohup	Allows you to log out without terminating processes running in the background. Some systems are set up this way by default. Refer to page 775 for information on the nohup builtin and the nohup utility.
notify	Causes the shell to notify you immediately when the status of one of your jobs changes (page 285).
onintr	Controls the action that an interrupt causes within a script (page 381). See "trap: Catches a Signal" on page 453 for information on the equivalent command in bash.
popd	Changes the working directory to the directory on the top of the directory stack and removes that directory from the directory stack (page 288).
printenv	Displays all environment variable names and values.

Table 9-10   tcsh builtins (continued)

Builtin	Function
pushd	Changes the working directory and places the new directory at the top of the directory stack (page 288).
rehash	Re-creates the internal tables used by the hash mechanism. Whenever a new instance of tcsh is invoked, the hash mechanism creates a sorted list of all available commands based on the value of **path**. After you add a command to a directory in **path**, use rehash to re-create the sorted list of commands. If you do not, tcsh may not be able to find the new command. Also refer to hashstat (page 389) and unhash (page 391).
repeat	Takes two arguments—a count and a simple command (no pipes or lists of commands)—and repeats the command the number of times specified by the count.
sched	Executes a command at a specified time. For example, the following command causes the shell to display the message **Dental appointment.** at 10 AM: `tcsh $ sched 10:00 echo "Dental appointment."` Without any arguments, sched displays the list of scheduled commands. When the time to execute a scheduled command arrives, tcsh executes the command just before it displays a prompt.
set	Declares, initializes, and displays local variables (page 365).
setenv	Declares, initializes, and displays environment variables (page 365).
shift	Analogous to the bash shift builtin (page 442). Without an argument, shift promotes the indexes of the **argv** array. You can use it with an argument of an array name to perform the same operation on that array.
source	Executes the shell script given as its argument: source does not fork another process. It is similar to the bash . (dot) builtin (page 274). The source builtin expects a TC Shell script so no leading #! is required in the script. The current shell executes source; thus the script can contain commands, such as set, that affect the current shell. After you make changes to your **.tcshrc** or **.login** file, you can use source to execute it from the shell, thereby putting the changes into effect without logging out and in. You can nest source builtins.
stop	Stops a job or process that is running in the background. The stop builtin accepts multiple arguments.
suspend	Stops the current shell and puts it in the background. It is similar to the suspend key, which stops jobs running in the foreground. This builtin will not suspend a login shell.
time	Executes the command you give it as an argument. It displays a summary of time-related information about the executed command, according to the **time** shell variable (page 374). Without an argument, time displays the times for the current shell and its children.

Table 9-10   tcsh builtins (continued)

Builtin	Function
umask	Identifies or changes the access permissions that tcsh assigns to files you create (page 870).
unalias	Removes an alias (page 357).
unhash	Turns off the hash mechanism. See also hashstat (page 389) and rehash (page 390).
unlimit	Removes limits (page 389) on the current process.
unset	Removes a variable declaration (page 365).
unsetenv	Removes an environment variable declaration (page 365).
wait	Causes the shell to wait for all child processes to terminate. When you give a wait command in response to a shell prompt, tcsh does not display a prompt until all background processes have finished execution. If you interrupt it with the interrupt key, wait displays a list of background processes before tcsh displays a prompt.
where	When given the name of a command as an argument, locates all occurrences of the command and, for each, tells you whether it is an alias, a builtin, or an executable program in your path.
which	Similar to where but reports on only the command that would be executed, not all occurrences. This builtin is much faster than the Linux which utility and reports on aliases and builtins.

CHAPTER SUMMARY

Like the Bourne Again Shell, the TC Shell is both a command interpreter and a programming language. The TC Shell, which is based on the C Shell that was developed at the University of California at Berkeley, includes popular features such as history, alias, and job control.

You may prefer to use tcsh as a command interpreter, especially if you are familiar with the C Shell. You can use chsh to change your login shell to tcsh. However, running tcsh as your interactive shell does *not* cause tcsh to run shell scripts; they will continue to be run by bash unless you explicitly specify another shell on the first line of the script or specify the script name as an argument to tcsh. Specifying the shell on the first line of a shell script ensures the behavior you expect.

If you are familiar with bash, you will notice some differences between the two shells. For instance, the syntax you use to assign a value to a variable differs. In addition, tcsh allows SPACEs around the equal sign. Both numeric and nonnumeric variables are created and given values using the set builtin. The @ builtin can evaluate numeric expressions for assignment to numeric variables.

setenv   Because there is no export builtin in tcsh, you must use the setenv builtin to create an environment (global) variable. You can also assign a value to the variable with the setenv command. The command unset removes both local and environment variables, whereas the command unsetenv removes only environment variables.

Aliases   The syntax of the tcsh alias builtin is slightly different from that of alias in bash. Unlike bash, the tcsh aliases permit you to substitute command-line arguments using the history mechanism syntax.

Most other tcsh features, such as history, word completion, and command-line editing, closely resemble their bash counterparts. The syntax of the tcsh control structures is slightly different but provides functionality equivalent to that found in bash.

Globbing   The term *globbing,* a carryover from the original Bourne Shell, refers to the matching of strings containing special characters (such as * and ?) to filenames. If tcsh is unable to generate a list of filenames matching a globbing pattern, it displays an error message. This behavior contrasts with that of bash, which simply leaves the pattern alone.

Standard input and standard output can be redirected in tcsh, but there is no straightforward way to redirect them independently. Doing so requires the creation of a subshell that redirects standard output to a file while making standard error available to the parent process.

EXERCISES

1. Assume that you are working with the following history list:

```
37  mail zach
38  cd /home/sam/correspondence/business/cheese_co
39  less letter.0321
40  vim letter.0321
41  cp letter.0321 letter.0325
42  grep hansen letter.0325
43  vim letter.0325
44  lpr letter*
45  cd ../milk_co
46  pwd
47  vim wilson.0321 wilson.0329
```

Using the history mechanism, give commands to

a. Send mail to Zach.

b. Use vim to edit a file named **wilson.0329**.

    c. Send **wilson.0329** to the printer.

    d. Send both **wilson.0321** and **wilson.0329** to the printer.

2. a. How can you display the aliases currently in effect?

    b. Write an alias named **homedots** that lists the names (only) of all hidden files in your home directory.

3. a. How can you prevent a command from sending output to the terminal when you start it in the background?

    b. What can you do if you start a command in the foreground and later decide that you want it to run in the background?

4. Which statement can you put in your **~/.tcshrc** file to prevent accidentally overwriting a file when you redirect output? How can you override this feature?

5. Assume that the working directory contains the following files:

```
adams.ltr.03
adams.brief
adams.ltr.07
abelson.09
abelson.brief
anthony.073
anthony.brief
azevedo.99
```

What happens if you press TAB after typing the following commands?

a. **less adams.l**

b. **cat a**

c. **ls ant**

d. **file az**

What happens if you press CONTROL-D after typing the following commands?

e. **ls ab**

f. **less a**

6. Write an alias named **backup** that takes a filename as an argument and creates a copy of that file with the same name and a filename extension of **.bak**.

7. Write an alias named **qmake** (quiet make) that runs make with both standard output and standard error redirected to the file named **make.log**. The command **qmake** should accept the same options and arguments as make.

8. How can you make tcsh always display the pathname of the working directory as part of its prompt?

ADVANCED EXERCISES

9. Which lines do you need to change in the Bourne Again Shell script **command_menu** (page 423) to turn it into a TC Shell script? Make the changes and verify that the new script works.

10. Users often find rm (and even **rm –i**) too unforgiving because this utility removes files irrevocably. Create an alias named **delete** that moves files specified by its argument(s) into the ~/.trash directory. Create a second alias named **undelete** that moves a file from the ~/.trash directory into the working directory. Put the following line in your ~/.logout file to remove any files that you deleted during the login session:

```
/bin/rm -f $HOME/.trash/* >& /dev/null
```

Explain what could be different if the following line were put in your ~/.logout file instead:

```
rm $HOME/.trash/*
```

11. Modify the **foreach_1** script (page 384) so that it takes the command to exec as an argument.

12. Rewrite the program **while_1** (page 385) so that it runs faster. Use the time builtin to verify the improvement in execution time.

13. Write your own version of find named **myfind** that writes output to the file **findout** but without the clutter of error messages, such as those generated when you do not have permission to search a directory. The **myfind** command should accept the same options and arguments as find. Can you think of a situation in which **myfind** does not work as desired?

14. When the **foreach_1** script (page 384) is supplied with 20 or fewer arguments, why are the commands following **toomany:** not executed? (Why is there no exit command?)

PART IV
PROGRAMMING TOOLS

10

PROGRAMMING THE BOURNE AGAIN SHELL

Chapter 5 introduced the shells and Chapter 8 went into detail about the Bourne Again Shell. This chapter introduces additional Bourne Again Shell commands, builtins, and concepts that carry shell programming to a point where it can be useful. Although you may make use of shell programming as a system administrator, you do not have to read this chapter to perform system administration tasks. Feel free to skip this chapter and come back to it if and when you like.

The first part of this chapter covers programming control structures, also called control flow constructs. These structures allow you to write scripts that can loop over command-line arguments, make decisions based on the value of a variable, set up menus, and more. The Bourne Again Shell uses the same constructs found in such high-level programming languages as C.

The next part of this chapter discusses parameters and variables, going into detail about array variables, local versus global variables, special parameters, and positional parameters. The exploration of builtin commands covers type, which displays information about a command, and read, which allows a shell script to accept user input. The section on the exec builtin demonstrates how to use exec to execute a command efficiently by replacing a process and explains how to use exec to redirect input and output from within a script.

The next section covers the trap builtin, which provides a way to detect and respond to operating system signals (such as the signal generated when you press CONTROL-C). The discussion of builtins concludes with a discussion of kill, which can abort a process, and getopts, which makes it easy to parse options for a shell script. Table 10-6 on page 459 lists some of the more commonly used builtins.

Next the chapter examines arithmetic and logical expressions as well as the operators that work with them. The final section walks through the design and implementation of two major shell scripts.

This chapter contains many examples of shell programs. Although they illustrate certain concepts, most use information from earlier examples as well. This overlap not only reinforces your overall knowledge of shell programming but also demonstrates how you can combine commands to solve complex tasks. Running, modifying, and experimenting with the examples in this book is a good way to become comfortable with the underlying concepts.

Do not name a shell script test

tip   You can unwittingly create a problem if you give a shell script the name **test** because a Linux utility has the same name. Depending on how the **PATH** variable is set up and how you call the program, you may run either your script or the utility, leading to confusing results.

This chapter illustrates concepts with simple examples, which are followed by more complex ones in sections marked "Optional." The more complex scripts illustrate traditional shell programming practices and introduce some Linux utilities often used in scripts. You can skip these sections without loss of continuity. Return to them when you feel comfortable with the basic concepts.

CONTROL STRUCTURES

The *control flow* commands alter the order of execution of commands within a shell script. The TC Shell uses a different syntax for these commands than the Bourne Again Shell does; see page 378. Control structures include the **if...then, for...in, while, until,** and **case** statements. In addition, the **break** and **continue** statements work in conjunction with the control structures to alter the order of execution of commands within a script.

if...then

The **if...then** control structure has the following syntax:

```
if test-command
    then
        commands
fi
```

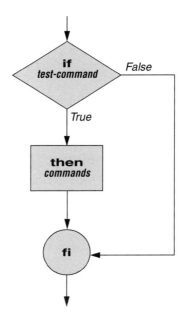

Figure 10-1 An **if...then** flowchart

The *bold* words in the syntax description are the items you supply to cause the structure to have the desired effect. The *nonbold* words are the keywords the shell uses to identify the control structure.

test builtin Figure 10-1 shows that the **if** statement tests the status returned by the ***test-command*** and transfers control based on this status. The end of the **if** structure is marked by a **fi** statement (*if* spelled backward). The following script prompts for two words, reads them, and then uses an **if** structure to execute commands based on the result returned by the test builtin (tcsh uses the test utility) when it compares the two words. (See page 854 for information on the test utility, which is similar to the test builtin.) The test builtin returns a status of *true* if the two words are the same and *false* if they are not. Double quotation marks around **$word1** and **$word2** make sure test works properly if you enter a string that contains a SPACE or other special character:

```
$ cat if1
echo -n "word 1: "
read word1
echo -n "word 2: "
read word2

if test "$word1" = "$word2"
    then
        echo "Match"
fi

echo "End of program."
```

```
$ ./if1
word 1: peach
word 2: peach
Match
End of program.
```

In the preceding example the *test-command* is **test "$word1" = "$word2"**. The **test** builtin returns a *true* status if its first and third arguments have the relationship specified by its second argument. If this command returns a *true* status (= 0), the shell executes the commands between the **then** and **fi** statements. If the command returns a *false* status (not = 0), the shell passes control to the statement following **fi** without executing the statements between **then** and **fi**. The effect of this **if** statement is to display **Match** if the two words are the same. The script always displays **End of program.**

Builtins   In the Bourne Again Shell, **test** is a builtin—part of the shell. It is also a stand-alone utility kept in **/usr/bin/test**. This chapter discusses and demonstrates many Bourne Again Shell builtins. Each **bash** builtin may or may not be a builtin in **tcsh**. You typically use the builtin version if it is available and the utility if it is not. Each version of a command may vary slightly from one shell to the next and from the utility to any of the shell builtins. See page 446 for more information on shell builtins.

Checking arguments   The next program uses an **if** structure at the beginning of a script to confirm that you have supplied at least one argument on the command line. The **test –eq** operator compares two integers; the **$#** special parameter (page 441) takes on the value of the number of command-line arguments. This structure displays a message and exits from the script with an exit status of 1 if you do not supply at least one argument:

```
$ cat chkargs
if test $# -eq 0
    then
        echo "You must supply at least one argument."
        exit 1
fi
echo "Program running."
$ ./chkargs
You must supply at least one argument.
$ ./chkargs abc
Program running.
```

A test like the one shown in **chkargs** is a key component of any script that requires arguments. To prevent the user from receiving meaningless or confusing information from the script, the script needs to check whether the user has supplied the appropriate arguments. Some scripts simply test whether arguments exist (as in **chkargs**). Other scripts test for a specific number or specific kinds of arguments.

You can use **test** to verify the status of a file argument or the relationship between two file arguments. After verifying that at least one argument has been given on the command line, the following script tests whether the argument is the name of an ordinary file (not a directory or other type of file) in the working directory. The test builtin with the –f option and the first command-line argument ($1) check the file:

```
$ cat is_ordfile
if test $# -eq 0
    then
        echo "You must supply at least one argument."
        exit 1
fi
if test -f "$1"
    then
        echo "$1 is an ordinary file in the working directory"
    else
        echo "$1 is NOT an ordinary file in the working directory"
fi
```

You can test many other characteristics of a file using test options; see Table 10-1.

Table 10-1   Options to the test builtin

Option	Tests file to see if it
–d	Exists and is a directory file
–e	Exists
–f	Exists and is an ordinary file (not a directory)
–r	Exists and is readable
–s	Exists and has a size greater than 0 bytes
–w	Exists and is writable
–x	Exists and is executable

Other test options provide ways to test relationships between two files, such as whether one file is newer than another. Refer to later examples in this chapter and to test on page 854 for more information.

Always test the arguments

tip   To keep the examples in this book short and focused on specific concepts, the code to verify arguments is often omitted or abbreviated. It is good practice to test arguments in shell programs that other people will use. Doing so results in scripts that are easier to run and debug.

[ ] is a synonym for test   The following example—another version of **chkargs**—checks for arguments in a way that is more traditional for Linux shell scripts. This example uses the bracket ([]) synonym for test. Rather than using the word test in scripts, you can surround the arguments to test with brackets. The brackets must be surrounded by white-space (SPACEs or TABs).

```
$ cat chkargs2
if [ $# -eq 0 ]
    then
        echo "Usage: chkargs2 argument..." 1>&2
        exit 1
fi
echo "Program running."
exit 0
$ ./chkargs2
Usage: chkargs2 argument...
$ ./chkargs2 abc
Program running.
```

Usage messages   The error message that **chkargs2** displays is called a *usage message* and uses the **1>&2** notation to redirect its output to standard error (page 275). After issuing the usage message, **chkargs2** exits with an exit status of 1, indicating an error has occurred. The **exit 0** command at the end of the script causes **chkargs2** to exit with a 0 status after the program runs without an error. The Bourne Again Shell returns a 0 status if you omit the status code.

The usage message is commonly employed to specify the type and number of arguments the script takes. Many Linux utilities provide usage messages similar to the one in **chkargs2**. If you call a utility or other program with the wrong number or wrong kind of arguments, it will often display a usage message. Following is the usage message that cp displays when you call it without any arguments:

```
$ cp
cp: missing file operand
Try 'cp --help' for more information.
```

if...then...else

The introduction of an **else** statement turns the **if** structure into the two-way branch shown in Figure 10-2. The **if...then...else** control structure (available in tcsh with a slightly different syntax) has the following syntax:

>*if **test-command***
>   *then*
>   *commands*
>   *else*
>   *commands*
>*fi*

Because a semicolon (;) ends a command just as a NEWLINE does, you can place **then** on the same line as **if** by preceding it with a semicolon. (Because **if** and **then** are separate builtins, they require a command separator between them; a semicolon and NEWLINE work equally well [page 282].) Some people prefer this notation for aesthetic reasons; others like it because it saves space.

>*if **test-command**; then*
>   *commands*
>   *else*
>   *commands*
>*fi*

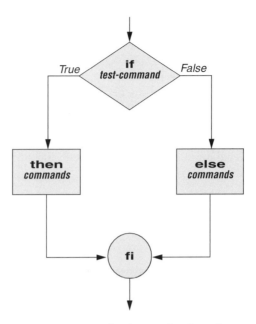

Figure 10-2   An **if...then...**else flowchart

If the **test-command** returns a *true* status, the **if** structure executes the commands between the **then** and **else** statements and then diverts control to the statement following **fi**. If the **test-command** returns a *false* status, the **if** structure executes the commands following the **else** statement.

When you run the **out** script with arguments that are filenames, it displays the files on the terminal. If the first argument is **–v** (called an option in this case), **out** uses less (page 48) to display the files one screen at a time. After determining that it was called with at least one argument, **out** tests its first argument to see whether it is **–v**. If the result of the test is *true* (the first argument is **–v**), **out** uses the shift builtin (page 442) to shift the arguments to get rid of the **–v** and displays the files using less. If the result of the test is *false* (the first argument is *not* **–v**), the script uses cat to display the files:

```
$ cat out
if [ $# -eq 0 ]
    then
        echo "Usage: out [-v] filenames..." 1>&2
        exit 1
fi

if [ "$1" = "-v" ]
    then
        shift
        less -- "$@"
    else
        cat -- "$@"
fi
```

optional   In **out** the –– argument to cat and less tells these utilities that no more options follow
on the command line and not to consider leading hyphens (–) in the following list as
indicating options. Thus –– allows you to view a file with a name that starts with a
hyphen. Although not common, filenames beginning with a hyphen do occasionally
occur. (You can create such a file by using the command **cat > –fname.**) The –– argument works with all Linux utilities that use the getopts builtin (page 456) to parse
their options; it does not work with more and a few other utilities. This argument is
particularly useful when used in conjunction with rm to remove a file whose name
starts with a hyphen (**rm –– –fname**), including any you create while experimenting
with the –– argument.

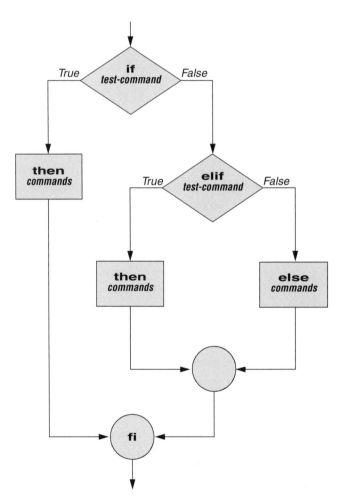

Figure 10-3   An **if**...**then**...**elif** flowchart

if...then...elif

The **if...then...elif** control structure (Figure 10-3; not available in tcsh) has the following syntax:

> *if test-command*
> > *then*
> > > *commands*
> > *elif test-command*
> > > *then*
> > > > *commands*
>
> . . .
>
> > *else*
> > > *commands*
>
> *fi*

The **elif** statement combines the **else** statement and the **if** statement and enables you to construct a nested set of **if...then...else** structures (Figure 10-3). The difference between the **else** statement and the **elif** statement is that each **else** statement must be paired with a **fi** statement, whereas multiple nested **elif** statements require only a single closing **fi** statement.

The following example shows an **if...then...elif** control structure. This shell script compares three words that the user enters. The first **if** statement uses the Boolean AND operator (**−a**) as an argument to test. The test builtin returns a *true* status only if the first and second logical comparisons are *true* (that is, **word1** matches **word2** and **word2** matches **word3**). If test returns a *true* status, the script executes the command following the next **then** statement, passes control to the statement following **fi**, and terminates:

```
$ cat if3
echo -n "word 1: "
read word1
echo -n "word 2: "
read word2
echo -n "word 3: "
read word3
if [ "$word1" = "$word2" -a "$word2" = "$word3" ]
    then
        echo "Match: words 1, 2, & 3"
    elif [ "$word1" = "$word2" ]
    then
        echo "Match: words 1 & 2"
    elif [ "$word1" = "$word3" ]
    then
        echo "Match: words 1 & 3"
    elif [ "$word2" = "$word3" ]
    then
        echo "Match: words 2 & 3"
    else
        echo "No match"
fi
```

```
$ ./if3
word 1: apple
word 2: orange
word 3: pear
No match
$ ./if3
word 1: apple
word 2: orange
word 3: apple
Match: words 1 & 3
$ ./if3
word 1: apple
word 2: apple
word 3: apple
Match: words 1, 2, & 3
```

If the three words are not the same, the structure passes control to the first **elif**, which begins a series of tests to see if any pair of words is the same. As the nesting continues, if any one of the **if** statements is satisfied, the structure passes control to the next **then** statement and subsequently to the statement following **fi**. Each time an **elif** statement is not satisfied, the structure passes control to the next **elif** statement. The double quotation marks around the arguments to echo that contain ampersands (&) prevent the shell from interpreting the ampersands as special characters.

optional   THE lnks SCRIPT

The following script, named **lnks**, demonstrates the **if...then** and **if...then...elif** control structures. This script finds hard links to its first argument, a filename. If you provide the name of a directory as the second argument, **lnks** searches for links in the directory hierarchy rooted at that directory. If you do not specify a directory, **lnks** searches the working directory and its subdirectories. This script does not locate symbolic links.

```
$ cat lnks
#!/bin/bash
# Identify links to a file
# Usage: lnks file [directory]

if [ $# -eq 0 -o $# -gt 2 ]; then
    echo "Usage: lnks file [directory]" 1>&2
    exit 1
fi
if [ -d "$1" ]; then
    echo "First argument cannot be a directory." 1>&2
    echo "Usage: lnks file [directory]" 1>&2
    exit 1
else
    file="$1"
fi
```

```
        if [ $# -eq 1 ]; then
                directory="."
            elif [ -d "$2" ]; then
                directory="$2"
            else
                echo "Optional second argument must be a directory." 1>&2
                echo "Usage: lnks file [directory]" 1>&2
                exit 1
        fi

        # Check that file exists and is an ordinary file
        if [ ! -f "$file" ]; then
            echo "lnks: $file not found or special file" 1>&2
            exit 1
        fi
        # Check link count on file
        set -- $(ls -l "$file")

        linkcnt=$2
        if [ "$linkcnt" -eq 1 ]; then
            echo "lnks: no other hard links to $file" 1>&2
            exit 0
        fi

        # Get the inode of the given file
        set $(ls -i "$file")

        inode=$1

        # Find and print the files with that inode number
        echo "lnks: using find to search for links..." 1>&2
        find "$directory" -xdev -inum $inode -print
```

Max has a file named **letter** in his home directory. He wants to find links to this file in his and other users' home directory file trees. In the following example, Max calls **lnks** from his home directory to perform the search. The second argument to **lnks**, **/home**, is the pathname of the directory where he wants to start the search. If you are running Mac OS X, substitute **/Users** for **/home**. The **lnks** script reports that **/home/max/letter** and **/home/zach/draft** are links to the same file:

```
$ ./lnks letter /home
lnks: using find to search for links...
/home/max/letter
/home/zach/draft
```

In addition to the **if...then...elif** control structure, **lnks** introduces other features that are commonly used in shell programs. The following discussion describes **lnks** section by section.

Specify the shell   The first line of the **lnks** script uses #! (page 280) to specify the shell that will execute the script:

```
#!/bin/bash
```

In this chapter, the #! notation appears only in more complex examples. It ensures that the proper shell executes the script, even when the user is running a different shell or the script is called from a script running a different shell.

Comments   The second and third lines of **lnks** are comments; the shell ignores text that follows a pound sign up to the next NEWLINE character. These comments in **lnks** briefly identify what the file does and explain how to use it:

```
# Identify links to a file
# Usage: lnks file [directory]
```

Usage messages   The first **if** statement tests whether **lnks** was called with zero arguments or more than two arguments:

```
if [ $# -eq 0 -o $# -gt 2 ]; then
    echo "Usage: lnks file [directory]" 1>&2
    exit 1
fi
```

If either of these conditions is *true,* **lnks** sends a usage message to standard error and exits with a status of 1. The double quotation marks around the usage message prevent the shell from interpreting the brackets as special characters. The brackets in the usage message indicate that the **directory** argument is optional.

The second **if** statement tests whether the first command-line argument (**$1**) is a directory (the **–d** argument to test returns *true* if the file exists and is a directory):

```
if [ -d "$1" ]; then
    echo "First argument cannot be a directory." 1>&2
    echo "Usage: lnks file [directory]" 1>&2
    exit 1
else
    file="$1"
fi
```

If the first argument is a directory, **lnks** displays a usage message and exits. If it is not a directory, **lnks** saves the value of **$1** in the **file** variable because later in the script set resets the command-line arguments. If the value of **$1** is not saved before the **set** command is issued, its value is lost.

Test the arguments   The next section of **lnks** is an **if...then...elif** statement:

```
if [ $# -eq 1 ]; then
        directory="."
    elif [ -d "$2" ]; then
        directory="$2"
    else
        echo "Optional second argument must be a directory." 1>&2
        echo "Usage: lnks file [directory]" 1>&2
        exit 1
fi
```

The first *test-command* determines whether the user specified a single argument on the command line. If the *test-command* returns 0 (*true*), the **directory** variable is assigned the value of the working directory (.). If the *test-command* returns *false,* the **elif** statement tests whether the second argument is a directory. If it is a directory, the **directory** variable is set equal to the second command-line argument, **$2.** If **$2** is not a directory, **lnks** sends a usage message to standard error and exits with a status of 1.

The next **if** statement in **lnks** tests whether **$file** does not exist. This test keeps **lnks** from wasting time looking for links to a nonexistent file. The **test** builtin, when called with the three arguments **!**, **–f**, and **$file**, evaluates to *true* if the file **$file** does *not* exist:

```
[ ! -f "$file" ]
```

The **!** operator preceding the **–f** argument to **test** negates its result, yielding *false* if the file **$file** *does* exist and is an ordinary file.

Next **lnks** uses **set** and **ls –l** to check the number of links **$file** has:

```
# Check link count on file
set -- $(ls -l "$file")

linkcnt=$2
if [ "$linkcnt" -eq 1 ]; then
    echo "lnks: no other hard links to $file" 1>&2
    exit 0
fi
```

The **set** builtin uses command substitution (page 340) to set the positional parameters to the output of **ls –l**. The second field in this output is the link count, so the user-created variable **linkcnt** is set equal to **$2.** The **––** used with **set** prevents **set** from interpreting as an option the first argument produced by **ls –l** (the first argument is the access permissions for the file and typically begins with –). The **if** statement checks whether **$linkcnt** is equal to 1; if it is, **lnks** displays a message and exits. Although this message is not truly an error message, it is redirected to standard error. The way **lnks** has been written, all informational messages are sent to standard error. Only the final product of **lnks**—the pathnames of links to the specified file—is sent to standard output, so you can redirect the output as you please.

If the link count is greater than 1, **lnks** goes on to identify the *inode* (page 959) for **$file**. As explained on page 107, comparing the inodes associated with filenames is a good way to determine whether the filenames are links to the same file. (On an HFS+ filesystem, the underlying data structures are different, but the system behaves comparably.) The **lnks** script uses **set** to set the positional parameters to the output of **ls –i**. The first argument to **set** is the inode number for the file, so the user-created variable named **inode** is assigned the value of **$1:**

```
# Get the inode of the given file
set $(ls -i "$file")

inode=$1
```

Finally **lnks** uses the find utility (page 688) to search for files having inode numbers that match **$inode**:

```
# Find and print the files with that inode number
echo "lnks: using find to search for links..." 1>&2
find "$directory" -xdev -inum $inode -print
```

The find utility searches the directory hierarchy rooted at the directory specified by its first argument (**$directory**) for files that meet the criteria specified by the remaining arguments. In this example, the remaining arguments send the names of files having inodes matching **$inode** to standard output. Because files in different filesystems can have the same inode number yet not be linked, find must search only directories in the same filesystem as **$directory**. The **–xdev** (cross-device) argument prevents find from searching directories on other filesystems. Refer to page 104 for more information about filesystems and links.

The echo command preceding the find command in **lnks**, which tells the user that find is running, is included because find can take a long time to run. Because **lnks** does not include a final exit statement, the exit status of **lnks** is that of the last command it runs, find.

DEBUGGING SHELL SCRIPTS

When you are writing a script such as **lnks**, it is easy to make mistakes. You can use the shell's **–x** option to help debug a script. This option causes the shell to display each command before it runs the command. Tracing a script's execution in this way can give you information about where a problem lies.

You can run **lnks** as in the previous example and cause the shell to display each command before it is executed. Either set the **–x** option for the current shell (**set –x**) so all scripts display commands as they are run or use the **–x** option to affect only the shell running the script called by the command line.

```
$ bash -x lnks letter /home
+ '[' 2 -eq 0 -o 2 -gt 2 ']'
+ '[' -d letter ']'
+ file=letter
+ '[' 2 -eq 1 ']'
+ '[' -d /home ']'
+ directory=/home
+ '[' '!' -f letter ']'
...
```

PS4 Each command the script executes is preceded by the value of the **PS4** variable—a plus sign (**+**) by default, so you can distinguish debugging output from script-produced output. You must export **PS4** if you set it in the shell that calls the script. The next command sets **PS4** to >>>> followed by a SPACE and exports it:

```
$ export PS4='>>>> '
```

You can also set the **–x** option of the shell running the script by putting the following **set** command near the beginning of the script:

```
set -x
```

Put **set –x** anywhere in the script you want to turn debugging on. Turn the debugging option off with a plus sign:

```
set +x
```

The **set –o xtrace** and **set +o xtrace** commands do the same things as **set –x** and **set +x**, respectively.

for...in

The **for...in** control structure (tcsh uses **foreach**) has the following syntax:

> for *loop-index* in *argument-list*
> do
>   *commands*
> done

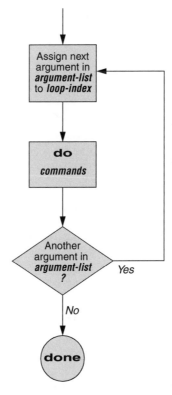

Figure 10-4   A **for...in** flowchart

The **for...in** structure (Figure 10-4, previous page) assigns the value of the first argument in the *argument-list* to the *loop-index* and executes the *commands* between the **do** and **done** statements. The **do** and **done** statements mark the beginning and end of the **for** loop.

After it passes control to the **done** statement, the structure assigns the value of the second argument in the *argument-list* to the *loop-index* and repeats the *commands*. It then repeats the *commands* between the **do** and **done** statements one time for each argument in the *argument-list*. When the structure exhausts the *argument-list*, it passes control to the statement following **done**.

The following **for...in** structure assigns **apples** to the user-created variable **fruit** and then displays the value of **fruit**, which is **apples**. Next the structure assigns **oranges** to **fruit** and repeats the process. When it exhausts the argument list, the structure transfers control to the statement following **done**, which displays a message.

```
$ cat fruit
for fruit in apples oranges pears bananas
do
    echo "$fruit"
done
echo "Task complete."

$ ./fruit
apples
oranges
pears
bananas
Task complete.
```

The next script lists the names of the directory files in the working directory by looping through the files in the working directory and using test to determine which are directory files:

```
$ cat dirfiles
for i in *
do
    if [ -d "$i" ]
        then
            echo "$i"
    fi
done
```

The ambiguous file reference character ***** matches the names of all files (except hidden files) in the working directory. Prior to executing the **for** loop, the shell expands the ***** and uses the resulting list to assign successive values to the index variable **i**.

for

The **for** control structure (not available in tcsh) has the following syntax:

for loop-index
do
    commands
done

In the **for** structure, the *loop-index* takes on the value of each of the command-line arguments, one at a time. The **for** structure is the same as the **for...in** structure (Figure 10-4) except in terms of where it gets values for the *loop-index*. The **for** structure performs a sequence of commands, usually involving each argument in turn.

The following shell script shows a **for** structure displaying each command-line argument. The first line of the script, **for arg**, implies **for arg in "$@"**, where the shell expands **"$@"** into a list of quoted command-line arguments **"$1" "$2" "$3"** and so on. The balance of the script corresponds to the **for...in** structure.

```
$ cat for_test
for arg
do
    echo "$arg"
done
$ for_test candy gum chocolate
candy
gum
chocolate
```

optional THE whos SCRIPT

The following script, named **whos**, demonstrates the usefulness of the implied **"$@"** in the **for** structure. You give **whos** one or more users' full names or usernames as arguments, and **whos** displays information about the users. The **whos** script gets the information it displays from the first and fifth fields in the **/etc/passwd** file. The first field contains a username, and the fifth field typically contains the user's full name. You can provide a username as an argument to **whos** to identify the user's name or provide a name as an argument to identify the username. The **whos** script is similar to the finger utility, although **whos** delivers less information. Mac OS X uses Open Directory in place of the **passwd** file; see page 926 for a similar script that runs under OS X.

```
$ cat whos
#!/bin/bash

if [ $# -eq 0 ]
    then
        echo "Usage: whos id..." 1>&2
        exit 1
fi
for id
do
    gawk -F: '{print $1, $5}' /etc/passwd |
    grep -i "$id"
done
```

In the next example, **whos** identifies the user whose username is **chas** and the user whose name is **Marilou Smith**:

```
$ ./whos chas "Marilou Smith"
chas Charles Casey
msmith Marilou Smith
```

Use of **"$@"**   The **whos** script uses a **for** statement to loop through the command-line arguments. In this script the implied use of **"$@"** in the **for** loop is particularly beneficial because it causes the **for** loop to treat an argument that contains a SPACE as a single argument. This example encloses **Marilou Smith** in quotation marks, which causes the shell to pass it to the script as a single argument. Then the implied **"$@"** in the **for** statement causes the shell to regenerate the quoted argument **Marilou Smith** so that it is again treated as a single argument.

gawk   For each command-line argument, **whos** searches the **/etc/passwd** file. Inside the **for** loop, the gawk utility (Chapter 12; awk and mawk will work the same way) extracts the first (**$1**) and fifth (**$5**) fields from each line in **/etc/passwd**. The **–F:** option causes mawk to use a colon (:) as a field separator when it reads **/etc/passwd**, allowing it to break each line into fields. The mawk command sets and uses the **$1** and **$5** arguments; they are included within single quotation marks and are not interpreted by the shell. Do not confuse these arguments with positional parameters, which correspond to command-line arguments. The first and fifth fields are sent to grep (page 719) via a pipe. The grep utility searches for **$id** (to which the shell has assigned the value of a command-line argument) in its input. The **–i** option causes grep to ignore case as it searches; grep displays each line in its input that contains **$id**.

| at the end of a line   An interesting syntactical exception that bash makes for the pipe symbol (**|**) appears on the line with the mawk command: You do not have to quote a NEWLINE that immediately follows a pipe symbol (that is, a pipe symbol that is the last character on a line) to keep the NEWLINE from executing a command. Try giving the command **who |** and pressing RETURN. The shell (not tcsh) displays a secondary prompt. If you then enter **sort** followed by another RETURN, you see a sorted who list. The pipe works even though a NEWLINE follows the pipe symbol.

while

The **while** control structure (not available in tcsh) has the following syntax:

> *while* **test-command**
> *do*
>   *commands*
> *done*

As long as the **test-command** (Figure 10-5) returns a *true* exit status, the **while** structure continues to execute the series of **commands** delimited by the **do** and **done** statements. Before each loop through the **commands**, the structure executes the **test-command**. When the exit status of the **test-command** is *false*, the structure passes control to the statement after the **done** statement.

test builtin   The following shell script first initializes the **number** variable to zero. The test builtin then determines whether **number** is less than 10. The script uses test with the **–lt** argument to perform a numerical test. For numerical comparisons, you must use **–ne** (not equal), **–eq** (equal), **–gt** (greater than), **–ge** (greater than or equal to), **–lt** (less than), or **–le** (less than or equal to). For string comparisons, use **=** (equal) or **!=** (not equal) when you are working with test. In this example, test has an exit status of 0 (*true*) as long as **number** is less than 10. As long as test returns *true*, the structure executes the

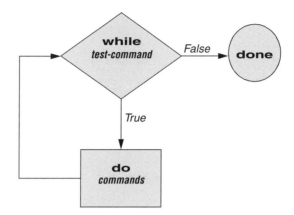

Figure 10-5 A while flowchart

commands between the **do** and **done** statements. See page 854 for information on the test utility, which is very similar to the test builtin.

```
$ cat count
#!/bin/bash
number=0
while [ "$number" -lt 10 ]
    do
        echo -n "$number"
        ((number +=1))
    done
echo
$ ./count
0123456789
$
```

The echo command following **do** displays **number**. The **–n** prevents echo from issuing a NEWLINE following its output. The next command uses arithmetic evaluation [((...)); page 460] to increment the value of **number** by 1. The **done** statement terminates the loop and returns control to the **while** statement to start the loop over again. The final echo causes **count** to send a NEWLINE character to standard output, so the next prompt occurs in the leftmost column on the display (rather than immediately following 9).

optional **THE** spell_check **SCRIPT**

The aspell utility checks the words in a file against a dictionary of correctly spelled words. With the **list** command, aspell (Linux only) runs in list mode: Input comes from standard input and aspell sends each potentially misspelled word to standard output. The following command produces a list of possible misspellings in the file **letter.txt**:

```
$ aspell list < letter.txt
quikly
portible
frendly
```

The next shell script, named **spell_check**, shows another use of a **while** structure. To find the incorrect spellings in a file, **spell_check** calls aspell to check a file against a system dictionary. But it goes a step further: It enables you to specify a list of correctly spelled words and removes these words from the output of aspell. This script is useful for removing words that you use frequently, such as names and technical terms, that do not appear in a standard dictionary. Although you can duplicate the functionality of **spell_check** by using additional aspell dictionaries, the script is included here for its instructive value.

The **spell_check** script requires two filename arguments: the file containing the list of correctly spelled words and the file you want to check. The first **if** statement verifies that the user specified two arguments. The next two **if** statements verify that both arguments are readable files. (The exclamation point negates the sense of the following operator; the **–r** operator causes test to determine whether a file is readable. The result is a test that determines whether a file is *not readable*.)

```
$ cat spell_check
#!/bin/bash
# remove correct spellings from aspell output

if [ $# -ne 2 ]
    then
        echo "Usage: spell_check file1 file2" 1>&2
        echo "file1: list of correct spellings" 1>&2
        echo "file2: file to be checked" 1>&2
        exit 1
fi

if [ ! -r "$1" ]
    then
        echo "spell_check: $1 is not readable" 1>&2
        exit 1
fi

if [ ! -r "$2" ]
    then
        echo "spell_check: $2 is not readable" 1>&2
        exit 1
fi

aspell list < "$2" |
while read line
do
    if ! grep "^$line$" "$1" > /dev/null
        then
            echo $line
    fi
done
```

The **spell_check** script sends the output from aspell (with the **list** argument, so it produces a list of misspelled words on standard output) through a pipe to standard input of a **while** structure, which reads one line at a time (each line has one word on it) from standard input. The *test-command* (that is, **read line**) returns a *true* exit status as long as it receives a line from standard input.

Inside the **while** loop, an **if** statement[1] monitors the return value of grep, which determines whether the line that was read is in the user's list of correctly spelled words. The pattern grep searches for (the value of **$line**) is preceded and followed by special characters that specify the beginning and end of a line (**^** and **$**, respectively). These special characters ensure that grep finds a match only if the **$line** variable matches an entire line in the file of correctly spelled words. (Otherwise, grep would match a string, such as **paul**, in the output of aspell if the file of correctly spelled words contained the word **paulson**.) These special characters, together with the value of the **$line** variable, form a regular expression (Appendix A).

The output of grep is redirected to **/dev/null** (page 131) because the output is not needed; only the exit code is important. The **if** statement checks the negated exit status of grep (the leading exclamation point negates or changes the sense of the exit status—*true* becomes *false,* and vice versa), which is 0 or *true* (*false* when negated) when a matching line is found. If the exit status is *not* 0 or *false* (*true* when negated), the word was *not* in the file of correctly spelled words. The echo builtin sends a list of words that are not in the file of correctly spelled words to standard output.

Once it detects the EOF (end of file), the read builtin returns a *false* exit status, control passes out of the **while** structure, and the script terminates.

Before you use **spell_check**, create a file of correct spellings containing words you use frequently but that are not in a standard dictionary. For example, if you work for a company named **Blinkenship and Klimowski, Attorneys,** you would put **Blinkenship** and **Klimowski** in the file. The following example shows how **spell_check** checks the spelling in a file named **memo** and removes **Blinkenship** and **Klimowski** from the output list of incorrectly spelled words:

```
$ aspell list < memo
Blinkenship
Klimowski
targat
hte
$ cat word_list
Blinkenship
Klimowski
$ ./spell_check word_list memo
targat
hte
```

Refer to page 607 for more information on aspell (Linux only).

---

1. This **if** statement can also be written as

```
if ! grep -qw "$line" "$1"
```

The **–q** option suppresses the output from grep so it returns only an exit code. The **–w** option causes grep to match only a whole word.

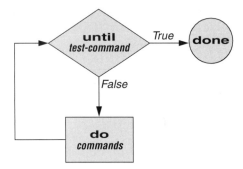

Figure 10-6   An **until** flowchart

until

The **until** (not available in tcsh) and **while** (available in tcsh with a slightly different syntax) structures are very similar, differing only in the sense of the test performed at the top of the loop. Figure 10-6 shows that **until** continues to loop *until* the *test-command* returns a *true* exit status. The **while** structure loops *while* the *test-command* continues to return a *true* or nonerror condition. The **until** control structure has the following syntax:

> *until **test-command***
> *do*
> > *commands*
> *done*

The following script demonstrates an **until** structure that includes read. When the user enters the correct string of characters, the *test-command* is satisfied and the structure passes control out of the loop.

```
$ cat until1
secretname=zach
name=noname
echo "Try to guess the secret name!"
echo
until [ "$name" = "$secretname" ]
do
    echo -n "Your guess: "
    read name
done
echo "Very good."

$ ./until1
Try to guess the secret name!

Your guess: helen
Your guess: barbara
Your guess: rachael
Your guess: zach
Very good
```

The following **locktty** script is similar to the lock command on Berkeley UNIX and the **Lock Screen** menu selection in GNOME. The script prompts for a key (password) and uses an **until** control structure to lock the terminal. The **until** statement causes the system to ignore any characters typed at the keyboard until the user types the key followed by a RETURN on a line by itself, which unlocks the terminal. The **locktty** script can keep people from using your terminal while you are away from it for short periods of time. It saves you from having to log out if you are concerned about other users using your login.

```
$ cat locktty
#! /bin/bash

trap '' 1 2 3 18
stty -echo
echo -n "Key: "
read key_1
echo
echo -n "Again: "
read key_2
echo
key_3=
if [ "$key_1" = "$key_2" ]
    then
        tput clear
        until [ "$key_3" = "$key_2" ]
        do
            read key_3
        done
    else
        echo "locktty: keys do not match" 1>&2
fi
stty echo
```

Forget your password for **locktty**?

tip   If you forget your key (password), you will need to log in from another (virtual) terminal and kill the process running **locktty**.

trap builtin   The trap builtin (page 453; not available in tcsh) at the beginning of the **locktty** script stops a user from being able to terminate the script by sending it a signal (for example, by pressing the interrupt key). Trapping signal 18 means that no one can use CONTROL-Z (job control, a stop from a tty) to defeat the lock. Table 10-5 on page 453 provides a list of signals. The **stty –echo** command (page 838) causes the terminal not to display characters typed at the keyboard, preventing the key the user enters from appearing on the screen. After turning off keyboard echo, the script prompts the user for a key, reads it into the user-created variable **key_1**, prompts the user to enter the same key again, and saves it in **key_2**. The statement **key_3=** creates a variable with a NULL value. If **key_1** and **key_2** match, **locktty** clears the screen (with the tput command) and starts an **until** loop. The **until** loop keeps attempting to read from the terminal and assigning the input to the **key_3** variable. Once the user types a string that matches one of the original keys (**key_2**), the **until** loop terminates and keyboard echo is turned on again.

break **AND** continue

You can interrupt a **for, while,** or **until** loop by using a **break** or **continue** statement. The **break** statement transfers control to the statement after the **done** statement, thereby terminating execution of the loop. The **continue** command transfers control to the **done** statement, continuing execution of the loop.

The following script demonstrates the use of these two statements. The **for...in** structure loops through the values 1–10. The first **if** statement executes its commands when the value of the index is less than or equal to 3 (**$index –le 3**). The second **if** statement executes its commands when the value of the index is greater than or equal to 8 (**$index –ge 8**). In between the two **if**s, echo displays the value of the index. For all values up to and including 3, the first **if** statement displays **continue**, executes a **continue** statement that skips echo $index and the second **if** statement, and continues with the next **for** statement. For the value of 8, the second **if** statement displays **break** and executes a **break** statement that exits from the **for** loop.

```
$ cat brk
for index in 1 2 3 4 5 6 7 8 9 10
    do
        if [ $index -le 3 ] ; then
            echo "continue"
            continue
        fi
#
    echo $index
#
    if [ $index -ge 8 ] ; then
        echo "break"
        break
    fi
done

$ ./brk
continue
continue
continue
4
5
6
7
8
break
```

case

The **case** structure (Figure 10-7, next page) is a multiple-branch decision mechanism. The path taken through the structure depends on a match or lack of a match between the *test-string* and one of the *patterns*. The **case** control structure (tcsh uses **switch**) has the following syntax:

> *case **test-string** in*
> > *pattern-1)*
> > > *commands-1*
> > > *;;*
> > *pattern-2)*
> > > *commands-2*
> > > *;;*
> > *pattern-3)*
> > > *commands-3*
> > > *;;*
> > . . .
> *esac*

The following **case** structure examines the character the user enters as the *test-string*. This value is held in the variable **letter**. If the *test-string* has a value of **A**, the structure executes the command following the *pattern* **A**. The right parenthesis is part of the **case** control structure, not part of the *pattern*. If the *test-string* has a value of **B** or **C**, the structure executes the command following the matching *pattern*. The asterisk (*) indicates *any string of characters* and serves as a catchall in case there is no match. If no *pattern* matches the *test-string* and if there is no catchall (*) *pattern*, control passes to the command following the **esac** statement, without the **case** structure taking any action.

```
$ cat case1
echo -n "Enter A, B, or C: "
read letter
case "$letter" in
    A)
        echo "You entered A"
        ;;
    B)
        echo "You entered B"
        ;;
    C)
        echo "You entered C"
        ;;
    *)
        echo "You did not enter A, B, or C"
        ;;
esac

$ ./case1
Enter A, B, or C: B
You entered B
```

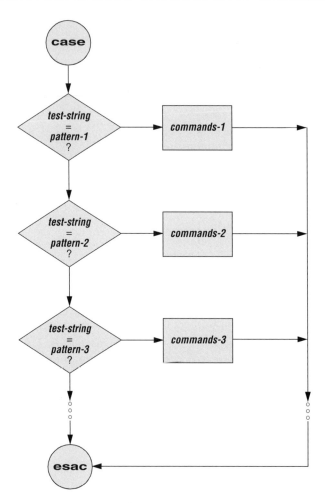

Figure 10-7　A **case** flowchart

The next execution of **case1** shows the user entering a lowercase **b**. Because the *test-string* **b** does not match the uppercase B *pattern* (or any other *pattern* in the **case** statement), the program executes the commands following the catchall *pattern* and displays a message:

```
$ ./case1
Enter A, B, or C: b
You did not enter A, B, or C
```

The *pattern* in the **case** structure is analogous to an ambiguous file reference. It can include any special characters and strings shown in Table 10-2.

The next script accepts both uppercase and lowercase letters:

```
$ cat case2
echo -n "Enter A, B, or C: "
read letter
case "$letter" in
    a|A)
        echo "You entered A"
        ;;
    b|B)
        echo "You entered B"
        ;;
    c|C)
        echo "You entered C"
        ;;
    *)
        echo "You did not enter A, B, or C"
        ;;
esac

$ ./case2
Enter A, B, or C: b
You entered B
```

Table 10-2   Patterns

Pattern	Function
*	Matches any string of characters. Use for the default case.
?	Matches any single character.
[...]	Defines a character class. Any characters enclosed within brackets are tried, one at a time, in an attempt to match a single character. A hyphen between two characters specifies a range of characters.
|	Separates alternative choices that satisfy a particular branch of the **case** structure.

optional   The following example shows how you can use the **case** structure to create a simple menu. The **command_menu** script uses echo to present menu items and prompt the user for a selection. (The **select** control structure [page 427] is a much easier way of coding a menu.) The **case** structure then executes the appropriate utility depending on the user's selection.

```
$ cat command_menu
#!/bin/bash
# menu interface to simple commands

echo -e "\n        COMMAND MENU\n"
echo "  a.  Current date and time"
echo "  b.  Users currently logged in"
echo "  c.  Name of the working directory"
echo -e "  d.  Contents of the working directory\n"
echo -n "Enter a, b, c, or d: "
read answer
echo
```

```
            #
            case "$answer" in
                a)
                    date
                    ;;
                b)
                    who
                    ;;
                c)
                    pwd
                    ;;
                d)
                    ls
                    ;;
                *)
                    echo "There is no selection: $answer"
                    ;;
            esac

$ ./command_menu

                COMMAND MENU

        a.  Current date and time
        b.  Users currently logged in
        c.  Name of the working directory
        d.  Contents of the working directory

Enter a, b, c, or d: a

Wed Jan  3 12:31:12 PST 2009
```

echo –e   The –e option causes echo to interpret \n as a NEWLINE character. If you do not include this option, echo does not output the extra blank lines that make the menu easy to read but instead outputs the (literal) two-character sequence \n. The –e option causes echo to interpret several other backslash-quoted characters (Table 10-3). Remember to quote (i.e., place double quotation marks around the string) the backslash-quoted character so the shell does not interpret it but passes the backslash and the character to echo. See **xpg_echo** (page 333) for a way to avoid using the –e option.

Table 10-3   Special characters in echo (must use **–e**)

Quoted character	echo **displays**
\a	Alert (bell)
\b	BACKSPACE
\c	Suppress trailing NEWLINE
\f	FORMFEED
\n	NEWLINE
\r	RETURN

Table 10-3	Special characters in echo (must use **–e**) (continued)
Quoted character	echo **displays**
\t	Horizontal TAB
\v	Vertical TAB
\\	Backslash
\nnn	The character with the ASCII octal code nnn; if nnn is not valid, echo displays the string literally

You can also use the **case** control structure to take various actions in a script, depending on how many arguments the script is called with. The following script, named **safedit**, uses a **case** structure that branches based on the number of command-line arguments (**$#**). It saves a backup copy of a file you are editing with vim.

```
$ cat safedit
#!/bin/bash

PATH=/bin:/usr/bin
script=$(basename $0)
case $# in

    0)
        vim
        exit 0
        ;;

    1)
        if [ ! -f "$1" ]
            then
                vim "$1"
                exit 0
            fi
        if [ ! -r "$1" -o ! -w "$1" ]
            then
                echo "$script: check permissions on $1" 1>&2
                exit 1
            else
                editfile=$1
            fi
        if [ ! -w "." ]
            then
                echo "$script: backup cannot be " \
                    "created in the working directory" 1>&2
                exit 1
            fi
        ;;
    *)
        echo "Usage: $script [file-to-edit]" 1>&2
        exit 1
        ;;
esac
```

```
        tempfile=/tmp/$$.$script
        cp $editfile $tempfile
        if vim $editfile
            then
                mv $tempfile bak.$(basename $editfile)
                echo "$script: backup file created"
            else
                mv $tempfile editerr
                echo "$script: edit error--copy of " \
                    "original file is in editerr" 1>&2
    fi
```

If you call **safedit** without any arguments, the **case** structure executes its first branch and calls vim without a filename argument. Because an existing file is not being edited, **safedit** does not create a backup file. (See the **:w** command on page 163 for an explanation of how to exit from vim when you have called it without a filename.) If you call **safedit** with one argument, it runs the commands in the second branch of the **case** structure and verifies that the file specified by **$1** does not yet exist or is the name of a file for which the user has read and write permission. The **safedit** script also verifies that the user has write permission for the working directory. If the user calls **safedit** with more than one argument, the third branch of the **case** structure presents a usage message and exits with a status of 1.

Set **PATH**   In addition to using a **case** structure for branching based on the number of command-line arguments, the **safedit** script introduces several other features. At the beginning of the script, the **PATH** variable is set to search **/bin** and **/usr/bin**. Setting **PATH** in this way ensures that the commands executed by the script are standard utilities, which are kept in those directories. By setting this variable inside a script, you can avoid the problems that might occur if users have set **PATH** to search their own directories first and have scripts or programs with the same names as the utilities the script calls. You can also include absolute pathnames within a script to achieve this end, although this practice can make a script less portable.

Name of the   The next line creates a variable named **script** and uses command substitution to
program   assign the simple filename of the script to it:

```
        script=$(basename $0)
```

The basename utility sends the simple filename component of its argument to standard output, which is assigned to the **script** variable, using command substitution. The **$0** holds the command the script was called with (page 441). No matter which of the following commands the user calls the script with, the output of basename is the simple filename **safedit**:

```
$ /home/max/bin/safedit memo
$ ./safedit memo
$ safedit memo
```

After the **script** variable is set, it replaces the filename of the script in usage and error messages. By using a variable that is derived from the command that invoked the script rather than a filename that is hardcoded into the script, you can create links to the script or rename it, and the usage and error messages will still provide accurate information.

Naming temporary files Another feature of **safedit** relates to the use of the $$ parameter in the name of a temporary file. The statement following the **esac** statement creates and assigns a value to the **tempfile** variable. This variable contains the name of a temporary file that is stored in the **/tmp** directory, as are many temporary files. The temporary filename begins with the PID number of the shell and ends with the name of the script. Using the PID number ensures that the filename is unique. Thus **safedit** will not attempt to overwrite an existing file, as might happen if two people were using **safedit** at the same time. The name of the script is appended so that, should the file be left in **/tmp** for some reason, you can figure out where it came from.

The PID number is used in front of—rather than after—**$script** in the filename because of the 14-character limit placed on filenames by some older versions of UNIX. Linux systems do not have this limitation. Because the PID number ensures the uniqueness of the filename, it is placed first so that it cannot be truncated. (If the **$script** component is truncated, the filename is still unique.) For the same reason, when a backup file is created inside the **if** control structure a few lines down in the script, the filename consists of the string **bak.** followed by the name of the file being edited. On an older system, if **bak** were used as a suffix rather than a prefix and the original filename were 14 characters long, **.bak** might be lost and the original file would be overwritten. The basename utility extracts the simple filename of **$editfile** before it is prefixed with **bak.**

The **safedit** script uses an unusual *test-command* in the **if** structure: **vim $editfile**. The *test-command* calls vim to edit **$editfile**. When you finish editing the file and exit from vim, vim returns an exit code. The **if** control structure uses that exit code to determine which branch to take. If the editing session completed successfully, vim returns 0 and the statements following the **then** statement are executed. If vim does not terminate normally (as would occur if the user killed [page 729] the vim process), vim returns a nonzero exit status and the script executes the statements following **else**.

select

The **select** control structure (not available in tcsh) is based on the one found in the Korn Shell. It displays a menu, assigns a value to a variable based on the user's choice of items, and executes a series of commands. The **select** control structure has the following syntax:

> select *varname [in arg . . .]*
> do
>   *commands*
> done

The **select** structure displays a menu of the *arg* items. If you omit the keyword **in** and the list of arguments, **select** uses the positional parameters in place of the *arg* items. The menu is formatted with numbers before each item. For example, a **select** structure that begins with

```
select fruit in apple banana blueberry kiwi orange watermelon STOP
```

displays the following menu:

```
1) apple       3) blueberry   5) orange      7) STOP
2) banana      4) kiwi        6) watermelon
```

The **select** structure uses the values of the **LINES** and **COLUMNS** variables to specify the size of the display. (**LINES** has a default value of 24; **COLUMNS** has a default value of 80.) With **COLUMNS** set to 20, the menu looks like this:

```
1) apple
2) banana
3) blueberry
4) kiwi
5) orange
6) watermelon
7) STOP
```

PS3   After displaying the menu, **select** displays the value of **PS3**, the **select** prompt. The default value of **PS3** is ?#, but it is typically set to a more meaningful value. When you enter a valid number (one in the menu range) in response to the **PS3** prompt, **select** sets *varname* to the argument corresponding to the number you entered. An invalid entry causes the shell to set *varname* to null. Either way **select** stores your response in the keyword variable **REPLY** and then executes the *commands* between **do** and **done**. If you press RETURN without entering a choice, the shell redisplays the menu and the **PS3** prompt.

The **select** structure continues to issue the **PS3** prompt and execute the *commands* until something causes it to exit—typically a **break** or **exit** statement. A **break** statement exits from the loop and an **exit** statement exits from the script.

The following script illustrates the use of **select**:

```
$ cat fruit2
#!/bin/bash
PS3="Choose your favorite fruit from these possibilities: "
select FRUIT in apple banana blueberry kiwi orange watermelon STOP
do
    if [ "$FRUIT" == "" ]; then
        echo -e "Invalid entry.\n"
        continue
    elif [ $FRUIT = STOP ]; then
        echo "Thanks for playing!"
        break
    fi
echo "You chose $FRUIT as your favorite."
echo -e "That is choice number $REPLY.\n"
done
```

```
$ ./fruit2
1) apple        3) blueberry   5) orange      7) STOP
2) banana       4) kiwi        6) watermelon
Choose your favorite fruit from these possibilities: 3
You chose blueberry as your favorite.
That is choice number 3.

Choose your favorite fruit from these possibilities: 99
Invalid entry.

Choose your favorite fruit from these possibilities: 7
Thanks for playing!
```

After setting the **PS3** prompt and establishing the menu with the **select** statement, **fruit2** executes the *commands* between **do** and **done**. If the user submits an invalid entry, the shell sets *varname* ($FRUIT) to a null value. If $FRUIT is null, echo displays an error; **continue** then causes the shell to redisplay the **PS3** prompt. If the entry is valid, the script tests whether the user wants to stop. If so, echo displays a message and **break** exits from the **select** structure (and from the script). If the user enters a valid response and does not want to stop, the script displays the name and number of the user's response. (See page 424 for information about the echo –e option.)

Here Document

A Here document allows you to redirect input to a shell script from within the shell script itself. A Here document is so named because it is *here*—immediately accessible in the shell script—instead of *there*, perhaps in another file.

The following script, named **birthday**, contains a Here document. The two less than symbols (<<) in the first line indicate a Here document follows. One or more characters that delimit the Here document follow the less than symbols—this example uses a plus sign. Whereas the opening delimiter must appear adjacent to the less than symbols, the closing delimiter must be on a line by itself. The shell sends everything between the two delimiters to the process as standard input. In the example it is as though you have redirected standard input to grep from a file, except that the file is embedded in the shell script:

```
$ cat birthday
grep -i "$1" <<+
Max     June 22
Barbara February 3
Darlene May 8
Helen   March 13
Zach    January 23
Nancy   June 26
+
$ ./birthday Zach
Zach    January 23
$ ./birthday june
Max     June 22
Nancy   June 26
```

When you run **birthday**, it lists all the Here document lines that contain the argument you called it with. In this case the first time **birthday** is run, it displays Zach's birthday because it is called with an argument of **Zach**. The second run displays all the birthdays in June. The –i argument causes grep's search not to be case sensitive.

optional   The next script, named **bundle**,[2] includes a clever use of a Here document. The **bundle** script is an elegant example of a script that creates a shell archive (**shar**) file. The script creates a file that is itself a shell script containing several other files as well as the code to re-create the original files:

```
$ cat bundle
#!/bin/bash
# bundle:  group files into distribution package

echo "# To unbundle, bash this file"
for i
do
    echo "echo $i 1>&2"
    echo "cat >$i <<'End of $i'"
    cat $i
    echo "End of $i"
done
```

Just as the shell does not treat special characters that occur in standard input of a shell script as special, so the shell does not treat the special characters that occur between the delimiters in a Here document as special.

As the following example shows, the output of **bundle** is a shell script, which is redirected to a file named **bothfiles**. It contains the contents of each file given as an argument to **bundle** (**file1** and **file2** in this case) inside a Here document. To extract the original files from **bothfiles**, you simply give it as an argument to a bash command. Before each Here document is a cat command that causes the Here document to be written to a new file when **bothfiles** is run:

```
$ cat file1
This is a file.
It contains two lines.
$ cat file2
This is another file.
It contains
three lines.

$ ./bundle file1 file2 > bothfiles
$ cat bothfiles
# To unbundle, bash this file
echo file1 1>&2
cat >file1 <<'End of file1'
```

2. Thanks to Brian W. Kernighan and Rob Pike, *The Unix Programming Environment* (Englewood Cliffs, N.J.: Prentice-Hall, 1984), 98. Reprinted with permission.

```
                    This is a file.
                    It contains two lines.
                    End of file1
                    echo file2 1>&2
                    cat >file2 <<'End of file2'
                    This is another file.
                    It contains
                    three lines.
                    End of file2
```

In the next example, **file1** and **file2** are removed before **bothfiles** is run. The **bothfiles** script echoes the names of the files it creates as it creates them. The ls command then shows that **bothfiles** has re-created **file1** and **file2**:

```
$ rm file1 file2
$ bash bothfiles
file1
file2
$ ls
bothfiles
file1
file2
```

FILE DESCRIPTORS

As discussed on page 275, before a process can read from or write to a file, it must open that file. When a process opens a file, Linux associates a number (called a *file descriptor*) with the file. A file descriptor is an index into the process's table of open files. Each process has its own set of open files and its own file descriptors. After opening a file, a process reads from and writes to that file by referring to its file descriptor. When it no longer needs the file, the process closes the file, freeing the file descriptor.

A typical Linux process starts with three open files: standard input (file descriptor 0), standard output (file descriptor 1), and standard error (file descriptor 2). Often these are the only files the process needs. Recall that you redirect standard output with the symbol **>** or the symbol **1>** and that you redirect standard error with the symbol **2>**. Although you can redirect other file descriptors, because file descriptors other than 0, 1, and 2 do not have any special conventional meaning, it is rarely useful to do so. The exception is in programs that you write yourself, in which case you control the meaning of the file descriptors and can take advantage of redirection.

Opening a file descriptor   The Bourne Again Shell opens files using the **exec** builtin as follows:

> *exec n> outfile*
> *exec m< infile*

The first line opens *outfile* for output and holds it open, associating it with file descriptor *n*. The second line opens *infile* for input and holds it open, associating it with file descriptor *m*.

Duplicating a
file descriptor

The **<&** token duplicates an input file descriptor; **>&** duplicates an output file descriptor. You can duplicate a file descriptor by making it refer to the same file as another open file descriptor, such as standard input or output. Use the following format to open or redirect file descriptor *n* as a duplicate of file descriptor *m*:

> *exec n<&m*

Once you have opened a file, you can use it for input and output in two ways. First, you can use I/O redirection on any command line, redirecting standard output to a file descriptor with **>&***n* or redirecting standard input from a file descriptor with **<&***n*. Second, you can use the read (page 447) and echo builtins. If you invoke other commands, including functions (page 327), they inherit these open files and file descriptors. When you have finished using a file, you can close it using

> *exec n<&–*

When you invoke the shell function in the next example, named **mycp**, with two arguments, it copies the file named by the first argument to the file named by the second argument. If you supply only one argument, the script copies the file named by the argument to standard output. If you invoke **mycp** with no arguments, it copies standard input to standard output.

A function is not a shell script

tip   The **mycp** example is a shell function; it will not work as you expect if you execute it as a shell script. (It will work: The function will be created in a very short-lived subshell, which is probably of little use.) You can enter this function from the keyboard. If you put the function in a file, you can run it as an argument to the . (dot) builtin (page 274). You can also put the function in a startup file if you want it to be always available (page 329).

```
function mycp ()
{
case $# in
    0)
        # Zero arguments
        # File descriptor 3 duplicates standard input
        # File descriptor 4 duplicates standard output
        exec 3<&0 4<&1
        ;;
    1)
        # One argument
        # Open the file named by the argument for input
        # and associate it with file descriptor 3
        # File descriptor 4 duplicates standard output
        exec 3< $1 4<&1
        ;;
    2)
        # Two arguments
        # Open the file named by the first argument for input
        # and associate it with file descriptor 3
        # Open the file named by the second argument for output
        # and associate it with file descriptor 4
        exec 3< $1 4> $2
        ;;
```

```
        *)
                echo "Usage: mycp [source [dest]]"
                return 1
                ;;
        esac

        # Call cat with input coming from file descriptor 3
        # and output going to file descriptor 4
        cat <&3 >&4

        # Close file descriptors 3 and 4
        exec 3<&- 4<&-
        }
```

The real work of this function is done in the line that begins with cat. The rest of the script arranges for file descriptors 3 and 4, which are the input and output of the cat command, to be associated with the appropriate files.

optional   The next program takes two filenames on the command line, sorts both, and sends the output to temporary files. The program then merges the sorted files to standard output, preceding each line by a number that indicates which file it came from.

```
$ cat sortmerg
#!/bin/bash
usage ()
{
if [ $# -ne 2 ]; then
    echo "Usage: $0 file1 file2" 2>&1
    exit 1
    fi
}

# Default temporary directory
: ${TEMPDIR:=/tmp}

# Check argument count
usage "$@"

# Set up temporary files for sorting
file1=$TEMPDIR/$$.file1
file2=$TEMPDIR/$$.file2

# Sort
sort $1 > $file1
sort $2 > $file2

# Open $file1 and $file2 for reading. Use file descriptors 3 and 4.
exec 3<$file1
exec 4<$file2

# Read the first line from each file to figure out how to start.
read Line1 <&3
status1=$?
read Line2 <&4
status2=$?
```

```
# Strategy: while there is still input left in both files:
#   Output the line that should come first.
#   Read a new line from the file that line came from.
while [ $status1 -eq 0 -a $status2 -eq 0 ]
    do
        if [[ "$Line2" > "$Line1" ]]; then
            echo -e "1.\t$Line1"
            read -u3 Line1
            status1=$?
        else
            echo -e "2.\t$Line2"
            read -u4 Line2
            status2=$?
        fi
    done

# Now one of the files is at end-of-file.
# Read from each file until the end.
# First file1:
while [ $status1 -eq 0 ]
    do
        echo -e "1.\t$Line1"
        read Line1 <&3
        status1=$?
    done
# Next file2:
while [[ $status2 -eq 0 ]]
    do
        echo -e "2.\t$Line2"
        read Line2 <&4
        status2=$?
    done

# Close and remove both input files
exec 3<&- 4<&-
rm -f $file1 $file2
exit 0
```

PARAMETERS AND VARIABLES

Shell parameters and variables were introduced on page 290. This section adds to the previous coverage with a discussion of array variables, global versus local variables, special and positional parameters, and expansion of null and unset variables.

ARRAY VARIABLES

The Bourne Again Shell supports one-dimensional array variables. The subscripts are integers with zero-based indexing (i.e., the first element of the array has the subscript 0). The following format declares and assigns values to an array:

name=(element1 element2 ...)

The following example assigns four values to the array **NAMES**:

```
$ NAMES=(max helen sam zach)
```

You reference a single element of an array as follows:

```
$ echo ${NAMES[2]}
sam
```

The subscripts [*] and [@] both extract the entire array but work differently when used within double quotation marks. An **@** produces an array that is a duplicate of the original array; an * produces a single element of an array (or a plain variable) that holds all the elements of the array separated by the first character in **IFS** (normally a SPACE). In the following example, the array **A** is filled with the elements of the **NAMES** variable using an *, and **B** is filled using an @. The declare builtin with the **–a** option displays the values of the arrays (and reminds you that bash uses zero-based indexing for arrays):

```
$ A=("${NAMES[*]}")
$ B=("${NAMES[@]}")

$ declare -a
declare -a A='([0]="max helen sam zach")'
declare -a B='([0]="max" [1]="helen" [2]="sam" [3]="zach")'
...
declare -a NAMES='([0]="max" [1]="helen" [2]="sam" [3]="zach")'
```

From the output of declare, you can see that **NAMES** and **B** have multiple elements. In contrast, **A**, which was assigned its value with an * within double quotation marks, has only one element: **A** has all its elements enclosed between double quotation marks.

In the next example, echo attempts to display element 1 of array **A**. Nothing is displayed because **A** has only one element and that element has an index of 0. Element 0 of array **A** holds all four names. Element 1 of **B** holds the second item in the array and element 0 holds the first item.

```
$ echo ${A[1]}

$ echo ${A[0]}
max helen sam zach
$ echo ${B[1]}
helen
$ echo ${B[0]}
max
```

You can apply the ${#*name*[*]} operator to array variables, returning the number of elements in the array:

```
$ echo ${#NAMES[*]}
4
```

The same operator, when given the index of an element of an array in place of *****, returns the length of the element:

```
$ echo ${#NAMES[1]}
5
```

You can use subscripts on the left side of an assignment statement to replace selected elements of the array:

```
$ NAMES[1]=max
$ echo ${NAMES[*]}
max max sam zach
```

LOCALITY OF VARIABLES

By default variables are local to the process in which they are declared. Thus a shell script does not have access to variables declared in your login shell unless you explicitly make the variables available (global). Under bash, export makes a variable available to child processes. Under tcsh, setenv (page 366) assigns a value to a variable and makes it available to child processes. The examples in this section use the bash syntax but the theory applies to both shells.

export   Once you use the export builtin with a variable name as an argument, the shell places the value of the variable in the calling environment of child processes. This *call by value* gives each child process a copy of the variable for its own use.

The following **extest1** shell script assigns a value of **american** to the variable named **cheese** and then displays its filename (**extest1**) and the value of **cheese**. The **extest1** script then calls **subtest**, which attempts to display the same information. Next **subtest** declares a **cheese** variable and displays its value. When **subtest** finishes, it returns control to the parent process, which is executing **extest1**. At this point **extest1** again displays the value of the original **cheese** variable.

```
$ cat extest1
cheese=american
echo "extest1 1: $cheese"
subtest
echo "extest1 2: $cheese"
$ cat subtest
echo "subtest 1: $cheese"
cheese=swiss
echo "subtest 2: $cheese"
$ ./extest1
extest1 1: american
subtest 1:
subtest 2: swiss
extest1 2: american
```

The **subtest** script never receives the value of **cheese** from **extest1**, and **extest1** never loses the value. In bash—unlike in the real world—a child can never affect its parent's attributes. When a process attempts to display the value of a variable that has not been declared, as is the case with **subtest**, the process displays nothing; the value of an undeclared variable is that of a null string.

The following **extest2** script is the same as **extest1** except it uses export to make **cheese** available to the **subtest** script:

```
$ cat extest2
export cheese=american
echo "extest2 1: $cheese"
subtest
echo "extest2 2: $cheese"
$ ./extest2
extest2 1: american
subtest 1: american
subtest 2: swiss
extest2 2: american
```

Here the child process inherits the value of **cheese** as **american** and, after displaying this value, changes *its copy* to **swiss**. When control is returned to the parent, the parent's copy of **cheese** retains its original value: **american**.

An export builtin can optionally include an assignment:

```
export cheese=american
```

The preceding statement is equivalent to the following two statements:

```
cheese=american
export cheese
```

Although it is rarely done, you can export a variable before you assign a value to it. You do not need to export an already-exported variable a second time after you change its value.

FUNCTIONS

Because functions run in the same environment as the shell that calls them, variables are implicitly shared by a shell and a function it calls.

```
$ function nam () {
> echo $myname
> myname=zach
> }

$ myname=sam
$ nam
sam
$ echo $myname
zach
```

In the preceding example, the **myname** variable is set to **sam** in the interactive shell. The **nam** function then displays the value of **myname** (**sam**) and sets **myname** to **zach**. The final echo shows that, in the interactive shell, the value of **myname** has been changed to **zach**.

Function local variables Local variables are helpful in a function written for general use. Because the function is called by many scripts that may be written by different programmers, you need to make sure the names of the variables used within the function do not conflict with (i.e., duplicate) the names of the variables in the programs that call the function. Local variables eliminate this problem. When used within a function, the typeset builtin declares a variable to be local to the function it is defined in.

The next example shows the use of a local variable in a function. It features two variables named **count**. The first is declared and assigned a value of 10 in the interactive shell. Its value never changes, as echo verifies after **count_down** is run. The other **count** is declared, using typeset, to be local to the function. Its value, which is unknown outside the function, ranges from 4 to 1, as the echo command within the function confirms.

The example shows the function being entered from the keyboard; it is not a shell script. See the tip "A function is not a shell script" on page 432.

```
$ function count_down () {
> typeset count
> count=$1
> while [ $count -gt 0 ]
> do
> echo "$count..."
> ((count=count-1))
> sleep 1
> done
> echo "Blast Off."
> }
$ count=10
$ count_down 4
4...
3...
2...
1...
Blast Off.
$ echo $count
10
```

The ((**count=count–1**)) assignment is enclosed between double parentheses, which cause the shell to perform an arithmetic evaluation (page 460). Within the double parentheses you can reference shell variables without the leading dollar sign (**$**).

SPECIAL PARAMETERS

Special parameters enable you to access useful values pertaining to command-line arguments and the execution of shell commands. You reference a shell special parameter by preceding a special character with a dollar sign (**$**). As with positional parameters, it is not possible to modify the value of a special parameter by assignment.

$$: PID NUMBER

The shell stores in the **$$** parameter the PID number of the process that is executing it. In the following interaction, echo displays the value of this variable and the ps utility confirms its value. Both commands show that the shell has a PID number of 5209:

```
$ echo $$
5209
$ ps
  PID TTY          TIME CMD
 5209 pts/1    00:00:00 bash
 6015 pts/1    00:00:00 ps
```

Because echo is built into the shell, the shell does not create another process when you give an echo command. However, the results are the same whether echo is a builtin or not, because the shell substitutes the value of **$$** *before* it forks a new process to run a command. Try using the echo utility (**/bin/echo**), which is run by another process, and see what happens. In the following example, the shell substitutes the value of **$$** and passes that value to cp as a prefix for a filename:

```
$ echo $$
8232
$ cp memo $$.memo
$ ls
8232.memo memo
```

Incorporating a PID number in a filename is useful for creating unique filenames when the meanings of the names do not matter; this technique is often used in shell scripts for creating names of temporary files. When two people are running the same shell script, having unique filenames keeps the users from inadvertently sharing the same temporary file.

The following example demonstrates that the shell creates a new shell process when it runs a shell script. The **id2** script displays the PID number of the process running it (not the process that called it—the substitution for **$$** is performed by the shell that is forked to run **id2**):

```
$ cat id2
echo "$0 PID= $$"
$ echo $$
8232
$ id2
./id2 PID= 8362
$ echo $$
8232
```

The first echo displays the PID number of the interactive shell. Then **id2** displays its name (**$0**) and the PID number of the subshell that it is running in. The last echo shows that the PID number of the interactive shell has not changed.

$! The shell stores the value of the PID number of the last process that ran in the background in $! (not available in tcsh). The following example executes sleep as a background task and uses echo to display the value of $!:

```
$ sleep 60 &
[1] 8376
$ echo $!
8376
```

$?: EXIT STATUS

When a process stops executing for any reason, it returns an *exit status* to its parent process. The exit status is also referred to as a *condition code* or a *return code*. The $? ($status under tcsh) variable stores the exit status of the last command.

By convention a nonzero exit status represents a *false* value and means the command failed. A zero is *true* and indicates the command executed successfully. In the following example, the first ls command succeeds and the second fails, as demonstrated by the exit status:

```
$ ls es
es
$ echo $?
0
$ ls xxx
ls: xxx: No such file or directory
$ echo $?
1
```

You can specify the exit status that a shell script returns by using the exit builtin, followed by a number, to terminate the script. If you do not use exit with a number to terminate a script, the exit status of the script is that of the last command the script ran.

```
$ cat es
echo This program returns an exit status of 7.
exit 7
$ es
This program returns an exit status of 7.
$ echo $?
7
$ echo $?
0
```

The es shell script displays a message and terminates execution with an exit command that returns an exit status of 7, the user-defined exit status in this script. The first echo then displays the value of the exit status of es. The second echo displays the value of the exit status of the first echo. This value is 0, indicating the first echo was successful.

POSITIONAL PARAMETERS

Positional parameters comprise the command name and command-line arguments. These parameters are called *positional* because within a shell script, you refer to them by their position on the command line. Only the set builtin (page 442) allows you to change the values of positional parameters. However, you cannot change the value of the command name from within a script. The tcsh set builtin does not change the values of positional parameters.

$#: NUMBER OF COMMAND-LINE ARGUMENTS

The $# parameter holds the number of arguments on the command line (positional parameters), not counting the command itself:

```
$ cat num_args
echo "This script was called with $# arguments."
$ ./num_args sam max zach
This script was called with 3 arguments.
```

$0: NAME OF THE CALLING PROGRAM

The shell stores the name of the command you used to call a program in parameter $0. This parameter is numbered zero because it appears before the first argument on the command line:

```
$ cat abc
echo "The command used to run this script is $0"
$ ./abc
The command used to run this script is ./abc
$ ~sam/abc
The command used to run this script is /home/sam/abc
```

The preceding shell script uses echo to verify the name of the script you are executing. You can use the basename utility and command substitution to extract and display the simple filename of the command:

```
$ cat abc2
echo "The command used to run this script is $(basename $0)"
$ ~sam/abc2
The command used to run this script is abc2
```

$1 – $n: COMMAND-LINE ARGUMENTS

The first argument on the command line is represented by parameter $1, the second argument by $2, and so on up to $n. For values of n greater than 9, the number must be enclosed within braces. For example, the twelfth command-line argument is represented by ${12}. The following script displays positional parameters that hold command-line arguments:

```
$ cat display_5args
echo First 5 arguments are $1 $2 $3 $4 $5

$ ./display_5args zach max helen
First 5 arguments are zach max helen
```

The **display_5args** script displays the first five command-line arguments. The shell assigns a null value to each parameter that represents an argument that is not present on the command line. Thus the $4 and $5 parameters have null values in this example.

shift: PROMOTES COMMAND-LINE ARGUMENTS

The shift builtin promotes each command-line argument. The first argument (which was $1) is discarded. The second argument (which was $2) becomes the first argument (now $1), the third becomes the second, and so on. Because no "unshift" command exists, you cannot bring back arguments that have been discarded. An optional argument to shift specifies the number of positions to shift (and the number of arguments to discard); the default is 1.

The following **demo_shift** script is called with three arguments. Double quotation marks around the arguments to echo preserve the spacing of the output. The program displays the arguments and shifts them repeatedly until no more arguments are left to shift:

```
$ cat demo_shift
echo "arg1= $1     arg2= $2     arg3= $3"
shift
echo "arg1= $1     arg2= $2     arg3= $3"
shift
echo "arg1= $1     arg2= $2     arg3= $3"
shift
echo "arg1= $1     arg2= $2     arg3= $3"
shift
$ ./demo_shift alice helen zach
arg1= alice    arg2= helen    arg3= zach
arg1= helen    arg2= zach     arg3=
arg1= zach     arg2=    arg3=
arg1=     arg2=    arg3=
```

Repeatedly using shift is a convenient way to loop over all command-line arguments in shell scripts that expect an arbitrary number of arguments. See page 403 for a shell script that uses shift.

set: INITIALIZES COMMAND-LINE ARGUMENTS

When you call the set builtin with one or more arguments, it assigns the values of the arguments to the positional parameters, starting with $1 (not available in tcsh). The following script uses set to assign values to the positional parameters $1, $2, and $3:

```
$ cat set_it
set this is it
echo $3 $2 $1
$ ./set_it
it is this
```

Combining command substitution (page 340) with the set builtin is a convenient way to get standard output of a command in a form that can be easily manipulated in a shell script. The following script shows how to use date and set to provide the date in a useful format. The first command shows the output of date. Then cat displays the contents of the **dateset** script. The first command in this script uses command substitution to set the positional parameters to the output of the date utility. The next command, **echo $***, displays all positional parameters resulting from the previous set. Subsequent commands display the values of parameters **$1**, **$2**, **$3**, and **$6**. The final command displays the date in a format you can use in a letter or report:

```
$ date
Wed Aug 13 17:35:29 PDT 2008
$ cat dateset
set $(date)
echo $*
echo
echo "Argument 1: $1"
echo "Argument 2: $2"
echo "Argument 3: $3"
echo "Argument 6: $6"
echo
echo "$2 $3, $6"
$ ./dateset
Wed Aug 13 17:35:34 PDT 2008

Argument 1: Wed
Argument 2: Aug
Argument 3: 13
Argument 6: 2008

Aug 13, 2008
```

You can also use the +*format* argument to date (page 655) to modify the format of its output.

When used without any arguments, set displays a list of the shell variables that are set, including user-created variables and keyword variables. Under bash, this list is the same as that displayed by declare and typeset when they are called without any arguments.

The set builtin also accepts options that let you customize the behavior of the shell (not available in tcsh). For more information refer to "set ±o: Turns Shell Features On and Off" on page 331.

$* AND $@: REPRESENT ALL COMMAND-LINE ARGUMENTS

The **$*** parameter represents all command-line arguments, as the **display_all** program demonstrates:

```
$ cat display_all
echo All arguments are $*

$ ./display_all a b c d e f g h i j k l m n o p
All arguments are a b c d e f g h i j k l m n o p
```

It is a good idea to enclose references to positional parameters between double quotation marks. The quotation marks are particularly important when you are using positional parameters as arguments to commands. Without double quotation marks, a positional parameter that is not set or that has a null value disappears:

```
$ cat showargs
echo "$0 was called with $# arguments, the first is :$1:."

$ ./showargs a b c
./showargs was called with 3 arguments, the first is :a:.
$ echo $xx

$ ./showargs $xx a b c
./showargs was called with 3 arguments, the first is :a:.
$ ./showargs "$xx" a b c
./showargs was called with 4 arguments, the first is ::.
```

The **showargs** script displays the number of arguments (**$#**) followed by the value of the first argument enclosed between colons. In the preceding example, **showargs** is initially called with three simple arguments. Next the echo command demonstrates that the **$xx** variable, which is not set, has a null value. In the final two calls to **showargs**, the first argument is **$xx**. In the first case the command line becomes **showargs a b c**; the shell passes **showargs** three arguments. In the second case the command line becomes **showargs "" a b c**, which results in calling **showargs** with four arguments. The difference in the two calls to **showargs** illustrates a subtle potential problem that you should keep in mind when using positional parameters that may not be set or that may have a null value.

"$*" versus "$@"   The **$*** and **$@** parameters work the same way except when they are enclosed within double quotation marks. Using "**$***" yields a single argument (with SPACEs or the value of the first character of **IFS** [page 301] between the positional parameters), whereas using "**$@**" produces a list wherein each positional parameter is a separate argument. This difference typically makes "**$@**" more useful than "**$***" in shell scripts.

The following scripts help explain the difference between these two special parameters. In the second line of both scripts, the single quotation marks keep the shell from interpreting the enclosed special characters so they are passed to echo and displayed as themselves. The **bb1** script shows that **set "$*"** assigns multiple arguments to the first command-line parameter:

```
$ cat bb1
set "$*"
echo $# parameters with '"$*"'
echo 1: $1
echo 2: $2
echo 3: $3
$ ./bb1 a b c
1 parameters with "$*"
1: a b c
2:
3:
```

The **bb2** script shows that **set "$@"** assigns each argument to a different command-line parameter:

```
$ cat bb2
set "$@"
echo $# parameters with '"$@"'
echo 1: $1
echo 2: $2
echo 3: $3

$ ./bb2 a b c
3 parameters with "$@"
1: a
2: b
3: c
```

EXPANDING NULL AND UNSET VARIABLES

The expression **${name}** (or just **$name** if it is not ambiguous) expands to the value of the **name** variable. If **name** is null or not set, bash expands **${name}** to a null string. The Bourne Again Shell provides the following alternatives to accepting the expanded null string as the value of the variable:

- Use a default value for the variable.

- Use a default value and assign that value to the variable.

- Display an error.

You can choose one of these alternatives by using a modifier with the variable name. In addition, you can use **set –o nounset** (page 333) to cause bash to display an error and exit from a script whenever an unset variable is referenced.

:– USES A DEFAULT VALUE

The **:–** modifier uses a default value in place of a null or unset variable while allowing a nonnull variable to represent itself:

${name:–default}

The shell interprets **:–** as "If *name* is null or unset, expand *default* and use the expanded value in place of *name*; else use *name*." The following command lists the contents of the directory named by the **LIT** variable. If **LIT** is null or unset, it lists the contents of **/home/max/literature**:

```
$ ls ${LIT:-/home/max/literature}
```

The default can itself have variable references that are expanded:

```
$ ls ${LIT:-$HOME/literature}
```

:= ASSIGNS A DEFAULT VALUE

The **:–** modifier does not change the value of a variable. However, you can change the value of a null or unset variable to its default in a script by using the **:=** modifier:

${name:=default}

The shell expands the expression *${name:=default}* in the same manner as it expands *${name:−default}* but also sets the value of *name* to the expanded value of *default*. If a script contains a line such as the following and **LIT** is unset or null at the time this line is executed, **LIT** is assigned the value **/home/max/literature**:

```
$ ls ${LIT:=/home/max/literature}
```

: (null) builtin   Shell scripts frequently start with the : (null) builtin followed on the same line by the := expansion modifier to set any variables that may be null or unset. The : builtin evaluates each token in the remainder of the command line but does not execute any commands. Without the leading colon (:), the shell evaluates and attempts to execute the "command" that results from the evaluation.

Use the following syntax to set a default for a null or unset variable in a shell script (a SPACE follows the first colon):

> :   *${name:=default}*

When a script needs a directory for temporary files and uses the value of **TEMPDIR** for the name of this directory, the following line assigns to **TEMPDIR** the value **/tmp** if **TEMPDIR** is null:

```
: ${TEMPDIR:=/tmp}
```

:? DISPLAYS AN ERROR MESSAGE

Sometimes a script needs the value of a variable but you cannot supply a reasonable default at the time you write the script. If the variable is null or unset, the **:?** modifier causes the script to display an error message and terminate with an exit status of 1:

> *${name:?message}*

If you omit *message*, the shell displays the default error message (**parameter null or not set**). Interactive shells do not exit when you use **:?**. In the following command, **TESTDIR** is not set so the shell displays on standard error the expanded value of the string following **:?**. In this case the string includes command substitution for date with the %T format, followed by the string **error, variable not set**.

```
cd ${TESTDIR:?$(date +%T) error, variable not set.}
bash: TESTDIR: 16:16:14 error, variable not set.
```

BUILTIN COMMANDS

Builtin commands, which were introduced in Chapter 5, do not fork a new process when you execute them. This section discusses the type, read, exec, trap, kill, and getopts builtins. Table 10-6 on page 459 lists many bash builtin commands. See Table 9-10 on page 387 for a list of tcsh builtins.

type: DISPLAYS INFORMATION ABOUT A COMMAND

The type builtin (use which under tcsh) provides information about a command:

```
$ type cat echo who if lt
cat is hashed (/bin/cat)
echo is a shell builtin
who is /usr/bin/who
if is a shell keyword
lt is aliased to 'ls -ltrh | tail'
```

The preceding output shows the files that would be executed if you gave **cat** or **who** as a command. Because cat has already been called from the current shell, it is in the *hash table* (page 957) and type reports that **cat is hashed**. The output also shows that a call to **echo** runs the echo builtin, **if** is a keyword, and **lt** is an alias.

read: ACCEPTS USER INPUT

One of the most common uses for user-created variables is storing information that a user enters in response to a prompt. Using read, scripts can accept input from the user and store that input in variables. See page 371 for information about reading user input under tcsh. The read builtin reads one line from standard input and assigns the words on the line to one or more variables:

```
$ cat read1
echo -n "Go ahead: "
read firstline
echo "You entered: $firstline"
$ ./read1
Go ahead: This is a line.
You entered: This is a line.
```

The first line of the **read1** script uses echo to prompt for a line of text. The **–n** option suppresses the following NEWLINE, allowing you to enter a line of text on the same line as the prompt. The second line reads the text into the variable **firstline**. The third line verifies the action of read by displaying the value of **firstline**. The variable is quoted (along with the text string) in this example because you, as the script writer, cannot anticipate which characters the user might enter in response to the prompt. Consider what would happen if the variable were not quoted and the user entered * in response to the prompt:

```
$ cat read1_no_quote
echo -n "Go ahead: "
read firstline
echo You entered: $firstline
$ ./read1_no_quote
Go ahead: *
You entered: read1 read1_no_quote script.1
$ ls
read1   read1_no_quote    script.1
```

The ls command lists the same words as the script, demonstrating that the shell expands the asterisk into a list of files in the working directory. When the variable **$firstline** is surrounded by double quotation marks, the shell does not expand the asterisk. Thus the **read1** script behaves correctly:

```
$ ./read1
Go ahead: *
You entered: *
```

REPLY   The read builtin includes several features that can make it easier to use. For example, when you do not specify a variable to receive read's input, bash puts the input into the variable named **REPLY**. You can use the **–p** option to prompt the user instead of using a separate echo command. The following **read1a** script performs exactly the same task as **read1**:

```
$ cat read1a
read -p "Go ahead: "
echo "You entered: $REPLY"
```

The **read2** script prompts for a command line, reads the user's response, and assigns it to the variable **cmd**. The script then attempts to execute the command line that results from the expansion of the **cmd** variable:

```
$ cat read2
read -p "Enter a command: " cmd
$cmd
echo "Thanks"
```

In the following example, **read2** reads a command line that calls the echo builtin. The shell executes the command and then displays **Thanks**. Next **read2** reads a command line that executes the who utility:

```
$ ./read2
Enter a command: echo Please display this message.
Please display this message.
Thanks
$ ./read2
Enter a command: who
max       pts/4        Jun 17 07:50   (:0.0)
sam       pts/12       Jun 17 11:54   (bravo.example.com)
Thanks
```

If **cmd** does not expand into a valid command line, the shell issues an error message:

```
$ ./read2
Enter a command: xxx
./read2: line 2: xxx: command not found
Thanks
```

The **read3** script reads values into three variables. The read builtin assigns one word (a sequence of nonblank characters) to each variable:

```
$ cat read3
read -p "Enter something: " word1 word2 word3
echo "Word 1 is: $word1"
echo "Word 2 is: $word2"
echo "Word 3 is: $word3"
```

```
$ ./read3
Enter something: this is something
Word 1 is: this
Word 2 is: is
Word 3 is: something
```

When you enter more words than read has variables, read assigns one word to each variable, assigning all leftover words to the last variable. Both **read1** and **read2** assigned the first word and all leftover words to the one variable the scripts each had to work with. In the following example, read assigns five words to three variables: It assigns the first word to the first variable, the second word to the second variable, and the third through fifth words to the third variable.

```
$ ./read3
Enter something: this is something else, really.
Word 1 is:  this
Word 2 is:  is
Word 3 is:  something else, really.
```

Table 10-4 lists some of the options supported by the read builtin.

Table 10-4   read options

Option	Function
–a *aname*	(array) Assigns each word of input to an element of array *aname*.
–d *delim*	(delimiter) Uses *delim* to terminate the input instead of NEWLINE.
–e	(Readline) If input is coming from a keyboard, uses the Readline Library (page 318) to get input.
–n *num*	(number of characters) Reads *num* characters and returns. As soon as the user types *num* characters, read returns; there is no need to press RETURN.
–p *prompt*	(prompt) Displays *prompt* on standard error without a terminating NEWLINE before reading input. Displays *prompt* only when input comes from the keyboard.
–s	(silent) Does not echo characters.

–u*n*	(file descriptor) Uses the integer *n* as the file descriptor that read takes its input from. Thus
	
	`    read –u4 arg1 arg2`
	
	is equivalent to
	
	`    read arg1 arg2 <&4`
	
	See "File Descriptors" (page 431) for a discussion of redirection and file descriptors.

The read builtin returns an exit status of 0 if it successfully reads any data. It has a nonzero exit status when it reaches the EOF (end of file).

The following example runs a **while** loop from the command line. It takes its input from the **names** file and terminates after reading the last line from **names**.

```
$ cat names
Alice Jones
Robert Smith
Alice Paulson
John Q. Public

$ while read first rest
> do
> echo $rest, $first
> done < names
Jones, Alice
Smith, Robert
Paulson, Alice
Q. Public, John
$
```

The placement of the redirection symbol (**<**) for the **while** structure is critical. It is important that you place the redirection symbol at the **done** statement and not at the call to read.

optional   Each time you redirect input, the shell opens the input file and repositions the read pointer at the start of the file:

```
$ read line1 < names; echo $line1; read line2 < names; echo $line2
Alice Jones
Alice Jones
```

Here each read opens **names** and starts at the beginning of the **names** file. In the following example, **names** is opened once, as standard input of the subshell created by the parentheses. Each read then reads successive lines of standard input:

```
$ (read line1; echo $line1; read line2; echo $line2) < names
Alice Jones
Robert Smith
```

Another way to get the same effect is to open the input file with **exec** and hold it open (refer to "File Descriptors" on page 431):

```
$ exec 3< names
$ read -u3 line1; echo $line1; read -u3 line2; echo $line2
Alice Jones
Robert Smith
$ exec 3<&-
```

exec: EXECUTES A COMMAND OR REDIRECTS FILE DESCRIPTORS

The exec builtin (not available in tcsh) has two primary purposes: to run a command without creating a new process and to redirect a file descriptor—including standard input, output, or error—of a shell script from within the script (page 431). When the shell executes a command that is not built into the shell, it typically creates a new process. The new process inherits environment (global or exported) variables from its parent but does not inherit variables that are not exported by the parent. (For more information refer to "Locality of Variables" on page 436.) In contrast, exec executes a command in place of (overlays) the current process.

exec: EXECUTES A COMMAND

The exec builtin used for running a command has the following syntax:

exec command arguments

exec versus . (dot) Insofar as exec runs a command in the environment of the original process, it is similar to the . (dot) command (page 274). However, unlike the . command, which can run only shell scripts, exec can run both scripts and compiled programs. Also, whereas the . command returns control to the original script when it finishes running, exec does not. Finally, the . command gives the new program access to local variables, whereas exec does not.

exec does not
return control Because the shell does not create a new process when you use exec, the command runs more quickly. However, because exec does not return control to the original program, it can be used only as the last command in a script. The following script shows that control is not returned to the script:

```
$ cat exec_demo
who
exec date
echo "This line is never displayed."

$ ./exec_demo
zach      pts/7    May 30  7:05 (bravo.example.com)
hls       pts/1    May 30  6:59 (:0.0)
Mon May 25 11:42:56 PDT 2009
```

The next example, a modified version of the **out** script (page 403), uses exec to execute the final command the script runs. Because **out** runs either cat or less and then terminates, the new version, named **out2**, uses exec with both cat and less:

```
$ cat out2
if [ $# -eq 0 ]
    then
        echo "Usage: out2 [-v] filenames" 1>&2
        exit 1
fi
if [ "$1" = "-v" ]
    then
        shift
        exec less "$@"
    else
        exec cat -- "$@"
fi
```

exec: REDIRECTS INPUT AND OUTPUT

The second major use of exec is to redirect a file descriptor—including standard input, output, or error—from within a script. The next command causes all subsequent input to a script that would have come from standard input to come from the file named **infile**:

```
exec < infile
```

Similarly the following command redirects standard output and standard error to **outfile** and **errfile**, respectively:

```
exec > outfile 2> errfile
```

When you use exec in this manner, the current process is not replaced with a new process, and exec can be followed by other commands in the script.

/dev/tty When you redirect the output from a script to a file, you must make sure the user sees any prompts the script displays. The **/dev/tty** device is a pseudonym for the screen the user is working on; you can use this device to refer to the user's screen without knowing which device it is. (The tty utility displays the name of the device you are using.) By redirecting the output from a script to **/dev/tty**, you ensure that prompts and messages go to the user's terminal, regardless of which terminal the user is logged in on. Messages sent to **/dev/tty** are also not diverted if standard output and standard error from the script are redirected.

The **to_screen1** script sends output to three places: standard output, standard error, and the user's screen. When run with standard output and standard error redirected, **to_screen1** still displays the message sent to **/dev/tty** on the user's screen. The **out** and **err** files hold the output sent to standard output and standard error.

```
$ cat to_screen1
echo "message to standard output"
echo "message to standard error" 1>&2
echo "message to the user" > /dev/tty

$ ./to_screen1 > out 2> err
message to the user
$ cat out
message to standard output
$ cat err
message to standard error
```

The following command redirects the output from a script to the user's screen:

```
exec > /dev/tty
```

Putting this command at the beginning of the previous script changes where the output goes. In **to_screen2**, exec redirects standard output to the user's screen so the **> /dev/tty** is superfluous. Following the exec command, all output sent to standard output goes to **/dev/tty** (the screen). Output to standard error is not affected.

```
$ cat to_screen2
exec > /dev/tty
echo "message to standard output"
echo "message to standard error" 1>&2
echo "message to the user" > /dev/tty

$ ./to_screen2 > out 2> err
message to standard output
message to the user
```

One disadvantage of using exec to redirect the output to **/dev/tty** is that all subsequent output is redirected unless you use exec again in the script.

You can also redirect the input to read (standard input) so that it comes from **/dev/tty** (the keyboard):

```
read name < /dev/tty
```

or

```
exec < /dev/tty
```

trap: CATCHES A SIGNAL

A *signal* is a report to a process about a condition. Linux uses signals to report interrupts generated by the user (for example, pressing the interrupt key) as well as bad system calls, broken pipes, illegal instructions, and other conditions. The trap builtin (tcsh uses onintr) catches (traps) one or more signals, allowing you to direct the actions a script takes when it receives a specified signal.

This discussion covers six signals that are significant when you work with shell scripts. Table 10-5 lists these signals, the signal numbers that systems often ascribe to them, and the conditions that usually generate each signal. Give the command **kill –l** (lowercase "ell"), **trap –l** (lowercase "ell"), or **man 7 signal** to display a list of all signal names.

Table 10-5 Signals

Type	Name	Number	Generating condition
Not a real signal	EXIT	0	Exit because of exit command or reaching the end of the program (not an actual signal but useful in trap)
Hang up	SIGHUP or HUP	1	Disconnect the line
Terminal interrupt	SIGINT or INT	2	Press the interrupt key (usually CONTROL-C)
Quit	SIGQUIT or QUIT	3	Press the quit key (usually CONTROL-SHIFT-| or CONTROL-SHIFT-\)
Kill	SIGKILL or KILL	9	The kill builtin with the **–9** option (cannot be trapped; use only as a last resort)
Software termination	SIGTERM or TERM	15	Default of the kill command
Stop	SIGTSTP or TSTP	20	Press the suspend key (usually CONTROL-Z)
Debug	DEBUG		Executes *commands* specified in the trap statement after each command (not an actual signal but useful in trap)
Error	ERR		Executes *commands* specified in the trap statement after each command that returns a nonzero exit status (not an actual signal but useful in trap)

When it traps a signal, a script takes whatever action you specify: It can remove files or finish other processing as needed, display a message, terminate execution immediately, or ignore the signal. If you do not use trap in a script, any of the six actual signals listed in Table 10-5 (not EXIT, DEBUG, or ERR) will terminate the script. Because a process cannot trap a KILL signal, you can use **kill –KILL** (or **kill –9**) as a last resort to terminate a script or other process. (See page 456 for more information on kill.)

The trap command has the following syntax:

*trap ['**commands**'] [signal]*

The optional ***commands*** specifies the commands that the shell executes when it catches one of the signals specified by ***signal***. The ***signal*** can be a signal name or number—for example, INT or 2. If ***commands*** is not present, trap resets the trap to its initial condition, which is usually to exit from the script.

Quotation marks   The trap builtin does not require single quotation marks around ***commands*** as shown in the preceding syntax, but it is a good practice to use them. The single quotation marks cause shell variables within the ***commands*** to be expanded when the signal occurs, rather than when the shell evaluates the arguments to trap. Even if you do not use any shell variables in the ***commands,*** you need to enclose any command that takes arguments within either single or double quotation marks. Quoting ***commands*** causes the shell to pass to trap the entire command as a single argument.

After executing the ***commands,*** the shell resumes executing the script where it left off. If you want trap to prevent a script from exiting when it receives a signal but not to run any commands explicitly, you can specify a null (empty) ***commands*** string, as shown in the **locktty** script (page 419). The following command traps signal number 15, after which the script continues:

```
trap '' 15
```

The following script demonstrates how the trap builtin can catch the terminal interrupt signal (2). You can use SIGINT, INT, or 2 to specify this signal. The script returns an exit status of 1:

```
$ cat inter
#!/bin/bash
trap 'echo PROGRAM INTERRUPTED; exit 1' INT
while true
do
    echo "Program running."
    sleep 1
done
$ ./inter
Program running.
Program running.
Program running.
CONTROL-C
PROGRAM INTERRUPTED
$
```

: (null) builtin The second line of **inter** sets up a trap for the terminal interrupt signal using INT. When trap catches the signal, the shell executes the two commands between the single quotation marks in the trap command. The echo builtin displays the message **PROGRAM INTERRUPTED**, exit terminates the shell running the script, and the parent shell displays a prompt. If exit were not there, the shell would return control to the **while** loop after displaying the message. The **while** loop repeats continuously until the script receives a signal because the true utility always returns a *true* exit status. In place of true you can use the **:** (null) builtin, which is written as a colon and always returns a 0 (*true*) status.

The trap builtin frequently removes temporary files when a script is terminated prematurely, thereby ensuring the files are not left to clutter the filesystem. The following shell script, named **addbanner**, uses two traps to remove a temporary file when the script terminates normally or owing to a hangup, software interrupt, quit, or software termination signal:

```
$ cat addbanner
#!/bin/bash
script=$(basename $0)

if [ ! -r "$HOME/banner" ]
    then
        echo "$script: need readable $HOME/banner file" 1>&2
        exit 1
fi

trap 'exit 1' 1 2 3 15
trap 'rm /tmp/$$.$script 2> /dev/null' 0

for file
do
    if [ -r "$file" -a -w "$file" ]
        then
            cat $HOME/banner $file > /tmp/$$.$script
            cp /tmp/$$.$script $file
            echo "$script: banner added to $file" 1>&2
        else
            echo "$script: need read and write permission for $file" 1>&2
    fi
done
```

When called with one or more filename arguments, **addbanner** loops through the files, adding a header to the top of each. This script is useful when you use a standard format at the top of your documents, such as a standard layout for memos, or when you want to add a standard header to shell scripts. The header is kept in a file named **~/banner**. Because **addbanner** uses the **HOME** variable, which contains the pathname of the user's home directory, the script can be used by several users without modification. If Max had written the script with **/home/max** in place of **$HOME** and then given the script to Zach, either Zach would have had to change it or **addbanner** would have used Max's **banner** file when Zach ran it (assuming Zach had read permission for the file).

The first trap in **addbanner** causes it to exit with a status of 1 when it receives a hangup, software interrupt (terminal interrupt or quit signal), or software termination signal. The second trap uses a 0 in place of **signal-number**, which causes trap to execute its command argument *whenever* the script exits because it receives an exit command or reaches its end. Together these traps remove a temporary file whether the script terminates normally or prematurely. Standard error of the second trap is sent to **/dev/null** whenever trap attempts to remove a nonexistent temporary file. In those cases rm sends an error message to standard error; because standard error is redirected, the user does not see the message.

See page 419 for another example that uses trap.

kill: ABORTS A PROCESS

The kill builtin sends a signal to a process or job; kill has the following syntax:

> *kill [–signal] PID*

where *signal* is the signal name or number (for example, INT or 2) and *PID* is the process identification number of the process that is to receive the signal. You can specify a job number (page 135) as %*n* in place of *PID*. If you omit *signal*, kill sends a TERM (software termination, number 15) signal. For more information on signal names and numbers, see Table 10-5 on page 453.

The following command sends the TERM signal to job number 1, regardless of whether it is in the foreground (running) or in the background (running or stopped):

```
$ kill -TERM %1
```

Because TERM is the default signal for kill, you can also give this command as **kill %1**. Give the command **kill –l** (lowercase "l") to display a list of signal names.

A program that is interrupted can leave matters in an unpredictable state: Temporary files may be left behind (when they are normally removed), and permissions may be changed. A well-written application traps, or detects, signals and cleans up before exiting. Most carefully written applications trap the INT, QUIT, and TERM signals.

To terminate a program, first try INT (press CONTROL-C, if the job running is in the foreground). Because an application can be written to ignore these signals, you may need to use the KILL signal, which cannot be trapped or ignored; it is a "sure kill." Refer to page 729 for more information on kill. See also killall (page 731).

getopts: PARSES OPTIONS

The getopts builtin (not available in tcsh) parses command-line arguments, making it easier to write programs that follow the Linux argument conventions. The syntax for getopts is

> *getopts optstring varname [arg ...]*

where *optstring* is a list of the valid option letters, *varname* is the variable that receives the options one at a time, and *arg* is the optional list of parameters to be processed. If *arg* is not present, getopts processes the command-line arguments. If *optstring* starts with a colon (:), the script must take care of generating error messages; otherwise, getopts generates error messages.

The getopts builtin uses the **OPTIND** (option index) and **OPTARG** (option argument) variables to track and store option-related values. When a shell script starts, the value of **OPTIND** is 1. Each time getopts is called and locates an argument, it increments **OPTIND** to the index of the next option to be processed. If the option takes an argument, bash assigns the value of the argument to **OPTARG**.

To indicate that an option takes an argument, follow the corresponding letter in *optstring* with a colon (:). The option string **dxo:lt:r** indicates that getopts should search for –d, –x, –o, –l, –t, and –r options and that the –o and –t options take arguments.

Using getopts as the *test-command* in a **while** control structure allows you to loop over the options one at a time. The getopts builtin checks the option list for options that are in *optstring*. Each time through the loop, getopts stores the option letter it finds in *varname*.

Suppose that you want to write a program that can take three options:

1. A **–b** option indicates that the program should ignore whitespace at the start of input lines.

2. A **–t** option followed by the name of a directory indicates that the program should store temporary files in that directory. Otherwise, it should use **/tmp**.

3. A **–u** option indicates that the program should translate all output to uppercase.

In addition, the program should ignore all other options and end option processing when it encounters two hyphens (––).

The problem is to write the portion of the program that determines which options the user has supplied. The following solution does not use getopts:

```
SKIPBLANKS=
TMPDIR=/tmp
CASE=lower
while [[ "$1" = -* ]] # [[ = ]] does pattern match
do
    case $1 in
        -b)     SKIPBLANKS=TRUE ;;
        -t)     if [ -d "$2" ]
                    then
                    TMPDIR=$2
                    shift
                else
                    echo "$0: -t takes a directory argument." >&2
                    exit 1
                fi ;;
        -u)     CASE=upper ;;
        --)     break   ;;      # Stop processing options
        *)      echo "$0: Invalid option $1 ignored." >&2 ;;
    esac
    shift
done
```

This program fragment uses a loop to check and shift arguments while the argument is not ––. As long as the argument is not two hyphens, the program continues to loop through a **case** statement that checks for possible options. The –– **case** label breaks out of the **while** loop. The ✻ **case** label recognizes any option; it appears as the last **case** label to catch any unknown options, displays an error message, and allows processing to continue. On each pass through the loop, the program uses shift to access the next argument. If an option takes an argument, the program uses an extra shift to get past that argument.

The following program fragment processes the same options, but uses getopts:

```
SKIPBLANKS=
TMPDIR=/tmp
CASE=lower

while getopts :bt:u arg
do
    case $arg in
        b)      SKIPBLANKS=TRUE ;;
        t)      if [ -d "$OPTARG" ]
                    then
                    TMPDIR=$OPTARG
                else
                    echo "$0: $OPTARG is not a directory." >&2
                    exit 1
                fi ;;
        u)      CASE=upper ;;
        :)      echo "$0: Must supply an argument to -$OPTARG." >&2
                exit 1 ;;
        \?)     echo "Invalid option -$OPTARG ignored." >&2 ;;
        esac
done
```

In this version of the code, the **while** structure evaluates the getopts builtin each time control transfers to the top of the loop. The getopts builtin uses the **OPTIND** variable to keep track of the index of the argument it is to process the next time it is called. There is no need to call shift in this example.

In the getopts version of the script, the **case** patterns do not start with a hyphen because the value of **arg** is just the option letter (getopts strips off the hyphen). Also, getopts recognizes –– as the end of the options, so you do not have to specify it explicitly, as in the **case** statement in the first example.

Because you tell getopts which options are valid and which require arguments, it can detect errors in the command line and handle them in two ways. This example uses a leading colon in *optstring* to specify that you check for and handle errors in your code; when getopts finds an invalid option, it sets *varname* to ? and **OPTARG** to the option letter. When it finds an option that is missing an argument, getopts sets *varname* to : and **OPTARG** to the option lacking an argument.

The \? **case** pattern specifies the action to take when getopts detects an invalid option. The : **case** pattern specifies the action to take when getopts detects a missing option argument. In both cases getopts does not write any error message but rather leaves that task to you.

If you omit the leading colon from *optstring*, both an invalid option and a missing option argument cause *varname* to be assigned the string ?. **OPTARG** is not set and getopts writes its own diagnostic message to standard error. Generally this method is less desirable because you have less control over what the user sees when an error occurs.

Using getopts will not necessarily make your programs shorter. Its principal advantages are that it provides a uniform programming interface and that it enforces standard option handling.

A Partial List of Builtins

Table 10-6 lists some of the bash builtins. You can use type (page 447) to see if a command runs a builtin. See "Listing bash builtins" on page 141 for instructions on how to display complete lists of builtins.

Table 10-6   bash builtins

Builtin	Function
:	Returns 0 or *true* (the null builtin; page 455)
. (dot)	Executes a shell script as part of the current process (page 274)
bg	Puts a suspended job in the background (page 287)
break	Exits from a looping control structure (page 420)
cd	Changes to another working directory (page 87)
continue	Starts with the next iteration of a looping control structure (page 420)
echo	Displays its arguments (page 57)
eval	Scans and evaluates the command line (page 329)
exec	Executes a shell script or program in place of the current process (page 450)
exit	Exits from the current shell (usually the same as CONTROL-D from an interactive shell; page 440)
export	Places the value of a variable in the calling environment (makes it global; page 436)
fg	Brings a job from the background into the foreground (page 286)
getopts	Parses arguments to a shell script (page 456)
jobs	Displays a list of background jobs (page 285)
kill	Sends a signal to a process or job (page 729)
pwd	Displays the name of the working directory (page 82)

Table 10-6   bash builtins (continued)

Builtin	Function
read	Reads a line from standard input (page 447)
readonly	Declares a variable to be readonly (page 295)
set	Sets shell flags or command-line argument variables; with no argument, lists all variables (pages 331, 366, and 442)
shift	Promotes each command-line argument (page 442)
test	Compares arguments (pages 399 and 854)
times	Displays total times for the current shell and its children
trap	Traps a signal (page 453)
type	Displays how each argument would be interpreted as a command (page 447)
umask	Returns the value of the file-creation mask (page 870)
unset	Removes a variable or function (page 294)
wait	Waits for a background process to terminate (page 391)

Expressions

An expression comprises constants, variables, and operators that the shell can process to return a value. This section covers arithmetic, logical, and conditional expressions as well as operators. Table 10-8 on page 463 lists the bash operators.

Arithmetic Evaluation

The Bourne Again Shell can perform arithmetic assignments and evaluate many different types of arithmetic expressions, all using integers. The shell performs arithmetic assignments in a number of ways. One is with arguments to the let builtin:

```
$ let "VALUE=VALUE * 10 + NEW"
```

In the preceding example, the variables **VALUE** and **NEW** contain integer values. Within a let statement you do not need to use dollar signs ($) in front of variable names. Double quotation marks must enclose a single argument, or expression, that contains SPACEs. Because most expressions contain SPACEs and need to be quoted, bash accepts *((expression))* as a synonym for *let "expression"*, obviating the need for both quotation marks and dollar signs:

```
$ ((VALUE=VALUE * 10 + NEW))
```

You can use either form wherever a command is allowed and can remove the SPACEs if you like. In the following example, the asterisk (*) does not need to be quoted because the shell does not perform pathname expansion on the right side of an assignment (page 293):

```
$ let VALUE=VALUE*10+NEW
```

Because each argument to let is evaluated as a separate expression, you can assign values to more than one variable on a single line:

```
$ let "COUNT = COUNT + 1" VALUE=VALUE*10+NEW
```

You need to use commas to separate multiple assignments within a set of double parentheses:

```
$ ((COUNT = COUNT + 1, VALUE=VALUE*10+NEW))
```

Arithmetic evaluation versus arithmetic expansion

tip Arithmetic evaluation differs from arithmetic expansion. As explained on page 338, arithmetic expansion uses the syntax *$((expression))*, evaluates *expression*, and replaces *$((expression))* with the result. You can use arithmetic expansion to display the value of an expression or to assign that value to a variable.

Arithmetic evaluation uses the *let expression* or *((expression))* syntax, evaluates *expression*, and returns a status code. You can use arithmetic evaluation to perform a logical comparison or an assignment.

Logical expressions   You can use the *((expression))* syntax for logical expressions, although that task is frequently left to *[[expression]]*. The next example expands the **age_check** script (page 338) to include logical arithmetic evaluation in addition to arithmetic expansion:

```
$ cat age2
#!/bin/bash
echo -n "How old are you? "
read age
if ((30 < age && age < 60)); then
        echo "Wow, in $((60-age)) years, you'll be 60!"
    else
        echo "You are too young or too old to play."
fi

$ ./age2
How old are you? 25
You are too young or too old to play.
```

The *test-statement* for the **if** structure evaluates two logical comparisons joined by a Boolean AND and returns 0 (*true*) if they are both *true* or 1 (*false*) otherwise.

LOGICAL EVALUATION (CONDITIONAL EXPRESSIONS)

The syntax of a conditional expression is

[[expression]]

where *expression* is a Boolean (logical) expression. You must precede a variable name with a dollar sign ($) within *expression*. The result of executing this builtin, as with the test builtin, is a return status. The *conditions* allowed within the brackets are almost a superset of those accepted by test (page 854). Where the test builtin uses **−a** as a Boolean AND operator, *[[expression]]* uses &&. Similarly, where test uses **−o** as a Boolean OR operator, *[[expression]]* uses ||.

To see how conditional expressions work, replace the line that tests **age** in the **age2** script with the following conditional expression. You must surround the [[and]] tokens with whitespace or a command terminator, and place dollar signs before the variables:

```
if [[ 30 < $age && $age < 60 ]]; then
```

You can also use test's relational operators –gt, –ge, –lt, –le, –eq, and –ne:

```
if [[ 30 -lt $age && $age -lt 60 ]]; then
```

String comparisons The test builtin tests whether strings are equal. The *[[expression]]* syntax adds comparison tests for string operators. The > and < operators compare strings for order (for example, "aa" < "bbb"). The = operator tests for pattern match, not just equality: *[[string = pattern]]* is *true* if **string** matches **pattern**. This operator is not symmetrical; the *pattern* must appear on the right side of the equal sign. For example, [[artist = a∗]] is *true* (= 0), whereas [[a∗ = artist]] is *false* (= 1):

```
$ [[ artist = a* ]]
$ echo $?
0
$ [[ a* = artist ]]
$ echo $?
1
```

The next example uses a command list that starts with a compound condition. The condition tests that the directory **bin** and the file **src/myscript.bash** exist. If this is *true*, cp copies **src/myscript.bash** to **bin/myscript**. If the copy succeeds, chmod makes **myscript** executable. If any of these steps fails, echo displays a message.

```
$ [[ -d bin && -f src/myscript.bash ]] && cp src/myscript.bash \
bin/myscript && chmod +x bin/myscript || echo "Cannot make \
executable version of myscript"
```

STRING PATTERN MATCHING

The Bourne Again Shell provides string pattern-matching operators that can manipulate pathnames and other strings. These operators can delete from strings prefixes or suffixes that match patterns. Table 10-7 lists the four operators.

Table 10-7 String operators

Operator	Function
#	Removes minimal matching prefixes
##	Removes maximal matching prefixes
%	Removes minimal matching suffixes
%%	Removes maximal matching suffixes

The syntax for these operators is

${varname op pattern}

where *op* is one of the operators listed in Table 10-7 and ***pattern*** is a match pattern similar to that used for filename generation. These operators are commonly used to manipulate pathnames to extract or remove components or to change suffixes:

```
$ SOURCEFILE=/usr/local/src/prog.c
$ echo ${SOURCEFILE#/*/}
local/src/prog.c
$ echo ${SOURCEFILE##/*/}
prog.c
$ echo ${SOURCEFILE%/*}
/usr/local/src
$ echo ${SOURCEFILE%%/*}

$ echo ${SOURCEFILE%.c}
/usr/local/src/prog
$ CHOPFIRST=${SOURCEFILE#/*/}
$ echo $CHOPFIRST
local/src/prog.c
$ NEXT=${CHOPFIRST%%/*}
$ echo $NEXT
local
```

Here the string-length operator, ${#***name***}, is replaced by the number of characters in the value of **name**:

```
$ echo $SOURCEFILE
/usr/local/src/prog.c
$ echo ${#SOURCEFILE}
21
```

OPERATORS

Arithmetic expansion and arithmetic evaluation in bash use the same syntax, precedence, and associativity of expressions as in the C language. Table 10-8 lists operators in order of decreasing precedence (priority of evaluation); each group of operators has equal precedence. Within an expression you can use parentheses to change the order of evaluation.

Table 10-8 Operators

Type of operator/operator	Function
Post	
var++ Postincrement	
var-- Postdecrement	
Pre	
++*var* Preincrement	
--*var* Predecrement	

Table 10-8 Operators (continued)

Type of operator/operator	Function
Unary	
	− Unary minus
	+ Unary plus
Negation	
	! Boolean NOT (logical negation)
	~ Complement (bitwise negation)
Exponentiation	
	** Exponent
Multiplication, division, remainder	
	* Multiplication
	/ Division
	% Remainder
Addition, subtraction	
	− Subtraction
	+ Addition
Bitwise shifts	
	<< Left bitwise shift
	>> Right bitwise shift
Comparison	
	<= Less than or equal
	>= Greater than or equal
	< Less than
	> Greater than
Equality, inequality	
	== Equality
	!= Inequality
Bitwise	
	& Bitwise AND
	^ Bitwise XOR (exclusive OR)
	| Bitwise OR

Table 10-8   Operators (continued)

Type of operator/operator	Function
Boolean (logical)	
&& Boolean AND	
|| Boolean OR	
Conditional evaluation	
? : Ternary operator	
Assignment	
=, *=, /=, %=, +=, –=, Assignment <<=, >>=, &=, ^=, |=	
Comma	
, Comma	

Pipe   The pipe token has higher precedence than operators. You can use pipes anywhere in a command that you can use simple commands. For example, the command line

```
$ cmd1 | cmd2 || cmd3 | cmd4 && cmd5 | cmd6
```

is interpreted as if you had typed

```
$ ((cmd1 | cmd2) || (cmd3 | cmd4)) && (cmd5 | cmd6)
```

Do not rely on rules of precedence: use parentheses

tip   Do not rely on the precedence rules when you use compound commands. Instead, use parentheses to explicitly state the order in which you want the shell to interpret the commands.

Increment and decrement   The postincrement, postdecrement, preincrement, and predecrement operators work with variables. The pre- operators, which appear in front of the variable name (as in **++COUNT** and **––VALUE**), first change the value of the variable (**++** adds 1; **––** subtracts 1) and then provide the result for use in the expression. The post- operators appear after the variable name (as in **COUNT++** and **VALUE––**); they first provide the unchanged value of the variable for use in the expression and then change the value of the variable.

```
$ N=10
$ echo $N
10
$ echo $((--N+3))
12
$ echo $N
9
$ echo $((N++ - 3))
6
$ echo $N
10
```

Remainder   The remainder operator (%) yields the remainder when its first operand is divided by its second. For example, the expression $((15\%7))$ has the value 1.

Boolean   The result of a Boolean operation is either 0 (*false*) or 1 (*true*).

The && (AND) and || (OR) Boolean operators are called *short-circuiting* operators. If the result of using one of these operators can be decided by looking only at the left operand, the right operand is not evaluated. The && operator causes the shell to test the exit status of the command preceding it. If the command succeeded, bash executes the next command; otherwise, it skips the remaining commands on the command line. You can use this construct to execute commands conditionally.

```
$ mkdir bkup && cp -r src bkup
```

This compound command creates the directory **bkup**. If mkdir succeeds, the contents of directory **src** is copied recursively to **bkup**.

The || separator also causes bash to test the exit status of the first command but has the opposite effect: The remaining command(s) are executed only if the first one failed (that is, exited with nonzero status).

```
$ mkdir bkup || echo "mkdir of bkup failed" >> /tmp/log
```

The exit status of a command list is the exit status of the last command in the list. You can group lists with parentheses. For example, you could combine the previous two examples as

```
$ (mkdir bkup && cp -r src bkup) || echo "mkdir failed" >> /tmp/log
```

In the absence of parentheses, && and || have equal precedence and are grouped from left to right. The following examples use the true and false utilities. These utilities do nothing and return *true* (0) and *false* (1) exit statuses, respectively:

```
$ false; echo $?
1
```

The $? variable holds the exit status of the preceding command (page 440). The next two commands yield an exit status of 1 (*false*):

```
$ true || false && false
$ echo $?
1
$ (true || false) && false
$ echo $?
1
```

Similarly the next two commands yield an exit status of 0 (*true*):

```
$ false && false || true
$ echo $?
0
$ (false && false) || true
$ echo $?
0
```

Because || and && have equal precedence, the parentheses in the two preceding pairs of examples do not change the order of operations.

Because the expression on the right side of a short-circuiting operator may never be executed, you must be careful when placing assignment statements in that location. The following example demonstrates what can happen:

```
$ ((N=10,Z=0))
$ echo $((N || ((Z+=1)) ))
1
$ echo $Z
0
```

Because the value of **N** is nonzero, the result of the || (OR) operation is 1 (*true*), no matter what the value of the right side is. As a consequence, ((**Z+=1**)) is never evaluated and **Z** is not incremented.

Ternary   The ternary operator, ? :, decides which of two expressions should be evaluated, based on the value returned by a third expression:

> *expression1 ? expression2 : expression3*

If *expression1* produces a *false* (0) value, *expression3* is evaluated; otherwise, *expression2* is evaluated. The value of the entire expression is the value of *expression2* or *expression3*, depending on which is evaluated. If *expression1* is *true*, *expression3* is not evaluated. If *expression1* is *false*, *expression2* is not evaluated.

```
$ ((N=10,Z=0,COUNT=1))
$ ((T=N>COUNT?++Z:--Z))
$ echo $T
1
$ echo $Z
1
```

Assignment   The assignment operators, such as **+=**, are shorthand notations. For example, **N+=3** is the same as ((**N=N+3**)).

Other bases   The following commands use the syntax *base#n* to assign base 2 (binary) values. First **v1** is assigned a value of 0101 (5 decimal) and then **v2** is assigned a value of 0110 (6 decimal). The echo utility verifies the decimal values.

```
$ ((v1=2#0101))
$ ((v2=2#0110))
$ echo "$v1 and $v2"
5 and 6
```

Next the bitwise AND operator (&) selects the bits that are on in both 5 (0101 binary) and 6 (0110 binary). The result is binary 0100, which is 4 decimal.

```
$ echo $(( v1 & v2 ))
4
```

The Boolean AND operator (&&) produces a result of 1 if both of its operands are nonzero and a result of 0 otherwise. The bitwise inclusive OR operator (|) selects the bits that are on in either 0101 or 0110, resulting in 0111, which is 7 decimal. The Boolean OR operator (||) produces a result of 1 if either of its operands is nonzero and a result of 0 otherwise.

```
$ echo $(( v1 && v2 ))
1
$ echo $(( v1 | v2 ))
7
$ echo $(( v1 || v2 ))
1
```

Next the bitwise exclusive OR operator (^) selects the bits that are on in either, but not both, of the operands 0101 and 0110, yielding 0011, which is 3 decimal. The Boolean NOT operator (!) produces a result of 1 if its operand is 0 and a result of 0 otherwise. Because the exclamation point in $((! v1)) is enclosed within double parentheses, it does not need to be escaped to prevent the shell from interpreting the exclamation point as a history event. The comparison operators produce a result of 1 if the comparison is *true* and a result of 0 otherwise.

```
$ echo $(( v1 ^ v2 ))
3
$ echo $(( ! v1 ))
0
$ echo $(( v1 < v2 ))
1
$ echo $(( v1 > v2 ))
0
```

SHELL PROGRAMS

The Bourne Again Shell has many features that make it a good programming language. The structures that bash provides are not a random assortment, but rather have been chosen to provide most of the structural features that are found in other procedural languages, such as C or Perl. A procedural language provides the following abilities:

- Declare, assign, and manipulate variables and constant data. The Bourne Again Shell provides string variables, together with powerful string operators, and integer variables, along with a complete set of arithmetic operators.

- Break large problems into small ones by creating subprograms. The Bourne Again Shell allows you to create functions and call scripts from other scripts. Shell functions can be called recursively; that is, a Bourne Again Shell function can call itself. You may not need to use recursion often, but it may allow you to solve some apparently difficult problems with ease.

- Execute statements conditionally, using statements such as **if**.

- Execute statements iteratively, using statements such as **while** and **for**.

- Transfer data to and from the program, communicating with both data files and users.

Programming languages implement these capabilities in different ways but with the same ideas in mind. When you want to solve a problem by writing a program, you must first figure out a procedure that leads you to a solution—that is, an *algorithm*. Typically you can implement the same algorithm in roughly the same way in different programming languages, using the same kinds of constructs in each language.

Chapter 8 and this chapter have introduced numerous bash features, many of which are useful for both interactive use and shell programming. This section develops two complete shell programs, demonstrating how to combine some of these features effectively. The programs are presented as problems for you to solve, with sample solutions provided.

A RECURSIVE SHELL SCRIPT

A recursive construct is one that is defined in terms of itself. Alternatively, you might say that a recursive program is one that can call itself. This concept may seem circular, but it need not be. To avoid circularity, a recursive definition must have a special case that is not self-referential. Recursive ideas occur in everyday life. For example, you can define an ancestor as your mother, your father, or one of their ancestors. This definition is not circular; it specifies unambiguously who your ancestors are: your mother or your father, or your mother's mother or father or your father's mother or father, and so on.

A number of Linux system utilities can operate recursively. See the **–R** option to the chmod (page 626), chown (page 631), and cp (page 640) utilities for examples.

Solve the following problem by using a recursive shell function:

Write a shell function named **makepath** that, given a pathname, creates all components in that pathname as directories. For example, the command **makepath a/b/c/d** should create directories **a**, **a/b**, **a/b/c**, and **a/b/c/d**. (The mkdir **–p** option creates directories in this manner. Solve the problem without using **mkdir –p**.)

One algorithm for a recursive solution follows:

1. Examine the path argument. If it is a null string or if it names an existing directory, do nothing and return.

2. If the path argument is a simple path component, create it (using mkdir) and return.

3. Otherwise, call **makepath** using the path prefix of the original argument. This step eventually creates all the directories up to the last component, which you can then create using mkdir.

In general, a recursive function must invoke itself with a simpler version of the problem than it was given until it is finally called with a simple case that does not need to call itself. Following is one possible solution based on this algorithm:

makepath
```
# This is a function
# Enter it at the keyboard, do not run it as a shell script
#
function makepath()
{
    if [[ ${#1} -eq 0 || -d "$1" ]]
        then
            return 0          # Do nothing
    fi
    if [[ "${1%/*}" = "$1" ]]
        then
            mkdir $1
            return $?
    fi
    makepath ${1%/*} || return 1
    mkdir $1
    return $?
}
```

In the test for a simple component (the **if** statement in the middle of the function), the left expression is the argument after the shortest suffix that starts with a / character has been stripped away (page 462). If there is no such character (for example, if **$1** is **max**), nothing is stripped off and the two sides are equal. If the argument is a simple filename preceded by a slash, such as **/usr**, the expression **${1%/*}** evaluates to a null string. To make the function work in this case, you must take two precautions: Put the left expression within quotation marks and ensure that the recursive function behaves sensibly when it is passed a null string as an argument. In general, good programs are robust: They should be prepared for borderline, invalid, or meaningless input and behave appropriately in such cases.

By giving the following command from the shell you are working in, you turn on debugging tracing so that you can watch the recursion work:

```
$ set -o xtrace
```

(Give the same command, but replace the hyphen with a plus sign (**+**) to turn debugging off.) With debugging turned on, the shell displays each line in its expanded form as it executes the line. A **+** precedes each line of debugging output.

In the following example, the first line that starts with **+** shows the shell calling **makepath**. The **makepath** function is initially called from the command line with arguments of **a/b/c**. It then calls itself with arguments of **a/b** and finally **a**. All the work is done (using mkdir) as each call to **makepath** returns.

```
$ ./makepath a/b/c
+ makepath a/b/c
+ [[ 5 -eq 0 ]]
+ [[ -d a/b/c ]]
+ [[ a/b = \a\/\b\/\c ]]
+ makepath a/b
+ [[ 3 -eq 0 ]]
+ [[ -d a/b ]]
+ [[ a = \a\/\b ]]
```

```
+ makepath a
+ [[ 1 -eq 0 ]]
+ [[ -d a ]]
+ [[ a = \a ]]
+ mkdir a
+ return 0
+ mkdir a/b
+ return 0
+ mkdir a/b/c
+ return 0
```

The function works its way down the recursive path and back up again.

It is instructive to invoke **makepath** with an invalid path and see what happens. The following example, which is run with debugging turned on, tries to create the path **/a/b**. Creating this path requires that you create directory **a** in the root directory. Unless you have permission to write to the root directory, you are not permitted to create this directory.

```
$ ./makepath /a/b
+ makepath /a/b
+ [[ 4 -eq 0 ]]
+ [[ -d /a/b ]]
+ [[ /a = \/\a\/\b ]]
+ makepath /a
+ [[ 2 -eq 0 ]]
+ [[ -d /a ]]
+ [[ '' = \/\a ]]
+ makepath
+ [[ 0 -eq 0 ]]
+ return 0
+ mkdir /a
mkdir: cannot create directory '/a': Permission denied
+ return 1
+ return 1
```

The recursion stops when **makepath** is denied permission to create the **/a** directory. The error returned is passed all the way back, so the original **makepath** exits with nonzero status.

Use local variables with recursive functions

tip   The preceding example glossed over a potential problem that you may encounter when you use a recursive function. During the execution of a recursive function, many separate instances of that function may be active simultaneously. All but one of them are waiting for their child invocation to complete.

Because functions run in the same environment as the shell that calls them, variables are implicitly shared by a shell and a function it calls. As a consequence, all instances of the function share a single copy of each variable. Sharing variables can give rise to side effects that are rarely what you want. As a rule, you should use typeset to make all variables of a recursive function be local variables. See page 437 for more information.

THE quiz SHELL SCRIPT

Solve the following problem using a bash script:

Write a generic multiple-choice quiz program. The program should get its questions from data files, present them to the user, and keep track of the number of correct and incorrect answers. The user must be able to exit from the program at any time and receive a summary of results to that point.

The detailed design of this program and even the detailed description of the problem depend on a number of choices: How will the program know which subjects are available for quizzes? How will the user choose a subject? How will the program know when the quiz is over? Should the program present the same questions (for a given subject) in the same order each time, or should it scramble them?

Of course, you can make many perfectly good choices that implement the specification of the problem. The following details narrow the problem specification:

- Each subject will correspond to a subdirectory of a master quiz directory. This directory will be named in the environment variable **QUIZDIR**, whose default will be **~/quiz**. For example, you could have the following directories correspond to the subjects engineering, art, and politics: **~/quiz/engineering**, **~/quiz/art**, and **~/quiz/politics**. Put the **quiz** directory in **/usr/games** if you want all users to have access to it (requires **root** privileges).

- Each subject can have several questions. Each question is represented by a file in its subject's directory.

- The first line of each file that represents a question holds the text of the question. If it takes more than one line, you must escape the NEWLINE with a backslash. (This setup makes it easy to read a single question with the read builtin.) The second line of the file is an integer that specifies the number of choices. The next lines are the choices themselves. The last line is the correct answer. Following is a sample question file:

  ```
  Who discovered the principle of the lever?
  4
  Euclid
  Archimedes
  Thomas Edison
  The Lever Brothers
  Archimedes
  ```

- The program presents all the questions in a subject directory. At any point the user can interrupt the quiz with CONTROL-C, whereupon the program will summarize the results so far and exit. If the user does not interrupt the program, the program summarizes the results and exits when it has asked all questions for the chosen subject.

- The program scrambles the questions in a subject before presenting them.

Following is a top-level design for this program:

1. Initialize. This involves a number of steps, such as setting the counts of the number of questions asked so far and the number of correct and wrong answers to zero. It also sets up the program to trap CONTROL-C.

2. Present the user with a choice of subjects and get the user's response.

3. Change to the corresponding subject directory.

4. Determine the questions to be asked (that is, the filenames in that directory). Arrange them in random order.

5. Repeatedly present questions and ask for answers until the quiz is over or is interrupted by the user.

6. Present the results and exit.

Clearly some of these steps (such as step 3) are simple, whereas others (such as step 4) are complex and worthy of analysis on their own. Use shell functions for any complex step, and use the trap builtin to handle a user interrupt.

Here is a skeleton version of the program with empty shell functions:

```
function initialize
{
# Initializes variables.
}

function choose_subj
{
# Writes choice to standard output.
}

function scramble
{
# Stores names of question files, scrambled,
# in an array variable named questions.
}

function ask
{
# Reads a question file, asks the question, and checks the
# answer. Returns 1 if the answer was correct, 0 otherwise. If it
# encounters an invalid question file, exit with status 2.
}

function summarize
{
# Presents the user's score.
}

# Main program
initialize                          # Step 1 in top-level design

subject=$(choose_subj)              # Step 2
[[ $? -eq 0 ]] || exit 2            # If no valid choice, exit
```

```
cd $subject || exit 2              # Step 3
echo                               # Skip a line
scramble                           # Step 4

for ques in ${questions[*]}; do    # Step 5
    ask $ques
    result=$?
    (( num_ques=num_ques+1 ))
    if [[ $result == 1 ]]; then
        (( num_correct += 1 ))
    fi
    echo                           # Skip a line between questions
    sleep ${QUIZDELAY:=1}
done

summarize                          # Step 6
exit 0
```

To make reading the results a bit easier for the user, a sleep call appears inside the question loop. It delays **$QUIZDELAY** seconds (default = 1) between questions.

Now the task is to fill in the missing pieces of the program. In a sense this program is being written backward. The details (the shell functions) come first in the file but come last in the development process. This common programming practice is called top-down design. In top-down design you fill in the broad outline of the program first and supply the details later. In this way you break the problem up into smaller problems, each of which you can work on independently. Shell functions are a great help in using the top-down approach.

One way to write the **initialize** function follows. The cd command causes **QUIZDIR** to be the working directory for the rest of the script and defaults to **~/quiz** if **QUIZDIR** is not set.

```
function initialize ()
{
trap 'summarize ; exit 0' INT      # Handle user interrupts
num_ques=0                         # Number of questions asked so far
num_correct=0                      # Number answered correctly so far
first_time=true                    # true until first question is asked
cd ${QUIZDIR:=~/quiz} || exit 2
}
```

Be prepared for the cd command to fail. The directory may be unsearchable or conceivably another user may have removed it. The preceding function exits with a status code of 2 if cd fails.

The next function, **choose_subj**, is a bit more complicated. It displays a menu using a **select** statement:

```
function choose_subj ()
{
subjects=($(ls))
PS3="Choose a subject for the quiz from the preceding list: "
select Subject in ${subjects[*]}; do
    if [[ -z "$Subject" ]]; then
        echo "No subject chosen.  Bye." >&2
        exit 1
    fi
    echo $Subject
    return 0
done
}
```

The function first uses an **ls** command and command substitution to put a list of subject directories in the **subjects** array. Next the **select** structure (page 427) presents the user with a list of subjects (the directories found by **ls**) and assigns the chosen directory name to the **Subject** variable. Finally the function writes the name of the subject directory to standard output. The main program uses command substitution to assign this value to the **subject** variable [**subject=$(choose_subj)**].

The **scramble** function presents a number of difficulties. In this solution it uses an array variable (**questions**) to hold the names of the questions. It scrambles the entries in an array using the **RANDOM** variable (each time you reference **RANDOM**, it has the value of a [random] integer between 0 and 32767):

```
function scramble ()
{
typeset -i index quescount
questions=($(ls))
quescount=${#questions[*]}              # Number of elements
((index=quescount-1))
while [[ $index > 0 ]]; do
    ((target=RANDOM % index))
    exchange $target $index
    ((index -= 1))
done
}
```

This function initializes the array variable **questions** to the list of filenames (questions) in the working directory. The variable **quescount** is set to the number of such files. Then the following algorithm is used: Let the variable index count down from **quescount − 1** (the index of the last entry in the array variable). For each value of **index**, the function chooses a random value target between 0 and **index**, inclusive. The command

```
((target=RANDOM % index))
```

produces a random value between 0 and **index − 1** by taking the remainder (the % operator) when $RANDOM is divided by **index**. The function then exchanges the elements of **questions** at positions **target** and **index**. It is convenient to take care of this step in another function named **exchange**:

```
function exchange ()
{
temp_value=${questions[$1]}
questions[$1]=${questions[$2]}
questions[$2]=$temp_value
}
```

The **ask** function also uses the **select** structure. It reads the question file named in its argument and uses the contents of that file to present the question, accept the answer, and determine whether the answer is correct. (See the code that follows.)

The **ask** function uses file descriptor 3 to read successive lines from the question file, whose name was passed as an argument and is represented by **$1** in the function. It reads the question into the **ques** variable and the number of questions into **num_opts**. The function constructs the variable **choices** by initializing it to a null string and successively appending the next choice. Then it sets **PS3** to the value of **ques** and uses a **select** structure to prompt the user with **ques**. The **select** structure places the user's answer in **answer**, and the function then checks that response against the correct answer from the file.

The construction of the **choices** variable is done with an eye toward avoiding a potential problem. Suppose that one answer has some whitespace in it—then it might appear as two or more arguments in **choices**. To avoid this problem, make sure that **choices** is an array variable. The **select** statement does the rest of the work:

quiz
```
$ cat quiz
#!/bin/bash

# remove the # on the following line to turn on debugging
# set -o xtrace

#===================
function initialize ()
{
trap 'summarize ; exit 0' INT      # Handle user interrupts
num_ques=0                          # Number of questions asked so far
num_correct=0                       # Number answered correctly so far
first_time=true                     # true until first question is asked
cd ${QUIZDIR:=~/quiz} || exit 2
}

#===================
function choose_subj ()
{
subjects=($(ls))
PS3="Choose a subject for the quiz from the preceding list: "
select Subject in ${subjects[*]}; do
    if [[ -z "$Subject" ]]; then
        echo "No subject chosen.  Bye." >&2
        exit 1
    fi
    echo $Subject
    return 0
done
}
```

```
#==================
function exchange ()
{
temp_value=${questions[$1]}
questions[$1]=${questions[$2]}
questions[$2]=$temp_value
}


#==================
function scramble ()
{
typeset -i index quescount
questions=($(ls))
quescount=${#questions[*]}              # Number of elements
((index=quescount-1))
while [[ $index > 0 ]]; do
    ((target=RANDOM % index))
    exchange $target $index
    ((index -= 1))
done
}


#==================
function ask ()
{
exec 3<$1
read -u3 ques || exit 2
read -u3 num_opts || exit 2

index=0
choices=()
while (( index < num_opts )) ; do
    read -u3 next_choice || exit 2
    choices=("${choices[@]}" "$next_choice")
    ((index += 1))
done
read -u3 correct_answer || exit 2
exec 3<&-

if [[ $first_time = true ]]; then
    first_time=false
    echo -e "You may press the interrupt key at any time to quit.\n"
fi

PS3=$ques"   "                          # Make $ques the prompt for select
                                        # and add some spaces for legibility.
select answer in "${choices[@]}"; do
    if [[ -z "$answer" ]]; then
            echo  Not a valid choice. Please choose again.
        elif [[ "$answer" = "$correct_answer" ]]; then
            echo "Correct!"
            return 1
        else
            echo "No, the answer is $correct_answer."
            return 0
    fi
done
}
```

```
#===================
function summarize ()
{
echo                                # Skip a line
if (( num_ques == 0 )); then
    echo "You did not answer any questions"
    exit 0
fi

(( percent=num_correct*100/num_ques ))
echo "You answered $num_correct questions correctly, out of \
$num_ques total questions."
echo "Your score is $percent percent."
}

#===================
# Main program
initialize                          # Step 1 in top-level design

subject=$(choose_subj)              # Step 2
[[ $? -eq 0 ]] || exit 2            # If no valid choice, exit

cd $subject || exit 2               # Step 3
echo                                # Skip a line
scramble                            # Step 4

for ques in ${questions[*]}; do     # Step 5
    ask $ques
    result=$?
    (( num_ques=num_ques+1 ))
    if [[ $result == 1 ]]; then
        (( num_correct += 1 ))
    fi
    echo                            # Skip a line between questions
    sleep ${QUIZDELAY:=1}
done

summarize                           # Step 6
exit 0
```

CHAPTER SUMMARY

The shell is a programming language. Programs written in this language are called shell scripts, or simply scripts. Shell scripts provide the decision and looping control structures present in high-level programming languages while allowing easy access to system utilities and user programs. Shell scripts can use functions to modularize and simplify complex tasks.

Control structures   The control structures that use decisions to select alternatives are **if...then**, **if...then...else**, and **if...then...elif**. The **case** control structure provides a multiway branch and can be used when you want to express alternatives using a simple pattern-matching syntax.

The looping control structures are **for...in**, **for**, **until**, and **while**. These structures perform one or more tasks repetitively.

The **break** and **continue** control structures alter control within loops: **break** transfers control out of a loop, and **continue** transfers control immediately to the top of a loop.

The Here document allows input to a command in a shell script to come from within the script itself.

File descriptors The Bourne Again Shell provides the ability to manipulate file descriptors. Coupled with the read and echo builtins, file descriptors allow shell scripts to have as much control over input and output as do programs written in lower-level languages.

Variables The typeset builtin assigns attributes, such as readonly, to bash variables. The Bourne Again Shell provides operators to perform pattern matching on variables, provide default values for variables, and evaluate the length of variables. This shell also supports array variables and local variables for functions and provides built-in integer arithmetic, using the let builtin and an expression syntax similar to that found in the C programming language.

Builtins Bourne Again Shell builtins include type, read, exec, trap, kill, and getopts. The type builtin displays information about a command, including its location; read allows a script to accept user input.

The exec builtin executes a command without creating a new process. The new command overlays the current process, assuming the same environment and PID number of that process. This builtin executes user programs and other Linux commands when it is *not* necessary to return control to the calling process.

The trap builtin catches a signal sent by Linux to the process running the script and allows you to specify actions to be taken upon receipt of one or more signals. You can use this builtin to cause a script to ignore the signal that is sent when the user presses the interrupt key.

The kill builtin terminates a running program. The getopts builtin parses command-line arguments, making it easier to write programs that follow standard Linux conventions for command-line arguments and options.

Utilities in scripts In addition to using control structures, builtins, and functions, shell scripts generally call Linux utilities. The find utility, for instance, is commonplace in shell scripts that search for files in the system hierarchy and can perform a vast range of tasks, from simple to complex.

Expressions There are two basic types of expressions: arithmetic and logical. Arithmetic expressions allow you to do arithmetic on constants and variables, yielding a numeric result. Logical (Boolean) expressions compare expressions or strings, or test conditions to yield a *true* or *false* result. As with all decisions within Linux shell scripts, a *true* status is represented by the value zero; *false,* by any nonzero value.

Good programming practices A well-written shell script adheres to standard programming practices, such as specifying the shell to execute the script on the first line of the script, verifying the number and type of arguments that the script is called with, displaying a standard usage message to report command-line errors, and redirecting all informational messages to standard error.

EXERCISES

1. Rewrite the **journal** script of Chapter 8 (exercise 5, page 346) by adding commands to verify that the user has write permission for a file named **journal-file** in the user's home directory, if such a file exists. The script should take appropriate actions if **journal-file** exists and the user does not have write permission to the file. Verify that the modified script works.

2. The special parameter "**$@**" is referenced twice in the **out** script (page 403). Explain what would be different if the parameter "**$***" was used in its place.

3. Write a filter that takes a list of files as input and outputs the basename (page 426) of each file in the list.

4. Write a function that takes a single filename as an argument and adds execute permission to the file for the user.

   a. When might such a function be useful?

   b. Revise the script so it takes one or more filenames as arguments and adds execute permission for the user for each file argument.

   c. What can you do to make the function available every time you log in?

   d. Suppose that, in addition to having the function available on subsequent login sessions, you want to make the function available in your current shell. How would you do so?

5. When might it be necessary or advisable to write a shell script instead of a shell function? Give as many reasons as you can think of.

6. Write a shell script that displays the names of all directory files, but no other types of files, in the working directory.

7. Write a script to display the time every 15 seconds. Read the **date** man page and display the time, using the **%r** field descriptor. Clear the window (using the **clear** command) each time before you display the time.

8. Enter the following script named **savefiles**, and give yourself execute permission to the file:

```
$ cat savefiles
#! /bin/bash
echo "Saving files in current directory in file savethem."
exec > savethem
for i in *
        do
        echo "=================================================="
        echo "File: $i"
        echo "=================================================="
        cat "$i"
        done
```

a. Which error message do you get when you execute this script? Rewrite the script so that the error does not occur, making sure the output still goes to **savethem**.

b. What might be a problem with running this script twice in the same directory? Discuss a solution to this problem.

9. Read the bash man or info page, try some experiments, and answer the following questions:

a. How do you export a function?

b. What does the hash builtin do?

c. What happens if the argument to exec is not executable?

10. Using the find utility, perform the following tasks:

a. List all files in the working directory and all subdirectories that have been modified within the last day.

b. List all files that you have read access to on the system that are larger than 1 megabyte.

c. Remove all files named **core** from the directory structure rooted at your home directory.

d. List the inode numbers of all files in the working directory whose filenames end in **.c**.

e. List all files that you have read access to on the root filesystem that have been modified in the last 30 days.

11. Write a short script that tells you whether the permissions for two files, whose names are given as arguments to the script, are identical. If the permissions for the two files are identical, output the common permission field. Otherwise, output each filename followed by its permission field. (*Hint:* Try using the cut utility.)

12. Write a script that takes the name of a directory as an argument and searches the file hierarchy rooted at that directory for zero-length files. Write the names of all zero-length files to standard output. If there is no option on the command line, have the script delete the file after displaying its name, asking the user for confirmation, and receiving positive confirmation. A −f (force) option on the command line indicates that the script should display the filename but not ask for confirmation before deleting the file.

ADVANCED EXERCISES

13. Write a script that takes a colon-separated list of items and outputs the items, one per line, to standard output (without the colons).

14. Generalize the script written in exercise 13 so that the character separating the list items is given as an argument to the function. If this argument is absent, the separator should default to a colon.

15. Write a function named **funload** that takes as its single argument the name of a file containing other functions. The purpose of **funload** is to make all functions in the named file available in the current shell; that is, **funload** loads the functions from the named file. To locate the file, **funload** searches the colon-separated list of directories given by the environment variable **FUNPATH**. Assume that the format of **FUNPATH** is the same as **PATH** and that searching **FUNPATH** is similar to the shell's search of the **PATH** variable.

16. Rewrite **bundle** (page 430) so the script it creates takes an optional list of filenames as arguments. If one or more filenames are given on the command line, only those files should be re-created; otherwise, all files in the shell archive should be re-created. For example, suppose all files with the filename extension **.c** are bundled into an archive named **srcshell**, and you want to unbundle just the files **test1.c** and **test2.c**. The following command will unbundle just these two files:

    ```
    $ bash srcshell test1.c test2.c
    ```

17. What kind of links will the **lnks** script (page 406) not find? Why?

18. In principle, recursion is never necessary. It can always be replaced by an iterative construct, such as **while** or **until**. Rewrite **makepath** (page 470) as a nonrecursive function. Which version do you prefer? Why?

19. Lists are commonly stored in environment variables by putting a colon (:) between each of the list elements. (The value of the **PATH** variable is an example.) You can add an element to such a list by catenating the new element to the front of the list, as in

    ```
    PATH=/opt/bin:$PATH
    ```

    If the element you add is already in the list, you now have two copies of it in the list. Write a shell function named **addenv** that takes two arguments: (1) the name of a shell variable and (2) a string to prepend to the list that is the value of the shell variable only if that string is not already an element of the list. For example, the call

    ```
    addenv PATH /opt/bin
    ```

would add **/opt/bin** to **PATH** only if that pathname is not already in **PATH**. Be sure that your solution works even if the shell variable starts out empty. Also make sure that you check the list elements carefully. If **/usr/opt/bin** is in **PATH** but **/opt/bin** is not, the example just given should still add **/opt/bin** to **PATH**. (*Hint:* You may find this exercise easier to complete if you first write a function **locate_field** that tells you whether a string is an element in the value of a variable.)

20. Write a function that takes a directory name as an argument and writes to standard output the maximum of the lengths of all filenames in that directory. If the function's argument is not a directory name, write an error message to standard output and exit with nonzero status.

21. Modify the function you wrote for exercise 20 to descend all subdirectories of the named directory recursively and to find the maximum length of any filename in that hierarchy.

22. Write a function that lists the number of ordinary files, directories, block special files, character special files, FIFOs, and symbolic links in the working directory. Do this in two different ways:

    a. Use the first letter of the output of **ls –l** to determine a file's type.

    b. Use the file type condition tests of the *[[expression]]* syntax to determine a file's type.

23. Modify the **quiz** program (page 476) so that the choices for a question are randomly arranged.

11

THE PERL SCRIPTING LANGUAGE

Larry Wall created the Perl (Practical Extraction and Report Language) programming language for working with text. Perl uses syntax and concepts from awk, sed, C, the Bourne Shell, Smalltalk, Lisp, and English. It was designed to scan and extract information from text files and generate reports based on that information. Since its introduction in 1987, Perl has expanded enormously—its documentation growing up with it. Today, in addition to text processing, Perl is used for system administration, software development, and general-purpose programming.

Perl code is portable because Perl has been implemented on many operating systems (see www.cpan.org/ports). Perl is an informal, practical, robust, easy-to-use, efficient, and complete language. It is a down-and-dirty language that supports procedural and object-oriented programming. It is not necessarily elegant.

One of the things that distinguishes Perl from many other languages is its linguistic origins. In English you say, "I will buy a car if I win the lottery." Perl allows you to mimic that syntax. Another distinction is that Perl has singular and plural variables, the former holding single values and the latter holding lists of values.

INTRODUCTION TO PERL

A couple of quotes from the manual shed light on Perl's philosophy:

> Many of Perl's syntactic elements are optional. Rather than requiring you to put parentheses around every function call and declare every variable, you can often leave such explicit elements off and Perl will frequently figure out what you meant. This is known as Do What I Mean, abbreviated DWIM. It allows programmers to be lazy and to code in a style with which they are comfortable.

> The Perl motto is "There's more than one way to do it." Divining how many more is left as an exercise to the reader.

One of Perl's biggest assets is its support by thousands of third-party modules. The Comprehensive Perl Archive Network (CPAN; www.cpan.org) is a repository for many of the modules and other information related to Perl. See page 523 for information on downloading, installing, and using these modules in Perl programs.

Install perl-doc

tip   The **perl-doc** package holds a wealth of information. Install this package before you start using Perl; see the next page for more information.

The best way to learn Perl is to work with it. Copy and modify the programs in this chapter until they make sense to you. Many system tools are written in Perl. The first line of most of these tools begins with **#!/usr/bin/perl**, which tells the shell to pass the program to Perl for execution. Most files that contain the string **/usr/bin/perl** are Perl programs. The following command uses grep to search the **/usr/bin** and **/usr/sbin** directories recursively (**–r**) for files containing the string **/usr/bin/perl**; it lists many local system tools written in Perl:

```
$ grep -r /usr/bin/perl /usr/bin /usr/sbin | head -4
/usr/bin/defoma-user:#! /usr/bin/perl -w
/usr/bin/pod2latex:#!/usr/bin/perl
/usr/bin/pod2latex:    eval 'exec /usr/bin/perl -S $0 ${1+"$@"}'
/usr/bin/splain:#!/usr/bin/perl
```

Review these programs—they demonstrate how Perl is used in the real world. Copy a system program to a directory you own before modifying it. Do not run a system program while running with **root** privileges unless you know what you are doing.

MORE INFORMATION

Local   man pages: See the perl and perltoc man pages for lists of Perl man pages

Web   Perl home page: www.perl.com
CPAN: www.cpan.org
blog: perlbuzz.com

Book *Programming Perl,* third edition, by Wall, Christiansen, & Orwant, O'Reilly & Associates (July 2000)

HELP

Perl is a forgiving language. As such, it is easy to write Perl code that runs but does not perform as you intended. Perl includes many tools that can help you find coding mistakes. The **–w** option and the **use warnings** statement can produce helpful diagnostic messages. The **use strict** statement (see the **perldebtut** man page) can impose order on a program by requiring, among other things, that you declare variables before you use them. When all else fails, you can use Perl's builtin debugger to step through a program. See the **perldebtut** and **perldebug** man pages for more information.

perldoc

You must install the **perl-doc** package before you can use perldoc.

The perldoc utility locates and displays local Perl documentation. It is similar to man (page 33) but specific to Perl. It works with files that include lines of **pod** (plain old documentation), a clean and simple documentation language. When embedded in a Perl program, **pod** enables you to include documentation for the entire program, not just code-level comments, in a Perl program.

Following is a simple Perl program that includes **pod**. The two lines following **=cut** are the program; the rest is **pod**-format documentation.

```
$ cat pod.ex1.pl
#!/usr/bin/perl

=head1 A Perl Program to Say I<Hi there.>

This simple Perl program includes documentation in B<pod> format.
The following B<=cut> command tells B<perldoc> that what follows
is not documentation.

=cut
# A Perl program
print "Hi there.\n";

=head1 pod Documentation Resumes with Any pod Command

See the B<perldoc.perl.org/perlpod.html> page for more information
on B<pod> and B<perldoc.perl.org> for complete Perl documentation.
```

You can use Perl to run the program:

```
$ perl pod.ex1.pl
Hi there.
```

Or you can use perldoc to display the documentation:

```
$ perldoc pod.ex1.pl
POD.EX1(1)              User Contributed Perl Documentation              POD.EX1(1)
```

A Perl Program to Say <u>Hi there.</u>
This simple Perl program includes documentation in **pod** format. The
following =**cut** command tells **perldoc** that what follows is not documentation.

pod Documentation Resumes with Any pod Command
See the **perldoc.perl.org/perlpod.html** page for more information on **pod**
and **perldoc.perl.org** for complete Perl documentation.

```
perl v5.10.0                  2008-10-14                        POD.EX1(1)
```

Most publicly distributed modules and scripts, as well as Perl itself, include
embedded **pod**-format documentation. For example, the following command displays information about the Perl **print** function:

```
$ perldoc -f print
    print FILEHANDLE LIST
    print LIST
    print  Prints a string or a list of strings. Returns true if success-
           ful.  FILEHANDLE may be a scalar variable name, in which case
           the variable contains the name of or a reference to the file-
           handle, thus introducing one level of indirection.  (NOTE: If
           FILEHANDLE is a variable and the next token is a term, it may
           ...
```

Once you have installed a module (page 523), you can use perldoc to display documentation for that module. The following example shows perldoc displaying
information on the locally installed **Timestamp::Simple** module:

```
$ perldoc Timestamp::Simple
Timestamp::Simple(3)  User Contributed Perl Documentation Timestamp::Simple(3)

NAME
        Timestamp::Simple - Simple methods for timestamping

SYNOPSIS
            use Timestamp::Simple qw(stamp);
            print stamp, "\n";
    ...
```

Give the command **man perldoc** or **perldoc perldoc** to display the perldoc man page
and read more about this tool.

Make Perl programs readable

tip Although Perl has many shortcuts that are good choices for one-shot programming, the code in
this chapter presents code that is easy to understand and easy to maintain.

TERMINOLOGY

This section defines some of the terms used in this chapter.

Module A Perl *module* is a self-contained chunk of Perl code, frequently containing several functions that work together. A module can be called from another module or from a Perl program. A module must have a unique name. To help ensure unique names, Perl provides a hierarchical *namespace* (page 967) for modules, separating components of a name with double colons (::). Example module names are **Timestamp::Simple** and **WWW::Mechanize**.

Distribution A Perl *distribution* is a set of one or more modules that perform a task. You can search for distributions and modules at search.cpan.org. Examples of distributions include **Timestamp-Simple** (the **Timestamp-Simple-1.01.tar.gz** archive file contains the **Timestamp::Simple** module only) and **WWW-Mechanize** (**WWW-Mechanize-1.34.tar.gz** contains the **WWW::Mechanize** module, plus supporting modules including **WWW::Mechanize::Link** and **WWW::Mechanize::Image**).

Package A *package* defines a Perl namespace. For example, in the variable with the name **$WWW::Mechanize::ex**, **$ex** is a scalar variable in the **WWW::Mechanize** package, where "package" is used in the sense of a namespace. Using the same name, such as **WWW::Mechanize**, for a distribution, a package, and a module can be confusing.

Block A *block* is zero or more statements, delimited by curly braces ({}), that defines a scope. The shell control structure syntax explanations refer to these elements as *commands*. See the **if...then** control structure on page 398 for an example.

Package variable A *package variable* is defined within the package it appears in. Other packages can refer to package variables by using the variable's fully qualified name (for example, **$Text::Wrap::columns**). By default, variables are package variables unless you define them as lexical variables.

Lexical variable A *lexical variable*, which is defined by preceding the name of a variable with the keyword **my** (see the tip on page 494), is defined only within the block or file it appears in. Other languages refer to a lexical variable as a local variable. Because Perl 4 used the keyword **local** with a different meaning, Perl 5 uses the keyword **lexical** in its place. When programming using bash, variables that are not exported (page 436) are local to the program they are used in.

List A *list* is a series of zero or more scalars. The following list has three elements—two numbers and a string:

```
(2, 4, 'Zach')
```

Array An *array* is a variable that holds a list of elements in a defined order. In the following line of code, **@a** is an array. See page 497 for more information about array variables.

```
@a = (2, 4, 'Zach')
```

Compound statement A *compound statement* is a statement made up of other statements. For example, the **if** compound statement (page 501) incorporates an **if** statement that normally includes other statements within the block it controls.

RUNNING A PERL PROGRAM

There are several ways you can run a program written in Perl. The **–e** option enables you to enter a program on the command line:

```
$ perl -e 'print "Hi there.\n"'
Hi there.
```

The **–e** option is a good choice for testing Perl syntax and running brief, one-shot programs. This option requires that the Perl program appear as a single argument on the command line. The program must immediately follow this option—it is an argument to this option. An easy way to write this type of program is to enclose the program within single quotation marks.

Because Perl is a member of the class of utilities that take input from a file or standard input (page 128), you can give the command **perl** and enter the program terminated by CONTROL-D (end of file). Perl reads the program from standard input:

```
$ perl
print "Hi there.\n";
CONTROL-D
Hi there.
```

The preceding techniques are useful for quick, one-off command-line programs but are not helpful for running more complex programs. Most of the time, a Perl program is stored in a text file. Although not required, the file typically has a filename extension of **.pl**. Following is the same simple program used in the previous examples stored in a file:

```
$ cat simple.pl
print "Hi there.\n";
```

You can run this program by specifying its name as an argument to Perl:

```
$ perl simple.pl
Hi there.
```

Most commonly and similarly to most shell scripts, the file containing the Perl program is executable. In the following example, chmod (page 278) makes the **simple2.pl** file executable. As explained on page 280, the **#!** at the start of the first line of the file instructs the shell to pass the rest of the file to **/usr/bin/perl** for execution.

```
$ chmod 755 simple2.pl
$ cat simple2.pl
#!/usr/bin/perl -w
print "Hi there.\n";

$ ./simple2.pl
Hi there.
```

In this example, the **simple2.pl** program is executed as **./simple2.pl** because the working directory is not in the user's **PATH** (page 297). The **–w** option tells Perl to issue warning messages when it identifies potential errors in the code.

PERL VERSION 5.10

All examples in this chapter were run under Perl 5.10. Give the following command to see which version of Perl the local system is running:

```
$ perl -v

This is perl, v5.10.0 built for i486-linux-gnu-thread-multi
...
```

use feature 'say'   The **say** function is a Perl 6 feature that is available in Perl 5.10. It works the same way as **print**, except it adds a NEWLINE (**\n**) at the end of each line it outputs. Some versions of Perl require you to tell Perl explicitly that you want to use **say**. The **use** function in the following example tells Perl to enable **say**. Try running this program without the **use** line to see if the local version of Perl requires it.

```
$ cat 5.10.pl
use feature 'say';
say 'Output by say.';
print 'Output by print.';
say 'End.'
$ perl 5.10.pl
Output by say.
Output by print.End.
$
```

Earlier versions of Perl   If you are running an earlier version of Perl, you will need to replace **say** in the examples in this chapter with **print** and terminate the **print** statement with a quoted **\n**:

```
$ cat 5.8.pl
print 'Output by print in place of say.', "\n";
print 'Output by print.';
print 'End.', "\n";

$ perl 5.8.pl
Output by print in place of say.
Output by print.End.
```

SYNTAX

This section describes the major components of a Perl program.

Statements   A Perl program comprises one or more *statements,* each terminated by a semicolon (;). These statements are free-form with respect to *whitespace* (page 987), except for whitespace within quoted strings. Multiple statements can appear on a single line, each terminated by a semicolon. The following programs are equivalent. The first occupies two lines, the second only one; look at the differences in the spacing around the equal and plus signs. See **use feature 'say'** (above) if these programs complain about **say** not being available.

```
$ cat statement1.pl
$n=4;
say "Answer is ", $n + 2;
$ perl statement1.pl
Answer is 6

$ cat statement2.pl
$n = 4; say "Answer is ", $n+2;
$ perl statement2.pl
Answer is 6
```

Expressions   The syntax of Perl expressions frequently corresponds to the syntax of C expressions, but is not always the same. Perl expressions are covered in examples throughout this chapter.

Quotation marks   All character strings must be enclosed within single or double quotation marks. Perl differentiates between the two types of quotation marks in a manner similar to the way the shell does (page 292): Double quotation marks allow Perl to interpolate enclosed variables and interpret special characters such as \n (NEWLINE), whereas single quotation marks do not. Table 11-1 lists some of Perl's special characters.

The following example demonstrates how different types of quotation marks, and the absence of quotation marks, affect Perl in converting scalars between numbers and strings. The single quotation marks in the first **print** statement prevent Perl from interpolating the **$string** variable and from interpreting the **\n** special character. The leading **\n** in the second **print** statement forces the output of that statement to appear on a new line.

```
$ cat string1.pl
$string="5";       # $string declared as a string, but it will not matter

print '$string+5\n';   # Perl displays $string+5 literally because of
                       # the single quotation marks
print "\n$string+5\n"; # Perl interpolates the value of $string as a string
                       # because of the double quotation marks
print $string+5, "\n"; # Lack of quotation marks causes Perl to interpret
                       # $string as a numeric variable and to add 5;
                       # the \n must appear between double quotation marks

$ perl string1.pl
$string+5\n
5+5
10
```

Slash   By default, regular expressions are delimited by slashes (/). The following example tests whether the string **hours** contains the pattern **our**; see page 518 for more information on regular expressions in Perl.

```
$ perl -e 'if ("hours" =~ /our/) {say "yes";}'
```

The local version of Perl may require **use feature 'say'** (page 491) to work properly:

```
$ perl -e 'use feature "say"; if ("hours" =~ /our/) {say "yes";}'
```

Backslash   Within a string enclosed between double quotation marks, a backslash escapes
(quotes) another backslash. Thus Perl displays "\\n" as \n. Within a regular expression, Perl does not expand a metacharacter preceded by a backslash. See the **string1.pl** program on the previous page.

Comments   As in the shell, a comment in Perl begins with a pound sign (#) and ends at the end
of the line (just before the NEWLINE character).

Special characters   Table 11-1 lists some of the characters that are special within strings in Perl. Perl
interpolates these characters when they appear between double quotation marks
but not when they appear between single quotation marks. Table 11-3 on page 520
lists metacharacters, which are special within regular expressions.

Table 11-1   Some Perl special characters

Character	When within double quotation marks, interpolated as
\0xx (zero)	The ASCII character whose octal value is **xx**
\a	An alarm (bell or beep) character (ASCII 7)
\e	An ESCAPE character (ASCII 27)
\n	A NEWLINE character (ASCII 10)
\r	A RETURN character (ASCII 13)
\t	A TAB character (ASCII 9)

VARIABLES

Like human languages, Perl distinguishes between singular and plural data. Strings
and numbers are singular; lists of strings or numbers are plural. Perl provides three
types of variables: *scalar* (singular), *array* (plural), and *hash* (plural; also called
associative arrays). Perl identifies each type of variable by a special character preceding its name. The name of a scalar variable begins with a dollar sign ($), an array
variable begins with an at sign (@), and a hash variable begins with a percent sign
(%). As opposed to the way the shell identifies variables, Perl requires the leading
character to appear each time you reference a variable, including when you assign a
value to the variable:

```
$ name="Zach" ; echo "$name"              (bash)
Zach

$ perl -e '$name="Zach" ; print "$name\n";'  (perl)
Zach
```

Variable names, which are case sensitive, can include letters, digits, and the underscore
character (_). A Perl variable is a package variable (page 489) unless it is preceded by

the keyword **my**, in which case it is a lexical variable (page 489) that is defined only within the block or file it appears in. See "Subroutines" on page 515 for a discussion of the locality of Perl variables.

Lexical variables overshadow package variables

caution   If a lexical variable and a package variable have the same name, within the block or file in which the lexical variable is defined, the name refers to the lexical variable and not to the package variable.

A Perl variable comes into existence when you assign a value to it—you do not need to define or initialize a variable, although it may make a program more understandable to do so. Normally, Perl does not complain when you reference an uninitialized variable:

```
$ cat variable1.pl
#!/usr/bin/perl
my $name = 'Sam';
print "Hello, $nam, how are you?\n"; # Typo, e left off of name

$ ./variable1.pl
Hello, , how are you?
```

use strict   Include **use strict** to cause Perl to require variables to be declared before being assigned values. See the **perldebtut man** page for more information. When you include **use strict** in the preceding program, Perl displays an error message:

```
$ cat variable1b.pl
#!/usr/bin/perl
use strict;
my $name = 'Sam';
print "Hello, $nam, how are you?\n"; # Typo, e left off of name

$ ./variable1b.pl
Global symbol "$nam" requires explicit package name at ./variable1b.pl line 4.
Execution of ./variable1b.pl aborted due to compilation errors.
```

Using my: lexical versus package variables

tip   In **variable1.pl**, **$name** is declared to be lexical by preceding its name with the keyword **my**; its name and value are known within the file **variable1.pl** only. Declaring a variable to be lexical limits its scope to the block or file it is defined in. Although not necessary in this case, declaring variables to be lexical is good practice. This habit becomes especially useful when you write longer programs, subroutines, and packages, where it is harder to keep variable names unique. Declaring all variables to be lexical is mandatory when you write routines that will be used within code written by others. This practice allows those who work with your routines to use whichever variable names they like, without regard to which variable names you used in the code you wrote.

The shell and Perl scope variables differently. In the shell, if you do not **export** a variable, it is local to the routine it is used in (page 436). In Perl, if you do not use **my** to declare a variable to be lexical, it is defined for the package it appears in.

The **−w** option and the **use warnings** statement perform the same function: They cause Perl to generate an error message when it detects a syntax error. In the following example, Perl displays two warnings. The first tells you that you have used the variable named **$nam** once, on line 3, which probably indicates an error. This message is helpful when you mistype the name of a variable. Under Perl 5.10, the second warning specifies the name of the uninitialized variable. This warning refers to the same problem as the first warning. Although it is not hard to figure out which of the two variables is undefined in this simple program, doing so in a complex program can take a lot of time.

```
$ cat variable1a.pl
#!/usr/bin/perl -w
my $name = 'Sam';
print "Hello, $nam, how are you?\n"; # Prints warning because of typo and -w

$ ./variable1a.pl
Name "main::nam" used only once: possible typo at ./variable1a.pl line 3.
Use of uninitialized value $nam in concatenation (.) or string at ./variable1a.pl line 3.
Hello, , how are you?
```

You can also use **−w** on the command line. If you use **−e** as well, make sure the argument that follows this option is the program you want to execute (e.g., **−e −w** does not work). See the tip on page 518.

```
$ perl -w -e 'my $name = "Sam"; print "Hello, $nam, how are you?\n"'
Name "main::nam" used only once: possible typo at -e line 1.
Use of uninitialized value $nam in concatenation (.) or string at -e line 1.
Hello, , how are you?
```

undef and defined An undefined variable has the special value **undef**, which evaluates to zero (0) in a numeric expression and expands to an empty string ("") when you print it. Use the **defined** function to determine whether a variable has been defined. The following example, which uses constructs explained later in this chapter, calls **defined** with an argument of **$name** and negates the result with an exclamation point (!). The result is that the **print** statement is executed if **$name** is *not* defined.

```
$ cat variable2.pl
#!/usr/bin/perl
if (!defined($name)) {
print "The variable '\$name' is not defined.\n"
};

$ ./variable2.pl
The variable '$name' is not defined.
```

Because the **−w** option causes Perl to warn you when you reference an undefined variable, using this option would generate a warning.

SCALAR VARIABLES

A scalar variable has a name that begins with a dollar sign ($) and holds a single string or number: It is a singular variable. Because Perl converts between the two when necessary, you can use strings and numbers interchangeably. Perl interprets scalar variables as strings when it makes sense to interpret them as strings, and as numbers when it makes sense to interpret them as numbers. Perl's judgment in these matters is generally good.

The following example shows some uses of scalar variables. The first two lines of code (lines 3 and 4) assign the string **Sam** to the scalar variable **$name** and the numbers 5 and 2 to the scalar variables **$n1** and **$n2**, respectively. In this example, multiple statements, each terminated with a semicolon (;), appear on a single line. See **use feature 'say'** on page 491 if this program complains about **say** not being available.

```
$ cat scalars1.pl
#!/usr/bin/perl -w

$name = "Sam";
$n1 = 5; $n2 = 2;

say "$name $n1 $n2";
say "$n1 + $n2";
say '$name $n1 $n2';
say $n1 + $n2, " ", $n1 * $n2;
say $name + $n1;

$ ./scalars1.pl
Sam 5 2
5 + 2
$name $n1 $n2
7 10
Argument "Sam" isn't numeric in addition (+) at ./scalers1.pl line 11.
5
```

Double quotation marks   The first **say** statement sends the string enclosed within double quotation marks to standard output (the screen unless you redirect it). Within double quotation marks, Perl expands variable names to the value of the named variable. Thus the first **say** statement displays the values of three variables, separated from each other by SPACEs. The second **say** statement includes a plus sign (**+**). Perl does not recognize operators such as **+** within either type of quotation marks. Thus Perl displays the plus sign between the values of the two variables.

Single quotation marks   The third **say** statement sends the string enclosed within single quotation marks to standard output. Within single quotation marks, Perl interprets all characters literally, so it displays the string exactly as it appears between the single quotation marks.

In the fourth **say** statement, the operators are not quoted, and Perl performs the addition and multiplication as specified. Without the quoted SPACE, Perl would catenate the two numbers (**710**). The last **say** statement attempts to add a string and a number; the **–w** option causes Perl to display an error message before displaying **5**. The **5** results from adding **Sam**, which Perl evaluates as 0 in a numerical context, to the number 5 (0 + 5 = 5).

ARRAY VARIABLES

An array variable is an ordered container of scalars whose name begins with an at sign (**@**) and whose first element is numbered zero (zero-based indexing). Because an array can hold zero or more scalars, it is a plural variable. Arrays are ordered; hashes (page 500) are unordered. In Perl, arrays grow as needed. If you reference an uninitialized element of an array, such as an element beyond the end of the array, Perl returns **undef**.

The first statement in the following program assigns the values of two numbers and a string to the array variable named **@arrayvar**. Because Perl uses zero-based indexing, the first **say** statement displays the value of the second element of the array (the element with the index 1). This statement specifies the variable **$arrayvar[1]** as a scalar (singular) because it refers to a single value. The second **say** statement specifies the variable **@arrayvar[1,2]** as a list (plural) because it refers to multiple values (the elements with the indexes 1 and 2).

```
$ cat arrayvar1.pl
#!/usr/bin/perl -w
@arrayvar = (8, 18, "Sam");
say $arrayvar[1];
say "@arrayvar[1,2]";

$ perl arrayvar1.pl
18
18 Sam
```

The next example shows a couple of ways to determine the length of an array and presents more information on using quotation marks within **print** statements. The first assignment statement in **arrayvar2.pl** assigns values to the first six elements of the **@arrayvar2** array. When used in a scalar context, Perl evaluates the name of an array as the length of the array. The second assignment statement assigns the number of elements in **@arrayvar2** to the scalar variable **$num**.

```
$ cat arrayvar2.pl
#!/usr/bin/perl -w
@arrayvar2 = ("apple", "bird", 44, "Tike", "metal", "pike");

$num = @arrayvar2;                      # number of elements in array
print "Elements: ", $num, "\n";         # two equivalent print statements
print "Elements: $num\n";

print "Last: $#arrayvar2\n";            # index of last element in array

$ ./arrayvar2.pl
Elements: 6
Elements: 6
Last: 5
```

The first two **print** statements in **arrayvar2.pl** display the string **Elements:**, a SPACE, the value of **$num**, and a NEWLINE, each using a different syntax. The first of these statements displays three values, using commas to separate them within the **print** statement. The second **print** statement has one argument and demonstrates that Perl expands a variable (replaces the variable with its value) when the variable is enclosed within double quotation marks.

$#*array* The final **print** statement in **arrayvar2.pl** shows that Perl evaluates the variable **$#*array*** as the index of the last element in the array named *array*. Because Perl uses zero-based indexing by default, this variable evaluates to one less than the number of elements in the array.

The next example works with elements of an array and uses a dot (.; the string catenation operator). The first two lines assign values to four scalar variables. The third line shows that you can assign values to array elements using scalar variables, arithmetic, and catenated strings. The dot operator catenates strings, so Perl evaluates **$va . $vb** as **Sam** catenated with **uel**—that is, as **Samuel** (see the output of the last **print** statement).

```
$ cat arrayvar3.pl
#!/usr/bin/perl -w
$v1 = 5; $v2 = 8;
$va = "Sam"; $vb = "uel";
@arrayvar3 = ($v1, $v1 * 2, $v1 * $v2, "Max", "Zach", $va . $vb);

print $arrayvar3[2], "\n";       # one element of an array is a scalar
print @arrayvar3[2,4], "\n";     # two elements of an array are a list
print @arrayvar3[2..4], "\n\n";  # a slice

print "@arrayvar3[2,4]", "\n";   # a list, elements separated by SPACEs
print "@arrayvar3[2..4]", "\n\n"; # a slice, elements separated by SPACEs

print "@arrayvar3\n";            # an array, elements separated by SPACEs

$ ./arrayvar3.pl
40
40Zach
40MaxZach

40 Zach
40 Max Zach

5 10 40 Max Zach Samuel
```

The first **print** statement in **arrayvar3.pl** displays the third element (the element with an index of 2) of the **@arrayvar3** array. This statement uses **$** in place of **@** because it refers to a single element of the array. The subsequent **print** statements use **@** because they refer to more than one element. Within the brackets that specify an array subscript, two subscripts separated by a comma specify two elements of an array. The second **print** statement, for example, displays the third and fifth elements of the array.

Array slice When you separate two elements of an array with two dots (**..**; the range operator), Perl substitutes all elements between and including the two specified elements. A portion of an array comprising elements is called a *slice*. The third **print** statement in the preceding example displays the elements with indexes 2, 3, and 4 (the third, fourth, and fifth elements) as specified by **2..4**. Perl puts no SPACEs between the elements it displays.

Within a **print** statement, when you enclose an array variable, including its subscripts, within double quotation marks, Perl puts a SPACE between each of the elements. The fourth and fifth **print** statements in the preceding example illustrate this syntax. The last **print** statement displays the entire array, with elements separated by SPACEs.

shift, push, The next example demonstrates several functions you can use to manipulate arrays.
pop, and splice The example uses the **@colors** array, which is initialized to a list of seven colors. The **shift** function returns and removes the first element of an array, **push** adds an element to the end of an array, and **pop** returns and removes the last element of an array. The **splice** function replaces elements of an array with another array; in the example, **splice** inserts the **@ins** array starting at index 1 (the second element), replacing two elements of the array. See **use feature 'say'** on page 491 if this program complains about **say** not being available. See the **perlfunc** man page for more information on the functions described in this paragraph.

```
$ cat ./shift1.pl
#!/usr/bin/perl -w

@colors = ("red", "orange", "yellow", "green", "blue", "indigo", "violet");

say "                        Display array: @colors";
say " Display and remove first element of array: ", shift (@colors);
say "       Display remaining elements of array: @colors";

push (@colors, "WHITE");
say "   Add element to end of array and display: @colors";

say " Display and remove last element of array: ", pop (@colors);
say "       Display remaining elements of array: @colors";

@ins = ("GRAY", "FERN");
splice (@colors, 1, 2, @ins);
say "Replace second and third elements of array: @colors";
```

```
$ ./shift1.pl
                        Display array: red orange yellow green blue indigo violet
 Display and remove first element of array: red
       Display remaining elements of array: orange yellow green blue indigo violet
   Add element to end of array and display: orange yellow green blue indigo violet WHITE
 Display and remove last element of array: WHITE
       Display remaining elements of array: orange yellow green blue indigo violet
Replace second and third elements of array: orange GRAY FERN blue indigo violet
```

Hash Variables

A hash variable, sometimes called an associative array variable, is a plural data structure that holds an array of key–value pairs. It uses strings as keys (indexes) and is optimized to return a value quickly when given a key. Each key must be a unique scalar. Hashes are unordered; arrays (page 497) are ordered. When you assign a hash to a list, the key–value pairs are preserved, but their order is neither alphabetical nor the order in which they were inserted into the hash; instead, the order is effectively random.

Perl provides two syntaxes to assign values to a hash. The first uses a single assignment statement for each key–value pair:

```
$ cat hash1.pl
#!/usr/bin/perl -w
$hashvar1{boat} = "tuna";
$hashvar1{"number five"} = 5;
$hashvar1{4} = "fish";

@arrayhash1 = %hashvar1;
say "@arrayhash1";

$ ./hash1.pl
boat tuna 4 fish number five 5
```

Within an assignment statement, the key is located within braces to the left of the equal sign; the value is on the right side of the equal sign. As illustrated in the preceding example, keys and values can take on either numeric or string values. You do not need to quote string keys unless they contain SPACEs. This example also shows that you can display the keys and values held by a hash, each separated from the next by a SPACE, by assigning the hash to an array variable and then printing that variable enclosed within double quotation marks.

The next example shows the other way of assigning values to a hash and illustrates how to use the **keys** and **values** functions to extract keys and values from a hash. After assigning values to the **%hash2** hash, **hash2.pl** calls the **keys** function with an argument of **%hash2** and assigns the resulting list of keys to the **@array_keys** array. The program then uses the **values** function to assign values to the **@array_values** array.

```
$ cat hash2.pl
#!/usr/bin/perl -w

%hash2 = (
    boat => "tuna",
    "number five" => 5,
    4 => "fish",
    );

@array_keys = keys(%hash2);
say "  Keys: @array_keys";

@array_values = values(%hash2);
say "Values: @array_values";
```

```
$ ./hash2.pl
  Keys: boat 4 number five
Values: tuna fish 5
```

Because Perl automatically quotes a single word that appears to the left of the **=>** operator, you do not need quotation marks around **boat** in the third line of this program. However, removing the quotation marks from around **number five** would generate an error because the string contains a SPACE.

CONTROL STRUCTURES

Control flow statements alter the order of execution of statements within a Perl program. Starting on page 398, Chapter 10 discusses bash control structures in detail and includes flow diagrams. Perl control structures perform the same functions as their bash counterparts, although the two languages use different syntaxes. The description of each control structure in this section references the discussion of the same control structure under bash.

In this section, the **bold italic** words in the syntax description are the items you supply to cause the structure to have the desired effect, the *nonbold italic* words are the keywords Perl uses to identify the control structure, and *{...}* represents a block (page 489) of statements. Many of these structures use an expression, denoted as *expr,* to control their execution. See **if/unless** (next) for an example and explanation of a syntax description.

if/unless

The **if** and **unless** control structures are compound statements that have the following syntax:

if (expr) {...}

unless (expr) {...}

These structures differ only in the sense of the test they perform. The **if** structure executes the block of statements *if expr* evaluates to *true*; **unless** executes the block of statements *unless expr* evaluates to *true* (i.e., if *expr* is *false*).

The *if* appears in nonbold type because it is a keyword; it must appear exactly as shown. The *expr* is an expression; Perl evaluates it and executes the block (page 489) of statements represented by *{...}* if the expression evaluates as required by the control structure.

File test operators   The *expr* in the following example, **–r memo1**, uses the **–r** file test operator to determine if a file named **memo1** exists in the working directory and if the file is readable. Although this operator tests only whether you have read permission for the file, the file must exist for you to have read permission; thus it implicitly tests that the file is present. (Perl uses the same file test operators as bash; see Table 10-1 on page 401.) If this expression evaluates to *true*, Perl executes the block of statements (in this case one statement) between the braces. If the expression evaluates to *false*, Perl skips the block of statements. In either case, Perl then exits and returns control to the shell.

```
$ cat if1.pl
#!/usr/bin/perl -w
if (-r "memo1") {
    say "The file 'memo1' exists and is readable.";
    }

$ ./if1.pl
The file 'memo1' exists and is readable.
```

Following is the same program written using the postfix **if** syntax. Which syntax you use depends on which part of the statement is more important to someone reading the code.

```
$ cat if1a.pl
#!/usr/bin/perl -w
say "The file 'memo1' exists and is readable." if (-r "memo1");
```

The next example uses a **print** statement to display a prompt on standard output and uses the statement **$entry = <>;** to read a line from standard input and assign the line to the variable **$entry**. Reading from standard input, working with other files, and use of the magic file handle (<>) for reading files specified on the command line are covered on page 510.

Comparison operators
Perl uses different operators to compare numbers from those it uses to compare strings. Table 11-2 lists numeric and string comparison operators. In the following example, the expression in the **if** statement uses the **==** numeric comparison operator to compare the value the user entered and the number **28**. This operator performs a numeric comparison, so the user can enter **28**, **28.0**, or **00028** and in all cases the result of the comparison will be *true*. Also, because the comparison is numeric, Perl ignores both the whitespace around and the NEWLINE following the user's entry. The **−w** option causes Perl to issue a warning if the user enters a nonnumeric value and the program uses that value in an arithmetic expression; without this option Perl silently evaluates the expression as *false*.

```
$ cat if2.pl
#!/usr/bin/perl -w
print "Enter 28: ";
$entry = <>;
if ($entry == 28) {                        # use == for a numeric comparison
    print "Thank you for entering 28.\n";
    }
print "End.\n";

$ ./if2.pl
Enter 28: 28.0
Thank you for entering 28.
End.
```

Table 11-2 Comparison operators

Numeric operators	String operators	Value returned based on the relationship between the values preceding and following the operator
==	eq	True if equal
!=	ne	True if not equal
<	lt	True if less than
>	gt	True if greater than
<=	le	True if less than or equal
>=	ge	True if greater than or equal
<=>	cmp	0 if equal, 1 if greater than, –1 if less than

The next program is similar to the preceding one, except it tests for equality between two strings. The **chomp** function (page 511) removes the trailing NEWLINE from the user's entry—without this function the strings in the comparison would never match. The **eq** comparison operator compares strings. In this example the result of the string comparison is *true* when the user enters the string **five**. Leading or trailing whitespace will yield a result of *false,* as would the string 5, although none of these entries would generate a warning because they are legitimate strings.

```
$ cat if2a.pl
#!/usr/bin/perl -w
print "Enter the word 'five': ";
$entry = <>;
chomp ($entry);
if ($entry eq "five") {             # use eq for a string comparison
    print "Thank you for entering 'five'.\n";
    }
print "End.\n";

$ ./if2a.pl
Enter the word 'five': five
Thank you for entering 'five'.
End.
```

if...else

The **if...else** control structure is a compound statement that is similar to the bash **if...then...else** control structure (page 402). It implements a two-way branch using the following syntax:

if (expr) {...} else {...}

die The next program prompts the user for two different numbers and stores those numbers in **$num1** and **$num2**. If the user enters the same number twice, an **if** structure executes a **die** function, which sends its argument to standard error and aborts program execution.

If the user enters different numbers, the **if...else** structure reports which number is larger. Because *expr* performs a numeric comparison, the program accepts numbers that include decimal points.

```
$ cat ifelse.pl
#!/usr/bin/perl -w
print "Enter a number: ";
$num1 = <>;
print "Enter another, different number: ";
$num2 = <>;

if ($num1 == $num2) {
    die ("Please enter two different numbers.\n");
    }
if ($num1 > $num2) {
    print "The first number is greater than the second number.\n";
    }
else {
    print "The first number is less than the second number.\n";
    }

$ ./ifelse.pl
Enter a number: 8
Enter another, different number: 8
Please enter two different numbers.

$ ./ifelse.pl
Enter a number: 5.5
Enter another, different number: 5
The first number is greater than the second number.
```

if...elsif...else

Similar to the bash **if...then...elif** control structure (page 405), the Perl **if...elsif...else** control structure is a compound statement that implements a nested set of **if...else** structures using the following syntax:

> *if (expr) {...} elsif {...} ... else {...}*

The next program implements the functionality of the preceding **ifelse.pl** program using an **if...elsif...else** structure. A **print** statement replaces the **die** statement because the last statement in the program displays the error message; the program terminates after executing this statement anyway. You can use the STDERR handle (page 510) to cause Perl to send this message to standard error instead of standard output.

```
$ cat ifelsif.pl
#!/usr/bin/perl -w
print "Enter a number: ";
$num1 = <>;
print "Enter another, different number: ";
$num2 = <>;
```

```
if ($num1 > $num2) {
        print "The first number is greater than the second number.\n";
        }
    elsif ($num1 < $num2) {
        print "The first number is less than the second number.\n";
        }
    else {
        print "Please enter two different numbers.\n";
        }
```

foreach/for

The Perl **foreach** and **for** keywords are synonyms; you can replace one with the other in any context. These structures are compound statements that have two syntaxes. Some programmers use one syntax with **foreach** and the other syntax with the **for**, although there is no need to do so. This book uses **foreach** with both syntaxes.

foreach: SYNTAX 1

The first syntax for the **foreach** structure is similar to the shell's **for...in** structure (page 411):

foreach|for [var] (list) {...}

where *list* is a list of expressions or variables. Perl executes the block of statements once for each item in *list*, sequentially assigning to *var* the value of one item in *list* on each iteration, starting with the first item. If you do not specify *var*, Perl assigns values to the $_ variable (page 509).

The following program demonstrates a simple **foreach** structure. On the first pass through the loop, Perl assigns the string **Mo** to the variable **$item** and the **say** statement displays the value of this variable followed by a NEWLINE. On the second and third passes through the loop, **$item** is assigned the value of **Larry** and **Curly**. When there are no items left in the list, Perl continues with the statement following the **foreach** structure. In this case, the program terminates. See **use feature 'say'** on page 491 if this program complains about **say** not being available.

```
$ cat foreach.pl
foreach $item ("Mo", "Larry", "Curly") {
    say "$item says hello.";
    }

$ perl foreach.pl
Mo says hello.
Larry says hello.
Curly says hello.
```

Using $_ (page 509), you can write this program as follows:

```
$ cat foreacha.pl
foreach ("Mo", "Larry", "Curly") {
    say "$_ says hello.";
    }
```

Following is the program using an array:

```
$ cat foreachb.pl
@stooges = ("Mo", "Larry", "Curly");
foreach (@stooges) {
    say "$_ says hello.";
    }
```

Following is the program using the **foreach** postfix syntax:

```
$ cat foreachc.pl
@stooges = ("Mo", "Larry", "Curly");
say "$_ says hello." foreach @stooges;
```

The loop variable (**$item** and **$_** in the preceding examples) references the elements in the *list* within the parentheses. When you modify the loop variable, you modify the element in the list. The **uc** function returns an upshifted version of its argument. The next example shows that modifying the loop variable **$stooge** modifies the **@stooges** array:

```
$ cat foreachd.pl
@stooges = ("Mo", "Larry", "Curly");
foreach $stooge (@stooges) {
    $stooge = uc $stooge;
    say "$stooge says hello.";
    }
say "$stooges[1] is uppercase"

$ perl foreachd.pl
MO says hello.
LARRY says hello.
CURLY says hello.
LARRY is uppercase
```

See page 513 for an example that loops through command-line arguments.

last **AND** next

Perl's **last** and **next** statements allow you to interrupt a loop; they are analogous to the Bourne Again Shell's **break** and **continue** statements (page 420). The **last** statement transfers control to the statement following the block of statements controlled by the loop structure, terminating execution of the loop. The **next** statement transfers control to the end of the block of statements, which continues execution of the loop with the next iteration.

In the following program, the **if** structure tests whether **$item** is equal to the string **two**; if it is, the structure executes the **next** command, which skips the **say** statement and continues with the next iteration of the loop. If you replaced **next** with **last**, Perl would exit from the loop and not display **three**. See **use feature 'say'** on page 491 if this program complains about **say** not being available.

```
$ cat foreach1.pl
foreach $item ("one", "two", "three") {
    if ($item eq "two") {
        next;
        }
    say "$item";
    }

$ perl foreach1.pl
one
three
```

foreach: SYNTAX 2

The second syntax for the **foreach** structure is similar to the C **for** structure:

foreach|for (expr1; expr2; expr3) {...}

The *expr1* initializes the **foreach** loop; Perl evaluates *expr1* one time, before it executes the block of statements. The *expr2* is the termination condition; Perl evaluates it before each pass through the block of statements and executes the block of statements if *expr2* evaluates as *true*. Perl evaluates *expr3* after each pass through the block of statements—it typically increments a variable that is part of *expr2*.

In the next example, the **foreach2.pl** program prompts for three numbers; displays the first number; repeatedly increments this number by the second number, displaying each result until the result would be greater than the third number; and quits. See page 510 for a discussion of the magic file handle (<>).

```
$ cat ./foreach2.pl
#!/usr/bin/perl -w

print "Enter starting number: ";
$start = <>;

print "Enter ending number: ";
$end = <>;

print "Enter increment: ";
$incr = <>;

if ($start >= $end || $incr < 1) {
    die ("The starting number must be less than the ending number\n",
    "and the increment must be greater than zero.\n");
    }

foreach ($count = $start+0; $count <= $end; $count += $incr) {
    say "$count";
    }
```

```
$ ./foreach2.pl
Enter starting number: 2
Enter ending number: 10
Enter increment: 3
2
5
8
```

After prompting for three numbers, the preceding program tests whether the starting number is greater than or equal to the ending number or if the increment is less than 1. The || is a Boolean OR operator; the expression within the parentheses following **if** evaluates to *true* if either the expression before or the expression after this operator evaluates to *true*.

The **foreach** statement begins by assigning the value of **$start+0** to **$count**. Adding 0 (zero) to the string **$start** forces Perl to work in a numeric context, removing the trailing NEWLINE when it performs the assignment. Without this fix, the program would display an extra NEWLINE following the first number it displayed.

while/until

The **while** (page 414) and **until** (page 418) control structures are compound statements that implement conditional loops using the following syntax:

> *while (**expr**) {...}*

> *until (**expr**) {...}*

These structures differ only in the sense of their termination conditions. The **while** structure repeatedly executes the block of statements *while **expr*** evaluates to *true*; **until** continues *until **expr*** evaluates to *true* (i.e., while **expr** remains *false*).

The following example demonstrates one technique for reading and processing input until there is no more input. Although this example shows input coming from the user (standard input), the technique works the same way for input coming from a file (see the example on page 512). The user enters CONTROL-D on a line by itself to signal the end of file.

In this example, *expr* is **$line = <>**. This statement uses the magic file handle (**<>**; page 510) to read one line from standard input and assigns the string it reads to the **$line** variable. This statement evaluates to *true* as long as it reads data. When it reaches the end of file, the statement evaluates to *false*. The **while** loop continues to execute the block of statements (in this example, only one statement) as long as there is data to read.

```
$ cat while1.pl
#!/usr/bin/perl -w
$count = 0;
while ($line = <>) {
    print ++$count, ". $line";
    }
print "\n$count lines entered.\n";
```

```
$ ./while1.pl
Good Morning.
1. Good Morning.
Today is Monday.
2. Today is Monday.
CONTROL-D

2 lines entered.
```

In the preceding example, **$count** keeps track of the number of lines the user enters. Putting the **++** increment operator before a variable (**++$count**; called a preincrement operator) increments the variable before Perl evaluates it. Alternatively, you could initialize **$count** to 1 and increment it with **$count++** (postincrement), but then in the final **print** statement **$count** would equal one more than the number of lines entered.

$.   The **$.** variable keeps track of the number of lines of input a program has read. Using **$.** you can rewrite the previous example as follows:

```
$ cat while1a.pl
#!/usr/bin/perl -w
while ($line = <>) {
        print $., ". $line";
        }
print "\n$. lines entered.\n";
```

$_**   Frequently you can simplify Perl code by using the **$_ variable. You can use **$_** many places in a Perl program—think of **$_** as meaning *it*, the object of what you are doing. It is the default operand for many operations. For example, the following section of code processes a line using the **$line** variable. It reads a line into **$line**, removes any trailing NEWLINE from **$line** using **chomp** (page 511), and checks whether a regular expression matches **$line**.

```
while (my $line = <>) {
    chomp $line;
    if ($line =~ /regex/) ...
}
```

You can rewrite this code by using **$_** to replace **$line**:

```
while (my $_ = <>) {
    chomp $_;
    if ($_ =~ /regex/) ...
}
```

Because **$_** is the default operand in each of these instances, you can also omit **$_** altogether:

```
while (<>) {          # read into $_
    chomp;            # chomp $_
    if (/regex/) ...  # if $_ matches regex
}
```

WORKING WITH FILES

Opening a file and assigning a handle A *handle* is a name that you can use in a Perl program to refer to a file or process that is open for reading and/or writing. When you are working with the shell, handles are referred to as *file descriptors* (page 431). As when you are working with the shell, the kernel automatically opens handles for standard input (page 123), standard output (page 123), and standard error (page 275) before it runs a program. The kernel closes these descriptors after a program finishes running. The names for these handles are **STDIN**, **STDOUT**, and **STDERR**, respectively. You must manually open handles to read from or write to other files or processes. The syntax of an **open** statement is

> *open (file-handle, ['mode',] "file-ref");*

where **file-handle** is the name of the handle or a variable you will use in the program to refer to the file or process named by **file-ref**. If you omit **mode** or specify a **mode** of <, Perl opens the file for input (reading). Specify **mode** as > to truncate and write to a file or as >> to append to a file.

See page 526 for a discussion of reading from and writing to processes.

Writing to a file The **print** function writes output to a file or process. The syntax of a **print** statement is

> *print [file-handle] "text";*

where **file-handle** is the name of the handle you specified in an **open** statement and **text** is the information you want to output. The **file-handle** can also be **STDOUT** or **STDERR**, as explained earlier. Except when you send information to standard output, you must specify a handle in a **print** statement. Do not place a comma after **file-handle**. Also, do not enclose arguments to **print** within parentheses because doing so can create problems.

Reading from a file The following expression reads one line, including the NEWLINE (\n), from the file or process associated with **file-handle**:

> *<file-handle>*

This expression is typically used in a statement such as

```
$line = <IN>;
```

which reads into the variable **$line** one line from the file or process identified by the handle **IN**.

Magic file handle (<>) To facilitate reading from files named on the command line or from standard input, Perl provides the *magic file handle*. This book uses this file handle in most examples. In place of the preceding line, you can use

```
$line = <>;
```

This file handle causes a Perl program to work like many Linux utilities: It reads from standard input unless the program is called with one or more arguments, in which case it reads from the files named by the arguments. See page 128 for an explanation of how this feature works with cat.

The **print** statement in the first line in the next example includes the optional handle **STDOUT**; the next **print** statement omits this handle; the final **print** statement uses the **STDERR** file handle, which causes **print**'s output to go to standard error. The first **print** statement prompts the user to enter something. The string that this statement outputs is terminated with a SPACE, not a NEWLINE, so the user can enter information on the same line as the prompt. The second line then uses a magic file handle to read one line from standard input, which it assigns to **$userline**. Because of the magic file handle, if you call **file1.pl** with an argument that is a filename, it reads one line from that file instead of from standard input. The command line that runs **file1.pl** uses **2>** (see "File descriptors" on page 275) to redirect standard error (the output of the third **print** statement) to the **file1.err** file.

```
$ cat file1.pl
print STDOUT "Enter something: ";
$userline = <>;
print "1>>>$userline<<<\n";
chomp ($userline);
print "2>>>$userline<<<\n";
print STDERR "3. Error message.\n";

$ perl file1.pl 2> file1.err
Enter something: hi there
1>>>hi there
<<<
2>>>hi there<<<

$ cat file1.err
3. Error message.
```

chomp/chop The two **print** statements following the user input in **file1.pl** display the value of **$userline** immediately preceded by greater than signs (>) and followed by less than signs (<). The first of these statements demonstrates that **$userline** includes a NEWLINE: The less than signs following the string the user entered appear on the line following the string. The **chomp** function removes a trailing NEWLINE, if it exists, from a string. After **chomp** processes **$userline**, the **print** statement shows that this variable no longer contains a NEWLINE. (The **chop** function is similar to **chomp**, except it removes *any* trailing character from a string.)

The next example shows how to read from a file. It uses an **open** statement to assign the lexical file handle **$infile** to the file **/usr/share/dict/words**. Each iteration of the **while** structure evaluates an expression that reads a line from the file represented by **$infile** and assigns the line to **$line**. When **while** reaches the end of file, the expression evaluates to *false*; control then passes out of the **while** structure. The block of one statement displays the line as it was read from the file, including the NEWLINE.

This program copies **/usr/share/dict/words** to standard output. A pipe (|; page 56) is then used to send the output through head (page 52), which displays the first four lines of the file (the first line is blank).

```
$ cat file2.pl
open (my $infile, "/usr/share/dict/words") or die "Cannot open dictionary: $!\n";
while ($line = <$infile>) {
    print $line;
    }

$ perl file2.pl | head -4

A
A's
AOL
```

$!**   The **$! variable holds the last system error. In a numeric context, it holds the system error number; in a string context, it holds the system error string. If the **words** file is not present on the system, **file2.pl** displays the following message:

> Cannot open dictionary: No such file or directory

If you do not have read permission for the file, the program displays this message:

> Cannot open dictionary: Permission denied

Displaying the value of **$!** gives the user more information about what went wrong than simply saying that the program could not open the file.

Always check for an error when opening a file

tip   When a Perl program attempts to open a file and fails, the program does not display an error message unless it checks whether **open** returned an error. In **file2.pl**, the **or** operator in the **open** statement causes Perl to execute **die** (page 503) if **open** fails. The **die** statement sends the message **Cannot open the dictionary** followed by the system error string to standard error and terminates the program.

@ARGV   The **@ARGV** array holds the arguments from the command line Perl was called with. When you call the following program with a list of filenames, it displays the first line of each file. If the program cannot read a file, **die** (page 503) sends an error message to standard error and quits. The **foreach** structure loops through the command-line arguments, as represented by **@ARGV**, assigning each argument in turn to **$filename**. The **foreach** block starts with an **open** statement. Perl executes the **open** statement that precedes the OR Boolean operator (**or**) or, if that fails, Perl executes the statement following the **or** operator (**die**). The result is that Perl either opens the file named by **$filename** and assigns IN as its handle or, if it cannot open that file, executes the **die** statement and quits. The **print** statement displays the name of the file followed by a colon and the first line of the file. When it accepts **$line = <IN>** as an argument to **print**, Perl displays the value of **$line** following the assignment. After reading a line from a file, the program closes the file.

```
$ cat file3.pl
foreach $filename (@ARGV) {
    open (IN, $filename) or die "Cannot open file '$filename': $!\n";
    print "$filename: ", $line = <IN>;
    close (IN);
    }
$ perl file3.pl f1 f2 f3 f4
f1: First line of file f1.
f2: First line of file f2.
Cannot open file 'f3': No such file or directory
```

The next example is similar to the preceding one, except it takes advantage of several Perl features that make the code simpler. It does not quit when it cannot read a file. Instead, Perl displays an error message and continues. The first line of the program uses **my** to declare **$filename** to be a lexical variable. Next, **while** uses the magic file handle to open and read each line of each file named by the command-line arguments; **$ARGV** holds the name of the file. When there are no more files to read, the **while** condition [(<>)] is *false,* **while** transfers control outside the **while** block, and the program terminates. Perl takes care of all file opening and closing operations; you do not have to write code to take care of these tasks. Perl also performs error checking.

The program displays the first line of each file named by a command-line argument. Each time through the **while** block, **while** reads another line. When it finishes with one file, it starts reading from the next file. Within the **while** block, **if** tests whether it is processing a new file. If it is, the **if** block displays the name of the file and the (first) line from the file and then assigns the new filename (**$ARGV**) to **$filename**.

```
$ cat file3a.pl
my $filename;
while (<>) {
    if ($ARGV ne $filename) {
        print "$ARGV: $_";
        $filename = $ARGV;
    }
}

$ perl file3a.pl f1 f2 f3 f4
f1: First line of file f1.
f2: First line of file f2.
Can't open f3: No such file or directory at file3a.pl line 3, <> line 3.
f4: First line of file f4.
```

Sort

reverse   The **sort** function returns elements of an array ordered numerically or alphabetically, based on the *locale* (page 963) environment. The **reverse** function is not related to **sort**; it simply returns the elements of an array in reverse order.

The first two lines of the following program assign values to the **@colors** array and display these values. Each of the next two pairs of lines uses **sort** to put the values in the **@colors** array in order, assign the result to **@scolors**, and display **@scolors**. These sorts put uppercase letters before lowercase letters. Observe the positions of **Orange** and **Violet**, both of which begin with an uppercase letter, in the sorted output. The first assignment statement in these two pairs of lines uses the full sort syntax, including the block {**$a cmp $b**} that tells Perl to use the **cmp** subroutine, which compares strings, and to put the result in ascending order. When you omit the block in a **sort** statement, as is the case in the second assignment statement, Perl also performs an ascending textual sort.

```
$ cat sort3.pl
@colors = ("red", "Orange", "yellow", "green", "blue", "indigo", "Violet");

say "@colors";

@scolors = sort {$a cmp $b} @colors;          # ascending sort with
say "@scolors";                               # an explicit block

@scolors = sort @colors;                      # ascending sort with
say "@scolors";                               # an implicit block

@scolors = sort {$b cmp $a} @colors;          # descending sort
say "@scolors";

@scolors = sort {lc($a) cmp lc($b)} @colors;  # ascending folded sort
say "@scolors";

$ perl sort3.pl
red Orange yellow green blue indigo Violet
Orange Violet blue green indigo red yellow
Orange Violet blue green indigo red yellow
yellow red indigo green blue Violet Orange
blue green indigo Orange red Violet yellow
```

The third sort in the preceding example reverses the positions of **$a** and **$b** in the block to specify a descending sort. The last sort converts the strings to lowercase before comparing them, providing a sort wherein the uppercase letters are folded into the lowercase letters. As a result, **Orange** and **Violet** appear in alphabetical order.

To perform a numerical sort, specify the **<=>** subroutine in place of **cmp**. The following example demonstrates ascending and descending numerical sorts:

```
$ cat sort4.pl
@numbers = (22, 188, 44, 2, 12);

print "@numbers\n";

@snumbers = sort {$a <=> $b} @numbers;
print "@snumbers\n";

@snumbers = sort {$b <=> $a} @numbers;
print "@snumbers\n";
```

```
$ perl sort4.pl
22 188 44 2 12
2 12 22 44 188
188 44 22 12 2
```

SUBROUTINES

All variables are package variables (page 489) unless you use the **my** function to define them to be lexical variables (page 489). Lexical variables defined in a subroutine are local to that subroutine.

The following program includes a main part and a subroutine named **add**(). This program uses the variables named **$one**, **$two**, and **$ans**, all of which are package variables: They are available to both the main program and the subroutine. The call to the subroutine does not pass values to the subroutine and the subroutine returns no values. This setup is not typical: It demonstrates that all variables are package variables unless you use **my** to declare them to be lexical variables.

The **subroutine1.pl** program assigns values to two variables and calls a subroutine. The subroutine adds the values of the two variables and assigns the result to another variable. The main part of the program displays the result.

```
$ cat subroutine1.pl
$one = 1;
$two = 2;
add();
print "Answer is $ans\n";

sub add {
    $ans =$one + $two
    }

$ perl subroutine1.pl
Answer is 3
```

The next example is similar to the previous one, except the subroutine takes advantage of a **return** statement to return a value to the main program. The program assigns the value returned by the subroutine to the variable **$ans** and displays that value. Again, all variables are package variables.

```
$ cat subroutine2.pl
$one = 1;
$two = 2;
$ans = add();
print "Answer is $ans\n";

sub add {
    return ($one + $two)
    }

$ perl subroutine2.pl
Answer is 3
```

Keeping variables local to a subroutine is important in many cases. The subroutine in the next example changes the values of variables and insulates the calling program from these changes by declaring and using lexical variables. This setup is more typical.

@_   When you pass values in a call to a subroutine, Perl makes those values available in the array named @_ in the subroutine. Although @_ is local to the subroutine, its elements are aliases for the parameters the subroutine was called with. Changing a value in the @_ array changes the value of the underlying variable, which may not be what you want. The next program avoids this pitfall by assigning the values passed to the subroutine to lexical variables.

The **subroutine3.pl** program calls the **addplusone**() subroutine with two variables as arguments and assigns the value returned by the subroutine to a variable. The first statement in the subroutine declares two lexical variables and assigns to them the values from the @_ array. The **my** function declares these variables to be lexical. (See the tip on lexical and package variables on page 494.) Although you can use **my** without assigning values to the declared variables, the syntax in the example is more commonly used. The next two statements increment the lexical variables **$lcl_one** and **$lcl_two**. The **print** statement displays the value of **$lcl_one** within the subroutine. The **return** statement returns the sum of the two incremented, lexical variables.

```
$ cat subroutine3.pl
$one = 1;
$two = 2;
$ans = addplusone($one, $two);
print "Answer is $ans\n";
print "Value of 'lcl_one' in main: $lcl_one\n";
print "Value of 'one' in main: $one\n";

sub addplusone {
    my ($lcl_one, $lcl_two) = @_;
    $lcl_one++;
    $lcl_two++;
    print "Value of 'lcl_one' in sub: $lcl_one\n";
    return ($lcl_one + $lcl_two)
    }

$ perl subroutine3.pl
Value of 'lcl_one' in sub: 2
Answer is 5
Value of 'lcl_one' in main:
Value of 'one' in main: 1
```

After displaying the result returned by the subroutine, the **print** statements in the main program demonstrate that **$lcl_one** is not defined in the main program (it is local to the subroutine) and that the value of **$one** has not changed.

The next example illustrates another way to work with parameters passed to a subroutine. This subroutine does not use variables other than the @_ array it was passed and does not change the values of any elements of that array.

```
$ cat subroutine4.pl
$one = 1;
$two = 2;
$ans = addplusone($one, $two);
print "Answer is $ans\n";
sub addplusone {
    return ($_[0] + $_[1] + 2);
    }

$ perl subroutine4.pl
Answer is 5
```

The final example in this section presents a more typical Perl subroutine. The subroutine **max**() can be called with any number of numeric arguments and returns the value of the largest argument. It uses the **shift** function to assign to **$biggest** the value of the first argument the subroutine was called with and to shift the rest of the arguments. After using **shift**, argument number 2 becomes argument number 1 (8), argument 3 becomes argument 2 (**64**), and argument 4 becomes argument 3 (**2**). Next, **foreach** loops over the remaining arguments (@_). Each time through the **foreach** block, Perl assigns to **$_** the value of each of the arguments, in order. The **$biggest** variable is assigned the value of **$_** if **$_** is bigger than **$biggest**. When **max**() finishes going through its arguments, **$biggest** holds the maximum value, which **max**() returns.

```
$ cat subroutine5.pl
$ans = max (16, 8, 64, 2);
print "Maximum value is $ans\n";

sub max {
    my $biggest = shift;  # Assign first and shift the rest of the arguments to max()
    foreach (@_) {        # Loop through remaining arguments
    $biggest = $_ if $_ > $biggest;
    }
return ($biggest);
}

$ perl subroutine5.pl
Maximum value is 64
```

REGULAR EXPRESSIONS

Appendix A defines and discusses regular expressions as you can use them in many Linux utilities. All of the material in Appendix A applies to Perl, except as noted. In addition to the facilities described in Appendix A, Perl offers regular expression features that allow you to perform more complex string processing. This section reviews some of the regular expressions covered in Appendix A and describes some of the additional features of regular expressions available in Perl. It also introduces the syntax Perl uses for working with regular expressions.

SYNTAX AND THE =~ OPERATOR

The –l option   The Perl **–l** option applies **chomp** to each line of input and places **\n** at the end of each line of output. The examples in this section use the Perl **–l** and **–e** (page 490) options. Because the program must be specified as a single argument, the examples enclose the Perl programs within single quotation marks. The shell interprets the quotation marks and does not pass them to Perl.

Using other options with –e

tip   When you use another option with **–e**, the program must immediately follow the **–e** on the command line. Like many other utilities, Perl allows you to combine options following a single hyphen; if **–e** is one of the combined options, it must appear last in the list of options. Thus you can use **perl –l –e** or **perl –le** but not **perl –e –l** or **perl –el**.

/ is the default   By default, Perl delimits a regular expression with slashes (**/**). The first program uses delimiter   the **=~** operator to search for the pattern **ge** in the string **aged**. You can think of the **=~** operator as meaning "contains." Using different terminology, the **=~** operator determines whether the regular expression **ge** has a match in the string **aged**. The regular expression in this example contains no special characters; the string **ge** is part of the string **aged**. Thus the expression within the parentheses evaluates to *true* and Perl executes the **print** statement.

```
$ perl -le 'if ("aged" =~ /ge/) {print "true";}'
true
```

You can achieve the same functionality by using a postfix **if** statement:

```
$ perl -le 'print "true" if "aged" =~ /ge/'
true
```

!~   The **!~** operator works in the opposite sense from the **=~** operator. The expression in the next example evaluates to *true* because the regular expression **xy** does *not* match any part of **aged**:

```
$ perl -le 'print "true" if ("aged" !~ /xy/)'
true
```

As explained on page 889, a period within a regular expression matches any single character, so the regular expression **a..d** matches the string **aged**:

```
$ perl -le 'print "true" if ("aged" =~ /a..d/)'
true
```

You can use a variable to hold a regular expression. The following syntax quotes *string* as a regular expression:

qr/*string*/

The next example uses this syntax to assign the regular expression **/a..d/** (including the delimiters) to the variable **$re** and then uses that variable as the regular expression:

```
$ perl -le '$re = qr/a..d/; print "true" if ("aged" =~ $re)'
true
```

If you want to include the delimiter within a regular expression, you must quote it. In the next example, the default delimiter, a slash (**/**), appears in the regular expression. To keep Perl from interpreting the **/** in **/usr** as the end of the regular expression, the **/** that is part of the regular expression is quoted by preceding it with a backslash (****). See page 891 for more information on quoting characters in regular expressions.

```
$ perl -le 'print "true" if ("/usr/doc" =~ /\/usr/)'
true
```

Quoting several characters by preceding each one with a backslash can make a complex regular expression harder to read. Instead, you can precede a delimited regular expression with **m** and use a paired set of characters, such as {}, as the delimiters. In the following example, the caret (**^**) anchors the regular expression to the beginning of the line (page 890):

```
$ perl -le 'print "true" if ("/usr/doc" =~ m{^/usr})'
true
```

You can use the same syntax when assigning a regular expression to a variable:

```
$ perl -le '$pn = qr{^/usr}; print "true" if ("/usr/doc" =~ $pn)'
true
```

Replacement string and assignment Perl uses the syntax shown in the next example to substitute a string (the *replacement string*) for a matched regular expression. The syntax is the same as that found in vim and sed. In the second line of the example, an **s** before the regular expression instructs Perl to substitute the string between the second and third slashes (**worst**; the replacement string) for a match of the regular expression between the first two slashes (**best**). Implicit in this syntax is the notion that the substitution is made in the string held in the variable on the left of the **=~** operator.

```
$ cat re10a.pl
$stg = "This is the best!";
$stg =~ s/best/worst/;
print "$stg\n";

$ perl re10a.pl
This is the worst!
```

Table 11-3 (on the next page) list some of the characters, called metacharacters, that are considered special within Perl regular expressions. Give the command **perldoc perlre** for more information.

Table 11-3   Some Perl regular expression metacharacters

Character	Matches
^ (caret)	Anchors a regular expression to the beginning of a line (page 890)
$ (dollar sign)	Anchors a regular expression to the end of a line (page 890)
(...)	Brackets a regular expression (page 521)
. (period)	Any single character except NEWLINE (**\n**; page 889)
****	A backslash (****)
\b	A word boundary (zero-width match)
\B	A nonword boundary (**[^\b]**)
\d	A single decimal digit (**[0–9]**)
\D	A single nondecimal digit (**[^0–9]** or **[^\d]**)
\s (lowercase)	A single whitespace character SPACE, NEWLINE, RETURN, TAB, FORMFEED
\S (uppercase)	A single nonwhitespace character (**[^\s]**)
\w (lowercase)	A single word character (a letter or digit; **[a–zA–Z0–9]**)
\W (uppercase)	A single nonword character (**[^\w]**)

GREEDY MATCHES

By default Perl performs *greedy matching*, which means a regular expression matches the longest string possible (page 891). In the following example, the regular expression /{.*} / matches an opening brace followed by any string of characters, a closing brace, and a SPACE (**{remove me} may have two {keep me}**). Perl substitutes a null string (//) for this match.

```
$ cat 5ha.pl
$string = "A line {remove me} may have two {keep me} pairs of braces.";
$string =~ s/{.*} //;
print "$string\n";

$ perl 5ha.pl
A line pairs of braces.
```

Nongreedy matches   The next example shows the classic way of matching the shorter brace-enclosed string from the previous example. This type of match is called *nongreedy* or *parsimonious matching*. Here the regular expression matches

1. An opening brace followed by

2. A character belonging to the character class (page 889) that includes all characters except a closing brace ([^}]) followed by

3. Zero or more occurrences of the preceding character (`*`) followed by

4. A closing brace followed by

5. A SPACE.

(A caret as the first character of a character class specifies the class of all characters that do not match the following characters, so [^}] matches any character that is not a closing brace.)

```
$ cat re5b.pl
$string = "A line {remove me} may have two {keep me} pairs of braces.";
$string =~ s/{[^}]*} //;
print "$string\n";

$ perl re5b.pl
A line may have two {keep me} pairs of braces.
```

Perl provides a shortcut that allows you to specify a nongreedy match. In the following example, the question mark in {.*?} causes the regular expression to match the shortest string that starts with an opening brace followed by any string of characters followed by a closing brace.

```
$ cat re5c.pl
$string = "A line {remove me} may have two {keep me} pairs of braces.";
$string =~ s/{.*?} //;
print "$string\n";

$ perl re5c.pl
A line may have two {keep me} pairs of braces.
```

BRACKETING EXPRESSIONS

As explained on page 892, you can bracket parts of a regular expression and recall those parts in the replacement string. Most Linux utilities use quoted parentheses [i.e., \(and \)] to bracket a regular expression. In Perl regular expressions, parentheses are special characters. Perl omits the backslashes and uses unquoted parentheses to bracket regular expressions. To specify a parenthesis as a regular character within a regular expression in Perl, you must quote it (page 891).

The next example uses unquoted parentheses in a regular expression to bracket part of the expression. It then assigns the part of the string that the bracketed expression matched to the variable that held the string in which Perl originally searched for the regular expression.

First the program assigns the string **My name is Sam** to **$stg**. The next statement looks for a match for the regular expression **/My name is (.*)/** in the string held by **$stg**. The part of the regular expression bracketed by parentheses matches **Sam**; the **$1** in the replacement string matches the first (and only in this case) matched bracketed portion of the regular expression. The result is that the string held in **$stg** is replaced by the string **Sam**.

```
$ cat re11.pl
$stg = "My name is Sam";
$stg =~ s/My name is (.*)/$1/;
print "Matched: $stg\n";
```

```
$ perl re11.pl
Matched: Sam
```

The next example uses regular expressions to parse a string for numbers. Two variables are initialized to hold a string that contains two numbers. The third line of the program uses a regular expression to isolate the first number in the string. The **\D*** matches a string of zero or more characters that does not include a digit: The **\D** special character matches any single nondigit character. The trailing asterisk makes this part of the regular expression perform a greedy match that does not include a digit (it matches **What is**). The bracketed regular expression **\d+** matches a string of one or more digits. The parentheses do not affect what the regular expression matches; they allow the **$1** in the replacement string to match what the bracketed regular expression matched. The final **.*** matches the rest of the string. This line assigns the value of the first number in the string to **$string**.

The next line is similar but assigns the second number in the string to **$string2**. The **print** statements display the numbers and the result of subtracting the second number from the first.

```
$ cat re8.pl
$string = "What is 488 minus 78?";
$string2 = $string;
$string =~ s/\D*(\d+).*/$1/;
$string2 =~ s/\D*\d+\D*(\d+).*/$1/;

print "$string\n";
print "$string2\n";
print $string - $string2, "\n";
```

```
$ perl re8.pl
488
78
410
```

The next few programs show some of the pitfalls of using unquoted parentheses in regular expressions when you do not intend to bracket part of the regular expression. The first of these programs attempts to match parentheses in a string with unquoted parentheses in a regular expression, but fails. The regular expression **ag(e** matches the same string as the regular expression **age** because the parenthesis is a special character; the regular expression does not match the string **ag(ed)**.

```
$ perl -le 'if ("ag(ed)" =~ /ag(ed)/) {print "true";} else {print "false";}'
false
```

The regular expression in the next example quotes the parentheses by preceding each with a backslash, causing Perl to interpret them as regular characters. The match is successful.

```
$ perl -le 'if ("ag(ed)" =~ /ag\(ed\)/) {print "true";} else {print "false";}'
true
```

Next, Perl finds an unmatched parenthesis in a regular expression:

```
$ perl -le 'if ("ag(ed)" =~ /ag(e/) {print "true";} else {print "false";}'
Unmatched ( in regex; marked by <-- HERE in m/ag( <-- HERE e/ at -e line 1.
```

When you quote the parenthesis, all is well and Perl finds a match:

```
$ perl -le 'if ("ag(ed)" =~ /ag\(e/) {print "true";} else {print "false";}'
true
```

CPAN MODULES

CPAN (Comprehensive Perl Archive Network) provides Perl documentation, FAQs, modules (page 489), and scripts on its Web site (www.cpan.org). It holds more than 16,000 distributions (page 489) and provides links, mailing lists, and versions of Perl compiled to run under various operating systems (ports of Perl). One way to locate a module is to visit search.cpan.org and use the search box or click one of the classes of modules listed on that page.

This section explains how to download a module from CPAN and how to install and run the module. Perl provides a hierarchical namespace for modules, separating components of a name with double colons (::). The example in this section uses the module named **Timestamp::Simple**, which you can read about and download from search.cpan.org/dist/Timestamp-Simple. The timestamp is the date and time in the format YYYYMMDDHHMMSS

To use a Perl module, you first download the file that holds the module. For this example, the search.cpan.org/~shoop/Timestamp-Simple-1.01/Simple.pm Web page has a link on the right side labeled **Download**. Click this link and save the file to the directory you want to work in. You do not need to work as a privileged user until the last step of this procedure, when you install the module.

Most Perl modules come as compressed tar files (page 63). With the downloaded file in the working directory, decompress the file:

```
$ tar xzvf Timestamp-Simple-1.01.tar.gz
Timestamp-Simple-1.01/
Timestamp-Simple-1.01/Simple.pm
Timestamp-Simple-1.01/Makefile.PL
Timestamp-Simple-1.01/README
Timestamp-Simple-1.01/test.pl
Timestamp-Simple-1.01/Changes
Timestamp-Simple-1.01/MANIFEST
Timestamp-Simple-1.01/ARTISTIC
Timestamp-Simple-1.01/GPL
Timestamp-Simple-1.01/META.yml
```

The **README** file in the newly created directory usually provides instructions for building and installing the module. Most modules follow the same steps.

```
$ cd Timestamp-Simple-1.01
$ perl Makefile.PL
Checking if your kit is complete...
Looks good
Writing Makefile for Timestamp::Simple
```

If the module you are building depends on other modules that are not installed on the local system, running **perl Makefile.PL** will display one or more warnings about prerequisites that are not found. This step writes out the makefile even if modules are missing. In this case the next step will fail, and you must build and install missing modules before continuing.

The next step is to run make on the makefile you just created. After you run **make**, run **make test** to be sure the module is working.

```
$ make
cp Simple.pm blib/lib/Timestamp/Simple.pm
Manifying blib/man3/Timestamp::Simple.3pm

$ make test
PERL_DL_NONLAZY=1 /usr/bin/perl "-Iblib/lib" "-Iblib/arch" test.pl
1..1
# Running under perl version 5.100000 for linux
# Current time local: Fri Sep  4 18:20:41 2009
# Current time GMT:   Sat Sep  5 01:20:41 2009
# Using Test.pm version 1.25
ok 1
ok 2
ok 3
```

Finally, running with **root** privileges, install the module:

```
# make install
Installing /usr/local/share/perl/5.10.0/Timestamp/Simple.pm
Installing /usr/local/man/man3/Timestamp::Simple.3pm
Writing /usr/local/lib/perl/5.10.0/auto/Timestamp/Simple/.packlist
Appending installation info to /usr/local/lib/perl/5.10.0/perllocal.pod
```

Once you have installed a module, you can use perldoc to display the documentation that tells you how to use the module. See page 487 for an example.

Some modules contain SYNOPSIS sections. If the module you installed includes such a section, you can test the module by putting the code from the SYNOPSIS section in a file and running it as a Perl program:

```
$ cat times.pl
use Timestamp::Simple qw(stamp);
print stamp, "\n";

$ perl times.pl
20090905182627
```

You can then incorporate the module in a Perl program. The following example uses the timestamp module to generate a unique filename:

```
$ cat fn.pl
use Timestamp::Simple qw(stamp);

# Save timestamp in a variable
$ts = stamp, "\n";

# Strip off the year
$ts =~ s/....(.*)/\1/;

# Create a unique filename
$fn = "myfile." . $ts;

# Open, write to, and close the file
open (OUTFILE, '>', "$fn");
print OUTFILE "Hi there.\n";
close (OUTFILE);

$ perl fn.pl
$ ls myf*
myfile.0905183010
```

substr   You can use the **substr** function in place of the regular expression to strip off the year. To do so, replace the line that starts with **$ts =~** with the following line. Here, **substr** takes on the value of the string **$ts** starting at position 4 and continuing to the end of the string:

```
$ts = substr ($ts, 4);
```

EXAMPLES

This section provides some sample Perl programs. First try running these programs as is, and then modify them to learn more about programming with Perl.

The first example runs under Linux and displays the list of groups that the user given as an argument is a member of. Without an argument, it displays the list of groups that the user running the program is a member of. In a Perl program, the **%ENV** hash holds the environment variables from the shell that called Perl. The keys in this hash are the names of environment variables; the values in this hash are the values of the corresponding variables. The first line of the program assigns a username to **$user**. The **shift** function (page 499) takes on the value of the first command-line argument and shifts the rest of the arguments, if any remain. If the user runs the program with an argument, that argument is assigned to **$user**. If no argument appears on the command line, **shift** fails and Perl executes the statement following the Boolean OR (||). This statement extracts the value associated with the **USER** key in **%ENV**, which is the name of the user running the program.

The third statement initializes the array **@list**. Although this statement is not
required, it is good practice to include it to make the code easier to read. The next
statement opens the **$fh** lexical handle. The trailing pipe symbol (|) in the *file-ref*
(page 510) portion of this **open** statement tells Perl to pass the command line preceding the pipe symbol to the shell for execution and to accept standard output
from the command when the program reads from the file handle. In this case the
command uses grep to filter the **/etc/group** file for lines containing the username
held in **$user**. The **die** statement displays an error message if Perl cannot open the
handle.

```
$ cat groupfind.pl
$user = shift || $ENV{"USER"};
say "User $user belongs to these groups:";
@list = ();
open (my $fh, "grep $user /etc/group |") or die "Error: $!\n";
while ($group = <$fh>) {
    chomp $group;
    $group =~ s/(.*?):.*/$1/;
    push @list, $group;
}
close $fh;
@slist = sort @list;
say "@slist";

$ perl groupfind.pl
User sam belongs to these groups:
adm admin audio cdrom dialout dip floppy kvm lpadmin ...
```

The **while** structure in **groupfind.pl** reads lines from standard output of grep and
terminates when grep finishes executing. The name of the group appears first on
each line in **/etc/group**, followed by a colon and other information, including the
names of the users who belong to the group. Following is a line from this file:

```
sam:x:1000:max,zach,helen
```

The line

```
$group =~ s/(.*?):.*/$1/;
```

uses a regular expression and substitution to remove everything except the name of
the group from each line. The regular expression .*: would perform a greedy match
of zero or more characters followed by a colon; putting a question mark after the
asterisk causes the expression to perform a nongreedy match (page 520). Putting
parentheses around the part of the expression that matches the string the program
needs to display enables Perl to use the string that the regular expression matches in
the replacement string. The final .* matches the rest of the line. Perl replaces the **$1**
in the replacement string with the string the bracketed portion of the regular expression (the part between the parentheses) matched and assigns this value (the name of
the group) to **$group**.

The **chomp** statement removes the trailing NEWLINE (the regular expression did not match this character). The **push** statement adds the value of **$group** to the end of the **@list** array. Without **chomp**, each group would appear on a line by itself in the output. After the **while** structure finishes processing input from grep, **sort** orders **@list** and assigns the result to **@slist**. The final statement displays the sorted list of groups the user belongs to.

opendir and readdir The next example introduces the **opendir** and **readdir** functions. The **opendir** function opens a directory in a manner similar to the way **open** opens an ordinary file. It takes two arguments: the name of the directory handle and the name of the directory to open. The **readdir** function reads the name of a file from an open directory.

In the example, **opendir** opens the working directory (specified by .) using the **$dir** lexical directory handle. If **opendir** fails, Perl executes the statement following the **or** operator: **die** sends an error message to standard error and terminates the program. With the directory opened, **while** loops through the files in the directory, assigning the filename that **readdir** returns to the lexical variable **$entry**. An **if** statement executes **print** only for those files that are directories (**–d**). The **print** function displays the name of the directory unless the directory is named **.** or **..** When **readdir** has read all files in the working directory, it returns *false* and control passes to the statement following the **while** block. The **closedir** function closes the open directory and **print** displays a NEWLINE following the list of directories the program displayed.

```
$ cat dirs2a.pl
#!/usr/bin/perl
print "The working directory contains these directories:\n";

opendir my $dir, '.' or die "Could not open directory: $!\n";
while (my $entry = readdir $dir) {
    if (-d $entry) {
        print $entry, ' ' unless ($entry eq '.' || $entry eq '..');
    }
}
closedir $dir;
print "\n";

$ ./dirs2a.pl
The working directory contains these directories:
two one
```

split The **split** function divides a string into substrings as specified by a delimiter. The syntax of a call to **split** is

split (/re/, string);

where *re* is the delimiter, which is a regular expression (frequently a single regular character), and *string* is the string that is to be divided. As the next example shows, you can assign the list that **split** returns to an array variable.

The next program runs under Linux and lists the usernames of users with UIDs greater than or equal to 100 listed in the **/etc/passwd** file. It uses a **while** structure to read lines from **passwd** into **$user,** and it uses **split** to break the line into substrings separated by colons. The line that begins with **@row** assigns each of these substrings to an element of the **@row** array. The expression the **if** statement evaluates is *true* if the third substring (the UID) is greater than or equal to 100. This expression uses the **>=** numeric comparison operator because it compares two numbers; an alphabetic comparison would use the **ge** string comparison operator.

The **print** statement sends the UID number and the associated username to the **$sortout** file handle. The **open** statement for this handle establishes a pipe that sends its output to **sort –n**. Because the sort utility (page 54) does not display any output until it finishes receiving all of the input, **split3.pl** does not display anything until it closes the **$sortout** handle, which it does when it finishes reading the **passwd** file.

```
$ cat split3.pl
#!/usr/bin/perl -w

open ($pass, "/etc/passwd");
open ($sortout, "| sort -n");
while ($user = <$pass>) {
    @row = split (/:/, $user);
    if ($row[2] >= 100) {
        print $sortout "$row[2] $row[0]\n";
        }
    }
close ($pass);
close ($sortout);

$ ./split3.pl
100 libuuid
101 syslog
102 klog
103 avahi-autoipd
104 pulse
...
```

The next example counts and displays the arguments it was called with, using **@ARGV** (page 512). A **foreach** structure loops through the elements of the **@ARGV** array, which holds the command-line arguments. The **++** preincrement operator increments **$count** before it is displayed.

```
$ cat 10.pl
#!/usr/bin/perl -w

$count = 0;
$num = @ARGV;
print "You entered $num arguments on the command line:\n";
foreach $arg (@ARGV) {
    print ++$count, ". $arg\n";
    }
```

```
$ ./10.pl apple pear banana watermelon
You entered 4 arguments on the command line:
1. apple
2. pear
3. banana
4. watermelon
```

CHAPTER SUMMARY

Perl was written by Larry Wall in 1987. Since that time Perl has grown in size and functionality and is now a very popular language used for text processing, system administration, software development, and general-purpose programming. One of Perl's biggest assets is its support by thousands of third-party modules, many of which are stored in the CPAN repository.

The perldoc utility locates and displays local Perl documentation. It also allows you to document a Perl program by displaying lines of **pod** (plain old documentation) that you include in the program.

Perl provides three types of variables: scalar (singular variables that begin with a **$**), array (plural variables that begin with an **@**), and hash (also called associative arrays; plural variables that begin with a **%**). Array and hash variables both hold lists, but arrays are ordered while hashes are unordered. Standard control flow statements allow you to alter the order of execution of statements within a Perl program. In addition, Perl programs can take advantage of subroutines that can include variables local to the subroutines (lexical variables).

Regular expressions are one of Perl's strong points. In addition to the same facilities that are available in many utilities, Perl offers regular expression features that allow you to perform more complex string processing.

EXERCISES

1. What are two different ways to turn on warnings in Perl?

2. What is the difference between an array and a hash?

3. In each example, when would you use a hash and when would you use an array?

   a. Counting the number of occurrences of an IP address in a log file.

   b. Generating a list of users who are over disk quota for use in a report.

4. Write a regular expression to match a quoted string, such as

   ```
   He said, "Go get me the wrench," but I didn't hear him.
   ```

5. Write a regular expression to match an IP address in a log file.

6. Many configuration files contain many comments, including commented-out default configuration directives. Write a program to remove these comments from a configuration file.

ADVANCED EXERCISES

7. Write a program that removes ***~** and ***.ico** files from a directory hierarchy. (*Hint*: Use the **File::Find** module.)

8. Describe a programming mistake that Perl's warnings do not report on.

9. Write a Perl program that counts the number of files in the working directory and the number of bytes in those files, by filename extension.

10. Describe the difference between quoting strings using single quotation marks and using double quotation marks.

11. Write a program that copies all files with a **.ico** filename extension in a directory hierarchy to a directory named **icons** in your home directory. (*Hint*: Use the **File::Find** and **File::Copy** modules.)

12. Write a program that analyzes Apache logs. Display the number of bytes served by each path. Ignore unsuccessful page requests. If there are more than ten paths, display the first ten only.

   Following is a sample line from an Apache access log. The two numbers following the HTTP/1.1 are the response code and the byte count. A response code of 200 means the request was successful. A byte count of – means no data was transferred.

```
__DATA__
92.50.103.52 - - [19/Aug/2008:08:26:43 -0400] "GET /perl/automated-testing/next_active.gif
HTTP/1.1" 200 980 "http://example.com/perl/automated-testing/navigation_bar.htm"
"Mozilla/5.0 (X11; U; Linux x86_64; en-US; rv:1.8.1.6) Gecko/20061201 Firefox/3.0.0.6
(Ubuntu-feisty); Blazer/4.0"
```

12

THE AWK PATTERN PROCESSING LANGUAGE

AWK is a pattern-scanning and processing language that searches one or more files for records (usually lines) that match specified patterns. It processes lines by performing actions, such as writing the record to standard output or incrementing a counter, each time it finds a match. Unlike *procedural* languages, AWK is *data driven*: You describe the data you want to work with and tell AWK what to do with the data once it finds it.

You can use AWK to generate reports or filter text. It works equally well with numbers and text; when you mix the two, AWK usually comes up with the right answer. The authors of AWK (Alfred V. Aho, Peter J. Weinberger, and Brian W. Kernighan) designed the language to be easy to use. To achieve this end they sacrificed execution speed in the original implementation.

AWK takes many of its constructs from the C programming language. It includes the following features:

- A flexible format
- Conditional execution
- Looping statements
- Numeric variables
- String variables
- Regular expressions
- Relational expressions
- C's **printf**
- Coprocess execution (gawk only)
- Network data exchange (gawk only)

SYNTAX

A gawk command line has the following syntax:

gawk [options] [program] [file-list]
gawk [options] –f program-file [file-list]

The gawk utility takes its input from files you specify on the command line or from standard input. An advanced command, **getline**, gives you more choices about where input comes from and how gawk reads it (page 558). Using a coprocess, gawk can interact with another program or exchange data over a network (page 560; not available under awk or mawk). Output from gawk goes to standard output.

ARGUMENTS

In the preceding syntax, *program* is a gawk program that you include on the command line. The *program-file* is the name of the file that holds a gawk program. Putting the program on the command line allows you to write short gawk programs without having to create a separate *program-file*. To prevent the shell from interpreting the gawk commands as shell commands, enclose the *program* within single quotation marks. Putting a long or complex program in a file can reduce errors and retyping.

The *file-list* contains the pathnames of the ordinary files that gawk processes. These files are the input files. When you do not specify a *file-list*, gawk takes input from standard input or as specified by **getline** (page 558) or a coprocess (page 560).

AWK has many implementations

tip   The AWK language was originally implemented under UNIX as the awk utility. Most Linux distributions provide gawk (the GNU implementation of awk) or mawk (a faster, stripped-down version of awk). Mac OS X provides awk. This chapter describes gawk. All the examples in this chapter work under awk and mawk except as noted; the exceptions make use of coprocesses (page 560). You can easily install gawk on most Linux distributions. See gawk.darwinports.com if you are running Mac OS X. For a complete list of gawk extensions, see **GNU EXTENSIONS** in the gawk man page or see the gawk info page.

OPTIONS

Options preceded by a double hyphen (––) work under gawk only. They are not available under awk and mawk.

––field-separator *fs*

    –F *fs*

        Uses *fs* as the value of the input field separator (**FS** variable; page 536).

––file *program-file*

    –f *program-file*

        Reads the gawk program from the file named ***program-file*** instead of the command line. You can specify this option more than once on a command line. See page 545 for examples.

––help –W help

        Summarizes how to use gawk (gawk only).

––lint –W lint

        Warns about gawk constructs that may not be correct or portable (gawk only).

––posix –W posix

        Runs a POSIX-compliant version of gawk. This option introduces some restrictions; see the gawk man page for details (gawk only).

––traditional –W traditional

        Ignores the new GNU features in a gawk program, making the program conform to UNIX awk (gawk only).

––assign *var=value*

    –v *var=value*

        Assigns ***value*** to the variable ***var***. The assignment takes place prior to execution of the gawk program and is available within the **BEGIN** pattern (page 535). You can specify this option more than once on a command line.

NOTES

See the tip on the previous page for information on AWK implementations.

For convenience many Linux systems provide a link from **/bin/awk** to **/bin/gawk** or **/bin/mawk**. As a result you can run the program using either name.

LANGUAGE BASICS

A gawk program (from *program* on the command line or from *program-file*) consists of one or more lines containing a *pattern* and/or *action* in the following format:

> *pattern { action }*

The *pattern* selects lines from the input. The gawk utility performs the *action* on all lines that the *pattern* selects. The braces surrounding the *action* enable gawk to differentiate it from the *pattern*. If a program line does not contain a *pattern*, gawk selects all lines in the input. If a program line does not contain an *action*, gawk copies the selected lines to standard output.

To start, gawk compares the first line of input (from the *file-list* or standard input) with each *pattern* in the program. If a *pattern* selects the line (if there is a match), gawk takes the *action* associated with the *pattern*. If the line is not selected, gawk does not take the *action*. When gawk has completed its comparisons for the first line of input, it repeats the process for the next line of input. It continues this process of comparing subsequent lines of input until it has read all of the input.

If several *patterns* select the same line, gawk takes the *actions* associated with each of the *patterns* in the order in which they appear in the program. It is possible for gawk to send a single line from the input to standard output more than once.

PATTERNS

~ and !~   You can use a regular expression (Appendix A), enclosed within slashes, as a *pattern*. The ~ operator tests whether a field or variable matches a regular expression (examples on page 543). The !~ operator tests for no match. You can perform both numeric and string comparisons using the relational operators listed in Table 12-1. You can combine any of the *patterns* using the Boolean operators || (OR) or && (AND).

Table 12-1   Relational operators

Relational operator	Meaning
<	Less than
<=	Less than or equal to
==	Equal to

Table 12-1 Relational operators (continued)

Relational operator	Meaning
!=	Not equal to
>=	Greater than or equal to
>	Greater than

BEGIN and END   Two unique *patterns*, **BEGIN** and **END**, execute commands before gawk starts processing the input and after it finishes processing the input. The gawk utility executes the *actions* associated with the **BEGIN** *pattern* before, and with the **END** *pattern* after, it processes all the input. See pages 545 and 546 for examples.

, (comma)   The comma is the range operator. If you separate two *patterns* with a comma on a single gawk program line, gawk selects a range of lines, beginning with the first line that matches the first *pattern*. The last line selected by gawk is the next subsequent line that matches the second *pattern*. If no line matches the second *pattern*, gawk selects every line through the end of the input. After gawk finds the second *pattern*, it begins the process again by looking for the first *pattern* again. See page 544 for examples.

ACTIONS

The *action* portion of a gawk command causes gawk to take that *action* when it matches a *pattern*. When you do not specify an *action*, gawk performs the default *action*, which is the **print** command (explicitly represented as {print}). This *action* copies the record (normally a line; see "Record separators" on the next page) from the input to standard output.

When you follow a **print** command with arguments, gawk displays only the arguments you specify. These arguments can be variables or string constants. You can send the output from a **print** command to a file (use > within the gawk program; page 549), append it to a file (>>), or send it through a pipe to the input of another program (|). A coprocess (|&) is a two-way pipe that exchanges data with a program running in the background (available under gawk only; page 560).

Unless you separate items in a **print** command with commas, gawk catenates them. Commas cause gawk to separate the items with the output field separator (**OFS**, normally a SPACE; page 536).

You can include several *actions* on one line by separating them with semicolons.

COMMENTS

The gawk utility disregards anything on a program line following a pound sign (#). You can document a gawk program by preceding comments with this symbol.

VARIABLES

Although you do not need to declare gawk variables prior to their use, you can assign initial values to them if you like. Unassigned numeric variables are initialized to 0; string variables are initialized to the null string. In addition to supporting user variables, gawk maintains program variables. You can use both user and program variables in the *pattern* and *action* portions of a gawk program. Table 12-2 lists a few program variables.

Table 12-2   Variables

Variable	Meaning
$0	The current record (as a single variable)
$1–$n	Fields in the current record
FILENAME	Name of the current input file (null for standard input)
FS	Input field separator (default: SPACE or TAB; page 550)
NF	Number of fields in the current record (page 554)
NR	Record number of the current record (page 546)
OFS	Output field separator (default: SPACE; page 547)
ORS	Output record separator (default: NEWLINE; page 554)
RS	Input record separator (default: NEWLINE)

In addition to initializing variables within a program, you can use the **--assign** (**-v**) option to initialize variables on the command line. This feature is useful when the value of a variable changes from one run of gawk to the next.

Record separators   By default the input and output record separators are NEWLINE characters. Thus gawk takes each line of input to be a separate record and appends a NEWLINE to the end of each output record. By default the input field separators are SPACEs and TABs; the default output field separator is a SPACE. You can change the value of any of the separators at any time by assigning a new value to its associated variable either from within the program or from the command line by using the **--assign** (**-v**) option.

FUNCTIONS

Table 12-3 lists a few of the functions gawk provides for manipulating numbers and strings.

Table 12-3   Functions

Function	Meaning
length(*str*)	Returns the number of characters in *str*; without an argument, returns the number of characters in the current record (page 545)
int(*num*)	Returns the integer portion of *num*
index(*str1*,*str2*)	Returns the index of *str2* in *str1* or 0 if *str2* is not present
split(*str*,*arr*,*del*)	Places elements of *str*, delimited by *del*, in the array *arr*[1]...*arr*[*n*]; returns the number of elements in the array (page 556)

Table 12-3 Functions (continued)

Function	Meaning
sprintf(*fmt*,*args*)	Formats *args* according to *fmt* and returns the formatted string; mimics the C programming language function of the same name
substr(*str*,*pos*,*len*)	Returns the substring of *str* that begins at *pos* and is *len* characters long
tolower(*str*)	Returns a copy of *str* in which all uppercase letters are replaced with their lowercase counterparts
toupper(*str*)	Returns a copy of *str* in which all lowercase letters are replaced with their uppercase counterparts

ARITHMETIC OPERATORS

The gawk arithmetic operators listed in Table 12-4 are from the C programming language.

Table 12-4 Arithmetic operators

Operator	Meaning
**	Raises the expression preceding the operator to the power of the expression following it
*	Multiplies the expression preceding the operator by the expression following it
/	Divides the expression preceding the operator by the expression following it
%	Takes the remainder after dividing the expression preceding the operator by the expression following it
+	Adds the expression preceding the operator to the expression following it
−	Subtracts the expression following the operator from the expression preceding it
=	Assigns the value of the expression following the operator to the variable preceding it
++	Increments the variable preceding the operator
−−	Decrements the variable preceding the operator
+=	Adds the expression following the operator to the variable preceding it and assigns the result to the variable preceding the operator
−=	Subtracts the expression following the operator from the variable preceding it and assigns the result to the variable preceding the operator
*=	Multiplies the variable preceding the operator by the expression following it and assigns the result to the variable preceding the operator
/=	Divides the variable preceding the operator by the expression following it and assigns the result to the variable preceding the operator
%=	Assigns the remainder, after dividing the variable preceding the operator by the expression following it, to the variable preceding the operator

ASSOCIATIVE ARRAYS

The *associative array* is one of gawk's most powerful features. These arrays use strings as indexes. Using an associative array, you can mimic a traditional array by using numeric strings as indexes. In Perl, an associative array is called a *hash* (page 500).

You assign a value to an element of an associative array using the following syntax:

array[string] = value

where *array* is the name of the array, *string* is the index of the element of the array you are assigning a value to, and *value* is the value you are assigning to that element.

Using the following syntax, you can use a **for** structure with an associative array:

for (elem in array) action

where *elem* is a variable that takes on the value of each element of the array as the **for** structure loops through them, *array* is the name of the array, and *action* is the action that gawk takes for each element in the array. You can use the *elem* variable in this *action*.

See page 551 for example programs that use associative arrays.

printf

You can use the **printf** command in place of **print** to control the format of the output gawk generates. The gawk version of **printf** is similar to that found in the C language. A **printf** command has the following syntax:

printf "control-string", arg1, arg2, ..., argn

The *control-string* determines how **printf** formats *arg1, arg2, ..., argn*. These arguments can be variables or other expressions. Within the *control-string* you can use **\n** to indicate a NEWLINE and **\t** to indicate a TAB. The *control-string* contains conversion specifications, one for each argument. A conversion specification has the following syntax:

%[–][x[.y]]conv

where – causes **printf** to left-justify the argument, *x* is the minimum field width, and *.y* is the number of places to the right of a decimal point in a number. The *conv* indicates the type of numeric conversion and can be selected from the letters in Table 12-5. See page 548 for example programs that use **printf**.

Table 12-5   Numeric conversion

conv	Type of conversion
d	Decimal
e	Exponential notation
f	Floating-point number

Table 12-5 Numeric conversion (continued)

conv	Type of conversion
g	Use **f** or **e**, whichever is shorter
o	Unsigned octal
s	String of characters
x	Unsigned hexadecimal

CONTROL STRUCTURES

Control (flow) statements alter the order of execution of commands within a gawk program. This section details the **if...else**, **while**, and **for** control structures. In addition, the **break** and **continue** statements work in conjunction with the control structures to alter the order of execution of commands. See page 398 for more information on control structures. You do not need to use braces around *commands* when you specify a single, simple command.

if...else

The **if...else** control structure tests the status returned by the *condition* and transfers control based on this status. The syntax of an **if...else** structure is shown below. The **else** part is optional.

> *if (condition)*
> > *{commands}*
> *[else*
> > *{commands}]*

The simple **if** statement shown here does not use braces:

```
if ($5 <= 5000) print $0
```

Next is a gawk program that uses a simple **if...else** structure. Again, there are no braces.

```
$ cat if1
BEGIN   {
        nam="sam"
        if (nam == "max")
                print "nam is max"
            else
                print "nam is not max, it is", nam
        }
$ gawk -f if1
nam is not max, it is sam
```

while

The **while** structure loops through and executes the *commands* as long as the *condition* is *true*. The syntax of a **while** structure is

> *while (condition)*
> > *{commands}*

The next gawk program uses a simple **while** structure to display powers of 2. This example uses braces because the **while** loop contains more than one statement. This program does not accept input; all processing takes place when gawk executes the statements associated with the BEGIN pattern.

```
$ cat while1
BEGIN{
    n = 1
    while (n <= 5)
        {
        print "2^" n, 2**n
        n++
        }
    }

$ gawk -f while1
1^2 2
2^2 4
3^2 8
4^2 16
5^2 32
```

for

The syntax of a **for** control structure is

> *for (init; condition; increment)*
> *{commands}*

A **for** structure starts by executing the ***init*** statement, which usually sets a counter to 0 or 1. It then loops through the ***commands*** as long as the ***condition*** remains *true*. After each loop it executes the ***increment*** statement. The **for1** gawk program does the same thing as the preceding **while1** program except that it uses a **for** statement, which makes the program simpler:

```
$ cat for1
BEGIN   {
        for (n=1; n <= 5; n++)
        print "2^" n, 2**n
        }
$ gawk -f for1
1^2 2
2^2 4
3^2 8
4^2 16
5^2 32
```

The gawk utility supports an alternative **for** syntax for working with associative arrays:

> *for (var in array)*
> *{commands}*

This **for** structure loops through elements of the associative array named *array,* assigning the value of the index of each element of *array* to *var* each time through the loop. The following line of code (from the program on page 551) demonstrates a **for** structure:

```
END     {for (name in manuf) print name, manuf[name]}
```

break

The **break** statement transfers control out of a **for** or **while** loop, terminating execution of the innermost loop it appears in.

continue

The **continue** statement transfers control to the end of a **for** or **while** loop, causing execution of the innermost loop it appears in to continue with the next iteration.

EXAMPLES

cars data file Many of the examples in this section work with the **cars** data file. From left to right, the columns in the file contain each car's make, model, year of manufacture, mileage in thousands of miles, and price. All whitespace in this file is composed of single TABs (the file does not contain any SPACES).

```
$ cat cars
plym     fury     1970    73      2500
chevy    malibu   1999    60      3000
ford     mustang  1965    45      10000
volvo    s80      1998    102     9850
ford     thundbd  2003    15      10500
chevy    malibu   2000    50      3500
bmw      325i     1985    115     450
honda    accord   2001    30      6000
ford     taurus   2004    10      17000
toyota   rav4     2002    180     750
chevy    impala   1985    85      1550
ford     explor   2003    25      9500
```

Missing pattern A simple gawk program is

```
{ print }
```

This program consists of one program line that is an *action.* Because the *pattern* is missing, gawk selects all lines of input. When used without any arguments the **print** command displays each selected line in its entirety. This program copies the input to standard output.

```
$ gawk '{ print }' cars
plym     fury     1970    73      2500
chevy    malibu   1999    60      3000
ford     mustang  1965    45      10000
volvo    s80      1998    102     9850
...
```

Missing action   The next program has a *pattern* but no explicit **action**. The slashes indicate that **chevy** is a regular expression.

```
/chevy/
```

In this case gawk selects from the input just those lines that contain the string **chevy**. When you do not specify an *action*, gawk assumes the *action* is **print**. The following example copies to standard output all lines from the input that contain the string **chevy**:

```
$ gawk '/chevy/' cars
chevy    malibu    1999    60    3000
chevy    malibu    2000    50    3500
chevy    impala    1985    85    1550
```

Single quotation marks   Although neither gawk nor shell syntax requires single quotation marks on the command line, it is still a good idea to use them because they can prevent problems. If the gawk program you create on the command line includes SPACEs or characters that are special to the shell, you must quote them. Always enclosing the program in single quotation marks is the easiest way to make sure you have quoted any characters that need to be quoted.

Fields   The next example selects all lines from the file (it has no *pattern*). The braces enclose the *action;* you must always use braces to delimit the *action* so gawk can distinguish it from the *pattern*. This example displays the third field ($3), a SPACE (the output field separator, indicated by the comma), and the first field ($1) of each selected line:

```
$ gawk '{print $3, $1}' cars
1970 plym
1999 chevy
1965 ford
1998 volvo
...
```

The next example, which includes both a *pattern* and an *action*, selects all lines that contain the string **chevy** and displays the third and first fields from the selected lines:

```
$ gawk '/chevy/ {print $3, $1}' cars
1999 chevy
2000 chevy
1985 chevy
```

In the following example, gawk selects lines that contain a match for the regular expression **h**. Because there is no explicit *action*, gawk displays all the lines it selects.

```
$ gawk '/h/' cars
chevy    malibu    1999    60    3000
ford     thundbd   2003    15    10500
chevy    malibu    2000    50    3500
honda    accord    2001    30    6000
chevy    impala    1985    85    1550
```

~ (matches operator) The next *pattern* uses the matches operator (~) to select all lines that contain the letter **h** in the first field:

```
$ gawk '$1 ~ /h/' cars
chevy   malibu   1999   60      3000
chevy   malibu   2000   50      3500
honda   accord   2001   30      6000
chevy   impala   1985   85      1550
```

The caret (^) in a regular expression forces a match at the beginning of the line (page 890) or, in this case, at the beginning of the first field:

```
$ gawk '$1 ~ /^h/' cars
honda   accord   2001   30      6000
```

Brackets surround a character class definition (page 889). In the next example, gawk selects lines that have a second field that begins with **t** or **m** and displays the third and second fields, a dollar sign, and the fifth field. Because there is no comma between the "$" and the $5, gawk does not put a SPACE between them in the output.

```
$ gawk '$2 ~ /^[tm]/ {print $3, $2, "$"  $5}' cars
1999 malibu $3000
1965 mustang $10000
2003 thundbd $10500
2000 malibu $3500
2004 taurus $17000
```

Dollar signs The next example shows three roles a dollar sign can play in a gawk program. First, a dollar sign followed by a number names a field. Second, within a regular expression a dollar sign forces a match at the end of a line or field (5$). Third, within a string a dollar sign represents itself.

```
$ gawk '$3 ~ /5$/ {print $3, $1, "$"  $5}' cars
1965 ford $10000
1985 bmw $450
1985 chevy $1550
```

In the next example, the equal-to relational operator (==) causes gawk to perform a numeric comparison between the third field in each line and the number **1985**. The gawk command takes the default *action*, **print**, on each line where the comparison is *true*.

```
$ gawk '$3 == 1985' cars
bmw     325i     1985   115     450
chevy   impala   1985   85      1550
```

The next example finds all cars priced at or less than $3,000.

```
$ gawk '$5 <= 3000' cars
plym    fury     1970   73      2500
chevy   malibu   1999   60      3000
bmw     325i     1985   115     450
toyota  rav4     2002   180     750
chevy   impala   1985   85      1550
```

Textual comparisons
When you use double quotation marks, gawk performs textual comparisons by using the ASCII (or other local) collating sequence as the basis of the comparison. In the following example, gawk shows that the *strings* 450 and 750 fall in the range that lies between the *strings* 2000 and 9000, which is probably not the intended result.

```
$ gawk '"2000" <= $5 && $5 < "9000"' cars
plym      fury      1970    73        2500
chevy     malibu    1999    60        3000
chevy     malibu    2000    50        3500
bmw       325i      1985    115       450
honda     accord    2001    30        6000
toyota    rav4      2002    180       750
```

When you need to perform a numeric comparison, do not use quotation marks. The next example gives the intended result. It is the same as the previous example except it omits the double quotation marks.

```
$ gawk '2000 <= $5 && $5 < 9000' cars
plym      fury      1970    73        2500
chevy     malibu    1999    60        3000
chevy     malibu    2000    50        3500
honda     accord    2001    30        6000
```

, (range operator)
The range operator (,) selects a group of lines. The first line it selects is the one specified by the *pattern* before the comma. The last line is the one selected by the *pattern* after the comma. If no line matches the *pattern* after the comma, gawk selects every line through the end of the input. The next example selects all lines, starting with the line that contains **volvo** and ending with the line that contains **bmw**.

```
$ gawk '/volvo/ , /bmw/' cars
volvo     s80       1998    102       9850
ford      thundbd   2003    15        10500
chevy     malibu    2000    50        3500
bmw       325i      1985    115       450
```

After the range operator finds its first group of lines, it begins the process again, looking for a line that matches the *pattern* before the comma. In the following example, gawk finds three groups of lines that fall between **chevy** and **ford**. Although the fifth line of input contains **ford**, gawk does not select it because at the time it is processing the fifth line, it is searching for **chevy**.

```
$ gawk '/chevy/ , /ford/' cars
chevy     malibu    1999    60        3000
ford      mustang   1965    45        10000
chevy     malibu    2000    50        3500
bmw       325i      1985    115       450
honda     accord    2001    30        6000
```

```
ford    taurus  2004    10      17000
chevy   impala  1985    85      1550
ford    explor  2003    25      9500
```

––file option   When you are writing a longer gawk program, it is convenient to put the program in a file and reference the file on the command line. Use the **–f** (**––file**) option followed by the name of the file containing the gawk program.

BEGIN   The following gawk program, which is stored in a file named **pr_header**, has two *actions* and uses the **BEGIN** *pattern*. The gawk utility performs the *action* associated with **BEGIN** before processing any lines of the data file: It displays a header. The second *action*, {**print**}, has no *pattern* part and displays all lines from the input.

```
$ cat pr_header
BEGIN   {print "Make    Model   Year    Miles   Price"}
        {print}

$ gawk -f pr_header cars
Make    Model   Year    Miles   Price
plym    fury    1970    73      2500
chevy   malibu  1999    60      3000
ford    mustang 1965    45      10000
volvo   s80     1998    102     9850
...
```

The next example expands the *action* associated with the **BEGIN** *pattern*. In the previous and the following examples, the whitespace in the headers is composed of single TABs, so the titles line up with the columns of data.

```
$ cat pr_header2
BEGIN   {
print "Make    Model   Year    Miles   Price"
print "------------------------------------"
}
        {print}

$ gawk -f pr_header2 cars
Make    Model   Year    Miles   Price
------------------------------------
plym    fury    1970    73      2500
chevy   malibu  1999    60      3000
ford    mustang 1965    45      10000
volvo   s80     1998    102     9850
...
```

length function   When you call the **length** function without an argument, it returns the number of characters in the current line, including field separators. The **$0** variable always contains the value of the current line. In the next example, gawk prepends the line length to each line and then a pipe sends the output from gawk to sort (the **–n** option specifies a numeric sort; page 817). As a result, the lines of the **cars** file appear in order of line length.

```
$ gawk '{print length, $0}' cars | sort -n
21 bmw    325i    1985    115    450
22 plym fury    1970    73    2500
23 volvo    s80    1998    102    9850
24 ford explor 2003    25    9500
24 toyota    rav4    2002    180    750
25 chevy    impala 1985    85    1550
25 chevy    malibu 1999    60    3000
25 chevy    malibu 2000    50    3500
25 ford taurus 2004    10    17000
25 honda    accord 2001    30    6000
26 ford mustang 1965    45    10000
26 ford thundbd 2003    15    10500
```

The formatting of this report depends on TABs for horizontal alignment. The three extra characters at the beginning of each line throw off the format of several lines; a remedy for this situation is covered shortly.

NR (record number)   The **NR** variable contains the record (line) number of the current line. The following *pattern* selects all lines that contain more than 24 characters. The *action* displays the line number of each of the selected lines.

```
$ gawk 'length > 24 {print NR}' cars
2
3
5
6
8
9
11
```

You can combine the range operator (,) and the **NR** variable to display a group of lines of a file based on their line numbers. The next example displays lines 2 through 4:

```
$ gawk 'NR == 2 , NR == 4' cars
chevy    malibu    1999    60    3000
ford     mustang 1965    45    10000
volvo    s80    1998    102    9850
```

END   The **END** *pattern* works in a manner similar to the **BEGIN** *pattern*, except gawk takes the *actions* associated with this pattern after processing the last line of input. The following report displays information only after it has processed all the input. The **NR** variable retains its value after gawk finishes processing the data file, so an *action* associated with an **END** *pattern* can use it.

```
$ gawk 'END {print NR, "cars for sale." }' cars
12 cars for sale.
```

The next example uses **if** control structures to expand the abbreviations used in some of the first fields. As long as gawk does not change a record, it leaves the entire record—including any separators—intact. Once it makes a change to a record, gawk changes all separators in that record to the value of the output field separator. The default output field separator is a SPACE.

```
$ cat separ_demo
        {
        if ($1 ~ /ply/)  $1 = "plymouth"
        if ($1 ~ /chev/) $1 = "chevrolet"
        print
        }

$ gawk -f separ_demo cars
plymouth fury 1970 73 2500
chevrolet malibu 1999 60 3000
ford      mustang 1965      45        10000
volvo    s80      1998      102       9850
ford      thundbd 2003      15        10500
chevrolet malibu 2000 50 3500
bmw      325i     1985      115       450
honda    accord   2001      30        6000
ford     taurus   2004      10        17000
toyota   rav4     2002      180       750
chevrolet impala 1985 85 1550
ford     explor   2003      25        9500
```

Stand-alone script Instead of calling gawk from the command line with the –f option and the name of the program you want to run, you can write a script that calls gawk with the commands you want to run. The next example is a stand-alone script that runs the same program as the previous example. The #!/bin/gawk –f command (page 280) runs the gawk utility directly. To execute it, you need both read and execute permission to the file holding the script (page 278).

```
$ chmod u+rx separ_demo2
$ cat separ_demo2
#!/bin/gawk -f
        {
        if ($1 ~ /ply/)  $1 = "plymouth"
        if ($1 ~ /chev/) $1 = "chevrolet"
        print
        }

$ ./separ_demo2 cars
plymouth fury 1970 73 2500
chevrolet malibu 1999 60 3000
ford      mustang 1965      45        10000
...
```

OFS variable You can change the value of the output field separator by assigning a value to the OFS variable. The following example assigns a TAB character to OFS, using the backslash escape sequence \t. This fix improves the appearance of the report but does not line up the columns properly.

```
$ cat ofs_demo
BEGIN   {OFS = "\t"}
        {
        if ($1 ~ /ply/)  $1 = "plymouth"
        if ($1 ~ /chev/) $1 = "chevrolet"
        print
        }
```

```
$ gawk -f ofs_demo cars
plymouth          fury    1970    73      2500
chevrolet         malibu  1999    60      3000
ford     mustang 1965    45      10000
volvo    s80     1998    102     9850
ford     thundbd 2003    15      10500
chevrolet         malibu  2000    50      3500
bmw      325i    1985    115     450
honda    accord  2001    30      6000
ford     taurus  2004    10      17000
toyota   rav4    2002    180     750
chevrolet         impala  1985    85      1550
ford     explor  2003    25      9500
```

printf   You can use **printf** (page 538) to refine the output format. The following example uses a backslash at the end of two program lines to quote the following NEWLINE. You can use this technique to continue a long line over one or more lines without affecting the outcome of the program.

```
$ cat printf_demo
BEGIN   {
    print "                              Miles"
    print "Make      Model      Year     (000)       Price"
    print \
    "-------------------------------------------------"
    }
    {
    if ($1 ~ /ply/)  $1 = "plymouth"
    if ($1 ~ /chev/) $1 = "chevrolet"
    printf "%-10s %-8s    %2d    %5d       $ %8.2f\n",\
        $1, $2, $3, $4, $5
    }
```

```
$ gawk -f printf_demo cars
                     Miles
Make      Model      Year     (000)         Price
-------------------------------------------------
plymouth   fury       1970      73     $   2500.00
chevrolet  malibu     1999      60     $   3000.00
ford       mustang    1965      45     $  10000.00
volvo      s80        1998     102     $   9850.00
ford       thundbd    2003      15     $  10500.00
chevrolet  malibu     2000      50     $   3500.00
bmw        325i       1985     115     $    450.00
```

```
honda      accord    2001    30    $  6000.00
ford       taurus    2004    10    $ 17000.00
toyota     rav4      2002   180    $   750.00
chevrolet  impala    1985    85    $  1550.00
ford       explor    2003    25    $  9500.00
```

Redirecting output   The next example creates two files: one with the lines that contain **chevy** and one with the lines that contain **ford**.

```
$ cat redirect_out
/chevy/    {print > "chevfile"}
/ford/     {print > "fordfile"}
END        {print "done."}

$ gawk -f redirect_out cars
done.

$ cat chevfile
chevy   malibu  1999   60    3000
chevy   malibu  2000   50    3500
chevy   impala  1985   85    1550
```

The **summary** program produces a summary report on all cars and newer cars. Although they are not required, the initializations at the beginning of the program represent good programming practice; gawk automatically declares and initializes variables as you use them. After reading all the input data, gawk computes and displays the averages.

```
$ cat summary
BEGIN   {
        yearsum = 0 ; costsum = 0
        newcostsum = 0 ; newcount = 0
        }
        {
        yearsum += $3
        costsum += $5
        }
$3 > 2000 {newcostsum += $5 ; newcount ++}
END     {
        printf "Average age of cars is %4.1f years\n",\
           2006 - (yearsum/NR)
        printf "Average cost of cars is $%7.2f\n",\
           costsum/NR
           printf "Average cost of newer cars is $%7.2f\n",\
              newcostsum/newcount
        }

$ gawk -f summary cars
Average age of cars is 13.1 years
Average cost of cars is $6216.67
Average cost of newer cars is $8750.00
```

The following gawk command shows the format of a line from a Linux **passwd** file that the next example uses:

```
$ awk '/mark/ {print}' /etc/passwd
mark:x:107:100:ext 112:/home/mark:/bin/tcsh
```

FS variable   The next example demonstrates a technique for finding the largest number in a field. Because it works with a Linux **passwd** file, which delimits fields with colons (**:**), the example changes the input field separator (**FS**) before reading any data. It reads the **passwd** file and determines the next available user ID number (field 3). The numbers do not have to be in order in the **passwd** file for this program to work.

The *pattern* (**$3 > saveit**) causes gawk to select records that contain a user ID number greater than any previous user ID number it has processed. Each time it selects a record, gawk assigns the value of the new user ID number to the **saveit** variable. Then gawk uses the new value of **saveit** to test the user IDs of all subsequent records. Finally gawk adds 1 to the value of **saveit** and displays the result.

```
$ cat find_uid
BEGIN           {FS = ":"
                 saveit = 0}
$3 > saveit     {saveit = $3}
END             {print "Next available UID is " saveit + 1}

$ gawk -f find_uid /etc/passwd
Next available UID is 1092
```

The next example produces another report based on the **cars** file. This report uses nested **if...else** control structures to substitute values based on the contents of the price field. The program has no *pattern* part; it processes every record.

```
$ cat price_range
    {
    if          ($5 <= 5000)              $5 = "inexpensive"
        else if (5000 < $5 && $5 < 10000) $5 = "please ask"
        else if (10000 <= $5)             $5 = "expensive"
    #
    printf "%-10s %-8s   %2d   %5d   %-12s\n",\
    $1, $2, $3, $4, $5
    }

$ gawk -f price_range cars
plym      fury      1970      73   inexpensive
chevy     malibu    1999      60   inexpensive
ford      mustang   1965      45   expensive
volvo     s80       1998     102   please ask
ford      thundbd   2003      15   expensive
chevy     malibu    2000      50   inexpensive
bmw       325i      1985     115   inexpensive
honda     accord    2001      30   please ask
ford      taurus    2004      10   expensive
toyota    rav4      2002     180   inexpensive
chevy     impala    1985      85   inexpensive
ford      explor    2003      25   please ask
```

Associative arrays | Next the **manuf** associative array uses the contents of the first field of each record in the **cars** file as an index. The array consists of the elements **manuf[plym]**, **manuf[chevy]**, **manuf[ford]**, and so on. Each new element is initialized to 0 (zero) as it is created. The **++** operator increments the variable it follows.

for structure | The *action* following the **END** *pattern* is a **for** structure, which loops through the elements of an associative array. A pipe sends the output through sort to produce an alphabetical list of cars and the quantities in stock. Because it is a shell script and not a gawk program file, you must have both read and execute permission to the **manuf** file to execute it as a command.

```
$ cat manuf
gawk ' {manuf[$1]++}
END     {for (name in manuf) print name, manuf[name]}
' cars |
sort

$ ./manuf
bmw 1
chevy 3
ford 4
honda 1
plym 1
toyota 1
volvo 1
```

The next program, **manuf.sh**, is a more general shell script that includes error checking. This script lists and counts the contents of a column in a file, with both the column number and the name of the file specified on the command line.

The first *action* (the one that starts with {**count**) uses the shell variable **$1** in the middle of the gawk program to specify an array index. Because of the way the single quotation marks are paired, the **$1** that appears to be within single quotation marks is actually not quoted: The two quoted strings in the gawk program surround, but do not include, the **$1**. Because the **$1** is not quoted, and because this is a shell script, the shell substitutes the value of the first command-line argument in place of **$1** (page 441). As a result, the **$1** is interpreted before the gawk command is invoked. The leading dollar sign (the one before the first single quotation mark on that line) causes gawk to interpret what the shell substitutes as a field number.

```
$ cat manuf.sh
if [ $# != 2 ]
    then
        echo "Usage: manuf.sh field file"
        exit 1
fi
gawk < $2 '
        {count[$'$1']++}
END     {for (item in count) printf "%-20s%-20s\n",\
            item, count[item]}' |
sort
```

```
$ ./manuf.sh
Usage: manuf.sh field file

$ ./manuf.sh 1 cars
bmw             1
chevy           3
ford            4
honda           1
plym            1
toyota          1
volvo           1

$ ./manuf.sh 3 cars
1965            1
1970            1
1985            2
1998            1
1999            1
2000            1
2001            1
2002            1
2003            2
2004            1
```

A way around the tricky use of quotation marks that allow parameter expansion within the gawk program is to use the **–v** option on the command line to pass the field number to gawk as a variable. This change makes it easier for someone else to read and debug the script. You call the **manuf2.sh** script the same way you call **manuf.sh**:

```
$ cat manuf2.sh
if [ $# != 2 ]
        then
                echo "Usage: manuf.sh field file"
                exit 1
fi
gawk -v "field=$1" < $2 '
                {count[$field]++}
END             {for (item in count) printf "%-20s%-20s\n",\
                        item, count[item]}' |
sort
```

The **word_usage** script displays a word usage list for a file you specify on the command line. The tr utility (page 864) lists the words from standard input, one to a line. The sort utility orders the file, putting the most frequently used words first. The script sorts groups of words that are used the same number of times in alphabetical order.

```
$ cat word_usage
tr -cs 'a-zA-Z' '[\n*]' < $1 |
gawk    '
        {count[$1]++}
END     {for (item in count) printf "%-15s%3s\n", item, count[item]}' |
sort +1nr +0f -1
```

```
$ ./word_usage textfile
the             42
file            29
fsck            27
system          22
you             22
to              21
it              17
SIZE            14
and             13
MODE            13
...
```

Following is a similar program in a different format. The style mimics that of a C program and may be easier to read and work with for more complex gawk programs.

```
$ cat word_count
tr -cs 'a-zA-Z' '[\n*]' < $1 |
gawk ' {
        count[$1]++
}
END     {
        for (item in count)
                {
                if (count[item] > 4)
                        {
                        printf "%-15s%3s\n", item, count[item]
                        }
                }
} ' |
sort +1nr +0f -1
```

The tail utility displays the last ten lines of output, illustrating that words occurring fewer than five times are not listed:

```
$ ./word_count textfile | tail
directories     5
if              5
information     5
INODE           5
more            5
no              5
on              5
response        5
this            5
will            5
```

The next example shows one way to put a date on a report. The first line of input to the gawk program comes from date. The program reads this line as record number 1 (**NR == 1**), processes it accordingly, and processes all subsequent lines with the *action* associated with the next *pattern* (**NR > 1**).

```
$ cat report
if (test $# = 0) then
    echo "You must supply a filename."
    exit 1
fi
(date; cat $1) |
gawk '
NR == 1      {print "Report for", $1, $2, $3 ", " $6}
NR > 1       {print $5 "\t" $1}'

$ ./report cars
Report for Mon Jan 31, 2010
2500     plym
3000     chevy
10000    ford
9850     volvo
10500    ford
3500     chevy
450      bmw
6000     honda
17000    ford
750      toyota
1550     chevy
9500     ford
```

The next example sums each of the columns in a file you specify on the command line; it takes its input from the **numbers** file. The program performs error checking, reporting on and discarding rows that contain nonnumeric entries. It uses the **next** command (with the comment **skip bad records**) to skip the rest of the commands for the current record if the record contains a nonnumeric entry. At the end of the program, gawk displays a grand total for the file.

```
$ cat numbers
10       20       30.3     40.5
20       30       45.7     66.1
30       xyz      50       70
40       75       107.2    55.6
50       20       30.3     40.5
60       30       45.0     66.1
70       1134.7   50       70
80       75       107.2    55.6
90       176      30.3     40.5
100      1027.45  45.7     66.1
110      123      50       57a.5
120      75       107.2    55.6
```

```
$ cat tally
gawk ' BEGIN   {
                ORS = ""
               }

NR == 1 {                                       # first record only
    nfields = NF                                # set nfields to number of
    }                                           # fields in the record (NF)
    {
```

```
    if ($0 ~ /[^0-9. \t]/)                    # check each record to see if it contains
        {                                      # any characters that are not numbers,
        print "\nRecord " NR " skipped:\n\t"   # periods, spaces, or TABs
        print $0 "\n"
        next                                   # skip bad records
        }
    else
        {
        for (count = 1; count <= nfields; count++) # for good records loop through fields
            {
            printf "%10.2f", $count > "tally.out"
            sum[count] += $count
            gtotal += $count
            }
        print "\n" > "tally.out"
        }
    }

END     {                                      # after processing last record
    for (count = 1; count <= nfields; count++)  # print summary
        {
        print "   -------" > "tally.out"
        }
    print "\n" > "tally.out"
    for (count = 1; count <= nfields; count++)
        {
        printf "%10.2f", sum[count] > "tally.out"
        }
    print "\n\n       Grand Total " gtotal "\n" > "tally.out"
} ' < numbers
```

```
                $ ./tally
                Record 3 skipped:
                        30      xyz     50      70

                Record 6 skipped:
                        60      30      45.0    66.1

                Record 11 skipped:
                        110     123     50      57a.5

                $ cat tally.out
                    10.00       20.00       30.30       40.50
                    20.00       30.00       45.70       66.10
                    40.00       75.00      107.20       55.60
                    50.00       20.00       30.30       40.50
                    70.00     1134.70       50.00       70.00
                    80.00       75.00      107.20       55.60
                    90.00      176.00       30.30       40.50
                   100.00     1027.45       45.70       66.10
                   120.00       75.00      107.20       55.60
                  -------     -------     -------     -------
                   580.00     2633.15      553.90      490.50

                    Grand Total 4257.55
```

The next example reads the **passwd** file, listing users who do not have passwords and users who have duplicate user ID numbers. (The pwck utility [Linux only] performs similar checks.) Because Mac OS X uses Open Directory (page 926) and not the **passwd** file, this example will not work under OS X.

```
$ cat /etc/passwd
bill::102:100:ext 123:/home/bill:/bin/bash
roy:x:104:100:ext 475:/home/roy:/bin/bash
tom:x:105:100:ext 476:/home/tom:/bin/bash
lynn:x:166:100:ext 500:/home/lynn:/bin/bash
mark:x:107:100:ext 112:/home/mark:/bin/bash
sales:x:108:100:ext 102:/m/market:/bin/bash
anne:x:109:100:ext 355:/home/anne:/bin/bash
toni::164:100:ext 357:/home/toni:/bin/bash
ginny:x:115:100:ext 109:/home/ginny:/bin/bash
chuck:x:116:100:ext 146:/home/chuck:/bin/bash
neil:x:164:100:ext 159:/home/neil:/bin/bash
rmi:x:118:100:ext 178:/home/rmi:/bin/bash
vern:x:119:100:ext 201:/home/vern:/bin/bash
bob:x:120:100:ext 227:/home/bob:/bin/bash
janet:x:122:100:ext 229:/home/janet:/bin/bash
maggie:x:124:100:ext 244:/home/maggie:/bin/bash
dan::126:100::/home/dan:/bin/bash
dave:x:108:100:ext 427:/home/dave:/bin/bash
mary:x:129:100:ext 303:/home/mary:/bin/bash
```

```
$ cat passwd_check
gawk < /etc/passwd '       BEGIN    {
    uid[void] = ""                      # tell gawk that uid is an array
    }
    {                                   # no pattern indicates process all records
    dup = 0                             # initialize duplicate flag
    split($0, field, ":")               # split into fields delimited by ":"
    if (field[2] == "")                 # check for null password field
        {
        if (field[5] == "")             # check for null info field
            {
            print field[1] " has no password."
            }
        else
            {
            print field[1] " ("field[5]") has no password."
            }
        }
    for (name in uid)                   # loop through uid array
        {
        if (uid[name] == field[3])      # check for second use of UID
            {
            print field[1] " has the same UID as " name " : UID = " uid[name]
            dup = 1                      # set duplicate flag
            }
        }
```

```
if (!dup)                               # same as if (dup == 0)
                                        # assign UID and login name to uid array
    {
    uid[field[1]] = field[3]
    }
}'
```

```
$ ./passwd_check
bill (ext 123) has no password.
toni (ext 357) has no password.
neil has the same UID as toni : UID = 164
dan has no password.
dave has the same UID as sales : UID = 108
```

The next example shows a complete interactive shell script that uses gawk to generate a report on the **cars** file based on price ranges:

```
$ cat list_cars
trap 'rm -f $$.tem > /dev/null;echo $0 aborted.;exit 1' 1 2 15
echo -n "Price range (for example, 5000 7500):"
read lowrange hirange

echo '
                              Miles
Make         Model      Year  (000)       Price
---------------------------------------------------' > $$.tem
gawk < cars '
$5 >= '$lowrange' && $5 <= '$hirange' {
        if ($1 ~ /ply/)  $1 = "plymouth"
        if ($1 ~ /chev/) $1 = "chevrolet"
        printf "%-10s %-8s    %2d    %5d    $ %8.2f\n", $1, $2, $3, $4,
$5
        }' | sort -n +5 >> $$.tem
cat $$.tem
rm $$.tem
```

```
$ ./list_cars
Price range (for example, 5000 7500):3000 8000

                              Miles
Make         Model      Year  (000)       Price
-------------------------------------------------
chevrolet    malibu     1999     60    $ 3000.00
chevrolet    malibu     2000     50    $ 3500.00
honda        accord     2001     30    $ 6000.00
```

```
$ ./list_cars
Price range (for example, 5000 7500):0 2000

                              Miles
Make         Model      Year  (000)       Price
-------------------------------------------------
bmw          325i       1985    115    $  450.00
toyota       rav4       2002    180    $  750.00
chevrolet    impala     1985     85    $ 1550.00
```

```
$ ./list_cars
Price range (for example, 5000 7500):15000 100000

                                 Miles
Make        Model       Year     (000)          Price
-------------------------------------------------------
ford        taurus      2004        10     $ 17000.00
```

optional

ADVANCED gawk PROGRAMMING

This section discusses some of the advanced features of AWK. It covers how to control input using the **getline** statement, how to use a coprocess to exchange information between gawk and a program running in the background, and how to use a coprocess to exchange data over a network. Coprocesses are available under gawk only; they are not available under awk and mawk.

getline: CONTROLLING INPUT

Using the **getline** statement gives you more control over the data gawk reads than other methods of input do. When you provide a variable name as an argument to **getline**, **getline** reads data into that variable. The **BEGIN** block of the **g1** program uses **getline** to read one line into the variable **aa** from standard input:

```
$ cat g1
BEGIN   {
        getline aa
        print aa
        }
$ echo aaaa | gawk -f g1
aaaa
```

The next few examples use the **alpha** file:

```
$ cat alpha
aaaaaaaaa
bbbbbbbbb
ccccccccc
ddddddddd
```

Even when **g1** is given more than one line of input, it processes only the first line:

```
$ gawk -f g1 < alpha
aaaaaaaaa
```

When **getline** is not given an argument, it reads input into $0 and modifies the field variables ($1, $2, . . .):

```
$ gawk 'BEGIN {getline;print $1}' < alpha
aaaaaaaaa
```

The **g2** program uses a **while** loop in the **BEGIN** block to loop over the lines in standard input. The **getline** statement reads each line into **holdme** and **print** outputs each value of **holdme**.

```
$ cat g2
BEGIN   {
        while (getline holdme)
            print holdme
        }
$ gawk -f g2 < alpha
aaaaaaaaa
bbbbbbbbb
ccccccccc
ddddddddd
```

The **g3** program demonstrates that gawk automatically reads each line of input into $0 when it has statements in its body (and not just a **BEGIN** block). This program outputs the record number (**NR**), the string $0:, and the value of $0 (the current record) for each line of input.

```
$ cat g3
        {print NR, "$0:", $0}

$ gawk -f g3 < alpha
1 $0: aaaaaaaaa
2 $0: bbbbbbbbb
3 $0: ccccccccc
4 $0: ddddddddd
```

Next **g4** demonstrates that **getline** works independently of gawk's automatic reads and $0. When **getline** reads data into a variable, it does not modify either $0 or any of the fields in the current record ($1, $2, . . .). The first statement in **g4**, which is the same as the statement in **g3**, outputs the line that gawk has automatically read. The **getline** statement reads the next line of input into the variable named **aa**. The third statement outputs the record number, the string **aa:**, and the value of **aa**. The output from **g4** shows that **getline** processes records independently of gawk's automatic reads.

```
$ cat g4
        {
        print NR, "$0:", $0
        getline aa
        print NR, "aa:", aa
        }

$ gawk -f g4 < alpha
1 $0: aaaaaaaaa
2 aa: bbbbbbbbb
3 $0: ccccccccc
4 aa: ddddddddd
```

The **g5** program outputs each line of input except for those lines that begin with the letter **b**. The first **print** statement outputs each line that gawk reads automatically. Next the /^b/ *pattern* selects all lines that begin with **b** for special processing. The *action* uses **getline** to read the next line of input into the variable **hold**, outputs the string **skip this line:** followed by the value of **hold**, and outputs the value of **$1**. The **$1** holds the value of the first field of the record that gawk read automatically, not the record read by **getline**. The final statement displays a string and the value of **NR**, the current record number. Even though **getline** does not change **$0** when it reads data into a variable, gawk increments **NR**.

```
$ cat g5
        # print all lines except those read with getline
        {print "line #", NR, $0}

# if line begins with "b" process it specially
/^b/    {
        # use getline to read the next line into variable named hold
        getline hold

        # print value of hold
        print "skip this line:", hold

        # $0 is not affected when getline reads data into a variable
        # $1 still holds previous value
        print "previous line began with:", $1
        }


        {
        print ">>>> finished processing line #", NR
        print ""
        }
$ gawk -f g5 < alpha
line # 1 aaaaaaaaa
>>>> finished processing line # 1

line # 2 bbbbbbbbb
skip this line: ccccccccc
previous line began with: bbbbbbbbb
>>>> finished processing line # 3

line # 4 ddddddddd
>>>> finished processing line # 4
```

COPROCESS: TWO-WAY I/O

A *coprocess* is a process that runs in parallel with another process. Starting with version 3.1, gawk can invoke a coprocess to exchange information directly with a background process. A coprocess can be useful when you are working in a client/server environment, setting up an *SQL* (page 980) front end/back end, or exchanging data with a remote system over a network. The gawk syntax identifies a coprocess by preceding the name of the program that starts the background process with a |& operator.

Only gawk supports coprocesses

tip The awk and mawk utilities do not support coprocesses. Only gawk supports coprocesses.

The coprocess command must be a filter (i.e., it reads from standard input and writes to standard output) and must flush its output whenever it has a complete line rather than accumulating lines for subsequent output. When a command is invoked as a coprocess, it is connected via a two-way pipe to a gawk program so you can read from and write to the coprocess.

to_upper   When used alone the tr utility (page 864) does not flush its output after each line. The **to_upper** shell script is a wrapper for tr that does flush its output; this filter can be run as a coprocess. For each line read, **to_upper** writes the line, translated to uppercase, to standard output. Remove the # before **set –x** if you want **to_upper** to display debugging output.

```
$ cat to_upper
#!/bin/bash
#set -x
while read arg
do
    echo "$arg" | tr '[a-z]' '[A-Z]'
done

$ echo abcdef | ./to_upper
ABCDEF
```

The **g6** program invokes **to_upper** as a coprocess. This gawk program reads standard input or a file specified on the command line, translates the input to uppercase, and writes the translated data to standard output.

```
$ cat g6
    {
    print $0 |& "to_upper"
    "to_upper" |& getline hold
    print hold
    }

$ gawk -f g6 < alpha
AAAAAAAAA
BBBBBBBBB
CCCCCCCCC
DDDDDDDDD
```

The **g6** program has one compound statement, enclosed within braces, comprising three statements. Because there is no *pattern,* gawk executes the compound statement once for each line of input.

In the first statement, **print $0** sends the current record to standard output. The **|&** operator redirects standard output to the program named **to_upper,** which is running as a coprocess. The quotation marks around the name of the program are required. The second statement redirects standard output from **to_upper** to a **getline** statement, which copies its standard input to the variable named **hold.** The third statement, **print hold,** sends the contents of the **hold** variable to standard output.

GETTING INPUT FROM A NETWORK

Building on the concept of a coprocess, gawk can exchange information with a process on another system via an IP network connection. When you specify one of the special filenames that begins with **/inet/**, gawk processes the request using a network connection. The format of these special filenames is

/inet/protocol/local-port/remote-host/remote-port

where *protocol* is usually **tcp** but can be **udp**, *local-port* is 0 (zero) if you want gawk to pick a port (otherwise it is the number of the port you want to use), *remote-host* is the *IP address* (page 960) or *fully qualified domain name* (page 955) of the remote host, and *remote-port* is the port number on the remote host. Instead of a port number in *local-port* and *remote-port*, you can specify a service name such as **http** or **ftp**.

The **g7** program reads the **rfc-retrieval.txt** file from the server at **www.rfc-editor.org**. On **www.rfc-editor.org** the file is located at **/rfc/rfc-retrieval.txt**. The first statement in **g7** assigns the special filename to the **server** variable. The filename specifies a TCP connection, allows the local system to select an appropriate port, and connects to **www.rfc-editor.org** on port 80. You can use **http** in place of 80 to specify the standard HTTP port.

The second statement uses a coprocess to send a **GET** request to the remote server. This request includes the pathname of the file gawk is requesting. A **while** loop uses a coprocess to redirect lines from the server to **getline**. Because **getline** has no variable name as an argument, it saves its input in the current record buffer **$0**. The final **print** statement sends each record to standard output. Experiment with this script, replacing the final **print** statement with gawk statements that process the file.

```
$ cat g7
BEGIN            {
    # set variable named server
    # to special networking filename
    server = "/inet/tcp/0/www.rfc-editor.org/80"

    # use coprocess to send GET request to remote server
    print "GET /rfc/rfc-retrieval.txt" |& server

    # while loop uses coprocess to redirect
    # output from server to getline
    while (server |& getline)
        print $0
}
```

```
$ gawk -f g7

            Where and how to get new RFCs
            ===============================

RFCs may be obtained via FTP or HTTP or email from many RFC repositories.
The official repository for RFCs is:

        http://www.rfc-editor.org/
...
```

CHAPTER SUMMARY

AWK is a pattern-scanning and processing language that searches one or more files for records (usually lines) that match specified patterns. It processes lines by performing actions, such as writing the record to standard output or incrementing a counter, each time it finds a match. AWK has several implementations, including awk, gawk, and mawk.

An AWK program consists of one or more lines containing a *pattern* and/or *action* in the following format:

> *pattern { action }*

The *pattern* selects lines from the input. An AWK program performs the *action* on all lines that the *pattern* selects. If a *program* line does not contain a *pattern*, AWK selects all lines in the input. If a program line does not contain an *action*, AWK copies the selected lines to standard output.

An AWK program can use variables, functions, arithmetic operators, associative arrays, control statements, and C's **printf** statement. Advanced AWK programming takes advantage of **getline** statements to fine-tune input, coprocesses to enable gawk to exchange data with other programs (gawk only), and network connections to exchange data with programs running on remote systems on a network (gawk only).

EXERCISES

1. Write an AWK program that numbers each line in a file and sends its output to standard output.

2. Write an AWK program that displays the number of characters in the first field followed by the first field and sends its output to standard output.

3. Write an AWK program that uses the **cars** file (page 541), displays all cars priced at more than $5,000, and sends its output to standard output.

4. Use AWK to determine how many lines in **/usr/share/dict/words** contain the string **abul**. Verify your answer using grep.

ADVANCED EXERCISES

5. Experiment with pgawk (available only with gawk). What does it do? How can it be useful?

6. Write a gawk (not awk or mawk) program named **net_list** that reads from the **rfc-retrieval.txt** file on **www.rfc-editor.org** (see "Getting Input from a Network" on page 562) and displays a the last word on each line in all uppercase letters.

7. Expand the **net_list** program developed in Exercise 6 to use **to_upper** (page 561) as a coprocess to display the list of cars with only the make of the cars in uppercase. The model and subsequent fields on each line should appear as they do in the **cars** file.

8. How can you get gawk (not awk or mawk) to neatly format—that is, "pretty print"—a gawk program file? (*Hint:* See the gawk man page.)

13

THE sed EDITOR

The sed (stream editor) utility is a batch (noninteractive) editor. It transforms an input stream that can come from a file or standard input. It is frequently used as a filter in a pipe. Because it makes only one pass through its input, sed is more efficient than an interactive editor such as ed. Most Linux distributions provide GNU sed; Mac OS X supplies BSD sed. This chapter applies to both versions.

Syntax

A sed command line has the following syntax:

sed [–n] program [file-list]
sed [–n] –f program-file [file-list]

The sed utility takes its input from files you specify on the command line or from standard input. Output from sed goes to standard output.

Arguments

The *program* is a sed program included on the command line. The first format allows you to write simple, short sed programs without creating a separate file to hold the sed program. The *program-file* in the second format is the pathname of a file containing a sed program (see "Editor Basics"). The *file-list* contains pathnames of the ordinary files that sed processes; these are the input files. When you do not specify a *file-list*, sed takes its input from standard input.

Options

Options preceded by a double hyphen (--) work under Linux (GNU sed) only. Options named with a single letter and preceded by a single hyphen work under Linux (GNU sed) and OS X (BSD sed).

--file *program-file*

    –f *program-file*

        Causes sed to read its program from the file named *program-file* instead of from the command line. You can use this option more than once on the command line.

--help   Summarizes how to use sed. `LINUX`

--in-place[=*suffix***]**

    –i[*suffix***]**

        Edits files in place. Without this option sed sends its output to standard output. With this option sed replaces the file it is processing with its output. When you specify a *suffix*, sed makes a backup of the original file. The backup has the original filename with *suffix* appended. You must include a period in *suffix* if you want a period to appear between the original filename and *suffix*.

--quiet *or* **–n** Causes sed not to copy lines to standard output except as specified by the Print
--silent   (**p**) instruction or flag.

EDITOR BASICS

A sed program consists of one or more lines with the following syntax:

[address[,address]] instruction [argument-list]

The *address*es are optional. If you omit the *address,* sed processes all lines of input. The *instruction* is an editing instruction that modifies the text. The *address*es select the line(s) the *instruction* part of the command operates on. The number and kinds of arguments in the *argument-list* depend on the *instruction.* If you want to put several sed commands on one line, separate the commands with semicolons (;).

The sed utility processes input as follows:

1. Reads one line of input from *file-list* or standard input.

2. Reads the first instruction from the *program* or *program-file.* If the *address*(es) select the input line, acts on the input line as the *instruction* specifies.

3. Reads the next instruction from the *program* or *program-file.* If the *address*(es) select the input line, acts on the input line (possibly modified by the previous instruction) as the *instruction* specifies.

4. Repeats step 3 until it has executed all instructions in the *program* or *program-file.*

5. Starts over with step 1 if there is another line of input; otherwise, sed is finished.

ADDRESSES

A line number is an address that selects a line. As a special case, the line number **$** represents the last line of input.

A regular expression (Appendix A) is an address that selects those lines containing a string that the regular expression matches. Although slashes are often used to delimit these regular expressions, sed permits you to use any character other than a backslash or NEWLINE for this purpose.

Except as noted, zero, one, or two addresses (either line numbers or regular expressions) can precede an instruction. If you do not specify an address, sed selects all lines, causing the instruction to act on every line of input. Specifying one address causes the instruction to act on each input line the address selects. Specifying two addresses causes the instruction to act on groups of lines. In this case the first address selects the first line in the first group. The second address selects the next subsequent line that it matches; this line is the last line in the first group. If no match for the second address is found, the second address points to the end of the file. After selecting the last line in a group, sed starts the selection process over, looking for the next line the first address matches. This line is the first line in the next group. The sed utility continues this process until it has finished going through the entire file.

INSTRUCTIONS

Pattern space   The sed utility has two buffers. The following commands work with the *Pattern space,* which initially holds the line of input that sed just read. The other buffer, the *Hold space,* is discussed on page 570.

a   (**append**) The Append instruction appends one or more lines to the currently selected line. If you precede an Append instruction with two addresses, it appends to each line that is selected by the addresses. If you do not precede an Append instruction with an address, it appends to each input line. An Append instruction has the following format:

> *[address[,address]] a*
> *text *
> *text *
> ...
> *text*

You must end each line of appended text, except the last, with a backslash, which quotes the following NEWLINE. The appended text concludes with a line that does not end with a backslash. The sed utility *always* writes out appended text, regardless of whether you use a **–n** flag on the command line. It even writes out the text if you delete the line to which you are appending the text.

c   (**change**) The Change instruction is similar to Append and Insert except it changes the selected lines so that they contain the new text. When you specify an address range, Change replaces the range of lines with a single occurrence of the new text.

d   (**delete**) The Delete instruction causes sed not to write out the lines it selects and not to finish processing the lines. After sed executes a Delete instruction, it reads the next input line and then begins anew with the first instruction from the *program* or *program-file.*

i   (**insert**) The Insert instruction is identical to the Append instruction except it places the new text *before* the selected line.

N   (**next without write**) The Next (**N**) instruction reads the next input line and appends it to the current line. An embedded NEWLINE separates the original line and the new line. You can use the **N** command to remove NEWLINEs from a file. See the example on page 575.

n   (**next**) The Next (**n**) instruction writes out the currently selected line if appropriate, reads the next input line, and starts processing the new line with the next instruction from the *program* or *program-file.*

p   (**print**) The Print instruction writes the selected lines to standard output, writing the lines immediately, and does not reflect the effects of subsequent instructions. This instruction overrides the –**n** option on the command line.

q   (**quit**) The Quit instruction causes sed to terminate immediately.

r *file*   (**read**) The Read instruction reads the contents of the specified file and appends it to the selected line. A single SPACE and the name of the input file must follow a Read instruction.

s   (**substitute**) The Substitute instruction in sed is similar to that in vim (page 176). It has the following format:

[address[,address]] s/pattern/replacement-string/[g][p][w **file***]*

The *pattern* is a regular expression (Appendix A) that traditionally is delimited by a slash (*/*); you can use any character other than a SPACE or NEWLINE. The *replacement-string* starts immediately following the second delimiter and must be terminated by the same delimiter. The final (third) delimiter is required. The *replacement-string* can contain an ampersand (&), which sed replaces with the matched *pattern.* Unless you use the **g** flag, the Substitute instruction replaces only the first occurrence of the *pattern* on each selected line.

The **g** (global) flag causes the Substitute instruction to replace all nonoverlapping occurrences of the *pattern* on the selected lines.

The **p** (print) flag causes sed to send all lines on which it makes substitutions to standard output. This flag overrides the –**n** option on the command line.

The **w** (write) flag is similar to the **p** flag but sends its output to the file specified by *file.* A single SPACE and the name of the output file must follow a **w** flag.

w *file*   (**write**) This instruction is similar to the Print instruction except it sends the output to the file specified by *file.* A single SPACE and the name of the output file must follow a Write instruction.

CONTROL STRUCTURES

!   (**NOT**) Causes sed to apply the following instruction, located on the same line, to each of the lines *not* selected by the address portion of the instruction. For example, **3!d** deletes all lines except line 3 and **$!p** displays all lines except the last.

{ }   (**group instructions**) When you enclose a group of instructions within a pair of braces, a single address or address pair selects the lines on which the group of instructions operates. Use semicolons (;) to separate multiple commands appearing on a single line.

Branch instructions   The GNU sed info page identifies the branch instructions as "Commands for sed gurus" and suggests that if you need them you might be better off writing your program in awk or Perl.

: *label*   Identifies a location within a sed program. The *label* is useful as a target for the **b** and **t** branch instructions.

b [*label*]   Unconditionally transfers control to *label*. Without *label*, skips the rest of the instructions for the current line of input and reads the next line of input.

t [*label*]   Transfers control to *label* only if a Substitute instruction has been successful since the most recent line of input was read (conditional branch). Without *label*, skips the rest of the instructions for the current line of input and reads the next line of input.

THE HOLD SPACE

The commands reviewed up to this point work with the *Pattern space,* a buffer that initially holds the line of input that sed just read. The *Hold space* can hold data while you manipulate data in the Pattern space; it is a temporary buffer. Until you place data in the Hold space, it is empty. This section discusses commands that move data between the Pattern space and the Hold space.

g   Copies the contents of the Hold space to the Pattern space. The original contents of the Pattern space is lost.

G   Appends a NEWLINE and the contents of the Hold space to the Pattern space.

h   Copies the contents of the Pattern space to the Hold space. The original contents of the Hold space is lost.

H   Appends a NEWLINE and the contents of the Pattern space to the Hold space.

x   Exchanges the contents of the Pattern space and the Hold space.

EXAMPLES

lines data file   The following examples use the **lines** file for input:

```
$ cat lines
Line one.
The second line.
The third.
This is line four.
Five.
This is the sixth sentence.
This is line seven.
Eighth and last.
```

Unless you instruct it not to, sed sends all lines—selected or not—to standard output. When you use the **–n** option on the command line, sed sends only certain lines, such as those selected by a Print (**p**) instruction, to standard output.

The following command line displays all lines in the **lines** file that contain the word **line** (all lowercase). In addition, because there is no **–n** option, sed displays all the lines of input. As a result, sed displays the lines that contain the word **line** twice.

```
$ sed '/line/ p' lines
Line one.
The second line.
The second line.
The third.
This is line four.
This is line four.
Five.
This is the sixth sentence.
This is line seven.
This is line seven.
Eighth and last.
```

The preceding command uses the address **/line/**, a regular expression that is a simple string. The sed utility selects each of the lines that contains a match for that pattern. The Print (**p**) instruction displays each of the selected lines.

The following command uses the **–n** option, so sed displays only the selected lines:

```
$ sed -n '/line/ p' lines
The second line.
This is line four.
This is line seven.
```

In the next example, sed displays part of a file based on line numbers. The Print instruction selects and displays lines 3 through 6.

```
$ sed -n '3,6 p' lines
The third.
This is line four.
Five.
This is the sixth sentence.
```

The next command line uses the Quit instruction to cause sed to display only the beginning of a file. In this case sed displays the first five lines of **lines** just as a **head –5 lines** command would.

```
$ sed '5 q' lines
Line one.
The second line.
The third.
This is line four.
Five.
```

program-file When you need to give sed more complex or lengthy instructions, you can use a *program-file*. The **print3_6** program performs the same function as the command line in the second preceding example. The **–f** option tells sed to read its program from the file named following this option.

```
$ cat print3_6
3,6 p

$ sed -n -f print3_6 lines
The third.
This is line four.
Five.
This is the sixth sentence.
```

Append The next program selects line 2 and uses an Append instruction to append a NEWLINE and the text **AFTER.** to the selected line. Because the command line does not include the **–n** option, sed copies all lines from the input file **lines**.

```
$ cat append_demo
2 a\
AFTER.

$ sed -f append_demo lines
Line one.
The second line.
AFTER.
The third.
This is line four.
Five.
This is the sixth sentence.
This is line seven.
Eighth and last.
```

Insert The **insert_demo** program selects all lines containing the string **This** and inserts a NEWLINE and the text **BEFORE.** before the selected lines.

```
$ cat insert_demo
/This/ i\
BEFORE.

$ sed -f insert_demo lines
Line one.
The second line.
The third.
BEFORE.
This is line four.
Five.
BEFORE.
This is the sixth sentence.
BEFORE.
This is line seven.
Eighth and last.
```

Change The next example demonstrates a Change instruction with an address range. When you specify a range of lines for a Change instruction, it does not change each line within the range but rather changes the block of lines to a single occurrence of the new text.

```
$ cat change_demo
2,4 c\
SED WILL INSERT THESE\
THREE LINES IN PLACE\
OF THE SELECTED LINES.

$ sed -f change_demo lines
Line one.
SED WILL INSERT THESE
THREE LINES IN PLACE
OF THE SELECTED LINES.
Five.
This is the sixth sentence.
This is line seven.
Eighth and last.
```

Substitute The next example demonstrates a Substitute instruction. The sed utility selects all lines because the instruction has no address. On each line **subs_demo** replaces the first occurrence of **line** with **sentence**. The **p** flag displays each line where a substitution occurs. The command line calls sed with the **–n** option, so sed displays only the lines the program explicitly specifies.

```
$ cat subs_demo
s/line/sentence/p

$ sed -n -f subs_demo lines
The second sentence.
This is sentence four.
This is sentence seven.
```

The next example is similar to the preceding one except that a **w** flag and filename (**temp**) at the end of the Substitute instruction cause sed to create the file named **temp**. The command line does not include the **–n** option, so it displays all lines in addition to writing the changed lines to **temp**. The cat utility displays the contents of the file **temp**. The word **Line** (starting with an uppercase L) is not changed.

```
$ cat write_demo1
s/line/sentence/w temp

$ sed -f write_demo1 lines
Line one.
The second sentence.
The third.
This is sentence four.
Five.
This is the sixth sentence.
This is sentence seven.
Eighth and last.

$ cat temp
The second sentence.
This is sentence four.
This is sentence seven.
```

The following bash script changes all occurrences of **REPORT** to **report**, **FILE** to **file**, and **PROCESS** to **process** in a group of files. Because it is a shell script and not a sed program file, you must have read and execute permission to the **sub** file to execute it as a command (page 278). The **for** structure (page 412) loops through the list of files on the command line. As it processes each file, the script displays each filename before processing the file with sed. This program uses embedded sed commands that span multiple lines. Because the NEWLINEs between the commands are quoted (they appear between single quotation marks), sed accepts multiple commands on a single, extended command line (within the shell script). Each Substitute instruction includes a **g** (global) flag to take care of the case where a string occurs more than once on a line.

```
$ cat sub
for file
do
        echo $file
        mv $file $$.subhld
        sed 's/REPORT/report/g
             s/FILE/file/g
             s/PROCESS/process/g' $$.subhld > $file
done
rm $$.subhld

$ sub file1 file2 file3
file1
file2
file3
```

In the next example, a Write instruction copies part of a file to another file (**temp2**). The line numbers **2** and **4**, separated by a comma, select the range of lines sed is to copy. This program does not alter the lines.

```
$ cat write_demo2
2,4 w temp2

$ sed -n -f write_demo2 lines

$ cat temp2
The second line.
The third.
This is line four.
```

The program **write_demo3** is similar to **write_demo2** but precedes the Write instruction with the NOT operator (**!**), causing sed to write to the file those lines *not* selected by the address.

```
$ cat write_demo3
2,4 !w temp3

$ sed -n -f write_demo3 lines
```

```
$ cat temp3
Line one.
Five.
This is the sixth sentence.
This is line seven.
Eighth and last.
```

Next (n)   The following example demonstrates the Next (**n**) instruction. When it processes the selected line (line 3), sed immediately starts processing the next line without displaying line 3.

```
$ cat next_demo1
3 n
p
```

```
$ sed -n -f next_demo1 lines
Line one.
The second line.
This is line four.
Five.
This is the sixth sentence.
This is line seven.
Eighth and last.
```

The next example uses a textual address. The sixth line contains the string **the**, so the Next (**n**) instruction causes sed not to display it.

```
$ cat next_demo2
/the/ n
p
```

```
$ sed -n -f next_demo2 lines
Line one.
The second line.
The third.
This is line four.
Five.
This is line seven.
Eighth and last.
```

Next (N)   The following example is similar to the preceding example except it uses the upper-case Next (**N**) instruction in place of the lowercase Next (**n**) instruction. Here the Next (**N**) instruction appends the next line to the line that contains the string **the**. In the **lines** file, sed appends line 7 to line 6 and embeds a NEWLINE between the two lines. The Substitute command replaces the embedded NEWLINE with a SPACE. The Substitute command does not affect other lines because they do not contain embedded NEWLINEs; rather, they are terminated by NEWLINEs. See page 926 for an example of the Next (**N**) instruction in a sed script running under OS X.

```
$ cat Next_demo3
/the/ N
s/\n/ /
p
```

```
$ sed -n -f Next_demo3 lines
Line one.
The second line.
The third.
This is line four.
Five.
This is the sixth sentence. This is line seven.
Eighth and last.
```

The next set of examples uses the **compound.in** file to demonstrate how sed instructions work together.

```
$ cat compound.in
1. The words on this page...
2. The words on this page...
3. The words on this page...
4. The words on this page...
```

The following example substitutes the string **words** with **text** on lines 1, 2, and 3 and the string **text** with **TEXT** on lines 2, 3, and 4. The example also selects and deletes line 3. The result is **text** on line 1, **TEXT** on line 2, no line 3, and **words** on line 4. The sed utility makes two substitutions on lines 2 and 3: **text** for **words** and **TEXT** for **text**. Then sed deletes line 3.

```
$ cat compound
1,3 s/words/text/
2,4 s/text/TEXT/
3 d

$ sed -f compound compound.in
1. The text on this page...
2. The TEXT on this page...
4. The words on this page...
```

The ordering of instructions within a sed program is critical. Both Substitute instructions are applied to the second line in the following example, as in the previous example, but the order in which the substitutions occur changes the result.

```
$ cat compound2
2,4 s/text/TEXT/
1,3 s/words/text/
3 d

$ sed -f compound2 compound.in
1. The text on this page...
2. The text on this page...
4. The words on this page...
```

In the next example, **compound3** appends two lines to line 2. The sed utility displays all lines from the file once because no **–n** option appears on the command line. The Print instruction at the end of the program file displays line 3 an additional time.

```
$ cat compound3
2 a\
This is line 2a.\
This is line 2b.
3 p

$ sed -f compound3 compound.in
1. The words on this page...
2. The words on this page...
This is line 2a.
This is line 2b.
3. The words on this page...
3. The words on this page...
4. The words on this page...
```

The next example shows that sed always displays appended text. Here line 2 is deleted but the Append instruction still displays the two lines that were appended to it. Appended lines are displayed even if you use the **–n** option on the command line.

```
$ cat compound4
2 a\
This is line 2a.\
This is line 2b.
2 d

$ sed -f compound4 compound.in
1. The words on this page...
This is line 2a.
This is line 2b.
3. The words on this page...
4. The words on this page...
```

The next example uses a regular expression as the pattern. The regular expression in the following instruction (^.) matches one character at the beginning of every line that is not empty. The replacement string (between the second and third slashes) contains a backslash escape sequence that represents a TAB character (\t) followed by an ampersand (&). The ampersand takes on the value of what the regular expression matched.

```
$ sed 's/^./\t&/' lines
        Line one.
        The second line.
        The third.
...
```

This type of substitution is useful for indenting a file to create a left margin. See Appendix A for more information on regular expressions.

You can also use the simpler form **s/^/\t/** to add TABs to the beginnings of lines. In addition to placing TABs at the beginnings of lines with text on them, this instruction places a TAB at the beginning of every empty line—something the preceding command does not do.

You may want to put the preceding sed instruction into a shell script so you do not have to remember it (and retype it) each time you want to indent a file. The chmod utility gives you read and execute permission to the **ind** file.

```
$ cat ind
sed 's/^./\t&/' $*
$ chmod u+rx ind
$ ind lines
        Line one.
        The second line.
        The third.
...
```

Stand-alone script When you run the preceding shell script, it creates two processes: It calls a shell, which in turn calls sed. You can eliminate the overhead associated with the shell process by putting the line **#!/bin/sed –f** (page 280) at the beginning of the script, which runs the sed utility directly. You need read and execute permission to the file holding the script.

```
$ cat ind2
#!/bin/sed -f
s/^./\t&/
```

In the following sed program, the regular expression (two SPACEs followed by ✳$) matches one or more SPACEs at the end of a line. This program removes trailing SPACEs at the ends of lines, which is useful for cleaning up files you created using vim.

```
$ cat cleanup
sed 's/ *$//' $*
```

The **cleanup2** script runs the same sed command as **cleanup** but stands alone: It calls sed directly with no intermediate shell.

```
$ cat cleanup2
#!/bin/sed -f
s/ *$//
```

Hold space The next sed program makes use of the Hold space to exchange pairs of lines in a file.

```
$ cat s1
h # Copy Pattern space (line just read) to Hold space.
n # Read the next line of input into Pattern space.
p # Output Pattern space.
g # Copy Hold space to Pattern space.
p # Output Pattern space (which now holds the previous line).

$ sed -nf s1 lines
The second line.
Line one.
This is line four.
```

```
The third.
This is the sixth sentence.
Five.
Eighth and last.
This is line seven.
```

The commands in the **s1** program process pairs of input lines. This program reads a line and stores it; reads another line and displays it; and then retrieves the stored line and displays it. After processing a pair of lines, the program starts over with the next pair of lines.

The next sed program adds a blank line after each line in the input file (i.e., it double-spaces a file).

```
$ sed 'G' lines
Line one.

The second line.

The third.

This is line four.

$
```

The **G** instruction appends a NEWLINE and the contents of the Hold space to the Pattern space. Unless you put something in the Hold space, it will be empty. Thus the **G** instruction appends a NEWLINE to each line of input before sed displays the line(s) from the Pattern space.

The **s2** sed program reverses the order of the lines in a file just as the tac utility does.

```
$ cat s2
2,$G  # On all but the first line, append a NEWLINE and the
      # contents of the Hold space to the Pattern space.
h     # Copy the Pattern space to the Hold space.
$!d   # Delete all except the last line.

$ sed -f s2 lines
Eighth and last.
This is line seven.
This is the sixth sentence.
Five.
This is line four.
The third.
The second line.
Line one.
```

This program comprises three commands: **2,$G**, **h**, and **$!d**. To understand this script it is important to understand how the address of the last command works: The **$** is the address of the last line of input and the **!** negates the address. The result is an address that selects all lines except the last line of input. In the same fashion you could replace the first command with **1!G**: It would select all lines except the first line for processing; the results would be the same.

Here is what happens as **s2** processes the **lines** file:

1. The sed utility reads the first line of input (**Line one.**) into the Pattern space.

    a. The **2,$G** does not process the first line of input—because of its address the **G** instruction starts processing at the second line.

    b. The **h** copies **Line one.** from the Pattern space to the Hold space.

    c. The **$!d** deletes the contents of the Pattern space. Because there is nothing in the Pattern space, sed does not display anything.

2. The sed utility reads the second line of input (**The second line.**) into the Pattern space.

    a. The **2,$G** adds what is in the Hold space (**Line one.**) to the Pattern space. The Pattern space now contains **The second line.**NEWLINE**Line one.**

    b. The **h** copies what is in the Pattern space to the Hold space.

    c. The **$!d** deletes the second line of input. Because it is deleted, sed does not display it.

3. The sed utility reads the third line of input (**The third.**) into the Pattern space.

    a. The **2,$G** adds what is in the Hold space (**The second line.**NEWLINE**Line one.**) to the Pattern space. The Pattern space now has **The third.**NEWLINE **The second line.**NEWLINE**Line one.**

    b. The **h** copies what is in the Pattern space to the Hold space.

    c. The **$!d** deletes the contents of the Pattern space. Because there is nothing in the Pattern space, sed does not display anything.

    . . .

8. The sed utility reads the eighth (last) line of input into the Pattern space.

    a. The **2,$G** adds what is in the Hold space to the Pattern space. The Pattern space now contains all the lines from **lines** in reverse order.

    b. The **h** copies what is in the Pattern space to the Hold space. This step is not necessary for the last line of input but does not alter the program's output.

    c. The **$!d** does not process the last line of input. Because of its address the **d** instruction does not delete the last line.

    d. The sed utility displays the contents of the Pattern space.

CHAPTER SUMMARY

The sed (stream editor) utility is a batch (noninteractive) editor. It takes its input from files you specify on the command line or from standard input. Unless you redirect the output from sed, it goes to standard output.

A sed program consists of one or more lines with the following syntax:

[address[,address]] instruction [argument-list]

The *address*es are optional. If you omit the *address,* sed processes all lines of input. The *instruction* is the editing instruction that modifies the text. The *address*es select the line(s) the *instruction* part of the command operates on. The number and kinds of arguments in the *argument-list* depend on the *instruction.*

In addition to basic instructions, sed includes some powerful advanced instructions. One set of these instructions allows sed programs to store data temporarily in a buffer called the Hold space. Other instructions provide unconditional and conditional branching in sed programs.

EXERCISES

1. Write a sed command that copies a file to standard output, removing all lines that begin with the word **Today.**

2. Write a sed command that copies only those lines of a file that begin with the word **Today** to standard output.

3. Write a sed command that copies a file to standard output, removing all blank lines (i.e., lines with no characters on them).

4. Write a sed program named **ins** that copies a file to standard output, changing all occurrences of **cat** to **dog** and preceding each modified line with a line that says **following line is modified:**

5. Write a sed program named **div** that copies a file to standard output, copies the first five lines to a file named **first**, and copies the rest of the file to a file named **last.**

6. Write a sed command that copies a file to standard output, replacing a single SPACE as the first character on a line with a 0 (zero) only if the SPACE is immediately followed by a number (0–9). For example:

   ```
   abc   →abc
    abc  →  abc
   85c   →085c
   55b   →55b
   000   →0000
   ```

7. How can you use sed to triple-space (i.e., add two blank lines after each line in) a file?

14

THE rsync SECURE COPY UTILITY

The rsync (remote synchronization) utility copies an ordinary file or directory hierarchy locally or from the local system to or from another system on a network. By default, this utility uses OpenSSH to transfer files and the same authentication mechanism as OpenSSH; therefore it provides the same security as OpenSSH. The rsync utility prompts for a password when it needs one. Alternatively, you can use the **rsyncd** daemon as a transfer agent.

SYNTAX

An rsync command line has the following syntax:

rsync [options] [[user@]from-host:]source-file [[user@]to-host:][destination-file]

The rsync utility copies files, including directory hierarchies, on the local system or between the local system and a remote system.

ARGUMENTS

The *from-host* is the name of the system you are copying files from; the *to-host* is the name of the system you are copying files to. When you do not specify a host, rsync assumes the local system. The *user* on either system defaults to the user who is giving the command on the local system; you can specify a different user with *user@*. Unlike scp, rsync *does not* permit copying between remote systems.

The *source-file* is the ordinary or directory file you are copying; the *destination-file* is the resulting copy. You can specify files as relative or absolute pathnames. On the local system, relative pathnames are relative to the working directory; on a remote system, relative pathnames are relative to the specified or implicit user's home directory. When the *source-file* is a directory, you must use the −−**recursive** or −−**archive** option to copy its contents. When the *destination-file* is a directory, each of the source files maintains its simple filename. If the *source-file* is a single file, you can omit *destination-file*; the copied file will have the same simple filename as *source-file* (useful only when copying to or from a remote machine).

A trailing slash (/) on *source-file* is critical

caution | When *source-file* is a directory, a trailing slash in *source-file* causes rsync to copy the contents of the directory. The slash is equivalent to /*; it tells rsync to ignore the directory itself and copy the files within the directory. Without a trailing slash, rsync copies the directory. See page 587.

OPTIONS

The Mac OS X version of rsync accepts long options

tip | Options for rsync preceded by a double hyphen (−−) work under Mac OS X as well as under Linux.

−−acls   −A   Preserves ACLs (page 99) of copied files.

−−archive   −a   Copies files including dereferenced symbolic links, device files, and special files recursively, preserving ownership, group, permissions, and modification times associated with the files. Using this option is the same as specifying the **--devices, --specials, --group, --links, --owner, --perms, --recursive,** and **--times** options. This option does not include the **--acls, --hard-links,** or **--xattrs** options; you must specify these options in addition to **--archive** if you want to use them. See page 588 for an example.

--backup –b Renames files that otherwise would be deleted or overwritten. By default, the rsync utility renames files by appending a tilde (~) to existing filenames. See **--backup-dir=***dir* if you want rsync to put these files in a specified directory instead of renaming them. See also **--link-dest=***dir*.

--backup-dir=*dir* When used with the **--backup** option, moves files that otherwise would be deleted or overwritten into the directory named *dir*. After moving the older version of the file in *dir*, rsync copies the newer version of the file from *source-file* to *destination-file*.

The directory named *dir* is located on the same system as *destination-file*. If *dir* is a relative pathname, it is relative to *destination-file*.

--copy-unsafe-links

(**partial dereference**) For each file that is a symbolic link that refers to a file outside the *source-file* hierarchy, copies the file the link points to, not the symbolic link itself. Without this option rsync copies all symbolic links, even if it does not copy the file the link refers to.

–D same as **--devices --specials**.

--delete Deletes files in the *destination-file* that are not in the *source-file*. This option can easily remove files you did not intend to remove; see the caution box on page 589.

--devices Copies device files (**root** user only).

--dry-run Runs rsync without writing to disk. With the **--verbose** option, this option reports on what rsync would have done had it been run without this option. Useful with the **--delete** option.

--group –g Preserves group associations of copied files.

--hard-links –H Preserves hard links of copied files.

--links –l (lowercase "l"; **no dereference**) For each file that is a symbolic link, copies the symbolic link, not the file the link points to, even if the file the link points to is not in the *source-file*.

--link-dest=*dir* If rsync would normally copy a file—that is, if the file exists in *source-file* but not in *destination-file* or is changed in *destination-file*—rsync looks in the directory named *dir* for the same file. If it finds an exact copy of the file in *dir*, rsync makes a hard link from the file in *dir* to *destination-file*. If it does not find an exact copy, rsync copies the file to *destination-file*. See page 592 for an example.

The directory named *dir* is located on the same system as *destination-file*. If *dir* is a relative pathname, it is relative to *destination-file*.

−−owner	−o	Preserves the owner of copied files (**root** user only).
−−perms	−p	Preserves the permissions of copied files.
−−recursive	−r	Recursively descends a directory specified in *source-file* and copies all files in the directory hierarchy. See page 587 for an example.
−−specials		Copies special files.
−−times	−t	Preserves the modification times of copied files. This option also speeds up copying files because it causes rsync not to copy a file that has the same modification time and size in both the *source-file* and the *destination-file*. See page 587 for an example.
−−update	−u	Skips files that are newer in the *destination-file* than in the *source-file*.
−−verbose	−v	Displays information about what rsync is doing. This option is useful with the −−dry-run option. See page 587 for an example.
−−xattrs	−X	Preserves the extended attributes of copied files. This option is not available with all compilations of rsync.
−−compress	−z	Compresses files while copying them.

NOTES

The rsync utility has many options. This chapter describes a few of them; see the rsync man page for a complete list.

OpenSSH By default, rsync copies files to and from a remote system using OpenSSH. The remote system must be running an OpenSSH server. If you can use ssh to log in on the remote system, you can use rsync to copy files to or from that system. If ssh requires you to enter a password, rsync will require a password. See "Copying Files to and from a Remote System" on page 590 for examples. See "Discussion" on page 829 for more information on setting up and using OpenSSH.

rsyncd daemon If you use a double colon (::) in place of a single colon (:) following the name of a remote system, rsync connects to the **rsyncd** daemon on the remote system (it does not use OpenSSH). See the rsync man page for more information.

MORE INFORMATION

man page: rsync
rsync home page: www.samba.org/rsync
Backup information: www.mikerubel.org/computers/rsync_snapshots

Backup tools: www.rsnapshot.org, backuppc.sourceforge.net
File synchronization: alliance.seas.upenn.edu/~bcpierce

EXAMPLES

--recursive
--verbose The first example shows rsync making a copy of a directory using the **--recursive** and **--verbose** options. Both the source and destination directories are in the working directory.

```
$ ls -l memos
total 12
-rw-r--r-- 1 max max 1500 Jun  6 14:24 0606
-rw-r--r-- 1 max max 6001 Jun  8 16:16 0608

$ rsync --recursive --verbose memos memos.copy
building file list ... done
created directory memos.copy
memos/
memos/0606
memos/0608

sent 7671 bytes  received 70 bytes  15482.00 bytes/sec
total size is 7501  speedup is 0.97

$ ls -l memos.copy
total 4
drwxr-xr-x 2 max max 4096 Jul 20 17:42 memos
```

In the preceding example, rsync copies the **memos** directory to the **memos.copy** directory. As the following ls command shows, rsync changed the modification times on the copied files to the time it made the copies:

```
$ ls -l memos.copy/memos
total 12
-rw-r--r-- 1 max max 1500 Jul 20 17:42 0606
-rw-r--r-- 1 max max 6001 Jul 20 17:42 0608
```

USING A TRAILING SLASH (/) ON *source-file*

Whereas the previous example copied a directory to another directory, you may want to copy the *contents* of a directory to another directory. A trailing slash (/) on the *source-file* causes rsync to act as though you had specified a trailing **/*** and causes rsync to copy the contents of the specified directory. A trailing slash on the *destination-file* has no effect.

--times The next example makes another copy of the **memos** directory, using **--times** to preserve modification times of the copied files. It uses a trailing slash on **memos**

to copy the contents of the **memos** directory—not the directory itself—to memos.copy2.

```
$ rsync --recursive --verbose --times memos/ memos.copy2
building file list ... done
created directory memos.copy2
./
0606
0608

sent 7665 bytes  received 70 bytes  15470.00 bytes/sec
total size is 7501  speedup is 0.97
$
$ ls -l memos.copy2
total 12
-rw-r--r-- 1 max max 1500 Jun  6 14:24 0606
-rw-r--r-- 1 max max 6001 Jun  8 16:16 0608
```

--archive   The **--archive** option causes rsync to copy directories recursively, dereferencing symbolic links (copying the files the links point to, not the symbolic links themselves), preserving modification times, ownership, group association of the copied files, and more. This option does not preserve hard links; use the **--hard-links** option for that purpose. See page 584 for more information on **--archive**. The following commands perform the same functions as the previous one:

```
$ rsync --archive --verbose memos/ memos.copy2
$ rsync -av memos/ memos.copy2
```

REMOVING FILES

--delete   The **--delete** option causes rsync to delete from *destination-file* files that are not in
--dry-run   *source-file*. Together, the **--dry-run** and **--verbose** options report on what an rsync command would do without the **--dry-run** option, without rsync taking any action. With the **--delete** option, the **--dry-run** and **--verbose** options can help you avoid removing files you did not intend to remove. This combination of options marks files rsync would remove with the word **deleting**. The next example uses these options in addition to the **--archive** option.

```
$ ls -l memos memos.copy3
memos:
total 20
-rw-r--r-- 1 max max 1500 Jun  6 14:24 0606
-rw-r--r-- 1 max max 6001 Jun  8 16:16 0608
-rw-r--r-- 1 max max 5911 Jun 10 12:02 0610

memos.copy3:
total 16
-rw-r--r-- 1 max max 1500 Jun  6 14:24 0606
-rw-r--r-- 1 max max 6001 Jun  8 16:16 0608
-rw-r--r-- 1 max max 1200 Jul 21 10:17 notes
```

```
$ rsync --archive --verbose --delete --dry-run memos/ memos.copy3
building file list ... done
deleting notes
./
0610

sent 125 bytes  received 32 bytes  314.00 bytes/sec
total size is 13412  speedup is 85.43
```

The rsync utility reports **deleting notes**, indicating which file it would remove if you ran it without the **––dry-run** option. It also reports it would copy the **0610** file.

Test to make sure ––delete is going to do what you think it will do

caution The **––delete** option can easily delete an entire directory tree if you omit a needed slash (/) or include an unneeded slash in *source-file*. Use **––delete** with the **––dry-run** and **––verbose** options to test an rsync command.

If you get tired of using the long versions of options, you can use the single-letter versions. The next rsync command is the same as the previous one (there is no short version of the ––delete option):

```
$ rsync -avn --delete memos/ memos.copy3
```

The next example runs the same rsync command, omitting the **––dry-run** option. The ls command shows the results of the rsync command: The **––delete** option causes rsync to remove the **notes** file from the *destination-file* (memos.copy3) because it is not in the *source-file* (memos). In addition, rsync copies the **0610** file.

```
$ rsync --archive --verbose --delete memos/ memos.copy3
building file list ... done
deleting notes
./
0610

sent 6076 bytes  received 48 bytes  12248.00 bytes/sec
total size is 13412  speedup is 2.19

$ ls -l memos memos.copy3
memos:
total 20
-rw-r--r-- 1 max max 1500 Jun  6 14:24 0606
-rw-r--r-- 1 max max 6001 Jun  8 16:16 0608
-rw-r--r-- 1 max max 5911 Jun 10 12:02 0610

memos.copy3:
total 20
-rw-r--r-- 1 max max 1500 Jun  6 14:24 0606
-rw-r--r-- 1 max max 6001 Jun  8 16:16 0608
-rw-r--r-- 1 max max 5911 Jun 10 12:02 0610
```

To this point, the examples have copied files locally, in the working directory. To copy files to other directories, replace the simple filenames with relative or absolute pathnames. On the local system, relative pathnames are relative to the working directory; on a remote system, relative pathnames are relative to the user's home directory. For example, the following command copies **memos** from the working directory to the **/backup** directory on the local system:

```
$ rsync --archive --verbose --delete memos/ /backup
```

COPYING FILES TO AND FROM A REMOTE SYSTEM

To copy files to or from a remote system, that system must be running an OpenSSH server or another transport mechanism rsync can connect to. For more information refer to "Notes" on page 586. To specify a file on a remote system, preface the filename with the name of the remote system and a colon. Relative pathnames on the remote system are relative to the user's home directory. Absolute pathnames are absolute (i.e., they are relative to the root directory). See page 83 for more information on relative and absolute pathnames.

In the next example, Max copies the **memos** directory from the working directory on the local system to the **holdfiles** directory in his working directory on the remote system named **coffee**. The ssh utility runs an ls command on **coffee** to show the result of the rsync command. The rsync and ssh utilities do not request a password because Max has set up OpenSSH-based utilities to log in automatically on **coffee** (page 830).

```
$ rsync --archive memos/ coffee:holdfiles
$ ssh coffee 'ls -l holdfiles'
total 20
-rw-r--r-- 1 max max 1500 Jun  6 14:24 0606
-rw-r--r-- 1 max max 6001 Jun  8 16:16 0608
-rw-r--r-- 1 max max 5911 Jun 10 12:02 0610
```

When copying from a remote system to the local system, place the name of the remote system before *source-file*:

```
$ rsync --archive coffee:holdfiles/ ~/memo.copy4
$ rsync --archive coffee:holdfiles/ /home/max/memo.copy5
```

Both of these commands copy the **holdfiles** directory from Max's working directory on **coffee** to his home directory on the local system. Under Mac OS X, replace **/home** with **/Users**.

MIRRORING A DIRECTORY

You can use rsync to maintain a copy of a directory. Because it is an exact copy, this type of copy is called a *mirror*. The mirror directory must be on an OpenSSH server (you must be able to connect to it using an OpenSSH utility such as ssh). If you want to run this script using crontab (page 649), you must set up OpenSSH so you can log in on the remote system automatically (without providing a password; page 830).

--compress
--update

The next example introduces the rsync **--compress** and **--update** options. The **--compress** option causes rsync to compress files as it copies them, usually making the transfer go more quickly. In some cases, such as a setup with a fast network connection and a slower CPU, compressing files can slow down the transfer. The **--update** option keeps rsync from overwriting a newer file with an older one.

As with all shell scripts, you must have read and execute access to the **mirror** script. To make it easier to read, each option in this script appears on a line by itself. Each line of each command except the last is terminated with a SPACE and a backslash (\). The SPACE separates one option from the next; the backslash quotes the following NEWLINE so the shell passes all arguments to rsync and does not interpret the NEWLINES as the end of the command.

```
$ cat mirror
rsync \
--archive \
--verbose \
--compress \
--update \
--delete \
~/mirrordir/ coffee:mirrordir

$ ./mirror > mirror.out
```

The **mirror** command in the example redirects output to **mirror.out** for review. Remove the **--verbose** option if you do not want the command to produce any output except for errors. The rsync command in **mirror** copies the **mirrordir** directory hierarchy from the user's home directory on the local system to the user's home directory on the remote (server) system. In this example the remote system is named **coffee**. Because of the **--update** option, rsync will not overwrite newer versions of files on the server with older versions of the same files from the local system. Although this option is not required if files on the server system are never changed manually, it can save you from grief if you accidentally update files on or add files to the server system. The **--delete** option causes rsync to remove files on the server system that are not present on the local system.

MAKING BACKUPS

After performing an initial full backup, rsync is able to perform subsequent incremental backups efficiently with regard to running time and storage space. By definition, an incremental backup stores only those files that have changed since the last backup; these are the only files that rsync needs to copy. As the following example shows, rsync, without using extra disk space, can make each incremental backup appear to be a full backup by creating hard links between the incremental backup and the unchanged files in the initial full backup.

--link-dest=*dir* The rsync **--link-dest=*dir*** option makes backups easy and efficient. It presents the user and/or system administrator with snapshots that appear to be full backups while taking minimal extra space in addition to the initial backup. The *dir* directory is always located on the machine holding the *destination-file*. If *dir* is a relative pathname, the pathname is relative to the *destination-file*. See page 585 for a description of this option.

Following is a simple rsync command that uses the **--link-dest=*dir*** option:

```
$ rsync --archive --link-dest=../backup source/ destination
```

When you run this command, rsync descends the **source** directory, examining each file it finds. For each file in the **source** directory, rsync looks in the **destination** directory to find an exact copy of the file.

- If it finds an exact copy of the file in the **destination** directory, rsync continues with the next file.

- If it does not find an exact copy of the file in the **destination** directory, rsync looks in the **backup** directory to find an exact copy of the file.

  - If it finds an exact copy of the file in the **backup** directory, rsync makes a hard link from the file in the **backup** directory to the **destination** directory.

  - If it does not find an exact copy of the file in the **backup** directory, rsync copies the file from the **source** directory to the **destination** directory.

Next is a simple example showing how to use rsync to make full and incremental backups using the **--link-dest=*dir*** option. Although the backup files reside on the local system, they could easily be located on a remote system.

As specified by the two arguments to rsync in the **bkup** script, rsync copies the **memos** directory to the **bu.0** directory. The **--link-dest=*dir*** option causes rsync to check whether each file it needs to copy exists in **bu.1**. If it does, rsync creates a link to the **bu.1** file instead of copying it.

The **bkup** script rotates three backup directories named **bu.0**, **bu.1**, and **bu.2** and calls rsync. The script removes **bu.2**, moves **bu.1** to **bu.2**, and moves **bu.0** to **bu.1**. The first time you run the script, rsync copies all the files from **memos** because they do not exist in **bu.0** or **bu.1**.

```
$ cat bkup
rm -rf bu.2
mv bu.1 bu.2
mv bu.0 bu.1
rsync --archive --link-dest=../bu.1 memos/  bu.0
```

Before you run **bkup** for the first time, **bu.0**, **bu.1**, and **bu.2** do not exist. Because of the **–f** option, rm does not display an error message when it tries to remove the nonexistent **bu.2** directory. Until **bkup** creates **bu.0** and **bu.1**, mv displays error messages saying there is **No such file or directory**.

In the following example, ls shows the **bkup** script and the contents of the **memos** directory. After running **bkup**, ls shows the contents of **memos** and of the new **bu.0** directory; **bu.0** holds exact copies of the files in **memos**. The rsync utility created no links because there were no files in **bu.1**: The directory did not exist.

```
$ ls -l *
-rwxr-xr-x 1 max max   87 Jul 22 11:23 bkup

memos:
total 20
-rw-r--r-- 1 max max 1500 Jun  6 14:24 0606
-rw-r--r-- 1 max max 6001 Jun  8 16:16 0608
-rw-r--r-- 1 max max 5911 Jun 10 12:02 0610

$ ./bkup
mv: cannot stat 'bu.1': No such file or directory
mv: cannot stat 'bu.0': No such file or directory

$ ls -l *
-rwxr-xr-x 1 max max   87 Jul 22 11:23 bkup

bu.0:
total 20
-rw-r--r-- 1 max max 1500 Jun  6 14:24 0606
-rw-r--r-- 1 max max 6001 Jun  8 16:16 0608
-rw-r--r-- 1 max max 5911 Jun 10 12:02 0610

memos:
total 20
-rw-r--r-- 1 max max 1500 Jun  6 14:24 0606
-rw-r--r-- 1 max max 6001 Jun  8 16:16 0608
-rw-r--r-- 1 max max 5911 Jun 10 12:02 0610
```

After working with the files in **memos**, ls shows **0610** has been removed and **newfile** has been added:

```
$ ls -l memos
total 20
-rw-r--r-- 1 max max 2100 Jul 22 14:31 0606
-rw-r--r-- 1 max max 6001 Jun  8 16:16 0608
-rw-r--r-- 1 max max 5251 Jul 22 14:32 newfile
```

After running **bkup** again, **bu.0** holds the same files as **memos** and **bu.1** holds the files that **bu.0** held before running **bkup**. The 0608 file has not changed, so rsync, with the **--link-dest=***dir* option, has not copied it but rather has made a link from the copy in **bu.1** to the copy in **bu.0**, as indicated by the **2** ls displays between the permissions and **max**.

```
$ ./bkup
mv: cannot stat 'bu.1': No such file or directory

$ ls -l bu.0 bu.1
bu.0:
total 20
-rw-r--r-- 1 max max 2100 Jul 22 14:31 0606
-rw-r--r-- 2 max max 6001 Jun  8 16:16 0608
-rw-r--r-- 1 max max 5251 Jul 22 14:32 newfile

bu.1:
total 20
-rw-r--r-- 1 max max 1500 Jun  6 14:24 0606
-rw-r--r-- 2 max max 6001 Jun  8 16:16 0608
-rw-r--r-- 1 max max 5911 Jun 10 12:02 0610
```

The beauty of this setup is that each incremental backup occupies only the space needed to hold files that have changed. Files that have not changed are stored as links, which take up minimal disk space. Yet users and the system administrator have access to a directory that appears to hold a full backup.

You can run a backup script such as **bkup** once an hour, once a day, or as often as you like. Storage space permitting, you can have as many backup directories as you like. If rsync does not require a password, you can automate this process by using crontab (page 649).

Chapter Summary

The rsync utility copies an ordinary file or directory hierarchy locally or between the local system and a remote system on a network. By default, this utility uses openSSH to transfer files and the same authentication mechanism as openSSH; therefore it provides the same security as openSSH. The rsync utility prompts for a password when it needs one.

Exercises

1. List three features of rsync.

2. Write an rsync command that copies the **backmeup** directory from your home directory on the local system to the **/tmp** directory on **coffee**, preserving file ownership, permissions, and modification times. Write a command that will copy the same directory to your home directory on **coffee**. Do not assume your working directory on the local system is your home directory.

3. You are writing an rsync command that includes the --delete option. Which options would you use to test the command without copying or removing any files?

4. What does the --archive option do? Why is it useful?

5. When running a script such as **bkup** (page 592) to back up files on a remote system, how could you rotate (rename) files on a remote system?

6. What effect does a trailing slash (/) on the *source-file* have?

PART V
COMMAND REFERENCE

COMMAND REFERENCE

The following tables list the utilities covered in this part of the book grouped by function and alphabetically within function. Although most of these are true utilities (programs that are separate from the shells), some are built into the shells (shell builtins). The sample utility on page 605 shows the format of the description of each utility in this part of the book.

Utilities That Display and Manipulate Files

aspell	Checks a file for spelling errors—page 607
bzip2	Compresses or decompresses files—page 615
cat	Joins and displays files—page 618
cmp	Compares two files—page 634
comm	Compares sorted files—page 636
cp	Copies files—page 640
cpio	Creates an archive, restores files from an archive, or copies a directory hierarchy—page 644
cut	Selects characters or fields from input lines—page 652
dd	Converts and copies a file—page 658
diff	Displays the differences between two text files—page 663
ditto	Copies files and creates and unpacks archives—page 671 **OS X**
emacs	Editor—page 205
find	Finds files based on criteria—page 688
fmt	Formats text very simply—page 697
grep	Searches for a pattern in files—page 719
gzip	Compresses or decompresses files—page 724
head	Displays the beginning of a file—page 727
less	Displays text files, one screen at a time—page 735
ln	Makes a link to a file—page 740
lpr	Sends files to printers—page 742
ls	Displays information about one or more files—page 745
man	Displays documentation for commands—page 759

mkdir	Creates a directory—page 763
mv	Renames or moves a file—page 771
od	Dumps the contents of a file—page 776
open	Opens files, directories, and URLs—page 780 *OS X*
otool	Displays object, library, and executable files—page 782 *OS X*
paste	Joins corresponding lines from files—page 784
pax	Creates an archive, restores files from an archive, or copies a directory hierarchy—page 786
plutil	Manipulates property list files—page 792 *OS X*
pr	Paginates files for printing—page 794
rm	Removes a file (deletes a link)—page 804
rmdir	Removes directories—page 806
sed	Edits a file noninteractively—page 565
sort	Sorts and/or merges files—page 817
split	Divides a file into sections—page 826
strings	Displays strings of printable characters—page 837
tail	Displays the last part (tail) of a file—page 843
tar	Stores or retrieves files to/from an archive file—page 846
touch	Creates a file or changes a file's access and/or modification time—page 862
uniq	Displays unique lines—page 872
vim	Editor—page 149
wc	Displays the number of lines, words, and bytes—page 876

Network Utilities

ftp	Transfers files over a network—page 704
rcp	Copies one or more files to or from a remote system—page 800
rlogin	Logs in on a remote system—page 803
rsh	Executes commands on a remote system—page 807
rsync	Copies files and directory hierarchies securely over a network—page 583
scp	Securely copies one or more files to or from a remote system—page 810
ssh	Securely executes commands on a remote system—page 828
telnet	Connects to a remote system over a network—page 852

Utilities That Display and Alter Status

cd	Changes to another working directory—page 620
chgrp	Changes the group associated with a file—page 622
chmod	Changes the access mode (permissions) of a file—page 626
chown	Changes the owner of a file and/or the group the file is associated with—page 631
date	Displays or sets the system time and date—page 655
df	Displays disk space usage—page 661
dscl	Displays and manages Directory Service information—page 674 *OS X*
dmesg	Displays kernel messages—page 673
du	Displays information on disk usage by directory hierarchy and/or file—page 677
file	Displays the classification of a file—page 686
finger	Displays information about users—page 695
GetFileInfo	Displays file attributes—page 717 *OS X*
kill	Terminates a process by PID—page 729
killall	Terminates a process by name—page 731
nice	Changes the priority of a command—page 773
nohup	Runs a command that keeps running after you log out—page 775
ps	Displays process status—page 796
renice	Changes the priority of a process—page 802
SetFile	Sets file attributes—page 813 *OS X*
sleep	Creates a process that sleeps for a specified interval—page 815
stat	Displays information about files—page 835
stty	Displays or sets terminal parameters—page 838
sysctl	Displays and alters kernel variables—page 842 *OS X*
top	Dynamically displays process status—page 858
umask	Establishes the file-creation permissions mask—page 870
w	Displays information about system users—page 874
which	Shows where in PATH a command is located—page 877
who	Displays information about logged-in users—page 879

Utilities That Are Programming Tools

awk	Searches for and processes patterns in a file—page 531
configure	Configures source code automatically—page 638
gawk	Searches for and processes patterns in a file—page 531
gcc	Compiles C and C++ programs—page 712
make	Keeps a set of programs current—page 753
mawk	Searches for and processes patterns in a file—page 531

Miscellaneous Utilities

at	Executes commands at a specified time—page 611
cal	Displays a calendar—page 617
crontab	Maintains crontab files—page 649
diskutil	Checks, modifies, and repairs local volumes—page 668 *OS X*
echo	Displays a message—page 680
expr	Evaluates an expression—page 682
fsck	Checks and repairs a filesystem—page 699
launchctl	Controls the **launchd** daemon—page 733 *OS X*
mkfs	Creates a filesystem on a device—page 764
Mtools	Uses DOS-style commands on files and directories—page 767
tee	Copies standard input to standard output and one or more files—page 851
test	Evaluates an expression—page 854
tr	Replaces specified characters—page 864
tty	Displays the terminal pathname—page 867
tune2fs	Changes parameters on an **ext2**, **ext3**, or **ext4** filesystem—page 868
xargs	Converts standard input to command lines—page 881

Standard Multiplicative Suffixes

Several utilities allow you to use the suffixes listed in Table V-1 following byte counts. You can precede a multiplicative suffix with a number that is a multiplier. For example, 5K means 5×2^{10}. The absence of a multiplier indicates that the multiplicative suffix is to be multiplied by 1. The utilities that allow these suffixes are marked as such.

Table V-1 Multiplicative suffixes

Suffix	Multiplicative value	Suffix	Multiplicative value
KB	1,000 (10^3)	PB	10^{15}
K	1,024 (2^{10})	P	2^{50}
MB	1,000,000 (10^6)	EB	10^{18}
M	1,048,576 (2^{20})	E	2^{60}
GB	1,000,000,000 (10^9)	ZB	10^{21}
G	1,073,741,824 (2^{30})	Z	2^{70}
TB	10^{12}	YB	10^{24}
T	2^{40}	Y	2^{80}

BLOCKSIZE Under Mac OS X, some utilities use the **BLOCKSIZE** environment variable to set a default block size. You can set **BLOCKSIZE** to a value that is a number of bytes or to a value that uses one of the K, M, or G suffixes. The text identifies utilities that use **BLOCKSIZE**.

Common Options

Several GNU utilities share the options listed in Table V-2. The utilities that use these options are marked as such.

Table V-2 Common command-line options

Option	Effect
–	A single hyphen appearing in place of a filename instructs the utility to accept standard input in place of the file.
––	A double hyphen marks the end of the options on a command line. You can follow this option with an argument that begins with a hyphen. Without this option the utility assumes that an argument that begins with a hyphen is an option.
––help	Displays a help message for the utility. Some of these messages are quite long; using a pipe, you can send the output through less to display it one screen at a time. For example, you could give the command **ls ––help | less**. Alternatively, you can send the output through a pipe to grep if you are looking for specific information. For example, you could give the following command to get information on the **–d** option to ls: **ls ––help | grep –– –d**. See the preceding entry in this table for information on the double hyphen.
––version	Displays version information for the utility.

The sample Utility

The following description of the sample utility shows the format that this part of the book uses to describe the utilities. These descriptions are similar to the man page descriptions (pages 33 and 759); however, most users find the descriptions in this book easier to read and understand. They emphasize the most useful features of the utilities and often leave out the more obscure features. For information about the less commonly used features, refer to the man and info pages or call the utility with the ––help option, which works with many utilities.

sample **OS X** ←*OS X in an oval indicates this utility runs under Mac OS X only.*

Brief description of what the utility does

sample [options] arguments

Following the syntax line is a description of the utility. The syntax line shows how to run the utility from the command line. Options and arguments enclosed in brackets (*[]*) are not required. Enter words that appear in *this italic typeface* as is. Words that you must substitute when you type appear in ***this bold italic typeface***. Words listed as arguments to a command identify single arguments (for example, ***source-file***) or groups of similar arguments (for example, ***directory-list***).

Arguments   This section describes the arguments you can use when you run the utility. The argument itself, as shown in the preceding syntax line, is printed in ***this bold italic typeface***.

Options   This section lists some of the options you can use with the command. Unless otherwise specified, you must precede options with one or two hyphens. Most commands accept a single hyphen before multiple options (page 119). Options in this section are ordered alphabetically by short (single-hyphen) options. If an option has only a long version (two hyphens), it is ordered by its long option. Following are some sample options:

--delimiter=*dchar*
  -d *dchar*

> This option includes an argument. The argument is set in a ***bold italic typeface*** in both the heading and the description. You substitute another word (filename, string of characters, or other value) for any arguments you see in ***this typeface***. Type characters that are in **bold type** (such as the **--delimiter** and **-d**) as is.

--make-dirs   -m   This option has a long and a short version. You can use either option; they are equivalent. This option description ends with **Linux** in a box, indicating it is available under Linux only. Options *not* followed by **Linux** or **OS X** are available under both operating systems. **LINUX**

  -t   (**table of contents**) This simple option is preceded by a single hyphen and not followed by arguments. It has no long version. The **table of contents** appearing in parentheses at the beginning of the description is a cue, suggestive of what the option letter stands for. This option description ends with **OS X** in a box, indicating it is available under OS X only. Options *not* followed by **Linux** or **OS X** are available under both operating systems. **OS X**

Discussion   This optional section describes how to use the utility and identifies any quirks it may have.

Notes   This section contains miscellaneous notes—some important and others merely interesting.

Examples   This section contains examples illustrating how to use the utility. This section is a tutorial, so it takes a more casual tone than the preceding sections of the description.

aspell

Checks a file for spelling errors

*aspell **check** [options] filename*
*aspell **list** [options] < filename*
*aspell **config***
*aspell **help***

The aspell utility checks the spelling of words in a document against a standard dictionary. You can use aspell interactively: It displays each misspelled word in context, together with a menu that gives you the choice of accepting the word as is, choosing one of aspell's suggested replacements for the word, inserting the word into your personal dictionary, or replacing the word with one you enter. You can also use aspell in batch mode so it reads from standard input and writes to standard output. The aspell utility is available under Linux only. `LINUX`

aspell **is not like other utilities regarding its input**

tip   Unlike many other utilities, aspell does not accept input from standard input when you do not specify a filename on the command line. Instead, the ***action*** specifies where aspell gets its input.

Actions

You must choose one and only one ***action*** when you run aspell.

check   –c   Runs aspell as an interactive spelling checker. Input comes from a single file named on the command line. Refer to "Discussion" on page 608.

config   Displays aspell's configuration, both default and current values. Send the output through a pipe to less for easier viewing, or use grep to find the option you are looking for (for example, **aspell config | grep backup**).

help   –?   Displays an extensive page of help. Send the output through a pipe to less for easier viewing.

list   –l   Runs aspell in batch mode (noninteractively) with input coming from standard input and output going to standard output.

Arguments

The *filename* is the name of the file you want to check. The aspell utility accepts this argument only when you use the **check** (**–c**) ***action**.* With the **list** (**–l**) ***action**,* input must come from standard input.

Options

The aspell utility has many options. A few of the more commonly used ones are listed in this section; see the aspell man page for a complete list. Default values of many options are determined when aspell is compiled (see the **config** ***action***).

You can specify options on the command line, as the value of the **ASPELL_CONF** shell variable, or in your personal configuration file (**~/.aspell.conf**). A user working with **root** privileges can create a global configuration file (**/etc/aspell.conf**). Put one option per line in a configuration file; separate options with a semicolon (;) in **ASPELL_CONF**. Options on the command line override those in **ASPELL_CONF**, which override those in your personal configuration file, which override those in the global configuration file.

The following list contains two types of options: Boolean and value. The Boolean options turn a feature on (enable the feature) or off (disable the feature). Precede a Boolean option with **dont–** to turn it off. For example, **––ignore-case** turns the **ignore-case** feature on and **––dont-ignore-case** turns it off.

Value options assign a value to a feature. Follow the option with an equal sign and a value—for example, **––ignore=4**.

For all options in a configuration file or in the **ASPELL_CONF** variable, drop the leading hyphens (**ignore-case** or **dont-ignore-case**).

aspell **options and leading hyphens**

caution   The way you specify options differs depending on whether you are specifying them on the command line, using the **ASPELL_CONF** shell variable, or in a configuration file.

On the command line, prefix long options with two hyphens (for example, **––ignore-case** or **––dont-ignore-case**). In **ASPELL_CONF** and configuration files, drop the leading hyphens (for example, **ignore-case** or **dont-ignore-case**).

––dont-backup	Does not create a backup file named *filename*.**bak** (default is **––backup** when *action* is **check**).
––ignore=*n*	Ignores words with *n* or fewer characters (default is 1).
––ignore-case	Ignores the case of letters in words being checked (default is **––dont-ignore-case**).
––lang=*cc*	Specifies the two-letter language code (*cc*). The language code defaults to the value of **LC_MESSAGES** (page 304).
––mode=*mod*	Specifies a filter to use. Select *mod* from **url** (default), **none, sgml,** and others. The modes work as follows: **url**: skips URLs, hostnames, and email addresses; **none**: turns off all filters; **sgml**: skips SGML, HTML, XHTML, and XML commands.
––strip-accents	Removes accent marks from all the words in the dictionary before checking words (default is **––dont-strip-accents**).

Discussion   The aspell utility has two basic modes of operation: batch and interactive. You specify batch mode by using the **list** or **–l** *action*. In batch mode, aspell accepts the document you want to check for spelling errors as standard input and sends the list of potentially misspelled words to standard output.

You specify interactive mode by using the **check** or **–c** *action*. In interactive mode, aspell displays a screen with the potentially misspelled word highlighted in context and a menu of choices. See "Examples" for an illustration. The menu includes various commands (Table V-3) as well as some suggestions of similar, correctly spelled words. You either enter one of the numbers from the menu to select a suggested word to replace the word in question or enter a letter to give a command.

Table V-3   aspell commands

Command	Action
SPACE	Takes no action and goes on to next the misspelled word.
n	Replaces the misspelled word with suggested word number *n*.
a	Adds the "misspelled" word to your personal dictionary.
b	Aborts aspell; does not save changes.
i *or* **I** (letter "i")	Ignores the misspelled word. **I** (uppercase "I") ignores all occurrences of this word; **i** ignores this occurrence only and is the same as SPACE.
l (lowercase "l")	Changes the "misspelled" word to lowercase and adds it to your personal dictionary.
r *or* **R**	Replaces the misspelled word with the word you enter at the bottom of the screen. **R** replaces all occurrences of this word; **r** replaces this occurrence only.
x	Saves the file as corrected so far and exits from aspell.

Notes

For more information refer to the aspell home page located at aspell.net and to the **/usr/share/doc/aspell** directory.

The aspell utility is not a foolproof way of finding spelling errors. It also does not check for misused, properly spelled words (such as *red* instead of *read*).

Spelling from emacs   You can make it easy to use aspell from emacs by adding the following line to your **~/.emacs** file (page 250). This line causes emacs' ispell functions to call aspell:

```
(setq-default ispell-program-name "aspell")
```

Spelling from vim   Similarly, you can make it easy to use aspell from vim by adding the following line to your **~/.vimrc** file (page 185):

```
map ^T :w!<CR>:!aspell check %<CR>:e! %<CR>
```

When you enter this line in **~/.vimrc** using vim, enter the **^T** as CONTROL-V CONTROL-T (page 169). With this line in **~/.vimrc**, CONTROL-T brings up aspell to spell check the file you are editing with vim.

Examples

The following examples use aspell to correct the spelling in the **memo.txt** file:

```
$ cat memo.txt
Here's a document for teh aspell utilitey
to check. It obviosly needs proofing
quiet badly.
```

The first example uses aspell with the **check** action and no options. The appearance of the screen for the first misspelled word, **teh,** is shown. At the bottom of the screen is the menu of commands and suggested words. Each of the numbered words differs slightly from the misspelled word:

```
$ aspell check memo.txt
```

```
Here's a document for teh aspell utilitey
to check. It obviosly needs proofing
quiet badly.
```

```
========================================================
1) the                          6) th
2) Te                           7) tea
3) tech                         8) tee
4) Th                           9) Ted
5) eh                           0) tel
i) Ignore                       I) Ignore all
r) Replace                      R) Replace all
a) Add                          1) Add Lower
b) Abort                        x) Exit
========================================================
?
```

Enter one of the menu choices in response to the preceding display; aspell will do your bidding and move the highlight to the next misspelled word (unless you choose to abort or exit). In this case, entering **1** (one) would change **teh** to **the** in the file.

The next example uses the **list** *action* to display a list of misspelled words. The word **quiet** is not in the list—it is not properly used but is properly spelled.

```
$ aspell list < memo.txt
teh
aspell
utilitey
obviosly
```

The last example also uses the **list** action. It shows a quick way to check the spelling of a word or two with a single command. The user gives the **aspell list** command and then enters **seperate temperature** into aspell's standard input (the keyboard). After the user presses RETURN and CONTROL-D (to mark the end of file), aspell writes the misspelled word to standard output (the screen):

```
$ aspell list
seperate temperatureRETURN
CONTROL-D
seperate
```

at

Executes commands at a specified time

*at [options] **time** [date | +increment]*
atq
*atrm **job-list***
batch [options] [time]

The at and batch utilities execute commands at a specified time. They accept commands from standard input or, with the **–f** option, from a file. Commands are executed in the same environment as the at or batch command. Unless redirected, standard output and standard error from commands are emailed to the user who ran the at or batch command. A *job* is the group of commands that is executed by one call to at. The batch utility differs from at in that it schedules jobs so they run when the CPU load on the system is low.

The atq utility displays a list of at jobs you have queued; atrm cancels pending at jobs.

Arguments   The *time* is the time of day when at runs the job. You can specify the *time* as a one-, two-, or four-digit number. One- and two-digit numbers specify an hour, and four-digit numbers specify an hour and minute. You can also give the time in the form **hh:mm**. The at utility assumes a 24-hour clock unless you place **am** or **pm** immediately after the number, in which case it uses a 12-hour clock. You can also specify *time* as **now, midnight, noon,** or **teatime** (4:00 PM).

The *date* is the day of the week or day of the month when you want at to execute the job. When you do not specify a day, at executes the job today if the hour you specify in *time* is greater than the current hour. If the hour is less than the current hour, at executes the job tomorrow.

You specify a day of the week by spelling it out or abbreviating it to three letters. You can also use the words **today** and **tomorrow**. Use the name of a month followed by the number of the day in the month to specify a date. You can follow the month and day number with a year.

The *increment* is a number followed by one of the following (both plural and singular are allowed): **minutes, hours, days,** or **weeks**. The at utility adds the *increment* to *time*. You cannot specify an increment for a date.

When using atrm, *job-list* is a list of one or more at job numbers. You can list job numbers by running at with the **–l** option or by using atq.

Options   The batch utility accepts options under OS X only. The **–c, –d,** and **–l** options are not for use when you initiate a job with at; use these options to determine the status of a job or to cancel a job only.

−c *job-list*

(**cat**) Displays the environment and commands specified by the job numbers in *job-list*.

−d *job-list*

(**delete**) Cancels jobs that you submitted with at. The *job-list* is a list of one or more at job numbers to cancel. If you do not remember the job number, use the **−l** option or run atq to list your jobs and their numbers. Using this option with at has the same effect as running atrm. This option is deprecated under OS X; use the **−r** option instead.

−f *file*

(**file**) Specifies that commands come from *file* instead of standard input. This option is useful for long lists of commands or commands that are executed repeatedly.

−l (**list**) Displays a list of your at jobs. Using this option with at has the same effect as running atq.

−m (**mail**) Sends you email after a job is run, even when nothing is sent to standard output or standard error. When a job generates output, at always emails it to you, regardless of this option.

−r *job-list*

(**remove**) Same as the **−d** option. *OS X*

Notes

The at utility uses **/bin/sh** to execute commands. Under Linux, this file is typically a link to bash or dash.

The shell saves the environment variables and the working directory at the time you submit an at job so they are available when at executes commands.

at.allow and **at.deny**   A user running with **root** privileges can always use at. The Linux **/etc/at.allow** (OS X uses **/var/at/at.allow**) and Linux **/etc/at.deny** (OS X uses **/var/at/at.deny**) files, which should be readable and writable by **root** only (mode 600), control which ordinary, local users can use at. When **at.deny** exists and is empty, all users can use at. When **at.deny** does not exist, only those users listed in **at.allow** can use at. Users listed in **at.deny** cannot use at unless they are also listed in **at.allow**.

Under Linux, jobs you submit using at are run by the **atd** daemon. This daemon stores jobs in **/var/spool/at** or **/var/spool/cron/atjobs** and stores their output in **/var/spool/at/spool** or **/var/spool/cron/atspool**. These files should be set to mode 700 and owned by the user named **daemon**.

Under Mac OS X, jobs you submit using at are run by atrun, which is called every 30 seconds by **launchd**. The atrun utility stores jobs in **/var/at/jobs** and stores their output in **/var/at/spool**, both of which should be set to mode 700 and owned by the user named **daemon**.

Under OS X 10.4 and later, the **atrun** daemon is disabled by default. Working as a privileged user, you can enable and disable **atrun** with the following commands:

```
# launchctl load -w /System/Library/LaunchDaemons/com.apple.atrun.plist
# launchctl unload -w /System/Library/LaunchDaemons/com.apple.atrun.plist
```

See launchctl (page 733) for more information.

Examples   You can use any of the following techniques to paginate and print **long_file** tomorrow at 2:00 AM. The first example executes the command directly from the command line; the last two examples use the **pr_tonight** file, which contains the necessary command, and execute that command using at. Prompts and output from different versions of at differ.

```
$ at 2am
at> pr long_file | lpr
at>CONTROL-D<EOT>
job 8 at 2009-08-17 02:00

$ cat pr_tonight
#!/bin/bash
pr long_file | lpr

$ at -f pr_tonight 2am
job 9 at 2009-08-17 02:00

$ at 2am < pr_tonight
job 10 at 2009-08-17 02:00
```

If you execute commands directly from the command line, you must signal the end of the commands by pressing CONTROL-D at the beginning of a line. After you press CONTROL-D, at displays a line that begins with **job** followed by the job number and the time at will execute the job.

If you run atq after the preceding commands, it displays a list of jobs in its queue:

```
$ atq
8        2009-08-17 02:00 a
9        2009-08-17 02:00 a
10       2009-08-17 02:00 a
```

The following command removes job number 9 from the queue:

```
$ atrm 9
$ atq
8        2009-08-17 02:00 a
10       2009-08-17 02:00 a
```

The next example executes **cmdfile** at 3:30 PM (1530 hours) one week from today:

```
$ at -f cmdfile 1530 +1 week
job 12 at 2009-08-23 15:30
```

The next at command executes a job at 7 PM on Thursday. This job uses find to create an intermediate file, redirects the output sent to standard error, and prints the file.

```
$ at 7pm Thursday
at> find / -name "core" -print >report.out 2>report.err
at> lpr report.out
at>CONTROL-D<EOT>
job 13 at 2009-08-18 19:00
```

The final example shows some of the output generated by the –c option when at is queried about the preceding job. Most of the lines show the environment; only the last few lines execute the commands:

```
$ at -c 13
#!/bin/sh
# atrun uid=500 gid=500
# mail     sam 0
umask 2
PATH=/usr/kerberos/bin:/usr/local/bin:/bin:/usr/bin:/usr/X11R6/bin:.;
export PATH
PWD=/home/sam/book.examples/99/cp; export PWD
EXINIT=set\ ai\ aw; export EXINIT
LANG=C; export LANG
PS1=\\\$\ ; export PS1
...
cd /home/sam/book\.examples/99/cp || {
        echo 'Execution directory inaccessible' >&2
        exit 1
}
find / -name "core" -print >report.out 2>report.err
lpr report.out
```

bzip2

Compresses or decompresses files

bzip2 [options] [file-list]
bunzip2 [options] [file-list]
bzcat [options] [file-list]
bzip2recover [file]

The bzip2 utility compresses files; bunzip2 restores files compressed with bzip2; and bzcat displays files compressed with bzip2.

Arguments The *file-list* is a list of one or more files (no directories) that are to be compressed or decompressed. If *file-list* is empty or if the special option – is present, bzip2 reads from standard input. The **––stdout** option causes bzip2 to write to standard output.

Options Under Linux, bzip2, bunzip2, and bzcat accept the common options described on page 603.

The Mac OS X version of bzip2 accepts long options

tip Options for bzip2 preceded by a double hyphen (––) work under Mac OS X as well as under Linux.

––stdout –c Writes the results of compression or decompression to standard output.

––decompress –d Decompresses a file compressed with bzip2. This option with bzip2 is equivalent to the bunzip2 command.

––fast *or* –*n* Sets the block size when compressing a file. The *n* is a digit from 1 to 9, where
––best 1 (**––fast**) generates a block size of 100 kilobytes and 9 (**––best**) generates a block size of 900 kilobytes. The default level is 9. The options **––fast** and **––best** are provided for compatibility with gzip and do not necessarily yield the fastest or best compression.

––force –f Forces compression even if a file already exists, has multiple links, or comes directly from a terminal. The option has a similar effect with bunzip2.

––keep –k Does not delete input files while compressing or decompressing them.

––quiet –q Suppresses warning messages; does display critical messages.

––test –t Verifies the integrity of a compressed file. Displays nothing if the file is OK.

––verbose –v For each file being compressed, displays the name of the file, the compression ratio, the percentage of space saved, and the sizes of the decompressed and compressed files.

Discussion   The bzip2 and bunzip2 utilities work similarly to gzip and gunzip; see the discussion of gzip (page 725) for more information. Normally bzip2 does not overwrite a file; you must use **--force** to overwrite a file during compression or decompression.

Notes   See page 62 for additional information on and examples of tar.

The bzip2 home page is bzip.org.

The bzip2 utility does a better job of compressing files than does gzip.

Use the **--bzip2** modifier with tar (page 847) to compress archive files with bzip2.

bzcat *file-list*   Works like cat except it uses bunzip2 to decompress *file-list* as it copies files to standard output.

bzip2recover   Attempts to recover a damaged file that was compressed with bzip2.

Examples   In the following example, bzip2 compresses a file and gives the resulting file the same name with a **.bz2** filename extension. The –v option displays statistics about the compression.

```
$ ls -l
total 728
-rw-r--r--  1 sam sam 737414 Feb 20 19:05 bigfile
$ bzip2 -v bigfile
  bigfile: 3.926:1, 2.037 bits/byte, 74.53% saved, 737414 in, 187806 out
$ ls -l
total 188
-rw-r--r--  1 sam sam 187806 Feb 20 19:05 bigfile.bz2
```

Next touch creates a file with the same name as the original file; bunzip2 refuses to overwrite the file in the process of decompressing **bigfile.bz2**. The **--force** option enables bunzip2 to overwrite the file.

```
$ touch bigfile
$ bunzip2 bigfile.bz2
bunzip2: Output file bigfile already exists.
$ bunzip2 --force bigfile.bz2
$ ls -l
total 728
-rw-r--r--  1 sam sam 737414 Feb 20 19:05 bigfile
```

cal

Displays a calendar

cal [options] [[month] year]

The cal utility displays a calendar.

Arguments The arguments specify the month and year for which cal displays a calendar. The *month* is a decimal integer from 1 to 12 and the *year* is a decimal integer. Without any arguments, cal displays a calendar for the current month. When you specify a single argument, it is taken to be the year.

Options –j (**Julian**) Displays Julian days—a calendar that numbers the days consecutively from January 1 (1) through December 31 (365 or 366).

–m (**Monday**) Makes Monday the first day of the week. Without this option, Sunday is the first day of the week. *LINUX*

–y (**year**) Displays a calendar for the current year. *LINUX*

–3 (**three months**) Displays the previous, current, and next months. *LINUX*

Notes Do not abbreviate the year. The year 05 is not the same as 2005.

The ncal (new cal) utility displays a more compact calendar.

Examples The following command displays a calendar for August 2007:

```
$ cal 8 2007<U>vim:
      August 2007
Su Mo Tu We Th Fr Sa
          1  2  3  4
 5  6  7  8  9 10 11
12 13 14 15 16 17 18
19 20 21 22 23 24 25
26 27 28 29 30 31
```

Next is a Julian calendar for 1949:

```
$ cal -j 1949
                    1949

         January              February
Su  Mo  Tu  We  Th  Fr  Sa  Su  Mo  Tu  We  Th  Fr  Sa
                         1              32  33  34  35  36
 2   3   4   5   6   7   8  37  38  39  40  41  42  43
 9  10  11  12  13  14  15  44  45  46  47  48  49  50
16  17  18  19  20  21  22  51  52  53  54  55  56  57
23  24  25  26  27  28  29  58  59
30  31
...
```

cat

Joins and displays files

cat [options] [file-list]

The cat utility copies files to standard output. You can use cat to display the contents of one or more text files on the screen.

Arguments   The *file-list* is a list of the pathnames of one or more files that cat processes. If you do not specify an argument or if you specify a hyphen (–) in place of a filename, cat reads from standard input.

Options   Under Linux, cat accepts the common options described on page 603. Options preceded by a double hyphen (––) work under Linux only. Except as noted, options named with a single letter and preceded by a single hyphen work under Linux and OS X.

––show-all   –A   Same as –vET. `LINUX`

––number-nonblank
              –b   Numbers all lines that are not blank as they are written to standard output.

              –e   (**end**) Same as –vE.

––show-ends   –E   Marks the ends of lines with dollar signs. `LINUX`

––number   –n   Numbers all lines as they are written to standard output.

––squeeze-blank –s   Removes extra blank lines so there are never two or more blank lines in a row.

              –t   (**tab**) Same as –vT.

––show-tabs   –T   Displays TABs as ^I. `LINUX`

––show-nonprinting
              –v   Displays CONTROL characters with the caret notation (^M) and displays characters that have the high bit set (META characters) with the M- notation (page 216). This option does not convert TABs and LINEFEEDs. Use –T (––show-tabs) if you want to display TABs as ^I. LINEFEEDs cannot be displayed as anything but themselves; otherwise, the line would be too long.

Notes   See page 125 for a discussion of cat, standard input, and standard output.

Use the od utility (page 776) to display the contents of a file that does not contain text (for example, an executable program file).

Use the tac utility to display lines of a text file in reverse order. See the tac info page for more information.

The name cat is derived from one of the functions of this utility, *catenate,* which means to join together sequentially, or end to end.

Set noclobber to avoid overwriting a file

caution Despite cat's warning message, the shell destroys the input file (**letter**) before invoking cat in the following example:

```
$ cat memo letter > letter
cat: letter: input file is output file
```

You can prevent overwriting a file in this situation by setting the **noclobber** variable (pages 129 and 377).

Examples

The following command displays the contents of the **memo** text file on the terminal:

```
$ cat memo
...
```

The next example catenates three text files and redirects the output to the **all** file:

```
$ cat page1 letter memo > all
```

You can use cat to create short text files without using an editor. Enter the following command line, type the text you want in the file, and press CONTROL-D on a line by itself:

```
$ cat > new_file
...
(text)
...
CONTROL-D
```

In this case cat takes input from standard input (the keyboard) and the shell redirects standard output (a copy of the input) to the file you specify. The CONTROL-D signals the EOF (end of file) and causes cat to return control to the shell.

In the next example, a pipe sends the output from who to standard input of cat. The shell redirects cat's output to the file named **output;** after the commands have finished executing, **output** contains the contents of the **header** file, the output of who, and **footer.** The hyphen on the command line causes cat to read standard input after reading **header** and before reading **footer.**

```
$ who | cat header - footer > output
```

cd

Changes to another working directory

cd [options] [directory]

The cd builtin makes *directory* the working directory.

Arguments   The *directory* is the pathname of the directory you want to be the new working directory. Without an argument, cd makes your home directory the working directory. Using a hyphen in place of *directory* changes to the previous working directory.

Options   The following options are available under bash and dash only.

−L   (**no dereference**) If *directory* is a symbolic link, cd makes the symbolic link the working directory (default).

−P   (**dereference**) If *directory* is a symbolic link, cd makes the directory the symbolic link points to the working directory.

Notes   The cd command is a bash, dash, and tcsh builtin.

See page 87 for a discussion of cd.

Without an argument, cd makes your home directory the working directory; it uses the value of the **HOME** (bash; page 297) or **home** (tcsh; page 372) variable to determine the pathname of your home directory.

With an argument of a hyphen, cd makes the previous working directory the working directory. It uses the value of the **OLDPWD** (bash) or **owd** (tcsh) variable to determine the pathname of the previous working directory.

The **CDPATH** (bash; page 302) or **cdpath** (tcsh; page 372) variable contains a colon-separated list of directories that cd searches. Within the list a null directory name (::) or a period (:.:) represents the working directory. If **CDPATH** or **cdpath** is not set, cd searches only the working directory for *directory*. If this variable is set and *directory* is not an absolute pathname (does not begin with a slash), cd searches the directories in the list; if the search fails, cd searches the working directory. See page 302 for a discussion of **CDPATH**.

Examples   A cd command without an argument makes a user's home directory the working directory. In the following example, cd makes Max's home directory the working directory and the pwd builtin verifies the change.

```
$ pwd
/home/max/literature
$ cd
$ pwd
/home/max
```

Under Mac OS X, home directories are stored in **/Users**, not **/home**.

The next command makes the **/home/max/literature** directory the working directory:

```
$ cd /home/max/literature
$ pwd
/home/max/literature
```

Next the cd utility makes a subdirectory of the working directory the new working directory:

```
$ cd memos
$ pwd
/home/max/literature/memos
```

Finally cd uses the .. reference to the parent of the working directory (page 88) to make the parent the new working directory:

```
$ cd ..
$ pwd
/home/max/literature
```

chgrp

Changes the group associated with a file

chgrp [options] group file-list
chgrp [options] --reference=rfile file-list   `LINUX`

The chgrp utility changes the group associated with one or more files. The second format works under Linux only.

Arguments

The *group* is the name or numeric group ID of the new group. The *file-list* is a list of the pathnames of the files whose group association is to be changed. The *rfile* is the pathname of a file whose group is to become the new group associated with *file-list*.

Options

Options preceded by a double hyphen (––) work under Linux only. Except as noted, options named with a single letter and preceded by a single hyphen work under Linux and OS X.

––changes   –c   Displays a message for each file whose group is changed. `LINUX`

––dereference   For each file that is a symbolic link, changes the group of the file the link points to, not the symbolic link itself. Under Linux, this option is the default. `LINUX`

––quiet *or*   –f   Suppresses warning messages about files whose permissions prevent you from
––silent   changing their group IDs.

––no-dereference   –h   For each file that is a symbolic link, changes the group of the symbolic link, not the file the link points to.

–H   (**partial dereference**) For each file that is a symbolic link, changes the group of the file the link points to, not the symbolic link itself. This option affects files specified on the command line; it does not affect files found while descending a directory hierarchy. This option treats files that are not symbolic links normally and works with –R only. See page 623 for an example of the use of the –H versus –L options.

–L   (**dereference**) For each file that is a symbolic link, changes the group of the file the link points to, not the symbolic link itself. This option affects all files, treats files that are not symbolic links normally, and works with –R only. See page 623 for an example of the use of the –H versus –L options.

–P   (**no dereference**) For each file that is a symbolic link, changes the group of the symbolic link, not the file the link points to (default). This option affects all files, treats files that are not symbolic links normally, and works with –R only. See page 625 for an example of the use of the –P option.

--recursive   **-R**   Recursively descends a directory specified in *file-list* and changes the group ID on all files in the directory hierarchy.

--reference=*rfile*   Changes the group of the files in *file-list* to that of *rfile*. `LINUX`

--verbose   **-v**   For each file, displays a message saying whether its group was retained or changed.

Notes

Only the owner of a file or a user working with **root** privileges can change the group association of a file.

Unless you are working with **root** privileges, you must belong to the specified *group* to change the group ID of a file to that *group*.

See page 631 for information on how to use chown to change the group associated with, as well as the owner of, a file.

Examples

The following command changes the group that the **manuals** file is associated with; the new group is **pubs**.

```
$ chgrp pubs manuals
```

-H versus **-L**   The following examples demonstrate the difference between the **-H** and **-L** options. Initially all files and directories in the working directory are associated with the **zach** group:

```
$ ls -lR
.:
total 12
-rw-r--r-- 1 zach zach  102 Jul  2 12:31 bb
drwxr-xr-x 2 zach zach 4096 Jul  2 15:34 dir1
drwxr-xr-x 2 zach zach 4096 Jul  2 15:33 dir4

./dir1:
total 4
-rw-r--r-- 1 zach zach  102 Jul  2 12:32 dd
lrwxrwxrwx 1 zach zach    7 Jul  2 15:33 dir4.link -> ../dir4

./dir4:
total 8
-rw-r--r-- 1 zach zach  125 Jul  2 15:33 gg
-rw-r--r-- 1 zach zach  375 Jul  2 15:33 hh
```

When you call chgrp with the **-R** and **-H** options (-H does not work without -R), chgrp dereferences only symbolic links you list on the command line, which includes symbolic links found in directories you list on the command line. That means chgrp changes the group association of the files these links point to. It does not dereference symbolic links it finds as it descends into directory hierarchies, nor does it change symbolic links themselves. While descending the **dir1** hierarchy, chgrp does not change **dir4.link**, but it does change **dir4**, the directory **dir4.link** points to.

```
$ chgrp -RH pubs bb dir1

$ ls -lR
.:
total 12
-rw-r--r-- 1 zach pubs  102 Jul  2 12:31 bb
drwxr-xr-x 2 zach pubs 4096 Jul  2 15:34 dir1
drwxr-xr-x 2 zach pubs 4096 Jul  2 15:33 dir4

./dir1:
total 4
-rw-r--r-- 1 zach pubs 102 Jul  2 12:32 dd
lrwxrwxrwx 1 zach zach   7 Jul  2 15:33 dir4.link -> ../dir4

./dir4:
total 8
-rw-r--r-- 1 zach zach 125 Jul  2 15:33 gg
-rw-r--r-- 1 zach zach 375 Jul  2 15:33 hh
```

The –H option under Mac OS X

caution The chgrp **–H** option works slightly differently under Mac OS X than it does under Linux. Under OS X, chgrp **–RH** changes the group of the symbolic link it finds in a directory listed on the command line and does not change the file the link points to. (It does not dereference the symbolic link.) When you run the preceding example under OS X, the group association of **dir4** is not changed, but the group association of **dir4.link** is.

If your program depends on how the **–H** option functions with a utility under OS X, test the option with that utility to determine exactly how it works.

When you call chgrp with the –R and –L options (–L does not work without –R), chgrp dereferences all symbolic links: those you list on the command line and those it finds as it descends the directory hierarchy. It does not change the symbolic links themselves. This command changes the files **dir4.link** points to:

```
$ chgrp -RL pubs bb dir1

$ ls -lR
.:
total 12
-rw-r--r-- 1 zach pubs  102 Jul  2 12:31 bb
drwxr-xr-x 2 zach pubs 4096 Jul  2 15:34 dir1
drwxr-xr-x 2 zach pubs 4096 Jul  2 15:33 dir4

./dir1:
total 4
-rw-r--r-- 1 zach pubs 102 Jul  2 12:32 dd
lrwxrwxrwx 1 zach zach   7 Jul  2 15:33 dir4.link -> ../dir4

./dir4:
total 8
-rw-r--r-- 1 zach pubs 125 Jul  2 15:33 gg
-rw-r--r-- 1 zach pubs 375 Jul  2 15:33 hh
```

−P When you call chgrp with the **−R** and **−P** options (**−P** does not work without **−R**), chgrp does not dereference symbolic links. It does change the group of the symbolic link itself.

```
$ ls -l bb*
-rw-r--r-- 1 zach zach 102 Jul  2 12:31 bb
lrwxrwxrwx 1 zach zach   2 Jul  2 16:02 bb.link -> bb

$ chgrp -PR pubs bb.link

$ ls -l bb*
-rw-r--r-- 1 zach zach 102 Jul  2 12:31 bb
lrwxrwxrwx 1 zach pubs   2 Jul  2 16:02 bb.link -> bb
```

chmod

Changes the access mode (permissions) of a file

chmod [*options*] *who operator permission file-list*   **symbolic**
chmod [*options*] *mode file-list*   **absolute**
chmod [*options*] *--reference=rfile file-list*   **referential** `LINUX`

The chmod utility changes the ways in which a file can be accessed by the owner of the file, the group the file is associated with, and/or all other users. You can specify the new access mode absolutely or symbolically. Under Linux you can also specify the mode referentially (third format). Under Mac OS X, you can use chmod to modify ACLs (page 932).

Arguments   Arguments specify which files are to have their modes changed in what ways. The *rfile* is the pathname of a file whose permissions are to become the new permissions of *file-list*.

Symbolic

You can specify multiple sets of symbolic modes (***who operator permission***) by separating each set from the next with a comma.

The chmod utility changes the access permission for the class of users specified by *who*. The class of users is designated by one or more of the letters specified in the *who* column of Table V-4.

Table V-4   Symbolic mode user class specification

who	User class	Meaning
u	User	Owner of the file
g	Group	Group the file is associated with
o	Other	All other users
a	All	Use in place of **ugo**

Table V-5 lists the symbolic mode *operators*.

Table V-5   Symbolic mode operators

operator	Meaning
+	Adds the permission for the specified user class
–	Removes the permission for the specified user class
=	Sets the permission for the specified user class; resets all other permissions for that user class

The access *permission* is specified by one or more of the letters listed in Table V-6.

Table V-6   Symbolic mode permissions

permission	Meaning
r	Sets read permission
w	Sets write permission
x	Sets execute permission
s	Sets the user ID or group ID (depending on the *who* argument) to that of the owner of the file while the file is being executed (For more information see page 96.)
t	Sets the sticky bit (Only a user working with **root** privileges can set the sticky bit, and it can be used only with **u**; see page 980.)
X	Makes the file executable only if it is a directory or if another user class has execute permission
u	Sets the specified permissions to those of the owner
g	Sets the specified permissions to those of the group
o	Sets the specified permissions to those of others

Absolute

You can use an octal number to specify the access mode. Construct the number by ORing the appropriate values from Table V-7. To OR two or more octal numbers from this table, just add them. (Refer to Table V-8 on the next page for examples.)

Table V-7   Absolute mode specifications

mode	Meaning
4000	Sets the user ID when the program is executed (page 96)
2000	Sets the group ID when the program is executed (page 96)
1000	Sticky bit (page 980)
0400	Owner can read the file
0200	Owner can write to the file
0100	Owner can execute the file
0040	Group can read the file
0020	Group can write to the file
0010	Group can execute the file
0004	Others can read the file
0002	Others can write to the file
0001	Others can execute the file

Table V-8 lists some typical modes.

Table V-8   Examples of absolute mode specifications

Mode	Meaning
0777	Owner, group, and others can read, write, and execute the file
0755	Owner can read, write, and execute the file; group and others can read and execute the file
0711	Owner can read, write, and execute the file; group and others can execute the file
0644	Owner can read and write the file; group and others can read the file
0640	Owner can read and write the file, group can read the file, and others cannot access the file

Options

Options preceded by a double hyphen (−−) work under Linux only. Except as noted, options named with a single letter and preceded by a single hyphen work under Linux and OS X.

−−changes −c Displays a message for each file whose permissions are changed. `LINUX`

−−quiet *or* −f Suppresses warning messages about files whose permissions prevent chmod
−−silent   from changing the permissions of the file.

−H (**partial dereference**) For each file that is a symbolic link, changes permissions of the file the link points to, not the symbolic link itself. This option affects files specified on the command line; it does not affect files found while descending a directory hierarchy. This option treats files that are not symbolic links normally and works with −R only. See page 623 for an example of the use of the −H versus −L options. `OS X`

−L (**dereference**) For each file that is a symbolic link, changes permissions of the file the link points to, not the symbolic link itself. This option affects all files, treats files that are not symbolic links normally, and works with −R only. See page 623 for an example of the use of the −H versus −L options. `OS X`

−P (**no dereference**) For each file that is a symbolic link, changes permissions of the symbolic link, not the file the link points to. This option affects all files, treats files that are not symbolic links normally, and works with −R only. See page 625 for an example of the use of the −P option. `OS X`

−−recursive −R Recursively descends a directory specified in *file-list* and changes the permissions on all files in the directory hierarchy.

−−reference=*rfile*   Changes the permissions of the files in *file-list* to that of *rfile*. `LINUX`

--verbose   **–v**   For each file, displays a message saying that its permissions were changed (even if they were not changed) and specifying the permissions. Use **––changes** to display messages only when permissions are actually changed.

Notes

Only the owner of a file or a user working with **root** privileges can change the access mode, or permissions, of a file.

When you use symbolic arguments, you can omit the *permission* from the command line when the *operator* is **=**. This omission takes away all permissions for the specified user class. See the second example in the next section.

Under Linux, chmod never changes the permissions of symbolic links.

Under Linux, chmod dereferences symbolic links found on the command line. In other words, chmod changes the permissions of files that symbolic links found on the command line point to; chmod does not affect files found while descending a directory hierarchy. This behavior mimics the behavior of the Mac OS X **–H** option.

See page 94 for another discussion of chmod.

See page 933 for a discussion of using chmod under Mac OS X to change ACLs.

Examples

See page 932 for examples of using chmod to change ACLs under Mac OS X.

The following examples show how to use the chmod utility to change the permissions of the file named **temp**. The initial access mode of **temp** is shown by ls. See "Discussion" on page 748 for information about the ls display.

```
$ ls -l temp
-rw-rw-r-- 1 max pubs 57 Jul 12 16:47 temp
```

When you do not follow an equal sign with a permission, chmod removes all permissions for the specified user class. The following command removes all access permissions for the group and all other users so only the owner has access to the file:

```
$ chmod go= temp
$ ls -l temp
-rw------- 1 max pubs 57 Jul 12 16:47 temp
```

The next command changes the access modes for all users (owner, group, and others) to read and write. Now anyone can read from or write to the file.

```
$ chmod a=rw temp
$ ls -l temp
-rw-rw-rw- 1 max pubs 57 Jul 12 16:47 temp
```

Using an absolute argument, **a=rw** becomes **666**. The next command performs the same function as the previous one:

```
$ chmod 666 temp
```

The next command removes write access permission for other users. As a result, members of the **pubs** group can read from and write to the file, but other users can only read from the file:

```
$ chmod o-w temp
$ ls -l temp
-rw-rw-r-- 1 max pubs 57 Jul 12 16:47 temp
```

The following command yields the same result, using an absolute argument:

```
$ chmod 664 temp
```

The next command adds execute access permission for all users:

```
$ chmod others temp
$ ls -l temp
-rwxrwxr-x 1 max pubs 57 Jul 12 16:47 temp
```

If **temp** is a shell script or other executable file, all users can now execute it. (The operating system requires read and execute access to execute a shell script but only execute access to execute a binary file.) The absolute command that yields the same result is

```
$ chmod 775 temp
```

The final command uses symbolic arguments to achieve the same result as the preceding one. It sets permissions to read, write, and execute for the owner and the group, and to read and execute for other users. A comma separates the sets of symbolic modes.

```
$ chmod ug=rwx,o=rx temp
```

chown

Changes the owner of a file and/or the group the file is associated with

chown [options] owner file-list
chown [options] owner:group file-list
chown [options] owner: file-list
chown [options] :group file-list
chown [options] --reference=rfile file-list   `LINUX`

The chown utility changes the owner of a file and/or the group the file is associated with. Only a user working with **root** privileges can change the owner of a file. Only a user working with **root** privileges or the owner of a file who belongs to the new group can change the group a file is associated with. The last format works under Linux only.

Arguments   The *owner* is the username or numeric user ID of the new owner. The *file-list* is a list of the pathnames of the files whose ownership and/or group association you want to change. The *group* is the group name or numeric group ID of the new group the file is to be associated with. The *rfile* is the pathname of a file whose owner and/or group association is to become the new owner and/or group association of *file-list*. Table V-9 shows the ways you can specify the new *owner* and/or *group*.

Table V-9   Specifying the new owner and/or group

Argument	Meaning
owner	The new owner of *file-list*; the group is not changed
owner:group	The new owner of and new group associated with *file-list*
owner:	The new owner of *file-list*; the group associated with *file-list* is changed to the new owner's login group
:group	The new group associated with *file-list*; the owner is not changed

Options   Under Linux, chown accepts the common options described on page 603. Options preceded by a double hyphen (--) work under Linux only. Except as noted, options named with a single letter and preceded by a single hyphen work under Linux and OS X.

--changes   –c Displays a message for each file whose ownership/group is changed. `LINUX`

--dereference   Changes the ownership/group of the files symbolic links point to, not the symbolic links themselves. Under Linux, this option is the default. `LINUX`

--quiet *or*   –f Suppresses error messages about files whose ownership and/or group association
--silent   chown cannot change.

–H (**partial dereference**) For each file that is a symbolic link, changes the owner and/or group association of the file the link points to, not the symbolic link itself. This option affects files specified on the command line; it does not affect files found while descending a directory hierarchy. This option treats files that are not symbolic links normally and works with **–R** only. See page 623 for an example of the use of the **–H** versus **–L** options.

––no-dereference **–h** For each file that is a symbolic link, changes the owner and/or group association of the symbolic link, not the file the link points to.

–L (**dereference**) For each file that is a symbolic link, changes the owner and/or group association of the file the link points to, not the symbolic link itself. This option affects all files, treats files that are not symbolic links normally, and works with **–R** only. See page 623 for an example of the use of the **–H** versus **–L** options.

–P (**no dereference**) For each file that is a symbolic link, changes the owner and/or group association of the symbolic link, not the file the link points to. This option affects all files, treats files that are not symbolic links normally, and works with **–R** only. See page 625 for an example of the use of the **–P** option.

––recursive **–R** When you include directories in the *file-list*, this option descends the directory hierarchy, setting the specified owner and/or group association for all files in the hierarchy.

––reference=*rfile* Changes the owner and/or group association of the files in the *file-list* to that of *rfile*. **LINUX**

––verbose **–v** Displays for each file a message saying whether its owner and/or group association was retained or changed.

Notes

The chown utility clears setuid and setgid bits when it changes the owner of a file.

Examples

The following command changes the owner of the **chapter1** file in the **manuals** directory. The new owner is Sam.

```
# chown sam manuals/chapter1
```

The following command makes Max the owner of, and Max's login group the group associated with, all files in the **/home/max/literature** directory and in all its subdirectories.

```
# chown -R max: /home/max/literature
```

Under Mac OS X, home directories are stored in **/Users**, not **/home**.

The next command changes the ownership of the files in **literature** to **max** and the group associated with these files to **pubs**:

```
# chown max:pubs /home/max/literature/*
```

The final example changes the group association of the files in **manuals** to **pubs** without altering their ownership. The owner of the files, who is executing this command, must belong to the **pubs** group.

```
$ chown :pubs manuals/*
```

cmp

Compares two files

cmp [options] file1 [file2 [skip1 [skip2]]]

The cmp utility displays the differences between two files on a byte-by-byte basis. If the files are the same, cmp is silent. If the files differ, cmp displays the byte and line number of the first difference.

Arguments   The *file1* and *file2* arguments are the pathnames of the files that cmp compares. If *file2* is omitted, cmp uses standard input instead. Using a hyphen (–) in place of *file1* or *file2* causes cmp to read standard input instead of that file.

The *skip1* and *skip2* arguments are decimal numbers indicating the number of bytes to skip in each file before beginning the comparison. You can use the standard multiplicative suffixes after *skip1* and *skip2*; see Table V-1 on page 603.

Options   Under Linux *and* OS X, cmp accepts the common options described on page 603. Options preceded by a double hyphen (––) work under Linux only. Options named with a single letter and preceded by a single hyphen work under Linux and OS X.

––print–bytes   **–b**   Displays more information, including filenames, byte and line numbers, and the octal and ASCII values of the first differing byte.

––ignore–initial=*n1*[:*n2*]
           –i *n1*[:*n2*]
           Without *n2*, skips the first *n1* bytes in both files before beginning the comparison. With *n1* and *n2*, skips the first *n1* bytes in *file1* and skips the first *n2* bytes in *file2* before beginning the comparison. You can follow *n1* and/or *n2* with one of the multiplicative suffixes listed in Table V-1 on page 603.

––verbose   **–l**   (lowercase "l") Instead of stopping at the first byte that differs, continues comparing the two files and displays both the location and the value of each byte that differs. Locations are displayed as decimal byte count offsets from the beginning of the files; byte values are displayed in octal. The comparison terminates when an EOF is encountered on either file.

––silent *or*   **–s**   Suppresses output from cmp; only sets the exit status (see "Notes").
––quiet

Notes   Byte and line numbering start at 1.

The cmp utility does not display a message if the files are identical; it only sets the exit status. This utility returns an exit status of 0 if the files are the same and an exit status of 1 if they are different. An exit status greater than 1 means an error occurred.

When you use *skip1* (and *skip2*), the offset values cmp displays are based on the byte where the comparison began.

Under Mac OS X, cmp compares data forks (page 929) of a file only. If you want to compare resource forks, you can manually compare the **..namedfork/rsrc** files (page 930) for the target files.

Unlike diff (page 663), cmp works with binary as well as ASCII files.

Examples   The examples use the files **a** and **b** shown below. These files have two differences. The first difference is that the word **lazy** in file **a** is replaced by **lasy** in file **b**. The second difference is more subtle: A TAB character appears just before the NEWLINE character in file **b**.

```
$ cat a
The quick brown fox jumped over the lazy dog.
$ cat b
The quick brown fox jumped over the lasy dog.TAB
```

The first example uses cmp without any options to compare the two files. The cmp utility reports that the files are different and identifies the offset from the beginning of the files where the first difference is found:

```
$ cmp a b
a b differ: char 39, line 1
```

You can display the values of the bytes at that location by adding the **–b** (**––print–bytes**) option:

```
$ cmp --print-bytes a b
a b differ: char 39, line 1 is 172 z 163 s
```

The **–l** option displays all bytes that differ between the two files. Because this option creates a lot of output if the files have many differences, you may want to redirect the output to a file. The following example shows the two differences between files **a** and **b**. The **–b** option displays the values for the bytes as well. Where file **a** has a CONTROL-J (NEWLINE), file **b** has a CONTROL-I (TAB). The message saying that the end of file on file **a** has been reached indicates that file **b** is longer than file **a**.

```
$ cmp -lb a b
39 172 z    163 s
46  12 ^J    11 ^I
cmp: EOF on a
```

In the next example, the **––ignore–initial** option is used to skip over the first difference in the files. The cmp utility now reports on the second difference. The difference is put at character 7, which is the 46th character in the original file **b** (7 characters past the ignored 39 characters).

```
$ cmp --ignore-initial=39 a b
a b differ: char 7, line 1
```

You can use *skip1* and *skip2* in place of the **––ignore–initial** option used in the preceding example:

```
$ cmp a b 39 39
a b differ: char 7, line 1
```

comm

Compares sorted files

comm [options] file1 file2

The comm utility displays a line-by-line comparison of two sorted files. The first of the three columns it displays lists the lines found only in **file1**, the second column lists the lines found only in **file2**, and the third lists the lines common to both files.

Arguments   The **file1** and **file2** arguments are pathnames of the files that comm compares. Using a hyphen (–) in place of **file1** or **file2** causes comm to read standard input instead of that file.

Options   You can combine the options. With no options, comm produces three-column output.

  –1 Does not display column 1 (does not display lines found only in **file1**).

  –2 Does not display column 2 (does not display lines found only in **file2**).

  –3 Does not display column 3 (does not display lines found in both files).

Notes   If the files have not been sorted, comm will not work properly.

Lines in the second column are preceded by one TAB, and those in the third column are preceded by two TABs.

The exit status indicates whether comm completed normally (0) or abnormally (not 0).

Examples   The following examples use two files, **c** and **d**. As with all input to comm, the files have already been sorted:

```
$ cat c
bbbbb
ccccc
ddddd
eeeee
fffff
$ cat d
aaaaa
ddddd
eeeee
ggggg
hhhhh
```

Refer to sort on page 817 for information on sorting files.

The following example calls comm without any options, so it displays three columns. The first column lists those lines found only in file **c**, the second column lists those found in **d**, and the third lists the lines found in both **c** and **d**:

```
$ comm c d
          aaaaa
bbbbb
ccccc
                    ddddd
                    eeeee
fffff
     ggggg
     hhhhh
```

The next example shows the use of options to prevent comm from displaying columns 1 and 2. The result is column 3, a list of the lines common to files **c** and **d**:

```
$ comm -12 c d
ddddd
eeeee
```

configure

Configures source code automatically

./configure [options]

The configure script is part of the GNU Configure and Build System. Software developers who supply source code for their products face the problem of making it easy for relatively naive users to build and install their software package on a wide variety of machine architectures, operating systems, and system software. To facilitate this process many software developers supply a shell script named configure with their source code.

When you run configure, it determines the capabilities of the local system. The data collected by configure is used to build the makefiles with which make (page 753) builds the executables and libraries. You can adjust the behavior of configure by specifying command-line options and environment variables.

Options

> **The Mac OS X version of configure accepts long options**
>
> tip Options for configure preceded by a double hyphen (--) work under Mac OS X as well as under Linux.

--disable-*feature* Works in the same manner as *--enable-feature* except it disables support for *feature*.

--enable-*feature* The *feature* is the name of a feature that can be supported by the software being configured. For example, configuring the Z Shell source code with the command **configure --enable-zsh-mem** configures the source code to use the special memory allocation routines provided with zsh instead of using the system memory allocation routines. Check the **README** file supplied with the software distribution to see the choices available for *feature*.

--help Displays a detailed list of all options available for use with configure. The contents of this list depends on the software you are installing.

--prefix=*directory*

By default configure builds makefiles that install software in the **/usr/local** directory hierarchy (when you give the command **make install**). To install software into a different directory, replace *directory* with the pathname of the desired directory.

--with-*package* The *package* is the name of an optional package that can be included with the software you are configuring. For example, if you configure the source code for the Windows emulator wine with the command **configure --with-dll**, the source code is configured to build a shared library of Windows emulation support. Check the **README** file supplied with the software you are installing to see the choices available for *package*. The command **configure --help** usually displays the choices available for *package*.

Discussion The GNU Configure and Build System allows software developers to distribute software that can configure itself to be built on a variety of systems. It builds a shell script named configure, which prepares the software distribution to be built and installed on a local system. The configure script searches the local system to find the dependencies for the software distribution and constructs the appropriate makefiles. Once you have run configure, you can build the software with a **make** command and install the software with a **make install** command.

The configure script determines which C compiler to use (usually gcc) and specifies a set of flags to pass to that compiler. You can set the environment variables **CC** and **CFLAGS** to override these values. See the "Examples" section.

Notes Each package that uses the GNU autoconfiguration utility provides its own custom copy of configure, which the software developer created using the GNU autoconf utility (www.gnu.org/software/autoconf). Read the **README** and **INSTALL** files that are provided with the software you are installing for information about the available options.

The configure scripts are self-contained and run correctly on a wide variety of systems. You do not need any special system resources to use configure.

The configure utility will exit with an error message if a dependency is not installed.

Examples The simplest way to call configure is to cd to the base directory for the software you are installing and then run the following command:

```
$ ./configure
```

The ./ is prepended to the command name to ensure you are running the configure script supplied with the software you are installing. For example, to cause configure to build makefiles that pass the flags **-Wall** and **-O2** to gcc, give the following command from bash:

```
$ CFLAGS="-Wall -O2" ./configure
```

If you are using tcsh, give the following command:

```
tcsh $ env CFLAGS="-Wall -O2" ./configure
```

cp

Copies files

cp [options] source-file destination-file
cp [options] source-file-list destination-directory

The cp utility copies one or more files. It can either make a copy of a single file (first format) or copy one or more files to a directory (second format). With the **–R** option, cp can copy directory hierarchies.

Arguments

The *source-file* is the pathname of the file that cp makes a copy of. The *destination-file* is the pathname that cp assigns to the resulting copy of the file.

The *source-file-list* is a list of one or more pathnames of files that cp makes copies of. The *destination-directory* is the pathname of the directory in which cp places the copied files. With this format, cp gives each copied file the same simple filename as its *source-file*.

The **–R** option enables cp to copy directory hierarchies recursively from the *source-file-list* into the *destination-directory*.

Options

Under Linux, cp accepts the common options described on page 603. Options preceded by a double hyphen (––) work under Linux only. Except as noted, options named with a single letter and preceded by a single hyphen work under Linux and OS X.

––archive –a Attempts to preserve the owner, group, permissions, access date, and modification date of source file(s) while copying recursively without dereferencing symbolic links. Same as **–dpR**. `LINUX`

––backup –b If copying a file would remove or overwrite an existing file, this option makes a backup copy of the file that would be overwritten. The backup copy has the same name as the *destination-file* with a tilde (~) appended to it. When you use both **––backup** and **––force**, cp makes a backup copy when you try to copy a file over itself. For more backup options, search for **Backup options** in the **core utils** info page. `LINUX`

–d For each file that is a symbolic link, copies the symbolic link, not the file the link points to. Also preserves hard links in *destination-files* that exist between corresponding *source-files*. This option is equivalent to **––no-dereference** and **––preserve=links**. `LINUX`

––force –f When the *destination-file* exists and cannot be opened for writing, causes cp to try to remove *destination-file* before copying *source-file*. This option is useful when the user copying a file does not have write permission to an existing *destination-file* but does have write permission to the directory containing the *destination-file.* Use this option with **–b** to back up a destination file before removing or overwriting it.

–H (**partial dereference**) For each file that is a symbolic link, copies the file the link points to, not the symbolic link itself. This option affects files specified on the command line; it does not affect files found while descending a directory hierarchy. This option treats files that are not symbolic links normally. Under OS X works with **–R** only. See page 623 for an example of the use of the **–H** versus **–L** options.

––interactive **–i** Prompts you whenever cp would overwrite a file. If you respond with a string that starts with **y** or **Y**, cp copies the file. If you enter anything else, cp does not copy the file.

––dereference **–L** (**dereference**) For each file that is a symbolic link, copies the file the link points to, not the symbolic link itself. This option affects all files and treats files that are not symbolic links normally. Under OS X works with **–R** only. See page 623 for an example of the use of the **–H** versus **–L** options.

––no-dereference **–P** (**no dereference**) For each file that is a symbolic link, copies the symbolic link, not the file the link points to. This option affects all files and treats files that are not symbolic links normally. Under OS X works with **–R** only. See page 625 for an example of the use of the **–P** option.

––preserve[=*attr*] **–p** Creates a *destination-file* with the same owner, group, permissions, access date, and modification date as the *source-file*. The **–p** option does not take an argument.

Without *attr*, **––preserve** works as described above. The *attr* is a comma-separated list that can include **mode** (permissions and ACLs), **ownership** (owner and group), **timestamps** (access and modification dates), **links** (hard links), and **all** (all attributes).

––parents Copies a relative pathname to a directory, creating directories as needed. See the "Examples" section. `LINUX`

––recursive **–R** *or* **–r**
Recursively copies directory hierarchies including ordinary files. Under Linux, the **––no-dereference** (**–d**) option is implied: With the **–R**, **–r**, or **––recursive** option, cp copies the links (not the files the links point to). The **–r** and **––recursive** options are available under Linux only.

––update **–u** Copies only when the *destination-file* does not exist or when it is older than the *source-file* (i.e., this option will not overwrite a newer destination file). `LINUX`

––verbose **–v** Displays the name of each file as cp copies it.

Notes   Under Linux, cp dereferences symbolic links unless you use one or more of the –R, –r, ––recursive, –P, –d, or ––no-dereference options. As explained on the previous page, under Linux the –H option dereferences only symbolic links listed on the command line. Under Mac OS X, without the –R option, cp always dereferences symbolic links; with the –R option, cp does not dereference symbolic links (–P is the default) unless you specify –H or –L.

Many options are available for cp under Linux. See the **coreutils** info page for a complete list.

If the *destination-file* exists before you execute a cp command, cp overwrites the file, destroying the contents but leaving the access privileges, owner, and group associated with the file as they were.

If the *destination-file* does not exist, cp uses the access privileges of the *source-file*. The user who copies the file becomes the owner of the *destination-file* and the user's login group becomes the group associated with the *destination-file*.

Using the –p option without any arguments causes cp to attempt to set the owner, group, permissions, access date, and modification date to match those of the *source-file*.

Unlike with the ln utility (page 740), the *destination-file* that cp creates is independent of its *source-file*.

Under Mac OS X version 10.4 and later, cp copies extended attributes (page 928).

Examples   The first command makes a copy of the file **letter** in the working directory. The name of the copy is **letter.sav**.

```
$ cp letter letter.sav
```

The next command copies all files with filenames ending in **.c** into the **archives** directory, which is a subdirectory of the working directory. Each copied file retains its simple filename but has a new absolute pathname. The –p (––**preserve**) option causes the copied files in **archives** to have the same owner, group, permissions, access date, and modification date as the source files.

```
$ cp -p *.c archives
```

The next example copies **memo** from Sam's home directory to the working directory:

```
$ cp ~sam/memo .
```

The next example runs under Linux and uses the ––**parents** option to copy the file **memo/thursday/max** to the **dir** directory as **dir/memo/thursday/max**. The find utility shows the newly created directory hierarchy.

```
$ cp --parents memo/thursday/max dir
$ find dir
dir
dir/memo
dir/memo/thursday
dir/memo/thursday/max
```

The following command copies the files named **memo** and **letter** into another directory. The copies have the same simple filenames as the source files (**memo** and **letter**) but have different absolute pathnames. The absolute pathnames of the copied files are **/home/sam/memo** and **/home/sam/letter**, respectively.

```
$ cp memo letter /home/sam
```

The final command demonstrates one use of the –f (--force) option. Max owns the working directory and tries unsuccessfully to copy **one** over another file (**me**) that he does not have write permission for. Because he has write permission to the directory that holds **me**, Max can remove the file but cannot write to it. The –f (--force) option unlinks, or removes, **me** and then copies **one** to the new file named **me**.

```
$ ls -ld
drwxrwxr-x    2 max max 4096 Oct 21 22:55 .
$ ls -l
-rw-r--r--    1 root root 3555 Oct 21 22:54 me
-rw-rw-r--    1 max max 1222 Oct 21 22:55 one
$ cp one me
cp: cannot create regular file 'me': Permission denied
$ cp -f one me
$ ls -l
-rw-r--r--    1 max max 1222 Oct 21 22:58 me
-rw-rw-r--    1 max max 1222 Oct 21 22:55 one
```

If Max had used the –b (--backup) option in addition to –f (--force), cp would have created a backup of **me** named **me~**. Refer to "Directory Access Permissions" on page 98 for more information.

cpio

Creates an archive, restores files from an archive, or copies a directory hierarchy

cpio --create|-o [options]
cpio --extract|-i [options] [pattern-list]
cpio --pass-through|-p [options] destination-directory

The cpio utility has three modes of operation: Create (copy-out) mode places multiple files into a single archive file, extract (copy-in) mode restores files from an archive, and pass-through (copy-pass) mode copies a directory hierarchy. The archive file cpio creates can be saved on disk, tape, other removable media, or a remote system.

Create mode reads a list of ordinary or directory filenames from standard input and writes the resulting archive file to standard output. You can use this mode to create an archive. Extract mode reads an archive from standard input and extracts files from that archive. You can restore all files from the archive or only those files whose names match a pattern. Pass-through mode reads a list of names of ordinary or directory files from standard input and copies the files to a specified directory.

Arguments

By default cpio in extract mode extracts all files found in the archive. You can choose to extract files selectively by supplying a *pattern-list*. If the name of a file in the archive matches one of the patterns in *pattern-list*, cpio extracts that file; otherwise, it ignores the file. The patterns in a cpio *pattern-list* are similar to shell wildcards (page 136) except that *pattern-list* match slashes (/) and a leading period (.) in a filename.

In pass-through mode you must give the name of the *destination-directory* as an argument to cpio.

Options

A major option specifies the mode in which cpio operates: create, extract, or pass-through.

Major Options

You must include exactly one of these options. Options preceded by a double hyphen (--) work under Linux only. Options named with a single letter and preceded by a single hyphen work under Linux and OS X.

--extract   -i (copy-in mode) Reads the archive from standard input and extracts files. Without a *pattern-list* on the command line, cpio extracts all files from the archive. With a *pattern-list*, cpio extracts only files with names that match one of the patterns in *pattern-list*. The following example extracts from the device mounted on **/dev/sde1** only those files whose names end in **.c**:

```
$ cpio -i \*.c < /dev/sde1
```

The backslash prevents the shell from expanding the * before it passes the argument to cpio.

--create   –o   (**copy-out mode**) Constructs an archive from the files named on standard input. These files may be ordinary or directory files, and each must appear on a separate line. The archive is written to standard output as it is built. The find utility frequently generates the filenames that cpio uses. The following command builds an archive of the entire local system and writes it to the device mounted on **/dev/sde1**:

```
$ find / -depth -print | cpio -o >/dev/sde1
```

The **–depth** option causes find to search for files in a depth-first search, thereby reducing the likelihood of permissions problems when you restore the files from the archive. See the discussion of this option on page 647.

--pass-through   –p   (**copy-pass mode**) Copies files from one place on the system to another. Instead of constructing an archive file containing the files named on standard input, cpio copies them to the ***destination-directory*** (the last argument on the cpio command line). The effect is the same as if you had created an archive with copy-out mode and then extracted the files with copy-in mode, except using pass-through mode avoids creating an archive. The following example copies the files in the working directory and all subdirectories into **~max/code**:

```
$ find . -depth -print | cpio -pdm ~max/code
```

Other Options

The following options alter the behavior of cpio. These options work with one or more of the preceding major options.

Options preceded by a double hyphen (––) work under Linux only. Except as noted, options named with a single letter and preceded by a single hyphen work under Linux and OS X.

--reset-access-time

  –a   Resets the access times of source files after copying them so they have the same access time after copying as they did before.

  –B   (**block**) Sets the block size to 5,120 bytes instead of the default 512 bytes. Under Linux this option affects input and output block sizes; under OS X it affects only output block sizes.

--block-size=*n*   Sets the block size used for input and output to *n* 512-byte blocks. **LINUX**

  –c   (**compatible**) Writes header information in ASCII so older (incompatible) cpio utilities on other systems can read the file. This option is rarely needed.

--make-directories

  –d   Creates directories as needed when copying files. For example, you need this option when you are extracting files from an archive with a file list generated by find with the **–depth** option. This option can be used only with the **–i** (**––extract**) and **–p** (**––pass-through**) options.

--pattern-file=*filename*
-E *filename*
Reads *pattern-list* from *filename,* one *pattern* per line. Additionally, you can specify *pattern-list* on the command line.

--file=*archive*   -F *archive*
Uses *archive* as the name of the archive file. In extract mode, reads from *archive* instead of standard input. In create mode, writes to *archive* instead of standard output. You can use this option to access a device on another system on a network; see the –f (--**file**) option to tar (page 847) for more information.

--nonmatching   –f   (**flip**) Reverses the sense of the test performed on *pattern-list* when extracting files from an archive. Files are extracted from the archive only if they do *not* match any of the patterns in the *pattern-list.*

--help   Displays a list of options. `LINUX`

--dereference   –L   For each file that is a symbolic link, copies the file the link points to (not the symbolic link itself). This option treats files that are not symbolic links normally.

--link   –l   When possible, links files instead of copying them.

--preserve-modification-time
–m   Preserves the modification times of files that are extracted from an archive. Without this option the files show the time they were extracted. With this option the created files show the time they had when they were copied into the archive.

--no-absolute-filenames
In extract mode, creates all filenames relative to the working directory—even files that were archived with absolute pathnames. `LINUX`

--rename   –r   Allows you to rename files as cpio copies them. When cpio prompts you with the name of a file, you respond with the new name. The file is then copied with the new name. If you press RETURN instead, cpio does not copy the file.

--list   –t   (**table of contents**) Displays a table of contents of the archive. This option works only with the –i (--**extract**) option, although no files are actually extracted from the archive. With the –v (--**verbose**) option, it displays a detailed table of contents in a format similar to that used by ls –l.

--unconditional   –u   Overwrites existing files regardless of their modification times. Without this option cpio will not overwrite a more recently modified file with an older one; it displays a warning message.

--verbose   –v   Lists files as they are processed. With the –t (--**list**) option, it displays a detailed table of contents in a format similar to that used by ls –l.

Discussion Without the **–u** (**––unconditional**) option, cpio will not overwrite a more recently modified file with an older file.

You can use both ordinary and directory filenames as input when you create an archive. If the name of an ordinary file appears in the input list before the name of its parent directory, the ordinary file appears before its parent directory in the archive as well. This order can lead to an avoidable error: When you extract files from the archive, the child has nowhere to go in the file structure if its parent has not yet been extracted.

Making sure that files appear after their parent directories in the archive is not always a solution. One problem occurs if the **–m** (**––preserve-modification-time**) option is used when extracting files. Because the modification time of a parent directory is updated whenever a file is created within it, the original modification time of the parent directory is lost when the first file is written to it.

The solution to this potential problem is to ensure that all files appear *before* their parent directories when creating an archive *and* to create directories as needed when extracting files from an archive. When you use this technique, directories are extracted only after all files have been written to them and their modification times are preserved.

With the **–depth** option, find generates a list of files, with all children appearing in the list before their parent directories. If you use this list to create an archive, the files are in the proper order. (Refer to the first example in the next section.) When extracting files from an archive, the **–d** (**––make-directories**) option causes cpio to create parent directories as needed and the **–m** (**––preserve-modification-time**) option does just what its name says. Using this combination of utilities and options preserves directory modification times through a create/extract sequence.

This strategy also solves another potential problem. Sometimes a parent directory may not have permissions set so that you can extract files into it. When cpio automatically creates the directory with **–d** (**––make-directories**), you can be assured that you have write permission to the directory. When the directory is extracted from the archive (after all the files are written into the directory), it is extracted with its original permissions.

Examples The first example creates an archive of the files in Sam's home directory, writing the archive to a USB flash drive mounted at **/dev/sde1**.

```
$ find /home/sam -depth -print | cpio -oB >/dev/sde1
```

The find utility produces the filenames that cpio uses to build the archive. The **–depth** option causes all entries in a directory to be listed before listing the directory name itself, making it possible for cpio to preserve the original modification times of directories (see the preceding "Discussion" section). Use the **–d** (**––make-directories**) and

–m (––preserve-modification-time) options when you extract files from this archive (see the following examples). The –B option sets the block size to 5,120 bytes.

Under Mac OS X, home directories are stored in /Users, not /home.

To check the contents of the archive file and display a detailed listing of the files it contains, give the following command:

```
$ cpio -itv < /dev/sde1
```

The following command restores the files that formerly were in the **memo** subdirectory of Sam's home directory:

```
$ cpio -idm /home/sam/memo/\* < /dev/sde1
```

The –d (––make-directories) option ensures that any subdirectories that were in the **memo** directory are re-created as needed. The –m (––preserve-modification-time) option preserves the modification times of files and directories. The asterisk in the regular expression is escaped to keep the shell from expanding it.

The next command is the same as the preceding command except it uses the Linux ––no-absolute-filenames option to re-create the **memo** directory in the working directory, which is named **memocopy**. The pattern does not start with the slash that represents the root directory, allowing cpio to create the files with relative pathnames.

```
$ pwd
/home/sam/memocopy
$ cpio -idm --no-absolute-filenames home/sam/memo/\* < /dev/sde1
```

The final example uses the –f option to restore all files in the archive except those that were formerly in the **memo** subdirectory:

```
$ cpio -ivmdf /home/sam/memo/\* < /dev/sde1
```

The –v option lists the extracted files as cpio processes the archive, verifying the expected files are extracted.

crontab

Maintains crontab files

*crontab [–u **user-name**] **filename***
*crontab [–u **user-name**] **option***

A crontab file associates periodic times (such as 14:00 on Wednesdays) with commands. The cron utility executes each command at the specified time. When you are working as yourself, the crontab utility installs, removes, lists, and allows you to edit your crontab file. A user working with **root** privileges can work with any user's crontab file.

Arguments   The first format copies the contents of ***filename*** (which contains crontab commands) into the crontab file of the user who runs the command or that of ***username***. When the user does not have a crontab file, this process creates a new one; when the user has a crontab file, this process overwrites the file. When you replace ***filename*** with a hyphen (–), crontab reads commands from standard input.

The second format lists, removes, or edits the crontab file, depending on which option you specify.

Options   Choose only one of the **–e**, **–l**, or **–r** options. A user working with **root** privileges can use **–u** with one of these options.

–e   (**edit**) Runs the text editor specified by the **VISUAL** or **EDITOR** shell variable on the crontab file, enabling you to add, change, or delete entries. This option installs the modified crontab file when you exit from the editor.

–l   (**list**) Displays the contents of the crontab file.

–r   (**remove**) Deletes the crontab file.

–u ***username***
(**user**) Works on ***username***'s crontab file. Only a user working with **root** privileges can use this option.

Notes   This section covers the versions of cron, crontab, and crontab files that were written by Paul Vixie—hence this version of cron is called *Vixie cron*. These versions are POSIX compliant and differ from an earlier version of Vixie cron as well as from the classic SVR3 syntax.

User crontab files are kept in the **/var/spool/cron** or **/var/spool/cron/crontabs** directory. Each file is named with the username of the user that it belongs to.

The system utility named cron reads the crontab files and runs the commands. If a command line in a crontab file does not redirect its output, all output sent to standard output and standard error is mailed to the user unless you set the **MAILTO** variable within the crontab file to a different username.

To make the system administrator's job easier, the directories named **/etc/cron.hourly**, **/etc/cron.daily**, **/etc/cron.weekly**, and **/etc/cron.monthly** hold crontab files that, on most systems, are run by run-parts, which in turn are run by the **/etc/crontab** file. Each of these directories contains files that execute system tasks at the interval named by the directory. A user working with **root** privileges can add files to these directories instead of adding lines to **root**'s crontab file. A typical **/etc/crontab** file looks like this:

```
$ cat /etc/crontab
SHELL=/bin/bash
PATH=/sbin:/bin:/usr/sbin:/usr/bin
MAILTO=root
HOME=/

# run-parts
01 * * * * root run-parts /etc/cron.hourly
02 4 * * * root run-parts /etc/cron.daily
22 4 * * 0 root run-parts /etc/cron.weekly
42 4 1 * * root run-parts /etc/cron.monthly
```

Each entry in a crontab file begins with five fields that specify when the command is to run (minute, hour, day of the month, month, and day of the week). The cron utility interprets an asterisk appearing in place of a number as a wildcard representing all possible values. In the day-of-the-week field, you can use either 7 or 0 to represent Sunday.

It is a good practice to start cron jobs a variable number of minutes before or after the hour, half-hour, or quarter-hour. When you start jobs at these times, it becomes less likely that many processes will start at the same time, thereby potentially overloading the system.

When cron starts (usually when the system is booted), it reads all of the crontab files into memory. The cron utility mostly sleeps but wakes up once a minute, reviews all crontab entries it has stored in memory, and runs whichever jobs are due to be run at that time.

cron.allow, cron.deny   By creating, editing, and removing the **cron.allow** and **cron.deny** files, a user working with **root** privileges determines which users can run crontab. Under Linux these files are kept in the **/etc** directory; under Mac OS X they are kept in **/var/at** (which has a symbolic link at **/usr/lib/cron**). When you create a **cron.deny** file with no entries and no **cron.allow** file exists, everyone can use crontab. When the **cron.allow** file exists, only users listed in that file can use crontab, regardless of the presence and contents of **cron.deny**. Otherwise, you can list in the **cron.allow** file those users who are allowed to use crontab and in **cron.deny** those users who are not allowed to use it. (Listing a user in **cron.deny** is not strictly necessary because, if a **cron.allow** file exists and the user is not listed in it, the user will not be able to use crontab anyway.)

Examples   The following example uses **crontab –l** to list the contents of Sam's crontab file
(**/var/spool/cron/sam**). All the scripts that Sam runs are in his **~/bin** directory. The
first line sets the **MAILTO** variable to **max** so that Max gets the output from commands run from Sam's crontab file that is not redirected. The **sat.job** script runs
every Saturday (day 6) at 2:05 AM, **twice.week** runs at 12:02 AM on Sunday and
Thursday (days 0 and 4), and **twice.day** runs twice a day, every day, at 10:05 AM
and 4:05 PM.

```
$ who am i
sam

$ crontab -l
MAILTO=max
05 02 * * 6        $HOME/bin/sat.job
00 02 * * 0,4      $HOME/bin/twice.week
05 10,16 * * *     $HOME/bin/twice.day
```

To add an entry to your crontab file, run the crontab utility with the –e (edit) option.
Some Linux systems use a version of crontab that does not support the –e option. If
the local system runs such a version, you need to make a copy of your existing
crontab file, edit it, and then resubmit it, as in the example that follows. The **–l** (list)
option displays a copy of your **crontab** file.

```
$ crontab -l > newcron
$ vim newcron
...
$ crontab newcron
```

cut

Selects characters or fields from input lines

cut [options] [file-list]

The cut utility selects characters or fields from lines of input and writes them to standard output. Character and field numbering start with 1.

Arguments   The *file-list* is a list of ordinary files. If you do not specify an argument or if you specify a hyphen (–) in place of a filename, cut reads from standard input.

Options   Under Linux, cut accepts the common options described on page 603. Options preceded by a double hyphen (––) work under Linux only. Options named with a single letter and preceded by a single hyphen work under Linux and OS X.

––characters=*clist*
> –c *clist*
>> Selects the characters given by the column numbers in *clist*. The value of *clist* is one or more comma-separated column numbers or column ranges. A range is specified by two column numbers separated by a hyphen. A range of *–n* means columns 1 through *n*; *n–* means columns *n* through the end of the line.

––delimiter=*dchar*
> –d *dchar*
>> Specifies *dchar* as the input field delimiter. Also specifies *dchar* as the output field delimiter unless you use the ––**output-delimiter** option. The default delimiter is a TAB character. Quote characters as necessary to protect them from shell expansion.

––fields=*flist*   –f *flist*
>> Selects the fields specified in *flist*. The value of *flist* is one or more comma-separated field numbers or field ranges. A range is specified by two field numbers separated by a hyphen. A range of *–n* means fields 1 through *n*; *n–* means fields *n* through the last field. The field delimiter is a TAB character unless you use the ––**delimiter** option to change it.

––output-delimiter=*ochar*
>> Specifies *ochar* as the output field delimiter. The default delimiter is the TAB character. You can specify a different delimiter by using the ––**delimiter** option. Quote characters as necessary to protect them from shell expansion.

--only-delimited   –s   Copies only lines containing delimiters. Without this option, cut copies—but does not modify—lines that do not contain delimiters.

Notes   Although limited in functionality, cut is easy to learn and use and is a good choice when columns and fields can be selected without using pattern matching. Sometimes cut is used with paste (page 784).

Examples   For the next two examples, assume that an ls –l command produces the following output:

```
$ ls -l
total 2944
-rwxr-xr-x  1 zach pubs      259 Feb  1 00:12 countout
-rw-rw-r--  1 zach pubs     9453 Feb  4 23:17 headers
-rw-rw-r--  1 zach pubs  1474828 Jan 14 14:15 memo
-rw-rw-r--  1 zach pubs  1474828 Jan 14 14:33 memos_save
-rw-rw-r--  1 zach pubs     7134 Feb  4 23:18 tmp1
-rw-rw-r--  1 zach pubs     4770 Feb  4 23:26 tmp2
-rw-rw-r--  1 zach pubs    13580 Nov  7 08:01 typescript
```

The following command outputs the permissions of the files in the working directory. The cut utility with the –c option selects characters 2 through 10 from each input line. The characters in this range are written to standard output.

```
$ ls -l | cut -c2-10
otal 2944
rwxr-xr-x
rw-rw-r--
rw-rw-r--
rw-rw-r--
rw-rw-r--
rw-rw-r--
rw-rw-r--
```

The next command outputs the size and name of each file in the working directory. The –f option selects the fifth and ninth fields from the input lines. The –d option tells cut to use SPACEs, not TABs, as delimiters. The tr utility (page 864) with the –s option changes sequences of more than one SPACE character into a single SPACE; otherwise, cut counts the extra SPACE characters as separate fields.

```
$ ls -l | tr -s ' ' ' ' | cut -f5,9 -d' '

259 countout
9453 headers
1474828 memo
1474828 memos_save
7134 tmp1
4770 tmp2
13580 typescript
```

The last example displays a list of full names as stored in the fifth field of the **/etc/passwd** file. The –d option specifies that the colon character be used as the field delimiter. Although this example works under Mac OS X, **/etc/passwd** does not contain information about most users; see "Open Directory" on page 926 for more information.

```
$ cat /etc/passwd
root:x:0:0:Root:/:/bin/sh
sam:x:401:50:Sam the Great:/home/sam:/bin/zsh
max:x:402:50:Max Wild:/home/max:/bin/bash
zach:x:504:500:Zach Brill:/home/zach:/bin/tcsh
hls:x:505:500:Helen Simpson:/home/hls:/bin/bash

$ cut -d: -f5 /etc/passwd
Root
Sam the Great
Max Wild
Zach Brill
Helen Simpson
```

date

Displays or sets the system time and date

date [options] [+format]
date [options] [newdate]

The date utility displays the time and date known to the system. A user working with **root** privileges can use date to change the system clock.

Arguments   The *+format* argument specifies the format for the output of date. The format string, which consists of field descriptors and text, follows a plus sign (+). The field descriptors are preceded by percent signs, and date replaces each one by its value in the output. Table V-10 lists some of the field descriptors.

Table V-10   Selected field descriptors

Descriptor	Meaning
%a	Abbreviated weekday—Sun to Sat
%A	Unabbreviated weekday—Sunday to Saturday
%b	Abbreviated month—Jan to Dec
%B	Unabbreviated month—January to December
%c	Date and time in default format used by date
%d	Day of the month—01 to 31
%D	Date in mm/dd/yy format
%H	Hour—00 to 23
%I	Hour—00 to 12
%j	Julian date (day of the year—001 to 366)
%m	Month of the year—01 to 12
%M	Minutes—00 to 59
%n	NEWLINE character
%P	AM or PM
%r	Time in AM/PM notation
%s	Number of seconds since the beginning of January 1, 1970
%S	Seconds—00 to 60 (the 60 accommodates leap seconds)

Table V-10   Selected field descriptors (continued)

Descriptor	Meaning
%t	TAB character
%T	Time in HH:MM:SS format
%w	Day of the week—0 to 6 (0 = Sunday)
%y	Last two digits of the year—00 to 99
%Y	Year in four-digit format (for example, 2009)
%Z	Time zone (for example, PDT)

By default date zero fills numeric fields. Placing an underscore (_) immediately following the percent sign (%) for a field causes date to blank fill the field. Placing a hyphen (–) following the percent sign causes date not to fill the field—that is, to left justify the field.

The date utility assumes that, in a format string, any character that is not a percent sign, an underscore or a hyphen following the percent sign, or a field descriptor is ordinary text and copies it to standard output. You can use ordinary text to add punctuation to the date and to add labels (for example, you can put the word **DATE:** in front of the date). Surround the *format* argument with single quotation marks if it contains SPACEs or other characters that have a special meaning to the shell.

Setting the system clock
When a user working with **root** privileges specifies *newdate,* the system changes the system clock to reflect the new date. The *newdate* argument has the format

$$nnddhhmm[[cc]yy][.ss]$$

where *nn* is the number of the month (01–12), *dd* is the day of the month (01–31), *hh* is the hour based on a 24-hour clock (00–23), and *mm* is the minutes (00–59). When you change the date, you must specify at least these fields.

The optional *cc* specifies the first two digits of the year (the value of the century minus 1), and *yy* specifies the last two digits of the year. You can specify *yy* or *ccyy* following *mm*. When you do not specify a year, date assumes that the year has not changed.

You can specify the number of seconds past the start of the minute with *.ss*.

Options

Under Linux, date accepts the common options described on page 603. Options preceded by a double hyphen (––) work under Linux only. Except as noted, options named with a single letter and preceded by a single hyphen work under Linux and OS X.

––date=*datestring*

–d *datestring*

Displays the date specified by *datestring*, not the current date. This option does not change the system clock. `LINUX`

--reference=*file*   –r *file*

Displays the modification date and time of *file* in place of the current date and time. `LINUX`

--utc *or*   –u Displays or sets the time and date using Universal Coordinated Time (UTC; page 986). UTC is also called Greenwich Mean Time (GMT).
--universal

Notes

If you set up a locale database, date uses that database to substitute terms appropriate to your *locale* (page 963).

Examples

The first example shows how to set the date for 2:07:30 PM on August 19 without changing the year:

```
# date 08191407.30
Fri Aug 19 14:07:30 PDT 2009
```

The next example shows the *format* argument, which causes date to display the date in a commonly used format:

```
$ date '+Today is %h %d, %Y'
Today is Aug 19, 2009
```

dd

Converts and copies a file

dd [arguments]

The dd (device-to-device copy) utility converts and copies a file. The primary use of dd is to copy files to and from hard disk files and removable media. It can operate on hard disk partitions and create block-for-block identical disk images. Often dd can handle the transfer of information to and from other operating systems when other methods fail. Its rich set of arguments gives you precise control over the characteristics of the transfer.

Arguments   Under Linux, dd accepts the common options described on page 603. By default dd copies standard input to standard output.

bs=*n*
(**block size**) Reads and writes *n* bytes at a time. This argument overrides the **ibs** and **obs** arguments.

cbs=*n*
(**conversion block size**) When performing data conversion during the copy, converts *n* bytes at a time.

conv=*type[,type...]*

By applying conversion *types* in the order given on the command line, converts the data being copied. The *types* must be separated by commas with no SPACEs. The types of conversions are shown in Table V-11.

count=*numblocks*
Restricts to *numblocks* the number of blocks of input that dd copies. The size of each block is the number of bytes specified by the **bs** or **ibs** argument.

ibs=*n*
(**input block size**) Reads *n* bytes at a time.

if=*filename*
(**input file**) Reads from *filename* instead of from standard input. You can use a device name for *filename* to read from that device.

obs=*n*
(**output block size**) Writes *n* bytes at a time.

of=*filename*
(**output file**) Writes to *filename* instead of to standard output. You can use a device name for *filename* to write to that device.

seek=*numblocks*
Skips *numblocks* blocks of output before writing any output. The size of each block is the number of bytes specified by the **bs** or **obs** argument.

skip=*numblocks*
Skips *numblocks* blocks of input before starting to copy. The size of each block is the number of bytes specified by the **bs** or **ibs** argument.

Table V-11   Conversion types

type	Meaning
ascii	Converts EBCDIC-encoded characters to ASCII, allowing you to read tapes written on IBM mainframe and similar computers.

Table V-11 Conversion types (continued)

type	Meaning
block	Each time a line of input is read (that is, a sequence of characters terminated with a NEWLINE character), outputs a block of text without the NEWLINE. Each output block has the size given by the **bs** or **obs** argument and is created by adding trailing SPACE characters to the text until it is the proper size.
ebcdic	Converts ASCII-encoded characters to EBCDIC, allowing you to write tapes for use on IBM mainframe and similar computers.
lcase	Converts uppercase letters to lowercase while copying data.
noerror	If a read error occurs, **dd** normally terminates. This conversion allows **dd** to continue processing data and is useful when you are trying to recover data from bad media.
notrunc	Does not truncate the output file before writing to it.
ucase	Converts lowercase letters to uppercase while copying data.
unblock	Performs the opposite of the block conversion.

Notes   Under Linux, you can use the standard multiplicative suffixes to make it easier to specify large block sizes. See Table V-1 on page 603. Under Mac OS X, you can use some of the standard multiplicative suffixes; however, OS X uses lowercase letters in place of the uppercase letters shown in the table. In addition, under OS X, dd supports **b** (block; multiply by 512) and **w** (word; multiply by the number of bytes in an integer).

Examples   You can use dd to create a file filled with pseudo-random bytes.

```
$ dd if=/dev/urandom of=randfile2 bs=1 count=100
```

The preceding command reads from the **/dev/urandom** file (an interface to the kernel's random number generator) and writes to the file named **randfile**. The block size is 1 and the count is 100, so **randfile** is 100 bytes long. For bytes that are more random, you can read from **/dev/random**. See the **urandom** and **random** man pages for more information. Under OS X, **urandom** and **random** behave identically.

You can also use dd to make an exact copy of a disk partition. Be careful however—the following command wipes out anything that was on the **/dev/sdb1** partition.

```
# dd if=/dev/sda1 of=/dev/sdb1
```

Wiping a file   You can use a similar technique to wipe data from a file before deleting it, making it almost impossible to recover data from the deleted file. You might want to wipe a file for security reasons; wipe a file several times for added security.

In the following example, ls shows the size of the file named **secret**; dd, with a block size of 1 and a count corresponding to the number of bytes in **secret**, then wipes the file. The **conv=notrunc** argument ensures that dd writes over the data in the file and not another place on the disk.

```
$ ls -l secret
-rw-rw-r--  1 max max 2494 Feb  6 00:56 secret
$ dd if=/dev/urandom of=secret bs=1 count=2494 conv=notrunc
2494+0 records in
2494+0 records out
$ rm secret
```

Copying a diskette You can use dd to make an exact copy of a floppy diskette. First copy the contents of the diskette to a file on the hard drive and then copy the file from the hard disk to a formatted diskette. This technique works regardless of what is on the floppy diskette. The next example copies a DOS-formatted diskette. (The filename for the floppy on the local system may differ from that in the example.) The mount, ls, umount sequences at the beginning and end of the example verify that the original diskette and the copy hold the same files. You can use the **floppy.copy** file to make multiple copies of the diskette.

```
# mount -t msdos /dev/fd0H1440 /mnt
# ls /mnt
abprint.dat  bti.ini      setup.ins    supfiles.z   wbt.z
adbook.z     setup.exe    setup.pkg    telephon.z
# umount /mnt
# dd if=/dev/fd0 ibs=512 > floppy.copy
2880+0 records in
2880+0 records out
# ls -l floppy.copy
-rw-rw-r--  1 max speedy 1474560 Oct 11 05:43 floppy.copy
# dd if=floppy.copy bs=512 of=/dev/fd0
2880+0 records in
2880+0 records out
# mount -t msdos /dev/fd0H1440 /mnt
# ls /mnt
abprint.dat  bti.ini      setup.ins    supfiles.z   wbt.z
adbook.z     setup.exe    setup.pkg    telephon.z
# umount /mnt
```

df

Displays disk space usage

df [options] [filesystem-list]

The df (disk free) utility reports on the total space and the free space on each mounted device.

Arguments When you call df without an argument, it reports on the free space on each of the devices mounted on the local system.

The ***filesystem-list*** is an optional list of one or more pathnames that specify the filesystems you want the report to cover. This argument works on Mac OS X and some Linux systems. You can refer to a mounted filesystem by its device pathname or by the pathname of the directory it is mounted on.

Options Options preceded by a double hyphen (−−) work under Linux only. Except as noted, options named with a single letter and preceded by a single hyphen work under Linux and OS X.

−−all −a Reports on filesystems with a size of 0 blocks, such as **/dev/proc**. Normally df does not report on these filesystems.

−−block-size=*sz* −B *sz*
  The *sz* specifies the units that the report uses (the default is 1-kilobyte blocks). The *sz* is a multiplicative suffix from Table V-1 on page 603. See also the −h (−−**human-readable**) and −H (−−**si**) options. `LINUX`

−g (**gigabyte**) Displays sizes in 1-gigabyte blocks. `OS X`

−−si −H Displays sizes in K (kilobyte), M (megabyte), and G (gigabyte) blocks, as is appropriate. Uses powers of 1,000.

−−human-readable
  −h Displays sizes in K (kilobyte), M (megabyte), and G (gigabyte) blocks, as is appropriate. Uses powers of 1,024.

−−inodes −i Reports the number of *inodes* (page 959) that are used and free instead of reporting on blocks.

−k (**kilobyte**) Displays sizes in 1-kilobyte blocks.

−−local −l Displays local filesystems only.

−m (**megabyte**) Displays sizes in 1-megabyte blocks. `OS X`

−−type=*fstype* −t *fstype*
  Reports information only about the filesystems of type *fstype,* such as DOS or NFS. Repeat this option to report on several types of filesystems. `LINUX`

−−exclude-type=*fstype*
  −x *fstype*
  Reports information only about the filesystems *not* of type *fstype*. `LINUX`

Notes   Under Mac OS X, the df utility supports the **BLOCKSIZE** environment variable
(page 603) and ignores block sizes smaller than 512 bytes or larger than 1 gigabyte.

Under Mac OS X, the count of used and free inodes (–i option) is meaningless on
HFS+ filesystems. On these filesystems, new files can be created as long as free space
is available in the filesystem.

Examples   In the following example, df displays information about all mounted filesystems on
the local system:

```
$ df
Filesystem         1k-blocks       Used Available Use% Mounted on
/dev/hda12          1517920       53264   1387548   4% /
/dev/hda1             15522        4846      9875  33% /boot
/dev/hda8           1011928      110268    850256  11% /free1
/dev/hda9           1011928       30624    929900   3% /free2
/dev/hda10          1130540       78992    994120   7% /free3
/dev/hda5           4032092     1988080   1839188  52% /home
/dev/hda7           1011928          60    960464   0% /tmp
/dev/hda6           2522048      824084   1569848  34% /usr
zach:/c             2096160     1811392    284768  86% /zach_c
zach:/d             2096450     1935097    161353  92% /zach_d
```

Next df is called with the –l and –h options, generating a human-readable list of
local filesystems. The sizes in this listing are given in terms of megabytes and
gigabytes.

```
$ df -lh
Filesystem         Size  Used Avail Use% Mounted on
/dev/hda12         1.4G   52M  1.3G   4% /
/dev/hda1           15M  4.7M  9.6M  33% /boot
/dev/hda8          988M  108M  830M  11% /free1
/dev/hda9          988M   30M  908M   3% /free2
/dev/hda10         1.1G   77M  971M   7% /free3
/dev/hda5          3.8G  1.9G  1.8G  52% /home
/dev/hda7          988M   60k  938M   0% /tmp
/dev/hda6          2.4G  805M  1.5G  34% /usr
```

The next example, which runs under Linux only, displays information about the
/free2 partition in megabyte units:

```
$ df -BM /free2
Filesystem         1M-blocks       Used Available Use% Mounted on
/dev/hda9                988         30       908   3% /free2
```

The final example, which runs under Linux only, displays information about NFS
filesystems in human-readable terms:

```
$ df -ht nfs
Filesystem         Size  Used Avail Use% Mounted on
zach:/c            2.0G  1.7G  278M  86% /zach_c
zach:/d            2.0G  1.8G  157M  92% /zach_d
```

diff

Displays the differences between two text files

diff [options] file1 file2
diff [options] file1 directory
diff [options] directory file2
diff [options] directory1 directory2

The diff utility displays line-by-line differences between two text files. By default diff displays the differences as instructions, which you can then use to edit one of the files to make it the same as the other.

Arguments The *file1* and *file2* are pathnames of ordinary text files that diff works on. When the *directory* argument is used in place of *file2*, diff looks for a file in *directory* with the same name as *file1*. It works similarly when *directory* replaces *file1*. When you specify two directory arguments, diff compares the files in *directory1* with the files that have the same simple filenames in *directory2*.

Options The diff utility accepts the common options described on page 603, with one exception: When one of the arguments is a directory and the other is an ordinary file, you cannot compare to standard input.

The Mac OS X version of diff accepts long options

tip Options for diff preceded by a double hyphen (--) work under Mac OS X as well as under Linux.

--ignore-blank-lines

    –B Ignores differences that involve only blank lines.

--ignore-space-change

    –b Ignores whitespace (SPACEs and TABs) at the ends of lines and considers other strings of whitespace to be equal.

--context[=*lines*] **–C** *[lines]*

Displays the sections of the two files that differ, including *lines* lines (the default is 3) around each line that differs to show the context. Each line in *file1* that is missing from *file2* is preceded by a hyphen (–); each extra line in *file2* is preceded by a plus sign (+); and lines that have different versions in the two files are preceded by an exclamation point (!). When lines that differ are within *lines* lines of each other, they are grouped together in the output.

--ed **–e** Creates and sends to standard output a script for the ed editor, which will edit *file1* to make it the same as *file2*. You must add **w** (Write) and **q** (Quit) instructions to the end of the script if you plan to redirect input to ed from the script. When you use **--ed**, diff displays the changes in reverse order: Changes to the end of the file are listed before changes to the top, preventing early changes from affecting later changes when the script is used as input to ed. For example, if a line near the top were deleted, subsequent line numbers in the script would be wrong.

--ignore-case –i Ignores differences in case when comparing files.

--new-file –N When comparing directories, when a file is present in one of the directories only, considers it to be present and empty in the other directory.

--show-c-function

–p Shows which C function, bash control structure, Perl subroutine, and so forth each change affects.

--brief –q Does not display the differences between lines in the files. Instead, diff reports only that the files differ.

--recursive –r When using diff to compare the files in two directories, causes the comparisons to descend through the directory hierarchies.

--unified[=*lines*] –U *lines* or –u

Uses the easier-to-read unified output format. See the discussion of diff on page 54 for more detail and an example. The *lines* argument is the number of lines of context; the default is three (the –u option does not take an argument and provides three lines of context).

--ignore-all-space

–w (**whitespace**) Ignores whitespace when comparing lines.

--width=*n* –W *n*

Sets the width of the columns that diff uses to display the output to *n* characters. This option is useful with the --side-by-side option. The sdiff utility (see the "Notes" section) uses a lowercase **w** to perform the same function: –w *n*.

--side-by-side –y Displays the output in a side-by-side format. This option generates the same output as sdiff. Use the --width=*columns* option with this option.

Notes The sdiff utility is similar to diff but its output may be easier to read. The diff --side-by-side option produces the same output as sdiff. See the "Examples" section and refer to the diff and sdiff man and info pages for more information.

Use the diff3 utility to compare three files.

Use cmp (page 634) to compare nontext (binary) files.

Discussion When you use diff without any options, it produces a series of lines containing Add (**a**), Delete (**d**), and Change (**c**) instructions. Each of these lines is followed by the lines from the file you need to add to, delete from, or change, respectively, to make the files the same. A *less than* symbol (**<**) precedes lines from *file1*. A *greater than* symbol (**>**) precedes lines from *file2*. The diff output appears in the format shown in Table V-12. A pair of line numbers separated by a comma represents a range of lines; a single line number represents a single line.

The diff utility assumes you will convert *file1* to *file2*. The line numbers to the left of each of the **a**, **c**, or **d** instructions always pertain to *file1*; the line numbers to the right of the instructions apply to *file2*. To convert *file2* to *file1*, run diff again, reversing the order of the arguments.

Table V-12   diff output

Instruction	Meaning (to change file1 to file2)
`line1 a line2,line3` `> lines from file2`	Append lines line2 through line3 from **file2** after line1 in **file1**.
`line1,line2 d line3` `< lines from file1`	Delete line1 through line2 from **file1**.

`line1,line2 c line3,line4`
`< lines from file1`
`---`
`> lines from file 2`
	Change line1 through line2 in **file1** to line3 through line 4 from **file2**.

Examples   The first example shows how diff displays the differences between two short, similar files:

```
$ cat m
aaaaa
bbbbb
ccccc
$ cat n
aaaaa
ccccc

$ diff m n
2d1
< bbbbb
```

The difference between files **m** and **n** is that the second line of file **m** (**bbbbb**) is missing from file **n**. The first line that diff displays (**2d1**) indicates that you need to delete the second line from *file1* (**m**) to make it the same as *file2* (**n**). The next line diff displays starts with a less than symbol (**<**), indicating that this line of text is from **file1**. In this example, you do not need this information—all you need to know is the line number so that you can delete the line.

The **--side-by-side** option and the sdiff utility, both with the output width set to 30 characters, display the same output. In the output, a less than symbol points to the extra line in file **m**; diff/sdiff leaves a blank line in file **n** where the extra line would go to make the files the same.

```
$ diff --side-by-side --width=30 m n
aaaaa           aaaaa
bbbbb         <
ccccc           ccccc

$ sdiff -w 30 m n
aaaaa           aaaaa
bbbbb         <
ccccc           ccccc
```

The next example uses the same **m** file and a new file, **p**, to show diff issuing an **a** (Append) instruction:

```
$ cat p
aaaaa
bbbbb
rrrrr
ccccc
$ diff m p
2a3
> rrrrr
```

In the preceding example, diff issues the instruction **2a3** to indicate you must append a line to file **m**, after line 2, to make it the same as file **p**. The second line diff displays indicates the line is from file **p** (the line begins with **>**, indicating **file2**). In this example, you need the information on this line; the appended line must contain the text **rrrrr**.

The next example uses file **m** again, this time with file **r**, to show how diff indicates a line that needs to be changed:

```
$ cat r
aaaaa
-q
ccccc

$ diff m r
2c2
< bbbbb
---
> -q
```

The difference between the two files appears in line 2: File **m** contains **bbbbb**, and file **r** contains **–q**. The diff utility displays **2c2** to indicate that you need to change line 2. After indicating a change is needed, diff shows you must change line 2 in file **m** (**bbbbb**) to line 2 in file **r** (**–q**) to make the files the same. The three hyphens indicate the end of the text in file **m** that needs to be changed and the beginning of the text in file **r** that is to replace it.

Comparing the same files using the side-by-side and width options (**–y** and **–W**) yields an easier-to-read result. The pipe symbol (**|**) indicates the line on one side must replace the line on the other side to make the files the same:

```
$ diff -y -W 30 m r
aaaaa           aaaaa
bbbbb         | -q
ccccc           ccccc
```

The next examples compare the two files **q** and **v**:

```
$ cat q         $ cat v
Monday          Monday
Tuesday         Wednesday
Wednesday       Thursday
Thursday        Thursday
Saturday        Friday
Sunday          Saturday
                Sundae
```

Running in side-by-side mode diff shows **Tuesday** is missing from file **v**, there is only one **Thursday** in file **q** (there are two in file **v**), and **Friday** is missing from file **q**. The last line is **Sunday** in file **q** and **Sundae** in file **v**: diff indicates these lines are different. You can change file **q** to be the same as file **v** by removing **Tuesday**, adding one **Thursday** and **Friday**, and substituting **Sundae** from file **v** for **Sunday** from file **q**. Alternatively, you can change file **v** to be the same as file **q** by adding **Tuesday**, removing one **Thursday** and **Friday**, and substituting **Sunday** from file **q** for **Sundae** from file **v**.

```
$ diff -y -W 30 q v
Monday          Monday
Tuesday       <
Wednesday       Wednesday
Thursday        Thursday
              > Thursday
              > Friday
Saturday        Saturday
Sunday        | Sundae
```

Context diff With the **--context** option (called a *context diff*), diff displays output that tells you how to turn the first file into the second file. The top two lines identify the files and show that **q** is represented by asterisks, whereas **v** is represented by hyphens. Following a row of asterisks that indicates the beginning of a hunk of text is a row of asterisks with the numbers **1,6** in the middle. This line indicates that the instructions in the first section tell you what to remove from or change in file **q**—namely, lines 1 through 6 (that is, all the lines of file **q**; in a longer file it would mark the first hunk). The hyphen on the second subsequent line indicates you need to remove the line with **Tuesday**. The line with an exclamation point indicates you need to replace the line with **Sunday** with the corresponding line from file **v**. The row of hyphens with the numbers **1,7** in the middle indicates that the next section tells you which lines from file **v**—lines 1 through 7—you need to add or change in file **q**. You need to add a second line with **Thursday** and a line with **Friday**, and you need to change **Sunday** in file **q** to **Sundae** (from file **v**).

```
$ diff --context q v
*** q   Mon Aug 24 18:26:45 2009
--- v   Mon Aug 24 18:27:55 2009
***************
*** 1,6 ****
  Monday
- Tuesday
  Wednesday
  Thursday
  Saturday
! Sunday
--- 1,7 ----
  Monday
  Wednesday
  Thursday
+ Thursday
+ Friday
  Saturday
! Sundae
```

diskutil **OS X**

Checks, modifies, and repairs local volumes

diskutil action [arguments]

The diskutil utility mounts, unmounts, and displays information about disks and partitions (volumes). It can also format and repair filesystems and divide a disk into partitions.

Arguments   The *action* specifies what diskutil is to do. Table V-13 lists common *actions* along with the argument each takes.

Table V-13   diskutil actions

Action	Argument	Description
eraseVolume	*type name device*	Reformats *device* using the format *type* and the label *name*. The *name* specifies the name of the volume; alphanumeric names are the easiest to work with.
		The filesystem *type* is typically HFS+, but can also be UFS or MS-DOS. You can specify additional options as part of the *type*. For example, a FAT32 filesystem (as used in Windows 98 and later) would have a type of MS-DOS FAT32. A journaled, case-sensitive, HFS+ filesystem would have a *type* of Case-sensitive Journaled HFS+.
info	*device*	Displays information about *device*. Does not require ownership of *device*.
list	*[device]*	Lists partitions on *device*. Without *device* lists partitions on all devices. Does not require ownership of *device*.
mount	*device*	Mounts *device*.
mountDisk	*device*	Mounts all devices on the disk containing *device*.
reformat	*device*	Reformats *device* using its current name and format.
repairVolume	*device*	Repairs the filesystem on *device*.
unmount	*device*	Unmounts *device*.
unmountDisk	*device*	Unmounts all devices on the disk containing *device*.
verifyVolume	*device*	Verifies the filesystem on *device*. Does not require ownership of *device*.

Notes   The diskutil utility provides access to the Disk Management framework, the support code used by the Disk Utility application. It allows some choices that are not supported from the graphical interface.

You must own *device*, or be working with **root** privileges, when you specify an *action* that modifies or changes the state of a volume.

fsck   The diskutil **verifyVolume** and **repairVolume** actions are analogous to the fsck utility on Linux systems. Under OS X, the fsck utility is deprecated except when the system is in single-user mode.

disktool   Some of the functions performed by diskutil were handled by disktool in the past.

Examples   The first example displays a list of disk devices and volumes available on the local system:

```
$ diskutil list
/dev/disk0
   #:                    type name              size       identifier
   0: Apple_partition_scheme                    *152.7 GB  disk0
   1:     Apple_partition_map                   31.5 KB    disk0s1
   2:            Apple_HFS Eva01                30.7 GB    disk0s3
   3:            Apple_HFS Users                121.7 GB   disk0s5
/dev/disk1
   #:                    type name              size       identifier
   0: Apple_partition_scheme                    *232.9 GB  disk1
   1:     Apple_partition_map                   31.5 KB    disk1s1
   2:          Apple_Driver43                   28.0 KB    disk1s2
   3:          Apple_Driver43                   28.0 KB    disk1s3
   4:       Apple_Driver_ATA                    28.0 KB    disk1s4
   5:       Apple_Driver_ATA                    28.0 KB    disk1s5
   6:         Apple_FWDriver                    256.0 KB   disk1s6
   7:      Apple_Driver_IOKit                   256.0 KB   disk1s7
   8:           Apple_Patches                   256.0 KB   disk1s8
   9:            Apple_HFS Spare                48.8 GB    disk1s9
  10:            Apple_HFS House                184.1 GB   disk1s10
```

The next example displays information about one of the mounted volumes:

```
$ diskutil info disk1s9
   Device Node:        /dev/disk1s9
   Device Identifier:  disk1s9
   Mount Point:        /Volumes/Spare
   Volume Name:        Spare

   File System:        HFS+
   Owners:             Enabled
   Partition Type:     Apple_HFS
   Bootable:           Is bootable
   Media Type:         Generic
```

```
Protocol:            FireWire
SMART Status:        Not Supported
UUID:                C77BB3DC-EFBB-30B0-B191-DE7E01D8A563

Total Size:          48.8 GB
Free Space:          48.8 GB

Read Only:           No
Ejectable:           Yes
```

The next example formats the partition at **/dev/disk1s8** as an HFS+ Extended (HFSX) filesystem and labels it **Spare2**. This command erases all data on the partition:

```
# diskutil eraseVolume 'Case-sensitive HFS+' Spare2 disk1s8
Started erase on disk disk1s10
Erasing
Mounting Disk
Finished erase on disk disk1s10
```

The final example shows the output of a successful **verifyVolume** operation:

```
$ diskutil verifyVolume disk1s9
Started verify/repair on volume disk1s9 Spare
Checking HFS Plus volume.
Checking Extents Overflow file.
Checking Catalog file.
Checking Catalog hierarchy.
Checking volume bitmap.
Checking volume information.
The volume Spare appears to be OK.
Mounting Disk
Verify/repair finished on volume disk1s9 Spare
```

ditto **OS X**

Copies files and creates and unpacks archives

ditto [options] source-file destination-file
ditto [options] source-file-list destination-directory
ditto –c [options] source-directory destination-archive
ditto –x [options] source-archive-list destination-directory

The ditto utility copies files and their ownership, timestamps, and other attributes, including extended attributes (page 928). It can copy to and from cpio and zip archive files, as well as copy ordinary files and directories.

Arguments   The *source-file* is the pathname of the file that ditto is to make a copy of. The *destination-file* is the pathname that ditto assigns to the resulting copy of the file.

The *source-file-list* specifies one or more pathnames of files and directories that ditto makes copies of. The *destination-directory* is the pathname of the directory that ditto copies the files and directories into. When you specify a *destination-directory*, ditto gives each of the copied files the same simple filename as its *source-file*.

The *source-directory* is a single directory that ditto copies into the *destination-archive*. The resulting archive holds copies of the contents of *source-directory*, but not the directory itself.

The *source-archive-list* specifies one or more pathnames of archives that ditto extracts into *destination-directory*.

Using a hyphen (–) in place of a filename or a directory name causes ditto to read from standard input or write to standard output instead of reading from or writing to that file or directory.

Options   You cannot use the –c and –x options together.

   –c   (**create archive**) Creates an archive file.

   ––help   Displays a help message.

   –k   (**pkzip**) Uses the zip format, instead of the default cpio (page 644) format, to create or extract archives. For morc information on zip, see the tip on page 62.

   ––norsrc   (**no resource**) Ignores extended attributes. This option causes ditto to copy only data forks (the default behavior under Mac OS X 10.3 and earlier).

   ––rsrc   (**resource**) Copies extended attributes, including resource forks (the default behavior under Mac OS X 10.4 and later). Also –rsrc and –rsrcFork.

   –V   (**very verbose**) Sends a line to standard error for each file, symbolic link, and device node ditto copies.

   –v   (**verbose**) Sends a line to standard error for each directory ditto copies.

−X   (**exclude**) Prevents ditto from searching directories in filesystems other than the filesystems that hold the files it was explicitly told to copy.

−x   (**extract archive**) Extracts files from an archive file.

−z   (**compress**) Uses gzip (page 724) or gunzip to compress or decompress cpio archives.

Notes   The ditto utility does not copy the locked attribute flag (page 931). The utility also does not copy ACLs.

By default ditto creates and reads *archives* (page 941) in the cpio (page 644) format.

The ditto utility cannot list the contents of archive files; it can only create or extract files from archives. Use pax or cpio to list the contents of cpio archives, and use unzip with the −l option to list the contents of zip files.

Examples   The following examples show three ways to back up a user's home directory, including extended attributes (except as mentioned in "Notes"), preserving timestamps and permissions. The first example copies Zach's home directory to the volume (filesystem) named **Backups**; the copy is a new directory named **zach.0228**:

```
$ ditto /Users/zach /Volumes/Backups/zach.0228
```

The next example copies Zach's home directory into a single cpio-format archive file on the volume named **Backups**:

```
$ ditto -c /Users/zach /Volumes/Backups/zach.0228.cpio
```

The next example copies Zach's home directory into a zip archive:

```
$ ditto -c -k /Users/zach /Volumes/Backups/zach.0228.zip
```

Each of the next three examples restores the corresponding backup archive into Zach's home directory, overwriting any files that are already there:

```
$ ditto /Volumes/Backups/zach.0228 /Users/zach
$ ditto -x /Volumes/Backups/zach.0228.cpio /Users/zach
$ ditto -x -k /Volumes/Backups/zach.0228.zip /Users/zach
```

The following example copies the **Scripts** directory to a directory named **Scripts-Backups** on the remote host **bravo**. It uses an argument of a hyphen in place of *source-directory* locally to write to standard output and in place of *destination-directory* on the remote system to read from standard input:

```
$ ditto -c Scripts - | ssh bravo ditto -x - ScriptsBackups
```

The final example copies the local startup disk (the root filesystem) to the volume named **Backups.root**. Because some of the files can be read only by **root**, the script must be run by a user with **root** privileges. The −X option keeps ditto from trying to copy other volumes (filesystems) that are mounted under /.

```
# ditto -X / /Volumes/Backups.root
```

dmesg

Displays kernel messages

dmesg [options]

The dmesg utility displays messages stored in the kernel ring buffer.

Options   −c   Clears the kernel ring buffer after running dmesg. `LINUX`

−M *core*
The *core* is the name of the (core dump) file to process (defaults to /dev/kmem). `OS X`

−N *kernel*
The *kernel* is the pathname of a kernel file (defaults to **/mach**). If you are displaying information about a core dump, *kernel* should be the kernel that was running at the time the core file was created. `OS X`

Discussion   When the system boots, the kernel fills its ring buffer with messages regarding hardware and module initialization. Messages in the kernel ring buffer are often useful for diagnosing system problems.

Notes   Under Mac OS X, you must run this utility while working with **root** privileges.

As a ring buffer, the kernel message buffer keeps the most recent messages it receives, discarding the oldest messages once it fills up. To save a list of kernel boot messages, give the following command immediately after booting the system and logging in:

```
$ dmesg > dmesg.boot
```

This command saves the kernel messages in the **dmesg.boot** file. This list can be educational and quite useful when you are having a problem with the boot process.

Under most Linux systems, after the system boots, the system records much of the same information as dmesg displays in **/var/log/messages** or a similar file.

Examples   The following command displays kernel messages in the ring buffer with the string **serial** in them, regardless of case:

```
$ dmesg | grep -i serial
Apple16X50PCI2: Identified 4 Serial channels at PCI SLOT-2 Bus=5 Dev=2 Func=0
```

dscl *OS X*

Displays and manages Directory Service information

dscl [options] [datasource [command]]

The dscl (Directory Service command line) utility enables you to work with Directory Service directory nodes. When you call dscl without arguments, it runs interactively.

Arguments   The *datasource* is a node name or a Mac OS X Server host specified by a hostname or IP address. A period (.) specifies the local domain.

Options   **–p**   (**prompt**) Prompts for a password as needed.

–q   (**quiet**) Does not prompt.

–u *user*
Authenticates as *user*.

Commands   Refer to the "Notes" section for definitions of some of the terms used here.

The hyphen (–) before a command is optional.

–list *path [key]*   (also **–ls**) Lists subdirectories in *path*, one per line. If you specify *key*, this command lists subdirectories that match *key*.

–read *[path [key]]*
(also **–cat** and **.**) Displays a directory, one property per line.

–readall *[path [key]]*
Displays properties with a given key.

–search *path key value*
Displays properties where *key* matches *value*.

Notes   When discussing Directory Service, the term *directory* refers to a collection of data (a database), not to a filesystem directory. Each directory holds one or more properties. Each property comprises a key/value pair, where there may be more than one value for a given key. In general, dscl displays a property with the key first, followed by a colon, and then the value. If there is more than one value, the values are separated by SPACEs. If a value contains SPACEs, dscl displays the value on the line following the key.

Under Mac OS X and Mac OS X Server, Open Directory stores information for the local system in key/value-formatted XML files in the **/var/db/dslocal** directory hierarchy.

The dscl utility is the command-line equivalent of NetInfo Manager (available on versions of Mac OS X prior to 10.5) or of Workgroup Manager on Mac OS X Server.

Examples   The dscl **–list** command displays a list of top-level directories when you specify a path of /:

```
$ dscl . -list /
AFPServer
AFPUserAliases
Aliases
AppleMetaRecord
Augments
Automount
...
SharePoints
SMBServer
Users
WebServer
```

The period as the first argument to dscl specifies the local domain as the data source. The next command displays a list of **Users** directories:

```
$ dscl . -list /Users
_amavisd
_appowner
_appserver
_ard
...
_www
_xgridagent
_xgridcontroller
daemon
max
nobody
root
```

You can use the dscl **–read** command to display information about a specific user:

```
$ dscl . -read /Users/root
AppleMetaNodeLocation: /Local/Default
GeneratedUID: FFFFEEEE-DDDD-CCCC-BBBB-AAAA00000000
NFSHomeDirectory: /var/root
Password: *
PrimaryGroupID: 0
RealName:
 System Administrator
RecordName: root
RecordType: dsRecTypeStandard:Users
UniqueID: 0
UserShell: /bin/sh
```

The following dscl **–readall** command lists all usernames and user IDs on the local system. The command looks for the **RecordName** and **UniqueID** keys in the **/Users** directory and displays the associated values. The dscl utility separates multiple values with SPACEs. See page 926 for an example of a shell script that calls dscl with the **–readall** command.

```
$ dscl . -readall /Users RecordName UniqueID
RecordName: _amavisd amavisd
UniqueID: 83
-
RecordName: _appowner appowner
UniqueID: 87
-
...
RecordName: daemon
UniqueID: 1
-
RecordName: sam
UniqueID: 501
-
RecordName: nobody
UniqueID: -2
-
RecordName: root
UniqueID: 0
```

The following example uses the dscl **–search** command to display all properties where the key **RecordName** equals **sam**:

```
$ dscl . -search / RecordName sam
Users/sam              RecordName = (
    sam
)
```

du

Displays information on disk usage by directory hierarchy and/or file

du [options] [path-list]

The du (disk usage) utility reports how much disk space is occupied by a directory hierarchy or a file. By default du displays the number of 1,024-byte blocks occupied by the directory hierarchy or file.

Arguments Without any arguments, du displays information about the working directory and its subdirectories. The *path-list* specifies the directories and files you want information on.

Options Options preceded by a double hyphen (––) work under Linux only. Except as noted, options named with a single letter and preceded by a single hyphen work under Linux and OS X.

Without any options, du displays the total storage used for each argument in *path-list*. For directories, du displays this total after recursively listing the totals for each subdirectory.

––all   **–a**   Displays the space used by all ordinary files along with the total for each directory.

––block-size=*sz*   **–B** *sz*

The *sz* argument specifies the units the report uses. It is a multiplicative suffix from Table V-1 on page 603. See also the **–H** (**––si**) and **–h** (**––human-readable**) options. `LINUX`

––total   **–c**   Displays a grand total at the end of the output.

––dereference-args

–D   (**partial dereference**) For each file that is a symbolic link, reports on the file the link points to, not the symbolic link itself. This option affects files specified on the command line; it does not affect files found while descending a directory hierarchy. This option treats files that are not symbolic links normally. `LINUX`

–d *depth*

Displays information for subdirectories to a level of *depth* directories. `OS X`

––si   **–H**   (**human readable**) Displays sizes in K (kilobyte), M (megabyte), and G (gigabyte) blocks, as appropriate. Uses powers of 1,000. In the future, the **–H** option will change to be the equivalent of **–D**. `LINUX`

–H   (**partial dereference**) For each file that is a symbolic link, reports on the file the link points to, not the symbolic link itself. This option affects files specified on the command line; it does not affect files found while descending a directory hierarchy. This option treats files that are not symbolic links normally. See page 623 for an example of the use of the **–H** versus **–L** options. `OS X`

--human-readable

      –h Displays sizes in K (kilobyte), M (megabyte), and G (gigabyte) blocks, as appropriate. Uses powers of 1,024.

      –k Displays sizes in 1-kilobyte blocks.

--dereference **–L** For each file that is a symbolic link, reports on the file the link points to, not the symbolic link itself. This option affects all files and treats files that are not symbolic links normally. The default is **–P** (**--no-dereference**). See page 623 for an example of the use of the **–H** versus **–L** options.

      –m Displays sizes in 1-megabyte blocks.

--no-dereference **–P** For each file that is a symbolic link, reports on the symbolic link, not the file the link points to. This option affects all files and treats files that are not symbolic links normally. This behavior is the default. See page 625 for an example of the use of the **–P** option.

--summarize **–s** Displays only the total size for each directory or file you specify on the command line; subdirectory totals are not displayed.

--one-file-system **–x** Reports only on files and directories on the same filesystem as that of the argument being processed.

Examples

In the first example, du displays size information about subdirectories in the working directory. The last line contains the grand total for the working directory and its subdirectories.

```
$ du
26       ./Postscript
4        ./RCS
47       ./XIcon
4        ./Printer/RCS
12       ./Printer
105      .
```

The total (105) is the number of blocks occupied by all plain files and directories under the working directory. All files are counted, even though du displays only the sizes of directories.

If you do not have read permission for a file or directory that du encounters, du sends a warning to standard error and skips that file or directory. Next, using the **–s** (summarize) option, du displays the total for each of the directories in **/usr** but does not display information for subdirectories:

```
$ du -s /usr/*
4        /usr/X11R6
260292   /usr/bin
10052    /usr/games
7772     /usr/include
1720468  /usr/lib
105240   /usr/lib32
0        /usr/lib64
```

```
du: cannot read directory `/usr/local/lost+found': Permission denied
...
130696  /usr/src
```

Add to the previous example the **–c** (total) option and du displays the same listing with a grand total at the end:

```
$ du -sc /usr/*
4         /usr/X11R6
260292    /usr/bin
...
130696    /usr/src
3931436 total
```

The following example uses the **–s** (summarize), **–h** (human-readable), and **–c** (total) options:

```
$ du -shc /usr/*
4.0K      /usr/X11R6
255M      /usr/bin
9.9M      /usr/games
7.6M      /usr/include
1.7G      /usr/lib
103M      /usr/lib32
...
128M      /usr/src
3.8G      total
```

The final example displays, in human-readable format, the total size of all files the user can read in the **/usr** filesystem. Redirecting standard error to **/dev/null** discards all warnings about files and directories that are unreadable.

```
$ du -hs /usr 2>/dev/null
3.8G      /usr
```

echo

Displays a message

echo [options] message

The echo utility copies its arguments, followed by a NEWLINE, to standard output. Both the Bourne Again and TC Shells have their own echo builtin that works similarly to the echo utility.

Arguments   The *message* consists of one or more arguments, which can include quoted strings, ambiguous file references, and shell variables. A SPACE separates each argument from the next. The shell recognizes unquoted special characters in the arguments. For example, the shell expands an asterisk into a list of filenames in the working directory.

Options   You can configure the tcsh echo builtin to treat backslash escape sequences and the –n option in different ways. Refer to **echo_style** in the tcsh man page. The typical tcsh configuration recognizes the –n option, enables backslash escape sequences, and ignores the –E and –e options.

   –E   Suppresses the interpretation of backslash escape sequences such as \n. Available with the bash builtin version of echo only.

   –e   Enables the interpretation of backslash escape sequences such as \n. Available with the bash builtin version of echo only.

   ––help   Gives a short summary of how to use echo. The summary includes a list of the backslash escape sequences interpreted by echo. This option works only with the echo utility; it does not work with the echo builtins. **LINUX**

   –n   Suppresses the NEWLINE terminating the *message*.

Notes   Suppressing the interpretation of backslash escape sequences is the default behavior of the bash builtin version of echo and of the echo utility.

   You can use echo to send messages to the screen from a shell script. See page 138 for a discussion of how to use echo to display filenames using wildcard characters.

   The echo utility and builtins provide an escape notation to represent certain non-printing characters in *message* (Table V-14). You must use the –e option for these backslash escape sequences to work with the echo utility and the bash echo builtin. Typically you do not need the –e option with the tcsh echo builtin.

Table V-14   Backslash escape sequences

Sequence	Meaning
\a	Bell
\c	Suppress trailing NEWLINE

Table V-14   Backslash escape sequences (continued)

Sequence	Meaning
\n	NEWLINE
\t	HORIZONTAL TAB
\v	VERTICAL TAB
\\	BACKSLASH

Examples   Following are some echo commands. These commands will work with the echo utility (**/bin/echo**) and the bash and tcsh echo builtins, except for the last, which may not need the –e option under tcsh.

```
$ echo "This command displays a string."
This command displays a string.
$ echo -n "This displayed string is not followed by a NEWLINE."
This displayed string is not followed by a NEWLINE.$ echo hi
hi
$ echo -e "This message contains\v a vertical tab."
This message contains
                      a vertical tab.
$
```

The following examples contain messages with the backslash escape sequence \c. In the first example, the shell processes the arguments before calling echo. When the shell sees the \c, it replaces the \c with the character c. The next three examples show how to quote the \c so that the shell passes it to echo, which then does not append a NEWLINE to the end of the message. The first four examples are run under bash and require the –e option. The final example runs under tcsh, which may not need this option.

```
$ echo -e There is a newline after this line.\c
There is a newline after this line.c

$ echo -e 'There is no newline after this line.\c'
There is no newline after this line.$

$ echo -e "There is no newline after this line.\c"
There is no newline after this line.$

$ echo -e There is no newline after this line.\\c
There is no newline after this line.$

$ tcsh
tcsh $ echo -e 'There is no newline after this line.\c'
There is no newline after this line.$
```

You can use the –n option in place of –e and \c.

expr

Evaluates an expression

*expr **expression***

The expr utility evaluates an expression and sends the result to standard output. It evaluates character strings that represent either numeric or nonnumeric values. Operators are used with the strings to form expressions.

Arguments The *expression* is composed of strings interspersed with operators. Each string and operator constitute a distinct argument that you must separate from other arguments with a SPACE. You must quote operators that have special meanings to the shell (for example, the multiplication operator, **∗**).

The following list of expr operators is given in order of decreasing precedence. Each operator within a group of operators has the same precedence. You can change the order of evaluation by using parentheses.

: (**comparison**) Compares two strings, starting with the first character in each string and ending with the last character in the second string. The second string is a regular expression with an implied caret (**^**) as its first character. If expr finds a match, it displays the number of characters in the second string. If expr does not find a match, it displays a zero.

∗ (**multiplication**)
/ (**division**)
% (**remainder**)
Work only on strings that contain the numerals 0 through 9 and optionally a leading minus sign. Convert strings to integer numbers, perform the specified arithmetic operation on numbers, and convert the result back to a string before sending it to standard output.

+ (**addition**)
– (**subtraction**)
Function in the same manner as the preceding group of operators.

< (**less than**)
<= (**less than or equal to**)
= *or* == (**equal to**)
!= (**not equal to**)
>= (**greater than or equal to**)
> (**greater than**)
Relational operators work on both numeric and nonnumeric arguments. If one or both of the arguments are nonnumeric, the comparison is nonnumeric, using the machine collating sequence (typically ASCII). If both arguments are

numeric, the comparison is numeric. The expr utility displays a 1 (one) if the comparison is *true* and a 0 (zero) if it is *false*.

    &   (**AND**) Evaluates both of its arguments. If neither is 0 or a null string, expr displays the value of the first argument. Otherwise, it displays a 0 (zero). You must quote this operator.

    | (**OR**) Evaluates the first argument. If it is neither 0 nor a null string, expr displays the value of the first argument. Otherwise, it displays the value of the second argument. You must quote this operator.

Notes

The expr utility returns an exit status of 0 (zero) if the expression evaluates to anything other than a null string or the number 0, a status of 1 if the expression is null or 0, and a status of 2 if the expression is invalid.

Although expr and this discussion distinguish between numeric and nonnumeric arguments, all arguments to expr are nonnumeric (character strings). When applicable, expr attempts to convert an argument to a number (for example, when using the **+** operator). If a string contains characters other than 0 through 9 and optionally a leading minus sign, expr cannot convert it. Specifically, if a string contains a plus sign or a decimal point, expr considers it to be nonnumeric. If both arguments are numeric, the comparison is numeric. If one is nonnumeric, the comparison is lexicographic.

Examples

In the following examples, expr evaluates constants. You can also use expr to evaluate variables in a shell script. The fourth command displays an error message because of the illegal decimal point in **5.3**:

```
$ expr 17 + 40
57
$ expr 10 - 24
-14
$ expr -17 + 20
3
$ expr 5.3 + 4
expr: non-numeric argument
```

The multiplication (*****), division (**/**), and remainder (**%**) operators provide additional arithmetic power. You must quote the multiplication operator (precede it with a backslash) so that the shell will not treat it as a special character (an ambiguous file reference). You cannot put quotation marks around the entire expression because each string and operator must be a separate argument.

```
$ expr 5 \* 4
20
$ expr 21 / 7
3
$ expr 23 % 7
2
```

The next two examples show how parentheses change the order of evaluation. You must quote each parenthesis and surround the backslash/parenthesis combination with SPACEs:

```
$ expr 2 \* 3 + 4
10
$ expr 2 \* \( 3 + 4 \)
14
```

You can use relational operators to determine the relationship between numeric or nonnumeric arguments. The following commands compare two strings to see if they are equal; expr displays a 0 when the relationship is *false* and a 1 when it is *true*.

```
$ expr fred == sam
0
$ expr sam == sam
1
```

In the following examples, the relational operators, which must be quoted, establish order between numeric or nonnumeric arguments. Again, if a relationship is *true*, expr displays a 1.

```
$ expr fred \> sam
0
$ expr fred \< sam
1
$ expr 5 \< 7
1
```

The next command compares 5 with **m**. When one of the arguments expr is comparing with a relational operator is nonnumeric, expr considers the other to be nonnumeric. In this case, because **m** is nonnumeric, expr treats 5 as a nonnumeric argument. The comparison is between the ASCII (on many systems) values of **m** and 5. The ASCII value of **m** is 109 and that of 5 is 53, so expr evaluates the relationship as *true*.

```
$ expr 5 \< m
1
```

In the next example, the matching operator determines that the four characters in the second string match the first four characters in the first string. The expr utility displays the number of matching characters (4).

```
$ expr abcdefghijkl : abcd
4
```

The & operator displays a 0 if one or both of its arguments are 0 or a null string; otherwise, it displays the first argument:

```
$ expr '' \& book
0

$ expr magazine \& book
magazine
```

```
$ expr 5 \& 0
0

$ expr 5 \& 6
5
```

The I operator displays the first argument if it is not 0 or a null string; otherwise, it displays the second argument:

```
$ expr '' \| book
book

$ expr magazine \| book
magazine

$ expr 5 \| 0
5

$ expr 0 \| 5
5

$ expr 5 \| 6
5
```

file

Displays the classification of a file

file [option] file-list

The file utility classifies files according to their contents.

Arguments   The *file-list* is a list of the pathnames of one or more files that file classifies. You can specify any kind of file, including ordinary, directory, and special files, in the *file-list*.

Options

The Mac OS X version of file accepts long options

tip   Options for file preceded by a double hyphen (−−) work under Mac OS X as well as under Linux.

−−files-from=*file*   **−f** *file*
Takes the names of files to be examined from *file* rather than from *file-list* on the command line. The names of the files must be listed one per line in *file*.

−−no-dereference   **−h**   For each file that is a symbolic link, reports on the symbolic link, not the file the link points to. This option treats files that are not symbolic links normally. This behavior is the default on systems where the environment variable **POSIXLY_CORRECT** is not defined (typical).

−−help   Displays a help message.

−−mime   **−I**   Displays *MIME* (page 966) type strings. **OS X**

−−mime   **−i**   Displays *MIME* (page 966) type strings. **LINUX**

−−dereference   **−L**   For each file that is a symbolic link, reports on the file the link points to, not the symbolic link itself. This option treats files that are not symbolic links normally. This behavior is the default on systems where the environment variable **POSIXLY_CORRECT** is defined.

−−uncompress   **−z**   (**zip**) Attempts to classify files within a compressed file.

Notes   The file utility can classify more than 5,000 file types. Some of the more common file types found on Linux systems, as displayed by file, follow:

```
archive
ascii text
c program text
commands text
core file
cpio archive
data
```

```
directory
ELF 32-bit LSB executable
empty
English text
executable
```

The file utility uses a maximum of three tests in its attempt to classify a file: file-system, magic number, and language tests. When file identifies the type of a file, it ceases testing. The filesystem test examines the return from a **stat**() system call to see whether the file is empty or a special file. The *magic number* (page 964) test looks for data in particular fixed formats near the beginning of the file. The language test, if needed, determines whether the file is a text file, which encoding it uses, and which language it is written in. Refer to the file man page for a more detailed description of how file works. The results of file are not always correct.

Examples   Some examples of file identification follow:

```
/etc/Muttrc:              ASCII English text
/etc/Muttrc.d:            directory
/etc/adjtime:             ASCII text
/etc/aliases.db:          Berkeley DB (Hash, version 9, native byte-order)
/etc/at.deny:             writable, regular file, no read permission
/etc/bash_completion:     ASCII Pascal program text
/etc/blkid.tab.old:       Non-ISO extended-ASCII text, with CR, LF line terminators
/etc/brltty.conf:         UTF-8 Unicode C++ program text
/etc/chatscripts:         setgid directory
/etc/magic:               magic text file for file(1) cmd
/etc/motd:                symbolic link to `/var/run/motd'
/etc/qemu-ifup:           POSIX shell script text executable
/usr/bin/4xml:            a python script text executable
/usr/bin/Xorg:            ELF 64-bit LSB executable, x86-64, version 1 (SYSV), for GNU/Linux
2.6.8, dynamically linked (uses shared libs), stripped
/usr/bin/debconf:         perl script text executable
/usr/bin/locate:          symbolic link to `/etc/alternatives/locate'
/usr/share/man/man7/hier.7.gz: gzip compressed data, was "hier.7", from Unix, last
modified: Thu Jan 31 03:06:00 2008, max compression
```

find

Finds files based on criteria

find [directory-list] [option] [expression]

The find utility selects files that are located in specified directory hierarchies and that meet specified criteria.

Arguments   The *directory-list* specifies the directory hierarchies that find is to search. When you do not specify a *directory-list*, find searches the working directory hierarchy.

The *option* controls whether find dereferences symbolic links as it descends directory hierarchies. By default find does not dereference symbolic links (it works with the symbolic link, not the file the link points to). Under Mac OS X, you can use the **–x** option to prevent find from searching directories in filesystems other than those specified in *directory-list*. Under Linux, the **–xdev** criterion performs the same function.

The *expression* contains criteria, as described in the "Criteria" section. The find utility tests each of the files in each of the directories in the *directory-list* to see whether it meets the criteria described by the *expression*. When you do not specify an *expression*, the *expression* defaults to **–print**.

A SPACE separating two criteria is a Boolean AND operator: The file must meet *both* criteria to be selected. A **–or** or **–o** separating the criteria is a Boolean OR operator: The file must meet one or the other (or both) of the criteria to be selected.

You can negate any criterion by preceding it with an exclamation point. The find utility evaluates criteria from left to right unless you group them using parentheses.

Within the *expression* you must quote special characters so the shell does not interpret them but rather passes them to find. Special characters that are frequently used with find include parentheses, brackets, question marks, and asterisks.

Each element within the *expression* is a separate argument. You must separate arguments from each other with SPACES. A SPACE must appear on both sides of each parenthesis, exclamation point, criterion, or other element.

Options   **–H**   (partial dereference) For each file that is a symbolic link, works with the file the link points to, not the symbolic link itself. This option affects files specified on the command line; it does not affect files found while descending a directory hierarchy. This option treats files that are not symbolic links normally. See page 623 for an example of the use of the **–H** versus **–L** options.

–L   (dereference) For each file that is a symbolic link, works with the file the link points to, not the symbolic link itself. This option affects all files and treats files that are not symbolic links normally. See page 623 for an example of the use of the –H versus –L options.

–P (**no dereference**) For each file that is a symbolic link, works with the symbolic link, not the file the link points to. This option affects all files and treats files that are not symbolic links normally. This behavior is the default. See page 625 for an example of the use of the –P option.

–x Causes find not to search directories in filesystems other than the one(s) specified by *directory-list*. Under Linux, use the –**xdev** criterion. (OS X)

Criteria

You can use the following criteria within the *expression*. As used in this list, ±*n* is a decimal integer that can be expressed as +*n* (more than *n*), –*n* (fewer than *n*), or *n* (exactly *n*).

–anewer *filename*
> (**accessed newer**) The file being evaluated meets this criterion if it was accessed more recently than *filename*.

–atime ±*n*
> (**access time**) The file being evaluated meets this criterion if it was last accessed ±*n* days ago. When you use this option, find changes the access times of directories it searches.

–depth
> The file being evaluated always meets this action criterion. It causes find to take action on entries in a directory before it acts on the directory itself. When you use find to send files to the cpio utility, the –**depth** criterion enables cpio to preserve the modification times of directories when you restore files (assuming you use the ––**preserve–modification–time** option to cpio). See the "Discussion" and "Examples" sections under cpio on page 647.

–exec *command* \;
> The file being evaluated meets this action criterion if the *command* returns a 0 (zero [*true*]) exit status. You must terminate the *command* with a quoted semicolon. A pair of braces ({}) within the *command* represents the name of the file being evaluated. You can use the –**exec** action criterion at the end of a group of other criteria to execute the *command* if the preceding criteria are met. Refer to the following "Discussion" section for more information. See the section on xargs on page 881 for a more efficient way of doing what this option does.

–group *name*
> The file being evaluated meets this criterion if it is associated with the group named *name*. You can use a numeric group ID in place of *name*.

–inum *n*
> The file being evaluated meets this criterion if its inode number is *n*.

–links ±*n*

The file being evaluated meets this criterion if it has **±***n* links.

–mtime ±*n*

(**modify time**) The file being evaluated meets this criterion if it was last modified **±***n* days ago.

–name *filename*

The file being evaluated meets this criterion if the pattern *filename* matches its name. The *filename* can include wildcard characters (*****, **?**, and **[]**) but these characters must be quoted.

–newer *filename*

The file being evaluated meets this criterion if it was modified more recently than *filename.*

–nogroup

The file being evaluated meets this criterion if it does not belong to a group known on the local system.

–nouser

The file being evaluated meets this criterion if it does not belong to a user known on the local system.

–ok *command* **\;**

This action criterion is the same as **–exec** except it displays each *command* to be executed enclosed in angle brackets as a prompt and executes the *command* only if it receives a response that starts with a **y** or **Y** from standard input.

–perm [±]*mode*

The file being evaluated meets this criterion if it has the access permissions given by *mode*. If *mode* is preceded by a minus sign (**–**), the file access permissions must include all the bits in *mode*. For example, if *mode* is 644, a file with 755 permissions will meet this criterion. If *mode* is preceded by a plus sign (**+**), the file access permissions must include at least one of the bits in *mode*. If no plus or minus sign precedes *mode,* the mode of the file must exactly match *mode*. You may use either a symbolic or octal representation for *mode* (see chmod on page 626).

–print

The file being evaluated always meets this action criterion. When evaluation of the *expression* reaches this criterion, find displays the pathname of the file it is evaluating. If **–print** is the only criterion in the *expression,* find displays the names of all files in the *directory-list*. If this criterion appears with other criteria, find displays the name only if the preceding criteria are met. If no action criteria appear in the *expression,* **–print** is assumed. (Refer to the following "Discussion" and "Notes" sections.)

–size ±*n*[c|k|M|G]

The file being evaluated meets this criterion if it is the size specified by **±*n***, measured in 512-byte blocks. Follow *n* with the letter **c** to measure files in characters, **k** to measure files in kilobytes, **M** to measure files in megabytes, or **G** to measure files in gigabytes.

–type *filetype*

The file being evaluated meets this criterion if its file type is specified by *filetype*. Select a *filetype* from the following list:

b	Block special file
c	Character special file
d	Directory file
f	Ordinary file
l	Symbolic link
p	FIFO (named pipe)
s	Socket

–user *name*

The file being evaluated meets this criterion if it belongs to the user with the username *name*. You can use a numeric user ID in place of *name*.

–xdev

The file being evaluated always meets this action criterion. It prevents find from searching directories in filesystems other than the one specified by *directory-list*. Also **–mount**. Under Mac OS X, use the **–x** option. `LINUX`

Discussion Assume **x** and **y** are criteria. The following command line never tests whether the file meets criterion **y** if it does not meet criterion **x**. Because the criteria are separated by a SPACE (the Boolean AND operator), once find determines that criterion **x** is not met, the file cannot meet the criteria so find does not continue testing. You can read the expression as "(test to see whether) the file meets criterion **x** *and* [SPACE means *and*] criterion **y**."

```
$ find dir x y
```

The next command line tests the file against criterion **y** if criterion **x** is not met. The file can still meet the criteria so find continues the evaluation. You can read the expression as "(test to see whether) the file meets criterion **x** *or* criterion **y**." If the file meets criterion **x**, find does not evaluate criterion **y** as there is no need to do so.

```
$ find dir x -or y
```

Action criteria Certain "criteria" do not select files but rather cause find to take action. The action is triggered when find evaluates one of these *action criteria*. Therefore, the position of an action criterion on the command line—not the result of its evaluation—determines whether find takes the action.

The **–print** action criterion causes find to display the pathname of the file it is testing. The following command line displays the names of *all* files in the **dir** directory (and all its subdirectories), regardless of whether they meet the criterion **x**:

```
$ find dir -print x
```

The following command line displays only the names of the files in the **dir** directory that meet criterion **x**:

```
$ find dir x -print
```

This use of **–print** after the testing criteria is the default action criterion. The following command line generates the same output as the previous one:

```
$ find dir x
```

Notes   You can use the **–a** operator between criteria to improve clarity. This operator is a Boolean AND operator, just as the SPACE is.

You may want to consider using pax (page 786) in place of cpio.

Examples   The simplest find command has no arguments and lists the files in the working directory and all subdirectories:

```
$ find
...
```

The following command finds the files in the working directory and subdirectories that have filenames beginning with **a**. The command uses a period to designate the working directory. To prevent the shell from interpreting the **a*** as an ambiguous file reference, it is enclosed within single quotation marks.

```
$ find . -name 'a*'
```

The **–print** criterion is implicit in the preceding command. If you omit the *directory-list* argument, find searches the working directory. The next command performs the same function as the preceding one without explicitly specifying the working directory:

```
$ find -name 'a*'
```

The next command sends a list of selected filenames to the cpio utility, which writes them to the device mounted on **/dev/sde1**. The first part of the command line ends with a pipe symbol, so the shell expects another command to follow and displays a secondary prompt (**>**) before accepting the rest of the command line. You can read this find command as "find, in the root directory and all subdirectories (**/**), ordinary files (**–type f**) that have been modified within the past day (**–mtime –1**), with the exception of files whose names are suffixed with .o (**! –name '*.o'**)." (An object file carries a .o suffix and usually does not need to be preserved because it can be re-created from the corresponding source file.)

```
$ find / -type f -mtime -1 ! -name '*.o' -print |
> cpio -oB > /dev/sde1
```

The following command finds, displays the filenames of, and deletes the files named **core** or **junk** in the working directory and its subdirectories:

```
$ find . \( -name core -o -name junk \) -print -exec rm {} \;
...
```

The parentheses and the semicolon following –**exec** are quoted so the shell does not treat them as special characters. SPACEs separate the quoted parentheses from other elements on the command line. Read this find command as "find, in the working directory and subdirectories (.), files named **core** (–**name core**) *or* (–**o**) **junk** (–**name junk**) [if a file meets these criteria, continue] *and* (SPACE) print the name of the file (–**print**) *and* (SPACE) delete the file (–**exec rm {}**)."

The following shell script uses find in conjunction with grep to identify files that contain a particular string. This script enables you to look for a file when you remember its contents but cannot remember its filename. The **finder** script locates files in the working directory and subdirectories that contain the string specified on the command line. The –**type f** criterion causes find to pass to grep only the names of ordinary files, not directory files.

```
$ cat finder
find . -type f -exec grep -l "$1" {} \;
$ finder "Executive Meeting"
./january/memo.0102
./april/memo.0415
```

When called with the string **Executive Meeting, finder** locates two files containing that string: **./january/memo.0102** and **./april/memo.0415**. The period (.) in the pathnames represents the working directory; **january** and **april** are subdirectories of the working directory. The **grep** utility with the ––**recursive** option performs the same function as the **finder** script.

The next command looks in two user directories for files that are larger than 100 blocks (–**size +100**) and have been accessed only more than five days ago—that is, files that have not been accessed within the past five days (–**atime +5**). This find command then asks whether you want to delete the file (–**ok rm {}**). You must respond to each query with **y** (for *yes*) or **n** (for *no*). The rm command works only if you have write and execute access permissions to the directory.

```
$ find /home/max /home/hls -size +100 -atime +5 -ok rm {} \;
< rm ... /home/max/notes >? y
< rm ... /home/max/letter >? n
...
```

In the next example, **/home/max/memos** is a symbolic link to Sam's directory named **/home/sam/memos**. When you use the –**follow** option with find, the symbolic link is followed, and that directory is searched.

```
$ ls -l /home/max
lrwxrwxrwx  1 max    pubs     17 Aug 19 17:07 memos -> /home/sam/memos
-rw-r--r--  1 max    pubs   5119 Aug 19 17:08 report

$ find /home/max -print
/home/max
/home/max/memos
/home/max/report
/home/max/.profile

$ find /home/max -follow -print
/home/max
/home/max/memos
/home/max/memos/memo.817
/home/max/memos/memo.710
/home/max/report
/home/max/.profile
```

finger

Displays information about users

finger [options] [user-list]

The finger utility displays the usernames of users, together with their full names, terminal device numbers, times they logged in, and other information. The *options* control how much information finger displays, and the *user-list* specifies which users finger displays information about. The finger utility can retrieve information from both local and remote systems.

Arguments   Without any arguments, finger provides a short (–s) report on users who are logged in on the local system. When you specify a *user-list*, finger provides a long (–l) report on each user in the *user-list*. Names in the *user-list* are not case sensitive.

If the name includes an at sign (@), the finger utility interprets the name following the @ as the name of a remote host to contact over the network. If a username appears in front of the @ sign, finger provides information about that user on the remote system.

Options   –l   (**long**) Displays detailed information (the default display when *user-list* is specified).

–m   (**match**) If a *user-list* is specified, displays entries only for those users whose username matches one of the names in *user-list*. Without this option the *user-list* names match usernames and full names.

–p   (**no plan, project, or pgpkey**) Does not display the contents of **.plan**, **.project**, and **.pgpkey** files for users. Because these files may contain backslash escape sequences that can change the behavior of the screen, you may not wish to view them. Normally the long listing displays the contents of these files if they exist in the user's home directory.

–s   (**short**) Provides a short report for each user (the default display when *user-list* is not specified).

Discussion   The long report provided by the finger utility includes the user's username, full name, home directory location, and login shell, plus information about when the user last logged in and how long it has been since the user last typed on the keyboard and read her email. After extracting this information from system files, finger displays the contents of the ~/**.plan**, ~/**.project**, and ~/**.pgpkey** files in the user's home directory. It is up to each user to create and maintain these files, which usually provide more information about the user (such as telephone number, postal mail address, schedule, interests, and PGP key).

The short report generated by finger is similar to that provided by the w utility; it includes the user's username, his full name, the device number of the user's terminal, the amount of time that has elapsed since the user last typed on the terminal keyboard, the time the user logged in, and the location of the user's terminal. If the user logged in over the network, finger displays the name of the remote system.

Notes   Not all Linux distributions install finger by default.

When you specify a network address, the finger utility queries a standard network service that runs on the remote system. Although this service is supplied with most Linux systems, some administrators choose not to run it (so as to minimize the load on their systems, eliminate possible security risks, or simply maintain privacy). If you try to use finger to get information on someone at such a site, the result may be an error message or nothing at all. The remote system determines how much information to share with the local system and in which format. As a result the report displayed for any given system may differ from the examples shown here. See also "finger: Lists Users on the System" on page 68.

A file named ~/.nofinger causes finger to deny the existence of the person whose home directory it appears in. For this subterfuge to work, the finger query must originate from a system other than the local host and the **fingerd** daemon must be able to see the .nofinger file (generally the home directory must have its execute bit for other users set).

Examples   The first example displays information on the users logged in on the local system:

```
$ finger
Login    Name             Tty     Idle Login Time  Office  Office Phone
max      Max Wild         tty1    13:29 Jun 25 21:03
hls      Helen Simpson    *pts/1  13:29 Jun 25 21:02 (:0)
sam      Sam the Great    pts/2         Jun 26 07:47 (bravo.example.com)
```

The asterisk (*) in front of the name of Helen's terminal (TTY) line indicates she has blocked others from sending messages directly to her terminal (see mesg on page 71). A long report displays the string **messages off** for users who have disabled messages.

The next two examples cause finger to contact the remote system named **kudos** over the network for information:

```
$ finger @kudos
[kudos]
Login    Name           Tty     Idle Login Time  Office  Office Phone
max      Max Wild       tty1    23:15 Jun 25 11:22
roy      Roy Wong       pts/2         Jun 25 11:22
```

```
$ finger watson@kudos
[kudos]
Login: max                        Name: Max Wild
Directory: /home/max              Shell: /bin/zsh
On since Sat Jun 25 11:22 (PDT) on tty1,  idle 23:22
Last login Sun Jun 26 06:20 (PDT) on ttyp2 from speedy
Mail last read Thu Jun 23 08:10 2005 (PDT)
Plan:
For appointments contact Sam the Great, x1963.
```

fmt

Formats text very simply

fmt [option] [file-list]

The fmt utility does simple text formatting by attempting to make all nonblank lines nearly the same length.

Arguments   The fmt utility reads the files in *file-list* and sends a formatted version of their contents to standard output. If you do not specify a filename or if you specify a hyphen (–) in place of a filename, fmt reads from standard input.

Options   Options preceded by a double hyphen (––) work under Linux only. Except as noted, options named with a single letter and preceded by a single hyphen work under Linux and OS X.

––split-only   –s   Splits long lines but does not fill short lines. `LINUX`

–s   Replaces multiple adjacent SPACE characters with a single SPACE. `OS X`

––tagged-paragraph
–t   Indents all but the first line of each paragraph. `LINUX`

–t *n*
Specifies *n* as the number of SPACEs per TAB stop. The default is eight. `OS X`

––uniform-spacing
–u   Changes the formatted output so that one SPACE appears between words and two SPACEs appear between sentences. `LINUX`

––width=*n*   –w *n*
Changes the output line length to *n* characters. Without this option, fmt keeps output lines close to 75 characters wide. You can also specify this option as *–n*.

Notes   The fmt utility works by moving NEWLINE characters. The indention of lines, as well as the spacing between words, is left intact.

You can use this utility to format text while you are using an editor, such as vim. For example, you can format a paragraph with the vim editor in command mode by positioning the cursor at the top of the paragraph and then entering !}fmt –60. This command replaces the paragraph with the output generated by feeding it through fmt, specifying a width of 60 characters. Type **u** immediately if you want to undo the formatting.

Examples

The following example shows how fmt attempts to make all lines the same length. The **–w 50** option gives a target line length of 50 characters.

```
$ cat memo
One factor that is important to remember while administering the dietary
intake of Charcharodon carcharias is that there is, at least from
the point of view of the subject,
very little
differentiating the prepared morsels being proffered from your digits.

In other words, don't feed the sharks!

$ fmt -w 50 memo
One factor that is important to remember while
administering the dietary intake of Charcharodon
carcharias is that there is, at least from the
point of view of the subject, very little
differentiating the prepared morsels being
proffered from your digits.

In other words, don't feed the sharks!
```

The next example demonstrates the **––split-only** option. Long lines are broken so that none is longer than 50 characters; this option prevents fmt from filling short lines.

```
$ fmt -w 50 --split-only memo
One factor that is important to remember while
administering the dietary
intake of Charcharodon carcharias is that there
is, at least from
the point of view of the subject,
very little
differentiating the prepared morsels being
proffered from your digits.

In other words, don't feed the sharks!
```

fsck

Checks and repairs a filesystem

fsck [options] [filesystem-list]

The fsck utility verifies the integrity of a filesystem and reports on and optionally repairs problems it finds. It is a front end for filesystem checkers, each of which is specific to a certain filesystem type. The fsck utility is available under Linux only; under OS X, use diskutil. **LINUX**

Arguments
Without the **–A** option and with no *filesystem-list*, fsck checks the filesystems listed in the **/etc/fstab** file one at a time (serially). With the **–A** option and with no *filesystem-list*, fsck checks all the filesystems listed in the **/etc/fstab** file in parallel if possible. See the **–s** option for a discussion of checking filesystems in parallel.

The *filesystem-list* specifies the filesystems to be checked. It can either specify the name of the device that holds the filesystem (for example, **/dev/hda2**) or, if the filesystem appears in **/etc/fstab**, specify the mount point (for example, **/usr**) for the filesystem. The *filesystem-list* can also specify the label for the filesystem from **/etc/fstab** (for example, **LABEL=home**).

Options
When you run fsck, you can specify both global options and options specific to the filesystem type that fsck is checking (for example, **ext2**, **ext3**, **msdos**, **reiserfs**). Global options must precede type-specific options.

Global Options

–A (**all**) Processes all filesystems listed in the **/etc/fstab** file, in parallel if possible. See the **–s** option for a discussion of checking filesystems in parallel. Do not specify a *filesystem-list* when you use this option; you can specify filesystem types to be checked with the **–t** option. Use this option with the **–a**, **–p**, or **–n** option so fsck does not attempt to process filesystems in parallel *interactively* (in which case you would have no way of responding to its multiple prompts).

–N (**no**) Assumes a *no* response to any questions that arise while processing a filesystem. This option generates the messages you would normally see but causes fsck to take no action.

–R (**root-skip**) With the **–A** option, does not check the root filesystem. This option is useful when the system boots, because the root filesystem may be mounted with read-write access.

–s (**serial**) Causes fsck to process filesystems one at a time. Without this option, fsck processes multiple filesystems that reside on separate physical disk drives in parallel. Parallel processing enables fsck to process multiple filesystems more quickly. This option is required if you want to process filesystems interactively. See the **–a**, **–p**, or **–N** (or **–n**, on some filesystems) option to turn off interactive processing.

–T   (**title**) Causes fsck not to display its title.

–t *fstype*

>   (**filesystem type**) A comma-separated list that specifies the filesystem type(s) to process. With the –**A** option, fsck processes all the filesystems in **/etc/fstab** that are of type *fstype*. Common filesystem types are **ext2, ext3, ext4, msdos,** and **reiserfs.** You do not typically check remote NFS filesystems.

–V   (**verbose**) Displays more output, including filesystem type-specific commands.

Filesystem Type-Specific Options

The following command lists the filesystem checking utilities available on the local system. Files with the same inode numbers are linked (page 107).

```
$ ls -i /sbin/*fsck*
63801 /sbin/dosfsck   63856 /sbin/fsck.cramfs   63801 /sbin/fsck.msdos
63763 /sbin/e2fsck    63763 /sbin/fsck.ext2     63801 /sbin/fsck.vfat
63780 /sbin/fsck      63763 /sbin/fsck.ext3
```

Review the man page or give the pathname of the filesystem checking utility to determine which options the utility accepts:

```
$ /sbin/fsck.ext3
Usage: /sbin/fsck.ext3 [-panyrcdfvstDFSV] [-b superblock] [-B blocksize]
                [-I inode_buffer_blocks] [-P process_inode_size]
                [-l|-L bad_blocks_file] [-C fd] [-j ext-journal]
                [-E extended-options] device

Emergency help:
 -p                     Automatic repair (no questions)
 -n                     Make no changes to the filesystem
 -y                     Assume "yes" to all questions
 -c                     Check for bad blocks and add them to the badblock list
 -f                     Force checking even if filesystem is marked clean
...
```

The following options apply to many filesystem types, including **ext2** and **ext3**:

–a   (**automatic**) Same as the –**p** option; kept for backward compatibility.

–f   (**force**) Forces fsck to check filesystems even if they are *clean*. A clean filesystem is one that was just successfully checked with fsck or was successfully unmounted and has not been mounted since then. Clean filesystems are skipped by fsck, which greatly speeds up system booting under normal conditions. For information on setting up periodic, automatic filesystem checking on **ext2, ext3,** and **ext4** filesystems, see tune2fs page 868.

–n   (**no**) Same as the –**N** global option. Does not work with all filesystems.

–p   (**preen**) Attempts to repair all minor inconsistencies it finds when processing a filesystem. If any problems are not repaired, fsck terminates with a nonzero exit status. This option runs fsck in batch mode; as a consequence, it does not ask whether to correct each problem it finds. The **–p** option is commonly used with the **–A** option when checking filesystems while booting Linux.

–r (**interactive**) Asks whether to correct or ignore each problem that is found. For many filesystem types, this behavior is the default. This option is not available on all filesystems.

–y (**yes**) Assumes a *yes* response to any questions that fsck asks while processing a filesystem. Use this option with caution, as it gives fsck free reign to do what it thinks is best to clean up a filesystem.

Notes

The fsck and fsck_hfs utilities are deprecated under Mac OS X version 10.5 and later. Apple suggests using diskutil (page 668) instead.

You can run fsck from a live or rescue CD.

When a filesystem is consistent, fsck displays a report such as the following:

```
# fsck -f /dev/sdb1
fsck 1.40.8 (13-Mar-2008)
e2fsck 1.40.8 (13-Mar-2008)
Pass 1: Checking inodes, blocks, and sizes
Pass 2: Checking directory structure
Pass 3: Checking directory connectivity
Pass 4: Checking reference counts
Pass 5: Checking group summary information
/dev/sdb1: 710/4153408 files (10.1% non-contiguous), 455813/8303589 blocks
```

Interactive mode You can run fsck either interactively or in batch mode. For many filesystems, unless you use one of the **–a**, **–p**, **–y**, or **–n** options, fsck runs in interactive mode. In interactive mode, if fsck finds a problem with a filesystem, it reports the problem and allows you to choose whether to repair or ignore it. If you repair a problem you may lose some data; however, that is often the most reasonable alternative.

Although it is technically feasible to repair files that are damaged and that fsck says you should remove, this action is rarely practical. The best insurance against significant loss of data is to make frequent backups.

Order of checking The fsck utility looks at the sixth column in the **/etc/fstab** file to determine if, and in which order, it should check filesystems. A **0** (zero) in this position indicates the filesystem should not be checked. A **1** (one) indicates that it should be checked first; this status is usually reserved for the root filesystem. A **2** (two) indicates that the filesystem should be checked after those marked with a **1**.

fsck is a front end Similar to mkfs (page 764), fsck is a front end that calls other utilities to handle various types of filesystems. For example, fsck calls e2fsck to check the widely used **ext2** and **ext3** filesystems. Refer to the e2fsck man page for more information. Other utilities that fsck calls are typically named **fsck.***type,* where *type* is the filesystem type. By splitting fsck in this manner, filesystem developers can provide programs to check their filesystems without affecting the development of other filesystems or changing how system administrators use fsck.

Boot time   Run fsck on filesystems that are unmounted or are mounted readonly. When Linux is booting, the root filesystem is first mounted readonly to allow it to be processed by fsck. If fsck finds no problems with the root filesystem, it is then remounted (using the **remount** option to the mount utility) read-write and fsck is typically run with the –A, –R, and –p options.

lost+found   When it encounters a file that has lost its link to its filename, fsck asks whether to reconnect it. If you choose to reconnect it, the file is put in a directory named **lost+found** in the root directory of the filesystem where the file was found. The reconnected file is given its inode number as a name. For fsck to restore files in this way, a **lost+found** directory must be present in the root directory of each filesystem. For example, if a system uses the **/**, **/usr**, and **/home** filesystems, you should have these three **lost+found** directories: **/lost+found**, **/usr/lost+found**, and **/home/lost+found**. Each **lost+found** directory must have unused entries in which fsck can store the inode numbers for files that have lost their links. When you create an **ext2/ext3/ext4** filesystem, mkfs (page 764) creates a **lost+found** directory with the required unused entries. Alternatively, you can use the mklost+found utility to create this directory in **ext2/ext3/ext4** filesystems if needed. On other types of filesystems, you can create the unused entries by adding many files to the directory and then removing them. Try using touch (page 862) to create 500 entries in the **lost+found** directory and then using rm to delete them.

Messages   Table V-15 lists fsck's common messages. In general fsck suggests the most logical way of dealing with a problem in the file structure. Unless you have information that suggests another response, respond to the prompts with **yes**. Use the system backup tapes or disks to restore data that is lost as a result of this process.

Table V-15   Common fsck messages

Phase (message)	What fsck checks
Phase 1 - Checking inodes, blocks, and sizes	Checks inode information.
Phase 2 - Checking directory structure	Looks for directories that point to bad inodes that fsck found in Phase 1.
Phase 3 - Checking directory connectivity	Looks for unreferenced directories and a nonexistent or full **lost+found** directory.
Phase 4 - Checking reference counts	Checks for unreferenced files, a nonexistent or full **lost+found** directory, bad link counts, bad blocks, duplicated blocks, and incorrect inode counts.
Phase 5 - Checking group summary information	Checks whether the free list and other filesystem structures are OK. If any problems are found with the free list, Phase 6 is run.
Phase 6 - Salvage free list	If Phase 5 found any problems with the free list, Phase 6 fixes them.

Cleanup

Once it has repaired the filesystem, fsck informs you about the status of the filesystem. The fsck utility displays the following message after it repairs a filesystem:

```
*****File System Was Modified*****
```

On **ext2/ext3/ext4** filesystems, fsck displays the following message when it has finished checking a filesystem:

filesys: *used/maximum* files *(percent* non-contiguous*)*, *used/maximum* blocks

This message tells you how many files and disk blocks are in use as well as how many files and disk blocks the filesystem can hold. The *percent non-contiguous* tells you how fragmented the disk is.

ftp

Transfers files over a network

ftp [options] [remote-system]

The ftp utility is a user interface to the standard File Transfer Protocol (FTP), which transfers files between systems that can communicate over a network. To establish an FTP connection, you must have access to an account (personal, guest, or anonymous) on the remote system.

Use FTP only to download public information

security FTP is not a secure protocol. The ftp utility sends your password over the network as cleartext, which is not a secure practice. You can use sftp as a secure replacement for ftp if the server is running OpenSSH. You can also use scp (page 810) for many FTP functions other than allowing anonymous users to download information. Because scp uses an encrypted connection, user passwords and data cannot be sniffed.

Arguments The *remote-system* is the name or network address of the server, running an FTP daemon (e.g., **ftpd**, **vsftpd**, or **sshd**), you want to exchange files with.

Options **–i** (**interactive**) Turns off prompts during file transfers with **mget** and **mput**. See also **prompt**.

–n (**no automatic login**) Disables automatic logins.

–p (**passive mode**) Starts ftp in passive mode (page 706).

–v (**verbose**) Tells you more about how ftp is working. Displays responses from the *remote-system* and reports transfer times and speeds.

Discussion The ftp utility is interactive. After you start it, ftp prompts you to enter commands to set parameters and transfer files. You can use a number of commands in response to the **ftp>** prompt; following are some of the more common ones.

![command] Escapes to (spawns) a shell on the local system; use CONTROL-D or **exit** to return to ftp when you are finished using the local shell. Follow the exclamation point with a command to execute that command only; ftp returns to the **ftp>** prompt when the command completes executing. Because the shell that ftp spawns with this command is a child of the shell that is running ftp, no changes you make in this shell are preserved when you return to ftp. Specifically, when you want to copy files to a local directory other than the directory that you started ftp from, you need to use the ftp **lcd** command to change the local working directory: Issuing a **cd** command in the spawned shell will not make the change'you desire. See page 709 for an example.

ascii Sets the file transfer type to ASCII. This command allows you to transfer text files from systems that end lines with a RETURN/LINEFEED combination and automatically strip off the RETURN. Such a transfer is useful when the remote computer is a DOS or MS Windows machine. The **cr** command must be ON for **ascii** to work.

binary   Sets the file transfer type to binary. This command allows you to transfer files that contain non-ASCII (unprintable) characters correctly. It also works for ASCII files that do not require changes to the ends of lines.

bye   Closes the connection to a remote system and terminates ftp. Same as **quit**.

cd *remote-directory*
Changes to the working directory named *remote-directory* on the remote system.

close   Closes the connection with the remote system without exiting from ftp.

cr   (**carriage return**) Toggles RETURN stripping when you retrieve files in ASCII mode. See **ascii**.

dir *[directory [file]]*
Displays a listing of the directory named *directory* from the remote system. When you do not specify *directory*, the working directory is displayed. When you specify a *file*, the listing is saved on the local system in a file named *file*.

get *remote-file [local-file]*
Copies *remote-file* to the local system under the name *local-file*. Without *local-file*, ftp uses *remote-file* as the filename on the local system. The *remote-file* and *local-file* names can be pathnames.

glob   Toggles filename expansion for the **mget** and **mput** commands and displays the current state (**Globbing on** or **Globbing off**).

help   Displays a list of commands recognized by the ftp utility on the local system.

lcd *[local_directory]*
(**local change directory**) Changes the working directory on the local system to *local_directory*. Without an argument, this command changes the working directory on the local system to your home directory (just as **cd** does without an argument).

ls *[directory [file]]* Similar to **dir** but produces a more concise listing on some remote systems.

mget *remote-file-list*
(**multiple get**) Unlike the **get** command, allows you to retrieve multiple files from the remote system. You can name the remote files literally or use wildcards (see **glob**). See also **prompt**.

mput *local-file-list*
(**multiple put**) The **mput** command allows you to copy multiple files from the local system to the remote system. You can name the local files literally or use wildcards (see **glob**). See also **prompt**.

open   Interactively specifies the name of the remote system. This command is useful if you did not specify a remote system on the command line or if the attempt to connect to the system failed.

passive   Toggles between the active (PORT—the default) and passive (PASV) transfer modes and displays the transfer mode. See "Passive versus active connections" under the "Notes" section.

prompt   When using **mget** or **mput** to receive or send multiple files, ftp asks for verification (by default) before transferring each file. This command toggles that behavior and displays the current state (**Interactive mode off** or **Interactive mode on**).

put *local-file [remote-file]*
Copies *local-file* to the remote system under the name *remote-file*. Without *remote-file*, ftp uses *local-file* as the filename on the remote system. The *remote-file* and *local-file* names can be pathnames.

pwd   Causes ftp to display the pathname of the remote working directory. Use **!pwd** to display the name of the local working directory.

quit   Closes the connection to a remote system and terminates ftp. Same as **bye**.

reget *remote-file*   Attempts to resume an aborted transfer. This command is similar to **get**, but instead of overwriting an existing local file, ftp appends new data to it. Not all servers support **reget**.

user *[username]*   If the ftp utility did not log you in automatically, you can specify your account name as *username*. If you omit *username*, ftp prompts you for a username.

Notes

A Linux or Mac OS X system running ftp can exchange files with any of the many operating systems that support the FTP protocol. Many sites offer archives of free information on an FTP server, although many of these FTP sites are merely alternatives to an easier-to-access Web site (for example, ftp://ftp.ibiblio.org/pub/Linux and http://www.ibiblio.org/pub/Linux). Most browsers can connect to and download files from FTP servers.

The ftp utility makes no assumptions about filesystem naming or structure because you can use ftp to exchange files with non-UNIX/Linux systems (whose filename conventions may be different).

Anonymous FTP   Many systems—most notably those from which you can download free software—allow you to log in as **anonymous**. Most systems that support anonymous logins accept the name **ftp** as an easier-to-spell and quicker-to-enter synonym for **anonymous**. An anonymous user is usually restricted to a portion of a filesystem set aside to hold files that are to be shared with remote users. When you log in as an anonymous user, the server prompts you to enter a password. Although any password may be accepted, by convention you are expected to supply your email address. Many systems that permit anonymous access store interesting files in the **pub** directory.

Passive versus active connections   A client can ask an FTP server to establish either a PASV (passive—the default) or PORT (active) connection for data transfer. Some servers are limited to one type of connection. The difference between passive and active FTP connections lies in whether the client or server initiates the data connection. In passive mode, the client initiates the data connection to the server (on port 20 by default); in active mode, the server initiates the data connection (there is no default port). Neither type of connection is inherently more secure. Passive connections are more common because a client behind a *NAT* (page 967) firewall can connect to a passive server and because it is simpler to program a scalable passive server.

Automatic login
You can store server-specific FTP username and password information so that you do not have to enter it each time you visit an FTP site. Each line of the ~/.netrc file identifies a server. When you connect to an FTP server, ftp reads ~/.netrc to determine whether you have an automatic login set up for that server. The format of a line in ~/.netrc is

*machine **server** login **username** password **passwd***

where **server** is the name of the server, **username** is your username, and **passwd** is your password on **server**. Replace *machine* with **default** on the last line of the file to specify a username and password for systems not listed in ~/.netrc. The **default** line is useful for logging in on anonymous servers. A sample ~/.netrc file follows:

```
$ cat ~/.netrc
machine bravo login max password mypassword
default login anonymous password max@example.com
```

To protect the account information in **.netrc**, make it readable by only the user whose home directory it appears in. Refer to the **netrc** man page for more information.

Examples

Following are two ftp sessions wherein Max transfers files from and to an FTP server named **bravo**. When Max gives the command **ftp bravo**, the local ftp client connects to the server, which asks for a username and a password. Because he is logged in on his local system as **max**, ftp suggests that he log in on **bravo** as **max**. To log in as **max**, Max could just press RETURN. His username on **bravo** is **watson**, however, so he types **watson** in response to the **Name (bravo:max):** prompt. Max responds to the **Password:** prompt with his normal (remote) system password, and the FTP server greets him and informs him that it is **Using binary mode to transfer files**. With ftp in binary mode, Max can transfer ASCII and binary files.

Connect and log in
```
$ ftp bravo
Connected to bravo.
220 (vsFTPd 2.0.7)
530 Please login with USER and PASS.
530 Please login with USER and PASS.
KERBEROS_V4 rejected as an authentication type
Name (bravo:max): watson
331 Please specify the password.
Password:
230 Login successful.
Remote system type is UNIX.
Using binary mode to transfer files.
ftp>
```

After logging in, Max uses the ftp **ls** command to display the contents of his remote working directory, which is his home directory on **bravo**. Then he cds to the **memos** directory and displays the files there.

ls and **cd**

```
ftp> ls
227 Entering Passive Mode (192,168,0,6,79,105)
150 Here comes the directory listing.
drwxr-xr-x    2 500       500          4096 Oct 10 23:52 expenses
drwxr-xr-x    2 500       500          4096 Oct 10 23:59 memos
drwxrwxr-x   22 500       500          4096 Oct 10 23:32 tech
226 Directory send OK.

ftp> cd memos
250 Directory successfully changed.

ftp> ls
227 Entering Passive Mode (192,168,0,6,114,210)
150 Here comes the directory listing.
-rw-r--r--    1 500       500          4770 Oct 10 23:58 memo.0514
-rw-r--r--    1 500       500          7134 Oct 10 23:58 memo.0628
-rw-r--r--    1 500       500          9453 Oct 10 23:58 memo.0905
-rw-r--r--    1 500       500          3466 Oct 10 23:59 memo.0921
-rw-r--r--    1 500       500          1945 Oct 10 23:59 memo.1102
226 Directory send OK.
```

Next Max uses the ftp **get** command to copy **memo.1102** from the server to the local system. His use of binary mode ensures that he will get a good copy of the file regardless of whether it is in binary or ASCII format. The server confirms that the file was copied successfully and notes the size of the file and the time it took to copy. Max then copies the local file **memo.1114** to the remote system. The file is copied into his remote working directory, **memos**.

get and **put**

```
ftp> get memo.1102
local: memo.1102 remote: memo.1102
227 Entering Passive Mode (192,168,0,6,194,214)
150 Opening BINARY mode data connection for memo.1102 (1945 bytes).
226 File send OK.
1945 bytes received in 7.1e-05 secs (2.7e+04 Kbytes/sec)

ftp> put memo.1114
local: memo.1114 remote: memo.1114
227 Entering Passive Mode (192,168,0,6,174,97)
150 Ok to send data.
226 File receive OK.
1945 bytes sent in 2.8e-05 secs (6.8e+04 Kbytes/sec)
```

After a while Max decides he wants to copy all the files in the **memos** directory on **bravo** to a new directory on the local system. He gives an **ls** command to make sure he is going to copy the right files, but ftp has timed out. Instead of exiting from ftp and giving another ftp command from the shell, Max gives ftp an **open bravo** command to reconnect to the server. After logging in, he uses the ftp **cd** command to change directories to **memos** on the server.

Timeout and open

```
ftp> ls
421 Timeout.
Passive mode refused.
ftp> open bravo
Connected to bravo (192.168.0.6).
220 (vsFTPd 1.1.3)
...
ftp> cd memos
250 Directory successfully changed.
```

lcd (local cd)   At this point, Max realizes he has not created the new directory to hold the files he wants to download. Giving an ftp **mkdir** command would create a new directory on the server, but Max wants a new directory on the local system. He uses an exclamation point (**!**) followed by a **mkdir memos.hold** command to invoke a shell and run mkdir on the local system, thereby creating a directory named **memos.hold** in his working directory on the local system. (You can display the name of your working directory on the local system with **!pwd**.) Next, because he wants to copy files from the server to the **memos.hold** on his local system, Max has to change his working directory on the local system. Giving the command **!cd memos.hold** will not accomplish what Max wants to do because the exclamation point spawns a new shell on the local system and the **cd** command would be effective only in the new shell, which is not the shell that ftp is running under. For this situation, ftp provides the **lcd** (local cd) command, which changes the working directory for ftp and reports on the new local working directory.

```
ftp> !mkdir memos.hold

ftp> lcd memos.hold
Local directory now /home/max/memos.hold
```

Max uses the ftp **mget** (multiple get) command followed by the asterisk (*****) wildcard to copy all the files from the remote **memos** directory to the **memos.hold** directory on the local system. When ftp prompts him for the first file, he realizes that he forgot to turn off the prompts, so he responds with **n** and presses CONTROL-C to stop copying files in response to the second prompt. The server checks whether he wants to continue with his **mget** command.

Next Max gives the ftp **prompt** command, which toggles the prompt action (turns it *off* if it is *on* and turns it *on* if it is *off*). Now when he gives an **mget *** command, ftp copies all the files without prompting him.

After getting the files he wants, Max gives a **quit** command to close the connection with the server, exit from ftp, and return to the local shell prompt.

mget and prompt

```
ftp> mget *
mget memo.0514? n
mget memo.0628? CONTROL-C
Continue with mget? n

ftp> prompt
Interactive mode off.
```

```
ftp> mget *
local: memo.0514 remote: memo.0514
227 Entering Passive Mode (192,168,0,6,53,55)
150 Opening BINARY mode data connection for memo.0514 (4770 bytes).
226 File send OK.
4770 bytes received in 8.8e-05 secs (5.3e+04 Kbytes/sec)
local: memo.0628 remote: memo.0628
227 Entering Passive Mode (192,168,0,6,65,102)
150 Opening BINARY mode data connection for memo.0628 (7134 bytes).
226 File send OK.
...
150 Opening BINARY mode data connection for memo.1114 (1945 bytes).
226 File send OK.
1945 bytes received in 3.9e-05 secs (4.9e+04 Kbytes/sec)
ftp> quit
221 Goodbye.
```

gawk

Searches for and processes patterns in a file

gawk [options] [program] [file-list]
gawk [options] –f program-file [file-list]

AWK is a pattern-scanning and processing language that searches one or more files for records (usually lines) that match specified patterns. It processes lines by performing actions, such as writing the record to standard output or incrementing a counter, each time it finds a match. As opposed to *procedural* languages, AWK is *data driven*: You describe the data you want to work with and tell AWK what to do with the data once it finds it.

See Chapter 12 for information on gawk

tip   See Chapter 12 starting on page 531 for information on the awk, gawk, and mawk implementations of the AWK language.

gcc

Compiles C and C++ programs

gcc [options] file-list [–larg]
g++ [options] file-list [–larg]

The Linux and Mac OS X operating systems use the GNU C compiler, gcc, to preprocess, compile, assemble, and link C language source files. The same compiler with a different front end, g++, processes C++ source code. The gcc and g++ compilers can also assemble and link assembly language source files, link object files only, or build object files for use in shared libraries.

These compilers take input from files you specify on the command line. Unless you use the –o option, they store the executable program in **a.out**.

The gcc and g++ compilers are part of GCC, the *GNU Compiler Collection*, which includes front ends for C, C++, Objective C, Fortran, Java, and Ada as well as libraries for these languages. Go to gcc.gnu.org for more information.

gcc **and** g++

tip   Although this section specifies the gcc compiler, most of it applies to g++ as well.

Arguments   The *file-list* is a list of files gcc is to process.

Options   Without any options gcc accepts C language source files, assembly language files, object files, and other files described in Table V-16 on page 715. The gcc utility preprocesses, compiles, assembles, and links these files as appropriate, producing an executable file named **a.out**. If gcc is used to create object files without linking them to produce an executable file, each object file is named by adding the extension .o to the basename of the corresponding source file. If gcc is used to create an executable file, it deletes the object files after linking.

Some of the most commonly used options are listed here. When certain filename extensions are associated with an option, you can assume gcc adds the extension to the basename of the source file.

–c   (**compile**) Suppresses the linking step of compilation. Compiles and/or assembles source code files and leaves the object code in files with the extension .o.

–D*name[=value]*
       Usually **#define** preprocessor directives are given in header, or include, files. You can use this option to define symbolic names on the command line instead. For example, **–DLinux** is equivalent to placing the line **#define Linux** in an include file, and **–DMACH=i586** is the same as **#define MACH i586**.

–E (**everything**) For source code files, suppresses all steps of compilation *except* preprocessing and writes the result to standard output. By convention the extension **.i** is used for preprocessed C source and **.ii** for preprocessed C++ source.

–fpic

Causes gcc to produce *position-independent* code, which is suitable for installing into a shared library.

–fwritable-strings

By default the GNU C compiler places string constants into *protected memory,* where they cannot be changed. Some (usually older) programs assume you can modify string constants. This option changes the behavior of gcc so that string constants can be modified.

–g (**gdb**) Embeds diagnostic information in the object files. This information is used by symbolic debuggers, such as gdb. Although this option is necessary only if you later use a debugger, it is a good practice to include it as a matter of course.

–I*directory*

Looks for include files in *directory* before looking in the standard locations. Give this option multiple times to look in more than one directory.

–l*arg*

(lowercase "l") Searches the directories **/lib** and **/usr/lib** for a library file named **lib***arg***.a**. If the file is found, gcc then searches this library for any required functions. Replace *arg* with the name of the library you want to search. For example, the **–lm** option normally links the standard math library **libm.a**. The position of this option is significant: It generally needs to appear at the end of the command line but can be repeated multiple times to search different libraries. Libraries are searched in the order in which they appear on the command line. The linker uses the library only to resolve undefined symbols from modules that *precede* the library option on the command line. You can add other library paths to search for **lib***arg***.a** using the **–L** option.

–L*directory*

Adds *directory* to the list of directories to search for libraries given with the **–l** option. Directories that are added to the list with **–L** are searched before gcc looks in the standard locations for libraries.

–o *file*

(**output**) Names the executable program that results from linking *file* instead of **a.out**.

–O*n*

(**optimize**) Attempts to improve (optimize) the object code produced by the compiler. The value of *n* may be **0, 1, 2,** or **3** (or **06** if you are compiling code for the Linux kernel). The default value of *n* is **1**. Larger values of *n* result in better optimization but may increase both the size of the object file and the time it takes gcc to run. Specify **–O0** to turn off optimization. Many related options control precisely the types of optimizations attempted by gcc when you use **–O**. Refer to the gcc info page for details.

–pedantic

The C language accepted by the GNU C compiler includes features that are not part of the ANSI standard for the C language. Using this option forces gcc to reject these *language extensions* and accept only standard C programming language features.

–Q   Displays the names of functions as gcc compiles them. This option also displays statistics about each pass.

–S   (**suppress**) Suppresses the assembling and linking steps of compilation on source code files. The resulting assembly language files have **.s** filename extensions.

–traditional

Causes gcc to accept only C programming language features that existed in the traditional Kernighan and Ritchie C programming language. With this option, older programs written using the traditional C language (which existed before the ANSI standard C language was defined) can be compiled correctly.

–Wall

Causes gcc to warn you about questionable code in the source code files. Many related options control warning messages more precisely.

Notes

The preceding list of options represents only a small fraction of the full set of options available with the GNU C compiler. See the gcc info page for a complete list.

Although the **–o** option is generally used to specify a filename in which to store object code, this option also allows you to name files resulting from other compilation steps. In the following example, the **–o** option causes the assembly language produced by the gcc command to be stored in the file **acode** instead of **pgm.s**, the default:

```
$ gcc -S -o acode pgm.c
```

The lint utility found in many UNIX systems is not available on Linux or Mac OS X. However, the **–Wall** option performs many of the same checks and can be used in place of lint.

Table V-16 summarizes the conventions used by the C compiler for assigning filename extensions.

Table V-16 Filename extensions

Extension	Type of file
.a	Library of object modules
.c	C language source file
.C, .cc, *or* .cxx	C++ language source file
.i	Preprocessed C language source file
.ii	Preprocessed C++ language source file
.o	Object file
.s	Assembly language source file
.S	Assembly language source file that needs preprocessing

Examples

The first example compiles, assembles, and links a single C program, **compute.c**. The executable output is stored in **a.out**. The gcc utility deletes the object file.

```
$ gcc compute.c
```

The next example compiles the same program using the C optimizer (–O option). It assembles and links the optimized code. The –o option causes gcc to store the executable output in **compute**.

```
$ gcc -O -o compute compute.c
```

Next a C source file, an assembly language file, and an object file are compiled, assembled, and linked. The executable output is stored in **progo**.

```
$ gcc -o progo procom.c profast.s proout.o
```

In the next example, gcc searches the standard math library found in **/lib/libm.a** when it is linking the **himath** program and stores the executable output in **a.out**:

```
$ gcc himath.c -lm
```

In the following example, the C compiler compiles **topo.c** with options that check the code for questionable source code practices (–**Wall** option) and violations of the ANSI C standard (–**pedantic** option). The –g option embeds debugging support in the executable file, which is saved in **topo** with the –o topo option. Full optimization is enabled with the –O3 option.

The warnings produced by the C compiler are sent to standard output. In this example the first and last warnings result from the –**pedantic** option; the other warnings result from the –**Wall** option.

```
$ gcc -Wall -g -O3 -pedantic -o topo topo.c
In file included from topo.c:2:
/usr/include/ctype.h:65: warning: comma at end of enumerator list
topo.c:13: warning: return-type defaults to 'int'
topo.c: In function 'main':
topo.c:14: warning: unused variable 'c'
topo.c: In function 'getline':
topo.c:44: warning: 'c' might be used uninitialized in this function
```

When compiling programs that rely on the X11 include files and libraries, you may need to use the –I and –L options to tell gcc where to locate those include files and libraries. The next example uses those options and instructs gcc to link the program with the basic X11 library:

```
$ gcc -I/usr/X11R6/include plot.c -L/usr/X11R6/lib -lX11
```

GetFileInfo **OS X**

Displays file attributes

GetFileInfo [option] file

The GetFileInfo utility displays file attributes (page 931), including the file's type and creator code, creation and last modification times, and attribute flags such as the invisible and locked flags.

Arguments The *file* specifies a single file or a directory that GetFileInfo displays information about.

Options The options for GetFileInfo correspond to the options for SetFile (page 813).

Without an option, GetFileInfo reports on the metadata of *file,* indicating the flags that are set, the file's type and creator codes, and its creation and modification dates. Missing data is omitted. When you specify an option, GetFileInfo displays the information specified by that option only. This utility accepts a single option; it silently ignores additional options.

–a*flag*
   (**attribute**) Reports the status of a single attribute flag named *flag*. This option displays **1** if *flag* is set and **0** if *flag* is not set. The *flag* must follow the –a immediately, without any intervening SPACEs. See Table D-2 on page 931 for a list of attribute flags.

–c (**creator**) Displays the creator code of *file*. If *file* is a directory and has no creator code, this option displays an error message.

–d (**date**) Displays the creation date of *file* as **mm/dd/yyyy hh:mm:ss**, using a 24-hour clock.

–m (**modification**) Displays the modification date of *file* as **mm/dd/yyyy hh:mm:ss**, using a 24-hour clock.

–P (**no dereference**) For each file that is a symbolic link, displays information about the symbolic link, not the file the link points to. This option affects all files and treats files that are not symbolic links normally. See page 625 for an cxample of the –P option.

–t (**type**) Displays the type code of *file*. If *file* is a directory and has no type code, this option displays an error message.

Discussion Without an option, GetFileInfo displays flags as the string **avbstclinmedz**, with uppercase letters denoting which flags are set. See page 931 for a discussion of attribute flags.

Notes
You can use the SetFile utility (page 813) to set file attributes. You can set Mac OS X permissions and ownership (page 93) using chmod (page 626) or chown (page 631), and you can display this information using ls (page 745) or stat (page 835).

Directories do not have type or creator codes, and they may not have all flags. The GetFileInfo utility cannot read special files such as device files.

Examples
The first example shows the output from GetFileInfo when you call it without an option.

```
$ GetFileInfo picture.jpg
file: "/private/tmp/picture.jpg"
type: "JPEG"
creator: "GKON"
attributes: avbstClinmedz
created: 07/18/2005 15:15:26
modified: 07/18/2005 15:15:26
```

The only uppercase letter on the **attributes** line is **C**, indicating that this flag is set. The **c** flag tells the Finder to look for a custom icon for this file. See Table D-2 on page 931 for a list of flags.

The next example uses the **–a** flag to display the attribute flags for a file:

```
$ GetFileInfo -a /Applications/Games/Alchemy/Alchemy
avBstclInmedz
```

The output shows that the **b** and **i** flags are set.

The GetFileInfo utility can process only one file each time you call it. The following multiline bash command uses a **for** loop (page 411) to display the creator codes of multiple files. The echo command displays the name of the file being examined because GetFileInfo does not always display the name of the file:

```
$ for i in *
> do echo -n "$i: "; GetFileInfo -c "$i"
> done
Desktop: Desktop is a directory and has no creator
Documents: Documents is a directory and has no creator
...
aa: ""
ab: ""
...
```

grep

Searches for a pattern in files

grep [options] pattern [file-list]

The grep utility searches one or more text files, line by line, for a *pattern*, which can be a simple string or another form of a regular expression. The grep utility takes various actions, specified by options, each time it finds a line that contains a match for the *pattern*. This utility takes its input either from files you specify on the command line or from standard input.

Arguments   The *pattern* is a regular expression, as defined in Appendix A. You must quote regular expressions that contain special characters, SPACEs, or TABs. An easy way to quote these characters is to enclose the entire expression within single quotation marks.

The *file-list* is a list of the pathnames of ordinary text files that grep searches. With the **–r** option, *file-list* may contain directories whose contents are searched.

Options   Without any options grep sends lines that contain a match for *pattern* to standard output. When you specify more than one file on the command line, grep precedes each line it displays with the name of the file it came from, followed by a colon.

Major Options

You can use only one of the following three options at a time. Normally you do not need to use any, because grep defaults to **–G**, which is regular grep.

–E   (**extended**) Interprets *pattern* as an extended regular expression (page 895). The command **grep –E** is the same as egrep. See the "Notes" section.

–F   (**fixed**) Interprets *pattern* as a fixed string of characters. The command **grep –F** is the same as fgrep.

–G   (**grep**) Interprets *pattern* as a basic regular expression. This is the default major option if you do not specify a major option.

Other Options

The grep utility accepts the common options described on page 603.

The Mac OS X version of grep accepts long options

tip   Options for grep preceded by a double hyphen (**––**) work under Mac OS X as well as under Linux.

––count   **–c**   Displays only the number of lines that contain a match in each file.

––context=*n*   **–C** *n*
Displays *n* lines of context around each matching line.

--file=*file*	–f *file*	Reads *file*, which contains one pattern per line, and finds lines in the input that match each of the patterns.
--no-filename	–h	Does not display the filename at the beginning of each line when searching through multiple files.
--ignore-case	–i	Causes lowercase letters in the pattern to match uppercase letters in the file, and vice versa. Use this option when you are searching for a word that may appear at the beginning of a sentence (that is, the word may or may not start with an uppercase letter).
--files-with-matches	–l	(lowercase "l"; **list**) Displays only the name of each file that contains one or more matches. A filename is displayed only once, even if the file contains more than one match.
--max-count=*n*	–m *n*	Stops reading each file, or standard input, after displaying *n* lines containing matches.
--line-number	–n	Precedes each line by its line number in the file. The file does not need to contain line numbers.
--quiet *or* --silent	–q	Does not write anything to standard output; only sets the exit code.
--recursive	–r *or* –R	Recursively descends directories in the *file-list* and processes files within these directories.
--no-messages	–s	(**silent**) Does not display an error message if a file in the *file-list* does not exist or is not readable.
--invert-match	–v	Causes lines *not* containing a match to satisfy the search. When you use this option by itself, grep displays all lines that do *not* contain a match for the *pattern*.
--word-regexp	–w	With this option, the *pattern* must match a whole word. This option is helpful if you are searching for a specific word that may also appear as a substring of another word in the file.
--line-regexp	–x	The *pattern* matches whole lines only.

Notes

The grep utility returns an exit status of 0 if it finds a match, 1 if it does not find a match, and 2 if the file is not accessible or the grep command contains a syntax error.

egrep and fgrep   Two utilities perform functions similar to that of grep. The egrep utility (same as **grep –E**) allows you to use *extended regular expressions* (page 895), which include a different set of special characters than basic regular expressions (page 893). The fgrep utility (same as **grep –F**) is fast and compact but processes only simple strings, not regular expressions.

GNU grep, which runs under Linux and Mac OS X, uses extended regular expressions in place of regular expressions. Thus egrep is virtually the same as grep. Refer to the grep info page for a minimal distinction.

Examples   The following examples assume that the working directory contains three files: **testa**, **testb**, and **testc**.

File testa	File testb	File testc
aaabb	aaaaa	AAAAA
bbbcc	bbbbb	BBBBB
ff-ff	ccccc	CCCCC
cccdd	ddddd	DDDDD
dddaa		

The grep utility can search for a pattern that is a simple string of characters. The following command line searches **testa** and displays each line containing the string **bb**:

```
$ grep bb testa
aaabb
bbbcc
```

The **–v** option reverses the sense of the test. The following example displays the lines in **testa** *without* **bb**:

```
$ grep -v bb testa
ff-ff
cccdd
dddaa
```

The **–n** option displays the line number of each displayed line:

```
$ grep -n bb testa
1:aaabb
2:bbbcc
```

The grep utility can search through more than one file. Here it searches through each file in the working directory. The name of the file containing the string precedes each line of output.

```
$ grep bb *
testa:aaabb
testa:bbbcc
testb:bbbbb
```

When the search for the string **bb** is done with the **–w** option, grep produces no output because none of the files contains the string **bb** as a separate word:

```
$ grep -w bb *
$
```

The search grep performs is case sensitive. Because the previous examples specified lowercase **bb**, grep did not find the uppercase string **BBBBB** in **testc**. The **–i** option causes both uppercase *and* lowercase letters to match either case of letter in the pattern:

```
$ grep -i bb *
testa:aaabb
testa:bbbcc
testb:bbbbb
testc:BBBBB
$ grep -i BB *
testa:aaabb
testa:bbbcc
testb:bbbbb
testc:BBBBB
```

The **–c** option displays the number of lines in each file that contain a match:

```
$ grep -c bb *
testa:2
testb:1
testc:0
```

The **–f** option finds matches for each pattern in a file of patterns. In the next example, **gfile** holds two patterns, one per line, and grep searches for matches to the patterns in **gfile**:

```
$ cat gfile
aaa
bbb
$ grep -f gfile test*
testa:aaabb
testa:bbbcc
testb:aaaaa
testb:bbbbb
```

The following command line searches **text2** and displays lines that contain a string of characters starting with **st**, followed by zero or more characters (.***** represents zero or more characters in a regular expression—see Appendix A), and ending in **ing**:

```
$ grep 'st.*ing' text2
...
```

The **^** regular expression, which matches the beginning of a line, can be used alone to match every line in a file. Together with the **–n** option, **^** can be used to display the lines in a file, preceded by their line numbers:

```
$ grep -n '^' testa
1:aaabb
2:bbbcc
3:ff-ff
4:cccdd
5:dddaa
```

The next command line counts the number of times **#include** statements appear in C source files in the working directory. The **–h** option causes grep to suppress the filenames from its output. The input to sort consists of all lines from ***.c** that match **#include**. The output from sort is an ordered list of lines that contains many duplicates. When uniq with the **–c** option processes this sorted list, it outputs repeated lines only once, along with a count of the number of repetitions in its input.

```
$ grep -h '#include' *.c | sort | uniq -c
9 #include "buff.h"
2 #include "poly.h"
1 #include "screen.h"
6 #include "window.h"
2 #include "x2.h"
2 #include "x3.h"
2 #include <math.h>
3 #include <stdio.h>
```

The final command calls the vim editor with a list of files in the working directory that contain the string **Sampson**. The **$(...)** command substitution construct (page 340) causes the shell to execute grep in place and supply vim with a list of filenames that you want to edit:

```
$ vim $(grep -l 'Sampson' *)
...
```

The single quotation marks are not necessary in this example, but they are required if the regular expression you are searching for contains special characters or SPACEs. It is generally a good habit to quote the pattern so the shell does not interpret any special characters the pattern may contain.

gzip

Compresses or decompresses files

gzip [options] [file-list]
gunzip [options] [file-list]
zcat [file-list]

The gzip utility compresses files, the gunzip utility restores files compressed with gzip, and the zcat utility displays files compressed with gzip.

Arguments   The *file-list* is a list of the names of one or more files that are to be compressed or decompressed. If a directory appears in *file-list* with no **--recursive** option, gzip/gunzip issues an error message and ignores the directory. With the **--recursive** option, gzip/gunzip recursively compresses/decompresses files within the directory hierarchy.

If *file-list* is empty or if the special option – (hyphen) is present, gzip reads from standard input. The **--stdout** option causes gzip and gunzip to write to standard output.

The information in this section also applies to gunzip, a link to gzip.

Options   The gzip, gunzip, and zcat utilities accept the common options described on page 603.

The Mac OS X versions of gzip, gunzip, and zcat accept long options

tip   Options for gzip, gunzip, and zcat preceded by a double hyphen (--) work under Mac OS X as well as under Linux.

--stdout   **-c**   Writes the results of compression or decompression to standard output instead of to *filename.gz*.

--decompress *or*   **-d**   Decompresses a file compressed with gzip. This option with gzip is equivalent
--uncompress   to the gunzip command.

--force   **-f**   Overwrites an existing output file on compression/decompression.

--list   **-l**   For each compressed file in *file-list,* displays the file's compressed and decompressed sizes, the compression ratio, and the name of the file before compression. Use this option with **--verbose** to display additional information.

--fast *or*   **-***n*   Controls the tradeoff between the speed of compression and the amount of com-
--best   pression. The *n* argument is a digit from 1 to 9; level 1 is the fastest (least) compression and level 9 is the best (slowest and most) compression. The default level is 6. The options **--fast** and **--best** are synonyms for –1 and –9, respectively.

--quiet   **-q**   Suppresses warning messages.

--recursive   **-r**   Recursively descends directories in *file-list* and compresses/decompresses files within these directories.

--test –t Verifies the integrity of a compressed file. This option displays nothing if the file is OK.

--verbose –v Displays the name of the file, the name of the compressed file, and the amount of compression as each file is processed.

Discussion

Compressing files reduces disk space requirements and shortens the time needed to transmit files between systems. When gzip compresses a file, it adds the extension **.gz** to the filename. For example, compressing the file **fname** creates the file **fname.gz** and, unless you use the **--stdout** (**–c**) option, deletes the original file. To restore **fname**, use the command **gunzip** with the argument **fname.gz**.

Almost all files become much smaller when compressed with gzip. On rare occasions a file will become larger, but only by a slight amount. The type of a file and its contents (as well as the *–n* option) determine how much smaller a file becomes; text files are often reduced by 60 to 70 percent.

The attributes of a file, such as its owner, permissions, and modification and access times, are left intact when gzip compresses and gunzip decompresses a file.

If the compressed version of a file already exists, gzip reports that fact and asks for your confirmation before overwriting the existing file. If a file has multiple links to it, gzip issues an error message and exits. The **--force** option overrides the default behavior in both of these situations.

Notes

Without the **--stdout** (**–c**) option, gzip removes the files in *file-list*.

The bzip2 utility (page 615) compresses files more efficiently than does gzip.

In addition to the gzip format, gunzip recognizes several other compression formats, enabling gunzip to decompress files compressed with compress.

To see an example of a file that becomes larger when compressed with gzip, compare the size of a file that has been compressed once with the same file compressed with gzip again. Because gzip complains when you give it an argument with the extension **.gz**, you need to rename the file before compressing it a second time.

The tar utility with the –z modifier (page 848) calls gzip.

The following related utilities display and manipulate compressed files. None of these utilities changes the files it works on.

zcat *file-list* Works like cat except that it uses gunzip to decompress *file-list* as it copies files to standard output.

zdiff [*options*] *file1* [*file2*]
Works like diff (page 663) except *file1* and *file2* are decompressed with gunzip as needed. The zdiff utility accepts the same options as diff. If you omit *file2*, zdiff compares *file1* with the compressed version of *file1*.

zless *file-list* Works like less except that it uses gunzip to decompress *file-list* as it displays files.

Examples   In the first example, gzip compresses two files. Next gunzip decompresses one of the files. When a file is compressed and decompressed, its size changes but its modification time remains the same:

```
$ ls -l
total 175
-rw-rw-r-- 1 max group 33557 Jul 20 17:32 patch-2.0.7
-rw-rw-r-- 1 max group 143258 Jul 20 17:32 patch-2.0.8
$ gzip *
$ ls -l
total 51
-rw-rw-r-- 1 max group 9693 Jul 20 17:32 patch-2.0.7.gz
-rw-rw-r-- 1 max group 40426 Jul 20 17:32 patch-2.0.8.gz
$ gunzip patch-2.0.7.gz
$ ls -l
total 75
-rw-rw-r-- 1 max group 33557 Jul 20 17:32 patch-2.0.7
-rw-rw-r-- 1 max group 40426 Jul 20 17:32 patch-2.0.8.gz
```

In the next example, the files in Sam's home directory are archived using cpio (page 644). The archive is compressed with gzip before it is written to the device mounted on **/dev/sde1**.

```
$ find ~sam -depth -print | cpio -oBm | gzip >/dev/sde1
```

head

Displays the beginning of a file

head [options] [file-list]

The head utility displays the beginning (head) of a file. This utility takes its input either from one or more files you specify on the command line or from standard input.

Arguments
The *file-list* is a list of the pathnames of the files that head displays. When you specify more than one file, head displays the filename before displaying the first few lines of each file. When you do not specify a file, head takes its input from standard input.

Options
Under Linux, head accepts the common options described on page 603. Options preceded by a double hyphen (––) work under Linux only. Except as noted, options named with a single letter and preceded by a single hyphen work under Linux and OS X.

––bytes=*n[u]* **–c *n[u]***
Displays the first *n* bytes (characters) of a file. Under Linux only, the *u* argument is an optional multiplicative suffix as described on page 602, except that head uses a lowercase **k** for kilobyte (1,024-byte blocks) and accepts **b** for 512-byte blocks. If you include a multiplicative suffix, head counts by this unit instead of by bytes.

––lines=*n* **–n *n***
Displays the first *n* lines of a file. You can use *–n* to specify *n* lines without using the **lines** keyword or the **–n** option. If you specify a negative value for *n*, head displays all but the last *n* lines of the file.

––quiet **–q** Suppresses header information when you specify more than one filename on the command line. `LINUX`

Notes
The head utility displays the first ten lines of a file by default.

Examples
The examples in this section are based on the following file:

```
$ cat eleven
line one
line two
line three
line four
line five
line six
line seven
line eight
line nine
line ten
line eleven
```

Without any arguments head displays the first ten lines of a file:

```
$ head eleven
line one
line two
line three
line four
line five
line six
line seven
line eight
line nine
line ten
```

The next example displays the first three lines (**–n 3**) of the file:

```
$ head -n 3 eleven
line one
line two
line three
```

The following example is equivalent to the preceding one:

```
$ head -3 eleven
line one
line two
line three
```

The next example displays the first six characters (**–c 6**) in the file:

```
$ head -c 6 eleven
line o$
```

The final example displays all but the last seven lines of the file:

```
$ head -n -7 eleven
line one
line two
line three
line four
```

kill

Terminates a process by PID

kill [option] PID-list
kill –l [signal-name | signal-number]

The kill utility sends a signal to one or more processes. Typically this signal terminates the processes. For kill to work, the processes must belong to the user executing kill, with one exception: A user working with **root** privileges can terminate any process. The –l (lowercase "l") option lists information about signals.

Arguments The *PID-list* is a list of process identification (PID) numbers of processes that kill is to terminate.

Options –l **(list)** Without an argument, displays a list of signals. With an argument of a *signal-name*, displays the corresponding *signal-number.* With an argument of a *signal-number,* displays the corresponding *signal-name.*

–*signal-name* | –*signal-number*
Sends the signal specified by *signal-name* or *signal-number* to *PID-list.* You can specify a *signal-name* preceded by **SIG** or not (e.g., **SIGKILL** or **KILL**). Without this option, kill sends a software termination signal (**SIGTERM**; signal number 15).

Notes See also killall on page 731.

See Table 10-5 on page 453 for a list of signals. The command **kill –l** displays a complete list of signal numbers and names.

In addition to the kill utility, a kill builtin is available in the Bourne Again and TC Shells. The builtins work similarly to the utility described here. Give the command **/bin/kill** to use the kill utility and the command **kill** to use the builtin. It does not usually matter which version you call.

The shell displays the PID number of a background process when you initiate the process. You can also use the ps utility to determine PID numbers.

If the software termination signal does not terminate a process, try sending a KILL signal (signal number 9). A process can choose to ignore any signal except KILL.

The kill utility/builtin accepts job identifiers in place of the *PID-list.* Job identifiers consist of a percent sign (%) followed by either a job number or a string that uniquely identifies the job.

To terminate all processes that the current login process initiated and have the operating system log you out, give the command **kill –9 0**.

root: do not run kill with arguments of –9 0 *or* KILL 0

caution   If you run the command **kill –9 0** while you are working with **root** privileges, you will bring the system down.

Examples   The first example shows a command line executing the file **compute** as a background process and the kill utility terminating it:

```
$ compute &
[2] 259
$ kill 259
$ RETURN
[2]+  Terminated               compute
```

The next example shows the ps utility determining the PID number of the background process running a program named **xprog** and the kill utility terminating **xprog** with the TERM signal:

```
$ ps
PID TTY          TIME CMD
 7525 pts/1    00:00:00 bash
14668 pts/1    00:00:00 xprog
14699 pts/1    00:00:00 ps

$ kill -TERM 14668
$
```

killall

Terminates a process by name

killall [option] name-list

The killall utility sends a signal to one or more processes executing specified commands. Typically this signal terminates the processes. For killall to work, the processes must belong to the user executing killall, with one exception: A user working with **root** privileges can terminate any process.

Arguments   The *name-list* is a SPACE-separated list of names of programs that are to receive signals.

Options   Options preceded by a double hyphen (––) work under Linux only. Except as noted, options named with a single letter and preceded by a single hyphen work under Linux and OS X.

––interactive   –i   Prompts for confirmation before killing a process. LINUX

––list   –l   Displays a list of signals (but **kill –l** displays a better list). With this option killall does not accept a *name-list*.

––quiet   –q   Does not display a message if killall fails to terminate a process. LINUX

–signal-name | –signal-number
Sends the signal specified by *signal-name* or *signal-number* to *name-list*. You can specify a *signal-name* preceded by **SIG** or not (e.g., **SIGKILL** or **KILL**). Without this option, kill sends a software termination signal (**SIGTERM**; signal number 15).

Notes   See also kill on page 729.

See Table 10-5 on page 453 for a list of signals. The command **kill –l** displays a complete list of signal numbers and names.

If the software termination signal does not terminate the process, try sending a KILL signal (signal number 9). A process can choose to ignore any signal except KILL.

You can use ps (page 796) to determine the name of the program you want to terminate.

Examples   You can give the following commands to experiment with killall:

```
$ sleep 60 &
[1] 23274
$ sleep 50 &
[2] 23275
$ sleep 40 &
[3] 23276
```

```
$ sleep 120 &
[4] 23277
$ killall sleep
$ RETURN
[1]   Terminated              sleep 60
[2]   Terminated              sleep 50
[3]-  Terminated              sleep 40
[4]+  Terminated              sleep 120
```

The next command, run by a user with **root** privileges, terminates all instances of the Firefox browser:

```
# killall firefox
```

launchctl OS X

Controls the **launchd** daemon

launchctl [command [options] [arguments]]

The launchctl utility controls the **launchd** daemon.

Arguments The *command* is the command that launchctl sends to **launchd**. Table V-17 lists some of the *commands* and the options and arguments each *command* accepts. Without a *command*, launchctl reads commands, options, and arguments from standard input, one set per line. Without a *command*, when standard input comes from the keyboard, launchctl runs interactively.

Table V-17 launchctl commands

Command	Argument	Description
help	None	Displays a help message
list	None	Lists jobs loaded into **launchd**
load [–w]	Job configuration file	Loads the job named by the argument
shutdown	None	Prepares for shutdown by removing all jobs
start	Job name	Starts the job named by the argument
stop	Job name	Stops the job named by the argument
unload [–w]	Job configuration file	Unloads the job named by the argument

Option Only the **load** and **unload** *commands* take an option.

–w (**write**) When loading a file, removes the **Disabled** key and saves the modified configuration file. When unloading a file, adds the **Disabled** key and saves the modified configuration file.

Discussion The launchctl utility is the user interface to **launchd**, which manages system daemons and background tasks (called jobs). Each job is described by a job configuration file, which is a property list file in the format defined by the **launchd.plist** man page.

For security reasons, users not working with **root** privileges cannot communicate with the system's primary **launchd** process, PID 1. When such a user loads jobs, OS X creates a new instance of **launchd** for that user. When all its jobs are unloaded, that instance of **launchd** quits.

Notes The launchctl utility and **launchd** daemon were introduced in Mac OS X version 10.4. Under version 10.3 and earlier, system jobs were managed by **init**, **xinetd**, and **cron**.

Examples   The first example, which is run by a user with **root** privileges, uses the **list** command to list **launchd** jobs running on the local system:

```
# launchctl list
PID       Status   Label
51479     –        0x109490.launchctl
50515     –        0x10a780.bash
50514     –        0x10a680.sshd
50511     –        0x108d20.sshd
22        –        0x108bc0.securityd
–         0        com.apple.launchctl.StandardIO
37057     –        [0x0-0x4e84e8].com.apple.ScreenSaver.Engine
27860     –        0x10a4e0.DiskManagementTo
27859     –        [0x0-0x3a23a2].com.apple.SoftwareUpdate
...
```

The next example enables the **ntalk** service. Looking at the **ntalk.plist** file before and after the launchctl command is executed shows that launchctl has modified the file by removing the **Disabled** key.

```
# cat /System/Library/LaunchDaemons/ntalk.plist
...
<dict>
        <key>Disabled</key>
        <true/>
        <key>Label</key>
        <string>com.apple.ntalkd</string>
...
# launchctl load -w /System/Library/LaunchDaemons/ntalk.plist
# cat /System/Library/LaunchDaemons/ntalk.plist
...
<dict>
        <key>Label</key>
        <string>com.apple.ntalkd</string>
...
```

Without any arguments, launchctl prompts for commands on standard input. Give a **quit** command or press CONTROL-D to exit from launchctl. In the last example, a user running with **root** privileges causes launchctl to display a list of jobs and then to stop the job that would launch **airportd**:

```
# launchctl
launchd% list
PID       Status   Label
8659      –        0x10ba10.cron
1         –        0x10c760.launchd
...
–         0        com.apple.airport.updateprefs
–         0        com.apple.airportd
–         0        com.apple.AirPort.wps
–         0        0x100670.dashboardadvisoryd
–         0        com.apple.launchctl.System
launchd% stop com.apple.airportd
launchd% quit
```

less

Displays text files, one screen at a time

less [options] [file-list]

The less utility displays text files, one screen at a time.

Arguments The *file-list* is the list of files you want to view. If there is no *file-list*, less reads from standard input.

Options The less utility accepts the common options described on page 603.

The Mac OS X version of less accepts long options

tip Options for less preceded by a double hyphen (––) work under Mac OS X as well as under Linux.

––clear-screen **–c** Repaints the screen from the top line down instead of scrolling.

––QUIT-AT-EOF **–E** (**exit**) Normally less requires you to enter **q** to terminate. This option exits automatically the *first* time less reads the end of file.

––quit-at-eof **–e** (**exit**) Similar to **–E**, except that less exits automatically the *second* time it reads the end of file.

––quit-if-one-screen
  –F Displays the file and quits if the file can be displayed on a single screen.

––ignore-case **–i** Causes a search for a string of lowercase letters to match both uppercase and lowercase letters. This option is ignored if you specify a pattern that includes uppercase letters.

––IGNORE-CASE
  –I Causes a search for a string of letters of any case to match both uppercase and lowercase letters, regardless of the case of the search pattern.

––long-prompt **–m** Each prompt reports the percentage of the file you have viewed. This option causes less to display a prompt similar to the prompt used by more. It reports byte numbers when less reads from standard input because less has no way of determining the size of the input file.

––LINE-NUMBERS
  –N Displays a line number at the beginning of each line.

––prompt=*prompt*
  –P*prompt*
      Changes the short prompt string (the prompt that appears at the bottom of each screen of output) to *prompt*. Enclose *prompt* in quotation marks if it contains SPACEs. You can include special symbols in *prompt*, which less will replace

with other values when it displays the prompt. For example, less displays the current filename in place of %f in *prompt*. See the less man page for a list of these special symbols and descriptions of other prompts. Custom prompts are useful if you are running less from within another program and want to give instructions or information to the person using the program. The default prompt is the name of the file displayed in reverse video.

--squeeze-blank-lines

   -s   Displays multiple, adjacent blank lines as a single blank line. When you use less to display text that has been formatted for printing with blank space at the top and bottom of each page, this option shortens these headers and footers to a single line.

--tabs=*n*   -x*n*

Sets tab stops *n* characters apart. The default is eight characters.

--window=*n*   -[z]*n*

Sets the scrolling size to *n* lines. The default is the height of the display in lines. Each time you move forward or backward a page, you move *n* lines. The z part of the option maintains compatibility with more and can be omitted.

+*command*

Any command you can give less while it is running can also be given as an option by preceding it with a plus sign (**+**) on the command line. See the "Commands" section. A command preceded by a plus sign on the command line is executed as soon as less starts and applies to the first file only.

++*command*

Similar to **+*command*** except that *command* is applied to every file in *file-list*, not just the first file.

Notes

The phrase "less is more" explains the origin of the name of this utility. The more utility is the original Berkeley UNIX pager (also available under Linux). The less utility is similar to more but includes many enhancements. (Under OS X, less and more are copies of the same file.) After displaying a screen of text, less displays a prompt and waits for you to enter a command. You can skip forward and backward in the file, invoke an editor, search for a pattern, or perform a number of other tasks.

See the **v** command in the next section for information on how you can edit the file you are viewing with less.

You can set the options to less either from the command line when you call less or by setting the **LESS** environment variable. For example, you can use the following command from bash to use less with the **–x4** and **–s** options:

```
$ export LESS="-x4 -s"
```

Normally you would set **LESS** in **~/.bash_profile** if you are using bash or in **~/.login** if you are using tcsh. Once you have set the **LESS** variable, less is invoked with the specified options each time you call it. Any options you give on the command line override the settings in the **LESS** variable. The **LESS** variable is used both when you call less from the command line and when less is invoked by another program, such as man. To specify less as the pager to use with man and other programs, set the environment variable **PAGER** to **less**. For example, with bash you can add the following line to **~/.bash_profile**:

```
export PAGER=less
```

Commands   Whenever less pauses, you can enter any of a large number of commands. This section describes some commonly used commands. Refer to the less man page for the full list of commands. The optional numeric argument *n* defaults to 1, with the exceptions noted. You do not need to follow these commands with a RETURN.

*n*b *or* *n*CONTROL-B   (**backward**) Scrolls backward *n* lines. The default value of *n* is the height of the screen in lines.

*n*d *or* *n*CONTROL-D   (**down**) Scrolls forward *n* lines. The default value of *n* is one-half the height of the screen in lines. When you specify *n*, it becomes the new default value for this command.

F   (**forward**) Scrolls forward. If the end of the input is reached, this command waits for more input and then continues scrolling. This command allows you to use less in a manner similar to **tail –f** (page 843), except that less paginates the output as it appears.

*n*g   (**go**) Goes to line number *n*. This command may not work if the file is read from standard input and you have moved too far into the file. The default value of *n* is 1.

h *or* H   (**help**) Displays a summary of all available commands. The summary is displayed using less, as the list of commands is quite long.

*n*RETURN *or* *n*j   (**jump**) Scrolls forward *n* lines. The default value of *n* is 1.

q *or* :q   Terminates less.

*n*u *or* *n*CONTROL-U   Scrolls backward *n* lines. The default value of *n* is one-half the height of the screen in lines. When you specify *n*, it becomes the default value for this command.

v   Brings the current file into an editor with the cursor on the current line. The less utility uses the editor specified in the **EDITOR** environment variable. If **EDITOR** is not set, less uses vi (which is typically linked to vim).

*n*w   Scrolls backward like *n*b, except that the value of *n* becomes the new default value for this command.

*n*y *or* *n*k   Scrolls backward *n* lines. The default value of *n* is 1.

*n*z   Displays the next *n* lines like *n*SPACE except that the value of *n*, if present, becomes the new default value for the **z** and SPACE commands.

*n*SPACE Displays the next *n* lines. Pressing the SPACE bar by itself displays the next screen of text.

/*regular-expression*

Skips forward in the file, looking for lines that contain a match for ***regular-expression***. If you begin ***regular-expression*** with an exclamation point (!), this command looks for lines that do *not* contain a match for ***regular-expression***. If ***regular-expression*** begins with an asterisk (❋), this command continues the search through ***file-list***. (A normal search stops at the end of the current file.) If ***regular-expression*** begins with an at sign (@), this command begins the search at the beginning of ***file-list*** and continues to the end of ***file-list***.

?*regular-expression*

This command is similar to the previous one but searches backward through the file (and ***file-list***). An asterisk (❋) as the first character in ***regular-expression*** causes the search to continue backward through ***file-list*** to the beginning of the first file. An at sign (@) causes the search to start with the last line of the last file in ***file-list*** and progress toward the first line of the first file.

{ *or* (*or* [If one of these characters appears in the top line of the display, this command scrolls forward to the matching right brace, parenthesis, or bracket. For example, typing { causes less to move the cursor forward to the matching }.

} *or*) *or*] Similar to the preceding commands, these commands move the cursor backward to the matching left brace, parenthesis, or bracket.

CONTROL-L Redraws the screen. This command is useful if the text on the screen has become garbled.

[*n*]:n Skips to the next file in ***file-list***. If *n* is given, skips to the *n*th next file in ***file-list***.

![*command line*] Executes ***command line*** under the shell specified by the **SHELL** environment variable or under sh (usually linked to or a copy of bash) by default. A percent sign (%) in ***command line*** is replaced by the name of the current file. If you omit ***command line***, less starts an interactive shell.

Examples

The following example displays the file **memo.txt**. To see more of the file, the user presses the SPACE bar in response to the less prompt at the lower-left corner of the screen:

```
$ less memo.txt
. . .
memo.txt SPACE
. . .
```

In the next example, the user changes the prompt to a more meaningful message and uses the –N option to display line numbers. Finally the user instructs less to skip forward to the first line containing the string **procedure**.

```
$ less -Ps"Press SPACE to continue, q to quit" -N +/procedure ncut.icn
   28  procedure main(args)
   29      local filelist, arg, fields, delim
   30
   31      filelist:=[]
...
   45      # Check for real field list
   46      #
   47      if /fields then stop("-fFIELD_LIST is required.")
   48
   49      # Process the files and output the fields
Press SPACE to continue, q to quit
```

ln

Makes a link to a file

ln [options] existing-file [new-link]
ln [options] existing-file-list directory

The ln utility creates hard or symbolic links to one or more files. You can create a symbolic link, but not a hard link, to a directory.

Arguments   In the first format the *existing-file* is the pathname of the file you want to create a link to. The *new-link* is the pathname of the new link. When you are creating a symbolic link, the *existing-file* can be a directory. If you omit *new-link,* ln creates a link to *existing-file* in the working directory, and uses the same simple filename as *existing-file*.

In the second format the *existing-file-list* is a list of the pathnames of the ordinary files you want to create links to. The ln utility establishes the new links in the *directory*. The simple filenames of the entries in the *directory* are the same as the simple filenames of the files in the *existing-file-list*.

Options   Options preceded by a double hyphen (––) work under Linux only. Except as noted, options named with a single letter and preceded by a single hyphen work under Linux and OS X.

––backup   **–b**   If the ln utility will remove a file, this option makes a backup by appending a tilde (~) to the filename. This option works only with **––force**. **LINUX**

––force   **–f**   Normally ln does not create the link if *new-link* already exists. This option removes *new-link* before creating the link. When you use **––force** and **––backup** together (Linux only), ln makes a copy of *new-link* before removing it.

––interactive   **–i**   If *new-link* already exists, this option prompts you before removing *new-link*. If you enter **y** or **yes**, ln removes *new-link* before creating the link. If you answer **n** or **no**, ln does not remove *new-link* and does not make a new link.

––symbolic   **–s**   Creates a symbolic link. When you use this option, the *existing-file* and the *new-link* may be directories and may reside on different filesystems. Refer to "Symbolic Links" on page 108.

Notes   For more information refer to "Links" on page 104. The ls utility with the **–l** option displays the number of hard links to a file (Figure 4-12, page 94).

Hard links   By default ln creates *hard links*. A hard link to a file is indistinguishable from the original file. All hard links to a file must be in the same filesystem. For more information refer to "Hard Links" on page 106.

Symbolic links   You can also use ln to create *symbolic links*. Unlike a hard link, a symbolic link can exist in a different filesystem from the linked-to file. Also, a symbolic link can point to a directory. For more information refer to "Symbolic Links" on page 108.

If *new-link* is the name of an existing file, ln does not create the link unless you use the **--force** option (Linux only) or answer **yes** when using the **-i** (**--interactive**) option.

Examples   The following command creates a link between **memo2** in the **literature** subdirectory of Zach's home directory and the working directory. The file appears as **memo2** (the simple filename of the existing file) in the working directory:

```
$ ln ~zach/literature/memo2 .
```

You can omit the period that represents the working directory from the preceding command. When you give a single argument to ln, it creates a link in the working directory.

The next command creates a link to the same file. This time the file appears as **new_memo** in the working directory:

```
$ ln ~zach/literature/memo2 new_memo
```

The following command creates a link that causes the file to appear in Sam's home directory:

```
$ ln ~zach/literature/memo2 ~sam/new_memo
```

You must have write and execute access permissions to the other user's directory for this command to work. If you own the file, you can use chmod to give the other user write access permission to the file.

The next command creates a symbolic link to a directory. The **ls -ld** command shows the link:

```
$ ln -s /usr/local/bin bin
$ ls -ld bin
lrwxrwxrwx  1 zach zach 14 Feb 10 13:26 bin -> /usr/local/bin
```

The final example attempts to create a symbolic link named **memo1** to the file **memo2**. Because the file **memo1** exists, ln refuses to make the link. When you use the **-i** (**--interactive**) option, ln asks whether you want to replace the existing **memo1** file with the symbolic link. If you enter **y** or **yes**, ln creates the link and the old **memo1** disappears.

```
$ ls -l memo?
-rw-rw-r--  1 zach group 224 Jul 31 14:48 memo1
-rw-rw-r--  1 zach group 753 Jul 31 14:49 memo2
$ ln -s memo2 memo1
ln: memo1: File exists
$ ln -si memo2 memo1
ln: replace 'memo1'? y
$ ls -l memo?
lrwxrwxrwx  1 zach group 5 Jul 31 14:49 memo1 -> memo2
-rw-rw-r--  1 zach group 753 Jul 31 14:49 memo2
```

Under Linux you can also use the **--force** option to cause ln to overwrite a file.

lpr

Sends files to printers

lpr [options] [file-list]
lpq [options] [job-identifiers]
lprm [options] [job-identifiers]

The lpr utility places one or more files into a print queue, providing orderly access to printers for several users or processes. This utility can work with printers attached to remote systems. You can use the lprm utility to remove files from the print queues and the lpq utility to check the status of files in the queues. Refer to "Notes" later in this section.

Arguments   The *file-list* is a list of one or more filenames for lpr to print. Often these files are text files, but many systems are configured so lpr can accept and properly print a variety of file types including PostScript and PDF files. Without a *file-list*, lpr accepts input from standard input.

The *job-identifiers* is a list of job numbers or usernames. If you do not know the job number, use lpq to display a list of print jobs.

Options   Some of the following options depend on which type of file is being printed as well as on how the system is configured for printing.

-h (**no header**) Suppresses printing of the header (burst) page. This page is useful for identifying the owner of the output in a multiuser setup, but printing it is a waste of paper when this identification is not needed.

-l (lowercase "l") Specifies that lpr should not preprocess (filter) the file being printed. Use this option when the file is already formatted for the printer.

-P *printer*
Routes the print jobs to the queue for the printer named *printer*. If you do not use this option, print jobs are routed to the default printer for the local system. The acceptable values for *printer* are found in the Linux file **/etc/printcap** and can be displayed by an **lpstat -t** command. These values vary from system to system.

-r (**remove**) Deletes the files in *file-list* after calling lpr.

-# *n*
Prints *n* copies of each file. Depending on which shell you are using, you may need to escape the # by preceding it with a backslash to keep the shell from interpreting it as a special character.

Discussion   The lpr utility takes input either from files you specify on the command line or from standard input; it adds these files to the print queue as *print jobs*. The utility assigns a unique identification number to each print job. The lpq utility displays the job numbers of the print jobs that lpr has set up; you can use the lprm utility to remove a job from the print queue.

lpq   The lpq utility displays information about jobs in a print queue. When called without any arguments, lpq lists all print jobs queued for the default printer. Use lpr's **–P** *printer* option with lpq to look at other print queues—even those for printers connected to remote systems. With the **–l** option, lpq displays more information about each job. If you give a username as an argument, lpq displays only the printer jobs belonging to that user.

lprm   One item displayed by lpq is the job number for each print job in the queue. To remove a job from the print queue, give the job number as an argument to lprm. Unless you are working with **root** privileges, you can remove only your own jobs. Even a user working with **root** privileges may not be able to remove a job from a queue for a remote printer. If you do not give any arguments to lprm, it removes the active printer job (that is, the job that is now printing) from the queue, if you own that job.

Notes   If you normally use a printer other than the system default printer, you can set up lpr to use another printer as your personal default by assigning the name of this printer to the environment variable **PRINTER**. For example, if you use bash, you can add the following line to **~/.bash_profile** to set your default printer to the printer named **ps**:

```
export PRINTER=ps
```

LPD and LPR   Traditionally, UNIX had two printing systems: the BSD Line Printer Daemon (LPD) and the System V Line Printer system (LPR). Linux adopted those systems at first, and both UNIX and Linux have seen modifications to and replacements for these systems. Today CUPS is the default printing system under Linux and OS X.

CUPS   CUPS is a cross-platform print server built around the Internet Printing Protocol (IPP), which is based on HTTP. CUPS provides a number of printer drivers and can print different types of files, including PostScript files. CUPS provides System V and BSD command-line interfaces and, in addition to IPP, supports LPD/LPR, HTTP, SMB, and JetDirect (socket) protocols, among others.

This section describes the LPD command-line interface that runs under CUPS and also in native mode on older systems.

Examples   The first command sends the file named **memo2** to the default printer:

```
$ lpr memo2
```

Next a pipe sends the output of ls to the printer named **deskjet**:

```
$ ls | lpr -Pdeskjet
```

The next example paginates and sends the file **memo** to the printer:

```
$ pr -h "Today's memo" memo | lpr
```

The next example shows a number of print jobs queued for the default printer. Max owns all the jobs, and the first one is being printed (it is active). Jobs 635 and 639 were created by sending input to lpr's standard input; job 638 was created by giving **ncut.icn** as an argument to the lpr command. The last column gives the size of each print job.

```
$ lpq
deskjet is ready and printing
Rank    Owner    Job  Files                    Total Size
active  max      635  (stdin)                  38128 bytes
1st     max      638  ncut.icn                  3587 bytes
2nd     max      639  (stdin)                   3960 bytes
```

The next command removes job 638 from the default print queue:

```
$ lprm 638
```

ls

Displays information about one or more files

ls [options] [file-list]

The ls utility displays information about one or more files. It lists the information alphabetically by filename unless you use an option that changes the order.

Arguments   When you do not provide an argument, ls displays the names of the visible files (those with filenames that do not begin with a period) in the working directory.

The *file-list* is a list of one or more pathnames of any ordinary, directory, or device files. It can include ambiguous file references.

When the *file-list* includes a directory, ls displays the contents of the directory. It displays the name of the directory only when needed to avoid ambiguity, such as when the listing includes more than one directory. When you specify an ordinary file, ls displays information about that one file.

Options   Options preceded by a double hyphen (--) work under Linux only. Except as noted, options named with a single letter and preceded by a single hyphen work under Linux and OS X.

The options determine the type of information ls displays, the manner in which it displays the information, and the order in which the information is displayed. When you do not use an option, ls displays a short list that contains just the names of files, in alphabetical order.

--almost-all   **-A**   The same as -a but does not list the . and .. directory entries.

--all   **-a**   Includes hidden filenames (those filenames that begin with a period; page 82) in the listing. Without this option ls does not list information about hidden files unless you include the name of a hidden file in the *file-list*. The * ambiguous file reference does not match a leading period in a filename (page 138), so you must use this option or explicitly specify a filename (ambiguous or not) that begins with a period to display hidden files.

--escape   **-b**   Displays nonprinting characters in a filename, using backslash escape sequences similar to those used in C language strings (Table V-18). Other nonprinting characters are displayed as a backslash followed by an octal number.

Table V-18   Backslash escape sequences

Sequence	Meaning
\b	BACKSPACE
\n	NEWLINE

Table V-18 Backslash escape sequences (continued)

Sequence	Meaning
\r	RETURN
\t	HORIZONTAL TAB
\v	VERTICAL TAB
\\	BACKSLASH

--color[=*when*] The ls utility can display various types of files in different colors but normally does not use colors (the same result as when you specify *when* as **none**). If you do not specify *when* or if you specify *when* as **always**, ls uses colors. When you specify *when* as **auto**, ls uses colors only when the output goes to a screen. See the "Notes" section for more information. `LINUX`

--directory   –d Displays directories without displaying their contents. This option does not dereference symbolic links; that is, for each file that is a symbolic link, this option lists the symbolic link, not the file the link points to.

–e Displays ACLs (page 934). `OS X`

--format=*word* By default ls displays files sorted vertically. This option sorts files based on *word*: **across** or **horizontal** (also **–x**), separated by **commas** (also **–m**), **long** (also **–l**), or **single-column** (also **–1**). `LINUX`

--classify   –F Displays a slash (/) after each directory, an asterisk (*) after each executable file, and an at sign (@) after a symbolic link.

--dereference-command-line
–H (**partial dereference**) For each file that is a symbolic link, lists the file the link points to, not the symbolic link itself. This option affects files specified on the command line; it does not affect files found while descending a directory hierarchy. This option treats files that are not symbolic links normally. See page 623 for an example of the use of the –H versus –L options.

--human-readable
–h With the –l option, displays sizes in K (kilobyte), M (megabyte), and G (gigabyte) blocks, as appropriate. This option works with the –l option only. It displays powers of 1,024. Under Mac OS X, it displays B (bytes) in addition to the preceding suffixes. See also --si.

--inode   –i Displays the inode number of each file. With the –l option, this option displays the inode number in column 1 and shifts other items one column to the right.

--dereference   –L (**dereference**) For each file that is a symbolic link, lists the file the link points to, not the symbolic link itself. This option affects all files and treats files that are not symbolic links normally. See page 623 for an example of the use of the –H versus –L options.

--format=long	–l	(lowercase "l") Lists more information about each file. This option does not dereference symbolic links; that is, for each file that is a symbolic link, this option lists the symbolic link, not the file the link points to. If standard output for a directory listing is sent to the screen, this option displays the number of blocks used by all files in the listing on a line before the listing. Use this option with –h to make file sizes more readable. See the "Discussion" section for more information.
--format=commas		
	–m	Displays a comma-separated list of files that fills the width of the screen.
	–P	(**no dereference**) For each file that is a symbolic link, lists the symbolic link, not the file the link points to. This option affects all files and treats files that are not symbolic links normally. See page 625 for an example of the use of the –P option. `OS X`
--hide-control-chars		
	–q	Displays nonprinting characters in a filename as question marks. When standard output is sent to the screen, this behavior is the default. Without this option, when standard output is sent to a filter or a file, nonprinting characters are displayed as themselves.
--recursive	–R	Recursively lists directory hierarchies.
--reverse	–r	Displays the list of filenames in reverse sorted order.
--size	–s	Displays the number of 1,024-byte (Linux) or 512-byte (Mac OS X) blocks allocated to the file. The size precedes the filename. With the –l option this option displays the size in column 1 and shifts other items one column to the right. If standard output for a directory listing is sent to the screen, this option displays the number of blocks used by all files in the listing on a line before the listing. You can include the –h option to make the file sizes easier to read.
		Under Mac OS X, you can use the **BLOCKSIZE** environment variable (page 603) to change the size of the blocks this option reports on.
--si		With the –l option, displays sizes in K (kilobyte), M (megabyte), and G (gigabyte) blocks, as appropriate. This option works with the –l option only. This option displays powers of 1,000. See also --**human-readable**. `LINUX`
--sort=time	–t	Displays files sorted by the time they were last modified.
--sort=*word*		By default ls displays files in ASCII order. This option sorts the files based on *word*: filename **extension** (–X; Linux only), **none** (–U; Linux only), file **size** (–S), **access** time (–u), or modification **time** (–t). See --**time** for an exception. `LINUX`
--time=*word*		By default ls with the –l option displays the modification time of a file. Set *word* to **atime** (–u) to display the access time or to **ctime** (–t) to display the modification time. The list is sorted by *word* when you also give the --**sort=time** option. `LINUX`

−−sort=access   **−u**   Displays files sorted by the time they were last accessed.

−−format=extension

−X   Displays files sorted by filename extension. Files with no filename extension are listed first. `LINUX`

−−format=across   **−x**   Displays files sorted by lines (the default display is sorted by columns).

−−format=single-column

−1   (one) Displays one file per line. This type of display is the default when you redirect the output from ls.

Discussion   The ls long listing (**−l** or **−−format=long** options) displays the columns shown in Figure 4-12 on page 94. The first column, which contains 10 or 11 characters, is divided as described in the following paragraphs. The character in the first position describes the type of file, as shown in Table V-19.

Table V-19   First character in a long ls display

Character	Meaning
−	Ordinary
b	Block device
c	Character device
d	Directory
p	FIFO (named pipe)
l	Symbolic link

The next nine characters of the first column describe the access permissions associated with the file. These characters are divided into three sets of three characters each.

The first three characters represent the owner's access permissions. If the owner has read access permission to the file, **r** appears in the first character position. If the owner is not permitted to read the file, a hyphen appears in this position. The next two positions represent the owner's write and execute access permissions. If **w** appears in the second position, the owner is permitted to write to the file; if **x** appears in the third position, the owner is permitted to execute the file. An **s** in the third position indicates the file has both setuid and execute permissions. An **S** in the third position indicates setuid permission without execute permission. A hyphen indicates that the owner does not have the access permission associated with the character position.

In a similar manner the second set of three characters represents the access permissions for the group the file is associated with. An **s** in the third position indicates the file has setgid permission with execute permission, and an **S** indicates setgid permission with no execute permission.

The third set of three characters represents the access permissions for other users. A **t** in the third position indicates that the file has the *sticky bit* (page 980) set.

Refer to chmod on page 626 for information on changing access permissions.

If ACLs (page 99) are enabled and a listed file has an ACL, ls –l displays a plus sign (+) following the third set of three characters.

Still referring to Figure 4-12 on page 94, the second column indicates the number of hard links to the file. Refer to page 104 for more information on links.

The third and fourth columns display the name of the owner of the file and the name of the group the file is associated with, respectively.

The fifth column indicates the size of the file in bytes or, if information about a device file is being displayed, the major and minor device numbers. In the case of a directory, this number is the size of the directory file, not the size of the files that are entries within the directory. (Use du [page 677] to display the sum of the sizes of all files in a directory.) Use the **–h** option to display the size of files in kilobytes, megabytes, or gigabytes.

The last two columns display the date and time the file was last modified and the filename, respectively.

Notes   By default, ls dereferences symbolic links: For each file that is a symbolic link, ls lists the file the link points to, not the symbolic link itself. Use the **–l** or **–d** option to reference symbolic links (display information on symbolic links, not the files the links point to).

For other than long listings (displayed by the **–l** option), when standard output goes to the screen, ls displays output in columns based on the width of the screen. When you redirect standard output to a filter or file, ls displays a single column.

Refer to page 136 for examples of using ls with ambiguous file references.

With the **--color** option, ls displays the filenames of various types of files in different colors. By default executable files are green, directory files are blue, symbolic links are cyan, archives and compressed files are red, and ordinary text files are black. The manner in which ls colors the various file types is specified in the **/etc/DIR_COLORS** file. If this file does not exist on the local system, ls will not color filenames. You can modify **/etc/DIR_COLORS** to alter the default color/filetype mappings on a systemwide basis. For your personal use, you can copy **/etc/DIR_COLORS** to the **~/.dir_colors** file in your home directory and modify it. For your login, **~/.dir_colors** overrides the systemwide colors established in **/etc/DIR_COLORS**. Refer to the **dir_colors** and dircolors man pages for more information.

Examples   The first example shows ls, without any options or arguments, listing the names of the files in the working directory in alphabetical order. The listing is sorted in columns (vertically):

```
$ ls
bin   calendar  letters
c     execute   shell
```

The next example shows the ls utility with the **−x** option, which sorts the files horizontally:

```
$ ls -x
bin      c        calendar
execute  letters  shell
```

The **−F** option appends a slash (**/**) to files that are directories, an asterisk to files that are executable, and an at sign (**@**) to files that are symbolic links:

```
$ ls -Fx
bin/     c/       calendar
execute* letters/ shell@
```

Next the **−l** (**long**) option displays a long list. The files are still in alphabetical order:

```
$ ls -l
total 20
drwxr-xr-x 2 sam pubs 4096 May 20 09:17 bin
drwxr-xr-x 2 sam pubs 4096 Mar 26 11:59 c
-rw-r--r-- 1 sam pubs  104 Jan  9 14:44 calendar
-rwxr-xr-x 1 sam pubs   85 May  6 08:27 execute
drwxr-xr-x 2 sam pubs 4096 Apr  4 18:56 letters
lrwxrwxrwx 1 sam sam     9 May 21 11:35 shell -> /bin/bash
```

The **−a** (**all**) option lists all files, including those with hidden names:

```
$ ls -a
.            bin       execute
..           c         letters
.profile     calendar  shell
```

Combining the **−a** and **−l** options displays a long listing of all files, including invisible files, in the working directory. This list is still in alphabetical order:

```
$ ls -al
total 32
drwxr-xr-x 5 sam sam  4096 May 21 11:50 .
drwxrwxrwx 3 sam sam  4096 May 21 11:50 ..
-rw-r--r-- 1 sam sam   160 May 21 11:45 .profile
drwxr-xr-x 2 sam pubs 4096 May 20 09:17 bin
drwxr-xr-x 2 sam pubs 4096 Mar 26 11:59 c
-rw-r--r-- 1 sam pubs  104 Jan  9 14:44 calendar
-rwxr-xr-x 1 sam pubs   85 May  6 08:27 execute
drwxr-xr-x 2 sam pubs 4096 Apr  4 18:56 letters
lrwxrwxrwx 1 sam sam     9 May 21 11:35 shell -> /bin/bash
```

When you add the **–r** (reverse) option to the command line, ls produces a list in reverse alphabetical order:

```
$ ls -ral
total 32
lrwxrwxrwx 1 sam sam      9 May 21 11:35 shell -> /bin/bash
drwxr-xr-x 2 sam pubs 4096 Apr  4 18:56 letters
-rwxr-xr-x 1 sam pubs   85 May  6 08:27 execute
-rw-r--r-- 1 sam pubs  104 Jan  9 14:44 calendar
drwxr-xr-x 2 sam pubs 4096 Mar 26 11:59 c
drwxr-xr-x 2 sam pubs 4096 May 20 09:17 bin
-rw-r--r-- 1 sam sam   160 May 21 11:45 .profile
drwxrwxrwx 3 sam sam  4096 May 21 11:50 ..
drwxr-xr-x 5 sam sam  4096 May 21 11:50 .
```

Use the **–t** and **–l** options to list files so the *most recently* modified file appears at the top of the list:

```
$ ls -tl
total 20
lrwxrwxrwx 1 sam sam      9 May 21 11:35 shell -> /bin/bash
drwxr-xr-x 2 sam pubs 4096 May 20 09:17 bin
-rwxr-xr-x 1 sam pubs   85 May  6 08:27 execute
drwxr-xr-x 2 sam pubs 4096 Apr  4 18:56 letters
drwxr-xr-x 2 sam pubs 4096 Mar 26 11:59 c
-rw-r--r-- 1 sam pubs  104 Jan  9 14:44 calendar
```

Together the **–r** and **–t** options cause the file you modified *least recently* to appear at the top of the list:

```
$ ls -trl
total 20
-rw-r--r-- 1 sam pubs  104 Jan  9 14:44 calendar
drwxr-xr-x 2 sam pubs 4096 Mar 26 11:59 c
drwxr-xr-x 2 sam pubs 4096 Apr  4 18:56 letters
-rwxr-xr-x 1 sam pubs   85 May  6 08:27 execute
drwxr-xr-x 2 sam pubs 4096 May 20 09:17 bin
lrwxrwxrwx 1 sam sam      9 May 21 11:35 shell -> /bin/bash
```

The next example shows ls with a directory filename as an argument. The ls utility lists the contents of the directory in alphabetical order:

```
$ ls bin
c   e   lsdir
```

To display information about the directory file itself, use the **–d** (directory) option. This option lists information about the directory only:

```
$ ls -dl bin
drwxr-xr-x 2 sam pubs 4096 May 20 09:17 bin
```

You can use the following command to display a list of all hidden filenames (those starting with a period) in your home directory. It is a convenient way to list the startup (initialization) files in your home directory.

```
$ ls -d ~/.*
/home/sam/.
/home/sam/..
/home/sam/.AbiSuite
/home/sam/.Azureus
/home/sam/.BitTornado
...
```

A plus sign (+) to the right of the permissions in a long listing denotes the presence of an ACL for a file:

```
$ ls -l memo
-rw-r--r--+ 1 sam pubs 19 Jul 19 21:59 memo
```

Under Mac OS X you can use the –le option to display an ACL:

```
$ ls -le memo
-rw-r--r-- + 1 sam pubs 19 Jul 19 21:59 memo
 0: user:jenny allow read
```

See page 934 for more examples of using ls under Mac OS X to display ACLs.

make

Keeps a set of programs current

make [options] [target-files] [arguments]

The GNU make utility keeps a set of executable programs current, based on differences in the modification times of the programs and the source files that each program is dependent on.

Arguments The *target-files* refer to targets on dependency lines in the makefile. When you do not specify a *target-file*, make updates the target on the first dependency line in the makefile. Command-line *arguments* of the form *name=value* set the variable *name* to *value* inside the makefile. See the "Discussion" section for more information.

Options If you do not use the –f option, make takes its input from a file named **GNUmakefile**, **makefile**, or **Makefile** (in that order) in the working directory. In this section, this input file is referred to as **makefile**. Many users prefer to use the name **Makefile** because it shows up earlier in directory listings.

The Mac OS X version of make accepts long options

tip   Options for make preceded by a double hyphen (––) work under Mac OS X as well as under Linux.

--directory=*dir* –C *dir*
Changes directories to *dir* before starting.

--debug –d Displays information about how make decides what to do.

--file=*file* –f *file*
(**input file**) Uses *file* as input instead of **makefile**.

--jobs[=*n*] –j [*n*]
(**jobs**) Runs up to *n* commands at the same time instead of the default of one command. Running multiple commands simultaneously is especially effective if you are working on a multiprocessor system. If you omit *n*, make does not limit the number of simultaneous jobs.

--keep-going –k Continues with the next file from the list of *target-files* instead of quitting when a construction command fails.

--just-print *or* --dry-run –n (**no execution**) Displays, but does not execute, the commands that make would execute to bring the *target-files* up-to-date.

--silent *or* --quiet –s Does not display the names of the commands being executed.

--touch –t Updates the modification times of target files but does not execute any construction commands. Refer to touch on page 862.

Discussion The make utility bases its actions on the modification times of the programs and the source files that each program depends on. Each of the executable programs, or *target-files*, depends on one or more prerequisite files. The relationships between *target-files* and prerequisites are specified on *dependency lines* in a makefile. Construction commands follow the dependency line, specifying how make can update the *target-files*. See page 756 for examples of makefiles.

Documentation Refer to www.gnu.org/software/make/manual/make.html and to the make info page for more information about make and makefiles.

Although the most common use of make is to build programs from source code, this general-purpose build utility is suitable for a wide range of applications. Anywhere you can define a set of dependencies to get from one state to another represents a candidate for using make.

Much of make's power derives from the features you can set up in a makefile. For example, you can define variables using the same syntax found in the Bourne Again Shell. *Always* define the variable **SHELL** in a makefile; set it to the pathname of the shell you want to use when running construction commands. To define the variable and assign it a value, place the following line near the top of a makefile:

```
SHELL=/bin/sh
```

Assigning the value **/bin/sh** to **SHELL** allows you to use a makefile on other computer systems. On Linux systems, **/bin/sh** is generally linked to **/bin/bash** or **/bin/dash**. Under Mac OS X, **/bin/sh** is a copy of bash that attempts to emulate the original Bourne Shell. The make utility uses the value of the environment variable **SHELL** if you do not set **SHELL** in a makefile. If **SHELL** does not hold the path of the shell you intended to use and if you do not set **SHELL** in a makefile, the construction commands may fail.

Following is a list of additional features associated with make:

- You can run specific construction commands silently by preceding them with an at sign (**@**). For example, the following lines will display a short help message when you run the command **make help**:

```
help:
    @echo "You can make the following:"
    @echo " "
    @echo "libbuf.a        -- the buffer library"
    @echo "Bufdisplay      -- display any-format buffer"
    @echo "Buf2ppm         -- convert buffer to pixmap"
```

Without the **@** signs in the preceding example, make would display each of the echo commands before executing it. This way of displaying a message works because no file is named **help** in the working directory. As a result make runs the construction commands in an attempt to build this file. Because the construction commands display messages but do not build the file **help**, you can run **make help** repeatedly with the same result.

- You can cause make to ignore the exit status of a command by preceding the command with a hyphen (–). For example, the following line allows make to continue regardless of whether the call to **/bin/rm** is successful (the call to **/bin/rm** fails if **libbuf.a** does not exist):

```
-/bin/rm libbuf.a
```

- You can use special variables to refer to information that might change from one use of make to the next. Such information might include files that need updating, files that are newer than the target, and files that match a pattern. For example, you can use the variable **$?** in a construction command to identify all prerequisite files that are newer than the target file. This variable allows you to print any files that have changed since the last time you printed those files out:

```
list:       .list
.list:      Makefile buf.h xtbuff_ad.h buff.c buf_print.c xtbuff.c
pr $? | lpr
date >.list
```

The target list depends on the source files that might be printed. The construction command **pr $? | lpr** prints only those source files that are newer than the file **.list**. The line **date > .list** modifies the **.list** file so it is newer than any of the source files. The next time you run the command **make list**, only the files that have been changed are printed.

- You can include other makefiles as if they were part of the current makefile. The following line causes make to read **Make.config** and treat the contents of that file as though it were part of the current makefile, allowing you to put information common to more than one makefile in a single place:

```
include Make.config
```

Note   Under Mac OS X, the make utility is part of the Developer Tools optional install.

Examples   The first example causes make to bring the *target-file* named **analysis** up-to-date by issuing three **cc** commands. It uses a makefile named **GNUmakefile**, **makefile**, or **Makefile** in the working directory.

```
$ make analysis
cc -c analy.c
cc -c stats.c
cc -o analysis analy.o stats.o
```

The following example also updates **analysis** but uses a makefile named **analysis.mk** in the working directory:

```
$ make -f analysis.mk analysis
'analysis' is up to date.
```

The next example lists the commands make would execute to bring the *target-file* named **credit** up-to-date. Because of the **–n** (**no-execution**) option, make does not execute the commands.

```
$ make -n credit
cc -c -O credit.c
cc -c -O accounts.c
cc -c -O terms.c
cc -o credit credit.c accounts.c terms.c
```

The next example uses the **–t** option to update the modification time of the *target-file* named **credit**. After you use this option, make thinks that **credit** is up-to-date.

```
$ make -t credit
$ make credit
'credit' is up to date.
```

Example makefiles   Following is a very simple makefile named **Makefile**. This makefile compiles a program named **morning** (the target file). The first line is a dependency line that shows **morning** depends on **morning.c**. The next line is the construction line: It shows how to create **morning** using the gcc C compiler. The construction line must be indented using a TAB, not SPACEs.

```
$ cat Makefile
morning: morning.c
TAB gcc -o morning morning.c
```

When you give the command **make**, make compiles **morning.c** if it has been modified more recently than **morning**.

The next example is a simple makefile for building a utility named ff. Because the cc command needed to build ff is complex, using a makefile allows you to rebuild ff easily, without having to remember and retype the cc command.

```
$ cat Makefile
# Build the ff command from the fastfind.c source
SHELL=/bin/sh

ff:
gcc -traditional -O2 -g -DBIG=5120 -o ff fastfind.c myClib.a

$ make ff
gcc -traditional -O2 -g -DBIG=5120 -o ff fastfind.c myClib.a
```

In the next example, a makefile keeps the file named **compute** up-to-date. The make utility ignores comment lines (lines that begin with a pound sign [#]); the first three lines of the following makefile are comment lines. The first dependency line shows that **compute** depends on two object files: **compute.o** and **calc.o**. The corresponding construction line gives the command make needs to produce **compute**. The second dependency line shows that **compute.o** depends not only on its C source file but also on the **compute.h** header file. The construction line for **compute.o** uses the C compiler optimizer (**–O3** option). The third set of dependency and construction lines is not required. In their absence, make infers that **calc.o** depends on **calc.c** and produces the command line needed for the compilation.

```
$ cat Makefile
#
# Makefile for compute
#
compute: compute.o calc.o
        gcc -o compute compute.o calc.o

compute.o: compute.c compute.h
        gcc -c -O3 compute.c

calc.o: calc.c
        gcc -c calc.c

clean:
    rm *.o *core* *~
```

There are no prerequisites for **clean,** the last target. This target is often used to
remove extraneous files that may be out-of-date or no longer needed, such as .o
files.

The next example shows a much more sophisticated makefile that uses features not
discussed in this section. Refer to the sources cited under "Documentation" on
page 754 for information about these and other advanced features.

```
$ cat Makefile
#########################################################
## build and maintain the buffer library
#########################################################
SHELL=/bin/sh

#########################################################
## Flags and libraries for compiling. The XLDLIBS are needed
#   whenever you build a program using the library. The CCFLAGS
#   give maximum optimization.
CC=gcc
CCFLAGS=-O2 $(CFLAGS)
XLDLIBS= -lXaw3d -lXt -lXmu -lXext -lX11 -lm
BUFLIB=libbuf.a

#########################################################
## Miscellaneous
INCLUDES=buf.h
XINCLUDES=xtbuff_ad.h
OBJS=buff.o buf_print.o xtbuff.o

#########################################################
## Just a 'make' generates a help message
help:   Help
        @echo "You can make the following:"
        @echo " "
        @echo " libbuf.a        -- the buffer library"
        @echo " bufdisplay      -- display any-format buffer"
        @echo " buf2ppm         -- convert buffer to pixmap"

#########################################################
```

```
## The main target is the library
libbuf.a:    $(OBJS)
    -/bin/rm libbuf.a

    ar rv libbuf.a $(OBJS)
    ranlib libbuf.a
###########################################################
## Secondary targets -- utilities built from the library
bufdisplay: bufdisplay.c libbuf.a
    $(CC) $(CCFLAGS) bufdisplay.c -o bufdisplay $(BUFLIB) $(XLDLIBS)

buf2ppm: buf2ppm.c libbuf.a
    $(CC) $(CCFLAGS) buf2ppm.c -o buf2ppm $(BUFLIB)


###########################################################
## Build the individual object units
buff.o: $(INCLUDES) buff.c
    $(CC) -c $(CCFLAGS) buff.c

buf_print.o:$(INCLUDES) buf_print.c
    $(CC) -c $(CCFLAGS) buf_print.c

xtbuff.o: $(INCLUDES) $(XINCLUDES) xtbuff.c
    $(CC) -c $(CCFLAGS) xtbuff.c
```

The make utility can be used for tasks other than compiling code. As a final example, assume you have a database that lists IP addresses and the corresponding hostnames in two columns and that the database dumps these values to a file named **hosts.tab**. You need to extract only the hostnames from this file and generate a Web page named **hosts.html** containing these names. The following makefile is a simple report writer:

```
$ cat makefile
#
SHELL=/bin/bash
#
hosts.html: hosts.tab
        @echo "<HTML><BODY>" > hosts.html
        @awk '{print $$2, "<br>"}' hosts.tab >> hosts.html
        @echo "</BODY></HTML>" >> hosts.html
```

man

Displays documentation for commands

man [options] [section] command
man –k keyword

The man (manual) utility provides online documentation for Linux and Mac OS X commands. In addition to user commands, documentation is available for many other commands and details that relate to Linux and OS X. Because many Linux and OS X commands come from GNU, the GNU info utility (page 36) frequently provides more complete information about them.

A one-line header is associated with each manual page. This header consists of a command name, the section of the manual in which the command is found, and a brief description of what the command does. These headers are stored in a database; thus you can perform quick searches on keywords associated with each man page.

Arguments   The *section* argument tells man to limit its search to the specified section of the manual (see page 34 for a listing of manual sections). Without this argument man searches the sections in numerical order and displays the first man page it finds. In the second form of the man command, the –k option searches for the *keyword* in the database of man page headers; man displays a list of headers that contain the *keyword*. A **man –k** command performs the same function as apropos (page 35).

Options   Options preceded by a double hyphen (––) work under Linux only. Not all options preceded by a double hyphen work under all Linux distributions. Options named with a single letter and preceded by a single hyphen work under Linux and OS X.

--all   –a   Displays man pages for all sections of the manual. Without this option man displays only the first page it finds. Use this option when you are not sure which section contains the desired information.

–K *keyword*
Searches for *keyword* in all man pages. This option can take a long time to run. It is not available under some Linux distributions.

--apropos   –k *keyword*
Displays manual page headers that contain the string *keyword*. You can scan this list for commands of interest. This option is equivalent to the apropos command (page 35).

--manpath=*path* –M *path*
Searches the directories in *path* for man pages, where *path* is a colon-separated list of directories. See "Discussion."

––troff   **–t**   Formats the page for printing on a PostScript printer. The output goes to standard output.

Discussion   The manual pages are organized in sections, each pertaining to a separate aspect of the Linux system. Section 1 contains user-callable commands and is the section most likely to be accessed by users who are not system administrators or programmers. Other sections of the manual describe system calls, library functions, and commands used by system administrators. See page 34 for a listing of the manual sections.

Pager   The man utility uses less to display manual pages that fill more than one screen. To use another pager, set the environment variable **PAGER** to the pathname of that pager. For example, adding the following line to the **~/.bash_profile** file allows a bash user to use more instead of less:

```
export PAGER=/usr/bin/less
```

Under OS X, less and more are copies of the same file. Because of the way each is called, they work slightly differently.

MANPATH   You can tell man where to look for man pages by setting the environment variable **MANPATH** to a colon-separated list of directories. For example, bash users running Linux can add the following line to **~/.bash_profile** to cause man to search the **/usr/man**, **/usr/local/man**, and **/usr/local/share/man** directories:

```
export MANPATH=/usr/man:/usr/local/man:/usr/local/share/man
```

Working as a privileged user, you can edit **/etc/manpath.config** or **/etc/man.config** (Linux) or **/etc/man.conf** (OS X) to further configure man. Refer to the man man page for more information.

Notes   See page 33 for another discussion of man.

The argument to man does not have to be a command name. For example, the command **man ascii** lists the ASCII characters and their various representations; the command **man –k postscript** lists man pages that pertain to PostScript.

The man pages are commonly stored in an unformatted, compressed form. When you request a man page, it has to be decompressed and formatted before being displayed. To speed up subsequent requests for that man page, man attempts to save the formatted version of the page.

Some utilities described in the manual pages have the same name as shell builtin commands. The behavior of the shell builtin may differ slightly from the behavior of the utility as described in the manual page. For information about shell builtins, see the man page for **builtin** or the man page for a specific shell.

References to man pages frequently use section numbers in parentheses. For example, **write(2)** refers to the man page for **write** in section 2 of the manual (page 34).

The first of the following commands uses the col utility to generate a simple text man page that does not include bold or underlined text. The second command generates a PostScript version of the man page.

```
$ man ls | col -b > ls.txt
$ man -t ls > ls.ps
```

Under Linux you can use ps2pdf to convert the PostScript file to a PDF file.

Examples   The following example uses man to display the documentation for the command write, which sends messages to another user's terminal:

```
$ man write
WRITE(1)                     BSD General Commands Manual                     WRITE(1)

NAME
     write - send a message to another user

SYNOPSIS
     write user [ttyname]

DESCRIPTION
     The write utility allows you to communicate with other users, by copying
     lines from your terminal to theirs.

     When you run the write command, the user you are writing to gets a mes-
     sage of the form:

          Message from yourname@yourhost on yourtty at hh:mm ...
...
```

The next example displays the man page for another command—the man command itself, which is a good starting place for someone learning about the system:

```
$ man man
MAN(1)                          Manual pager utils                          MAN(1)

NAME
     man - an interface to the on-line reference manuals

SYNOPSIS
     man  [-c|-w|-tZ] [-H[browser]] [-T[device]] [-X[dpi]] [-adhu7V] [-i|-I]
     [-m system[,...]] [-L locale] [-p string] [-C file] [-M path] [-P
     pager] [-r prompt] [-S list] [-e extension] [--warnings [warnings]]
     [[section] page ...] ...
...

DESCRIPTION
     man  is  the  system's manual pager. Each page argument given to man is
     normally the name of a program, utility or function.  The  manual  page
     associated  with each of these arguments is then found and displayed. A
...
```

You can also use the man utility to find the man pages that pertain to a certain topic. In the next example, **man –k** displays man page headers containing the string **latex**. The apropos utility functions similarly to **man –k**.

```
$ man -k latex
elatex (1) [latex]    - structured text formatting and typesetting
latex (1)             - structured text formatting and typesetting
mkindex (1)           - script to process LaTeX index and glossary files
pdflatex (1)          - PDF output from TeX
pod2latex (1)         - convert pod documentation to latex format
Pod::LaTeX (3perl)    - Convert Pod data to formatted Latex
...
```

The search for the keyword entered with the –k option is not case sensitive. Although the keyword entered on the command line is all lowercase, it matches the last header, which contains the string **LaTeX** (uppercase and lowercase). The **3perl** entry on the last line indicates the man page is from Section 3 (Subroutines) of the Linux System Manual and comes from the *Perl Programmers Reference Guide* (it is a Perl subroutine; see Chapter 11 for more information on the Perl programming language).

mkdir

Creates a directory

mkdir [option] directory-list

The mkdir utility creates one or more directories.

Arguments The *directory-list* is a list of pathnames of directories that mkdir creates.

Options Under Linux, mkdir accepts the common options described on page 603. Options preceded by a double hyphen (––) work under Linux only. Options named with a single letter and preceded by a single hyphen work under Linux and OS X.

––mode=*mode* –m *mode*
> Sets the permission to *mode*. You can represent the *mode* absolutely using an octal number (Table V-7 on page 627) or symbolically (Table V-4 on page 626).

––parents –p Creates directories that do not exist in the path to the directory you wish to create.

––verbose –v Displays the name of each directory created. This option is helpful when used with the –p option.

Notes You must have permission to write to and search (execute permission) the parent directory of the directory you are creating. The mkdir utility creates directories that contain the standard hidden entries (. and ..).

Examples The following command creates the **accounts** directory as a subdirectory of the working directory and the **prospective** directory as a subdirectory of **accounts**:

```
$ mkdir -p accounts/prospective
```

Without changing working directories, the same user now creates another subdirectory within the **accounts** directory:

```
$ mkdir accounts/existing
```

Next the user changes the working directory to the **accounts** directory and creates one more subdirectory:

```
$ cd accounts
$ mkdir closed
```

The last example shows the user creating another subdirectory. This time the **––mode** option removes all access permissions for the group and others:

```
$ mkdir -m go= accounts/past_due
```

mkfs

Creates a filesystem on a device

mkfs [options] device

The mkfs utility creates a filesystem on a device such as a floppy diskette or a partition of a hard disk. It acts as a front end for programs that create filesystems, each specific to a filesystem type. The mkfs utility is available under Linux only. `LINUX`

mkfs **destroys all data on a device**

caution   Be careful when using mkfs: It destroys all data on a device.

Arguments

The *device* is the name of the device that you want to create the filesystem on. If the device name is in **/etc/fstab**, you can use the mount point of the device instead of the device name (e.g., **/home** in place of **/dev/sda2**).

Options

When you run mkfs, you can specify both global options and options specific to the filesystem type that mkfs is creating (e.g., **ext2, ext3, ext4, msdos, reiserfs**). Global options must precede type-specific options.

Global Options

−t *fstype*

(**type**) The *fstype* is the type of filesystem you want to create—for example, **ext2, ext3, msdos,** or **reiserfs**. The default filesystem varies.

−v   (**verbose**) Displays more output. Use −**V** for filesystem-specific information.

Filesystem Type-Specific Options

The options described in this section apply to many common filesystem types, including **ext2** and **ext3**. The following command lists the filesystem creation utilities available on the local system:

```
$ ls /sbin/mkfs.*
/sbin/mkfs.bfs      /sbin/mkfs.ext2  /sbin/mkfs.minix   /sbin/mkfs.reiserfs
/sbin/mkfs.cramfs   /sbin/mkfs.ext3  /sbin/mkfs.msdos   /sbin/mkfs.vfat
```

There is frequently a link to **/sbin/mkfs.ext2** at **/sbin/mke2fs**. Review the man page or give the pathname of the filesystem creation utility to determine which options the utility accepts.

```
$ /sbin/mkfs.ext3
Usage: mkfs.ext3 [-c|-l filename] [-b block-size] [-f fragment-size]
        [-i bytes-per-inode] [-I inode-size] [-J journal-options]
        [-N number-of-inodes] [-m reserved-blocks-percentage] [-o creator-os]
        [-g blocks-per-group] [-L volume-label] [-M last-mounted-directory]
        [-O feature[,...]] [-r fs-revision] [-E extended-option[,...]]
        [-T fs-type] [-jnqvFSV] device [blocks-count]
```

–b *size*

(**block**) Specifies the size of blocks in bytes. On **ext2**, **ext3**, and **ext4** filesystems, valid block sizes are 1,024, 2,048, and 4,096 bytes.

–c (**check**) Checks for bad blocks on the device before creating a filesystem. Specify this option twice to perform a slow, destructive, read-write test.

Discussion

Before you can write to and read from a hard disk or floppy diskette in the usual fashion, there must be a filesystem on it. Typically a hard disk is divided into *partitions* (page 970), each with a separate filesystem. A floppy diskette normally holds a single filesystem. Refer to Chapter 4 for more information on filesystems.

Notes

Under Mac OS X, use diskutil (page 668) to create a filesystem.

You can use tune2fs (page 868) with the –j option to change an existing **ext2** filesystem into a *journaling filesystem* (page 961) of type **ext3**. (See the "Examples" section.) You can also use tune2fs to change how often fsck (page 699) checks a filesystem.

mkfs is a front end
Much like fsck, mkfs is a front end that calls other utilities to handle various types of filesystems. For example, mkfs calls mke2fs (which is typically linked to mkfs.ext2 and mkfs.ext3) to create the widely used **ext2** and **ext3** filesystems. Refer to the mke2fs man page for more information. Other utilities that mkfs calls are typically named **mkfs.***type,* where *type* is the filesystem type. By splitting mkfs in this manner, filesystem developers can provide programs to create their filesystems without affecting the development of other filesystems or changing how system administrators use mkfs.

Examples

In the following example, mkfs creates a filesystem on the device at **/dev/hda8**. In this case the default filesystem type is **ext2**.

```
# /sbin/mkfs /dev/sda5
mke2fs 1.41.4 (27-Jan-2009)
Filesystem label=
OS type: Linux
Block size=1024 (log=0)
Fragment size=1024 (log=0)
122880 inodes, 489948 blocks
24497 blocks (5.00%) reserved for the super user
First data block=1
Maximum filesystem blocks=67633152
60 block groups
8192 blocks per group, 8192 fragments per group
2048 inodes per group
Superblock backups stored on blocks:
        8193, 24577, 40961, 57345, 73729, 204801, 221185, 401409

Writing inode tables: done
Writing superblocks and filesystem accounting information: done

This filesystem will be automatically checked every 37 mounts or
180 days, whichever comes first.  Use tune2fs -c or -i to override.
```

Next the administrator uses tune2fs to convert the **ext2** filesystem to an **ext3** journaling filesystem:

```
# /sbin/tune2fs -j /dev/sda5
tune2fs 1.41.4 (27-Jan-2009)
Creating journal inode: done
This filesystem will be automatically checked every 37 mounts or
180 days, whichever comes first.  Use tune2fs -c or -i to override.
```

Mtools

Uses DOS-style commands on files and directories

mcd [directory]
mcopy [options] file-list target
mdel file-list
mdir [–w] directory
mformat [options] device
mtype [options] file-list

These utilities mimic DOS commands and manipulate Linux, Mac OS X, or DOS files. The mcopy utility provides an easy way to move files between a Linux/OS X filesystem and a DOS disk. The default drive for all commands is **/dev/fd0** or **A:**.

Utilities   Table V-20 lists some of the utilities in the Mtools collection.

Table V-20   The Mtools collection

Utility	Function
mcd	Changes the working directory on the DOS disk
mcopy	Copies DOS files from one directory to another
mdel	Deletes DOS files
mdir	Lists the contents of DOS directories
mformat	Adds DOS formatting information to a disk
mtype	Displays the contents of DOS files

Arguments   The *directory*, which is used with mcd and mdir, must be the name of a directory on a DOS disk. The *file-list*, which is used with mcopy and mtype, is a SPACE-separated list of filenames. The *target*, which is used with mcopy, is the name of a regular file or a directory. If you give mcopy a *file-list* with more than one filename, *target* must be the name of a directory. The *device*, which is used with mformat, is the DOS drive letter containing the disk to be formatted (for example, **A:**).

Options   mcopy

–n   Automatically replaces existing files without asking. Normally mcopy asks for verification before overwriting a file.

–p   (**preserve**) Preserves the attributes of files when they are copied.

–s   (**recursive**) Copies directory hierarchies.

–**t** (**text**) Converts DOS text files for use on a Linux/OS X system, and vice versa. Lines in DOS text files are terminated with the character pair RETURN–NEWLINE; lines in Linux/OS X text files end in NEWLINE. This option removes the RETURN character when copying from a DOS file and adds it when copying from a Linux file.

mdir

–**w** (**wide**) Displays only filenames and fits as many as possible on each line. By default mdir lists information about each file on a separate line, showing the filename, size, and creation time.

mformat

–**f 1440**

Specifies a 1,440K 3.5-inch HD floppy diskette.

–**f 2880**

Specifies a 2,880K 3.5-inch ED floppy diskette.

–**v** *vol*

(**label**) Puts *vol* as the volume label on the newly formatted DOS disk.

mtype

–**t** (**text**) Similar to the **–t** option for mcopy, this option replaces each RETURN–NEWLINE character pair in the DOS file with a single NEWLINE character before displaying the file.

Discussion   Although these utilities mimic their DOS counterparts, they do not attempt to match those tools exactly. In most cases the restrictions imposed by DOS are removed. For example, the ambiguous file reference represented by the asterisk (✶) matches all filenames (as it does under Linux/OS X), including those filenames that DOS would require ✶.✶ to match.

Notes   In this discussion, the term **DOS disk** refers to either a DOS partition on a hard disk or a DOS floppy diskette.

If Mtools is not available in a Linux distribution repository, you can download Mtools from the Mtools home page (www.gnu.org/software/mtools). Under Mac OS X, follow these steps to download and compile Mtools:

1. Install MacPorts.

2. Exit from any running terminals.

3. Start a terminal and run **sudo port install Mtools**.

If the local kernel is configured to support DOS filesystems, you can mount DOS disks on a Linux/OS X filesystem and manipulate the files using Linux/OS X utilities. Although this feature is handy and reduces the need for Mtools, it may not be practical or efficient to mount and unmount DOS filesystems each time you need to access a DOS file. These tasks can be time-consuming, and some systems are set up so regular users cannot mount and unmount filesystems.

Use caution when using Mtools. Its utilities may not warn you if you are about to overwrite a file. Using explicit pathnames—not ambiguous file references—reduces the chance of overwriting a file.

The Mtools utilities are most commonly used to examine files on DOS floppy diskettes (mdir) and to copy files between a DOS floppy diskette and the Linux filesystem (mcopy). You can identify DOS disks by using the usual DOS drive letters: **A:** for the first floppy drive, **C:** for the first hard disk, and so on. To separate filenames in paths use either the Linux forward slash (**/**) or the DOS backslash (****). You need to escape backslashes to prevent the shell from interpreting them before passing the pathname to the utility you are using.

Each of the Mtools utilities returns an exit code of 0 on success, 1 on complete failure, and 2 on partial failure.

Examples   In the first example, mdir displays the contents of a DOS floppy diskette in **/dev/fd0**:

```
$ mdir
 Volume in drive A is DOS UTY
 Directory for A:/

ACAD     LIF       419370     5-10-09    1:29p
CADVANCE LIF        40560     2-08-08   10:36a
CHIPTST  EXE         2209     4-26-09    4:22p
DISK     ID            31    12-27-09    4:49p
GENERIC  LIF        20983     2-08-08   10:37a
INSTALL  COM          896     7-05-09   10:23a
INSTALL  DAT        45277    12-27-09    4:49p
KDINSTAL EXE       110529     8-13-09   10:50a
LOTUS    LIF        44099     1-18-09    3:36p
PCAD     LIF        17846     5-01-09    3:46p
READID   EXE        17261     5-07-09    8:26a
README   TXT         9851     4-30-09   10:32a
UTILITY  LIF        51069     5-05-09    9:13a
WORD     LIF        16817     7-01-09    9:58a
WP       LIF        57992     8-29-09    4:22p
      15 File(s)      599040 bytes free
```

The next example uses mcopy to copy the ***.TXT** files from the DOS floppy diskette to the working directory on the local filesystem. Because only one file has the extension **.TXT**, only one file is copied. Because **.TXT** files are usually text files under

DOS, the **–t** option strips the unnecessary RETURN characters at the end of each line. The ambiguous file reference ✳ is escaped on the command line to prevent the shell from attempting to expand it before passing the argument to mcopy. The mcopy utility locates the file **README.TXT** when given the pattern ✳**.txt** because DOS does not differentiate between uppercase and lowercase letters in filenames.

```
$ mcopy -t a:\*.txt .
Copying README.TXT
```

Finally, the DOS floppy diskette is reformatted using mformat, which wipes all data from the diskette. If the diskette has not been low-level formatted, you need to use fdformat before giving the following command:

```
$ mformat a:
```

A check with mdir shows the floppy diskette is empty after formatting:

```
$ mdir a:
Can't open /dev/fd0: No such device or address
Cannot initialize 'A:'
```

mv

Renames or moves a file

mv [options] existing-file new-filename
mv [options] existing-file-list directory
mv [options] existing-directory new-directory

The mv utility, which renames or moves one or more files, has three formats. The first renames a single file with a new filename that you supply. The second renames one or more files so that they appear in a specified directory. The third renames a directory. The mv utility physically moves the file if it is not possible to rename it (that is, if you move the file from one filesystem to another).

Arguments   In the first form, the *existing-file* is a pathname that specifies the ordinary file you want to rename. The *new-filename* is the new pathname of the file.

In the second form, the *existing-file-list* is a list of the pathnames of the files you want to rename and the *directory* specifies the new parent directory for the files. The files you rename will have the same simple filenames as each of the files in the *existing-file-list* but new absolute pathnames.

The third form renames the *existing-directory* with the *new-directory* name. This form works only when the *new-directory* does not already exist.

Options   Under Linux, mv accepts the common options described on page 603. Options preceded by a double hyphen (−−) work under Linux only. Except as noted, options named with a single letter and preceded by a single hyphen work under Linux and OS X.

−−backup   −b   Makes a backup copy (by appending ~ to the filename) of any file that would be overwritten. `LINUX`

−−force   −f   Causes mv *not* to prompt you if a move would overwrite an existing file that you do not have write permission for. You must have write permission for the directory holding the existing file.

−−interactive   −i   Prompts for confirmation if mv would overwrite a file. If your response begins with a y or Y, mv overwrites the file; otherwise, mv does not move the file.

−−update   −u   If a move would overwrite an existing file—not a directory—this option causes mv to compare the modification times of the source and target files. If the target file has a more recent modification time (the target is newer than the source), mv does not replace it. `LINUX`

−−verbose   −v   Lists files as they are moved.

Notes

When GNU mv copies a file from one filesystem to another, mv is implemented as cp (with the –a option) and rm: It first copies the *existing-file* to the *new-file* and then deletes the *existing-file*. If the *new-file* already exists, mv may delete it before copying.

As with rm, you must have write and execute access permissions to the parent directory of the *existing-file*, but you do not need read or write access permission to the file itself. If the move would overwrite a file that you do not have write permission for, mv displays the file's access permissions and waits for a response. If you enter **y** or **Y**, mv overwrites the file; otherwise, it does not move the file. If you use the –f option, mv does not prompt you for a response but simply overwrites the file.

Although earlier versions of mv could move only ordinary files between filesystems, mv can now move any type of file, including directories and device files.

Examples

The first command renames **letter**, a file in the working directory, as **letter.1201**:

```
$ mv letter letter.1201
```

The next command renames the file so it appears with the same simple filename in the user's **~/archives** directory:

```
$ mv letter.1201 ~/archives
```

The following command moves all files in the working directory whose names begin with **memo** so they appear in the **/p04/backup** directory:

```
$ mv memo* /p04/backup
```

Using the –u option prevents mv from replacing a newer file with an older one. After the **mv –u** command shown below is executed, the newer file (**memo2**) has not been overwritten. The **mv** command without the –u option overwrites the newer file (**memo2**'s modification time and size have changed to those of **memo1**).

```
$ ls -l
-rw-rw-r--  1 sam sam 22 Mar 25 23:34 memo1
-rw-rw-r--  1 sam sam 19 Mar 25 23:40 memo2
$ mv -u memo1 memo2
$ ls -l
-rw-rw-r--  1 sam sam 22 Mar 25 23:34 memo1
-rw-rw-r--  1 sam sam 19 Mar 25 23:40 memo2
$ mv memo1 memo2
$ ls -l
-rw-rw-r--  1 sam sam 22 Mar 25 23:34 memo2
```

nice

Changes the priority of a command

nice [option] [command-line]

The nice utility reports the priority of the shell or alters the priority of a command. An ordinary user can decrease the priority of a command. Only a user working with **root** privileges can increase the priority of a command. The nice builtin in the TC Shell has a different syntax. Refer to the "Notes" section for more information.

Arguments   The *command-line* is the command line you want to execute at a different priority. Without any options or arguments, nice displays the priority of the shell running nice.

Options   Without an option, nice defaults to an adjustment of 10, lowering the priority of the command by 10—typically from 0 to 10. As you raise the priority value, the command runs at a lower priority.

The option preceded by a double hyphen (−−) works under Linux only. The option named with a single letter and preceded by a single hyphen works under Linux and OS X.

−−adjustment=*value*
   −n *value*

Changes the priority by the increment (or decrement) specified by ***value***. The priorities range from −20 (the highest priority) to 19 (the lowest priority). A positive ***value*** lowers the priority, whereas a negative ***value*** raises the priority. Only a user working with **root** privileges can specify a negative ***value***. When you specify a value outside this range, the priority is set to the limit of the range.

Notes   You can use renice (page 802) or top's **r** command (page 860) to change the priority of a running process.

Higher (more positive) priority values mean that the kernel schedules a job less often. Lower (more negative) values cause the job to be scheduled more often.

When a user working with **root** privileges schedules a job to run at the highest priority, this change can affect the performance of the system for all other jobs, including the operating system itself. For this reason you should be careful when using nice with negative values.

The TC Shell includes a nice builtin. Under tcsh, use the following syntax to change the priority at which *command-line* is run. The default priority is 4. You must include the plus sign for positive values.

nice [±value] command line

The tcsh nice builtin works differently from the nice utility: When you use the builtin, **nice −5** decrements the priority at which *command-line* is run. When you use the utility, **nice −n −5** increments the priority at which *command-line* is run.

Examples   The following command executes find in the background at the lowest possible priority. The **ps −l** command displays the nice value of the command in the **NI** column:

```
# nice -n 19 find / -name core -print > corefiles.out &
[1] 422
# ps -l
F S   UID   PID  PPID  C PRI  NI ADDR SZ WCHAN  TTY          TIME CMD
4 R     0   389  8657  0  80   0 -  4408 -       pts/4    00:00:00 bash
4 D     0   422   389 28  99  19 -  1009 -       pts/4    00:00:04 find
0 R     0   433   389  0  80   0 -  1591 -       pts/4    00:00:00 ps
```

The next command finds very large files and runs at a high priority (−15):

```
# nice -n -15 find / -size +50000k
```

nohup

Runs a command that keeps running after you log out

nohup **command line**

The nohup utility executes a command line such that the command keeps running after you log out. In other words, nohup causes a process to ignore a SIGHUP signal. Depending on how the local shell is configured, it may kill your background processes when you log out. The TC Shell includes a nohup builtin. Refer to the "Notes" section for more information.

Arguments   The **command line** is the command line you want to execute.

Notes   Under Linux, nohup accepts the common options described on page 603.

If you do not redirect the output from a command you execute using nohup, both standard output *and* standard error are sent to the file named **nohup.out** in the working directory. If you do not have write permission for the working directory, nohup sends output to **~/nohup.out**.

Unlike the nohup utility, the TC Shell's nohup builtin does not send output to **nohup.out**. Background jobs started from tcsh continue to run after you log out.

Examples   The following command executes find in the background, using nohup:

```
$ nohup find / -name core -print > corefiles.out &
[1] 14235
```

od

Dumps the contents of a file

od [options] [file-list]

The od (octal dump) utility dumps the contents of a file. The dump is useful for viewing executable (object) files and text files with embedded nonprinting characters. This utility takes its input from the file you specify on the command line or from standard input. The od utility is available under Linux only. **LINUX**

Arguments   The *file-list* specifies the pathnames of the files that od displays. When you do not specify a *file-list*, od reads from standard input.

Options   The od utility accepts the common options described on page 603.

--address-radix=*base*   **–A** *base*

Specifies the base used when displaying the offsets shown for positions in the file. By default offsets are given in octal. Possible values for *base* are **d** (decimal), **o** (octal), **x** (hexadecimal), and **n** (no offsets printed).

--skip-bytes=*n*   **–j** *n*

Skips *n* bytes before displaying data.

--read-bytes=*n*   **–N** *n*

Reads a maximum of *n* bytes and then quits.

--strings=*n*   **–S** *n*

Outputs from the file only those bytes that contain runs of *n* or more printable ASCII characters that are terminated by a NULL byte.

--format=*type[n]*

–t *type[n]*

Specifies the output format for displaying data from a file. You can repeat this option with different format *types* to see the file in several different formats. Table V-21 lists the possible values for *type*.

By default od dumps a file as 2-byte octal numbers. You can specify the number of bytes od uses to compose each number by specifying a length indicator, *n*. You can specify a length indicator for all types except **a** and **c**. Table V-23 lists the possible values of *n*.

Table V-21   Output formats

type	Type of output
a	Named character. Displays nonprinting control characters using their official ASCII names. For example, FORMFEED is displayed as **ff**.

Table V-21   Output formats (continued)

type	Type of output
c	ASCII character. Displays nonprinting control characters as backslash escape sequences (Table V-22) or three-digit octal numbers.
d	Signed decimal.
f	Floating point.
o	Octal (default).
u	Unsigned decimal.
x	Hexadecimal.

Table V-22   Output format type **c** backslash escape sequences

Sequence	Meaning
\0	NULL
\a	BELL
\b	BACKSPACE
\f	FORMFEED
\n	NEWLINE
\r	RETURN
\t	HORIZONTAL TAB
\v	VERTICAL TAB

Table V-23   Length indicators

n	Number of bytes to use
Integers (types d, o, u, and x)	
C (character)	Uses single characters for each decimal value
S (short integer)	Uses 2 bytes
I (integer)	Uses 4 bytes
L (long)	Uses 4 bytes on 32-bit machines and 8 bytes on 64-bit machines

Table V-23   Length indicators (continued)

Floating point (type f)

F	(float)	Uses 4 bytes
D	(double)	Uses 8 bytes
L	(long double)	Typically uses 8 bytes

Notes

To retain backward compatibility with older, non-POSIX versions of od, the od utility includes the options listed in Table V-24 as shorthand versions of many of the preceding options.

Table V-24   Shorthand format specifications

Shorthand	Equivalent specification
–a	–t a
–b	–t oC
–c	–t c
–d	–t u2
–f	–t fF
–h	–t x2
–i	–t d2
–l	–t d4
–o	–t o2
–x	–t x2

Examples

The file **ac**, which is used in the following examples, contains all of the ASCII characters. In the first example, the bytes in this file are displayed as named characters. The first column shows the offset of the first byte on each line of output from the start of the file. The offsets are displayed as octal values.

```
$ od -t a ac
0000000 nul soh stx etx eot enq ack bel bs ht nl vt ff cr so si
0000020 dle dc1 dc2 dc3 dc4 nak syn etb can em sub esc fs gs rs us
0000040 sp ! " # $ % & ' ( ) * + , - . /
0000060 0 1 2 3 4 5 6 7 8 9 : ; < = > ?
0000100 @ A B C D E F G H I J K L M N O
0000120 P Q R S T U V W X Y Z [ \ ] ^ _
0000140 ` a b c d e f g h i j k l m n o
0000160 p q r s t u v w x y z { | } ~ del
0000200 nul soh stx etx eot enq ack bel bs ht nl vt ff cr so si
0000220 dle dc1 dc2 dc3 dc4 nak syn etb can em sub esc fs gs rs us
0000240 sp ! " # $ % & ' ( ) * + , - . /
```

```
0000260 0 1 2 3 4 5 6 7 8 9 : ; < = > ?
0000300 @ A B C D E F G H I J K L M N O
0000320 P Q R S T U V W X Y Z [ \ ] ^ _
0000340 ` a b c d e f g h i j k l m n o
0000360 p q r s t u v w x y z { | } ~ del
0000400 nl
0000401
```

In the next example, the bytes are displayed as octal numbers, ASCII characters, or printing characters preceded by a backslash (refer to Table V-22 on page 777):

```
$ od -t c ac
0000000 \0 001 002 003 004 005 006 \a \b \t \n \v \f \r 016 017
0000020 020 021 022 023 024 025 026 027 030 031 032 033 034 035 036 037
0000040  !  "  #  $  %  &  '  (  )  *  +  ,  -  .  /
0000060 0 1 2 3 4 5 6 7 8 9 : ; < = > ?
0000100 @ A B C D E F G H I J K L M N O
0000120 P Q R S T U V W X Y Z [ \ ] ^ _
0000140 ` a b c d e f g h i j k l m n o
0000160 p q r s t u v w x y z { | } ~ 177
0000200 200 201 202 203 204 205 206 207 210 211 212 213 214 215 216 217
0000220 220 221 222 223 224 225 226 227 230 231 232 233 234 235 236 237
0000240 240 241 242 243 244 245 246 247 250 251 252 253 254 255 256 257
0000260 260 261 262 263 264 265 266 267 270 271 272 273 274 275 276 277
0000300 300 301 302 303 304 305 306 307 310 311 312 313 314 315 316 317
0000320 320 321 322 323 324 325 326 327 330 331 332 333 334 335 336 337
0000340 340 341 342 343 344 345 346 347 350 351 352 353 354 355 356 357
0000360 360 361 362 363 364 365 366 367 370 371 372 373 374 375 376 377
0000400 \n
0000401
```

The final example finds in the file **/usr/bin/who** all strings that are at least three characters long (the default) and are terminated by a null byte. See strings on page 837 for another way of displaying a similar list. The offset positions are given as decimal offsets instead of octal offsets.

```
$ od -A d -S 3 /usr/bin/who
...
0028455 /usr/share/locale
0028473 Michael Stone
0028487 David MacKenzie
0028503 Joseph Arceneaux
0028520 6.10
0028525 GNU coreutils
0028539 who
0028543 abdlmpqrstuwHT
0028558 %Y-%m-%d %H:%M
0028573 %b %e %H:%M
0028585 extra operand %s
0028602 all
0028606 count
0028612 dead
0028617 heading
0028625 ips
0028629 login
...
```

open *OS X*

Opens files, directories, and URLs

open [option] [file-list]

The open utility opens one or more files, directories, or URLs.

Arguments   The *file-list* specifies the pathnames of the files, directories, or URLs that open is to open.

Options   Without any options, open opens the files in *file-list* as though you had double-clicked each of the files' icons in the Finder.

–a *application*

Opens *file-list* using *application*. This option is equivalent to dragging *file-list* to the *application*'s icon in the Finder.

–b *bundle*

Opens *file-list* using the application with bundle identifier *bundle*. A bundle identifier is a string, registered with the system, that identifies an application that can open files. For example, the bundle identifier **com.apple.TextEdit** specifies the TextEdit editor.

–e   (**edit**) Opens *file-list* using the TextEdit application.

–f   (**file**) Opens standard input as a file in the default text editor. This option does not accept *file-list*.

–t   (**text**) Opens *file-list* using the default text editor (see the "Discussion" section).

Discussion   Opening a file brings up the application associated with that file. For example, opening a disk image file mounts it. The open command returns immediately, without waiting for the application to launch.

LaunchServices is a system framework that identifies applications that can open files. It maintains lists of available applications and user preferences about which application to use for each file type. LaunchServices also keeps track of the default text editor used by the **–t** and **–f** options.

Notes   When a file will be opened by a GUI application, you must run open from Terminal or another terminal emulator that is running under a GUI. Otherwise, the operation will fail.

Examples   The first example mounts the disk image file **backups.dmg**. The disk is mounted in **/Volumes**, using the name it was formatted with.

```
$ ls /Volumes
House    Spare    Leopard
$ open backups.dmg
$ ls /Volumes
Backups    House       Spare       Leopard
```

The next command opens the file **picture.jpg**. You must run this and the following example from a textual window within a GUI (e.g., Terminal). The application selected depends on the file attributes. If the file's type and creator code specify a particular application, open opens the file using that application. Otherwise, open uses the system's default program for handling **.jpg** files.

```
$ open picture.jpg
```

The final example opens the **/usr/bin** directory in the Finder. The **/usr** directory is normally hidden from the Finder because its **invisible** file attribute flag (page 931) is set. However, the open command can open any file you can access from the shell, even if it is not normally accessible from the Finder.

```
$ open /usr/bin
```

otool *OS X*

Displays object, library, and executable files

*otool **options file-list***

The otool utility displays information about, or part of, object, library, and executable files.

Arguments   The *file-list* specifies the pathnames of files that otool is to display.

Options   You must use at least one of the –L, –M, –t, or –T options to specify which part of each file in *file-list* otool is to display.

–L   (**libraries**) Displays the names and version numbers of the shared libraries an object file uses.

–M   (**module**) Displays the module table of a shared library.

–p *name*
(**print**) Begins output at the symbol named *name*. This option requires the –t option and either the –v or –V option.

–T   (**table of contents**) Displays the table of contents of a shared library.

–t   (**text**) Displays the TEXT section of an object file.

–V   (**very verbose**) Displays even more data (than the –v option) symbolically. When displaying code, this option causes otool to display the names of called routines instead of their addresses.

–v   (**verbose**) Displays data symbolically. When displaying code, this option causes otool to display the names of instructions instead of numeric codes.

Discussion   The otool utility displays information about the contents and dependencies of object files. This information can prove helpful when you are debugging a program. For example, when you are setting up a chroot jail, otool can report which libraries are needed to run a given program.

Some options are useful only with certain types of object modules. For example, the –T option does not report anything for a typical executable file.

Notes   The otool utility is part of the Developer Tools optional install.

An **otool –L** command performs a function similar to the ldd utility on systems using the ELF binary format.

Examples   The examples in this section use the compiled version of the following C program:

```
$ cat myname.c
#include <stdio.h>
int main(void) {
    printf("My name is Sam.\n");
    return 0;
}
```

In the first example, otool displays the libraries the program is linked with:

```
$ otool -L myname
myname:
        /usr/lib/libmx.A.dylib (compatibility version 1.0.0, current version 92.0.0)
        /usr/lib/libSystem.B.dylib (compatibility version 1.0.0, current version 88.0.0)
```

In some cases, a library used by a program will depend on other libraries. You can use **otool -L** on a library to see whether it uses other libraries:

```
$ otool -L /usr/lib/libmx.A.dylib /usr/lib/libSystem.B.dylib
/usr/lib/libmx.A.dylib:
        /usr/lib/libmx.A.dylib (compatibility version 1.0.0, current version 92.0.0)
        /usr/lib/libSystem.B.dylib (compatibility version 1.0.0, current version 88.0.0)
/usr/lib/libSystem.B.dylib:
        /usr/lib/libSystem.B.dylib (compatibility version 1.0.0, current version 88.0.0)
        /usr/lib/system/libmathCommon.A.dylib (compatibility version 1.0.0, current ...
```

The next example disassembles the code for the **main** function. When compiling programs, the compiler sometimes modifies symbol names. The compiler gives functions, such as **main**, a leading underscore; thus the symbol name is **_main**.

```
$ otool -Vt -p _main myname
myname:
(__TEXT,__text) section
_main:
00002ac0        mfspr   r0,lr
00002ac4        stmw    r30,0xfff8(r1)
00002ac8        stw     r0,0x8(r1)
00002acc        stwu    r1,0xffb0(r1)
00002ad0        or      r30,r1,r1
00002ad4        bcl     20,31,0x2ad8
00002ad8        mfspr   r31,lr
00002adc        addis   r2,r31,0x0
00002ae0        addi    r3,r2,0x4b8
00002ae4        bl      _printf$LDBLStub
00002ae8        li      r0,0x0
00002aec        or      r3,r0,r0
00002af0        lwz     r1,0x0(r1)
00002af4        lwz     r0,0x8(r1)
00002af8        mtspr   lr,r0
00002afc        lmw     r30,0xfff8(r1)
00002b00        blr
...
```

paste

Joins corresponding lines from files

paste [option] [file-list]

The paste utility reads lines from the *file-list* and joins corresponding lines in its output. By default output lines are separated by a TAB character.

Arguments   The *file-list* is a list of ordinary files. When you omit the *file-list*, paste reads from standard input.

Options   Under Linux, paste accepts the common options described on page 603. Options preceded by a double hyphen (--) work under Linux only. Options named with a single letter and preceded by a single hyphen work under Linux and OS X.

--delimiter=*dlist*   -d *dlist*

> The *dlist* is a list of characters used to separate output fields. If *dlist* contains a single character, paste uses that character instead of the default TAB character to separate fields. If *dlist* contains more than one character, the characters are used in turn to separate fields and are then reused from the beginning of the list as necessary.

--serial   -s   Processes one file at a time; pastes horizontally. See the "Examples" section.

Notes   The paste utility is often used to rearrange the columns of a table. A utility, such as cut, can place the desired columns in separate files, and then paste can join them in any order.

Examples   The following example uses the files **fnames** and **acctinfo**. You can create these files using cut (page 652) and the **/etc/passwd** file. The paste command puts the full-name field first, followed by the remaining user account information. A TAB character separates the two output fields. Although this example works under Mac OS X, **/etc/passwd** does not contain information about most users; see "Open Directory" on page 926 for more information.

```
$ cat fnames
Sam the Great
Max Wild
Zach Brill
Helen Simpson

$ cat acctinfo
sam:x:401:50:/home/sam:/bin/zsh
max:x:402:50:/home/max:/bin/bash
zach:x:504:500:/home/zach:/bin/tcsh
hls:x:505:500:/home/hls:/bin/bash
```

```
$ paste fnames acctinfo
Sam the Great    sam:x:401:50:/home/sam:/bin/zsh
Max Wild         max:x:402:50:/home/max:/bin/bash
Zach Brill       zach:x:504:500:/home/zach:/bin/tcsh
Helen Simpson    hls:x:505:500:/home/hls:/bin/bash
```

The next examples use the files **p1, p2, p3,** and **p4.** In the last example in this group, the **–d** option gives paste a list of characters to use to separate output fields:

```
$ cat p1
1
one
ONE
$ cat p2
2
two
TWO
extra
$ cat p3
3
three
THREE
$ cat p4
4
four
FOUR

$ paste p4 p3 p2 p1
4       3       2       1
four    three   two     one
FOUR    THREE   TWO     ONE
                extra

$ paste -d="+-=" p3 p2 p1 p4
3+2-1=4
three+two-one=four
THREE+TWO-ONE=FOUR
+extra-=
```

The final example uses the **––serial** option to paste the files one at a time:

```
$ paste --serial p1 p2 p3 p4
1       one     ONE
2       two     TWO     extra
3       three   THREE
4       four    FOUR
```

pax

Creates an archive, restores files from an archive, or copies a directory hierarchy

pax [options] [pattern-list]
pax –w [options] [source-files]
pax –r [options] [pattern-list]
*pax –rw [options] [source-files] **destination-directory***

The pax utility has four modes of operation: List mode displays the list of files in an archive, create mode places multiple files into a single archive file, extract mode restores files from an archive, and copy mode copies a directory hierarchy. The archive files created by pax can be saved on disk, removable media, or a remote system.

A major option determines the mode pax runs in. List mode (absence of a major option) reads an archive from standard input and displays a list of files stored in the archive. Create mode (–w for *write*) reads a list of ordinary or directory filenames from the command line or standard input and writes the resulting archive file to standard output. Extract mode (–r for *read*) reads an archive from standard input and extracts files from that archive; you can restore all files from the archive or only those files whose names match a pattern. Copy mode (–rw) reads a list of ordinary or directory filenames from the command line or standard input and copies the files to an existing directory.

Arguments   In create mode, pax reads the names of files that will be included in the archive from *source-files* on the command line. If *source-files* is not present, pax reads the names from standard input, one filename per line.

By default, in extract mode pax extracts, and in list mode pax displays the names of, all files in the archive it reads from standard input. You can choose to extract or display the names of files selectively by supplying a *pattern-list*. If the name of a file in the archive matches a pattern in the *pattern-list*, pax extracts that file or displays that filename; otherwise, it ignores the file. The pax patterns are similar to shell wildcards (page 136) except they match slashes (/) and a leading period (.) in a filename. See the fnmatch man page for more information about pax patterns (OS X only).

In copy mode, pax does not create *destination-directory*. Thus *destination-directory* must exist before you give pax a copy mode command.

Options   A major option specifies the mode in which pax operates: create, extract, or copy.

Major Options

Three options determine the mode in which pax operates. You must include zero or one of these options. Without a major option, pax runs in list mode.

–r   (**read**) Reads the archive from standard input and extracts files. Without a *pattern-list* on the command line, pax extracts all files from the archive. With a *pattern-list,* pax extracts only those files whose names match one of the patterns in the *pattern-list.* The following example extracts from the **root.pax** archive file on an external drive only those files whose names end in **.c**:

```
$ pax -r \*.c < /Volumes/Backups/root.pax
```

The backslash prevents the shell from expanding the * before it passes the argument to pax.

–w (**write**) Constructs an archive from the files named on the command line or standard input. These files may be ordinary or directory files. When the files come from standard input, each must appear on a separate line. The archive is written to standard output. The find utility frequently generates the filenames that pax uses. The following command builds an archive of the **/Users** directory and writes it to the archive file named **Users.pax** on **/Volumes/Backups**:

```
# find -d /Users -print | pax -w > /Volumes/Backups/Users.pax
```

The **–d** option causes find to search for files in a depth-first manner, reducing the likelihood of permissions problems when you restore the files from the archive. See the discussion of this find option on page 647.

–rw (**copy**) Copies files named on the command line or standard input from one place on the system to another. Instead of constructing an archive file containing the files named on standard input, pax copies them to the *destination-directory* (the last argument on the pax command line). The effect is the same as if you had created an archive in create mode and then extracted the files in extract mode, except using copy mode avoids creating an archive.

The following example copies the working directory hierarchy to the **/Users/max/code** directory. The **code** directory must exist before you give this command. Make sure that **~max/code** is not a subdirectory of the working directory or you will perform a recursive copy.

```
$ pax -rw . ~max/code
```

Other Options

The following options alter the behavior of pax. These options work with one or more of the major options.

–c (**complement**) Reverses the sense of the test performed on *pattern-list.* Files are listed or put in the archive only if they do *not* match any of the patterns in *pattern-list.*

–f *archive*

(**file**) Uses *archive* as the name of the archive file. In list and extract modes, this option reads from *archive* instead of standard input. In create mode, it writes to *archive* instead of standard output. You can use this option to access a device on another system on a network; see the **--file** option to tar (page 847) for more information.

–H (**partial dereference**) For each file that is a symbolic link, copies the file the link points to, not the symbolic link itself. This option affects files specified on the command line; it does not affect files found while descending a directory hierarchy. This option treats files that are not symbolic links normally. See page 623 for an example of the use of the **–H** versus **–L** options.

–L (**dereference**) For each file that is a symbolic link, copies the file the link points to, not the symbolic link itself. This option affects all files and treats files that are not symbolic links normally. See page 623 for an example of the use of the **–H** versus **–L** options.

–l (**link**) In copy mode, when possible, makes hard links instead of copying files.

–P (**no dereference**) For each file that is a symbolic link, copies the symbolic link, not the file the link points to. This option affects all files and treats files that are not symbolic links normally. This behavior is the default for **pax**. See page 625 for an example of the use of the **–P** option.

–p *preserve-list*

Preserves or discards the file attributes specified by *preserve-list*. The *preserve-list* is a string of one or more letters as shown in Table V-25. By default **pax** preserves file access and modification times but does not preserve ownership or file permissions. This option works in extract and copy modes only.

Table V-25   Preserve flags

Letter	Meaning
a	Discard the access time
e	Preserve everything
m	Discard the modification time
o	Preserve ownership
p	Preserve permissions

–s *subcmd*

Executes *subcmd*, a substitution command, on filenames while storing them in any of the modes. The *subcmd* has the following format:

   s/search-string/replacement-string/[gp]

The **pax** utility replaces occurrences of the regular expression *search-string* with *replacement-string*. A trailing **g** indicates a global replacement; without it **pax** replaces only the first instance of *search-string* in each filename. A trailing **p** (for print) causes **pax** to display each substitution it makes. The *subcmd* is similar to vim's search and replace feature described on page 178, except it lacks an address.

-v (**verbose**) In list mode, displays output similar to that produced by **ls –l**. In other modes, displays a list of files being processed.

–**X** In copy and create modes, prevents **pax** from searching directories in filesystems other than those holding *source-files*.

–**x** *format*

In create mode, writes the archive in *format* format, as shown in Table V-26. If you do not specify a format, **pax** writes a (POSIX) tar format file (**ustar** in the table).

–**z** (**gzip**) In create mode, compresses archives using gzip. In extract mode, decompresses archives using gunzip.

Table V-26   Archive formats

format	Description
cpio	The format specified for cpio archives in POSIX
sv4cpio	The format used for cpio archives under UNIX System V, release 4
tar	The historical Berkeley tar format
ustar	The POSIX tar format (default)

Discussion

The pax utility is a general replacement for tar, cpio, and other archive programs.

In create and copy modes, pax processes specified directories recursively. In list and extract modes, if a pattern in the *pattern-list* matches a directory name, pax lists or extracts the files from the named directory.

Notes

There is no native pax format. Instead, the pax utility can read and write archives in a number of formats. By default it creates POSIX tar format archives. See Table V-26 for the list of formats pax supports.

The pax utility determines the format of an archive file; it does not allow you to specify an archive format (–x option) in list or extract mode.

Under Mac OS X version 10.4 and later, pax copies extended attributes (page 928).

Examples

In the first example, pax creates an archive named **corres.0901.pax**. This archive stores the contents of the **corres** directory.

```
$ pax -w corres > corres.0901.pax
```

The –**w** option puts pax in create mode, where the list of files to be put in an archive is supplied by command-line arguments (**corres** in the preceding example) or from standard input. The pax utility sends the archive to standard output. The preceding example redirects that output to a file named **corres.0901.pax**.

Next, without any options, pax displays a list of files in the archive it reads from standard input:

```
$ pax < corres.0901.pax
corres
corres/hls
corres/max
corres/max/0823
corres/max/0828
corres/max/0901
corres/memo1
corres/notes
```

The following command uses the **–f** option to name the input file and performs the same function as the preceding command:

```
$ pax -f corres.0901.pax
```

When pax reads an archive file, as in the previous examples, it determines the format of the file. You do not have to (nor are you allowed to) specify the format.

The next example, run under Mac OS X, attempts to create an archive of the **/etc** directory hierarchy in the default tar format. In this case pax is run by a user with **root** privileges because some of the files in this hierarchy cannot be read by ordinary users. Because pax does not follow (dereference) symbolic links by default, and because under Mac OS X **/etc** is a symbolic link, pax copies the link and not the directory that the link points to. The first command creates the archive, the second command shows the link in the archive, and the third command uses the **–v** option to show that it is a link:

```
# pax -w -f /tmp/etc.tar /etc
# pax -f /tmp/etc.tar
/etc
# pax -v -f /tmp/etc.tar
lrwxr-xr-x  1 root      admin          0 May 21 01:48 /etc => private/etc
pax: ustar vol 1, 1 files, 10240 bytes read, 0 bytes written.
```

The **–L** option follows (dereferences) links. In the next example, pax creates the desired archive of **/etc**:

```
# pax -wLf /tmp/etc.tar /etc
# pax -f /tmp/etc.tar
/etc
/etc/6to4.conf
/etc/AFP.conf
/etc/afpovertcp.cfg
/etc/aliases
/etc/aliases.db
/etc/amavisd.conf
/etc/amavisd.conf.personal
/etc/appletalk.cfg
...
```

The next example uses pax to create a backup of the **memos** directory, preserving ownership and file permissions. The destination directory must exist before you give pax a copy mode command.

```
$ mkdir memos.0625
$ pax -rw -p e memos memos.0625
$ ls memos.0625
memos
```

The preceding example copies the **memos** directory into the destination directory. You can use pax to make a copy of a directory in the working directory without putting it in a subdirectory. In the next example, the **–s** option causes pax to replace the name of the **memos** directory with the name . (the name of the working directory) as it writes files to the **memos.0625** directory:

```
$ pax -rw -p e -s /memos/./ memos memos.0625
```

The final example uses find to build a list of files that begin with the string **memo** and that are located in the working directory hierarchy. The pax utility writes these files to an archive in cpio format. The output from pax goes to standard output, which is sent through a pipe to bzip2, which compresses it before writing it to the archive file.

```
$ find . -type f -name "memo*" | pax -w -x cpio | bzip2 > memos.cpio.bz2
```

plutil *OS X*

Manipulates property list files

plutil [options] file-list

The plutil utility converts property list files between formats and checks their syntax.

Arguments   The *file-list* specifies the pathnames of one or more files that plutil is to manipulate.

Options
−convert *format*
　　Converts *file-list* to *format*, which must be either **xml1** or **binary1**.

−e *extension*
　　Gives output files a filename extension of ***extension***.

−help
　　Displays a help message.

−lint
　　Checks the syntax of files (default).

−o *file*
　　(**output**) Names the converted file ***file***.

−s　(**silent**) Does not display any messages for successfully converted files.

Discussion   The plutil utility converts files from the XML property list format to binary format, and vice versa. The plutil utility can read—but not write—the older plain-text property list format.

Notes   The plutil utility accepts a double hyphen (−−) to mark the end of the options on the command line. For more information refer to "Common Options" on page 603.

Examples   The following example checks the syntax of the file named **java.plist**:

```
$ plutil java.plist
java.plist: OK
```

The next example shows the output of plutil as it checks a damaged property list file:

```
$ plutil broken.plist
broken.plist:
XML parser error:
        Encountered unexpected element at line 2 (plist can only include one object)
Old-style plist parser error:
        Malformed data byte group at line 1; invalid hex
```

The next example converts the file **StartupParameters.plist** to binary format, overwriting the original file:

```
$ plutil -convert binary1 StartupParameters.plist
```

The final example converts the binary format property list file **loginwindow.plist** in the working directory to XML format and, because of the **–o** option, puts the converted file in **/tmp/lw.p**:

```
$ plutil -convert xml1 -o /tmp/lw.p loginwindow.plist
```

pr

Paginates files for printing

pr [options] [file-list]

The pr utility breaks files into pages, usually in preparation for printing. Each page has a header with the name of the file, date, time, and page number.

The pr utility takes its input from files you specify on the command line or from standard input. The output from pr goes to standard output and is frequently redirected through a pipe to a printer.

Arguments   The *file-list* is a list of the pathnames of text files that you want pr to paginate. When you omit the *file-list*, pr reads from standard input.

Options   Under Linux, pr accepts the common options described on page 603. Options preceded by a double hyphen (––) work under Linux only. Except as noted, options named with a single letter and preceded by a single hyphen work under Linux and OS X.

You can embed options within the *file-list*. An embedded option affects only those files following it on the command line.

––show-control-chars

   –c   Displays control characters with a caret (^; for example, ^H). Displays other nonprinting characters as octal numbers preceded by a backslash. `LINUX`

––columns=*col*   –*col*
   Displays output in *col* columns with a default of one. This option may truncate lines and cannot be used with the –m (––merge) option.

––double-space   –d   Double-spaces the output.

––form-feed   –F   Uses a FORMFEED character to skip to the next page rather than filling the current page with NEWLINE characters.

––header=*head*   –h *head*
   Displays *head* at the top of each page instead of the filename. If *head* contains SPACEs, you must enclose it within quotation marks.

––length=*lines*   –l *lines*
   Sets the page length to *lines* lines. The default is 66 lines.

––merge   –m   Displays all specified files simultaneously in multiple columns. This option cannot be used with the –*col* (––columns) option.

––number-lines=*[c[num]]*
         –n*[c[num]]*
   Numbers the lines of output. The pr utility appends the character *c* to the

number to separate it from the contents of the file (the default is a TAB). The *num* specifies the number of digits in each line number (the default is 5).

--indent=*spaces*   –o *spaces*
　　　　　Indents the output by *spaces* characters (specifies the left margin).

--separator=*c*   –s[*c*]
　　　　　Separates columns with the single character *c* (defaults to TAB when you omit *c*). By default pr uses TABs as separation characters to align columns unless you use the –w option, in which case nothing separates the columns.

--omit-header   –t   Causes pr not to display its five-line page header and trailer. The header that pr normally displays includes the name of the file, the date, time, and page number. The trailer is five blank lines.

--width=*num*   –w *num*
　　　　　Sets the page width to *num* columns. This option is effective only with multi-column output (the –m [--merge] or –col [--columns] option).

--pages=*firstpage[:lastpage]*
　　　　　+*firstpage[:lastpage]*
　　　　　Output begins with the page numbered *firstpage* and ends with *lastpage*. Without *lastpage,* pr outputs through the last page of the document. The short version of this option begins with a plus sign, not a hyphen. Mac OS X does not accept the *lastpage* argument; printing always continues through the end of the document.

Notes　　When you use the –col (--columns) option to display the output in multiple columns, pr displays the same number of lines in each column (with the possible exception of the last).

Examples　　The first command shows pr paginating a file named **memo** and sending its output through a pipe to lpr for printing:

```
$ pr memo | lpr
```

Next **memo** is sent to the printer again, this time with a special heading at the top of each page. The job is run in the background.

```
$ pr -h 'MEMO RE: BOOK' memo | lpr &
[1] 4904
```

Finally pr displays the **memo** file on the screen, without any header, starting with page 3:

```
$ pr -t +3 memo
...
```

ps

Displays process status

ps [options] [process-list]

The ps utility displays status information about processes running on the local system.

Arguments   The *process-list* is a comma- or SPACE-separated list of PID numbers. When you specify a *process-list,* ps reports on just the processes in that list.

Options   Under Linux, the ps utility accepts three types of options, each preceded by a different prefix. You can intermix the options. See the ps man page for details.

Two hyphens: GNU (long) options
One hyphen: UNIX98 (short) options
No hyphens: BSD options

Options preceded by a double hyphen (−−) or no hyphen work under Linux only. Options named with a single letter and preceded by a single hyphen work under Linux and OS X.

−A   (**all**) Reports on all processes. Also **−e**.

−e   (**everything**) Reports on all processes. Also **−A**.

−f   (**full**) Displays a listing with more columns of information.

−−forest   **f**   Displays the process tree (no hyphen before the **f**). `LINUX`

−l   (**long**) Produces a long listing showing more information about each process. See the "Discussion" section for a description of the columns this option displays.

−−no-headers   Omits the header. This option is useful if you are sending the output to another program. `LINUX`

−−user *usernames*   **−u***usernames*
Reports on processes being run by *usernames*, a comma-separated list of the names or UIDs of one or more users on the local system.

−w   (**wide**) Without this option ps truncates output lines at the right side of the screen. This option extends the display to 132 columns; it wraps around one more line, if needed. Use this option twice to extend the display to an unlimited number of columns, which is the default if you redirect the output of ls.

Discussion   Without any options, ps displays the statuses of all active processes controlled by your terminal or screen. Table V-27 lists the heading and content of each of the four columns ps displays.

Table V-27   Column headings I

Heading	Meaning
PID	The process identification number.
TTY (terminal)	The name of the terminal that controls the process.
TIME	The number of hours, minutes, and seconds the process has been running.
CMD	The command line the process was called with. The command is truncated to fit on one line. Use the **–w** option to see more of the command line.

The columns that ps displays depend on your choice of options. Table V-28 lists the headings and contents of the most common columns.

Table V-28   Column headings II

The column titles differ, depending on the type of option you use. This table shows the headings for UNIX98 (one-hyphen) options.

Heading	Meaning
%CPU	The percentage of total CPU time the process is using. Because of the way Linux/OS X handles process accounting, this figure is approximate, and the total of %CPU values for all processes may exceed 100%.
%MEM (memory)	The percentage of RAM the process is using.
COMMAND *or* **CMD**	The command line the process was called with. The command is truncated to fit on one line. Use the **–w** option to see more of the command line. This column is always displayed last on a line.
F (flags)	The flags associated with the process.
NI (nice)	The nice value of the process (page 773).
PID	The process identification number.
PPID (parent PID)	The process identification number of the parent process.
PRI (priority)	The priority of the process.
RSS (resident set size)	The number of blocks of memory the process is using.
SIZE *or* **SZ**	The size, in blocks, of the core image of the process.
STIME *or* **START**	The date the process started.

Table V-28   Column headings II (continued)

Heading	Meaning
STAT *or* **S** (status)	The status of the process as specified by one or more letters from the following list:

<	High priority
D	Sleeping and cannot be interrupted
L	Pages locked in memory (real-time and custom I/O)
N	Low priority
R	Available for execution (in the run queue)
S	Sleeping
T	Either stopped or being traced
W	Has no pages resident in RAM
X	Dead
Z	Zombie process that is waiting for its child processes to terminate before it terminates

Heading	Meaning
TIME	The number of minutes and seconds that the process has been running.
TTY (terminal)	The name of the terminal controlling the process.
USER *or* **UID**	The username of the user who owns the process.
WCHAN (wait channel)	If the process is waiting for an event, the address of the kernel function that caused the process to wait. This value is 0 for processes that are not waiting or sleeping.

Notes

Use top (page 858) to display process status information dynamically.

Examples

The first example shows ps, without any options, displaying the user's active processes. The first process is the shell (bash), and the second is the process executing the ps utility.

```
$ ps
  PID TTY          TIME CMD
 2697 pts/0    00:00:02 bash
 3299 pts/0    00:00:00 ps
```

With the **–l** (long) option, ps displays more information about the processes:

```
$ ps -l
  F S   UID   PID  PPID  C PRI  NI ADDR    SZ WCHAN  TTY          TIME CMD
000 S   500  2697  2696  0  75   0    -   639 wait4  pts/0    00:00:02 bash
000 R   500  3300  2697  0  76   0    -   744 -      pts/0    00:00:00 ps
```

The **–u** option shows information about the specified user:

```
$ ps -u root
  PID TTY          TIME CMD
    1 ?        00:00:01 init
    2 ?        00:00:00 kthreadd
    3 ?        00:00:00 migration/0
    4 ?        00:00:01 ksoftirqd/0
    5 ?        00:00:00 watchdog/0
  ...
```

The **--forest** option causes ps to display what the man page describes as an "ASCII art process tree." Processes that are children of other processes appear indented under their parents, making the process hierarchy, or tree, easier to see.

```
$ ps -ef --forest
UID         PID  PPID  C STIME TTY          TIME CMD
root          1     0  0 Jul22 ?        00:00:03 init
root          2     1  0 Jul22 ?        00:00:00 [keventd]
...
root        785     1  0 Jul22 ?        00:00:00 /usr/sbin/apmd -p 10 -w 5 -W -P
root        839     1  0 Jul22 ?        00:00:01 /usr/sbin/sshd
root       3305   839  0 Aug01 ?        00:00:00  \_ /usr/sbin/sshd
max        3307  3305  0 Aug01 ?        00:00:00      \_ /usr/sbin/sshd
max        3308  3307  0 Aug01 pts/1    00:00:00          \_ -bash
max        3774  3308  0 Aug01 pts/1    00:00:00              \_ ps -ef --forest
...
root       1040     1  0 Jul22 ?        00:00:00 login -- root
root       3351  1040  0 Aug01 tty2     00:00:00  \_ -bash
root       3402  3351  0 Aug01 tty2     00:00:00      \_ make modules
root       3416  3402  0 Aug01 tty2     00:00:00          \_ make -C drivers CFLA
root       3764  3416  0 Aug01 tty2     00:00:00              \_ make -C scsi mod
root       3773  3764  0 Aug01 tty2     00:00:00                  \_ ld -m elf_i3
```

ps and kill The next sequence of commands shows how to use ps to determine the PID number of a process running in the background and how to terminate that process using kill. In this case it is not necessary to use ps because the shell displays the PID number of the background processes. The ps utility verifies the PID number.

The first command executes find in the background. The shell displays the job and PID numbers of the process, followed by a prompt.

```
$ find ~ -name memo -print > memo.out &
[1] 3343
```

Next ps confirms the PID number of the background task. If you did not already know this number, using ps would be the only way to obtain it.

```
$ ps
  PID TTY          TIME CMD
 3308 pts/1    00:00:00 bash
 3343 pts/1    00:00:00 find
 3344 pts/1    00:00:00 ps
```

Finally kill (page 729) terminates the process:

```
$ kill 3343
$ RETURN
[1]+  Terminated              find ~ -name memo -print >memo.out
$
```

rcp

Copies one or more files to or from a remote system

rcp [options] source-file destination-file
rcp [options] source-file-list destination-directory

The rcp utility copies one or more ordinary files between two systems that can communicate over a network.

rcp **is not secure**

security   The rcp utility uses host-based trust, which is not secure, to authorize files to be copied. Use scp (page 810) when it is available.

Arguments   The *source-file*, *source-file-list*, and *destination-file* are pathnames of the ordinary files, and the *destination-directory* is the pathname of a directory file. A pathname that does not contain a colon (**:**) is the name of a file on the local system. A pathname of the form *name@host:path* names a file on the remote system named *host*. The *path* is relative to the home directory of the user *name* (unless *path* is an absolute pathname). When you omit the *name@* portion of the destination, a relative pathname is relative to the home directory on the *host* of the user giving the rcp command.

Like cp, rcp has two modes of operation: The first copies one file to another, and the second copies one or more files to a directory. The *source-file[-list]* is a list of the name(s) of the file(s) that rcp will copy; *destination-file* is the name rcp assigns to the resulting copy of the file, or *destination-directory* is the name of the directory rcp puts the copied files in. When rcp copies files to a *destination-directory*, the files maintain their original simple filenames.

Options   –p   (preserve) Sets the modification times and file access permissions of each copy to match those of the *source-file*. When you do not use **–p**, rcp uses the file-creation mask (umask; see page 870) on the remote system to modify the access permissions.

–r   (recursive) When a file in the *source-file-list* is a directory, copies the contents of that directory and any subdirectories into the *destination-directory*. You can use this option only when the destination is a directory.

Notes   You must have an account on the remote system to copy files to or from it using rcp. The rcp utility does not prompt for a password but rather uses several alternative methods to verify you have the authority to read or write files on the remote system.

One method requires that the name of the local system be specified in the **/etc/hosts.equiv** file on the remote system. If the name is there, rcp allows you to copy files *if* your usernames are the same on both systems *and* your account on the remote system has the necessary permissions to access files there.

Authorization can also be specified on a per-user basis. With this method the remote user's home directory must contain a file named **~/.rhosts** that lists trusted remote systems and users. Your local and remote user names do not have to match but your local username must appear on the line in the remote **~/.rhosts** file that starts with the name of the local system. See page 803 for a sample **.rhosts** file.

If you use a wildcard (such as *) in a remote pathname, you must quote the wildcard character or pathname so the wildcard is interpreted by the shell on the remote system and not by the local shell. As with cp, if the **destination-file** exists before you execute rcp, rcp overwrites the file.

Examples   The first example copies the files with filenames ending in .c into the **archives** directory on the remote system named **bravo**. Because the command does not specify a username, rcp uses the local user's username on the remote system. Because the command does not specify the full pathname of the **archives** directory, rcp assumes it is a subdirectory of the user's home directory on **bravo**. Each of the copied files retains its simple filename.

```
$ rcp *.c bravo:archives
```

The next example copies **memo** from the **/home/sam** directory on **bravo** to the working directory on the local system:

```
$ rcp bravo:/home/sam/memo .
```

Next rcp copies the files named **memo.new** and **letter** to Sam's home directory on the remote system **bravo**. The absolute pathnames of the copied files on **bravo** are **/home/sam/memo.new** and **/home/sam/letter**, respectively:

```
$ rcp memo.new letter bravo:/home/sam
```

The final command copies all the files in Sam's **reports** directory on **bravo** to the **oldreports** directory on the local system, preserving the original modification dates and file access permissions on the copies:

```
$ rcp -p 'bravo:reports/*' oldreports
```

renice

Changes the priority of a process

renice **priority process-list**
renice –n **increment process-list**

The renice utility alters the priority of a running process. An ordinary user can decrease the priority of a process that he owns. Only a user running with **root** privileges can increase the priority of a process or alter the priority of another user's process.

Arguments The *process-list* specifies the PID numbers of the processes that are to have their priorities altered. Each process has its priority set to *priority* or, using the second format, has its priority incremented by a value of *increment* (which can be negative).

Options The options, which you can specify throughout the *process-list*, change the interpretation of the arguments that follow them on the command line.

–p (**process**) Interprets the following arguments as process ID (PID) numbers (default).

–u (**user**) Interprets the following arguments as usernames or user ID numbers.

Notes The range of priorities is from –20 (the highest priority) to +20 (the lowest priority). Higher (more positive) priority values mean the kernel schedules a job less often. Lower (more negative) values cause the job to be scheduled more often.

When a user running with **root** privileges schedules a job to run at the highest priority, this change can affect the performance of the system for all other jobs, including the operating system itself. For this reason you should be careful when using renice with negative values.

See nice (page 773) if you want to start a process with a nondefault priority.

Examples The first example decreases the priority of all tasks owned by Zach:

```
$ renice -n 5 -u zach
```

In the following example, **root** uses ps to check the priority of the process running find. The **NI** (nice) column shows a value of 19 and the administrator decides to increase the priority by 5:

```
# ps -l
UID   PID  PPID CPU PRI NI    VSZ    RSS WCHAN  STAT  TT      TIME COMMAND
501  9705  9701   0  31  0   27792    856 -      Ss    p1   0:00.15 -bash
501 10548  9705   0  12 19   27252    516 -      RN    p1   0:00.62 find /
# renice -n -5 10548
```

rlogin

Logs in on a remote system

rlogin [option] remote-system

The rlogin utility establishes a login session on a remote system over a network.

rlogin **is not secure**

security The rlogin utility uses host-based trust, which is not secure, to authorize your login. Alternatively, it sends your password over the network as cleartext, which is not a secure practice. Use ssh (page 828) when it is available.

Arguments The *remote-system* is the name of a system the local system can reach over a network.

Options −l*username*
> (**login**) Logs you in on the remote system as the user specified by *username*.

Notes If the file named **/etc/hosts.equiv** located on the remote system specifies the name of the local system, the remote system will not prompt you to enter your password. Systems that are listed in the **/etc/hosts.equiv** file are considered to be just as secure as the local system.

An alternative way to specify a trusted relationship is on a per-user basis. Each user's home directory can contain a file named **~/.rhosts** that holds a list of trusted remote systems and users. See the "Examples" section for a sample **.rhosts** file.

Examples The following example illustrates the use of rlogin. On the local system, Max's username is **max**; on the remote system **bravo**, his username is **watson**. The remote system prompts Max to enter a password because he is logging in using a username different from the one he uses on the local system.

```
$ who am i
max          tty06         Oct 14 13:26
$ rlogin -l watson bravo
Password:
```

~/.rhosts file If the local system is named **hurrah**, the following **.rhosts** file on **bravo** allows the user **max** to log in as the user **watson** without entering a password:

```
$ cat ~watson/.rhosts
hurrah max
```

rm

Removes a file (deletes a link)

rm [options] file-list

The rm utility removes hard and/or symbolic links to one or more files. When you remove the last hard link to a file, the file is deleted.

Be careful when you use rm **with wildcards**

caution Because this utility enables you to remove a large number of files with a single command, use rm cautiously, especially when you are working with ambiguous file references. If you have any doubts about the effect of an rm command with an ambiguous file reference, first use echo with the same file reference and evaluate the list of files the reference generates. Alternatively, you can use the **–i** (**––interactive**) option.

Arguments   The *file-list* is a list of the files rm will delete.

Options   Under Linux, rm accepts the common options described on page 603. Options preceded by a double hyphen (––) work under Linux only. Options named with a single letter and preceded by a single hyphen work under Linux and OS X.

––force   **–f** Without asking for your consent, removes files for which you do not have write access permission. This option also suppresses informative messages if a file does not exist.

––interactive   **–i** Asks before removing each file. If you use **––recursive** with this option, rm also asks you before examining each directory.

––recursive   **–r** Deletes the contents of the specified directory, including all its subdirectories, and the directory itself. Use this option with caution.

––verbose   **–v** Displays the name of each file as it is removed.

Notes   To delete a file, you must have execute and write access permission to the parent directory of the file, but you do not need read or write access permission to the file itself. If you are running rm interactively (that is, if rm's standard input is coming from the keyboard) and you do not have write access permission to the file, rm displays your access permission and waits for you to respond. If your response starts with a y or Y, rm deletes the file; otherwise, it takes no action. If standard input is not coming from a keyboard, rm deletes the file without querying you.

Refer to page 106 for information on hard links and page 108 for information on symbolic links. Page 110 includes a discussion about removing links. Refer to the rmdir utility (page 806) if you need to remove an empty directory.

When you want to remove a file that begins with a hyphen, you must prevent rm from interpreting the filename as an option. One way to do so is to give the special option -- (double hyphen) before the name of the file. This option tells rm that no more options follow: Any arguments that come after it are filenames, even if they look like options.

Use shred to remove a file securely

security   Using rm does not securely delete a file—it is possible to recover a file deleted with rm. Use the shred utility to delete files more securely. See the example "Wiping a file" on page 659 for another method of deleting files more securely.

Examples   The following commands delete files both in the working directory and in another directory:

```
$ rm memo
$ rm letter memo1 memo2
$ rm /home/sam/temp
```

The next example asks the user before removing each file in the working directory and its subdirectories:

```
$ rm -ir .
```

This command is useful for removing filenames that contain special characters, especially SPACEs, TABs, and NEWLINEs. (You should not create filenames containing these characters on purpose, but it may happen accidentally.)

rmdir

Removes directories

rmdir directory-list

The rmdir utility deletes empty directories.

Arguments   The *directory-list* is a list of pathnames of empty directories that rmdir removes.

Options   Under Linux, rmdir accepts the common options described on page 603. Options preceded by a double hyphen (––) work under Linux only. Except as noted, options named with a single letter and preceded by a single hyphen work under Linux and OS X.

––ignore-fail-on-non-empty
> Suppresses the message rmdir normally displays when it fails because a directory is not empty. With the ––**parents** option, rmdir does not quit when it finds a directory that is not empty. `LINUX`

––parents   –p   Removes a hierarchy of empty directories.

––verbose   –v   Displays the names of directories as they are removed. `LINUX`

Notes   Use the rm utility with the –**r** option if you need to remove directories that are not empty, together with their contents.

Examples   The following command deletes the empty **literature** directory from the working directory:

```
$ rmdir literature
```

The next command removes the **letters** directory, using an absolute pathname:

```
$ rmdir /home/sam/letters
```

The final command removes the **letters**, **march**, and **05** directories, assuming the directories are empty except for other directories named in the path:

```
$ rmdir -p letters/march/05
```

rsh

Executes commands on a remote system

rsh [option] host [command-line]

The rsh utility runs ***command-line*** on ***host*** by starting a shell on the remote system. Without a ***command-line***, rsh calls rlogin, which logs you in on the remote system.

rsh **is not secure**

The rsh utility uses host-based trust, which is not secure, to authorize your login. Alternatively, it sends your password over the network as cleartext, which is not a secure practice. Use ssh (page 828) when it is available.

Arguments

The ***host*** is the name of the remote system. The rsh utility runs ***command-line*** on the remote system. You must quote special characters in ***command-line*** so the local shell does not expand them prior to passing them to rsh.

Options

–l*username*
    (**login**) Logs you in on the remote system as the user specified by ***username***.

Notes

If the file named **/etc/hosts.equiv** located on the remote system specifies the name of the local system, the remote system will not prompt you to enter your password. Systems that are listed in the **/etc/hosts.equiv** file are considered as secure as the local system.

An alternative way to specify a trusted relationship is on a per-user basis. Each user's home directory can contain a file named **~/.rhosts** that holds a list of trusted remote systems and users. See "Examples" under rlogin (page 803) for a sample **.rhosts** file.

Examples

In the first example, Max uses rsh to obtain a listing of the files in his home directory on **bravo**:

```
$ rsh bravo ls
cost_of_living
info
preferences
work
```

Next the output of the previous command is redirected to the file **bravo.ls**. Because the redirection character (**>**) is not escaped, it is interpreted by the local shell and the file **bravo.ls** is created on the local system.

```
$ rsh bravo ls > bravo_ls
$ cat bravo_ls
cost_of_living
info
preferences
work
```

The next example quotes the redirection character (>) so the file **bravo.ls** is created on the remote system (**bravo**), as shown by ls run on **bravo**:

```
$ rsh bravo ls ">" bravo.ls
$ rsh bravo ls
bravo.ls
cost_of_living
info
preferences
work
```

In the final example, rsh without *command-line* logs in on the remote system. Max has used the **–l watson** option to log in on **bravo** as **watson**. The **~watson/.rhosts** file must be configured to allow Max to log in on the account in this manner. See "Examples" under rlogin (page 803) for a sample **.rhosts** file.

```
$ rsh -l watson bravo
Last login: Sat Jul 30 16:13:53 from kudos
$ hostname
bravo
$ exit
rlogin: connection closed.
```

rsync

Copies files and directory hierarchies securely over a network

rsync [options] [[user@]from-host:]source-file [[user@]to-host:][destination-file]

The rsync (remote synchronization) utility copies an ordinary file or directory hierarchy locally or from the local system to or from another system on a network. By default, this utility uses OpenSSH to transfer files and the same authentication mechanism as OpenSSH; as a consequence, it provides the same security as OpenSSH. The rsync utility prompts for a password when it needs one. Alternatively you can use the **rsyncd** daemon as a transfer agent.

See Chapter 14 for information on rsync

tip   See Chapter 14 starting on page 583 for information on rsync.

scp

Securely copies one or more files to or from a remote system

scp [[user@]from-host:]source-file [[user@]to-host:][destination-file]

The scp (secure copy) utility copies an ordinary or directory file from one system to another on a network. This utility uses ssh to transfer files and the same authentication mechanism as ssh; as a consequence, it provides the same security as ssh. The scp utility prompts for a password when it needs one.

Arguments   The *from-host* is the name of the system you are copying files from and the *to-host* is the system you are copying to. When you do not specify a host, scp assumes the local system. The *user* on either system defaults to the user on the local system who is giving the command; you can specify a different user with *user@*. The scp utility permits you to copy between two remote systems.

The *source-file* is the file you are copying, and the *destination-file* is the resulting copy. You can specify plain or directory files as relative or absolute pathnames. A relative pathname is relative to the specified or implicit user's home directory. When the *source-file* is a directory, you must use the –r option to copy its contents. When the *destination-file* is a directory, each of the source files maintains its simple filename. If *source-file* is a single file, you can omit *destination-file* and the copied file will have the same simple filename as *source-file*.

Options   –P*port*

Connects to port *port* on the remote system. Be aware that ssh uses (lowercase) –p to specify a port.

–p   (**preserve**) Preserves the modification and access times as well as the permissions of the original file.

–q   (**quiet**) Does not display the progress meter.

–r   (**recursive**) Recursively copies a directory hierarchy.

–v   (**verbose**) Displays debugging messages about the connection and transfer. This option is useful if things are not going as expected.

Notes   The scp utility belongs to the OpenSSH suite of secure network connectivity tools. See the "Discussion" section on page 829 for a discussion of OpenSSH security. Refer to "First-time authentication" on page 829 for information about a message you may get when using scp to connect to a remote system for the first time.

Using this utility, you can copy files from or to the local system or between two remote systems. Make sure you have read permission for the file you are copying and write permission for the directory you are copying it into.

You must quote a wildcard character (such as *) in a remote pathname so it is interpreted by the shell on the remote system and not by the local shell.

As with cp, if the *destination-file* exists before you run scp, scp overwrites the file.

Examples   The first example copies the files with filenames ending in .c from the working directory on the local system into the ~sam/archives directory on **bravo**. The wildcard character is not quoted so the local shell will expand it. Because **archives** is a relative pathname, scp assumes it is a subdirectory of Sam's home directory on **bravo**. Each of the copied files retains its simple filename.

```
$ scp *.c sam@bravo:archives
```

Next Max copies the directory structure under ~**max/memos** on the system named **bravo** to ~**sam/max.memos.bravo** on **kudos**. He must have the necessary permissions to write to Sam's home directory on **kudos**.

```
$ scp -r bravo:memos sam@kudos:max.memos.bravo
```

Finally Max copies the files with filenames ending in .c from Sam's **archives** directory on **bravo** to the **sam.c.bravo** directory in his working directory. The wildcard character is quoted to protect it from expansion by the local shell; it will be interpreted by the remote system, **bravo**.

```
$ scp -r 'sam@bravo:archives/*.c' sam.c.bravo
```

Whenever you copy multiple files or directories, the destination—either local or remote—must be an existing directory and not an ordinary or nonexistent file.

sed

Edits a file noninteractively

*sed [–n] **program** [**file-list**]*
*sed [–n] –f **program-file** [**file-list**]*

The sed (stream editor) utility is a batch (noninteractive) editor. It transforms an input stream that can come from a file or standard input. It is frequently used as a filter in a pipe. Because it makes only one pass through its input, sed is more efficient than an interactive editor such as ed. Most Linux distributions provide GNU sed; Mac OS X supplies BSD sed. Chapter 13 applies to both versions.

See Chapter 13 for information on sed

tip   See Chapter 13 starting on page 565 for information on sed.

SetFile *OS X*

Sets file attributes

SetFile [options] file-list

The SetFile utility sets file attributes (page 931), including the file's type and creator codes, creation and last modification times, and attribute flags such as the invisible and locked flags.

Arguments   The *file-list* specifies the pathnames of one or more files that SetFile works on.

Options   The options for SetFile correspond to the options for GetFileInfo (page 717).

-a *flags*

(**attribute**) Sets the attribute flags specified by *flags*. An uppercase letter for a flag sets that flag and a lowercase letter unsets the flag. The values of unspecified flags are not changed. See Table D-2 on page 931 or the SetFile man page for a list of attribute flags.

-c *creator*

Sets the creator code to *creator*.

-d *date*

Sets the creation date to *date*. You must format the *date* as **mm/dd/[yy]yy [hh:mm:[:ss] [AM | PM]]**. If you do not specify **AM** or **PM**, SetFile assumes a 24-hour clock. You must enclose a *date* string that contains SPACEs within quotation marks.

-m *date*

(**modification**) Sets the modification date to *date*. The format of *date* is the same as that used with the -d option.

-P   (**no dereference**) For each file that is a symbolic link, sets information about the symbolic link, not the file the link points to. This option affects all files and treats files that are not symbolic links normally. See page 625 for an example of the -P option.

-t *type*

Sets the type code to *type*.

Notes   The SetFile utility is part of the Developer Tools optional install.

The options to SetFile and the corresponding options to GetFileInfo have minor differences. For example, you can specify multiple attribute flags with the -a option to SetFile but only a single flag with GetFileInfo. Also, SetFile requires a SPACE between the -a option and the list of flags; GetFileInfo does not allow a SPACE there.

Examples   The first example sets the type and creator codes of the file named **arch** to **SIT5** and **SIT!**, respectively, indicating that it is a StuffIt archive. The GetFileInfo utility displays these codes.

```
$ SetFile -t SIT5 -c SIT! arch
$ GetFileInfo -c arch
"SIT!"
$ GetFileInfo -t arch
"SIT5"
```

The next example marks the file named **secret** as invisible and locked. The file will not be visible in the Finder, and most OS X applications will be unable to overwrite it.

```
$ SetFile -a VL secret
```

The final example clears the invisible attribute flag from every file in the working directory:

```
$ SetFile -a v *
```

sleep

Creates a process that sleeps for a specified interval

sleep **time**
sleep **time-list** `LINUX`

The sleep utility causes the process executing it to go to sleep for the time specified.

Arguments Traditionally the amount of time a process sleeps is given as a single integer argument, *time*, which denotes a number of seconds. The *time* does not have to be an integer, however: You can specify a decimal fraction. Under Linux you can also append a unit specification to *time:* **s** (seconds), **m** (minutes), **h** (hours), or **d** (days).

Under Linux you can construct a ***time-list*** by including several times on the command line: The total time the process sleeps is the sum of these times. For example, if you specify **1h 30m 100s**, the process will sleep for 91 minutes and 40 seconds.

Examples You can use sleep from the command line to execute a command after a period of time. The following example executes in the background a process that reminds you to make a phone call in 20 minutes (1,200 seconds):

```
$ (sleep 1200; echo "Remember to make call.") &
[1] 4660
```

Alternatively, under Linux, you could give the following command to get the same reminder:

```
$ (sleep 20m; echo "Remember to make call.") &
[2] 4667
```

You can also use sleep within a shell script to execute a command at regular intervals. For example, the **per** shell script executes a program named **update** every 90 seconds:

```
$ cat per
#!/bin/bash
while true
do
    update
    sleep 90
done
```

If you execute a shell script such as **per** in the background, you can terminate it only by using kill.

The final shell script accepts the name of a file as an argument and waits for that file to appear on the disk. If the file does not exist, the script sleeps for 1 minute and 45 seconds before checking for the file again.

```
$ cat wait_for_file
#!/bin/bash

if [ $# != 1 ]; then
    echo "Usage: wait_for_file filename"
    exit 1
fi

while true
do
    if [ -f "$1" ]; then
        echo "$1 is here now"
        exit 0
    fi
    sleep 1m 45
done
```

Under Mac OS X replace **1m 45** with **105**.

sort

Sorts and/or merges files

sort [options] [file-list]

The sort utility sorts and/or merges one or more text files.

Arguments The *file-list* is a list of pathnames of one or more ordinary files that contain the text to be sorted. If the *file-list* is omitted, sort takes its input from standard input. Without the **–o** option, sort sends its output to standard output. This utility sorts and merges files unless you use the **–m** (merge only) or **–c** (check only) option.

Options When you do not specify an option, sort orders the file in the machine collating sequence (usually ASCII). Without a **––key** option, sort orders a file based on full lines. Use **––key** to specify sort fields within a line. You can follow a **––key** option with additional options without a leading hyphen; see the "Discussion" section for more information.

The Mac OS X version of sort accepts long options

tip Options for sort preceded by a double hyphen (––) work under Mac OS X as well as under Linux.

––**ignore-leading-blanks**

–b Blanks (TAB and SPACE characters) normally mark the beginning of fields in the input file. Without this option, sort considers leading blanks to be part of the field they precede. This option ignores leading blanks within a field, so sort does not consider these characters in sort comparisons.

––**check** **–c** Checks whether the file is properly sorted. The sort utility does not display anything if everything is in order. It displays a message if the file is not in sorted order and returns an exit status of 1.

––**dictionary-order**

–d Ignores all characters that are not alphanumeric characters or blanks. For example, sort does not consider punctuation with this option.

––**ignore-case** **–f** (**fold**) Considers all lowercase letters to be uppercase letters. Use this option when you are sorting a file that contains both uppercase and lowercase letters.

––**ignore-nonprinting**

–i Ignores nonprinting characters. This option is overridden by the **––dictionary-order** option.

––**key=**_start[,stop]_

–k *start[,stop]*

Specifies a sort field within a line. Without this option sort orders a file based on full lines. The sort field starts at the position on the line specified by *start* and ends at *stop*, or the end of the line if *stop* is omitted. The *start* and *stop* positions are in the format *f[.c]*, where *f* is the field number and *c* is the optional character within the field. Numbering starts with 1. When *c* is omitted from *start*, it defaults to the first character in the field; when *c* is omitted from *stop*, it defaults to the last character in the field. See the "Discussion" section for further explanation of sort fields and the "Examples" section for illustrations of their use.

--merge   –m   Assumes that each of the multiple input files is in sorted order and merges them without verifying they are sorted.

--numeric-sort   –n   Sorts in arithmetic sequence; does not order lines or sort fields in the machine collating sequence. With this option, minus signs and decimal points take on their arithmetic meaning.

--output=*filename*

–o *filename*

Sends output to *filename* instead of standard output; *filename* can be the same as one of the names in the *file-list*.

--reverse   –r   Reverses the sense of the sort (for example, **z** precedes **a**).

--field-separator=*x*

–t *x*

Specifies *x* as the field separator. See the "Discussion" section for more information on field separators.

--unique   –u   Outputs repeated lines only once. When you use this option with **--check**, sort displays a message if the same line appears more than once in the input file, even if the file is in sorted order.

Discussion

Without any options, sort bases its ordering on full lines.

In the following description, a *field* is a sequence of characters in a line of input. Without the **--field-separator** option, fields are bounded by the empty string preceding a group of one or more blanks (TAB and SPACE characters). You cannot see the empty string that delimits the fields; it is an imaginary point between two fields. Fields are also bounded by the beginning and end of the line. The line shown in Figure V-1 holds the fields **Toni**, SPACE**Barnett**, and SPACESPACESPACESPACE**55020**. These fields define sort fields. Sometimes fields and sort fields are the same.

Sort field   A *sort field* is a sequence of characters that sort uses to put lines in order. A sort field can contain all or part of one or more fields (Figure V-1).

The **--key** option specifies pairs of pointers that define subsections of each line (sort fields) for comparison. See the **--key** option (page 817) for details.

Leading blanks   The **–b** option causes sort to ignore leading blanks in a sort field. If you do not use this option, sort considers each leading blank to be a character in the sort field and includes it in the sort comparison.

Options   You can specify options that pertain only to a given sort field by immediately following the *stop* pointer (or the *start* pointer if there is no *stop* pointer) with one

Field   Field   Field

Toni Barnett   55020

Possible
sort fields

Figure V-1 Fields and sort fields

of the options **b**, **d**, **f**, **i**, **n**, or **r**. In this case you must *not* precede the option with a hyphen.

Multiple sort fields   When you specify more than one sort field, sort examines them in the order you specify them on the command line. If the first sort field of two lines is the same, sort examines the second sort field. If these are again the same, sort looks at the third field. This process continues for all the sort fields you specify. If all the sort fields are the same, sort examines the entire line.

Examples

The examples in this section demonstrate some of the features and uses of the sort utility. The examples assume the following **list** file is in the working directory:

```
$ cat list
Tom Winstrom        94201
Janet Dempsey       94111
Alice MacLeod       94114
David Mack          94114
Toni Barnett        95020
Jack Cooper         94072
Richard MacDonald   95510
```

This file contains a list of names and ZIP codes. Each line of the file contains three fields: the first name field, the last name field, and the ZIP code field. For the examples to work, the blanks in the file must be SPACEs, and not TABs.

The first example demonstrates sort without any options—the only argument is the name of the input file. In this case sort orders the file on a line-by-line basis. If the first characters on two lines are the same, sort looks at the second characters to determine the proper order. If the second characters are the same, sort looks at the third characters. This process continues until sort finds a character that differs between the lines. If the lines are identical, it does not matter which one sort puts first. In this example, sort needs to examine only the first three characters (at most) of each line. It displays a list that is in alphabetical order by first name.

```
$ sort list
Alice MacLeod       94114
David Mack          94114
Jack Cooper         94072
Janet Dempsey       94111
Richard MacDonald   95510
Tom Winstrom        94201
Toni Barnett        95020
```

You can instruct sort to skip any number of fields and characters on a line before beginning its comparison. Blanks normally mark the beginning of a field. The next example sorts the same list by last name, the second field: The **--key=2** argument instructs sort to begin its comparison with the this field. Because there is no second pointer, the sort field extends to the end of the line. Now the list is almost in last-name order, but there is a problem with **Mac**.

```
$ sort --key=2 list
Toni Barnett          95020
Jack Cooper           94072
Janet Dempsey         94111
Richard MacDonald     95510
Alice MacLeod         94114
David Mack            94114
Tom Winstrom          94201
```

In the preceding example, **MacLeod** comes before **Mack**. After finding that the sort fields of these two lines were the same through the third letter (**Mac**), sort put **L** before **k** because it arranges lines based on ASCII character codes, in which upper-case letters come before lowercase ones.

The **--ignore-case** option makes sort treat uppercase and lowercase letters as equals and fixes the problem with **MacLeod** and **Mack**:

```
$ sort --ignore-case --key=2 list
Toni Barnett          95020
Jack Cooper           94072
Janet Dempsey         94111
Richard MacDonald     95510
David Mack            94114
Alice MacLeod         94114
Tom Winstrom          94201
```

The next example attempts to sort **list** on the third field, the ZIP code. In this case sort does not put the numbers in order but rather puts the shortest name first in the sorted list and the longest name last. The **--key=3** argument instructs sort to begin its comparison with the third field, the ZIP code. A field starts with a blank and includes subsequent blanks. In the case of the **list** file, the blanks are SPACEs. The ASCII value of a SPACE character is less than that of any other printable character, so sort puts the ZIP code that is preceded by the most SPACEs first and the ZIP code that is preceded by the fewest SPACEs last.

```
$ sort --key=3 list
David Mack            94114
Jack Cooper           94072
Tom Winstrom          94201
Toni Barnett          95020
Janet Dempsey         94111
Alice MacLeod         94114
Richard MacDonald     95510
```

The **–b** (**--ignore-leading-blanks**) option causes sort to ignore leading SPACEs within a field. With this option, the ZIP codes come out in the proper order. When sort determines that **MacLeod** and **Mack** have the same ZIP codes, it compares the entire lines, putting **Alice MacLeod** before **David Mack** (because **A** comes before **D**).

```
$ sort -b --key=3 list
Jack Cooper            94072
Janet Dempsey          94111
Alice MacLeod          94114
David Mack             94114
Tom Winstrom           94201
Toni Barnett           95020
Richard MacDonald      95510
```

To sort alphabetically by last name when ZIP codes are the same, sort needs to make a second pass that sorts on the last name field. The next example shows how to make this second pass by specifying a second sort field and uses the –f (––ignore-case) option to keep the **Mack/MacLeod** problem from cropping up again:

```
$ sort -b -f --key=3 --key=2 list
Jack Cooper            94072
Janet Dempsey          94111
David Mack             94114
Alice MacLeod          94114
Tom Winstrom           94201
Toni Barnett           95020
Richard MacDonald      95510
```

The next example shows a **sort** command that skips not only fields but also characters. The –k 3.4 option (equivalent to ––key=3.4) causes sort to start its comparison with the fourth character of the third field. Because the command does not define an end to the sort field, it defaults to the end of the line. The sort field is the last two digits in the ZIP code.

```
$ sort -fb -k 3.4 list
Tom Winstrom           94201
Richard MacDonald      95510
Janet Dempsey          94111
Alice MacLeod          94114
David Mack             94114
Toni Barnett           95020
Jack Cooper            94072
```

The problem of how to sort by last name within the last two digits of the ZIP code is solved by a second pass covering the last name field. The f option following the –k 2 affects the second pass, which orders lines by last name only.

```
$ sort -b -k 3.4 -k 2f list
Tom Winstrom           94201
Richard MacDonald      95510
Janet Dempsey          94111
David Mack             94114
Alice MacLeod          94114
Toni Barnett           95020
Jack Cooper            94072
```

The next set of examples uses the **cars** data file. From left to right, the columns in this file contain each car's make, model, year of manufacture, mileage, and price:

```
$ cat cars
plym     fury     1970    73       2500
chevy    malibu   1999    60       3000
ford     mustang  1965    45       10000
volvo    s80      1998    102      9850
ford     thundbd  2003    15       10500
chevy    malibu   2000    50       3500
bmw      325i     1985    115      450
honda    accord   2001    30       6000
ford     taurus   2004    10       17000
toyota   rav4     2002    180      750
chevy    impala   1985    85       1550
ford     explor   2003    25       9500
```

Without any options sort displays a sorted copy of the file:

```
$ sort cars
bmw      325i     1985    115      450
chevy    impala   1985    85       1550
chevy    malibu   1999    60       3000
chevy    malibu   2000    50       3500
ford     explor   2003    25       9500
ford     mustang  1965    45       10000
ford     taurus   2004    10       17000
ford     thundbd  2003    15       10500
honda    accord   2001    30       6000
plym     fury     1970    73       2500
toyota   rav4     2002    180      750
volvo    s80      1998    102      9850
```

The objective of the next example is to sort by manufacturer and by price within manufacturer. Unless you specify otherwise, a sort field extends to the end of the line. The **–k 1** sort field specifier sorts from the beginning of the line. The command line instructs sort to sort on the entire line and then make a second pass, sorting on the fifth field all lines whose first-pass sort fields were the same (**–k 5**):

```
$ sort -k 1 -k 5 cars
bmw      325i     1985    115      450
chevy    impala   1985    85       1550
chevy    malibu   1999    60       3000
chevy    malibu   2000    50       3500
ford     explor   2003    25       9500
ford     mustang  1965    45       10000
ford     taurus   2004    10       17000
ford     thundbd  2003    15       10500
honda    accord   2001    30       6000
plym     fury     1970    73       2500
toyota   rav4     2002    180      750
volvo    s80      1998    102      9850
```

Because no two lines are the same, sort makes only one pass, sorting on each entire line. (If two lines differed only in the fifth field, they would be sorted properly on the first pass anyway, so the second pass would be unnecessary.) Look at the lines containing **taurus** and **thundbd**. They are sorted by the second field rather than by the fifth field, demonstrating that sort never made a second pass and so never sorted on the fifth field.

The next example forces the first-pass sort to stop at the end of the first field. The **–k 1,1** option specifies a *start* pointer of the first character of the first field and a *stop* pointer of the last character of the first field. When you do not specify a character within a *start* pointer, it defaults to the first character; when you do not specify a character within a *stop* pointer, it defaults to the last character. Now **taurus** and **thundbd** are properly sorted by price. But look at **explor**: It is less expensive than the other Fords, but sort has it positioned as the most expensive. The sort utility put the list in ASCII collating sequence order, not in numeric order: **9500** comes after **10000** because **9** comes after **1**.

```
$ sort -k 1,1 -k 5 cars
bmw     325i    1985    115     450
chevy   impala  1985    85      1550
chevy   malibu  1999    60      3000
chevy   malibu  2000    50      3500
ford    mustang 1965    45      10000
ford    thundbd 2003    15      10500
ford    taurus  2004    10      17000
ford    explor  2003    25      9500
honda   accord  2001    30      6000
plym    fury    1970    73      2500
toyota  rav4    2002    180     750
volvo   s80     1998    102     9850
```

The **–n** (numeric) option on the second pass puts the list in the proper order:

```
$ sort -k 1,1 -k 5n cars
bmw     325i    1985    115     450
chevy   impala  1985    85      1550
chevy   malibu  1999    60      3000
chevy   malibu  2000    50      3500
ford    explor  2003    25      9500
ford    mustang 1965    45      10000
ford    thundbd 2003    15      10500
ford    taurus  2004    10      17000
honda   accord  2001    30      6000
plym    fury    1970    73      2500
toyota  rav4    2002    180     750
volvo   s80     1998    102     9850
```

The next example again demonstrates that, unless you instruct it otherwise, sort orders a file starting with the field you specify and continuing to the end of the line. It does not make a second pass unless two of the first sort fields are the same. Because there is no *stop* pointer on the first sort field specifier, the sort field for the first pass includes the third field through the end of the line. Although this example sorts the cars by years, it does not sort the cars by model within manufacturer within years (**ford thundbd** comes before **ford explor**, these lines should be reversed).

```
$ sort -k 3 -k 1 cars
ford    mustang 1965    45      10000
plym    fury    1970    73      2500
bmw     325i    1985    115     450
chevy   impala  1985    85      1550
volvo   s80     1998    102     9850
chevy   malibu  1999    60      3000
chevy   malibu  2000    50      3500
honda   accord  2001    30      6000
toyota  rav4    2002    180     750
ford    thundbd 2003    15      10500
ford    explor  2003    25      9500
ford    taurus  2004    10      17000
```

Specifying an end to the sort field for the first pass allows sort to perform its secondary sort properly:

```
$ sort -k 3,3 -k 1 cars
ford    mustang 1965    45      10000
plym    fury    1970    73      2500
bmw     325i    1985    115     450
chevy   impala  1985    85      1550
volvo   s80     1998    102     9850
chevy   malibu  1999    60      3000
chevy   malibu  2000    50      3500
honda   accord  2001    30      6000
toyota  rav4    2002    180     750
ford    explor  2003    25      9500
ford    thundbd 2003    15      10500
ford    taurus  2004    10      17000
```

The next examples demonstrate important sorting techniques: putting a list in alphabetical order, merging uppercase and lowercase entries, and eliminating duplicates. The unsorted list follows:

```
$ cat short
Pear
Pear
apple
pear
Apple
```

Following is a plain sort:

```
$ sort short
Apple
Pear
Pear
apple
pear
```

The following folded sort is a good start, but it does not eliminate duplicates:

```
$ sort -f short
Apple
apple
Pear
Pear
pear
```

The **–u** (unique) option eliminates duplicates but without the **–f** the uppercase entries come first:

```
$ sort -u short
Apple
Pear
apple
pear
```

When you attempt to use both **–u** and **–f**, some of the entries get lost:

```
$ sort -uf short
apple
Pear
```

Two passes is the answer. Both passes are unique sorts, and the first folds lowercase letters onto uppercase ones:

```
$ sort -u -k 1f -k 1 short
Apple
apple
Pear
pear
```

split

Divides a file into sections

split [options] [filename [prefix]]

The split utility breaks its input into 1,000-line sections named **xaa, xab, xac,** and so on. The last section may be shorter. Options can change the sizes of the sections and lengths of the names.

Arguments The *filename* is the pathname of the file that split processes. If you do not specify an argument or if you specify a hyphen (–) instead of the *filename*, split reads from standard input. The *prefix* is one or more characters that split uses to prefix the names of the files it creates; the default is **x.**

Options Under Linux, split accepts the common options described on page 603. Options preceded by a double hyphen (––) work under Linux only. Options named with a single letter and preceded by a single hyphen work under Linux and OS X.

––suffix-length=*len*

      –a *len*
> Specifies that the filename suffix is *len* characters long (the default is 2).

––bytes=*n[u]*   –b *n[u]*
> Breaks the input into files that are *n* bytes long. The *u* is an optional unit of measure that can be **k** (kilobyte or 1,024-byte blocks) or **m** (megabyte or 1,048,576-byte blocks). If you include the unit of measure, split counts by this unit in place of bytes. Under Linux, *u* can be **b** (512-byte blocks) or any of the suffixes listed in Table V-1 on page 603.

––numeric-suffixes
>   –d Specifies numeric suffixes instead of alphabetic suffixes.

––lines=*num*   –l *num*
> Breaks the input into files that are *num* lines long (the default is 1,000).

Discussion By default split names the first file it creates **xaa.** The **x** is the default prefix. You can change the prefix with the *prefix* argument on the command line. You can change the number of characters in each filename following the prefix with the ––**suffix-length** option.

Examples By default split breaks a file into 1,000-line sections with the names **xaa, xab, xac,** and so on. The wc utility with the –l option shows the number of lines in each file. The last file, **xar,** is smaller than the rest.

```
$ split /usr/share/dict/words
$ wc -l *
   1000 xaa
   1000 xab
   1000 xac
...
   1000 xdt
    569 xdu
  98569 total
```

The next example uses the *prefix* argument to specify a filename prefix of **SEC** and uses −c (−−**suffix-length**) to change the number of letters in the filename suffix to 3:

```
$ split -a 3 /usr/share/dict/words SEC
$ ls
SECaaa  SECaak  SECaau  SECabe  SECabo  SECaby  SECaci  SECacs  SECadc  SECadm
SECaab  SECaal  SECaav  SECabf  SECabp  SECabz  SECacj  SECact  SECadd  SECadn
...
SECaaj  SECaat  SECabd  SECabn  SECabx  SECach  SECacr  SECadb  SECadl
```

ssh

Securely executes commands on a remote system

ssh [option] [user@]host [command-line]

The ssh utility logs in on a remote system and starts a shell. Optionally, ssh executes a command on the remote system and logs off. The ssh utility, which can replace rsh and rlogin, provides secure, encrypted communication between two systems over an unsecure network.

Arguments   The *host* is the system you want to log in or run a command on. Unless you have one of several kinds of authentication established, ssh prompts you for a username and password for the remote system. When ssh is able to log in automatically, it logs in as the user running the ssh command or as *user* if you specify *user@* on the ssh command line.

The *command-line* runs on the remote system. Without *command-line,* ssh logs in on the remote system. You must quote special characters in *command-line* if you do not want the local shell to expand them.

Options   **–f**   (**not foreground**) Sends ssh to the background after asking for a password and before executing *command-line*. This option is useful when you want to run the *command-line* in the background but must supply a password. Its use implies **–n**.

–l *user*
    (**login**) Attempts to log in as *user*. This option is equivalent to using *user@* on the command line.

–n   (**null**) Redirects standard input to ssh to come from **/dev/null**. See **–f**.

–p *port*
    Connects to port *port* on the remote system. Be aware that scp uses (uppercase) **–P** to specify a port.

–q   (**quiet**) Suppresses warning and diagnostic messages.

–t   (**tty**) Allocates a pseudo-tty to the ssh process on the remote system. Without this option, when you run a command on a remote system, ssh does not allocate a tty (terminal) to the process. Instead, ssh attaches standard input and standard output of the remote process to the ssh session—that is normally, but not always, what you want. This option forces ssh to allocate a tty on the remote system so programs that require a tty will work.

–v   (**verbose**) Displays debugging messages about the connection and transfer. This option is useful if things are not going as expected.

–X (**X11**) Turns on X11 forwarding. You may not need this option—X11 forwarding may be turned on in a configuration file.

–x (**X11**) Turns off X11 forwarding.

Discussion

OpenSSH Using public key encryption, OpenSSH provides two levels of authentication: server and client/user. First the client verifies that it is connected to the correct server. Then OpenSSH encrypts communication between the systems. Once a secure, encrypted connection has been established, OpenSSH makes sure the user is authorized to log in on or copy files to and from the server. After verifying the system and user, OpenSSH can allow various services to pass through the connection, including interactive shell sessions (ssh), remote command execution (ssh), file copying (scp), FTP services (sftp), X11 client/server connections, and TCP/IP port tunneling.

ssh The ssh utility allows you to log in on a remote system over a network. For example, you might choose to use a remote system to access a special-purpose application or to take advantage of a device that is available only on that system, or you might use a remote system because you know it is faster or less busy than the local system. While they are traveling, many businesspeople use ssh on a laptop to log in on a system at company headquarters. From a GUI you can use several systems simultaneously by logging in on each one from a different terminal emulator window.

X11 forwarding With trusted X11 forwarding turned on, it is a simple matter to run an X11 program over an ssh connection: Run ssh from a terminal emulator running on an X11 server and give an X11 command such as **xclock**; the graphical output appears on the local display. To turn on trusted X11 forwarding, set ForwardX11Trusted to **yes** in the **/etc/ssh/ssh_config** configuration file. To increase security (and in some cases reduce usability) set ForwardX11Trusted to **no**.

known_hosts, Two files list the hosts the local system has connected to and positively identified:
ssh_known_hosts **~/.ssh/known_hosts** (user) and **/etc/ssh/ssh_known_hosts** (global). No one except the owner (a user working with **root** privileges in the case of the second file) should be able to write to either of these files. No one except the owner should have any access to a **~/.ssh** directory.

First-time authentication When you connect to an OpenSSH server for the first time, the OpenSSH client prompts you to confirm you are connected to the right system. This check can help prevent a man-in-the-middle attack:

```
The authenticity of host 'plum (192.168.0.10)' can't be established.
RSA key fingerprint is d1:9d:1b:5b:97:5c:80:e9:4b:41:9a:b7:bc:1a:ea:a1.
Are you sure you want to continue connecting (yes/no)? yes
Warning: Permanently added 'plum,192.168.0.10' (RSA) to the list of
known hosts.
```

Before you respond to the preceding query, make sure you are logging in on the correct system and not on an imposter. If you are not sure, a telephone call to someone who logs in on that system locally can help verify you have accessed the right system. When you answer **yes** (you must spell it out), the client appends the server's public host key (the single line in the **/etc/ssh/ssh_host_rsa_key.pub** or **/etc/ssh/ssh_host_dsa_key.pub** file on the server) to the user's **~/.ssh/known_hosts** file on the local system, creating the **~/.ssh** directory if necessary. To ensure that it can keep track of which line in **known_hosts** applies to which server, OpenSSH prepends the name of the server and the server's IP address to the line.

When you subsequently use OpenSSH to connect to that server, the client verifies it is connected to the correct server by comparing this key to the one supplied by the server.

After a remote system's public key is stored in one of the known-hosts files, if the remote system supplies a different fingerprint when the systems connect, OpenSSH displays the following message and does not complete the connection:

```
@@@@@@@@@@@@@@@@@@@@@@@@@@@@@@@@@@@@@@@@@@@@@@@@@@@@@@@@@@@
@    WARNING: REMOTE HOST IDENTIFICATION HAS CHANGED!     @
@@@@@@@@@@@@@@@@@@@@@@@@@@@@@@@@@@@@@@@@@@@@@@@@@@@@@@@@@@@
IT IS POSSIBLE THAT SOMEONE IS DOING SOMETHING NASTY!
Someone could be eavesdropping on you right now (man-in-the-middle attack)!
It is also possible that the RSA host key has just been changed.
The fingerprint for the RSA key sent by the remote host is
f1:6f:ea:87:bb:1b:df:cd:e3:45:24:60:d3:25:b1:0a.
Please contact your system administrator.
Add correct host key in /home/sam/.ssh/known_hosts to get rid of this message.
Offending key in /home/sam/.ssh/known_hosts:1
RSA host key for plum has changed and you have requested strict checking.
Host key verification failed.
```

If you see this message, you may be the subject of a man-in-the-middle attack. More likely, however, something on the remote system has changed, causing it to supply a new fingerprint. Check with the remote system's administrator. If all is well, remove the offending key from the specified file (the third line from the bottom in the preceding example points to the line you need to remove) and try connecting again. You can use ssh-keygen with the **–R** option followed by the name of a host to remove a hashed entry. In this scenario you will be subject to first-time authentication (page 829) again as OpenSSH verifies you are connecting to the correct system. Follow the same steps as when you initially connected to the remote host.

Authorized keys: automatic login   You can configure OpenSSH so you do not have to enter a password each time you connect to a server (remote system). To set up this feature, you need to generate a personal authentication key on the client (local system), place the public part of the key on the server, and keep the private part of the key on the client. When you connect to the server, it issues a challenge based on the public part of the key. The private part of the key must then respond properly to this challenge. If the client provides the appropriate response, the server logs you in.

The first step in setting up an automatic login is to generate your personal authentication keys. First check whether these authentication keys already exist on the local system (client) by looking in **~/.ssh** for either **id_dsa** and **id_dsa.pub** or **id_rsa** and **id_rsa.pub**. If one of these pairs of files is present, skip the next step (i.e., do not create a new key).

On the client, the ssh-keygen utility creates the public and private parts of an RSA key. The key's randomart image is a visual representation of the public key; it is designed to be easy to recall. Display of the randomart image by a client is controlled by the **VisualHostKey** declaration in the **ssh_config** file.

ssh-keygen

```
$ ssh-keygen -t rsa
Generating public/private rsa key pair.
Enter file in which to save the key (/home/sam/.ssh/id_rsa):RETURN
Enter passphrase (empty for no passphrase):RETURN
Enter same passphrase again:RETURN
Your identification has been saved in /home/sam/.ssh/id_rsa.
Your public key has been saved in /home/sam/.ssh/id_rsa.pub.
The key fingerprint is:
f2:eb:c8:fe:ed:fd:32:98:e8:24:5a:76:1d:0e:fd:1d sam@peach
The key's randomart image is:
+--[ RSA 2048]----+
|              oE|
|     o .      . o|
|    . o +      ..|
|    .   + o    o |
...
```

Replace **rsa** with **dsa** to generate DSA keys. In this example, the user pressed RETURN in response to each query. You have the option of specifying a passphrase (10–30 characters is a good length) to encrypt the private part of the key. There is no way to recover a lost passphrase. See the following security tip for more information about the passphrase.

When you encrypt your personal key

security   The private part of the key is kept in a file that only you can read. If a malicious user compromises your account, an account that can use sudo to gain **root** privileges, or the **root** account on the local system, that user then has access to your account on the remote system because she can read the private part of your personal key.

Encrypting the private part of your personal key protects the key and, therefore, restricts access to the remote system should someone compromise your local account. However, if you encrypt your personal key, you must supply the passphrase you used to encrypt the key each time you use the key, negating the benefit of not having to type a password when logging in on the remote system. Also, most passphrases that you can easily remember can be cracked quite quickly by a powerful computer.

A better idea is to store the private keys on a removable medium, such as a USB flash drive, and use your **~/.ssh** directory as the mount point for the filesystem stored on this drive. You may want to encrypt these keys with a passphrase in case you lose the flash drive.

The ssh-keygen utility generates two keys: a private key or identification in **~/.ssh/id_rsa** and a public key in **~/.ssh/id_rsa.pub**. No one except the owner should be able to write to either of these files, and only the owner should be able to read from the private key file.

authorized_keys   To enable you to log in on or copy files to and from another system without supplying a password, first create a **~/.ssh** directory with permissions set to 700 on the server (remote system). Next copy **~/.ssh/id_rsa.pub** from the client (local system) to a file named **~/.ssh/authorized_keys** on the server (remote system). Set its permissions to 600 so that no one except the owner can read from or write to this file. Now when you run ssh or scp to access the server, you do not have to supply a password. To make the server even more secure, you can disable password authentication by setting PasswordAuthentication to **no** in **/etc/ssh/sshd_config** (remove the **#** from the beginning of the PasswordAuthentication line and change the **yes** to **no**).

Examples   In the first example, Max uses ssh to display a list of the files in his home directory on **kudos**:

```
$ ssh kudos ls
max@kudos's password:
Work
code
graphs
reports
```

Next the output of the previous command is redirected to the file **kudos_ls**. Because the redirection character (**>**) is not escaped, it is interpreted by the local shell, and the file **kudos_ls** is created on the local system.

```
$ ssh kudos ls > kudos_ls
max@kudos's password:
$ cat kudos_ls
Work
code
graphs
reports
```

The next example quotes the entire command that will run on the remote system. As a result, the local shell does not interpret the redirection character (**>**) but rather passes it to the remote shell. The file **kudos.ls** is created on the remote system (**kudos**), as shown by ls run on **kudos**:

```
$ ssh kudos "ls > kudos.ls"
max@kudos's password:
$ ssh kudos ls
max@kudos's password:
Work
code
graphs
kudos.ls
reports
```

The next command does not quote the pipe symbol (|). As a result the pipe is interpreted by the local shell, which sends the output of the remote ls to standard input of less on the local system:

```
$ ssh kudos ls | less
```

Next ssh executes a series of commands, connected with pipes, on a remote system. The commands are enclosed within single quotation marks so the local shell does not interpret the pipe symbols and all the commands are run on the remote system.

```
$ ssh kudos 'ps -ef | grep nmbd | grep -v grep | cut -c10-15 |xargs kill -1'
```

The output of ps is piped through grep, which passes all lines containing the string **nmbd** to another invocation of grep. The second grep passes all lines *not* containing the string **grep** to cut (page 652). The cut utility extracts the process ID numbers and passes them to xargs (page 881), which kills the listed processes by calling kill to issue a HUP signal (**kill −1**).

In the following example, ssh without *command-line* logs in on the remote system. Here Max has used **watson@kudos** to log in on **kudos** as **watson**:

```
$ ssh watson@kudos
watson@kudos's password:
Last login: Sat Sep 17 06:51:59 from bravo
$ hostname
kudos
$ exit
```

Max now decides to change the password for his **watson** login on **kudos**:

```
$ ssh watson@kudos passwd
watson@kudos's password:
(current) UNIX password: por
```

Max stops as soon as he sees passwd (running on **kudos**) displaying his password: He knows something is wrong. For the passwd to work, it must run with a tty (terminal) so it can turn off character echo (**stty −echo**); then it will not display passwords as the user enters them. The **−t** option solves the problem by associating a pseudo-tty with the process running passwd on the remote system:

```
$ ssh -t watson@kudos passwd
watson@kudos's password:
Changing password for watson
(current) UNIX password:
New UNIX password:
Retype new UNIX password:
passwd: all authentication tokens updated successfully
Connection to kudos closed.
$
```

The **−t** option is also useful when you are running a program that uses a character-based/pseudographical interface.

The following example uses tar (page 846) to create an archive file of the contents of the working directory hierarchy. The **f –** option causes tar to send its output to standard output. A pipe sends the output of tar running on the local system, via ssh, to dd (page 658) running on the remote system.

```
$ cat buwd
#! /bin/bash
# back up the working directory to the user's
# home directory on the remote system specified
# by $machine

# remote system:
machine=speedy

dir=$(basename $(pwd))
filename=$$.$dir.tar

echo Backing up $(pwd) to your home directory on $machine
tar -cf - . | ssh $machine "dd obs=256k of=$filename"
echo done. Name of file on $machine is $filename
```

stat

Displays information about files

stat [*options*] [*file-list*]

The stat utility displays information about files.

Arguments   The *file-list* specifies the pathnames of one or more files that stat displays information about. Without a *file-list*, stat displays information about standard input.

Options   Options preceded by a double hyphen (−−) work under Linux only. Except as noted, options named with a single letter and preceded by a single hyphen work under Linux and OS X.

Without any options, stat displays all available information about each file it processes.

−−format=*fmt* −c *fmt*
  Formats output using *fmt*. See the stat man page for more information. **LINUX**

  −F (**file type**) Displays a slash (**/**) after each directory, an asterisk (*****) after each executable file, an at sign (**@**) after a symbolic link, an equal sign (**=**) after a socket, and a pipe (**l**) after a FIFO. **OS X**

  −f (**filesystem**) Displays filesystem information instead of file information. **LINUX**

  −f *format*
  Formats output using *format*. The *format* string is similar to that used by printf. See the stat man page for more information. **OS X**

−−dereference −L For each file that is a symbolic link, displays information about the file the link points to, not the symbolic link itself. This option treats files that are not symbolic links normally.

  −l (**long**) Uses the same format as ls −l (page 93). **OS X**

  −q (**quiet**) Suppresses error messages. **OS X**

  −s (**shell**) Displays information in a format that can be used to initialize shell variables. See the "Examples" section. **OS X**

  −x (**Linux**) Displays a more verbose format that is compatible with the version of stat found on Linux. **OS X**

Examples   The Linux and Mac OS X versions of stat display different information. The examples show the output from the Linux version.

The first example displays information about the **/bin/bash** file:

```
$ stat /bin/bash
  File: `/bin/bash'
  Size: 813912          Blocks: 1600        IO Block: 4096    regular file
Device: 812h/2066d      Inode: 146674       Links: 1
Access: (0755/-rwxr-xr-x)  Uid: ( 1003/      sam)  Gid: ( 1002/     pubs)
Access: 2009-05-28 11:36:01.000000000 -0700
Modify: 2008-05-12 11:36:49.000000000 -0700
Change: 2009-05-21 11:34:41.000000000 -0700
```

The next example displays information about the root filesystem:

```
$ stat -f /
  File: "/"
    ID: 586ac700c664ac38 Namelen: 255       Type: ext2/ext3
Block size: 4096        Fundamental block size: 4096
Blocks: Total: 960602     Free: 703655      Available: 654858
Inodes: Total: 488640     Free: 467723
```

strings

Displays strings of printable characters

strings [options] file-list

The strings utility displays strings of printable characters from object and other nontext files.

Arguments The *file-list* is a list of files that strings processes.

Options Options preceded by a double hyphen (––) work under Linux only. Except as noted, options named with a single letter and preceded by a single hyphen work under Linux and OS X.

––**all** –**a** Processes whole files. Without this option strings processes only the initialized and loaded parts of an object file.

––**print-file-name** –**f** Precedes each string with the name of the file that the string comes from. `LINUX`

––**bytes=***min* –*min*

Displays strings of characters that are at least *min* characters long (the default is 4).

Discussion The strings utility can help you determine the contents of nontext files. One notable application for strings is determining the owner of files in a **lost+found** directory.

Examples The following example displays strings of four or more printable characters in the executable file for the man utility. If you did not know what this file was, these strings could help you determine that it was the man executable.

```
$ strings /usr/bin/man
...
--Man-- next: %s [ view (return) | skip (Ctrl-D) | quit (Ctrl-C) ]
format: %d, save_cat: %d, found: %d
cannot write to %s in catman mode
creating temporary cat for %s
can't write to temporary cat for %s
can't create temporary cat for %s
cat-saver exited with status %d
found ultimate source file %s
...
```

stty

Displays or sets terminal parameters

stty [options] [arguments]

Without any arguments, stty displays parameters that affect the operation of the terminal or terminal emulator. For a list of some of these parameters and an explanation of each, see the "Arguments" section. The arguments establish or change parameters.

Options   Under Linux, stty accepts the common options described on page 603. Options preceded by a double hyphen (––) work under Linux only. Except as noted, options named with a single letter and preceded by a single hyphen work under Linux and OS X.

––all   –a   Reports on all parameters. This option does not accept arguments.

––file=*device*   –F *device*

Affects *device*. Without this option stty affects the device attached to standard input. You can change the characteristics of a device only if you own its device file or if you are working with **root** privileges. **LINUX**

–f *device*

Affects *device*. Performs the same function as –F. **OS X**

––save   –g   Generates a report of the current settings in a format you can use as arguments to another stty command. This option does not accept arguments.

Arguments   The arguments to stty specify which terminal parameters stty is to alter. To turn on each of the parameters that is preceded by an optional hyphen (indicated in the following list as [–]) specify the parameter without the hyphen. To turn it off, use the hyphen. Unless specified otherwise, this section describes the parameters in their *on* states.

Special Keys and Characteristics

columns *n*   Sets the line width to *n* columns.

ek   (**erase kill**) Sets the erase and line kill keys to their default values. Many systems use DELETE and CONTROL-U, respectively, as the defaults.

erase *x*   Sets the erase key to *x*. To specify a control character, precede *x* with CONTROL-V (for example, use CONTROL-V CONTROL-H to indicate CONTROL-H) or use the notation **^h**, where **^** is a caret (SHIFT-6 on most keyboards).

intr *x*   Sets the interrupt key to *x*. See **erase *x*** for conventions.

kill *x*   Sets the line kill key to *x*. See **erase *x*** for conventions.

rows *n*   Sets the number of screen rows to *n*.

sane   Sets the terminal parameters to values that are usually acceptable. The **sane** argument is useful when several stty parameters have changed, making it difficult to use the terminal to run stty to set things right. If **sane** does not appear to work, try entering the following characters:

        CONTROL-J **stty sane** CONTROL-J

susp *x*   (**suspend**) Sets the suspend (terminal stop) key to *x*. See **erase** *x* for conventions.

werase *x*   (**word erase**) Sets the word erase key to *x*. See **erase** *x* for conventions.

Modes of Data Transmission

[–]cooked   See **raw**. `LINUX`

cooked   See **sane**. `OS X`

[–]cstopb   (**stop bits**) Selects two stop bits (**–cstopb** specifies one stop bit).

[–]parenb   (**parity enable**) Enables parity on input and output. When you specify **–parenb**, the system does not use or expect a parity bit when communicating with the terminal.

[–]parodd   (**parity odd**) Selects odd parity (**–parodd** selects even parity).

[–]raw   The normal state is **–raw**. When the system reads input in its raw form, it does not interpret the following special characters: erase (usually DELETE), line kill (usually CONTROL-U), interrupt execution (CONTROL-C), and EOF (CONTROL-D). In addition, the system does not use parity bits. Reflecting the humor that is typical of Linux's heritage, under Linux you can also specify **–raw** as **cooked**.

Treatment of Characters

[–]echo   Echoes characters as they are typed (full-duplex operation). If a terminal is half-duplex and displays two characters for each one it should display, turn the **echo** parameter off (**–echo**). Use **–echo** when the user is entering passwords.

[–]echoe   (**echo erase**) The normal setting is **echoe**, which causes the kernel to echo the character sequence BACKSPACE SPACE BACKSPACE when you use the erase key to delete a character. The effect is to move the cursor backward across the line, removing characters as you delete them.

[–]echoke   (**echo kill erase**) The normal setting is **echoke**. When you use the kill character to delete a line while this option is set, all characters back to the prompt are erased on the current line. When this option is negated, pressing the kill key moves the cursor to the beginning of the next line.

[–]echoprt   (**echo print**) The normal setting is **–echoprt**, which causes characters to disappear as you erase them. When you set **echoprt**, characters you erase are displayed between a backslash (\) and a slash (/). For example, if you type the word **sort** and then erase it by pressing BACKSPACE four times, Linux displays **sort\tros/** when **echoprt** is set. If you use the kill character to delete the entire line, having **echoprt** set causes the entire line to be displayed as if you had BACKSPACEd to the beginning of the line.

[–]lcase   For uppercase-only terminals, translates all uppercase characters into lowercase as they are entered (also [–]LCASE). LINUX

[–]nl   Accepts only a NEWLINE character as a line terminator. With **–nl** in effect, the system accepts a RETURN character from the terminal as a NEWLINE but sends a RETURN followed by a NEWLINE to the terminal in place of a NEWLINE.

[–]tabs   Transmits each TAB character to the terminal as a TAB character. When **tabs** is turned off (**–tabs**), the kernel translates each TAB character into the appropriate number of SPACEs and transmits them to the terminal (also [–]tab3).

Job Control Parameters

[–]tostop   Stops background jobs if they attempt to send output to the terminal (**–tostop** allows background jobs to send output to the terminal).

Notes   The name stty is an abbreviation for *set teletypewriter,* or *set tty* (page 867), the first terminal UNIX was run on. Today stty is commonly thought of as meaning *set terminal.*

The shells retain some control over standard input when you use them interactively. As a consequence, a number of the options available with stty appear to have no effect. For example, the command **stty –echo** appears to have no effect under tcsh:

```
tcsh $ stty -echo
tcsh $ date
Thu May 28 16:53:01 PDT 2009
```

While **stty –echo** does work when you are using bash interactively, **stty –echoe** does not. However, you can still use these options to affect shell scripts and other utilities.

```
$ cat testit
#!/bin/bash
stty -echo
echo -n "Enter a value: "
read a
echo
echo "You entered: $a"
stty echo

$ ./testit
Enter a value:
You entered: 77
```

The preceding example does not display the user's response to the **Enter a value:** prompt. The value is retained by the **a** variable and is displayed by the **echo "You entered: $a"** statement.

Examples   The first example shows that stty without any arguments displays several terminal operation parameters. (Your system may display more or different parameters.) The character following the **erase =** is the erase key. A ^ preceding a character indicates a CONTROL key. In the example the erase key is set to CONTROL-H. If stty does not display the erase character, it is set to its default value of DELETE. If it does not display a kill character, it is set to its default of ^U.

```
$ stty
speed 38400 baud; line = 0;
erase = ^H;
```

Next the **ek** argument returns the erase and line kill keys to their default values:

```
$ stty ek
```

The next display verifies the change. The stty utility does not display either the erase character or the line kill character, indicating both are set to their default values:

```
$ stty
speed 38400 baud; line = 0;
```

The next example sets the erase key to CONTROL-H. The CONTROL-V quotes the CONTROL-H so that the shell does not interpret it and it is passed to stty unchanged:

```
$ stty erase CONTROL-V CONTROL-H
$ stty
speed 38400 baud; line = 0;
erase = ^H;
```

Next stty sets the line kill key to CONTROL-X. This time the user entered a caret (^) followed by an **x** to represent CONTROL-X. You can use either a lowercase or uppercase letter.

```
$ stty kill ^X
$ stty
speed 38400 baud; line = 0;
erase = ^H; kill = ^X;
```

Now stty changes the interrupt key to CONTROL-C:

```
$ stty intr CONTROL-V CONTROL-C
```

In the following example, stty turns off TABs so the appropriate number of SPACEs is sent to the terminal in place of a TAB. Use this command if a terminal does not automatically expand TABs.

```
$ stty -tabs
```

If you log in under Linux and everything appears on the terminal in uppercase letters, give the following command and then check the CAPS LOCK key. If it is set, turn it off.

```
$ STTY -LCASE
```

Turn on **lcase** if you are using a very old terminal that cannot display lowercase characters.

Although no one usually changes the suspend key from its default of CONTROL-Z, you can. Give the following command to change the suspend key to CONTROL-T:

```
$ stty susp ^T
```

sysctl *OS X*

Displays and alters kernel variables

sysctl [options] [variable-list]
sysctl [options] –w [var=value ...]

The sysctl utility displays and alters kernel variables, including kernel tuning parameters.

Arguments

The *variable-list* is a list of kernel variables whose values sysctl displays. In the second format, each *value* is assigned to the variable named *var*.

Options

–a   (**all**) Displays all kernel variables.

–b   (**binary**) Displays kernel variables as binary data without terminating NEWLINEs.

–n   (**no label**) Displays variables without labels.

Discussion

The sysctl utility provides access to a number of kernel variables, including the maximum number of processes the kernel will run at one time, the filename used for core files, and the system security level. Some variables cannot be altered or can be altered only in certain ways. For example, you can never lower the security level.

Examples

The sysctl utility is commonly used for tuning the kernel. The process limits can be displayed by anyone, but can be altered only by a user who is working with **root** privileges. The following example shows a user changing the maximum number of processes per UID:

```
$ sysctl -a | grep proc
kern.maxproc = 532
kern.maxfilesperproc = 10240
kern.maxprocperuid = 266
kern.aioprocmax = 16
kern.proc_low_pri_io = 0
...
# sysctl -w kern.maxprocperuid=200
kern.maxprocperuid: 266 -> 200
```

tail

Displays the last part (tail) of a file

tail [options] [file-list]

The tail utility displays the last part, or end, of a file.

Arguments The *file-list* is a list of pathnames of the files that tail displays. When you specify more than one file, tail displays the filename of each file before displaying lines from that file. If you do not specify an argument or, under Linux, if you specify a hyphen (–) instead of a filename, tail reads from standard input.

Options Under Linux, tail accepts the common options described on page 603. Options preceded by a double hyphen (––) work under Linux only. Except as noted, options named with a single letter and preceded by a single hyphen work under Linux and OS X.

–b *[+]n*

Counts by 512-byte blocks instead of lines. The *n* argument is an integer that specifies the number of blocks. Thus the command **tail –b 5** displays the last five blocks of a file. See the note about using a plus sign (**+**) in the next option. *OS X*

––bytes=*[+]n[u]*   **–c** *[+]n[u]*

Counts by bytes (characters) instead of lines. The *n* argument is an integer that specifies the number of bytes. Thus the command **tail –c 5** displays the last five bytes of a file. Under Linux only, the *u* is an optional multiplicative suffix as described on page 602, except that tail uses a lowercase **k** for kilobyte (1,024-byte blocks). If you include a multiplicative suffix, tail counts by this unit instead of by bytes.

If you put a plus sign (**+**) in front of *n,* tail counts from the start of the file instead of the end. The tail utility still *displays characters through the end* of the file, even though it *starts counting* from the beginning. Thus **tail –c +5** causes tail to display from the fifth character through the end of the file.

––follow   **–f** After copying the last line of the file, tail enters an endless loop, waiting and copying additional lines from the file if the file grows. If you specify multiple files in *file-list* with this option, tail includes a new header each time it displays output from a different file so you know which file is being added to. This option is useful for tracking the progress of a process that is running in the background and sending its output to a file. The tail utility continues to wait indefinitely, so you must use the interrupt key to terminate it. See also the **–s** option.

**--lines=*[+]n[u]*   −n *[+]n[u]*

> Counts by lines (the default). The *n* argument is an integer that specifies the number of lines. Under Linux, the *u* is an optional unit of measure; see the −c (−−**bytes**) option for an explanation of its use. Although it is not documented, you can use ±*n* to specify a number of lines without using this option.
>
> If you put a plus sign (+) in front of *n,* tail counts from the start of the file instead of the end. The tail utility still *displays lines through the end* of the file, even though it *starts counting* from the beginning. Thus **tail −n +5** causes tail to display from the fifth line through the last line of the file.

--quiet   −q   Suppresses header information when you specify multiple files in *file-list.* `LINUX`

--sleep-interval=*n*   −s *n*

> When used with **−f,** causes tail to sleep for *n* seconds between checks for additional output. `LINUX`

Notes

The tail utility displays the last ten lines of its input by default.

Examples

The examples are based on the **eleven** file:

```
$ cat eleven
line one
line two
line three
line four
line five
line six
line seven
line eight
line nine
line ten
line eleven
```

First tail displays the last ten lines of the **eleven** file (no options):

```
$ tail eleven
line two
line three
line four
line five
line six
line seven
line eight
line nine
line ten
line eleven
```

Next it displays the last three lines (**−n 3** or **−−lines 3**) of the file:

```
$ tail -n 3 eleven
line nine
line ten
line eleven
```

The following example displays the file starting at line 8 (+8):

```
$ tail -n +8 eleven
line eight
line nine
line ten
line eleven
```

The next example displays the last six characters in the file (**–c 6** or **––bytes 6**). Only five characters are evident (**leven**); the sixth is a NEWLINE.

```
$ tail -c 6 eleven
leven
```

The final example demonstrates the **–f** option. Here tail tracks the output of a make command, which is being sent to the file **accounts.out**:

```
$ make accounts > accounts.out &
$ tail -f accounts.out
        cc -c trans.c
        cc -c reports.c
...
CONTROL-C
$
```

In the preceding example, running tail with **–f** displays the same information as running make in the foreground and not redirecting its output to a file. However, using tail offers some advantages. First, the output of make is saved in a file. (The output would not be saved if you did not redirect its output.) Second, if you decide to do something else while make is running, you can kill tail and the screen will be free for you to use while make continues running in the background. When you are running a large job such as compiling a large program, you can use tail with the –f option to check on its progress periodically.

tar

Stores or retrieves files to/from an archive file

tar option [modifiers] [file-list]

The tar (tape archive) utility creates, adds to, lists, and retrieves files from an archive file.

Arguments   The *file-list* is a list of pathnames of the files that tar archives or extracts.

Options   Use only one of the following options to indicate which action you want tar to take. You can alter the action of the option by following it with one or more *modifiers*.

The Mac OS X version of tar accepts long options

tip   Options for tar preceded by a double hyphen (−−) work under Mac OS X as well as under Linux.

−−create   −c   Creates an archive. This option stores the files named in *file-list* in a new archive. If the archive already exists, tar destroys it before creating the new archive. If a *file-list* argument is a directory, tar copies the directory hierarchy into the archive. Without the −−file option, tar writes the archive to standard output.

−−compare *or*   −d   Compares an archive with the corresponding disk files and reports on the
−−diff   differences.

−−help   Displays a list of options and modifiers, along with short descriptions of each.

−−append   −r   Writes the files named in *file-list* to the end of the archive. This option leaves files that are already in the archive intact, so duplicate copies of files may appear in the archive after tar finishes. When tar extracts the files, the most recent copy of a file in the archive is the one that ends up on the disk.

−−list   −t   (**table of contents**) Without a *file-list,* this option produces a table of contents listing all files in an archive. With a *file-list,* it displays the name of each file in the *file-list* each time it occurs in the archive. You can use this option with the −−verbose option to display detailed information about each file in an archive.

−−update   −u   Adds the files from *file-list* if they are not already in the archive or if they have been modified since they were last written to the archive. Because of the additional checking required, tar runs more slowly when you specify this option.

−−extract   −x   Extracts *file-list* from the archive and writes it to the disk, overwriting existing files with the same names. Without a *file-list,* this option extracts all files from the archive. If the *file-list* includes a directory, tar extracts the directory hierarchy. The tar utility attempts to keep the owner, modification time, and access privileges the same as those of the original file. If tar reads the same file more than once, the last version read will appear on the disk when tar is finished.

Modifiers

--blocking-factor *n*

-b *n*

Uses *n* as the blocking factor for creating an archive. Use this option only when tar is creating an archive directly to removable media. (When tar reads an archive, it automatically determines the blocking factor.) The value of *n* is the number of 512-byte blocks to write as a single block on the removable media.

--directory *dir*   **-C** *dir*

Changes the working directory to *dir* before processing.

--checkpoint

Displays periodic messages. This option lets you know tar is running without forcing you to view all the messages displayed by **--verbose**.

--exclude=*file*

Does not process the file named *file*. If *file* is a directory, no files or directories in that directory hierarchy are processed. The *file* can be an ambiguous file reference; quote special characters as needed.

--file *filename*   **-f** *filename*

Uses *filename* as the name of the file the archive is created in or extracted from. The *filename* can be the name of an ordinary file or a device (e.g., a CD or USB flash drive). You can use a hyphen (–) instead of the *filename* to refer to standard input when creating an archive and to standard output when extracting files from an archive. The following two commands are equivalent ways of creating a compressed archive of the files in the **/home** directory hierarchy on **/dev/sde1**:

```
$ tar -zcf /dev/sde1 /home
$ tar -cf - /home | gzip > /dev/sde1
```

--dereference   **-h**   For each file that is a symbolic link, archives the file the link points to, not the symbolic link itself.

--ignore-failed-read

When creating an archive, tar normally quits with a nonzero exit status if any of the files in *file-list* is unreadable. This option causes tar to continue processing, skipping unreadable files.

--bzip2   **-j**   Uses bzip2 (pages 60 and 615) to compress/decompress files when creating an archive and extracting files from an archive.

--tape–length *n*   **-L** *n*

Asks for a new medium after writing $n * 1,024$ bytes to the current medium. This feature is useful when you are building archives that are too big to fit on a single USB flash drive, partition, CD, or other storage device.

--touch   **-m**   Sets the modification time of the extracted files to the time of extraction. Without this option tar attempts to maintain the modification time of the original file.

--one-file-system   When a directory name appears in *file-list* while it is creating an archive, tar recursively processes the files and directories in the named directory hierarchy. With this option tar stays in the filesystem that contains the named directory and does not process directories in other filesystems. Under OS X, you can use –l (lowercase "l") in place of --one-file-system. Under Linux, –l is used for a different purpose.

--absolute-names –P   The default behavior of tar is to force all pathnames to be relative by stripping leading slashes from them. This option disables this feature, so absolute pathnames remain absolute.

--sparse –S   Linux allows you to create *sparse files* (large, mostly empty files). The empty sections of sparse files do not take up disk space. When tar extracts a sparse file from an archive, it normally expands the file to its full size. As a result, when you restore a sparse file from a tar backup, the file takes up its full space and may no longer fit in the same disk space as the original. This option causes tar to handle sparse files efficiently so they do not take up unnecessary space either in the archive or when they are extracted.

--verbose –v   Lists each file as tar reads or writes it. When combined with the –t option, –v causes tar to display a more detailed listing of the files in the archive, showing their ownership, permissions, size, and other information.

--interactive –w   Asks you for confirmation before reading or writing each file. Respond with y if you want tar to take the action. Any other response causes tar not to take the action.

--exclude-from *filename*
–X *filename*
   Similar to the **--exclude** option, except *filename* specifies a file that contains a list of files to exclude from processing. Each file listed in *filename* must appear on a separate line.

--compress *or* **–Z**   Uses compress when creating an archive and uncompress when extracting files
--uncompress   from an archive.

--gzip *or* **–z**   Causes tar to use gzip to compress an archive while it is being created and to
--gunzip   decompress an archive when extracting files from it. This option also works to extract files from archives that have been compressed with the compress utility.

Notes

The **--help** option displays all tar options and modifiers; the **--usage** option provides a brief summary of the same information. The info page on tar provides extensive information, including a tutorial for this utility.

You can use ambiguous file references in *file-list* when you create an archive but not when you extract files from an archive.

The name of a directory file within the *file-list* references the directory hierarchy (all files and directories within that directory).

The file that tar sends its output to by default is compilation specific; typically it goes to standard output. Use the **–f** option to specify a different filename or device to hold the archive.

When you create an archive using a simple filename in *file-list,* the file appears in the working directory when you extract it. If you use a relative pathname when you create an archive, the file appears with that relative pathname, starting from the working directory when you extract it. If you use the **–P** option and an absolute pathname when you create an archive, and if you use the **–P** option when you extract files from the archive, tar extracts the file with the same pathname.

Leading hyphens · The tar utility does not require leading hyphens on options and modifiers. However, it behaves slightly differently with regard to the order of options and modifiers it requires with and without the hyphen.

You can specify one or more modifiers following an option. With a leading hyphen, the following tar command generates an error:

```
$ tar -cbf 10 /dev/sde1 memos
tar: f: Invalid blocking factor
Try `tar --help' or `tar --usage' for more information.
```

The error occurs because the **–b** modifier takes an argument but is not the last modifier in a group. The same command works correctly if you omit the leading hyphen.

You must use leading hyphens if you separate options:

```
$ tar -cb 10 -f /dev/sde1 memos
```

Examples   The following example makes a copy of the **/home/max** directory hierarchy on a USB flash drive mounted at **/dev/sde1**. The **v** modifier causes the command to list the files it writes to the device. This command erases anything that was already on the device. The message from tar explains that the default action is to store all pathnames as relative paths instead of absolute paths, thereby allowing you to extract the files into a different directory on the disk.

```
$ tar -cvf /dev/sde1 /home/max
tar: Removing leading '/' from member names.
/home/max/
/home/max/.bash_history
/home/max/.bash_profile
...
```

In the next example, the same directory is saved on the device mounted on **/dev/sde1** with a blocking factor of 100. Without the **v** modifier, tar does not display the list of files it is writing to the device. The command runs in the background and displays any messages after the shell issues a new prompt.

```
$ tar -cb 100 -f /dev/sde1 /home/max &
[1] 4298
$ tar: Removing leading '/' from member names.
```

The next command displays the table of contents of the archive on the device mounted on **/dev/sde1**:

```
$ tar -tvf /dev/sde1
drwxrwxrwx max/group          0 Jun 30 21:39 2008 home/max/
-rw-r--r-- max/group        678 Aug  6 14:12 2009 home/max/.bash_history
-rw-r--r-- max/group        571 Aug  6 14:06 2009 home/max/.bash_profile
drwx------ max/group          0 Nov  6 22:34 2009 home/max/mail/
-rw------- max/group       2799 Nov  6 22:34 2009 home/max/mail/sent-mail
...
```

Next, Max creates a gzipped tar archive in **/tmp/max.tgz**. This approach is a popular way to bundle files that you want to transfer over a network or otherwise share with others. Ending a filename with **.tgz** is one convention for identifying gzipped tar archives. Another convention is to end the filename with **.tar.gz**.

```
$ tar -czf /tmp/max.tgz literature
```

The final command lists the files in the compressed archive **max.tgz**:

```
$ tar -tzvf /tmp/max.tgz
...
```

tee

Copies standard input to standard output and one or more files

tee [options] file-list

The tee utility copies standard input to standard output *and* to one or more files.

Arguments The *file-list* is a list of the pathnames of files that receive output from tee. If a file in *file-list* does not exist, tee creates it.

Options Options preceded by a double hyphen (−−) work under Linux only. Options named with a single letter and preceded by a single hyphen work under Linux and OS X. Without any options, tee overwrites the output files if they exist and responds to interrupts.

−−**append** −a Appends output to existing files rather than overwriting them.

        −i Causes tee not to respond to the **SIGINT** interrupt. *OS X*

−−**ignore-interrupts**
        −i Causes tee not to respond to interrupts. *LINUX*

Examples In the following example, a pipe sends the output from make to tee, which copies that information to standard output and to the file **accounts.out**. The copy that goes to standard output appears on the screen. The cat utility displays the copy that was sent to the file.

```
$ make accounts | tee accounts.out
        cc -c trans.c
        cc -c reports.c
...
$ cat accounts.out
        cc -c trans.c
        cc -c reports.c
...
```

Refer to page 845 for a similar example that uses **tail −f** rather than tee.

telnet

Connects to a remote system over a network

telnet [options] [remote-system]

The telnet utility implements the TELNET protocol to connect to a remote system over a network.

telnet **is not secure**

security The telnet utility is not secure. It sends your username and password over the network as clear-text, which is not a secure practice. Use ssh (page 828) when it is available.

Arguments The *remote-system* is the name or IP address of the remote system that telnet connects to. When you do not specify a *remote-system,* telnet works interactively and prompts you to enter one of the commands described in this section.

Options **–a** Initiates automatic login (the default behavior under Mac OS X).

–e *c*
(**escape**) Changes the escape character from CONTROL-] to the character *c*.

–K Prevents automatic login. This option is available under Mac OS X and some Linux distributions (it is the default behavior under Linux).

–l *username*
Attempts an automatic login on the remote system using *username.* If the remote system understands how to handle automatic login with telnet, it prompts for a password.

Discussion After telnet connects to a remote system, you can put telnet into command mode by typing the escape character (usually CONTROL-]). The remote system typically reports the escape character it recognizes. To leave command mode, type RETURN on a line by itself.

In command mode, telnet displays the **telnet>** prompt. You can use the following commands in command mode:

? (**help**) Displays a list of commands recognized by the telnet utility on the local system.

close Closes the connection to the remote system. If you specified the name of a system on the command line when you started telnet, **close** has the same effect as **quit**: The telnet program quits, and the shell displays a prompt. If you used the **open** command instead of specifying a remote system on the command line, **close** returns telnet to command mode.

logout Logs you out of the remote system; similar to **close**.

open *remote-computer*
> If you did not specify a remote system on the command line or if the attempt to connect to the system failed, you can specify the name of a remote system interactively with the **open** command.

quit Quits the telnet session.

z Suspends the telnet session. When you suspend a session, you return to the login shell on the local system. To resume the suspended telnet session, type **fg** at a shell prompt.

Notes

Under Linux, telnet does not attempt to log in automatically. Under OS X, telnet attempts to log in automatically. When telnet attempts to log in automatically, it uses your username on the local system unless you specify a different name using the –l option.

Many computers, including non-Linux/OS X systems, support the TELNET protocol. The telnet utility is a user interface to this protocol for Linux/OS X systems that allows you to connect to many different types of systems. Although you typically use telnet to log in, the remote computer may offer other services through telnet, such as access to special databases.

Examples

In the following example, the user connects to the remote system named **bravo**. After running a few commands, the user escapes to command mode and uses the **z** command to suspend the telnet session so he can run a few commands on the local system. The user gives an **fg** command to the shell to resume using telnet. The **logout** command on the remote system ends the telnet session, and the local shell displays a prompt.

```
kudos% telnet bravo
Trying 192.168.0.55 ...
Connected to bravo.
Escape character is '^]'.

login: watson
Password:
Last login: Wed Jul 31 10:37:16 from kudos
bravo $
...
bravo $CONTROL-]
telnet> z

[1]+ Stopped    telnet bravo
kudos $
...
kudos $fg
telnet bravo

bravo$ logout
Connection closed by foreign host.
kudos $
```

test

Evaluates an expression

test expression
[expression]

The test utility evaluates an expression and returns a condition code indicating the expression is either *true* (0) or *false* (not 0). You can place brackets ([]) around the expression instead of using the word **test** (second format).

Arguments The *expression* contains one or more criteria (see the following list) that test evaluates. A –a separating two criteria is a Boolean AND operator: Both criteria must be *true* for test to return a condition code of *true*. A –o is a Boolean OR operator. When –o separates two criteria, one or the other (or both) of the criteria must be *true* for test to return a condition code of *true*.

You can negate any criterion by preceding it with an exclamation point (!). You can group criteria with parentheses. If there are no parentheses, –a takes precedence over –o, and test evaluates operators of equal precedence from left to right.

Within the *expression* you must quote special characters, such as parentheses, so the shell does not interpret them but rather passes them to test unchanged.

Because each element, such as a criterion, string, or variable within the **expression**, is a separate argument, you must separate each element from other elements with a SPACE. Table V-29 lists the criteria you can use within the *expression*. Table V-30 on page 856 lists test's relational operators.

Table V-29   Criteria

Criterion	Meaning
string	*True* if *string* has a length greater than zero. **LINUX**
	True if *string* is not a null string. **OS X**
–n *string*	*True* if *string* has a length greater than zero.
–z *string*	*True* if *string* has a length of zero.
string1 = *string2*	*True* if *string1* is equal to *string2*.
string1 != *string2*	*True* if *string1* is not equal to *string2*.
int1 relop int2	*True* if integer *int1* has the specified algebraic relationship to integer *int2*. The *relop* is a relational operator from Table V-30. As a special case, –l *string*, which gives the length of *string*, may be used for *int1* or *int2*.

Table V-29   Criteria (continued)

Criterion	Meaning
file1 −ef *file2*	*True* if *file1* and *file2* have the same device and inode numbers.
file1 −nt *file2*	*True* if *file1* was modified after *file2* (the modification time of *file1* is newer than that of *file2*).
file1 −ot *file2*	*True* if *file1* was modified before *file2* (the modification time of *file1* is older than that of *file2*).
−b *filename*	*True* if the file named *filename* exists and is a block special file.
−c *filename*	*True* if the file named *filename* exists and is a character special file.
−d *filename*	*True* if the file named *filename* exists and is a directory.
−e *filename*	*True* if the file named *filename* exists.
−f *filename*	*True* if the file named *filename* exists and is an ordinary file.
−g *filename*	*True* if the file named *filename* exists and its setgid bit (page 96) is set.
−G *filename*	*True* if the file named *filename* exists and is associated with the group that is the primary group of the user running the command (same effective group ID).
−k *filename*	*True* if the file named *filename* exists and its sticky bit (page 980) is set.
−L *filename*	*True* if the file named *filename* exists and is a symbolic link.
−O *filename*	*True* if the file named *filename* exists and is owned by the user running the command (same effective user ID).
−p *filename*	*True* if the file named *filename* exists and is a named pipe.
−r *filename*	*True* if the file named *filename* exists and the user running the command has read permission for it.
−s *filename*	*True* if the file named *filename* exists and contains information (has a size greater than 0 bytes).
−t *file-descriptor*	*True* if *file-descriptor* is open and associated with the screen or keyboard. The *file-descriptor* for standard input is 0, for standard output is 1, and for standard error is 2.
−u *filename*	*True* if the file named *filename* exists and its setuid bit (page 96) is set.
−w *filename*	*True* if the file named *filename* exists and you have write permission for it.
−x *filename*	*True* if the file named *filename* exists and you have execute/search permission for it.

Table V-30   Relational operators

Relational operator	Meaning
−eq	Equal to
−ge	Greater than or equal to
−gt	Greater than
−le	Less than or equal to
−lt	Less than
−ne	Not equal to

Notes   The test command is built into the Bourne Again and TC Shells.

Examples   The following examples demonstrate the use of the test utility in Bourne Again Shell scripts. Although test works from a command line, it is more commonly employed in shell scripts to test input or verify access to a file.

The first example prompts the user, reads a line of input into a variable, and uses the synonym for test, [], to see whether the user entered **yes**:

```
$ cat user_in
echo -n "Input yes or no: "
read user_input
if [ "$user_input" = "yes" ]
    then
        echo You input yes.
fi
```

The next example prompts for a filename and then uses the synonym for test, [], to see whether the user has read access permission (−r) for the file *and* (−a) whether the file contains information (−s):

```
$ cat validate
echo -n "Enter filename: "
read filename
if [ -r "$filename" -a -s "$filename" ]
    then
        echo File $filename exists and contains information.
        echo You have read access permission to the file.
fi
```

The −t 1 criterion checks whether the process running test is sending standard output to the screen. If it is, the test utility returns a value of *true* (0). The shell stores the exit status of the last command it ran in the **$?** variable. The following script tests whether its output is going to a terminal:

```
$ cat term
test -t 1
echo "This program is (=0) or is not (=1)
sending its output to a terminal:" $?
```

First **term** is run with the output going to the terminal:

```
$ term
This program is (=0) or is not (=1)
sending its output to a terminal: 0
```

The next example runs **term** and redirects its output to a file. The contents of the file **temp** show that test returned 1, indicating its output was not going to a terminal.

```
$ term > temp
$ cat temp
This program is (=0) or is not (=1)
sending its output to a terminal: 1
```

top

Dynamically displays process status

top [options]

The top utility displays information about the status of the local system, including information about current processes.

Options

Although top does not require the use of hyphens with options, it is a good idea to include them for clarity and consistency with other utilities. You can cause top to run as though you had specified any of the options by giving commands to the utility while it is running. See the "Discussion" section for more information.

–ca Causes top to run in accumulative mode. In this mode, times and events are counted cumulatively since top started. See the top man page if you want to use the **–c** option to run top in another mode. `OS X`

–d *ss.tt*

(**delay**) Specifies *ss.tt* as the number of seconds and tenths of seconds of delay from one display update to the next. The default is 3 seconds. `LINUX`

–i Ignores idle and *zombie processes* (processes without a parent). `LINUX`

–n *n*

(**number**) Specifies the number of iterations: top updates the display *n* times and exits. `LINUX`

–p *n*

(**PID**) Monitors the process with a PID of *n*. You can use this option up to 20 times on a command line or specify *n* as a comma-separated list of up to 20 PID numbers. `LINUX`

–S (**sum**) Causes top to run in cumulative mode. In cumulative mode, the CPU times reported for processes include forked processes and CPU times accumulated by child processes that are now dead. `LINUX`

–s (**secure**) Runs top in secure mode, restricting the commands you can use while top is running to those that pose less of a security risk. `LINUX`

–s *ss*

(**seconds**) Specifies *ss* as the number of seconds of delay from one display update to the next. The default is 1 second. `OS X`

Discussion

The first few lines top displays summarize the status of the local system. You can turn each of these lines on or off with the toggle switches (interactive command keys) specified in the following descriptions. The first line is the same as the output of the uptime utility and shows the current time, the amount of time the local system has been running since it was last booted, the number of users logged in, and the load averages from the last 1, 5, and 15 minutes (toggle l [lowercase "l"]). The second line indicates the number of running processes (toggle t). The next three lines report on CPU (also toggle t), memory (toggle m), and swap space (also toggle m) use.

The rest of the display reports on individual processes, which are listed in order by descending CPU usage (i.e., the most CPU-intensive process is listed first). By default top displays the number of processes that fit on the screen.

Table V-31 describes the meanings of the fields displayed for each process.

Table V-31   Field names

Name	Meaning
PID	Process identification number
USER	Username of the owner of the process
PR	Priority of the process
NI	nice value (page 773)
VIRT	Number of kilobytes of virtual memory used by the process
RES	Number of kilobytes of physical (nonswapped) memory used by the process
SHR	Number of kilobytes of shared memory used by the process
S	Status of the process (see **STAT** on page 798)
%CPU	Percentage of the total CPU time the process is using
%MEM	Percentage of physical memory the process is using
TIME[+]	Total CPU time used by the process
COMMAND	Command line that started the process or name of the program (toggle with **c**)

While top is running, you can issue the following commands to modify its behavior:

 h   (**help**) Displays a summary of the commands you can use while top is running. `LINUX`

 ?   (**help**) Displays a summary of the commands you can use while top is running. `OS X`

 k   (**kill**) Allows you to kill a process. Unless you are working with **root** privileges, you can kill only processes you own. When you use this command, top prompts you for the PID of the process and the signal to send to the process. You can enter either a signal number or a name. (See Table 10-5 on page 453 for a list of signals.) This command is disabled when you are working in secure mode. `LINUX`

n (**number**) When you give this command, top asks you to enter the number of processes you want it to display. If you enter 0 (the default), top shows as many processes as fit on the screen.

q (**quit**) Terminates top.

r (**renice**) Changes the priority of a running process (refer to renice on page 802). Unless you are working with **root** privileges, you can change the priority of only your own processes and even then only to lower the priority by entering a positive value. A user working with **root** privileges can enter a negative value, increasing the priority of the process. This command is disabled when you are working in secure mode. *LINUX*

S (**switch**) Toggles top between cumulative mode and regular mode. See the –S option for details. *LINUX*

s (**seconds**) Prompts for the number of seconds to delay between updates to the display (3 is the default). You may enter an integer, a fraction, or 0 (for continuous updates). Under Linux, this command is disabled when you are working in secure mode.

W (**write**) Writes top's current configuration to your personal configuration file (**~/.toprc**). *LINUX*

SPACE
Refreshes the screen.

Notes

The Linux and OS X versions of top are very different. Although it applies to both versions, this coverage of top is oriented toward the Linux version. Refer to the OS X top man page for more information about the OS X version.

The top utility is similar to ps but periodically updates the display, enabling you to monitor the behavior of the local system over time.

This utility shows only as much of the command line for each process as fits on a line. If a process is swapped out, top replaces the command line with the name of the command in parentheses.

Under Linux, the top utility uses the **proc** filesystem. When **proc** is not mounted, top does not work.

Requesting continuous updates is almost always a mistake. The display is updated too quickly and the system load increases dramatically.

Example

The following display is the result of a typical execution of top:

```
top - 17:48:53 up  6:21,  1 user,  load average: 0.71, 1.00, 0.80
Tasks: 178 total,   1 running, 176 sleeping,   0 stopped,   1 zombie
Cpu(s): 16.2%us, 3.0%sy, 0.0%ni, 80.4%id, 0.0%wa, 0.3%hi, 0.0%si, 0.0%st
Mem:   8188664k total,  8122636k used,    66028k free,   127200k buffers
Swap: 11912112k total,        0k used, 11912112k free,  7217728k cached

  PID USER      PR  NI  VIRT  RES  SHR S %CPU %MEM    TIME+  COMMAND
 7841 mark      20   0  108m  29m  12m S   15  0.4  5:14.62 npviewer.bin
 7810 mark      20   0  675m 175m  27m S    8  2.2 24:07.87 firefox
12084 mark      20   0  568m  70m  32m S    7  0.9  5:14.39 amarokapp
13428 mark      10 -10 1715m  74m  62m S    5  0.9  6:25.19 vmware-vmx
 7147 root      20   0  449m 102m  14m S    4  1.3 57:57.59 Xorg
 7676 mark      20   0  159m  17m  11m S    1  0.2  0:05.14 konsole
13437 root      20   0  300m  18m  10m S    1  0.2  0:21.14 firestarter
16542 mark      20   0 18992 1332  940 R    1  0.0  0:00.16 top
 7672 mark      20   0  323m  21m  10m S    0  0.3  1:09.47 artsd
 7747 mark      20   0  306m  45m  25m S    0  0.6  1:20.28 vmware
    1 root      20   0  4020  876  592 S    0  0.0  0:01.24 init
    2 root      15  -5     0    0    0 S    0  0.0  0:00.00 kthreadd
    3 root      RT  -5     0    0    0 S    0  0.0  0:00.00 migration/0
    4 root      15  -5     0    0    0 S    0  0.0  0:03.04 ksoftirqd/0
...
```

touch

Creates a file or changes a file's access and/or modification time

touch [options] file-list

The touch utility changes the access and/or modification time of a file to the current time or a time you specify. You can also use touch to create a file.

Arguments   The *file-list* is a list of the pathnames of the files that touch will create or update.

Options   Under Linux, touch accepts the common options described on page 603. Options preceded by a double hyphen (––) work under Linux only. Except as noted, options named with a single letter and preceded by a single hyphen work under Linux and OS X. Without any options, touch changes the access and modification times to the current time. When you do not specify the –c (––no-create) option, touch creates files that do not exist.

–a   Updates the access time only, leaving the modification time unchanged.

––no–create   –c   Does not create files that do not exist.

––date=*datestring*   –d *datestring*

Updates times with the date specified by *datestring*. Most familiar formats are permitted for *datestring*. Components of the date and time not included in *datestring* are assumed to be the current date and time. This option may not be used with –t. `LINUX`

–m   Updates the modification time only, leaving the access time unchanged.

––reference=*file*   –r *file*

Updates times with the times of *file*.

–t [[*cc*]*yy*]*nnddhhmm*[.*ss*]

Changes times to the date specified by the argument. The *nn* argument is the number of the month (01–12), *dd* is the day of the month (01–31), *hh* is the hour based on a 24-hour clock (00–23), and *mm* is the minutes (00–59). You must specify at least these fields. You can specify the number of seconds past the start of the minute with .*ss*.

The optional *cc* specifies the first two digits of the year (the value of the century minus 1), and *yy* specifies the last two digits of the year. When you do not specify a year, touch assumes the current year. When you do not specify *cc*, touch assumes 20 for *yy* in the range 0–68 and 19 for *yy* in the range 69–99.

This option may not be used with –d.

Examples   The first three commands show touch updating an existing file. The ls utility with the –l option displays the modification time of the file. The last three commands show touch creating a file.

```
$ ls -l program.c
-rw-r--r--   1 max group 5860 Apr 21 09:54 program.c
$ touch program.c
$ ls -l program.c
-rw-r--r--   1 max group 5860 Aug 13 19:01 program.c

$ ls -l read.c
ls: read.c: No such file or directory
$ touch read.c
$ ls -l read.c
-rw-rw-r--   1 max group 0 Aug 13 19:01 read.c
```

The first of the following ls commands displays the file *modification* times; the second ls (with the –lu options) displays the file *access* times:

```
$ ls -l
-rw-r--r-- 1 max group  552 Jan 10 19:44 cases
-rw-r--r-- 1 max group 2209 Apr 18 04:24 excerpts

$ ls -lu
-rw-r--r-- 1 max group  552 May 29 15:28 cases
-rw-r--r-- 1 max group 2209 May 29 15:28 excerpts
```

The next example works on the two files shown above and demonstrates the use of the –a option to change the access time only and the –t option to specify a date for touch to use instead of the current date and time. After the touch command is executed, ls shows that the access times of the files **cases** and **excerpts** have been updated but the modification times remain the same.

```
$ touch -at 02040608 cases excerpts

$ ls -l
-rw-r--r-- 1 max group  552 Jan 10 19:44 cases
-rw-r--r-- 1 max group 2209 Apr 18 04:24 excerpts

$ ls -lu
-rw-r--r-- 1 max group  552 Feb  4 06:08 cases
-rw-r--r-- 1 max group 2209 Feb  4 06:08 excerpts
```

tr

Replaces specified characters

tr [options] string1 [string2]

The tr utility reads standard input and, for each input character, either maps it to an alternate character, deletes the character, or leaves the character as is. This utility reads from standard input and writes to standard output.

Arguments

The tr utility is typically used with two arguments, *string1* and *string2*. The position of each character in the two strings is important: Each time tr finds a character from *string1* in its input, it replaces that character with the corresponding character from *string2*.

With one argument, *string1,* and the **–d** (**––delete**) option, tr deletes the characters specified in *string1*. The option **–s** (**––squeeze-repeats**) replaces multiple sequential occurrences of characters in *string1* with single occurrences (for example, **abbc** becomes **abc**).

Ranges

A range of characters is similar in function to a character class within a regular expression (page 889). GNU tr does not support ranges (character classes) enclosed within brackets. You can specify a range of characters by following the character that appears earlier in the collating sequence with a hyphen and the character that comes later in the collating sequence. For example, **1–6** expands to **123456**. Although the range A–Z expands as you would expect in ASCII, this approach does not work when you use the EBCDIC collating sequence, as these characters are not sequential in EBCDIC. See "Character Classes" for a solution to this issue.

Character Classes

A tr character class is not the same as the character class described elsewhere in this book. (GNU documentation uses the term *list operator* for what this book calls a *character class.*) You specify a character class as '*[:class:]*', where *class* is one of the character classes from Table V-32. You must specify a character class in *string1* (and not *string2*) unless you are performing case conversion (see the "Examples" section) or you use the **–d** and **–s** options together.

Table V-32   Character classes

Class	Meaning
alnum	Letters and digits
alpha	Letters

Table V-32   Character classes (continued)

Class	Meaning
blank	Whitespace
cntrl	CONTROL characters
digit	Digits
graph	Printable characters but not SPACES
lower	Lowercase letters
print	Printable characters including SPACES
punct	Punctuation characters
space	Horizontal or vertical whitespace
upper	Uppercase letters
xdigit	Hexadecimal digits

Options

Options preceded by a double hyphen (––) work under Linux only. Except as noted, options named with a single letter and preceded by a single hyphen work under Linux and OS X.

––complement –c   Complements *string1*, causing tr to match all characters *except* those in *string1*.

––delete –d   Deletes characters that match those specified in *string1*. If you use this option with the –s (**––squeeze-repeats**) option, you must specify both *string1* and *string2* (see "Notes").

––help   Summarizes how to use tr, including the special symbols you can use in *string1* and *string2*. `LINUX`

––squeeze-repeats –s   Replaces multiple sequential occurrences of a character in *string1* with a single occurrence of the character when you call tr with only one string argument. If you use both *string1* and *string2*, the tr utility first translates the characters in *string1* to those in *string2*; it then replaces multiple sequential occurrences of a character in *string2* with a single occurrence of the character.

––truncate-set1 –t   Truncates *string1* so it is the same length as *string2* before processing input. `LINUX`

Notes

When *string1* is longer than *string2*, the initial portion of *string1* (equal in length to *string2*) is used in the translation. When *string1* is shorter than *string2*, tr uses the last character of *string1* to extend *string1* to the length of *string2*. In this case tr departs from the POSIX standard, which does not define a result.

If you use the **–d** (**––delete**) and **–s** (**––squeeze-repeats**) options at the same time, tr first deletes the characters in *string1* and then replaces multiple sequential occurrences of a character in *string2* with a single occurrence of the character.

Examples   You can use a hyphen to represent a range of characters in *string1* or *string2*. The two command lines in the following example produce the same result:

```
$ echo abcdef | tr  'abcdef' 'xyzabc'
xyzabc
$ echo abcdef | tr  'a-f' 'x-za-c'
xyzabc
```

The next example demonstrates a popular method for disguising text, often called ROT13 (rotate 13) because it replaces the first letter of the alphabet with the thirteenth, the second with the fourteenth, and so forth.

```
$ echo The punchline of the joke is ... |
> tr 'A-M N-Z a-m n-z' 'N-Z A-M n-z a-m'
Gur chapuyvar bs gur wbxr vf ...
```

To make the text intelligible again, reverse the order of the arguments to tr:

```
$ echo Gur chapuyvar bs gur wbxr vf ... |
> tr 'N-Z A-M n-z a-m' 'A-M N-Z a-m n-z'
The punchline of the joke is ...
```

The **––delete** option causes tr to delete selected characters:

```
$ echo If you can read this, you can spot the missing vowels! |
> tr --delete 'aeiou'
If y cn rd ths, y cn spt th mssng vwls!
```

In the following example, tr replaces characters and reduces pairs of identical characters to single characters:

```
$ echo tennessee | tr -s 'tnse' 'srne'
serene
```

The next example replaces each sequence of nonalphabetic characters (the complement of all the alphabetic characters as specified by the character class **alpha**) in the file **draft1** with a single NEWLINE character. The output is a list of words, one per line.

```
$ tr -c -s '[:alpha:]' '\n' < draft1
```

The next example uses character classes to upshift the string **hi there**:

```
$ echo hi there | tr '[:lower:]' '[:upper:]'
HI THERE
```

tty

Displays the terminal pathname

tty [option]

The tty utility displays the pathname of standard input if it is a terminal and displays **not a tty** if it is not a terminal. The exit status is 0 if standard input is a terminal and 1 if it is not.

Arguments There are no arguments.

Options Under Linux, tty accepts the common options described on page 603. The option preceded by a double hyphen (––) works under Linux only. The option named with a single letter and preceded by a single hyphen works under Linux and OS X.

––silent *or* –s Causes tty not to print anything. The exit status of tty is set.
––quiet

Notes The term *tty* is short for *teletypewriter*, the terminal device on which UNIX was first run. This command appears in UNIX, and Linux has kept it for the sake of consistency and tradition.

Examples The following example illustrates the use of tty:

```
$ tty
/dev/pts/11
$ echo $?
0
$ tty < memo
not a tty
$ echo $?
1
```

tune2fs

Changes parameters on an **ext2**, **ext3**, or **ext4** filesystem

tune2fs [options] device

The tune2fs utility displays and modifies filesystem parameters on **ext2**, **ext3**, and **ext4** filesystems. This utility can also set up journaling on an **ext2** filesystem, turning it into an **ext3** filesystem. With typical filesystem permissions, tune2fs must be run by a user working with **root** privileges. The tune2fs utility is available under Linux only. `LINUX`

Arguments

The *device* is the name of the device, such as **/dev/sda8**, that holds the filesystem whose parameters you want to display or modify.

Options

–C *n*

(**count**) Sets the number of times the filesystem has been mounted without being checked to *n*. This option is useful for staggering filesystem checks (see "Discussion") and for forcing a check the next time the system boots.

–c *n*

(**max count**) Sets the maximum number of times the filesystem can be mounted between filesystem checks to *n*. Set *n* to **0** (zero) to disregard this parameter.

–e *behavior*

(**error**) Specifies what the kernel will do when it detects an error. Set *behavior* to **continue** (continues execution), **remount-ro** (remounts the filesystem read-only), or **panic** (causes a kernel panic). Regardless of how you set this option, an error will cause fsck to check the filesystem next time the system boots.

–i *n[u]*

(**interval**) Sets the maximum time between filesystem checks to *n* time periods. Without *u* or with *u* set to **d**, the time period is days. Set *u* to **w** to set the time period to weeks; use **m** for months. Set *n* to **0** (zero) to disregard this parameter. Because a filesystem check is forced only when the system is booted, the time specified by this option may be exceeded.

–j (**journal**) Adds an **ext3** journal to an **ext2** filesystem. For more information on journaling filesystems see page 961.

–l (**list**) Lists information about the filesystem.

–T *date*

(**time**) Sets the time the filesystem was last checked to *date*. The *date* is the time and date in the format *yyyynndd[hh[mm]ss]]]*. Here *yyyy* is the year, *nn* is the number of the month (01–12), and *dd* is the day of the month (01–31). You must specify at least these fields. The *hh* is the hour based on a 24-hour clock (00–23), *mm* is the minutes (00–59), and *.ss* is the number of seconds past the start of the minute. You can also specify *date* as **now**.

Discussion Checking a large filesystem can take a long time. When all filesystem checks occur at the same time, the system may boot slowly. Use the –C and/or –T options to stagger filesystem checks so they do not all happen at the same time.

Example Following is the output of tune2fs run with the –l option on a typical **ext3** filesystem:

```
# /sbin/tune2fs -l /dev/sda1
tune2fs 1.41.4 (27-Jan-2009)
Filesystem volume name:   <none>
Last mounted on:          <not available>
Filesystem UUID:          b6d9714e-ed5d-45b8-8023-716a669c16d8
Filesystem magic number:  0xEF53
Filesystem revision #:    1 (dynamic)
Filesystem features:      has_journal ext_attr resize_inode dir_index
    filetype needs_recovery sparse_super large_file
Filesystem flags:         signed_directory_hash
Default mount options:    (none)
Filesystem state:         clean
Errors behavior:          Continue
Filesystem OS type:       Linux
Inode count:              624624
Block count:              2498099
Reserved block count:     124904
Free blocks:              1868063
Free inodes:              509355
First block:              0
Block size:               4096
Fragment size:            4096
Reserved GDT blocks:      609
Blocks per group:         32768
Fragments per group:      32768
Inodes per group:         8112
Inode blocks per group:   507
Filesystem created:       Mon Apr 27 09:41:43 2009
Last mount time:          Tue May  5 03:54:59 2009
Last write time:          Tue May  5 03:54:59 2009
Mount count:              4
Maximum mount count:      31
Last checked:             Mon Apr 27 09:41:43 2009
Check interval:           15552000 (6 months)
Next check after:         Sat Oct 24 09:41:43 2009
Reserved blocks uid:      0 (user root)
Reserved blocks gid:      0 (group root)
First inode:              11
Inode size:               256
Required extra isize:     28
Desired extra isize:      28
Journal inode:            8
First orphan inode:       308701
Default directory hash:   half_md4
Directory Hash Seed:      bceae349-a46f-4d45-a8f1-a21b1ae8d2bd
Journal backup:           inode blocks
```

umask

Establishes the file-creation permissions mask

umask [mask]

The umask builtin specifies the mask the system uses to set access permissions when you create a file. This builtin works slightly differently in each of the shells.

Arguments The *mask* can be a three-digit octal number (bash and tcsh) or a symbolic value (bash) such as you would use with chmod (page 626). The *mask* specifies the permissions that are *not* allowed.

When *mask* is an octal number, the digits correspond to the permissions for the owner of the file, members of the group the file is associated with, and everyone else. Because the *mask* specifies the permissions that are *not* allowed, the system subtracts each of these digits from 7 when you create a file. The resulting three octal numbers specify the access permissions for the file (the numbers you would use with chmod). A *mask* you specify as a symbolic value also specifies the permissions that are *not* allowed. See the "Notes" section.

Without any arguments, umask displays the file-creation permissions mask.

Option –S (**symbolic**) Displays the file-creation permissions mask symbolically.

Notes Most utilities and applications do not attempt to create files with execute permissions, regardless of the value of *mask*; they assume you do not want an executable file. As a result, when a utility or application such as touch creates a file, the system subtracts each of the digits in *mask* from 6. An exception occurs with mkdir, which does assume that you want the execute (access in the case of a directory) bit set. See the "Examples" section.

The umask program is a builtin in bash and tcsh and generally goes in the initialization file for your shell (~/.bash_profile [bash] or ~/.login [tcsh]).

Under bash the argument **u=rwx,go=r** turns *off* all bits in the *mask* for the owner and turns *off* the read bit in the *mask* for groups and other users (the mask is 0033), causing those bits to be *on* in file permissions (744 or 644). Refer to chmod on page 626 for more information about symbolic permissions.

Examples The following commands set the file-creation permissions mask and display the mask and its effect when you create a file and a directory. The mask of 022, when subtracted from 777, gives permissions of 644 (**rw–r––r––**) for a file and 755 (**rwxr–xr–x**) for a directory:

```
$ umask 022
$ umask
0022
$ touch afile
$ mkdir adirectory
$ ls -ld afile adirectory
drwxr-xr-x  2 max max 4096 Jul 24 11:25 adirectory
-rw-r--r--  1 max max 0 Jul 24 11:25 afile
```

The next example sets the same mask using symbolic values. The **–S** option displays the mask symbolically:

```
$ umask u=rwx,g=rx,o=rx
$ umask
0022
$ umask -S
u=rwx,g=rx,o=rx
```

uniq

Displays unique lines

uniq [options] [input-file] [output-file]

The uniq utility displays its input, removing all but one copy of successive repeated lines. If the file has been sorted (see sort on page 817), uniq ensures that no two lines it displays are the same.

Arguments When you do not specify the *input-file*, uniq reads from standard input. When you do not specify the *output-file*, uniq writes to standard output.

Options Under Linux, uniq accepts the common options described on page 603. Options preceded by a double hyphen (−−) work under Linux only. Except as noted, options named with a single letter and preceded by a single hyphen work under Linux and OS X. A *field* is a sequence of characters bounded by SPACEs, TABs, NEWLINEs, or a combination of these characters.

−−count   **−c** Precedes each line with the number of occurrences of the line in the input file.

−−repeated   **−d** Displays one copy of lines that are repeated; does not display lines that are not repeated.

−−skip-fields=*nfield*
   −f *nfield*
   Ignores the first *nfield* blank-separated fields of each line. The uniq utility bases its comparison on the remainder of the line, including the leading blanks of the next field on the line (see the **−s** [**−−skip-chars**] option).

−−ignore-case   **−i** Ignores case when comparing lines.

−−skip-chars=*nchar*
   −s *nchar*
   Ignores the first *nchar* characters of each line. If you also use the **−f** (**−−skip-fields**) option, uniq ignores the first *nfield* fields followed by *nchar* characters. You can use this option to skip over leading blanks of a field.

−−unique   **−u** Displays only lines that are *not* repeated.

−−check-chars=*nchar*
   −w *nchar*
   Compares up to *nchars* characters on a line after honoring the **−f** (**−−skip-fields**) and **−s** (**−−skip-chars**) options. By default uniq compares the entire line. **LINUX**

Examples These examples assume the file named **test** in the working directory contains the following text:

```
$ cat test
boy took bat home
boy took bat home
girl took bat home
dog brought hat home
dog brought hat home
dog brought hat home
```

Without any options, uniq displays only one copy of successive repeated lines:

```
$ uniq test
boy took bat home
girl took bat home
dog brought hat home
```

The –c (––count) option displays the number of consecutive occurrences of each line in the file:

```
$ uniq -c test
      2 boy took bat home
      1 girl took bat home
      3 dog brought hat home
```

The –d (––repeated) option displays only lines that are consecutively repeated in the file:

```
$ uniq -d test
boy took bat home
dog brought hat home
```

The –u (––unique) option displays only lines that are *not* consecutively repeated in the file:

```
$ uniq -u test
girl took bat home
```

In the next example, the –f (––skip-fields) option skips the first field in each line, causing the lines that begin with **boy** and the one that begins with **girl** to appear to be consecutive repeated lines. The uniq utility displays only one occurrence of these lines:

```
$ uniq -f 1 test
boy took bat home
dog brought hat home
```

The next example uses both the –f (––skip-fields) and –s (––skip-chars) arguments first to skip two fields and then to skip two characters. The two characters this command skips include the SPACE that separates the second and third fields and the first character of the third field. Ignoring these characters, all the lines appear to be consecutive repeated lines containing the string **at home**. The uniq utility displays only the first of these lines:

```
$ uniq -f 2 -s 2 test
boy took bat home
```

w

Displays information about system users

w [options] [username]

The w utility displays the names of users who are currently logged in, together with their terminal device numbers, the times they logged in, the commands they are running, and other information.

Arguments   The *username* restricts the display to information about that user.

Options
-f   (**from**) Removes the **FROM** column. For users who are directly connected, this field contains a hyphen. `LINUX`

-h   (**no header**) Suppresses the header line.

-s   (**short**) Displays less information: username, terminal device, idle time, and command. `LINUX`

Discussion   The first line w displays is the same as that displayed by uptime. This line includes the time of day, how long the system has been running (in days, hours, and minutes), how many users are logged in, and how busy the system is (load average). From left to right, the load averages indicate the number of processes that have been waiting to run in the past 1 minute, 5 minutes, and 15 minutes.

The columns of information that w displays have the following headings:

```
USER TTY FROM LOGIN@ IDLE JCPU PCPU WHAT
```

The **USER** is the username of the user. The **TTY** is the device name for the line that the user logged in on. The **FROM** is the system name that a remote user is logged in from; it is a hyphen for a local user. The **LOGIN@** gives the date and time when the user logged in. The **IDLE** indicates how many minutes have elapsed since the user last used the keyboard. The **JCPU** is the CPU time used by all processes attached to the user's tty, not including completed background jobs. The **PCPU** is the time used by the process named in the **WHAT** column. The **WHAT** is the command that user is running.

Examples   The first example shows the full list produced by the w utility:

```
$ w
 10:26am  up 1 day, 55 min,  6 users,  load average: 0.15, 0.03, 0.01
 USER     TTY      FROM         LOGIN@   IDLE   JCPU   PCPU  WHAT
 max      tty1     -            Fri 9am  20:39m  0.22s  0.01s vim td
 max      tty2     -            Fri 5pm  17:16m  0.07s  0.07s -bash
 root     pts/1    -            Fri 4pm  14:28m  0.20s  0.07s -bash
 sam      pts/2    -            Fri 5pm  3:23    0.08s  0.08s /bin/bash
 hls      pts/3    potato       10:07am  0.00s   0.08s  0.02s w
```

In the next example, the **–s** option produces an abbreviated listing:

```
$ w -s
 10:30am  up 1 day, 58 min,  6 users,  load average: 0.15, 0.03, 0.01
USER     TTY     FROM            IDLE  WHAT
max      tty1    -              20:43m  vim td
max      tty2    -              17:19m  -bash
root     pts/1   -              14:31m  -bash
sam      pts/2   -               0.20s  vim memo.030125
hls      pts/3   potato          0.00s  w -s
```

The final example requests information only about Max:

```
$ w max
 10:35am  up 1 day,  1:04,  6 users,  load average: 0.06, 0.01, 0.00
USER     TTY     FROM             LOGIN@   IDLE   JCPU   PCPU  WHAT
max      tty1    -              Fri 9am 20:48m  0.22s  0.01s  vim td
max      tty2    -              Fri 5pm 17:25m  0.07s  0.07s  -bash
```

wc

Displays the number of lines, words, and bytes

wc [options] [file-list]

The wc utility displays the number of lines, words, and bytes in its input. When you specify more than one file on the command line, wc displays totals for each file as well as totals for all files.

Arguments   The *file-list* is a list of the pathnames of one or more files that wc analyzes. When you omit *file-list*, wc takes its input from standard input.

Options   Under Linux, wc accepts the common options described on page 603. Options preceded by a double hyphen (––) work under Linux only. Except as noted, options named with a single letter and preceded by a single hyphen work under Linux and OS X.

––bytes	–c	Displays only the number of bytes in the input.
––max-line-length	–L	Displays the length of the longest line in the input. `LINUX`
––lines	–l	(lowercase "l") Displays only the number of lines (that is, NEWLINE characters) in the input.
––chars	–m	Displays only the number of characters in the input.
––words	–w	Displays only the number of words in the input.

Notes   A *word* is a sequence of characters bounded by SPACEs, TABs, NEWLINEs, or a combination of these characters.

Examples   The following command analyzes the file named **memo**. The numbers in the output represent the number of lines, words, and bytes in the file.

```
$ wc memo
      5      31     146 memo
```

The next command displays the number of lines and words in three files. The line at the bottom, with the word **total** in the right column, contains the sum of each column.

```
$ wc -lw memo1 memo2 memo3
     10      62 memo1
     12      74 memo2
     12      68 memo3
     34     204 total
```

which

Shows where in **PATH** a command is located

which **command-list**

For each command in ***command-list***, the which utility searches the directories in the **PATH** variable (page 297) and displays the absolute pathname of the first file it finds whose simple filename is the same as the command.

Arguments The ***command-list*** is a list of one or more commands (utilities) that which searches for. For each command, which searches the directories listed in the **PATH** environment variable, in order, and displays the full pathname of the first command (executable file) it finds. If which does not locate a command, it displays a message.

Options Options preceded by a double hyphen (−−) work under Linux only; not all of these options are available under all Linux distributions. Except as noted, options named with a single letter and preceded by a single hyphen work under Linux and OS X.

−−all **−a** Displays all matching executable files in **PATH**, not just the first.

−−read-alias **−i** Reads aliases from standard input and reports on matching aliases in addition to executable files in **PATH** (turn off with **−−skip-alias**). *LINUX*

−−read-functions Reads shell functions from standard input and reports on matching functions in addition to executable files in **PATH** (turn off with **−−skip-functions**). *LINUX*

−−show-dot Displays ./ in place of the absolute pathname when a directory in **PATH** starts with a period and a matching executable file is in that directory (turn off with **−−skip-dot**). *LINUX*

−−show-tilde Displays a tilde (~) in place of the absolute pathname of the user's home directory where appropriate. This option is ignored when a user working with **root** privileges runs which. *LINUX*

−−tty-only Does not process more options (to the right of this option) if the process running which is not attached to a terminal. *LINUX*

Notes Some distributions define an alias for which such as the following:

```
$ alias which
alias which='alias | /usr/bin/which --tty-only --read-alias --show-dot --show-tilde'
```

If which is not behaving as you would expect, verify that you are not running an alias. The preceding alias causes which to be effective only when it is run interactively (**−−tty-only**) and to display aliases, display the working directory as a period when appropriate, and display the name of the user's home directory as a tilde.

The TC Shell includes a which builtin (see the tcsh man page) that works slightly differently from the which utility (**/usr/bin/which**). Without any options, the which utility does not locate aliases, functions, and shell builtins because these do not appear in **PATH**. In contrast, the tcsh which builtin locates aliases, functions, and shell builtins.

Examples   The first example quotes the first letter of the command (**\which**) to prevent the shell from invoking the alias (page 326) for which:

```
$ \which vim dir which
/usr/bin/vim
/bin/dir
/usr/bin/which
```

The next example, which works on some Linux systems only, is the same as the first but uses the alias for which (which it displays):

```
$ which vim dir which
alias which='alias | /usr/bin/which --tty-only --read-alias --show-dot --show-tilde'
        /usr/bin/which
/usr/bin/vim
/usr/bin/dir
```

The final example is the same as the previous one except it is run from tcsh. The tcsh which builtin is used instead of the which utility:

```
tcsh $ which vim dir which
/usr/bin/vim
/bin/dir
which: shell built-in command.
```

who

Displays information about logged-in users

who [options]
who am i

The who utility displays information about users who are logged in on the local system. This information includes each user's username, terminal device, login time, and, if applicable, the corresponding remote hostname.

Arguments

When given two arguments (traditionally, **am i**), who displays information about the user giving the command. If applicable, the username is preceded by the hostname of the system running who (as in **kudos!max**).

Options

Under Linux, who accepts the common options described on page 603. Options preceded by a double hyphen (−−) work under Linux only. Except as noted, options named with a single letter and preceded by a single hyphen work under Linux and OS X.

−−all	**−a**	Displays a lot of information. `LINUX`
−−boot	**−b**	Displays the date and time when the system was last booted. `LINUX`
−−heading	**−H**	Displays a header.
−−login	**−l**	(lowercase "l") Lists devices waiting for a user to log in. `LINUX`
−−count	**−q**	(**quick**) Lists the usernames only, followed by the number of users logged in on the system.
−−mesg	**−T**	Appends after each user's username a character that shows whether that user has messages enabled. A plus (**+**) means that messages are enabled, a hyphen (**−**) means that they are disabled, and a question mark (**?**) indicates that who cannot find the device. If messages are enabled, you can use write to communicate with the user. Refer to "mesg: Denies or Accepts Messages" on page 71.
−−users	**−u**	Includes each user's idle time in the display. If the user has typed on her terminal in the past minute, a period (.) appears in this field. If no input has occurred for more than a day, the word **old** appears. In addition, this option includes the PID number and comment fields. See the "Discussion" section.

Discussion

The line who displays has the following syntax:

user [messages] line login-time [idle] [PID] comment

The *user* is the username of the user. The *messages* argument indicates whether messages are enabled or disabled (see the **–T** [**--mesg**] option). The *line* is the device name associated with the line the user is logged in on. The *login-time* is the date and time when the user logged in. The *idle* argument is the length of time since the terminal was last used (the *idle time;* see the **–u** [**--users**] option). The *PID* is the process identification number. The *comment* is the name of the remote system that the user is logged in from (it is blank for local users).

Notes

The finger utility (pages 68 and 695) provides information similar to that given by who.

Examples

The following examples demonstrate the use of the who utility:

```
$ who
hls        tty1     Jul 30 06:01
sam        tty2     Jul 30 06:02
max        ttyp3    Jul 30 14:56 (bravo)

$ who am i
bravo!max       ttyp3      Jul 30 14:56 (bravo)

$ who -HTu
USER          LINE      TIME           IDLE        PID COMMENT
hls         - tty1      Jul 30 06:01 03:53       1821
sam         + tty2      Jul 30 06:02 14:47       2235
max         + ttyp3     Jul 30 14:56   .         14777   (bravo)
```

xargs

Converts standard input to command lines

xargs [options] [command]

The xargs utility is a convenient, efficient way to convert standard output of one command into arguments for another command. This utility reads from standard input, keeps track of the maximum allowable length of a command line, and avoids exceeding that limit by repeating *command* as needed. Finally xargs executes the constructed command line(s).

Arguments   The *command* is the command line you want xargs to use as a base for the command it constructs. If you omit *command*, it defaults to echo. The xargs utility appends to *command* the arguments it receives from standard input. If any arguments should precede the arguments from standard input, you must include them as part of *command*.

Options   Options preceded by a double hyphen (––) work under Linux only. Except as noted, options named with a single letter and preceded by a single hyphen work under Linux and OS X.

–I *[marker]*
> (**replace**) Allows you to place arguments from standard input anywhere within *command*. All occurrences of *marker* in *command* for xargs are replaced by the arguments generated from standard input of xargs. With this option, xargs executes *command* for each input line. The –l (––**max-lines**) option is ignored when you use this option.

––max-lines*[=num]*
–l *[num]*
> (lowercase "l") Executes *command* once for every *num* lines of input (*num* defaults to 1). `LINUX`

––max-args=*num*   **–n** *num*
> Executes *command* once for every *num* arguments in the input line.

––max-procs=*num*
–P *num*
> Allows xargs to run up to *maxprocs* instances of *command* simultaneously. (The default is 1, which runs *commands* sequentially.) This option may improve the throughput if xargs is running on a multiprocessor system.

––interactive   **–p**   Prompts prior to each execution of *command*.

––no-run-if-empty
–r   Causes xargs not to execute *command* if standard input is empty. Ordinarily xargs executes *command* at least once, even if standard input includes only blanks. `LINUX`

Discussion The xargs utility reads arguments to *command* from standard input, interpreting each whitespace-delimited string as a separate argument. It then constructs a command line from *command* and a series of arguments. When the maximum command line length would be exceeded by adding another argument, xargs runs the command line it has built. If there is more input, xargs repeats the process of building a command line and running it. This process continues until all input has been read.

Notes The xargs utility is often used as an efficient alternative to the **–exec** option of find (page 689). If you call find with the **–exec** option to run a command, it runs the command once for each file it processes. Each execution of the command creates a new process, which can drain system resources when you are processing many files. By accumulating as many arguments as possible, xargs can greatly reduce the number of processes needed. The first example in the "Examples" section shows how to use xargs with find.

Examples To locate and remove all files with names ending in .o from the working directory and its subdirectories, you can use the find **–exec** option:

```
$ find . -name \*.o -exec rm --force {} \;
```

This approach calls the rm utility once for each .o file that find locates. Each invocation of rm requires a new process. If a lot of .o files exist, the system must spend a significant amount of time creating, starting, and then cleaning up these processes. You can reduce the number of processes by allowing xargs to accumulate as many filenames as possible before calling rm:

```
$ find . -name \*.o -print | xargs rm --force
```

In the next example, the contents of all ***.txt** files located by find are searched for lines containing the word **login**. All filenames that contain **login** are displayed by grep.

```
$ find . -name \*.txt -print | xargs grep -w -l login
```

The next example shows how to use the **–I** option to cause xargs to embed standard input within *command* instead of appending it to *command*. This option also causes *command* to be executed each time a NEWLINE character is encountered in standard input; **–l** (**––max-lines**) does not override this behavior.

```
$ cat names
Tom,
Dick,
and Harry

$ xargs echo "Hello," < names
Hello, Tom, Dick, and Harry
```

```
$ xargs -I xxx echo "Hello xxx. Join me for lunch?" < names
Hello Tom,. Join me for lunch?
Hello Dick,. Join me for lunch?
Hello and Harry. Join me for lunch?
```

The final example uses the same input file as the previous examples as well as the **–n** (**––max-args**) and **–l** (**––max-lines**) options:

```
$ xargs -n 1 echo "Hi there" < names
Hi there Tom,
Hi there Dick,
Hi there and
Hi there Harry

$ xargs -l 2 echo "Hi there" < names
Hi there Tom, Dick,
Hi there and Harry
```

See page 833 for another example of the use of xargs.

PART VI
Appendixes

REGULAR EXPRESSIONS

A *regular expression* defines a set of one or more strings of characters. A simple string of characters is a regular expression that defines one string of characters: itself. A more complex regular expression uses letters, numbers, and special characters to define many different strings of characters. A regular expression is said to *match* any string it defines.

This appendix describes the regular expressions used by ed, vim, emacs, grep, awk/mawk/gawk, sed, Perl, and many other utilities. Refer to page 517 for more information on Perl regular expressions. The regular expressions used in shell ambiguous file references are different and are described in "Filename Generation/Pathname Expansion" on page 136.

CHARACTERS

As used in this appendix, a *character* is any character *except* a NEWLINE. Most characters represent themselves within a regular expression. A *special character,* also called a *metacharacter,* is one that does not represent itself. If you need to use a special character to represent itself, you must quote it as explained on page 891.

DELIMITERS

A character called a *delimiter* usually marks the beginning and end of a regular expression. The delimiter is always a special character for the regular expression it delimits (that is, it does not represent itself but marks the beginning and end of the expression). Although vim permits the use of other characters as a delimiter and grep does not use delimiters at all, the regular expressions in this appendix use a forward slash (/) as a delimiter. In some unambiguous cases, the second delimiter is not required. For example, you can sometimes omit the second delimiter when it would be followed immediately by RETURN.

SIMPLE STRINGS

The most basic regular expression is a simple string that contains no special characters except the delimiters. A simple string matches only itself (Table A-1). In the examples in this appendix, the strings that are matched are underlined and look like this.

Table A-1   Simple strings

Regular expression	Matches	Examples
/ring/	ring	ring, spring, ringing, stringing
/Thursday/	Thursday	Thursday, Thursday's
/or not/	or not	or not, poor nothing

SPECIAL CHARACTERS

You can use special characters within a regular expression to cause the regular expression to match more than one string. A regular expression that includes a special character always matches the longest possible string, starting as far toward the beginning (left) of the line as possible.

PERIODS

A period (.) matches any character (Table A-2).

Table A-2   Periods

Regular expression	Matches	Examples
/ .alk/	All strings consisting of a SPACE followed by any character followed by <u>alk</u>	will <u>talk</u>, may <u>balk</u>
/.ing/	All strings consisting of any character preceding <u>ing</u>	<u>sing</u> song, <u>ping</u>, before <u>inglenook</u>

BRACKETS

Brackets ([]) define a *character class*[1] that matches any single character within the brackets (Table A-3). If the first character following the left bracket is a caret (^), the brackets define a character class that matches any single character not within the brackets. You can use a hyphen to indicate a range of characters. Within a character-class definition, backslashes and asterisks (described in the following sections) lose their special meanings. A right bracket (appearing as a member of the character class) can appear only as the first character following the left bracket. A caret is special only if it is the first character following the left bracket. A dollar sign is special only if it is followed immediately by the right bracket.

Table A-3   Brackets

Regular expression	Matches	Examples
/[bB]ill/	Member of the character class <u>b</u> and <u>B</u> followed by <u>ill</u>	<u>bill</u>, <u>Bill</u>, <u>bill</u>ed
/t[aeiou].k/	<u>t</u> followed by a lowercase vowel, any character, and a <u>k</u>	<u>talka</u>tive, <u>stink</u>, <u>teak</u>, <u>tank</u>er
/# [6–9]/	<u>#</u> followed by a SPACE and a member of the character class <u>6</u> through <u>9</u>	<u># 6</u>0, <u># 8</u>:, get <u># 9</u>
/[^a–zA–Z]/	Any character that is not a letter (ASCII character set only)	<u>1</u>, <u>7</u>, <u>@</u>, <u>.,</u> <u>}</u>, Stop<u>!</u>

---

1. GNU documentation calls these List Operators and defines Character Class operators as expressions that match a predefined group of characters, such as all numbers (see Table V-32 on page 864).

Asterisks

An asterisk can follow a regular expression that represents a single character (Table A-4). The asterisk represents *zero* or more occurrences of a match of the regular expression. An asterisk following a period matches any string of characters. (A period matches any character, and an asterisk matches zero or more occurrences of the preceding regular expression.) A character-class definition followed by an asterisk matches any string of characters that are members of the character class.

Table A-4   Asterisks

Regular expression	Matches	Examples
/ab*c/	a followed by zero or more b's followed by a c	ac, abc, abbc, debbcaabbbc
/ab.*c/	ab followed by zero or more characters followed by c	abc, abxc, ab45c, xab 756.345 x cat
/t.*ing/	t followed by zero or more characters followed by ing	thing, ting, I thought of going
/[a–zA–Z]*/	A string composed only of letters and SPACES	1. any string without numbers or punctuation!
/(.*)/	As long a string as possible between (and)	Get (this) and (that);
/([^)]*)/	The shortest string possible that starts with (and ends with)	(this), Get (this and that)

Carets and Dollar Signs

A regular expression that begins with a caret (^) can match a string only at the beginning of a line. In a similar manner, a dollar sign ($) at the end of a regular expression matches the end of a line. The caret and dollar sign are called anchors because they force (anchor) a match to the beginning or end of a line (Table A-5).

Table A-5   Carets and dollar signs

Regular expression	Matches	Examples
/^T/	A T at the beginning of a line	This line..., That Time..., In Time
/^+[0–9]/	A plus sign followed by a digit at the beginning of a line	+5 +45.72, +759 Keep this...
/:$/	A colon that ends a line	...below:

QUOTING SPECIAL CHARACTERS

You can quote any special character (but not parentheses [except in Perl; page 521] or a digit) by preceding it with a backslash (Table A-6). Quoting a special character makes it represent itself.

Table A-6   Quoted special characters

Regular expression	Matches	Examples
/end\./	All strings that contain <u>end</u> followed by a period	The <u>end.</u>, s<u>end.</u>, pret<u>end.</u>mail
/ \\/	A single backslash	\
/ */	An asterisk	*.c, an asterisk (*)
/ \[5\]/	<u>[5]</u>	it was five <u>[5]</u>
/and\/or/	<u>and/or</u>	<u>and/or</u>

RULES

The following rules govern the application of regular expressions.

LONGEST MATCH POSSIBLE

A regular expression always matches the longest possible string, starting as far toward the beginning of the line as possible. Perl calls this type of mach a *greedy match* (page 520). For example, given the string

    This (rug) is not what it once was (a long time ago), is it?

the expression **/Th.*is/** matches

    This (rug) is not what it once was (a long time ago), is

and **/(.*)/** matches

    (rug) is not what it once was (a long time ago)

However, **/([^)]*)/** matches

    (rug)

Given the string

    singing songs, singing more and more

the expression **/s.*ing/** matches

    singing songs, singing

and **/s.*ing song/** matches

    singing song

Empty Regular Expressions

Within some utilities, such as vim and less (but not grep), an empty regular expression represents the last regular expression you used. For example, suppose you give vim the following Substitute command:

```
:s/mike/robert/
```

If you then want to make the same substitution again, you can use the following command:

```
:s//robert/
```

Alternatively, you can use the following commands to search for the string **mike** and then make the substitution

```
/mike/
:s//robert/
```

The empty regular expression (**//**) represents the last regular expression you used (**/mike/**).

Bracketing Expressions

You can use quoted parentheses, \(and \), to *bracket* a regular expression. (However, Perl uses unquoted parentheses to bracket regular expressions; page 521.) The string that the bracketed regular expression matches can be recalled, as explained in "Quoted Digit." A regular expression does not attempt to match quoted parentheses. Thus a regular expression enclosed within quoted parentheses matches what the same regular expression without the parentheses would match. The expression **/\(rexp\)/** matches what **/rexp/** would match; **/a\(b*\)c/** matches what **/ab*c/** would match.

You can nest quoted parentheses. The bracketed expressions are identified only by the opening \(, so no ambiguity arises in identifying them. The expression **/\([a–z]\([A–Z]*\)x\)/** consists of two bracketed expressions, one nested within the other. In the string **3 t dMNORx7 l u**, the preceding regular expression matches **dMNORx**, with the first bracketed expression matching **dMNORx** and the second matching **MNOR**.

The Replacement String

The vim and sed editors use regular expressions as search strings within Substitute commands. You can use the ampersand (**&**) and quoted digits (**\n**) special characters to represent the matched strings within the corresponding replacement string.

AMPERSAND

Within a replacement string, an ampersand (&) takes on the value of the string that the search string (regular expression) matched. For example, the following vim Substitute command surrounds a string of one or more digits with **NN**. The ampersand in the replacement string matches whatever string of digits the regular expression (search string) matched:

    :s/[0-9][0-9]*/NN&NN/

Two character-class definitions are required because the regular expression [0–9]* matches *zero* or more occurrences of a digit, and *any* character string constitutes zero or more occurrences of a digit.

QUOTED DIGIT

Within the search string, a bracketed regular expression, \(**xxx**\) [(**xxx**) in Perl], matches what the regular expression would have matched without the quoted parentheses, **xxx**. Within the replacement string, a quoted digit, *n*, represents the string that the bracketed regular expression (portion of the search string) beginning with the *n*th \(matched. (Perl accepts a quoted digit for this purpose, but Perl's preferred style is to precede the digit with a dollar sign [$*n*; page 521]). For example, you can take a list of people in the form

    last-name, first-name initial

and put it in the form

    first-name initial last-name

with the following vim command:

    :1,$s/\([^,]*\), \(.*\)/\2 \1/

This command addresses all lines in the file (**1,$**). The Substitute command (**s**) uses a search string and a replacement string delimited by forward slashes. The first bracketed regular expression within the search string, \([^,]*\), matches what the same unbracketed regular expression, [^,]*, would match: zero or more characters not containing a comma (the **last-name**). Following the first bracketed regular expression are a comma and a SPACE that match themselves. The second bracketed expression, \(.*\), matches any string of characters (the **first-name** and **initial**).

The replacement string consists of what the second bracketed regular expression matched (\2), followed by a SPACE and what the first bracketed regular expression matched (\1).

EXTENDED REGULAR EXPRESSIONS

This section covers patterns that use an extended set of special characters. These patterns are called *full regular expressions* or *extended regular expressions*. In addition to ordinary regular expressions, Perl and vim provide extended regular expressions. The three utilities egrep, grep when run with the –E option (similar to egrep), and mawk/gawk provide all the special characters included in ordinary regular expressions, except for \(and \), as well those included in extended regular expressions.

Two of the additional special characters are the plus sign (+) and the question mark (?). They are similar to *, which matches *zero* or more occurrences of the previous character. The plus sign matches *one* or more occurrences of the previous character, whereas the question mark matches *zero* or *one* occurrence. You can use any one of the special characters *, +, and ? following parentheses, causing the special character to apply to the string surrounded by the parentheses. Unlike the parentheses in bracketed regular expressions, these parentheses are not quoted (Table A-7).

Table A-7   Extended regular expressions

Regular expression	Matches	Examples
/ab+c/	a followed by one or more b's followed by a c	yabcw, abbc57
/ab?c/	a followed by zero or one b followed by c	back, abcdef
/(ab)+c/	One or more occurrences of the string ab followed by c	zabcd, ababc!
/(ab)?c/	Zero or one occurrence of the string ab followed by c	xc, abcc

In full regular expressions, the vertical bar (|) special character is a Boolean OR operator. Within vim, you must quote the vertical bar by preceding it with a backslash to make it special (\|). A vertical bar between two regular expressions causes a match with strings that match the first expression, the second expression, or both. You can use the vertical bar with parentheses to separate from the rest of the regular expression the two expressions that are being ORed (Table A-8).

Table A-8   Full regular expressions

Regular expression	Meaning	Examples
/ab|ac/	Either ab or ac	ab, ac, abac (***abac*** *is two matches of the regular expression*)
/^Exit|^Quit/	Lines that begin with Exit or Quit	Exit, Quit, No Exit
/(D|N)\. Jones/	D. Jones or N. Jones	P.D. Jones, N. Jones

APPENDIX SUMMARY

A regular expression defines a set of one or more strings of characters. A regular expression is said to match any string it defines.

In a regular expression, a special character is one that does not represent itself. Table A-9 lists special characters.

Table A-9   Special characters

Character	Meaning
.	Matches any single character
*	Matches zero or more occurrences of a match of the preceding character
^	Forces a match to the beginning of a line
$	A match to the end of a line
\	Quotes special characters
\<	Forces a match to the beginning of a word
\>	Forces a match to the end of a word

Table A-10 lists ways of representing character classes and bracketed regular expressions.

Table A-10   Character classes and bracketed regular expressions

Class	Defines
[*xyz*]	Defines a character class that matches *x*, *y*, or *z*
[^ *xyz*]	Defines a character class that matches any character except *x*, *y*, or *z*
[*x–z*]	Defines a character class that matches any character *x* through *z* inclusive
\(*xyz*\)	Matches what *xyz* matches (a bracketed regular expression; not Perl)
(*xyz*)	Matches what *xyz* matches (a bracketed regular expression; Perl only)

In addition to the preceding special characters and strings (excluding quoted parentheses, except in vim), the characters in Table A-11 are special within full, or extended, regular expressions.

Table A-11   Extended regular expressions

Expression	Matches
+	Matches one or more occurrences of the preceding character
?	Matches zero or one occurrence of the preceding character

Table A-11   Extended regular expressions (continued)

Expression	Matches
(*xyz*)+	Matches one or more occurrences of what *xyz* matches
(*xyz*)?	Matches zero or one occurrence of what *xyz* matches
(*xyz*) *	Matches zero or more occurrences of what *xyz* matches
xyz|*abc*	Matches either what *xyz* or what *abc* matches (use \\| in vim)
(*xy*|*ab*)*c*	Matches either what *xyc* or what *abc* matches (use \\| in vim)

Table A-12 lists characters that are special within a replacement string in sed, vim, and Perl.

Table A-12   Replacement strings

String	Represents
&	Represents what the regular expression (search string) matched
n	A quoted number, *n*, represents what the *n*th bracketed regular expression in the search string matched
$*n*	A number preceded by a dollar sign, *n*, represents what the *n*th bracketed regular expression in the search string matched (Perl only)

B

HELP

You need not be a user or system administrator in isolation. A large community of Linux and OS X experts is willing to assist you in learning about, helping you solve problems with, and getting the most out of a Linux or OS X system. Before you ask for help, however, make sure you have done everything you can to solve the problem yourself. No doubt, someone has experienced the same problem before you and the answer to your question exists somewhere on the Internet. Your job is to find it. This appendix lists resources and describes methods that can help you in that task.

SOLVING A PROBLEM

Following is a list of steps that can help you solve a problem without asking someone for help. Depending on your understanding of and experience with the hardware and software involved, these steps may lead to a solution.

1. Linux and OS X come with extensive documentation. Read the documentation on the specific hardware or software you are having a problem with. If it is a GNU product, use info; otherwise, use man to find local information. Also look in **/usr/share/doc** for documentation on specific tools. For more information refer to "Where to Find Documentation" on page 33.

2. When the problem involves some type of error or other message, use a search engine, such as Google (www.google.com) or Google Groups (groups.google.com), to look up the message on the Web. If the message is long, pick a unique part of the message to search for; 10 to 20 characters should be enough. Enclose the search string within double quotation marks. See "Using the Internet to Get Help" on page 39 for an example of this kind of search.

3. Check whether the Linux Documentation Project (www.tldp.org) has a HOWTO or mini-HOWTO on the subject in question. Search its site for keywords that relate directly to the product and problem. Read the FAQs.

4. See Table B-1 on page 900 for other sources of documentation.

5. Use Google or Google Groups to search on keywords that relate directly to the product and problem.

6. When all else fails (or perhaps before you try anything else), examine the system logs in **/var/log**. First look at the end of the **messages** (Linux) or **system.log** (OS X) file using one of the following commands:

```
# tail -20 /var/log/messages
# tail -20 /var/log/system.log
```

If **messages** or **system.log** contain nothing useful, run the following command. It displays the names of the log files in chronological order, with the most recently modified files appearing at the bottom of the list:

```
$ ls -ltr /var/log
```

Look at the files at the bottom of the list first. If the problem involves a network connection, review the **secure** or **auth.log** file (some systems use a different name) on the local and remote systems. Also look at **messages** or **system.log** on the remote system.

7. The **/var/spool** directory contains subdirectories with useful information: **cups** holds the print queues; **postfix, mail**, or **exim4** holds the user's mail files. Other subdirectories of **/var** contain similarly useful files.

If you are unable to solve a problem yourself, a thoughtful question to an appropriate newsgroup (page 902) or mailing list (page 903) can often elicit useful information. When you send or post a question, make sure you describe the problem and identify the local system carefully. Include the version numbers of the operating system and any software packages that relate to the problem. Describe the hardware, if appropriate. There is an etiquette to posting questions—see www.catb.org/~esr/faqs/smart-questions.html for a good paper by Eric S. Raymond and Rick Moen titled "How To Ask Questions the Smart Way."

The author's home page (www.sobell.com) contains corrections to this book, answers to selected chapter exercises, and pointers to other Linux and OS X sites.

THE APPLE WEB SITE

The Apple Web site is a rich source of Mac OS X information. Following is a list of some locations that may be of interest:

- Manuals for Apple operating systems and products are available at www.info.apple.com/support/manuals.html.

- General support material is available at www.apple.com/support.

- Apple support forums are online discussions about Apple-related issues. Forums are dedicated to specific applications or OS versions, specific Macintosh models, and so on. Go to discussions.info.apple.com to browse through the forums.

- Mailing lists are hosted by Apple; see lists.apple.com for a list of mailing lists.

- Even if you are not using Mac OS X Server, the documentation for Server has a lot of material on OS X command-line usage.

FINDING LINUX AND OS X–RELATED INFORMATION

Linux and OS X come with reference pages stored online. You can read these documents by using the man (page 33) or info (page 36) utility. Under Mac OS X, you can use the documentation browser in Xcode or the Mac Help application. You can read man and info pages to get more information about specific topics while reading this book or to determine which features are available with Linux or OS X. To search for topics, use the apropos utility (see page 35 or give the command **man apropos**). The Apple support site (www.apple.com/support) has many useful Mac OS X links.

DOCUMENTATION

Good books are available on various aspects of using and managing UNIX systems in general and Linux and OS X systems in particular. In addition, you may find the sites listed in Table B-1 useful.[1]

Table B-1   Documentation

Site	About the site	URL
Apple Manuals	Apple manuals (look under **Software Manuals/Mac OS X** in a box on the right)	www.apple.com/support/manuals
freedesktop.org	Creates standards for interoperability between open-source desktop environments	freedesktop.org
GNOME	GNOME home page	www.gnome.org
GNU Manuals	GNU manuals	www.gnu.org/manual
info	Instructions for using the info utility	www.gnu.org/software/texinfo/manual/info
Internet FAQ Archives	Searchable FAQ archives	www.faqs.org
KDE Documentation	KDE documentation	www.kde.org/documentation
KDE News	KDE news	dot.kde.org
Linux Documentation Project	All things related to Linux documentation (in many languages): HOWTOs, guides, FAQs, man pages, and magazines. This site is the best overall source for Linux documentation. Make sure to visit the Links page.	www.tldp.org
RFCs	Requests for comments; see *RFC* (page 975)	www.rfc-editor.org
System Administrators Guild (SAGE)	SAGE is a group for system administrators	www.sage.org

---

1. The right-hand columns of most of the tables in this appendix show Internet addresses (URLs). All sites have an implicit http:// prefix unless ftp:// or https:// is shown. Refer to "URLs (Web addresses)" on page 25.

USEFUL LINUX AND OS X SITES

Sometimes the sites listed in Table B-2 are so busy that you cannot connect to them. In this case, you are usually given a list of alternative, or *mirror*, sites to try.

Table B-2   Useful Linux and OS X sites

Site	About the site	URL
Accelerate Your Mac	Covers improving system performance mostly through hardware upgrades	xlr8yourmac.com
Apple Developer Connection	A site for OS X developers	developer.apple.com developer.apple.com/opensource
Command-Line Fu	The place to record those command-line gems you return to again and again	www.commandlinefu.com
DistroWatch	A survey of Linux distributions, including news, reviews, and articles	distrowatch.com
Fedora Forums	A forum about everything Fedora	fedoraforum.org
Gentoo Forums	A forum about everything Gentoo	forums.gentoo.org
GNU	GNU Project home page	www.gnu.org
ibiblio	A large library and digital archive. Formerly Metalab; formerly Sunsite.	www.ibiblio.org www.ibiblio.org/pub/linux www.ibiblio.org/pub/historic-linux
Linux Standard Base (LSB)	A group dedicated to standardizing Linux	www.linuxfoundation.org/collaborate/workgroups/lsb
MacFixit	A user site full of tips, trivia, and troubleshooting help for Macintosh systems	www.macfixit.com
Mac Forums	Forums about everything Mac, official and unofficial	discussions.apple.com macosx.com/forums
Mac Hints	Mac tips	www.macosxhints.com
MacLife	A magazine with reviews, tips, and articles about Macintosh systems	www.maclife.com
Mac User Groups	Apple's registry of Macintosh user groups; includes a searchable database	www.apple.com/usergroups www.apple.com/usergroups/find

Table B-2   Useful Linux and OS X sites (continued)

Site	About the site	URL
MacWorld	A magazine dedicated to the Mac	www.macworld.com
Notes from the Field	A blog by Charles Edge with coverage of Mac innards and tips for enhancing the Mac experience	krypted.com
OS X VersionTracker	A searchable site covering new releases of OS X software packages	www.versiontracker.com/macosx
Psychocats	Tutorials and random pages for Ubuntu users	www.psychocats.net/ubuntu
System Administrators Guild (SAGE)	SAGE is a group for system administrators	www.sage.org
Sobell	The author's home page contains useful links, errata for this book, code for many of the examples in this book, and answers to selected exercises	www.sobell.com
Threads	Linux Documentation Project threads FAQ	tldp.org/FAQ/Threads-FAQ
Ubuntu Forums	A forum about everything Ubuntu; in some cases discusses other distributions	ubuntuforums.org
USENIX	A large, well-established UNIX group. This site has many links, including a list of conferences.	www.usenix.org
X.Org	The X Window System home	www.x.org

Linux and OS X Newsgroups

One of the best ways of getting specific information is through a newsgroup. You can often find the answer to a question by reading postings to the newsgroup. Try using Google Groups (groups.google.com) to search through newsgroups to see whether the question has already been asked and answered. Alternatively, open a newsreader program and subscribe to appropriate newsgroups. If necessary, you can post a question for someone to answer. Before you do so, make sure you are posting to the correct group and that your question has not already been answered.

The **comp.os.linux.answers** (Linux) and **comp.sys.mac.system** (OS X) newsgroups provide postings of solutions to common problems and periodic postings of the most up-to-date versions of FAQ and HOWTO documents. The **comp.os.linux.misc** newsgroup has answers to miscellaneous Linux-related questions.

Apple Discussions (discussions.apple.com) has a list of online forums, including a section on **Mac OS X and Related Software**.

Mailing Lists

Subscribing to a mailing list allows you to participate in an electronic discussion. With most lists, you can send and receive email dedicated to a specific topic to and from a group of users. Moderated lists do not tend to stray as much as unmoderated lists, assuming the list has a good moderator. The disadvantage of a moderated list is that some discussions may be cut off when they get interesting if the moderator deems that the discussion has gone on for too long. Mailing lists described as bulletins are unidirectional: You cannot post information to these lists but can only receive periodic bulletins. If you have the subscription address for a mailing list but are not sure how to subscribe, put the word **help** in the body and/or header of email you send to the address. You will usually receive instructions via return email. You can also use a search engine to search for **mailing list linux** or **mailing list os x**.

You can find Red Hat and Fedora mailing lists at www.redhat.com/mailman/listinfo, Ubuntu mailing lists at www.ubuntu.com/support/community/mailinglists, and Debian mailing lists at www.debian.org/MailingLists/subscribe.

Apple supports many mailing lists. Visit www.lists.apple.com/mailman/listinfo to display a list of Mac OS X mailing lists; click on the name of a list to display subscription information.

Words

Many dictionaries, thesauruses, and glossaries are available online. Table B-3 lists a few of them.

Table B-3   Looking up words

Site	About the site	URL
DICT.org	Multiple-database search for words	www.dict.org
Dictionary.com	Everything related to words	dictionary.reference.com
DNS Glossary	DNS glossary	www.menandmice.com/knowledgehub/dnsglossary
FOLDOC	The Free On-Line Dictionary of Computing	foldoc.org
GNOME Controls	Defines many GUI controls (widgets)	developer.gnome.org/projects/gup/hig/2.0/controls.html
The Jargon File	An online version of *The New Hacker's Dictionary*	www.catb.org/~esr/jargon
Merriam-Webster	English language	www.merriam-webster.com
OneLook	Multiple-site word search with a single query	www.onelook.com
Roget's Thesaurus	Thesaurus	humanities.uchicago.edu/forms_unrest/ROGET.html
Webopedia	Commercial technical dictionary	www.webopedia.com

Table B-3 Looking up words (continued)

Site	About the site	URL
Wikipedia	An open-source (user-contributed) encyclopedia project	wikipedia.org
Wordsmyth	Dictionary and thesaurus	www.wordsmyth.net
Yahoo Reference	Search multiple sources at the same time	education.yahoo.com/reference

SOFTWARE

There are many ways to learn about interesting software packages and their availability on the Internet. Table B-4 lists sites you can download software from. Another way to learn about software packages is through a newsgroup (page 902).

Table B-4 Software

Site	About the site	URL
afp548	OS X essays and tools	www.afp548.com
BitTorrent	BitTorrent efficiently distributes large amounts of static data	azureus.sourceforge.net www.transmissionbt.com
bombich.com	Home of OS X Carbon Copy Center and other useful tools	bombich.com
CVL	Concurrent Versions Librarian, a GUI for CVS under OS X	www.sente.ch/software/cvl
CVS	CVS (Concurrent Versions System) is a version control system	www.nongnu.org/cvs
ddd	The ddd utility is a graphical front-end for command-line debuggers such as gdb	www.gnu.org/software/ddd
fink	The fink utility builds and installs OS X software automatically	www.finkproject.org
Firefox	Web browser	www.mozilla.com/firefox
Free Software Directory	Categorized, searchable lists of free software	directory.fsf.org
Free the Software!	A Red Hat site that hosts many open-source projects	sourceware.org
Freshmeat	A large index of UNIX and cross-platform software and themes	freshmeat.net
gcc	Home page for the GNU C compiler	gcc.gnu.org

Table B-4 Software (continued)

Site	About the site	URL
gdb	The gdb utility is a command-line debugger	www.gnu.org/software/gdb
GNOME Project	Links to all GNOME projects	projects.gnome.org
IceWALKERS	Categorized, searchable lists of free software	www.icewalkers.com
kdbg	The kdbg utility is a graphical user interface to gdb	freshmeat.net/projects/kdbg
Linux Software Map	A database of packages written for, ported to, or compiled for Linux	www.boutell.com/lsm
MacPorts Project	A system for compiling, installing, and upgrading command-line, X11, or Aqua-based open-source software	www.macports.org
Mtools	A collection of utilities to access DOS floppy diskettes from Linux without mounting the diskettes (page 767)	www.gnu.org/software/mtools
Network Calculators	Subnet mask calculator	www.subnetmask.info
NTFS driver	Driver that enables Linux to read from and write to Windows NTFS filesystems (available in the **ntfs-3g** package)	www.ntfs-3g.org
Savannah	Central point for development, distribution, and maintenance of free software	savannah.gnu.org
SourceForge	A development Web site with a large repository of open-source code and applications	sourceforge.net
splint	C program verifier (replaces lint)	www.splint.org
strace	The strace utility is a system call trace debugging tool	sourceforge.net/projects/strace
Thunderbird	Mail application	www.mozillamessaging.com
TkCVS	A CVS GUI	www.twobarleycorns.net/tkcvs.html
ups	The ups utility is a graphical source-level debugger	ups.sourceforge.net
versiontracker	A large index of OS X software	www.versiontracker.com/macosx

OFFICE SUITES AND WORD PROCESSORS

Several office suites and many word processors are available for Linux. Table B-5 lists a few of them. If you are exchanging documents with people using Windows, make sure the import from and export to MS Word functionality covers your needs.

Table B-5 Office suites and word processors

Product name	What it does	URL
AbiWord	Word processor	www.abisource.com
KOffice	Integrated suite of office applications, including the KWord word processing program	www.koffice.org
NeoOffice	OpenOffice tailored for the Mac with native look and feel	www.neooffice.org
OpenOffice	A multiplatform and multilingual office suite	www.openoffice.org www.gnome.org/projects/ooo

SPECIFYING A TERMINAL

Because vim, emacs, and other textual and pseudographical programs take advantage of features specific to various kinds of terminals and terminal emulators, you must tell these programs the name of the terminal you are using or the terminal the terminal emulator is emulating. Most of the time the terminal name is set for you. If the terminal name is not specified or is not specified correctly, the characters on the screen will be garbled or, when you start a program, the program will ask which type of terminal you are using.

Terminal names describe the functional characteristics of a terminal or terminal emulator to programs that require this information. Although terminal names are referred to as either Terminfo or Termcap names, the difference relates to the method each system uses to store the terminal characteristics internally—not to the manner in which you specify the name of a terminal. Terminal names that are often used with terminal emulators and with graphical monitors while they are run in textual mode include **ansi**, **linux**, **vt100**, **vt102**, **vt220**, and **xterm**.

When you are running a terminal emulator, you can specify the type of terminal you want to emulate. Set the emulator to either **vt100** or **vt220**, and set **TERM** to the same value.

When you log in, you may be prompted to identify the type of terminal you are using:

```
TERM = (vt100)
```

You can respond to this prompt in one of two ways. First you can press RETURN to set your terminal type to the name in parentheses. Alternatively, if that name does not describe the terminal you are using, you can enter the correct name and then press RETURN.

```
TERM = (vt100) ansi
```

You may also receive the following prompt:

```
TERM = (unknown)
```

This prompt indicates that the system does not know which type of terminal you are using. If you plan to run programs that require this information, enter the name of the terminal or terminal emulator you are using before you press RETURN.

TERM If you do not receive a prompt, you can give the following command to display the value of the **TERM** variable and check whether the terminal type has been set:

```
$ echo $TERM
```

If the system responds with the wrong name, a blank line, or an error message, set or change the terminal name. From the Bourne Again Shell (bash), enter a command similar to the following to set the **TERM** variable so the system knows which type of terminal you are using:

export TERM=name

Replace *name* with the terminal name of the terminal you are using, making sure you do not put a SPACE before or after the equal sign. If you always use the same type of terminal, you can place this command in your ~/**.bashrc** file (page 271), causing the shell to set the terminal type each time you log in. For example, give the following command to set the terminal name to **vt100**:

```
$ export TERM=vt100
```

Use the following format under the TC Shell (tcsh):

setenv TERM name

Replace *name* with the terminal name for the terminal you are using. Under tcsh you can place this command in your ~/**.login** file (page 352). For example, under tcsh you can give this command to set your terminal name to **vt100**:

```
$ setenv TERM vt100
```

LANG For some programs to display information correctly, you may need to set the **LANG** variable (page 304). Frequently you can set this variable to C. Under bash use the command

```
$ export LANG=C
```

and under tcsh use

```
$ setenv LANG C
```

C

KEEPING THE SYSTEM UP-TO-DATE

The apt-get and yum utilities both fill the same role: They install and update software packages. Both utilities compare the files in a repository (generally on the Internet) with those on the local system and update the files on the local system according to your instructions. Both utilities automatically install and update any additional files that a package depends on (dependencies). Most Linux distributions come with apt-get or yum. Debian-based systems such as Ubuntu are set up to use apt-get, which works with **deb** packages. Red Hat and Fedora use yum, which works with **rpm** packages. There are also versions of apt-get that work with **rpm** packages. On a Mac OS X system it is easiest to use the software update GUI to kccp the system up-to-date.

To facilitate the update process, apt-get and yum keep locally a list of packages that are held in each of the repositories they use. Any software you want to install or update must reside in a repository.

When you give apt-get or yum a command to install a package, they look for the package in a local package list. If the package appears in the list, apt-get or yum fetches both that package and any packages the package you are installing depends on and installs the packages.

The yum examples in this section are from a Fedora system and the apt-get examples are from an Ubuntu system. Although the files, input, and output on the local system may look different, how you use the tools—and the results—will be the same.

In contract to apt-get and yum, BitTorrent efficiently distributes large amounts of static data, such as installation ISO images. It does not examine files on the local system and does not check for dependencies.

USING yum

Early releases of Linux did not include a tool for managing updates. Although the rpm utility could install or upgrade individual software packages, it was up to the user to locate a package and any packages it depended on. When Terra Soft produced its Red Hat–based Linux distribution for the PowerPC, named Yellow Dog, the company created the Yellow Dog Updater to fill this gap. This program has since been ported to other architectures and distributions. The result is named Yellow Dog Updater, Modified (yum; yum.baseurl.org).

rpm packages   The yum utility works with **rpm** packages. When yum installs or upgrades a software package, it also installs or upgrades packages that the package depends on.

Repositories   The yum utility downloads package headers and packages from servers called repositories. Frequently, yum is set up to use copies of repositories kept on mirror sites. See "Configuring yum" on page 914 for information on selecting a repository.

USING yum TO INSTALL, REMOVE, AND UPDATE PACKAGES

Installing packages   The behavior of yum depends on the options you specify. To install a new package together with the packages it depends on, while working with **root** privileges give the command **yum install**, followed by the name of the package. After yum determines what it needs to do, it asks for confirmation. The next example installs the **tcsh** package:

```
# yum install tcsh
Loaded plugins: refresh-packagekit
Setting up Install Process
Resolving Dependencies
--> Running transaction check
---> Package tcsh.i586 0:6.15-8.fc11 set to be updated
--> Finished Dependency Resolution

Dependencies Resolved

================================================================================
 Package           Arch          Version            Repository          Size
================================================================================
Installing:
 tcsh              i586          6.15-8.fc11        fedora             477 k

Transaction Summary
================================================================================
Install       1 Package(s)
Update        0 Package(s)
Remove        0 Package(s)
```

```
                      Total download size: 477 k
                      Is this ok [y/N]: y
                      Downloading Packages:
                      tcsh-6.15-8.fc11.i586.rpm                                    | 477 kB     00:00
                      Running rpm_check_debug
                      Running Transaction Test
                      Finished Transaction Test
                      Transaction Test Succeeded
                      Running Transaction
                        Installing     : tcsh-6.15-8.fc11.i586                                    1/1

                      Installed:
                        tcsh.i586 0:6.15-8.fc11

                      Complete!
```

Removing packages You can also use yum to remove packages, using a similar syntax. The following example removes the **tcsh** package:

```
                      # yum remove tcsh
                      Loaded plugins: refresh-packagekit
                      Setting up Remove Process
                      Resolving Dependencies
                      --> Running transaction check
                      ---> Package tcsh.i586 0:6.15-8.fc11 set to be erased
                      --> Finished Dependency Resolution

                      Dependencies Resolved

                      ================================================================================
                      Package          Arch          Version              Repository         Size
                      ================================================================================
                      Removing:
                       tcsh            i586          6.15-8.fc11          installed          1.1 M

                      Transaction Summary
                      ================================================================================
                      Install      0 Package(s)
                      Update       0 Package(s)
                      Remove       1 Package(s)

                      Is this ok [y/N]: y
                      Downloading Packages:
                      Running rpm_check_debug
                      Running Transaction Test
                      Finished Transaction Test
                      Transaction Test Succeeded
                      Running Transaction
                        Erasing        : tcsh-6.15-8.fc11.i586                                    1/1

                      Removed:
                        tcsh.i586 0:6.15-8.fc11

                      Complete!
```

Updating packages The **update** option, without additional parameters, updates all installed packages. It downloads summary files that hold information about package headers for installed packages, determines which packages need to be updated, prompts to continue, and downloads and installs the updated packages. Unlike the situation with apt-get, the yum **upgrade** command is very similar to yum **update**.

In the following example, yum determines that two packages, **at** and **firefox**, need to be updated and checks dependencies. Once it has determined what it needs to do, yum advises you of the action(s) it will take, prompts with **Is this ok [y/N]**, and, if you approve, downloads and installs the packages.

```
# yum update
Loaded plugins: refresh-packagekit
Setting up Update Process
Resolving Dependencies
--> Running transaction check
---> Package at.i586 0:3.1.10-31.fc11 set to be updated
---> Package firefox.i586 0:3.5.1-3.fc11 set to be updated
--> Finished Dependency Resolution

Dependencies Resolved

================================================================================
 Package          Arch           Version              Repository          Size
================================================================================
Updating:
 at               i586           3.1.10-31.fc11       updates             63 k
 firefox          i586           3.5.1-3.fc11         updates             15 M

Transaction Summary
================================================================================
Install       0 Package(s)
Update        2 Package(s)
Remove        0 Package(s)

Total download size: 15 M
Is this ok [y/N]: y
Downloading Packages:
(1/2): at-3.1.10-31.fc11.i586.rpm                        |  63 kB     00:00
(2/2): firefox-3.5.1-3.fc11.i586.rpm                     |  15 MB     00:10
--------------------------------------------------------------------------------
Total                                         1.3 MB/s |  15 MB     00:11
Running rpm_check_debug
Running Transaction Test
Finished Transaction Test
Transaction Test Succeeded
Running Transaction
  Updating       : firefox-3.5.1-3.fc11.i586                               1/4
  Updating       : at-3.1.10-31.fc11.i586                                  2/4
  Cleanup        : firefox-3.5.1-1.fc11.i586                               3/4
  Cleanup        : at-3.1.10-30.fc11.i586                                  4/4

Updated:
  at.i586 0:3.1.10-31.fc11                     firefox.i586 0:3.5.1-3.fc11

Complete!
```

You can update individual packages by specifying the names of the packages on the command line following the word **update**.

OTHER yum COMMANDS

Many yum commands and options are available. A few of the more useful commands are described here. The yum man page contains a complete list.

check-update   Lists packages installed on the local system that have updates available in the yum repositories.

clean all   Removes header files that yum uses for resolving dependencies. Also removes cached packages—yum does not automatically remove packages once they have been downloaded and installed, unless you set **keepcache** (page 914) to 0.

clean metadata   Removes the files yum uses to determine remote package availability. Using this option forces yum to download all metadata the next time you run it.

list available   Lists all packages that can be installed from the yum repositories.

search *word* Searches for *word* in the package description, summary, packager, and name.

yum GROUPS

In addition to working with single packages, yum can work with groups of packages. The next example shows how to display a list of installed and available package groups:

```
$ yum grouplist
Loaded plugins: refresh-packagekit
Setting up Group Process
Installed Groups:
    Administration Tools
    Arabic Support
    Armenian Support
    Assamese Support
    Base
...
    Web Server
    X Window System
Available Groups:
...
    Italian Support
    Java
    Java Development
    KDE (K Desktop Environment)
    KDE Software Development
    Kashmiri Support
Done
```

The command **yum groupinfo** followed by the name of a group displays information about the group, including a description of the group and a list of mandatory, default, and optional packages. The next example displays information about the Web Server group of packages. If the name of the package includes a SPACE, you must quote it.

```
$ yum groupinfo "Web Server"
Loaded plugins: refresh-packagekit
Setting up Group Process

Group: Web Server
 Description: These tools allow you to run a Web server on the system.
 Mandatory Packages:
    httpd
 Default Packages:
    crypto-utils
    distcache
    httpd-manual
    mod_perl
    mod_python
...
 Optional Packages:
    Pound
    apachetop
    awstats
    boa
    cherokee
```

To install a group of packages, give the command **yum groupinstall** followed by the name of the group.

DOWNLOADING rpm PACKAGE FILES WITH yumdownloader

The yumdownloader utility locates and downloads—but does not install—**rpm** package files. If this utility is not available on the local system, use yum to download and install the **yum-utils** package before you attempt to run yumdownloader.

The following example downloads the **samba rpm** file to the working directory:

```
$ yumdownloader samba
Loaded plugins: refresh-packagekit
fedora/primary_db                              | 8.4 MB      00:12
updates/primary_db                             | 2.6 MB      00:07
samba-3.3.2-0.33.fc11.i586.rpm                 | 4.4 MB      00:08
```

Downloading source files
You can use yumdownloader with the **--source** option to download **rpm** source package files. The yumdownloader utility automatically enables the necessary source repositories. The following example downloads in the working directory the **rpm** file for the latest version of the kernel source code for the installed release:

```
$ yumdownloader --source kernel
Loaded plugins: refresh-packagekit
Enabling updates-source repository
updates-source/metalink                        | 5.7 kB      00:00
updates-source                                 | 3.3 kB      00:00
updates-source/primary_db                      | 620 kB      00:02
Enabling fedora-source repository
fedora-source/metalink                         |  14 kB      00:00
fedora-source                                  | 2.7 kB      00:00
fedora-source/primary_db                       | 2.4 MB      00:04
kernel-2.6.29.6-213.fc11.src.rpm               |  56 MB      02:37
```

Without the **--source** option, yumdownloader downloads the executable kernel **rpm** file.

CONFIGURING yum

Most Linux distributions that use yum for updating files come with yum ready to use; you do not need to configure it. This section describes the yum configuration files for those users who want to modify them. The primary configuration file, **/etc/yum.conf**, holds global settings. The first example shows a typical **yum.conf** file:

```
$ cat /etc/yum.conf
[main]
cachedir=/var/cache/yum
keepcache=0
debuglevel=2
logfile=/var/log/yum.log
exactarch=1
obsoletes=1
gpgcheck=1
```

```
plugins=1
installonly_limit=3
...
# PUT YOUR REPOS HERE OR IN separate files named file.repo
# in /etc/yum.repos.d
```

The section labeled [main] defines global configuration options. The cachedir specifies the directory in which yum stores downloaded packages, although with keepcache set to 0, yum does not store headers and packages after installing them. The amount of information logged is specified by debuglevel, with a value of 10 producing the most information. The logfile specifies where yum keeps its log.

Setting exactarch to 1 causes yum to update packages only with packages of the same architecture, thereby preventing an i686 package from replacing an i386 package, for example. You can use retries to specify the number of times yum will try to retrieve a file before returning an error (the default is 6). Set this parameter to 0 to cause yum to continue trying forever.

Setting obsoletes to 1 causes yum to replace obsolete packages when performing an update; it has no effect during an install. When gpgcheck is set to 1, yum checks the GPG (GNU Privacy Guard; GnuPG.org) signatures on packages it installs. This check verifies the authenticity of the packages. Setting plugins to 1 enables yum plugins, which extend yum functionality. (See wiki.linux.duke.edu/YumPlugins and yum in section 8 of the man pages for more information on yum plugins.) The installonly parameter specifies packages that yum is to install but never upgrade, such as the kernel. The installonly_limit specifies the number of versions of a given installonly package that are to be installed at one time.

Although the balance of the yum configuration information, which specifies the yum repositories, can appear in the yum.conf file, this information is frequently kept in the /etc/yum.repos.d directory. A parameter set in a repository section overrides the same parameter set in the [main] section. Following is a listing for a yum.repos.d directory on a Fedora system:

```
$ ls /etc/yum.repos.d
fedora-rawhide.repo          fedora-updates.repo
fedora-updates-testing.repo  fedora.repo
```

Each of these files contains a header, such as [fedora], which provides a unique name for the repository. The name of the file is generally similar to the repository name, with the addition of a fedora- (or similar) prefix and a .repo filename extension. On a Fedora system, commonly used repositories include fedora (held in the fedora.repo file), which contains the packages present on the installation DVD; updates (held in the fedora-updates.repo file), which contains updated versions of the stable packages; updates-testing (held in the fedora-updates-testing.repo file), which contains updates that are not ready for release; and rawhide (held in fedora.rawhide.repo), which contains a daily snapshot of the latest build versions of Fedora packages. The last two repositories are not enabled; do not enable either of these repositories unless you are testing unstable packages. Never enable them on a production system.

Each ❖ .repo file can specify several repositories

tip Each ❖.**repo** file includes specifications for several related repositories, which are usually disabled. For example, the **fedora.repo** file holds **[fedora-debuginfo]** and **[fedora-source]** in addition to **[fedora]**.

You cannot download source files using yum. Instead, use yumdownloader (page 914) for this task.

The next example shows part of the **fedora.repo** file that specifies the parameters for the **fedora** repository:

```
$ cat /etc/yum.repos.d/fedora.repo
[fedora]
name=Fedora $releasever - $basearch
failovermethod=priority
#baseurl=http://download.fedoraproject.org/pub/fedora/linux/releases/$releasever/Everythng/$basearch/os/
mirrorlist=https://mirrors.fedoraproject.org/metalink?repo=fedora-$releasever&arch=$basearch
enabled=1
metadata_expire=7d
gpgcheck=1
gpgkey=file:///etc/pki/rpm-gpg/RPM-GPG-KEY-fedora-$basearch
...
```

Repository specification Each repository specification contains the name of the repository enclosed in brackets ([]), a **name**, a **failovermethod**, a **baseurl**, and a **mirrorlist**. The **name** provides an informal name for the repository that yum displays. The **failovermethod** determines the order in which yum contacts an initial mirror site and additional mirror sites if the first one fails; **priority** selects the sites in the order in which they appear, while **roundrobin** selects sites randomly. The **baseurl** indicates the location of the main repository; it is normally commented out. The **mirrorlist** specifies the URL of a file that holds a list of **baseurl**s, or mirrors of the main repository. The mirror list server uses geoip (geolocation; www.geoiptool.com) to attempt to return the nearest mirrors for yum to try. Only **baseurl** or **mirrorlist** can be enabled at one time. These definitions use two variables: yum sets **$basearch** to the architecture of the system and **$releasever** to the version of the release (such as **11** for Fedora 11).

The repository described by the file is enabled (yum will use it) if **enabled** is set to **1** and is disabled if **enabled** is set to **0**. As described earlier, **gpgcheck** determines whether yum checks GPG signatures on files it downloads. The **gpgkey** specifies the location of the GPG key. Refer to the **yum.conf** man page for more options.

USING apt-get

APT (Advanced Package Tool) is a collection of utilities that download, install, remove, upgrade, and report on software packages. APT utilities download packages and call **dpkg** utilities to manipulate the packages once they are on the local system. For more information refer to www.debian.org/doc/manuals/apt-howto.

Updating the   The primary APT command is apt-get; its arguments determine what the command
package list   does. Working with **root** privileges, give the command **apt-get update** to update the
local package list:

```
# apt-get update
Get:1 http://dl.google.com stable Release.gpg [191B]
Get:2 http://dl.google.com testing Release.gpg [191B]
Get:3 http://dl.google.com stable Release [1308B]
Get:4 http://dl.google.com testing Release [1297B]
Get:5 http://dl.google.com stable/non-free Packages [966B]
Hit http://archive.canonical.com hardy Release.gpg
Hit http://us.archive.ubuntu.com hardy Release.gpg
Hit http://us.archive.ubuntu.com hardy-updates Release.gpg
Hit http://security.ubuntu.com hardy-security Release.gpg
Get:6 http://dl.google.com testing/non-free Packages [734B]
Hit http://archive.canonical.com hardy Release
Hit http://us.archive.ubuntu.com hardy Release
...
Fetched 4687B in 1s (2895B/s)
Reading package lists... Done
```

Check the   The apt-get utility does not tolerate a broken dependency tree. To check the status of
dependency tree the local dependency tree, give the command **apt-get check**:

```
# apt-get check
Reading package lists... Done
Building dependency tree
Reading state information... Done
```

The easiest way to fix errors that apt-get reveals is to remove the offending packages
and then reinstall them using apt-get.

USING apt-get TO INSTALL, REMOVE, AND UPDATE PACKAGES

Installing packages   The following command uses apt-get to install the **zsh** package:

```
# apt-get install zsh
Reading package lists... Done
Building dependency tree
Reading state information... Done
Suggested packages:
  zsh-doc
The following NEW packages will be installed:
  zsh
0 upgraded, 1 newly installed, 0 to remove and 0 not upgraded.
Need to get 3892kB of archives.
After this operation, 11.6MB of additional disk space will be used.
Get:1 http://us.archive.ubuntu.com hardy/main zsh 4.3.4-24ubuntu1 [3892kB]
Fetched 3892kB in 23s (165kB/s)
Selecting previously deselected package zsh.
(Reading database ... 192924 files and directories currently installed.)
Unpacking zsh (from .../zsh_4.3.4-24ubuntu1_amd64.deb) ...
Setting up zsh (4.3.4-24ubuntu1) ...
```

Removing packages Remove a package the same way you install a package, substituting **remove** for
install:

```
# apt-get remove zsh
Reading package lists... Done
Building dependency tree
Reading state information... Done
The following packages will be REMOVED:
  zsh
0 upgraded, 0 newly installed, 1 to remove and 0 not upgraded.
After this operation, 11.6MB disk space will be freed.
Do you want to continue [Y/n]? y
(Reading database ... 193880 files and directories currently installed.)
Removing zsh ...
```

To ensure you can later reinstall a package with the same configuration, the apt-get
remove command does not remove configuration files from the /etc directory hierarchy. Although it is not recommended, you can use the **purge** command instead of
remove to remove all the package files, including configuration files. Alternatively,
you can move these files to an archive so you can restore them later if necessary.

USING apt-get TO UPGRADE THE SYSTEM

Two arguments cause apt-get to upgrade all packages on the system: **upgrade**
upgrades all packages on the system that do not require new packages to be
installed and **dist-upgrade** upgrades all packages on the system, installing new packages as needed; this argument will install a new version of the operating system if
one is available.

The following command updates all packages on the system that depend only on
packages that are already installed:

```
# apt-get upgrade
Reading package lists... Done
Building dependency tree
Reading state information... Done
The following packages will be upgraded:
cups cups-bsd cups-client cups-common firefox firefox-3.0 firefox-3.0-branding firefox-3.0-gnome
support firefox-gnome-support
9 upgraded, 0 newly installed, 0 to remove and 0 not upgraded.
Need to get 4764kB of archives.
After this operation, 0B of additional disk space will be used.
Do you want to continue [Y/n]? y
Get:1 http://us.archive.ubuntu.com jaunty-updates/main cups-common 1.3.9-17ubuntu3.2 [1165kB]
...
Get:8 http://us.archive.ubuntu.com jaunty-updates/main firefox 3.0.12+build1+nobinonly-0ubuntu0.9.04.1
[69.3kB]
Get:9 http://us.archive.ubuntu.com jaunty-updates/main firefox-gnome-support 3.0.12+build1+nobinonly-
0ubuntu0.9.04.1 [69.2kB]
Fetched 4764kB in 44s (107kB/s)
Preconfiguring packages ...
(Reading database ... 123035 files and directories currently installed.)
Preparing to replace cups-common 1.3.9-17ubuntu3 (using .../cups-common_1.3.9-17ubuntu3.2_all.deb) ...
Unpacking replacement cups-common ...
Preparing to replace cups 1.3.9-17ubuntu3 (using .../cups_1.3.9-17ubuntu3.2_i386.deb) ...
* Stopping Common Unix Printing System: cupsd
[ OK ]
```

```
Unpacking replacement cups ...
...
Setting up firefox (3.0.12+build1+nobinonly-0ubuntu0.9.04.1) ...
Setting up firefox-gnome-support (3.0.12+build1+nobinonly-0ubuntu0.9.04.1) ...
```

When apt-get asks if you want to continue, enter **Y** to upgrade the listed packages; otherwise, enter **N**. Packages that are not upgraded because they depend on packages that are not already installed are listed as **kept back**.

Use **dist-upgrade** to upgrade all packages, including packages that depend on packages that are not installed. This command also installs dependencies.

OTHER apt-get COMMANDS

autoclean Removes old archive files.

check Checks for broken dependencies.

clean Removes archive files.

dist-upgrade Upgrades packages on the system, installing new packages as needed. If a new version of the operating system is available, this option upgrades to the new version.

purge Removes a package and all its configuration files.

source Downloads source files.

update Retrieves new lists of packages.

upgrade Upgrades all packages on the system that do not require new packages to be installed.

REPOSITORIES

Repositories hold collections of software packages and related information, including headers that describe each package and provide information on other packages the package depends on. Typically, a Linux distribution maintains repositories for each of its releases.

Software package categories — Software packages are frequently divided into several categories. Ubuntu uses the following categories:

- **main**—Ubuntu-supported open-source software
- **universe**—Community-maintained open-source software
- **multiverse**—Software restricted by copyright or legal issues
- **restricted**—Proprietary device drivers
- **backports**—Packages from later releases of Ubuntu that are not available for an earlier release

The apt-get utility selects packages from repositories it searches based on the categories specified in the **sources.list** file.

sources.list: SPECIFIES REPOSITORIES FOR apt-get TO SEARCH

The **/etc/apt/sources.list** file specifies the repositories apt-get searches when you ask it to find or install a package. You must modify the **sources.list** file to enable apt-get to download software from nondefault repositories. Typically, you do not need to configure apt-get to install supported software.

Each line in **sources.list** describes one repository and has the following format:

> *type URI repository category-list*

where *type* is **deb** for packages of executable files and **deb-src** for packages of source files; *URI* is the location of the repository, usually **cdrom** or an Internet address that starts with **http://**; *repository* is the name of the repository apt-get is to search; and *category-list* is a SPACE-separated list of categories apt-get selects packages from. Comments begin with a pound sign (#) anywhere on a line and end at the end of the line.

The following line from **sources.list** on an Ubuntu system causes apt-get to search the Jaunty archive located at us.archive.ubuntu.com/ubuntu for **deb** packages that contain executable files. It accepts packages that are categorized as **main, restricted,** and **multiverse:**

```
deb http://us.archive.ubuntu.com/ubuntu/ jaunty main restricted multiverse
```

Replace **deb** with **deb-src** to search for packages of source files in the same manner. Use the apt-get **source** command to download source packages.

Default repositories   The default **sources.list** file on an Ubuntu system includes repositories such as **jaunty** (Jaunty as originally released), **jaunty-updates** (major bug fixes after the release of Jaunty), **jaunty-security** (critical security-related updates), and **backports** (newer, less-tested software that is not reviewed by the Ubuntu security team). Some repositories in **sources.list** may be commented out. Remove the leading pound sign (#) on the lines of the repositories you want to enable. After you modify **sources.list**, give the command **apt-get update** (page 917) to update the local package indexes.

The next line, which was added to **sources.list**, enables apt-get to search a third-party repository (but see the following security tip):

```
deb http://download.skype.com/linux/repos/debian/ stable non-free
```

In this case, the repository is named **stable** and the category is **non-free.** Although the code is compiled for Debian, it runs on Ubuntu, as is frequently the case.

Use repositories you trust

security   There are many repositories of software packages. Be selective in which repositories you add to **sources.list**: When you add a repository, you are trusting the person who runs the repository not to put malicious software in packages you may download. In addition, unsupported packages may conflict with other packages or cause upgrades to fail.

BitTorrent

The BitTorrent protocol implements a hybrid client/server and *P2P* (page 970) file transfer mechanism. BitTorrent efficiently distributes large amounts of static data, such as the Linux installation ISO images. It can replace protocols such as anonymous FTP, where client authentication is not required. Each BitTorrent client that downloads a file provides additional bandwidth for uploading the file, thereby reducing the load on the initial source. In general, BitTorrent downloads proceed more rapidly than FTP downloads. Unlike protocols such as FTP, BitTorrent groups multiple files into a single package: a BitTorrent file.

Tracker, peer, seed, and swarm BitTorrent, like other P2P systems, does not use a dedicated server. Instead, the functions of a server are performed by the tracker, peers, and seeds. The *tracker* is a server that allows clients to communicate with each other. Each client—called a *peer* when it has downloaded part of the BitTorrent file and a *seed* once it has downloaded the entire BitTorrent file—acts as an additional source for the BitTorrent file. Peers and seeds are collectively called a *swarm*. As with a P2P network, a member of a swarm uploads to other clients the sections of the BitTorrent file it has already downloaded. There is nothing special about a seed: It can be removed at any time once the torrent is available for download from other seeds.

The torrent The first step in downloading a BitTorrent file is to locate or acquire the *torrent*, a file with the filename extension of **.torrent**. A torrent contains pertinent information (metadata) about the BitTorrent file to be downloaded, such as its size and the location of the tracker. You can obtain a torrent by accessing its URI, or you can acquire it via the Web, an email attachment, or other means. The BitTorrent client can then connect to the tracker to learn the locations of other members of the swarm that it can download the BitTorrent file from.

Manners Once you have downloaded a BitTorrent file (i.e., the local system has become a seed), it is good manners to allow the local BitTorrent client to continue to run so peers (clients that have not downloaded the entire BitTorrent file) can download *at least* as much information as you have downloaded.

Prerequisites

If necessary, use yum (page 910) or apt-get (page 916) to install the **bittorrent** package. With this package installed, the command **apropos bittorrent** displays a list of BitTorrent utilities. See **/usr/share/doc/bittorrent** for more information. You may want to try BitTornado, an experimental BitTorrent client with additional features (**bittornado** package; see bittornado.com)

Because the BitTorrent utilities are written in Python and run on any platform with a Python interpreter, they do not depend on system architecture. Python is installed in **/usr/bin/python** and is available in the **python** package.

USING BITTORRENT

The btdownloadcurses utility is a textual BitTorrent client that provides a pseudo-graphical interface. Once you have a torrent, give a command such as the following, substituting the name of the torrent you want to download for the Ubuntu torrent in the example:

```
$ btdownloadcurses ubuntu-9.04-desktop-i386.iso.torrent
```

In the preceding command, the torrent specifies that the BitTorrent file be saved as **ubuntu-9.04-desktop-i386.iso** in the working directory. The name of the BitTorrent file is not always the same as the name of the torrent. In the case of a multifile torrent, the BitTorrent files may be stored in a directory, also named by the torrent. Depending on the speed of the Internet connection and the number of seeds, downloading a large BitTorrent file can take anywhere from hours to days. Following is what btdownloadcurses looks like when it is running:

```
------------------------------------------------
| file:     ubuntu-9.04-desktop-i386.iso        |
| size:     732,909,568 (699.0  M)              |
| dest:     /p02/ubuntu-9.04-desktop-i386.iso   |
| progress: ########_____ |
| status:   finishing in 0:21:13 (23.6%)        |
| speed:    449.7  K/s down -                   |
| totals:    23.6  M   down -                   |
| error(s):                                     |
|                                               |
------------------------------------------------
```

You can abort the download by pressing **q** or CONTROL-C. The download will automatically resume from where it left off when you download the same torrent to the same location again.

Make sure you have enough room to download the torrent

caution   Some torrents are huge. Make sure the partition you are working in has enough room to hold the BitTorrent file you are downloading.

See the btdownloadcurses man page for a list of options. One of the most useful options is **--max_upload_rate**, which limits how much bandwidth the swarm can use while downloading the torrent *from you*. The default is 0, meaning there is no limit to the upload bandwidth. The following command prevents BitTorrent from using more than 10 kilobytes per second of upstream bandwidth:

```
$ btdownloadcurses --max_upload_rate 10 ubuntu-9.04-desktop-i386.iso.torrent
```

BitTorrent usually allows higher download rates for members of the swarm that upload more data, so it is to your advantage to increase this value if you have spare bandwidth. You need to leave enough free upstream bandwidth for the acknowledgment packets from your download to get through or else the download will be very slow. By default, btdownloadcurses uploads to a maximum of seven other clients at once. You can change this number by using the **−−max_uploads** argument, followed by the number of concurrent uploads you wish to permit. If you are downloading over a modem, try setting **−−max_upload_rate** to 3 and **−−max_uploads** to **2**.

The name of the file or directory that BitTorrent saves a file or files in is specified by the torrent. You can specify a different file or directory name by using the **−−saveas** option. The btshowmetainfo utility displays the name the BitTorrent file will be saved as, the size of the file, the name of the torrent (**metainfo file**), and other information:

```
$ btshowmetainfo ubuntu-9.04-desktop-i386.iso.torrent
btshowmetainfo 20021207 - decode BitTorrent metainfo files

metainfo file.: ubuntu-9.04-desktop-i386.iso.torrent
info hash.....: 60d5d82328b4547511fdeac9bf4d0112daa0ce00
file name.....: ubuntu-9.04-desktop-i386.iso
file size.....: 732909568 (1397 * 524288 + 479232)
announce url..: http://torrent.ubuntu.com:6969/announce
```

D

MAC OS X NOTES

This appendix is a brief guide to Mac OS X features that differ from those of Linux. See Chapter 1 for a history of UNIX, Linux, and OS X.

OPEN DIRECTORY

Open Directory replaced the monolithic NetInfo database in Mac OS X version 10.5. The ni* utilities, including nireport and nidump, were replaced by dscl (page 674). The work the **lookupd** daemon did is now done by the **DirectoryService** daemon.

For information on the local system, both Mac OS X and Mac OS X Server now use a hierarchy of small *.plist XML files called *nodes*, which are stored in the **/var/db/dslocal** hierarchy. Many of these files are human readable. On Mac OS X Server, a network-wide Open Directory is based on OpenLDAP, Kerberos, and the SASL-based Password Server.

/etc/passwd   Because OS X does not use the **/etc/passwd** file to store most user information, examples in this book that use this file do not run under OS X. In most cases you must use dscl to extract information from the **passwd** database. As an example, the **whos2** program (following) is a version of **whos** (page 413) that runs under OS X 10.5 and later.

whos2   For each command-line argument, **whos2** searches the **passwd** database. Inside the **for** loop, the dscl (page 674) –readall command lists all usernames and user IDs on the local system. The command looks for the **RealName** keys in the **/Users** directory and displays the associated values. The four-line sed (page 565) command deletes lines containing only a dash (**/^-$/ d**), finds lines containing only **RealName:** (**/^RealName:$/**), reads and appends the next line (**N**; page 568), and substitutes a semicolon for the NEWLINE (**s/\n/; /**). Finally, grep (page 719) selects lines containing the ID the program was called with.

```
$ cat whos2
#!/bin/bash

if [ $# -eq 0 ]
    then
        echo "Usage: whos id..." 1>&2
        exit 1
fi

for id
do
    dscl . -readall /Users RealName |
    sed '/^-$/ d
        /^RealName:$/N;s/\n//
        N
        s/\n/; /'                    |
    grep -i "$id"
done
```

/etc/group   *Groups* (page 956) allow users to share files or programs without allowing all system users access to them. This scheme is useful if several users are working with files that are not public. In a Linux system, the **/etc/group** file associates one or more usernames with each group (number). Mac OS X 10.5 and later rely on

Open Directory (page 926) to provide group information. OS X 10.4 and earlier use NetInfo for this task.

FILESYSTEMS

Mac OS X supports several types of filesystems. The most commonly used is the default HFS+ (Hierarchical File System plus). Introduced under Mac OS 8.1 to support larger disks, HFS+ is an enhanced version of the original HFS filesystem. When it was introduced in OS 3.0 in 1986, HFS stood in contrast to the then-standard MFS (Macintosh File System). Some applications will not run correctly under filesystems other than HFS+. HFS+ filesystems do not have *inodes* (page 959) but, through an elaborate scheme, appear to have inodes.

HFS+ is different from Linux filesystems, but because Linux offers a standardized filesystem interface, the differences are generally transparent to the user. The most significant difference lies in the handling of extended attributes (page 928).

OS X also supports Linux filesystems such as UFS (UNIX File System), which it inherited from Berkeley UNIX. Other supported filesystems include FAT16 and FAT32, which were originally used in MS-DOS and Windows. These filesystems are typically used on removable media, such as digital camera storage cards. Also supported is ISO9660, which is used on CD-ROMs, and the related UDF filesystem, which is used on DVDs.

NONDISK FILESYSTEMS

Mac OS X supports filesystems that do not correspond to a physical volume such as a partition on a hard disk or a CD-ROM. A **.dmg** (disk image) file is one example (you can mount a disk image file so you can access the files it holds by double-clicking it in the Finder). Another example is a virtual filesystem in which the filenames represent kernel functionality. For example, the **/Network** virtual filesystem holds a directory tree representing the local network; most network filesystem protocols use this filesystem. Also, you can use the Disk Utility to create encrypted or password-protected **.iso** (*ISO9660*; page 961) image files you can mount.

CASE SENSITIVITY

The default OS X filesystem, HFS+, is case preserving but not case sensitive. *Case preserving* means the filesystem remembers which capitalization you used when you created a file and displays the filename with that capitalization, but accepts any capitalization to refer to the file. Thus, under HFS+, files named **JANUARY**, **January**, and **january** refer to the same file. The HFS+ Extended (HFSX) filesystem is case sensitive and is fully supported under Mac OS X Server only. Because HFSX is case sensitive, the three example filenames refer to three different files.

/Volumes

Each physical hard disk in a Mac OS X system is typically divided into one or more logical sections (partitions) that, when formatted, are called *volumes*. On a Linux system they are called *filesystems*.

Startup disk   Each OS X system has a volume, called the *startup disk,* that the system boots from. By default the startup disk is named **Macintosh HD**. When the system boots, **Macintosh HD** is mounted as the root directory (**/**).

The root directory always has a subdirectory named **Volumes**. For historical reasons, every volume other than the startup disk is mounted in the **/Volumes** directory. The pathname of a disk labeled **MyPhotos** is **/Volumes/MyPhotos**.

To simplify access, **/Volumes** holds a symbolic link (page 108) to the startup disk (the root directory). Assuming that the startup disk is named **Macintosh HD**, **/Volumes/Macintosh HD** is a symbolic link to **/**.

```
$ ls -ld '/Volumes/Macintosh HD'
lrwxr-xr-x   1 root   admin  1 Jul 12 19:03 /Volumes/Macintosh HD -> /
```

The system automatically mounts all volumes in **/Volumes**. The desktop presented by the Finder contains an icon for each mounted disk and for files in the user's **Desktop** directory, making the **/Volumes** directory the effective root (top level or **/**) for the Finder and other applications. The Finder presents the pre-UNIX Mac OS view of the filesystem. The files in **/Volumes** are the same as the first components of Carbon pathnames.

CARBON PATHNAMES

Carbon pathnames differ from OS X pathnames and are discussed here because many applications use them. Some operating system features are accessible through Carbon API calls only.

The Carbon environment uses the historical Macintosh model of a *desktop* holding mounted disks, which does not correspond well to the Linux filesystem's single-directory hierarchy. Furthermore, the Carbon environment represents pathnames differently from the Linux environment. Carbon pathnames use a colon (**:**) as a separator, instead of a slash (**/**). No top-level root exists for Carbon pathnames; instead, they start with the name of a disk. For example, the Linux-style pathname **/Volumes/Images/backups** equates to the Carbon-style pathname **Images:backups**.

Know which kind of pathname you are using

caution   If you enter a Linux pathname when a Carbon pathname is expected, or vice versa, the system may display an error message, not retrieve the correct file, or save the file in the wrong location.

EXTENDED ATTRIBUTES

Mac OS X files have *extended attributes,* which include file attributes used by the Finder, Access Control Lists, and resource forks. Not all utilities recognize extended attributes. This section describes extended attributes, which include resource forks, file attributes, and ACLs.

Resource forks and file attributes are native to the HFS+ filesystem. Mac OS X emulates resource forks and file attributes on other types of filesystems. These features are not found on Linux filesystems.

Some utilities do not process extended attributes

caution   Some third-party programs and most utilities under Mac OS X 10.3 and earlier do not support extended attributes. Some utilities require options to process extended attributes.

Some utilities, on systems with ACLs enabled, have a bug involving extended attributes. For more information, see the "Enabling ACLs may cause errors" caution on page 932.

See also the tip "Redirection does not support resource forks" on page 930.

FILE FORKS

Forks are segments of a single file, each holding different content. Mac OS has supported file forks since its inception. The most widely used are the *data fork* and the *resource fork*.

Data forks   The data fork is equivalent to a Linux file. It consists of an unstructured stream of bytes. Many files have only a data fork.

Resource forks   The resource fork holds a database that allows random access to resources, each of which has a type and identifier number. Modifying, adding, or deleting one resource has no effect on the other resources. Resource forks can store different types of information—some critical and some merely useful. For example, a Mac OS graphics program might save a smaller copy of an image (a preview or thumbnail) in a resource fork. Also, text files created with the BBEdit text editor store display size and tab stop information in the file's resource fork. Because this program is a text editor and not a word processor, this type of information cannot be stored in the data fork. Losing a resource fork that holds a thumbnail or display information is at most an inconvenience because, for example, the thumbnail can be regenerated from the original image. Other programs store more important data in the resource fork or create files that contain only a resource fork, which contains all the file's information. In this case, losing the resource fork is just as bad as losing the data fork. It may even be worse: You may not notice a resource fork is missing because the data fork is still there. You might notice the loss only when you try to use the file.

A Linux filesystem associates each filename with a single stream of bytes. Forks do not fit this model. As a result, many Linux utilities do not process resource forks, but instead process only data forks. Most of the file utilities provided with OS X 10.4 and later support resource forks. Many third-party utilities do not support resource forks.

Pipes do not work with resource forks

caution   Pipes work with the data fork of a file only; they do not work with resource forks.

Redirection does not support resource forks

caution   When you redirect input to or output from a utility (page 126), only the information in the data fork is redirected. Information in the resource fork is not redirected. For example, the following command copies the data fork of **song.ogg** only:

```
$ cat song.ogg > song.bak.ogg
```

optional
..namedfork   You can verify the existence of file forks on an HFS+ filesystem. The **..namedfork** pseudodirectory, as a subdirectory of a file, holds files that correspond to a file's forks. The two most common files are **data**, which holds the data fork, and **rsrc**, which holds the resource fork. The following example shows how to use **..namedfork** to verify the existence of and display the size of the data and resource forks associated with the **pic.jpg** file. You cannot list the **..namedfork** pseudodirectory.

```
$ ls -l pic.jpg
-rwxr-xr-x   1 max   max   13432 Jul 18 15:15 pic.jpg
$ ls -l pic.jpg/..namedfork
ls: pic.jpg/..namedfork: Not a directory
$ ls -l pic.jpg/..namedfork/data
-rwxr-xr-x   1 max   max   13432 Jul 18 15:15 pic.jpg/..namedfork/data
$ ls -l pic.jpg/..namedfork/rsrc
-rwxr-xr-x   1 max   max   140622 Jul 18 15:15 pic.jpg/..namedfork/rsrc
```

The **data** file is human readable if the underlying file is human readable. The **rsrc** file is not in a strictly human-readable format, although you may be able to garner some information by viewing these files.

If you are unsure whether a program supports resource forks, test it before relying on this functionality. Make a backup copy using the Finder, ditto, or, under version 10.4 and later, cp. Then check whether the copied file works correctly.

Table D-1 lists utilities that manipulate resource forks. These utilities are installed with the Developer Tools package. Consult the respective man pages for detailed descriptions.

Table D-1   Utilities that manipulate resource forks

Utility	Function
Rez	Creates a resource fork from a resource description file
DeRez	Creates a resource description file from a resource fork
RezWack	Converts a file with forks to a single flat file that holds all the forks
UnRezWack	Converts a flat file that holds forks to a file with forks
SplitForks	Converts a file with forks to multiple files, each holding a fork

FILE ATTRIBUTES

A file contains data. Information about the file is called *metadata*. Examples of metadata include ownership information and permissions for a file. Mac OS X stores more metadata than Linux stores. This section discusses *file attributes*, the metadata stored by Mac OS X.

File attributes include the following:

- Attribute flags
- Type codes
- Creator codes

The same caveats apply to file attributes as apply to resource forks: Some utilities may not preserve them when copying or manipulating files, and many utilities do not recognize attribute flags. Loss of file attributes is particularly common when you move files to non-Macintosh systems.

ATTRIBUTE FLAGS

Attribute flags (Table D-2) hold information that is distinct from Linux permissions. Two attribute flags are the invisible flag (which keeps a file from being displayed in file dialogs and in the Finder) and the locked flag (which keeps a file from being modified). Flags are generally ignored by command-line utilities and affect only GUI applications. The ls utility lists files that have the invisible flag set. See GetFileInfo on page 717 and SetFile on page 813 for information on displaying, setting, and clearing attribute flags.

Table D-2   Attribute flags

Flag	Can the flag be set on a directory?	Description
a	No	Alias file
c	Yes	Custom icon
l	No	Locked
t	No	Stationery pad file
v	Yes	Invisible

CREATOR CODES AND TYPE CODES

Type codes and creator codes are 32-bit integers, generally displayed as 4-character words, that specify the type and creator of a file. The creator code specifies the application that created a document, not the user who created it. An application can typically open documents that have the same creator code as the application, but cannot open documents with other creator codes.

Creator codes   Creator codes generally correspond to vendors or product lines. The operating system—and in particular the Finder—uses creator codes to group related files. For example, the AppleWorks application file and its document files have the creator code **BOBO**. In the file browser in an application's open file dialog box, grayed-out files generally indicate files that have a different creator code from the application. The open utility (page 780) also looks at creator codes when it opens a file.

Type codes   Type codes indicate how a file is used. The type code **APPL** indicates an application, a program used to open other files. For example, an AppleWorks word processor document has the type code **CWWP**, a mnemonic for Claris Works Word Processor (AppleWorks used to be named Claris Works). While a few type codes, such as the application type, are standardized, vendors are free to invent new type codes for their programs. A single application may support several document types. For example, AppleWorks supports spreadsheet files (**CWSS**), word processor documents (**CWWP**), and drawings (**CWGR**). Similarly a graphics program will typically support many document types. Data files used by an application may also have the same creator code as the application, even though they cannot be opened as documents. For example, the dictionary used by a spelling checker cannot be opened as a document but typically uses the same creator code as the spelling checker.

Filename extensions   Filename extensions (page 81) can substitute for type and creator codes. For example, an AppleWorks word processor document is saved with an extension of **.cwk**. Also, if open cannot determine which application to use to open a file using the file's creator code, it reverts to using the file's filename extension.

FINDER ALIASES VERSUS SYMBOLIC LINKS

A Macintosh Finder alias is similar to a symbolic link or a Windows shortcut, but a Finder alias is *not* a symbolic link. Conversely, the Finder recognizes a symbolic link as though it were a Finder alias. A Finder alias points to a pathname, no matter where it is. Only if no target remains at the pathname does a Finder alias fall back to the file ID. Finder aliases work like resilient symbolic links as long as the target file is still on the same volume.

ACLs

ACLs (Access Control Lists) are discussed on page 99. This section discusses how to enable and work with ACLs under Mac OS X.

Enabling ACLs may cause errors

caution   Enabling ACLs on a filesystem prevents some programs that handle extended attributes (page 928) from working correctly. If a file has a resource fork but no ACL, attempts to copy it may fail with an error message such as the following:

```
$ pax -w -f arch.pax picture.jpg
pax: Unable to open ._picture.jpg to read <No such file or directory>
```

Some utilities, such as cp, are not affected by this problem.

fsaclctl: ENABLING AND DISABLING ACLs

Under Mac OS X, the fsaclctl (file system ACL control) utility can report on or change ACL support status on one or more volumes (filesystems).

With the **–p** option, fsaclctl reports on the support status for the volume you specify as an argument to **–p**:

```
$ fsaclctl -p /
Access control lists are supported on /.
```

Use the **–a** option without an argument to display the support status for all mounted volumes.

You must use the **–p** option to specify a volume when you change the status of a volume. The fsaclctl **–e** option enables ACL support on the specified volume(s); the **–d** option disables ACL support. You must work using **root** privileges to enable and disable ACL support.

The following example first disables (**–d**) ACL support on the root filesystem (**/**) and then verifies support is disabled. Next it enables (**–e**) support and again verifies the change.

```
$ sudo fsaclctl -p / -d
$ fsaclctl -p /
Access control lists are not supported or currently disabled on /.

$ sudo fsaclctl -p / -e
$ fsaclctl -p /
Access control lists are supported on /.
```

chmod: WORKING WITH ACLs

Under Mac OS X, you can use chmod (page 626) to create, modify, and delete ACL rules. A chmod command used for this purpose has the following format:

chmod option[# n] "who allow|deny permission-list" file-list

where *option* is **+a** (add rule), **–a** (remove rule), or **=a** (change rule); *n* is an optional rule number; *who* is a username, user ID number, group name, or group ID number; *permission-list* is one or more comma-separated file access permissions selected from **read**, **write**, **append**, and **execute**; and *file-list* is the list of files the rule is applied to. The quotation marks are required. In the first example, Sam adds a rule that grants Helen read and write access to the **memo** file:

```
$ chmod +a "helen allow read,write" memo
```

The chmod utility displays an error message if you forget the quotation marks:

```
$ chmod +a max deny write memo
chmod: Invalid entry format -- expected allow or deny
```

ls –l   An ls –l command displays a plus sign (+) following the permissions for a file that has an ACL (see also Figure 4-12 on page 94):

```
$ ls -l memo
-rw-r--r--+ 1 sam   staff  1680 May 12 13:30 memo
```

ls –le   Under Mac OS X, the ls –e option displays ACL rules:

```
$ ls -le memo
-rw-r--r--+ 1 sam   staff  1680 May 12 13:30 memo
 0: user:helen allow read,write
```

For each rule, the –e option displays from left to right the rule number followed by a colon, **user:** or **group:** followed by the name of the user or group the rule pertains to, **allow** or **deny** depending on whether the rule grants or denies permissions, and a list of the permissions that are granted or denied.

The kernel processes multiple rules in an ACL in rule number order. The kernel does not necessarily number rules in the order you enter them. In general, rules denying permissions come before rules granting permissions. You can override the default order by assigning a number to a rule using the **+a#** *n* syntax. The following command bumps rule 0 from the previous example to rule 1 and replaces it with a rule that denies Max write access to **memo**:

```
$ chmod +a# 0 "max deny write" memo
$ ls -le memo
-rw-r--r--+ 1 sam   staff  1680 May 12 13:30 memo
 0: user:max deny write
 1: user:helen allow read,write
```

There are two ways to remove access rules. First, you can specify a rule by using its number:

```
$ chmod -a# 1 memo
$ ls -le memo
-rw-r--r--+ 1 sam   staff  1680 May 12 13:30 memo
 0: user:max deny write
```

Second, you can specify a rule by using the string you used when you added it:

```
$ chmod -a "max deny write" memo
$ ls -le memo
-rw-r--r--  1 sam   staff  1680 May 12 13:30 memo
```

After you remove the last rule, **memo** does not have an ACL. (There is no **+** in the line ls –le displays.) When you specify an ACL operation that chmod cannot complete, it displays an error message:

```
$ chmod -a# 0 memo
chmod: No ACL present
```

In the next example, Sam restores Helen's read and write permission to **memo**:

```
$ chmod +a "helen allow read,write" memo
$ ls -le memo
-rw-r--r--+ 1 sam  staff  1680 May 12 13:30 memo
 0: user:helen allow read,write
```

Sam then removes the write permissions he just gave Helen. When you remove one of several access permissions from a rule, the other permissions remain unchanged:

```
$ chmod -a "helen allow write" memo
$ ls -le memo
-rw-r--r--+ 1 sam  staff  1680 May 12 13:30 memo
 0: user:helen allow read
```

The next example shows that chmod inserts rules in an ACL in a default order. Even though Sam added the **allow** rule before the **deny** rule, the **allow** rule appears first. The rule controlling permission for Helen, which was added before either of the other rules, appears last.

```
$ chmod +a "max allow read" memo
$ chmod +a "max deny read" memo
$ ls -le memo
-rw-r--r--+ 1 sam  staff  1680 May 12 13:30 memo
 0: user:max deny read
 1: user:max allow read
 2: user:helen allow read
```

You can replace a rule using the **=a** syntax. In the following example, Sam changes rule 2 to grant Helen read and write permission to **memo**:

```
$ chmod =a# 2 "helen allow read,write" memo
$ ls -le memo
-rw-r--r--+ 1 sam  staff  1680 May 12 13:30 memo
 0: user:max deny read
 1: user:max allow read
 2: user:helen allow read,write
```

ACTIVATING THE META KEY

Under Mac OS X, in the Terminal utility, you can make the OPTION (or ALT) key work as the META key. From the Terminal utility **File** menu, select **Window Settings** to display the Terminal Inspector window. This window provides a drop-down menu of properties you can change. Select **Keyboard**, check the box labeled **Use option key as meta key**, and click **Use Settings as Defaults**. This procedure causes the OPTION key (on Mac keyboards) or the ALT key (on PC keyboards) to function as the META key *while you are using the* Terminal *utility*.

STARTUP FILES

Both Mac OS and application documentation refer to startup files as *configuration files* or *preference files*. Many Mac OS X applications store startup files in the **Library** and **Library/Preferences** subdirectories of a user's home directory, which are created when an account is set up. Most of these files do not have invisible filenames.

REMOTE LOGINS

By default Mac OS X does not allow remote logins. You can enable remote logins via ssh by enabling remote login in the **Services** tab of the Sharing pane of the Preferences window. OS X does not support telnet logins.

MANY UTILITIES DO NOT RESPECT APPLE HUMAN INTERFACE GUIDELINES

By default rm under Mac OS X does not act according to the Apple Human Interface Guidelines, which state that an operation should either be reversible or ask for confirmation. In general, Mac OS X command-line utilities do not ask whether you are sure of what you are doing.

MAC OS X IMPLEMENTATION OF LINUX FEATURES

Table D-3 explains how some Linux features are implemented under Mac OS X.

Table D-3   Mac OS X implementation of Linux features

Linux feature	OS X implementation
/bin/sh	The **/bin/sh** is a copy of bash (**/bin/bash**); it is not a link to **/bin/bash** as it is on most Linux systems. The original Bourne Shell does not exist under OS X. When you call bash using the command sh, bash tries to mimic the behavior of the original Bourne Shell as closely as possible.
Core files	By default OS X does not save core files. When core files are saved, they are kept in **/cores**, not in the working directory.
Developer tools	The Developer Tools package, which includes the gcc compiler, is not installed by default.

Table D-3   Mac OS X implementation of Linux features (continued)

Linux feature	OS X implementation
Development APIs	Mac OS X uses three software development APIs: Cocoa, Carbon, and BSD UNIX.
Dynamic linker ld.so	The OS X dynamic linker is **dyld**, not ld.so.
ELF and **a.out** binary formats	The primary binary format under OS X is Mach-O, not ELF or **a.out**.
/etc/group	Mac OS X uses OpenDirectory (page 926), not **/etc/group**, to store group information.
/etc/passwd	Mac OS X uses OpenDirectory (page 926), not **/etc/passwd**, to store user accounts.
Filesystem structure **/etc/fstab**	Instead of filesystems being mounted according to settings in **/etc/fstab**, filesystems are automatically mounted in the **/Volumes** directory (page 928).
finger	By default, Mac OS X disables remote finger support.
LD_LIBRARY_PATH	The variable used to control the dynamic linker is **DYLD_LIBRARY_PATH**, not **LD_LIBRARY_PATH**.
System databases	Some system databases, such as **passwd** and **group**, are stored by Open-Directory (page 926), not in the **/etc** directory (page 92). You can work with OpenDirectory databases using the **dscl** utility (page 674).
vi editor	As with many Linux distributions, when you call the vi editor, Mac OS X 10.3 and later run vim (page 149) because the file **/usr/bin/vi** is a link to **/usr/bin/vim**.

GLOSSARY

All entries marked with ^{FOLDOC} are based on definitions in the Free On-Line Dictionary of Computing (www.foldoc.org), Denis Howe, editor. Used with permission.

10.0.0.0	See *private address space* on page 972.
172.16.0.0	See *private address space* on page 972.
192.168.0.0	See *private address space* on page 972.
802.11	A family of specifications developed by IEEE for wireless LAN technology, including 802.11 (1–2 megabits per second), 802.11a (54 megabits per second), 802.11b (11 megabits per second), and 802.11g (54 megabits per second).
absolute pathname	A pathname that starts with the root directory (represented by /). An absolute pathname locates a file without regard to the working directory.
access	In computer jargon, a verb meaning to use, read from, or write to. To access a file means to read from or write to the file.
Access Control List	See *ACL*.
access permissions	Permission to read from, write to, or execute a file. If you have write access permission to a file (usually just called *write permission*), you can write to the file. Also *access privilege*.
ACL	Access Control List. A system that performs a function similar to file permissions but with much finer-grain control.
active window	On a desktop, the window that receives the characters you type on the keyboard. Same as *focus, desktop* (page 955).
address mask	See *subnet mask* on page 981.
alias	A mechanism of a shell that enables you to define new commands.
alphanumeric character	One of the characters, either uppercase or lowercase, from A to Z and 0 to 9, inclusive.
ambiguous file reference	A reference to a file that does not necessarily specify any one file but can be used to specify a group of files. The shell expands an ambiguous file reference into a list of filenames. Special characters represent single characters (?), strings of zero or more characters (*), and character classes ([]) within ambiguous file references. An ambiguous file reference is a type of *regular expression* (page 975).
angle bracket	A left angle bracket (<) and a right angle bracket (>). The shell uses < to redirect a command's standard input to come from a file and > to redirect the standard output. The shell uses the characters << to signify the start of a Here document and >> to append output to a file.
animate	When referring to a window action, means that the action is slowed down so the user can view it. For example, when you minimize a window, it can disappear all at once (not animated) or it can slowly telescope into the panel so you can get a visual feel for what is happening (animated).

anti-aliasing   Adding gray pixels at the edge of a diagonal line to get rid of the jagged appearance and thereby make the line look smoother. Anti-aliasing sometimes makes type on a screen look better and sometimes worse; it works best on small and large fonts and is less effective on fonts from 8 to 15 points. See also *subpixel hinting* (page 981).

API   Application program interface. The interface (calling conventions) by which an application program accesses an operating system and other services. An API is defined at the source code level and provides a level of abstraction between the application and the kernel (or other privileged utilities) to ensure the portability of the code.^{FOLDOC}

append   To add something to the end of something else. To append text to a file means to add the text to the end of the file. The shell uses **>>** to append a command's output to a file.

applet   A small program that runs within a larger program. Examples are Java applets that run in a browser and panel applets that run from a desktop panel.

archive   A file that contains a group of smaller, typically related, files. Also, to create such a file. The tar and cpio utilities can create and read archives.

argument   A number, letter, filename, or another string that gives some information to a command and is passed to the command when it is called. A command-line argument is anything on a command line following the command name that is passed to the command. An option is a kind of argument.

arithmetic expression   A group of numbers, operators, and parentheses that can be evaluated. When you evaluate an arithmetic expression, you end up with a number. The Bourne Again Shell uses the expr command to evaluate arithmetic expressions; the TC Shell uses @, and the Z Shell uses let.

array   An arrangement of elements (numbers or strings of characters) in one or more dimensions. The Bourne Again, TC, and Z Shells and mawk/gawk can store and process arrays.

ASCII   American Standard Code for Information Interchange. A code that uses seven bits to represent both graphic (letters, numbers, and punctuation) and CONTROL characters. You can represent textual information, including program source code and English text, in ASCII code. Because ASCII is a standard, it is frequently used when exchanging information between computers. See the file **/usr/pub/ascii** or give the command **man ascii** to see a list of ASCII codes.

Extensions of the ASCII character set use eight bits. The seven-bit set is common; the eight-bit extensions are still coming into popular use. The eighth bit is sometimes referred to as the metabit.

ASCII terminal   A textual terminal. Contrast with *graphical display* (page 956).

ASP   Application service provider. A company that provides applications over the Internet.

asynchronous event

An event that does not occur regularly or synchronously with another event. Linux system signals are asynchronous; they can occur at any time because they can be initiated by any number of nonregular events.

attachment

A file that is attached to, but is not part of, a piece of email. Attachments are frequently opened by programs (including your Internet browser) that are called by your mail program so you may not be aware that they are not an integral part of an email message.

authentication

The verification of the identity of a person or process. In a communication system, authentication verifies that a message comes from its stated source. Methods of authentication on a Linux system include the **/etc/passwd** and **/etc/shadow** files, LDAP, Kerberos 5, and SMB authentication.FOLDOC

automatic mounting

A way of demand mounting directories from remote hosts without having them hard configured into **/etc/fstab**. Also called *automounting*.

avoided

An object, such as a panel, that should not normally be covered by another object, such as a window.

back door

A security hole deliberately left in place by the designers or maintainers of a system. The motivation for creating such holes is not always sinister; some operating systems, for example, come out of the box with privileged accounts intended for use by field service technicians or the vendor's maintenance programmers.

Ken Thompson's 1983 Turing Award lecture to the ACM revealed the existence, in early UNIX versions, of a back door that may be the most fiendishly clever security hack of all time. The C compiler contained code that would recognize when the **login** command was being recompiled and would insert some code recognizing a password chosen by Thompson, giving him entry to the system whether or not an account had been created for him.

Normally such a back door could be removed by removing it from the source code for the compiler and recompiling the compiler. But to recompile the compiler, you have to *use* the compiler, so Thompson arranged that the compiler would *recognize when it was compiling a version of itself.* It would insert into the recompiled compiler the code to insert into the recompiled **login** the code to allow Thompson entry, and, of course, the code to recognize itself and do the whole thing again the next time around. Having done this once, he was then able to recompile the compiler from the original sources; the hack perpetuated itself invisibly, leaving the back door in place and active but with no trace in the sources.

Sometimes called a wormhole. Also *trap door.*FOLDOC

background process

A process that is not run in the foreground. Also called a *detached process*, a background process is initiated by a command line that ends with an ampersand (**&**). You do not have to wait for a background process to run to completion before giving the shell additional commands. If you have job control, you can move background processes to the foreground, and vice versa.

basename	The name of a file that, in contrast with a pathname, does not mention any of the directories containing the file (and therefore does not contain any slashes [/]). For example, **hosts** is the basename of **/etc/hosts**.^{FOLDOC}
baud	The maximum information-carrying capacity of a communication channel in symbols (state transitions or level transitions) per second. It coincides with bits per second only for two-level modulation with no framing or stop bits. A symbol is a unique state of the communication channel, distinguishable by the receiver from all other possible states. For example, it may be one of two voltage levels on a wire for a direct digital connection, or it might be the phase or frequency of a carrier.^{FOLDOC}
	Baud is often mistakenly used as a synonym for bits per second.
baud rate	Transmission speed. Usually used to measure terminal or modem speed. Common baud rates range from 110 to 38,400 baud. See *baud*.
Berkeley UNIX	One of the two major versions of the UNIX operating system. Berkeley UNIX was developed at the University of California at Berkeley by the Computer Systems Research Group and is often referred to as *BSD* (Berkeley Software Distribution).
BIND	Berkeley Internet Name Domain. An implementation of a *DNS* (page 951) server developed and distributed by the University of California at Berkeley.
BIOS	Basic Input/Output System. On PCs, *EEPROM*-based (page 953) system software that provides the lowest-level interface to peripheral devices and controls the first stage of the *bootstrap* (page 944) process, which loads the operating system. The BIOS can be stored in different types of memory. The memory must be nonvolatile so that it remembers the system settings even when the system is turned off. Also BIOS ROM.
bit	The smallest piece of information a computer can handle. A *bit* is a binary digit: either 1 or 0 (*on* or *off*).
bit depth	Same as *color depth* (page 947).
bit-mapped display	A graphical display device in which each pixel on the screen is controlled by an underlying representation of zeros and ones.
blank character	Either a SPACE or a TAB character, also called *whitespace* (page 987). In some contexts, NEWLINEs are considered blank characters.
block	A section of a disk or tape (usually 1,024 bytes long but shorter or longer on some systems) that is written at one time.
block device	A disk or tape drive. A block device stores information in blocks of characters. A block device is represented by a block device (block special) file. Contrast with *character device* (page 946).
block number	Disk and tape *blocks* are numbered so that Linux can keep track of the data on the device.

blocking factor The number of logical blocks that make up a physical block on a tape or disk. When you write 1K logical blocks to a tape with a physical block size of 30K, the blocking factor is 30.

Boolean The type of an expression with two possible values: *true* and *false*. Also, a variable of Boolean type or a function with Boolean arguments or result. The most common Boolean functions are AND, OR, and NOT.FOLDOC

boot See *bootstrap*.

boot loader A very small program that takes its place in the *bootstrap* process that brings a computer from off or reset to a fully functional state.

bootstrap Derived from "Pull oneself up by one's own bootstraps," the incremental process of loading an operating system kernel into memory and starting it running without any outside assistance. Frequently shortened to *boot*.

Bourne Again Shell bash. GNU's command interpreter for UNIX, bash is a POSIX-compliant shell with full Bourne Shell syntax and some C Shell commands built in. The Bourne Again Shell supports emacs-style command-line editing, job control, functions, and online help.FOLDOC

Bourne Shell sh. This UNIX command processor was developed by Steve Bourne at AT&T Bell Laboratories.

brace A left brace ({) and a right brace (}). Braces have special meanings to the shell.

bracket A *square bracket* (page 980) or an *angle bracket* (page 940).

branch In a tree structure, a branch connects nodes, leaves, and the root. The Linux filesystem hierarchy is often conceptualized as an upside-down tree. The branches connect files and directories. In a source code control system, such as SCCS or RCS, a branch occurs when a revision is made to a file and is not included in subsequent revisions to the file.

bridge Typically a two-port device originally used for extending networks at layer 2 (data link) of the Internet Protocol model.

broadcast A transmission to multiple, unspecified recipients. On Ethernet a broadcast packet is a special type of multicast packet that has a special address indicating that all devices that receive it should process it. Broadcast traffic exists at several layers of the network stack, including Ethernet and IP. Broadcast traffic has one source but indeterminate destinations (all hosts on the local network).

broadcast address The last address on a subnet (usually 255), reserved as shorthand to mean all hosts.

broadcast network A type of network, such as Ethernet, in which any system can transmit information at any time, and all systems receive every message.

BSD	See *Berkeley UNIX* on page 943.
buffer	An area of memory that stores data until it can be used. When you write information to a file on a disk, Linux stores the information in a disk buffer until there is enough to write to the disk or until the disk is ready to receive the information.
bug	An unwanted and unintended program property, especially one that causes the program to malfunction.[FOLDOC]
builtin (command)	A command that is built into a shell. Each of the three major shells—the Bourne Again, TC, and Z Shells—has its own set of builtins.
byte	A component in the machine data hierarchy, usually larger than a bit and smaller than a word; now most often eight bits and the smallest addressable unit of storage. A byte typically holds one character.[FOLDOC]
C programming language	A modern systems language that has high-level features for efficient, modular programming as well as lower-level features that make it suitable for use as a systems programming language. It is machine independent so that carefully written C programs can be easily transported to run on different machines. Most of the Linux operating system is written in C, and Linux provides an ideal environment for programming in C.
C Shell	csh. The C Shell command processor was developed by Bill Joy for BSD UNIX. It was named for the C programming language because its programming constructs are similar to those of C. See *shell* on page 978.
cable modem	A type of modem that allows you to access the Internet by using your cable television connection.
cache	Holding recently accessed data, a small, fast memory designed to speed up subsequent access to the same data. Most often applied to processor-memory access but also used for a local copy of data accessible over a network, from a hard disk, and so on.[FOLDOC]
calling environment	A list of variables and their values that is made available to a called program. Refer to "Executing a Command" on page 308.
cascading stylesheet	See *CSS* on page 949.
cascading windows	An arrangement of windows such that they overlap, generally with at least part of the title bar visible. Opposite of *tiled windows* (page 983).
case sensitive	Able to distinguish between uppercase and lowercase characters. Unless you set the **ignorecase** parameter, vim performs case-sensitive searches. The grep utility performs case-sensitive searches unless you use the –i option.
catenate	To join sequentially, or end to end. The Linux cat utility catenates files: It displays them one after the other. Also *concatenate*.

chain loading   The technique used by a boot loader to load unsupported operating systems. Used for loading such operating systems as DOS or Windows, it works by loading another boot loader.

character-based   A program, utility, or interface that works only with *ASCII* (page 941) characters. This set of characters includes some simple graphics, such as lines and corners, and can display colored characters. It cannot display true graphics. Contrast with *GUI* (page 956).

character-based terminal   A terminal that displays only characters and very limited graphics. See *character-based*.

character class   In a regular expression, a group of characters that defines which characters can occupy a single character position. A character-class definition is usually surrounded by square brackets. The character class defined by [**abcr**] represents a character position that can be occupied by **a**, **b**, **c**, or **r**. Also *list operator*.

In POSIX, used to refer to sets of characters with a common characteristic, denoted by the notation [:*class*:]; for example, [:upper:] denotes the set of uppercase letters.

This book uses the term character class as explained under "Brackets" on page 889.

character device   A terminal, printer, or modem. A character device stores or displays characters one at a time. A character device is represented by a character device (character special) file. Contrast with *block device* (page 943).

check box   A GUI widget, usually the outline of a square box with an adjacent caption, that a user can click to display or remove a *tick* (page 983). When the box holds a tick, the option described by the caption is on or true. Also *tick box*.

checksum   A computed value that depends on the contents of a block of data and is transmitted or stored along with the data to detect corruption of the data. The receiving system recomputes the checksum based on the received data and compares this value with the one sent with the data. If the two values are the same, the receiver has some confidence that the data was received correctly.

The checksum may be 8, 16, or 32 bits, or some other size. It is computed by summing the bytes or words of the data block, ignoring overflow. The checksum may be negated so that the total of the data words plus the checksum is zero.

Internet packets use a 32-bit checksum.FOLDOC

child process   A process that is created by another process, the parent process. Every process is a child process except for the first process, which is started when Linux begins execution. When you run a command from the shell, the shell spawns a child process to run the command. See *process* on page 972.

CIDR   Classless Inter-Domain Routing. A scheme that allocates blocks of Internet addresses in a way that allows summarization into a smaller number of routing table entries. A CIDR block is a block of Internet addresses assigned to an ISP by the Internic.FOLDOC

CIFS   Common Internet File System. An Internet filesystem protocol based on *SMB* (page 978). CIFS runs on top of TCP/IP, uses DNS, and is optimized to support slower dial-up Internet connections. SMB and CIFS are used interchangeably.[FOLDOC]

CIPE   Crypto IP *Encapsulation* (page 953). This *protocol* (page 973) *tunnels* (page 984) IP packets within encrypted *UDP* (page 984) packets, is lightweight and simple, and works over dynamic addresses, *NAT* (page 967), and *SOCKS* (page 979) *proxies* (page 973).

cipher (cypher)   A cryptographic system that uses a key to transpose/substitute characters within a message, the key itself, or the message.

ciphertext   Text that is encrypted. Contrast with *plaintext* (page 971).

Classless Inter-Domain Routing   See *CIDR* on page 946.

cleartext   Text that is not encrypted. Also *plaintext*. Contrast with *ciphertext*.

CLI   Command-line interface. See also *character-based* (page 946). Also *textual interface*.

client   A computer or program that requests one or more services from a server.

CODEC   Coder/decoder or compressor/decompressor. A hardware and/or software technology that codes and decodes data. MPEG is a popular CODEC for computer video.

color depth   The number of bits used to generate a pixel—usually 8, 16, 24, or 32. The color depth is directly related to the number of colors that can be generated. The number of colors that can be generated is 2 raised to the color-depth power. Thus a 24-bit video adapter can generate about 16.7 million colors.

color quality See *color depth*.

combo box   A combination of a *drop-down list* (page 952) and *text box* (page 983). You can enter text in a combo box. Or, you can click a combo box, cause it to expand and display a static list of selections for you to choose from.

command   What you give the shell in response to a prompt. When you give the shell a command, it executes a utility, another program, a builtin command, or a shell script. Utilities are often referred to as commands. When you are using an interactive utility, such as vim or mail, you use commands that are appropriate to that utility.

command line A line containing instructions and arguments that executes a command. This term usually refers to a line that you enter in response to a shell prompt on a character-based terminal or terminal emulator.

command substitution   Replacing a command with its output. The shells perform command substitution when you enclose a command between $(and) or between a pair of back ticks (` `), also called grave accent marks.

component architecture   A notion in object-oriented programming where "components" of a program are completely generic. Instead of having a specialized set of methods and fields, they have generic methods through which the component can advertise the functionality it supports to the system into which it is loaded. This strategy enables completely dynamic loading of objects. JavaBeans is an example of a component architecture.^{FOLDOC}

concatenate   See *catenate* on page 945.

condition code   See *exit status* on page 953.

connection-oriented protocol   A type of transport layer data communication service that allows a host to send data in a continuous stream to another host. The transport service guarantees that all data will be delivered to the other end in the same order as sent and without duplication. Communication proceeds through three well-defined phases: connection establishment, data transfer, and connection release. The most common example is *TCP* (page 982).

Also called connection-based protocol and stream-oriented protocol. Contrast with *connectionless protocol* and *datagram* (page 950).^{FOLDOC}

connectionless protocol   The data communication method in which communication occurs between hosts with no previous setup. Packets sent between two hosts may take different routes. There is no guarantee that packets will arrive as transmitted or even that they will arrive at the destination at all. *UDP* (page 984) is a connectionless protocol. Also called packet switching. Contrast with circuit switching and *connection-oriented protocol*.^{FOLDOC}

console   The main system terminal, usually directly connected to the computer and the one that receives system error messages. Also *system console* and *console terminal*.

console terminal   See *console*.

control character   A character that is not a graphic character, such as a letter, number, or punctuation mark. Such characters are called control characters because they frequently act to control a peripheral device. RETURN and FORMFEED are control characters that control a terminal or printer.

The word CONTROL is shown in this book in THIS FONT because it is a key that appears on most terminal keyboards. Control characters are represented by ASCII codes less than 32 (decimal). See also *nonprinting character* on page 969.

control structure   A statement used to change the order of execution of commands in a shell script or other program. Each shell provides control structures (for example, **if** and **while**) as well as other commands that alter the order of execution (for example, **exec**). Also *control flow commands*.

cookie   Data stored on a client system by a server. The client system browser sends the cookie back to the server each time it accesses that server. For example, a catalog shopping service may store a cookie on your system when you place your first order. When you return to the site, it knows who you are and can supply your name and address for subsequent orders. You may consider cookies to be an invasion of privacy.

CPU Central processing unit. The part of a computer that controls all the other parts. The CPU includes the control unit and the arithmetic and logic unit (ALU). The control unit fetches instructions from memory and decodes them to produce signals that control the other parts of the computer. These signals can cause data to be transferred between memory and ALU or peripherals to perform input or output. A CPU that is housed on a single chip is called a microprocessor. Also *processor* and *central processor*.

cracker An individual who attempts to gain unauthorized access to a computer system. These individuals are often malicious and have many means at their disposal for breaking into a system. Contrast with *hacker* (page 956).ᶠᵒˡᵈᵒᶜ

crash The system suddenly and unexpectedly stops or fails. Derived from the action of the hard disk heads on the surface of the disk when the air gap between the two collapses.

cryptography The practice and study of encryption and decryption—encoding data so that only a specific individual or machine can decode it. A system for encrypting and decrypting data is a cryptosystem. Such systems usually rely on an algorithm for combining the original data (plaintext) with one or more keys—numbers or strings of characters known only to the sender and/or recipient. The resulting output is called *ciphertext* (page 947).

The security of a cryptosystem usually depends on the secrecy of keys rather than on the supposed secrecy of an algorithm. Because a strong cryptosystem has a large range of keys, it is not possible to try all of them. Ciphertext appears random to standard statistical tests and resists known methods for breaking codes.ᶠᵒˡᵈᵒᶜ

.cshrc file In your home directory, a file that the TC Shell executes each time you invoke a new TC Shell. You can use this file to establish variables and aliases.

CSS Cascading stylesheet. Describes how documents are presented on screen and in print. Attaching a stylesheet to a structured document can affect the way it looks without adding new HTML (or other) tags and without giving up device independence. Also *stylesheet*.

current (process, line, character, directory, event, etc.) The item that is immediately available, working, or being used. The current process is the program you are running, the current line or character is the one the cursor is on, and the current directory is the working directory.

cursor A small lighted rectangle, underscore, or vertical bar that appears on a terminal screen and indicates where the next character will appear. Differs from the *mouse pointer* (page 966).

daemon   A program that is not invoked explicitly but lies dormant, waiting for some condition(s) to occur. The perpetrator of the condition need not be aware that a daemon is lurking (although often a program will commit an action only because it knows that it will implicitly invoke a daemon). From the mythological meaning, later rationalized as the acronym Disk And Execution MONitor..ꜰᴏʟᴅᴏᴄ

data structure   A particular format for storing, organizing, working with, and retrieving data. Frequently, data structures are designed to work with specific algorithms that facilitate these tasks. Common data structures include trees, files, records, tables, arrays, etc.

datagram   A self-contained, independent entity of data carrying sufficient information to be routed from the source to the destination computer without reliance on earlier exchanges between this source and destination computer and the transporting network. *UDP* (page 984) uses datagrams; *IP* (page 960) uses *packets* (page 970). Packets are indivisible at the network layer; datagrams are not.ꜰᴏʟᴅᴏᴄ See also *frame* (page 955).

dataless   A computer, usually a workstation, that uses a local disk to boot a copy of the operating system and access system files but does not use a local disk to store user files.

dbm   A standard, simple database manager. Implemented as **gdbm** (GNU database manager), it uses hashes to speed searching. The most common versions of the **dbm** database are **dbm**, **ndbm**, and **gdbm**.

DDoS attack   Distributed denial of service attack. A *DoS attack* (page 952) from many systems that do not belong to the perpetrator of the attack.

debug   To correct a program by removing its bugs (that is, errors).

default   Something that is selected without being explicitly specified. For example, when used without an argument, ls displays a list of the files in the working directory by default.

delta   A set of changes made to a file that has been encoded by the Source Code Control System (SCCS).

denial of service   *See DoS attack* on page 952.

dereference   When speaking of symbolic links, follow the link rather than working with the reference to the link. For example, the –L or ––dereference option causes ls to list the entry a symbolic link points to, not the symbolic link (the reference) itself.

desktop   A collection of windows, toolbars, icons, and buttons, some or all of which appear on your display. A desktop comprises one or more *workspaces* (page 988).

desktop manager   An icon- and menu-based user interface to system services that allows you to run applications and use the filesystem without using the system's command-line interface.

detached process	See *background process* on page 942.
device	A disk drive, printer, terminal, plotter, or other input/output unit that can be attached to the computer. Short for *peripheral device*.
device driver	Part of the Linux kernel that controls a device, such as a terminal, disk drive, or printer.
device file	A file that represents a device. Also *special file*.
device filename	The pathname of a device file. All Linux systems have two kinds of device files: block and character device files. Linux also has FIFOs (named pipes) and sockets. Device files are traditionally located in the **/dev** directory.
device number	See *major device number* (page 964) and *minor device number* (page 966).
DHCP	Dynamic Host Configuration Protocol. A protocol that dynamically allocates IP addresses to computers on a LAN.ᶠᴼᴸᴰᴼᶜ
dialog box	In a GUI, a special window, usually without a titlebar, that displays information. Some dialog boxes accept a response from the user
directory	Short for *directory file*. A file that contains a list of other files.
directory hierarchy	A directory, called the root of the directory hierarchy, and all the directory and ordinary files below it (its children).
directory service	A structured repository of information on people and resources within an organization, facilitating management and communication.ᶠᴼᴸᴰᴼᶜ
disk partition	See *partition* on page 970.
diskless	A computer, usually a workstation, that has no disk and must contact another computer (a server) to boot a copy of the operating system and access the necessary system files.
distributed computing	A style of computing in which tasks or services are performed by a network of cooperating systems, some of which may be specialized.
DMZ	Demilitarized zone. A host or small network that is a neutral zone between a LAN and the Internet. It can serve Web pages and other data to the Internet and allow local systems access to the Internet while preventing LAN access to unauthorized Internet users. Even if a DMZ is compromised, it holds no data that is private and none that cannot be easily reproduced.
DNS	Domain Name Service. A distributed service that manages the correspondence of full hostnames (those that include a domain name) to IP addresses and other system characteristics.
DNS domain name	See *domain name* on page 952.

document object model	See *DOM*.
DOM	Document Object Model. A platform-/language-independent interface that enables a program to update the content, structure, and style of a document dynamically. The changes can then be made part of the displayed document. Go to www.w3.org/DOM for more information.
domain name	A name associated with an organization, or part of an organization, to help identify systems uniquely. Technically, the part of the *FQDN* (page 955) to the right of the leftmost period. Domain names are assigned hierarchically. The domain berkeley.edu refers to the University of California at Berkeley, for example; it is part of the top-level edu (education) domain. Also DNS domain name. Different than *NIS domain name* (page 968).
Domain Name Service	See *DNS*.
door	An evolving filesystem-based *RPC* (page 976) mechanism.
DoS attack	Denial of service attack. An attack that attempts to make the target host or network unusable by flooding it with spurious traffic.
DPMS	Display Power Management Signaling. A standard that can extend the life of CRT monitors and conserve energy. DPMS supports four modes for a monitor: Normal, Standby (power supply on, monitor ready to come to display images almost instantly), Suspend (power supply off, monitor takes up to ten seconds to display an image), and Off.
drag	The motion part of *drag-and-drop*.
drag-and-drop	To move an object from one position or application to another within a GUI. To drag an object, the user clicks a mouse button (typically the left one) while the mouse pointer *hovers* (page 958) over the object. Then, without releasing the mouse button, the user drags the object, which stays attached to the mouse pointer, to a different location. The user can then drop the object at the new location by releasing the mouse button.
drop-down list	A *widget* (page 987) that displays a static list for a user to choose from. When the list is not active, it appears as text in a box, displaying the single selected entry. When a user clicks the box, a list appears; the user can move the mouse cursor to select an entry from the list. Different from a *list box* (page 963).
druid	In role-playing games, a character that represents a magical user. Red Hat uses the term *druid* at the ends of names of programs that guide you through a task-driven chain of steps. Other operating systems call these types of programs *wizards*.
DSA	Digital Signature Algorithm. A public key cipher used to generate digital signatures.

DSL	Digital Subscriber Line/Loop. Provides high-speed digital communication over a specialized, conditioned telephone line. See also *xDSL* (page 988).
Dynamic Host Configuration Protocol	See *DHCP* on page 951.
editor	A utility, such as vim or emacs, that creates and modifies text files.
EEPROM	Electrically erasable, programmable, readonly memory. A *PROM* (page 972) that can be written to.
effective user ID	The user ID that a process appears to have; usually the same as the user ID. For example, while you are running a setuid program, the effective user ID of the process running the program is that of the owner of the program.
element	One thing; usually a basic part of a group of things. An element of a numeric array is one of the numbers stored in the array.
emoticon	See *smiley* on page 978.
encapsulation	See *tunneling* on page 984.
environment	See *calling environment* on page 945.
EOF	End of file.
EPROM	Erasable programmable readonly memory. A *PROM* (page 972) that can be written to by applying a higher than normal voltage.
escape	See *quote* on page 973.
Ethernet	A type of *LAN* (page 962) capable of transfer rates as high as 1,000 megabits per second.
event	An occurrence, or happening, of significance to a task or program—for example, the completion of an asynchronous input/output operation, such as a keypress or mouse click.[FOLDOC]
exabyte	2^{60} bytes or about 10^{18} bytes. See also *large number* (page 962).
exit status	The status returned by a process; either successful (usually 0) or unsuccessful (usually 1).
exploit	A security hole or an instance of taking advantage of a security hole.[FOLDOC]
expression	See *logical expression* (page 964) and *arithmetic expression* (page 941).
extranet	A network extension for a subset of users (such as students at a particular school or engineers working for the same company). An extranet limits access to private information even though it travels on the public Internet.

failsafe session A session that allows you to log in on a minimal desktop in case your standard login does not work well enough to allow you to log in to fix a login problem.

FDDI Fiber Distributed Data Interface. A type of *LAN* (page 962) designed to transport data at the rate of 100 million bits per second over fiberoptic cable.

file A collection of related information referred to with a *filename* and frequently stored on a disk. Text files typically contain memos, reports, messages, program source code, lists, or manuscripts. Binary or executable files contain utilities or programs that you can run. Refer to "Directory Files and Ordinary Files" on page 78.

filename The name of a file. A filename refers to a file.

filename completion Automatic completion of a filename after you specify a unique prefix.

filename extension The part of a filename following a period.

filename generation What occurs when the shell expands ambiguous file references. See *ambiguous file reference* on page 940.

filesystem A *data structure* (page 950) that usually resides on part of a disk. All Linux systems have a root filesystem, and many have other filesystems. Each filesystem is composed of some number of blocks, depending on the size of the disk partition that has been assigned to the filesystem. Each filesystem has a control block, named the superblock, that contains information about the filesystem. The other blocks in a filesystem are inodes, which contain control information about individual files, and data blocks, which contain the information in the files.

filling A variant of maximizing in which window edges are pushed out as far as they can go without overlapping another window.

filter A command that can take its input from standard input and send its output to standard output. A filter transforms the input stream of data and sends it to standard output. A pipe usually connects a filter's input to standard output of one command, and a second pipe connects the filter's output to standard input of another command. The grep and sort utilities are commonly used as filters.

firewall A device for policy-based traffic management used to keep a network secure. A firewall can be implemented in a single router that filters out unwanted packets, or it can rely on a combination of routers, proxy servers, and other devices. Firewalls are widely used to give users access to the Internet in a secure fashion and to separate a company's public WWW server from its internal network. They are also employed to keep internal network segments more secure.

Recently the term has come to be defined more loosely to include a simple packet filter running on an endpoint machine.

See also *proxy server* on page 973.

firmware	Software built into a computer, often in *ROM* (page 976). May be used as part of the *bootstrap* (page 944) procedure.
focus, desktop	On a desktop, the window that is active. The window with the desktop focus receives the characters you type on the keyboard. Same as *active window* (page 940).
footer	The part of a format that goes at the bottom (or foot) of a page. Contrast with *header* (page 957).
foreground process	When you run a command in the foreground, the shell waits for the command to finish before giving you another prompt. You must wait for a foreground process to run to completion before you can give the shell another command. If you have job control, you can move background processes to the foreground, and vice versa. See *job control* on page 961. Contrast with *background process* (page 942).
fork	To create a process. When one process creates another process, it forks a process. Also *spawn*.
FQDN	Fully qualified domain name. The full name of a system, consisting of its hostname and its domain name, including the top-level domain. Technically the name that **gethostbyname**(2) returns for the host named by **gethostname**(2). For example, **speedy** is a hostname and **speedy.example.com** is an FQDN. An FQDN is sufficient to determine a unique Internet address for a machine on the Internet.^{FOLDOC}
frame	A data link layer packet that contains, in addition to data, the header and trailer information required by the physical medium. Network layer packets are encapsulated to become frames.^{FOLDOC} See also *datagram* (page 950) and *packet* (page 970).
free list	In a filesystem, the list of blocks that are available for use. Information about the free list is kept in the superblock of the filesystem.
free space	The portion of a hard disk that is not within a partition. A new hard disk has no partitions and contains all free space.
full duplex	The ability to receive and transmit data simultaneously. A *network switch* (page 968) is typically a full-duplex device. Contrast with *half-duplex* (page 956).
fully qualified domain name	See *FQDN*.
function	See *shell function* on page 978.
gateway	A generic term for a computer or a special device connected to more than one dissimilar type of network to pass data between them. Unlike a router, a gateway often must convert the information into a different format before passing it on. The historical usage of gateway to designate a router is deprecated.
GCOS	*See GECOS on page 956.*

GECOS   General Electric Comprehensive Operating System. For historical reasons, the user information field in the **/etc/passwd** file is called the GECOS field. Also GCOS.

gibibyte   Giga binary byte. A unit of storage equal to 2^{30} bytes = 1,073,741,824 bytes = 1024 *mebibytes* (page 965). Abbreviated as GiB. Contrast with *gigabyte*.

gigabyte   A unit of storage equal to 10^9 bytes. Sometimes used in place of *gibibyte*. Abbreviated as GB. See also *large number* on page 962.

glyph   A symbol that communicates a specific piece of information nonverbally. A *smiley* (page 978) is a glyph.

GMT   Greenwich Mean Time. See *UTC* on page 986.

graphical display   A bitmapped monitor that can display graphical images. Contrast with *ASCII terminal* (page 941).

graphical user interface   See *GUI*.

group (of users)   A collection of users. Groups are used as a basis for determining file access permissions. If you are not the owner of a file and you belong to the group the file is assigned to, you are subject to the group access permissions for the file. A user can simultaneously belong to several groups.

group (of windows)   A way to identify similar windows so they can be displayed and acted on similarly. Typically windows started by a given application belong to the same group.

group ID   A unique number that identifies a set of users. It is stored in the password and group databases (**/etc/passwd** and **/etc/group** files or their NIS equivalents). The group database associates group IDs with group names. Also *GID*.

GUI   Graphical user interface. A GUI provides a way to interact with a computer system by choosing items from menus or manipulating pictures drawn on a display screen instead of by typing command lines. Under Linux, the X Window System provides a graphical display and mouse/keyboard input. GNOME and KDE are two popular desktop managers that run under X. Contrast with *character-based* (page 946).

hacker   A person who enjoys exploring the details of programmable systems and learning how to stretch their capabilities, as opposed to users, who prefer to learn only the minimum necessary. One who programs enthusiastically (even obsessively) or who enjoys programming rather than just theorizing about programming.[FOLDOC] Contrast with *cracker* (page 949).

half-duplex   A half-duplex device can only receive or transmit at a given moment; it cannot do both. A *hub* (page 958) is typically a half-duplex device. Contrast with *full duplex* (page 955).

hard link   A directory entry that contains the filename and inode number for a file. The inode number identifies the location of control information for the file on the disk, which in turn identifies the location of the file's contents on the disk. Every file has at least one hard link, which locates the file in a directory. When you remove the last hard link to a file, you can no longer access the file. See *link* (page 963) and *symbolic link* (page 982).

hash A string that is generated from another string. See *one-way hash function* on page 969. When used for security, a hash can prove, almost to a certainty, that a message has not been tampered with during transmission: The sender generates a hash of a message, encrypts the message and hash, and sends the encrypted message and hash to the recipient. The recipient decrypts the message and hash, generates a second hash from the message, and compares the hash that the sender generated to the new hash. When they are the same, the message has probably not been tampered with. Hashed versions of passwords can be used to authenticate users. A hash can also be used to create an index called a *hash table*. Also *hash value*.

hash table An index created from hashes of the items to be indexed. The hash function makes it highly unlikely that two items will create the same hash. To look up an item in the index, create a hash of the item and search for the hash. Because the hash is typically shorter than the item, the search is more efficient.

header When you are formatting a document, the header goes at the top, or head, of a page. In electronic mail the header identifies who sent the message, when it was sent, what the subject of the message is, and so forth.

Here document A shell script that takes its input from the file that contains the script.

hesiod The nameserver of project Athena. Hesiod is a name service library that is derived from *BIND* (page 943) and leverages a DNS infrastructure.

heterogeneous Consisting of different parts. A heterogeneous network includes systems produced by different manufacturers and/or running different operating systems.

hexadecimal number A base 16 number. Hexadecimal (or *hex*) numbers are composed of the hexadecimal digits 0–9 and A–F. See Table G-1, next page.

hidden filename A filename that starts with a period. These filenames are called hidden because the ls utility does not normally list them. Use the **–a** option of ls to list all files, including those with hidden filenames. The shell does not expand a leading asterisk (*) in an ambiguous file reference to match files with hidden filenames. Also *hidden file*, *invisible file*.

hierarchy An organization with a few things, or thing—one at the top—and with several things below each other thing. An inverted tree structure. Examples in computing include a file tree where each directory may contain files or other directories, a hierarchical network, and a class hierarchy in object-oriented programming.[FOLDOC] Refer to "The Hierarchical Filesystem" on page 78.

Table G-1   Decimal, octal, and hexadecimal numbers

Decimal	Octal	Hex	Decimal	Octal	Hex
1	1	1	17	21	11
2	2	2	18	22	12
3	3	3	19	23	13
4	4	4	20	24	14
5	5	5	21	25	15
6	6	6	31	37	1F
7	7	7	32	40	20
8	10	8	33	41	21
9	11	9	64	100	40
10	12	A	96	140	60
11	13	B	100	144	64
12	14	C	128	200	80
13	15	D	254	376	FE
14	16	E	255	377	FF
15	17	F	256	400	100
16	20	10	257	401	101

history   A shell mechanism that enables you to modify and reexecute recent commands.

home directory   The directory that is the working directory when you first log in. The pathname of this directory is stored in the **HOME** shell variable.

hover   To leave the mouse pointer stationary for a moment over an object. In many cases hovering displays a *tooltip* (page 984).

HTML   Hypertext Markup Language. A *hypertext* document format used on the World Wide Web. Tags, which are embedded in the text, consist of a less than sign (<), a directive, zero or more parameters, and a greater than sign (>). Matched pairs of directives, such as <TITLE> and </TITLE>, delimit text that is to appear in a special place or style.ᶠᴼᴸᴰᴼᶜ For more information on HTML, go to www.htmlhelp.com/faq/html/all.html.

HTTP   Hypertext Transfer Protocol. The client/server TCP/IP protocol used on the World Wide Web for the exchange of *HTML* documents.

hub   A multiport repeater. A hub rebroadcasts all packets it receives on all ports. This term is frequently used to refer to small hubs and switches, regardless of the device's intelligence. It is a generic term for a layer 2 shared-media networking device. Today the term *hub* is sometimes used to refer to small intelligent devices, although that was not its original meaning. Contrast with *network switch* (page 968).

hypertext	A collection of documents/nodes containing (usually highlighted or underlined) cross-references or links, which, with the aid of an interactive browser program, allow the reader to move easily from one document to another.[FOLDOC]
Hypertext Markup Language	See *HTML*.
Hypertext Transfer Protocol	See *HTTP*.
i/o device	Input/output device. See *device* on page 951.
IANA	Internet Assigned Numbers Authority. A group that maintains a database of all permanent, registered system services (www.iana.org).
ICMP	Internet Control Message Protocol. A type of network packet that carries only messages, no data.
icon	In a GUI, a small picture representing a file, directory, action, program, and so on. When you click an icon, an action, such as opening a window and starting a program or displaying a directory or Web site, takes place. From miniature religious statues.[FOLDOC]
iconify	The process of changing a window into an *icon*. Contrast with *restore* (page 975).
ignored window	A state in which a window has no decoration and therefore no buttons or titlebar to control it with.
indentation	See *indention*.
indention	The blank space between the margin and the beginning of a line that is set in from the margin.
inode	A *data structure* (page 950) that contains information about a file. An inode for a file contains the file's length, the times the file was last accessed and modified, the time the inode was last modified, owner and group IDs, access privileges, number of links, and pointers to the data blocks that contain the file itself. Each directory entry associates a filename with an inode. Although a single file may have several filenames (one for each link), it has only one inode.
input	Information that is fed to a program from a terminal or other file. See *standard input* on page 980.
installation	A computer at a specific location. Some aspects of the Linux system are installation dependent. Also *site*.
interactive	A program that allows ongoing dialog with the user. When you give commands in response to shell prompts, you are using the shell interactively. Also, when you give commands to utilities, such as vim and mail, you are using the utilities interactively.

interface	The meeting point of two subsystems. When two programs work together, their interface includes every aspect of either program that the other deals with. The *user interface* (page 985) of a program includes every program aspect the user comes into contact with: the syntax and semantics involved in invoking the program, the input and output of the program, and its error and informational messages. The shell and each of the utilities and built-in commands have a user interface.
International Organization for Standardization	See *ISO* on page 961.
internet	A large network that encompasses other, smaller networks.
Internet	The largest internet in the world. The Internet (uppercase "I") is a multilevel hierarchy composed of backbone networks (ARPANET, NSFNET, MILNET, and others), midlevel networks, and stub networks. These include commercial (**.com** or **.co**), university (**.ac** or **.edu**), research (**.org** or **.net**), and military (**.mil**) networks and span many different physical networks around the world with various protocols, including the Internet Protocol (IP). Outside the United States, country code domains are popular (**.us**, **.es**, **.mx**, **.de**, and so forth), although you will see them used within the United States as well.
Internet Protocol	See *IP*.
Internet service provider	See *ISP*.
intranet	An inhouse network designed to serve a group of people such as a corporation or school. The general public on the Internet does not have access to the intranet.
invisible file	See *hidden filename* on page 957.
IP	Internet Protocol. The network layer for TCP/IP. IP is a best-effort, packet-switching, *connectionless protocol* (page 948) that provides packet routing, fragmentation, and reassembly through the data link layer. *IPv4* is slowly giving way to *IPv6*.<small>FOLDOC</small>
IP address	Internet Protocol address. A four-part address associated with a particular network connection for a system using the Internet Protocol (IP). A system that is attached to multiple networks that use the IP will have a different IP address for each network interface.
IP multicast	See *multicast* on page 967.

IP spoofing   A technique used to gain unauthorized access to a computer. The would-be intruder sends messages to the target machine. These messages contain an IP address indicating that the messages are coming from a trusted host. The target machine responds to the messages, giving the intruder (privileged) access to the target.

IPC   Interprocess communication. A method to communicate specific information between programs.

IPv4   *IP* version 4. See *IP* and *IPv6*.

IPv6   *IP* version 6. The next generation of Internet Protocol, which provides a much larger address space (2^{128} bits versus 2^{32} bits for IPv4) that is designed to accommodate the rapidly growing number of Internet addressable devices. IPv6 also has built-in autoconfiguration, enhanced security, better multicast support, and many other features.

ISDN   Integrated Services Digital Network. A set of communications standards that allows a single pair of digital or standard telephone wires to carry voice, data, and video at a rate of 64 kilobits per second.

ISO   International Organization for Standardization. A voluntary, nontreaty organization founded in 1946. It is responsible for creating international standards in many areas, including computers and communications. Its members are the national standards organizations of 89 countries, including the American National Standards Institute.[FOLDOC]

ISO9660   The *ISO* standard defining a filesystem for CD-ROMs.

ISP   Internet service provider. Provides Internet access to its customers.

job control   A facility that enables you to move commands from the foreground to the background and vice versa. Job control enables you to stop commands temporarily.

journaling filesystem   A filesystem that maintains a noncached log file, or journal, which records all transactions involving the filesystem. When a transaction is complete, it is marked as complete in the log file.

The log file results in greatly reduced time spent recovering a filesystem after a crash, making it particularly valuable in systems where high availability is an issue.

JPEG   Joint Photographic Experts Group. This committee designed the standard image-compression algorithm. JPEG is intended for compressing either full-color or gray-scale digital images of natural, real-world scenes and does not work as well on nonrealistic images, such as cartoons or line drawings. Filename extensions: **.jpg**, **.jpeg**.[FOLDOC]

justify   To expand a line of type in the process of formatting text. A justified line has even margins. A line is justified by increasing the space between words and sometimes between letters on the line.

Kerberos   An MIT-developed security system that authenticates users and machines. It does not provide authorization to services or databases; it establishes identity at logon, which is used throughout the session. Once you are authenticated, you can open as many terminals, windows, services, or other network accesses as you like until your session expires.

kernel   The part of the operating system that allocates machine resources, including memory, disk space, and *CPU* (page 949) cycles, to all other programs that run on a computer. The kernel includes the low-level hardware interfaces (drivers) and manages *processes* (page 972), the means by which Linux executes programs. The kernel is the part of the Linux system that Linus Torvalds originally wrote (see the beginning of Chapter 1).

kernelspace   The part of memory (RAM) where the kernel resides. Code running in kernelspace has full access to hardware and all other processes in memory. See the *KernelAnalysis-HOWTO*.

key binding   A *keyboard* key is said to be bound to the action that results from pressing it. Typically keys are bound to the letters that appear on the keycaps: When you press **A**, an **A** appears on the screen. Key binding usually refers to what happens when you press a combination of keys, one of which is CONTROL, ALT, META, or SHIFT, or when you press a series of keys, the first of which is typically ESCAPE.

keyboard   A hardware input device consisting of a number of mechanical buttons (keys) that the user presses to input characters to a computer. By default a keyboard is connected to standard input of a shell.FOLDOC

kilo-   In the binary system, the prefix *kilo-* multiplies by 2^{10} (i.e., 1,024). Kilobit and kilobyte are common uses of this prefix. Abbreviated as *k*.

Korn Shell   ksh. A command processor, developed by David Korn at AT&T Bell Laboratories, that is compatible with the Bourne Shell but includes many extensions. See also *shell* on page 978.

LAN   Local area network. A network that connects computers within a localized area (such as a single site, building, or department).

large number   Visit mathworld.wolfram.com/LargeNumber.html for a comprehensive list.

LDAP   Lightweight Directory Access Protocol. A simple protocol for accessing online directory services. LDAP is a lightweight alternative to the X.500 Directory Access Protocol (DAP). It can be used to access information about people, system users, network devices, email directories, and systems. In some cases, it can be used as an alternative for services such as NIS. Given a name, many mail clients can use LDAP to discover the corresponding email address. See *directory service* on page 951.

leaf   In a tree structure, the end of a branch that cannot support other branches. When the Linux filesystem hierarchy is conceptualized as a tree, files that are not directories are leaves. See *node* on page 969.

least privilege, concept of
Mistakes made by a user working with **root** privileges can be much more devastating than those made by an ordinary user. When you are working on the computer, especially when you are working as the system administrator, always perform any task using the least privilege possible. If you can perform a task logged in as an ordinary user, do so. If you must work with **root** privileges, do as much as you can as an ordinary user, log in as **root** or give an **su** or **sudo** command so you are working with **root** privileges, do as much of the task that has to be done with **root** privileges, and revert to being an ordinary user as soon as you can.

Because you are more likely to make a mistake when you are rushing, this concept becomes more important when you have less time to apply it.

Lightweight Directory Access Protocol
See *LDAP*.

link
A pointer to a file. Two kinds of links exist: *hard links* (page 956) and *symbolic links* (page 982) also called *soft links*. A hard link associates a filename with a place on the disk where the contents of the file is located. A symbolic link associates a filename with the pathname of a hard link to a file.

Linux-PAM
See *PAM* on page 970.

Linux-Pluggable Authentication Modules
See *PAM* on page 970.

list box
A *widget* (page 987) that displays a static list for a user to choose from. The list appears as multiple lines with a *scrollbar* (page 977) if needed. The user can scroll the list and select an entry. Different from a *drop-down list* (page 952).

loadable kernel module
See *loadable module*.

loadable module
A portion of the operating system that controls a special device and that can be loaded automatically into a running kernel as needed to access that device.

local area network
See *LAN*.

locale
The language; date, time, and currency formats; character sets; and so forth that pertain to a geopolitical place or area. For example, en_US specifies English as spoken in the United States and dollars; en_UK specifies English as spoken in the United Kingdom and pounds. See the **locale** man page in section 5 of the system manual for more information. Also the locale utility.

log in To gain access to a computer system by responding correctly to the **login:** and **Password:** prompts. Also *log on, login.*

log out To end your session by exiting from your login shell. Also *log off.*

logical expression A collection of strings separated by logical operators (>, >=, =, !=, <=, and <) that can be evaluated as *true* or *false.* Also *Boolean* (page 944) *expression.*

.login file A file in a user's home directory that the TC Shell executes when you log in. You can use this file to set environment variables and to run commands that you want executed at the beginning of each session.

login name See *username* on page 985.

login shell The shell that you are using when you log in. The login shell can fork other processes that can run other shells, utilities, and programs.

.logout file A file in a user's home directory that the TC Shell executes when you log out, assuming that the TC Shell is your login shell. You can put in the **.logout** file commands that you want run each time you log out.

MAC address Media Access Control address. The unique hardware address of a device connected to a shared network medium. Each network adapter has a globally unique MAC address that it stores in ROM. MAC addresses are 6 bytes long, enabling 256^6 (about 300 trillion) possible addresses or 65,536 addresses for each possible IPv4 address.

A MAC address performs the same role for Ethernet that an IP address performs for TCP/IP: It provides a unique way to identify a host.

machine collating sequence The sequence in which the computer orders characters. The machine collating sequence affects the outcome of sorts and other procedures that put lists in alphabetical order. Many computers use ASCII codes so their machine collating sequences correspond to the ordering of the ASCII codes for characters.

macro A single instruction that a program replaces by several (usually more complex) instructions. The C compiler recognizes macros, which are defined using a #define instruction to the preprocessor.

magic number A magic number, which occurs in the first 512 bytes of a binary file, is a 1-, 2-, or 4-byte numeric value or character string that uniquely identifies the type of file (much like a DOS 3-character filename extension). See **/usr/share/magic** and the **magic** man page for more information.

main memory Random access memory (RAM), an integral part of the computer. Although disk storage is sometimes referred to as memory, it is never referred to as main memory.

major device number A number assigned to a class of devices, such as terminals, printers, or disk drives. Using the ls utility with the –l option to list the contents of the **/dev** directory displays the major and minor device numbers of many devices (as major, minor).

MAN	Metropolitan area network. A network that connects computers and *LANs* (page 962) at multiple sites in a small regional area, such as a city.
masquerade	To appear to come from one domain or IP address when actually coming from another. Said of a packet (iptables) or message. See also *NAT* on page 967.
MD5	Message Digest 5. A *one-way hash function* (page 969). The *SHA1* (page 977) algorithm has supplanted MD5 in many applications.
MDA	Mail delivery agent. One of the three components of a mail system; the other two are the *MTA* (page 966) and *MUA* (page 966). An MDA accepts inbound mail from an MTA and delivers it to a local user.
mebibyte	Mega binary byte. A unit of storage equal to 2^{20} bytes = 1,048,576 bytes = 1,024 kibibytes. Abbreviated as MiB. Contrast with *megabyte*.
megabyte	A unit of storage equal to 10^6 bytes. Sometimes used in place of *mebibyte*. Abbreviated as MB.
memory	See *RAM* on page 974.
menu	A list from which the user may select an operation to be performed. This selection is often made with a mouse or other pointing device under a GUI but may also be controlled from the keyboard. Very convenient for beginners, menus show which commands are available and facilitate experimenting with a new program, often reducing the need for user documentation. Experienced users usually prefer keyboard commands, especially for frequently used operations, because they are faster to use.[FOLDOC]
merge	To combine two ordered lists so that the resulting list is still in order. The sort utility can merge files.
META key	On the keyboard, a key that is labeled META or ALT. Use this key as you would the SHIFT key. While holding it down, press another key. The emacs editor makes extensive use of the META key.
metacharacter	A character that has a special meaning to the shell or another program in a particular context. Metacharacters are used in the ambiguous file references recognized by the shell and in the regular expressions recognized by several utilities. You must quote a metacharacter if you want to use it without invoking its special meaning. See *regular character* (page 975) and *special character* (page 979).
metadata	Data about data. In data processing, metadata is definitional data that provides information about, or documentation of, other data managed within an application or environment.
	For example, metadata can document data about data elements or attributes (name, size, data type, and so on), records or *data structures* (page 950) (length, fields, columns, and so on), and data itself (where it is located, how it is associated, who

owns it, and so on). Metadata can include descriptive information about the context, quality and condition, or characteristics of the data.^{FOLDOC}

metropolitan area network See *MAN* on page 965.

MIME Multipurpose Internet Mail Extension. Originally used to describe how specific types of files that were attached to email were to be handled. Today MIME types describe how a file is to be opened or worked with, based on its contents, determined by its *magic number* (page 964), and filename extension. An example of a MIME *type* is **image/jpeg**: The MIME *group* is **image** and the MIME *subtype* is **jpeg**. Many MIME groups exist, including application, audio, image, inode, message, text, and video.

minimize See *iconify* on page 959.

minor device number A number assigned to a specific device within a class of devices. See *major device number* on page 964.

modem Modulator/demodulator. A peripheral device that modulates digital data into analog data for transmission over a voice-grade telephone line. Another modem demodulates the data at the other end.

module See *loadable module* on page 963.

mount To make a filesystem accessible to system users. When a filesystem is not mounted, you cannot read from or write to files it contains.

mount point A directory that you mount a local or remote filesystem on.

mouse A device you use to point to a particular location on a display screen, typically so you can choose a menu item, draw a line, or highlight some text. You control a pointer on the screen by sliding a mouse around on a flat surface; the position of the pointer moves relative to the movement of the mouse. You select items by pressing one or more buttons on the mouse.

mouse pointer In a GUI, a marker that moves in correspondence with the mouse. It is usually a small black **x** with a white border or an arrow. Differs from the *cursor* (page 949).

mouseover The action of passing the mouse pointer over an object on the screen.

MTA Mail transfer agent. One of the three components of a mail system; the other two are the *MDA* and *MUA*. An MTA accepts mail from users and MTAs.

MUA Mail user agent. One of the three components of a mail system; the other two are the *MDA* (page 965) and *MTA*. An MUA is an end-user mail program such as KMail, mutt, or Outlook.

multiboot specification Specifies an interface between a boot loader and an operating system. With compliant boot loaders and operating systems, any boot loader should be able to load any operating system. The object of this specification is to ensure that different operating systems will work on a single machine. For more information, go to odin-os.sourceforge.net/guides/multiboot.html.

multicast   A multicast packet has one source and multiple destinations. In multicast, source hosts register at a special address to transmit data. Destination hosts register at the same address to receive data. In contrast to *broadcast* (page 944), which is LAN-based, multicast traffic is designed to work across routed networks on a subscription basis. Multicast reduces network traffic by transmitting a packet one time, with the router at the end of the path breaking it apart as needed for multiple recipients.

multitasking   A computer system that allows a user to run more than one job at a time. A multitasking system, such as Linux, allows you to run a job in the background while running a job in the foreground.

multiuser system   A computer system that can be used by more than one person at a time. Linux is a multiuser operating system. Contrast with *single-user system* (page 978).

namespace   A set of names (identifiers) in which all names are unique.ᶠᴼᴸᴰᴼᶜ

NAT   Network Address Translation. A scheme that enables a LAN to use one set of IP addresses internally and a different set externally. The internal set is for LAN (private) use. The external set is typically used on the Internet and is Internet unique. NAT provides some privacy by hiding internal IP addresses and allows multiple internal addresses to connect to the Internet through a single external IP address. See also *masquerade* on page 965.

NBT   NetBIOS over TCP/IP. A protocol that supports NetBIOS services in a TCP/IP environment. Also *NetBT*.

negative caching   Storing the knowledge that something does not exist. A cache normally stores information about something that exists. A negative cache stores the information that something, such as a record, does not exist.

NetBIOS   Network Basic Input/Output System. An *API* (page 941) for writing network-aware applications.

netboot   To boot a computer over the network (as opposed to booting from a local disk).

netiquette   The conventions of etiquette—that is, polite behavior—recognized on Usenet and in mailing lists, such as not (cross-)posting to inappropriate groups and refraining from commercial advertising outside the business groups.

The most important rule of netiquette is "Think before you post." If what you intend to post will not make a positive contribution to the newsgroup and be of interest to several readers, do not post it. Personal messages to one or two individuals should not be posted to newsgroups; use private email instead.ᶠᴼᴸᴰᴼᶜ

netmask   A 32-bit mask (for IPv4), that shows how an Internet address is to be divided into network, subnet, and host parts. The netmask has ones in the bit positions in the 32-bit address that are to be used for the network and subnet parts and zeros for the host part.

	The mask should contain at least the standard network portion (as determined by the address class). The subnet field should be contiguous with the network portion.^FOLDOC
network address	The network portion (**netid**) of an IP address. For a class A network, it is the first byte, or segment, of the IP address; for a class B network, it is the first two bytes; and for a class C network, it is the first three bytes. In each case the balance of the IP address is the host address (**hostid**). Assigned network addresses are globally unique within the Internet. Also *network number*.
Network Filesystem	See *NFS*.
Network Information Service	See *NIS*.
network number	See *network address*.
network segment	A part of an Ethernet or other network on which all message traffic is common to all nodes; that is, it is broadcast from one node on the segment and received by all others. This commonality normally occurs because the segment is a single continuous conductor. Communication between nodes on different segments is via one or more routers.^FOLDOC
network switch	A connecting device in networks. Switches are increasingly replacing shared media hubs in an effort to increase bandwidth. For example, a 16-port 10BaseT hub shares the total 10 megabits per second bandwidth with all 16 attached nodes. By replacing the hub with a switch, both sender and receiver can take advantage of the full 10 megabits per second capacity. Each port on the switch can give full bandwidth to a single server or client station or to a hub with several stations. Network switch refers to a device with intelligence. Contrast with *hub* (page 958).
Network Time Protocol	See *NTP* on page 969.
NFS	Network Filesystem. A remote filesystem designed by Sun Microsystems, available on computers from most UNIX system vendors.
NIC	Network interface card (or controller). An adapter circuit board installed in a computer to provide a physical connection to a network.^FOLDOC
NIS	Network Information Service. A distributed service built on a shared database to manage system-independent information (such as usernames and passwords).
NIS domain name	A name that describes a group of systems that share a set of NIS files. Different from *domain name* (page 952).
NNTP	Network News Transfer Protocol.

node In a tree structure, the end of a branch that can support other branches. When the Linux filesystem hierarchy is conceptualized as a tree, directories are nodes. See *leaf* on page 962.

nonprinting character See *control character* on page 948. Also *nonprintable character*.

nonvolatile storage A storage device whose contents are preserved when its power is off. Also NVS and persistent storage. Some examples are CD-ROM, paper punch tape, hard disk, *ROM* (page 976), *PROM* (page 972), *EPROM* (page 953), and *EEPROM* (page 953). Contrast with *RAM* (page 974).

NTP Network Time Protocol. Built on top of TCP/IP, NTP maintains accurate local time by referring to known accurate clocks on the Internet.

null string A string that could contain characters but does not. A string of zero length.

octal number A base 8 number. Octal numbers are composed of the digits 0–7, inclusive. Refer to Table G-1 on page 958.

one-way hash function A one-way function that takes a variable-length message and produces a fixed-length hash. Given the hash, it is computationally infeasible to find a message with that hash; in fact, you cannot determine any usable information about a message with that hash. Also *message digest function*. See also *hash* (page 957).

open source A method and philosophy for software licensing and distribution designed to encourage use and improvement of software written by volunteers by ensuring that anyone can copy the source code and modify it freely.

The term *open source* is now more widely used than the earlier term *free software* (promoted by the Free Software Foundation; www.fsf.org) but has broadly the same meaning—free of distribution restrictions, not necessarily free of charge.

OpenSSH A free version of the SSH (secure shell) protocol suite that replaces TELNET, rlogin, and more with secure programs that encrypt all communication—even passwords—over a network.

operating system A control program for a computer that allocates computer resources, schedules tasks, and provides the user with a way to access resources.

option A command-line argument that modifies the effects of a command. Options are usually preceded by hyphens on the command line and traditionally have single-character names (such as **–h** or **–n**). Some commands allow you to group options following a single hyphen (for example, **–hn**). GNU utilities frequently have two arguments that do the same thing: a single-character argument and a longer, more descriptive argument that is preceded by two hyphens (such as **––show-all** and **––invert-match**).

ordinary file A file that is used to store a program, text, or other user data. See *directory* (page 951) and *device file* (page 951).

output
Information that a program sends to the terminal or another file. See *standard output* on page 980.

P2P
Peer-to-Peer. A network that does not divide nodes into clients and servers. Each computer on a P2P network can fulfill the roles of client and server. In the context of a file-sharing network, this ability means that once a node has downloaded (part of) a file, it can act as a server. BitTorrent implements a P2P network.

packet
A unit of data sent across a network. *Packet* is a generic term used to describe a unit of data at any layer of the OSI protocol stack, but it is most correctly used to describe network or application layer data units ("application protocol data unit," APDU).FOLDOC See also *frame* (page 955) and *datagram* (page 950).

packet filtering
A technique used to block network traffic based on specified criteria, such as the origin, destination, or type of each packet. See also *firewall* (page 954).

packet sniffer
A program or device that monitors packets on a network. See *sniff* on page 979.

pager
A utility that allows you to view a file one screen at a time (for example, less and more).

paging
The process by which virtual memory is maintained by the operating system. The contents of process memory is moved (paged out) to the *swap space* (page 982) as needed to make room for other processes.

PAM
Linux-PAM or Linux-Pluggable Authentication Modules. These modules allow a system administrator to determine how various applications authenticate users.

parent process
A process that forks other processes. See *process* (page 972) and *child process* (page 946).

partition
A section of a (hard) disk that has a name so you can address it separately from other sections. A disk partition can hold a filesystem or another structure, such as the swap area. Under DOS and Windows, partitions (and sometimes whole disks) are labeled C:, D:, and so on. Also *disk partition* and *slice*.

passive FTP
Allows FTP to work through a firewall by allowing the flow of data to be initiated and controlled by the client FTP program instead of the server. Also called PASV FTP because it uses the FTP PASV command.

passphrase
A string of words and characters that you type in to authenticate yourself. A passphrase differs from a *password* only in length. A password is usually short—6 to 10 characters. A passphrase is usually much longer—up to 100 characters or more. The greater length makes a passphrase harder to guess or reproduce than a password and therefore more secure.FOLDOC

password
To prevent unauthorized access to a user's account, an arbitrary string of characters chosen by the user or system administrator and used to authenticate the user when attempting to log in.FOLDOC See also *passphrase*.

PASV FTP
See *passive FTP*.

pathname	A list of directories separated by slashes (/) and ending with the name of a file, which can be a directory. A pathname is used to trace a path through the file structure to locate or identify a file.
pathname, last element of a	The part of a pathname following the final /, or the whole filename if there is no /. A simple filename. Also *basename*.
pathname element	One of the filenames that forms a pathname.
peripheral device	See *device* on page 951.
persistent	Data that is stored on nonvolatile media, such as a hard disk.
phish	An attempt to trick users into revealing or sharing private information, especially passwords or financial information. The most common form is email purporting to be from a bank or vendor that requests that a user fill out a form to "update" an account on a phoney Web site disguised to appear legitimate. Generally sent as *spam* (page 979).
physical device	A tangible device, such as a disk drive, that is physically separate from other, similar devices.
PID	Process identification, usually followed by the word *number*. Linux assigns a unique PID number as each process is initiated.
pipe	A connection between programs such that standard output of one program is connected to standard input of the next. Also *pipeline*.
pixel	The smallest element of a picture, typically a single dot on a display screen.
plaintext	Text that is not encrypted. Also *cleartext*. Contrast with *ciphertext* (page 947).
Pluggable Authentication Modules	See *PAM* on page 970.
point-to-point link	A connection limited to two endpoints, such as the connection between a pair of modems.
port	A logical channel or channel endpoint in a communications system. The *TCP* (page 982) and *UDP* (page 984) transport layer protocols used on Ethernet use port numbers to distinguish between different logical channels on the same network interface on the same computer.
	The **/etc/services** file (see the beginning of this file for more information) or the *NIS* (page 968) **services** database specifies a unique port number for each application program. The number links incoming data to the correct service (program). Standard, well-known ports are used by everyone: Port 80 is used for HTTP (Web) traffic. Some protocols, such as TELNET and HTTP (which is a special form of

TELNET), have default ports specified as mentioned earlier but can use other ports as well.^{FOLDOC}

port forwarding
The process by which a network *port* on one computer is transparently connected to a port on another computer. If port X is forwarded from system A to system B, any data sent to port X on system A is sent to system B automatically. The connection can be between different ports on the two systems. See also *tunneling* (page 984).

portmapper
A server that converts TCP/IP port numbers into *RPC* (page 976) program numbers.

printable character
One of the graphic characters: a letter, number, or punctuation mark. Contrast with a nonprintable, or CONTROL, character. Also *printing character*.

private address space
IANA (page 959) has reserved three blocks of IP addresses for private internets or LANs:

```
10.0.0.0 - 10.255.255.255
172.16.0.0 - 172.31.255.255
192.168.0.0 - 192.168.255.255
```

You can use these addresses without coordinating with anyone outside of your LAN (you do not have to register the system name or address). Systems using these IP addresses cannot communicate directly with hosts using the global address space but must go through a gateway. Because private addresses have no global meaning, routing information is not stored by DNSs and most ISPs reject privately addressed packets. Make sure that your router is set up not to forward these packets onto the Internet.

privileged port
A *port* (page 971) with a number less than 1024. On Linux and other UNIX-like systems, only a process running with **root** privileges can bind to a privileged port. Any user on Windows 98 and earlier Windows systems can bind to any port. Also *reserved port*.

procedure
A sequence of instructions for performing a particular task. Most programming languages, including machine languages, enable a programmer to define procedures that allow the procedure code to be called from multiple places. Also *subroutine*.^{FOLDOC}

process
The execution of a command by Linux.

.profile file
A startup file in a user's home directory that the Bourne Again or Z Shell executes when you log in. The TC Shell executes **.login** instead. You can use the **.profile** file to run commands, set variables, and define functions.

program
A sequence of executable computer instructions contained in a file. Linux utilities, applications, and shell scripts are all programs. Whenever you run a command that is not built into a shell, you are executing a program.

PROM
Programmable readonly memory. A kind of nonvolatile storage. *ROM* (page 976) that can be written to using a PROM programmer.

prompt   A cue from a program, usually displayed on the screen, indicating that it is waiting for input. The shell displays a prompt, as do some of the interactive utilities, such as mail. By default the Bourne Again and Z Shells use a dollar sign ($) as a prompt, and the TC Shell uses a percent sign (%).

protocol   A set of formal rules describing how to transmit data, especially across a network. Low-level protocols define the electrical and physical standards, bit and byte ordering, and transmission, error detection, and correction of the bit stream. High-level protocols deal with data formatting, including message syntax, terminal-to-computer dialog, character sets, and sequencing of messages.FOLDOC

proxy   A service that is authorized to act for a system while not being part of that system. See also *proxy gateway* and *proxy server*.

proxy gateway   A computer that separates clients (such as browsers) from the Internet, working as a trusted agent that accesses the Internet on their behalf. A proxy gateway passes a request for data from an Internet service, such as HTTP from a browser/client, to a remote server. The data that the server returns goes back through the proxy gateway to the requesting service. A proxy gateway should be transparent to the user.

A proxy gateway often runs on a *firewall* (page 954) system and acts as a barrier to malicious users. It hides the IP addresses of the local computers inside the firewall from Internet users outside the firewall.

You can configure browsers, such as Mozilla/Firefox and Netscape, to use a different proxy gateway or to use no proxy for each URL access method including FTP, netnews, SNMP, HTTPS, and HTTP. See also *proxy*.

proxy server   A *proxy gateway* that usually includes a *cache* (page 945) that holds frequently used Web pages so that the next request for that page is available locally (and therefore more quickly). The terms proxy server and proxy gateway are frequently interchanged so that the use of cache does not rest exclusively with the proxy server. See also *proxy*.

Python   A simple, high-level, interpreted, object-oriented, interactive language that bridges the gap between C and shell programming. Suitable for rapid prototyping or as an extension language for C applications, Python supports packages, modules, classes, user-defined exceptions, a good C interface, and dynamic loading of C modules. It has no arbitrary restrictions. For more information, see www.python.org.FOLDOC

quote   When you quote a character, you take away any special meaning that it has in the current context. You can quote a character by preceding it with a backslash. When you are interacting with the shell, you can also quote a character by surrounding it with single quotation marks. For example, the command **echo *** or **echo '*'** displays *. The command **echo *** displays a list of the files in the working directory. See *ambiguous file reference* (page 940), *metacharacter* (page 965), *regular character* (page 975), *regular expression* (page 975), and *special character* (page 979). See also *escape* on page 953.

radio button   In a GUI, one of a group of buttons similar to those used to select the station on a car radio. Radio buttons within a group are mutually exclusive; only one button can be selected at a time.

RAID   Redundant array of inexpensive/independent disks. Two or more (hard) disk drives used in combination to improve fault tolerance and performance. RAID can be implemented in hardware or software.

RAM   Random access memory. A kind of volatile storage. A data storage device for which the order of access to different locations does not affect the speed of access. Contrast with a hard disk or tape drive, which provides quicker access to sequential data because accessing a nonsequential location requires physical movement of the storage medium and/or read/write head rather than just electronic switching. Contrast with *nonvolatile storage* (page 969). Also *memory.*<small>FOLDOC</small>

RAM disk   *RAM* that is made to look like a floppy diskette or hard disk. A RAM disk is frequently used as part of the *boot* (page 944) process.

RAS   Remote access server. In a network, a computer that provides access to remote users via analog modem or ISDN connections. RAS includes the dial-up protocols and access control (authentication). It may be a regular fileserver with remote access software or a proprietary system, such as Shiva's LANRover. The modems may be internal or external to the device.

RDF   Resource Description Framework. Being developed by W3C (the main standards body for the World Wide Web), a standard that specifies a mechanism for encoding and transferring *metadata* (page 965). RDF does not specify what the metadata should or can be. It can integrate many kinds of applications and data, using XML as an interchange syntax. Examples of the data that can be integrated include library catalogs and worldwide directories; syndication and aggregation of news, software, and content; and collections of music and photographs. Go to www.w3.org/RDF for more information.

redirection   The process of directing standard input for a program to come from a file rather than from the keyboard. Also, directing standard output or standard error to go to a file rather than to the screen.

reentrant   Code that can have multiple simultaneous, interleaved, or nested invocations that do not interfere with one another. Noninterference is important for parallel processing, recursive programming, and interrupt handling.

It is usually easy to arrange for multiple invocations (that is, calls to a subroutine) to share one copy of the code and any readonly data. For the code to be reentrant, however, each invocation must use its own copy of any modifiable data (or synchronized access to shared data). This goal is most often achieved by using a stack and allocating local variables in a new stack frame for each invocation. Alternatively, the caller may pass in a pointer to a block of memory that that invocation can use (usually for output), or the code may allocate some memory on a heap, especially if the data must survive after the routine returns.

Reentrant code is often found in system software, such as operating systems and teleprocessing monitors. It is also a crucial component of multithreaded programs, where the term *thread-safe* is often used instead of reentrant.ᶠᴼᴸᴰᴼᶜ

regular character	A character that always represents itself in an ambiguous file reference or another type of regular expression. Contrast with *special character*.
regular expression	A string—composed of letters, numbers, and special symbols—that defines one or more strings. See Appendix A.
relative pathname	A pathname that starts from the working directory. Contrast with *absolute pathname* (page 940).
remote access server	See *RAS* on page 974.
remote filesystem	A filesystem on a remote computer that has been set up so that you can access (usually over a network) its files as though they were stored on your local computer's disks. An example of a remote filesystem is NFS.
remote procedure call	See *RPC* on page 976.
resolver	The TCP/IP library software that formats requests to be sent to the *DNS* (page 951) for hostname-to-Internet address conversion.ᶠᴼᴸᴰᴼᶜ
Resource Description Framework	See *RDF* on page 974.
restore	The process of turning an icon into a window. Contrast with *iconify* (page 959)
return code	See *exit status* on page 953.
RFC	Request for comments. Begun in 1969, one of a series of numbered Internet informational documents and standards widely followed by commercial software and freeware in the Internet and UNIX/Linux communities. Few RFCs are standards but all Internet standards are recorded in RFCs. Perhaps the single most influential RFC has been RFC 822, the Internet electronic mail format standard.
	The RFCs are unusual in that they are floated by technical experts acting on their own initiative and reviewed by the Internet at large rather than being formally promulgated through an institution such as ANSI. For this reason they remain known as RFCs, even after they are adopted as standards. The RFC tradition of pragmatic, experience-driven, after-the-fact standard writing done by individuals or small working groups has important advantages over the more formal, committee-driven process typical of ANSI or ISO. For a complete list of RFCs, go to www.rfc-editor.org.ᶠᴼᴸᴰᴼᶜ
roam	To move a computer between *wireless access points* (page 987) on a wireless network without the user or applications being aware of the transition. Moving

between access points typically results in some packet loss, although this loss is transparent to programs that use TCP.

ROM Readonly memory. A kind of nonvolatile storage. A data storage device that is manufactured with fixed contents. In general, ROM describes any storage system whose contents cannot be altered, such as a phonograph record or printed book. When used in reference to electronics and computers, ROM describes semiconductor integrated circuit memories, of which several types exist, and CD-ROM.

ROM is nonvolatile storage—it retains its contents even after power has been removed. ROM is often used to hold programs for embedded systems, as these usually have a fixed purpose. ROM is also used for storage of the *BIOS* (page 943) in a computer. Contrast with *RAM* (page 974)._{FOLDOC}

root directory The ancestor of all directories and the start of all absolute pathnames. The root directory has no name and is represented by / standing alone or at the left end of a pathname.

root filesystem The filesystem that is available when the system is brought up in single-user or recovery mode. This filesystem is always represented by /. You cannot unmount or mount the root filesystem. You can remount root to change its mount options.

root login Usually the username of *Superuser* (page 982).

root (user) Another name for *Superuser* (page 982).

root window Any place on the desktop not covered by a window, object, or panel.

rotate When a file, such as a log file, gets indefinitely larger, you must keep it from taking up too much space on the disk. Because you may need to refer to the information in the log files in the near future, it is generally not a good idea to delete the contents of the file until it has aged. Instead you can periodically save the current log file under a new name and create a new, empty file as the current log file. You can keep a series of these files, renaming each as a new one is saved. You will then *rotate* the files. For example, you might remove **xyzlog.4**, **xyzlog.3** →**xyzlog.4**, **xyzlog.2** →**xyzlog.3**, **xyzlog.1** →**xyzlog.2**, **xyzlog** →**xyzlog.1**, and create a new **xyzlog** file. By the time you remove **xyzlog.4**, it will not contain any information more recent than you want to remove.

router A device (often a computer) that is connected to more than one similar type of network to pass data between them. See *gateway* on page 955.

RPC Remote procedure call. A call to a *procedure* (page 972) that acts transparently across a network. The procedure itself is responsible for accessing and using the network. The RPC libraries make sure that network access is transparent to the application. RPC runs on top of TCP/IP or UDP/IP.

RSA A public key encryption technology that is based on the lack of an efficient way to factor very large numbers. Because of this lack, it takes an extraordinary amount of computer processing time and power to deduce an RSA key. The RSA algorithm is the de facto standard for data sent over the Internet.

run   To execute a program.

Samba   A free suite of programs that implement the Server Message Block (SMB) protocol. See *SMB* (page 978).

schema   Within a GUI, a pattern that helps you see and interpret the information that is presented in a window, making it easier to understand new information that is presented using the same schema.

scroll   To move lines on a terminal or window up and down or left and right.

scrollbar   A *widget* (page 987) found in graphical user interfaces that controls (scrolls) which part of a document is visible in the window. A window can have a horizontal scrollbar, a vertical scrollbar (more common), or both.FOLDOC

server   A powerful centralized computer (or program) designed to provide information to clients (smaller computers or programs) on request.

session   The lifetime of a process. For a desktop, it is the desktop session manager. For a character-based terminal, it is the user's login shell process. In KDE, it is launched by kdeinit. A session may also be the sequence of events between when you start using a program, such as an editor, and when you finish.

setgid   When you execute a file that has setgid (set group ID) permission, the process executing the file takes on the privileges of the group the file belongs to. The ls utility shows setgid permission as an **s** in the group's executable position. See also *setuid*.

setuid   When you execute a file that has setuid (set user ID) permission, the process executing the file takes on the privileges of the owner of the file. As an example, if you run a setuid program that removes all the files in a directory, you can remove files in any of the file owner's directories, even if you do not normally have permission to do so. When the program is owned by **root,** you can remove files in any directory that a user working with **root** privileges can remove files from. The ls utility shows setuid permission as an **s** in the owner's executable position. See also *setgid*.

sexillion   In the British system, 10^{36}. In the American system, this number is named *undecillion*. See also *large number* (page 962).

SHA1   Secure Hash Algorithm 1. The SHA family is a set of cryptographic *hash* (page 957) algorithms that were designed by the National Security Agency (NSA). The second member of this family is SHA1, a successor to *MD5* (page 965). See also *cryptography* on page 949.

share   A filesystem hierarchy that is shared with another system using *SMB* (page 978). Also *Windows share* (page 987).

shared network topology	A network, such as Ethernet, in which each packet may be seen by systems other than its destination system. *Shared* means that the network bandwidth is shared by all users.
shell	A Linux system command processor. The three major shells are the *Bourne Again Shell* (page 944), the *TC Shell* (page 982), and the *Z Shell* (page 988).
shell function	A series of commands that the shell stores for execution at a later time. Shell functions are like shell scripts but run more quickly because they are stored in the computer's main memory rather than in files. Also, a shell function is run in the environment of the shell that calls it (unlike a shell script, which is typically run in a subshell).
shell script	An ASCII file containing shell commands. Also *shell program.*
signal	A very brief message that the UNIX system can send to a process, apart from the process's standard input. Refer to "trap: Catches a Signal" on page 453.
simple filename	A single filename containing no slashes (/). A simple filename is the simplest form of pathname. Also the last element of a pathname. Also *basename* (page 943).
single-user system	A computer system that only one person can use at a time. Contrast with *multiuser system* (page 967).
slider	A *widget* (page 987) that allows a user to set a value by dragging an indicator along a line. Many sliders allow the user also to click on the line to move the indicator. Differs from a *scrollbar* (page 977) in that moving the indicator does not change other parts of the display.
SMB	Server Message Block. Developed in the early 1980s by Intel, Microsoft, and IBM, SMB is a client/server protocol that is the native method of file and printer sharing for Windows. In addition, SMB can share serial ports and communications abstractions, such as named pipes and mail slots. SMB is similar to a remote procedure call (*RPC*, page 976) that has been customized for filesystem access. Also *Microsoft Networking.*FOLDOC
SMP	Symmetric multiprocessing. Two or more similar processors connected via a high-bandwidth link and managed by one operating system, where each processor has equal access to I/O devices. The processors are treated more or less equally, with application programs able to run on any or all processors interchangeably, at the discretion of the operating system.FOLDOC
smiley	A character-based *glyph* (page 956), typically used in email, that conveys an emotion. The characters :-) in a message portray a smiley face (look at it sideways). Because it can be difficult to tell when the writer of an electronic message is saying something in jest or in seriousness, email users often use :-) to indicate humor. The two original smileys, designed by Scott Fahlman, were :-) and :-(. Also *emoticon, smileys,* and *smilies.* For more information search on **smiley** on the Internet.

smilies   *See smiley.*

SMTP   Simple Mail Transfer Protocol. A protocol used to transfer electronic mail between computers. It is a server-to-server protocol, so other protocols are used to access the messages. The SMTP dialog usually happens in the background under the control of a message transport system such as **sendmail** or **exim4**.ᶠᵒᴸᴰᴼᶜ

snap (windows)   As you drag a window toward another window or edge of the workspace, it can move suddenly so that it is adjacent to the other window/edge. Thus the window *snaps* into position.

sneakernet   Using hand-carried magnetic media to transfer files between machines.

sniff   To monitor packets on a network. A system administrator can legitimately sniff packets and a malicious user can sniff packets to obtain information such as usernames and passwords. See also *packet sniffer* (page 970).

SOCKS   A networking proxy protocol embodied in a SOCKS server, which performs the same functions as a *proxy gateway* (page 973) or *proxy server* (page 973). SOCKS works at the application level, requiring that an application be modified to work with the SOCKS protocol, whereas a *proxy* (page 973) makes no demands on the application.

SOCKSv4 does not support authentication or UDP proxy. SOCKSv5 supports a variety of authentication methods and UDP proxy.

sort   To put in a specified order, usually alphabetic or numeric.

SPACE **character**   A character that appears as the absence of a visible character. Even though you cannot see it, a SPACE is a printable character. It is represented by the ASCII code 32 (decimal). A SPACE character is considered a *blank* or *whitespace* (page 987).

spam   Posting irrelevant or inappropriate messages to one or more Usenet newsgroups or mailing lists in deliberate or accidental violation of *netiquette* (page 967). Also, sending large amounts of unsolicited email indiscriminately. This email usually promotes a product or service. Another common purpose of spam is to *phish* (page 971). Spam is the electronic equivalent of junk mail. From the Monty Python "Spam" song.ᶠᵒᴸᴰᴼᶜ

sparse file   A file that is large but takes up little disk space. The data in a sparse file is not dense (thus its name). Examples of sparse files are core files and dbm files.

spawn   *See fork* on page 955.

special character   A character that has a special meaning when it occurs in an ambiguous file reference or another type of regular expression, unless it is quoted. The special characters most commonly used with the shell are * and ?. Also *metacharacter* (page 965) and *wildcard*.

special file   See *device file* on page 951.

spin box   In a GUI, a type of *text box* (page 983) that holds a number you can change by typing over it or using the up and down arrows at the end of the box. Also *spinner*.

spinner   See *spin box*.

spoofing   See *IP spoofing* on page 961.

spool   To place items in a queue, each waiting its turn for some action. Often used when speaking about printers. Also used to describe the queue.

SQL   Structured Query Language. A language that provides a user interface to relational database management systems (RDBMS). SQL, the de facto standard, is also an ISO and ANSI standard and is often embedded in other programming languages.^{FOLDOC}

square bracket   A left square bracket ([) or a right square bracket (]). These special characters define character classes in ambiguous file references and other regular expressions.

SSH Communications Security   The company that created the original SSH (secure shell) protocol suite (www.ssh.com). Linux uses *OpenSSH* (page 969).

standard error   A file to which a program can send output. Usually only error messages are sent to this file. Unless you instruct the shell otherwise, it directs this output to the screen (that is, to the device file that represents the screen).

standard input   A file from which a program can receive input. Unless you instruct the shell otherwise, it directs this input so that it comes from the keyboard (that is, from the device file that represents the keyboard).

standard output   A file to which a program can send output. Unless you instruct the shell otherwise, it directs this output to the screen (that is, to the device file that represents the screen).

startup file   A file that the login shell runs when you log in. The Bourne Again and Z Shells run **.profile**, and the TC Shell runs **.login**. The TC Shell also runs **.cshrc** whenever a new TC Shell or a subshell is invoked. The Z Shell runs an analogous file whose name is identified by the **ENV** variable.

status line   The bottom (usually the twenty-fourth) line of the terminal. The vim editor uses the status line to display information about what is happening during an editing session.

sticky bit   Originally, an access permission bit that caused an executable program to remain on the swap area of the disk. Today, Linux and Mac OS X kernels do not use the sticky bit for this purpose but rather use it to control who can remove files from a directory. In this new capacity, the sticky bit is called the *restricted deletion flag*. If this bit is set on a directory, a file in the directory can be removed or renamed only by a user who is working with **root** privileges or by a user who has write permission for the directory *and* who owns the file or the directory.

streaming tape   A tape that moves at a constant speed past the read/write heads rather than speeding up and slowing down, which can slow the process of writing to or reading from the tape. A proper blocking factor helps ensure that the tape device will be kept streaming.

streams   See *connection-oriented protocol* on page 948.

string   A sequence of characters.

stylesheet   *See CSS* on page 949.

subdirectory   A directory that is located within another directory. Every directory except the root directory is a subdirectory.

subnet   Subnetwork. A portion of a network, which may be a physically independent network segment, that shares a network address with other portions of the network and is distinguished by a subnet number. A subnet is to a network as a network is to an internet.^FOLDOC

subnet address   The subnet portion of an IP address. In a subnetted network, the host portion of an IP address is split into a subnet portion and a host portion using a subnet mask (also address mask). See also *subnet number*.

subnet mask   A bit mask used to identify which bits in an IP address correspond to the network address and subnet portions of the address. Called a subnet mask because the network portion of the address is determined by the number of bits that are set in the mask. The subnet mask has ones in positions corresponding to the network and subnet numbers and zeros in the host number positions. Also *address mask*.

subnet number   The subnet portion of an IP address. In a subnetted network, the host portion of an IP address is split into a subnet portion and a host portion using a *subnet mask*. Also *address mask*. See also *subnet address*.

subpixel hinting   Similar to *anti-aliasing* (page 941) but takes advantage of colors to do the anti-aliasing. Particularly useful on LCD screens.

subroutine   See *procedure* on page 972.

subshell   A shell that is forked as a duplicate of its parent shell. When you run an executable file that contains a shell script by using its filename on the command line, the shell forks a subshell to run the script. Also, commands surrounded with parentheses are run in a subshell.

superblock   A block that contains control information for a filesystem. The superblock contains housekeeping information, such as the number of inodes in the filesystem and free list information.

superserver   The extended Internet services daemon.

Superuser   A user working with **root** privileges. This user has access to anything any other system user has access to and more. The system administrator must be able to become Superuser (work with **root** privileges) to establish new accounts, change passwords, and perform other administrative tasks. The username of Superuser is usually **root**. Also *root* or *root user*.

swap   The operating system moving a process from main memory to a disk, or vice versa. Swapping a process to the disk allows another process to begin or continue execution.

swap space   An area of a disk (that is, a swap file) used to store the portion of a process's memory that has been paged out. Under a virtual memory system, the amount of swap space—rather than the amount of physical memory—determines the maximum size of a single process and the maximum total size of all active processes. Also *swap area* or *swapping area*.^{FOLDOC}

switch   See *network switch* on page 968.

symbolic link   A directory entry that points to the pathname of another file. In most cases a symbolic link to a file can be used in the same ways a hard link can be used. Unlike a hard link, a symbolic link can span filesystems and can connect to a directory.

system administrator   The person responsible for the upkeep of the system. The system administrator has the ability to log in as **root** or use sudo to work with **root** privileges. See also *Superuser*.

system console   See *console* on page 948.

system mode   The designation for the state of the system while it is doing system work. Some examples are making system calls, running NFS and autofs, processing network traffic, and performing kernel operations on behalf of the system. Contrast with *user mode* (page 985).

System V   One of the two major versions of the UNIX system.

TC Shell   tcsh. An enhanced but completely compatible version of the BSD UNIX C shell, csh.

TCP   Transmission Control Protocol. The most common transport layer protocol used on the Internet. This connection-oriented protocol is built on top of *IP* (page 960) and is nearly always seen in the combination TCP/IP (TCP over *IP*). TCP adds reliable communication, sequencing, and flow control and provides full-duplex, process-to-process connections. *UDP* (page 984), although connectionless, is the other protocol that runs on top of *IP*.^{FOLDOC}

tera-   In the binary system, the prefix *tera-* multiplies by 2^{40} (1,099,511,627,776). Terabyte is a common use of this prefix. Abbreviated as *T*. See also *large number* on page 962.

termcap   Terminal capability. The **/etc/termcap** file contains a list of various types of terminals and their characteristics. *System V* replaced the function of this file with the *terminfo* system.

terminal	Differentiated from a *workstation* (page 988) by its lack of intelligence, a terminal connects to a computer that runs Linux. A workstation runs Linux on itself.
terminfo	Terminal information. The **/usr/lib/terminfo** directory contains many subdirectories, each containing several files. Each of those files is named for and holds a summary of the functional characteristics of a particular terminal. Visually oriented textual programs, such as vim, use these files. An alternative to the **termcap** file.
text box	A GUI *widget* (page 987) that allows a user to enter text.
theme	Defined as an implicit or recurrent idea, *theme* is used in a GUI to describe a look that is consistent for all elements of a desktop. Go to themes.freshmeat.net for examples.
thicknet	A type of coaxial cable (thick) used for an Ethernet network. Devices are attached to thicknet by tapping the cable at fixed points.
thinnet	A type of coaxial cable (thin) used for an Ethernet network. Thinnet cable is smaller in diameter and more flexible than *thicknet* cable. Each device is typically attached to two separate cable segments by using a T-shaped connector; one segment leads to the device ahead of it on the network and one to the device that follows it.
thread-safe	See *reentrant* on page 974.
thumb	The movable button in the *scrollbar* (page 977) that positions the image in the window. The size of the thumb reflects the amount of information in the buffer. Also *bubble*.
tick	A mark, usually in a *check box* (page 946), that indicates a positive response. The mark can be a check mark (✔) or an **x**. Also *check mark* or *check*.
TIFF	Tagged Image File Format. A file format used for still-image bitmaps, stored in tagged fields. Application programs can use the tags to accept or ignore fields, depending on their capabilities._{FOLDOC}
tiled windows	An arrangement of windows such that no window overlaps another. The opposite of *cascading windows* (page 945).
time to live	See *TTL*.
toggle	To switch between one of two positions. For example, the ftp **glob** command toggles the **glob** feature: Give the command once, and it turns the feature on or off; give the command again, and it sets the feature back to its original state.
token	A basic, grammatically indivisible unit of a language, such as a keyword, operator, or identifier._{FOLDOC}
token ring	A type of *LAN* (page 962) in which computers are attached to a ring of cable. A token packet circulates continuously around the ring. A computer can transmit information only when it holds the token.

tooltip   A minicontext help system that a user activates by allowing the mouse pointer to *hover* (page 958) over an object (such as those on a panel).

transient window   A dialog or other window that is displayed for only a short time.

Transmission Control Protocol   See *TCP* on page 982.

Trojan horse   A program that does something destructive or disruptive to your system. Its action is not documented, and the system administrator would not approve of it if she were aware of it.

The term *Trojan horse* was coined by MIT-hacker-turned-NSA-spook Dan Edwards. It refers to a malicious security-breaking program that is disguised as something benign, such as a directory lister, archive utility, game, or (in one notorious 1990 case on the Mac) a program to find and destroy viruses. Similar to *back door* (page 942).ᶠᴼᴸᴰᴼᶜ

TTL   Time to live.

1. All DNS records specify how long they are good for—usually up to a week at most. This time is called the record's *time to live*. When a DNS server or an application stores this record in *cache* (page 945), it decrements the TTL value and removes the record from cache when the value reaches zero. A DNS server passes a cached record to another server with the current (decremented) TTL guaranteeing the proper TTL, no matter how many servers the record passes through.

2. In the IP header, a field that indicates how many more hops the packet should be allowed to make before being discarded or returned.

TTY   Teletypewriter. The terminal device that UNIX was first run from. Today TTY refers to the screen (or window, in the case of a terminal emulator), keyboard, and mouse that are connected to a computer. This term appears in UNIX, and Linux has kept the term for the sake of consistency and tradition.

tunneling   Encapsulation of protocol A within packets carried by protocol B, such that A treats B as though it were a data link layer. Tunneling is used to transfer data between administrative domains that use a protocol not supported by the internet connecting those domains. It can also be used to encrypt data sent over a public internet, as when you use ssh to tunnel a protocol over the Internet.ᶠᴼᴸᴰᴼᶜ See also *VPN* (page 986) and *port forwarding* (page 972).

UDP   User Datagram Protocol. The Internet standard transport layer protocol that provides simple but unreliable datagram services. UDP is a *connectionless protocol* (page 948) that, like *TCP* (page 982), is layered on top of *IP* (page 960).

Unlike *TCP*, UDP neither guarantees delivery nor requires a connection. As a result it is lightweight and efficient, but the application program must handle all error processing and retransmission. UDP is often used for sending time-sensitive data that is not particularly sensitive to minor loss, such as audio and video data.FOLDOC

UID   User ID. A number that the **passwd** database associates with a username.

undecillion   In the American system, 10^{36}. In the British system, this number is named *sexillion*. See also *large number* (page 962).

unicast   A packet sent from one host to another host. Unicast means one source and one destination.

Unicode   A character encoding standard that was designed to cover all major modern written languages with each character having exactly one encoding and being represented by a fixed number of bits.

unmanaged window   See *ignored window* on page 959.

URI   Universal Resource Identifier. The generic set of all names and addresses that are short strings referring to objects (typically on the Internet). The most common kinds of URIs are *URLs*.FOLDOC

URL   Uniform (was Universal) Resource Locator. A standard way of specifying the location of an object, typically a Web page, on the Internet. URLs are a subset of *URIs*.

usage message   A message displayed by a command when you call the command using incorrect command-line arguments.

User Datagram Protocol   See *UDP*.

User ID   See *UID*.

user interface   See *interface* on page 960.

user mode   The designation for the state of the system while it is doing user work, such as running a user program (but not the system calls made by the program). Contrast with *system mode* (page 982).

username   The name you enter in response to the **login:** prompt. Other users use your username when they send you mail or write to you. Each username has a corresponding user ID, which is the numeric identifier for the user. Both the username and the user ID are stored in the **passwd** database (**/etc/passwd** or the NIS equivalent). Also *login name*.

userspace   The part of memory (RAM) where applications reside. Code running in userspace cannot access hardware directly and cannot access memory allocated to other applications. Also *userland*. See the *KernelAnalysis-HOWTO*.

UTC   Coordinated Universal Time. UTC is the equivalent to the mean solar time at the prime meridian (0 degrees longitude). Also called Zulu time (Z stands for longitude zero) and GMT (Greenwich Mean Time).

UTF-8   An encoding that allows *Unicode* (page 985) characters to be represented using sequences of 8-bit bytes.

utility   A program included as a standard part of Linux. You typically invoke a utility either by giving a command in response to a shell prompt or by calling it from within a shell script. Utilities are often referred to as commands. Contrast with *builtin (command)* (page 945).

UUID   Universally Unique Identifier. A 128-bit number that uniquely identifies an object on the Internet. Frequently used on Linux systems to identify an **ext2** or **ext3** disk partition.

variable   A name and an associated value. The shell allows you to create variables and use them in shell scripts. Also, the shell inherits several variables when it is invoked, and it maintains those and other variables while it is running. Some shell variables establish characteristics of the shell environment; others have values that reflect different aspects of your ongoing interaction with the shell.

viewport   Same as *workspace* (page 988).

virtual console   Additional consoles, or displays, that you can view on the system, or physical, console.

virus   A *cracker* (page 949) program that searches out other programs and "infects" them by embedding a copy of itself in them, so that they become *Trojan horses* (page 984). When these programs are executed, the embedded virus is executed as well, propagating the "infection," usually without the user's knowledge. By analogy with biological viruses.FOLDOC

VLAN   Virtual LAN. A logical grouping of two or more nodes that are not necessarily on the same physical network segment but that share the same network number. A VLAN is often associated with switched Ethernet.FOLDOC

VPN   Virtual private network. A private network that exists on a public network, such as the Internet. A VPN is a less expensive substitute for company-owned/leased lines and uses encryption to ensure privacy. A nice side effect is that you can send non-Internet protocols, such as AppleTalk, IPX, or *NetBIOS* (page 967), over the VPN connection by *tunneling* (page 984) them through the VPN IP stream.

W2K   Windows 2000 Professional or Server.

W3C   World Wide Web Consortium (www.w3.org).

WAN   Wide area network. A network that interconnects *LANs* (page 962) and *MANs* (page 965), spanning a large geographic area (typically states or countries).

WAP   Wireless access point. A bridge or router between wired and wireless networks. WAPs typically support some form of access control to prevent unauthorized clients from connecting to the network.

Web ring   A collection of Web sites that provide information on a single topic or group of related topics. Each home page that is part of the Web ring has a series of links that let you go from site to site.

whitespace   A collective name for SPACEs and/or TABs and occasionally NEWLINEs. Also *white space*.

wide area network   See *WAN*.

widget   The basic objects of a graphical user interface. A button, *combo box* (page 947), and *scrollbar* (page 977) are examples of widgets.

wildcard   See *metacharacter* on page 965.

Wi-Fi   Wireless Fidelity. A generic term that refers to any type of *802.11* (page 940) wireless network.

window   On a display screen, a region that runs or is controlled by a particular program.

window manager   A program that controls how windows appear on a display screen and how you manipulate them.

Windows share   See *share* on page 977.

WINS   Windows Internet Naming Service. The service responsible for mapping NetBIOS names to IP addresses. WINS has the same relationship to NetBIOS names that DNS has to Internet domain names.

WINS server   The program responsible for handling WINS requests. This program caches name information about hosts on a local network and resolves them to IP addresses.

wireless access point   See *WAP*.

word   A sequence of one or more nonblank characters separated from other words by TABs, SPACEs, or NEWLINEs. Used to refer to individual command-line arguments. In vim, a word is similar to a word in the English language—a string of one or more characters bounded by a punctuation mark, a numeral, a TAB, a SPACE, or a NEWLINE.

Work buffer   A location where vim stores text while it is being edited. The information in the Work buffer is not written to the file on the disk until you give the editor a command to write it.

working directory	The directory that you are associated with at any given time. The relative pathnames you use are *relative to* the working directory. Also *current directory*.
workspace	A subdivision of a *desktop* (page 950) that occupies the entire display.
workstation	A small computer, typically designed to fit in an office and be used by one person and usually equipped with a bit-mapped graphical display, keyboard, and mouse. Differentiated from a *terminal* (page 983) by its intelligence. A workstation runs Linux on itself while a terminal connects to a computer that runs Linux.
worm	A program that propagates itself over a network, reproducing itself as it goes. Today the term has negative connotations, as it is assumed that only *crackers* (page 949) write worms. Compare to *virus* (page 986) and *Trojan horse* (page 984). From **Tapeworm** in John Brunner's novel, *The Shockwave Rider,* Ballantine Books, 1990 (via XEROX PARC).FOLDOC
WYSIWYG	What You See Is What You Get. A graphical application, such as a word processor, whose display is similar to its printed output.
X server	The X server is the part of the *X Window System* that runs the mouse, keyboard, and display. (The application program is the client.)
X terminal	A graphics terminal designed to run the X Window System.
X Window System	A design and set of tools for writing flexible, portable windowing applications, created jointly by researchers at MIT and several leading computer manufacturers.
XDMCP	X Display Manager Control Protocol. XDMCP allows the login server to accept requests from network displays. XDMCP is built into many X terminals.
*x***DSL**	Different types of *DSL* (page 953) are identified by a prefix, for example, ADSL, HDSL, SDSL, and VDSL.
Xinerama	An extension to X.org. Xinerama allows window managers and applications to use the two or more physical displays as one large virtual display. Refer to the Xinerama-HOWTO.
XML	Extensible Markup Language. A universal format for structured documents and data on the Web. Developed by *W3C* (page 986), XML is a pared-down version of SGML. See www.w3.org/XML and www.w3.org/XML/1999/XML-in-10-points.
XSM	X Session Manager. This program allows you to create a session that includes certain applications. While the session is running, you can perform a *checkpoint* (saves the application state) or a *shutdown* (saves the state and exits from the session). When you log back in, you can load your session so that everything in your session is running just as it was when you logged off.
Z Shell	zsh. A *shell* (page 978) that incorporates many of the features of the *Bourne Again Shell* (page 944), *Korn Shell* (page 962), and *TC Shell* (page 982), as well as many original features.
Zulu time	See *UTC* on page 986.

FILE TREE INDEX

A light page number such as *456* indicates a brief mention.

UTILITY INDEX

A light page number such as 456 indicates a brief mention. Page numbers followed by the letter t refer to tables.

Main Index

An italic page number such as *123* indictes a definition. A light page number such as 456 indicates a brief mention. Page numbers followed by the letter **t** refer to tables. Only variables that must always appear with a leading dollar sign are indexed with a leading dollar sign. Other variables are indexed without a leading dollar sign.

Symbols

R

ALSO AVAILABLE FROM MARK G. SOBELL AND PRENTICE HALL

Best-Selling Author Mark G. Sobell's Complete Reference for Ubuntu Linux

A *Practical Guide to Ubuntu Linux, Second Edition,* is the most comprehensive, authoritative reference to installing, configuring, and working with Ubuntu Linux: 8.04 (Hardy Heron) and 8.10 (Intrepid Ibex). This is a thorough update of the first edition, which earned universal raves and rocketed to the top of the Ubuntu list.

You will find everything that makes Sobell's books so extraordinary, including: complete coverage of administration from both GUI and command line, allowing you to gain deep insights into what's going on beneath the surface; extensive coverage of using Ubuntu as a server, including coverage of DNS, LDAP, Apache, exim4, and Samba; and a DVD containing a complete version of 8.10 Intrepid Ibex

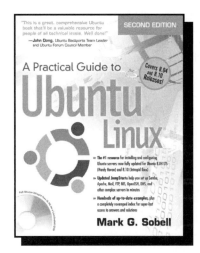

ISBN-13: 978-0-13-700388-4
1,272 pages • © 2009

The book provides comprehensive coverage of installation, configuration, and use—with the best coverage of Ubuntu servers available anywhere and innovative new indexes to deliver even faster access to answers.

FREE Online Edition

Your purchase of **A Practical Guide to Linux® Commands, Editors, and Shell Programming, Second Edition,** includes access to a free online edition for 45 days through the Safari Books Online subscription service. Nearly every Prentice Hall book is available online through Safari Books Online, along with more than 5,000 other technical books and videos from publishers such as Addison-Wesley Professional, Cisco Press, Exam Cram, IBM Press, O'Reilly, Que, and Sams.

SAFARI BOOKS ONLINE allows you to search for a specific answer, cut and paste code, download chapters, and stay current with emerging technologies.

Activate your FREE Online Edition at www.informit.com/safarifree

> **STEP 1:** Enter the coupon code: SYYIQVH.

> **STEP 2:** New Safari users, complete the brief registration form.
> Safari subscribers, just log in.